THE ESSAYS OF
MONTAIGNE

THE ESSAYS OF MONTAIGNE

TRANSLATED BY
E. J. TRECHMANN

WITH AN INTRODUCTION
BY THE RT. HON.
J. M. ROBERTSON
*Author of 'Montaigne
and Shakespeare'*

In two volumes
Volume I

OXFORD UNIVERSITY PRESS
NEW YORK & LONDON

LITHOGRAPHED IN UNITED STATES OF AMERICA

TO THE MEMORY OF
MY EXCELLENT COLLABORATORS
JOHN FLORIO
1553–1625

AND

CHARLES COTTON
1630–1687
THIS TRANSLATION IS
GRATEFULLY AND RESPECTFULLY
DEDICATED

CONTENTS

Translator's Preface	xi
Introduction	xix

BOOK I

To the Reader	1
1. By various means we arrive at the same end . .	3
2. Of Sadness	7
3. Our feelings continue beyond this life . . .	10
4. How the soul relieves its feelings on the wrong objects, when the real are wanting	17
5. Whether the Governor of a place besieged should go out to parley	19
6. The hour of parleying is dangerous	22
7. That the Intention is judge of our actions . . .	24
8. Of Idleness	26
9. Of Liars	27
10. Of quick or slow Speech	33
11. Of Prognostications	35
12. Of Steadfastness	39
13. Ceremony at the meeting of Kings	41
14. That the taste of Good and Evil depends, for a good part, upon the opinion we have of them . . .	43
15. One does not with impunity defend a place obstinately and against reason	63
16. Of the punishment of Cowardice	64
17. A characteristic of some Ambassadors . . .	66
18. Of Fear	69
19. That we should not judge of our Happiness till after Death	72
20. To Philosophize is to learn to die	75
21. Of the power of Imagination	91
22. One man's gain is another man's loss . . .	102
23. Of Custom, and that an established Law is not lightly to be changed	103
24. Of different results of the same counsel . . .	120

CONTENTS

25.	Of Pedantry	130
26.	Of the Education of Boys	142
27.	It is folly to measure the True and the False by our own capacity	178
28.	Of Friendship	182
29.	Dedication of Sonnets to Madame de Grammont	195
30.	Of Moderation	196
31.	Of Cannibals	202
32.	That we should soberly meddle with judging the Divine ordinances	215
33.	Of fleeing from Pleasures at the price of life	217
34.	Fortune is often met hand in hand with Reason	219
36.	Of a Want in our administration	222
36.	Of the custom of wearing Clothes	224
37.	Of Cato the Younger	227
38.	How we cry and laugh for the same thing	231
39.	Of Solitude	234
40.	A Consideration upon Cicero	246
41.	Of not communicating one's Honour	252
42.	Of the Inequality that is amongst us	254
43.	Of Sumptuary Laws	263
44.	Of Sleeping	265
45.	Of the Battle of Dreux	268
46.	Of Names	269
47.	Of the Uncertainty of our Judgement	275
48.	Of War-Horses	281
49.	Of Ancient Customs	289
50.	Of Democritus and Heraclitus	293
51.	Of the Vanity of Words	297
52.	Of the Parsimony of the Ancients	300
53.	Of a saying of Caesar	301
54.	Of vain Subtleties	302
55.	Of Smells	305
56.	Of Prayers	307
57.	Of Age	316

BOOK II

1. Of the Inconsistency of our actions 320
2. Of Drunkenness 327
3. A Custom of the Island of Cea 336
4. Time enough for business to-morrow 351
5. Of Conscience 354
6. Of Preparation 357
7. Of Rewarding Honour 368
8. Of the Affection of Fathers for their Children . . 372
9. Of the Arms of the Parthians 394
10. Of Books 397
11. Of Cruelty 412
12. Apology for Raimond Sebond 428

TRANSLATOR'S PREFACE

THE first English translation of Montaigne's Essays appeared in 1603, the work of John Florio, a contemporary and perhaps a friend of Shakespeare. His father was Italian, he had been partially brought up in France, and he was a teacher of languages at Oxford; he appears therefore to have been well equipped for his formidable task. A third edition of this translation was published in 1632, and no other appeared for two hundred and fifty years. In 1685 a much more accurate translation was made by Charles Cotton. By that time Florio seems to have so fallen into oblivion that Pierre Coste, who in 1724 published an edition of the Essays in French, with many notes and comments, apparently had no knowledge of him. Coste was a Huguenot refugee who passed most of his life in England, and is the most eminent of the earlier editors and commentators of Montaigne. He makes frequent and appreciative mention of Cotton as *the* English translator, whose version was many times republished during the eighteenth century, and no doubt became the favourite reading of many a Squire Thorne of Ullathorne.

Some fifty years ago Florio was discovered or rediscovered by the late Professor Henry Morley, who issued a one-volume edition of him in 1885. It was like the finding of a valuable piece of old furniture. The lively style and the racy Elizabethan flavour made an immediate appeal, and Florio has since held the field as first favourite with discriminating readers. But style and flavour are not everything. In his laudatory preface Morley concludes with these words: 'This book that was enjoyed by Shakespeare and Ben Jonson will always bring us nearer to Montaigne than the best possible translation by a later hand.' If this means anything, it is sheer nonsense. Montaigne is translatable into any language, whether Elizabethan or Georgian, and that of the twentieth century will obviously bring him nearer to the modern reader, in the sense of making him better understood, than that of a century so far back as the sixteenth. That language has many fine qualities, but that of the present day need not necessarily be despised.

In any case it seems a pity that Florio has never been subjected to a little 'editing'. His numerous elementary blunders (e. g. *poisson* : poison), inaccuracies and misrepresentations (he makes Montaigne say that he was 'altogether ignorant in the holy Scripture', whereas Montaigne in the same essay quotes the Bible at least sixteen times) must be very perplexing to the reader. He is besides generally published in a very unattractive form. Like the earliest edition of the French original, Florio's work, as it is still repeatedly issued, flows on in one continuous stream, with no breaks except where the poetical quotations occur. Every chapter is a paragraph. In an author like Montaigne, who digresses on every page, this is a great disadvantage, and leaves the reader very much at sea.

Cotton, on the other hand, whose mistakes are legion, though greatly outnumbered by Florio's, has been two or three times very well revised. In 1842 William Hazlitt published a very fine and complete, though rather unwieldy, edition in one volume of Montaigne's Works, including his most interesting Travel diary. Hazlitt concludes his preface with these words : 'I have no hesitation in expressing the opinion that the present edition of the Essays of Montaigne fully comes up to the definition of a good translation suggested by Lord Woodhouselea, viz.: "That in which the merit of the original work is so completely transfused into another language as to be as distinctly apprehended, and as strongly felt, by a native of the country to which that language belongs, as it is to those who speak the language of the original work." Here indeed, as in the case of Ozell's *Rabelais*, the position might even be more strongly put.' A bold opinion ! It would perhaps have been more becoming in Hazlitt if he had substituted the word *hope* for *opinion*. It may be safely said that a translation of Montaigne in which the errors are to be numbered only by hundreds is a good translation, and Hazlitt's revised version of Cotton, to which we may still allow that claim, greatly exceeds that estimate.

The same may be said of the younger Hazlitt's revision, which was issued in three volumes. W. C. Hazlitt besides introduced an innovation which is anything but an improvement. Instead of following up the numerous Latin and other poetical quotations with metrical translations, as his predecessors had done, he followed the example of the French editors in relegating his renderings, and that in bald prose, to the foot-notes. To some people there is nothing more detestable than a prose version of poetry.

I may remark parenthetically that in my search for poetical translations of the Latin poets I have found them sadly wanting. With the exception of Horace, Virgil, Lucretius and perhaps Martial, none appear to have been translated in full by modern hands. Those of the seventeenth century are too free, too inaccurate, and altogether unsatisfactory. Even Juvenal and Persius suffer from this lack.

The first edition of the original Essays, comprising two books only, appeared in two small volumes in 1580 at Bordeaux, probably published at Montaigne's own expense ('in Guienne I buy the printers, elsewhere they buy me'), with the title 'Essais de Messire Michel Seigneur de Montaigne Chevalier de l'Ordre du Roy & Gentilhomme Ordinaire de sa Chambre'. A single copy is in existence which bears the simple title 'Essais de Michel de Montaigne'. In order to account for this single copy, it is assumed that this was the copy sent to the author for correction, according to the custom of the day, the *errata* being all printed on a separate sheet; and that by Montaigne's directions a new title-page was printed with the full titles. A second, revised and slightly augmented, edition appeared in 1582, with the addition on the title-page of 'Maire & Gouverneur de Bordeaux'. In 1588, a new edition, with the addition of a third book and many other additions (600, according to the title-page), was published in Paris. The title was now simplified to 'Essais de Michel Seigneur de Montaigne'. No need to flaunt his titles now that he was so well known! His view with regard to good taste had besides undergone a change. He had come to see the vanity of 'covering with these (titles of honour) the title-page and inscription of the books we print'. It would be uncharitable to suggest that it was a case of *post hoc ergo propter hoc*, since he admittedly very often changes his opinions.

When he died in 1592, Montaigne left a copy of this edition with numerous corrections, and additions written on the margins, which when printed made the book half as long again as the preceding edition. This copy, which is now in the Municipal Library at Bordeaux, is known as the Bordeaux copy (*Exemplaire de Bordeaux*), or the 'Bordeaux Manuscript', and from it was published, by the care of Mademoiselle de Gournay, assisted by the poet Pierre de Brach, the posthumous edition of 1595. (A facsimile page of the 'Bordeaux MS.' will be found in the second volume of this work.) Marie de Gournay was a 'jeune fille' who had enjoyed a thorough classical education, and was an enthusiastic admirer of the essayist. When he was in Paris in 1588, for the purpose of seeing his book through the press, she called upon her idol, and a close friendship sprang up between the two. She became henceforth his 'daughter' (*fille d'alliance*), and she referred to him as her 'father'.

The 1595 edition does not strictly follow the Bordeaux copy throughout, the editor having made many slight and not very important alterations, chiefly in the wording, and a few additions, with regard to which it is impossible to decide whether they were written by Montaigne or not. These additions are in the present translation enclosed in square brackets. Among the alterations is one very significant omission, that of the word 'miracles' in the chapter on the 'Power of the Imagination'. Montaigne wrote: 'It is likely that *miracles*, visions, enchantments, and the like extraordinary phenomena, derive their credit chiefly from the power of the imagination, acting principally on the more impressionable minds of the common people. Their credulity is so easily imposed upon that they think they see what they do not see.'

Among the additions is the eulogy of Mlle de Gournay at the end of the seventeenth chapter of the second book. It has been suggested that this passage was crowded out and written by Montaigne on a separate sheet, but, since there was more than enough margin on the page where it should have appeared, that explanation is not convincing. It has also been rather ungallantly hinted that it might have been written by the lady herself; that, however, is hard to believe. In the folio edition of 1635, which was also prepared by Mlle de Gournay, the passage appears in an altered and abridged form. This also needs explanation. We are thus reduced to leaving the question of authenticity in doubt.

The present translation (apart from the few additions above mentioned) is entirely based upon the Bordeaux copy, which should obviously be accepted as the only authoritative text.

Whilst engaged on the pleasant task, begun four years ago, of turning this author into English, the present translator was flattering himself on being the first in the field, after a lapse of some two hundred and forty years, with a new version, when the startling announcement reached him of a new American translation of the complete Essays. On examination, however, he discovered that it was not, strictly speaking, complete, since many passages have been left in the original French, including the greater part of the long fifth chapter of Book III, which treats mostly of sex matters, and which neither Florio nor Cotton had shirked.

The question of bowdlerization is one on which opinions differ. For entire suppression something might be said; but to publish the outspoken passages in their original is like hiding a thing behind a curtain that may be easily drawn aside. The curiosity aroused by this mystification is the greater, and one expects something worse than the reality. Montaigne did not, like Rabelais (and especially his English translators), revel in coarseness. Although he does not agree with the convention which forbids speaking of actions which are 'natural, necessary and legitimate', he always does so guardedly and apologetically. In these days of outspokenness prudery appears to be particularly out of season.

As a fellow-labourer in the same vineyard who knows perhaps better than anybody the difficulty of the task of doing into English an author like Montaigne, it is not for me to criticize Mr. Ives' achievement. I can only remark that we differ in very many interpretings.

A characteristic of our author which is neglected generally by his editors and translators is his keen sense of humour. They all sin in treating him too seriously. He tells us himself, 'j'ai naturellement un style comique (*humorous, playful, facetious*) et privé (*familiar, conversational*).' He admits besides, in reply to his critics, 'that he often jests; that people think him serious when he is pretending; that he uses words of Gascon growth, and risky expressions, and that he avoids no words that are used in the streets of Paris' (the word *argot* was not in his day used in the modern sense, or he would probably have admitted using *argot*). It is sometimes difficult to know whether he is serious or jesting, as when in his last chapter he becomes eloquent on the many privileges enjoyed by a sufferer from that most painful disease, stone in the bladder, when compared with those who suffer from other maladies. He is rather fond of 'pulling his reader's leg', as when, after relating how a swarm of bees routed a hostile army, he adds that when the swarm returned to its hive not a single bee was missing. He enjoys a joke at his doctor's expense, and is not above making a bad pun. In fact he seldom dismisses a subject without finishing on a humorous or naughty note.

Another point that cannot be too much emphasized is Montaigne's modernness. Every fresh reading of the Essays reveals some detail which shows how much he was in advance of his time; he is indeed often in advance of the present time. When all the world believed in witchcraft, and when Jean Bodin threatened the disbeliever in the witch with the fate of the witch, Montaigne alone raised his voice in defence of those unfortunate victims of popular superstition; after examining some of them he came to the conclusion that they 'needed a dose of hellebore rather than of hemlock'. His attitude towards torture, especially judicial torture, is the same; everything that is over and above simple death he regarded as cruel: a sentiment that was censured by the Holy See. Even a criminal should not be vivisected to satisfy the medical thirst for knowledge. He took the common-sense view of natural infirmities and monstrosities, which were commonly regarded as 'judgements of God' and punishment for sin. The gloom of mourning was an abomination to him, and he would prefer to see white instead of black funerals, as was the usage in ancient Rome. And did he not declare that 'male and female are cast in the same mould'?

In these days he would be among the Simplified Spellers. Orthography in his day was not so cut and dried a thing as it is now, but there were many conventions, one of which consisted in writing words with letters which had been reintroduced from their Latin originals, and that were not intended to be pronounced. He spelled simply and more or less phonetically, and his spelling was retained in the earliest editions; he is not responsible for all the 'quaint' spellings of the later editions, in which his *avec* is lengthened into *avecques*, and his *conu* appears as *cogneu*. It was for this reason no doubt that the late Bayle St. John declared that he 'generally spelt like an ignorant soldier'.

I have to acknowledge with thanks the permission of Messrs. J. M. Dent & Sons to use extracts from the translations, published by them, of Mr. W. E. Leonard's *Lucretius*, of the late E. Fairfax Taylor's *Aeneid*, and Mr. T. F. Royds' *Georgics*; and I cannot sufficiently express my obligation and thanks to Mr. J. M. Robertson, not only for his admirable introduction, but also for his valuable suggestions after most carefully going through the proofs with the original.

E. J. T.

INTRODUCTION

I

IT is a singular fact that an author who, after nearly three and a half centuries, is seen to have an ever-widening audience alike in his own country and in others, began to write only in middle age, after having long counted on a life of action which came to nothing ; and, even then, only after years of desultory note-taking by way of pastime proceeded to find himself and to express himself. Montaigne has won and kept the ear of the world by reason, largely, of having never planned to gain it. Having as little vocation for systematic thinking or teaching as for the arts of poetry and drama and fiction, he sought none of those fields. He never even strove to cultivate the 'literary' style of his time. Happily nourished on the Latin classics, he found in them practically all the artistic literature he wanted, though he read Italian poetry for his pleasure. What he began to write was not literature. What he came to write was literature of a new and enduring kind.

This development can be seen to take place by the quite spontaneous reaction of a strongly marked intellectual bias under pressure of a series of political events. More than most writers, Montaigne is to be understood in the light of the public life of his time. An outline of his life is thus a first step to the general comprehension and valuation of the famous Essays.

Michel Eyquem de Montaigne was born in 1533, the third child of a successful and esteemed country gentleman of the district of Périgord in Gascony, a good Catholic, who came of a stock of traders raised to modest affluence by diligence in business. The aristocratic Joseph Scaliger was not inaccurate in affirming that the ancestors of the essayist had sold salted herrings ; but they were not limited to that important 'line'. Michel's great-grandfather, Ramon Eyquem, bought the estate of Montaigne in 1477, which brought the right to the name 'de Montaigne'; and the family acquired other estates, which were distributed among the uncles and brothers of Michel. His father, Pierre Eyquem, though also a trader and always closely connected with the business life of Bordeaux, of which he became Mayor, played the part of a French squire, and served as a young man in the wars of Francis the First in Italy. Thereafter he married Antoinette de Lopez or Louppe, a young woman of Jewish birth, whose family, as was not uncommon among educated Jews in that period and region, had become Protestants. Of the marriage were born eight or nine (some say eleven) children, of whom two, his brother Beauregard, sieur de St. Martin, and his youngest sister Jeanne (who became Madame Lestonnat), adopted the Protestantism of their mother.

Pierre, it is clear, cannot have been a fanatic. Michel, in his youth, had some small leaning of that kind; and it may be (though there is another possible explanation) that a certain early domestic dissidence on that score is the reason why, in the Essays, although he gives many admiring accounts of his father, there is only one passing mention of his mother. On the other hand, the circumstance that there were three Protestants in his home circle may account for the fact that his early Catholic zeal led him but a little way, and was soon recoiled from, though he always stood by the old forms, on a principle of practical conservatism.

His upbringing was remarkable. Pierre Eyquem had a notably original cast of mind, and is recorded by his son to have schemed for town-dwellers a kind of labour exchange, making known the needs of buyers and sellers, travellers, employers and men out of work. Himself unlearned, though not uninterested in books, Pierre had inquired much concerning methods of education, and reached the happy idea of making Michel learn Latin as his mother tongue. The child accordingly had a German tutor, a cultured physician who knew no French; and the servants who looked after him had to find Latin words enough for any talk they had with him. Father and mother alike learned to talk Latin when necessary; and the fashion partly spread to the neighbourhood. Another of Pierre's original notions was to have the child awakened every morning, after the cradle stage, by music, thus giving his infancy a certain aspect of luxury, though, in accordance with an old French custom, which is found recurring long afterwards in the case of Montesquieu, the father gave his boy a peasant godfather and godmother, and had him suckled by a peasant woman in her home, by way of keeping him in kindly touch with the people. Pierre's educational ideas were thus all of an attractive kind; and perhaps all were fruitful. The child learned Latin without tears, hearing no French until he was six; and he never lost his friendly feeling for the peasantry. It is not unlikely, too, that his morning harmony developed his imaginative life; though he does not seem ever to have cultivated music. But it is not impossible, on the other hand, that those six years of childhood in which the mother was substantially excluded from her child's life may have developed on her part a certain aloofness from the boy who had thus been taken out of her hands. It may be suspected, too, that she knew Pierre to have taken the course he did in order to prevent Michel's being made a Protestant.

Speaking Latin ' as a native ', Michel was sent, at the age of six, to the then famous college of Guienne at Bordeaux, where he made friends of ' noble ' status. His exceptional preparation, though it placed him in an upper form, naturally did not admit of his being dealt with in a class by himself, ahead of all the other pupils. But though he was put through an established drudgery of which he has no good to say, he was conducted by a wise tutor through Latin literature with an uncommon facility, and always retained an easy hold of it, avowing as he does in his latter years that he knew it better than French, though he professed to have lost all facility in speaking and writing it. Among the little we learn of his college life is his account of how he figured brilliantly in Latin plays, including some by George Buchanan and Muret and others of his learned masters. Buchanan, he tells us, was much impressed by his upbringing, and proposed to advocate the method.

Destined by his father for the law, he probably studied it to some extent after leaving school at thirteen; and Toulouse is considered the likeliest place. In those days 'magistracies' were bought offices; and in that fashion he was entered by his father in 1554 at the new and short-lived Cour des Aides of Périgueux, founded by Henry II to raise funds by the sale of new offices; but, that institution being speedily suppressed, in the following year he accompanied his father, then Mayor of Bordeaux, to Paris, where Pierre was skilfully advocating the restoration of the privileges of his municipality, which had been lost by popular rioting against the salt-tax some years before. Michel acquired a love for Paris which never left him; but in 1557 he took up his law work at the Parlement of Bordeaux, in which the Cour of Périgueux was embodied; winning, however, no distinction, and apparently small practice, in that capacity, though he acted for his Périgueux colleagues in claiming their rights. Much more important to his mental life was the instantaneous and intense friendship he formed with another young lawyer, Étienne de la Boëtie, a personality in some ways as remarkable, perhaps, as Montaigne's own, and still remembered in respect of some of his political writings, as well as of that singularly ardent friendship. It lasted till the death of La Boëtie, which occurred in 1563, under circumstances movingly described in a long letter by Montaigne to his father.

La Boëtie's estimate of his young friend helps us to realize Michel's temperament. The essayist in later years tells us that in youth he was in large measure dull and inert, or, as we should say, incorrigibly lazy. Also, however, he describes his adult self as vehement, though not quarrelsome, in debate. La Boëtie, describing him as somewhat prone to the gratification of his passions, counsels him in a Latin poem against that proclivity.

At this stage Michel's ambitions were towards a more distinguished career than that of the provincial magistracy.

It is clear that he readily attracted and impressed men in high place; and in 1559 we find him, by his own account, at Bar-le-Duc with the court of Francis II, and again at Rouen in 1560 at the celebration of the majority of Charles IX. There it was that he saw the 'cannibals' brought from Brazil, who moved him to some of the reflections which constitute his essay under that title, though it was not penned till nineteen years later, when he had read an account of the conquest of the New World. But what exactly he was doing, or hoped to do, about 1560, we cannot tell. He, who has professed to reveal himself to the full in his Essays, and has indeed done it to an exceptional degree in respect of his tastes, habits, ideals, opinions, affections, follies, and preferences, tells us nothing of his life at Court, or of his hopes and frustrations. All that we know in that connexion is that he won the special esteem of both Charles IX and Henry III, as well as of Henry of Navarre; that he had done (as we gather from several passages in the Essays) some campaigning, but apparently no fighting; that in 1561 he carried to the Court at Paris a report from the authorities at Bordeaux of religious rioting there; that so late as 1574 he was employed to negotiate an agreement between the Duc de Guise and Henry of Navarre; that in that year he carried an official message from the royalist commander at the camp of St. Hermine to the Parlement of Bordeaux; that he further mediated between the two Henries; and that he grew more and more in the estimation of the King of Navarre, whom he in turn valued above all his predecessors.

At an early stage of his connexion with court affairs, it would seem, he began to feel that it would prove for him a blind alley. His friend La Boëtie died at the age of thirty-two, leaving him his library and papers; and after mourning for his dead friend as intensely as he had loved him, he married in his own thirty-third year Françoise de la Chassaigne, daughter of one of his colleagues at the Parlement of Bordeaux. At this stage, though the marriage proved a substantially happy one, he had not renounced the hope of a public career, but the fates disposed otherwise. In 1568 his father died, aged 72, leaving him a well-found estate and château, Pierre having been as careful an administrator as his son was confessedly lax. It appears to be now agreed among the biographers that Michel was the eldest son; though it was long taken for granted that he had two elder brothers who predeceased him. What is certain is that, desolated alike by the loss of his friend and the desperate aspect of the affairs of the nation, and failing to obtain a high employment which he seems to have hoped for in 1570, when he spent some time at Paris, he retired to country life, resigning or selling his function as magistrate at Bordeaux. The surviving brothers were provided for by other family estates, but Michel had a sufficiency in that of Montaigne.

We can partly guess at his thwarted ambitions from the fact that he has set up a mystification by calling himself, first in his line, simply 'de Montaigne', dropping from his signature the 'Eyquem', which his father had always used. He further provoked the gibe of Scaliger by alleging (Essays, III, ix, and elsewhere) that 'most of his ancestors' had been 'de Montaigne', and had there been buried; which was not the fact. There is thus a certain touch of worldly self-importance in the famous Latin declaration which he caused to be incribed, in 1571, on the walls of his little study, opening on the library in the tower of his château :

'In the year of Christ 1571, at the age of 38, the eve of the Calends of March, his birthday, Michel de Montaigne [*Mich. Montanus*], long wearied of the slavery of the courts and of public functions, while still in health [*dum se integer*] retires to the bosom of the learned Virgins, where in quiet and security he hopes, if the fates allow, to pass what may be left him of a life already more than half spent, consecrating this ancestral dwelling and sweet retreat to his liberty and tranquillity and leisure.'

Even at that stage, probably, he would have taken a post at Court had it been offered him on tolerable terms. The Order of St. Michael, conferred on him by Charles IX with a highly flattering letter, in October 1571, had been greatly coveted by him in his youth ; he has warmly avowed his love for Paris ; he had confessedly no vocation for a rural life ; and his profession of weariness, though it seems to refer mainly to his duties as magistrate, tells of some considerable past share in public affairs. The inference has been drawn that he found it impossible to lend himself to the political methods of Catherine de Médicis, who habitually sought to overrule the measures of her sons, always intriguing and always playing false. One student has summed up that in the Queen's and her sons' counsels at that time there was ' perhaps not one honest man '. Montaigne's own love of straight dealing, which was never affected by any of his rules of worldly wisdom, is shown by his dedication, in 1570, of the small volume of La Boëtie's Latin verses to Michel de L'Hôpital, who had been ' disgraced ' from his Chancellorship in 1568. But, when all is said, it has to be recognized that Montaigne had not the cast of mind and temperament needed to fit a man for the tasks of political life in his period. In one of his most intimate Essays (III, ix) he suggests that he might have developed that way if he would, but comes down heavily on the side of avowal of his repugnances.

Doubtless he knew that men like Brantôme mocked him, regarding him as a dabbler in State affairs, thinking to play that tremendous game, with its countless crises and appalling surprises, its desperate cross currents and its incalculable risks, by way of common sense and good feeling. Montaigne was a hater of cruelty in a cruel age, sickened by the sight of executions when executions were of daily occurrence, loathing massacres, yearning for order and legality among men vowed to illegality and deadly feud. His desultory work even as a magistrate irked and burdened him. He saw a vast mass of complicated laws, uncomprehended by the people and administered by magistrates who made their incomes by their fees, doing justice or injustice as their skill or their ignorance prevailed. Loathing the stupidity of judicial torture, he had to face it as part of the received jurisprudence. For such a spirit, impatient of drudgery, incapable of systematic toil, chronically sunk in reveries on the follies and madnesses of men, statecraft was even less practicable than the taskwork of law ; and he inevitably gravitated to another way of life.

The issue, in separate volumes, of the writings and translations of La Boëtie, in commemoration of the dead friend, had followed on the publication in 1569 of Montaigne's translation of the Latin *Theologia Naturalis* of Raymond Sebond or Sebon, a task laid upon him by his father some time before the latter's death. So far there was no sign of any craving for authorship on Montaigne's own part, save for a hint in one of his dedications of the writings of La Boëtie. It was not till 1572, the year of the Massacre of St. Bartholomew's Day, after which de L'Hôpital died broken-hearted, that he began to jot down small essays of commentary on matters that had struck him in his reading ; and it was after the Massacre that his thoughts began to take a written shape determined by that frightful episode and the new harvest of national evil which followed.

In such early essays as those on Goods and Evils, on Learning to Die, on Custom, and on The Cannibals, in Book I, we see him already at that standpoint of agnostic and anti-dogmatic sanity which is the essential note of his message to his time. He had been forced back on his own soul for a philosophy of life in an age which was visibly going from bad to worse in a series of murderous strifes over matters of church government ; and he was feeling his way towards ruling conceptions by which men and States could maintain a better life. In the years 1573-6 men of his general way of political thinking, who can be classed as Liberal Catholics, planned for a new settlement ; and in 1574, as we learn from the historian De Thou, who highly esteemed him, he personally mediated between the two outstanding leaders of the great factions, the Duc de Guise and Henry of Navarre. But in 1576 Henry escaped from the Louvre, where he had been in informal detention since the Massacre ; and in that year was formed the new Catholic League against the party of Protestant Reform, initiating a new period of furious warfare. The publication in 1574 of the *Discours sur la Servitude Volontaire* of La Boëtie, which greatly fomented the new Protestant movement, has been held to be a result of the communication of the manuscript by Montaigne, who had abstained thus far from publishing it. It is indeed, despite its lame conclusion, a singularly bold performance, setting forth, in a fashion that savours much of Montaigne's own forthright dialectic, how the power of the autocrat is given him by those who obey and abet him—a classic truth more calmly formulated by Hume two hundred years later.

In his own person, however, Montaigne was no advocate of either innovation or insurrection. He simply desired peace and quietness on conservative lines; and he early saw that the hope of France lay in the unfanatical Henry of Navarre, from whom in 1577 he accepted the honour of the post of Gentleman Ordinary of the King's Chamber— this though he already held the same status with Charles IX. But henceforth he took no share either in the fighting or in diplomacy, keeping in touch both with Navarre and the Court, but also keeping as far as possible free from all embroilments with his neighbours, some of whom made the task hard for him.

His house, being undefended, was once entered; but his tranquil self-possession discountenanced the intruders. Once, in a time of truce, he was captured and pillaged; but in that case also he extricated himself by his cool courage. In a time of plague he had to leave his château for six months and harbour his household as best he could elsewhere; but he weathered the storm.

His life's leisurely task was now the writing of the Essays, in the light of varying but ever maturing thought. A large part was evidently played in his intellectual life by the new French translation, by Jacques Amyot (1559-72), of the *Lives* and the *Moralia* of Plutarch, in which the strifes and the meditations of antiquity yield so much light and leading for the modern world. It is chiefly through Plutarch that he intellectually relates to Greek life and thought. We see him at times reacting strongly against both Plato and Aristotle; and he is not always firm in his homage to Socrates. But Plutarch always holds him, as a treasury of the lore of life and action and ethical feeling.

We can picture him doing his thinking, as he tells us, chiefly on his rides, or over his books in his secluded study life, so vividly set forth in a late Essay (III, iii), alone among his books and his papers, looking up occasionally at his pictures and his Latin mottoes—a very characteristic miscellany from Ecclesiastes, Ecclesiasticus, Sextus Empiricus, Stobaeus, Solomon's Proverbs, the Psalms, St. Paul's Epistles, Isaiah, Homer, Plato, Epictetus, Herodotus, Horace, Terence, Lucretius, and other ancient stores of wisdom. Fifty-four sentences, thus extracted, have been deciphered from forty-six joists and two transverse beams of the library. They are the gnomic forms of the conception of human life expounded throughout the Essays. 'There is no reason which is not opposed by an equal reason'; 'Rejoice in the present life: all else is beyond thee'; 'I determine nothing; I do not comprehend things; I suspend judgement; I examine'; 'Guiding ourselves by custom and the senses'; 'All is vanity'; 'God made men like to a shadow, of which who, after sunset, shall judge?'; 'All: the heavens and the earth and the waters, are as nothing beside the immensity of the universe'; 'Man, a fragile vase'; 'No man hath known, and none shall know, aught with certitude'; 'The human race is too greedy of fables'; 'Woe to you who are wise in your own eyes'; 'Men are tormented by their opinions of things, not by the things themselves'; 'The beautiful is worthy of admiration'.

And inasmuch as his library of a thousand volumes was gathered on the nucleus of that left him by La Boëtie, he caused to be inscribed on the frieze, in Latin, this tribute to the never-forgotten friend:

'Unhappily deprived of the sweetest, the kindest, and the closest comrade, than whom our age has seen nothing better, nothing more learned, nothing more lovable, nothing more perfect, Michel Montaigne [*Montanus*] mindful of that mutual love which conjoined them, greatly desiring to erect a monument thereof than which nothing could be more significant, set up this special furniture of learning, in which is his joy.'

Thus surrounded, and thus inspired by emotion and discursive reading, he gradually passed from unpretending comments on historic episodes to an unfolding of his thoughts and feelings on the whole panorama of human experience, past and present, collective and individual, connecting it all by the living thread of his personality, till he could claim that always he was but revealing and propounding himself, his ' Me ', seeing himself in mankind and mankind in himself. Writing as the mood took him, through years of apparently insuperable strife, living in one of the most violently troubled regions of a France perpetually convulsed, yet contriving to pass unscathed through the whole evil time, he could not but keep his thoughts adjusted to that tempest outside, however peacefully he passed his days with his books and his pen. Thus it came about that he penned a singularly vital book, a *livre de bonne foi*, coming home, in Bacon's phrase, to the business and bosoms of men with a curiously discursive directness.

It first appeared in 1580, in two small volumes, representing only about a third part of what it was to become. Then, having had it carefully printed at Bordeaux, he rested for a time from his labours. In 1579 he had had his first attack of the malady of the stone, which he had inherited from his father, who died of it ; and, with his book off his hands, he bethought himself of seeing the world outside France, doubting whether he had many years of life before him. Accordingly he set out upon his travels, which lasted for seventeen months, and of which he preserved an exact itinerary, in large part dictated to his valet. At Paris he presented himself to Henry III, to whom he had previously sent a copy of the *Essais*; and the King, who always regarded him amicably, bestowed due compliments.

Leaving Paris in June 1580, he went to the siege of La Fère, whence he transported to Soissons the body of his friend, the intimate companion of Henry of Navarre,

Philibert de Grammont, who had been killed in that siege. Thence he passed through Switzerland and Germany to Rome, where he was courteously received, though his *Essais* had been subjected to the ecclesiastical censure, and he was politely invited to make certain changes. Some changes (not all of those promised) he did make in the second edition, but they were of such a kind as appear to posterity to deepen the heresy imputed. Long afterwards, this was recognized by the Papal authorities; and in 1676 the *Essais* were placed on the Papal Index of Prohibited Books.[1] But in Italy his behaviour was carefully correct; and at Loretto he installed a silver *ex-voto* group of figures, representing himself, his wife and his daughter, kneeling before the Virgin. At Lucca the essayist learned that he was to be elected Mayor of Bordeaux, as his father had been before him, an honour probably resulting from the intervention of both Henry III and Henry of Navarre. Returning to Bordeaux, he received there a letter from Henry III which left him no choice but to accept the mayoralty.

However remiss he may have been as a magistrate, he seems to have been an efficient Mayor. He took action against the Jesuits, who had been fanatically mismanaging matters in the town, and also took steps to create a municipal service to look after destitute children. In 1583 he was re-elected Mayor for two more years, continuing to be active against the seditious Leaguers, and mediating, not without good effect, between Henry of France and Henry of Navarre.

In 1584, by the death of the Duc d'Alençon, last surviving brother of Henry III, Henry of Navarre became legitimate heir to the throne; and one of his journeys was to the château of Montaigne, where, with his retinue, he stayed two days, paying his host the compliment of eating without the 'examen of aliments' which was still customary in the

---

[1] It has been inferred that the special cause was his insistence on crediting animals with reason, whereas the Cartesian philosophy, which in 1676 was dominant, represented them as automata. Montaigne's doctrine was held to imperil that of human immortality.

life of kings in that age. In the following year Montaigne incurred a modern charge of neglect of public duty by not residing at Bordeaux during a visitation of the plague. No contemporary, however, expected him to do so. Two years later, in 1587, the King of Navarre, now victor of Coutras, again passed two days at Montaigne's château.

By this time Montaigne had put together the greatly expanded fourth edition of his *Essais*, the solid foundation of his fame. The two 'books' had become three, and the two earlier had undergone much enlargement. Going to Paris to have the new edition published there, he had the memorable experience of being cast into prison, on grounds of private malice, by the Catholic League, a durance from which he was released after eight hours by the intervention of Catherine de Médicis. Returning from Paris, he attended the fateful 'États Généraux' at Blois, and had the luck to leave before the assassination of the Duc de Guise, which was to be avenged in the following year by the assassination of Henry III; an event which left Henry of Navarre the legitimate king.

But Montaigne was not fated to live to see the triumph of his chosen hero. In two letters, written in 1590, he declares his joyful adherence, and vows to go to Henry at Paris, if his strength permits, as soon as the king enters his capital; refusing incidentally to accept offers of money which Henry had made him. Not till 1594 did Henry, turned Catholic, enter Paris. On the 13th of September, 1592, with France still agonizing in a religious war, the essayist had passed away, after a brief illness, in the course of which he quietly took leave of his friends. True to his practice, he received the sacrament, dying immediately afterwards.

In the last two years of his life he had made two new friends, one the ecclesiastic Pierre Charron, who became his devoted disciple, the other Mademoiselle Marie de Gournay, no less devoted, of whom the essayist affectionately spoke as his adopted daughter. Dying, he left behind him a revised copy of the 1588 edition of the Essays, with many additions and corrections; and in 1595 there resulted the publication of the definitive edition, which Mlle de Gournay supervised. To this day, disputes continue as to the faithfulness of her editing at certain points; though at the hands of vigilant editors there has latterly emerged an authoritative text. But the posthumous edition found reception as a classic. Montaigne, writing *sans façon*, with no thought of immortality, had at once created for himself a monument 'more enduring than brass', and wrought for his country a service which even then thoughtful men could see to be inestimable.

II

Pascal and the other recluses of Port-Royal, who in the seventeenth century censured Montaigne for 'putting all things in doubt', do not seem ever to have asked themselves what parts they themselves would or could have played in the world of furious strife in which Montaigne's lot was laid. It is well said that we should be cautious as to how we condemn a past age in relation to our own; but even those who give the warning confess that the age of the religious wars in France was one of the very worst in modern history. Montaigne is the witness, as he is the monitor. For a full generation, after a hideous epidemic of heretic-burning, there went on an almost continuous war of religions, producing an immense dissolution of all the normal moralities between man and man, their place being taken by the lawless impulses of fanaticism, faction, and hate. Religious passions wrought, as do race hatreds, to make men abnormally cruel and unscrupulous. Again and again does Montaigne indicate how perjury and treachery and massacre and savage cruelty came to be regarded as fitting expedients in such a protracted struggle. Everything that Thucydides has said of the corruption of Greek character in the Peloponnesian war is true for the France of Montaigne's lifetime in a far higher degree.

In one grave paragraph (vol. II, p. 421) he presents a

picture which impresses more than any statistical record of crime and slaughter :

'I see not one action, or three, or a hundred, but a commonly accepted state of morality so unnatural, especially as regards inhumanity and treachery, which are to me the worst of all sins, that I have not the heart to think of them without horror ; and they excite my wonder almost as much as my detestation. The practice of these egregious villanies bears as much the mark of strength and vigour of soul as of error and disorder.'

It was a world in which men had come to make evil their good ; and it was for that age of anarchy that Montaigne shaped his curiously skilful counsels of doubt. Any one who should have sought to do the work by a frontal attack, directly antagonizing the established faith as such, would but have put himself in mortal danger. Rabelais, in a previous generation, had need to cover his assaults on bigotry by an exuberant parade of buffoonery; and when Montaigne doubtfully spoke of Rabelais's books as merely amusing —a term which has dissatisfied many good Rabelaisians —he was probably not blind to Rabelais's real service, but simply careful not to lay significant stress on it. It suited at once Montaigne's ultimate purpose and his cast of mind to set out by challenging in particular the Protestant innovators in religion and the unbelievers. The 'Apology for Raymond Sebond' begins by professing to vindicate that respectable theologian, who had methodically vindicated theism, providence, and revelation, against all who called them in question. Montaigne naturally leant to the side of his father, who had enjoined upon him the translation of Sebond's Latin treatise into French ; and he professes to have retained his own orthodoxy intact in the face of all assaults upon it. But his charge against heretics and unbelievers is not that they lack faith and orthodoxy ; it is that they are unwarrantably confident in the inerrancy of reason.

This again was a strictly orthodox line of attack : 'philosophic' scepticism was already an established weapon against rationalism and in the defence of the Catholic faith ; as it was later in the hands of Huet and others. But no one, perhaps, ever employed it so vigorously against any form of reasoned religious or irreligious conviction as does Montaigne. Sebond, writing about a century and a half earlier, had placed man high in the scheme of things, extolling reason as a divine gift. Montaigne, at this stage full of the Pyrrhonism he had drawn from Sextus Empiricus, will allow no virtue to reason save as a means of discrediting reason. Having scouted its constructive pretensions, he proceeds, under the flag of faith, to turn his battery on the very convictions which ostensibly underlie faith, putting every species of *a priori* belief on one footing. Thus all forms of dogmatism are alike discredited as phases of the same folly of certitude on matters essentially uncertain.

And there was no counsel that the age more needed. For a whole generation, men had grown more and more indurated in enmity over issues of creed and formula, church government, ritual and doctrine, till it seemed as if France were realizing Armageddon. As early as 1580, it was estimated that 800,000 lives had been destroyed in battle and massacre, nine towns razed, 250 villages burned, and 128,000 houses ruined, with brigandage everywhere on foot. After 1580 there was much further fighting, bloodshed, and destruction. And still nothing was settled. The Protestants had set out to challenge the established system with all the asperity of earnest theologians, utterly convinced of their own rightness and of the wrongness of what they attacked. In the Sacred Books they felt they had at once a basis that could not be shaken and a guidance which could not mislead ; and the resistance they encountered was for them that of men clinging to temporalities and blind to any other consideration. Broadly speaking, perhaps, this was true. The most resented heresies were always those which endangered church revenues and churchmen's power. But in the nature of things the Protestant divines also sought, and needed, power and revenue ; and the transference to them of the Catholic endowments in a large part of Switzerland, to say nothing of the secularization of

Church property in England, precluded any great pretence of unworldliness on the side of the new opinion.

Montaigne had quite sincerely resented the unending turmoil created by the Reform doctrines. For him they were but reckless enforcements of new dogmas against old, by men no better qualified to dogmatize than their fathers had been, and culpably heedless of the frightful social consequences of their demands. In this mood, he was little concerned to plead for toleration for their forms of worship, which, indeed, with the accompanying system of new Church government, promised an ultimate state of things wherein, as in Geneva and England and Scotland, scanty tolerance would be shown to Catholics. That Montaigne should have taken the oath of the fanatical Paris Parlement in 1562 speaks rather ill for his judgement at that stage—if indeed it was not practically dictated to him; but many men not lacking in judgement have pronounced that the dream of mutual toleration then cherished by the great Chancellor de L'Hôpital was that of a man who simply could not realize the nature of the forces facing him. Montaigne, nevertheless, came to respect him deeply as a great man and a true patriot.

Whether or not Montaigne had any painful searchings of heart after taking the oath of 1562, he has not told us. But he has abundantly revealed how he recoiled from the ever-intensifying fury of the later Leaguers, and that the Massacre of St. Bartholomew's Day was for him a profoundly shattering and revolting experience, fixing his determination to keep aloof to the utmost of his power from the party principles which led to such practice. Some of the burning phrases in the 'Apology' (Book II, xii) are evidently struck from him by that frightful memory. Thenceforth it was clear to him that the one thing he could do for his country was to undermine as he best might the deadly certitudes that had turned France into a scene of savagery and desolation. Though he repeats, and never retracts, his keen indictment of the Huguenots for having plunged their country into the whirlpool of civil war, he so bore himself latterly that he was by many reckoned one of their party. As he tells us, he met such charges with mockery, disdaining to exculpate himself. In his book, his vehement censure of the Reformers could best gain him the ear of the Catholics; and so he compassed his end.

No line of policy that might have been proposed to kings and chiefs of faction could avail. The kings and the Protestant faction-leaders were not the main determining forces. It is clear that Charles IX and Henry III, and Catherine de Médicis before them, were alike willing to come to terms with the Protestants, seeing in the Catholic faction headed by the Guises a more dangerous enemy to their dynasty. By the zealots behind them they were baffled and driven to worse courses, till finally Henry III was assassinated. On the other hand, as Montaigne knew, Henry of Navarre was no fanatical Protestant, but one who had to go warily lest he should alienate his more zealous followers. It was the general spirit of fierce fanatical certitude, on both sides, that maintained the state of chronic civil war, the continuous demoralization of civil life, the anarchy and the deepening impoverishment of the whole realm. Montaigne early learned to see in Henry of Navarre the hope of the future; but Henry would be powerless in a France of unimpaired fanaticism. It was for Montaigne, then, to play the sapper and miner of the old order of things; and this purpose, once fortuitously formed, can be seen to underlie at length the bulk of his writing.

In the 'Apology for Raymond Sebond' he can be seen as it were giving out, under cover of orthodoxy, his own reaction, in his first years of retreat, against all the dogmatism of his age. It appears to have been written at intervals round 1576, when he had a medal struck with his effigy and the inscription *Que sçay je?* 'What know I?' Portions cannot be of earlier date than 1578. The result is a treatise in which credulity and incredulity, faith in tradition and derision of common belief, insistence on scientific doubt and disparagement of all science, oddly alternate. But the total effect is a discrediting of the normal religious certitudes.

That ethics are matters of custom ; that creeds are matters of place of birth ; that Moslem faith is the twin of Christian faith ; that religious zeal turns men into savages ; that wars are matters of mere nationality or of mere partisanship ; that men in the mass are for ever ignorantly sure of what they know nothing about, and childishly heedless of how they risk life and well-being for vain causes—such is the burden of Montaigne's 'sceptical' polemic, addressed to a generation that had brought France nigh to both moral and material ruin by stress of the certitudes in question.

It is forcing an open door to retort that Montaigne, parading universal 'doubt', was no consistent sceptic. Of course he was not, as he expressly avows ; though for a time he sought to be, sawing at the bough on which he sat. For a time, perhaps, he had little confidence in any abstract moral proposition ; and, living in an age whose 'science' had its hinder parts embedded in delusion, he was always dubious about science, new and old. When certitude spelt havoc, such a rebounding spirit as his might touch the state of universal uncertainty which some of his earlier essays profess. But his large and sane understanding and his searching thought soon brought him to steady moral bearings. When he had re-made his philosophy of life for himself, he was full of hearty certitudes, moral, educational, political, and literary. The certitudes he distrusted and deprecated were mainly those which made men anti-moral, disloyal, internecine, barbarian, decivilized. That these things were bad, he never doubted. A sceptic in the strict theoretic sense, indeed, a doubter of all things, a consistent 'Pyrrhonist', never existed, as Montaigne himself observes. Pyrrho at his start evoked the challenging and unanswerable question whether he doubted that he doubted ; and Montaigne's polemic was but a shrewd yet artless strategy to turn fierce believers into sobered doubters on one side, by showing them that the enduring certitudes lay with the vital pieties of human relationship, which were being utterly lost in the desperate maintenance of the other sort.

It is not to be pretended that he was all along clear and

consistent in his thought. His dialectic often outgoes his own conviction, and clashes flatly with his profession of faith. And though it may be argued, as by his latest and most accomplished editor, the veteran Dr. Armaingaud, that some of his self-contradictions are deliberate and strategic, some are not so describable. Just as he at times contradicts himself, within a page, on concrete matters, through sheer change of mood or stress of argument, he varies in his philosophic positions. Few men of his day, indeed, passed their intuitions and their prepossessions so energetically through the alembic of thought; but to the last he exhibits some that have not undergone the process. He shaped his philosophy as he went along, expressing himself differently at different times, constantly avowing, even in excess of the fact, that he was 'undulating and diverse' in his thinking. This was at once his security and half the secret of his influence. Had he been the confident framer of a new system of precise doctrine, he would have aroused hot hostility where in his own way he disarmed it. His congenital conservatism, making him dubious about Copernicanism and many other 'upsetting' notions, gave him a footing with many who might easily have been alienated by any large show of faith in 'new-fangled' doctrines. His flouting of innovation won him their ear for his counsels against dogmatism. The outcome was that on the wasting fever of French fanaticism Montaigne sprinkled cool reason, and thus wrought incalculably to prepare for the better life that was to come with the advent of Henry of Navarre, the king who thought that 'Paris was well worth a Mass', entered it without a siege, and made peace by declaring himself a Catholic while securing for Protestants complete liberty of worship. That was the king for Montaigne, who would have given him a delighted acclamation had he lived to see his crowning.

To note the evolution is to realize at once the sagacity and the efficacy of Montaigne's literary course. He has been on the one hand censured for circuitous tactics, and on the other praised for pioneering hardihood. Both views have their measure of justification. Montaigne's tactic was the only one that in his day could have to any important extent carried his point. He was, in fact, playing with fire, and could succeed only by protesting that he was but playing. Yet he writes at times with an astonishing temerity ; and not least audaciously when he humorously hints that he means more than he says. It is to be suspected, on the other hand, that the tissue of trivialities which he spins in the closing essay was inserted by way of giving an air of slightness to the whole, as well as of covering the mordancy of some sayings in that very essay. How dangerous it was to do the same work in a systematic and dead-serious fashion was seen in the decade after his death, when his friend and disciple, the churchman Charron, put into his treatise *Of Wisdom*, in close order, the gist of Montaigne's teaching, unwittingly bringing out the contradictions in startling relief. The disciple was execrated and persecuted where the master had gone scot-free. The famous *Satyre Ménippée*, a witty composition which in 1593 brought to the work of pacification the powerful weapon of ridicule, wielded by *politiques*—Catholics who were tired of Spanish fomenting of French strifes—has been disparaged as ' belated ' in relation to Montaigne's pioneering. But before Montaigne had cooled the old fervours, direct ridicule of Catholic fanaticism would have been as impracticable, in orthodox circles, as direct impeachment of Catholic beliefs. The *Satyre*, which ran through three editions in three weeks, was the practical corollary of Montaigne's subtle permeation ; and the whole movement culminated in Henry's coronation and in the establishment of toleration by the Edict of Nantes.

If we turn aside from the course of State life to that of philosophic thought, we see the influence of Montaigne at work in another fashion. The reconsideration of faith and dogma had of course begun long before him : the very treatise of Raymond Sebond was a reaction against it in the previous century ; and such writings as those of Bonaventure des Périers were partly co-operant with those of

Montaigne in his own day. But the 'Apology for Raymond Sebond', and the recurrent pressure of the same course of thought in Montaigne's later essays, constituted the most effective impulse of the kind that had yet arisen. The covert humour of Montaigne outdid the humorism of Des Périers. The once famous treatise of Sanchez (1581) *Quod Nihil Scitur*, 'That Nothing is to be Known,' is thoroughly sceptical; but to read it is to listen to the click of logical castanets, and to turn away unmoved. Montaigne's impact is vital. It is accordingly a warrantable statement that Montaigne is the spiritual father of Descartes, as Descartes in turn was the spiritual father of Spinoza. This does not seem to have been fully realized in Descartes' own day, by reason of the complete contrast between his grave methodic ways and the gaily unmethodic fashion of Montaigne, as well as of the conflict of their views on reason in animals; but in retrospect it seems clear enough. And the fact that Montaigne was not soon recognized as a philosophic force is the decisive proof of the completeness with which he had achieved his practical end, the undermining of active fanaticism, the lowering of men's blood pressures, the change of mood which put peace and progress in place of wholly destructive strife.

He had at once reached the audience that he required. From the first he was the favourite author of country squires; and he professed to grumble over the fact that ladies read him for pastime. It was thus that he was civilizing his nation. Not all at once, of course, and not at all completely. In the next century, Madame de Sévigné professed to adore him; and she doubtless enjoyed the *Essais* greatly, being herself a woman of genius, with the gift of putting things adhesively. Yet, with the ruck of her generation, she acclaimed the Revocation, by Louis XIV, of the Edict of Nantes, the enactment of which by Henry IV in 1598 had been the benign solution of the Wars of Religion, and would as such have been hailed by Montaigne had he been then alive. Madame de Sévigné hailed its undoing. That is the way of women, as of men. But nevertheless the humane wisdom of Montaigne had entered into the life-blood of France, and of the world. In his essay on the upbringing of boys there is a picture of a mother rejoicing in the spectacle of her boy wringing, in manly fashion, the neck of a chicken. You will find it subtly reproduced by Shakespeare, in *Coriolanus*, where the victim is a butterfly. Montaigne had touched a kindred spirit on that issue.

III

His quiet success was the outcome of three factors, his manifold matter, his unmethodical method, and his unmannered manner. His serious counsel was the febrifuge that most men needed. But it was blended with a vast variety of expatiation on a hundred topics of human interest, the talk of a widely read and widely interested man, chatting with his fellows as having no axe to grind, but merely delivering himself of most of the thoughts and comments on life that came to him in the chances of his discursive reading and his daily experience. No such mass of diversely interesting discourse had been put forth by any modern before the appearance of the expanded edition of the Essays in 1588.

It was indeed no small range of fascinating talk that won for Montaigne the ear of his countrymen in an age in which such serious counsels as his were by so many viewed askance. They were won by a quite novel vivacity of discussion of life in all its aspects, in which the perilous thoughts passed in the crowd of others. And he whose main service to his age was to calm passions that are now obsolescent is just as readable in ours by force of his vividness, his variety, his reality. In the age of Sidney he spontaneously acted on Sidney's counsel to the English rhymers. He looked in his heart and wrote.

Hence the Essays differed vitally from the most famous work of previous publicists, such as Petrarch and Erasmus and Lipsius, in respect of a new simplicity and spontaneity, a disregard of all academic artifice, alike in style and in structure. And this course was not taken for lack of literary instinct, but because of an instinct freshly alive. No man knew better than Montaigne the force of style at its best. In one essay, of equivocal inspiration, he breaks away in a truly well-inspired excursus on the potency of the right choice of words as made by the old masters of the art—the cry of a reader who from youth up had been progressively bored by the arts of the schooled virtuosi in prose and verse.

Montaigne's main literary secret is the resort to the mood of animated conversation for his driving force; the fit method of one who never planned an essay as it came to be finished, and who to the last was capable of inserting new blocks of matter in old discourses, with small concern for the sequence of the paragraphs. As against the essayists of the desk, he is the essayist of the armchair. He does not conceal his secret. 'The style I like', he writes (I, xxvi), 'is one that is simple and unaffected, the same in writing as on the tongue; a succulent and nervous style, terse and packed; not so much elegant and trimmed as vehement and brusque.' In his case, the style was truly the man. In reading many serious authors of that and previous centuries we have a sense as of listening to falsetto, or to the 'intoning' of the pulpit. In Montaigne we get always the living voice. And thus he adds to the effect of his utterance that of urgent personality, which is one of the vitalizing forces of literature. When matter and manner thus coalesce, as for instance in the essay just cited, there results an impact on the reader's whole perceptive faculties such as no writer on education before or since has surpassed, even though the doctrine be classic.

Launched at last on the enterprise of expressing his 'me' in as many of its facets as he was concerned to expose—and they were many, though not all—he utters himself with the stress and vivacity which, as he tells us, belonged to his conversation. He confesses to a vehement exuberance of asseveration in his talk, a characteristic still notable in Frenchmen of the south, whether gifted or ungifted as writers. To be direct, straightforward, keeping insistently to the point, he tells us, was his habit in talking to the great. He has paid his readers the compliment of talking to them in the same fashion; though with a breadth and range of discourse, and at times of impropriety, beyond the normal limits of spoken converse.

That conforms spontaneously to his character. Rhetoric he recognizes as the stock-in-trade of the conventional thinker and the professional demagogue. At the outset, despite his appreciation of skilled style, he places Cicero, the master of rhetoric, lower than Seneca, the man specially concerned for conduct; and Seneca, finally, he ranks below Plutarch (so pleasantly translated for him by Amyot), the writer who is so sure of his principles that he is content to let them be carried on the stream either of biography or essay, with a minimum of scholastic argumentation. Plutarch's essays, if any, are Montaigne's models after he has settled down to his work as an essayist.

But no essayist of any age has talked about himself and everything else with such radiant energy as fills his page after he has got into his stride. Of all his classics he makes literary booty; but no collector of quotations—unless it be, on a more dusty pilgrimage, our own Robert Burton (who seems to have invented many of *his* citations)—has ever so assimilated his learning to his purpose, so impressed his own spirit on all his gathered material. Perhaps he is less than fair (Book III, viii) to Commines and others when he taxes them with putting as their own the sententious sayings of classic writers. That he has himself done many a time. But, influenced by others, as he confessedly had been, to multiply quotations in his later editions, he could defend himself by saying that his own habit and intention is to give his quotation rather than to conceal his source, while claiming that the old thoughts are his thoughts also. 'It is no more according to Plato than according to me,' as he himself puts it: the wisdom of the ancients has become his wisdom, and it reaches us with a new life in his distillation. If the classics served him well, he no less well served the classics. More readers, probably, have through him come to relish the wisdom of antiquity than through any competing form of instruction. In Montaigne, the men of the past and those of the present are of one family and of one speech; the men of Plutarch are his friends and intimates as nearly as his neighbours and his readers.

It is this living utterance, and this unlimited interest in everything human, that gives him his hold on all the generations since his time. In his quite different way, he conveys that sense of universality of outlook that we find in Shakespeare, and call Shakespearian. The two minds are alike cosmopolitan, open-eyed on all sides, responsive to all human concerns, cognizant of the sins of the great and the virtues of the poor, and of the littlenesses and the absurdities of all.

It was the most natural thing in the world that the Essays, as translated by his acquaintance, 'resolute John Florio,' should be conned by Shakespeare even before the folio of them was printed off in 1603; and that we should find in his plays of that period a multitude of echoes of their thought and phrase. All the alert spirits of the time must have responded to Montaigne in England as in France. Bacon, Ben Jonson, Chapman, Daniel, Webster, all paid him heed. The lax use of the word 'debt' in this connexion, seeming to overlook the fact that Montaigne's own 'debts' were overwhelming, has aroused a needless resentment among some Shakespearians, who superfluously argue that Shakespeare could think his own thoughts, and had his genius in his own right. They had better have employed Montaigne's own retort and said, 'It is no more according to Montaigne than according to Shakespeare'. But it was not for nothing that Montaigne was steeped in the didactic classics from childhood to age. Half the time the communicated thought is according to the ancients, new minted by Montaigne, and newly relished through him by Shakespeare as by more learned readers. The genius of rhythmic utterance, by which the poet turned all thought at once to beauty and to dramatic illustration, is a new enhancement of the Frenchman's vibrating prose. But the highest ' debt ' we can owe to an author is to be moved by him to think better ; and it is no rash guess that Shakespeare was stirred by Montaigne's frequent extolling of ' Nature ' above ' Art ' to reach the larger truth that the art which is thought to outgo Nature ' is an art that Nature makes '. Montaigne, schooled by the Stoics and faced by a society often evilly sophisticated, did not steadily see, though he at times clearly glimpsed, the scientific truth that ' Nature ' is just everything, and that the new is good and bad as the old was.

It is assuredly no disparagement to Shakespeare that he should have been stirred and stimulated by a writer who so affected many of his best contemporaries in his own land, and has so influenced ten generations of French and English men of letters since. If only he could have been effectually assimilated in time, Montaigne might have done for England as a whole, in the next generation, some such service as he had done to France. But the dread fever of fanatical strife was to break out first in Germany, and soon afterwards in the island realm ; and not till that age was over did the essayist effectively come into his own with Englishmen. When he did, he served to prelude and introduce a new era of tolerance.

As early as 1685, Charles Cotton, the friend of Izaak Walton, translating the Essays anew with much more nearly exact scholarship and vigilance than had been bestowed on the work by the brave Florio, championed Montaigne against French dissentient criticism with a cordial force which won for him in England a new and enduring vogue, and this before the message of the Essays had created a new school of Montaignists in eighteenth-century France. In the nineteenth century, Montaigne came more and more fully into his own, Emerson being for the English-reading world his most effective herald ; till latterly the propaganda has been swelled by four competent English monographs, two of them by women students. Between such expositions and those of the eminent French scholars who have in the last half-century newly elucidated and edited the Essays,

Montaigne is to-day better understood and more widely read than ever before.

Hence the need for a new English translation. Florio's will always be a pleasant field for the lovers of Elizabethan English, with its rich 'crusted' vocabulary and its large prosody ; but Florio makes mistakes past counting, and hardly in any Essay does he fail to make a little nonsense somewhere. It is no shame to him. Professor Dowden has declared that Montaigne is at once the most translatable and the most untranslatable of writers ; but if the first clause is to suggest that his meaning is always apparent, it must be challenged. Charles Cotton modestly wrote :

> 'In truth, both Mr. Florio and I are to be excused, where we miss the sense of the author, whose language is such in many places as grammar cannot reconcile, which renders it the hardest book to make a justifiable version of that I yet ever saw in that or any other language I understand ; insomuch that though I do think, and am pretty confident, I understand French as well as many men, I have yet sometimes been forced to grope at his meaning. Peradventure the greatest critic would in some places have found my author abstruse enough.'

It is indeed no shame to the modest Cotton to have miscarried oftener than he suspected, or to his emendators to have left some of his errors standing, when we have the expert French testimony of Professor Pierre Villey that 'Our experience of university lectures has taught us that the language of Montaigne, even for instructed readers, lends itself to constant and serious contradictions of meaning.'

To be often obscure is a characteristic of Montaigne as of Shakespeare ; the difference here being that the text is rarely to be suspected of mere press corruption—though he tells us that that did happen—and that the difficulties are mainly of Montaigne's own making. He is not only highly idiomatic but Gascon, and old Gascon at that ; his hurrying thought at times entangles itself in the most perplexing way ; and now and then by an unrevised alteration he contrives to say the opposite of what can be seen to have been his meaning. A text, in fine, the interpretation of which frequently gives trouble to accomplished French specialists, must be often hard to render aright in English. It is safe to say of the translation of Mr. Trechmann, revised in the light of the preceding ones and of the best French editions and interpretations of recent years, that none has been more patiently and more watchfully made, and none brought nearer to all-round accuracy.

The result is that, as regards Montaigne's meaning, the English reader is now abreast of the French student, aided by the latest expert scholarship. And if it be argued, in the sense of Professor Dowden's second clause, that the savour and flavour of Montaigne cannot really be conveyed in another tongue, the answer is that his prose at least loses much less by translation than does most great poetry ; and that in point of meaning he is here made more continuously clear than he is in the original for any one but a close student. And that is much.. Montaigne, once more be it said, is not a consistent or systematic thinker. His very vivacity involved exaggeration, so that we find him on one leaf accusing his countrymen of a dissembling avoidance of argument because they cannot endure it, and on the next scolding them for the habitual violence of their disputes. And this is not a solitary sample. When his devoted exponent, Dr. Armaingaud, is fain to argue that his vindication of ignorance is not sincere, we must indeed avow that at times he writes, as aforesaid, with strategy. But we are on safer ground when we say that he is a man of shifting moods, sometimes setting up what he has deposed. And still he remains one of the most acute of all writers on life and opinion, action and impulse, the folly, the wisdom, and the potentialities for good inherent in erring humanity of all grades ; and to realize exactly what he means is eminently worth the while of all who read him at all. A 'bedside book' for many, as he was for Thackeray, he is also fitly to be read with the most alert attention.

Ranging from the frankest coarseness (outdone only by our own Chaucer and some of our later clerical classics, as

Donne, Herrick, and Swift), to the most earnest brooding on life and death, the most heart-searching study of the human soul, he is one of the living voices of the past for all to whom the past is voiceful. If he offends at one time, he makes good at another. At times disrespectful to women, he can treat them at others with the true respect which counts them equally interested with men in the main concerns of life; and he has had as many appreciative women students as any bookman of his age. And if it is his special distinction to be intellectually more akin to later ages than to his own, in respect of his agnostic outlook on ultimate problems, he is none the less acceptable to multitudes who adhere to the old ways. More than one student has undertaken, with what success it is needless to inquire, the vindication of his orthodoxy, in defiance of the ban of Pascal. The moral would seem to be that nothing human was to him alien; and that the recluse who professed to turn his back on the world remained one of its most intimate correspondents, as he is one of its most universally laurelled names.

He certainly lends himself to gainsaying. No man of his power ever dilated so largely in small talk. Some readers never get over the shock of his incidental remark that he had lost two or three children (there were really five who so died!) at nurse; and that though he sorrowed he did not lastingly grieve. Others find his *insouciant* attitude towards his wife and daughter a matter for charges of egoism, and indeed it would not be surprising if they did not warmly cherish his memory. But, though his latest editor is probably right in deciding that the essayist is concealing much family affection under airs of carelessness, charges of egoism would not in the least have discomposed Montaigne. Was he not making a frank parade of it? All those avowals are made with the ever-implicit comment: 'See what I am; see what men are: let us have no concealments'. When the personal details are most egoistic he is perfectly aware of the part he is playing, even if there be a latent concern for the friendly interest of the reader. One thing he will not have : he will not cater for esteem on false pretences. And it is not ultimately esteem on any grounds that he is seeking : it is the unfaltering presentment of the truth about all things, so far as a man may speak in the days of the wars of religion, and preserve (save in Latin) the irreducible proprieties—none other being recognized.

And the result is that, as Miss Sichel has put it, ' he who has read Montaigne is, if he be candid, never quite the same man again : while he thinks he has only been gossiped with, he has had his outlook changed '. And this involves the just judgement, first put by Miss Lowndes, that Montaigne is not to be called a ' Representative Man '—the label under which Emerson laxly classed him in his otherwise vivid presentment. The great essayist is not a representative man at all, in any practical sense—if there be any—of that phrase. Yet he is a man of many affinities ; and Emerson, who likes him even to the point of condoning his grossnesses, a thing he would not do for Gibbon, had with him many mental features in common, down to that of chronic loss of hold on syntax. By simply being himself, and revealing himself, Montaigne has made a unique contribution to the literature of the world.

But it would be an injustice to him, and a disservice to literature, to convey the notion that he has made his effect by disregarding the art of writing. When all is said, it is as an admirable writer that he lives for us. And whatever he may say in the Essay ' A Consideration upon Cicero ' (I, xl) of his resentment at being praised for his style, which he perversely represents as a way of disparaging his matter, he took in his own fashion as much pains with his style as he well could. The reader of English translations of him should know, what is made obvious in the later French editions with textual notes, that the *Essais* were revised and expanded at a thousand points, the process continuing after the main expansion of 1588. Few great books have been so abundantly retouched and amended ; and to read it in the edition of Villey or of Armaingaud is to see its whole growth, from the purposeless and perfunctory beginnings to the ever firmer and more daring deliverance of his thought, in so far as it was avowable. In the end he reaches a finesse and a humorous mastery of his undertaking that may be said to constitute him a modern of the moderns. Three elements, broadly speaking, go to the making of enduring literature, the factors of style (in the widest sense), of impact of personality, and of vital purport. In Montaigne these are all at work in a high degree; the second, perhaps, in the highest; but the first in a degree not before attained in post-classic prose. And so, whatever we may think of him and his doctrine, he is a permanent figure in the world of books.

J. M. ROBERTSON.

To the Reader

THIS is a sincere book, Reader. It forewarns you at the outset that in writing it I had no other but a private and family end in view. I thought neither of being serviceable to you, nor of my own fame. My powers are not equal to such a design. I intended it solely for the solace of my kinsfolk and friends: that, when they have lost me (as they must do before long), they may recover in it some lines of my character and humours, and by this means more fully and vividly cherish me in their memory.

Had my intention been to court the world's favour, I should have trimmed myself more bravely, and stood before it in a studied attitude. I desire to be seen in my simple, natural, and everyday dress, without artifice or constraint; for it is myself I portray. My faults may therein be read to the life, and my native form, as far as my respect to the public has permitted.

For, if my lot had been cast among those nations who are said to be still living in the sweet freedom of Nature's first laws, I assure you that I should have been quite prepared to give a full-length, and quite naked, portrait of myself.

So, Reader, I am myself the subject of my book; it is not reasonable to expect you to waste your leisure on a matter so frivolous and empty.

Farewell then, from MONTAIGNE, this first day of March, 1580.

Book the First

CHAPTER 1

BY VARIOUS MEANS WE ARRIVE AT THE SAME END

THE most common way to soften the hearts of those we have offended, when they have us at their mercy and are able to take revenge, is to move them to pity and commiseration by submission. Nevertheless, bravery and fortitude, quite contrary means, have sometimes wrought the same effect.

Edward, Prince of Wales, the same who was so long Regent in our Guienne, a personage who, by nature and fortune, had many and noteworthy attributes of greatness, having been grievously offended by the Limousins, and having taken their city by force, could not be stayed by the cries of the inhabitants, including women and children, given over to slaughter, throwing themselves at his feet and imploring his mercy, until, penetrating further into the town, he perceived three French gentlemen who, with incredible valour, were alone resisting the onslaught of his victorious army. Admiration and respect for this remarkable bravery at once blunted the edge of his anger, and, beginning with these three, he showed mercy to all the other inhabitants of the city.[1]

Scanderbeg, Prince of Epirus,[2] was pursuing one of his soldiers with intent to kill him, and the latter, having tried in vain to appease him by humble prayers and supplications, determined in his extremity to await him with sword in hand. This bold attitude put a sudden end to his master's fury, who received him into grace for his noble bearing. This example might be differently interpreted by such as

[1] This incident, which took place in 1370, is told by Froissart, who remarks however that the generosity of the Black Prince towards the three noblemen did not arrest the sacking of the city.

[2] George Castriot, an Albanian prince surnamed Scanderbeg (1414–67), an inveterate adversary of the Turks.

have not read of the prodigious strength and bravery of that prince.

The Emperor Conrad the Third having besieged Guelph,[1] Duke of Bavaria, though offered the most abject submission, would condescend to no milder conditions than that the gentlewomen who were besieged with the Duke should alone be allowed to leave the city on foot, with their honour unsullied, and with only so much as they were able to carry on their persons. The ladies showed their greatness of heart by loading on their backs their husbands, their children, and the Duke himself. The Emperor was so pleased with their pretty courage that he wept for joy, and put away all the bitterness and mortal enmity which he had borne against the Duke, and from that moment he treated him and his people with all humanity.

For my part, I could easily be moved by either of these means, for I am weakly and strangely inclined to mercy and indulgence; to such a degree that I imagine I should more naturally yield to compassion than to admiration. Yet the Stoics look upon pity as a fault: we should succour the afflicted, they hold, without being moved so far as to suffer with them.

Now these examples seem the more appropriate as we observe these souls, assailed and tried in these two several ways, resisting the one without weakening, and bowing to the other. It may be said that to break one's heart in commiseration is the mark of an easy, soft, and gentle nature, whence it comes that the weaker natures, as those of women, children, and the common people, are most subject to it; but that, after disdaining tears and prayers, to give way solely to respect for the sacred image of valour, is the mark of a strong and unyielding soul, that loves and honours a manly and obstinate courage.

Nevertheless, admiration and astonishment may similarly affect less generous natures: witness the people of Thebes who, having put their captains, Pelopidas and Epaminondas, on trial for a capital offence, which was that they had continued their charge beyond the time prescribed to them, were with great difficulty persuaded to absolve Pelopidas who, bowing under the weight of his accusations, relied on

---

[1] At Weinsberg in 1140. The incident forms the subject of a poem by Schiller, *Die Weiber von Weinsberg*.

appeals and supplications to save himself; whereas Epaminondas magniloquently recounted the deeds he had performed in their service, flinging them, as it were, in the face of the people with a haughty and arrogant mien, with the result that they had not the heart even to take the ballot-balls in hand, and the assembly broke up with loud praises for the lofty courage of that general.

Dionysius the Elder having, after a long and extremely difficult siege, taken the city of Rhegium and with it the captain Phyto, a great and worthy man, who had offered so stubborn a defence, was resolved to take a tragic and exemplary revenge on him. He first told him how he had the day before drowned his son and all his kindred, to which Phyto merely replied, 'that they were a day nearer happiness than he'. He then had him seized, stripped, and dragged through the town by his executioners, whilst he himself mercilessly and ignominiously whipped him, loading him at the same time with cruel insults. Phyto did not lose heart; but, on the contrary, with raised voice and unmoved countenance, recalled the glorious and honourable cause of his death, namely that he would not deliver his country into the hands of a tyrant, and threatened him with the speedy punishment of the gods. Dionysius, reading in the eyes of most of his soldiers that, far from being incensed by the bravado of this vanquished enemy and his contempt for their chief and his triumph, they were not only moved to astonishment by this show of valour, but even half inclined to rise in mutiny and on the point of snatching Phyto out of the hands of his minions, made an end of his martyrdom and sent him secretly to be drowned in the sea.

Truly man is a marvellously vain, fickle, and unstable creature, on whom it is difficult to found a certain and uniform judgement. Here we see Pompey pardoning the whole city of the Mamertines, with whom he was greatly angered, in consideration of the valour and magnanimity of the citizen Sthenon, who took upon himself the whole guilt of the people, and demanded no other favour but to bear alone the punishment; yet Sylla's host, who showed a like valour in the city of Perusia,[1] gained nothing either for himself or his fellow-citizens.

---

[1] Should be Praeneste, a city of Latium, and not Perusia. This

And, in direct contradiction to my first examples, Alexander, the boldest of men and so gracious to the vanquished, having, after many and great difficulties, forced the city of Gaza, came upon Beltis, who was in command there, and of whose valour he had during the siege experienced some wonderful proofs, now alone, abandoned by his troops, his arms broken in pieces, covered with blood and wounds, still fighting in the midst of a number of Macedons, who were belabouring him on all sides. Provoked by so dearly bought a victory (for among other injuries, he had received two fresh wounds on his person), Alexander said to him, ' You shall not die as you have wished, Beltis ; be sure that you shall suffer all the torments that may be invented for a captive ' ; to which menace the other returned no other answer but a proud and haughty look. Alexander then, observing his fierce and stubborn silence, ' Has he bent a knee ? has any suppliant voice escaped him ? Truly I will conquer this silence, and if I cannot wrest a word from him, I will at least wrest a groan ', and, his rage turning to fury, he ordered his heels to be pierced and had him dragged alive, torn and dismembered, at a cart's tail.

Can it have been that fearlessness was so familiar to him that he respected it the less for not being able to admire it ? Or that he esteemed it so peculiar to himself that he could not suffer to see it in so high a degree in another without vexation and envy ? Or was it that the natural impetuosity of his anger could brook no opposition ? In truth, if he had been capable of curbing it, we may believe that he would have done so at the capture and desolation of the city of Thebes, when he saw so many valiant men, lost and totally destitute of common defence, put to the sword. For no less than six thousand were killed, not one of whom was seen to fly or cry for quarter ; on the contrary, they sought, some here, some there, throughout the streets of the city, to confront the victorious enemy, provoking them to put them to an honourable death. Not one was seen so disheartened by wounds but he still tried with his last breath to avenge himself, and, with the weapons of despair, to find consolation for his own death in the death of an

error appeared in the first edition of Amyot's *Plutarch*, but was afterwards rectified.

enemy. The distress shown in their valour, however, found no pity, and the length of a day was not sufficient to quench Alexander's thirst for revenge ; the carnage continued until there was not a drop of blood left to shed, and was not stayed till all were killed except the unarmed, old men, women and children, who were enslaved to the number of thirty thousand.

CHAPTER 2
OF SADNESS

I AM more free from this feeling than most men,[1] neither loving nor admiring it, although the world has agreed, as if by common consent, to honour it with particular favour. They clothe therewith wisdom, virtue, and conscience : a foolish and unsightly ornament ! The Italians have more suitably bestowed the name on *malignity*,[2] for it is a quality ever hurtful, ever foolish. The Stoics will not allow their sage to entertain this feeling, as being always degrading and cowardly.

But the story goes that Psammenitus, King of Egypt, being defeated and taken prisoner by Cyrus, King of Persia, and seeing his captive daughter, dressed as a slave, pass him on her way to draw water, and all his friends weeping and wailing around him, kept his eyes fixed on the ground without uttering a word ; presently seeing his son led to his death, he continued in the same attitude, but when he saw one of his intimate friends led among the captives, he began in an excess of grief to beat his head.

This incident might be matched with what recently happened to one of our princes,[3] who, being at Trent and receiving news of the death of his eldest brother, but a brother who was the pride and support of his whole house, and soon after of that of a younger brother, the second hope of the family, sustained both these blows with an exemplary fortitude ; when, however, one of his men died a few days

---

[1] Montaigne means that he is not of a melancholy disposition.
[2] Italian *tristezza* means ' malignity ' as well as ' sadness '.
[3] The Cardinal de Lorraine who, at the Council of Trent, heard of the tragic death of the Duc de Guise on the 24th February 1563, and that of François de Lorraine, Grand Prior of France, on the 6th March following.

later, he was driven out of his firm attitude and abandoned himself to sorrow and tears. Some have argued that this last shock alone had touched him to the quick; but the truth is that, being already full to overflowing with sorrow, the slightest addition broke down the barriers of his endurance. The same interpretation, I say, might be put on our first story, if it had not been added that, Cambyses questioning Psammenitus as to why, though unmoved by the fate of his son and daughter, he bore so impatiently that of a friend, he replied, 'that the last calamity alone could find a vent in tears, the two first being quite beyond the power of expression'.

Perhaps the same idea was in the mind of a certain painter[1] who, in a picture representing the sacrifice of Iphigenia, attempted to depict the grief of the onlookers according to the degree of concern which each might feel over the fate of the beautiful and innocent girl. When he came to the maiden's father, having exhausted the resources of his art, he painted him with his face covered, thereby indicating that no expression was capable of doing justice to a parent's sorrow. For the same reason the poets, when they sing of Niobe, the wretched mother who lost seven sons and immediately after as many daughters, imagine her as turning to a rock,

> petrified by evils, (OVID.)

thereby to express that dull and mute and deaf stupefaction which paralyses us when crushed by a calamity that exceeds our power of endurance.

Indeed, the effect of an affliction, when extreme, must of necessity be to stun the whole soul and hinder its freedom of action; so it happens that, when alarmed by a piece of very bad news, we are seized, paralysed, and as it were crippled in all our movements, until the soul, after melting into tears and lamentations, appears to disengage and unravel itself, and become more at ease and free to act:

> Till speech, half choked with sorrow, finds a way. (VIRGIL.)

In the war which King Ferdinand waged, around Buda, against the widow of King John of Hungary, Raïsciac, a

---

[1] According to Quintilian, the painter was Timanthes of Cythnos, a contemporary of Zeuxis and Parrhasios.

German captain, seeing the body of a trooper being brought in, whose exceeding bravery in the fray had been observed by all, joined in the general lament; moved by the common curiosity, he came near to see who it was, and, the armour having been removed from the body, recognized his own son. Whilst all were moved to tears he alone stood there, dry-eyed and without a word, fixedly staring at the corpse until the violence of sorrow froze his life's blood, and he fell stark dead to earth.

> He knows not what it is to burn
> Who can his flame in words express, (PETRARCH.)

say the lovers, to describe an unbearable passion.

> All-conquering Lesbia, thine eyes
> Have ravished from me all my faculties:
> At the first glance of their victorious ray
> I was so struck I knew not what to say;
> Nor had a tongue to speak; a subtle flame
> Crept through my veins; my tingling ears became
> Deaf without noise, and my poor eyes I found
> With a black veil of double darkness bound. (CATULLUS.)

For it is not in the greatest heat of a paroxysm that we are fit to express our complaints and persuasions; the soul is then weighted with heavy thoughts and the body struck down and languishing with love. Hence there comes sometimes that sudden faintness which so unseasonably surprises the lover, and that chill which seizes him, by force of extreme ardour, even in the very lap of enjoyment. A passion which may be relished and digested is but a poor thing.

> Light cares find words, but heavy ones are dumb. (SENECA.)

The surprise of an unexpected joy may have a like stunning effect:

> Distracted with amaze
> She saw me, as the Trojan arms shone plain;
> Heat leaves her frame; she stiffens with the gaze,
> She swoons—and scarce at length these faltering words essays.
> (VIRGIL.)

Besides the examples of the Roman matron who died with joy on her son's unexpected return from the rout at Cannae, of Sophocles and Dionysius the tyrant, who were both killed by joy, and of Thalna who died in Corsica, reading the news of the honours which the Roman Senate had bestowed upon him, we hear, in modern times, of Pope Leo the Tenth, who fell into such an excess of joy on hearing of the taking of Milan, which he had so ardently desired, that he took a fever and died. And as a more notable testimony of human weakness it is recorded by the ancients that Diodorus the dialectician suddenly succumbed to a fit of shame for being unable to reply, in his school and before a public audience, to his adversary's arguments.

I am little subject to these violent passions, being naturally slow to apprehend, and this tendency becomes every day more crusted over and hardened by reason.

CHAPTER 3

OUR FEELINGS CONTINUE BEYOND THIS LIFE

THEY who accuse us of ever gaping after future things, and teach us to grasp and rest content with the good things of the present, as having no hold on what is to come, less indeed than we have on what is past, touch upon the most common of human errors, if they dare to call that an error to which Nature leads us in the service of continuing her handiwork. Being more jealous of what we do than of what we know, she stamps that wrong idea and many others on our minds.

We are never at home with, but always beyond, ourselves. Fear, desire, and hope impel us into the future, and rob us of the sense and consideration of that which is, in order to keep us musing over that which will be, even when we shall cease to be. *The mind is unhappy that is anxious about the future* (Seneca).

This great precept is often urged by Plato: 'Do thy business and know thyself.' Each of the two members of this precept generally comprises all our duty, and in like manner comprises its companion. He who does his own work will see that his first lesson is to know what he is, and what is proper to himself, and he who knows himself will not regard another's business as his; he will love and cultivate himself before anything else, and will eschew superfluous occupations as well as unprofitable thoughts and purposes. *As folly is not satisfied when its wishes are granted, so wisdom is contented with that which is present, and is never displeased with itself* (Cicero).

Epicurus releases his sage from foresight and anxiety for the future.

Among those laws which relate to the departed, I regard that one as very sound which decrees that the doings of Princes shall be investigated after their death. They are the equals, if not the masters, of the laws, and it is right that justice, which had no control over their lives, should have control over their reputation and the estates of their successors, things which we often value above life. That is a practice which brings singular advantages to those countries in which it is observed, and is to be desired by all good rulers who have reason to complain that the wicked and the good are held in like memory.

We owe submission and obedience to all kings alike, for that concerns their office; but they should not command our esteem, any more than our affection, unless they be worthy. Let us grant that it is necessary for public order that, though unworthy, they be suffered patiently, that their vices be concealed, that their indifferent actions be assisted by our approval, as long as their authority needs our support. But when our relations are ended, there is no reason why, in the name of justice and our freedom, we should not express our true feelings; and especially why good subjects should be denied the credit of having faithfully and reverently served a master whose imperfections were so well known to them; thus depriving posterity of so useful an example. And those who, because of some private obligation, wrongly espouse the memory of a prince who was undeserving of praise, do a private justice at the expense of public justice. Livy says truly 'that the language of men bred under royalty is always full of vain ostentation and false testimony', each of them indifferently exalting his king to the extreme limit of worth and sovereign greatness.

Some may reprove the high-mindedness of those two soldiers who defied Nero to his face, one of whom, asked by him why he wished him ill, replied, ' I loved you as long as you deserved my love; but since you are become a parricide, incendiary, mountebank and charioteer, I hate you as you deserve.' The other, asked why he wished to kill him, replied, 'Because I can think of no other remedy against your continual misdeeds.' But what man of sound judgement can reprove the universal publication of the evidence which was given after his death, and which will be given for ever against him and all wicked rulers like him, of his abominable and tyrannical conduct?

I am sorry that a government as pure as that of Sparta should have sanctioned this hypocritical ceremony: at the death of a king, all the confederates and neighbours, all the helots, men, women, pell-mell, slit[1] their foreheads in token of sorrow, and with cries and lamentations declared him, whatever he might have been, as the best of all their kings; thus attributing to rank the praise due to merit, and to the lowest and meanest rank that which is due to the highest merit.

Aristotle, who stirs up all questions, wonders, touching the saying of Solon, 'that no man can be declared happy before his death', whether even he who has lived and died according to his own desire may be called happy, if he has left an evil reputation, and if his posterity is wretched. Whilst we have life and motion, we may convey ourselves by anticipation whithersoever we please, but when we cease to be, we have no communication with that which is. And it would have been better said by Solon that a man is never happy, since he is not so until after he is no more.

> He plucks himself with all his roots from life,
> And casts that self away, quite unawares,
> Feigning that some remainder's left behind,
> ... removing not the self enough
> From the body flung away. (LUCRETIUS.)

Bertrand du Guesclin died at the siege of the castle of Randon, near to Le Puy in Auvergne; the besieged were, after capitulating, ordered to bring the keys of the place on the body of the dead man.

When Bartolomeo d'Alviano, general of the Venetian army, died in the service of the Republic in Brescia, and his body had to be carried back to Venice through the territory of Verona, an enemy country, the majority in the army were of opinion that a safe-conduct should be requested of

---

[1] Apparently a misreading of Herodotus; Rawlinson's translation has *smote*.

the Veronese. But Teodoro Trivulcio was against the proposal, choosing rather to cross by force of arms, at risk of a battle : ' It was not fit, he said, that the man who never in his life was afraid of his enemies should appear to fear them when dead.'

In a kindred matter, in fact, according to the Greek laws, he who begged of an enemy a body to be interred renounced the victory and forfeited the liberty of erecting a trophy to the dead, and he of whom it was requested was entitled to claim the victory. In this way it was that Nicias lost the advantage which he had clearly won over the Corinthians, and that Agesilaus, on the other hand, confirmed that which he had very doubtfully acquired over the Boeotians.

These facts might appear strange, but that there has prevailed from time immemorial not only the custom of taking care of the dead beyond the grave, but also a belief that the favours of heaven very often accompany us to the tomb, and continue to be extended to our remains. Of this there are so many examples in ancient history, leaving aside those of modern times, that there is no need to dwell on them.

Edward the First, King of England, having had experience, in his long wars with the Scottish King Robert, of the great advantage which his presence gave to his cause, since he was always victorious in what he undertook in person ; when he died, bound his son by solemn oath, that being dead he should cause his body to be boiled, until the flesh fell from the bones, and carefully keeping the latter, after burying the flesh, should always carry them about with him and his army, whenever he was at war with the Scots, as if his destiny had fatally annexed victory to his limbs.

John Ziska, who disturbed the state of Bohemia in his defence of Wyclif's heresies, left orders that they should flay his body after his death, and of his skin make a drum to be carried in the war against his enemies, believing that by this means the advantages he had gained over them in war would be continued after his death. In like manner certain Indians used to carry into battle against the Spaniards the bones of one of their chiefs, in consideration of the good fortune which had attended him in life. And other tribes in that same hemisphere drag into the war the bodies of the braves who have died in battle, in order to hearten them and bring them luck.

In the former examples only the reputation gained by past actions is reserved from the grave; in the latter a certain active power is attributed to the remains.

The case of Captain Bayard[1] has a better appearance: Feeling himself wounded to death by an arquebus shot, and being advised to withdraw from the fray, he replied that he would not begin at the end of his life to turn his back on the enemy; having then fought to the utmost of his strength, and feeling himself faint and slipping from his saddle, he commanded his steward to lay him down at the foot of a tree, but in such a way that he should die with his face to the enemy; which he did.

I must add yet another example, which is as remarkable in this connexion as any of the preceding. The Emperor Maximilian, great-grandfather of the King Philip who is now ruling, was a prince fully endowed with great qualities, among others a singular beauty of person. Among his humours was one which was not shared by those princes who, in the dispatch of important business, are wont to make a throne of their close-stool; this humour was that he would not permit even the valet who was most closely attached to his person to see him in his closet. He would retire into privacy to make water, being as scrupulous as any maid about showing the parts which are usually kept concealed, whether to a physician or any other person. Though so shameless in speech, I have by nature a touch of this kind of modesty: except when obliged by necessity or voluptuousness I exhibit to no eyes the members and actions which custom ordains to be covered. I feel more constraint in this matter than is befitting a man, especially a man who professes my views. But Maximilian's modesty was carried to such a pitch of superstition, that in his will he expressly ordered that after death his parts should be hidden by drawers. He ought to have added, by codicil, that the man who put them on should be blindfold.

The command that Cyrus left to his children, that neither they nor any other person should either look upon or touch

[1] Generally known as the Chevalier Bayard, 'le chevalier sans peur et sans reproche', whose real name was Pierre de Terrail. He was killed at the battle of Romagnano in 1524.

his body after the soul had left it, I attribute to some sort of religious sentiment. For both his historian [1] and he, among other great qualities, strewed the whole course of their lives with a singular care and reverence for religion.

I was displeased with a story told me by a prince about a kinsman of mine, a man very well known both in peace and war : when dying at an advanced age in his court, though painfully tormented by the stone, he wasted his last hours in arranging, with anxious care, the pomp and ceremony of his interment. He pressed all the nobles who visited him to promise that they would be present at his funeral, and earnestly entreated even the prince, who was with him at his last gasp, to command his household to attend, adducing many examples and reasons to show that it was a mark of respect due to a man of his rank. Having obtained this promise and arranged his obsequies to his satisfaction, he seemed to die content. I have seldom heard of such persistent vanity.

The contrary solicitude, of which I could cite an example among my own friends, seems germane to the matter, that, namely, of restricting one's funeral anxiously and parsimoniously to a single servant and a lantern. I have seen this humour commended in the case of Marcus Emilius Lepidus, who gave orders to his heirs forbidding them to carry out at his death the ceremonies that are customary on such occasions. Is it after all moderation and frugality to avoid an expense and gratification that we shall neither know nor feel ? An easy reform that, and of little cost. Assuming the need of ordering these matters, my advice is that in this, as in all actions of life, every man should be guided by his fortune. And the philosopher Lycon wisely left it to his friends to dispose of his body as they might think best, so long as his funeral rites were carried out without either meanness or superfluity.

In my own case I shall simply leave it to custom to arrange this ceremony, and [2] rely on the discretion of the persons, whoever they may be, to whom I shall become a burden. *This is a matter that we should despise for ourselves,*

---

[1] Xenophon.
[2] These words, which follow in the 1588 edition, were afterwards cancelled : ' saving the things requisite for the service of my religion, if it should be in a place where it is necessary to enjoin them.'

but not neglect for our friends (Cicero). A holy man has said: *The ordonnance of funerals, the choice of burial, the pomp of obsequies, are rather a consolation to the living than a benefit to the dead* (Saint Augustine). Socrates, accordingly, in reply to Crito who asked him at his last moment how he desired to be buried, said, 'As you will.' If I were to trouble myself any further with the matter, I should consider it more gentlemanlike to imitate those who are resolved, whilst they live and breathe, to enjoy the arrangement and honours of their burial, and are pleased to see their dead countenance in marble. Happy are they who can rejoice and gratify their senses by insensibility, and live in their death!

I could almost conceive an implacable hatred against all democratic rule, although it appears to me the most natural and equitable, when I call to mind the inhuman injustice of the Athenian people in sentencing to death, without remission, and without consenting even to hear their defence, those brave captains who had just won, against the Lacedemonians, the naval battle near the Arginusian Isles, the most vigorously contested battle that the Greeks had ever fought at sea with their own forces; for the reason that, after the victory, they had pursued the advantage that the rules of war offered them, instead of staying to gather and bury their dead. And this execution is rendered more odious by the bearing of Diomedon, one of the condemned, a man of notable worth both military and political. Coming forward to speak at the first opportunity of a calm hearing, which was after he had heard the sentence, instead of pleading his cause and exposing the evident malice of such a cruel decision, he only showed a concern for the preservation of his judges, praying the Gods to turn this judgement to their good, and not to visit their anger on them, in consideration of the non-fulfilment of the vows which he and his companions had offered up in their gratitude for such illustrious good fortune. After stating what these vows were, and without any hesitation, he walked with a firm step to his punishment.

Fortune a few years later paid them in their own coin, for Chabrias, captain-general of the Athenian naval forces, having had the best of the combat against Pollis the Spartan admiral at the island of Naxos, lost the net and clear profit of his victory, one of great importance for their affairs, through not wishing to incur the penalty of this example. In order not to lose the few dead bodies of his friends floating on the sea he allowed a host of living enemies to sail away in safety, who afterwards made them pay dearly for this troublesome superstition.

> Dost ask where thou shalt lie when dead ?
> Where they lie that were never born. (SENECA.)

This other restores the sense of repose to a body without soul : *Let him have no sepulchre to receive him, nor a haven where, after having shuffled off this mortal coil, his body may rest from its woes !* (Ennius.)

Thus does Nature let us see that many dead things still have occult relations with life. Wine turns sour in the cellar according to certain changes in the vintage season, and the flesh of venison changes its condition and flavour in the salting-tub, according to the laws of the living flesh, as it is said.

CHAPTER 4

HOW THE SOUL RELIEVES ITS FEELINGS ON THE WRONG OBJECTS, WHEN THE REAL ARE WANTING

A GENTLEMAN of these parts, who was uncommonly subject to the gout, being urged by his physicians to abstain from all kinds of salt meats, was wont to reply very humorously, that in the throes of his affliction he must needs have somebody or something to lay the blame upon, and that if he could shout and curse the Bologna sausage, or the ham, or the ox-tongues, he felt very much better.

But, in good sooth, when the hand is raised to strike we feel hurt if it misses its aim and falls on the empty air ; so also, if the sight is to have a pleasant prospect, it must not be lost and scattered on vacant space, but have an object to sustain it at a reasonable distance,

> As the tempests lose
> Their strength by sturdy forests unopposed,
> Diffused on empty space. (LUCAN.)

So it would seem as if the soul, when moved and shaken, were lost in itself if it is given no hold ; it must always be provided with an object to aim at and work upon. Plutarch says, speaking of those who lavish their affection on apes and little dogs, that the amorous part that is in us, for want of a legitimate object, rather than remain unsatisfied, will forge a false and frivolous one. And we see that the soul in its passions is wont to cheat itself by setting up a false and fanciful object, even against its own belief, rather than not have something to act upon. So it is that animals in their rage attack the stone or weapon that has hurt them, and with vicious teeth wreak their vengeance on themselves for the pain they feel :

> Not otherwise a bear
> Pannonian, fiercer for the wound received,
> Maddened by dart from Libyan thong propelled,
> Turns circling on her wound, and still pursues
> The weapon fleeing as she whirls around. (LUCAN.)

What causes do we not invent for the misfortunes that befall us ? What will we not blame, rightly or wrongly, that we may have something to fight with ? It was not those fair tresses that you tear, nor the whiteness of that bosom that in your anger you so cruelly beat, that with an unlucky bullet killed your beloved brother : wreak your vengeance elsewhere.

Of the Roman army in Spain, after the loss of their two great captains, who were brothers,[1] Livy says, *they all at once began to weep and beat their heads.* It is a common practice. And did not the philosopher Bion say humorously of the king who tore his hair in his grief, 'Does this man think that a bald head will assuage his sorrow ? ' Who has not seen a man chew and swallow the cards, or gorge himself with a box of dice, to avenge himself on anything for the loss of his money ? Xerxes scourged the waters of the Hellespont, placed it in chains and heaped insults upon it, and wrote a challenge to Mount Athos ; and Cyrus delayed a whole army for many days to avenge himself on the river Gyndus, for the fright he had had in crossing it ; and Caligula demolished a very fine mansion on account of the pleasure [2] which his mother had taken in it.

When I was young the people used to say that one of our neighbouring kings, for a cudgelling received from God,

---

[1] Publius and Cneius Scipio.
[2] *Plaisir* was evidently a misprint for *déplaisir*, for Seneca says that Caligula demolished a mansion in the Hercules quarter, because his mother had been detained there as a sort of prisoner.

swore to be revenged, and commanded that for ten years no man should pray to him, nor speak of him, nor, as far as lay in his power, believe in him. This story was intended to describe not so much the folly as the vainglory natural to the nation to which it referred.

These two faults always go together, but such actions truly partake more of the nature of overweeningness than of stupidity. Augustus Caesar, having been tossed about in a storm at sea, set about defying the god Neptune, and in celebrating the Circensian games commanded his statue to be removed from among the other deities, as a token of revenge. Wherein he has less excuse than the preceding, and less than he had later, when, after losing a battle under Quintilius Varus in Germany, he ran about in anger and despair, knocking his head against the walls and exclaiming, 'O Varus, give me back my legions!' For they are more than foolish, since they add impiety to their folly, who direct their anger against God himself, or against Fortune, as if she had ears to be assailed by our batteries; such as the Thracians, for instance, who, when it thunders or lightens, start shooting at heaven with Titanian vengeance, as if they could bring God to reason by a flight of arrows. Now, as the ancient poet says in Plutarch,

> 'Tis vain to be angered with things,
> They care not a rap for our wrath.

But when our minds are disordered we can never utter insults enough.

CHAPTER 5

WHETHER THE GOVERNOR OF A PLACE BESIEGED SHOULD GO OUT TO PARLEY

LUCIUS MARCIUS,[1] Roman legate in the war against Perseus, King of Macedon, wishing to gain the time he still needed to complete his preparations, set afoot some overtures of accommodation, whereby the King being lulled to security, granted a truce of several days, thus giving his enemy opportunity and leisure to reinforce his army, and preparing his own final ruin. Yet the old men of the Senate, mindful of their fathers' ways, condemned this

---

[1] Livy calls him Quintus Marcius.

proceeding as contrary to their ancient practice, which was, they said, to combat by valour and not by cunning, by surprises or night-encounters, by feigned flights and unexpected rallies; never entering upon a war without first declaring it, and often after appointing time and place for the battle. In the same conscientious spirit they sent back to Pyrrhus his treacherous physician, and to the Phalisci their disloyal schoolmaster.

Those were the true Roman methods, which had nothing in common with Greek subtlety or the cunning of the Carthaginians, who regarded victory by force as less glorious than victory by fraud. Deceit may serve for the nonce; but he alone acknowledges defeat who knows he has been overcome neither by craft nor by chance, but by valour, man to man, in fair and open warfare. The words of those honest old men show clearly that they had not yet accepted this fine maxim,

> Craft or courage, which,
> Who cares to ask in dealing with a foe ?   (VIRGIL.)

The Achaians, says Polybius, detested every kind of deceit in their wars, never esteeming themselves victorious except when the courage of the enemy was fairly subdued. *A wise and virtuous man will know that only where honour and good faith are untarnished is a real victory gained*, says another (Florus).

> Whether to you or me dame Fortune will
> The victory grant; or what the chance of war,
> Shall courage try.   (ENNIUS.)

In the kingdom of Ternate,[1] among those people whom we so complacently call barbarians, the custom holds of never beginning a war without having first declared it, with ample declaration of the means to be employed, the quality and number of men, the munitions and arms, whether offensive or defensive. But, that being done, if their enemies do not yield or come to an agreement, they claim the right to do their worst, and to employ, without fear of being accused of treachery or cunning, any means which will help them to victory.

The ancient Florentines were so far from seeking to gain

[1] One of the Moluccas.

advantage over their enemies by surprise, that they would warn them, a whole month before placing their army in the field, by the continual ringing of the bell they called *Martinella*.

As to ourselves, who, not being so overscrupulous, give the honour of the war to him who has the profit of it, and who say, with Lysander, that 'when the lion's skin is too short, we must eke it out with a bit from that of the fox', the most usual occasions of surprise are derived from this exercise of cunning; and there is no moment, we say, when a chief should be more wide-awake, than that of parleys and treaties of accommodation. For this reason a rule is current in the mouths of all the warriors of our days, 'that never must the governor of a besieged place himself go out to parley'. In the days of our fathers this was made a reproach against the Seigneurs de Montmord and de l'Assigni, when defending Mouson[1] against the Count de Nansaut.[1] But on this reckoning he would be excusable who went out in such a way that the safety and advantage still lay on his side, as Count Guy de Rangon did at the town of Reggio (if we are to believe du Bellay, for Guicciardini says it was himself), when the Seigneur de l'Escut approached to parley with him; for he stepped out such a little way from the stronghold that, a disturbance having arisen during the parley, not only did Monsieur de l'Escut and the men who accompanied him find themselves to be the weaker party, so that Alessandro Trivulcio was killed, but he himself was obliged for greater safety to follow the Count and, relying on the word of the latter, to take shelter from the shots within the town.

Eumenes, when pressed by Antigonus, who was besieging him in the town of Nora, to come out and treat with him, alleging among other reasons that that was only right and proper, since he (Antigonus) was the greater and stronger of the two, returned this noble answer, 'I shall never esteem a man greater than myself as long as I have my sword in my hand', and would not consent to come out until Antigonus acceded to his demand to deliver his own nephew Ptolemaeus as a hostage.

And yet there are some who have done very well to come

[1] Mouzon (Ardennes), not Pont-à-Mousson, as usually supposed. For Nansaut read Nassau.

out to parley, on the word of the assailant being given. Witness Henri de Vaux, a knight of Champagne, who being besieged in the castle of Commercy by the English, and Barthelemy de Brunes, who commanded the besieging army, having so undermined the greater part of the castle from the outside, that only a spark was needed to bury the besieged under the ruins, summoned the said Henri to come out to parley for his own good, which he did with three others. Seeing with his own eyes that his ruin was certain, he felt singularly obliged to his enemy; for after surrendering with his company to his discretion, fire was applied to the mine, the wooden props soon began to give way, and the castle was completely demolished.

I am easily persuaded to trust another's good faith; but I should less willingly do so if I gave him to understand that I did it in despair and from lack of courage, rather than in freedom and trust to his loyalty.

CHAPTER 6

THE HOUR OF PARLEYING IS DANGEROUS

RECENTLY, however, I saw at Mussidan[1] in this neighbourhood, how those who had been forcibly dislodged from the town by our army, together with others of their side, cried out treachery, because during the negotiations and whilst the truce was still in force, they had been surprised and cut in pieces: a protest which in another age might perhaps have appeared quite reasonable. But, as I have already said, our methods are entirely removed from those rules of conduct, and we must not expect any mutual trust until the last seal has been affixed to the bond. Even that is not enough, and it is always a dangerous decision to trust to the licence of a victorious army to observe the oath given to a town that has just surrendered upon easy and favourable conditions, and in the heat of victory to allow the free entry of the soldiery.

L. Emilius Regillus, the Roman praetor, after wasting his time in attempting to take the town of Phocaea by storm, by reason of the singular prowess shown by the inhabitants in

[1] A little town in Périgord (Dordogne) about seventeen miles from the château of Montaigne. The date is 1569.

their own defence, agreed to receive them as friends of the
Roman people, and to enter the town as into a confederate
city, thus removing all fear of hostile action. But having,
in order to appear with the greater pomp, introduced his
army with him, it was not in his power, in spite of all
efforts, to keep his soldiers in check, so that, the laws of
greed and revenge overcoming those of military discipline
and authority, he saw a good part of the city ransacked
before his very eyes.

Cleomenes said that whatever injury a man could do to an
enemy in time of war was above justice and not subject to
it, either in the eyes of gods or of men. And, having concluded a truce with the Argives for seven days, on the third
night he attacked them in their sleep and destroyed them,
his excuse being that in the truce there was no mention of
nights. But the gods avenged this subtle perfidy.

During a parley, and whilst they were pondering over
their sureties, the town of Casilinum [1] was seized by
surprise, and that in an age of the justest captains and the
most perfect Roman military discipline. For it is not said
that, time and place permitting, we are not allowed to take
advantage of the folly of our enemies, as we do of their
cowardice. And doubtless war has naturally many reasonable privileges, to the prejudice of reason; and here the
rule fails, *that no man should endeavour to prey upon another's
ignorance* (Cicero). But I am astonished at the freedom
allowed by Xenophon, both by the words and the example
of divers exploits of his perfect Emperor [2]: an author of
remarkable weight in such matters, as well as a great
captain, and as a philosopher one of the first of Socrates'
disciples. And I cannot consent to such a measure of
dispensation as he allows in all things and all places.

Monsieur d'Aubigny besieging Capua, and having subjected it to a furious battering, the Signor Fabrizio Colonna,
governor of the town, having begun to parley from the top
of a bastion, whilst his soldiers were more than usually
slack in their guard, our men took possession and put them
all to the sword. And in more recent memory, at Ivoy,[3]
the Signor Giuliano Romero, taking a step only worthy of
a clerk, in going out to parley with Monsieur the Constable,

---

[1] A town in Campania. [2] Cyrus.
[3] An error; the incident took place at Dinant in 1554.

at his return found his place taken. But, that we might not go scot-free, when the Marquis de Pescara was besieging Genoa, where the Duke Ottaviano Fregosa was in command, under our protection, the agreement being so far advanced that it was regarded as accomplished and on the point of being concluded, the Spaniards, having slipped in, took advantage of it to gain a complete victory. And since, at Ligny in Barrois, where the Count de Brienne was in command, the Emperor having beleaguered the place in person, and Bertheville, the said Count's lieutenant, being come out to negotiate, the town was seized during the parley. As the poet says:

> Whether by skill or ingenuity,
> To conquer always is a glorious thing. (ARIOSTO.)

But the philosopher Chrysippus would not have been of that opinion, and no more am I; for he used to say that they who run a race should use their best speed, but by no means are they at liberty to lay a hand on their adversary to stop him, or to stretch out a leg to trip him up.

And still more generous was the answer of the great Alexander to Polypercon, who was persuading him to take advantage of the darkness of night to attack Darius: 'By no means, he said; it is not for me to steal a victory: *I had rather complain of fortune than blush for a victory*' (Quintus Curtius).

> Orodes fled; Mezentius marks his flight,
> And scorns with lance a covert blow to deal,
> But face to face confronts him in the fight,
> Courage, not craft, prevails, and might o'ermatches might.
> (VIRGIL.)

CHAPTER 7

THAT THE INTENTION IS JUDGE OF OUR ACTIONS

DEATH, they say, releases us from all our obligations. I know of some who have taken this saying in a different sense. Henry the Seventh, King of England, made an agreement with Don Philip, son of the Emperor Maximilian, or, to place him more honourably, father of the Emperor Charles the Fifth, whereby the said Philip was to deliver into his hands the Duke of Suffolk of the White Rose, his enemy, who had fled and withdrawn into the Low Countries,

Henry promising to make no attempt on the life of the said Duke; when he came to die, however, he commanded his son in his will to put him to death immediately after his own decease.

More recently, in that tragedy which the Duke of Alva presented to us at Brussels in the persons of the Counts Horn and Egmont, there was an abundance of remarkable incidents; among others, that Count Egmont, on whose word and assurance the said Count Horn had surrendered to the Duke of Alva, very earnestly prayed that he might be the first to die, to the end that his death might release him from the obligation he was under to the said Count Horn.

To me it seems that death did not acquit the former of his given word, and that the latter was discharged from it, even without dying. We cannot be bound beyond our strength and means, for this reason, that effect and performance are not in our power, for nothing is really in our power except the will; on this are necessarily founded and established all the rules of the duty of man. Therefore Count Egmont, deeming his soul and will to be indebted to his promise, though it was not in his power to redeem it, was without doubt absolved from his duty, even if he had survived Count Horn.

But the King of England, intentionally failing to keep his word, is not to be excused for having delayed the performance of his disloyal action until after his death; any more than was the mason in Herodotus, who, having loyally kept during his lifetime the secret of the treasures of his master the King of Egypt, revealed it at his death to his children.

I have known several in my time who, convicted by their conscience of withholding others' property, arranged to satisfy it by their last will and after their decease. But their act avails them naught, either by fixing a term for so urgent a matter or by trying to redeem an injury at so little cost to their feelings and their purse. They owe something of what is really their own. And the more burdensome and inconvenient the restitution, the more just and meritorious is the satisfaction. Penitence demands a burden.

They do still worse who reserve for their last will the declaration of some spiteful intention against a neighbour after having concealed it during life; thereby manifesting little regard for their own honour, since they irritate the offended against their memory, and less for their conscience, not having been able, even out of respect to death itself, to let their ill-will die down, but extending the life of their hatred beyond their own. Unjust judges, who defer judgement to a time when the case is beyond their jurisdiction!

I shall see to it, if I can, that my death discovers nothing that my life has not first declared [and that openly].

CHAPTER 8

OF IDLENESS

AS we see land that has been lying idle, if rich and fertile, abounding in a hundred thousand kinds of wild and useless herbs, and which, to be rightly utilized, must be kept in order and sown with certain crops for our service; and as we see women, quite alone, bringing forth shapeless lumps of flesh, who with a different kind of seed would bear good and natural offspring: so it is with the mind. If it be not occupied with a certain subject that will keep it in check and under restraint, it will cast itself aimlessly, hither and thither, into the vague field of imaginations.

> As waters in a brazen urn flash bright,
> Smit by the sunbeam or the moon's pale rays,
> And round the chamber flits the trembling light,
> And darts aloft and on the ceiling plays. (VIRGIL.)

And there is no foolish or idle fancy that it will not bring forth in this restless state.

> They frame vain figures like a sick man's dreams. (HORACE.)

If the mind have no fixed aim, it loses itself, for, as they say, to be everywhere is to be nowhere;

> He dwells just nowhere that dwells everywhere. (MARTIAL.)

When lately I withdrew to my own home, resolved, as far as in me lay, to think only of spending in rest and retirement the little time I still have to live, it seemed to me that I could do my mind no greater favour than to allow it, in idleness, to entertain itself, to dwell and settle in itself, which I hoped that thenceforth it might be able to do more easily, having in course of time become more steady and mature; but I find that,

> as idle days breed wandering thoughts (LUCAN.)

on the other hand, like a horse that has escaped into freedom, it will run a hundred times more for itself than it did for others; that it brings forth so many chimeras and fantastic monsters, the one on top of the other, without order or design, that, in order to contemplate at my leisure their strangeness and absurdity, I have begun to set them down in writing, hoping in time to make it ashamed of them.[1]

CHAPTER 9

OF LIARS

THERE is no man whom it would so little become to boast of his memory as myself, for I can hardly show a trace of it, and I do not think that there is another in the world so marvellously defective as mine. All my other faculties are mean and ordinary, but in this I think I am singular and quite a rarity, deserving of a name and reputation.

Besides the natural inconvenience I suffer by it (for truly, seeing its necessity, Plato is right in calling it a 'great and powerful Goddess'), in my part of the country, when they mean that a man has no sense, they say that he has no memory; and when I complain of the defect of mine, they take me up and will not believe me, as though I were accusing myself of being a fool. They can see no alternative between memory and intelligence.

This is spoiling my market. But they do me wrong, for experience rather shows, on the contrary, that an excellent memory is, more often than not, coupled with an infirm judgement. They do me wrong also in this, since I am nothing if not a good friend, that the very words that accuse my infirmity stand for ingratitude. They doubt my affection on account of my memory, and turn a natural defect into a lack of conscience. 'He has forgotten, they

---

[1] This was written in 1571. Montaigne had retired from active life, as member of the Parlement of Bordeaux; but he was fated to be drawn into it again, rather against his will, as Mayor of Bordeaux, which office he held for four years, with great credit, during very troublous times.

say, this request or that promise ; He does not remember his friends ; He has forgotten to say this, to do that, or to conceal something else, for my sake.' Certainly I am apt to forget, but as for neglecting, through indifference, a thing that a friend has charged me with, that is not in my nature. Let them be satisfied with my misfortune without making it a kind of ill-will, and an ill-will that is so foreign to my temper !

I find some comfort. Firstly, in the reflection that it is an evil which has provided me with the principal reason for correcting a worse evil, which might easily have grown on me, to wit, ambition ; for the want of memory is an intolerable defect in one who would encumber himself with the world's affairs ;

That, as several like examples of the progress of Nature show, she has generally strengthened my other faculties in proportion as this has weakened, and my mind and judgement could be easily led to follow indolently in the foot-prints of others, without exercising its own power, as is the way of the world, had the discoveries and opinions of others been present with me, by the gift of memory ;

That my speech is the briefer, for the store-house of the memory is apt to be better furnished with matter than that of invention.

Had mine been faithful to me, I should have deafened all my friends with my chatter, the subjects arousing in me the little faculty I possess for handling and employing them, drawing out and warming my eloquence. That would be a pity, as I have experienced in the case of some of my intimate friends : according as their memory supplies them with a full and present view of their subject-matter, they carry their narrative so far back, and stuff it with so many needless details that, if the story be good, they stifle its goodness ; if it is not good, you begin to curse either their good fortune in having such a memory, or their misfortune in having such a poor judgement. And when once you are on the high road of a narrative, it is difficult to stop and cut it short. There is nothing in which a horse's power is better seen than in a neat and dead stop.

Even among those who keep to the point I know some who are unable, though willing, to stop short in their career. While searching about in their mind for a point of conclusion, they go maundering on, dragging their feet like a man faint from weakness. Especially dangerous are old men, who retain the memory of things past and have lost the memory of their repetitions. I have known very amusing stories, told by a lord, become very wearisome, each of the company having been drenched with them a hundred times.

Secondly, I find a comfort in the reflection that I am the less mindful of offences received; as that ancient writer said of somebody.[1] I should need a reminder, like Darius who, in order not to forget the injury he had received at the hands of the Athenians, instructed a page, whenever he sat down to table, to sing into his ear three times, ' Sire, remember the Athenians ! ' On the other hand, places and books that I see again always smile upon me with a fresh novelty.

Not without reason do they say that he who is not very strong in memory should not meddle with lying. I know that the grammarians make a distinction between telling an untruth and lying, and say that to tell an untruth is to tell a thing that is false, but which one thinks to be true, and that by its derivation the word *lie* in Latin (*mentiri*), whence comes our French word (*mentir*), means as much as to go against one's conscience,[2] and that it consequently applies only to those who say what is contrary to what they know, and of whom I am now speaking.

Now these either invent the whole, pith and all, or they alter and disguise something that has a true foundation. When they disguise and alter, and are often made to repeat the same story, they can hardly avoid tripping themselves up, because the real facts, as first lodged in the memory and imprinted upon it by the medium of conception and knowledge, cannot but present themselves to the imagination, dislodging the false, which cannot have so firm and settled a foothold; and the circumstances as originally learned, ever and again stealing into the mind, will make them lose the memory of those added details that are false and adulterated.

---

[1] Thou forgettest nothing, except injuries. (CICERO.)

[2] *Contra mentem ire* was perhaps at the back of Montaigne's mind; or he recalled an expression of Cornelius Nepos : *contra id quod in mente est loqui*.

In what they wholly invent, inasmuch as there is no contrary impression to clash with their falsehood, there seems to be less fear of tripping. Yet even this, because it is an empty body without any substance, is apt to escape the memory, if it be not very sure. Of this I have often had amusing experience at the expense of such as profess only to adapt their speech to the matter in hand, and to humour the great persons with whom they are speaking. For, those circumstances to which they are ready to enslave their faith and conscience being subject to many changes, their speech must needs vary accordingly. Whence it happens that they will speak of one thing as now grey, now yellow; to this man in one way, to that in another; and if by any chance these men bring back their booty and compare their contradictory information, what becomes of that fine art? Moreover, they so often trip themselves up when off their guard; for what memory could suffice them to recall the many different shapes in which they have forged one and the same subject? I have known several in my day who craved a reputation for this fine sort of caution; they do not see that if the reputation be there, the results cannot be there.

Lying is indeed an accursed vice. We are human beings, and hold together, only by speech. If we knew the horror of it, and the gravity, we should pursue it with fire, and more justly so than other crimes.

I find that people usually waste their energies in chastising children, very improperly, for innocent faults, and torment them for thoughtless acts which make no impression and are of no consequence. Lying alone, and stubbornness, which stands on a little lower level, are, in my opinion, those faults whose birth and progress should be most earnestly combated. As the child grows, they grow with it; and when once the tongue has been started in this wrong direction, it is marvellous how impossible it is to pull it back. Whence it comes that we find men subject and enslaved to this vice who are honest in every other respect. I have a good fellow of a tailor whom I have never known to speak the truth, not even when it could serve him a good turn. If falsehood, like truth, had but one face, we should know better where we are, for we should then take for certain the opposite of what the liar tells us. But the reverse of the truth has a hundred thousand shapes and a boundless field.

The good, according to the Pythagoreans, is certain and finite; evil is infinite and uncertain. A thousand ways deviate from, only one leads to, the bull's eye. I am by no means sure that I could tell a solemn and barefaced lie to save myself from an evident and extreme danger. An ancient father [1] says that a dog we know is better company than a man whose language we do not understand, *as a foreigner cannot be a man to a foreigner* (Pliny the Elder). And how much less sociable is false speaking than silence!

King Francis the First boasted of having, by this means, put on the rack one Francesco Taverna, ambassador of Francesco Sforza, Duke of Milan, a man of great fame in the art of talking. This man had been dispatched to excuse his master to his Majesty on account of a thing of great importance, which was this: The King, in order to keep up some communication with Italy, whence he had been recently driven, and especially with the duchy of Milan, had thought it expedient to have a gentleman to represent him at the Duke's court, an ambassador in effect, but ostensibly a private gentleman who resided there under the pretence of being engaged in his own affairs; for, being much more dependent on the Emperor, it was greatly against the interest of the Duke (especially at that time when he was negotiating a marriage with his niece, daughter of the King of Denmark, now Dowager of Lorraine) to be discovered having any intercourse and dealings with us. A fit and proper person for this charge was found in one Merveille, a Milanese gentleman and an equerry of the King's stables. Dispatched with secret credentials and ambassadorial instructions, and, for a cloak and appearance, with other letters of recommendation to the Duke to further him in his private concerns, this man was so long at the Duke's court that the Emperor had some inkling of it, which, as we think, was the occasion of what followed after, which was that, under colour of some murder, behold him one dark night decapitated by the Duke's orders, and his hash settled in a couple of days!

Messer Francesco being come, ready with a lengthy and made-up account of this affair (for the King had written,

[1] Saint Augustine.

to demand satisfaction, to all the princes in Christendom, and to the Duke himself), had audience at the morning's sitting of the Council, and there, to bolster up his case, very ingeniously put forward several plausible explanations of the deed : that his master had never regarded our man as any other than a private gentleman and a subject of his, who had come to Milan on his own business, and had never resided there in any other capacity ; that he denied any knowledge of his being of the King's household or even known to the King, much less that he was his ambassador. The King, in his turn, after pressing him with divers questions and objections, and attacking him on every quarter, at last cornered him on the matter of the execution carried out by night, and as it were by stealth. To which the poor man, in his embarrassment, assuming the part of the courtier, replied that out of respect to his Majesty the Duke would have been loath that the execution should have taken place in the daytime. We may all imagine how he was caught up, having tripped so clumsily in the presence of such a nose as that of King Francis.[1]

Pope Julius the Second sent an ambassador to the King of England to stir him up against King Francis.[2] After he had delivered himself of his charge, the King in his reply dwelt on the difficulties he would find in making the necessary preparations for fighting so powerful a king, and urged several other reasons, whereupon the ambassador very inopportunely answered that he also had considered these difficulties, and had represented them to the Pope. From these words, so foreign to his purpose, which was to incite him to immediate war, the King at once inferred, what he afterwards found to be the case, that this ambassador privately inclined to the side of France. Of which his master having been informed, his property was confiscated, and he himself barely escaped with his life.

[1] A glance at the portrait of King Francis will sufficiently explain the humour of this remark.
[2] Actually King Louis XII.

CHAPTER 10

OF QUICK OR SLOW SPEECH

NEVER yet was one man gifted with all graces (Étienne de la Boëtie). So we see that, in the gift of eloquence, some have facility and promptness, and so ready a repartee, as they say, that they are prepared for any emergency, whilst others, more sluggish, are never able to speak without elaborate premeditation.

As we advise ladies to take up those games and bodily exercises which will show off their particular beauty to the best advantage, so I would give the same advice with regard to those two advantages in eloquence, which in our age the preachers and lawyers seem principally to profess. The slow speaker should, methinks, make the better preacher, and the other the better lawyer, because the profession of the former gives him as much leisure as he desires to prepare himself ; besides that he runs his course along a straight and constant line without interruption, whilst the advocate's freedom obliges him at any moment to enter the lists, and, the unexpected replies of his adversary throwing him out of his stride, to take up a new position on the spur of the moment.

Yet, at the interview between Pope Clement and King Francis at Marseilles, it happened, quite on the contrary, that Monsieur Poyet,[1] a man trained all his life for the Bar and held in great repute, having been charged to deliver the address to the Pope, and having thought it out long beforehand, nay, according to some, brought it ready-made from Paris ; on the very day when it was to be delivered, the Pope, fearing lest something might be said which might give offence to the ambassadors of the other princes attending him, proposed to the King a subject which seemed to him most befitting the time and place, but which happened to differ entirely from that upon which Monsieur Poyet had been labouring. His speech was consequently of no use, and another had to be quickly prepared ; but, he finding himself unequal to the task, Monsieur the Cardinal du Bellay had to undertake it.

The lawyer's is a more difficult part than the preacher's,

[1] A celebrated lawyer, Chancellor of France, 1538–42.

and yet it seems to me that we shall find more passable lawyers than preachers, at least in France.

It appears to be rather of the essence of wit to be quick and sudden in its operation, and of the judgement to be slow and deliberate. But the man who remains quite dumb unless he have leisure to prepare himself, and he who cannot speak any better for having leisure, are equally at sea.

They tell of Severus Cassius that he spoke better without any premeditation, that he owed more to chance than to his diligence, that it was an advantage to him to be interrupted in speaking, and that his adversaries were afraid to nettle him, lest his anger should make him doubly eloquent. I know by experience that natural disposition which is impatient of earnest and laborious premeditation, and which will produce nothing good unless allowed to run merrily and free. We say of a work that it smells of the oil and the lamp, to account for a certain roughness and awkwardness which results from a too laborious handling. But besides this, the anxiety to do well, and that striving of a mind too strained and intent on its purpose, balks and hampers it, just as water by its own pressure and abundance cannot find a ready outlet through the open mouth of a bottle.

In this disposition of Nature of which I am speaking there is this besides, that it does not require to be shaken and spurred by those strong passions, such as Cassius's anger (for such a movement would be too violent); it needs to be, not shaken, but wooed; it needs to be roused and warmed up by outside, present, and fortuitous occasions. If it be left alone it flags and languishes; excitement is its life and charm.

I do not show to advantage when in complete possession of myself, and when left to my own disposition. The chance of accident can claim more credit for anything I say than myself. The occasion, the company, the very ring of my voice will draw more from my wit than I can find in it when I sound and exercise it apart. Hence my spoken words are better than my writings, if there can be a preference where there is no value.

This also happens to me, that I do not find myself when I seek myself, and I find myself more by accident than by a searching of my judgement. Say that I have launched some subtle remark in writing, I mean one that, though pointless to another, appears pointed to myself (away with this modesty! every one speaks like that according to his power): I have so completely lost the point, that I do not know what I meant to say, and a stranger has sometimes discovered it before me. If I were to use the erasing-knife wherever that happens, I should suppress the whole book. At some other time an accident will throw a light upon it, more brilliant than that of noon, and I shall wonder at my doubt.

CHAPTER 11
OF PROGNOSTICATIONS

WITH regard to oracles, it is certain that a good while before the coming of Jesus Christ they had begun to lose their credit, for we see that Cicero is at pains to find the cause of their decline, and these words are his: *Why are oracles no longer uttered at Delphi, so that, not only in this age of ours, but for a long time past, nothing is more despised?* But with regard to other prognostics, drawn from the anatomy of beasts at sacrifices, for which purpose Plato thinks that the natural constitution of the intestines of those animals were partly intended, from the scraping of fowls, the flight of birds—*We think there are birds expressly created for the purpose of augury* (Cicero)—from thunder, from the windings of rivers—*The Aruspices discern many things, the Augurs foresee many things, many things are announced by oracles, by vaticinations, by dreams and portents* (Cicero)—and others, upon which the ancients relied for most of their enterprises, both public and private, our religion has abolished them. And although there still remain among us certain means of divination, in the stars, in spirits, in the shapes of bodies, in dreams and elsewhere: a notable example of the senseless curiosity of our nature, wasting time in anticipating future things, as if we had not enough to do to digest the present:

> How seemed it just to thee, Olympus' king,
> That suffering mortals at thy doom should know,
> By dreadful omens, massacres to come?
>
> . . . . . .
>
> Whate'er be truth, keep thou the future veiled
> From mortal vision, and amid their fears
> Let men still hope, (LUCAN.)

we gain nothing by knowing what will happen in the future, for it is a miserable thing to torment oneself in vain (Cicero), yet the fact remains that they have much less authority.

That is why the example of François, Marquis de Salusses, appeared to me remarkable, who, being lieutenant of King Francis in his army beyond the mountains, enjoyed immense favour at our court and was beholden to the King even for the marquisate which had been confiscated from his brother. Without any occasion for turning his coat, and even in opposition to his feelings, he suffered himself, as has been averred, to be so terrified by the fine prognostics that were then current everywhere in favour of the Emperor Charles the Fifth and to our disadvantage (especially in Italy, where these silly prophecies gained so much ground that at Rome large sums of money changed hands on the chances of our ruin), that, after having often bewailed to his intimates the misfortunes that he saw inevitably impending over the crown of France and his friends there, he revolted and changed sides; to his own great hurt, however, constellations or no constellations. But he behaved in this affair as a man beset by divers passions. For, having both towns and forces in his hands, with the enemy's army under Antonio de Leyva only three steps away, and we without any suspicion of his action, he had it in his power to do worse than he did. For, in spite of his treachery we lost neither man nor city, excepting Fossano, and that only after a long struggle.

> Most wisely Jove in thickest night
> The issues of the future veils,
> And laughs at the self-torturing wight
> Who with imagined terrors quails.
>
> . . . .
>
> Lord of himself that man will be,
> And happy in his life alway,
> Who still at eve can say with free,
> Contented soul, ' I've lived to-day;
> Let Jove to-morrow, if he will,
> With blackest clouds the welkin fill,
> Or flood it all with sunlight pure!' (HORACE.)

Those, on the other hand, who believe this saying, believe wrongly: *These are reciprocal: if there be divination, there are Gods, and if there be Gods, there is divination* (Cicero). Much more wisely Pacuvius,

> All those who understand the speech of birds
> And hearts of victims better than their own,
> May be just listened to, but not obeyed.

That so celebrated art of divination of the Tuscans had the following origin : A ploughman, striking deep into the earth with his ploughshare, saw Tages arise out of it, a demigod with a child's face but with the wisdom of an old man. All the people hastened to see, and his words and knowledge, embodying the principles and the means to attain this art, were gathered and preserved for several centuries : a birth in conformity with its progress !

I would much rather regulate my affairs by a throw of the dice than by such dreams.

And indeed in every state a good deal of authority has always been allotted to chance. Plato, in the civil government that he frames according to his fancy, leaves to chance the decision of many things of importance, and among others ordains that marriages be made by lot among good citizens ; and he attaches so much weight to this accidental selection as to decree that the children born of these unions shall be brought up in the country, and those born of bad unions shall be cast out. Should, however, any of the banished ones by any chance show any hopeful signs when growing up, they may be recalled, whilst any among those retained may be exiled if they turn out hopeless in their youth.

I see some studying and glossing their almanacs, and quoting them as authorities on things that occur. Saying so much, they must tell both the truth and falsehood : *for who will shoot all day without sometimes hitting the mark ?* (Cicero.) I think never the better of them though they sometimes light upon the truth. There would be more certainty of getting at the truth if it were the rule that they always lie. Besides, nobody records their miscalculations, although they are usual and numberless ; and their correct prophecies are the more credited for being rare, incredible, and amazing. So Diagoras, who was surnamed the Atheist, to one who showed him in the temple of Samothrace numerous votive tablets of those who had escaped shipwreck, with the words, 'Well! you who think that the Gods care naught about human affairs, what say you to so many saved through their favour?' replied, 'It is explained thus: those who were drowned are not depicted here, though much more numerous.'

Cicero says that Xenophon the Colophonian alone, of all the philosophers who have acknowledged the Gods, endeavoured to uproot all manner of divination. The less is it to be wondered at that we have seen some of our princely souls wasting time, sometimes to their prejudice, on these vanities.

I should much like to have seen with my own eyes those two marvels, the book of Joachim the Calabrian abbot which foretold all the future popes, their names and characters; and that of the Emperor Leo, who predicted all the emperors and patriarchs of Greece.

This I have witnessed with my own eyes, that in public disturbances the people, stunned by their turns of fortune, rush headlong into all manner of superstitions and search the heavens for the ancient causes and menaces of their calamities. And they have been so strangely lucky in my time, that I am convinced (this being a pastime of acute and idle minds) that those who are versed in the subtleties of tying and untying these mysteries are capable of finding whatever they want to find in any writings whatever. But their task is made particularly easy by the obscure, ambiguous, and fantastic style of the prophetic jargon, to which its authors give no clear meaning, to the end that posterity may apply and interpret them according to its own fancy.

The daimon of Socrates was perhaps a certain impulse of will, which arose in him without awaiting the consent of his reason. In a soul as purified as his, and prepared by continual exercise of wisdom and virtue, it is probable that these inclinations, though sudden and ill-defined, were always serious and worthy of being followed. Every man is conscious within himself of some image of such stirrings of a prompt, vehement, and fortuitous opinion. I am well qualified to allow them some authority, who allow so little to our wisdom, and I have experienced some of them, equally weak in reason and violent in persuasion, or in dissuasion (which was more usual with Socrates), by which

I have been carried away so profitably and so happily, that they might be supposed to partake somewhat of divine inspiration.

CHAPTER 12

OF STEADFASTNESS

THE law of resolution and steadfastness does not imply that we should not, as far as lies in our power, take cover against the ills and discomforts which threaten us, nor does it, by inference, forbid the fear of being taken by them unawares. On the contrary, all honourable means of securing ourselves from harm are not only allowed, but commendable, and the game of steadfastness is chiefly played by resolutely supporting those ills which cannot be remedied. So that no bodily activity or wielding of hand-weapons is to be condemned, if it serve to protect us from the blow that is aimed at us.

Some very warlike nations, when fighting, found their chief advantage in flight, and showed their backs to the enemy more dangerously than their faces. The Turks still to some extent practise this ruse.

Socrates in Plato ridicules Laches for defining courage as 'standing firm in the ranks against the enemy'. 'What! he said, can it be cowardice to beat them by yielding ground?' and he cites Homer, who commends the art of flight in Aeneas. And when Laches, on better consideration, admits this practice in the Scythians and more generally in all who fight mounted on horseback, he again cites the example of the Lacedemonian foot-soldiers, a nation trained above others to maintain their ground in fighting, who, at the battle of Plataea, being unable to force an opening into the Persian phalanx, decided to disperse and fall back, in order that the compact mass of the enemy, thinking they were in flight, might be broken and dissolved in pursuit. By this means they gained the victory.

Speaking of the Scythians, it is recorded that Darius, when he went out to subdue them, sent a message to their king, bitterly taunting him for always recoiling and shunning a hand-to-hand battle. To which Idanthyrses, for that was his name, replied, 'That it was not for fear of him or any man living, but that it was the method of proceeding of his nation, who had neither cultivated lands, nor cities nor houses to defend, and so had no fear of the enemy's gaining any profit. But if Darius was so hungry for a bite, let him approach and see their ancient places of sepulture, and there he would meet with somebody to talk with.'

In a cannonade, however, when a man is exposed to the fire, as often happens in war, it is an unbecoming thing to wince before the menacing shot, the more so as by reason of its impetus and velocity we account it unavoidable. And many a man, by raising his hand or ducking his head, has at least provided his comrades with a good laugh. And yet, in the expedition which the Emperor Charles the Fifth conducted against us in Provence, the Marquis de Guast, going to reconnoitre the city of Arles, and coming from behind a windmill under cover of which he had been approaching, was perceived by the Seigneur de Bonneval and the Seneschal d'Agenois, who were promenading on the Amphitheatre. These gentlemen pointing him out to the Sieur de Villier, commissary of the artillery, he aimed a culverin so accurately that, had not the said Marquis, seeing him apply the match, leapt to one side, he would have got it full in the body.

And in like manner, some years before, Lorenzo dei Medici, Duke of Urbino, father of the Queen-mother of the King, laying siege to Mondolfo, a place in Italy, in the territory called the Vicariat, seeing the match being applied to a piece of artillery that was pointed at him, did well to 'play the duck', else he would doubtless have had the ball, which only grazed the top of his head, right in the stomach.

To tell the truth, I do not think that these movements are the result of calculation, for how can you judge a high or low aim in so sudden a matter? It is much easier to believe that Fortune favoured their fright, and that on some other occasion the same movement might bring them into the line of fire, instead of avoiding it.

I cannot deny that if the loud report of an arquebus suddenly strikes on my ear in a place where I have no reason to expect it, I am startled; which I have seen happen to others more valorous than I.

And the Stoics do not claim that the soul of their sage can be proof against the first ideas and fancies that surprise him; but, as we are all by nature subject to them, they acquiesce rather in his yielding, even so far as to be convulsed and to turn pale, to a loud crash in the sky, for example, or the collapse of a building. And so with the other feelings, provided that his judgement remain sound and entire, that his reason be not thrown off its balance, and that it yield no consent to his fright or suffering. With regard to the man who is not a philosopher, it is the same in the first stage, but quite otherwise in the second. For in his case feelings make not a merely superficial impression, but penetrate to the seat of his reason, infecting and corrupting it. He judges according to his feelings, and is guided by them. The state of the Stoic sage is fully and elegantly expressed in this line :

Though tears may flow, the mind remains unmoved. (VIRGIL.)

The Peripatetic sage is not exempt from perturbations of mind, but he moderates them.

CHAPTER 13

CEREMONY AT THE MEETING OF KINGS

THERE is no subject, however trivial, that does not deserve a place in this rhapsody. According to our ordinary rules it would be a notable discourtesy, both to an equal and still more to a person of eminence, to fail to be at home when he has given notice of his intention to visit you. Nay, on this point Queen Margaret of Navarre further adds that it would be incivility in a nobleman to leave his house, as is most frequently done, to meet one who is coming to see him, however great he might be, and that it is more civil and respectful to wait and receive him, if it be only from fear of missing him on the road ; and that it is enough to accompany him on his departure.

For my part, I often neglect both of these empty formalities, since I curtail all ceremony in my own house. If any take offence, what shall I do ? Better to offend him once than myself every day ; that would be a perpetual slavery.

What is the object of flying from the slavishness of the court, if we drag it into our own den ?

It is also a common rule in all meetings for the lesser to

be first at the place of appointment, since it is the privilege of the more eminent person to make others wait for him. Nevertheless, at the meeting which was arranged between Pope Clement and King Francis at Marseilles, the King, after ordering the necessary preparations, withdrew from the town, in order to give the Pope two or three days' leisure to install himself and recuperate, before he paid his visit. And similarly, at the entry of the Pope and the Emperor [1] into Bologna, the Emperor gave the Pope an opportunity to be there first, himself arriving later. It is, they say, the usual custom, when two such princes come together to confer, for the greater to be at the appointed place before the other, even before the person on whose domain the meeting takes place ; and they understand it in this way, that this formality is intended to make it appear as if it were the person of lesser degree that is visiting and paying his court to the greater, and not vice versa.

Not only every country, but every city and every profession has its particular form of civility. I was rather carefully drilled in this in my boyhood, and have lived in sufficiently good company not to be ignorant of the rules of our French courtesy, and could keep a school in it. I like to follow these rules, but not so timorously as to put a restraint upon my whole life. Some of them are so irksome that to neglect them, provided it be done out of discretion and not from ignorance, is no less graceful an act. I have often seen men become uncivil by dint of too much civility, and tiresome in their courtesy.

The study of good manners is on the whole a very useful study. Like grace and beauty, it smooths over the first approaches to sociability and friendliness, and consequently opens the door of instruction by the example of others, teaching us to cultivate and set an example ourselves, if it has anything instructive and communicable.

---

[1] The same Pope Clement VII and Charles V, in 1532.

CHAPTER 14

THAT THE TASTE OF GOOD AND EVIL DEPENDS, FOR A GOOD PART, UPON THE IDEA WE FORM OF THEM [2]

MEN, says an ancient Greek maxim, are tormented by the ideas they form of things, not by the things themselves.[3] It would be a great point gained for the solace of our miserable human condition, if this proposition could be established as true, everywhere and in all things. For if evils enter into us only through our judgement, it would seem to be in our power to despise them, or to turn them to good. If things deliver themselves to our mercy, why shall we not dispose of them, and employ them to our advantage? If what we call evil and affliction are neither evil nor affliction in themselves, but it is only our imagination that gives them those qualities, it is in us to change them. And having the choice, if there is no compulsion, we are strangely foolish to persist in the course that is most painful to us, and to give to sickness, want, and contempt a bitter and evil taste, when we can give them a good one; and if, when Fortune simply provides the matter, it is in our power to give it form. Now let us see whether it can be maintained that what we call evil is not in itself evil; or at least, it being what it is, that it depends upon us to give it another savour and complexion, for it all comes to the same thing.

If the original essence of those things that we fear had the power to take up its abode in us by its own authority, it would dwell alike and the same in all; for men are all of one species, and are provided, more or less, with the like tools and instruments for judging and understanding. But the diversity of opinions we entertain of those things clearly proves that they only enter into us by consent; one man

---

[1] In all the editions of the Essays published after Montaigne's death, except the most recent, this chapter, for no known reason, appeared as Chapter 40. It is here restored to its rightful place.

[2] 'There is nothing either good or bad, but thinking makes it so.' (*Hamlet*). These words first appear in the Shakespeare folio of 1623.

[3] This is one of about forty maxims which Montaigne had inscribed on the joists of the ceiling in his library at Montaigne, where they may still be seen.

perhaps harbours them in their true essence, but a thousand others harbour them in a new and contrary form.

We hold death, poverty, and pain to be our principal enemies. Now this death, which some call 'of all things dreadful the most dreadful', who does not know that others call it 'the only haven from the tempests of this life, the sovereign good of nature, sole support of our freedom, and the prompt and universal remedy for all ills'? And as some await her in fear and trembling, others support her more easily than life. This one complains of her complaisance,

> Ah death! wouldst thou but let the coward live
> And grant the brave alone the prize to die! (LUCAN.)

But let us not speak of those vainglorious hearts. Theodorus replied to Lysimachus, who was threatening to kill him, 'Thou wilt do a great thing in doing what a Spanish fly [1] could do!' Most of the philosophers are seen to have either designedly anticipated, or hastened and aided their own death. How many men of the people we see led to their death, and that not a simple death, but attended with ignominy and sometimes with cruel tortures, and exhibiting such assurance, the one through stubbornness, the other through a natural simplicity, that we may perceive no change from their ordinary demeanour; settling their domestic affairs, commending themselves to their friends, singing, preaching, and talking to the people, nay, sometimes jesting and drinking to their acquaintances, as cheerfully as Socrates.

A man who was being led to the gibbet said 'For goodness' sake don't go by such and such a street, where I shall run the risk of being collared by a tradesman for an old debt'. Another entreated the hangman 'not to touch his neck, for he was so ticklish he would shake with laughter'. Another replied to his confessor, who was promising him that he should sup that night with our Lord, 'You may go yourself, for I am fasting'. Another, having called for drink, and the hangman drinking before him, said he would not drink after him for fear of catching the pox. Everybody has heard the story of the man of Picardy who, when on the

---

[1] The Spanish fly seems to have been credited, whether rightly or not, with a deadly sting.

ladder, was presented with a girl, with the offer (as our justice sometimes permits) that, if he would marry her, his life should be spared ; he, having considered her for a while and perceived that she halted, said, ' Tie up ! Tie up ! she limps.' The same tale is current of a man in Denmark who was condemned to lose his head ; being on the scaffold he was offered the same condition, but refused it on the ground that the girl they offered him had flabby cheeks and too sharp a nose. A serving-man at Toulouse, being accused of heresy, gave as his only excuse that he shared the faith of his master, a young student who was in prison with him, and preferred to die rather than be persuaded that his master could err. We read of the people of the city of Arras that, when King Louis the Eleventh took it, there was a goodly number among them who, rather than say ' Vive le Roy ', suffered themselves to be hanged.

And among those base-souled buffoons there were some who would not leave their jesting even in death. One man exclaimed, as the hangman set him swinging, ' Vogue la gallée ! '[1] which was his usual refrain. And another, who, when on the point of giving up the ghost, had been laid on a mattress along the hearth-stone, and when the physician asked him where he had a pain, replied, ' Between the bench and the fire '. And when the priest came to administer the extreme unction and felt for his feet, which by reason of his malady were cramped and drawn up, he said, ' You will find them at the end of my legs '. Of a man who exhorted him to commend himself to God, he asked, ' Who is going there ? ' and the other replying, ' You will be with him shortly, if it is his pleasure '. ' Supposing I were there to-morrow evening ? ' he rejoined. ' Just commend yourself to him ; you will be with him soon.' ' In that case I had better carry my commendation with me.'

In the kingdom of Narsinga,[2] the wives of the priests are to this day buried alive with their husbands' bodies. All other widows are burned alive on the funeral pyre of their husbands, and that not only with fortitude, but with cheerfulness. When the body of their deceased king is

---

[1] *Vogue la galère !* (Come what may !) : Row the galley (FLORIO) ; Launch the galley ! (COTTON).

[2] There are several places in India with a similar name, as Narsingpur (Bengal), &c.

burned, his wives and concubines, his minions and officers and slaves of all kinds, who comprise quite a people, hasten with such alacrity to cast themselves into the fire with their master, that they appear to regard it as a great honour to share his death.

During our late Milanese wars, there were so many takings and retakings that the people, becoming impatient at such divers changes of fortune, were so firmly resolved to die, that I have heard my father say that he saw a calculation made of quite five and twenty heads of families who had made away with themselves in one week. An incident not unlike that which happened at Xanthos, where the inhabitants, besieged by Brutus, rushed forward pell-mell, men, women, and children, with so passionate a desire to die, that there is nothing done to fly from death that these did not do to fly from life : so much so that Brutus had difficulty in saving a very small number.

Any opinion is strong enough to be espoused at the price of life. The first article in that valiant oath which Greece swore and kept in the Median war, was that every man would sooner exchange life for death than their own laws for those of Persia. How many people we may see in the war between the Turks and the Greeks accepting the most cruel of deaths rather than be decircumcised and receive baptism ! An example which no kind of religion is incapable of following.

The kings of Castile having banished the Jews from their dominions, King John of Portugal sold to them, in consideration of eight crowns per head, a retreat in his kingdom for a certain time, on condition that they should depart when the term was expired, and promising to furnish them with vessels to transport them to Africa. The day having come, which being lapsed it was ordained that those who had not obeyed should remain slaves, the ships were provided in niggardly fashion, and those who embarked in them treated harshly and villainously by the passengers,[1] who, amongst many other indignities, kept them at sea, cruising backwards and forwards, until they had consumed all their provisions, and were constrained to buy of them ; but for so long a time and at so high a price that they were not landed until they had all been reduced to their shirts. The news of this inhumanity having been brought to those who were on land,

[1] No doubt Montaigne meant the crew.

the greater part of them resolved to accept slavery, and some made a show of changing their religion. When Emmanuel came to the throne, he at first set them at liberty, but afterwards, changing his mind, he commanded them to leave his country within a certain time, assigning to them three ports for their departure. He hoped, says Bishop Osorius, the best Latin historian of our times, that, the favour of the freedom he had granted them having failed to convert them to Christianity, the hard prospect of being delivered over, like their friends, to the mercy of the thievish seamen after leaving a country they were now become habituated to and were grown very rich in, to be landed in strange and unknown regions, would bring them to it. But seeing himself disappointed in his expectation, and that they were all resolved upon the voyage, he cut off two of the ports he had promised them, in order that the length and the inconveniences of the journey might induce some of them to think better of it, or that he might be enabled, by crowding them all into one place, to execute with greater convenience his purpose. Which was that he commanded all the children under the age of fourteen to be torn from their parents' arms, and removed out of their sight and company to a place where they could be instructed in our religion.[1]

They say that the sequel was horrible to see : the natural affection between parents and children, added to their zeal for their ancient faith, contending with this violent decree. It was quite common to see fathers and mothers making away with themselves, and—a still ruder test—driven by love and pity, throwing their young children into the wells, to evade the law. As to the remainder, the allotted time having expired, for want of resources they returned to slavery. Some of them became Christians ; but of their sincerity or that of their race in general few of the Portuguese are assured even to this day, a hundred years after ; although custom and length of time are much better counsellors than any compulsion. *How often have not only our leaders, but whole armies, hastened to certain death?* (Cicero).

[In the town of Castelnau Darry fifty heretical Albigenses, with a resolute courage, suffered themselves to be burned

---

[1] Mariana, the celebrated Spanish historian, who was a Jesuit, says that the children were baptized by force, and he protests very strongly against the cruelty of the whole affair.

alive together, in one fire, before they would renounce their religion.]

I have seen one of my intimate friends forcibly courting death with a real affection, that had become rooted in his heart by divers specious arguments that I was unable to refute; and, as soon as it presented itself crowned with a halo of honour, rush at it with fierce and ardent hunger, but no apparent reason.

We have many examples in our own time of people, even children, who, from fear of some slight inconvenience, have taken their lives.[1] And an ancient writer (Seneca) says in this connexion, 'What shall we not fear, if we fear that which cowardice itself has chosen for its refuge?'

If I were here to string together a long bead-roll of those, of both sexes and all conditions and sects, during the happiest ages, who have either awaited death with firmness or voluntarily sought it, and sought it not only to flee the ills of this life, but some merely to flee the satiety of living, and others in hope of a better condition in another place, I should never have done. The number of them is so infinite, that I should truly find it cheaper to take into account those who have feared it.

This only: Pyrrho the philosopher, being one very stormy day in a boat, pointed out to those he saw most terrified around him, to encourage them by its example, a pig which happened to be there, quite unconcerned about the storm.

Shall we then venture to say that this privilege of Reason, that we make such a fuss about, and because of which we think ourselves lords and emperors of the rest of creation, has been given to us for our torment? What avails the knowledge of things, if we lose thereby the tranquillity and repose we should enjoy without it, and if it reduces us to a worse condition than that of Pyrrho's pig? The intelligence which was given to us for our greatest good, shall we employ it for our ruin, setting ourselves against Nature's design and the universal order of things, which ordains that each of us shall use his tools and means to his advantage?

Very well, it may be said, let your rule hold with regard to death, but what will you say of want? And what will you

---

[1] Note by Dr. Armaingaud, the latest editor of Montaigne's works: 'It is the same to-day in France. From January 1895 to January 1905, 695 children committed suicide for absolutely futile reasons.'

say of pain, which Aristippus, Hieronymus, and most of the sages regarded as the worst of evils? And those who denied it in words confessed it in action. Posidonius, being extremely tormented by an acute and painful malady, Pompey came to see him, and excused himself for having chosen so unseasonable an hour to hear him discourse on philosophy. ' God forbid, said Posidonius, that pain should gain such a power over me as to prevent my talking and discussing philosophy ! ' and he fell upon this same theme of contempt of pain. But meanwhile it was playing its part and afflicting him unceasingly, whereupon he exclaimed : ' You may do your worst, pain ! yet will I not say that you are an evil.'

This tale that they make such a pother about, how does it prove the contempt of pain ? It only disputes the word, and meanwhile if those pangs do not move him, why does he break off his discourse ? Why does he think he does so great a thing in not calling it Evil ?

Here it is not all imagination. We conjecture the rest ; it is here that certain knowledge plays its part. Our senses themselves are judges of it :

If senses be not true, all reason then is false. (LUCRETIUS.)

Shall we make our skin believe that it is only tickled by the blows of a stirrup-leather, and our palate that aloes is *vin de Graves* ? Pyrrho's pig is here in the same boat with us. It is true that he is not afraid of death, but if you beat him he will rush about and squeal. Shall we force the universal law of Nature, which is seen in every living thing under heaven, and which ordains that we tremble under pain ? The very trees seem to groan when they are hurt. Death is only felt by thinking, seeing that it is the motion of an instant :

'Tis coming or 'tis past, but present it is never. (LA BOËTIE.)

Death deferred more painful is than death. (OVID.)

A thousand beasts, a thousand men, are sooner dead than threatened. And indeed, what we say we principally fear in death is pain, her usual forerunner.

However, if we are to believe a holy father, *that only which follows death makes death an evil* (Saint Augustine). And I should say besides, with more likelihood, that neither that which goes before nor that which comes after is of the adjuncts of death. We excuse ourselves falsely. I have found by experience that it is rather because we cannot bear the idea of death that we are unable to bear pain, and that we find it doubly grievous because it threatens us with death. But when reason accuses us of cowardice in fearing a thing so sudden, so unavoidable, so little felt, we grasp at that other more excusable pretence.

All the afflictions that have no other danger but the affliction itself we declare to be without danger: toothache and the gout, however painful they may be, as long as they do not kill a man, who accounts them diseases? Now let us suppose that in death we chiefly regard the pain. And poverty besides has nothing to fear except that it throws us into the arms of pain through thirst, hunger, cold, fever, and sleeplessness, to which it exposes us.

Let us then deal with pain alone. I grant you, and willingly, that it is the worst thing that can happen to us, for if there is a man in the world who hates it and runs away from it, it is myself, the more so as I have hitherto, thank God, had little to do with it. But it is in us, if not to annihilate it, at least to lessen it by patience, and, though the body may be disturbed by it, nevertheless to keep the soul and reason in good trim.

And if it were not so, how should it come about that virtue, valour, strength, magnanimity, and resolution are held in honour? Where would they play their part, if there were no more pain to be defied? *Virtue is greedy of peril* (Seneca). If there were no such thing as sleeping on the hard ground, enduring in full panoply the heat of noon, feeding on the flesh of horses and asses, seeing ourselves cut up and a bullet extracted from out our bones, suffering ourselves to be stitched up, probed and cauterized, how could we acquire the advantage we think we have over the common run of people?

There is a great difference between avoiding evil and pain and what the sages say, 'that of actions equally good, that is the most desirable which is attended with most pains'. *For austere men are not made happy by gaiety, pleasure, laughter and play, the companion of frivolity, but often by firmness and endurance* (Cicero). And for that reason it was impossible to persuade our fathers that the conquests carried out by bodily strength in the hazard of war were not more honourable than those gained in all security by intrigues and negotiations.

> An honest deed is sweetened by its cost. (LUCAN.)

Moreover, this should be our consolation, that naturally *if the pain be violent, it is short ; if it be long, it is easy* (Cicero). Thou wilt not feel it very long if thou feelest it too much : it will put an end to itself or to thee : both come to the same thing. If thou dost not bear it, it will bear thee away. *Remember that the greatest pains are ended by death ; the lighter ones have many intervals of rest : we may master the more moderate ones : so that if they are bearable we shall bear them ; if not, we can go out of life as from a theatre when the play ceases to please* (Cicero).

What makes us suffer pain with so much impatience is that we are not accustomed to find our chief contentment in the soul, and that we do not sufficiently rely upon her, who is sole and sovereign mistress of our condition and conduct. The body has, saving in greater or less proportion, but one course and one bent. The soul is variable in all manner of forms, and subjects to herself and to her empire, whether it be great or small, the feelings of the body and all other accidents. Therefore we should study our soul, examine her forces, and stir up her all-powerful springs of action. There is neither reason, prescription, nor force that will avail against her inclination and her choice. Of so many thousands of expedients that she has at her disposal, if we grant her one proper to our repose and preservation, then shall we be not only covered against any injury, but gratified even, and pleased, if it seem good to her, with evils and injuries. She makes her profit indifferently out of all things. Error, dreams, usefully serve her purpose, as rightful matter to bring us into safety and contentment.

It is easy to see that it is the working of our mind that gives an edge to our pains and pleasures. The beasts, that keep the mind under control, leave to their body their sensations, free and natural, and consequently almost one and the same in each species, as appears in the conformity of their movements. If we did not disturb in our members the jurisdiction that appertains to them in this, it may be believed that we should be the better for it, and that Nature has given them a right and moderate temper in face of pleasure and pain. And it cannot fail to be right, being the same in all of us. But, since we have emancipated ourselves from her rules, to indulge the vagabond freedom of our fancies, let us at least help to incline them to the most agreeable side.

Plato fears our hard bondage to pain and pleasure, because it too strictly binds and attaches the soul to the body. I rather, on the contrary, because it detaches and unbinds it. Just as the enemy is made more fierce by our flight, so pain is puffed up with pride to see us tremble under her. She will surrender on much better terms to one who makes head against her. We must brace ourselves and resist. By backing and giving ground, we attract and call down upon ourselves the destruction that threatens us. As the body by stiffening itself resists attack more firmly, so does the soul.

But let us come to the examples, which are the proper game for weak-backed fellows like me : in them we shall find that it is with pain as with those precious stones which take on a higher or a duller lustre according to the foil on which they are set, and that it has no more room in us than we allow it. *The more they gave way to pain the more did they feel it* (Saint Augustine). We are more sensible to the touch of the surgeon's lancet than to ten sword-cuts in the heat of battle. The pains of childbirth, deemed to be great by physicians and by God himself, which are attended with so many ceremonies, there are entire nations that make no account of them. I say nothing of the Spartan women ; but in the Swiss women in the camps of our foot-soldiers, what change will you find, except that you may see them to-day trudging after their husbands and carrying a child on their back which yesterday they bore in their womb ? And those ill-favoured Gipsy women, herding in our country-side, will themselves wash their new-born infants, and bathe in the nearest river.

Besides the many young girls who every day conceal the delivery as they did the conception of their babes, the modest wife of Sabinus, a Roman patrician, in consideration of others endured alone, without aid, without raising her voice or uttering a groan, the labour of bearing twins.[1]

---

[1] A pretty story of wifely affection, which may be read in Plutarch's essay on *Love*.

SPARTAN COURAGE

A simple Spartan boy, having stolen a fox (for they feared the disgrace of a theft stupidly carried out more than we do the penalty), and having put it under his cape, suffered it to gnaw his bowels rather than betray himself. And another, while offering incense at a sacrifice, let himself be burned to the bone by an ember fallen into his sleeve, in order not to disturb the mystery. And a great number have been seen, as a mere test of valour, in accordance with their system of education, who at the age of seven years suffered flogging to death without changing countenance. And Cicero saw men fighting by companies, with fists, feet, and teeth, until they swooned, before admitting themselves vanquished. *Never could custom conquer Nature, for she is ever unconquerable ; but we have corrupted the soul with pretences, luxuries, idleness, languor, indifference ; evil opinions and habits have made it effeminate* (Cicero).

Everybody knows the story of Scaevola who, having slipped into the camp of the enemy to kill the general and failed in his attempt, by a stranger fiction, to repair his fault and deliver his country, not only confessed his intention to Porsenna, the king whom he thought to slay, but added that in his camp there was a great number of Romans, confederates in his enterprise and as good men as himself. And to show what kind of man he was, having requested a brazier to be brought, he saw and suffered his arm to be grilled and roasted, till the enemy himself, struck with horror, commanded the brazier to be removed.

What of the man who deigned not to interrupt the reading of his book whilst he was being lanced ? And the man who persisted in laughing and sneering in contempt of the pain he was enduring ; so that the executioners who held him, provoked to greater cruelty, inflicted one after another every torture they could invent, until they were obliged to own themselves beaten ? But that was a philosopher. What of Caesar's gladiator who endured, laughing all the while, the probing and cutting of his wounds ? *Where is the gladiator, even the meanest, who ever uttered a groan or changed countenance ? Which of them ever disgraced himself, either withstanding his adversary or succumbing ? Which of them, when down and ordered to be slain with the sword, ever withdrew his neck ?* (Cicero).

Now for the ladies ! Who has not heard tell of the lady

in Paris who, solely to acquire a fresher complexion and a new skin, had herself flayed ? Some have had live and sound teeth drawn, to have them arranged in better order, or to render their voice softer and richer. How many examples we may see in this sex of contempt of pain! What are they not capable of, what do they fear, as long as they have any hope of improving their beauty ?

> Root out the tell-tale grey hairs from their place;
> Remove the skin to renovate the face. (TIBULLUS.)

I have known them to swallow sand and ashes, and set about purposely to ruin their digestion in order to acquire a pale complexion. For a slender figure *à l'Espagnole* what tortures will they not endure, their ribs forcibly strapped and laced into large splints, which enter the living flesh, nay, sometimes even cause death.

It is a common practice nowadays among many nations for people to wound themselves purposely, in order to give credit to their words, and our King [1] tells of some remarkable examples of this which he witnessed in Poland, and also with respect to himself. But, besides others that, to my knowledge, imitated this proceeding in France, I have seen a girl, as a proof of the sincerity of her promises and of her constancy, give herself four or five good stabs in the arm with a bodkin she wore in her hair, so that the skin cracked and blood flowed in good earnest. The Turks tear great holes in their flesh in honour of their ladies, and, that the mark may remain, immediately apply fire to the wound, holding it there an incredible time, to stop the blood and form a scar. People who have witnessed this have written to me and sworn to it. But for ten aspers [2] you may any day find one among them who will deal himself a deep gash in his arm or thighs.

I am very glad that evidence is more ready to hand where we have most need of it, for Christianity provides it in abundance. And there have been people in plenty who, following the example of our blessed Guide, have been willing, in their religious zeal, to bear the cross. We learn from a witness very worthy of belief [3] that the sainted King

---

[1] Henry III, who was also King of Poland from 1573 to 1574.
[2] Asper, a Turkish coin worth about a halfpenny.
[3] The Sire de Joinville, in his *Life of Saint Louis*.

Louis the Ninth wore the hair-shirt until, in his old age, his confessor gave him dispensation ; and that every Friday he had his shoulders scourged by his priest with five little iron chains which for that purpose he always carried in a box.

William, our last Duke of Guienne, father of that Eleanor who transmitted the duchy to the houses of France and England, by way of penance wore continually, during the last ten or twelve years of his life, a corselet under a monk's habit. Foulques, Count of Anjou, went all the way to Jerusalem in order to have himself scourged there by two of his varlets, with a rope round his neck, before our Lord's sepulchre. But on any Good Friday can we not see, in divers places, a great number of men and women flogging themselves, till they lacerate and cut the flesh to the bones ? That I have often witnessed, and without being enchanted ; and they used to say (for they go masked) that there were some among them who, for money payment, would undertake in this way to safeguard the religion of others, with a contempt for pain so much the greater, as the incentives to devotion are more powerful than those of avarice.

Q. Maximus buried his son when he was a consul, M. Cato his son who was praetor-elect, and L. Paulus two of his within a few days, with unmoved countenance and giving no signs of grief. I once said jestingly of some man that he had flouted divine justice ; for the violent death of three of his grown-up sons having been visited upon him in one day as a rude scourge, as may be supposed, he all but accepted it as a favour. I have lost two or three (but they were infants in arms), if not without grief, at least without brooding over the loss.[1] Yet there is hardly any mischance that cuts one more to the quick. I can think of many other common causes of affliction which, if they happened to me, I should hardly feel ; and some I have despised, when they have visited me, which to the world appear so atrocious, that I should not dare to boast of it before people without a blush. *From which we may understand that grief is not in nature, but in opinion* (Cicero).

---

[1] This apparent callousness has been much commented on. It must be remembered that, in accordance with the custom of the times, infants were sent out to neighbouring farms to be nursed, and that the father seldom if ever set eyes on them. But he should have remembered the number, which was actually four !

Belief is a powerful factor, bold and incalculable. Who ever sought security and repose as greedily as Alexander and Caesar sought uneasiness and hardships ? Teres, the father of Sitalces,[1] used to say, ' When he was not at war he could see very little difference between himself and his groom.'

Cato the consul, having, to make sure of certain cities in Spain, only forbidden the inhabitants to bear arms, a great number of them killed themselves : *a fierce race that thought they could not live without arms* (Livy). How many do we not know of who have fled the sweets of a tranquil life in their home, among their acquaintance, in pursuit of the horrors of uninhabitable deserts ; and who have eagerly courted humiliations, degradations and the contempt of the world, and taken a pleasure in them that amounted to affectation ! Cardinal Borromeo,[2] who recently died at Milan, in the midst of the debaucheries to which his noble rank, his great wealth, the air of Italy and his youth invited him, lived so austerely, that the same robe he wore in summer served him in winter ; that he slept on straw, and spent his spare hours, after performing his official duties, in continual study, planted on his knees, with a little bread and water at the side of his book, which was all that he provided for his repasts, and on which he wasted no time. I have known some who have knowingly derived profit and advancement from cuckoldry, the mere mention of which frightens so many people.[3]

If sight is not the most necessary of our senses, it at least gives us most pleasure ; but the most pleasant and useful of our members seem to be those which serve for procreation ; yet many people have conceived a mortal hatred of them, and have cast them off because they were so prized. As much thought he of his eyes who put them out.[4]

The generality of men, and the sanest of them, hold an abundance of children to be a piece of great good fortune ; I and some others regard the want of them as equally fortunate ; and when Thales is asked why he does not marry,

---

[1] King of Thrace.
[2] Archbishop of Milan, better known as St. Charles Borromeo, 1538–84.
[3] O word of fear
Unpleasing to a married ear ! (*Love's Labour's Lost*).
[4] Democritus ; but the fact seems to be very doubtful.

he replies that 'he has no mind to leave any posterity behind him'.

That it is our opinion that gives value to things may be seen in the great number which we consider not only from the point of view of their intrinsic value, but of their value to ourselves ; and we consider not their qualities nor their usefulness, but only what it cost us to procure them, as if that were a part of their substance ; and we call value in them, not what they bring to us but what we bring to them. Which brings to my mind that we are great husbanders of our outlay. It serves us according to its weight, and merely because it weighs. Our opinion will never allow it to be undervalued. The purchase gives value to the diamond, difficulty to virtue, suffering to devotion, and unpleasantness to physic.

A certain man, to acquire poverty, threw his money into the very same sea which so many others search all over in fishing for riches. Epicurus says that 'to be rich is not an end, but a change, of troubles'. Truly it is not want but abundance that creates avarice. I will relate my experience in this matter.

Since my childhood I have lived in three different states of mind. The first period, which continued nearly twenty years, I spent with only casual means, and depending on the direction and assistance of others, without any definite or prescribed revenue. I spent my money the more cheerfully and carelessly through relying over-boldly on Fortune. I was never better off. I never chanced to find my friends' purses closed to me, having convinced myself of the necessity, beyond any other necessity, never to miss the term I had fixed for payment, which they have a thousand times extended, in consideration of the efforts I made to satisfy them : so that I repaid them with a thrifty and somewhat guileful loyalty.

I naturally feel a certain pleasurable satisfaction in paying : it is as if I were unloading my shoulders of a troublesome burden, and of that image of slavery, besides that there is a certain satisfaction that flatters me in performing a just action and in satisfying another. I make an exception of payments where there is any calculation or haggling to be done ; for, unless I can find somebody to undertake the charge, I put them off, to my own shame and to others' prejudice, as long as I can, dreading that altercation which is quite incompatible with my humour and my way of speaking. There is nothing I hate more than driving a bargain. It is a pure interchange of trickery and impudence; after an hour of disputing and wrangling each party withdraws his word and his oaths for a betterment of five sous. And so I used to borrow at a disadvantage; for, not having the courage to make my request in person, I committed it to the hazard of paper, which is not a very successful advocate, and lends itself very easily to a refusal. I left the conduct of my needs to the stars more freely and more cheerfully than I have since done to my providence and my common sense.

Most good managers think it dreadful to live in this uncertainty, and they do not consider, Firstly, that the majority of the people in the world live thus. How many worthy men have carelessly cast away their whole fixed income, and do so every day, to court the wind of kings' and Fortune's favours! Caesar ran into debt to the extent of a million in gold over and above what he was worth, in order to become Caesar. And how many merchants found their traffic on the proceeds of the sale of their farms, which they send to the Indies

> Across so many stormy seas! (CATULLUS.)

And in this present great drouth of devotion we have a thousand and a thousand colleges [1] where they spend their life comfortably, expecting every day from the liberality of heaven what they need for their dinner.

Secondly, they do not consider that that certainty on which they rely is not much less uncertain and hazardous than hazard itself. I can see want as near to me, at the other end of an income of two thousand crowns, as if it were within touch. For, besides that fate has the power of opening a thousand gaps to poverty through our wealth, there being often no mean between the highest and the lowest fortune,

> Fortune is glass, and breaks when best it shines, (PUBLIUS SYRUS.)

and of turning all our defences and ramparts topsy-turvy, I find that, from divers causes, indigence as commonly dwells with those who possess worldly goods as with those who possess none; and that perhaps it is somewhat less in-

[1] Congregations or convents.

convenient when alone than when it is accompanied with riches. Wealth comes from good management rather than from revenue : *every man is his fortune's artisan* (Sallust). And it seems to me that a wealthy man who is uneasy, hard-up, and overwhelmed in business is more miserable than he who is simply poor. *Indigence in the lap of riches is the most grievous kind of poverty* (Seneca). The greatest and richest princes are, through poverty and want, commonly driven to the extremest necessity ; for can there be any more extreme than to become tyrants and unjust usurpers of their subjects' goods ?

My second state was to have money ; having acquired a taste for which, I soon laid by some considerable reserve funds, considering my circumstances : reflecting that a man possesses only that which is over and above his ordinary outlay, and that he cannot rely on the revenue which he still only expects to receive, however clear his expectation may be. For, I would say, what if I were overtaken by such and such a calamity ? And after such vain and pernicious imaginings I would exercise my ingenuity in providing, by means of this superfluous reserve, against all emergencies ; and to any man who objected that the number of emergencies was too infinite, I could still reply that if I could not provide against all, I could provide against some and many.

This did not go on without painful anxiety. I kept it very close ; and, though so bold in speaking of myself, I only lied about my money, like those rich men who call themselves poor, and those poor men who pretend to be rich, and dispense their conscience from ever giving a true account of their means : a ridiculous and shameful caution ! Was I starting on my travels ? I never seemed to be sufficiently provided. And the more I burdened myself with coin, the more did I burden myself with fear, now about the safety of the roads, now about the fidelity of those who conveyed my baggage, of which, like others I know, I was never sufficiently sure as long as it was out of my sight. Did I leave my box at my lodgings ? how many suspicions and perplexing ideas, which, to make the matter worse, I dared not communicate to another ! My mind was always with that box. Taking everything into account, there is more trouble in keeping money than in getting it. If I did not do all that I am saying here, it used at least to cost me an effort to keep myself from doing so.

I gained little or no satisfaction: though I had more means to spend, they weighed no less on my mind. For, as Bion says, 'The man with a good head of hair will resent it no less than the bald man, if you pull one out.' And, when once you have fixed your fancy on a certain pile and become accustomed to its possession, it is no longer at your service : you will not dare to make a hole in it. It is a building which, you think, will crumble to pieces if you touch it. You will not break into it till necessity takes you by the throat. So I would sooner and with much less constraint and less reluctance pawn my clothes or sell a horse, than make a breach in that favourite purse which I had laid by. But the danger is that it is not easy to set certain bounds to this passion (they are hard to find in things that one thinks good) and to fix a limit to economy. One ever goes on adding to this heap, and increasing it by one sum after another, to the extent of sordidly depriving oneself of the enjoyment of one's own property, finding one's pleasure in its safe-keeping, without making any use of it.

According to this kind of usage, the richest people, from the money point of view, are those who are set to guard the gates and walls of a good city. Every monied man is avaricious in my opinion.

Plato arranges the corporal or human goods in this order : health, beauty, strength, wealth ; and wealth, he says, is not blind, but very clear-sighted when enlightened by wisdom.

Dionysius the son [1] did a graceful thing. He was informed that one of his Syracusans had hidden a treasure in the ground. He sent word to the man to bring it to him, which he did, while secretly keeping back some part of it, with which he went to another town, where, having lost his appetite for hoarding, he began to live more generously. Hearing of which, Dionysius restored to him the remainder of his treasure, saying that, since he had learned how to use it, he gave it back willingly.

I was for some years in this state of mind.[2] I know not

---

[1] Or rather the father, according to Plutarch.
[2] The edition of 1588 says four or five years. Of his travels here

what good demon most beneficially threw me out of it, like the Syracusan, and my habit of saving was dropped; the pleasure of a certain very costly journey having set its foot on that very foolish fancy. In consequence of this I fell into a third kind of living (I speak as I feel about it), certainly much more agreeable and better regulated in that I make my expenses run abreast with my receipts; now one goes ahead, now the other, but they are never far apart. I live from day to day, and am content with having sufficient for present and ordinary needs; for the extraordinary all the provision in the world will not suffice. And it is madness to expect that Fortune could ever sufficiently arm us against herself. With our own arms must we fight her. Casual arms will betray us when the need is greatest. If I save up it is only in the hope of making some purchase in the near future; not to buy lands, of which I have no need, but to buy pleasure. *Not to be covetous is money; not to be keen to buy is revenue* (Cicero). I am little afraid of running short, and have no desire to increase my store. *The fruit of riches is in abundance, and content declares abundance* (Cicero). And I am singularly pleased that this reformation came to me at an age that is naturally inclined to avarice, and that I see myself rid of this disease so common to old men, and the most ridiculous of human follies.

Feraulez, who had experienced both kinds of fortune, and discovered that increase of substance did not mean an increased appetite for eating, drinking, sleeping, and embracing his wife, and who, on the other hand, was beginning to feel exacting household cares weighing upon his shoulders, as they do on mine, decided to gratify a poor young man, his faithful friend, who was barking after riches: he made him a gift of all his exceeding great possessions, and of those besides which he was accumulating every day through the liberality of Cyrus, his good master, and through the war; in return for which the other was to board and lodge him handsomely as his guest and friend. They thus lived ever after very happily, and equally satisfied with the change in their condition. That is an act I could very heartily imitate.

And I greatly commend the fortune of an aged prelate

mentioned, which took him through Germany, Switzerland, and Italy in 1580–1, Montaigne compiled a Journal, not published till 1774.

whom I know, who has so entirely given over his purse, his receipts and expenses, now to one chosen servant, now to another, that he has lived many tranquil years, as regardless of his household affairs as any stranger. Trust in others' goodness is no slight testimony of one's own goodness; wherefore does God willingly favour it. And with regard to the man I speak of, I know of no household that is more worthily and more stably managed than his. Happy is he who has regulated his needs in so just a measure, that his wealth may sufficiently provide for them without any care and trouble on his part, and without its acquisition and disposal disturbing his other, more suitable, more tranquil, and more congenial occupations!

Ease and indigence therefore depend on the opinion of each man; and neither riches nor fame and health have any more beauty and pleasure than he attributes to them by whom they are possessed. Every man is well or badly off as he thinks himself to be. The man is content who believes himself to be content, not he whom the world believes to be so. And that belief alone makes it real and true.

Fortune does us neither good nor harm: she only holds out to us the seed and the matter of good or harm, which our soul, more powerful than she, turns and applies as she pleases, being sole cause and mistress of her happy or unhappy condition.

External accessories take savour and colour from the internal constitution, as clothes keep us warm, not by their heat, but by our own, which they are adapted to keep in and cherish; he who would protect a cold body with them would do the same service for the cold, for thus are snow and ice preserved.

Truly, just as study is a torment to the sluggard, abstinence from wine to a drunkard, as frugality is a punishment to a man of riotous living, and exercise a torture to a tenderly-reared and lazy person, so with the rest. Things are not so painful or difficult in themselves; it is our weakness and laxity that make them so. To judge of great and sublime things needs a soul of the same quality, else we shall attribute to them the faults which are ours. A straight oar appears bent in the water. The important thing is not merely that we see the thing, but *how* we see it.

Well then, why, among so many reasons which diversely

persuade men to despise death and endure pain, do we not find one that makes for our purpose ? And among the many kinds of fancies which have persuaded others to do so, why does not each man apply one to himself, the most conformable to his humour ? If he cannot digest the strong and purgative drug to eradicate the evil, let him at least take a lenitive to ease it. *With regard to pain no less than to pleasure we are so weak and effeminate, we are so enervated and softened by luxury that we cannot without shouting endure the sting of a bee. It is all a matter of self-control* (Cicero).

For the rest, we do not escape Philosophy by stressing beyond measure the sharpness of pain and human weakness, for we constrain her to fall back on these unanswerable replies : ' If it is bad to live in need, there is at least no need to live in need.' ' No man suffers long but by his own fault.' ' He who has not the courage to suffer either death or life, he who will neither resist nor fly, what should we do with him ? '

CHAPTER 15

ONE DOES NOT WITH IMPUNITY DEFEND A PLACE OBSTINATELY AND AGAINST REASON

LIKE other virtues, valour has its limits, which being overstepped, it is in the way of becoming a vice, in the sense that it leads to temerity, obstinacy, and madness in one who cannot observe, which it is indeed not easy to do, the line where the one ends and the other begins. From this consideration is born the custom which we have in wartime of punishing, even with death, those who obstinately persist in defending a place which by the rules of warfare cannot be held. Otherwise, in the hope of impunity, there is not a hen-roost but could hold up an army.

Monsieur the Constable de Montmorency, having, at the siege of Pavia, been charged to cross the Ticino and take up his quarters in the suburb of S. Antonio, was held up by a tower at the end of the bridge, which obstinately held out until reduced by a battery ; the defenders were all hanged to a man. After that again, accompanying Monsieur the Dauphin in his expedition beyond the mountains, and taking the castle of Villano by assault, all those within were cut in pieces by the fury of the soldiers, the captain and ensign excepted, who were hanged and strangled for the same reason; the same thing was done by Captain Martin du Bellay, then governor of Turin in the same country, to the Captain de S. Bony, the rest of his men having been massacred at the taking of the place.

But, inasmuch as the strength and weakness of a place is measured by the estimate and comparison of the attacking forces (for a man might reasonably hold out against a couple of culverins who would be mad to abide a battery of thirteen pieces of cannon), where we also take into account the greatness of the conquering prince, his reputation and the respect that is due to him, there is the danger of pressing the scales a little on that side. And it may happen, by the same reasoning, that some are possessed with so great an opinion of themselves and their power that, deeming it contrary to reason to consider any place as worthy to hold its own against them, they use the knife on all wherever they meet with resistance, as long as their good fortune endures; as we may see in the form of summons and challenge, so full of pride, arrogance, and barbarian tyranny, in use among the Oriental princes and their present successors.

And in the quarter of the globe where the Portuguese first attacked the Indians, they found some states where it was a universal and inviolable law that every enemy vanquished by the king in person, or by his lieutenant, is shut out from both ransom and mercy.

So that above all things a man should take heed, if he can, against falling into the hands of an enemy judge who is victorious and armed.

CHAPTER 16

OF THE PUNISHMENT OF COWARDICE

I ONCE heard a prince, who was a very great captain, maintain that a soldier could not be condemned to death for faint-heartedness; he had just been told, whilst sitting at table, of the trial of the Seigneur de Vervins who was condemned to death for having surrendered Boulogne.[1]

[1] To Henry VIII of England, who was present at the siege.

It is reasonable indeed to see great difference between those faults which are the result of our weakness, and those which proceed from wickedness. For in the latter we knowingly oppose the laws of reason that Nature has imprinted in us, whereas in the former, it seems to me, we may justify ourselves by making that same Nature responsible for leaving us so weak and imperfect. So that many people have thought that we could be blamed only for the things we do against our conscience; and upon this rule is partly founded the opinion of those who condemn capital punishment for heretics and unbelievers, and that which maintains that an advocate and a judge are not accountable for having failed in their charge through ignorance.

But as to cowardice, it is certain that the most common custom is to chastise it by shame and ignominy. It is thought that this method was first introduced by the law-giver Charondas; that before him those who fled from battle were by the Greek laws punished with death, instead of which he ordained that they should only be seated for three days in the middle of the public square, dressed in a woman's gown, in the hope that by this disgrace their courage might come back to them, and they could still be of service: *Rather bring the blood into a man's cheek than shed it* (Tertullian). It seems too that in ancient times the Roman laws also punished with death those who ran away, for Ammianus Marcellinus says that the Emperor Julian condemned ten of his soldiers, who during a charge had turned their backs to the Parthians, to degradation and afterwards death, following, he says, the ancient laws. On another occasion however, for a like offence, he condemned others merely to be kept among the prisoners, under the baggage ensign. The severe punishment inflicted by the Roman people upon the soldiers who ran away at Cannae, and those who, in the same war, accompanied Cn. Fulvius in his defeat, did not extend to death. Yet it is to be feared lest disgrace may drive a man to despair and turn him, not merely into a cool friend, but an enemy.

In the time of our fathers, the Seigneur de Franget, formerly the lieutenant of Monsieur the Maréchal de Chastillon's company, having been appointed by Monsieur the Maréchal de Chabannes governor of Fuentarabia in the place of Monsieur du Lude, and having surrendered that place to the Spaniards, was condemned to be degraded from the nobility, and both he and his posterity were declared commoners, liable to pay taxes and incapable of bearing arms; which severe sentence was carried out at Lyons. Since then the same punishment was borne by all the noblemen who were in Guise, when the Count of Nassau entered that town, and by others again after that.

When however ignorance or cowardice is so gross and apparent that it exceeds the ordinary, it is but right to regard them as sufficient proof of malice and wickedness, and to punish them as such.

CHAPTER 17

A CHARACTERISTIC OF SOME AMBASSADORS

ON my travels I observe this practice, in order to be always learning something by intercourse with others (which is one of the best schools that can be), that I always lead those with whom I am conversing to speak of the things they know best;

> Let the sailor tell of storms,
>   The ploughman praise his ox,
> The warrior count his wounds,
>   The shepherd count his flocks. (PROPERTIUS.)

For most frequently it is the other way: every one prefers to talk about another's trade rather than his own, thinking thereby to acquire a new reputation; witness the reproof of Archidamus to Periander, that he was renouncing the fame of a good physician to gain that of a bad poet.

Observe how largely Caesar spreads himself out to explain to us his contrivances in building bridges and engines of war, and how concise he is by comparison when speaking of the business of his profession, of his valour and the conduct of his military affairs. His exploits sufficiently prove him to be an eminent general; he endeavours to make himself known as an excellent engineer: a somewhat extraneous quality.

A gentleman of the legal profession who was brought the other day to see a study furnished with all kinds of books dealing with his own calling and of every other sort, found there nothing to interest him. But he stopped to criticize, in a rude and authoritative tone, a balustrade fixed at the head of the winding staircase of the study, a thing which a hundred captains and soldiers will observe any day without remark or offence.

The elder Dionysius was a very great war-lord, as befitted his fortune, but he laboured to recommend himself principally by his poetry, in which he had no skill.

> The lumbering ox for housings longs ; the steed
> Thinks that to plough were happiness indeed. (HORACE.)

In this way you will never achieve anything worth doing.

We should therefore always bring back the architect and the painter each to his calling, the cobbler to his last, and so with the rest.

Being on this theme, when I read history, which is written by all sorts and conditions of men, I usually consider what kind of man the author is : if his profession is that of letters only, he teaches me principally style and language ; if he is a physician, I am the more ready to believe what he says of the temperature of the air, of the health and constitution of princes, of wounds and maladies ; if a lawyer, we must accept his observations on controversies about rights, laws and the establishment of civil government, and the like ; if a theologian, on the affairs of the church, on ecclesiastical censures, dispensations and marriages ; if a courtier, on manners and ceremonies ; if a soldier, on that which appertains to his profession, and principally his account of the exploits in which he was personally engaged ; if an ambassador, on intrigues, negotiations, and agreements, and the manner of conducting them.

For this reason I have marked and weighed in the history of the Seigneur de Langey, a man of great judgement in such matters, what I should have passed over without comment in another, which is that, after telling of the fine address which the Emperor Charles the Fifth delivered in the consistory at Rome, in the presence of the Bishop of Macon and the Seigneur du Velly, our ambassadors, in the course of which he made several insulting remarks against our nation, and amongst others that, if his own captains, soldiers and subjects had given no better proofs of their fidelity and military skill than those of our King, he would immediately put a rope round his neck and go and sue for his mercy (and it seems that he partly meant what he said, for two or three times in his life since then he happened to repeat the same words); he added that he challenged the King to fight him in his shirt, with sword and dagger, in a boat. The said Seigneur de Langey adds in his history that the ambassadors, in the dispatch which they sent to the King on this affair, disguised the greater part of it and even kept silence on the two preceding passages.

Now I have thought it very strange that it should be in the power of an ambassador to decide what warnings he ought to convey to his master, especially when of such consequence, coming from such a person, and uttered in so great an assembly. I should have thought it to be the duty of the servant to give a full and faithful account of things, exactly as they occurred, in order that the liberty of disposing, judging, and selecting might remain with the master. For to distort or conceal the truth, in the fear that he might take it otherwise than he should, and be driven to some evil step, and meanwhile to leave him in ignorance of his affairs, should methinks belong to him who gives the law and not to him who receives it, to the guardian and schoolmaster, and not to him who ought to regard himself as an inferior, not only in authority but also in wisdom and good counsel. However that may be, I should not like to be served thus in my little concerns.

We are so ready to evade authority upon some pretext or other, and to usurp the mastery; every man aspires so naturally to freedom and power, that to a superior nothing can be so dear as a simple and natural obedience in his servants.

The office of the commander is degraded when he is obeyed at discretion and not through subjection. And P. Crassus, the same whom the Romans reputed five times happy,[1] when he was consul in Asia, having sent word to a Greek engineer to bring him the taller of two ships' masts that he had seen at Athens, for some battering machine that he intended to make, the other, claiming the right of an expert, took upon himself to choose differently and brought the smaller and, by the rules of his art, the more suitable

[1] Five times happy, because he was very rich, very noble, very eloquent, very learned in the law, and Pontifex Maximus.

of the two. Crassus, after patiently listening to his reasons, had him well flogged, esteeming the interest of discipline to be greater than that of the work.

On the other hand, however, one might consider that such strict obedience is due only to a command that is precisely limited. Ambassadors have a freer hand and in many cases follow their own discretion; they do not merely execute, but by their counsel form and direct the master's will. I have in my time known of persons in command who were checked for obeying the words of a king's letter instead of adapting their measures according to their more intimate knowledge of the matter.

Men of understanding condemn the custom of the kings of Persia of cutting up their directions to their agents and lieutenants so small that they are obliged to refer to them in the smallest matters ; the delay caused by this proceeding, in so vast an extent of dominion, having often notably prejudiced their affairs. And did not Crassus, in writing to a man of the trade and advising him of the use for which the mast was designed, appear to call him into consultation, and invite him to interpose his own opinion ?

CHAPTER 18

OF FEAR

Aghast I stood, tongue-tied, with stiffening hair. (VIRGIL.)

I AM not a good Naturalist (as they call it), and know not by what springs fear works in us, but so much is true that it is a strange feeling, and the physicians say that there is none that more easily throws our judgement off its proper balance. Indeed I have known of many people going mad through fear, and it is certain that it will produce even in the most sober-minded, as long as the fit is on them, a fearful bewilderment. I leave aside the uneducated, in whom it takes the form, now of their great-grandfathers rising out of their graves wrapped in their shrouds, now of were-wolves, hobgoblins, and monsters ; but even in soldiers, who should be less liable to it, how often has it not transformed a flock of sheep into a squadron of mail-coats, reeds and bulrushes into lancers and men-at-arms, friends into enemies, the white cross into the red?[1]

When Monsieur de Bourbon took Rome, an ensign who was on guard at the Borgo San Pietro was seized with such terror at the first alarm that, with his colours in his hand, he rushed through a hole in a ruin out of the town and straight into the enemy, thinking that he was making for the centre of the city; at last, seeing Monsieur de Bourbon's company rallying to oppose him, who for their part thought that those of the town were making a sortie, he had no sooner come to himself than, facing about, he re-entered by the same hole through which he had advanced three hundred paces into the country. It by no means fell out so happily with the ensign of Captain Juille when St-Pol was taken from us by the Comte de Bures and Monsieur du Reu, for, distracted with fright, he rushed, flag and all, through a loop-hole out of the town, and was cut to pieces by the attacking party. The same siege was remembered for the fear that so seized, contracted, and froze the heart of a nobleman, that he fell without any wound stone dead in the breach.

At times a whole multitude will be seized with a like fear. In one of the encounters between Germanicus and the Germans, two large bodies of troops in their fright ran in opposite directions, the one from the place whence the other had fled.

Sometimes it lends wings to the heels, as in the two first cases; sometimes it nails and shackles our feet, as we read of the Emperor Theophilus who, in a battle which he lost against the Agarenes, was so benumbed and stupefied that he could not make up his mind to flee, *so much does fear dread even the means of safety!* (Quintus Curtius), until Manuel, one of the chief commanders of his army, had tugged and shaken him, as if to rouse him from a deep sleep, saying, 'If you do not follow me, I will kill you, for it is better that you should lose your life than, by being taken prisoner, the empire.'

Fear manifests its utmost power when, under its influence, we are driven to a deed of valour which our duty and honour had refused. In the first regular battle which the Romans lost to Hannibal under the Consul Sempronius, a

[1] i.e. the Frenchman into a Spaniard.

body of fully ten thousand foot-soldiers, being seized with terror and seeing no other outlet for their cowardice, threw themselves into the thick of the enemy, whom they charged through with wonderful energy and with a great slaughter of Carthaginians, thus purchasing an ignominious flight at the same price that a glorious victory would have cost them.

It is fear that I stand most in fear of; in sharpness it exceeds every other feeling. [What distress could be sharper and more reasonable than that of Pompey's friends who, in his ship, were spectators of that horrible massacre? Yet the fear of the Egyptian sails which were then approaching stifled that feeling to such an extent, that it was observed that they thought only of urging the sailors to make what speed they could and escape by strength of oars until, being arrived at Tyre and delivered from fear, they had leisure to turn their thoughts to their late loss and give a loose rein to the tears and lamentations which the other stronger feeling had suspended:

> Then dread discharged all wisdom from my mind. (ENNIUS.)][1]

They who have had a good drubbing in a fight may be led back to the charge on the morrow, though still wounded and bleeding; but if they have been given a good fright by the enemy, you will not induce them even to look at them. Such as are oppressed by the fear of losing their property or of being banished or enslaved, live in continual anguish, to the point of losing appetite and sleep, whereas the poor, the exiled, the slaves, often live as merrily as other folk. And the many people who, in their impatience of the prickings of fear, have hanged or drowned themselves, or hurled themselves from a precipice, have plainly taught us that it is even more importunate and more insupportable than death.

The Greeks distinguish another kind of fear, which is not due to an error of judgement, arising, as they say, without any apparent cause and from a celestial impulse. Whole nations are often seized with it, and entire armies. Of that kind was the terror which brought a miraculous desolation upon Carthage, when the air was filled with cries and terrified voices, and the inhabitants were seen to rush out

---

[1] It is doubtful whether Montaigne wrote the passage in square brackets, as it does not appear in the 'Bordeaux Manuscript', nor in the earlier editions.

of their houses as to an alarm-bell, and to charge, wound, and kill one another as if they had been enemies come to occupy their city. All was disorder and tumult until with prayers and sacrifices they had appeased the ire of the gods. They call that a *panic terror*.

CHAPTER 19

THAT WE SHOULD NOT JUDGE OF OUR HAPPINESS TILL AFTER DEATH

> But ah! who dares,
> Ere the last day of life hath set, and death
> And funeral rite from an ill-hap insure,
> Call any happy? (OVID.)

EVERY schoolboy knows the story of King Croesus on this subject, who, being taken prisoner by Cyrus and condemned to death, on the point of execution cried out, 'O Solon! Solon!' When this was reported to Cyrus and he inquired of him what he meant, he gave him to understand that he was now verifying to his cost the warning that Solon had once given him, 'that man, however much Fortune may smile upon him, cannot be called happy until the last day of his life has passed', by reason of the uncertainty and mutability of things human, which, by a very slight movement, may change from one state to an entirely different one. And therefore Agesilaus, to one who was saying how happy was the King of Persia for having in early youth come to so powerful a station, made answer, 'Yes, but neither was Priam unhappy at that age'. Now we may see kings of Macedon, successors of the great Alexander, become joiners and scriveners at Rome, and tyrants of Sicily, schoolmasters at Corinth.[1] A conqueror of half the world and emperor of so many armies becomes a miserable suppliant to the beggarly officers of a king of Egypt: so much did the prolongation of five or six months of life cost the great Pompey!

And in our fathers' day that Lodovico Sforza,[2] tenth Duke of Milan, under whom all Italy had so long staggered, was seen to die a prisoner at Loches, but not till he had lived there ten years, which was the worst of his bargain.

[1] An allusion to Philip, son of Perseus, and the elder Dionysius.
[2] Imprisoned in an iron cage by Louis XII in 1500, where he died in 1510.

The fairest queen, widow of the greatest king in Christendom, has she not just died at the hands of the executioner ? [Shameful and barbarous cruelty !][1] And a thousand such examples ; for it seems that, as storms and tempests are exasperated against the pride and haughtiness of our buildings, so there are spirits up above that are envious of the grandeurs here below ;

> Ah, so irrevocably some hidden power
> Betramples evermore affairs of men,
> And visibly grindeth with its heel in mire
> The lictors' glorious rods and axes dire,
> Having them in derision !   (LUCRETIUS.)

And it would seem that Fortune is sometimes purposely on the watch for the last day of our life, to show her power in overthrowing in a moment what she has built up during many years, making us cry out with Laberius,

> Too long I've lived to-day by this one day !   (MACROBIUS.)

In this sense may the good warning of Solon be reasonably taken. But, as he is of the race of philosophers, with whom the favours or disfavours of Fortune rank neither as happiness nor as unhappiness, and greatness and power are accidents of a quality wellnigh indifferent, I think it probable that he looked farther ahead, and meant to say that this same happiness of our life, which depends on the tranquillity and contentment of a well-born mind and the resolution and assurance of a well-ordered soul, must never be attributed to man, until we have seen him play the last, and doubtless the most difficult, act of his comedy. In all the rest there may be some play-acting : either our fine philosophical talk is only a mask, or our misfortunes do not try us so hard but that we may still preserve a serene countenance. But in this last act, where death and ourselves each play their part, there must be no more pretending : we must speak French,[2] and disclose what there is of good and clean at the bottom of the pot.

> For then alone
> Are the true voices conjured from his breast,
> The mask off-stripped, reality behind.   (LUCRETIUS.)

---

[1] Mary, Queen of Scots, widow of Francis II, executed in February 1587, the year before the third edition of the Essays appeared. The comment was apparently an addition by Mademoiselle de Gournay, Montaigne's 'fille d'alliance', who saw the 1595 edition through the press.

[2] As we should say, ' speak plain English '.

Therefore it is that at this our last breath all the other actions of our life should be proved on the touchstone. It is the master-day, the day that is judge of all the other days; it is the day, says one of the ancients, that must judge all my past years (Seneca). To death I leave the testing of all the fruit of my studies. It will then be seen if my words proceed from the mouth or the heart.

I have seen many by their death give a good or an ill repute to their whole life. Scipio, the father-in-law of Pompey, by a good death redeemed the bad opinion in which he had been hitherto held. Epaminondas, being asked which of the three he esteemed most, of Chabrias, Iphicrates, or himself, replied, 'You must see us die before being able to decide.' In truth we should rob him of much if we weighed him without the honour and greatness of his end.

God has willed it as it has best pleased him; but in my time, three men, the most execrable persons I have known in all abomination of life, and the most infamous, died an orderly death and in every way composed even to perfection.

There are brave and fortunate deaths. I have seen death cut the thread of the progress of a prodigious advancement, that was in the flower of its growth, in one whose end was so magnificent, that in my opinion the ambitions and courageous designs of the dying man could show nothing so lofty as their interruption. He reached his goal, without making for it, more grandly and gloriously than he could have hoped or desired, and by his fall anticipated the power and the name to which in his career he aspired.[1]

In judging the life of another I always observe how he bore himself in the end, and one of the chief studies of my own life is that I may bear myself well in the end, that is to say, peacefully and without fuss.

---

[1] This has generally been assumed to refer to Montaigne's great friend Etienne de la Boëtie, who died in his arms in 1563. It has been suggested, with more likelihood perhaps, that it refers to the Duc de Guise, assassinated by order of Henry III in 1588, with whom Montaigne was personally acquainted. The passage first appears in the 1595 edition, which seems to favour the latter supposition. The latest commentator, M. Armaingaud, after weighing the pros and cons, prefers to leave the question in doubt.

CHAPTER 20

THAT TO PHILOSOPHIZE IS TO LEARN TO DIE

CICERO says that philosophizing is nothing more than preparing for death. That is as much as to say that study and contemplation in some sort withdraw our soul outside of us, and keep it occupied apart from the body, and this is a kind of apprenticeship and resemblance to death; or perhaps, that all the wisdom and reason in the world converge in one point, to teach us not to fear death. In truth either reason is a mockery, or it must aim only at our contentment, and all its labour must tend in brief to make us live well and joyfully, as Holy Scripture says.[1] All opinions in the world agree in this, that pleasure is our end, although they differ as to the means of attaining it; otherwise they would be rejected at the outset, for who would give ear to him that should set up pain and misery as our goal? The dissensions of the philosophic sects in this case are verbal. *Let us skip over those subtle trifles* (Seneca). There is more obstinacy and wrangling than is consistent with so time-honoured a profession; but whatever part a man may undertake to play, he always brings in his own personality.

Whatever they may say, the last object we aim at, even in virtue, is voluptuousness. It amuses me to beat this word about their ears, which goes so much against their stomach. And if it signifies some supreme pleasure and excessive satisfaction, it is more due to the aid of Virtue than to any other. This pleasure, for being more lusty, more sinewy, more robust and virile, is the more seriously voluptuous. And to virtue we ought to give the name of pleasure, as being more suitable, sweeter, and more natural, and not that of vigour, from which it takes its name.[2] That other and baser kind of voluptuousness, if it could deserve the fair name of pleasure, should bear it by way of competition and not of privilege. I find it less free from crosses and troubles than virtue. Besides that the taste of it is more fleeting, thinner, and more feeble, it has its vigils, its fasts, and its pains, both sweat and blood, and

[1] Ecclesiastes, iii. 12–13.
[2] Montaigne derives *virtus* (virtue) from *vis* (strength, vigour).

moreover particularly its keen-edged sufferings of so many kinds and so dull a repletion attending it, that it is equivalent to penance.

We are greatly mistaken if we think that these incommodities serve as a sting and a condiment to its sweetness (as in nature a contrary is quickened by its contrary), or if we say, when we come to Virtue, that she is overwhelmed by the like consequences and difficulties and is rendered austere and inaccessible; whereas, much more really than in voluptuousness, they ennoble, sharpen, and enhance the divine and perfect pleasure that she procures us. He is certainly very unworthy to know her who weighs the cost against the fruit, and knows neither her charms nor her use. They who go about to instruct us that her quest is rugged and laborious, her fruition agreeable, what do they mean by that but that she is always disagreeable? For what human means ever arrived at its enjoyment? The most perfect have been well contented to aspire to and approach her, without possessing her. But they deceive themselves, seeing that of all the pleasures that we know, the very pursuit of her is pleasing. The attempt savours of the quality of the thing it aims at, for it is a good part of the effect, and consubstantial with it. The felicity and beatitude which glitters in virtue fills all its appurtenances and avenues, even to the first entry and utmost limit.

Now, one of the principal blessings of virtue is the contempt of death, by means of which our life is furnished with a soft tranquillity, and we are given a pure and loving taste for it, without which every other voluptuousness is extinct. For which reason all the rules meet and concur in this point.[1] And although they all in like manner lead us with one accord to despise pain, poverty, and the other calamities to which the life of man is subject, they do not do so with the same solicitude, as well because these calamities are not so inevitable (the greater part of mankind passing their lives without tasting of poverty, and some also without experience of pain and sickness, like Xenophilus the musician[2] who lived a hundred and six years in perfect health), as also

---

[1] The earlier editions have: 'all the philosophical sects meet and concur in this point of teaching us to despise death.'

[2] A slight confusion. Xenophilus was a philosopher; it was the musician Aristoxenes who recorded the fact.

DEATH IS EVERYWHERE

because, at the worst, death can, when we please, cut short and put an end to all other discomforts. But as to death, it is inevitable :

> One road, and to one bourne
> We all are goaded. Late
> Or soon will issue from the urn
> Of unrelenting Fate
> The lot that in yon bark exiles us all
> To undiscovered shores, from which is no recall. (HORACE.)

And consequently, if it frights us, we are subject to continual torment which can be in no way eased. There is no quarter from which it does not blow ; we may turn our heads this way or that way without ceasing, as in a suspected country : *ever like Tantalus' rock it hangs over us* (Cicero). Our parliaments[1] often send criminals to be executed on the spot where the crime was committed. Take them on their way past fine houses, entertain them with as good cheer as you please ;

> Not feasts Sicilian shall
> With all their cates recall
> That zest the simplest fare could once inspire,
> Nor song of birds, nor music of the lyre
> Shall his lost sleep restore : (HORACE)

do you think that they can rejoice in them, and that the final purpose of their journey, being continually before their eyes, will not have dried up their palate and sickened them with all such delights ?

> He hearkens as he goes and counts the days,
> The length of route is measure of his life ;
> His soul is racked by thoughts of coming doom. (CLAUDIAN.)

The end of our race is death ; it is the necessary object of our aim : if it frightens us, how is it possible to go a step forward without a fit of ague ? The remedy of the vulgar is not to think of it, but from what brutish stupidity can proceed so gross a blindness ? We must bridle their ass by the tail ;

> With forward head he wends his backward way. (LUCRETIUS.)

It is no wonder if they are so often caught in the snare. You will frighten those people by the mere mention of

---

[1] See *infra*, note, p. 138.

death, and most of them cross themselves as if we had spoken of the devil. And because a will is not made without a reference to death, you must not expect them to set their hand to it until the physician has given his last verdict; and God knows then, what with pain and terror, how much judgement they will bring to the concocting of it!

Because this syllable struck upon their ears too rudely, and the sound of it seemed unlucky, the Romans had learned to tone it down or extend it into a periphrasis. Instead of saying 'he is dead', they say 'he has ceased to live, he has lived'. So it be life, be it past or no, they are comforted. We have borrowed the same idea in our *feu Maistre Jehan*.[1]

Perhaps it is because, as the saying is, 'the delay is worth my money'. I was born between eleven o'clock and noon on the last day of February, one thousand five hundred and thirty-three, according to our present computation, beginning the year in January.[2] It is just a fortnight since I cleared thirty-nine years; I should live at least as many more. Meantime it were folly to encumber myself with thoughts of a thing so far off. But what! young and old leave their lives on the same terms. None departs this life otherwise than if he were presently entering into it. Added to which, there is no man so decrepit but thinks, as long as he has the example of Methuselah before his eyes, that he still has twenty years in his body. Moreover, poor fool that thou art, who has set a term to thy life? Thou reliest on physicians' tales; look rather at experience and facts. According to the ordinary course of things, thou hast long been living by extraordinary favour. Thou hast passed the ordinary term of life. And that that is so, reckon up among thy acquaintance how many more have died before thy age than have reached it; make a record of those even who have ennobled their lives by renown, and I will lay a wager that thou wilt find more who have died before than after thirty-five. It is consistent with reason and piety to take example by the humanity of Jesus Christ: he ended his life at

[1] The late Master John; probably Montaigne derived *feu* from *fut* = was.

[2] Under the first race of kings in France the year began on the 1st March; under the second, on Christmas Day; under the third, on Easter Day until, in 1563, Charles IX fixed the 1st January as the beginning.

thirty-three. The greatest man who was merely man, Alexander, died at the same age.

How many several ways has death to surprise us!

> No mortal due provision makes
> 'Gainst ills which any hour may fall. (HORACE.)

I leave aside fevers and pleurisies. Who would ever have imagined that a Duke of Brittany could be crushed to death in a crowd as that Duke was, at the entry of Pope Clement, my neighbour,[1] into Lyons ? Hast thou not seen one of our kings killed at play ? And did not one of his ancestors die through being charged by a hog ? In vain did Aeschylus, threatened[2] by the fall of a house, keep out of doors : behold him felled by the roof of a tortoise that had escaped from the talons of an eagle flying in the air ! The other met his death through a grape-stone ; an emperor from the scratch of a comb whilst combing his hair ; Emilius Lepidus through knocking his foot against the threshold of his door ; and Aufidius through colliding with the door on entering the council-chamber ; and between the thighs of women, Cornelius Gallus the praetor, Tigellinus, captain of the watch at Rome, Lodovico, son of Guido di Gonzaga, Marquis of Mantua, and, of still worse example, Speusippus the Platonic philosopher, and one of our popes.

Poor Bebius, a judge, whilst he is granting a term of eight days to a litigant, behold him taken with a seizure, and his own term of life expired ! And Caius Julius, a physician, anointing the eyes of a patient, when behold death closes his own ! And if I may bring in myself, a brother of mine, Captain Saint-Martin, twenty-three years old, who had already given sufficient proof of his valour, whilst playing at tennis was struck by a ball a little above the right ear. There being no sign of a wound or contusion, he did not sit down to rest, but five or six hours later he died of an apoplexy caused by this blow. When such frequent and ordinary examples pass before our eyes, how can we possibly help thinking of death and fancying every moment that he is gripping us by the throat ?

---

[1] Bertrand de Got, Pope Clement V and Archbishop of Bordeaux, hence 'my neighbour'. King Henri II was mortally wounded in a tournament ; his ancestor was Philip, eldest son of Louis le Gros.

[2] That is to say, threatened by a prophecy, which came true, metaphorically. 'The other' was Anacreon.

What matter, you will say, how it comes about, as long as one does not torment oneself? I am of this mind, and whatever means one may adopt to shelter from the blows, though it were under a calf's skin, I am not the man to despise them. For it is enough if I pass my life in comfort; and I steer the safest course that I can, though it be as little glorious and exemplary as you will.

> For my own part, I rather would be thought
> Dull as a writer, possibly distraught,
> Nor could I but take pleasure in my faults,
> Nor see where meaning or where music halts,
> Than be of mine own failings quite aware
> And gnash my teeth in impotent despair. (HORACE.)

But it is folly to think by that way to come to it. They go, they come, they trot, they dance, but of death, never a word! All that is very fine, but then, when it comes either to themselves or to their wives, their children or friends, surprising them on a sudden and unprepared, what torments, what outcries, what rage and despair overwhelms them! Did you ever see any one so dejected, so changed, so bewildered? We must look to it earlier, and that bestial nonchalance, even though it should lodge in the head of a man of intelligence, which seems to me utterly impossible, sells us its merchandise too dear. Were it an enemy that could be avoided, I should advise borrowing the weapons of cowardice. But since that cannot be, since he will overtake you whether you be a runaway poltroon or a man of honour,

> And death the coward slaves that fly
> Pursues with steps as fleet,
> Nor spares the loins and backs of those
> Unwarlike youths who shun their foes, (HORACE.)

and since no cuirass, however well-tempered, will cover you,

> Though brass and steel encase the wary wight,
> Death drags his head from forth his mask of mail, (PROPERTIUS.)

let us learn with firm foot to resist and fight him. And, to deprive him of the greatest advantage he has over us, let us first adopt a course quite contrary to the usual. Let us disarm him of his strangeness, let us become familiar and conversant with him, and keep nothing so frequently in our thoughts as death. At all times let us bring him before our imagination in his every shape. At the stumbling of a horse, at the fall of a tile, at the least prick of a pin, let us straightway ruminate: 'Well! and what if it had been death himself?' and thereupon stiffen and fortify ourselves. Amidst feasting and jollity let us ever repeat this refrain to remember our condition, and let us not be so carried away by our pleasures as not to remember, now and then, in how many ways our merriment is a mark for death, in how many ways he threatens to grip us. This the Egyptians did, who, in the midst of their banquets and at the height of their merriment, had the dry anatomy of a human corpse brought in, to serve as a warning to the guests.

> Regard each day as if it were thy last;
> The next day's joyful light thine eyes shall see,
> And unexpected will more welcome be. (HORACE.)

Where death is waiting for us is uncertain; let us await him everywhere. Premeditation of death is premeditation of freedom. He who has learned to die has unlearned to be a slave. The knowing how to die frees us from all subjection and constraint. There is no evil in life for him who has rightly understood that privation of life is no evil. Paulus Emilius, to a messenger sent by his prisoner, the wretched King of Macedon, to entreat him not to lead him in his triumph, replied, 'Let him make that request to himself'.

Indeed, if Nature lend not a hand, art and industry can hardly advance in any way. I am by nature not melancholic but a dreamer. Ever since I can remember, nothing has occupied my imagination more than death, yea, even in the most licentious season of my life,

> When gladsome spring my youthful eye rejoiced. (CATULLUS.)

When in the company of ladies and at games, many a man has thought I was disturbed by inward digestion of some jealousy, or the uncertainty of some hope, the while I was meditating on some one or other who had been overtaken, a few days before, by a burning fever and by his end, and after leaving a similar entertainment, his head full of idle fancies, love, and a 'good time', as mine was then, and thinking that I was in the same parlous state.

> Brief is this fruit of joy to paltry man,
> Soon, soon departed, and thereafter, no,
> It may not be recalled. (LUCRETIUS.)

Yet did not this thought wrinkle my brow any more than any other. It is impossible but we must at the outset feel the prickings of such imaginations, but by turning them over and over again in our minds, we may no doubt in the long run make them familiar. Otherwise I, for my part, should be in a perpetual fright and frenzy, for no man was ever more mistrustful of his life, no man ever counted less on its duration. Neither does my health, which hitherto has been with little interruption very robust, prolong, nor sickness curtail, my hope. Every minute I think may be my last, and this is my constant refrain: ' Whatever can be done another day can be done to-day.' Hazards and dangers bring us, indeed, little or no nearer to our end, and when we consider how many millions more remain and hang over our heads, not to speak of the calamity that seems most to threaten us, we shall find that, lusty or feverish, at sea or at home, in battle or in repose, it is equally near: *No man is more frail than another, no man more certain of to-morrow* (Seneca). To finish what I have to do before dying, were it but an hour's work, the longest leisure appears to me short.

The other day somebody, turning over my tablets, found a memorandum of something I wished to be done after my death. I told him, what was true, that being but a league's distance from my house, and healthy and robust, I had hastened to write it down on the spot, because I could not be certain even of reaching home. Continually brooding over my thoughts and turning them inwardly as I do, I am every moment about as prepared as I can ever be. And the unexpected coming of death can tell me nothing new.

We must be ever booted and ready to start, as far as in us lies, and above all we must see to it that we have no business with any but ourselves;

> Why should we still project and plan,
> We creatures of an hour ? (Horace.)

For that will keep us busy enough without any addition. One man will lament, not so much that he has to die, but that his death will interrupt the course of a fine victory, another that he has to quit before having married his daughter or arranged his children's education ; one regrets losing the society of his wife, another that of his son, as the principal comfort of his life.

I am at this hour in such a condition, thank God, that I can quit whenever it shall please him, without any repining whatever, except it be for life, if the prospect of losing it happens to weigh me down. I disengage myself on all sides; my farewells are half taken, of all except of myself. Never did man more fully and absolutely prepare to quit the world and cut himself adrift from all things, than I propose to do. [The deadest deaths are the soundest.]

> Poor wretch, they say, one hostile hour hath ta'en
> Wretchedly from thee all life's many guerdons. (LUCRETIUS.)

And the builder,

> The frowning battlements neglected lie,
> And lofty scaffolding that threats the sky. (VIRGIL.)

A man should design nothing so far ahead, or at least with no such passionate intent to see it accomplished. We are born for action:

> But when I die, would I might die in harness. (OVID.)

I agree that we should work and prolong the functions of life as far as we can, and hope that Death may find me planting my cabbages, but indifferent to him and still more to the unfinished state of my garden. I witnessed the death of one who, at his last gasp, incessantly lamented that Destiny was cutting the thread of a history that he had in hand, at the fifteenth or sixteenth of our kings.

> They add not, 'yet no longer unto thee
> Remains a remnant of desire for them'. (LUCRETIUS.)

We must throw off these vulgar and hurtful humours. Even as they laid out our cemeteries adjoining the churches and the most frequented parts of the city, in order, as Lycurgus said, to accustom the common people, the women and children, not to be scared at the sight of a corpse, and to the end that this continual spectacle of bones, tombs, and funeral processions might warn us of our condition;

> A custom 'twas to cheer the guests
> With bloody brawls and slaughter dire
> Of men contending with the sword.
> The dying fell among the cups
> And splashed the board with plenteous gore;
> (SILIUS ITALICUS.)

and as the Egyptians, after their banquets, presented to the sight of the company a large image of death, while one called out, 'Drink and be merry, for such shall you be when you are dead'; so it has been my custom to have death continually not only in my mind, but on my lips. And there is nothing about which I am so desirous of gathering information, as the death of men, their words, their looks, their behaviour, nor any passages in history that I remark so attentively. It may be seen in the cramming of my book with examples that I have a particular fancy for this subject. If I were a maker of books I should compile a register, with comments, of different deaths. He who should teach men to die, would teach them to live. Dicearchus wrote one with a title of that kind, but to another and less profitable purpose.

I may be told that the reality so far exceeds our imagination that the best fencing is of no avail when it comes to the point. Let them say; premeditation without doubt gives one a great advantage. And then, is it nothing to go at least so far without disturbance and tremor? What is more, Nature herself lends us a hand and gives us courage. If the death be short and violent, we have no leisure to fear it; if otherwise, I am conscious that, as the malady gains on me, I naturally conceive a certain disdain of life. I find it much more difficult to digest this resolution to die when I am in good health, than when I am in a fever. As I become less strongly attached to the amenities of life, by reason of beginning to lose the enjoyment and pleasure of them, so do I look upon death with much less terror. That makes me hope that the farther I am removed from the former, and the nearer I approach to the latter, the more easily shall I become reconciled to the exchange. Even as I have experienced on several occasions that, as Caesar says, objects often appear larger at a distance than near at hand, so I have found that when in good health I had a much greater horror of sickness than when afflicted by it. The cheerful humour, the vigour and pleasure that I enjoy, make the other state appear so disproportionate to the present one, that in imagination I magnify those afflictions by one half, and conceive them to be heavier than I find them when they are on my shoulders. I hope that it will be the same in death.

Let us see, in these ordinary changes and declines that we suffer, how Nature hides from us the taste of our loss and decay. What remains to an old man of the vigour of his youth and his past life?

> Alas, in age how little joy of life! (MAXIMIAN.)

Caesar, to a jaded and broken-down soldier of his guard, who came to him in the street to ask his leave to be put to death, looking at his decrepit appearance, humorously replied, 'You think then that you are alive?' Should we fall into this condition all of a sudden, I do not believe that we should be able to endure so great a change. But, led by the hand of Nature down a gentle and almost imperceptible slope, little by little, step by step, she rolls us into this miserable state, and makes us familiar with it, so that we feel not the shock when youth dies in us, which is, in truth and reality, a harder death than the complete death of a languishing life, than the death of old age, inasmuch as the leap from an evil existence to a non-existence is not so heavy as that from a pleasant and flourishing existence to a grievous and painful one.

A body that is bent and bowed has less strength to support a burden; so it is with the soul: it must be raised and straightened against the power of this enemy. For, as it is impossible for the soul to be at rest as long as the fear of him is on her, so, if she can once gain assurance, she may boast (a thing almost surpassing the power of man) that it is impossible that disquiet, torment, fear, even the least trouble, should dwell in her.

> Nor hath the tyrant's menace skill
> His fixed resolve to shake;
> Nor Auster, at whose wild command
> The Adriatic billows lash,
> Nor Jove's dread thunder-launching hand. (HORACE.)

She is become mistress of her passions and lusts, mistress of indigence, shame, poverty, and all other of Fortune's harms. Let us gain this advantage, those of us who can: this is the true and sovereign freedom, which enables us to snap our fingers in the face of violence and injustice, and to laugh at prisons and chains;

> 'In a dungeon cell
> I'll keep you bound with gyve and manacle.'
> 'A God will set me free whene'er I please.'
> Meaning, methinks, Death as the God who frees—
> Death that shuts up the sum of all our miseries. (HORACE.)

Our religion has no surer human foundation than the contempt of life. Not only the discourse of reason invites us to it, for why should we fear to lose a thing, which being lost cannot be lamented ; and, since we are menaced by death in so many shapes, is it not a greater evil to fear them all than to endure one ?

What matters it when it shall come to pass, since it is inevitable ? To him who announced to Socrates that the thirty tyrants [1] had condemned him to death, he replied, ' And Nature, them '.

What folly to torment ourselves about passing into a state of exemption from all torment ! As our birth brought us the birth of all things, so will our death bring us the death of all things. Wherefore it is as foolish to weep because a hundred years from now we shall not be alive, as to weep because we were not living a hundred years ago. Death is the origin of another life. So did we weep, so much did it cost us to enter into this life, so did we strip off our former veil on entering into it.

Nothing can be grievous that is but once. Is it reasonable to fear for so long a time of such brief duration ? Long life and short life are by death made all one ; for the long and the short are not in things that are no more. Aristotle tells us that there are little creatures on the river Hypanis that live but a day. The one that dies at eight o'clock in the morning dies in its youth, that which dies at five in the afternoon dies in its decrepitude. Which of us would not think it absurd to see this moment of duration put into the consideration of weal or woe ? The greater or lesser duration of our lives, if we compare it with eternity, or yet with that of mountains, rivers, stars, trees, or even of some animals, is no less ridiculous.

But Nature compels us to it. ' Go out of this world, she says, as you entered into it. The same way you came from death to life, without fear or passion, return from life to death. Your death is of one piece with the order of the universe, it is of one piece with the life of the world.

> We live as mortals by eternal give and take,
> . . . . .
> And like to runners hand the lamp of life
> One to another. (LUCRETIUS.)

---

[1] Not the thirty tyrants, but the Athenians.

'Why should I alter for you this beautiful disposition of things? Death is the condition of your creation, it is a part of you; you are flying from yourself. This being that you enjoy is equally divided between death and life. The first day of your birth starts you on the road to death as well as to life.

> The hour which gave us life begins our death. (SENECA.)
>
> As we are born to die, our lots are cast,
> And our first hour disposeth of our last. (MANILIUS.)

'Every day that you live you purloin from life; you live at the expense of life. The perpetual work of your life is to build up death. You are in death whilst you are in life; for you are after death when you are no more in life. Or, if you prefer it this way, you are dead after life, but dying while you live, and death handles the dying much more rudely than the dead, and more perceptibly and sharply.

'If you have made your profit out of life you are fed up with it; go your way satisfied.

> Why not,
> Even like a banqueter, depart the halls,
> Laden with life? (LUCRETIUS.)

'If you have not known how to make the best of it, if it has been unprofitable to you, what matters it to you that you have lost it? To what end do you still desire to keep it?

> Why seekest more to add—which in its turn
> Will perish foully and fall out in vain? (LUCRETIUS.)

'Life in itself is neither a good nor an evil; it is the scene of good and evil, as you arrange it. And if you have lived a day, you have seen all; one day is like all days. There is no other light, there is no other night. This sun, this moon, these stars, this order, are the very same that your ancestors enjoyed and that will rejoice your great-grandchildren:

> No other saw our sires of old,
> No other shall our sons behold. (MANILIUS.)

'And if it comes to the worst, the distribution and variety of all the acts of my comedy are performed in a year. If you have taken heed of the swing of my four seasons, they embrace the childhood, the youth, the virility, and the old age of the world. It has played its part, and knows no other cunning but to begin again. It will be always the same thing.

> Besides we're busied with the same device,
> Ever and ever. (LUCRETIUS.)
>
> The year revolves and ay its steps retraces. (VIRGIL.)

'I do not purpose to create for you any new pastimes:

> For all I may devise or find
> To pleasure thee is nothing: all things are
> The same forever. (LUCRETIUS.)

'Give place to others, as others have given place to you. Equality is the first part of equity. Who can complain of being comprehended where all are comprehended? So, live as long as you can, you shall by nothing shorten the time you are to be dead; it is all to no purpose: you will be as long in that state which you fear as if you had died at your nurse's breast:

> Therefore, O man, by living on, fulfil
> As many generations as you may:
> Eternal death shall there be waiting still. (LUCRETIUS.)

'And yet I will place you in such a condition that you will have no cause to be displeased;

> Thou knowest not
> That in true death there is no second self
> Alive and able to sorrow for self destroyed,
> Or stand lamenting that the self lies there. (LUCRETIUS.)

'Nor shall you so much as wish for the life that you so much regret;

> For no one then demands his self or being.
>
> Without desire of any selfhood more. (LUCRETIUS.)

'Death is less to be feared than nothing, if there were anything less than nothing:

> Death is, then, to us
> Much less—if there can be a less than that
> Which is itself a nothing. (LUCRETIUS.)

'Dead or alive, it concerns you not: alive, because you exist; dead, because you exist no more.

'No man dies before his hour. The time you leave behind

you was no more yours than that which elapsed before you were born, and concerns you no more,

> Look back:
> Nothing to us was all fore-passed eld
> Of time the eternal, ere we had a birth. (LUCRETIUS.)

'Wherever your life ends, it is all there. The profit of life is not in its length but in the use we put it to : many a man has lived long, who has lived little ; see to it as long as you are here. It lies in your will, not in the number of years, to make the best of life. Did you think never to arrive at a place you were incessantly making for ? Yet there is no road but has an end. And if society is any comfort to you, is not the world going the selfsame way as you ?

> And these, their life completed, follow you. (LUCRETIUS.)

'Do not all dance the same dance as you ? Is there a thing that does not age with you ? A thousand men, a thousand animals, and a thousand other creatures die at the same moment that you die :

> No night a day, no dawn a night hath followed
> That heard not, mingling with the small birth-cries,
> The wild laments, companions old of death
> And the black rites. (LUCRETIUS.)

'Why do you recoil, if you cannot draw back ? You have seen men enough who were the better for dying, thereby escaping great miseries. But have you known of any who were the worse off ? Hence it shows great simplicity to condemn a thing that you have proved neither in your own person nor in another's. Why dost thou complain of me and of destiny ? Do we do thee any wrong ? Is it for thee to govern us, or for us to govern thee ? Though thy age be not yet accomplished, thy life is. A little man is an entire man as well as a big one : neither men nor their lives are measured by the ell.

'Chiron refused immortality, being informed of the conditions thereof by the god of time and duration himself, his father Saturn. Imagine, indeed, how much more grievous and insupportable everlasting life would be to man than the life I have given him. If you had not death you would eternally curse me for having deprived you of it. I have knowingly mingled a little bitterness with it, to prevent you, seeing the advantage of it, from embracing it too eagerly and unwisely. To keep you in that middle state, which I require of you, where you neither fly life nor again fly death, I have tempered both one and the other between sweetness and bitterness.

'I taught Thales, the first of your sages, that to live and to die are indifferent, which made him answer very wisely one who asked him why then he did not die, "Because it is indifferent".

'Water, air, earth, fire and the other members of this my edifice, are no more instruments of thy life than instruments of thy death. Why dost thou fear thy last day? It contributes no more to thy death than does every other day. The last step does not cause the lassitude: it declares it. All days journey towards death; the last arrives there.'

These are the good lessons of our mother Nature.

Now, I have often wondered how it is that in war the face of death, whether we see it in ourselves or in others, appears incomparably less dreadful than at home in our houses (if it were not so, an army would be made up of physicians and whiners); and that, although death is everywhere the same, we find much more assurance in villagers and people of humble condition than in others. I believe indeed that it is the dismal faces and the appalling ceremony with which we surround death that frighten us more than the thing itself: a quite new way of living, the cries of mothers, wives and children, a crowd of visiting friends numb and dazed with grief, and servants pale and blubbering, a chamber from which the sun is excluded, lighted by tapers, our bedside besieged by doctors and preachers; to sum up, nothing around us but horrors and bugbears.[1] Behold us already shrouded and buried! Children are frightened even by friends, if they see them masked, and so are we. We must strip the mask from things and persons, which being removed, we shall see beneath it that same death which a varlet or simple chambermaid suffered the other day without any fear. Happy the death that leaves no time for all these ceremonious preparations!

[1] '*Pompa mortis magis terret quam mors ipsa.* Groans and convulsions, and a discoloured face, and friends weeping, and blacks, and obsequies, and the like, show death terrible.'—Bacon, Essay on *Death*.

CHAPTER 21

OF THE POWER OF IMAGINATION

A POWERFUL imagination begets the thing itself, say the clerks. I am of those who feel the strong arm of imagination; every one is struck by it, and some are knocked down. Its influence on me is profound. I contrive to avoid it, not to oppose it. I would live surrounded only by healthy and cheerful people. The sight of another's anguish gives me physical anguish, and my sensations often usurp the sensations of a third person. A perpetual cough in another irritates my lungs and throat. I am less fond of visiting a sick man under a sense of dutiful interest than one to whom I owe less attention and consideration. I catch the malady which gives me concern, and it takes root in me. I do not wonder that imagination brings on fevers and death in those who give it a free hand and encourage it.

Simon Thomas was a great physician in his day. I remember meeting him one day [at Toulouse] in the house of a rich old consumptive patient, and, discussing with him the best means of curing the invalid, he informed him that one remedy was for me to take a pleasure in his company: if he concentrated his gaze on my ruddy countenance, and his thoughts on the cheerfulness and robustness of my superabundant youth, and filled all his senses with the blooming health that I enjoyed, his habit of body might be improved. But he forgot to say that mine might be impaired.

Gallus Vibius so effectually bent his mind on understanding and imagining the nature and motions of madness,[1] that his judgement was thrown off its balance, so that he never after recovered it; he could boast of having become mad through wisdom. There are some who through terror anticipate the hand of the hangman; and one whose eyes were being unbandaged to have his pardon read to him, was found stark dead on the scaffold, killed by the mere stroke of his imagination. We sweat, we tremble, we turn pale and blush through the shock of our imagination, and lying back

---

[1] A slight inaccuracy. The story goes that he bent his mind on imitating the gestures of madmen, in order to impress his hearers, he being a rhetorician.

in our feather-bed we feel our body agitated by its power, sometimes to the point of expiring. Exuberant youth, when fast asleep, becomes so heated as in a dream to satisfy its amorous desires:

> So that, as it were
> With all the matter acted duly out,
> They pour the billows of a potent stream
> And stain their garment. (LUCRETIUS.)

And although it is no new thing to see a man grow horns in the night who had none when he went to bed, yet what befell Cippus, King of Italy,[1] is memorable: having one day been a very interested spectator at a bullfight, and having all night dreamed that he had horns on his head, he produced them on his forehead by the force of imagination.

Passion gave to the son of Croesus the voice that nature had denied him. And Antiochus contracted a fever through having the beauty of Stratonice too vividly imprinted on his mind. Pliny declares having seen Lucius Cossitius changed from a woman into a man on his wedding-day. Pontanus and others tell of similar transformations taking place in Italy in these latter ages. And, through his and his mother's vehement desire,

> Iphis the boy the offering pays
> Which Iphis the maid had vowed. (OVID.)

Passing through Vitry le François, I was enabled to see a man whom the bishop of Soissons had called Germain in confirmation, and whom all the inhabitants of the place had known and seen as a girl till the age of twenty-two, called Marie. He was now an old man with a full beard and unmarried. Straining himself when leaping, he said, his male member came forth; and the maids of the place to this day sing a song, wherein they warn each other not to take too great strides, for fear of becoming boys, like Marie Germain. It is not so much to be wondered at that this sort of accident is frequently met with, for if the imagination have any power in such things, it is so continually and vigorously fastened on this subject, that, to obviate so frequent a relapse into the same thoughts and violence of desire it were

---

[1] According to Valerius Maximus, Cippus was not King of Italy but a Roman praetor, of whom the oracles declared that he would be king if he returned to Rome; but he preferred to remain in exile.

cheaper once for all to incorporate this virile part into the maids.

Some attribute the scars of King Dagobert and the stigmata of Saint Francis to the force of imagination. It is said that bodies will sometimes be removed by it from their places. And Celsus tells of a priest whose soul would be ravished into such an ecstasy that his body would remain for a long time without sense and breathing. Saint Augustine makes mention of another who, if he but heard lamentable and plaintive cries, would suddenly fall into a swoon, and be so forcibly carried out of himself that it was in vain to bawl into his ear, to shake, pinch or scorch him until he had recovered ; he then used to say that he had heard voices, but appearing to be far away, and felt the bruisings and scorchings. And that this was no obstinate fancy assumed in defiance of his sense of feeling was shown by his having all the while neither pulse nor breath.

It is likely that miracles,[1] visions, enchantments, and the like extraordinary phenomena derive their credit chiefly from the power of imagination, acting principally on the more impressionable minds of the common people. Their credulity is so easily imposed upon that they think they see what they do not see.

I am still of opinion that those absurd ' ligatures ',[2] by which our world is so much obsessed that nothing else is talked of, are usually impressions of fear and apprehension, for I know by experience that so and so, for whom I can answer as for myself, and on whom no suspicion could fall of impotence or of being influenced by sorcery, having heard a friend of his tell of an extraordinary languor which had befallen him at a moment when he had least need of it, and being in a like situation, his imagination was so rudely and suddenly struck by the horror of this tale, that he found himself in a similar plight ; and from that time forward, the scurvy remembrance of his disaster possessing him and

---

[1] In the 1595 edition the word ' miracles ' was, no doubt purposely, omitted. In the next paragraph ' I am still of opinion that ' was toned down to ' I am still in doubt whether '.

[2] ' *Les nouements d'aiguillettes*, as they were called, knots tied by some person, at a wedding, in a thread of cotton, silk or leather which, when passed through the wedding-ring, were supposed to have the magical effect of preventing a consummation of the marriage, until they were untied.'—Louandre, *La Sorcellerie*, Paris, 1853.

tyrannizing over him, he was liable to relapse into the same misfortune. For this fancy he found some remedy in another fancy. By himself confessing and declaring beforehand this tyranny he was subject to, the strain on his mind was relieved by the reflection that, his evil being expected, his duty was thereby diminished, and weighed less on his mind. When he was at leisure and could choose his time (his thoughts being free and unfettered, and his body in proper trim), to have it then first tried, seized, and taken unawares in the knowledge of the other party, he was completely cured of this infirmity.

When a man has once been capable with a person, he is not again incapable with her, except through an excusable weakness.

This disaster is not to be feared but in an enterprise where the mind is excited beyond measure by desire or diffidence, and especially when the opportunity is of an unforeseen and pressing nature; there is no way then of recovering from this trouble. I have known of one who found it of service to bring his body to it half-sated from elsewhere, to abate the ardour of his fury, and of one who, by reason of his age, is the less impotent for being less vigorous. And a certain other who was well served by being assured by a friend that he had a counter-battery of enchantments certain to save him. It is best for me to tell how this came about.

A count of very good family, with whom I was very intimate, being married to a fair lady who had been courted by one who assisted at the feast, his friends were in great trouble about him; an old lady his kinswoman, who presided at the wedding and at whose house it took place, was particularly afraid of those spells, and she told me of her fears. I bade her rely upon me. I chanced to have in my coffers a certain little flat piece of gold engraved with celestial characters, a charm against sunstroke and headache if applied exactly to the suture of the skull; to keep it in place it was sewn upon a ribbon to be tied under the chin. A vain imagination that is germane to the matter in hand! This singular object had been presented to me by Jacques Peletier[1] [when he was living in my house]. It occurred to me that it might come in useful. I said to the count that he might possibly incur the same danger as others had done,

[1] A celebrated physician who died in 1582.

since there were men present who were not loath to 'lend him one', but that he might confidently go to bed; that I would do him a friendly turn, and, if need were, not spare a miracle which it was in my power to perform, provided that he promised me on his honour faithfully to keep it a secret. If things had not gone well with him he was only to give me a certain sign when we brought him the caudle at midnight. His mind and ears had been so beset with fancies, that he found himself fettered by a disturbed imagination, and at the appointed time gave me his sign. I then whispered to him to get up under pretence of turning us out, and playfully to take the night-gown I had on me (we were much about the same height), and wear it until he had carried out my instructions, which were, that, as soon as we had left the chamber, he should go aside to make water, that he should repeat three times certain prayers and go through certain movements, that each time he should tie the ribbon I gave him around his middle, and very carefully place the medallion which was attached to it over his kidneys, with the figures in such and such a position; that being done, and having at the third time secured the ribbon very tightly that it might not shift or become untied, he could confidently return to his business, not forgetting to throw my gown on his bed in such a way as to cover them both.

These monkey-tricks are the main thing: we cannot deliver our minds from the thought that means so strange proceed from some abstruse science. Their silliness lends them weight and an air of reverence. To sum up, it is certain that my talisman proved itself more Venerian than Solar,[1] more active than preventive. It was a sudden and curious humour that suggested this action, which was so foreign to my nature. I am an enemy to all subtle and pretended actions, and hate to practise cunning, not only in sport but for profit. If the action is not vicious, the road is.

Amasis, King of Egypt, married Laodice, a very beautiful Greek, and he, who had proved himself a gallant companion on all other occasions, fell short of enjoying her, and threatened to kill her, thinking there was some witchcraft in it. As in matters which rest on fancy, she referred him to religion, and, having made his vows and promises to Venus,

[1] Against the sunstroke.

he found himself divinely recovered on the very first night after his offerings and sacrifices.

Now, they are wrong to entertain us with their coy, mincing, and querulous affectations, which stifle and kindle our ardour at the same time. The daughter-in-law of Pythagoras [1] said that the woman who lies with a man should put off her modesty with her skirt, and put it on again with her petticoat. The mind of the assailant, disturbed by many several alarms, is easily dismayed, and if his imagination has once made him suffer this shame (he suffers it only at the first encounters, the more so as they are more fierce and impetuous, and also because in this first intimacy one is much more afraid of failure), having made a bad beginning, he falls into a fever of vexation at this mishap, which is apt to continue on the following occasions.

Married men, time being at their command, should not attempt or hasten the action if they are not ready; it is better to fail ingloriously to handsel the nuptial couch, which fills one with feverish agitation, and to await some other more intimate and less alarmed opportunity, than to fall into perpetual misery through being disturbed and made desperate by the first refusal. Before possession be taken, the patient should, by sallies and at different times, make light essays and overtures, without any pique and persistence in trying definitely to convince himself. Such as know their members to be naturally docile, let them only take care to counter-beguile their fancies.

One has reason to remark on the unruly liberty of this member that so importunately asserts itself when we have no need of it, and so inopportunely fails us when we have most need of it, so imperiously contesting in authority with our will, so proudly and obstinately refusing our solicitations, both mental and manual.

If, however, on being scolded for his rebellion and condemned on that score, he were to fee me to plead his cause, I might peradventure arraign our other members, his fellows, of having purposely got up this quarrel against him, out of pure envy of the importance and pleasure attached to his function, and of having plotted to arm the world against him, by maliciously charging him alone with their

---

[1] Theano, a famous Pythagorean, the wife and not the daughter-in-law of Pythagoras.

common offence. For I ask you to consider whether there is a single part of our body that does not often refuse to operate at our will, and does not often exercise its functions in defiance of our will. They have every one of them feelings of their own, which arouse them and send them to sleep without our permission. How often our involuntary facial motions testify to the thoughts we were keeping secret, and betray us to those around! The same cause that animates this member also animates, without our consent, the heart, the lungs, and pulse; the sight of a pleasing object imperceptibly diffusing over our countenance a flame of feverish emotion. Is it these muscles and veins alone that swell and flag without the consent, not only of our will, but of our thoughts? We do not command our hair to stand on end, nor our skin to shiver with desire or fear. The hand often goes whither it is not sent, the tongue is tied and the voice thickens at their own time. Even when, having nothing to fry, we would fain forbid it, the appetite for food and drink does not forbear to stir up the parts that are subject to it, any more nor any less than does that other appetite, and in like manner unseasonably forsakes us whenever it is so disposed. The instruments which serve to discharge the belly have their dilatations and compressions, beyond and against our intent, as well as those which discharge the kidneys. And when Saint Augustine declares, as a proof of the all-power of our will, having seen one who commanded his posterior to break wind as often as he pleased, and Vives, his commentator, overbids him with another case of his time, of one who could break wind in time with the lines spoken,[1] we are not to infer an absolute obedience in that member; for can there be anything that is usually more indiscreet and tumultuous? To which I may add that I know of one so turbulent and intractable that for forty years he has been keeping his master continually at it, with a constant and unremitting tyranny, thus bringing him to his grave. [Would to God that I only knew from

---

[1] The English translation of this passage from the *City of God* rather differs from this, and is equally quaint: 'There are that can break wind backward so artificially, that you would think they sung'; to which Vives adds: 'There was such an one, a Germane, about Maximilians court, and his son Phillips, that would have rehearsed any verse whatsoever with his taile.'

stories how often our belly, by one refusal, may bring us to the gates of a most painful death, and that the Emperor[1] who gave us leave to vent everywhere, had also given us the power!]

But our will, on whose behalf we are preferring this accusation, with how much more probability can we brand her with mutiny and sedition, on account of her irregularity and disobedience! Does she always will what we should wish her to will? Does she not often will what we forbid her to will, and that to our manifest prejudice? Does she let herself be guided by the conclusions of our reason?

To conclude, I will urge on behalf of Monsieur my client, that it please you to consider that though his cause, in this matter, is inseparably and indiscriminately joined to that of a consort, yet he alone is accused, and that by arguments and accusations which, seeing the conditions of the parties, cannot concern or be charged to his said consort. [For the latter may be said at times to invite inopportunely, but to refuse, never; and to invite, moreover, tacitly and quietly.] Wherefore the animosity and illegality of his accusers are manifest.

Be that as it may, whilst protesting that advocates and judges wrangle and sentence in vain, Nature will meanwhile go her own way, who had done but right if she had endowed this member with a particular privilege: author of the sole immortal work of mortals. Wherefore to Socrates generation is a divine action; and love, a desire for immortality, and itself an immortal Daimon.

Peradventure a man may, by the force of imagination, leave behind him here the king's evil, which his fellow will carry back to Spain. For that reason it is customary in such cases to require a prepared mind. Why do the physicians begin by playing on the credulity of their patients with so many false promises of cure, if not to the end that the power of imagination may assist the imposture of their decoctions? They know that one of the masters of their craft has given it in writing that there have been people on whom the mere sight of physic would work.

And this fanciful humour has just come into my mind through the recollection of a story told me by a domestic apothecary of my departed father, a simple fellow and a

---

[1] The Emperor Claudius, according to Suetonius, only *intended* to authorize by an edict this singular privilege.

Swiss, a nation little given to vanity and lying, of a tradesman he had long known at Toulouse, a valetudinarian afflicted with the stone, who often had need of enemas, of which he had several sorts prescribed by the physicians according to the incidence of his infirmity. When they were brought, none of the usual forms were omitted, and sometimes he would feel if they were too hot. Behold him then lying prone on his bed, the usual operation performed, except that no injection was made ! The apothecary having retired after this mummery, and the patient made comfortable, he felt the same effect as if he had really taken a clyster. And if the physician found that the operation was not sufficient, he would give him two or three doses in the same manner. My witness swears that in order to save the expense (for he paid for them as if he had really taken them), the patient's wife sometimes tried the same operation with warm water only, but the fraud was betrayed by the want of effect ; this having proved inoperative, the former method had to be resorted to.

A woman, imagining that she had swallowed a pin with her bread, shouted and raved as if she had an intolerable pain in her throat, where she thought she felt it sticking ; an ingenious fellow, perceiving neither swelling nor any other external alteration, and judging that it was all fancy and imagination, caused by a crumb pricking her in its passage, made her sick and, unseen, threw a bent pin into her vomit. The woman, thinking she had thrown up the pin, immediately felt herself eased of her pain.

I know of a gentleman who, having entertained a goodly company at his house, boasted three or four days afterwards by way of a jest (for there was nothing in it), that he had made them eat a cat-pasty, at which a lady of the company became so horrified, that she was taken with a looseness of the bowels, accompanied by fever, and it was found impossible to save her. Even animals are like ourselves subject to the force of imagination, witness those dogs that die of grief for the loss of their masters. We see them bark and tremble in their dreams, and horses will neigh and kick.

But all this may be attributed to the close affinity between mind and body intercommunicating their fortunes ; it is another thing when the imagination acts, as it sometimes does, not only on its own body, but on the body of another. And, just as a body will communicate its malady to another body, as we see in the case of the plague, the pox, and the diseases of the eyes that discharge themselves from one to another :

> Eyes become sore by looking at sore eyes ;
> And many ills are by infection caught, (OVID.)

so the imagination, being vehemently shaken, shoots out shafts which may hurt the foreign object. In ancient times it was believed that certain women of Scythia, when angered and stirred up against anybody, could kill them with a glance. Tortoises and ostriches hatch their eggs by sight alone : a sign that their eyes have some ejaculatory virtue. And the eyes of sorcerers are said to be noxious and baneful :

> Over my tender lambs some eye is casting a spell. (VIRGIL.)

I put very little faith in magicians. Yet we see by experience that women transfer the marks of their fancy to the bodies of the children they carry in their womb : witness her that gave birth to the Blackamoor. And there was presented to Charles, King of Bohemia and Emperor, a girl from near Pisa who was all rough and hairy, whom her mother said to be so conceived by reason of an image of Saint John the Baptist hanging in her bed.

With animals it is the same, witness Jacob's sheep, and the hares and partridges that the snow turns white on the mountains. Somebody the other day saw a cat near my house watching a bird on the branch of a tree ; after they had fixedly gazed at each other for some time, the bird fell apparently dead between the cat's claws, either intoxicated by its own imagination, or drawn by some attractive power of the cat. They who are fond of hawking must have heard of the falconer who, persistently fixing with his eyes a kite on the wing, wagered that he could bring her down by the sole power of his sight, which he did, so they say ; for the tales which I borrow I charge them upon the conscience of those from whom I get them.

The conclusions are my own and rely on the evidence of common sense, not of experience ; every one may add his own examples, and if he has none he may be sure that they exist, seeing the number and variety of things that occur. If I cite examples that do not exactly fit the matter in hand, another may substitute more fitting ones.

MONTAIGNE NOT A HISTORIAN

Besides, in this study which treats of our manners and movements, fabulous testimonies, provided they are possible, serve as well as true ones. Whether they happened or no, at Rome or Paris, to John or Peter, they are all within the compass of human capacity, of which I am profitably advised by this narrative. I see it and profit by it both in shadow and substance. And of the divers readings that the histories often afford I make use of that which is most rare and memorable. There are authors whose aim it is to tell of things that have happened. Mine, if I could attain to it, would be to tell of what may happen. Schools are rightly permitted to suppose similitudes where none exist. I do not do so, however, and on that side I surpass in religious scrupulousness all historical fidelity. In the examples that I here bring in of what I have [read], heard, done or said, I have refrained from daring to alter even the smallest and most indifferent circumstances. My conscience falsifies not an iota ; for my knowledge I cannot answer.

On this subject, it sometimes occurs to me whether it can be very befitting a theologian, a philosopher, and the like men who combine an exact and tender conscience with prudence, to write history. How can they pledge their word on a popular belief ? How can they be responsible for the opinions of men they do not know, and give out their conjectures as current coin ? Of actions performed by several persons in their presence they would refuse to give evidence upon oath before a judge, nor would they undertake full responsibility for the intentions of any man, however intimately known to them. I hold it to be less hazardous to write of things of the past than of things of the present, inasmuch as the writer has only to give an account of a borrowed truth.

It has been suggested to me that I should chronicle the events of my time, by some who regard me as one who sees them with eyes less impaired by passion than others, and from a nearer point of view, by reason of the access which Fortune has given me to the heads of different factions. But they do not say, That for all Sallust's fame I would not undertake such a task, sworn enemy as I am to obligation, assiduity and perseverance ; That there is nothing so foreign to my style as a continuous narrative : I so often have to pull up for want of breath ; I have neither composition nor exposition worth anything, being ignorant beyond a child of the phrases and terms which serve for the most common things; for which reason I have undertaken only to say what I am able to say, accommodating the matter to my capacity. If I took one to be my guide, my pace might fall short of his. Besides, being so free in my freedom, I might publish judgements which, even in my own opinion and according to reason, are unlawful and punishable.

Plutarch would readily tell us that if, in his work, the examples are always and in every way true, the credit is due to others; but that if they be profitable to posterity and presented with a lustre that will light us on our path to virtue, the credit is his own. Whether an ancient story be so or so, there is no danger in it, as there is in a medicinal drug.

CHAPTER 22

ONE MAN'S GAIN IS ANOTHER MAN'S LOSS

DEMADES, an Athenian, condemned a man of his city whose trade it was to sell the necessaries for funerals, on the score that he demanded too much profit, and that this profit could only come to him by the death of many people. This judgement seems to be ill-grounded, inasmuch as no profit is made but at others' expense, and that by this reckoning profit of any kind must be condemned.

The tradesman thrives only by the extravagance of youth, the husbandman by the dearness of grain, the architect by the ruin of houses, the officers of justice by lawsuits and men's quarrels; even the honour and practice of ministers of religion depend on our death and our vices. No physician delights in the good health even of his friends, says the ancient Greek comic dramatist, nor does a soldier in the peace of his city; and so with the rest. And, what is worse, if each of us sounds his conscience, he will find that his inmost wishes are for the most part born and nourished at the expense of others.

Considering which, it has come into my fancy that Nature in this does not belie her general policy, for natural philosophers hold that the birth, nourishment, and increase of each thing is the alteration and corruption of another:

For change of anything from out its bounds
Means instant death of that which was before. (LUCRETIUS.)

CHAPTER 23

OF CUSTOM, AND THAT AN ESTABLISHED LAW IS NOT LIGHTLY TO BE CHANGED

THAT man, methinks, had a very good idea of the force of habit who first invented the tale of the village woman, who, beginning to fondle and carry a calf in her arms from the hour of its birth, and continuing to do so every day, by this habit became so strong that she was still able to carry it when grown into an ox. For habit is indeed a tyrannical and insidious schoolmistress. Stealthily and little by little she sets the foot of her authority upon us; but having, by this meek and humble beginning, fixed and planted it with the aid of time, she presently uncovers a furious and tyrannical countenance, to which we are no more at liberty even to raise our eyes. We see her at every turn violating the laws of Nature: *Use is in all things the most efficient schoolmaster* (Pliny the Elder).

I rely upon the cave in Plato's *Republic*, and believe those physicians to be right who so often allow to habit an authoritative share in their art. I believe in that king [1] who by habit disposed his stomach to live on poison, as well as the girl who, as Albertus Magnus tells us, accustomed herself to live on spiders.

In that world of the New Indies they found great nations, and in very different climates, who lived on spiders, after storing and fattening them, as well as on grasshoppers, ants, lizards and bats (a toad was sold for six crowns in a time of famine); these are cooked and prepared with various sauces. There were other nations to whom our meat and other viands were deadly poison. *Great is the force of habit: hunters will sleep out in the snow or suffer heat on the mountains; pugilists, bruised with the cestus, will utter never a groan* (Cicero).

These examples, though foreign to us, are not strange, if we consider, as our experience often tells us, how custom dulls the senses. We need not go so far as the people we are told of who live near the cataracts of the Nile, or to the

---

[1] Mithridates.

explanation the philosophers give of the celestial music, that the bodies of those spheres, being smooth and solid, licking and rubbing against each other in their revolutions, cannot fail to create a wonderful harmony, the changes and cadences of which cause the revolutions and changing dances of the stars ; but that the sense of hearing of all creatures here below, being, like that of the Egyptians, lulled to sleep by the continuance of the sound, cannot perceive it, however loud it may be. Shoesmiths, millers, and armourers could not live in the din that strikes their ears, if they were stunned by it as we are.

My jerkin of perfumed leather gratifies my nose, but, after I have worn it three days together, it gratifies only the noses of the bystanders. This is more strange, that, notwithstanding long intervals and interruptions, custom should have the power to unite and render permanent the effect of its impression on our senses, which is the experience of those who live near church steeples. When at home I live in a tower, in which every day, at the reveille and the tattoo, a very big bell rings out the *Ave Maria*. The jangling of it makes even my tower shake with fright, and, though during the first days it seems unbearable, in a short time it becomes so familiar to me, that I can hear it without being annoyed, and often without being awakened by it.

Plato reproved a boy who was playing knuckle-bones : ' You chide me for a little thing ', answered he. ' Habit, replied Plato, is not a little thing.'[1]

I believe that our greatest vices take their ply from our tenderest childhood, and that the most important part of our education is in the hands of our nurses. Some mothers think it good sport to see their boy wring a chicken's neck and wound a dog or cat in play, and many a father is so fondly foolish as to look upon it as a good omen, and indicating a martial spirit, to see his son punching and insulting a peasant or a lackey who cannot defend himself, and a sign of a pretty wit if he overreaches his playfellow by some malicious treachery and deceit. Yet these are the true seeds and roots of cruelty, tyranny, and treason : there they sprout and presently shoot up vigorously, and thrive luxuri-

---

[1] Diogenes Laertius, from whom this anecdote is taken, says the boy, or rather the young man, was playing at dice, a rather more serious matter.

antly in the hands of custom. And it denotes a very dangerous education to excuse these ugly propensities by urging the tenderness of their age and the triviality of the subject. In the first place it is Nature that speaks, and her voice is most pure and strong when it is most thin. Secondly, the ugliness of cheating depends not on the difference between crowns and pins; it depends on itself. I hold it more correct to conclude thus: 'Why should he not cheat in crowns, since he cheats in pins?' than thus, as some people do: 'It was only with pins; he would not think of doing it with crowns.' We must carefully teach children to hate those vices which are inborn, and point out their natural ugliness, that they may avoid them not only in deed, but especially in their hearts. Whatever mask they may wear, the mere thought of them should be odious.

I know well that from having been trained from my boyhood always to tread the level high-road, and from having had an aversion to mingling trickery and cunning in my childish games (and it should be noted that the games of children are not games, but rather to be regarded as their most serious actions), there is no pastime, however trivial, to which I do not bring, inwardly and from a natural propensity and without effort, an extreme dislike of deceit. I handle the cards, and keep as strict account, when playing for a couple of sous, as when playing for double doubloons; when playing against my wife or daughter I am indifferent about winning or losing, as when I am playing in good earnest. At all times and in all places my own eyes are sufficient to keep me straight; by no others am I watched so closely, and there are none that I fear more.

I have just seen in my house a little man, a native of Nantes, who was born without arms, and who has so thoroughly trained his feet to perform the services that his hands owed him, that they have in truth half forgotten their natural functions. In fact he calls them his hands; he carves, he loads a pistol and fires it off, he threads a needle, he sews, he writes, he doffs his bonnet, he combs his hair, he plays at cards and dice, and will shuffle and rattle them as dexterously as any man; the money I gave him (for he earns his living by showing himself) he carried away in his foot as we do in our hands. I have seen another who, being yet a boy, wielded a two-handed sword, and a halberd, by bending the instep, for want of hands, tossed them up into the air and caught them again, hurled a dagger, and cracked a whip as well as any wagoner in France.

But the effects of custom are far better discovered in the strange impressions she makes on our minds, where she meets with less resistance. What can she not impose on our judgements and beliefs? Is there any opinion so fantastic (I leave aside the gross impostures of religion, by which so many great nations and so many worthy persons have been besotted; for, they being beyond the reach of our human reason, to go astray in them is more excusable in such as are not extraordinarily illuminated by divine favour)—but, of other opinions, is there any too extravagant for her to implant and establish by laws, in whatever regions she pleases? And that exclamation of an ancient is very just: *Is the natural philosopher, that is, the observer and hunter of nature, not ashamed to seek testimony of the truth in minds enslaved by custom?* (Cicero.)

I believe that no fancy, however crazy, can enter into the human imagination, of which we do not find an example in some popular usage, and which consequently is not founded on and supported by our reason. There are countries where the people are accustomed to turn their backs on those they salute, and never look at the man they intend to honour. In one nation, when the king spits, the most favoured of the ladies of the court stretches out her hand, and in another the most eminent about him stoop to collect his ordure in a linen cloth.[1]

Let us here steal room for a story. A French gentleman with a reputation for witty sayings used always to blow his nose into his fingers, a thing very inimical to our custom; in justifying himself for so doing, he asked me what privilege that unclean excrement enjoyed that we should go and provide a dainty piece of linen to receive it, and, what is more, that we should wrap it up and keep it carefully about us; he maintained that that should sicken and horrify us more than to see it thrown away, wherever it may be, like all the other evacuations. It seemed to me that he spoke not altogether without reason; custom had prevented my

---

[1] Almost all the information respecting customs in the following pages is derived from a Spanish *General History of the Indies*, by Lopez de Gomara, translated into French in 1586.

perceiving the oddity of that proceeding, which we should think so hideous when told of another country.

Miracles are in accordance with our ignorance of Nature, not according to the essence of Nature. Being accustomed to a thing blinds the eye of judgement. Barbarians are in no way more wonderful to us than we are to them, nor with more reason, as every one would allow if, after going over those newly discovered examples, he could reflect upon his own and sanely compare them. Human reason is a tincture infused, in about equal measure, into all our opinions and manners, whatever form they may take, infinite in matter, infinite in diversity. I return to our theme.

There are countries where no one, except his wife and children, speak to the king except through a tube.[1] In one and the same nation young girls openly show their parts, and the married women carefully hide them. To this custom is related another practised elsewhere : chastity is prized only in wedlock, for the girls may abandon themselves at their pleasure and, when pregnant, openly procure an abortion by means of special drugs. And, in another place, if a tradesman marries, all the other tradesmen invited to the wedding anticipate him with the bride, and the more there are of them, the more is she honoured and commended for her vigour and capacity ; if an officer marries, it is the same, and the same in the case of a noble, and so with the rest, except that if he be a labourer or a man of mean condition, it is the part of his lord to do it. And yet in that place strict fidelity is recommended during marriage.

In some countries there are public brothels of males, and even marriages between them. There are countries where women go to the wars together with their husbands and share not only in the fighting, but in the command. Where they wear not only rings through their noses, lips, cheeks, and on their toes, but very heavy gold rods thrust through their breasts and buttocks. Where, when eating, they wipe their fingers on their thighs, their testicles, and the soles of their feet. Where the inheritance goes, not to the children, but to brothers and nephews, and elsewhere to the nephews only, saving in the succession of the prince. Where, to regulate the community of goods that is there practised, certain chief magistrates take in hand the cultivation of all

---

[1] Perhaps meant metaphorically : ' through an intermediary '.

the lands and the distribution of the fruits, according to
each one's needs. Where they mourn at the death of children, and feast when the old men die. Where they sleep in
beds ten or a dozen together with their wives. Where
women who lose their husbands by a violent death may
remarry, but not the others. Where women are so little
esteemed, that female children are killed at birth, and men
buy women of their neighbours, for their need. Where
husbands may repudiate their wives without showing any
cause, but the women may not do so for any cause whatever.
Where the husbands are permitted to sell them if they are
barren. Where they boil the body of a deceased person and
then pound it to a pulp, which is then mixed with their wine
and drunk. Where the most desirable sepulture is to be
devoured by dogs, in other places by birds. Where they
believe that the souls of the blessed live, in all freedom, in
pleasant fields furnished with all good things, and that from
them proceeds the echo we hear. Where they fight in the
water, and draw their bow with sure aim whilst swimming.
Where, as a sign of subjection, they have to raise their
shoulders and bow their heads, and remove their shoes when
entering the king's palace. Where the eunuchs who guard
the religious women are minus nose and lips, that they may
not inspire love ; and the priests put out their own eyes, in
order to communicate with their demons and receive their
oracles. Where every man makes to himself a god of what
he pleases : the hunter of a lion or a fox, the fisherman of
a certain fish ; and idols are made of every human action or
passion : the sun, moon, and earth are the principal gods,
and the form of taking an oath is to touch the earth whilst
looking at the sun, and flesh and fish are eaten raw. Where
the most solemn oath is to swear by the name of some dead
person who was held in good repute in the country, the
while touching his tomb with one hand. Where the New
Year's gift the king sends every year to his vassal princes
is fire ; when the ambassador brings it, the old fire is
extinguished in the whole house ; and this new fire the
people depending on the prince are obliged to fetch each man
for himself, upon pain of the crime of high treason. Where
the king, in order to give himself entirely to his devotions, retires from his office, which often happens ; his first
successor is then obliged to do the same, and hands on the

right of ruling to the third successor. Where they vary the form of government as their affairs require : they depose the king when it seems good to them, substituting certain elders to take the helm of the state, and sometimes leaving it in the hands of the commonalty. Where men and women are both circumcised, and likewise baptized. Where the soldier who, in one or several engagements, has been so fortunate as to present to his king seven of the enemies' heads, is made a noble. Where they live under that belief, so uncommon and uncivil,[1] in the mortality of the soul. Where the women are delivered without terror and without complaining. Where the women on both legs wear copper greaves, and if they are bitten by a louse, are bound by the duty of magnanimity to bite it again ; and dare not marry till first they have made the king a tender of their virginity, if he please to accept it. Where they salute each other by putting a finger to the ground and then raising it to heaven. Where the men carry burdens on their heads, and the women on their shoulders ; the women make water standing, and the men squatting. Where they send some of their blood in token of friendship, and offer incense to the men they would honour, as if they were gods. Where kinship in marriage is forbidden not only to the fourth, but to a more remote degree. Where children are four years at nurse, and often twelve ; and among the same people it is accounted fatal to give a child suck on the very first day. Where the fathers undertake the chastisement of boys, and the mothers, apart, of the girls, the punishment being to smoke them hanging by their feet. Where they circumcise women. Where they eat all kinds of herbs, without any other discretion than to reject those which they think have an evil smell. Where everything is open, and the houses, however rich and handsome they may be, are without doors, windows, or chests that lock ; thieves are there punished double what they are elsewhere. Where they kill lice with their teeth, like apes, and think it horrible to see them crushed under their nails. Where they cut neither hair nor nails throughout life ; in another place they pare the nails of the right hand only, those of the left being allowed to grow as a pretty ornament. Where they let all the hair on the right hand of

[1] As Montaigne shared that belief, it is not clear what he means by 'incivile'. The 1595 edition has 'insociable'.

the body grow as long as it can, and shave the other side ; while in one of the neighbouring provinces the hair in front is left to grow, in another that behind, the opposite side being shaved. Where fathers lend their children, and husbands their wives, for the enjoyment of their guests, in return for payment. Where a man may, without scandal, get his mother with child, and fathers consort with their daughters and sons. Where at their festive gatherings they lend one another their children [without any distinction of parenthood].

Here they live on human flesh ; there it is a pious duty to kill your father at a certain age; elsewhere the father ordains which of his children are to be kept and reared, which to be killed and abandoned, whilst they are yet in their mother's womb. In another place the old husbands lend their wives to be enjoyed by young men ; in another again they are held in common, without sin ; nay, in one country they edge their garments, as a mark of honour, with pretty tassels corresponding to the number of men they have known. Moreover, has not custom made a separate commonwealth of women ? has it not put arms into their hands, and made them raise armies and fight battles ? And does she not, by her ordinance alone, teach the rudest people what no philosophy is able to implant in the heads of the wisest ? for we know of entire nations where death was not only despised, but welcomed ; where children seven years old suffered themselves to be scourged to death without changing countenance ; where riches were held in such contempt, that the meanest citizen in the town would not have stooped to pick up a purse full of crowns. And we know of regions very fertile in all manner of products, where, however, the most ordinary and most tasty dishes were bread, nasturtiums, and water.

Did she not, moreover, work that miracle in Chios that in seven hundred years no wife or maid had within living memory failed against her honour ?

To sum up, in my opinion there is nothing that custom does not or cannot do, and with reason does Pindar, as I have been told, call her the 'Queen and Empress of the world'.

A man that was seen to beat his father replied that it was the custom of his house, that his father had in like manner beaten his grandfather, his grandfather his great-grandfather, and added, pointing to his son, ' He will beat me when he shall have come to my age '.

And a father, whom his son was mauling and tugging along the street, ordered him to stop at a certain door, for he, he said, had dragged his father no further than that door, which was the boundary of the hereditary ill-treatment that the sons, in their family, meted out to their fathers. It is habit, says Aristotle, as often as disease that makes women pull out their hair, bite their nails, eat earth and charcoal ; and as much by custom as by nature males cohabit with males.

The laws of conscience, which we say are born of Nature, are born of custom : as every man holds in inward veneration the opinions and manners received and approved around him, he is unable to let go his hold on them without remorse, or to cling to them without approval.

When the people of Crete, in times past, wished to curse a man, they prayed the gods to enslave him to some bad habit.

But the principal effect of the force of custom is to seize and grip us so firmly, that we are scarce able to escape from its grasp, and to regain possession of ourselves sufficiently to discuss and reason out its commands. In truth, since we imbibe them with our mother's milk, and the world shows the same face to our infant eyes, we seem to be born to follow this same path ; and the common ideas that we find current around us, and infused into our souls with the seed of our fathers, appear to be general and natural. Whence it comes that what is off the hinges of custom we believe to be off the hinges of reason : God knows how unreasonably for the most part !

If, as we who study ourselves have learned to do, every man who hears a true maxim would straightway observe how it touches him personally, he would find that it is not so much a good saying as a good lash of the whip to the ordinary stupidity of his judgement. But the precepts and admonitions of truth are taken as if addressed to people in general, and never to ourselves ; and instead of applying them to our own manners, each of us foolishly and very unprofitably commits them to memory. Let us return to the sovereignty of custom.

The nations that have been bred up to liberty and self-rule look upon every other sort of government as abnormal and contrary to nature; those that are accustomed to a monarchy do the like. And, whatever facility Fortune may afford them to effect a change, even when they have with great difficulty rid themselves of a troublesome master, they hasten with all speed, and with equal difficulty, to set up a new one; being unable to make up their minds to hate a domineering rule.

[Custom makes every one content with the spot where Nature has planted him: the savages of Scotland have no use for Touraine, nor the Scythians for Thessaly.]

Darius asked some Greeks how much would induce them to adopt the Indian custom of eating their deceased fathers (for that was their usage, thinking they could not give them a more acceptable tomb than their own insides); they replied that for nothing in the world would they do it; but, when he also tried to persuade the Indians to drop their habit and, after the Greek manner, burn the bodies of their fathers, they were still more horrified. All are alike, since custom hides from us the true aspect of things.

> And nought soe'er that's great to such degree,
> Nor wonderful so far, but all mankind
> Little by little abandon their surprise. (LUCRETIUS.)

Having once had occasion to justify one of our observances, and one that was accepted with absolute authority in the far-outlying districts surrounding us, and not content, as most men are, to find it established merely by force of laws and examples, but searching still further into its origin, I found that it was built on so weak a foundation, that I, who had to encourage it in others, was all but disgusted.

It was by this remedy, which he esteems of first-rate and sovereign virtue, that Plato undertook to banish the unnatural amours of his time, namely, that public opinion should condemn them, that the poets, that every one, should invent horrible tales about them: a recipe by means of which the fairest daughters shall no more attract their fathers' love, nor brothers excelling in beauty that of their sisters; the very fables of Thyestes, Oedipus, and Macareus having, with the charm of the poetry, infused this wholesome belief into the tender brains of children.

Pudicity is indeed a beautiful virtue, the utility of which is sufficiently known ; but to treat of it and justify it in accordance with Nature is as difficult as it is easy to justify it by usage, laws, and precepts. The primary and universal reasons are difficult to investigate, and our masters pass over them skimmingly, or else, not daring even to touch them, they at once fly to the sanctuary of custom : there they can puff themselves and enjoy an easy triumph. Those who persist in seeking the original source fail still more completely, and commit themselves to wild theories : witness Chrysippus who, in so many passages scattered throughout his writings, showed the little account he made of incestuous unions of whatsoever kind.

He who would rid himself of this violent prejudice of custom will find that many things are accepted with undoubting resolve, which have no support but in the hoary beard and wrinkles of the usage which attends them ; but, the mask once torn away, if he will refer the matter to truth and reason, he will feel his judgement turned as it were topsy-turvy, and yet restored to a condition of greater sureness. I will therefore ask him, for example, what can be more incongruous than to see a nation obliged to obey laws that they have never understood, bound in all their domestic affairs, in marriages, donations, wills, sales, and purchases, by rules of which they can have no knowledge, being neither written nor published in their own tongue, and whose interpretations and use they must of necessity buy ? Not according to the ingenious idea of Isocrates, who counsels his king to make the trafficking and negotiations of his subjects free, open and lucrative, and their disputes and quarrels onerous, and burdened with heavy subsidies ; but to put a price on justice itself, and to make the laws a saleable commodity : a monstrous suggestion ! I thank my stars that, as our historians tell us, it was a Gascon gentleman and a countryman of mine who first opposed Charlemagne when he wished to give us Latin and imperial laws.

What can be more barbarous than to see a nation where, by lawful custom, the office of a judge is sold, and judgements are paid for in good ready money, and where justice is by law denied to him who has not the wherewithal to pay for it ; where this merchandise is held in so great repute, that a fourth estate of men, who manage lawsuits, is established in a government and added to the three ancient ones of the Church, Nobility, and the People; which estate, having the laws in their charge, and sovereign authority over lives and property, forms a body apart from that of the nobility? Whence it comes to pass that there are double laws, those of honour and those of justice, in many things very contradictory, the former as rigorously condemning a lie taken, as the latter do a lie revenged. By the duty of arms he is degraded from honour and nobility who puts up with an affront, and by civil duty he who avenges himself for the same incurs a capital penalty; he who appeals to the laws in order to obtain satisfaction for an offence done to his honour, dishonours himself, and he who does not so appeal is corrected and punished by the laws. And of those two so different professions, which are, however, responsible to a single head,[1] the one has peace, the other war, in its keeping; the one has gain, the other honour; the one, knowledge, the other, virtue; the one, words, the other, actions; the one, justice, the other, valour; the one, right, the other, might; the one, the long robe, the other, the short, for its share.

With regard to indifferent things like clothes, should any one wish to refer them back to their true purpose, which is the service and comfort of the body, on which depend their original grace and comeliness, I will give him among others the most fantastic that to my mind can be imagined, our square birettas, that long tail of plaited velvet that hangs from our women's heads, with its motley trappings, and that vain and useless model of a member we cannot decently so much as name, which, however, we show and parade in public. These considerations do not, however, deter a man of intelligence from following the common style. But, on the other hand, methinks that all peculiar and out-of-the-way fashions proceed rather from folly or ambitious affectation, than from true reason; and that the wise man should, in respect of his inward thoughts and opinions, withdraw his mind from the common crowd, and keep it at liberty and with power to judge freely of things; but, in respect of his exterior, that he should wholly follow accepted forms and fashions. Society in general has no business with our

---

[1] i.e. the King.

thoughts, but as for the rest, such as our actions, our labours, our fortunes, and our own lives, they should be given over entirely to its service, and to common opinions: as that great and good Socrates refused to save his life by disobedience to the magistracy, and a very unjust and very iniquitous magistracy at that; for it is the rule of rules, and universal law of laws, that every man shall observe those of the place wherein he lives:

'Tis good to obey one's country's laws. (Greek tragedy.)

Here is something from another cask. It is much to be doubted whether the manifest advantage of changing an established law, be it ever so bad, outweighs the evil involved in the removing of it, inasmuch as a government is a structure of various parts so closely joined together, that it is impossible to shake one part without the whole body feeling the concussion. The lawgiver of the Thurians decreed that whoever should propose to abolish one of the old laws or establish a new one should present himself before the people with a rope round his neck, to the end that, if the innovation were not approved by all, he might immediately be strangled. And the Lacedemonian legislator made it his life's task to extort from the citizens a sure promise not to infringe any of his ordinances. The Ephor who so rudely cut the two strings that Phrynis had added to the cithara, does not trouble himself to think whether it is the better for the change, or whether the chords are the fuller; to him the fact that it is the alteration of an old fashion is a sufficient reason for condemning it. That was the meaning of that rusty sword of justice at Marseilles.[1]

I dislike innovation in any disguise whatever, and have reason to do so, for I have witnessed its very injurious effects. The one which has lain so heavily upon us for so many years has not been directly accountable for all, but it may be said, with some colour of truth, that accidentally it has produced and begotten all, even the ruin and mischief that have since happened, without it, and against it: that innovation may take all the blame on its shoulders;

Alas! the wounds by my own shafts are made. (OVID.)

They who shake the foundations of a state are liable to

[1] According to Valerius Maximus, this sword had been preserved from the time of the foundation of the city, as an emblem of unchangeableness.

be the first involved in its downfall. The fruits of the disturbance are seldom reaped by the disturber ; he beats and troubles the waters for other fishermen. The unity and fabric of this monarchy, this great edifice, having been broken up and dissolved, notably in its old age, by this innovation, a free entrance has been opened to similar evils. The fall of the royal majesty, says an ancient writer, from the top to the middle is less easily brought about than its precipitation from the middle to the foundation.

But if the innovators are the more mischievous, the imitators are more in error in eagerly following examples the horror and mischief of which they have felt and punished.[1] And if there be any degree of honour, even in ill-doing, these latter must yield to the others the glory of contriving and the courage of making the first attempt.

All sorts of new disorders easily draw, from this original and prolific source, examples and models for disturbing our government. We read in our very laws, drawn up to remedy the first evil, the instructions and excuse for all sorts of wicked enterprises; and that befalls us which Thucydides tells of the civil wars of his time, that to excuse the public vices they were baptized with new and milder names, their true titles being falsified and toned down. The object, however, was to reform our consciences and our beliefs ; *fine words indeed !* (Terence). But the best pretext for innovation is very dangerous : *so dangerous it is to move anything out of its old grooves !* (Livy). And so, to speak openly, it argues, to my mind, great self-conceit and presumption in a man to rate his opinions so highly that, to put them in practice, he would overthrow a public peace, and introduce into his own country, in a matter of such great import, so many inevitable evils and so horrible a corruption of manners, as civil wars and government changes bring in their train. [Is it not bad husbandry to advance so many certain and known vices in order to combat errors that are contested and debatable ? Is there any worse kind of vice than that which shocks a man's own conscience and his natural insight ?][2]

---

[1] An allusion to the excesses of the Catholics who rebelled in imitation of the Protestants.

[2] The last two sentences appear on the margin of the Bordeaux copy of 1588, but they are not in Montaigne's handwriting. They are obviously an addition by Mlle de Gournay.

The Senate, in the difference between it and the people about the ministry of their religion, was bold enough to pay them with this evasion, *That this matter appertained more to the gods than to them; they would see to it that their sacred mysteries were not profaned* (Livy). This was in conformity with the reply which the oracle made to the men of Delphi, in the Median war. Fearing the invasion of the Persians, they asked the god what they were to do with the sacred treasures of his temple, whether they should hide them or remove them. He made reply that they should remove nothing, but look to themselves; that he was able to look after his own affairs.

The Christian religion has all the marks of the utmost justice and utility, but none more apparent than its strict recommendation of obedience to the authorities, and the maintenance of civil administration. What a wonderful example of this the divine wisdom has left us, which, to assure the salvation of the human race, and to conduct its glorious victory over death and sin, willed to do it only under favour of our political order, committing its progress and the issue of so high and salutary a work to the blindness and injustice of our customs and observances, sacrificing the innocent blood of so many of its favoured elect, and suffering a long waste of years to mature this inestimable fruit!

There is a great difference between the cases of one who follows the forms and laws of his country, and one who attempts to change and lord it over them. The former pleads simplicity, obedience, and example for his excuse; whatever he may do, it cannot be imputed to malice; at the worst it is but his misfortune. *For who could not but respect an antiquity sealed and attested by the most famous monuments?* (Cicero). Besides what Isocrates says, that defect is more akin to moderation than excess.

The other is in a much ruder case. For he who meddles with choosing and altering usurps the authority of a judge, and must feel strong in his assurance that he sees the defect of that which he abolishes, and the good of that which he introduces.

This very ordinary consideration strengthened me in my attitude, and restrained me in my youth, even when most inclined to be foolhardy, from loading my shoulders with so great a burden as to render myself responsible for knowledge of so great importance, and in this to dare what with sound judgement I could not dare in the easiest of those sciences wherein I had been instructed, and wherein rashness of judgement can do no harm ; since it seems to me most iniquitous to attempt to subject public and firmly established institutions and observances to the instability of a private fancy (for private reason has but a private jurisdiction), and to treat the divine laws in a way that no government would tolerate in the case of the civil laws, which, although human reason has much more to do with them, are yet sovereign judges of their judges ; their extreme sufficiency serves to explain their wide currency and to extend it, and obviates any diversion or innovation. If, at any time, divine providence has overridden the rules to which it has necessarily bound us, it was not intended as a dispensation to us to do the same. It was a master-stroke of the divine hand, which we may admire but not imitate, and an extraordinary example and mark of an express and particular approval, of the nature of a miracle, offered to us as a testimony of its all-power, above our orders and powers, which it would be folly and impiety to try to imitate, and which we are not to follow, but to contemplate with wonder. Acts of its personality, not of ours.

Cotta very appropriately declares : *When religion is in question, I follow T. Coruncanius, P. Scipio, P. Scevola, the sovereign pontiffs, not Zeno, Cleanthes or Chrysippus* (Cicero). God knows, in our present conflict, where there are a hundred articles, great and profound articles, to be removed and altered, how many there are who can boast of having accurately understood the grounds and reasons of both factions. It is a number, if they are a number, that would not give us much cause to be disturbed. But all that other throng, whither is it going ? under what ensign does it stray from the flock ? It is with theirs as with other weak and badly administered medicines : the humours that it professed to purge in us are only inflamed, exasperated and intensified by the conflict, and yet the physic still remains in our bodies. By reason of its weakness it was incapable of purging us, and has meanwhile left us enfeebled, in such a manner that we cannot void it any more than before, and its operation has had the effect of giving us prolonged intestinal pains.

MISTAKE OF OCTAVIUS AND CATO

Nevertheless Fortune, still reserving her authority over and above our reason, sometimes presents to us a necessity so urgent, that the laws must needs yield a little and give way to her.

And to resist the encroachments of an innovation which forces its way by violence is a dangerous obligation for one who, everywhere and in all things, holds himself in check and bound by rules; it places him at a disadvantage when faced with one who assumes all freedom to act, who regards everything as lawful that will serve his own designs, who knows no restraint and whose only law is to follow up his own advantage:

> Trust in a traitor gives him power to hurt. (SENECA.)

For the ordinary discipline of a state in a healthy condition does not provide against these extraordinary accidents; it presupposes a body that supports itself in its principal members and offices, and a general consent to observe and obey it. A legitimate procedure is a cool, deliberate, and restrained procedure, unable to make head against a licentious and unbridled course.

We know that it is still made a reproach against those two great men, Octavius and Cato, in the civil wars of Sylla on the one hand and Caesar on the other, that rather than help their country at the expense of the laws or change any of them, they allowed it to suffer the last extremities. For, of a truth, in these emergencies, when there is no other remedy, it would be wiser perhaps to bow the head and allow the blow to fall, than, by obstinately holding on without the possibility of doing good, to give violent men occasion to trample all under foot; it would be better to let the laws will what they can, since they cannot do what they will. After this manner did he who decreed that they should lie dormant for twenty-four hours;[1] he who, for this one occasion, removed a day from the calendar; and that other who of the month of June made a second month of May.[1]

Even the Lacedemonians, who were such scrupulous observers of the laws of their country, being restrained by that law which forbade them twice to choose the same man for admiral, and on the other hand, their affairs urgently

---

[1] Agesilaus and Alexander the Great.

requiring that Lysander should again assume that office, made one Aracus admiral and Lysander superintendent of the navy. And, with the same subtlety, one of their ambassadors being sent to the Athenians to recommend a change in some law, and Pericles pointing out to them that it was forbidden to remove a tablet on which a law had once been set down, he advised him simply to turn it round, since that was not forbidden. It was for this that Plutarch commends Philopoemen, that, being born to command, he was able to command not only according to the laws, but the laws themselves, when public necessity so required.

CHAPTER 24

OF DIFFERENT RESULTS OF THE SAME COUNSEL

JACQUES AMYOT, Grand Almoner of France, one day told me this story to the honour of one of our princes (and ours he was deservedly, although of foreign origin),[1] that during our first civil war, at the siege of Rouen, this Prince had been warned, by the Queen-mother of the King, of an attempt that was to be made on his life ; she particularly mentioned in her letters the person who was to carry out the design. This was a gentleman of Anjou, or of Maine, who with this end in view frequently visited the house of the Prince. He communicated this intelligence to no one, but, walking next day on the Mont Ste Catherine, from whence our battery played on Rouen (for it was at the time we were besieging it), with the aforesaid Lord Grand Almoner and another bishop at his side, he perceived the gentleman who had been denounced to him, and sent for him. When he came into his presence, he spoke to him thus, seeing him already turning pale and trembling at the alarms of his conscience : 'Monsieur So-and-so, you no doubt suspect why I wish to see you, and your face shows it. You have nothing to hide from me, for I am so well informed of your business, that you would only make things worse for yourself by trying to conceal it. You know very well such and such a thing (mentioning the ins and outs of

[1] The Duke François de Guise, of the house of Lorraine. The siege of Rouen took place in 1562 ; the Duke, who was on very friendly terms with Montaigne, was assassinated in the following year.

the most secret circumstances of this conspiracy); fail not, on your life, to confess to me the whole truth of the plot.' When the poor man saw himself caught and convicted (for the whole plot had been discovered to the Queen by one of the accomplices), he could but join his hands and implore the Prince's pardon and mercy, and would have cast himself at his feet, but that the Prince prevented him, and continued as follows: 'Come hither; have I at any time done you an injury? Have I, in private feud, offended any of your kin? I have hardly known you three weeks; what reason could have induced you to attempt my death?' The gentleman replied, with trembling voice, that it was not for any private motive, but the general interest of his party's cause; and that he had been persuaded by some that it would be a very pious deed to extirpate, by any means whatsoever, so powerful an enemy to their religion. 'Now, continued the Prince, I will prove to you how much more humane is the religion I hold than that which you profess. Yours counsels you to kill me without being heard, though you have suffered no wrong at my hands; and mine commands me to pardon you, convicted though you be of having intended to murder me without reason. Get you gone, withdraw; let me see you no more; and if you are wise, you will henceforth choose better men to advise you.'

When the Emperor Augustus was in Gaul, he received certain information of a plot that was being brewed against him by Lucius Cinna; he decided on revenge, and to that end summoned a council of his friends for the next morning. But he passed the night between in great uneasiness of mind, considering that he was about to put to death a young man of good family and a nephew of the great Pompey, and in his trouble he turned various considerations over in his mind: 'What! said he to himself, shall it be ordained that I am to remain in a state of fear and alarm, and let my murderer meanwhile walk abroad at his pleasure? Shall he go quit, who is aiming at my head, which I have carried safe and sound through so many civil wars, so many battles by sea and land, and after having established the universal peace of the world? Shall he be absolved who has conspired not only to murder, but to sacrifice me?' (for the plot was to kill him in the act of sacrificing.) Then, after a short silence, he began again in a louder voice, and took himself to task: 'Why dost thou live, if so many people are interested in thy death? Shall there be no end to thy vengeances and cruelties? Is thy life worth all the evil that is done to preserve it?'

Livia, his wife, hearing him in his anguish, said to him: 'And will a woman's counsel be taken? Do as the physicians do, who, when the customary remedies are of no avail, try the contrary ones. You have hitherto gained nothing by severity: Lepidus has followed Salvidienus; Murena, Lepidus; Cepio, Murena; Egnatius, Cepio. Begin now and try how mildness and clemency will succeed. Cinna is convicted; pardon him; injure you henceforth he cannot, and it will be to your glory.' Augustus was well pleased to have found an advocate of his own mind, and having thanked his wife and countermanded his friends whom he had called in council, he commanded Cinna to be brought to him all alone. Having ordered all his attendants to leave his chamber, and bidden Cinna to be seated, he spoke to him in this wise: 'In the first place I ask you, Cinna, to hear me in peace: do not interrupt me; I shall give you time and leisure to reply. You know, Cinna, that having taken you, a prisoner in my enemies' camp, though you not merely became, but were born my enemy, I gave you your life, I put you in possession of all your goods, and made you in short so comfortable and well off, that the victorious are envious of the condition of the vanquished. I granted you the priestly office you asked of me, after refusing it to others whose fathers had always fought on my side. After so many obligations you have plotted to kill me.' To which Cinna exclaiming that he was very far from such a wicked thought: 'You do not keep your promise, Cinna, continued Augustus; you assured me that I should not be interrupted. Yes, you have conspired to kill me in such a place, on such a day, in such company and in such a manner.' And seeing him paralysed at these words and struck dumb, not on account of keeping his bargain to be silent, but with the weight of conscience: 'Why, he added, do you do it? Is it in order to be emperor? Truly the Republic is in a bad way, if I alone hinder you from coming to empire. You cannot even defend your house, and the other day you lost a lawsuit, thanks to the efforts of a mere freedman. What! can you use your resources to no better purpose than to attack

Caesar ? I will throw up the game, if it is I alone who obstruct your hopes. Do you think that Paulus, that Fabius, that the Cossii and the Servilii will tolerate you, not to speak of a great number of nobles, not only nobles in name, but who, by their virtue, are a credit to their nobility ? ' After much more to the same effect (for he spoke for more than two full hours), he said : ' Now go, Cinna ; that life which I once gave you as to an enemy, I give as to a traitor and parricide ; friendship shall commence from this day between us, and let us strive which of us shall show the better faith, I who have given you life, or you who have received it.' And thus he parted from him. Some time after this he gave him the consulship, complaining that he had not dared to ask for it. Ever afterwards he had in Cinna a firm friend, and was made by him sole heir to his estates.

Now, after this event, which befell Augustus in the fortieth year of his age, there was never any attempt or conspiracy made against his life, and he received a just reward for his clemency. But it did not so happen to our Prince, for his humane action could not save him from afterwards falling into the toils of a like treason.[1] So vain and unavailing a thing is human wisdom ! and throughout all our plans, projects, and precautions Fortune is ever the mistress of events.

We call a physician lucky when he is successful in a case ; as if his art were the only one that could not stand upon its own legs, and whose foundations were too weak to support it by their own strength, and as if it alone had need of the helping hand of Fortune in its operations. My opinion of the art of physic is as bad or as good as you please, for we have, thank God ! no traffic together. My attitude towards it is quite the contrary to that of others ; for I ever despise it indeed, but when I am sick, instead of becoming reconciled with it, I begin to hate and fear it as well ; and to those who urge me to take physic I reply that they may wait at least until I am restored to health and strength, in order to be better able to support the effect and the danger of their potions. I allow Nature to work, and suppose her to be armed with teeth and claws to defend herself against

---

[1] He was, after all, assassinated by a gentleman of Angoumois called Poltrot de Méré, and from the same motive.

the assaults that are made upon her, and to maintain this frame whose dissolution she fears. I fear lest, instead of assisting her, when she is at grips and struggling with disease, I might assist her adversary instead of her, and put fresh burdens on her shoulders.

Now, I say that not only in medicine but in several more certain arts, there is a good deal of luck. Why should we not attribute the poetic flights which ravish and transport their author out of himself to his good luck, since he himself confesses that they exceed his power and ability, and acknowledges them to proceed from something else than himself, and to be no more within his power than those extraordinary emotions and agitations of orators, which, as they say, impel them beyond their intention?

It is the same with painting, for it sometimes happens that touches escape from the brush of the artist that so far exceed his conception and his art as to excite his own admiration and astonishment. But Fortune still more evidently shows the share that she has in all these works, by the charm and beauty which enter into them, not only in spite of the intention, but without even the knowledge of the workman. A competent reader will often discover in the writings of others perfections other than the author intended or perceived, and lend them a fairer face and a richer meaning.

With regard to military enterprises, every one knows how great a hand Fortune has in them. Even in our plannings and deliberations there must truly be mingled something of chance and good luck, for all that our wit can do is no great matter; the quicker and more acute it is, so much the weaker does it think itself to be, and so much the more does it distrust itself. I am of Sylla's way of thinking,[1] and when I closely examine the most famous exploits of war, I seem to see that they who conduct them only deliberate and take counsel as a matter of form, and leave the better part of their enterprise to Fortune; and, relying on her aid, at every turn go beyond the limits of all reason. There ensue, in their deliberations, accidental exhilarations and extraordinary fits of frenzy, which impel them most often to

[1] Sylla, according to Plutarch, 'disarmed envy by often commending his good fortune, and finally took the surname of *Faustinus*, the Fortunate'.

adopt a course that is apparently least founded on prudence, and which swell their courage beyond all reason. Whence it has come about that some of the great captains of old, to justify their foolhardy resolutions, declared to their soldiers that they were commanded by some inspiration, some sign or prognostic.

Wherefore, in the uncertainty and perplexity brought upon us by our inability to discern and choose the most proper course, by reason of the difficulties which the various accidents and circumstances of each thing bring along with them, the surest way, in my opinion, even though no other consideration should invite us to it, is to cast oneself on that side where there is most honesty and justice; and, when in doubt about the nearest path, to choose always the straight one; as in those two examples I have just cited, there can be no doubt that it was more noble and generous in him who had received the offence to pardon it, than to do otherwise. If the former came to grief, it must not be put down to his good intention; nor do we know whether, had he adopted the contrary course, he would have escaped the end to which his destiny called him, and then he would have forfeited the glory of so humane an action.

In history we read of many men who were possessed by this fear, the greater part of whom followed the course of meeting and anticipating the conspiracies formed against them by vengeance and punishment, but I read of very few who benefited by this remedy: witness so many Roman emperors. He who finds himself in this danger must not put too much faith either in his power or his vigilance. For how difficult it is to guard ourselves against an enemy who puts on the mask of the most assiduous friend we have, and to know the inner thoughts and intentions of those who serve us! It is of no avail to have a guard of foreigners, and to be continually surrounded by a hedge of armed men; any man who disregards his own life always has the power of disposing of another's. And then, that continual suspicion which makes a prince distrustful of all the world, must be a strange torment to him.

Therefore it was that Dion, being advised that Callipus was watching his opportunity to put him to death, never had the heart to make further inquiries, saying that he would rather die than live in the misery of having to be on his guard, not only against his enemies, but against his friends. This attitude of mind was much more vividly and more undauntedly acted upon by Alexander. Having had information by letter from Parmenio that Philippus, his favourite physician, had been bribed by Darius's money to poison him, he gave the letter to Philippus to read, and at the same moment swallowed the potion he had brought him. Was not this to express a resolution that, if his friends desired to kill him, he was willing to give them an opportunity to do so? This prince is the supreme pattern of hazardous deeds, yet I know not whether in all his life he showed an act of more resolute courage than this, or a beauty of mind so illustrious from every point of view.

They who preach to princes so vigilant a distrust, under cover of preaching security, preach their ruin and shame. No noble thing can be done without risk. I know one who is by nature very spirited and enterprising, whose good fortune is every day marred by persuasions such as these : 'That he should keep himself closely surrounded by his friends ; That he should give ear to no reconciliation with his old enemies ; That he should stand aloof, and never trust himself to any stronger than himself, whatever promises may be made to him, whatever advantages he may see in that course.' I know another who has unexpectedly advanced his fortune by following quite contrary counsels.[1]

Courage, the reputation for which is so eagerly sought after, may, when the need arises, make as magnificent a show in a doublet as in a chain armour, in a cabinet as in the field, with arms pendent as with raised arm.

Caution so tender and circumspect is a deadly enemy to lofty deeds. Scipio, in order to win over Syphax, was able to leave his army, abandoning the newly conquered and still doubtful country of Spain, and cross over into Africa in only two ships, to commit himself, in hostile territory, to the power of a barbarian king, to an unknown faith, without bond or hostage, under the sole security of his great personal bravery, his good fortune, and the promise of his high hopes. *Trust sometimes forces trust* (Livy).

But in a life of ambition and glory it is necessary not to give way to suspicion, but to keep a tight rein upon it : fear and

[1] This last sentence is supposed to refer to Montaigne's particular hero, Henry of Navarre, afterwards Henry IV of France.

distrust draw and invite attack. The most mistrustful of our kings carried his point principally by voluntarily abandoning and committing his life and liberty into the hands of his enemies, thus showing his entire confidence in them, in order that they might place the same trust in him.[1] When his legions armed and mutinied against him, Caesar confronted them with the sole authority of his countenance and his proud words : he had so great confidence in himself and his fortune, that he felt no fear in abandoning and committing it to a seditious and rebellious army :

> Upon a turfy mound unmoved he stood,
> And, since he feared not, worthy to be feared. (LUCAN.)

But it is most true that this powerful assurance cannot show forth fully and naturally except in one who is not affrighted by the image of death, and by the worst that might in the end happen to him ; for if it appear tremulous, doubtful, and uncertain, in the service of an important reconciliation, it can effect nothing to any purpose. An excellent way to win the heart and goodwill of another is to submit to and trust him, as long as it is done freely and without the constraint of any necessity, and on condition that one brings to it a full and clear confidence, with a brow at least free from all doubt.

In my boyhood I saw a nobleman, the commandant of a large town,[2] hard put to it by the sedition of a furious populace. To quell this beginning of disturbance, he decided to leave a very secure shelter and place himself at the mercy of a mutinous mob ; but it was his undoing, for he was miserably slain. But his mistake, I think, was not so much that for which he is usually blamed, namely, that he went out, as that he put on an air of meekness and submission, and attempted to lull the storm by obeying rather than by guiding, by entreaty rather than by remonstrance ; and I believe that a gracious severity combined with an air of military command, assured and confident as befitted his rank and the dignity of his office, would have been attended with greater success, at least with more honour and seemli-

---

[1] A reference to the interview between Louis XI and Charles the Bold at Péronne in 1468.
[2] This was M. de Monneins, governor of Bordeaux ; the incident occurred in 1548.

ness. Anything is to be expected from that monster in a state of commotion sooner than humanity and gentleness; it is much more likely to be moved by fear and awe. I should have represented to him also that, having taken a resolution (to my mind brave rather than foolhardy) to cast himself, weak and in his doublet, into this tempestuous sea of madmen, he should have swallowed the whole draught, and not have quitted the part he had assumed; whereas what happened was that, after he saw the danger near at hand, he began to bleed at the nose,[1] and the humble and wheedling mien he had so far put on was exchanged for one of terror: by charging his voice and eyes with consternation and penitence, and by trying, as it were, to scuttle away like a rabbit and hide himself, he inflamed and invited their fury.

A general muster of different armed troops was being discussed (these are the occasions of secret revenges, and nowhere can they be executed with greater safety). There were public and evident signs that it was not safe for certain men on whom devolved the chief and necessary duty of reviewing them. The matter being of weight and consequence, but difficult to decide, various proposals were put forward. My advice was that we should above everything show no sign of apprehension, but put in an appearance, and mix with the rank and file, with head erect and open countenance, and instead of cutting out anything (which was the chief purport of the other opinions), that we should, on the contrary, entreat the captains to command the soldiers to fire off fine and brave salvos in honour of the spectators, and not to spare their powder This pleased and gratified the suspected troops, and henceforth begat a mutual and wholesome confidence.[2]

The method of Julius Caesar I regard as the best that could be followed. In the first place, he tried by mildness and clemency to make himself beloved even by his enemies, contenting himself, when a conspiracy was disclosed to him,

[1] Idiomatic; he 'got cold feet', as we should say.
[2] This passage throws an interesting side-light on Montaigne's character, which has sometimes been described as 'unheroic'. A careful study of his life and work seems to show that he was undoubtedly a man of courage. The incident mentioned here took place in May 1585, during his second term of office as Mayor of Bordeaux.

with simply declaring that he was already informed of it; that done, he adopted the noble resolution of awaiting, without fear or anxiety, whatever might betide him, resignedly committing himself to the protection of the gods and fate; for undoubtedly he was in this state when he was assassinated.

A stranger having declared and published abroad that he could teach Dionysius, tyrant of Syracuse, a way to scent and discover with all certainty any conspiracies which his subjects might be hatching against him, in consideration of a round sum of money, Dionysius, being informed of it, sent for him, in order to be enlightened on an art so necessary to his preservation. The stranger told him that his art was no other than that he should hand over to him a talent, and then make boast of having learned a rare secret. Dionysius approved of the idea, and ordered six hundred crowns to be counted out to him. It did not seem likely that he should have given so great a sum to an unknown person but as a return for a very useful piece of knowledge, and this reputation served to keep his enemies in awe.

Princes therefore do wisely in publishing the warnings they receive of conspiracies directed against their life, in order to make believe that they are well informed, and that no attempt can be made upon them of which they have not wind. The Duke of Athens did many foolish things when establishing his recent tyranny over Florence, but this is the most remarkable that, having received the first notification of the intrigues that his people were hatching against him, from Matteo di Morozo, one of the accomplices, he put him to death in order to suppress the information, and not to let it be known that any one in the city found his just dominion irksome.

I remember having once read the story of some Roman, a person of dignity who, fleeing the tyranny of the Triumvirate, had by his craft and ingenuity escaped a thousand times from the hands of his pursuers. It happened one day that a troop of horsemen, who had been charged to take him, passed quite near a thicket in which he was crouching, and just missed discovering him; but he, reflecting at this point on the troubles and difficulties he had already so long endured, in evading the close and continued search that was everywhere made for him, the little pleasure he could hope for from such a life, and how much better it would be for him once for all to 'pass over', than to remain for ever in this trance of fear, himself called them back and disclosed his hiding-place, and voluntarily delivered himself up to their cruelty, to relieve both them and himself from further trouble.

To appeal to the hand of the enemy is a somewhat heroic counsel, yet I believe it would be better to take that course than to remain in a constant fever of fear of a calamity for which there is no remedy. But since the precautions one may take to that end are full of unquiet and uncertainty, it is better with good assurance to prepare for the worst that can happen, and draw some comfort from the reflection that one is not sure that it really will happen.

CHAPTER 25

OF PEDANTRY

I WAS often vexed as a boy to see the *pedante* or pedagogue always held up as the butt or laughing-stock in the Italian comedies, and that the title of Magister was not held in much greater estimation among us. For, having been placed under their charge and tuition, what could I do less than be jealous for their reputation? I tried indeed to excuse them by considering the natural difference that exists between the common sort and those rare men who excel them both in learning and judgement, seeing that their ways lie in entirely opposite directions. But I 'lost my Latin' when I saw that it was the finest gentlemen who most despised them; witness our good Du Bellay:

> The thing I most do hate is learned pedantry.

And that habit of so regarding them goes back to antiquity, for Plutarch tells us that *Greek* and *Scholar* were terms of reproach and contempt among the Romans.

As I grew older I found that they were most profoundly right, and that *magis magnos clericos non sunt magis magnos sapientes*.[1] But how it could happen that a mind that is

---

[1] 'Our late abbot used to say that it was a monstrous thing to see a learned monk. Pardieu, my friend, *magis magnos etc.*' Rabelais's Friar John, a typical monk of his time, thus excuses his ignorance.

rich with the knowledge of so many things should not become quicker and more wide-awake, and that a coarse and vulgar mind can, without being improved, find room within itself for the words and opinions of the most eminent minds that the world has borne, I am yet in doubt.

To receive so many and so great and powerful brains of others, as a lady (*fille*), the first of our Princesses,[1] said to me, speaking of somebody, his own would have to press and squeeze itself into a smaller compass, to make room for the others.

I should be inclined to say that, just as a plant is drowned by too much moisture and a lamp by too much oil, so is the mind drowned by too much study and matter, for, being occupied and clogged with a great variety of things, it must lose the power of freeing itself, and the weight of them must keep it bent and doubled up. But it is quite otherwise, for our mind expands the more it is filled, and in the examples of the olden time it may be seen, quite to the contrary, that men competent in the management of public affairs, great captains and great councillors in matters of state, have at the same time been very learned.

And as to the Philosophers, holding aloof from all public occupation, they have indeed also been sometimes despised in the outspoken comedies of their day, since their way of living and their opinions exposed them to ridicule. Would you make them judges of the merits of a lawsuit or of men's actions? They are quite ready to undertake it. They will besides go into the question, if there be life, if there be motion, if man be other than an ox, what is action and suffering, what kind of beasts law and justice are? Do they speak of a magistrate, or do they speak with him? They will do so with a disrespectful and discourteous freedom. Do they hear their prince, or a king, praised? To them he is a shepherd or herdsman, as idle as they, occupied in milking or shearing his beasts, but much more roughly than the shepherd or herdsman. Do you esteem somebody the greater for possessing two thousand acres of land? They will laugh at the idea, accustomed as they are to embrace the whole world as their possession. Do you boast of your nobility for being able to count up seven rich ancestors?

---

[1] Perhaps Margaret, wife of King Henry of Navarre, who, though married at the time this was written, was a ' Fille de France '.

They will look down on you, as being unable to conceive that all Nature is alike, and that every one of us has had the same number of ancestors, rich, poor, kings, varlets, Greeks, barbarians. And though you were the fiftieth descendant of Hercules, they will think you vain for making so much account of this gift of Fortune. So the vulgar sort despised them, as men ignorant of elementary and ordinary things, as presumptuous and insolent.

But our pedants are far from resembling this Platonic picture. Those were envied as being above the common run, as despising public activities, as having set before themselves a particular and inimitable life, regulated by definite lofty and uncommon ideals. These are despised as being below the common run, as incapable of public duties, as dragging out a life of mean and base habits in the tail of the vulgar crowd:

> How odious the idle, useless wight,
> Whose mouth is stuffed with philosophic saws! (PACUVIUS.)

As for those philosophers, I say, great as they were in knowledge, they were still greater in every kind of action. And even as they tell of that geometrician of Syracuse,[1] that, having been diverted from his contemplations to put some of the results of them in practice for the defence of his country, he straightway set in motion some terrifying engines of war, with results surpassing all human belief; himself all the while holding all this handiwork of his in disdain, and thinking he had thereby debased the dignity of his art, of which his works were but the apprenticeship and the pastime; so they, being sometimes put to the test of action, have been seen to fly with so lofty a wing, that it appeared indeed as if their hearts and souls had become wonderfully enlarged and enriched by the understanding of things.

But some of them, seeing the seat of political government in possession of incapable men, have retired within themselves; and a man who asked Crates how long he should study philosophy, received this answer: 'Till the time when our armies are no longer led by ass-drivers.' Heraclitus resigned the monarchy to his brother, and to the

---

[1] Archimedes, who by his inventions for three years kept the Romans in check, who were besieging Syracuse.

Ephesians who reproved him for spending his time playing with the boys before the temple, he replied: 'Is it not better to do this than to sit at the helm of affairs in your company?'

Others, with their ideas raised above worldly fortunes, looked upon the seats of justice and even the thrones of kings as base and contemptible. Empedocles went so far as to refuse the royal throne offered him by the people of Agrigentum. Thales, inveighing now and then against the pains that people devoted to getting rich in business, and being met with the retort that he was doing after the manner of the fox, being unable to succeed in it, he had a mind to try the experiment as a pastime; and, having for the nonce degraded his learning to the service of profit and gain, he set a traffic on foot which within a year brought him so great riches, that the most experienced in that trade were hardly able in all their lifetime to make as much.

What Aristotle relates of certain persons, that they called Thales and Anaxagoras, and their like, wise but not prudent, for not caring sufficiently about more profitable things (besides that I do not quite digest that verbal distinction), that will not excuse my pedantic friends; and, to see the humble and necessitous fortune wherewith they are content, we should rather have reason to declare them neither wise nor prudent.

I quit this first reason, and prefer to say that the evil proceeds from their taking a wrong view of learning, and that, seeing how we are taught, it is no marvel if neither scholars nor masters show any more intelligence, though they become more learned. In truth, the care and expense which our fathers devote to our education have no other aim but to furnish our heads with knowledge; of judgement and virtue, not a word! Exclaim to our people, of one who passes by: 'O what a learned man!' and of another: 'O what a good man!' they will be sure to direct their eyes and their respect to the first. There ought to be a third crier: 'O what blockheads!' We are apt to inquire: 'Does he know Greek or Latin? Does he write poetry or prose?' But whether he is become better or wiser, which is the main thing, that question is left unspoken. We should inquire who knows best, not who knows most.

We labour but to cram our memory, and leave the understanding and the conscience empty. Even as the birds sometimes fly in search of grain, and bring it in their beaks without tasting it, to feed their young, so do our pedants go picking knowledge out of books, carrying it at the end of their lips, only to spit it out and scatter it to the winds.

It is remarkable how aptly I come in to exemplify this folly. Am I not doing the same thing in the most part of this composition? I go sniffing about among books, now here now there, for the sentences which please me, not to store them, for I have no storehouse, but to transplant them to this book where, to tell the truth, they are no more mine than they were before. We can, I believe, know only the things that are going on at present, not those of the past any more than those of the future.

But, and this is the worst part of it, their scholars and their little ones are not fed nor nourished by this knowledge; rather it is passed from hand to hand, to the sole end of making a show of it, to entertain others, and to make up stories of it. It is like a counterfeit coin that has no value in commerce, and is useful only as a counter for casting up. *They have learned to speak with others, not with themselves* (Cicero). *It is no time for talking, but for steering* (Seneca).

Nature, to show that there is nothing barbarous in her conduct of affairs, will often, in nations least cultivated by art, engender productions of the mind that will vie with the most artistic productions. How prettily appropriate to the matter is the Gascon proverb, ' *Bouha prou bouha, mas à remuda lous dits qu'em?* We may blow and blow, but when it comes to using the fingers, where are we? ' taken from a shepherd's song.[1]

We can say: ' Cicero said thus; these are the morals of Plato; those are the very words of Aristotle; ' but what do we ourselves say? what do we judge? what do we do? A parrot could say as much.

This manner of regarding knowledge puts me in mind of that wealthy Roman who, with much trouble and at great expense, procured men learned in every branch of knowledge, whom he kept continually around his person, to the end that, when there fell among his friends any occasion to

---

[1] It is conceivable that these words suggested the scene of the 'recorders' in Hamlet. Florio translates them, 'You may blow long enough, but if once you stir your fingers, you may go seek.'

speak of something or other, these scholars might take his place and be quite prepared to supply him, one with a dissertation, another with a line of Homer, and so forth, each according to his trade; thinking this knowledge to be his own, because it was contained in the brains of men in his employment; as they also do whose fullness is lodged in their sumptuous libraries.

I know one who, when I question him on what he knows, asks me for a book to show it me, and will not venture to tell me that he has an itchy backside without straightway consulting his lexicon to find the meaning of 'itchy' and of 'backside'.

We take the opinions and the learning of others into our keeping, and that is all. We should make them our own. We are, properly speaking, like a man who, having need of fire, goes to his neighbour's house to fetch it, and, finding there a fine and large blaze, stops to warm himself and forgets to take any home. What does it avail us to have a paunch full of meat if it be not digested, if it be not transformed within us, if it do not strengthen us and increase our growth? Do we imagine that Lucullus, who by reading became so great a captain, though without any experience, set about it after this manner?

We lean so heavily on others' arms, that our own strength vanishes. Would I arm myself against the fear of death? I do so at Seneca's expense. Would I extract consolation for myself or another? I borrow it of Cicero. I might have found it in myself, if I had been trained to do so. I do not like this dependent and mendicant fullness.

Though we may be learned with another's learning, wise, at least, we cannot be but by our own wisdom.

> Him I despise
> Who in his own concern is never wise. (EURIPIDES.)

Whence Ennius: The wise man knows nothing who cannot profit by his wisdom (quoted by Cicero).

> If covetous and vain,
> And soft as lambs on fair Euganea's plain. (JUVENAL.)

For wisdom is not only to be acquired, but to be used (Cicero).

Dionysius[1] laughed at those grammarians who anxiously

---

[1] Diogenes the Cynic is the person meant.

inquire into the sufferings of Ulysses, and know nothing of their own: musicians who tune their flutes, and do not tune their morals; orators who study to talk justice, not to do it.

If our soul go not the better pace, if our judgement be not the sounder, I should wish as dearly that my scholar had spent his time in playing tennis: his body at least would be the more active. See him returning after fifteen or sixteen years employed in study: you can find none so unfit to be put to any occupation. All the progress you discover in him is that his Latin and Greek have made him more proud and conceited than he was before he left home. He should have brought back a full mind, and he only brings a puffed-up one; instead of enlarging it, he has only inflated it.

These masters, as Plato says of their cousins the Sophists, are, of all men, they who promise to be most useful to mankind, and they alone, of all men, not only do not improve what is committed to their charge, as a carpenter does, or a mason, but make it worse, and demand payment for making it worse.

If the rule that Protagoras proposed to his pupils were followed, ' either that they should pay him according to his demand, or swear in the temple how high they estimated the profit they had gained from his teaching, and satisfy him accordingly for his pains ', my pedagogues would find themselves done, if they stood to the sworn testimony of my experience.

In the patois of my Périgord they very wittily call these wiseacres *Lettre-ferits*, as you might say *Lettre-ferus*[1] (*letter-struck*), men whom letters had given, so to say, a hammer-blow. Indeed for the most part they seem to have stepped down even from common sense. For you may see the peasant and the shoemaker go their way simply and naturally, speaking of what they know; whereas these, trying to strut and swagger with the learning that floats on the surface of their brains, perpetually entangle and trip themselves up. Fine words escape them, but let another fit them. They know Galen indeed, but they know nothing of their patient. They have already filled your ears with laws, yet they have not even understood the crux of the case. They

[1] *Ferit* and *feru* were different forms of the past participle of the obsolete verb *ferir*, Lat. *ferire*, strike.

know the theory of all things, but you may seek in vain for one who will put it in practice.

I have heard a friend of mine, when arguing with one of these gentlemen in my house, invent, by way of a jest, a nonsensical jargon, words without rhyme or reason, a tissue of patchwork, saving that he often interlarded some words having a relation to their dispute, and so keep the blockhead for a whole day debating and all the time thinking that he was answering the objections raised against him; and yet he was a man of letters and reputation, and wore a fine gown.

> Patricians great,
> To a blind occiput condemned by fate,
> Prevent, while yet we may, the rabble's glee,
> And tremble at the scoff ye cannot see! (PERSIUS.)

Whoever shall closely observe this kind of people, who are scattered far and wide, will agree with me that for the most part they neither understand others nor themselves, and that, though their memory be full enough, their judgement is completely hollow, except when their nature itself has fashioned it otherwise: as I observed in Adrianus Turnebus, who made no other profession but that of letters, in which he was in my opinion the greatest man that has been seen these thousand years, who had, however, nothing of the pedant about him but the wearing of his gown, and a certain outward fashion that could not be civilized to courtier ways, which are things of no account. (And I hate your people that will sooner tolerate a soul than a gown that is awry, and will judge a man by his bow, his bearing, and his boots.) For his inmost soul was the most polished on earth. I have often purposely led him to speak of matters far removed from his profession; he had an insight so clear, so quick an apprehension, so sound a judgement, that you would have thought that he had never carried on any other profession but the conducting of wars and affairs of state. Those are fine and strong natures,

> Just here and there a heart with hand benign
> Prometheus forms, perhaps of clay more fine. (JUVENAL.)

which survive a bad education. Now it is not enough that our education should not spoil us; it must change us for the better.

Some of our parliaments,[1] when they have to admit candidates, examine them only on their learning ; others add a test of intelligence, by submitting to them the decision of some law-case. The latter appears to me a better proceeding, and, although both qualifications are necessary, and it is requisite that they should be defective in neither, yet learning is indeed of less value than judgement. The latter may make shift without the former, but not the former without the latter. For, as this Greek line says, *of what avail is learning, if not attended by understanding?* (Author unknown.) Would to God that, for the good of our justice, these bodies were as well furnished with understanding and conscience as they are with learning ! *We learn not for life but for the lecture-room* (Seneca). Now it is not enough to tie knowledge to the soul, it should be incorporated with it ; it should not be merely sprinkled, but dyed with it ; and if that does not change it and ameliorate its imperfect state, it is certainly much better to leave it alone. It is a dangerous sword that will hamper and wound its master, if wielded by a feeble hand that knows not how to use it ; *so that it were better not to have learned at all* (Cicero).

It is perhaps for this reason that neither we nor theology require much learning of women, and that Francis, Duke of Brittany, son of John the Fifth, when they approached him about his marriage with Isabel, a Scottish princess, and added that she had been brought up simply and without any instruction in letters, replied, ' that he liked her the better for it, and that a woman was learned enough when she knew the difference between her husband's shirt and his doublet '.[2]

So it is not so great a wonder as they now make of it, that our ancestors made no great account of learning, and that even to-day it is not found, except by chance, in the chief councils of our kings ; and if the goal, which is the only one we now set up before us, of getting rich by means of law, physic, teaching, and even theology, did not uphold it in credit, you would doubtless see it in as beggarly condition

---

[1] ' *Parlement*, a supreme or sovereign Court or Session of Justice, established in eight capital Cities of France, viz. Paris, Grenoble, Toulouse, Dijon, Rouen, Aix, Rennes and Bordeaux.' Cotgrave's French-English Dictionary, 1632.

[2] Chrysale, in Molière's *Femmes savantes*, echoed this opinion ; see Act I, sc. 7.

as ever it was. What loss would this be, if they teach us neither to think well, nor to do well ? *Now that the learned have become so numerous, good men are wanting* (Seneca). All other knowledge is hurtful to him who has not the knowledge of goodness.

But the reason that I sought for but now, can it not also proceed from this, that our studies in France having hardly any aim but profit, if we except those men who, by nature born for offices more honourable than lucrative, devote themselves to letters, if at all, only for so short a time (having, before acquiring a taste for them, taken up a profession that has nothing to do with books), there usually remain no others to apply themselves wholly to study but people of mean fortune, who seek their livelihood in it. And the minds of these men being, by nature, by home education, and by example, of the meanest alloy, they bring forth false fruits of knowledge. For knowledge is not capable of giving light to the soul of him that has none, or of making a blind man see : its business is not to furnish him with sight, but to direct it, and to regulate its goings, provided it have feet of its own and straight and capable legs.[1]

Knowledge is a good drug, but no drug is strong enough to preserve itself from change and corruption by the taint of the vessel that contains it. Many a man has a clear sight that cannot see straight, and in consequence sees the good and does not follow it, and sees knowledge without making use of it. Plato's principal ordinance in his *Republic* is to ' give to his citizens their employment according to their nature '. Nature can do all, and does all. Cripples are ill-adapted for bodily exercises, as are crippled souls for the exercises of the mind ; bastard and vulgar souls are unworthy of philosophy. When we see a man who is badly shod, we say that it is no wonder, if he is a shoemaker. In like manner experience often seems to show that a physician is worse physicked, a divine less reformed, and [usually] a scholar less competent than any other.

Aristo of Chius had reason to say in olden times that the philosophers did their hearers harm, seeing that most minds are not fit to profit by such instruction which, if not beneficial, is harmful ; *the school of Aristippus sent forth debauchees, that of Zeno crabbed minds* (Cicero).

---

[1] A good example of a mixed metaphor.

In that admirable education that Xenophon ascribes to the Persians, we find that they taught their children virtue, as in other nations they teach them letters. Plato says that the eldest son in their royal succession was thus brought up: after his birth he was given into the hands, not of women, but of eunuchs of the highest authority about the kings, by reason of their virtue. On these devolved the charge of rendering him sound and beautiful in body, and after seven years they trained him to ride and hunt. When he arrived at the age of fourteen, they entrusted him to the hands of four, the wisest, the justest, the most temperate, and the most valiant, in the nation. The first taught him religion; the second, to be always truthful; the third, to make himself master of his lusts; the fourth, to fear nothing.

It is a thing worthy of very great consideration that, in Lycurgus' excellent plan of government, which is indeed a pattern of perfection, though so solicitous about the bringing up of children as its principal concern, and that in the very seat of the Muses, so little mention is made of learning; whence it appears that those noble youths, disdaining any other yoke but that of virtue, had to be provided, not with masters of science, as with us, but only with masters to teach them valour, wisdom, and justice: an example that Plato followed in his *Laws*. The manner of their teaching was to put to them questions on the judgement of men and their actions; if they condemned or praised this person or that deed, they had to reason out their decision; by this means they sharpened their intellect and at the same time learned what was right. Astyages, in Xenophon's *Cyropedia*, asks Cyrus to give an account of his last lesson: 'It is, he says, that in our school a big boy, having a little coat, gave it to one of his comrades who was not so tall, and took from him his bigger coat. Our teacher having made me judge of this dispute, I decided that it was best to leave the matter as it stood, and that each of them seemed to be better suited in that way; whereupon he pointed out to me that I had done ill, for I had confined myself to considering the fitness where I should in the first place have looked at the justice of the matter, which required that no one should be forced in regard to what belonged to him.' And he adds that he was whipped for it, as we are in our villages for forgetting the first aorist of τύπτω.

My pedant would have to deliver a fine harangue *in genre demonstrativo* before he could persuade me that his school is as good as that. They tried the short cut; and since it is true that the sciences, even when they are directly studied, cannot but teach us wisdom, honesty, and resolution, they tried at the outset to bring their children in touch with results, and to instruct them not by hearsay, but by the test of action, by forming and moulding them, in a living way, not only by words and precepts, but chiefly by examples and works, to the end that their learning might become not merely a knowledge lodged in the mind, but its disposition and habit, not an acquisition but a natural possession. When somebody asked Agesilaus what he thought that children should learn, he replied: 'What they should do being men.' It is no wonder if such an education produced such admirable results.

They used to go, it is said, to the other cities of Greece to find rhetoricians, painters, and musicians, but to Lacedemon for lawgivers, magistrates, and army generals. At Athens they learned to speak well, and here to do well; there, to disentangle themselves from a sophistical argument and to confound the imposture of words captiously interlaced; here, to disentangle themselves from the snares and baits of pleasure, and with great courage to frustrate the menaces of fate and death; those busied themselves about words, these about things; there we find a continual exercising of the tongue, here a continual exercising of the soul. Wherefore it is not strange that, when Antipater demanded of them fifty children as hostages, they made answer, quite contrary to what we should do, that they would rather give him twice as many grown men: so much did they value the loss of their country's education! When Agesilaus invites Xenophon to send his children to be brought up at Sparta, it was not to learn rhetoric and dialectics, but, he says, ' to learn the finest of all sciences, to wit, the science of obeying and commanding '.

It is very amusing to see Socrates, after his manner, rallying Hippias, who tells him how he earned, especially in certain little townships of Sicily, a good sum of money by teaching, and that at Sparta he earned not a sou; that they are an idiotic people who can neither measure nor count, that they make no account of grammar and rhythm, wasting

lely on learning the succession of kings, the
nd the decay of states, and such trashy tales.
d of all this Socrates, after making him admit,
the excellence of their form of public govern-
ppiness and virtue of their private life, leaves
guess the conclusion of the futility of his arts.
teach us, both in that martial government and
in others of a like kind, that the study of the sciences makes
the hearts of men soft and effeminate rather than strong and
warlike. The strongest state that we see in the present-day
world is that of the Turks, a people equally trained to
esteem arms and to despise letters. I find that Rome was
more valiant before she became learned. The most warlike
nations nowadays are the most rude and ignorant. The
Scythians, the Parthians, Tamerlane, may serve as a proof
of this. When the Goths ravaged Greece, what saved all
the libraries from being committed to the flames was that
one of them disseminated the advice that they should leave
the enemy in full possession of that kind of furniture, as
being proper to divert them from military exercises, and
keep them in idle and sedentary occupations. When our
King Charles the Eighth, without drawing his sword from
the scabbard, saw himself master of the kingdom of Naples
and of a good part of Tuscany, the gentlemen of his suite
attributed that unexpected facility of conquest to this, that
the princes and nobles of Italy spent more time in making
themselves learned and clever than vigorous and warlike.

CHAPTER 26

OF THE EDUCATION OF BOYS

To Madame Diane de Foix, Comtesse de Gurson

I NEVER yet knew a father who, though his son were a
hunchback and scald-headed, refused to own him; that is
not to say, however, unless he were quite infatuated by his
affection, that he would not perceive his defects, but the
fact remains that he is his own. So it is with me: I see
better than any other that these Essays are but the idle
fancies of a man who has nibbled only the upper crust of
the sciences in his boyhood, and has retained only a general
and formless image of them, a little of each, and nothing

thoroughly, after our French manner. For, to sum it up, I know that there is medicine, jurisprudence, four parts of mathematics, and roughly, what these aim at, and perhaps I know besides how much the sciences in general have helped us in our lives ; but as to diving deeper, as to biting my nails in the study of Aristotle, the monarch of modern science, or stubbornly pursuing some particular branch of knowledge, I have never done it ; nor is there any art of which I could trace even the first lineaments. And there is not a boy of the middle forms who could not claim to be more learned than I, who am not sufficiently equipped to examine him on his first lesson, at least as long as I confined myself to the subject of it. And if I am forced to it, I find myself constrained rather awkwardly to draw upon some matter of universal interest, upon which to test his natural judgement: a lesson as strange to boys as theirs would be to me.

I have never had regular dealings with any solid book, unless it be Plutarch or Seneca, from whom I draw as did the Danaïds, unceasingly filling up and pouring out. Some of it sticks to this paper ; to me, as good as nothing.

History is the game I hunt, or poetry, which I love with a particular affection. For, as Cleanthes said, just as sound, forced through the narrow channel of a trumpet, comes out sharper and stronger, so it seems to me that a thought, concentrated within the harmonious feet of poetry, darts out much more briskly and strikes upon my ear with a more lively resonance. As to the natural faculties which are in me, of which this is the essay, I feel them bending under the burden. My conceptions and my judgements grope their way, staggering, stumbling, and tripping, and when I have gone as far as I can, I am yet by no means satisfied : I still see country beyond, but with a sight so dimmed and foggy, that I cannot clearly distinguish it. And when I attempt to speak indiscriminately of whatever enters my fancy, employing therein only my proper and natural resources, if I happen, as I often do, to light by a happy chance, in the good authors, upon those same subjects that I have attempted to treat, as I have done just now in Plutarch, where he speaks of the *power of imagination* ; when I see myself, in comparison with those men, so weak and puny, so dull and heavy, I hold myself in pity and contempt.

Yet I flatter myself that my opinions often have the

honour to jump with theirs, and that I at least go with them, though a long way behind, saying, 'How true that is!' Also that I have this advantage, which is not shared by everybody, that I can recognize the vast difference there is between them and myself. And yet I allow my ideas to run on in the poor and feeble form in which they have been produced, without mending and plastering up the defects that this comparison has laid bare to me.

A man had need of very strong loins to attempt to walk abreast with those men. Those injudicious writers of our century who, amongst their worthless productions, go scattering whole passages from the ancient authors, in order to gain credit, do the very opposite. For the infinitely greater brilliance of the latter makes their own stuff appear so pale, sallow and ugly, that it loses thereby more than it gains.

Here are two contrary fancies: the philosopher Chrysippus mixed into his books, not passages merely, but entire works of other authors, and in one of them the *Medea* of Euripides; and Apollodorus said that, if you cut out of them all the foreign matter, there would remain only the blank sheets. Epicurus, on the other hand, in three hundred volumes that he left behind him, did not insert a single quotation from another.[1]

I happened the other day to light upon a passage of the kind: I had been languidly crawling after French words, so fleshless, so bloodless, so void of matter and sense, that they were truly only French words; at the end of a long and tedious journey I came across a passage that was rich, sublime, and elevated to the very clouds. If I had found the declivity easy and the ascent a little gradual, it would have been excusable: it was a precipice so perpendicular and abrupt that, at the first six words, I knew that I was flying into another world. From thence I descried the quagmire from which I had come, so low and deep, that I never since had the heart to descend to it again. Were I to stuff one of my essays with those rich spoils, it would throw too strong a light on the stupidity of the others.

To reprehend my own faults in others appears to me no more incongruous than to reprehend, as I often do, those of

[1] This paragraph is a marginal interpolation, and breaks the continuity of Montaigne's reflections. The following paragraph should be read in connexion with that preceding the interpolation.

others in myself. They should be everywhere denounced and deprived of every sanctuary. Hence I know how audaciously I myself at every turn attempt to equal myself to my filchings, and to go hand in hand with them, not without a rash hope of deceiving the eyes of judges from discovering them ; but it is as much by the favour of my application as of my invention and power. And besides, I do not compete wholesale with those old champions, and body to body ; I do so by repetitions, by frequent and light attacks. I do not stubbornly grapple with them, but only try their strength, and if I try to keep pace with them, I do so hesitatingly. If I could hold my own with them I should be somebody, for I only attack their steepest points.

As for doing what I have seen others do, covering themselves with another's armour so as not to show so much as a finger's end, carrying out their design (an easy thing for a savant in an ordinary subject), in the guise of original ideas of ancient authors pieced together here and there, that would be, as long as they attempt to conceal them and pass them off as their own, in the first place a piece of injustice and meanness, in that, having no capital of their own wherewith to commend themselves, they seek to hide behind a purely borrowed value ; and secondly a great piece of folly, for, if they are satisfied with acquiring by trickery the ignorant approbation of the vulgar, they discredit themselves in the eyes of men of understanding, whose praise alone has any weight and who wrinkle their noses at your borrowed incrustations.

For my part I would do anything rather than that. When I quote others I do so in order to express my own ideas more clearly.

This does not apply to those centos which are published as centos,[1] and I have in my time seen some very ingenious ones, among others one published under the name of Capilupus, besides the ancients. They show themselves to be men of genius both in these and other works ; as, for example, Lipsius in that learned and laborious compilation, the *Politica*.

---

[1] A cento was a literary triviality in the form of a poem manufactured by putting together distinct lines or passages of one or several authors, thus producing a new poem with a different meaning. Montaigne seems to have thought more highly of these productions than they deserved.

Be that as it may, (I mean to say), and however good or bad these futilities may be, I have resolved not to hide them under a bushel, just as I should not think of concealing any bald and grizzled portrait of mine in which the painter has depicted, not a perfect face, but my own. For these are my humours and opinions; I give them as representing what I myself believe, not as what I expect others to believe. I aim here only at disclosing myself, who may peradventure be a different self to-morrow, if anything newly learned shall have changed me. I claim no authority, nor do I desire it, to be taken at my word, being too conscious of my lack of instruction to instruct others.

Now somebody said to me the other day in my house, after seeing the preceding article, that I should have enlarged a little on the subject of the education of children. Well, Madame, if I had any competence on that subject, I could not employ it better than to make a present of it to the little man who threatens shortly to come happily out of you (you are too nobly born to begin otherwise than with a male). For, having had so great a share in the conclusion of your marriage, I have by rights some interest in the greatness and prosperity of all that shall issue from it; besides that the ancient claim that you have on my service sufficiently obliges me to wish all honour, welfare, and advantage to all that you are concerned in. But indeed all that I mean is this, that the most difficult and important branch of human knowledge appears to be that which treats of the rearing and education of children.

In agriculture the operations which precede the planting, and the planting itself, are certain and easy; but as soon as that which is planted comes to life, there are many and difficult ways of cultivating it. So it is with human beings: little industry is needed in the planting, but as soon as they are born, we are charged with a great variety of cares, accompanied by a plenitude of troubles and fears, in training and bringing them up.

The display of their inclinations at that early age is so slight and obscure, the promises are so uncertain and misleading, that it is hard to ground any positive conjecture upon them. Look at Cimon, look at Themistocles and a thousand others, how they belied their promise. The young of bears and dogs show their natural disposition, but men, being very soon influenced by customs, opinions, and laws, easily change or disguise their nature.

And yet it is difficult to force natural propensities. Whence it comes to pass that, by reason of having chosen the wrong path, we often labour in vain and expend much time in training children for a calling to which they cannot settle down. In this difficulty, however, my advice is to guide them ever to the best and most profitable things, and to pay little heed to those uncertain divinations and prognostics which we draw from their childish actions. It seems to me that Plato in his *Republic* gives too much authority to them.

Madame, knowledge is a great ornament and an instrument of wonderful utility, especially in persons raised to such a degree of fortune as you are. And in truth it is not rightly used in the hands of people of mean and base condition. It takes more pride in lending its aid in the conduct of wars, in the ruling of a nation, in negotiating the friendship of a prince or a foreign people, than in formulating a dialectical argument, in pleading in an appeal, or in prescribing a box of pills. Wherefore, Madame, because I believe that you will not neglect this point in the education of your children, you who have tasted the sweets of it, and who come of a lettered race (for we still possess the writings of those ancient Counts of Foix, from whom Monsieur the Count your husband and yourself are descended; and François Monsieur de Candale your uncle every day brings forth others that will make this quality in your family known to many generations to come), I will acquaint you with one idea of mine on the subject that is at variance with common usage, and that is all that I am able in this matter to contribute to your service.

The charge of the governor whom you select for your son, upon the choice of whom depends the whole success of his education, will comprise several other important duties, but I will not touch upon them, being unable to make any valuable suggestions; and in this particular matter on which I presume to give him advice he will take it in so far as he approves of it. For a child of good family who seeks learning, not for gain (for so mean an object is unworthy of the grace and favour of the Muses, and besides, it looks to and depends on others), and not so much for external advantages as for his own good, to enrich and furnish himself within, since you would desire to turn out a man of parts rather than a scholar, I would have you be careful to choose as his director one with a well-made rather than a well-filled head, and to seek one who possesses both, but not so much learning as character and intelligence ; and he should exercise his charge after a new method.

The usual way is to keep bawling into the pupil's ears as one pours water into a funnel, the pupil's business being merely to repeat what he has been told. I would have the tutor amend this method, and at the outset, in order to test the capacity of the mind he has charge of, he should put it on trial, making his pupil to taste of things, and to discern and choose them of his own accord, sometimes opening out the path to him, and sometimes leaving him to open it out to himself. I would not have him always to start the subject and monopolize the speaking, but to listen while the pupil speaks in his turn. Socrates, and after him Arcesilaus, first made their disciples speak, and then spoke to them. *The authority of the teachers is generally prejudicial to those who desire to learn* (Cicero).

It is well that he should make him trot before him, to judge his paces, and see how far he must step down and adapt himself to his powers. For want of this proportion we spoil all ; and to be able to choose this and be guided by it in due measure, is one of the hardest tasks I know ; and it is the mark of a lofty and very powerful mind to be able to fall in with the child's gait and to guide it. I walk with a surer and firmer step up hill than down.

When, according to our custom, a teacher undertakes, in one and the same lesson, and with one measure of guidance, to train many minds differing so largely in kind and capacity, it is no wonder if, in a whole multitude of children, he hardly come upon two or three who can reap any real fruit from their teaching.

Let the tutor demand of him an account not only of the words of his lesson, but of their meaning and substance, and let him estimate the profit he has gained, not by the testimony of his memory, but of his life. Let him show what he has just learned from a hundred points of view, and adapt it to as many different subjects, to see if he has yet rightly taken it in and made it his own, taking stock of his progress according to Plato's disciplinary method.[1] It is a sign of crudeness and indigestion to disgorge meat as it has been swallowed. The stomach has not performed its operation, unless it has altered the form and condition of what has been given to it to cook.

Our mind only works on trust, bound and compelled to follow the appetite of another's fancy, a slave and captive to the authority of his teaching. We have been so much subjected to leading-strings, that we no longer have the power of walking freely. Our vigour and liberty are extinct. *They never cease to be under guardianship* (Seneca).

At Pisa I had a private interview with a worthy man, but such an Aristotelian that the most universal of his dogmas was: 'That the touchstone and measure of all sound opinions and of every truth is conformity to the teaching of Aristotle; that outside of that there is nothing but chimeras and foolishness; That he had seen all and said all.' This proposition of his, through having been interpreted a little widely and unjustly, once brought him and for a long time kept him in great danger of the Inquisition at Rome.

We must let him pass everything through a sieve, and store nothing in his head on mere authority and trust. To him Aristotle's principles should be no more principles than those of the Stoics and Epicureans; let their various theories be put to him, and he will choose, if he is able; if not, he will remain in doubt. Only fools are certain and cocksure.

> For doubting pleases me no less than knowing. (DANTE.)

For if he embraces the opinions of Xenophon and Plato by his own reasons, they will be no more theirs: they will be his. He who follows another follows nothing; he finds nothing, nay, he seeks nothing. *We are under no king; let each one look to himself* (Seneca). Let him know that he knows at least. He must imbibe their modes of thought, not learn their precepts. Let him boldly forget, if he likes, whence he has them, but he must be able to appropriate them. Truth and reason are common to every man, and belong no more to him who first gave them utterance than to him who repeats them after him. It is no more according to Plato than according to me, since he and I understand it

---

[1] Or more probably, perhaps, 'adopting Plato's method of questions and answers in his Dialogues'.

and see it alike. The bee rifles the flowers here and there, but she afterwards makes honey of what she has gathered, which is all her own: it is no longer thyme or marjoram; so the things borrowed from others he will transform and blend so as to make a work all his own, to wit, his judgement. His instruction, labour, and study shall have no other aim but the forming of that judgement.

Let him conceal all whereby he has been aided, and show only what he has made of it. The pillagers, the borrowers, parade their buildings, their purchases, but not what they extract from others. You do not see the spices[1] of the member of Parliament, but you see the alliances he has gained and the honours he has won for his children. None of them renders any public account of his takings, but every one displays his acquisitions.

The profit of our studies lies in our having become the better and wiser for them.

It is, said Epicharmus, the understanding that sees and hears, it is the understanding that turns everything to account, that orders all, that acts, sways, and reigns; all other things are blind, deaf, and soulless. Truly we make it servile and cowardly by not allowing it the freedom to do anything of itself. Who ever asked his pupil what he thinks of rhetoric and grammar, of such and such a saying of Cicero? They clap them into our memory ready feathered[2]; like oracles, where the letters and the syllables are of the substance of the thing. To know by heart is not to know; it is to retain what has been given in keeping to our memory. What we rightly know we can dispose of, without regard to the pattern, without turning our eyes to the book. What a poor, paltry competence is a mere bookish competence! I would have it serve as an ornament, not as a foundation, according to Plato's opinion, who says: 'Constancy, faith,

---

[1] 'Espices. Spices, or Spice; also, the fees that be taken by the (French) Judges, and their assistants, for Bookes perused, Consultations had, and sentence giuen, in a cause; (from the aunctient manner of gratefull suitors; who, hauing preuailed, were woont to present the Judges, or the Reporters, of their causes, with Comfets, or other Jonkets; which gratuitie they afterwards turned into money, and by degrees haue suffered it to become a dutie, and (as it is at this day) the only, or best, reuenew belonging to Judiciall places).'—COTGRAVE.

[2] Like an arrow; or better perhaps, 'with all their feathers', like a fowl thrown unplucked into the cooking-pot.

sincerity, are the true philosophy; the other sciences, that are directed to other ends, are but face-paint.'

I should like to have seen Paluel or Pompey,[1] those fine dancers of our day, teach us to dance caprioles by merely allowing us to watch them, without making us stir from our seats, as those men pretend to form our understanding without stirring it up. I should like to see any man teach us to manage a horse, or a pike, or a lute, or our voice, without practising them, as these men pretend to teach us to speak well and form a good judgement, without exercising us in speaking or forming a judgement. Now, in my apprenticeship, whatever we see is sufficient book : a page's mischief, a varlet's stupidity, conversation at table, these are so many new matters.

To this end human intercourse is marvellously well adapted, as well as travel in foreign countries, not after the manner of our French nobles, merely to report on how many paces the Santa Rotonda[2] measures, or on the richness of the Signora Livia's drawers; or, like some others, how much longer or broader the face of Nero is in some old ruin of that city than that on some similar medallion ; but to report chiefly on the intellectual characteristics and the manners of those nations, and to rub and file our brains in contact with those of others. I should wish that he might be taken abroad in his early childhood, and first, to kill two birds with one stone, to those neighbouring countries where the language is least like our own, to which the tongue will not bend itself unless it be formed in good time.

It is besides a generally accepted opinion that it is not right to bring up a child in its parents' lap. Their natural love makes them too soft and tender, even the wisest of them. They are neither capable of chastising his faults nor of seeing him reared coarsely as he should be, and hazardously. They could not bear to see him returning, all dust and sweat, from his exercises, drinking hot, drinking cold, or riding a skittish horse, or opposed to a rude antagonist, armed with

---

[1] Ludovico Palvalli and Pompeo Diobono, two eminent Milanese dancing-masters at the court of Henri III.

[2] The Pantheon of Agrippa, now used as a church. The Signora Livia was perhaps a ballet-dancer, as a commentator suggests, who adds that these 'caleçons' were afterwards introduced into France by Mlle du Parc of Molière's company.

a foil or any old arquebus. For there is no help for it : if he is to become a man of parts, there is no doubt that we must not spare him in his youth, and must often transgress the rules of physic :

> To live alert at danger's call
> Encamped on heath or down. (HORACE.)

It is not enough to stiffen his soul, we must also stiffen his muscles. The soul is too constrained if it be not backed up, and has too hard a task to discharge, alone, two offices. I know how mine groans in partnership with a body so tender, so delicate, and that leans so heavily upon her. And often in my readings I perceive that my masters commend, in their writings, as examples of magnanimity and stoutness of heart, men who are generally remarkable for thickness of skin and hardness of bones.

I have seen men, women, and children so constituted that a cudgelling with a stick is less to them than a fillip to me ; who will stir neither tongue nor eyebrow under the blows. When athletes imitate the philosophers in endurance, it is rather strength of nerves than of heart. Now, to be accustomed to endure labour is to be accustomed to endure pain : *labour hardens us against pain* (Cicero). He must be broken in to the pain and hardship of exercises, so as to be drilled to the pain and hardship of a dislocation, the colic, cauteries, and imprisonment as well as torture. For he may even be in danger of the two latter, which, seeing the times we live in, threaten both the good and the bad. We are now experiencing this : whoever combats the laws threatens the best of men with the scourge and the halter.

And moreover the governor's authority, which should be paramount over him, is checked and hindered by the presence of the parents ; to which may be added that the respect which the household pays him, and a consciousness of the power and greatness of his house are, in my opinion, no small disadvantages at that age.

In this school of human intercourse I have often remarked this error, that instead of taking stock of other men, we only labour to discover ourselves to them, and are more at pains to retail our wares than to acquire new ones. Silence and modesty are very becoming qualities in social intercourse. Our boy will be trained to save and husband his accomplishments, when he has acquired them ; not to take exception at the stories and foolish things that may be spoken in his presence, for he is an uncivil and tiresome person who falls foul of everything that is not to his liking. Let him be satisfied with correcting himself, and not to appear to reprove in others all that he declines to do, and be a censor of public morals : *He may be wise without ostentation, without exciting envy* (Seneca). Let him avoid those authoritative and unmannerly airs and that puerile ambition of trying to appear more clever, because he is different, and to gain a reputation for being critical and original. As it is becoming only in great poets to indulge in poetical licence, so to assume unconventional privileges is tolerable only in great and illustrious souls. *If Socrates and Aristippus have failed to observe the rules of good conduct and custom, let him not imagine that he is licensed to do the same ; their great and divine merits authorized that liberty* (Cicero).

He shall be taught to enter into no dispute or argument but where he sees a champion worthy to wrestle with, and even then not to employ all the turns that may serve him, but only those that may serve him best. He shall be taught to be particular in choosing and sifting his reasons, to prefer pertinence, and consequently brevity. Instruct him above all to quit his arms and surrender in the face of truth as soon as he perceives it, whether it appear in his opponent's arguments or in his own, through being better advised. For he will not be sitting in a professor's chair to read a prepared lecture. He is not pledged to any cause but in so far as he approves of it. Nor will he be of that profession in which the liberty of repenting and acknowledging one's errors is sold for good ready money. *Nor is he obliged by any necessity to defend all the things that have been prescribed and recommended to him* (Cicero).

If his governor be of my way of thinking, he will make him desire to be a very loyal, a very affectionate, and a very brave servant to his prince ; but he will cool in him any desire to become attached to him by any but public duty. Not to speak of many other disadvantages which greatly impair our freedom through these private obligations, the judgement of a man who is bought and salaried is either less free and unalloyed, or is tainted by imprudence and ingratitude. A courtier can have neither free choice nor will to think and speak otherwise than favourably of a master who has chosen him from among so many thousands of other subjects, to feed and raise him with his own hand. This favour and advantage will corrupt, not without some reason, his freedom, and dazzle him. Therefore we see the language of those people to differ ordinarily from any other language in the state, and little to be trusted in such matters.

Let his conscience and his virtue shine forth in his speech, and be guided solely by reason. Make him understand that to confess the error he discovers in his own reasoning, though he himself alone perceive it, is a mark of judgement and honesty, which are the chief qualities he aims at; that obstinacy and contention are vulgar qualities, most apparent in the basest minds; that to correct oneself and change one's mind, and in the heat of ardour to abandon a weak position, is a sign of strong, rare, and philosophical qualities.

Let him be advised, when in company, to have his eyes everywhere, for I have found that the chief places are commonly seized upon by the least capable men, and that greatness of fortune is seldom combined with ability. I have observed that whilst at the high end of a table the conversation has turned upon the beauty of a tapestry or the flavour of a Malmsey wine, many witty things spoken at the other end have been lost to them.

He will sound the depths of every man: a neatherd, a mason, a passing stranger; he should utilize and borrow from each according to his wares, for everything is of use in the household; he will learn something even from the follies and weaknesses of others. By observing the graces and manners of each, he will plant in himself the seeds of emulation of the good, and contempt of the bad.

Suggest to his fancy an honest curiosity that will make him inquire into all things; he should see everything uncommon in his surroundings: a building, a fountain, a man, the scene of an ancient battle, the passage of Caesar or of Charlemagne:

> What land's adust with heat, what numb'd with snow,
> And all the winds to Italy that blow. (PROPERTIUS.)

He will inquire into the character, the resources and the alliances of this and that prince: things very pleasant to learn and very useful to know.

His intercourse with men will comprise, as I understand it, and principally, those who live only in the memory of books. Through the medium of histories he will hold converse with the great souls of the best ages. That is an empty study, if a man list, but also, if a man list, it is a study of inestimable fruit, and the only study, as Plato tells us, that the Lacedemonians had reserved for their share. What profit will he not reap, to that end, by reading the Lives of our Plutarch ? But let my tutor remember the object of his charge, and impress upon his pupil not so much the date of the ruin of Carthage as the character of Hannibal and Scipio, not so much where Marcellus died, as why it was unworthy of his duty to die there. Let him not so much teach him history as to give his opinions on it. This is in my opinion of all subjects that to which we apply our minds most diversely. I have read in Livy a hundred things that another has not read in him. Plutarch has read in him a hundred besides what I have been able to read, and perhaps besides what the author put there. To some he is a purely grammatical study, to others the analysis of a philosophy in which the most abstruse parts of our nature penetrate.

There are in Plutarch many ample treatises most worthy to be known, for he is, to my mind, the master-worker in such matters ; but there are a thousand subjects that he has merely touched upon : he merely points with his finger the way we may go, if we please, and sometimes contents himself with giving a mere dig at the heart of a subject. We have to extract it and exhibit it in the open market-place. As an example, that saying of his, ' That the inhabitants of Asia served one man through being unable to pronounce one single syllable, which was No ', perhaps suggested to La Boëtie the matter and occasion for his *Servitude Volontaire*. Only to see Plutarch pick out a trivial action in a man's life, or a word which seems of no import, that in itself is a treatise. It is a pity that men of understanding are so fond of brevity ; no doubt their reputation gains by it, but it is our loss. Plutarch had rather that we applaud him for his judgement than for his knowledge, he would rather leave us with an appetite for him, than satiated. He knew that even of good things we may say too many, and that Alexandridas justly reproved him who was delivering a very good harangue to the Ephors, but which was too long : ' O stranger, you say what you should, but otherwise than you should.' They who have a slender body make it stouter with padding ; they whose matter is thin thicken it with words.

Mixing with society has a marvellous effect in clearing up a man's judgement. We are all compressed and heaped up within ourselves, and our sight is shortened to the length of our noses. Some one asked Socrates whence he was. He did not answer ' Of Athens ', but ' Of the world '. He, whose imagination was fuller and wider, embraced the universe as his city, extended his acquaintance, his society, and his affection over all mankind ; he was not as we are, who look no further than our feet. When the vines in my village are nipped by the frost, my priest argues therefrom God's anger with the human race, and concludes that the Cannibals are already dying of thirst.[1] Who is there that, seeing our civil wars, does not cry out that this machine, the world, is being overthrown, and that the day of judgement is seizing us by the throat, without calling to mind that many worse things have happened, and that, notwithstanding, ten thousand parts of the world are meanwhile having a merry time ? For my part, considering the licence and impunity they enjoy, I wonder to see them so gentle and moderate. To one who feels the hail coming down on his head, the whole hemisphere seems to be in storm and tempest. And a Savoyard said that ' if that fool of a French king had been well able to look after his own interest, he might have become steward to the household of my Duke '. His imagination could picture nothing higher and greater than his own master. We are all unconsciously in this error, an error fraught with great consequence and harm. But whoever shall conjure up in his fancy, as in a picture, that great form of our mother Nature, in her full majesty ; whoever reads in her face so universal and so constant a variety ; whoever observes himself therein, and not only himself, but a whole kingdom, to be no bigger than a point made with a very delicate brush, he alone estimates things according to their true proportion.

This great world, which some yet multiply as a species under one genus, is the mirror wherein we are to behold our-

[1] Literally, ' have got the pip '.

selves, in order to know ourselves from the right point of view. In a word, I should wish it to be my pupil's book. So many ways of looking at things, so many sects, judgements, opinions, laws and customs, teach us to form a sound estimate of our own, and teach our judgement to discover its own imperfection and its natural feebleness; and that is no small apprenticeship. So many disturbances of State and changes in public fortune instruct us to make no great miracle of our own. So many names, so many victories and conquests buried in oblivion, render ridiculous the hope of eternalizing our name by the capture of half a score of arquebusiers or of a wretched hovel that is only known to those that took it. The pride and arrogance of so many foreign pomps and ceremonies, the inflated majesty of so many courts and grandeurs, assures and fortifies our eyes to bear, without blinking, the brilliance of ours. So many millions of men interred before our time, encourage us to have no fear of finding as good company in the other world; and so with the rest.

Our life, said Pythagoras, may be likened to the great and populous assembly of the Olympic games. Some exercise their bodies to win fame in the contests; others bring merchandise to sell for profit. There are some, and they are not the worst, who seek no other fruit but to look on and see how and why everything is done, and to be spectators of the lives of other men, in order to consider and regulate their own.

Examples may fitly illustrate all the most profitable discourses of philosophy, which should be the touchstone of human actions and by which they should be ruled. He shall be told,

> What to wish with unreproved desires:
> How far the genuine use of wealth extends;
> And the just claims of country, kindred, friends;
> What heaven would have us be, and where our stand,
> In this great whole, is fixed by high command.
> . . . . .
> Learn what we are, and for what purpose born; (PROPERTIUS.)

what is knowledge and what is ignorance; what ought to be the aim of study; what valour, temperance, and justice are; what the difference is between ambition and avarice, servitude and subjection, licence and liberty; by what token a man may know true and solid contentment ; how far we should fear death, pain, and disgrace ;

> What toils to shun, what dangers to despise ;   (VIRGIL.)

by what springs we are moved, and the cause of so many different stirrings in us. For it seems to me that the first ideas with which we should soak his mind ought to be those which regulate his conduct and his understanding, which will teach him to know himself and how to die well and live a good life.

Among the liberal arts let us begin with the art which gives us liberty. They are all indeed of some service in instructing us in the right conduct of our life, as all other things do in some sort. But let us choose that which directly and professedly serves that end.

If we knew how to restrict the functions of our life within their just and natural limits, we should find that the better part of the sciences in use are of no use to us, and that even in those which are, there are many very unnecessary lengths and depths, and that we should do better to leave them alone ; and, following Socrates' system of education, limit the course of our studies to those where utility is needed :

> So, then, have courage to be wise ! Begin !
> He that would mend his life, yet still delays
> To set to work, is like the boor who stays
> Till the broad stream that bars his way is gone ;
> But on still flows the stream, and ever will flow on.   (HORACE.)

It is very silly and foolish to teach our children,

> The circling Fishes and the Lion brave,
> And Capricorn, that wades the Western wave,   (PROPERTIUS.)

the knowledge of the stars and the motion of the eighth sphere, before teaching them their own movements :

> A fig for Pleiads or Boötes' stars !   (ANACREON.)

Anaximenes writes to Pythagoras : ' What sense is there in musing over the secret of the stars, when death and slavery are ever present to mine eyes ? ' (for at that time the kings of Persia were preparing to wage war against his country). Every one should say thus : ' A prey to ambition, avarice, temerity, superstition, and having within me other such enemies of life, am I to go about dreaming of the world's revolution ? '

After he has been taught what will make him wiser and

better, his tutor will explain to him the nature of Logic, Physics, Geometry, Rhetoric, and, his judgement having been already formed, he will soon master the science that he has chosen. His lessons will be carried on, now by conversation, now by book ; sometimes the governor will put into his hands the author suited to the purpose, at other times he will give him the substance and marrow ready masticated. If the governor is not himself sufficiently familiar with books to discover in them all the fine teachings for his purpose, you may associate with him some man of letters, who will provide the necessary munitions to be dealt out and dispensed to his nursling. And who will doubt but that this kind of lesson will be easier and more natural than those of Gaza ?[1] There we have precepts so thorny and unattractive, words so empty and fleshless, that there is no getting hold of them, nothing to quicken the understanding. Here, on the other hand, is something for the mind to bite and feed on. The fruit of it will be incomparably greater, and also sooner matured.

It is a great pity that things have come to such a pass in our time, that Philosophy, even with men of intelligence, is become a mere name, empty and fanciful, a thing of no use and no value, either in people's opinion or in reality. I believe the cause of this to be the sophistries which have seized and blocked the approaches to her. It is very wrong to paint her as a thing inaccessible to children, of a surly, frowning, and repulsive aspect. Who, I should like to know, has disguised her under this false, pale, and hideous mask ? There can be nothing more blithe and cheerful, more lusty and, I might almost say, more wanton. She preaches nothing but merry-making and a good time. A melancholy and hang-dog look is a clear sign that she dwells not there.

Demetrius the grammarian, coming upon a group of philosophers seated together in the temple at Delphi, said to them : ' Either I am much deceived or, to judge by your calm and cheerful looks, you are not engaged in very serious converse.' To which one of them, Heracleon of Megara, replied : ' It-is for those who are inquiring whether the future of the verb $\beta\acute{a}\lambda\lambda\omega$ has a double λ, or searching the derivation of the comparatives $\chi\epsilon\hat{\iota}\rho o\nu$ and $\beta\acute{\epsilon}\lambda\tau\iota o\nu$, and the superlatives

---

[1] One of the many Greek scholars who came to Italy in the fifteenth century, and author of a Greek grammar, which is here referred to.

χείριστον and βέλτιστον, to knit their brows when discussing their science. But as to philosophical discussions, they are wont to make glad and rejoice those who carry them on, not to make them look sour and gloomy.'

> Detect we oft the torments of the mind,
> In the sick frame which love to lurk behind;
> Oft of supprest delight the lines we trace,
> Marked on the plastic features of the face. (JUVENAL.)

The soul that harbours philosophy ought, by reason of its healthfulness, to render the body healthful too. She should make her tranquillity and happiness to shine forth; should fashion the outward behaviour to her own mould, and so arm it with a graceful assurance, an active and joyous carriage, a serene and contented countenance. The most evident sign of wisdom is a constant cheerfulness; her state is ever serene, like the things beyond the moon. It is *Baroco* and *Baralipton*[1] that make their devotees look smoke-dried and muddy, and not she; they know her only by hearsay. Why! she makes it her object to still the tempest of the soul, to teach hunger and fever to laugh, not by a few imaginary epicycles, but by natural and palpable reasons. She has Virtue for her end, which is not, as they say in the schools, set on the summit of a precipitous, rugged and inaccessible mountain. Such as have approached her hold her to be, on the contrary, settled on a beautiful table-land, fertile and flourishing, from whence she sees all things below her; but it may be reached pleasantly, by one who knows the direction, by shady, green, and fragrant ways, and by a smooth and easy incline, like that of the heavenly vaults. Through not being familiar with this supreme, beautiful, triumphant, loving, delicious as well as courageous Virtue, this professed and implacable enemy to bitterness, displeasure, fear and constraint, having Nature for her guide, Fortune and Pleasure for her companions, they have gone, and in their feeble imagination created that foolish, melancholy, quarrelsome, spiteful, threatening and frowning image, and set it up on an isolated rock among the brambles: a ghost to frighten people!

---

[1] Two of a series of artificial words used in scholastic logic, the vowels of which denote certain forms of syllogism. See any elementary book on Logic.

My tutor, who knows it to be his duty to store his pupil's mind as much, or rather more, with affection than with awe and reverence for virtue, will be able to tell him that the poets are in agreement with the general view, and make it palpable to him that the gods have made it a more sweaty toil to approach Venus's bower than the chambers of Pallas. And when he begins to have feelings, and is introduced to a Bradamante or an Angelica,[1] as a mistress to be enjoyed, on the one hand a natural, active, generous, and virile beauty, though no virago, and on the other a soft, effeminate, coquettish, and artificial beauty; the one disguised as a youth, wearing a shining helmet, the other dressed as a girl with a pearl-embroidered head-dress, he will look upon even his love as a manly one, if he chooses differently to that effeminate Phrygian shepherd.[2]

He will give him this new lesson : That the grandeur and value of true virtue lies in the facility, the pleasure, and usefulness of its practice : it is so far from being difficult that children as well as men, the simple as well as the subtle, may possess it. The means of attaining it is moderation, not effort. Socrates, her first favourite, consciously abandons effort, to glide towards her by easy and natural stages. She is the nursing-mother of human joys. By making them righteous she makes them pure and certain. By moderating them she keeps them in breath and appetite. By curtailing those she denies, she whets our desire for those she allows, and like a mother abundantly leaves us all that nature requires, even to satiety, if not to lassitude (unless peradventure we mean to say that the regimen that stops the toper before he is drunk, the glutton before he is surfeited, the lecher before he loses his hair, is an enemy to our pleasures). If she misses the happy lot of the vulgar she will escape its consequences ; or she will do without them and will invent others, wholly her own, no longer fleeting and unsteady. She can be rich and powerful and learned, and lie on perfumed mattresses. She loves life, she loves beauty and glory and health. But her own particular duty is to know how to use these blessings temperately, and to lose them bravely : a duty much more noble than laborious, without which the whole course of life is unnatural, turbulent, and

---

[1] See Ariosto's *Orlando Furioso*.
[2] Alluding to the Judgement of Paris.

deformed, and such a life is more really dotted with those dangerous reefs, thickets, and monsters.

If this pupil happens to be of so wayward a disposition, that he would rather listen to a fictitious tale than to the narrative of some fine voyage or a wise conversation, when he chances to hear it ; if he be one who, at the beat of a drum that arms the youthful ardour of his companions, turns from it to another that invites him to the tricks of the mountebanks ; who, when he has the choice, does not find more pleasure and delight in returning, a dust-covered victor, from a battle-field, than from the tennis-court or the dance, with the prizes of that exercise, I see no other remedy but that his governor should take an early opportunity to choke him off, if there are no witnesses,[1] or bind him prentice to a pastry-cook in some good town, though he were the son of a duke ; in accordance with Plato's precept, ' that children should be placed, not according to the resources of their father, but according to the resources of their mind.'

Since it is philosophy that teaches us to live, and since childhood finds its lessons there as well as the other ages, why is it not communicated to children ?

> As clay thou art so moist, so pliant still,
> Adapted now to any shape at will—
> Then take the wheel, this constant labour thine,
> Thy shape to form, thy ruggedness to fine. (PERSIUS.)

We are taught to live, when life is past. A hundred scholars have caught the pox before they have come to read Aristotle *On Temperance*. That is wrong. Cicero said that though he should live the lives of two men, he would not give himself the leisure to study the lyric poets. And to me those sophisters are still more deplorably unprofitable. Our child has much less time to spare : he owes the schoolmaster only the first fifteen or sixteen years of his life ; the rest he owes to action. Let us employ that short time in the necessary instructions. Banish all those thorny subtleties of logic, by which our lives cannot be amended ; take the simple teachings of philosophy, know how to choose and treat them

---

[1] These last words, which obviously were not to be taken seriously, seem to have so disturbed Montaigne's literary executors that they suppressed them. They have not hitherto appeared in any except the latest critical editions.

aright: they are easier to understand than a tale of Boccaccio. A child is capable of doing so on leaving his nurse, much more so than of learning to read and write. Philosophy has teachings for the infancy as well as the decrepitude of man.

I am of Plutarch's mind, that Aristotle did right in not wasting his great pupil's time teaching him the trick of composing syllogisms or the elements of geometry, but rather furnished him with good precepts touching valour, prowess, magnanimity, and temperance, and the assurance to fear nothing; and, with this ammunition, sent him, as yet a boy, to subjugate the empire of the world, with only thirty thousand foot, four thousand horse, and forty thousand crowns. As for the other arts and sciences, he says, Alexander honoured them no doubt, and commended their excellence and fascinations, but, for all the pleasure he might take in them, he was not to be easily surprised into loving them and wishing to cultivate them.

> Old and young, let these your thoughts engage,
> They give the mind support, and cheer old age. (PERSIUS.)

As Epicurus writes at the beginning of his letter to Menicius: 'Let not the youngest turn away from the study of philosophy, nor the oldest weary of it.' He who does otherwise seems to say, either that it is not yet time, or no longer time, to live happily.

For all those reasons I would not have this youth kept a prisoner; I would not hand him over to the melancholy humours of a hot-tempered schoolmaster. I would not break his spirit by keeping him, as some others do, to hard labour and the torture for fourteen or fifteen hours a day, like a porter. Nor should I think it well, if, in consequence of a disposition to solitude and melancholy, he were found to be addicted to a too close application to his books, to encourage that tendency in him: that renders them unfit for society and conversation, and diverts them from better occupations. How many men have I not seen in my time dulled by this injudicious avidity for learning! Carneades was so infatuated with it that he had no leisure to comb his hair and pare his nails.

Nor would I spoil his noble manners by contact with the uncivilized and barbarous manners of others. French wisdom was of old proverbially known as a wisdom that took root early but had no stay. Indeed, we still see that nothing can compare in pretty manners with the little children in France ; but they generally disappoint the hopes that have been conceived of them, and when they are grown men we do not see them excel in anything. I have heard intelligent men declare that they are made as dull as they are by being sent to those colleges which so abound in this country.

For our boy a closet, a garden, the table and bed, solitude, company, morning and evening, all hours shall be one to him, all places shall be his study ; for Philosophy which, since it forms our judgement and character, shall be his principal study, has this privilege of having a hand in everything. The orator Isocrates having been entreated at a banquet to speak of his art, he was right, as we all believe, to reply : ' Now is not the time to do what I can do ; and that which it is now time to do, I cannot do.' For to deliver harangues and disputations on rhetoric to a company assembled for laughter and good cheer, would be a too inharmonious mixture. And as much might be said of all the other sciences. But with regard to Philosophy, in that part of it which treats of man and his duties and functions, it has been the common opinion of all the sages that, on account of the sweetness of her conversation, she should be excluded neither from sports nor banquets. And Plato having invited her to his *Symposium* we may see how she entertains the company, how pleasant and well-suited to the time and place is her discourse, although it is one of his loftiest and most salutary dissertations ;

> To grow proficient in the wisdom which
> Is precious equally to poor and rich—
> Which, if neglected, young and old will find,
> Leaves a long train of pain and loss behind. (HORACE.)

Thus he will be without doubt less idle than others. But, as in pacing a gallery, though we walk three times as much, we do not become so weary as in a set journey, so our lesson, coming by chance, without being tied to time and place, and mingling with all our actions, will slip by easily and insensibly. Even games and exercises will form a good part of his study, running, wrestling, music, dancing, the chase, the management of a horse and use of weapons. I would have a graceful exterior combined with tactful manners ; the body and the mind should be fashioned at the same time. It is not a soul, it is not a body that is being trained : it is a man ; they must not be separated. And, as Plato says, we must not train the one without the other, but drive them abreast, like a pair of horses harnessed to one pole. And, to hear him, does he not appear to give more time and more care to bodily exercises, and to hold that the mind is exercised at the same time, and not the contrary ?

For the rest, this education is to be conducted with a mild severity, contrary to the usual practice. Instead of making study attractive to children, they only suggest to their minds horrors and cruelties. Away with violence and compulsion ! There is nothing to my mind more calculated to deaden and brutalize a generous nature. If you wish him to fear shame and chastisement do not harden him to them. Harden him to sweat and cold, wind and sun, and the dangers that he is to despise ; wean him from all effeminacy and delicacy in clothing and bedding, in eating and drinking ; accustom him to everything. Let him not be a pretty and namby-pamby youth, but a fresh and sturdy boy. As boy and man I have ever been of this belief and opinion, and am so still in my old age.

But, among other things, I have always disliked the discipline of most of our colleges. They would perhaps have failed less disastrously by inclining to the side of indulgence. It is a regular jail of imprisoned youth. They become undisciplined by being punished before they are so. Go there at lesson time : you will hear nothing but crying and shouting, both of boys under execution and of masters drunk with rage. What a way to arouse an appetite for learning in those tender and timid souls, to drive them to it with a terrifying scowl and hands armed with rods ! An iniquitous and pernicious system ! Besides that, as Quintilian has very well observed, this imperious authority is attended with dangerous consequences, and especially in the matter of punishment. How much more becomingly would their class-room be strewn with flowers and green boughs, instead of with bloody stumps of birch ! I would have pictures of Joy and Gladness, of Flora and the Graces, such as the philosopher Speusippus had in his school. Where their profit is, there let also their recreation be. The viands that are wholesome for children should be sweetened, and the harmful ones made bitter with gall.

It is wonderful how solicitous Plato shows himself, in his Laws, about the gaiety and pastimes of the youth of his city, and how much he dwells on their races, games, songs, leaps, and dances, of which he says that antiquity has given the ordering and patronage to the gods themselves, Apollo, Minerva, and the Muses. He gives a thousand precepts for his gymnasia, but wastes very little time over literary studies, and seems to recommend poetry chiefly for the sake of the music.

Everything singular and unconventional in our manners and bearing is to be avoided as inimical to social intercourse, and as abnormal. Who would not be astonished at the constitution of Demophon, the steward of Alexander's household, who sweated in the shade and shivered in the sun? I have known one who would fly from the smell of an apple sooner than from the shot of an arquebus; I have seen others frightened by a mouse, others vomit at the sight of cream or the tousling of a feather-bed; and Germanicus could endure neither the sight nor the crowing of a cock. To account for this there may perhaps be some hidden quality, but it could, I think, be subdued by any one who set about it in good time. Training has done this for me, not indeed without some pains: my appetite accommodates itself indifferently to all things that men feed on, excepting beer.

The body being still supple should be bent to every fashion and custom, and, provided that he keep his appetite and will under control, a young man should boldly adapt himself to all nations and companies, even to the point of excess and licentiousness, if need be. In practice he should follow usage: let him be able to do all things, and love to do only the good. The philosophers themselves do not commend Callisthenes for losing the good graces of his master Alexander by refusing to hold his own with him in drinking. He shall laugh, he shall wanton, he shall live riotously with his prince. Even in the latter I would see him outdo his fellows in strength and vigour; and if he refrains from doing ill, let it be, not from lack of power and knowledge, but from lack of will: *there is a great difference between not wishing to sin, and not knowing how to sin* (Seneca).[1]

[1] The above paragraph was condemned by the Sacred College in Rome,

I thought I was passing a compliment on a lord, one who was as far removed from such excesses as any man in France, by asking him, in a company of good fellows, how often in his life he had got drunk in the interests of his king's affairs, in Germany. He took it in the same spirit and replied ' three times ', and related the circumstances. I have known some who, from lack of that faculty, have got into great trouble, when they had to associate with people of that nation. I have often had occasion to remark with great admiration the marvellous nature of Alcibiades, who was so easily able to suit himself to such diverse fashions, without prejudice to his health, now outdoing the Persians in pomp and sumptuousness, now the Lacedemonians in frugality and austerity : as chaste in Sparta as he was voluptuous in Ionia.

> Wealthy or poor, in high or humble place,
> All sat on Aristippus with a grace. (HORACE.)

So would I form my pupil :

> But lift a man into a higher sphere
> Who in a blanket wrapt his lore austere,
> And 'twill surprise me greatly, if he bear
> His change of life with a becoming air. (HORACE.)

These are my lessons ; he who puts them in practice has profited better than he who knows them. If you see it, you hear it ; if you hear it, you see it.

God forbid, says somebody in Plato, that philosophizing should mean learning many things and discoursing on the arts ! *This art of living well, which is of all the arts the greatest, they have followed in their lives rather than in their studies* (Cicero).

Leo, a prince of the Phliasians, inquiring of Heraclides Ponticus[1] what science, what art he professed, he replied : ' I know neither art nor science, but I am a philosopher.'

Some one reproachfully asking Diogenes why, being ignorant, he meddled with philosophy, he said : ' I meddle with it to so much the better purpose.' Hegesias entreated him to read some book to him, whereupon he replied : ' You

---

when Montaigne was there in 1580. He promised to correct it, but appears to have forgotten his promise.

[1] Actually, Pythagoras ; but the saying is quoted by Cicero from Heraclides of Pontus.

are jesting : you choose real and natural figs, not painted ones ; why do you not also choose real and natural exercises, instead of written ones ? '

He should not so much say his lesson, as do it. He should repeat it in his actions. We shall see if there is prudence in his enterprises, if there is goodness and justice in his behaviour, if there is judgement and grace in his speaking, manliness in his maladies, soberness in his play, temperance in his pleasures, indifference in his tastes, whether meat, fish, wine, or water, order in his economy ; *if his learning serves, not to show off his knowledge, but to regulate his life ; if he obeys himself and acts in conformity with his principles* (Cicero).

The true mirror of our speech is the course of our lives.

Zeuxidamus replied, to one who asked him why the Lacedemonians did not draw up in writing their rules of prowess, and give them to their young men to read : ' Because we desire to accustom them to deeds, not words.' Compare with our pupil at the end of fifteen or sixteen years one of your college Latinists, who has spent the same time on merely learning to speak. The world is all babble, and I never saw the man who did not rather say more than less than he should. And yet the half of our lives goes that way : we are kept four or five years listening to words and stitching them into sentences, as many again in proportioning them into a great body, extending into four or five parts, another five at least in learning to mix and interweave them briefly in some subtle fashion.[1] Let us leave that to those who make express profession of it.

One day on my way to Orleans I met, in the plain on this side of Cléry, two college professors who were coming to Bordeaux, about fifty paces distant from one another. Further behind them I saw a company with their lord at their head, who was the late Monsieur le Comte de la Rochefoucault. One of my men inquired of the foremost of the teachers who was the gentleman coming after him. Not seeing the retinue that followed after, and thinking his colleague was meant, he replied humorously : ' That is not a gentleman ; he is a grammarian, and I am a logician.'[2]

---

[1] Montaigne here gives an outline of the school curriculum of those days : five years in the ' classes de grammaire ', five in the ' classe des humanités ', and five in the ' classe de logique '.

[2] i. e., a professor of grammar and a professor of logic.

Now our object is, on the contrary, to make a gentleman and not a grammarian or a logician ; let them abuse their spare time : our business lies elsewhere. But if our pupil is well furnished with matter, words will follow soon enough ; if they are not willing to follow, he will drag them. I hear some making excuses for being unable to express themselves ; they put on an air of having their brains well filled with many fine ideas which, for want of eloquence, they are unable to bring to the light of day : that is all bluff. Do you know what I think ? They are shadows thrown by some shapeless conceptions, which they are unable to clear up and unravel within their minds, and consequently to produce out of them ; they do not yet understand themselves. See them with their little stammer when on the point of giving birth, and you will conclude that their travail is not at the delivery stage, but at that of conception, and that they are only licking that unfinished matter.[1] For my part I hold, and Socrates lays it down as an axiom, that he who has a clear and vivid idea in his mind will express it in some language or other, though it be the Bergamask patois, or, if he be dumb, by signs :

> Once master that and words will freely follow. (HORACE.)

And, as another no less poetically said in his prose, *when matter occupies the mind, words come of themselves* (Seneca) ; and another, *the things themselves carry words along with them* (Cicero).

He knows nothing of ablatives, conjunctives, substantives, or grammar, but no more does his lackey or a herring-wife of the Petit Pont, and yet they will talk to you to your heart's content, if you wish to hear them, and will perhaps stumble as little over the rules of their language as the best master of arts in France. He knows no rhetoric, nor is he able, in a preface, to captivate the goodwill of the 'gentle reader', and he does not care to know it. In truth all those artificial colours are easily eclipsed by the light of a simple and artless truth. Those pretty tricks serve only to beguile the vulgar, who are incapable of taking in a stronger and more solid meat ; as Aper very clearly shows in Tacitus. The ambassadors of Samos were come to Cleomenes, King of Sparta, prepared with a long and elegant harangue, to

---

[1] As a bear was supposed to lick its cubs into shape.

incite him to war against the tyrant Polycrates. After allowing them to have their say he replied : ' As to the commencement and exordium, I no more remember it, nor consequently the middle ; and as for your conclusion, I will do nothing of the kind.' There we see a fine answer, methinks, and speechifiers finely snubbed !

And what about this other ? The Athenians were about to choose between two architects to carry out a large building contract. The first and more affected came forward with a very elegant speech ready prepared on the subject of his work, and carried the verdict of the people in his favour. But the other, in three words : ' O Athenian lords, what this man has said, I will do.'

When Cicero was at the height of his eloquence many were carried away by admiration ; but Cato only laughed and said : ' We have an amusing consul.'[1] Whether it comes before or after, a useful maxim and a clever saying are always in season : if it does not go well with that which precedes, nor with that which follows, it is well in itself. I am not one of those who think that a good rhythm makes a good poem : let him make a short syllable long, if he pleases ; that matters little : if the original ideas please me, if the wit and judgement have done their office well, then we have a good poet, I shall say, but a poor versifier,

> With humour delicate, the lines are hard. (HORACE.)

Though this poet's work, says Horace, lose all its seams and measures,

> Take from Lucilius' verses, or from mine,
> The cadences and measures of the line ;
> Then change their order, and the words transpose . . .
> And still the poet's scattered limbs it shows ; (HORACE.)

he will not on that account belie his promise : the pieces in themselves will be fine. That is what Menander meant when, being taunted, as the day drew near for which he had promised a comedy, that he had not yet set his hand to it, he replied : ' It is composed and ready ; it only remains to

---

[1] Montaigne's memory has again played him false. Cicero is defending Murena against Cato, who has accused him of bribery, and, after the manner of defending counsel, is purposely making the judges laugh by casting ridicule on Cato's Stoical philosophy, when Cato remarks with a smile to the bystanders, ' We have indeed a most laughable consul.'

add the verses.' Having the matter and the details arranged in his mind, he made little account of the rest. Now that Ronsard and Du Bellay have brought our French poetry to honour, every little prentice rimester is swelling with words, and arrays his rhythms almost as well as they: *more sound than sense* (Seneca). In the eyes of the vulgar there never were so many poets. But, in proportion to the ease with which they copy their rhythms, they fall short of imitating the rich descriptions of the one and the delicate inventions of the other.

Yes, but what will he do if he be hard driven by the sophistic subtlety of some syllogism? 'Ham makes us drink; drink quenches our thirst: therefore ham quenches our thirst.' Let him snap his fingers at it: that will show more subtlety than any reply.

Let him borrow that witty counter-finesse of Aristippus: 'Why should I untie it, since, tied as it is, it gives me trouble?' Some one, debating with Cleanthes, was talking dialectical subtleties, whereupon Chrysippus said: 'Play these juggling tricks with children, and do not divert the serious thoughts of a man of years.' If these silly quibbles, *twisted and thorny sophisms* (Cicero), are intended to inculcate a falsehood, they are dangerous; but if they remain without effect and only move him to laughter, I do not see why he should be on his guard against them. There are some so foolish that they will turn aside from their path for a quarter of a league to run after a fine word, *or who fit not words to things, but search for things, quite out of the purpose, to fit their words* (Quintilian). And, as another says, *there are some who, attracted by some word that takes their fancy, are led to something they had no intention to treat of* (Seneca). I am more ready to twist a good sentence, in order to sew it upon myself, than to unwind my thread to go in search of it.[1] On the contrary, it is the duty of words to obey and follow, and if French words cannot get there, Gascon words may succeed. Things should be paramount and they should so fill the mind of the hearer that he thinks no more of the words. The speech that I like is simple and natural speech, the same on paper as on the lips: a succulent, nervous,

[1] Perhaps the meaning of this obscure sentence is: I would sooner alter the words of a thought to incorporate it into my prose than modify the course of my ideas in order to be able to introduce it.

short, and concise manner of speaking, not dainty and nicely combed so much as vehement and brisk:

> The words that strike the ear will please me most;
> (*From an epitaph on Lucan.*)

difficult rather than tedious, free from affectation, loose, irregular, and bold; every piece to form a body in itself; not in the manner of the professor, the preaching friar or the pleading advocate, but rather soldier-like, as Suetonius called Caesar's style; and yet I do not quite see why he called it so.[1]

I have been wont to copy that disorder in dress affected by our young men: a cloak worn negligently, the hood on one shoulder, ungartered hose, showing a haughty disdain of those foreign adornments, and careless of all art. But I find this carelessness still better applied to the style of speaking. Every kind of affectation, especially in the French gaiety and freedom, is unbecoming a courtier. And in a monarchy every gentleman should be trained to bear himself like a courtier. Wherefore we do well to bear a little to the side of the natural and contemptuous.

I do not like a texture that shows the knots and the seams, just as in a handsome body we must not be able to count the bones and veins. *Let the language that is devoted to truth be simple and artless* (Seneca). *Who can speak so elaborately without falling into affectation?* (Seneca).

The eloquence that diverts us to itself prejudices its subject-matter.

As in our dress it is the sign of a little mind to seek distinction by some particular and unusual fashion, so in language the search after novel phrases and little-known words proceeds from a puerile and pedantic ambition. O that I could use no other but those in use in the market-halls in Paris! Aristophanes the grammarian showed no sense when he blamed Epicurus for the simplicity of his language and the aim of his oratory, which was nothing more than perspicuity of speech. A whole nation is able at once to imitate speech on account of its facility, but to imitate judgement and invention is not so easy. Most readers, having found

---

[1] The edition of Suetonius's *Life of Caesar* which Montaigne used had a faulty reading of the passage in question. Suetonius made no such remark, and Montaigne's doubt goes the way of the faulty reading.

the gown that fits, very falsely imagine that they hold the body that fits it.

Strength and sinews cannot be borrowed; the cloak and attire may be borrowed.

Most of those who associate with me speak the same language as these *Essays*, but I know not if they think the same thoughts.

The Athenians, says Plato, have for their share the study of fullness and elegance in speech, the Lacedemonians that of brevity, the Cretans that of fertility of conception rather than of language: these are the best. Zeno used to say that he had two kinds of disciples: those he called φιλολόγους, curious to learn things, who were his favourites; and those he called λογοφίλους, who cared only about language. This is not to say that to speak well is not a good and fine thing, but it is not as good as some make it, and it vexes me that we make that the business of our whole life. I should like in the first place to know my own language well, and that of my neighbours with whom I have most to do.

There is no doubt that Greek and Latin are a great and fine accomplishment, but they are bought too dearly. I will here tell of a method by which they may be acquired more cheaply than they usually are, and which was tried on myself. Let him who will make use of it.

My late father, having made all possible inquiries among men of learning and understanding with regard to a perfect system of education, became aware of the disadvantages of the methods then in use: they told him that the length of time we spend in learning the languages of the ancient Greeks and Romans, which cost them no labour, was the sole reason why we could not attain to the knowledge and greatness of soul of those nations. I do not believe that to be the sole cause. However, the result of my father's inquiries was that he hit upon this expedient: whilst still in the nurse's hands, and, before the first unloosening of my tongue, he placed me in charge of a German,[1] who afterwards died a famous physician in France, entirely ignorant of our language, and very well versed in Latin. This man, whom he had expressly sent for to this end, and who was engaged at a very high salary, had me continually on his

[1] One Dr. Horstanus, who afterwards was a professor at the Collège de Guienne at Bordeaux.

hands. With him were joined two others, less learned than he, who had to attend me and relieve him. These spoke to me no other language but Latin. As to the rest of the household, it was an inviolable rule that neither my father nor my mother, nor any valet or housemaid, ever spoke in my presence any but the few Latin words which each had learned to jargon with me. It is wonderful how much they all profited by it. My father and mother learned enough Latin to understand it, and acquired a sufficient knowledge of it to use it in case of need, as did also the other domestics who were most attached to my service. In short we all became so latinized, that it overflowed to our villages around, where to this day may be heard several Latin names of artisans and tools, which through frequent use have taken root. As for myself I was more than six years old before I understood any more French or Périgordin than I did Arabic.

And so, without any artificial means, without any book, without grammar or teaching, without any rod and without tears, I learned a Latin quite as pure as that of my schoolmaster. For with me it was never mixed or adulterated. If, as a test, they desired to set me an exercise after the college fashion, where others were given a French one, I had a piece of bad Latin to turn into good. And Nicolas Grouchi, who wrote *De Comitiis Romanorum*, Guillaume Guerente, who annotated Aristotle, George Buchanan, that great Scottish poet, Marc Antoine Muret, whom France and Italy have acknowledged as the best orator of his time, my private tutors, have often said to me that in my childhood I had that language so ready and handy, that they were afraid of accosting me. Buchanan, whom I afterwards saw in attendance on the late Monsieur the Maréchal de Brissac, told me that he was engaged in writing a book on the education of children, and that he took mine as a model; for at that time he had charge of that Count de Brissac who has since shown himself so brave and valorous.[1]

As for Greek, of which I have as good as no knowledge whatever, my father designed to have me taught by artificial means, but in a new way: in the form of recreation and exercise. We bandied our declensions about, after the

[1] He was killed at the siege of Mussidan, quite near to Montaigne's residence, in 1569.

manner of those who, with the help of certain games played on boards, learned arithmetic and geometry. For, among other things, he had been advised to give me a relish for knowledge and duty, not by forcing my will, but by my own desire, and to train my mind in all freedom and indulgence, without rigour or constraint. He carried out this idea so religiously that, because some hold that it disturbs the tender brains of children to wake them in the morning with a start, and to drag them suddenly and violently out of their sleep (in which they are much more deeply plunged than we are), he had me awakened by the sound of some instrument; and he was never without a man [1] for this purpose.

This example may sufficiently enable one to judge of the rest, and to bring into favourable notice the wisdom and affection of so good a father, who is by no means to be blamed if he did not gather any fruit corresponding to so excellent a culture. Two things were the cause of this: firstly, the sterile and unsuitable soil; for, though of a sound and healthy constitution and at the same time of a gentle and tractable nature, I was withal so heavy, soft, and sluggish, that they could not shake me out of my sloth, not even to get me out to play. What I saw, I saw plainly, and beneath this heavy constitution nourished some bold ideas and opinions in advance of my age. I had a slow wit that would go no farther than it was led, a tardy apprehension, a weak initiative, and, with it all, an incredible defect of memory. It is no wonder then that he could extract nothing good from all this.

Secondly, like those who, impelled by a frantic desire to be cured, follow any kind of advice, the good man, in his extreme fear of failing in a matter he had so much at heart, suffered himself at last to be overborne by the prevailing opinion, which always, like the cranes, follows a leader, and fell in with custom. Being no longer in touch with those who had given him those first ideas that he had brought from Italy, he sent me, at about six years of age, to the Collège de Guienne, which was very flourishing at that time, and the best school in France. And there he took every possible care, both in choosing competent tutors and in all

---

[1] The first edition had: 'a man who played the spinet'.

matters appertaining to my bringing-up, at the same time reserving several particular privileges contrary to school usage. Not but that it was still a school. My Latin forthwith grew corrupt, of which I afterwards, through want of practice, lost the entire use. And that novel education of mine was only of service to me in that it enabled me at the outset to jump the first forms ; for, at the age of thirteen, when I left college I had finished my course (as they call it), and in truth without any gain that I could at present put to my account.

The first relish I had for books came to me from the pleasure I had in the fables of Ovid's *Metamorphoses*. For at the age of about seven or eight I would steal away from every other pleasure to read them ; seeing that the language was my mother-tongue and the book the easiest I knew, and, by reason of the subject, the most suited to my tender age. For of the Lancelots of the Lake, of the Amadis', and the Huons of Bordeaux and such rubbishy books on which boys waste their time, I knew not even the names, as I am still ignorant of their matter : so strict was my discipline ! But I became more negligent in the study of my other prescribed lessons.

And well did it fall out to my purpose that I had to deal with a tutor who was a man of good sense, who could cleverly connive at this and similar irregularities. For thereby I was able, without a stop, to run through Virgil's *Aeneid*, and then Terence, and then Plautus, as well as some Italian comedies, always allured by the attractiveness of the subject. If he had been so foolish as to cross this course, I imagine that I should only have left college with a hatred of books, as do nearly all our nobles. Herein he behaved with ingenuity. Pretending to see nothing of what I was doing, he whetted my appetite by letting me devour those books in secret and at the same time insensibly kept me in humour for the other and regular studies. For the chief qualities that my father sought in those who were given charge of me, were a complaisant and easy-going disposition. And my disposition had no other vices but languor and laziness. The danger was not that I should do ill, but that I should do nothing. Nobody predicted that I might become wicked, but only useless ; they foresaw a do-nothing nature, but not a bad nature.

I am sensible that matters have turned out as predicted. The complaints that make my ears tingle are these: 'Idle, cool in the offices of friendship and kinship, and in public functions; too reserved.' Even the most offensive say, not, 'Why has he taken? why has he not paid?' but, 'Why does he not let go? why does he not give?'

I should take it as a favour that men should expect of me only such works of supererogation. But they are unjust to exact of me what I do not owe, much more rigorously than they exact of themselves what they do owe. By that demand they deny the gratuitous character of the action, and so they deny me the gratitude that should be my due: whereas my active well-doing should be the more appreciated in consideration of the fact that I have never been the recipient of any beneficence. I may the more freely dispose of my fortune the more it is my own. However, if I were a great blazoner of my actions, I might peradventure repel these reproaches, and inform some, that they are not so much offended that I do not do enough, as that I am able to do a great deal more than I do.

At the same time my mind none the less, when left to itself, was not wanting in correct impressions, firm and broad opinions about those things it was able to comprehend, and could digest them without any help. And, among other things, I believe indeed that it was wholly incapable of yielding to force and violence.

Shall I put to my credit this faculty of my boyhood: an assurance of countenance and a flexibility of voice and gesture in acting the parts I undertook? For, in advance of my age,

The twelfth year's kiss had scarce yet touched my brow, (VIRGIL.)

I sustained the leading parts in the Latin tragedies of Buchanan, Guerente, and Muret, which were worthily performed in our college of Guienne.

In this matter of dramatic performances Andreas Goveanus, our principal, was, as in all other matters appertaining to his charge, without comparison the greatest principal in France; and I was considered therein a master-worker. It is a practice which I do not disapprove in young boys of good family, and I have since seen our princes honourably and commendably taking an active part therein, after the example of some of the ancients.

In Greece it was permissible even in men of quality to make a profession of it: *He disclosed his plan to the tragic actor Aristo. This was a man distinguished both by birth and fortune; nor did his art prejudice him, for it was not considered any disgrace in Greece* (Livy).

For I have always taxed with want of judgement those who condemn these recreations, and with injustice those who refuse to admit into our good towns those comedians who are worth seeing, and begrudge the people these public pleasures. Well-governed corporations take care to assemble and unite the citizens, not only for serious and devotional offices, but also for plays and sports; sociability and friendship are thereby increased. One could not besides concede to them more orderly pastimes than those which take place in presence of all, and even under the eyes of the authorities. And I should think it only right that the magistracy and the prince should from time to time gratify the community with such spectacles at their own expense, out of a sort of paternal goodness and affection; and that in populous towns there might be places intended and arranged for these shows, as some diversion from worse and secret actions.

To return to my subject, there is nothing like alluring the appetite and affections: else we shall produce only asses laden with books. With the whip we give them their pocketful of learning to keep, which, to do any good, we should not only harbour within us, but espouse.

CHAPTER 27

IT IS FOLLY TO MEASURE THE TRUE AND THE FALSE BY OUR OWN CAPACITY

IT is not perhaps without reason that we attribute a readiness to believe and be persuaded to simplicity and ignorance, for I seem to have once learned that belief is a kind of impression made on our mind; and that the softer and more yielding it is, the more easily does it take that impression. *As the scale of the balance necessarily gives way to the weight placed on it, so must the mind yield to things that are evident* (Cicero). The more empty a mind is, and the less subject to counterpoise, the more easily will it sink under the weight of the first impression. That is why children, the common people, women and the sick, are the most liable to be led by the ears. But then, on the other side, it is foolish presumption to go about disdaining and condemning as false what does not appear likely to us ; which is a common fault in those who think themselves uncommonly clever.

I was once like that : if I heard talk of returning spirits, of prognostics of future things, of enchantments and witchcraft, or any story that I could not bite,

> Dreams, hags, magic sleights,
> Thessalian spells and ghosts that walk o'nights, (HORACE.)

I felt a pity for the poor people who were taken in by those foolish things. And now I find that I was to be pitied at least as much as they : not that experience has since shown me anything transcending my first beliefs, and certainly curiosity was not wanting ; but reason has taught me that thus absolutely to condemn a thing as false and impossible, is to imagine our own brains to possess the privilege of knowing the bounds and limits of God's will and of the power of our mother Nature ; and that there is no more evident folly in the world than to measure those things by the rule of our capacity and ability. If we apply the name of prodigy or miracle to things that are beyond the reach of our reason, how many of these there are continually appearing before our eyes ! Let us consider through what clouds and how blindfold we are brought to the knowledge of most of the things that we are possessed of ; truly we shall find that it is familiarity rather than knowledge that takes away their strangeness in our eyes ;

> The which o'erwearied to behold, to-day
> None deigns look upward to those lucent realms : (LUCRETIUS.)

and that those very things, were they newly presented to us, would appear as incredible, or more so, than any others.

> If now they first for mortals were,
> If unforeseen now first asudden shown,
> What might there be more wonderful to tell,
> What that the nations would before have dared
> Less to believe might be ? (LUCRETIUS.)

He that had never seen a river imagined the first one he came across to be the ocean. And the things that are the greatest within our knowledge we conclude to be the extremes that Nature can do in that kind :

> Huge many a river seems
> To him that erstwhile ne'er a larger saw ;
> Thus huge seems tree or man ; and everything
> Which mortal sees the biggest of each class,
> That he imagines to be ' huge '. (LUCRETIUS.)

The habitual sight of things makes them familiar to the mind, which neither wonders nor inquires about the things seen every day (Cicero).

It is the novelty rather than the greatness of things that incites us to seek after their cause.

We must judge of the infinite power of Nature[1] with more reverence and with more acknowledgement of our ignorance and weakness. How many things of small likelihood there are, testified by trustworthy people, which, if we cannot be persuaded to believe, we should at least leave in suspense ! For to condemn them as impossible is to pretend, with rash presumption, to know how far possibility can go. If we rightly understood the difference between the impossible and the unusual, between that which is contrary to the ordinary course of nature and that which is contrary to the common opinion of men, whilst not believing rashly nor lightly disbelieving, we should observe the rule of *Nothing too much*, enjoined by Chilo.[2]

When we read in Froissart that the Comte de Foix knew, in Béarn, the defeat of King John of Castile at Juberoth, the morrow after it took place, and of the way he said he came by the knowledge, we may be inclined to ridicule it ; as also that which our annals tell, that Pope Honorius, the very same day that King Philip Augustus died at Mantes, publicly solemnized his funeral rites, and commanded the same to be done throughout Italy. For the authority of those witnesses does not perhaps rank high enough to hold us in check. But what ! if Plutarch, besides several ancient examples which he cites, tells us that he knows for certain that, in the time of Domitian, the news of the battle lost by

[1] In the copy of the 1588 edition with Montaigne's MS. notes and corrections, ' Nature ' is here substituted for the original ' Dieu '.
[2] This maxim has also been attributed to Solon and others.

Antony in Germany was published at Rome, many days' journey from thence, and dispersed throughout the world, the very day it was lost; and if Caesar maintains that it has often happened that the report anticipated the occurrence, shall we say that those simple people allowed themselves to be gulled like the common sort, through not being so clear-sighted as we are? Can there be anything clearer, more keen and discriminating than Pliny's judgement, when he is pleased to set it at work; anything more remote from want of balance? I leave aside his surpassing knowledge, of which I make less account. In which of those two respects do we surpass him? True it is however that there is no schoolboy, however young, who could not convict him of falsehood, and who is not prepared to give him a lesson on the progress of Nature's works.

When we read in Bouchet of the miracles wrought by the relics of Saint Hilary, let it go: his credit is not sufficiently great to bar us the liberty of disbelieving him. But to condemn wholesale all those and similar stories seems to me a singular impudence. The great Saint Augustine testifies to having seen a blind child restored to sight upon the relics of Saint Gervaise and Saint Protasius at Milan; a woman cured at Carthage of a cancer by the sign of the cross made upon her by a woman newly baptized; Hesperius, a familiar friend of his, driving out the spirits that infested his house, with a little earth from the sepulchre of our Lord, and, this earth being afterwards transported to the church, a paralytic immediately cured by it; a woman in a procession, after touching the shrine of Saint Stephen with a nosegay and then rubbing her eyes with the same, recovering her long-lost sight; together with many other miracles of which he says he was himself an eyewitness. Of what are we to accuse him and two holy bishops, Aurelius and Maximinus, whom he calls upon to confirm his statements? Shall it be of ignorance, simplicity, credulity, or of knavery and imposture? Is there any man in our day so impudent as to think himself comparable to them, either in virtue and piety, or in knowledge, judgement, and ability? *Who, though they should allege no reason, might persuade me by their sole authority* (Cicero).

It is a presumption of great danger and consequence, not to mention the absurd temerity it implies, to contemn what we cannot conceive. For after you have, with your fine understanding, established the limits of truth and falsehood, and you find that you are bound to believe things stranger even than those you deny, you have already obliged yourself to abandon them. Now, what seems to me to bring so much trouble to our conscience, in these times of religious commotion, is the way in which the Catholics surrender their beliefs. They imagine themselves to be acting the part of moderate and intelligent men when they cede to their opponents some of the articles in dispute. But, besides that they do not see what an advantage it is to the attacking party when you begin to give ground and retire, and how much he is thereby encouraged to pursue his point, those articles which they select as being the most indifferent are sometimes most important. Either we must submit wholly to the authority of our ecclesiastical polity, or entirely dispense with it. It is not for us to determine what portion of obedience we owe to it.

And I may say this moreover, from experience, having in days gone by exercised the same liberty of picking and choosing on my own behalf, regarding as indifferent certain points in the observances of our Church which appeared to me either too singular or too meaningless; when I came to communicate these points to men of learning I found them to have a substantial and very solid foundation, and that it is mere stupidity and ignorance that leads us to accept them with less reverence than the rest. Why do we not remember how much contradiction we are conscious of even in our own judgement? how many things there are which yesterday were to us articles of faith and to-day are but fables? Vainglory and curiosity are the two scourges of our soul. The latter prompts us to thrust our noses into everything, and the former forbids us to leave anything unresolved and undecided.

CHAPTER 28

OF FRIENDSHIP

AS I was considering the way in which a painter in my employment planned his work, I had a mind to imitate him. He chooses the fairest spots, the middle of each wall, for a picture that is elaborated with all his talent, and the vacant space around it he fills in with grotesques, that is to say, fantastic paintings whose only charm lies in their variety and extravagance.

And what are these essays but grotesque and monstrous bodies, pieced together of different members, without any definite shape, without any order, coherence, or proportion, except they be accidental?

> Like a woman, lovely as a wish,
> Tailing off into a loathsome fish. (HORACE.)

In the second point indeed I go with my painter, but I fall short in the other and better part; for my talent is not such that I could presume to attempt a picture that is rich, finished, and formed in accordance with art. It has occurred to me to borrow one of Étienne de la Boëtie, which will cast a lustre on all the rest of this work. It is a dissertation to which he gave the name *La Servitude Volontaire*, but some who did not know this have since very appropriately renamed it *Le Contre Un*. He wrote it by way of essay in his early youth,[1] in honour of liberty against tyrants. It has long been circulating among men of understanding, not without great and well-merited commendation, for it is elegant, and as full as can be. Yet it is far from being the best that he was capable of, and if, at the more mature age at which I knew him, he had adopted my plan of setting down his ideas in writing, we should see many rare things that would very nearly rival the writings of antiquity; for particularly in respect of natural gifts I know of no man who can compare with him. But he left behind him nothing besides this treatise (and it survived by chance, nor do I think he ever saw it after it left his hands), and a few memoranda on that Edict of January,[2] made famous by our civil wars, which will perhaps yet find a place elsewhere. These are all I have been able to recover of what he left (I, to whom, with such loving recommendation, when in the clutches of death, he bequeathed by will his library and papers), excepting the little volume of his works which I

---

[1] Montaigne originally added, 'having not yet reached the eighteenth year of his age.' At the end of this chapter he calls him a 'boy of sixteen'.

[2] The Edict, issued in 1571, which granted the Huguenots the public exercise of their religion.

have already published.[1] And I am particularly obliged to this piece of work, since it was the medium of our first acquaintance. For it was shown to me long before I had set eyes on him, and first brought his name to my notice, thus paving the way to that friendship, which we cherished, as long as God willed it, so perfect and entire, that surely the like of it is seldom read of, and no sign of any such friendship is to be seen in the men of our day. It needs so many chances to build it up, that it is much if Fortune can bring it about once in three centuries.

There is nothing to which Nature seems so much to have inclined us as to society. And Aristotle says that good lawgivers had more respect to friendship than to justice. Now the supreme point of its perfection is this. For, speaking generally, all those amities that are created and nourished by pleasure or profit, public or private needs, are so much the less noble and beautiful, and so much the less friendships, as they introduce some other cause and design and fruit into friendship, than itself.

Neither do the four kinds which antiquity knew, the natural, the social, the hospitable, and the venerean, either separately or conjointly, come up to the ideal friendship. That of children to their fathers is rather respect. Friendship is kept alive by communication, which, by reason of too great disparity, cannot exist between them, and would haply conflict with natural duties. For neither can all the secret thoughts of the father be communicated to his son, in order not to beget an unseemly familiarity, nor can the admonitions and corrections, which are among the first offices of friendship, be administered by the son to the father. There have been nations where it was the custom for children to kill their fathers, and others where the fathers killed their children, to avoid their becoming at some time a hindrance to each other; and by the law of Nature the one depends on the destruction of the other. Some philosophers have been known to disdain their natural tie: witness Aristippus, who, being close pressed about the affection he owed to his children, as being come out of him, began to spit, saying that that had also come out of him, and that

[1] Containing translations of two minor works of Xenophon and Plutarch, and a collection of French poems; published in two volumes in 1571.

we also breed lice and worms. And that other whom Plutarch tried to reconcile with his brother: 'I do not think any the better of him, he said, for having come out of the same orifice.'

Truly the name of brother is a beautiful name, and full of affection, and on that model did he and I form our alliance.[1] But that intervention of worldly goods, those divisions, and the fact that the wealth of the one is the other's poverty, have a wonderful effect in softening and loosening the brotherly solder. Brothers having to conduct the progress of their advancement along the same path and at the same rate, they must of necessity often jostle and clash with one another. Moreover the agreement and the relation which beget those true and perfect friendships, why should they be found in natural brothers? The father and son may be of entirely different dispositions, and brothers too. He is my son, he is my kinsman, but he is sullen, ill-natured, or a fool. And besides, the more these friendships are imposed upon us by law and natural obligation, the less is there of our voluntary choice and freedom. And our voluntary freedom produces nothing more properly its own than affection and friendship. Not but that I have experienced on that side all that can possibly be experienced, having had the best father that ever was, and the most indulgent, even in his extreme old age; and one who from father to son was descended from a family famed and exemplary in this respect of brotherly concord:

> Known
> For loving-kindness father-like
> To all his brothers shown. (HORACE.)

As to comparing it with our affection towards women, though it be born of our choice, we cannot do it, nor include it in this category. Its fire, I confess,

> No stranger to the Goddess I,
> Who blends with pain our bitter-sweet delight, (CATULLUS.)

is more active, fiercer, and more fervent. But it is a precipitate and volatile fire, fickle, and wavering, a feverish fire, subject to fits and returns, that holds us only by one corner.

---

[1] They became *frères d'alliance*, and called each other 'brother'. So afterwards Mlle de Gournay became Montaigne's *fille d'alliance*.

In friendship it is a general and universal warmth, tempered besides and equal, a constant and settled warmth, all gentleness and smoothness, with no sharp sting. What is more, in sexual love there is but a frantic desire for that which flies from us :

> Like hunters that the flying hare pursue
> O'er hill and dale, through heat and morning dew,
> Which being taken, the quarry they despise,
> Being only pleased in following that which flies. (ARIOSTO.)

As soon as it enters into the terms of friendship, that is to say into a conformity of wills, it flags and vanishes. Enjoyment destroys it, as having only a fleshly end and being subject to satiety. Friendship, on the other hand, is enjoyed in proportion as it is desired; it is bred, nourished, and increased only by enjoyment, as being spiritual, and the soul becoming refined by practice. During this perfect friendship those fleeting affections once found a place in me, not to speak of him, who only too clearly confesses them in his poetry. Thus I harboured those two passions, each known to the other, but to be compared, never ! the first steadily soaring in proud and haughty flight, and disdainfully looking down upon the other going its way far, far below.

As concerning marriage, besides that it is a bargain to which only the entrance is free (its continuance being forced and constrained, and depending on something other than our will), a bargain moreover that is usually concluded to other ends, there supervene a thousand extraneous entanglements to unravel, sufficient to break the thread and disturb the course of a lively affection ; whereas in friendship there is no traffic or business except with itself. Besides, to tell the truth, women are ordinarily not capable of responding to this communion and fellowship, the nurse of this sacred bond ; neither does their soul appear firm enough to support the strain of so hard and durable a knot. And truly, if that were not so, if such a free and voluntary familiarity could be established, where not only the souls might have their complete enjoyment, but the bodies also shared in the alliance, in which the entire man was engaged, it is certain that the friendship would be the fuller and more perfect. But the sex has never yet, by any example, been able to attain to it, and, by common agreement of the ancient schools, is shut out from it.

And that other Greek licence is rightly abhorred by our moral conscience. For, there being, according to their practice, so necessary a disparity of ages and difference of services between the lovers, it no more answered sufficiently to the perfect union and harmony that we here require, than the other : *For what love is this of friendship ? Why does no man love either a deformed youth, or a handsome old man ?* (Cicero). For even the picture which the Academy draws of it will not belie me, I think, when I say this on its behalf : That this first frenzy inspired by the son of Venus in the heart of the lover at sight of a youth in his tender bloom, to which they allow all the insolent and passionate actions produced by an immoderate ardour, was simply founded on an external beauty, the false image of corporeal generation. For it could not be founded on the mind, the proof of which yet lay concealed, being but at its birth and before the age of budding ; That if this frenzy took possession of a base heart, the means of its pursuit was riches, presents, favour in advancement to dignities, and such other base merchandise which one disapproves. If it fell on a more generous heart, the means of corruption were likewise generous : philosophical instruction, precepts to reverence religion, to obey the laws, to die for the good of one's country, examples of valour, wisdom, justice ; the lover studying to render himself acceptable by the good grace and beauty of his soul, that of his body being long decayed, and hoping, by this mental fellowship, to establish a firmer and more durable contract.

When this courtship had its effect in due season (for that which they do not require in the lover, that he should bring leisure and discretion to his pursuit, they strictly require in the loved one, since he had to judge of an internal beauty, difficult to know and, being hidden, hard to discover), there was born in the loved one the desire of a spiritual conception by the mediation of a spiritual beauty. The latter was the main thing ; corporeal beauty was accidental and secondary : quite the contrary to the case of the lover. For this reason they prefer the loved one, and aver that the gods also prefer him ; and they greatly reprove the poet Aeschylus for having, in the love of Achilles and Patroclus, given the lover's part to Achilles, who was in the first and beardless bloom of youth, and the handsomest of the Greeks.

This general fellowship being established, the chief and more worthy partner in it exercising his functions and predominating, they say that there proceeded fruits very profitable to the private and public weal; that it constituted the strength of the countries where the custom prevailed, and the chief defence of equity and freedom: witness the salutary loves of Harmodius and Aristogiton. Therefore they call it sacred and divine. And, by their account, only the violence of tyrants and the cowardice of the people are inimical to it. In short, all that can be said in favour of the Academy is that it is a love terminating in friendship, which definition agrees well enough with that of the Stoics: *That love is the attempt to gain the friendship of one to whom we are attracted by beauty* (Cicero).

I return to my description of a more even and respectable kind of friendship. *They only are to be reputed friendships when the character is fortified and matured by age* (Cicero). For the rest, what we commonly call friends and friendship are no more than acquaintanceships and intimacies contracted by chance or for some advantage, by means of which our souls come together. In the friendship I speak of, our souls blend and melt so entirely, that there is no more sign of the seam which joins them. If I am pressed to say why I loved him, I feel that I can only express myself by answering, 'Because it was he, because it was I.'

There is, over and above my reason and all that I am able particularly to say, I know not what inexplicable power of fate, as mediator of this union. We sought one another before we met, from reports we had each heard of the other, which wrought upon our affections more than reports are, in reason, supposed to do; I believe by some heavenly ordinance. We embraced one another by our names. And at our first meeting, which chanced to be at a great feast and town gathering, we found ourselves so taken with one another, so well acquainted, so bound together, that from that moment nothing could be so close as we were to one another. He wrote an excellent Latin satire,[1] which is published, in which he excuses and explains the precipitancy

---

[1] A didactic poem, rather than a satire in our sense of the word, of 332 lines, in which he admonishes his younger friend (by about two years), to be on his guard against the allurements of pleasure, to which Montaigne was in his opinion a little too much addicted.

of our mutual understanding, so suddenly come to perfection. Having begun so late, and with so little chance of a long duration (for we were both grown men and he several years my senior), our friendship had no time to lose; and it was not of the kind to conform to the regular pattern of mild friendships, which need all the precautions of a long preliminary intercourse. This one had no other model than itself, and can only be compared with itself. This is no one special consideration, nor two, nor three, nor four, nor a thousand: it is I know not what quintessence of all this mixture, which, having taken possession of my whole will, carried it to plunge and lose itself in his; which, having taken possession of his whole will, carried it to plunge and lose itself in mine, with a like hunger and emulation. I may truly say lose, reserving as we did nothing to ourselves, that was either his or mine.

When Lelius, in the presence of the Roman consuls, who, after Tiberius Gracchus was condemned, persecuted all those who had been in secret intelligence with him, came to ask Caius Blossius (who was his chief friend), what he would have done for him, he replied, 'Everything.' 'What means everything? answered Lelius; what if he had commanded you to set fire to our temples?' 'He would never have commanded that.' 'But supposing he had done so?' 'I should have obeyed him,' answered Blossius. If he was so perfect a friend to Gracchus as the historians say, he was not justified in offending the consuls by this bold and extreme confession, and should not have given up the assurance he had of Gracchus's intentions. Those however who accuse him of answering seditiously do not well understand this mystery, nor do they presuppose, as was the case, that he had Gracchus's will in his sleeve, both by his influence and knowledge. They were friends first, then citizens, more friends to one another than friends or enemies of their country, or than friends of ambition or sedition. Having wholly given themselves up to one another, they absolutely held the reins of one another's inclination; and if you suppose this team to have been guided by virtue and led by reason (without which it would be quite impossible to harness it), Blossius's answer was such as it should be. If their actions lost their handle, they were neither, according to my measure, friends to one another nor friends to themselves.

For the rest, this answer does not ring any more true than would mine if some one questioned me in this fashion : ' If your will commanded you to kill your daughter, would you kill her ? ' and I assented. For that would be no evidence of a consent to do it, because I am in no doubt with regard to my will, and just as little in regard to that of such a friend. All the arguments in the world cannot possibly dispossess me of the certainty I have of my friend's intentions and opinions. Not one of his actions could be reported to me, whatever aspect it might bear, but that I could immediately discover its motive. Our souls travelled together in such unity, they regarded each other with so ardent an affection, and with a like affection saw into the very depths of each other's hearts, that not only did I know his heart as well as my own, but I should certainly have trusted him in any matter concerning myself, sooner than myself.

I cannot allow those other common friendships to be placed in the same line with ours. I have as much knowledge of them as another, and of the most perfect of their kind, but I should not advise any one to measure them with the same rule ; he would be much mistaken. In those other friendships one has to walk with the bridle in one's hand, prudently and cautiously : the knot is not tied so tightly but that it will cause some misgiving. 'Love him, said Chilo, as if you had one day to hate him ; hate him, as if you had to love him.' This precept, which is so abominable in this sovereign and commanding friendship, is of salutary use in the common and customary friendships, to which must be applied the saying that Aristotle was so fond of, 'O my friends ! there is no friend.'

In this noble intercourse, good offices and benefits, the feeders of other friendships, deserve not even to be taken into account, by reason of the complete blending of our wills. For even as the love I bear to myself is not increased by the succour I give myself in time of need, whatever the Stoics may say, and as I feel no gratitude to myself for the service I do myself ; so the union of such friends, being truly perfect, makes them lose the sense of such duties, and hate and banish from their minds these words that imply separation and distinction : benefit, obligation, gratitude, request, thanks, and the like. Everything being actually in common between them, wills, thoughts, opinions, possessions, wives, children, honour, and life, and their agreement being such that they are but one soul in two bodies, according to the very apt definition of Aristotle, they can neither lend nor give anything to one another. That is why the makers of laws, in order to honour marriage with some imaginary resemblance to this divine alliance, interdict all donations between husband and wife; meaning to infer therefrom that all should belong to each of them, and that they have nothing to divide and share out between them.

If, in the friendship of which I speak, one could give to the other, it would be the one who received the benefit that lays his friend under an obligation. For, as each of them studies above all to benefit the other, it is he who furnishes the matter and occasion that plays the liberal part, by giving his friend the satisfaction of doing that to him which he most desires.

When the philosopher Diogenes was in want of money he used to say that he redemanded it of his friends, not that he demanded it. And to show how that works in practice, I will relate a singular example from antiquity.

Eudamidas of Corinth had two friends, Charixenus a Sicyonian and Aretheus a Corinthian. When on his death-bed, being poor, and his two friends rich, he made his will after this manner: 'My legacy to Aretheus is that he maintain my mother and support her in her old age; to Charixenus, that he give my daughter in marriage, and provide her with as good a dowry as he is able to afford; and in case one of them chance to die I appoint his survivor to take his place.' They who first saw this testament laughed at it; but when the heirs were informed of it, they accepted it with a singular satisfaction. And one of them, Charixenus, dying five days later, leaving Aretheus at liberty to take his place, the latter supported the mother with great care, and of five talents he had in his estate, he gave two and a half as a marriage portion to his only daughter, and two and a half to the daughter of Eudamidas; and the two weddings took place on the same day.

This example is very complete, except for one objection, namely the number of friends. For that perfect friendship of which I speak is indivisible: each one gives himself so wholly to his friend, that there remains to him nothing to divide with another; on the contrary he grieves that he is not double, triple, or fourfold, and that he has not several souls and several wills, to confer them all on the object of his love.

Common friendships are capable of being shared : we may love one for his handsome exterior, another for his easygoing manners, another again for his liberality ; this one for his fatherly and that one for his brotherly ways, and so forth ; but this friendship which possesses the soul and dominates it with absolute power, cannot possibly be split in two. If two at the same time entreated your assistance, to which of them would you hasten ? If they required of you opposite services, how would you arrange it ? If one of them imparted to you a secret that it would be useful for the other to know, how would you solve the difficulty ?

The unique and paramount friendship dissolves all other obligations. The secret that I have sworn not to reveal to another, I may without perjury communicate to one who is not another : that is myself. It is miracle enough to divide oneself into two, and they know not the greatness of it who speak of dividing oneself into three. Nothing is extreme that has its like. And he who supposes that I can equally love each of two, and that they can love one another and me as much as I love them, makes a multiple brotherhood of a thing that is most one and united, and of which even one is the rarest thing in the world to find.

The sequel of that story agrees very well with what I was saying, for Eudamidas makes it a kindness and a favour to his friends to employ them for his needs. He leaves them heirs to his liberality, which consists in giving into their hands the means of benefiting him. And without doubt the power of friendship is much more richly evident in his action than in that of Aretheus.

In short, these are delights which are not to be imagined by one who has not tasted them ; and therefore I highly honour the answer of a young soldier to Cyrus, who inquired of him what he would take for a horse that had just enabled him to win the prize in a race, and whether he would exchange it for a kingdom : ' No indeed, Sire, but I would willingly part with it to gain a friend, if I could find a man worthy of such alliance.' Not a bad answer, ' if I could find ' ; for it is easy to find men fit for a superficial acquaintance. But in the other kind, where we exhibit the very depths of our heart and make no reservations, truly all the springs of action must be perfectly clear and true.

In alliances that have but one end, we need only to provide against the imperfections which particularly concern that end. It matters little to me what religion my physician professes, or my lawyer. This consideration has nothing to do with the friendly offices that they owe me. In the domestic relations that arise between me and those who serve me, it is the same. I am little curious to know whether my footman is chaste, so long as he is assiduous. And I am less afraid to engage a muleteer who is a gambler, than one who is an idiot, or a cook who swears than an ignorant one. I do not meddle with telling people what they are to do in the world (there are plenty of others who do that); I only say what I do myself.

> I do what pleases me, do thou the like. (TERENCE.)

With the familiarity of the table I associate amusement, and not wisdom; in bed, beauty comes before goodness; in serious conversation, ability, even should sincerity be wanting; and the like elsewhere.

As he who was discovered astride on a stick playing with his children begged the man who surprised him at it not to speak of it until he was himself a father, supposing that the affection that would arise in his heart would make him a fair judge of such actions; so I should wish to speak to people who have had experience of what I say. But knowing how far from common, nay how rare, is such a friendship, I have no expectation of finding a competent judge. For even the dissertations which the writers of antiquity have left us on the subject appear to me weak and flat in comparison with my own sentiments. And in this particular the reality surpasses even the precepts of philosophy:

> Nothing, no, nothing on this earth,
> Whilst I have reason, shall I e'er
> With a true-hearted friend compare! (HORACE.)

The old poet Menander declared that man to be happy who had been able to meet with but the shadow of a friend. He was truly right in saying so, especially if he spoke from experience. For, in truth, when I compare all the rest of my life, although by the grace of God it has been spent in ease and comfort, and, saving the loss of so dear a friend, free from any grievous affliction, and in great tranquillity of mind ; having been well compensated with my natural and original advantages, without seeking any others ; when I compare all that, I say, with the four years which were granted me to enjoy the sweet companionship and society of that man, it is all smoke, a dark and wearisome night. From the day when I lost him,

> The day which heaven hath willed to be
> Sacred for evermore, but ever sad to me, (VIRGIL.)

my life has dragged on wearily, and the very pleasures which it offers me, instead of solacing me, redouble my grief for his loss. We were co-partners in everything, and it seems to me that I am robbing him of his share :

> Nor is it just to taste of pleasure here
> Till he return in safety to partake on't. (TERENCE.)

I was already grown so accustomed to being always and everywhere his second self, that I seem to be no more than a moiety :

> Ah, since untimely fate hath snatched thee hence,
>   Thee, of my soul a part,
> Why should I linger on, with deadened sense
>   And ever-aching heart,
> A worthless fragment of a fallen shrine ?
> No, no, one day hath seen thy death and mine. (HORACE.)

In all my actions and dreams I miss him, as he would indeed have missed me. For as he infinitely surpassed me in all other virtues and talents, so he did in the duties of friendship.

> Why blush that for a friend so dear we grieve,
> Why stint our tears ? (HORACE.)

> But, brother, what with mirth was once so rife
>   Is turned to sadness by the timeless doom ;
> Dead with thy death is all that cheered my life,
>   And all our house is buried in thy tomb !

> Gone are the joys that, whilst thou yet wert here,
>   Were by thy sweet affection fanned and fed,
> All studies, all delights, that once were dear,
>   I've banished from my soul since thou art dead.

> Oh, is thy voice for ever hushed and still ?
>   O brother, dearer far than life, shall I
> Behold thee never ? But in sooth I will
>   For ever love thee, as in days gone by. (CATULLUS.)

But let us give a little hearing to this boy of sixteen.

Having found that this work [1] has been since published, and with an evil intention, by those who seek to disturb and change the state of our government, without caring whether they improve it or not, and that they have mixed it up with some of their own scribblings, I have revoked my intention of inserting it in this place. And in order that the memory of the author may not be prejudiced in the eyes of such as cannot have had a real knowledge of his opinions and actions, I will inform them that this subject was handled by him in his early youth merely by way of an exercise, as a common theme that had been worn threadbare by a thousand other writers. I make no doubt that he believed what he wrote, for he was too conscientious to lie even in jest. And I know besides that, if he had had the choice, he would rather have been born in Venice than at Sarlac,[2] and with good reason. But he had another maxim, sovereignly imprinted on his soul, which was to obey and submit very religiously to the laws under which he was born. There never was a better citizen, nor one more interested in the tranquillity of his country, nor one more hostile to the commotions and innovations of his time. He would much rather have used his talents in suppressing them than in providing occasion for more mischief. His mind was moulded to a pattern of other ages than this.

Now, in place of that serious work I will substitute another, a product of that same season of his life, more gallant and lively.

CHAPTER 29

(Dedication of twenty-nine Sonnets of Étienne de la Boëtie)

TO MADAME DE GRAMMONT, COMTESSE DE GUISSEN

MADAME, I offer you nothing of my own, either because it is already yours, or because I can see nothing in my writings that is worthy of you. But I desire that these verses, wherever they may appear, shall bear your name at their head, on account of the honour that will accrue to

---

[1] *La Servitude Volontaire*, mentioned at the beginning of the chapter.
[2] Venice was then a republic; Sarlac or Sarlat in Périgord was La Boëtie's birthplace.

them from having the great Corisande d'Andouins[1] for their safe-conduct. I have deemed this to be a very suitable present for you, seeing that there are few ladies in France who have a better judgement in poetry, or who can write it more tellingly, than you; and none who is as capable of giving life and spirit to it with those rich and beautiful notes, with which, among a million other charms, Nature has gifted you. Madame, these verses deserve to be cherished by you, for you will agree with me that none have come out of Gascony to surpass them in ingenuity and gracefulness, or that give evidence of having proceeded from a richer vein. And be not jealous that you have only the remainder of what I published some time ago under the patronage of your good kinsman, Monsieur de Foix;[2] for these certainly have an indefinable something more lively and ebullient, as he composed them in his greenest youth, kindled by a noble and beautiful flame about which, Madame, I will one day whisper in your ear. The others were written later, when he was a suitor for marriage, in honour of his wife, and already smack somewhat of marital coolness. And I am one of those who hold that poetry is nowhere so smiling as on a wanton and irregular subject.

These poems may be seen elsewhere.[3]

CHAPTER 30

OF MODERATION

AS if our touch were infectious we, by our handling, corrupt the things which in themselves are good and beautiful. We may grasp virtue in such a manner that she will become vicious, if we embrace her with too violent and fierce a desire. Those who say that there is never excess in

---

[1] 'La belle Corisande d'Andouins', as the poets called her (her real name was Diane de Louvigny), was an ancestress of the Grammont of Hamilton's Memoirs. It seems that the King of Navarre, afterwards Henry IV of France, was enamoured of the fair lady in her widowhood, and had the intention of marrying her.

[2] A collection of about a dozen French poems published in 1572.

[3] In Montaigne's revised copy of the 1588 edition the Sonnets are deleted by his own hand, clearly showing his intention that they should not appear in the projected new edition.

virtue, inasmuch as it is no longer virtue if there be excess in it, only play upon words:

> Note this too: push even virtue to excess
> And right grows wrong, and wisdom foolishness. (HORACE.)

This is a subtle consideration of philosophy. We may both love virtue too much, and carry a just action to excess. The divine voice fits this bias, 'Be not wiser than you should, but be soberly wise.'[1]

I have known a certain prince to harm his reputation for religion by showing himself religious beyond every example of men of his sort.[2]

I like temperate and middle natures. Want of moderation, even in the direction of the good, if it does not offend me, astonishes me, and I am at pains how to baptize it. The action of Pausanias' mother, who gave the first information and brought the first stone for her son's death, and that of the dictator Posthumius, who put his own son to death because his youthful ardour had, with happy results, impelled him towards the enemy a little in front of the ranks, appear to me more extraordinary than right. And I am inclined neither to counsel nor to imitate a virtue so ruthless and so costly.

The archer who overshoots his mark misses as well as he who falls short of it. And my eyes trouble me equally when I suddenly mount up into a strong light and when I descend into the shadow. Callicles, in Plato, declares philosophy, when carried to extremes, to be hurtful, and advises us not to plunge into it beyond the limits of the useful; that taken in moderation it is pleasing and profitable, but that in the end it makes a man vicious and unsociable, contemptuous of religions and the common laws, an enemy of intercourse with his fellows, an enemy to human pleasures, incapable of all political administration, and of being helpful to others as well as to himself: a man to have his ears boxed with impunity. He speaks the truth; for in its excess it en-

---

[1] St. Paul, Romans xii. 3. The Authorized Version has: 'For I say ... to every man that is among you, not to think of himself more highly than he ought to think, but to think soberly, &c.'

[2] It is supposed that Montaigne was thinking of Henry III of France, of whom Pope Sixtus V said to Cardinal Joyeuse: 'Your king has done everything possible to be a monk, and I have done everything possible not to be one.'

slaves our natural freedom, and by an importunate subtlety, turns us from the fair and plain path that Nature traces out for us.

The love we bear to our wives is very lawful; which has not, however, prevented theology from curbing and restraining it. I seem to have once read in Saint Thomas, in a passage where he condemns the marriage of kinsfolk within the prohibited degrees, this reason among others, that there is a danger that the love one bears to a wife so nearly related may become excessive: for, if the marital love is whole and perfect as it should be, and there is added thereto that which is due to kinship, there is no doubt that this super-increase will carry such a husband beyond the bounds of reason.

The sciences which regulate human morals, such as theology and philosophy, have their say in everything. There is no action ever so private and secret that it escapes their cognizance and jurisdiction. Those are very simple and ignorant who would condemn their meddling. They are like those women who expose their parts as much as you will in order to wanton; shame forbidding them to do so to the physician. I will then, in the name of philosophy and religion, teach husbands this, if there are yet any who are too eager: that even those pleasures they enjoy in knowing their wives are to be condemned, unless they observe moderation therein; and that in this connexion there is as much scope for licentiousness and debauchery as in an illicit connexion. Those shameless caresses which the first heat suggests to us in this sport, are not only indecently but detrimentally practised on our wives. If they must learn shamelessness let it be from others. They are always sufficiently lively for our need. I have always followed Nature's simple instructions.

Marriage is a religious and holy bond; wherefore the pleasure we derive from it must be a restrained and serious pleasure, mixed with some austerity; it should be a somewhat discreet and conscientious voluptuousness. And because its chief end is generation, there are some who question whether, when we have no hope of such fruit, or when they are beyond the age or pregnant, it is permissible to seek their embraces. It is a homicide according to Plato. Certain nations, among others the Mohammedans, abominate any connexion with a pregnant woman ; many also with one who is in her courses. Zenobia received her husband but for one charge ; that done, she let him go free during the whole time of her conception, only then giving him permission to recommence: a brave and generous example of marriage.

It was of some needy poet who was famished for this delight that Plato borrowed this story : That Jupiter one day attacked his wife so impetuously that, too impatient to wait till she had gained her couch, he threw her on the floor, and in the vehemence of his pleasure forgot the great and important resolutions he had but recently taken with the other gods in his celestial court ; and he boasted that he found this encounter as good as when he first deflowered her by stealth and unknown to their parents.[1]

The kings of Persia used to invite their wives to share in their banquets, but when the wine began to heat them in good earnest, and when they felt the need of giving an entirely loose rein to voluptuousness, they sent them back to their private apartments, that they might not participate in their immoderate appetites, sending for other women to take their places, to whom they were not obliged to show the same respect.

Not all pleasures and gratifications are becoming in all classes of persons. Epaminondas committed to prison a boy of debauched habits ; Pelopidas entreated him, as a favour to himself, to set him at liberty. He refused, but granted the same request to a young girl his mistress, saying, ' that it was a gratification due to a sweetheart, but not to a captain.' Sophocles, when a partner in the Praetorship with Pericles, seeing a handsome youth who happened to be passing, said to Pericles, ' There goes a handsome youth ! ' ' That, said Pericles, might be very well in one who is not a Praetor, who should have not only his hands, but his eyes, chaste.'

The Emperor Aelius Verus replied to his wife, when she complained that he went after the love of other women, ' that he did so from conscientious motives, seeing that marriage was a name implying honour and dignity, not wanton and lascivious lust '. And our ancient ecclesiastical writers make honourable mention of a woman who repudiated her husband, not desiring to second his too lascivious

[1] Homer, *Iliad*, xiv. 294.

and immoderate embraces. There is, in short, no pleasure, however legitimate, in which excess and intemperance are not to be condemned.

But, to speak seriously, is not man a miserable creature? Scarcely is it in his power, constituted as he is by nature, to enjoy a single pure and entire pleasure, yet he is at pains, by reasoning about it, to curtail it: he is not wretched enough, except by art and study he augment his misery:

> By art we multiply the woes of Fortune. (PROPERTIUS.)

Man in his wisdom very foolishly exercises his ingenuity in lessening the number and sweetness of the pleasures that we have a right to; as he industriously and successfully employs his artifices in tricking out and disguising the ills and alleviating the sense of them.

Had I ruled the roast, I should have taken another more natural course, which is to say, a true, meet, and holy one, and I should perhaps have made myself strong enough to set bounds to it. What of our spiritual and bodily physicians, who, as if conspiring together, find no cure or remedy for the maladies of body and soul, except by way of misery, pain, and torment? Vigils, fasts, hair-shirts, remote and solitary exiles, perpetual imprisonments, scourges, and other afflictions, have been introduced to that end; the understanding being that they shall be really afflictions, with bitterness and sting; and that it shall not fall out as in the case of one Gallio, who had been banished to the isle of Lesbos. News having been brought to Rome that he was giving himself a good time, and that what had been imposed on him as a penance was turned to his advantage, they changed their minds and recalled him home to his wife and family, and commanded him to stay in his house, in order to make him fittingly sensible to their punishment. For, to a man whose health and cheerfulness are sharpened by fasting, or to whom fish is more appetizing than flesh, these would cease to be salutary remedies; just as in the other kind of medicine drugs have no effect on him who takes them with appetite and pleasure. The bitternesses and the reluctance are helpful to the operation. The constitution that would accept rhubarb as a familiar food would frustrate its use: it must be something that gives pain to the stomach, if it is to effect a cure; and here the common rule is at fault, that things are cured by their contraries; for here the evil cures the evil.

This idea has some relation to that other very ancient belief, which was universally embraced in all religions, that Heaven and Nature are gratified by our massacres and homicides. So recently as in the time of our fathers, Amurath, at the taking of the Isthmus, immolated six hundred young Greeks to his father's soul, in order that this blood might serve as a propitiation to expiate the sins of the defunct. And in those lands newly discovered in our time, which are still pure and virgin compared with ours, this is everywhere in some measure an accepted custom; all their idols are drenched with human blood, not unaccompanied in many cases by horrible cruelties. They are burned alive, and when half roasted are withdrawn from the brazier in order to have their hearts and entrails plucked out. In other places even women are flayed alive, and in the skins thus dripping with blood others are clothed and disguised. Nor are there wanting examples of fortitude and resolution. For those poor sacrificial victims, old men, women, children, themselves go about a few days before, begging alms for an offering at their sacrifice; and they present themselves to the butchery singing and dancing with the spectators.

The ambassadors of the King of Mexico, to give Fernando Cortez an idea of their master's greatness, after telling him that he had thirty vassals, each one of whom was able to assemble a hundred thousand combatants, and that he resided in the most beautiful and the most strongly fortified city under heaven, added that he had to sacrifice to the gods every year fifty thousand men. Indeed it is said that he kept up a state of warfare with certain great neighbouring nations, not only to exercise the young men of his country, but principally to provide himself with sufficient prisoners of war for his sacrifices. At a certain town in another country, as a welcome to Cortez, they sacrificed fifty men at once.

I will tell one more story: Some of these people, having been beaten by him, sent to acknowledge his rule and seek his friendship. The messengers brought him three kinds of gifts, with these words: 'Lord, here are five slaves: if you are a cruel god and feed on flesh and blood, eat them and we will bring you more; if you are a gentle god, here are incense and feathers; if you are a man, take these birds and fruits.'

CHAPTER 31

OF CANNIBALS

WHEN King Pyrrhus passed over into Italy, after acknowledging the good order that prevailed in the army that the Romans had sent to meet him, he said, ' I know not what barbarians are these (for so the Greeks called all foreign nations), but the disposition of this army I see is by no means barbarous '. The Greeks said the same of the army which Flaminius brought into their country, as did also Philip, on viewing from an eminence the orderly distribution of the Roman camp, in his kingdom, under Publius Sulpicius Galba. Thereby we may see how we should be on our guard against clinging to vulgar opinions, and how we should judge things by the light of reason, and not from common rumour.

I had living with me for a long time a man who had lived for ten or twelve years in that other world which was discovered in our century, in that place where Villegaignon landed,[1] which he called *Antarctic France*. This discovery of an unbounded country seems to me worthy of consideration. I do not know that I could pledge myself that some other discovery may not be made in the future, so many persons greater than we having been mistaken about this one. I fear our eyes are greater than our bellies, and that we have more curiosity than capacity. We embrace all, but we clasp only wind.

Plato introduces Solon, telling how he had learned of the priests of the city of Saïs in Egypt that, in days of old and before the Deluge, there was a large island named Atlantis, directly at the mouth of the Strait of Gibraltar, which contained more countries than all Asia and Africa together; and that the kings of that region, who not only possessed that island, but had extended their dominion so far into the mainland, that of the breadth of Africa they held as far as Egypt, and of the length of Europe as far as Tuscany, attempted to stride even into Asia, and to subjugate all the nations that border on the Mediterranean Sea as far as the gulf of the Greater Sea [2]; and to that end traversed the Spains, Gaul, Italy, as far as Greece, where the Athenians stood up against them; but that some time after both the

---

[1] In Brazil, in 1557.   [2] The Black Sea.

Athenians and they and their island were swallowed up by the Flood.

It is most likely that that extreme watery devastation has caused some wonderful alterations in the habitations of the earth, as it is thought that the sea cut off Sicily from Italy,

> These lands, 'tis said, one continent of yore
> (Such change can ages work) an earthquake tore
> Asunder; in with havoc rushed the main,
> And far Sicilia from Hesperia bore,
> And now, where leapt the parted lands in twain,
> The narrow tide pours through, 'twixt severed town and plain;
> (VIRGIL.)

Cyprus from Syria, the island of Negropont from the mainland of Boeotia; and elsewhere joined lands which were divided, by filling up the channels between them with sand and mud:

> Swamps, sterile long, all plashy, rank and drear,
> Groan 'neath the plough, and feed whole cities near. (HORACE.)

But it does not appear very likely that that great island was the new world that we have lately discovered, for it almost touched Spain, and it would have been an incredible result of an inundation to have removed it as far back as it is, more than twelve hundred leagues; besides that our modern navigators have already almost discovered it to be no island, but a firm land holding together with the East Indies on the one hand, and on the other with the lands which lie under the two poles; or, if it is separated from them, it is by so narrow a strait and interval, that it does not on that account deserve to be called an island.

It would seem that there are movements, some natural, others diseased, in those great bodies as well as in our own. When I consider the inroads that my river, the Dordogne, is making even in my time, upon the right bank in its descent, and that in twenty years it has gained so much ground, and robbed many buildings of their foundations, I plainly see that an extraordinary disturbance is going on; for if it had always been going on at this rate, or were to do so in the future, the face of the world would be entirely altered. But rivers are subject to changes: now they overflow in one direction, now in another, now they keep within their beds. I do not speak of the sudden inundations whose causes are manifest. In Médoc, along the sea-shore, my brother the Sieur d'Arsac sees an estate of his buried beneath the sands that the sea vomits before it; the tops of several buildings are still visible; his rents and domains have been converted into very poor pasturage. The inhabitants say that the sea has been for some time pushing so strongly towards them, that they have lost four leagues of land. These sands are its harbingers, and we see great dunes of moving sand, that march half a league before it, and are gaining ground.

The other testimony from antiquity, from which some infer this discovery, is in Aristotle, if at least that little book *Of Unheard-of Marvels* be his. He there relates how certain Carthaginians, having ventured across the Atlantic Sea, outside the Strait of Gibraltar, and navigated a long time, had at last discovered a large fertile island, all clothed in woods, and watered by broad and deep rivers, far remote from any mainland; and that they, and others after them, attracted by the goodness and fertility of the soil, had gone thither with their wives and children and begun to settle there. The lords of Carthage, seeing that their country was gradually becoming depopulated, expressly forbade any more to go there, on pain of death, and drove out those new settlers, fearing, it is said, lest in course of time they might multiply to such an extent as to supplant themselves and ruin their state. This narration of Aristotle no more agrees with our new-found lands than the other.

This man I had was a simple and ignorant fellow: hence the more fit to give true evidence; for your sophisticated men are more curious observers, and take in more things, but they glose them; to lend weight to their interpretations and induce your belief, they cannot help altering their story a little. They never describe things as they really are, but bend them and mask them according to the point of view from which they see things, and, to make their judgements the more credible and attractive, they are not loath to add a little to their matter, and to spin out and amplify their tale. Now we need either a very truthful man, or one so simple that he has not the art of building up and giving an air of probability to fictions, and is wedded to no theory. Such was my man; and he has besides at different times brought several sailors and traders to see me, whom he had known on that voyage. So I shall content myself with his information, without troubling myself about what the cosmographers may say about it.

We need topographers who would give us an exact account of the places which they have visited. But because they have this advantage over us that they have seen Palestine, they claim to enjoy the privilege of telling us new things of all the rest of the world. I would have every man write about what he knows, and no more than he knows, not only in this but on all other subjects. For a man may have some particular knowledge or experience of the nature of a river or a fountain, who otherwise knows no more than what everybody knows. Yet he will undertake, in order to circulate this little scrap of knowledge, to write a book on the whole science of physics. From this fault spring many great abuses.

Now, to return to my subject, from what I have heard of that nation, I can see nothing barbarous or uncivilized about it, except that we all call barbarism that which does not fit in with our usages. And indeed we have no other level of truth and reason but the example and model of the opinions and usages of the country we live in. There we always see the perfect religion, the perfect government, the perfect and accomplished manner of doing all things. Those people are wild in the sense in which we call wild the fruits that Nature has produced by herself and in her ordinary progress ; whereas in truth it is those we have altered artificially and diverted from the common order, that we should rather call wild. In the first we still see, in full life and vigour, the genuine and most natural and useful virtues and properties, which we have bastardized in the latter, and only adapted to please our corrupt taste. And yet in some of the uncultivated fruits of those countries there is a delicacy of flavour that is excellent even to our taste, and rivals even our own. It is not reasonable that art should gain the point of honour over our great and powerful mother Nature. We have so overburdened the beauty and richness of her works with our inventions, that we have quite smothered her. And yet, wherever she shines in her purity, she marvellously puts to shame our vain and trivial efforts,

> Uncared, unmarked the ivy blossoms best ;
> Midst desert rocks the ilex clusters still ;
> And sweet the wild bird's untaught melody. (PROPERTIUS.)

With all our efforts we are unable even to copy the nest of the smallest of little birds, its contexture, its beauty and convenience ; not so much as the web of the poor spider.

All things, says Plato, are produced either by Nature, or by chance, or by art : the greatest and most beautiful by one or other of the two first ; the least and most imperfect by the latter.

Those nations, then, appear to me so far barbarous in this sense, that their minds have been formed to a very slight degree, and that they are still very close to their original simplicity. They are still ruled by the laws of Nature, and very little corrupted by ours ; but they are still in such a state of purity, that I am sometimes vexed that they were not known earlier, at a time when there were men who could have appreciated them better than we do.

I am sorry that Lycurgus and Plato had no knowledge of them, for it seems to me that what we have learned by contact with those nations surpasses not only all the beautiful colours in which the poets have depicted the golden age, and all their ingenuity in inventing a happy state of man, but also the conceptions and desires of Philosophy herself. They were incapable of imagining so pure and native a simplicity, as that which we see by experience ; nor could they have believed that human society could have been maintained with so little human artifice and solder. This is a nation, I should say to Plato, which has no manner of traffic ; no knowledge of letters ; no science of numbers ; no name of magistrate or statesman ; no use for slaves ; neither wealth nor poverty ; no contracts ; no successions ; no partitions ; no occupation but that of idleness ; only a general respect of parents ; no clothing ; no agriculture ; no metals ; no use of wine or corn. The very words denoting falsehood, treachery, dissimulation, avarice, envy, detraction, pardon, unheard of.[1] How far removed from this perfection would he find the ideal republic he imagined ! *Men newly come from the hands of the gods* (Seneca).

These manners first by nature taught. (VIRGIL.)

For the rest, they live in a region with a very agreeable and very temperate climate, so that, according to my witnesses, a sick man is rarely seen ; and they assured me that

---

[1] This is the passage which Shakespeare, through Florio's translation, reproduced almost word for word in *The Tempest*, Act II, sc. i.

they had never seen any man shaking with palsy, or with dripping eyes, toothless or bent with age. They are settled along the sea-coast, and closed in on the land side by large and high mountains, the land between them and the sea extending for a hundred leagues or thereabouts. They have great abundance of fish and flesh, which bear no resemblance to ours, and they eat them roasted without any other preparation. The first man who brought a horse thither, although he had associated with them on several previous voyages, so horrified them in the riding posture, that they shot him dead with arrows before recognizing him.

Their buildings are very long, capable of holding two or three hundred souls, covered with the bark of tall trees, the strips resting by one end on the ground, and leaning to and supporting one another at the top, after the manner of some of our barns, the coverings of which slope down to the ground and serve as side-walls. They have a wood so hard that they can cut with it, of which they make their swords, and gridirons to roast their meat. Their beds are made of cotton tissue, suspended from the roof like those in our ships, each one having his own : for the women sleep apart from their husbands.

They rise with the sun and eat immediately after rising, for the whole day : for they have no other meal. They drink nothing with that meal, like some other Eastern peoples of whom Suidas tells us, who drank apart from eating ; but they drink several times a day, and to excess. Their drink is made of some root, and is of the colour of our claret wines,[1] and they only drink it warm. This beverage will keep only two or three days ; it has a slightly pungent taste, is anything but heady, good for the stomach, and laxative for such as are not used to it, but a very pleasant drink for those who are. For bread they use a certain white material resembling preserved coriander. I have tried some of it : it is sweet but rather tasteless.

The whole day is spent in dancing. The younger men hunt animals with bows. Some of the women meanwhile spend their time warming their drink, which is their chief duty. One of their old men, in the morning before they begin to eat, preaches to the whole barnfull of people in

[1] *Vin clairet,* claret wine (is commonly made of white and red grapes mingled, or growing together).—COTGRAVE.

common, walking from one end to the other, repeating the same words several times, until he has finished the round (for the buildings are quite a hundred paces in length). He recommends only two things, valour against the enemy and love to their wives. And they never fail to stress this obligation, which forms their refrain, ' that it is they who keep their wine warm and seasoned '.

In several places, among others in my house, may be seen the formation of their beds, of their ropes, their wooden swords and bracelets, with which they cover their wrists in battle, and large canes open at one end, by the sound of which they keep the time and rhythm of their dances. They are close shaven all over, and remove the hair much more neatly than we do, although their razors are only made of wood or stone. They believe the soul to be immortal, and that those who have deserved well of the gods are lodged in that part of the heaven where the sun rises, and those who are damned in the west.

They have some kind of priest and prophet, who very seldom appears among the people, having his dwelling in the mountains. On his arrival there is a great feast and a solemn assembly of several villages (each barn, as I have described it, forms a village, and they are about a French league distant one from the other). This prophet speaks to them in public, exhorting them to virtue and their duty; but their whole ethical science comprises only these two articles: an unfaltering courage in war and affection to their women. This man foretells things to come, and the issue they are to expect from their enterprises; urges them to war, or holds them back; but he does so on the understanding that, where he fails to prophesy correctly, and if things turn out otherwise than he has predicted, he is cut into a thousand pieces if he is caught, and condemned for a false prophet. For that reason he who has once miscalculated is seen no more.

Divination is a gift of God, wherefore to abuse it ought to be regarded as a punishable imposture. Among the Scythians, when the prophets failed to hit the mark, they were laid, shackled hand and foot, on a little cart filled with heather and drawn by oxen, on which they were burned. They who take in hand such matters as depend on the conduct of human capacity are to be excused if they do their best.

But those others who come and delude us with assurances of an extraordinary faculty that is beyond our ken, should they not be punished when they fail to carry out what they promise, and for the temerity of their imposture?

They have their wars with the nations beyond their mountains, further back on the mainland, to which they go quite naked, with no other weapons but bows or wooden swords pointed at one end, after the fashion of the tongues of our boar-spears. It is marvellous with what obstinacy they fight their battles, which never end but in massacre and bloodshed : for of routs and terrors they know not even the meaning. Each man brings back as a trophy the head of the enemy he has slain, and fixes it over the entrance to his dwelling. After treating his prisoner well for a considerable time, and giving him all that hospitality can devise, his captor convokes a great gathering of his acquaintance. He ties a cord to one of his prisoner's arms, holding him at some distance for fear of being hurt, and gives the other arm to be held in the same way by his best friend ; and these two, in presence of the whole assembly, dispatch him with their swords. This done, they roast and eat him in common, and send bits of him to their absent friends. Not, as one might suppose, for nourishment, as the ancient Scythians used to do, but to signify an extreme revenge.

And that it is so, may be seen from this : having perceived that the Portuguese, who had allied themselves with their adversaries, inflicted a different kind of death on their prisoners, which was to bury them up to the waist, shoot the upper part of the bodies full of arrows, and afterwards to hang them ; they imagined that these people of another world (seeing that they had sown the knowledge of a great many vices among their neighbours, and were much greater masters than themselves in every kind of wickedness) had some reason for adopting this kind of vengeance, and that it must be more painful than their own ; wherefore they began to give up their old method, and followed this one.

I am not so much concerned that we should remark on the horrible barbarity of such acts, as that, whilst rightly judging their errors, we should be so blind to our own. I think there is more barbarity in eating a live than a dead man, in tearing on the rack and torturing the body of a man still full of feeling, in roasting him piecemeal and giving him to be bitten and mangled by dogs and swine (as we have not only read, but seen within fresh memory, not between old enemies, but between neighbours and fellow citizens, and, what is worse, under the cloak of piety and religion), than in roasting and eating him after he is dead.

Chrysippus and Zeno, the leaders of the Stoic sect, thought indeed that there was no harm in making use of our carrion for any purpose in case of necessity, and of extracting nourishment from it. And our ancestors, when besieged by Caesar in the city of Alexia, decided to relieve the famine during the siege by eating the bodies of the old men, women, and other persons incapable of fighting ;

> Time was, the Gascons, as old tales relate,
> Thus fed, contended long with cruel fate. (JUVENAL.)

And physicians are not afraid of using it in all sorts of ways as cures, either for inward or outward application. But no man's brain was ever so disordered that he would excuse treachery, disloyalty, cruelty, tyranny, which are our ordinary vices.

We may therefore well call those people barbarians in respect to the rules of reason, but not in respect to ourselves, who surpass them in every kind of barbarity.

Their warfare is entirely noble and generous, and is as fair and excusable as can be expected in that human disease : their only motive being a zeal for valour. They do not strive to conquer new territory, for they still enjoy that luxuriance of nature which provides them, without labour and pains, with all necessary things in such abundance, that they have no need to enlarge their borders. They are still in that happy state of not desiring more than their natural needs demand : all that is over and above it is for them superfluity.

They generally call each other, if of the same age, brothers ; if younger, children ; and the old men are fathers to all the others. These latter leave to their heirs in common the full and undivided possession of their property, without any but that pure title that Nature gives to her creatures, by bringing them into the world. If their neighbours cross the mountains to attack them, and gain the victory over them, the acquisition of the victor is the glory and advantage of having proved himself the superior in valour and virtue, for otherwise they have no need for the spoils of the vanquished ; and so they return to their own country, where they have no want of any necessaries, nor even of that great portion, which is to know how to enjoy happily their condition, and be content with it. These do the same in their turn. They ask of their prisoners no other ransom but a confession and acknowledgement of being vanquished. But you will not find one in a whole century who would not rather die than yield, either by word or look, one tittle of an invincible greatness of courage ; not one who would not rather be killed and eaten than even pray to be spared. They are very liberal in their treatment of their prisoners, in order to make life the more dear to them, and usually entertain them with threats of their impending death, the torments they will suffer, the preparations made to that end, the cutting up of their limbs, and the banquet that will be made at their expense. All this is done with the sole purpose of extorting from them a weak or spiritless word, or to give them a desire to escape, in order to gain the advantage of having terrified them and shaken their firmness. For indeed, if rightly taken, therein alone lies the real victory :

> The victor's wreath no triumphs more attest
> Than when the foe's subjection is confest. (CLAUDIAN.)

The Hungarians, very bellicose fighters, did not formerly pursue their advantage further than making their enemy cry for mercy. For, after forcing from them that confession, they let them go without hurt or ransom, except, at the most, making them pledge their word not again to take up arms against them.

We often enough gain an advantage over our enemy which is a borrowed advantage, and to which we have no real claim. To have more muscular arms and legs is the quality of a porter, not a sign of valour ; skill is a dead and corporal quality : it is a stroke of fortune that causes our adversary to stumble or to be dazzled by the glare of the sun ; it is a trick of art and science that makes an able fencer, who may easily be a coward and an insignificant fellow.

A man's value and estimation consists in heart and will : there lies his true honour. Valour is strength, not of legs and arms, but of heart and soul ; it lies not in the goodness of our horse, or our weapons, but in our own. He who falls fighting with obstinate courage, *if his legs fail him, he fights on his knees* (Seneca). He who, in spite of being in danger of imminent death, abates nothing of his assurance, who, in yielding up his soul, still fixes on his enemy a firm and scornful glance, is vanquished, not by us, but by Fortune : he is slain but not conquered.

The most valiant are sometimes the most unfortunate. Hence there are triumphant defeats that vie in glory with victories. Neither did those four sister victories, the most glorious that the sun has ever beheld with its eyes, of Salamis, Plataea, Mycale, and Sicily, ever dare to oppose their combined glories to the glory of the discomfiture of King Leonidas and his comrades at the pass of Thermopylae.

What man ever hastened with a more glorious and ambitious desire to the winning, than Captain Ischolas did to the losing, of a battle ? What man ever used more care and ingenuity to secure his own safety than he did to ensure his destruction ? He was charged to defend a certain pass in the Peloponnesus against the Arcadians. But knowing that he was wholly unable to do so, on account of the nature of the place and the inequality of the forces, and being sure that every man who confronted the enemy must needs remain on the spot ; on the other hand, deeming it unworthy both of his own virtue and magnanimity, and of the name of a Spartan, to fail in his charge, he adopted a middle course between these two extremes, which was in this manner : the youngest and most active of his band he reserved for the service and defence of their country, and sent them home ; and with those whose loss would be of less account he decided to hold the pass, and with their death make the enemy purchase their entry as dear as possible. And so it fell out : for, being presently surrounded on every side by the Arcadians, after a great butchery of them he and his comrades were all put to the sword. Was ever a trophy raised to a victor that was not rather due to these vanquished men ? The part that true victory plays is the struggle, not the coming off safe ; and the honour of virtue consists in combating, not in beating.[1]

To return to our narrative. Far from giving in, in spite of all they suffer, these prisoners, on the contrary, during

[1] *A combattre, non à battre* ; Montaigne is very fond of this kind of *jeux de mots*.

the two or three months that they are held in captivity, bear a cheerful countenance; they urge their captors to hasten to put them to the proof, defy them, insult them, reproach them with their cowardice and the number of battles lost against their own countrymen.

I have a song composed by a prisoner, which contains this outburst: ' Come boldly, every one of you, and assemble together to dine off me, for you shall at the same time eat your fathers and grandfathers, whose flesh has served to feed and nourish this body. These muscles, this flesh and these veins are yours, poor fools that you are! can you not see that they still contain the substance of your ancestors' limbs ? Relish them well, you will find that they have the flavour of your own flesh.' A fiction that by no means savours of barbarity. On the pictures which represent these prisoners being executed or at the point of death, they are seen spitting in the face of their slayers or making mouths at them. Indeed they never cease to challenge and defy them by word and look until the breath is out of their body. Verily here we see men who are indeed savages if we compare them with ourselves: for either they must be so in good sooth, or we; there is a wonderful distance between their character and ours.

The men there have several wives, and the higher their reputation for valour the greater is the number of their wives. It is a remarkably beautiful feature in their marriages, that the same jealousy that our wives have to keep us from the love and favours of other women, they have to an equal degree to procure it. Being more solicitous for their husbands' honour than for anything else, they use their best endeavours to have as many companions as they can, seeing that that is a proof of their husbands' worth.

Ours will cry ' miracle ', but it is not so. It is after all a proper matrimonial virtue, but of the highest order. And in the Bible, Leah, Rachel, Sarah, and Jacob's wives [1] accommodated their husbands with their fair handmaids; and Livia gratified Augustus' appetites to her own detriment; and Stratonice, the wife of King Deiotarus, not only lent her husband the use of a very beautiful young chamber-

---

[1] These inaccuracies must be put down to Montaigne's defective memory, not to ignorance; he did not profess to be one of your savants who verify every statement they make by looking up the authorities.

maid in her service, but carefully brought up her children, and gave them a shoulder in succeeding to their father's estates.

And, that it may not be supposed that all this is done through a simple and slavish obligation to follow usage, and under the weight of authority of their ancient customs, without reasoning or judgement, and because their minds are too dull to imagine any other, I must give a few proofs of their intellectual capacity. Besides the warlike song I have just cited I have another, of an amorous nature, which begins thus : 'Adder, stay ; stay, adder, that thy colours may serve as a pattern for my sister to work a rich girdle to give to my love : thus shall thy beauty and the disposition of thy spots be preferred for all time to all other serpents.' This first verse is the burden of the song. Now, I have enough knowledge of poetry to judge this much : that not only is there nothing barbarous in this idea, but that it is altogether Anacreontic. Their language, by the way, is a soft language, with an agreeable tone, and their terminations resemble the Greek.

Three men of this nation, not knowing how dear, in tranquillity and happiness, it will one day cost them to know the corruptions of this side of the world, and that this intercourse will be the cause of their ruin, which indeed I imagine is already advanced (poor wretches, to be allured by the desire to see new things and to leave their own serene sky to come and see ours!), were at Rouen at a time when the late King Charles the Ninth was there. The King had a long talk with them. They were shown our ways, our pomp, the form of a fine city. After that somebody asked their opinion, desiring to know what they most wondered at. They mentioned three things, the third of which I am sorry to have forgotten, but I still remember two. They said that in the first place they thought it very strange that so many big men with beards, strong and armed, who were about the King (they were probably thinking of the Swiss who formed his guard) should submit to obey a child, and that they did not rather choose one of their own number to command them. Secondly (they have a way of speaking of men as if they were halves of one another), that they had observed that there were men amongst us, full and gorged with all kinds of good things, and that their halves were begging at their doors, emaciated with hunger and poverty ;

and they thought it strange how these necessitous halves could suffer such injustice, and that they did not seize the others by the throat, or set fire to their houses.

I had a long talk with one of them; but I had an interpreter who followed my meaning so badly, and was at such a loss, in his stupidity, to take in my ideas, that I could get little satisfaction out of him. When I asked the native, 'What he gained from his superior position among his people?' (for he was a captain, and our sailors called him a king), he said it was 'to march foremost in war'. How many men did he lead? He pointed to a piece of ground, to signify as many as that space could hold: it might be four or five thousand men. Did all his authority lapse with the war? He said 'that this remained, that, when he visited the villages that were dependent on him, they made paths through their thickets, by which he might pass at his ease.' All this does not sound too ill; but hold! they don't wear trousers.

CHAPTER 32

THAT WE SHOULD SOBERLY MEDDLE WITH JUDGING THE DIVINE ORDINANCES

THE true field and subject of imposture are things unknown, because, in the first place, mere strangeness induces belief; and moreover, as they do not come within our ordinary experience, we lose the means of combating them. For that reason, says Plato, it is much easier to satisfy people when speaking of the nature of the gods, than when speaking of the nature of men: because the ignorance of the hearers gives us a fine and wide range and every freedom to discuss hidden matters.

Whence it comes that nothing is so firmly believed as that of which we know least, and that there are no people so confident as those who entertain us with fictions, such as Alchemists, Prognosticators, Astrologers, Palm-readers, Physicians, *id genus omne*. To whom I should like to join, if I dared, a pack of people, interpreters and ordinary recordkeepers of the designs of God, who profess to find out the causes of every event, to see into the secrets of the divine will and discover the incomprehensible motives of its works; and, although the variety and continual discordance of events drive them from corner to corner,[1] from east to west, still persist in following their ball, and with the same chalk paint black and white.

In a certain Indian nation they observe this commendable custom: When they have had the worst in a battle or encounter, they publicly ask pardon of the sun, which is their god, as if they had committed an unjust action: attributing their good or evil fortune to the divine reason, and submitting to it their own reason and judgement.

It is enough for a Christian to believe that all things come from God, to accept them with acknowledgement of his divine and inscrutable wisdom, taking them, however, as well meant, in whatsoever form they may be sent to him. But I disapprove the common practice of trying to confirm and bolster up our religion by the success and prosperity of our enterprises. Our faith has other foundations enough, without authorizing it by results; for when a people is accustomed to hear arguments which are so plausible and so much to their liking, there is a danger lest, when events turn out to their disadvantage and contrary to their expectation, their faith be shaken. As in our present wars of religion, those who had the best of it in the engagement at La Rochelabeille, loudly rejoicing over this accidental success and regarding their good fortune as a certain approbation of their cause; when they afterwards came to excuse their misfortune at Montcontour and Jarnac, by saying that if they had not a people wholly at their mercy it was because they were being chastised and scourged by a fatherly hand, they make it quite clear that they are taking double payment for grinding one sack of corn, and blowing hot and cold with the same breath.[2] It would be better to explain to them the true foundations of truth.

It was a fine naval victory that was won a few months ago against the Turks under the leadership of Don John of Austria;[3] but it has pleased God at other times to let us see other such, to our loss.

---

[1] As in a tennis-court.

[2] At La Rochelabeille the Huguenots defeated the Catholics; in the other two engagements they were defeated. Jarnac came first, so that the word 'afterwards' is misleading.

[3] By the combined fleets of Spain, Venice, and the Pope, on the 7th October 1571, in the Gulf of Lepanto. It was in this engagement that the author of the immortal *Don Quixote* was seriously wounded.

In short, it is a hard matter to reduce divine things to our scale, without their suffering waste. And he that would take upon himself to give reasons for Arius and Leo his Pope, the principal leaders of that heresy, dying, at different times, so similar and so strange a death (for they both, after withdrawing from the debate, with a pain in the bowels, to their closet, suddenly gave up the ghost), and declare that the divine vengeance was aggravated by the circumstance of the place, might very well add the death of Heliogabalus, who was also killed in a privy. But what about Irenaeus, who was involved in the same fate ?

God, desiring to teach us that the good have something else to hope for, and the wicked something else to fear, than the fortunes and misfortunes of this world, controls and allots these according to his occult disposition, and deprives us of any occasion for foolishly explaining them to our advantage. And they deceive themselves who endeavour, by human reasonings, to make themselves out the better. They never score a hit with their rapier, but they get two in return. Saint Augustine proves it finely against his adversaries. It is a conflict that is decided by the weapons of memory rather than by those of reason.

We must be content with the light which it pleases the sun to communicate to us by its rays ; and he who lifts up his eyes to receive more light into his body, let him not think it strange if, as a punishment for his overweeningness, he loses his sight. *For what man is he that can know the counsel of God ? or who can think what the will of the Lord is ?*[1]

CHAPTER 33
OF FLEEING FROM PLEASURES AT THE PRICE OF LIFE

I HAD indeed observed that most of the ancients agree on this point : That it is time to die when there is more evil than good in living ; and that to preserve our life to our torment and discomfort, is to offend against the very laws of Nature, as the old precepts tell us :

   Or live without distress, or die in happiness.
   'Tis good for us to die, when life brings infamy.
   O better far to die, than live in misery ! (*Gnomic poets.*)

But as for carrying contempt for death to such a degree as

---

[1] Book of Wisdom ix. 13, in the Apocrypha.

to make it a reason for withdrawing from the honours, riches, dignities, and other favours and blessings of Fortune, as we call them, as if Reason had not enough to do in persuading us to abandon them without thrusting this new charge upon her; I had never seen it either enjoined or practised, until that passage of Seneca fell into my hands, where, counselling Lucilius, a powerful personage and of great authority with the Emperor, to give up his life of pleasure and ostentation, and retire from worldly ambitions to a life of solitude and philosophic repose, to which Lucilius opposed some difficulties, he said: 'My advice is, that either you quit this life you are leading, or life altogether; I do indeed counsel you to follow the easier path, and to untie rather than cut the knot you have tied so badly, provided that you cut it, if it cannot be otherwise untied. There is no man so cowardly but that he would rather fall once for all than be always tottering.' I should have expected this advice to be conformable to the hard doctrines of the Stoics, but it is more strange that it should be borrowed of Epicurus, who writes in a similar vein and on a like occasion to Idomeneus.

Yet I think I have observed some sentiments of the same nature in men of our own religion, but expressed with Christian moderation. Saint Hilary, Bishop of Poitiers, that famous enemy of the Arian heresy, being in Syria, was informed that Abra his only daughter, whom he had left at home with her mother, was sought in marriage by the most eminent lords of the country, she being a beautiful, rich, and very well educated damsel in the flower of her age. He wrote to her (as we may see) that she should withdraw her affections from all those pleasures and advantages which were set before her eyes; that on his travels he had found a much greater and more worthy match, a bridegroom of much greater power and magnificence, who would bestow upon her gifts of robes and jewels of inestimable price. His design was to make her lose the appetite and use of mundane pleasures, and wed her wholly to God; but as the shortest and surest means to that end appeared to him to be the death of his daughter, he did not cease, by vows, prayers, and orisons, to beseech God to take her from this world, and call her to him. And so it happened, for soon after his return she departed from him, whereat he exhibited a singular joy.

This man seems to outbid the others, since from the very outset he has recourse to this means, which the others only adopt subsidiarily ; and besides, it concerned his only daughter.

But I will not omit the end of this story, although it is not to the point. Saint Hilary's wife, having heard from him how by his will and design he had brought about the death of their daughter, and how much happier she was in being removed from this world than in being in it, conceived such a lively apprehension of the eternal and celestial beatitude, that she begged her husband most earnestly to do the same for her. And God, having soon after taken her to him in response to their combined prayers, it was a death embraced with a singular and mutual contentment.

CHAPTER 34

FORTUNE IS OFTEN MET HAND IN HAND WITH REASON

THE inconsistency of the various swings of Fortune [1] makes her necessarily show herself in all sorts of disguises. Can any act of justice be more clearly expressed than this ? The Duc de Valentinois,[2] having resolved to poison Adrian, Cardinal of Corneto, with whom his father Pope Alexander the Sixth and himself were going to sup at the Vatican, sent one ahead of him with a bottle of poisoned wine and strict injunctions to the butler to take charge of it very carefully. The Pope arriving before his son and calling for drink, the butler, who supposed that this wine had only been recommended to him on account of its excellence, poured out some of it for the Pope ; and the Duke himself arriving just in time for the meal, and relying upon his bottle not having been touched, drank some in his turn : with the result that the father died on the spot, and the son, after being long tormented by sickness, was reserved for another and worse fate.

Sometimes she seems to mock us of set purpose. The Seigneur d'Estrées, at that time ensign to Monsieur de

---

[1] Montaigne's frequent use of the word Fortune instead of Providence was censured by the Papal authorities at Rome.
[2] Caesar Borgia.

Vendôme, and the Seigneur de Licques, lieutenant in the company of the Duc d'Ascot, being both servants [1] of the sister of the Sieur de Fouquerolles, although they were on different sides (as sometimes happens among frontier neighbours), the Sieur de Licques carried off the prize; but on the very wedding-day, and, what was worse, before going to bed, the bridegroom, being desirous to break a lance in honour of his young bride, went out to a skirmish near St. Omer, where the Sieur d'Estrées, being the stronger, made him prisoner; and, to make his advantage the more triumphant, the damsel was fain—

> When forced from her endearments to unclasp
> The spouse so lately welcomed to her bower;
> Forced, ere a second winter's long, sweet nights
> Could to her hungry love such rapture give,—(CATULLUS.)

to entreat him of his courtesy to give up his prisoner, which he did: since the French noble never denies anything to a lady.

Does it not appear as if fate were an artist? Constantine, son of Helen, founded the empire of Constantinople; and so many centuries later, Constantine, a son of Helen, ended it.

Sometimes she is pleased to outdo our miracles. We have it on record that when King Clovis was besieging Angoulême, the walls fell of themselves by divine favour; and Bouchet borrows from some authority that King Robert, laying siege to a city, and having stolen away to solemnize the feast of Saint Aignan at Orleans, being at his devotions at a certain part of the Mass, the walls of the besieged city fell to ruin without any effort on the part of the besiegers. She acted quite against the grain in our wars against Milan. For Captain Rense, laying siege on our behalf to the town of Eronne, and having sprung a mine under a large stretch of wall, it was lifted bodily from its base; but it dropped back all of a piece and so straight into its foundation, that the besieged were no worse off than before.

Sometimes she practises medicine. Jason Phereus, being given up by the doctors for an abscess on the chest, and desirous to be rid of it, at least by death, desperately hurled himself into the thick of the enemy in a battle, where he

i.e. suitors for the hand of.

received a wound in the body so pat, that his abscess burst and he was cured.

Did she not surpass the painter Protogenes in knowledge of his art ? This man, having finished the picture of a weary and spent hound, to his own satisfaction in every respect except that he was unable to paint the foam and slaver to his liking ; vexed with his work, he took his sponge, and, soaked as it was in various colours, hurled it against the picture, with intent utterly to deface it ; Fortune most aptly directed the throw to the right spot on the dog's jaw, and accomplished what his art had been unable to effect.

Does she not sometimes correct and amend our counsels ? Isabel, Queen of England, having to recross from Zealand to her own kingdom with an army, to assist her son against her husband, had been lost if she had landed at the port she intended, as her enemies were lying in wait for her there ; but Fortune cast her to another place against her will, and there she came to land in safety. And that ancient, hurling a stone at a dog, hit and killed his step-mother, had he not good reason to give utterance to this line :

> Fortune is better advised than we ? (MENANDER.)

Icetes had suborned two soldiers to kill Timoleon, while he was sojourning at Adrana in Sicily. They chose the time when he should be offering sacrifice, and, mingling with the crowd, they were making signs to one another that the moment was propitious for their business, when behold a third soldier who, dealing one of them a heavy blow on the head with his sword, strikes him dead to earth, and escapes. His fellow, supposing himself discovered and undone, ran to seek sanctuary at the altar, promising to tell the whole truth. As he was telling the story of the conspiracy, behold the third man again, who had been caught and was being pushed and kicked for a murderer through the crowd towards Timoleon and the most eminent persons in the assembly. There he cries for mercy, saying he had justly killed his father's assassin, verifying his assertion on the spot with the help of witnesses with whom his good fortune very opportunely provided him, that his father had in truth been slain in the city of the Leontines by him on whom he had taken vengeance. He was awarded ten Attic minae for having had the good fortune to make the death of his own father the occasion of saving from death the common father of the Sicilians. In this case the justice of Fortune surpasses all the laws established by human wisdom.

To make an end of it. Does not the following fact disclose a very manifest application of her favour, goodness, and singular piety? The two Ignatii, father and son, having been proscribed by the Triumvirs at Rome, nobly resolved to deliver their lives into each other's hands, and thus frustate the cruelty of the tyrants. They ran upon one another sword in hand; Fortune directed their points and caused the two thrusts to be equally fatal, and, adding to the honour of so noble a love, left them just enough strength to withdraw their armed and blood-stained hands from the wounds and clasp each other in so tight an embrace, that the executioners severed both their heads at one blow, leaving their bodies still fast linked together in this noble bond, and their wounds so joined that they lovingly drank in each other's blood and remnant of life.

CHAPTER 35

OF A WANT IN OUR ADMINISTRATION

MY late father, a man of a very clear judgement though aided by nature and experience alone, said to me one day that he had wished to organize a scheme to establish in the towns a certain fixed place, to which they might resort who had need of anything, and have their business entered by an official appointed for that purpose; such as, 'I have pearls for sale; I want to buy pearls; So-and-so desires a companion to go with him to Paris; So-and-so wants a servant with such and such qualifications; So-and-so wants a master; So-and-so a labourer; one this, another that, each according to his need.' And it seems to me that this method of informing one another of one's wants would be of no slight advantage in public intercourse; for at all times there are conditions that are in need of one another, and, for want of mutual understanding, people are left in great necessity.[1]

I have heard, with a feeling of great shame for the age we

---

[1] This idea was realized not very long after, in 1631, by the founding of the *Gazette de France*, the first French daily paper.

live in, that under our very eyes two most excellent men of great learning have died in a condition of not having enough to eat, Lilius Gregorius Giraldus in Italy, and Sebastianus Castalio in Germany ; and I believe that there are a thousand who would have invited them to their houses under very advantageous circumstances, or succoured them where they were, if they had known.

The world is not so generally corrupt but that I know of a man [1] who would very heartily wish that the means that had been placed in his hands by his forbears might be used, as long as it should please Fortune to allow him to enjoy them, in sheltering from want persons eminent and distinguished in any kind of excellence, who are sometimes driven to extremes by misfortune ; who would at least set them up in such a way that they would be lacking in good sense if they were not content.

In his economic administration my father had this system, which I commend but am quite incapable of following : besides the daybook of household transactions, in which were entered the petty accounts, payments, and bargains which did not require the hand of a notary, which daybook was kept by a receiver ; he entrusted to the man who did his writing business, a daily paper in which he set down all the happenings of any note, and day by day the memoirs of the family history : very pleasant to read when time begins to efface the remembrance of them, and often very handy for clearing up any doubts : 'When this business was begun, when finished ; What visitors came, with what retinue, and how long they stopped : Our travels, our absences, marriages, deaths ; The receiving of good or bad tidings ; Change of principal servants ; such and such matters.' An ancient usage which I consider good to revive, by each man in his own home. And I think myself a fool to have neglected it.[2]

---

[1] Montaigne perhaps meant himself. There is other evidence that there was in him a good deal of the milk of human kindness.

[2] But Montaigne carried out the idea on his travels through Germany and Italy in 1580-1, when he kept a diary written partly by a secretary, partly by himself, portions of which are intensely interesting.

CHAPTER 36
OF THE CUSTOM OF WEARING CLOTHES

WHATEVER I may be aiming at, I am obliged to force some barrier of custom : so carefully has she barred all our approaches ! I was considering within myself in this chilly season, whether the fashion of going about quite naked, in those lately discovered nations, is a fashion imposed by the warm temperature of the air, as we say of the Indians and the Moors, or whether it is the original custom of mankind. Inasmuch as all things under heaven, as the holy word declares,[1] are subject to the same laws, men of understanding are wont, in considerations such as these, where we must distinguish the natural laws from those which have been invented, to have recourse to the general polity of the world, where there can be nothing counterfeit.

Now, all other creatures being fittingly provided with needle and thread, to maintain their being, it is really not to be believed that we alone should have been brought into the world in this defective and indigent state, in a state that cannot be maintained without foreign aid. So I hold that, as plants, trees, animals, all that lives, are by Nature equipped with sufficient covering to protect them against the injury of the weather,

> And therefore almost all
> Are covered either with hides, or else with shells,
> Or with the horny callus, or with bark, (LUCRETIUS.)

so were we ; but, like those who with artificial light extinguish the light of day, we have extinguished our proper means with borrowed means. And it is easy to see that it is custom that makes impossible to us, what is not so : for among those nations that have no knowledge of clothes, there are some that dwell in much the same climate as we do ; and moreover, the most delicate parts of us are those which are always uncovered, the eyes, the mouth, the nose, the ears ; in the case of our peasants, as with our ancestors, the pectoral and ventral parts. If we had been born on condition of wearing farthingales and galligaskins, I make no doubt but that Nature would have armed with a thicker

[1] Ecclesiastes ix. 2, 3.

skin what she has exposed to the battery of the seasons, as she has done the finger-ends and the soles of the feet.

Why does this seem hard to believe? Between my habit of clothing and that of a peasant of my country-side there is a much greater distance than between his and that of a man who is clothed only in his skin.

How many men, especially in Turkey, go naked as a matter of religion! Somebody or other asked one of our beggars whom he saw in his shirt in the depth of winter, as merry as a grig and feeling the cold as little as many a man who is muffled up to the ears in sable, how he could patiently bear it. 'And you, sir, he replied, you have your face uncovered; now, I am all face.' The Italians tell a tale of, I think, the Duke of Florence's fool, that his master asking him how, being so poorly clad, he could bear the cold, which he himself was hardly able to do: 'Follow my recipe, he replied, and pile on all the garments you have, like me, and you will feel the cold no more than I do.' King Massinissa could not be induced, even in his extreme old age, to go with his head covered, were it ever so cold, stormy or rainy. The same is told of the Emperor Severus.

In the battles fought between the Egyptians and the Persians, Herodotus says that both he and others remarked that, of those who were left dead on the field, the skulls of the Egyptians were without comparison harder than those of the Persians, by reason that the latter always have their heads covered, first with biggins and afterwards with turbans, and the former are shaven from infancy and uncovered.

And King Agesilaus observed the habit, until his decrepitude, of wearing the same clothing in winter as in summer. Caesar, says Suetonius, always marched at the head of his army, and most often on foot, bareheaded, whether in sunshine or rain; and the same is said of Hannibal;

Bareheaded then he braved the raging storm. (SILIUS ITALICUS.)

A Venetian, who had long resided in the kingdom of Pegu, and has but lately returned from thence, writes that both the men and women of that country always go barefoot, even on horseback, the rest of their body being clothed.

And Plato gives this wonderful advice, that, to keep the

whole body in health, we should give the feet and head no covering but that which Nature has provided.

The man who, following our King, was chosen King of Poland,[1] and who is indeed one of the greatest princes of our age, never wears gloves, nor does he change, however severe the weather in winter, the bonnet he wears indoors. Just as I cannot go loose and unbuttoned, the labourers round about here would feel fettered if they had to button up. Varro contends that, when it was ordained that we should uncover in presence of the gods or the magistracy, it was rather for our health's sake, and to harden us against the inclemency of the weather, than upon the account of reverence.

And since we are on the subject of cold, and being Frenchmen accustomed to array ourselves in motley colours (not I myself, for like my father I seldom wear any but black or white), let me add, in another connexion, that Captain Martin du Bellay relates how, on the march to Luxemburg, he experienced so sharp a frost that the munition wine was cut with an axe or hatchet, and distributed among the soldiers by weight, and that they carried it away in baskets; and Ovid, as near as can be,

> The frozen wines retain the vessel's shape,
> Of which, instead of draughts, they pieces take.

The frosts are so severe at the mouth of the Palus Maeotides,[2] that at the same place where Mithridates' lieutenant had fought a battle, dry-footed, with the enemy and defeated them, when summer was come he again won a naval battle against them. The Romans suffered a great disadvantage, in the engagement they fought with the Carthaginians near to Placentia, in going to the charge with blood stiffened and limbs benumbed with cold; whilst Hannibal had distributed fire throughout his host to warm his soldiers, and each company was provided with oil, wherewith anointing themselves they might render their sinews more supple and active, and encrust their pores against the blasts of air and the icy wind that was then blowing.

The retreat of the Greeks from Babylon to their own country is become famous on account of the hardships and discomforts which they had to surmount. One of them was

---

[1] Henri III and Stephen Bathori.   [2] The Sea of Azov.

that, being met in the mountains of Armenia by a terrible snowstorm, they lost all knowledge of the country and the roads ; and, being thus suddenly besieged, they were a day and night without food, most of their cattle dead, many of themselves dead, many blinded by the driving hail and the dazzling snow, many crippled in their extremities, many stiff, paralysed and unable to move through cold, though in full possession of their senses.

Alexander saw a nation where they bury their fruit-trees in winter to protect them from the frost [; and we may also see the same thing].

Apropos of clothing, the King of Mexico would change his raiment four times a day, never putting on the same again, using his cast-off clothing for his continual charities and rewards ; and neither pot, nor dish, nor other kitchen or table utensil served more than once.

CHAPTER 37

OF CATO THE YOUNGER

I DO not share that common error of judging another by myself. I can readily appreciate in him qualities differing from my own. Although I am tied down to one line of conduct, I do not, as others do, oblige the world to follow it ; and I believe in and conceive a thousand contrary ways of life ; and, unlike the common run of men, I more readily admit our differences than our resemblances. I can excuse, as much as any one could wish, another from possessing my qualities or following my principles, and consider him simply in himself, without relation to others, moulding him to his own model. Though not myself continent, I can none the less sincerely acknowledge the continence of the Feuillants [1] and the Capuchins, and approve their way of life ; I can very easily imagine myself in their place, and love and honour them the more for being other than myself.

I am singular in my desire that we should all be judged apart from others, and that I may not be expected to con-

---

[1] A religious order founded in 1574, about the time this was written, near Toulouse. The monks observed the Cistercian rule, with the addition of several other austerities, such as drinking out of human skulls and eating on the ground.

form to the general pattern. My own weakness in no way alters the good opinion I ought to have of the strength and vigour of those who deserve it: *There are men who praise no action that they are not themselves able to imitate* (Cicero). Crawling in the slime of the earth, I do not fail to exalt even to the clouds the inimitable greatness of some heroic souls. It is a great point in my favour to have a well regulated judgement, though it may not appear in my actions, and to keep at least this sovereign quality free from corruption. It is something to have a good intention when my legs fail me. This age in which we live, in this part of the world at least, is so dull and leaden that, I will not say the exercise, but the mere conception of virtue is lacking: it would seem to be no more than a piece of college jargon;

> Virtue's a phrase, and morals verbal tricks,
> They think, just as a grove is merely sticks; (Horace.)

which they ought to reverence, even though they are unable to comprehend it (Cicero). It is a trinket to hang in a cabinet, or at the tip of the tongue, or to be worn like an ear-ring for ornament.

Virtuous actions are no longer recognized: those which bear the face of them have not the essence, for it is profit, glory, fear, custom, and other such extraneous motives that impel us to perform them. The justice, valour, and courtesy that we exercise under their influence may be so named in respect to others and for the appearance they bear in public; but in the doer they can in no wise be virtuous: they have another end in view, and another motive cause. Now, Virtue will acknowledge nothing that is not done through and for herself alone.

In that great battle of Potidaea[1] which the Greeks under Pausanias gained against Mardonius and the Persians, the victors, according to their custom, coming to divide among them the glory of the exploit, attributed to the Spartan nation the pre-eminence of valour in that encounter. The Spartans, excellent judges of valour, when they came to decide to what individual should be given the honour of having done best on that day, concluded that Aristodemus had hazarded his life more courageously than any; they did not, however, award him the prize, since his virtue had

---

[1] Montaigne wrote Potidaea in mistake for Plataea.

been incited by the desire to cleanse himself of the reproach he had incurred at the action of Thermopyle, and by a craving to die bravely to retrieve his past disgrace.

Our judgement is still sick, and follows the depravity of our manners. I observe most of the wits of my time exercising their ingenuity in obscuring the glory of the noble and generous actions of the ancients, putting some base interpretation on them and inventing for them empty causes and occasions : a great subtlety ! Give me the most excellent and blameless action, and I will straightway provide it with fifty vicious intentions, all having a semblance of likelihood. God knows, if one tried to multiply them, how many different interpretations may be placed on our real intentions ! In all their calumnies their ingenuity is not so much malicious as clumsy and ignorant.

The same pains they take to detract from those great names, and the same licence, I would willingly take to hoist them to a higher plane. I should not dissemble in restoring to honour, as far as my invention will permit, in all the circumstances of favourable interpretation, those rare figures that have been sifted out by the general consent of the wise, as examples to the world. But it may be believed that the efforts of our invention will fall far short of their merit. It is the office of an honest man to paint Virtue in as beautiful colours as he is able, and it would not become us ill if feeling carried us a little beyond ourselves in favour of such time-honoured figures.

What those people do to the contrary they do either out of malice or from the vice of adjusting their belief to their capacity, of which I have just spoken ; or, as I am rather inclined to think, because their sight is not strong and clear enough, or sufficiently trained, to conceive the splendour of Virtue in its native purity. So Plutarch asserts that in his time some attributed the cause of the death of the younger Cato to the fear in which he stood of Caesar ; whereat he is naturally angry, and we may judge from that how much more he would have been offended with those who attributed it to ambition. Foolish people ! He would indeed sooner have performed a noble, just, and generous action with ignominy than for glory. That man was verily a pattern that Nature chose to show to what height human virtue and constancy can reach.

But I am not prepared in this place to discuss so pregnant a theme. My only intention is to match the judgements of five Latin poets contending in their praise of Cato, both in the interest of Cato's fame, and incidentally of their own. Now, a well instructed boy must find the two first rather languid compared with the others; the third more fresh and vigorous, but overcome by the extravagance of his own power; he will conclude that there is still room for one or two degrees of invention to reach up to the fourth, in respect of whom he will raise his hands in admiration. At the last, but first by a long interval, which interval, he will swear, is not to be filled up by any human wit, he will be astounded, he will be speechless.

It is matter for astonishment that we have many more poets than critics and interpreters of poetry. It is easier to write than to recognize it. At a certain low stage it may be judged by precepts and by art. But the good, the supreme, the divine, is above rules and reason. Whoever is able to discern the beauty of it with firm and steady sight sees it no more than he sees the splendour of a lightning flash. It does not beguile our judgement, it transports and overwhelms it. The frenzy that spurs him who is able to penetrate into it also strikes a third person on hearing him discuss and recite it; as a magnet not only attracts a needle, but infuses into it the power of attracting others. This is more clearly seen in the theatre, where the sacred inspiration of the Muses, having first stirred the poet to anger, grief, hatred, and transported him at their will outside of himself, through the poet again strikes the actor, and through the actor consecutively a whole people. It is the chain of our needles hanging one from the other.

From my earliest childhood poetry has had this power to transpierce and transport me. But this very vivid feeling which is natural to me has been differently affected by different styles, not so much higher and lower (for they were always the highest in each kind), as differing in colour: firstly, a gay and ingenious fluency; then a sublime and penetrating subtlety; lastly, a mature and constant power. The examples will tell more: Ovid, Lucan, Virgil. But here are our competitors in the arena.

> Let Cato in life greater than Caesar be! (MARTIAL.)

says one;

> Death vanquished, Cato is invincible, (MANILIUS.)

says the second. And the third, speaking of the civil wars between Pompey and Caesar,

> Each for his cause can vouch a judge supreme:
> The victor, heaven; the vanquished, Cato, thee. (LUCAN.)

And the fourth, on the praises of Caesar,

> And the whole orb of earth subdued,
> Save Cato's unrelenting soul. (HORACE.)

And the master-singer, after displaying on his picture the names of the greatest Romans, ends in this wise:

> There Cato stands, dealing the laws divine. (VIRGIL.)

CHAPTER 38

HOW WE CRY AND LAUGH FOR THE SAME THING

WHEN we read in history that Antigonus was very angry with his son when he produced the head of Pyrrhus, his enemy, whom he had only just fought and slain, and that at the sight of it he began to weep very bitterly; and that the Duke René of Lorraine also lamented the death of Duke Charles of Burgundy, whom he had just defeated, and wore mourning at his funeral; and that at the battle of Auray, which the Comte de Montfort won against Charles de Blois, his competitor for the duchy of Brittany, the victor, coming across the dead body of his enemy, exhibited signs of deep grief, there is no need straightway to exclaim,

> Thus doth the mind oft variously conceal
> Its several passions by a different veil,
> Now with a countenance that's sad, now gay. (PETRARCH.)

When Pompey's head was brought to Caesar, we are told in history that he turned his eyes away, as from an ugly and unpleasant sight. They had been so long intimately associated in the management of public affairs, they had so long shared the same fortunes, so many mutual services had they done to each other, and there had been so many alliances between them, that it must not be believed that that countenance was entirely false and put on, as this other supposes:

> Then when the truth was sure,
> Dissembling love he rose, and tears he shed
> Which flowed at his command, and, glad in heart,
> Forced from his breast a groan. (LUCAN.)

For, although the most part of our actions are in truth but a mask and a veneer, and it may sometimes be true that

> The smiles of heirs are hid behind the mask; (PUBLIUS.)

yet, in judging these manifestations, we must consider how often our soul is stirred by different feelings. And even as our bodies are said to harbour a multitude of conflicting humours, of which that one is mistress which is most usually predominant within us, according to our disposition: so, although our soul be stirred by different impulses, yet there must be one that remains in possession of the field. Not, however, with so absolute a dominion but that, considering its pliancy and mutability, the weaker ones occasionally make a little onslaught in their turn and regain the place. Hence not only do we see children, who in all innocence follow the bidding of Nature, often crying and laughing at the same time; but there is not one of us who can boast, however much he has set his heart on a journey he is starting upon, that, on taking leave of his family and friends, he does not find his courage waver a little; and, though he may not actually shed tears, he will at least put his foot into the stirrup with a sad and gloomy countenance.

Again, however gentle the flame that warms the heart of a well-born maiden, yet has she to be forcibly torn from her mother's neck to be delivered up to her husband, in spite of what this boon companion may say,

> Are the endearments of their plighted lord
> By new-made brides detested and abhorred?
> Sincere the tears, which they profusely pour,
> Soon as they pass the nuptial chamber-door,
> To dash their parents' joy? No! False, I swear
> By all the gods, such tears and such despair! (CATULLUS.)

So it is not strange that a man should lament the death of one whom he would not on any account have alive.

When I scold my valet I scold him with all my heart: my imprecations are real and not feigned; but when the fumes

have passed over, let him but need my help, I willingly
grant it him ; I instantly turn the leaf. When I call him a
silly fool, a calf, I have no intention of sewing those labels
on him for ever ; nor do I think I give myself the lie when
presently after I call him an honest fellow.

There is no one quality that covers us purely and universally. If it were not that it makes one look like a madman to talk to oneself, I should confess that hardly a day
passes on which I may not be heard growling to myself,
' Confound the idiot ! ' And yet I do not intend that to be
my definition.

Whoever imagines, seeing me looking at my wife now
coldly, now fondly, that either look is feigned, is a fool.
Nero, taking leave of his mother whom he was sending to
be drowned, was still sensible of emotion at this maternal
farewell, and had a feeling of horror and pity.

They say that the light of the sun is not continuous, but
that it darts new rays one upon the other so thick and incessantly, that we cannot perceive the intervals :

> The abounding well-spring of the liquid light,
> The ethereal sun, doth flood the heaven o'er
> With constant flux of radiance ever new,
> And with fresh light supplies the place of light,
> Upon the instant. (LUCRETIUS.)

Thus diversely and imperceptibly does our soul dart its
rays.

Artabanus, taking his nephew Xerxes unawares, chid him
for the sudden alteration of his countenance. He was reflecting on the immensity of his army as it was crossing the
Hellespont for the expedition against Greece. He was first
thrilled with joy at the sight of so many thousands of men
in his service, and showed it in his gay and festive looks.
And suddenly, in an instant, his thought suggesting to him
how many lives would wither and die within a century at
the furthest, he knit his brows and was saddened to tears.

We have with resolute will pursued our vengeance for an
injury, and felt a singular satisfaction in the victory, and
yet we weep. It is not for that we weep : there is nothing
changed ; but our mind looks at the matter with a different
eye, and imagines it under another aspect ; for every object
has many angles and throws off many lights. Kinships, old
acquaintances, and friendships seize upon our imagination,

and strongly affect it for the moment, according to their condition; but the turn is so quick that it escapes us.

> Nothing is seen to happen with such speed
> As what the mind proposes and begins;
> Therefore the same bestirs itself more swiftly
> Than aught whose nature's palpable to eyes. (LUCRETIUS.)

And for that reason we are wrong in trying to piece together all these successive feelings. When Timoleon weeps over the murder he has committed with such noble and mature deliberation, he weeps not for the freedom restored to his country, he weeps not for the tyrant, but he weeps for his brother. One part of his duty is performed; let us allow him to perform the other.

CHAPTER 39

OF SOLITUDE

WE will not enter into a lengthy comparison between the active and the solitary life, and as for those fine words under which ambition and avarice take cover, 'That we were not born for our individual selves, but for the public,' let us boldly appeal to those who are in the thick of the dance; and let them cudgel their conscience and ask themselves if on the contrary those positions, those offices, and that hurly-burly of the world are not rather sought after with a view to making private profit at the public expense. The evil means we adopt to push ourselves in these days very clearly show that the end cannot be worth much. Let us reply to ambition, That it is she herself that gives us a taste for solitude; for what does she shun so much as society? What does she seek so much as elbow-room? We may find opportunities anywhere for doing good or evil. However, if the saying of Bias be true, 'that the wicked are in a majority', or that of the Preacher, 'that there is not one good out of a thousand',[1]

> The just are rare, a race so small,
> The gates of Thebes would more than equal all,
> Or the seven mouths of Nile, (JUVENAL.)

the danger of contact with the crowd is great. We must either imitate the vicious or hate them. There is danger,

---

[1] Ecclesiastes vii. 28.

both of resembling them because they are many, and of hating many of them, because they are unlike.[1]

And the traders who go to sea are right to take care that those who join the same ships are not dissolute, blasphemous, and wicked, regarding such company as unlucky. Wherefore Bias said humorously to his shipmates who, during a violent storm at sea, were calling on the gods for help : ' Be silent ; let them not know that you are here with me.' And, in a more urgent case, Albuquerque, Viceroy in the Indies for Emmanuel, King of Portugal, when in extreme peril of shipwreck at sea, took upon his shoulders a young boy, to the sole end that, being partners in fortune, the child's innocence might serve him as a safeguard, and a recommendation to the divine favour to spare his life.

Not but that the wise man can live contented everywhere, and be alone even in a palace crowd ; but if he has the choice, he will flee, he says, the very sight of it. He will endure, if need be, the former, but if it be left to him, he will choose the latter. He will not think himself sufficiently quit of vices, if he still has to contend with those of other men.

Charondas chastised as wicked men those who were convicted of keeping bad company.

There is nothing so unsociable and so sociable as man : the one by his vice, the other by his nature. And Antisthenes does not, in my opinion, give a satisfactory answer to that man who reproved him for associating with the wicked, when he said ' that physicians live indeed with the sick ' : for if they help to restore the sick to health, they impair their own by continually seeing and coming in contact with diseases.

Now the aim of all solitude, I take it, is the same, to live more at one's ease and leisure. But one does not always seek the right way. A man often thinks he has given up business, when he has only exchanged it for another. There is little less worry in governing a household than a whole state ; whatever the mind is busied with, it gives itself entirely up to ; and though domestic occupations be less important, they are no less importunate. Moreover, though

[1] ' But both courses are to be avoided ; you should not copy the bad, simply because they are many, nor should you hate the many, because they are unlike you.'—SENECA, Ep. VII (Gummere's translation).

we are rid of the court and the market-place, we are not rid of the chief vexations of our life :

> Ease and tranquillity of mind are due
> To plain good sense, not to a grand sea-view. (HORACE.)

Ambition, avarice, irresolution, fear and the lusts do not leave us, though we have changed our country ;

> Behind the horseman sits black care. (HORACE.)

They will often follow us even into the cloister and the school of philosophy. Neither deserts, nor rocky caves, nor hair-shirts, nor fastings will rid us of them :

> The fatal shaft sticks in the wounded side. (VIRGIL.)

Somebody said to Socrates that a certain man had not in any way been improved by his travels. 'I quite believe it, he replied ; he took himself along with him.'

> Why quit home to find
> Lands warmed by other suns ? Who, self-exiled,
> Leaves self behind ? (HORACE.)

If we do not at once unburden ourselves and our souls of the load that oppresses us, the motion will make it weigh more heavily : as a ship's cargo is less cumbrous when it has settled down. You do a sick man more harm than good by removing him to another place. The motion shakes the evil down into the sack ; as stakes sink deeper and more firmly into the ground by being stirred and shaken. Wherefore it is not enough to get away from the people ; it is not enough to change to another place : we must get away from the gregarious conditions that are within us ; we must sequester and regain possession of ourselves.

> Can you for that exclaim, ' I've burst my chain ' ?
> No ! for the struggling dog the rope may break,
> Yet as he flies it dangles from his neck. (PERSIUS.)

We carry our fetters along with us : it is not full freedom ; we still turn our eyes to that we have left behind ; our fancy is full of it.

> Unless the breast be purged, what conflicts then,
> What perils, must bosom, in our own despite !
> O then how great and keen the cares of lust
> That split the man distraught ! How great the fears !
> And lo, the pride, grim greed, and wantonness—
> How great the slaughters in their train ! and lo,
> Debaucheries and every breed of sloth ! (LUCRETIUS.)

Our disease is rooted in our soul, and the soul cannot escape from herself ;

> The soul is in fault, which never escapes from itself. (HORACE.)

Therefore the soul must be brought back, and must retire within itself : that is the true solitude, which may be enjoyed in the midst of cities and kings' courts ; but it is enjoyed more comfortably apart.

Now, since we are endeavouring to live alone, and to dispense with society, let us make our contentment to depend on ourselves ; let us cut ourselves adrift from all the ties that bind us to others ; let us so conquer ourselves as to be able to live really alone and then live contentedly.

Stilpo having escaped from the burning of his city, in which he had lost wife, children, and substance, Demetrius Poliorcetes, seeing him amidst the ruins of his home, with face unmoved by fright, asked him if he had not suffered loss. He replied, ' No ; thanks to God, he had lost nothing of his.' [1] The same idea was expressed by the philosopher Antisthenes when he said wittily, ' That man should furnish himself with provisions that float on the water, then he might save them and himself from the shipwreck by swimming.'

Truly the sensible man has lost nothing, if he have himself. When the city of Nola was ruined by the barbarians, Paulinus, who was bishop of that place, having lost everything and being himself their prisoner, prayed to God as follows : ' Lord, keep me from feeling this loss ; for thou knowest that they have yet touched nothing of that which is mine.' The riches that made him rich, and the goods that made him good, were yet in their integrity. See what it is rightly to choose treasures that may be kept from injury, and to hide them in a place where no man comes, and which cannot be betrayed but by ourselves !

We should have wife, children, worldly goods, and, above all, health, if we can ; but not be so strongly attached to them that our happiness depends on them. We must reserve a little back-shop, all our own, entirely free, wherein to establish our true liberty and principal retreat and soli-

---

[1] According to Seneca ; but neither Plutarch nor Diogenes Laertius, when relating this anecdote, mentions the loss of wife and children. The Stoic Seneca exaggerates the resignation of the philosopher.

tude. In this retreat we should keep up our ordinary converse with ourselves, and so private, that no acquaintance or outside communication may find a place there ; there to talk and laugh, as if we had neither wife, nor children, nor worldly goods, retinue or servants : to the end that, should we happen to lose them, it may be no new thing to do without them. We have a soul that can turn upon itself, that can keep company with itself ; it has the wherewithal to attack and defend, to receive and give : let us not fear that in this solitude we shall stagnate in tedious idleness,

> And seem a world with solitude around. (TIBULLUS.)

Virtue, says Antisthenes, is content with herself, without rules, without words, without deeds.

Of our customary actions there is not one in a thousand that concerns ourself. The man that you see scaling that wall in ruins, furious and beside himself, exposed to so many musket-shots ; and that other, all scarred, pale and half-dead with hunger, determined to perish rather than open the gates to him, do you think they are there on their own account ? For one, peradventure, whom they have never set eyes on, and who is quite unconcerned about their fate, and is all the time wallowing in idleness and pleasure.

This other, dirty, dripping from eyes and nose, that you see leaving his study after midnight, do you think he is searching among his books how to become a better, wiser, or more contented man ? Not a bit of it. He will die or he will teach posterity the metre of a line of Plautus, or the correct spelling of a Latin word. Who is there that will not readily exchange health, tranquillity and life for reputation and glory, the most useless, worthless, and false coin in use ? Our own death has not sufficiently frightened us ; let us burden ourselves also with that of our wives, our children and dependants. Our own affairs have not given us sufficient anxiety ; let us also torment and beat our brains over those of our neighbours and friends.

> Good heavens ! That a man
> Should dote so much, or suffer any one
> To wind himself so close about his heart
> As to be dearer to him than himself ! (TERENCE.)

Solitude, I think, is more becoming and more reasonable

in one who has given to the world the most active and vigorous period of his life, after the example of Thales.

We have lived enough for others; let us live for ourselves, at least this remaining bit of life. Let us bring back our thoughts and intentions to ourselves and our comfort. It is no small business to prepare securely one's retirement: it gives us enough to do without the intrusion of any other concerns. Since God gives us permission to arrange for our removal, let us prepare for it; let us pack up our belongings, take leave betimes of the company, and shake off those violent holdfasts that engage us elsewhere and estrange us from ourselves. We must undo those powerful bonds, and from this day forth we may love this and that, but be wedded only to ourselves. That is to say, let the rest be ours, but not joined and glued so firmly to us that it cannot be detached without taking our skin along with it, and tearing away a piece of us. The greatest thing in the world is to know how to belong to ourselves.

It is time to break our ties with society, since we can contribute nothing to it. And he who cannot lend must beware of borrowing. Our powers are failing us: let us withdraw them and concentrate them on ourselves. He who can transmute and turn upon himself the offices of friendship and fellowship, let him do so. In this fallen state which makes him useless, irksome, and troublesome to others, let him take care not to be troublesome to himself, as well as irksome and useless. Let him indulge and cherish, and above all govern himself, respecting and fearing his reason and his conscience to such a degree, that he cannot without shame make a false step in their presence. *For it is a rare thing to see one that sufficiently respects himself* (Quintilian).

Socrates says [1] that the young should be instructed, that grown men should exercise themselves, in well-doing; that the old men should retire from all civil and military employments, living at their discretion without being tied to any fixed office.

There are some natures that are more adapted than others to follow these precepts of retirement. Such as are of weak and slow apprehension, fastidious of taste and inclination, and reluctant to take service or office, whereof I

[1] Not Socrates, but the Pythagoreans.

am one, both by natural disposition and on reflection, will sooner comply with that advice than those active and busy minds that embrace all things, engage themselves everywhere, enter passionately into everything, who offer, who come forward and give themselves on all occasions. We should use those accidental opportunities that lie outside of us, so far as they are agreeable to us, but without making them our mainstay; they are not so: neither reason nor nature desires it.

Why should we, contrary to the laws of reason and nature, make our contentment subject to another's power? To anticipate, moreover, the accidents of fortune; to deprive ourselves of the good things we possess, as many have done from religious motives, and some philosophers in accordance with the dictates of reason; to be slaves to ourselves, to lie hard, to put out our eyes, throw our riches into the river, to court pain (either, as some do, to win the beatitude of another life by torturing ourselves in this, or, like others, to be safe from falling anew by standing on the lowest step), all such are acts of an excessive virtue. Let the strongest and most unbending natures make their hiding-place itself glorious and exemplary:

> When no better I see,
> Oh, the simple, the homely, the humble for me!
> I'm a Stoic with nothing to tempt me. But say
> Something rich or more toothsome shall come in my way,
> 'They only are wise and live well, I protest,
> Who in fine country-places their money invest.' (HORACE.)

I find difficulties enough without going so far as that. It is enough for me, while under Fortune's favours, to prepare for her disfavours, and to picture to myself, whilst I am well off, the ill that is to come, as far as my imagination can reach: just as we exercise ourselves in jousts and tournaments, and mimic wars, in the midst of peace.

I do not regard the philosopher Arcesilaus as less virtuous because he used vessels of gold and silver, as long as the condition of his fortune allowed him to do so; and I esteem him more highly for having used them moderately and liberally, than if he had done away with them.

I know how far our natural necessities extend, and when I see the poor man begging at my door, often more cheerful and healthy than myself, I can imagine myself in his place:

I try to clothe my mind after his measure. And, thus running over all the other examples in my mind, although I may imagine death, poverty, contempt, and disease to be treading on my heels, I easily resolve not to stand in terror of what a meaner man than I accepts with so much patience. And I refuse to believe that a mean understanding can do more than a vigorous one, or that reason cannot attain the same results as habit. And knowing how unstable are these temporary blessings, I do not fail, whilst in the full enjoyment of them, to make it my sovereign request to God to make me content with myself and the good things I bring forth.

I see young men who, notwithstanding their robust health, keep a supply of pills in their trunks, to take when afflicted by a cold, which they fear the less for thinking that they have their remedy near at hand. This must we do ; and, moreover, if we feel ourselves subject to a more serious malady, provide ourselves with drugs to deaden and relieve the part affected.

The occupation we should choose for such a life should be neither laborious nor tedious, otherwise our object in seeking retirement would be frustrated. That depends on the particular taste of each one : mine cannot in any way adapt itself to husbandry. They who love it should apply themselves to it with moderation,

> And strive by outward circumstance to be
> No more controlled, but make it bend to them. (HORACE.)

Agriculture is besides an occupation fit for slaves, as Sallust calls it. Some of its branches are more excusable, such as the care of gardens, to which, according to Xenophon, Cyrus was devoted, and a mean may be found between that abject and servile solicitude, that intense anxiety we see in men who are entirely immersed in it, and that extreme and rooted negligence that allows things to go to rack and ruin, that we may see in others :

> Why marvel we if, whilst his soul,
> Of body heedless, swept the pole,
> Democritus allowed his beeves
> Make havoc of his plants and sheaves ? (HORACE.)

But let us give ear to the counsel that the younger Pliny gives to his friend Caninius Rufus, on this matter of solitude: 'I counsel you, in the full and prosperous retreat wherein you are, to leave to your slaves the humble and sordid cares of managing your estate, and devote yourself to the study of letters, in order to derive something from them that shall be entirely your own.' He means reputation; he is of a like mind with Cicero, when he said he would employ his solitude and retirement from public affairs in acquiring by his writings an immortal life:

> Is then your knowledge absolutely nought
> Unless another know you have that knowledge? (PERSIUS.)

It seems only reasonable, when a man speaks of retiring from the world, that he should look outside of it. These people only half do it. They indeed arrange all their affairs for the time when they shall be no longer here; but, by a ridiculous contradiction, they still expect to reap the fruit of their action from the world on which they have turned their backs.

The idea of those who seek solitude from religious motives, filling their hearts with the certainty of the divine promises in the next life, is much more consistent with sanity. They keep God before their eyes, as an object infinite in goodness and power; there the soul has the wherewithal to satisfy its desires in all freedom. Pain and affliction come to them as a gain, being suffered for the acquisition of eternal health and gladness; death as a thing wished for, as a passage to so perfect a state. The asperity of their rules of discipline is at once made smooth by habit; and the carnal appetites are lulled and kept down by being denied, for nothing keeps them active but use and exercise. This prospect alone of another happily immortal life truly deserves that we should abandon the comforts and sweets of this our present life. And he who can really and constantly kindle his soul with the flame of that living faith and hope, builds himself in solitude a delicious and voluptuous life, transcending any other kind of life.

I am satisfied therefore neither with the end nor the means of that advice [1]: it still only means falling out of an ague into a burning fever.

Occupation with books is as laborious as any other, and as great an enemy to health, which should be the chief con-

---

[1] Pliny's advice to Rufus.

sideration. And we should not allow ourselves to be lulled to sleep by the pleasure we take in it: it is the same pleasure that ruins the economist, the miser, the voluptuary, and the man of ambition. The sages teach us often enough to beware of the treachery of our appetites, and to distinguish the true and entire pleasures from pleasures that are mixed and interlarded with more pain. For most of our pleasures, they say, caress and embrace us only to strangle us, like the thieves the Egyptians called Philistas.[1] And if the headache preceded the intoxication we should take care not to drink too much. But pleasure, to deceive us, walks before and conceals her retinue.

Books are pleasant companions, but if by associating with them we end by losing gaiety and health, our best possessions, let us leave them. I am one of those who believe that our enjoyment of them cannot outweigh this loss. As men who, having long felt themselves weakened by some indisposition, at length place themselves at the mercy of physicians, and have certain rules of living prescribed to them by art, which are not to be transgressed: so he who retires, wearied and disgusted with everyday life, must model this retired life by the rules of reason, arrange and order it with premeditation and reflection. He must take leave of every kind of labour, in any shape or form, and flee, in general, the passions that hinder the tranquillity of body and soul,

And choose the way that suits his humour best. (PROPERTIUS.)

From husbandry, study, the chase, and any other pursuit he should get all the pleasure he possibly can, but beware of being drawn into them any further, where the pleasure begins to be a labour. He must reserve only so much business and occupation as is needful to keep him in breath, and save him from the evil consequences which the other extreme of slack and sleepy idleness brings with it.

There are sterile and thorny sciences, for the most part invented for public life; we must leave them to those who are engaged in the service of the world. For my part, I love such books as are either easy and entertaining, and that tickle

---

[1] *Philistas,* an error on the part of Montaigne or his printers for *Philetas,* as they were called by the Egyptians, according to Seneca.

my fancy, or such as give me comfort, and offer counsel in reordering my life and death;

> Sauntering silent through the healthful woods,
> In lonely reveries devising what
> May best engage a wise and good man's thought. (HORACE.)

Wiser men, possessed of a strong and vigorous soul, may create for themselves a wholly spiritual repose. I, with my commonplace soul, have to bring my bodily advantages to my aid; and age having of late robbed me of those pleasures that were more to my fancy, I train and sharpen my appetite to those that remain and are more fitting to this later season. We must cling tooth and nail to the pleasures of life, which our years tear, one after another, from our hands:

> Pluck we life's sweets; to-morrow we shall be
> A little dust, a ghost, a gossip's tale. (PERSIUS.)

Now, as to setting up glory as a goal, as Pliny and Cicero do, that is very far from my reckoning. The humour that is most incompatible with retirement is ambition. Glory and repose are two things that cannot lie in the same bed. As far as I can see, those two men have only their arms and legs out of the throng; their souls and intentions are more than ever in the thick of it:

> Dost thou in thy advancing years
> Cull dainty bits for others' ears? (PERSIUS.)

They have only stepped back to take a better jump and to hurl themselves with a stronger impetus further into the crowd. Would you see how they shoot short by a grain's length? Let us counterbalance their advice with that of two philosophers,[1] of two very different sects, writing, the one to Idomeneus, the other to Lucilius, their friends, to induce them to give up the management of public affairs and their high positions, and retire into solitude. 'You have hitherto, they say, lived swimming and floating; come now and die in harbour. You have given the first part of your life to light; give the other remaining part to the shade. It is impossible to give up your occupations, if you do not give up the fruits of them; therefore put away all care for reputation and glory. There is a danger lest the

---

[1] Epicurus and Seneca.

light of your past actions may dazzle you too much, and follow you even into your den. Quit with the other pleasures that which comes from others' approval; and as to your learning and talents, give yourself no concern about them: they will not lose their effect, if you yourselves are the better for them. Remember the man who, when he was asked to what purpose he took so much pains in an art which would come to the knowledge of few persons, replied: Few will suffice me; one, nay, less than one will suffice me. He spoke truly. You and a companion are a sufficient stage for one another, or you for yourself. Let the people be to you one, and let one be to you a whole people. It is a poor ambition to wish to extract glory from our idleness and hiding-place. We should do like those animals that remove the traces of their footsteps at the entrance to their lair. What you should concern yourself about is not that the world should talk about you, but how you should talk to yourself. Retire within yourself; but first prepare to receive yourself there: it would be madness to trust to yourself if you cannot govern yourself. There are ways of going wrong in solitude as well as in company. Until you have made yourself such that you dare not trip in your own presence, and until you are ashamed and stand in awe of yourself,—*let noble ideas be present to your mind* (Cicero);— keep ever before your mind Cato, Phocion, and Aristides, in whose presence the very fools would hide their errors, and appoint them controllers of all your intentions; should these get off the track, your reverence for those will set them right again. They will keep you in the way to be contented with yourself, to borrow nothing but of yourself, to keep your mind firmly fixed on definite and limited thoughts in which it may take pleasure; and, having understood the true blessings that one enjoys the more one understands them, to rest content with them, without any desire to prolong life and reputation.'

That is the counsel of true and natural philosophy, not of ostentatious and prating philosophy, like that of the first two.[1]

[1] Pliny the younger and Cicero.

CHAPTER 40

A CONSIDERATION UPON CICERO

ONE more point in the comparison of these two pairs of writers.[1] From the writings of Cicero and of this Pliny (who in my opinion takes little after his uncle in disposition), we may gather numberless evidences of a nature ambitious beyond measure, among others that, as all the world knows, they solicit the historians of their time not to forget them in their annals, and Fortune, as if in spite, has preserved till our day the vanity of these requests, and has long ago consigned those histories to perdition. But what exceeds every kind of vulgarity in men of their rank is their endeavouring to extract any great fame from gossip and tittle-tattle, and going so far as to publish, with that end in view, their private letters to their friends;[2] with the result that, when some of these letters, having missed their opportunity, were never sent, they were published all the same, with this worthy excuse that the writers were unwilling to lose their labour and midnight oil. Is it not a becoming thing for two Roman consuls, sovereign magistrates of the empress republic of the world, to employ their leisure time in daintily piecing together and arranging a pretty missive, to gain a reputation for having a good command of the language of their nurses! What could a simple schoolmaster do worse, who was making a living by it? If the deeds of Xenophon and Caesar had not by a long way surpassed their eloquence, I do not think they would ever have recorded them in writing. They sought to recommend, not their sayings, but their doings.

And if the perfection of fine speech could bring any glory befitting a great personage, certainly Scipio and Laelius would not have resigned the honour of their comedies, and all the charms and daintinesses of the Latin tongue, to an African slave: for that that work was theirs is sufficiently testified by its beauty and excellence, and Terence himself

---

[1] Pliny and Cicero, Epicurus and Seneca.

[2] Montaigne appears to be doing Cicero an injustice, in accusing him of writing his letters with a view to publication. This is especially true of the seventy letters he wrote to Atticus, the only ones he himself preserved. In Book II, Chapter 10, Montaigne again refers to Cicero's letters.

admits it.[1] And I should be highly displeased to be dispossessed of this belief.

It is a kind of mockery and insult to try to make a man's worth depend on qualities unbecoming his rank, though they may be otherwise commendable, and on qualities also which ought not to be his chief qualities ; as if a king were praised for being a good painter or a good architect, or even a good marksman or ring-tilter. These praises bring no honour, unless they be presented in the lump, and after those which are appropriate to him, to wit, justice and the art of leading his people in peace and war. From this point of view agriculture does honour to Cyrus, eloquence and the knowledge of good letters to Charlemagne. In my time I have known eminent men, who were writers by title and calling, to disown in stronger terms their apprenticeship, to corrupt their style, affect an ignorance of so vulgar an accomplishment (which is held by our people to be hardly compatible with learning), and recommend themselves by better qualities.

The companions of Demosthenes in the embassy to Philip praised that prince for his beauty, his eloquence, and his prowess in drinking ; Demosthenes said that those were praises more appropriate to a woman, a lawyer, and a sponge, than to a king ;

> First still in war, may he when war is done
> The conquered spare ! (HORACE.)

It is not his profession to be a good hunter or a good dancer :

> Let others plead their causes at the law
> More deftly, trace the motions of the skies
> With learned rod, and tell the stars that rise.
> Let this man rule, and o'er the world proclaim
> The ways of peace. (VIRGIL.)

Plutarch says besides that to appear so proficient in these less necessary accomplishments is to produce testimony against oneself of having made a bad use of one's leisure and study, which should be employed in more

---

[1] Montaigne here goes a little too far. The charge brought against Terence by his enemies, he tells us in his Prologue to the *Adelphi*, was that certain 'homines nobiles' assisted him and wrote with him, and this he says he regarded as his greatest merit. It would be interesting to know what would have been Montaigne's attitude in the Bacon-Shakespeare controversy.

necessary and profitable things. So Philip, King of Macedon, hearing the great Alexander, his son, sing at a banquet, in emulation with the best musicians, said to him, 'Are you not ashamed to sing so well?' And to this same Philip a musician with whom he was disputing about his art said, 'God forbid, Sire, that such a misfortune should ever befall you as to understand these things better than I!'

A king should be able to reply as Iphicrates did to an orator who showered invectives upon him, in this manner: 'Well! and what are you, that you should hector it thus? are you a man-at-arms? are you an archer? are you a pikeman?' 'I am none of all these; but I am one who can command them all.'

And Antisthenes, hearing Ismenias being extolled as an excellent flute-player, argued that he could not be much good at anything else.

I know well, when I hear some one expatiating on the style of these Essays, that I would rather he held his peace. It is not so much to extol the words as to depreciate the sense; and the more indirectly it is done, the more galling it is. Yet I am mistaken if there are many others who offer their readers a matter more fertile in reflections, and if any writer has scattered more material, whether good or bad, or at least has scattered it as thickly, on his paper. I amass only the heads of ideas, in order to include more. For if I should draw the conclusions from them, I should multiply this volume several times over. And how many stories have I not spread over the book, which tell us nothing, but in which any one who analyses them a little more skilfully will find matter for numberless essays! Neither those tales nor my quotations are always intended merely as examples, as authorities or embellishments. I do not regard them solely for the use I make of them. They often bear, outside of my purpose, the seeds of a richer and bolder matter; and obliquely sound a more subtle note, both for myself, who am not going to be more explicit, and for those who will catch my meaning.[1]

To come back to the talkative virtue, I find no great

---

[1] A difficult passage, but very significant. It is in fact a word to the wise, and a hint that they must often read between the lines, since in political and religious matters Montaigne was obliged to observe a certain reticence. The whole paragraph is an interpolation.

choice between being able to speak only badly, and being able to speak only well. *Elegance of style is no ornament worthy of a man* (Seneca). The wise say that with regard to knowledge only philosophy, and with regard to actions only virtue, are generally suited to all ranks and classes.

There is something in common between our two letter-writers and those other two philosophers,[1] for these too promise immortality to the letters they write to their friends; but in a different way, and by flattering, for a good end, the vanity of others: for they send them word that, if it is desire for renown and being known to future ages that still makes them cling to the management of public affairs, and fear the solitude and retirement to which they would invite them, they may set their minds at rest, inasmuch as the writers have sufficient credit with posterity to guarantee that the letters alone which they write to them will make their names as famous and well known as any of their own public actions could do. There is this difference too, that these letters are not empty and marrowless epistles, that are merely held together by a delicate choice of words heaped up and disposed in correct rhythmic order, but discourses stuffed with sage counsel, by reading which we may become wiser if not more eloquent, and learn, not to speak well, but to do well. Fie on that eloquence which makes us love itself and not its matter! Unless we admit that Cicero's, being so extremely perfect, gives itself body and substance.

I may here add a tale that we read about him and which is to the point, as it enables us to lay a finger on his real nature. He had to deliver a harangue in public, and was a little pressed for time to prepare it at leisure. Eros, one of his slaves, came and informed him that the meeting was postponed till the next day. He was so rejoiced that in return for the good news he gave him his freedom.

On the subject of letter-writing I may say a word, namely, that it is a kind of work in which my friends maintain that I have some ability. And I should have preferred publishing my fancies in that form, if I had had somebody to converse with. I needed, what I once had,[2] a certain interchange of ideas that would lead me on, that would sustain

[1] Epicurus and Seneca.
[2] A reference, no doubt, to his friend Étienne de la Boëtie.

and lift me up. For, as for talking at random, as others do, or inventing empty names to discourse with on a serious matter, I could only do so in dreams, sworn enemy as I am to every kind of falsification. I could have addressed myself with more confidence and attention to a person I loved and respected, than I now do, having to consider the various tastes of a public audience. And, if I am not mistaken, I should have been more successful. I have naturally a humorous and familiar style, but of a form quite my own, ill adapted for public transactions, as indeed my language is in every way, being too compact, irregular, disconnected and individual; and I have no skill in writing letters of ceremony that have no other substance but a fine string of courteous phrases. I have neither taste nor faculty for those long-drawn-out offers of service and affection. I do not sufficiently believe in them, and dislike saying much more than I myself believe. This is very remote from the present practice, for there never was so abject and servile a prostitution of compliments: Life, Soul, Devotion, Worship, Servant, Slave, all these words are in such common circulation that when they wish sincerely to profess a more positive and respectful feeling, they have no more words to express it.

I have a mortal hatred of being thought a flatterer, and for that reason I naturally drop into a dry, plain, and blunt way of speaking, which to one who does not otherwise know me may appear a little disdainful. I honour most those on whom I expend the fewest marks of honour; and, where my soul walks with a great joy, I forget to control my looks and outward demeanour. My protestations to those whom I regard as friends are meagre but bold. I pay the fewest compliments to those I am most devoted to: I feel that they should read them in my heart, and understand that my expressed words fall short of my meaning.

In welcoming, in taking leave, in thanking and greeting, in offering my services and such like wordy compliments which the ceremonious laws of our civility enjoin, I know of nobody who is so stupidly barren of words as I am. And I have never been asked for a letter of favour or recommendation but he for whom it was written thought it dry and lukewarm.

The Italians are great printers of letters. I have, I should

CH. 40 HATRED OF FLATTERY AND COMPLIMENTS

think, a hundred several volumes of them; those of Annibale Caro seem to me the best. If all the paper I have once besmeared for the ladies, when my hand was really carried away by my passion, were now in existence, there might peradventure be found a page or two worthy to be communicated to our idle youth who are infatuated with this mania.

I always write my letters post-haste, and so hurriedly that, although my hand is intolerably bad,[1] I prefer writing myself rather than employ another, for I cannot find any one able to follow me, and I never transcribe. I have accustomed the great ones who know me to tolerate my scratching out words and substituting others, and a paper without fold or margin. Those that cost me most trouble are the most worthless: when once they begin to drag, it is a sign that my heart is not in them. I usually begin without any plan: the first word begets the second. The letters of this age consist more in embroideries and in preambles than in matter. As I would rather compose two letters than close and fold up one, which charge I always resign to another; so, when I have come to the end of the substance of my letter, I would gladly commission another to add all those long declarations, offers, and prayers that we tack on to the end. I could wish that some new custom would relieve us of all that, as well as of inscribing them with a tiresome enumeration of titles and qualities. In order not to stumble in these I have many a time refrained from writing, especially to lawyers and financiers. There are so many newly created offices, so difficult a distribution and arrangement of different titles of honour, which, having been so dearly bought, cannot be confused or forgotten without giving offence. I likewise regard it as bad taste to cover with these the title-pages and inscriptions of the books we print.[2]

---

[1] Montaigne's handwriting is, on the contrary, perfectly legible.

[2] Montaigne was not always of this opinion. When he published his first Essays he seemed particularly anxious to display all his titles on the title-page.

CHAPTER 41

OF NOT COMMUNICATING ONE'S HONOUR

OF all the visionary ideas in the world, the most universally received is the solicitude about reputation and glory, to which we are so wedded that we are ready to abandon wealth, repose, life and health, which are real and substantial blessings, in order to follow that vain phantom and simple sound, which has neither body nor substance.[1]

> That fame that charms with sweet alluring sound
> Proud mortals, and appears to them so fair,
> Is but an echo, a dream, the shadow of a dream,
> Dispersed abroad by every breath of air. (TASSO.)

And of the irrational humours of men it would seem that even the philosophers put away this one more tardily and more reluctantly than any other.

It is the most intractable and stubborn of all, *because it ceases not to assail even well disciplined minds* (St. Augustine). There is perhaps not another whose vanity is so clearly condemned by reason, but it has such live roots in us, that I know not if any man has been able ever to tear himself clean away from it. Even if you have voiced and believed all the arguments for rejecting it, it will produce within you, in opposition to your reason, so inward a bias, that you will have little power to withstand it.

For, as Cicero says, the very men who combat it still desire that the books they write about it shall bear their names on their titles, and endeavour to derive glory from the contempt of glory. All other things become interchangeable: we lend our goods and our lives to our friends' needs; but to communicate one's honour and bestow one's glory on another, that is rarely seen.

Catulus Luctatius, in the war against the Cimbrians, having done his utmost to check his soldiers who were fleeing before the enemy, joined the fugitives and played the coward, that they might appear to be following their captain rather than flying from the enemy: that was to abandon his reputation to cover others' disgrace.

When the Emperor Charles the Fifth entered Provence

[1] 'What is honour? a word. What is that word honour? air. A trim reckoning.' (Falstaff in *King Henry IV*, Pt. I.)

in the year 1537, it is thought that Antonio de Leyva, although he saw that his master was resolved upon this expedition, and believed that it would add very greatly to his glory, yet expressed the contrary opinion and counselled him against it; to the end that all the honour and glory of the plan might be attributed to his master, and that it might be said that his good judgement and foresight had been such, that he had carried out such a noble enterprise against the advice of all: which was to honour his master at his own expense.

The Thracian ambassadors, condoling with Archileonida, the mother of Brasidas, on the death of her son, and praising him so highly as to say that he had not left his like behind him, she rejected that private and particular praise, to give it back to the public: 'Do not tell me that, she replied; I know that the city of Sparta has many greater and more valiant citizens than he was.'

At the battle of Crécy, the Prince of Wales, still a very young man, was in charge of the vanguard, and the chief stress of the encounter lay in his quarter. The lords who accompanied him, finding themselves very hard pressed, sent word to King Edward to approach and succour them. He inquired about his son's condition, and being answered that he was alive and on horseback, he said: 'I should do him wrong now to rob him of the honour of victory in this combat that he has so long sustained; whatever be the risk he is running, it shall be all his own.' And he would neither go nor send, knowing that, if he had gone, it would have been said that all was lost without his aid: *it is always the last weight added that has the credit of turning the balance* (Livy).

Many at Rome thought, and would commonly tell each other, that the chief of Scipio's fine deeds were in part due to Lelius, who, however, always went about promoting and seconding the greatness and glory of Scipio, without any care about his own. And Theopompus, King of Sparta, to one who said that the Republic remained on its feet because he could rule well, replied: 'Say rather because the people know how to obey well.'

Like those women who, having succeeded to a peerage, had the right, notwithstanding their sex, to attend and vote in the cases which appertained to the jurisdiction of the peers ; so also the ecclesiastical peers, notwithstanding their profession, were bound to assist our kings in their wars, not only with their friends and retainers, but also in person. The Bishop of Beauvais, being with Philip Augustus at the battle of Bouvines, very bravely participated in the success; but he regarded it as his duty not to touch the fruit and glory of this bloody and violent practice of fighting. With his own hand he forced many of the enemy to surrender to him on that day, and delivered them to the first gentleman he came across, to cut their throats or make them prisoners, resigning to him the whole execution. Thus he delivered William, Earl of Salisbury, to Messire Jean de Nesle. With a like subtlety of conscience he was willing to club a man to death, but not to wound him, and for that reason only fought with a mace.

Somebody in my time being reproved by the King for having laid hands on a priest, he strongly and stoutly denied it, meaning that he had only cudgelled and kicked him.

CHAPTER 42

OF THE INEQUALITY THAT IS AMONGST US

PLUTARCH says somewhere that he does not find so great a difference between one animal and another as between one man and another. He is speaking of the perfections and internal qualities of the soul. In truth I can see such a distance between Epaminondas, as I imagine him, and certain men I know, I mean men capable of common sense, that I should be inclined to overbid Plutarch and say that there is more difference between this man and that man than between this man and that animal;

> Ye Gods, how much one man excels another! (TERENCE.)

and that there are as many degrees in minds as there are cubits between here and heaven, and as innumerable.

But, speaking of the estimate of men, it is strange that, excepting ourselves, nothing is estimated but by its proper qualities. We praise a horse for its strength and speed,

> Is it not thus we praise the impatient steed,
> Whose easy triumph and transcendent speed
> Palm after palm proclaim—while victory
> In the hoarse Circus stands exulting by! (JUVENAL.)

not on account of its harness ; a greyhound for its swiftness
and not its collar ; a hawk for its wing and not for its jesses
and bells. Why then do we not value a man for what is his ?
He has a great retinue, a fine palace, so much influence, so
much income : all that is around him, not within him. You
do not buy a cat in a bag. If you bargain over a horse, you
remove its trappings, you see it bare and uncovered ; or, if it
is covered, as they were formerly shown to princes for sale,
it is only as to the less important parts, that you may not
waste your admiration on the beauty of its colour or the
breadth of its crupper, but pay attention chiefly to its legs,
its eyes and feet, which are the most useful parts,

> The custom is with princes not to buy
> A steed uncovered, lest they be deceived
> By crupper round, short head and ample chest
> Planted upon soft hooves and groggy legs. (HORACE.)

Why, when estimating a man, do you estimate him all
wrapped and muffled up ? He exhibits only those parts
which are in no wise his, and conceals from us those by
which alone we may really judge of his value. It is the price
of the sword you seek to know, not of the scabbard. You
will perhaps not give a farthing for him when you see him
stripped. We must judge him by himself, not by his attire.
And, as one of the ancients [1] says very wittily : ' Do you
know why you think him tall ? you are counting in the
height of his pattens.' The pedestal is no part of the
statue. Measure him without his stilts : let him lay aside
his riches and his honours, and show himself in his shirt.
Has he a body equal to his functions, sound and active ?
What mind has he ? is it beautiful, capable, happily furnished with all its parts ? Is it rich with its own store, or
with that of others ? has fortune nothing to do with it ?
Will his soul with open eyes face a naked sword ? does she
care how life goes from her, whether by the mouth or by
the throat ? is she sedate, even-tempered, contented ?
That is what we should consider, and thereby judge of the
extreme differences that lie between us. Is he

> The wise man, who
> Can at all times himself subdue,—
> Whom neither want, nor death, nor chains
> Appal,—who manfully restrains

[1] Seneca.

> His appetites, nor cares to win
> Titles or honours, and, within,
> Himself self-centred and complete,
> Life's chance and change can frankly meet—
> Yea, front the heaviest blows of fate
> With courage constant and sedate ? (HORACE.)

such a man is five hundred cubits above kingdoms and duchies ; he is an empire in himself.

> That man indeed is wise
> Who his own fortune can devise. (PLAUTUS.)

What more can he desire ?

> O not to see that nature for herself
> Barks after nothing, save that pain keep off,
> Disjoined from the body, and that mind enjoy
> Delightsome feeling, far from care and fear ! (LUCRETIUS.)

Compare him with the ruck of mankind, stupid, degraded, servile, unstable, and continually fluctuating in the storm of varying passions, which drive him hither and thither, and entirely dependent on others : there is a greater distance than between heaven and earth ; and yet we are so blinded by custom, that we make little or no account of it ; whereas, if we look at a peasant and a king, a noble and a serf, a magistrate and a private individual, a rich man and a poor, there immediately appears to our eyes an extreme disparity, although they differ, in a manner of speaking, only in their breeches.

In Thrace the king was distinguished from his people in a ludicrous and very exclusive way. He had a religion to himself, a god all his own, whom it was not meet for his subjects to worship : that was Mercury ; and he for his part disdained their gods, Mars, Bacchus, and Diana.

Yet they are but coats of paint that make no essential difference. For, like the actors in a comedy, you see them upon the platform putting on the airs of a duke or an emperor ; but immediately after behold them again become wretched varlets and porters, which is their true and original condition.

So the Emperor, whose pomp dazzled you in public,

> And (as ye may be sure)
> Big emeralds of green light are set in gold ;
> And rich sea-purple dress by constant wear
> Grows shabby and all soaked with Venus' sweat ; (LUCRETIUS.)

see him behind the curtain: he is nothing but an ordinary mortal, and perchance meaner than the least of his subjects. *This one is inwardly happy; the other's happiness is on the surface* (Seneca). He is moved by cowardice, irresolution, ambition, spite and envy, like any other man;

> For hoarded treasures cannot keep
> Disquietudes at bay,
> Nor can the Consul's lictor drive away
> The brood of dark solicitudes, that sweep
> Round gilded ceilings gay; (HORACE.)

and fear and anxiety hold him by the throat in the midst of his armies;

> And of a truth man's dread, with cares at heels,
> Fears not these sounds of arms, these savage swords,
> But among kings and lords of all the world
> Mingles undaunted, nor is overawed
> By gleam of gold. (LUCRETIUS.)

Do fevers, the megrims, and the gout spare him any more than they do us? When old age weighs upon his shoulders, will the archers of his guard relieve him of it? When he is paralysed by the fear of death, will he be reassured by the presence of the gentlemen of his chamber? When he is in a jealous and capricious mood, will our bonnetings compose him? That bed-tester, all bloated with gold and pearls, has no virtue to allay the gripings of an acute colic:

> Nor yet the quicker will hot fevers go
> If on a pictured tapestry thou toss,
> Or purple robe, than if 'tis thine to lie
> Upon the poor man's bedding. (LUCRETIUS.)

The flatterers of the great Alexander made him believe that he was a son of Jupiter; one day, being wounded and seeing the blood flow from his wound, he said, 'Well, what say you? is not this a crimson and purely human blood? It is not of the thickness of that which Homer makes to flow from the wounds of the gods.' Hermodorus the poet had written some lines in honour of Antigonus, in which he called him son of the sun; but he contradicted him, saying: 'The man who empties my stool knows very well that I am nothing of the kind.'

When all's said he is but a man, and if he be of ignoble birth, the empire of the universe could not reclothe him.

> Let maidens fly his smiles to greet,
> And roses spring about his feet! (PERSIUS.)

What if after all his soul be gross and stupid ? Even pleasure and happiness are not felt without vigour and spirit.

> Yet these all take their value from the mind
> Of the possessor : he that knows their use
> To him they're blessings ; he that knows it not
> To him misuse converts them into curses. (TERENCE.)

The blessings of fortune of every kind yet require the right sense to relish them. It is the enjoying, not the possessing, that makes us happy :

> Nor house, nor lands, nor brass, nor golden store
> Can of its fire the fevered brain relieve,
> Or make the care-fraught spirit cease to grieve.
> Sound, mind and body both, should be his health
> To true account who hopes to turn his wealth.
> Fortune nor home not more the man can cheer,
> Who lives a prey to covetise or fear,
> Than may a picture's richest hues delight
> Eyes that with dropping rheum are thick of sight,
> Or warm soft lotions soothe a gout-racked foot. (HORACE.)

He is a fool, his palate is blunt and dulled ; he no more enjoys what he has than one with a cold in the head can appreciate the mellowness of Greek wine, or a horse the richness of the trappings that adorn it ; just as, according to Plato, health, beauty, strength, riches, and everything we call good, are as great an evil to the unjust as they are a blessing to the just ; and the evil contrariwise.

And then, where body and mind are in evil plight, what avail these external advantages, seeing that the least prick of a pin and suffering of the soul is enough to rob us of the pleasure of being monarch of the world ? At the first twitch of the gout, in spite of his Sire and Majesty,

> All bloated with silver, all bloated with gold, (TIBULLUS.)

will he not forget all about his palaces and his grandeurs ? If he is in anger, will his princedom keep him from turning red or pale, from grinding his teeth like a madman ? Now, if he be a man of parts and well-endowed by Nature, royalty will add little to his happiness :

> Let your digestion be but sound,
> Your side unwrung by spasm or stitch,
> Your foot unconscious of a twitch ;
> Then could you be more truly blest,
> Though you the wealth of kings possest ? (HORACE.)

he will see that it is all a snare and a delusion. Yea, he

would peradventure agree with King Seleucus, 'That if a man knew the weight of a sceptre, he would not stoop to pick it up if he saw it lying on the ground.' He was thinking of the great and laborious charges incumbent upon a good king.

Truly it is no little thing to have to rule others, since ruling ourselves presents so many difficulties. As for commanding, which appears so smooth, I am strongly of opinion, considering the imbecility of human judgement and the difficulty of choice in things that are new and doubtful, that it is much easier and more pleasant to follow than to guide; and that it is very restful to the mind to have to keep to a beaten track, and to have itself alone to answer for:

> So better far in quiet to obey,
> Than to desire chief mastery of affairs
> And ownership of empires. (LUCRETIUS.)

Add to this that saying of Cyrus, that no man is fit to rule who is not better than those he rules.

But King Hiero, in Xenophon, says further, that in the enjoyment even of pleasures, kings are worse off than private individuals, inasmuch as the ease and facility rob them of the bitter-sweet sting we find in them.

> Fat love and too much fulsome me annoys,
> Even as sweet meat a glutted stomach cloys. (OVID.)

Do you think that the chorister-boys take a great pleasure in music? Satiety rather makes it tedious to them. Feasts, dances, masquerades, and tourneys delight such as seldom see them and have desired to see them; but to him to whom they are an ordinary fare they become stale and unpleasant. Nor do the ladies gratify him who has his fill of them. He who does not give himself time to be thirsty, can take no pleasure in drinking. The farces of the mountebanks delight us, but to the actors they are a drudgery. And that this is so we may see in the diversions of princes, to whom it is a great treat to be able sometimes to put on disguise, and stoop to a low and plebeian way of living:

> It is the rich who relish best
>   To dwell at times from state aloof;
> And simple suppers, neatly dressed,
>   Beneath a poor man's humble roof,
> With neither pall nor purple there,
> Have smoothed ere now the brow of care. (HORACE.)

There is nothing so clogging and so distasteful as abundance. What desire would not be repelled to see three hundred women at its disposal, such as the Grand Turk has in his seraglio ? And what relish for sport and what form of it can that ancestor of his have retained who never went a-hunting without seven thousand falconers ?

Moreover, I believe that this lustre of grandeur is attended with no small drawbacks in the enjoyment of the more delightful pleasures : the great are too much in the limelight and exposed to the public view. And, I know not for what reason, we expect them, more than we do others, to cover up and hide their errors. For what in us is indiscretion, in them the people deem to be tyranny, contempt and slighting of the laws ; and, besides their proclivity to vice, it would seem that they take an additional pleasure in reviling public observances and treading them under foot. Plato, indeed, in his *Gorgias*, defines a Tyrant as one who has a licence to do all that pleases him in a city. And often, for that reason, the public display of the vices offends more than the vice itself. Every man fears being spied upon and overlooked ; princes, even as regards their demeanour and their thoughts, are under observation, since all the people think they have a right and an interest in judging them ; besides that blemishes are magnified according to the eminence and brightness of the place where they are set : as a mole or wart on the forehead is more conspicuous than a scar in any other place.

For that reason the poets imagine the amours of Jupiter to be conducted under different disguises ; of all the amorous adventures ascribed to him there is only one, it seems to me, where he appears in his majesty and grandeur.

But let us return to Hiero : he also tells of the many disadvantages he is sensible of in his kingship, in being unable to go about and travel in freedom, in being as it were a prisoner within the bounds of his country, and in finding himself encircled in all his actions by an importunate crowd. In truth, to see our kings all alone at table, besieged by so many talkers and strange onlookers, I have often been moved to pity rather than envy of them.

King Alphonso used to say that in this respect asses were better off than kings : their masters allow them to graze in peace, whilst kings cannot obtain that favour of their own servants.

And I have never been able to imagine why it should be so remarkable a convenience in the life of an intelligent man to have a score of people overlooking his close-stool; nor why the services of a man with an income of ten thousand pounds, or who has taken Casale or defended Siena, should be more convenient and acceptable than those of a good and experienced footman.

Princely advantages are quasi-imaginary advantages. Every degree of fortune has some semblance of principality: Caesar called all the lords in France who administered justice in his time, kinglets. Indeed, saving the title of 'Sire', we are coming very near to being kings. Consider, in the provinces remote from the court, taking Brittany as an example, the retinue, the vassals, the officers, the occupations, the services and ceremonies of a retired and home-keeping lord, brought up among his servants. And look at the flight of his imagination, than which there is nothing more regal. He hears speak of his master once in a year, as he might of the King of Persia, and only acknowledges him by some ancient cousinship of which his secretary keeps a record. In truth our laws are free enough, and the weight of sovereignty is hardly felt twice in a lifetime by a French nobleman. The real and actual subjection only concerns those of us who agree to accept it and who prefer to gain honours and riches by such service: for he who is content to live in obscurity by his own fireside, and is able to manage his house and family without quarrels and lawsuits, is as free as the Doge of Venice. *Slavery holds few; more hold fast to slavery* (Seneca).

But especially does Hiero emphasize the fact that he is deprived of all reciprocal friendship and comradeship, wherein consists the sweetest and most perfect fruit of human life. For what evidence of affection and goodwill can I extract from one who, willy-nilly, owes to me all his power? Can I make any account of his humble address and his courteous homage, seeing that it is not in his power to refuse them? The honour we receive from those who fear us is no honour: those respects are due to royalty, not to me.[1]

> The greatest good is this
> Of royal power, that men are forced to praise
> Their monarch's deeds as well as bear them. (Seneca.)

[1] Montaigne is putting himself in the place of a king.

Do I not see that the wicked and the good king, he who is hated and he who is loved, are paid the same honour and respect, one as much as the other? The same outward show, the same ceremonies, attended my predecessor, and will attend my successor. If my subjects do not offend me, that is no evidence of any great affection: why should I take it in that sense, since they could not do so, even if they would? None follows me on account of any friendship that may exist between him and me: for no friendship can be knit where there is so little relation and correspondence. My elevation has placed me above human intercourse; there is too much disparity and disproportion. Their obedience is a posture and a habit: it is given to my fortune rather than to myself, to increase their own. All they say and do to me is but face-paint. Their freedom being bridled on all sides by the great power I have over them, I see nothing around me but what is covered and masked.

Julian the Emperor was one day praised by his courtiers for his good administration of justice: 'I might be puffed up with pride by this praise, he said, if it came from persons who would dare to condemn or disapprove my contrary actions, should I commit any.'

All the real advantages which princes enjoy are shared by men of mean fortune (it is for the gods to ride on winged steeds and feed on ambrosia): for their sleep and their appetites differ in no way from ours; their steel is of no finer temper than that with which we are armed; their crown shelters them from neither sun nor rain. Diocletian, who wore one so revered and fortunate, resigned it in order to retire to the joys of private life; and some time after, the urgency of public affairs requiring his return to resume his charge, he replied to those who were entreating him to do so: 'You would not attempt to persuade me to do this, if you had seen the beautiful order of the trees I have myself planted at home, and the fine melons[1] I have sown.'

In the opinion of Anacharsis the happiest state of government would be that in which, all other things being equal, precedence should be measured out to virtue, and the refuse to vice.

When King Pyrrhus was preparing to invade Italy,

---

[1] Diocletian said 'cabbages', but Montaigne had a particular weakness for melons.

Cineas, his wise counsellor, desiring to bring home to him the vanity of his ambition, asked him: 'Well, Sire, to what end are you directing this great enterprise?' 'To make myself master of Italy,' he replied immediately. 'And then, continued Cineas, that being done?' 'I will pass over into Gaul and Spain,' said the other. 'And after that?' 'I will go and subdue Africa; and, at the end of it all, when I shall have brought the world under my subjection, I will take mine ease and live contented and happy.' 'In God's name! Sire, Cineas then retorted, tell me how it is that you are not at this moment, if you will, in that state? why do you not at this very hour settle yourself in the state you say you aspire to, and save yourself all the labour and hazard you interpose?'[1]

> Because, of very truth, he hath not learnt
> What the true end of getting is, nor yet
> At all how far true pleasure may increase. (LUCRETIUS.)

I will close this passage with a line from an ancient writer which I think singularly fine and to the purpose:

> Every man his own good fortune frames. (CORNELIUS NEPOS.)

CHAPTER 43

OF SUMPTUARY LAWS

THE way in which our laws attempt to regulate the vain and foolish expenses of the table and wardrobe appears to defeat their purpose. The right method would be to create in humanity a contempt for gold and silk, as vain and useless things; and we enhance the honour and value of those things in people's eyes, which is a very inept way of giving them a distaste for them. For to say thus, That only princes shall eat turbot, and be allowed to wear velvet and gold braid, and to forbid the people those things, what is that but to put a price on them and to increase every man's desire to have them? Let kings boldly abandon those marks of grandeur: they have others enough besides; such excesses are more excusable in any other than a prince. We may learn from the example of several nations better ways enough of distinguishing ourselves externally from one

---

[1] The same story, elaborated with much humour, is told by Rabelais in his first book, chapter 33.

another, according to our degrees (which I conceive in truth to be very requisite in a state), without fostering to that end such corruption and manifest inconveniences.

It is marvellous how easily and quickly custom puts down the foot of her authority in these indifferent things. Scarce had we worn cloth for a year at court, as mourning for King Henry the Second, when it is certain that silk had already become so cheap in general opinion, that, if you saw any one clothed in it, you at once set him down as one of the middle class. Silk had fallen to the lot of physicians and surgeons; and although all were clothed pretty much alike, yet there were sufficient other distinctions to make apparent the different ranks of men.[1]

How quickly do dirty doublets of chamois and linen become a mark of honour in our armies, and richness and elegance of clothing a mark of reproach and contempt!

Let kings make a beginning of leaving off these expenses, and in a month, without edict or decree, the thing will be done: we shall all follow after. The law should say, on the contrary, that crimson and gold ornaments are forbidden to all kinds of people, excepting mountebanks and courtesans.

With this kind of ingenuity did Zaleucus mend the corrupt manners of the Locrians. These were his ordinances: 'That the woman of free condition may not be followed by more than one maid, unless she be drunk; nor may she go outside the city by night, nor wear jewels of gold about her person, nor wear a richly embroidered robe, if she be not a public prostitute; That, excepting keepers of brothels, no man shall wear a ring of gold on his finger, nor a flimsy robe, as are those made of the cloth woven in the city of Miletus.' And thus, by these shameful exceptions, he ingeniously drew his citizens away from these superfluities and pernicious luxuries. It was a very useful way to attract men, by honour and ambition, to their obedience.

Our kings can do anything they please towards such external reforms: their inclination will serve as a law. *Whatever princes do, they seem to command* (Quintilian). The rest of France adopts as its rule the rule of the court. Let them discourage those villainous cod-pieces which so openly show

---

[1] Montaigne seems to be thinking of the upper classes only, and not of the 'people'.

our secret parts; those heavy puffed-out doublets, which make us look so unlike ourselves, and are so inconvenient when putting on armour; those long, effeminate tresses of hair; that custom of kissing what we present to our friends, and each others' hands, when greeting, a ceremony formerly due only to princes; of a gentleman appearing, in a place where respect should be shown, without his sword at his side, all disordered and untidy, as if he were coming from his closet; of our standing bare-headed, contrary to the custom of our fathers and the particular privilege of the nobility of this kingdom, at a long distance around them, wherever they may be, and not only around them, but around a hundred others, so many semi-kings and demi-semi-kings [1] have we now: likewise other similar vicious and newly-introduced fashions: we shall immediately see them decried and vanish. Those are superficial errors, yet of evil presage: we are warned that the solid masonry is giving way when we see the cement and plaster of our walls cracking.

Plato, in his Laws, thinks there could be no plague more pernicious to his city than to allow the young men to take the liberty of changing from one fashion to another in their dress, behaviour, dances, exercises, and songs; shifting their opinions from one basis to another, running after new things and honouring their inventors; whereby morals are corrupted, and all ancient institutions fall into contempt and disdain. In all things, saving the bad only, change is to be feared: the change of seasons, winds, food, and opinions. And no laws are truly honoured excepting those to which God has given some duration, so old that nobody knows of their birth, or that they were ever different.

CHAPTER 44

OF SLEEPING

REASON commands us ever to walk along the same path, but not at the same pace; and, although the wise man should not permit his human passions to turn him from the right course, he may indeed, without prejudice to his duty, leave it to them to hasten or retard his steps and not plant

[1] *Tiercelets et quartelets de roys*: petty-kings and petty-petty-kinglets (Florio); tiercelets and quartelets of kings (Cotton).

himself like an immovable and impassive Colossus. Though Virtue herself should put on flesh and blood, I believe her pulse would beat more strongly when marching to an attack than when going to dinner: nay, it is necessary that she should be subject to emotion and heat. For that reason I have remarked as a rare thing to see great men, when engaged in the loftiest enterprises and the most important affairs, keep themselves so entirely in trim, as not even to curtail their sleep.

Alexander the Great, on the day assigned to that furious battle against Darius, slept so profoundly and so late in the morning, that Parmenion was obliged to enter his chamber, and, approaching his bed, call him two or three times by name to awaken him, the moment to go to battle being so urgent.

The Emperor Otho, having resolved to kill himself, on that same night, when he had settled his domestic affairs, divided his money among his servants, and sharpened the edge of a sword wherewith he intended to take his own life, staying only to know if each of his friends had retired in safety, fell into so sound a sleep, that his chamber-servants heard him snore.

The death of that Emperor has many points in common with that of the great Cato, and particularly that just mentioned: for, Cato being ready to make away with himself, whilst awaiting news to be brought to him whether the Senators whom he was sending away had evacuated the port of Utica, began to sleep so soundly that he could be heard breathing from the next room; and when the man he had sent to the port awakened him to tell him that the Senators were prevented by a storm from conveniently setting sail, he sent yet another, and, resettling himself in his bed, again began to slumber until the second messenger assured him of their departure.

We may also compare with that of Alexander his behaviour in that great and dangerous storm which threatened him through the sedition of Metellus the Tribune, when the latter insisted on publishing the decree recalling Pompey with his army to the city, on the occasion of Catiline's conspiracy; which decree Cato alone opposing, high words and violent threats passed between him and Metellus in the Senate. But it was on the next day that the matter was to be put into execution in the Forum, where Metellus, besides being favoured by the common people and by Caesar, then conspiring in Pompey's interest, was to appear accompanied by many alien slaves and desperate gladiators, Cato being fortified by his courage alone. His friends and relations and many worthy people were consequently in great anxiety about him, some of whom spent the night together without any desire to sleep, eat or drink, on account of the danger they saw threatening him; his wife and sisters especially did nothing but weep and fret in his house, whilst he, on the contrary, comforted everybody, and, after having supped in his usual manner, retired to his couch, and slept a very sound sleep till morning, when one of his fellow tribunes roused him to go to the skirmish.

The knowledge we possess of the greatness of this man's courage, throughout the rest of his life, may enable us to judge in all sureness that his conduct proceeded from a soul so far raised above such accidents, that he disdained to allow this one to cause him any more uneasiness than any ordinary event.

In the naval battle which Augustus won against Sextus Pompeius in Sicily, when on the point of entering into conflict, he was sunk in so deep a sleep, that his friends had to rouse him to give the signal for attack. This gave occasion to M. Antonius to reproach him afterwards, that he had not had the heart even to behold with open eyes the array of his army, and that he had not dared to appear before his soldiers, until Agrippa came to announce to him the victory he had gained over his enemies.

But as to the young Marius, who did still worse, for on the day of his last battle against Sylla, after having marshalled his army and given the word and signal for battle, he lay down to rest in the shade of a tree, and slept so heavily that he could hardly be awakened by the rout and flight of his own men, having seen nothing of the battle; they say it was because he was so extremely spent with fatigue and the want of sleep, that nature could hold out no longer.

On the subject of sleep, the physicians will determine whether it is so necessary that our life depends on it: for we hear indeed that King Perseus of Macedon, when a prisoner at Rome, was brought to his death by being prevented from sleeping ; but Pliny instances cases of people who lived a long time without sleep. In Herodotus we read of nations where men sleep and wake by half-years.[1] And they who wrote the life of the sage Epimenides say that he slept for fifty-seven years on end.

CHAPTER 45

OF THE BATTLE OF DREUX

OUR battle of Dreux[2] was crowded with uncommon incidents ; but they who do not greatly favour the reputation of Monsieur de Guise are fond of maintaining that he cannot be excused for having made a halt and temporized with the forces under his command, while Monsieur le Connétable, the commander-in-chief of the army, was being knocked to pieces by artillery ; and that it had been better for him to risk taking the enemy in the flank, than to suffer so heavy a loss by waiting for the advantage of seeing their rear. But, besides that the result proved this, he who will debate the matter without passion will, I think, readily admit that the end and aim, not only of a captain, but of every soldier, should be the victory as a whole ; and that no particular occurrences, of whatever interest to himself, should divert him from that goal.

Philopoemen, in an encounter with Machanidas, having sent forward, to begin the skirmish, a good force of bowmen and archers, the enemy, after routing these, wasted their strength, after their victory, in pursuing them at full speed, passing along the battalion where Philopoemen was standing. Although his soldiers were very excited, he thought it best not to budge from the spot, nor face the enemy to succour his men ; but, having permitted them to be hunted and cut to pieces before his eyes, began to charge the enemy in the battalion of their infantry, when he saw them entirely abandoned by their horsemen. And, although they were Lacedemonians, since he attacked them at the moment when, being sure of victory, they began to fall into disorder, he easily overcame them ; and having done so went in

[1] Herodotus had it on hearsay, but declares positively that he does not believe it.
[2] December 1562, in which the Catholics, commanded by the Duc de Guise and the Constable de Montmorency, defeated the Protestants.

pursuit of Machanidas. This case is germane to that of Monsieur de Guise.

In that hard-fought battle of Agesilaus against the Beotians, which Xenophon, who was present, said was the fiercest he had ever witnessed, Agesilaus refused the advantage that Fortune offered him of allowing the battalion of the Beotians to pass and charging them in the rear, however certain the victory he foresaw, regarding that course as more artful than valiant ; and to show his prowess, he chose rather to attack them in the front, which he did with marvellous ardour of courage. But he was well beaten and wounded, and was obliged at last to extricate himself and adopt the course he had at first refused, opening his ranks to give passage to that torrent of Beotians ; then, when they had passed, taking notice that they were marching in disorder, like men who thought themselves well out of all danger, he followed and charged them in the flank. But, for all that, he was unable to turn their retreat into a rout ; rather they withdrew slowly and by degrees, still showing their teeth, until they had reached safety.

CHAPTER 46
OF NAMES

HOWEVER great the diversity in herbs, we wrap them all up under the name of salad. In like manner, under the consideration of names, I am going to make up a gallimaufry of divers articles.

Every nation has a few names which, I know not why, are taken in a bad sense, as, with us, Jean, Guillaume, Benoît.[1]

Item, there seem to be, in the genealogy of princes, certain ill-fated names : as in the case of the Ptolemies among the Egyptians, the Henries in England, the Charles' in France, the Baudouins in Flanders, and in our ancient Aquitania the Guillaumes, from which the name of Guienne is said to come ;[2] by a loose coincidence, if there were not as crude even in Plato.

Item, it is a trifling matter, worthy to be remembered,

[1] *Guillaume*, a nickname for a gull, dolt, fop, fool. *Benoist* or *Benet*, a simple, plaine doltish fellow ; a noddipeake, a ninnyhammer, a peagoose, a coxe, a silly companion (Cotgrave).

[2] Guienne does not derive from Guillaume, but from Aquitania, the stages being somewhat as follows : l'Aquitaine, l'Aquienne, la Guienne.

however, for its strangeness, and recorded by an eyewitness, that Henry, Duke of Normandy, son of Henry the Second, King of England, giving a feast in France, the assembly of nobles was so great, that having, as a pastime, sorted themselves into companies according to the resemblance of names, in the first company, which was that of the Williams, there were seated at table a hundred and ten knights, without counting simple gentlemen and servants.

It is as amusing to distribute the tables according to the names of the persons present, as it was to the Emperor Geta to distribute the courses of his dishes according to the first letter of the names of the viands: they served together those beginning with M: *mouton, marcassin* (young wild boar), *merlus* (hake), *marsouin* (porpoise), and so with the rest.

Item, they say that it is good to have a good name, that is to say, credit and reputation; but it is in truth also an advantage to have a good-sounding name, and one that it is easy to pronounce and remember; for kings and grandees will the more easily recognize, and be less apt to forget us; and even of our own servants we more usually call and employ those whose names come the more readily to the tongue. I have observed that King Henry the Second was never able to call by his right name a gentleman of this part of Gascony; and to a maid of the Queen he himself proposed to give the general name of her family, because that of her father's house seemed to him too uncouth.

And Socrates thinks it worthy of a father's care to give well-sounding names to his children.

Item, the foundation of Notre-Dame la Grand at Poitiers is said to have this origin, that a dissipated young man living in that place, having procured a young girl and immediately after asked her name, which was Marie, felt himself so suddenly struck with religious awe at that sacrosanct name of the virgin mother of our Saviour, that not only did he at once drive her away, but was reformed for the rest of his life; and that in consideration of this miracle there was built on the spot where this young man's house stood, a chapel dedicated to our Lady, and afterwards the church we see there.

This pious, vocal and auricular reproof aimed straight at the soul; this other, of a similar nature, insinuated itself through the bodily senses: Pythagoras, being in the company of some young men whom, heated with feasting, he overheard conspiring to go and violate a house of chaste women, ordered the minstrel-girl to change the tune, and with a heavy, grave, and spondaic music gradually charmed their ardour and lulled it to sleep.

Item, will not posterity say that our present-day reformers have been scrupulous and exact in having not only combated errors and vices, and filled the world with devotion and humility, obedience, peace, and every kind of virtue, but also in having proceeded to make war upon our old baptismal names, Charles, Louis, François, to people the world with Methuselahs, Ezekiels, Malachis, which savour much more strongly of the faith ? A gentleman, a neighbour of mine, casting up the advantages of the olden times in comparison with our own, did not neglect to take into account the stately and pompous names of the nobles of those days, Don Grumedan, Quedragan, Agesilan, the mere sound of which made him feel that they must have been a very different kind of men to Pierre, Guillot, and Michel.

Item, I feel very grateful to Jacques Amyot for having, in the course of a French oration, left the Latin names in their entirety,[1] without changing and disguising them in order to give them a French cadence. It seemed a little harsh at first, but usage, by the authority of his Plutarch, has already robbed it of all its strangeness. I have often wished that those who write histories in Latin would leave our names such as they are ; for, by turning Vaudemont into Vallemontanus and metamorphosing them in order to give them a Greek or Roman garb, we know not where we are, and fail to recognize them.

To close our account, it is a vile custom, and of very bad consequence in our France, to call every man by the name of his estate and lordship, and is the chief cause of our mixing up and losing sight of families. A cadet of a good family, having received for his appanage an estate, by the name of which he has been known and honoured, cannot honestly abandon it. Ten years after his death the estate goes to a stranger who does the same thing : you may guess how much we are at sea in trying to distinguish these men. We need look no further, in quest of other examples, than

---

[1] Montaigne did not always follow Amyot's example, e.g. when he wrote *Plaute, Pline, Terence*, &c.

to our royal house, where the rule is : so many divisions, so many surnames ; meanwhile the original of the stock has escaped us.

There is so much liberty in these changes, that I have not in my time seen any one raised by Fortune to some extraordinary eminence, but that he has forthwith been saddled with new genealogical titles, of which his father knew naught, and finds himself grafted on to some illustrious stock. And, by good luck, the obscurest families are the most susceptible of falsification. How many gentlemen have we not in France who, according to their own account, are of royal race ? They number more, I think, than those who are not.

Was this not a delightful reproof uttered by one of my friends ? A number of gentlemen were gathered together to discuss a quarrel between two lords, one of whom indeed had some prerogative of titles and alliances above the ordinary nobility. The question of prerogative having arisen, every one, seeking to make himself out his equal, alleged, one of them one origin, another another, the third a resemblance of names, the fourth of arms, the fifth an old family document ; the least of them was a descendant of some overseas king. When they came to sit down to dinner, my friend, instead of taking his place, retreating with profound bows towards the door, entreated the company to excuse him for having had the boldness hitherto to associate with them on equal terms ; but that having been newly informed of their ancient rank, he would begin to honour them according to their several degrees, and that it was not for him to sit down among so many princes. After this bit of comedy he abused them roundly : ' In God's name let us be content with that which contented our fathers, and with what we are ; we are great enough, if we rightly know how to maintain our state. Let us not disown the rank and position of our grandfathers ; let us cast aside those silly pretensions, which any one can put forward who has the impudence to do so.'

Arms have no more security than surnames. I bear azure powdered with trefoils or, with a lion's paw of the same, armed gules in fesse. What privilege has this coat to remain particularly in my house ? A son-in-law will transport it into another family ; some paltry purchaser will make it his first coat of armour. There is nothing in which we find more change and confusion.

But this consideration drags me perforce into another field. Let us probe a little deeper, and in God's name consider on what foundation we erect that glory and reputation for which the world is turned upside down. Whereon do we establish that renown that we so laboriously go searching after? It is in the end Peter or William who bears it, who takes possession of it, and whom it concerns. O what a brave faculty is hope which, in a mortal subject and in a moment, goes usurping infinity, immensity, eternity and, to the best of her power, [arbitrarily endowing her indigent master with all he may imagine and desire]! There Nature has given us a delightful toy to play with. And this Peter or William, what is it after all but a sound, what is it but three or four dashes with the pen, so easy to vary in the first place, that I should be inclined to ask, To whom is to fall the honour of so many victories, to Guesquin, to Glesquin, or to Gueaquin.[1] There is much more in this than in Lucian's quarrel of the Greek letters, where Σ goes to law with T; for

> For no mean stake or sportive prize they play. (VIRGIL.)

It is no laughing matter. The question is, which of these letters is to be credited with so many sieges, battles, wounds, prisons, and services done to the crown of France by her famous Constable.

Nicolas Denisot[2] concerned himself only with the letters forming his name, and entirely rearranged them to build up the *Conte d'Alsinois*, whom he presented with the glory of his poetry and painting. And the historian Suetonius liked only the meaning of his name, and, having robbed Lenis of it, which was his father's surname, left Tranquillus to succeed to the reputation of his writings.[3]

Who would believe that Captain Bayard[4] should have no honour but that which he borrows from the deeds of Pierre

---

[1] It has been observed that the name of the famous du Guesclin has been found in fourteen different forms: du Guéclin, du Guayaquin, du Guesquin, Guesquinius, &c.

[2] A poet and painter, born at Mans in 1515; the assumed name is an anagram of his own.

[3] C. Tranquillus Suetonius, author of the *Lives of the Twelve Caesars*. It is not, I think, recorded that he changed his name from Lenis to Tranquillus, which bears a similar meaning.

[4] Pierre Terrail was the name of the famous Chevalier Bayard.

Terrail? and that Antoine Escalin[1] should allow himself to be robbed, before his very eyes, of so many navigations and charges, by sea and land, by a Captain Poulin and a Baron de La Garde?

Secondly, these same dashes of the pen are common to a thousand people. How many persons are there in every clan with the same name and surname? And how many in different clans, ages and countries? History has known of three Socrates', five Platos, eight Aristotles, seven Xenophons, twenty Demetrius', twenty Theodores, and you may guess how many there are unknown to history.

What prevents my groom from calling himself Pompey the Great? But, after all, by what means, by what power are that glorified sound and those so honoured dashes of the pen joined and associated with my deceased groom or that other man who was decapitated in Egypt, that they should derive any advantage from them?

> Dost think such cares affect the shades below? (VIRGIL.)

Of the two companions in greatest esteem among men, how can Epaminondas feel the beauty of this glorious line in his praise, which has [for so many ages] been on our lips,

> The wings of Sparta's pride my counsels clipt;
> (Quoted by CICERO.)

and Africanus, of these other lines,

> Who, from beyond Meotis to the place
> Where the sun rises, deeds like mine can trace?
> (Quoted by CICERO.)

The survivors are tickled by the sweetness of these sounds and, incited by them to jealousy and desire, with inconsiderate fancy transfer to the deceased this their own feeling; and, with a luring hope, flatter themselves that they will in their turn be capable of it. God knows!

However,

> Greek, Roman and Barbarian, all have sought
> The warrior's wreath, by toils and perils bought;
> No other motive knew, no other cause,
> Than what we thirst for most of all—Applause!
> Applause more prized than virtue! (JUVENAL.)

---

[1] Antonius Iscalinus Adhemarus, Polinius Garda, as he is called in de Thou's history, was an officer of fortune with a distinguished military and ambassadorial career. He took the name Paulin from his birthplace, and that of de La Garde from a corporal of that name, who carried him away in his youth.

CHAPTER 47

OF THE UNCERTAINTY OF OUR JUDGEMENT

WHAT this line says, is well said : *There is much to be said, everywhere, on both sides* (Homer). For example :

> Hannibal conquered oft, but never knew
> The fruits and gain of victory to get. (PETRARCH.)

He who will agree with this point of view and impress on our people the error of not having pursued our advantage recently at Moncontour ; or who will condemn the King of Spain for not knowing how to make the most of the advantage he had over us at St. Quentin, may say that this error proceeded from a soul drunk with its success, and from a spirit which, full and gorged with this beginning of good fortune, loses its appetite for increasing it, being already too glutted to digest what it has taken in. He has his arms full and can embrace no more, unworthy of the great good that Fortune has placed in his hands ; for what profit does he reap if he nevertheless gives his enemy the means of recovering ? What hope can one have of his again daring to attack them when rallied and recovered and newly armed with anger and revenge, who dared not or knew not how to pursue them when routed and dismayed ?

> While Fortune glowed and terror filled the plain. (LUCAN.)

But, after all, what better can he expect than what he has just lost ? It is not as in a fencing-match, where the number of hits decides the victory : as long as the enemy is on his feet, it is a matter of beginning over again ; it is no victory if it do not make an end of the war. In that skirmish in which Caesar had the worst near the city of Oricum, he taunted the soldiers of Pompey, telling them that he had been lost if their captain had known how to vanquish ; and he made him clap on his spurs to much greater purpose when it came to his own turn.

But why can we not also say on the other hand, That it is the effect of a headlong and insatiable spirit not to be able to set bounds to one's greed ; That it is abusing God's favours to try to stretch them beyond the limit he has set them ; That to plunge back into danger after victory is to recommit it once more to the mercy of Fortune ; That it is one of the greatest marks of discretion in military art not to drive your enemy to despair? Sylla and Marius, having defeated the Marsians in the Civil War, and seeing yet a remnant of troops returning to attack them with the desperation of wild beasts, thought it prudent not to await them. If Monsieur de Foix had not been carried away by his ardour to pursue too fiercely the survivors of the victory of Ravenna, he would not have sullied it with his death. Yet the recent memory of his example helped to save Monsieur d'Anguien from a like mischance at Sérisolles.

It is dangerous to attack a man whom you have cut off from every other means of escape but that of fighting; for necessity is a violent schoolmistress: *most dangerous are the bites of enraged necessity* (Porcius Latro).

Who braves his foe will sell his life most dear. (LUCAN.)

That is why Pharax prevented the King of Lacedemon, who had just won the battle against the Mantineans, from provoking the thousand Argives who had escaped from the discomfiture unharmed, but rather left them free to slip away, in order not to put to the test a valour nettled and enraged by misfortune. Clodomir, King of Aquitania, pursuing after his victory Gondemar, King of Burgundy, vanquished and a fugitive, forced him to face about; but his obstinacy robbed him of the fruit of his victory, for he lost his life.

Likewise, if one had to choose between keeping one's soldiers richly and sumptuously armed, and arming them for necessity, it might be argued for the first course, which was favoured by Sertorius, Brutus, Caesar, and others, that it is always a spur to honour and glory for a soldier to see himself in brave attire, and an occasion for displaying greater obstinacy in the combat, since he would have to save his arms, as being his goods and inheritance: a reason, says Xenophon, why the Asiatics took their wives and concubines, with their dearest jewels and possessions, along with them to the wars.

But it might be argued on the other side that we should make the soldier less rather than more careful about saving his skin: that by that means he will doubly fear the risk. To this may be added that the enemy's desire for victory will be increased by the prospect of rich spoils, and it has been remarked that that prospect was once a marvellous encouragement to the Romans in their encounter with the Samnites. Antiochus, showing Hannibal the army he was preparing against them, splendid and magnificent in every kind of equipment, and asking him : ' Will the Romans be content with this army ? ' ' Will they be content ? he replied, I should think so indeed, were they never so greedy.' Lycurgus forbade his soldiers not only sumptuousness in their equipment, but also the despoiling of the vanquished enemies ; desiring, he said, that their poverty and frugality should be as conspicuous as everything else in the battle.

In sieges and elsewhere where opportunity brings us into touch with the enemy, we are wont to give the soldiers full licence to defy, despise, and insult them with all manner of taunts, and not without some colour of reason. For it is no small matter to deprive the enemy of all hope of mercy and conciliation, by giving them to understand that it is no longer in the order of the day to expect it of those they have so grievously outraged, and that victory is their only remedy. Yet it is true that in this respect Vitellius made a blunder ; for, having to deal with Otho, who was weaker in the quality of his soldiers, long unaccustomed to warfare and softened by town pleasures, he in the end so provoked them by his stinging words, taunting them with pusillanimity and their regret for the ladies and feasts they had but lately left behind at Rome, that by this means he sent their hearts back into their stomachs, which no exhortations had been able to do, and drew them down upon himself, where no one had been able to push them. And indeed, when they are insults that touch one to the quick, they may easily make him who went faint-heartedly to work in his king's quarrel fall to with another sort of mettle in his own.

Considering how important is the preservation of the leader of an army, and that the enemy's aim is chiefly levelled at the head on which all others depend, there seems to be no reason to doubt the wisdom of that course, which we see adopted by many great captains, of disguising and masking themselves when on the point of entering into the fray. Yet the disadvantage one incurs by this proceeding is no less than that one thinks to avoid : for the captain being unrecognized by his men, the courage they derive from his example and presence begins to fail them at the same time, and, having lost sight of his well-known marks and insignia, they conclude either that he is dead, or that in despair of the business, he has stolen away. With regard to experience, it goes to show that now the one, now the other course is favoured. That which befell Pyrrhus, in his battle against the Consul Levinus in Italy, will serve to illustrate both points of view, for, by concealing himself under the armour of Megacles, and giving him his own, he did no doubt save his own life, but he came very near incurring the other mishap of losing the battle. Alexander, Caesar, Lucullus, loved to make themselves conspicuous in the battle by their rich armour and accoutrements, of particular colour and lustre; Agis, Agesilaus, and that great Gilippus, on the other hand, went to war obscurely covered and without imperial ornament.

At the battle of Pharsalia, among the things for which Pompey was blamed is that he halted his army to await the enemy with firm foot : ' Caesar condemned this measure (I will steal the very words of Plutarch, which are better than mine), as not only tending to lessen the vigour of the blows, which is always greatest in the assailants, but also to damp the fire and spirit of the men ; whereas those who advance with impetuosity and animate each other with shouts, are filled with an enthusiastic valour and superior ardour.' That is what he says with regard to this line of conduct. But if Caesar had lost, might we not as well say, That on the other hand the strongest and tightest foothold is that where a man stands planted without budging ; and, That he who has come to a standstill in the march, laying by and saving up his strength within himself against a time of need, has a great advantage over him who is in motion, and has already wasted half his breath in running ? Besides that it is impossible for an army, being a body of so many several members, to move under this excitement with so exact a motion as not to alter and break its battle array, so that the most active will be at grips with the enemy before his comrade can succour him.

In that villainous battle between the two Persian brothers,[1] Clearchus, a Lacedemonian, who commanded the Greeks on the side of Cyrus, led them quite deliberately to the attack, without any haste ; but at fifty paces from the enemy he set them on the run, hoping, in the shortness of the distance,

[1] Cyrus and Artaxerxes Mnemon.

both to keep the lines and husband their breath, giving them at the same time the advantage of the impetus, both for their persons and their missile arms. Others have settled the doubt in their armies in this fashion : 'If the enemy rush upon you, await them with firm foot ; if they await with firm foot, rush upon them.'

When the Emperor Charles the Fifth passed over into Provence, King Francis was placed in the dilemma of choosing whether to go to meet him in Italy, or to await his coming in his own territory ; and, although he considered, How great an advantage it is to keep one's house pure and undefiled by the troubles of war, in order that, unimpaired in its resources, it may continue to furnish the necessary money and succour ;

That warfare always of necessity implies a laying waste of the country, to which our own estates cannot take so kindly, and that the peasant will not so meekly endure this havoc at the hands of his own side as at the enemy's, so that sedition and disturbance may easily be kindled among our people ;

That the licence to pillage and plunder, which is not to be tolerated at home, has great sustaining power against the fatigues and hardships of war, and that it is difficult to keep a man to his duty who has no other hope of gain but his pay, being but a few steps from his wife and home ;

That he who lays the cloth always pays for the feast ;

That it is more cheering to attack than to defend ; and

That the shock caused by the loss of a battle on our intestines is so violent that it is bound to shake the whole body, seeing that no passion is as contagious as that of fear, so readily taken on trust and so quick to spread, and that the towns that have heard the rattle of the tempest at their gates, and have received their captains and soldiers still trembling and out of breath, are in great danger, in this heat of fury, of being rushed into some mischievous course of action.—Yet, in spite of all these reasons, Francis chose to recall the forces he had beyond the mountains, and to await the enemy's approach.

For he may have argued on the other hand, That, being at home among his friends, he could not fail to have abundance of all commodities : the rivers and passes, being devoted to him, would convey to him provisions and money in all security, and without need of escort ;

That the proximity of the danger would increase the affection of his subjects :

That, having so many towns and barriers to fall back upon, the choice of battle would devolve upon him, according to his opportunity and advantage ; and

That, if he were pleased to temporize, he might in sheltered ease see his enemy catching cold and defeating himself with the difficulties he had to contend against, being engaged on hostile territory, where before him and behind him, and on every side, war would be made upon him ; where he would have no opportunity of renewing or increasing his army, should sickness supervene, nor of placing his wounded under cover ; no money, no provisions, but at the point of the lance ; no leisure to repose and take breath, no knowledge of the places or the country to secure him from ambushes and surprises ; and if he came to lose a battle, no means of saving the remnant.[1] And there was no lack of examples of both courses.

Scipio thought it much better to attack his enemy's territory in Africa, than to defend his own and fight in Italy, where he was ; and it was well for him that he did so. But on the other hand, Hannibal, in that same war, ruined himself through abandoning the conquest of a foreign country to go and defend his own. The Athenians, having left the enemy in their lands in order to cross over into Sicily, had Fortune against them ; but Agathocles, King of Syracuse, found her favourable when he crossed to Africa and left the war at home.

And so we are wont to say, and with reason, that events and issues for the most part depend, especially in war, on Fortune, who will not yield and submit to our reason and prudence, as these lines say,

> The ill-advised may win, and prudence fail,
> For Fortune probes no cause, nor does she aid
> The better side alway. She roves at will
> With undiscerning step. A higher power
> There is that rules our fate and to its laws
> Subjects all mortal things.   (MANILIUS.)

But, to take it aright, it would seem that our counsels and

---

[1] The above passage is taken almost word for word from a speech delivered in council by Francis I, as recorded in the Memoirs of Guillaume du Bellay.

deliberations also depend just as much on Fortune, and that she involves even our reason in her confusion and uncertainty. 'We reason rashly and at random,' says Timaeus in Plato, 'because, like ourselves, our reason largely participates in chance.'

CHAPTER 48

OF WAR-HORSES

HERE you see me turned grammarian, who have never learned a language except by rote, and do not even know what is an adjective, a conjunctive, or an ablative. I seem to have heard that the Romans had horses they called *Funales* or *Dextrarios*,[1] which were led on the right-hand side, or taken in relays, so as to be quite fresh when needed : whence it comes that we call service-horses *Destriers*. And in our romances we generally find the word *adestrer* instead of *accompagner*. They also called *Desultorios equos* certain horses that were trained in such a way that, coupled abreast and running at full speed, without saddle or bridle, the Roman nobles, even fully armed, would leap from one to the other and back again, in full career. The Numidian men-at-arms used to lead a second horse by the hand, to change in the heat of the fray : *who were trained to manage two horses at the same time like circus-riders and, when the battle was at the hottest, were in the habit of jumping fully armed off the wearied horse on to the fresh one; such were the agility of the riders and the docility of the horses!* (Livy).

Many horses are trained to help their masters, to rush upon those who threaten them with a naked sword, and throw themselves with hoofs and teeth on those who face and attack them ; but they more often hurt their friends than their enemies. Besides that, when once they have grappled with the enemy, you cannot at will loose them from their hold, and so you remain at the mercy of their combativeness.

Artibius, general of the Persian army, made a clumsy mistake when, in a hand-to-hand fight against Onesilus, King of Salamis, he was mounted on a horse fashioned in that school ; for it was the cause of his death, Onesilus'

---

[1] *Dextrarius* is, however, not found in classical Latin authors, but appears first in the Middle Ages.

poniard-bearer having attacked him between the shoulders with a falchion, as the horse reared up against his master. And there is the story which the Italians tell of the king's steed at the battle of Fornova, that by kicking and plunging it rid its master of the enemies by whom he was hard pressed, without which aid he would have perished : that, if true, was a great stroke of chance.

The Mamelukes boast of having the cleverest cavalry horses of any in the world : they say that they are trained, by nature and habit, in obedience to certain words or signs, to pick up the lances and javelins with their teeth, and offer them to their master, in full *mêlée*, and to know and distinguish the enemy.

They tell of Caesar and also of the great Pompey, that among their other excellent accomplishments they were very good horsemen ; and of Caesar, that in his youth, mounted bareback and without bridle, he would ride at full gallop with his hands turned behind his back. As Nature designed to make of him and of Alexander two miracles of military art, so you might say that she also exerted herself to equip them in extraordinary fashion, for every one knows that Alexander's charger Bucephalus had a head resembling a bull's, that he would suffer no one to mount him but his master, that he could be broken only by him, and that he was honoured after his death and had a city built to his name. Caesar too had one with fore-feet like a man's, the hoofs being divided in the shape of toes ; he could be mounted and broken by Caesar alone, who after his death dedicated his statue to the goddess Venus.

I am loath to dismount when I am in the saddle, for it is the place where I am most at home, whether I am well or ill. Plato recommends riding for health's sake, and Pliny says it is good for the stomach and the joints. Let us then pursue the subject, since we are here.

We read in Xenophon of the law which forbids any one who possesses a horse to travel on foot. Trogus and Justinus say that the Parthians were wont not only to wage war but also to do all their public and private business on horseback, such as trading, conversing, disputing, taking the air ; and that with them the most noteworthy difference between the free and the slaves was that the former rode and the latter went on foot : an institution born of King Cyrus.

There are several examples in Roman history (and Suetonius notes it more particularly of Caesar) of captains commanding their horsemen to dismount on pressing occasions, to leave the soldiers no hope of flight, and for the advantage they expected from this kind of fighting : *wherein, without doubt, the Romans excel*, as Livy says. For this reason it was that the first precautionary measures the Romans took to bridle the rebellion of newly conquered nations was to deprive them of arms and horses, and that we so often read in Caesar : *he commands arms to be produced, horses to be brought out, hostages to be given.*

The Grand Turk to this day permits neither Christian nor Jew under his rule to possess a horse of his own.

Our ancestors, notably at the time of the English war, in all serious engagements and pitched battles, all fought most part of the time on foot, since they would not trust so dear a thing as honour and life to anything but their own strength and the vigour of their own courage and their own limbs. Whatever Chrysanthes and Xenophon may say, you stake your worth and your fortune on that of your horse : his wounds and death involve your own as a consequence ; his terror or his impetuosity make you either craven or rash ; if he minds neither bit nor spur, your honour will have to answer for it. For that reason I do not think it strange if those battles were more fast and furious than those that are fought on horseback :

> The ghastly fight
> Raves, as in turn they perish or prevail,
> Vanquished or victor, for none dreams of flight. (VIRGIL.)

Their battles were much better contested ; nowadays they are but routs ; *the first shout and onrush decides the matter* (Livy). And whatever we call upon to share so great a danger with us should be, as far as possible, at our command. Wherefore I should advise the choice of the shortest weapons, and such as we can best guarantee. A sword that we hold in the fist is manifestly more reliable than the bullet which escapes from our pistol, in which there are several parts, the powder, the flint, the wheel-lock, whereof if the least fail, your fortune will fail with it. The blow conducted by the air is unsurely dealt,

> But as the winds may suffer, from afar
> They draw their bows at venture. Brave men love

> The sword which, wielded by a stalwart arm,
> Drives home the blow and makes the battle sure. (LUCAN.)

But with regard to that weapon, I shall speak of it more fully when I compare the arms of the ancients with ours,[1] and saving the shock to the ears, with which every one is now familiarized, I regard it as a weapon of very little effect, and hope that we shall one day abandon the use of it.

That which the Italians used, at once a missile and a fire-arm, was more terrifying. They gave the name *Phalarica* to a certain kind of javelin, armed with an iron point three feet long, that could pierce an armed man through and through; it was hurled, now by hand in the field, now by means of machines to defend besieged places; the shaft, wrapped around with tow soaked in oil and pitch, flamed up in its flight and, sticking in a human body or a buckler, left limbs and weapons useless. It seems to me, however, that for coming to close quarters it might also hinder the assailant, and that the field strewn with these burning stumps might in the fray bring disaster to both sides:

> No dart for him; no dart his life had ta'en.
> A spear phalaric, thundering, pierced his side. (VIRGIL.)

They had other devices, in the use of which they were drilled, and which to us, from inexperience, seem incredible, wherewith they made up for the want of the powder and shot that we use. They hurled their javelins with such velocity that they would often pierce two bucklers and two armed men and join them together as with a needle. Their slings also carried far and with no less certain effect: *accustomed to throw out to sea the round pebbles of the beach with their slings and to hit a circle of moderate circumference from a great distance, they were able not only to wound their enemies in the head, but in any part of the head they aimed at* (Livy). Their battering machines produced not only the effect but also the din of our cannon: *the battering of the walls, performed with terrible noise, aroused fear and trembling* (Livy). Our cousins, the Gauls in Asia,[2] hated those treacherous flying weapons, being trained to fight hand to hand with more courage. *They are not so much afraid of*

---

[1] This intention was apparently not fulfilled, except perhaps in the two or three following paragraphs, which were an addition to the 1588 edition.
[2] The Galatians.

gaping wounds. . . . When the wound is wider than it is deep, they glory in it as a sign of valour; but when the sting of an arrow or a ball, with a small wound to show, galls them inwardly, then they throw themselves on the ground in shame and fury that so slight a hurt should kill them (Livy): which very nearly describes the shot of an arquebus.

The ten thousand Greeks, on their long and famous retreat, came across a nation that made wonderful havoc among them with large and strong bows, and arrows so long that if picked up by hand they could be hurled back in the manner of a javelin, piercing a buckler and an armed man through and through. The machines [1] that Dionysius invented at Syracuse for shooting big heavy bolts and stones of terrible size, which flew so far and with such velocity, came very near our inventions.

But we must not forget what an amusing figure was cut by one Master Pierre Pol, a doctor of theology, of whom Monstrelet tells that he used to ride about the city of Paris, sitting his mule sideways like a woman. He also tells us, in another place, that the Gascons had terrible horses, trained to wheel about while running, of which the French, Picards, Flemings, and Brabanters, made a great wonder, ' for not being used to see them ': those are his words.

Caesar, speaking of the people of Sweden,[2] says: ' In their encounters on horseback they often leap to the ground to fight on foot, their horses being trained not to stir from the spot in the meantime, so that they may quickly remount in case of need; and according to their way of thinking nothing is so base and contemptible as the use of saddles and pads: their contempt of those who use them is so great that, though themselves very few in number, they fear not to attack a great number of them.'

What I once wondered at, to see a horse trained in such a way as to perform all kinds of tricks in obedience to the touch of a switch, with the reins hanging down over its ears,[3]

[1] The catapult.
[2] *Suede*, found in all the editions, probably a misprint for *Sueve*, the modern *Swabia*, the *Suevorum gens* of Caesar. Montaigne no doubt knew that Sweden was unknown to the Romans in Caesar's time.
[3] In his *Journal de Voyage* Montaigne describes this feat performed in the Terme of Diocletian at Rome, by an Italian who had been for many years in Turkey.

was usual with the Massilians, who rode their horses without saddle or bridle.

> And those whose coursers, unrestrained by bit
> Or saddle, yet obey the rider's hand
> Which wields the guiding switch. (LUCAN.)

Without a bridle a horse runs ungracefully, with rigid neck and head thrust forward (Livy).

King Alfonso,[1] the same who instituted the Order of the Knights of the Band or Scarf, laid down a rule, among others, that they should never ride either a mule or hinny, on penalty of a fine of a silver mark, as I have just learned from Guevara's Letters, of which they who called them *Golden* formed a very different opinion to mine. *The Courtier*[2] says that before his time it was a disgrace for a gentleman to ride a mule. The Abyssinians, on the other hand, the greater and the nearer they are to the person of Prester John, their master, the more do they love the dignity of riding on mules.

Xenophon tells us that the Assyrians always kept their horses hobbled in their stables, so skittish and bad-tempered were they; and that it took so much time to untie and harness them, that, lest the delay should harm them in war, if they happened to be taken by surprise and unprepared by the enemy, they never took up their quarters in a camp that was not fortified by ditches and earthworks.

His Cyrus, who was so great a master of horsemanship, treated his horses as he did himself, and never allowed them to be given their fodder till they had earned it by the sweat of some exercise.

The Scythians, when pressed by necessity in war, drew blood from their steeds for their drink and food:

> The Scythian comes, who feeds on flesh of horse. (MARTIAL.)

The people of Crete, when besieged by Metellus, were so hard pinched for any other beverage, that they were constrained to drink their horses' urine.

To prove how much more cheaply the Turkish armies are maintained and transported than ours, they say that, besides that the soldiers drink only water and eat only rice

---

[1] Alfonso XI, King of Leon and Castile, who died in 1350.
[2] *Il Libro del Cortegiano*, 1528, an Italian book by Baldesar Castiglione.

and salt meat reduced to a powder, of which each man can easily carry about him a month's supply, they are also able to live on the blood of their horses, like the Tartars and Muscovites, and they salt it.

Those new peoples of the Indies, when the Spaniards first came there, imagined both men and horses to be either gods or animals of a nobility above their nature. Some of them, after being vanquished and coming to entreat peace and pardon of the men and bring them gold and viands, failed not to offer the same to the horses, addressing the same speeches to them as to the men, and interpreting their neighing as the language of truce and conciliation.

In the nearer Indies, the principal and royal honour was anciently to ride an elephant; the second, to go in a coach drawn by four horses; the third, to ride a camel; the last and meanest degree, to be carried or drawn by one horse only.

Somebody of our time writes of having seen, in that climate, countries where they bestride oxen with little pack-saddles, stirrups and bridles, and very comfortably mounted they are!

Quintus Fabius Maximus Rullianus, fighting against the Samnites, seeing that his cavalry had, after three or four charges, failed to break through the enemy's battalion, decided as follows: that they should unbridle their horses and clap spurs on them with all their might, with the result that, there being nothing to check their course through arms and prostrate men, they opened out a way for their infantry, who completed a very sanguinary defeat.

A like command was given by Q. Fulvius Flaccus against the Celtiberians: '*You will do it, he said, with greater impetus, if you urge your horses unbridled upon the enemy; which it is recorded that the Roman knights have often done with great glory.' Their bits being removed, they twice charged through them and back again, with great slaughter of the enemy, breaking down all their spears* (Livy).

The Duke of Muscovy formerly had to pay homage to the Tartars in this way: when they sent ambassadors to him he advanced on foot to meet them and presented them with a goblet of mare's milk (which they consider a delicious drink); and if, while drinking, a drop should fall on their horses' mane, he was bound to lick it up with his tongue.

The army that the Emperor Bajazet sent into Russia was overwhelmed by so dreadful a snow-storm that, to find shelter and save themselves from the cold, many bethought themselves to kill and disembowel their horses and then creep inside them, in order to benefit by that vital heat.

After the fierce battle in which his army was routed by Tamerlane, Bajazet, speeding off on an Arab steed, would have escaped if he had not been obliged to allow her to drink her fill in crossing a stream, which made her so cold and heavy that he was easily overtaken by his pursuers. They say indeed that to let a horse stale makes him slack, but I should have thought that drinking would rather refresh and put more vigour into him.

Croesus, passing along the city of Sardis, found some waste land in which was a great number of snakes, which the horses of his army devoured with a good appetite: a bad omen for his business, says Herodotus.

We call a horse entire when it has mane and ear, and no others will pass muster. The Lacedemonians, having defeated the Athenians in Sicily, returning in state after the victory to the city of Syracuse, amongst other bravados sheared the captured horses and thus led them in triumph. Alexander fought with a nation, the Dahae: they went to war armed and mounted two by two, but in the fray one of them alighted, and they fought, now on foot, now on horseback, one after the other.

I do not think that any nation excels us in skill and gracefulness in riding. To be a good horseman, according to our way of speaking, seems to imply courage rather than agility. The cleverest man to manage a horse rightly, who had the surest seat and the most pleasing manner, that I have known was, to my mind, Monsieur de Carnevalet, who served our King Henry the Second in that capacity.

I have seen a man ride full speed with both feet on the saddle, take off the saddle and on his return pick it up again, readjust it and resume his seat, the horse galloping all the while with reins hanging loose; having ridden over a cap, shooting backwards with a bow he pierced it with arrows. He would pick up anything he pleased, setting one foot on the ground and keeping the other in the stirrup; and other monkey-tricks, whereby he made his living.

In Constantinople the following tricks have been witnessed in my time : two men on one horse leaping by turns to the ground and back into the saddle, and that at full gallop. A man who bridled and harnessed his horse with his teeth only. Another who rode full career between two horses, with one foot on each saddle and carrying a man on his arms ; the second man standing bolt upright, shooting with certain aim as they ran with his bow. Several who rode full speed with their legs in the air, and their heads planted on their saddles between the points of cimetars attached to the harness. In my boyhood the Prince of Sulmona, at Naples, performed all kinds of feats on a rough horse, holding Spanish coins under his knees and toes as firmly as if they were nailed, to show the firmness of his seat.

CHAPTER 49

OF ANCIENT CUSTOMS

I WOULD willingly excuse my countrymen for having no other rule and pattern of perfection but their own manners and usages, for it is a common weakness, not of the vulgar only but of practically all men, not to look beyond the ways they have been born to. I could understand the ordinary man, should he see Fabricius or Laelius,[1] regarding their looks and bearing as barbarous, since they are neither clothed nor fashioned according to our mode. But I do complain of his particular unwisdom in being so completely blinded and deluded by the authority of the fashion of the day as to be capable of altering his mind and opinion every month, if custom requires it, and of judging himself so diversely.

When it was the fashion to wear the busk [2] of the doublet as high as the chest, he would maintain with heated arguments that it was in its proper place ; a few years after behold it slipping down as low as the thighs, then he laughs at the other fashion, finding it absurd and intolerable. The present fashion of dress makes him forthwith condemn the old so decidedly and unanimously that you might imagine it were some kind of mania that makes his understanding

[1] Meaning presumably the ancient Romans ; the 1588 edition originally had *Scipio*, corrected to *Laelius*.
[2] *Busc*, or *buste* : the long, small (or sharp-pointed) and hard-quilted belly of a doublet (Cotgrave).

thus turn heels over head. Our changes in this matter being so quick and sudden that the ingenuity of all the tailors in the world could not provide us with enough novelties, the despised fashions are very often bound to come into favour again, and these very same ones soon after fall into contempt; and one and the same thing will, with incredible levity and inconsistency, within the space of fifteen or twenty years, be the subject of two or three not only different but contrary judgements. Not one of us is so knowing but he will suffer himself to be hoodwinked into this contradiction, and both his outward and inward eyes to be insensibly blinded.

I will here scrape together a few ancient customs that I have in my memory, some of them resembling ours, others different; in order that, bearing in mind the continual variation in human things, our judgement concerning them may be clearer and more settled.

What we call fighting with rapier and cloak was already practised by the Romans, according to Caesar, who says: *they wrap their mantle around their left arms and draw their swords*. And even then he remarks on an uncivil custom in our country, which still prevails, namely that we stop travellers we meet on the road and oblige them to tell us who they are, and take it as an insult and an excuse for a quarrel if they refuse to answer.

At the baths, which the ancients took every day before meals, and which with them was as habitual as washing the hands is with us, they at first washed only their arms and legs; but afterwards they adopted the custom, which continued for centuries and in most countries of the world, of washing quite naked in water mixed with perfume; and they regarded it as evidence of great simplicity to wash in pure water. The most dainty and dandified perfumed their whole body three or four times a day. They often had all the hair of the body pulled out with tweezers, as the women of France have for some time been in the habit of treating their foreheads:

From breast and thighs and arms you pluck the hair; (MARTIAL.)

although they had unguents proper for that purpose:

With unguents shines her skin, and chalk in acid steept. (MARTIAL.)

They loved to lie soft, and spoke of sleeping on a mattress

as if it were a sign of endurance. They took their meals reclining on couches, in much the same posture as the Turks of our days :

> Then from his lofty couch Father Aeneas began. (VIRGIL.)

And it is related of Cato the younger that after the battle of Pharsalia, being in mourning on account of the evil condition of public affairs, he always ate seated, and adopted a more austere mode of life.

They kissed the hands of the great as a mark of honour and affection ; and friends saluted each other with a kiss, as do the Venetians :

> And kindest words I would with kisses mix. (OVID.)

When saluting or proffering a request to a great person they touched his knees. Pasicles the philosopher, brother of Crates, laid his hands on the genitals instead of the knee. When a man he was addressing rudely repelled him he replied : ' What, is not this yours as well as the knees ? '

They ended their meals with fruit, as we do.

In the privy (that foolish squeamishness about words may be left to the women) they used a sponge ; for which reason *spongia* is an indecent word in Latin ; and this sponge was fastened to the end of a stick, as evidenced by the story of the man who, as he was being led along to be thrown to the beasts in presence of the people, asked permission to go and do his business, and, finding no other means of killing himself, thrust this stick and sponge down his throat and choked himself. After doing they used a piece of perfumed flannel :

> At tibi nil faciam ; sed lota mentula lana.[1] (MARTIAL.)

Where the streets met in Rome they placed vessels and small tubs for urinals :

> And oft the innocent young,
> By sleep o'ermastered, think they lift their dress
> By pail or public jordan. (LUCRETIUS.)

They used to take snacks between meals. In summer there were sellers of snow to cool their wine ; and some there were who used snow in winter, their wine even then not being cold enough for them. The great had their cup-

---

[1] Both the last two statements appear to be founded on insufficient evidence. In the quotation from Martial the correct reading seems to be *laeva* and not *lana*, and the line is variously interpreted.

bearers and carvers, and their buffoons to make them merry. In winter their food was served up on chafing dishes which were brought to the table ; and portable kitchens were used, such as I have seen, which followed them about with all that was necessary for serving a meal.

> Keep for yourselves your ambulatory feasts,
> Ye epicures, for me they have no charms. (MARTIAL.)

In summer they often had, in their lower rooms, fresh clear water flowing through pipes beneath them, in which was great store of live fish, which the guests would choose and catch with their hands, to be prepared according to the taste of each. Fish has ever had this privilege, and still enjoys it, that the great presume to know how to dress it ; and it has indeed a more exquisite taste than flesh, at least to me.

But in every kind of magnificence, debauchery, effeminacy, and ingenuity in devising new and expensive pleasures, we are in truth doing our utmost to equal them ; we have the will, which is as corrupt as theirs, but we have not the ability to succeed. We have not the power to compete with them either in their vices or their virtues, for both proceed from an intellectual vigour which was incomparably greater in them than it is in us ; for the weaker a soul is, the less power has it to do either very well or very ill.

The high end with them was the middle.[1] The before and after, in writing and speaking, did not imply greatness, as is evident in their writings : they will say Oppius and Caesar as often as Caesar and Oppius, and indifferently Me and Thee or Thee and Me. Which made me once note, in the life of Flaminius in the French Plutarch,[2] a passage in which the author, speaking of the jealousy between the Aetolians and the Romans for the glory of having won a battle in which they shared the victory, seems to attach some weight to the fact that in the Greek songs the Aetolians were mentioned before the Romans ; unless there be ambiguity in the French words.

The ladies used to receive men in the vapour-baths, and even employed men-servants to rub and anoint them :

---

[1] Montaigne probably means that the guest of honour at a feast reclined on the middle couch of the *triclinium*. Florio translates oddly : 'The chiefest aim amongst them was a mean or mediocrity.'

[2] That is to say, in Amyot's translation of Plutarch.

> A slave, his middle girt with apron black,
> Stands by while nude you revel in your bath. (MARTIAL.)

They sprinkled themselves with some powder to suppress perspiration.

The ancient Gauls, says Sidonius Apollinaris, wore their hair long in front, whilst the back of the head was shorn: a fashion which is being revived in the effeminate and vicious usage of this age.

The Romans used to pay the boatman's fare as soon as they entered the boat, which we do not do till after returning to port:

> Thus while the mule is harnessed, and we pay
> Our fares, an hour in wrangling slips away. (HORACE.)

The women used to lie on the side of the bed next the wall; this explains why Caesar was called *spondam regis Nicomedis*.[1] They took breath while drinking. They baptized their wine:

> What active boy from sparkling spring
> Water to soothe the heat will bring
> Of our Falernian wine? (HORACE.)

And they also knew those rascally cunning looks of our lackeys:

> O Janus, whom no stork can peck behind,
> Whom none can mock by making asses' ears
> Or thrusting out a red derisive tongue
> As long as that of dogs in summer's heat. (PERSIUS.)

The ladies of Rome and Argos wore white mourning as ours used to do, and would continue to do if they took my advice.

But there are whole books written on this matter.

CHAPTER 50

OF DEMOCRITUS AND HERACLITUS

THE judgement is a tool adapted to all subjects, and meddles with everything. Therefore, for these trials I make of it I grasp at any kind of opportunity. If it is a subject I do not understand, I try my judgement upon it for

---

[1] For an explanation of this passage, see Suetonius's *Life of Julius Caesar*, § 49. The words there used are: *spondam interiorem regiae lecticae*, the inner side of the royal couch.

that very reason, sounding the ford from a distance; and
then, if I find it too deep for my stature, I keep to the bank.
And this acknowledgement of being unable to cross is a sign
of its power, yea, one it is most proud of. At times, in an
empty and unsubstantial subject, my judgement tries to see
if it is able to give body to it, to support and stanchion it.
At other times it rambles over a time-honoured and outworn
subject in which there is scope for originality, the path being
so beaten that it can only walk on others' tracks. There it
finds amusement in choosing the road that seems best, and
of a thousand paths it points to this or that as being the best
chosen.

I take the first subject that chance offers. They are all
equally good to me. And I never purpose to treat them
exhaustively, for I cannot overlook the whole of any one
thing; neither can they who promise to let us see it. Of a
hundred members and aspects that each thing has, I take
one, now merely licking it, now scraping the surface and
sometimes pinching it to the bone. I give it a stab, not as
wide but as deep as I can. And most often I love to catch
it from an unusual point of view. I might venture to go to
the bottom of a subject if I did not know my limitations
better. Scattering a word here, another there, samples
taken from their piece, separated without design and without
promise, I am not bound to answer for them, or to keep
to them, without varying when it suits my purpose, without
surrendering to doubt and uncertainty and to my predominating
defect, which is ignorance.

Every movement lays us bare. That same mind of
Caesar which we see commanding and directing the battle
of Pharsalia, we also see directing its idle and amorous
affairs. We judge a horse not only by its pace on a race-course,
but also by its walk, nay, when resting in its stable.

Among the functions of the soul are some that are lowly:
if we do not also see her exercising those, we cannot fully
know her. And perhaps we can observe her best when she
goes her simple way. The winds of passion most often catch
her in her lofty moods. Besides that she applies herself
wholly to each matter, and exercises her whole power upon
it, and never treats more than one at a time. And she treats
it, not according to itself, but according to herself.

Things in themselves perhaps have their own weight,

their own measures and conditions ; but when they enter within us she fashions them according to her own conception. Death is terrible to Cicero, desirable to Cato, indifferent to Socrates. Health, conscience, authority, knowledge, riches, beauty, and their contraries, are stripped on entry, and receive from the soul a new raiment tinted according to her liking, brown, green, light, dark, bitter, sweet, deep, superficial, according to the liking of each of them : for they have not agreed together upon their styles, rules, and shapes ; each one is a queen in her state. Wherefore let us not find excuse in ourselves for the external quality of things ; it is for us to account to ourselves for them. Our good and our ill depend on ourselves alone. To ourselves let us offer our offerings and our vows, not to Fortune : she has no power over our moral nature ; on the contrary, that drags her in its train, and casts her in its own mould.

Why shall I not judge Alexander at table, talking and drinking to excess, or when he is fingering the chess-men ? What chord of his mind is not touched and kept employed by this silly and puerile game ? I hate it and avoid it because it is not play enough, and because it is too serious as an amusement, being ashamed to give it the attention which would suffice for some good thing. He was never more busy in directing his glorious expedition to the Indies ; nor is this other man in unravelling a passage on which depends the salvation of the human race. See how our mind swells and magnifies this ridiculous amusement ; how it strains all its nerves over it ! How fully does this game enable every one to know and form a right opinion of himself ! In no other situation do I see and test myself more thoroughly than in this. What passion is not stirred up by this game : anger, spite, hatred, impatience, and a vehement ambition to win in a thing in which an ambition to be beaten would be more excusable ! For a rare pre-eminence, above the common, in a frivolous matter, is unbefitting a man of honour. What I say in this example may be said in all others. Every particle, every occupation of a man betrays him and shows him up as well as any other.

Democritus and Heraclitus were two philosophers, the former of whom, looking upon the state of man as vain and ridiculous, never went abroad without a mocking and laughing countenance; Heraclitus, feeling pity and compassion for this same condition of ours, appeared always with a sorrowful face and eyes filled with tears:

> One always, when he o'er his threshold stept,
> Laughed at the world; the other always wept. (JUVENAL.)

I prefer the first humour; not because it is pleasanter to laugh than to weep, but because it expresses more disdain, and condemns us more than the other; and it seems to me that we can never be despised more than we deserve. Lamentation and commiseration are mixed with some esteem for the things we lament; the things we scorn we regard as of no value. I do not think there is so much unhappiness in us as there is frivolity, nor so much wickedness as folly. We are not so full of mischief as of inanity; we are not so wretched as we are vile.

So Diogenes, who played the fool to himself, rolling his tub and wrinkling his nose at the great Alexander, accounting us no better than flies or wind-filled bladders, was a sharper and more caustic judge, and consequently more just, to my humour, than Timon, who was surnamed the Misanthrope. For what we hate we take seriously. The latter wished us ill, was passionately desirous of our ruin, fled our intercourse as dangerous, as of men wicked and depraved by nature. The other held us in so little esteem, that our contact could neither disturb nor corrupt him; he left us to our own company, not because he feared, but because he disdained, our society. He held us incapable of doing either good or ill.

Of the same stamp was the answer of Statilius, with whom Brutus spoke to induce him to join the conspiracy against Caesar. He thought the enterprise was just, but he did not think men were worth taking any trouble about: in conformity with the teaching of Hegesias, who said that the wise man should do nothing but for himself, seeing that he alone was worth doing anything for; and that of Theodorus: 'That it is not just that the wise man should risk his life for the good of his country, and imperil wisdom for fools.'

In our own peculiar condition we are as capable of exciting laughter as of laughing.

CHAPTER 51

OF THE VANITY OF WORDS

A RHETORICIAN of old said his trade was 'To make little things appear and be thought great'. There you have a shoemaker who can make big shoes for little feet. In Sparta he would have been given the whip for professing a lying and deceitful art. And I believe that Archidamus, who was king of that country, heard not without astonishment the reply of Thucydides,[1] when he asked him which was the stronger wrestler, Pericles or he : 'That, he said, would be difficult to decide ; for when I have thrown him in wrestling, he will persuade the onlookers that he has had no fall, and will carry off the prize.'

They who paint and mask the women do less harm, for little is lost by not seeing them in their natural state ; whilst those make a profession of deceiving, not our eyes, but our judgement, and of corrupting and adulterating the essence of things. The states that maintained themselves in a well-ordered and well-governed condition, like those of Crete and Lacedemon, made little account of orators.

Aristo wisely defines rhetoric as 'a science to persuade the people ' ; Socrates and Plato as ' the art of deceiving and flattering '. And they who deny the general definition verify it throughout in their precepts.

The Mohammedans forbade their children to be instructed in the art, on account of its uselessness.

And the Athenians, having perceived how pernicious was the practice of it, though it was held in high esteem in their city, ordained that the principal part, the appeal to the passions, should be abolished, together with the exordiums and perorations.

It is a tool invented for handling and stirring up a mob and an unruly community ; and it is a tool that is only employed for sick states, like medicine. In those where the vulgar, where the ignorant, where all were all-powerful, as in Athens, Rhodes, and Rome, and where things have been in a perpetual turmoil, there orators have abounded. And indeed we see few persons in those republics who have

---

[1] Not the historian, but one of the leaders of the aristocratic party opposed to Pericles, and exiled by him.

pushed themselves to high honours without the aid of eloquence. Pompey, Caesar, Crassus, Lucullus, Lentulus, Metellus, made it their principal ladder for mounting to that authoritative eminence to which they at last attained, and found it of greater help than arms ; contrary to the opinion of the best times, for L. Volumnius, speaking publicly in favour of Q. Fabius and P. Decius, who had been nominated for the consulship, said, ' These men are born commanders, great in action, unskilled in wordy contest, truly consular minds. The clever, the eloquent, and learned are good for the city, to admininster justice as Praetors.'

Eloquence was most flourishing at Rome when affairs were in the worst condition, and agitated by the storm of civil wars ; as a free and untamed field bears the most lusty herbs. From which it would appear that monarchal governments are less in need of it than others : for the stupidity and credulity we find in the common people, which renders them liable to be handled and twisted by the ears by the sweet sound of this harmony, without weighing and knowing the truth of things by the force of reason : this credulity, I say, is not so readily found in an individual, who is more easily safeguarded, by good education and advice, against the influence of that poison. There was never any orator of renown known to come out of Macedon or Persia.

What I have here said was suggested to me by a talk I had lately with an Italian who was in the service of the late Cardinal Caraffa until his death, in the capacity of majordomo. I made him tell me about his office. He entertained me with a dissertation on the science of the gullet with the gravity and demeanour of a schoolmaster, as if he were discussing some important point in theology. He minutely explained that there was a difference in appetites : that which we have when fasting, that which comes after the second and third course ; the means, now of simply gratifying it, now of arousing and stimulating it ; the organization of sauces : firstly in general, then particularizing the qualities of the ingredients and their effects ; the different salads according to the season, that which should be warmed, that which requires to be served cold, the manner of adorning and embellishing them to make them pleasing to the sight also. After that he entered upon the order of the courses, full of beautiful and important considerations:

> For, believe me, 'tis no light affair
> To carve a fowl or dissect a hare. (JUVENAL.)

And all this with such a mouthful of rich and magnificent words, as one might use in discussing the government of an empire. It reminded me of my Terence:

> This is too salt, this overdone, this not too clean:
> This is just right, bear that in mind; then I,
> According to my lights, admonish him:
> To make the dish as bright as mirror's face,
> And all the feast serve up in proper style.

And after all even the Greeks highly commended the order and disposition which Paulus Emilius observed in the feast he gave them on his return from Macedon. But I am now speaking, not of deeds, but of words.

I know not whether others feel as I do, but when I hear architects filling their mouths with big words like Pilasters, Architraves, Cornices, Corinthian, and Dorian work, and suchlike jargon, I cannot help my imagination being forthwith possessed with the palace of Apollidon[1]; and after all I find that they are the paltry parts of my kitchen-door.

Just listen to people talking of Metonymy, Metaphor, Allegory, and other such grammatical names; does it not seem as if they were using some rare and exotic form of language? And yet they do no more than describe your housemaid's chatter.

It is a trickery of a like kind to call the offices of our state by the superb titles of the Romans, although they have no resemblance in respect of function, and still less of authority and power. And this too, which will one day, I doubt not, be regarded as evidence of singular conceit in our age, to bestow undeservedly, upon whom we think fit, the most glorious surnames with which antiquity honoured one or two persons in several centuries. Plato has carried off that epithet of *Divine*, by universal consent, which no one has thought of begrudging him; and the Italians, who boast, and rightly so, of usually having a more lively wit and

---

[1] A palace built by the art of the necromancer Apollidon in the old romance of *Amadis of Gaul*, beloved by Don Quixote. One is inclined to doubt whether Montaigne was as ignorant of the subject of this book as he would make out in his chapter on Education.

a sounder judgement than the other nations of their time, have lately made a present of that title to Aretino,[1] in whom, saving a turgid style, boiling over with conceits, ingenious indeed but far-fetched and fantastic, and his eloquence, such as it may be, I can see nothing superior to the ordinary authors of his time ; so far is he from approaching that ancient divinity.

And the surname of *Great* we apply to princes in whom there is nothing transcending the greatness of the common people.

CHAPTER 52

OF THE PARSIMONY OF THE ANCIENTS

ATTILIUS Regulus, General of the Roman army in Africa, at the height of his fame and of his victories against the Carthaginians, wrote to the Republic that a farm-labourer whom he had left as sole manager of his estate, comprising seven acres of land all told, had run away and stolen his work-tools ; he requested leave to return home to look after his affairs, lest his wife and children should suffer from this mishap. The Senate appointed another to manage his estate, caused his loss to be made good, and decreed that his wife and children should be maintained at the public expense.

The elder Cato, returning as Consul from Spain, sold his service-horse to save the money it would have cost him to bring it back by sea to Italy ; and, being governor of Sardinia, he made his rounds on foot, with no retinue but an officer of the Republic who carried his gown and a sacrificial vessel ; and for most of the time he carried his own baggage. He made a boast of never having had a gown that cost him more than ten crowns, or spent more than ten sous a day in the market ; and that not one of his houses in the country was plastered and rough-cast on the outside.

Scipio Emilianus, after two triumphs and two consulships, went on a legation attended only by seven servants.

---

[1] Pietro Aretino, 1492–1551, dramatist and satirist, and writer of licentious and shameless sonnets. ' Nothing in the history of Italian literature is more extraordinary than that this coarse, dissolute, and comparatively ignorant man should have been praised, courted, and almost worshipped as he was ' (*Chambers' Encyclopedia*). Montaigne's critical acumen was seldom at fault.

Homer is said to have had never more than one, Plato three, Zeno, the leader of the Stoic sect, not one.

Tiberius Gracchus, going on a special mission in the service of the Republic, was voted only five and a half sous a day,[1] although he was at that time the first among the Romans.

CHAPTER 53

OF A SAYING OF CAESAR

IF we would bestow a little consideration on ourselves now and then, and employ, in probing ourselves, the time we spend finding fault with others and prying into things that do not concern us, we should soon become conscious how all this fabric of ours is built up of weak and decaying pieces. Is it not a singular testimony of imperfection to be unable to fix our contentment on any one thing, and that even in desire and imagination it is beyond our power to choose what we stand in need of? This fact is well proved by the great contention which the philosophers have carried on from all times, that still endures and will endure for ever without agreement or solution, regarding the sovereign good of man.

> But whilst the thing we long for
> Is lacking, that seems good above all else;
> Thereafter, when we've touched it, something else
> We long for; ever one equal thirst of life
> Grips us agape. (LUCRETIUS.)

Whatever it be that we know and enjoy, we feel that it does not satisfy us and we follow open-mouthed after things to come and unknown, inasmuch as those of the present do not satiate us; not that they have not, in my judgement, the power of satiating us, but that our hold upon them is infirm and ill-regulated:

> For when he [2] saw that wellnigh everything
> Which needs of man most urgently require
> Was ready to hand for mortals, and that life,
> As far as might be, was established safe,
> That men were lords in riches, honour, praise,
> And eminent in goodly fame of sons,
> And that they yet, O yet, within the home,

---

[1] Nine obols, according to Plutarch. This was hardly a case in point, for Plutarch remarks that 'they took every opportunity to insult him in the Senate'.
[2] Epicurus.

>   Still had the anxious heart which vexed life
>   Unpausingly with torments of the mind,
>   And raved perforce with angry plaints, then he,
>   Then he, the master, did perceive that 'twas
>   The vessel itself which worked the bane, and all,
>   However wholesome, which from here or there
>   Was gathered into it, was by that bane
>   Spoilt from within.   (LUCRETIUS.)

Our appetite is irresolute and uncertain: it can neither possess nor enjoy anything in the right way. Man, thinking that the fault lies in the thing he possesses, feeds on and fills himself with other things that he neither knows nor understands, on which he fixes his desires and hopes, holding them in honour and reverence; as Caesar says, *it happens by a common defect of nature, that we most trust and fear the things we have not seen, which are hidden and unknown to us*

CHAPTER 54

OF VAIN SUBTLETIES

THERE are certain vain and frivolous subtleties, by means of which men sometimes seek to earn applause, as do those poets who compose entire poems made up of lines beginning with the same letter. We may see old Greek poems shaped in such a way, by making the measure of the lines longer or shorter, as to represent such and such a figure, as an egg, a ball, a wing, or a hatchet. Equally vain was the industry of the man who wasted his time computing in how many ways the letters of the alphabet could be arranged, and found that they came to that incredible number that we may read in Plutarch.

I agree with the opinion of him [1] who had a man brought before him that had trained himself to throw a grain of millet so dexterously as never to miss the eye of a needle, and being entreated for a gift to reward him for so rare an accomplishment very wittily and, to my mind, very rightly, ordered this labourer to be given two or three pecks of millet, that so noble an art might not lapse for want of exercise. It is a marvellous testimony of the feebleness of our judgement, that it values things, which are neither good

---
[1] Alexander the Great.

nor useful, for their rarity and novelty, or even for their difficulty.

We have only just been playing in my house[1] at who could think of the most things that meet together at the two extreme ends, such as *Sire*, which is a form of address to the most exalted person in our State, the King, and is also used in speaking to the common sort, such as tradesmen,[2] but not to those between the two. Women of quality are called *Dames*, those of the middle class *Damoiselles*, and those on the lowest rung are again called *Dames*.

Those canopies which are stretched over tables are permitted only in the houses of princes and in taverns.

Democritus used to say that gods and animals have more acute senses than men, who are in the middle stage. The Romans wore the same attire on days of mourning and on feast-days. It is certain that extreme fear and extreme ardour of courage equally disturb and relax the bowels.

The sobriquet of *The Trembler*, which was a surname of Sancho, the twelfth King of Navarre, tells us that boldness as well as fear makes the limbs quake. One whose attendants were arming him, and, observing that his skin was quivering, tried to reassure him by minimizing the danger which he was about to face, said to them : ' You know me ill : if my flesh knew how far my courage is presently going to lead it, it would be paralysed stiff'.

That impotence which is the result of coolness or disgust in the exercises of Venus, is also occasioned by too vehement a desire and an inordinate heat. Extreme cold and extreme heat cook and roast. Aristotle says that pigs of lead will melt and run with the cold and in the rigour of winter, as well as with a fierce heat. Desire and satiety fill the stages above and below voluptuousness with pain.

Stupidity and wisdom equally feel, and are equally firm in the suffering of, human calamities. The wise curb and control evil, the others know it not : the latter are, in a manner of speaking, on this side of accidents, the others are beyond them ; for, after well weighing and considering their nature, after measuring and judging them to be such as they are, they soar above them by dint of a strong courage.

---

[1] A very rare glimpse into Montaigne's home-life.

[2] ' Or ça, sire Grégoire, que gagnez-vous par an ? ' (La Fontaine, *Le Savetier et le Financier*). Grégoire was a cobbler.

They disdain them and tread them under foot, possessing as they do a strong and steadfast soul against which the shafts of Fortune, when they hit, must needs rebound and become blunted, meeting a body on which they can make no impression. The ordinary and middle condition of men lies between these two extremes, which is that of those who perceive evils, feel them, and are unable to support them. Infancy and decrepitude meet together in a debility of brain; avarice and extravagance meet together in a like desire to grasp and acquire.

It may be said, with some appearance of truth, that there is an ABC ignorance that preceded knowledge, and another, a doctoral ignorance that comes after it : an ignorance that knowledge creates and engenders, just as it uncreates and destroys the former.

Simple minds, less curious and less instructed, make good Christians, who, through reverence and obedience, believe simply and submit to the laws. Minds of middle strength and middle capacity beget erroneous opinions : they follow the first probable meaning, and have some claim to be right when they interpret as simplicity and stupidity our keeping in the old rut, meaning those of us who are not instructed by study. Great minds, more sedate and more clear-sighted, form a different category of true believers, who, after long and reverent investigation, penetrate to a deeper and more abstruse knowledge of the Scriptures, and perceive the mysterious and divine secret of our ecclesiastical polity. There are some, however, who have arrived at this last stage through the second, with marvellous profit and confirmation, as at the extreme limit of Christian intelligence, and in the enjoyment of their victory feel comforted, grateful for divine favours, morally reformed, and truly humble. With these I do not intend to rank those others who, to cleanse themselves of the suspicion of their past error and to gain our assurance, become extreme, unwise, and unjust in the conduct of our cause, and stain it with infinite reproaches of violence.

The simple peasants are honest people, and honest people are the philosophers, or, as far as can be expected of them in these days, strong and clear natures, enriched with an ample store of useful knowledge. The half-breeds, who despise the first stage of ignorance of letters, and have not been able to join the others (with their seat between two stools, to whom I belong with so many others), are dangerous, foolish, and troublesome: it is they that disturb the world. Therefore, for my part, I retreat as far as I am able to the first and natural stage, which I vainly tried to depart from.

The popular and purely natural poetry has a charm and artlessness, in which it may compare in its principal beauty with poetry perfected by art; as we see in the *villanelles* of Gascony and the songs which are brought to us from nations which have no knowledge of any science, even of the art of writing. The mediocre poetry, which halts between the two, is disdained, worthless, and dishonoured.

But because, after a passage had been opened to the mind, I found, as usually happens, that what we had taken for a difficult exercise, and in an uncommon subject, was nothing of the kind; and that after our inventiveness has been warmed up, it discovers an infinite number of like examples, I will add only this one: That if these Essays were worthy of being judged, it might fall out, in my opinion, that they would not find much favour, either with common and vulgar minds, or with uncommon and eminent ones: the former would not find enough in them, the latter would find too much; they might manage to live somewhere in the middle region.

CHAPTER 55

OF SMELLS

IT is recorded of some people, as of Alexander the Great, that their sweat, in consequence of some rare and extraordinary constitution, emitted a sweet odour, the cause of which Plutarch and others investigated. But the nature of most bodies is the opposite, and at their best they are free from smell. Even the purest breath has nothing more excellent than to be without offensive odour, like that of very healthy children. Wherefore, as Plautus says,

> She sweetest smells who smelleth not at all,

as they say that the best odour of her actions is when they are unperceived and noiseless. And those pleasant foreign perfumes may rightly be suspected in such as use them, and considered as being intended to cover some natural defect

of that kind. Whence these paradoxes of the ancient poets :
To smell good is to stink,

> You laugh at me because I use no scents ;
> I'd rather than smell sweet smell not at all ;

and in another place :

> He smells not sweet who always uses scents,
> O Posthumus. (MARTIAL.)

I am, however, very fond of being regaled with sweet odours and have an unbounded hatred of bad ones, which attack me from a much greater distance than they do any other person :

> Sooner shall I detect a polypus,
> Or goaty odours that from arm-pits flow,
> Than will keen-scented hound a hidden boar. (HORACE.)

The simplest and most natural odours appear to me the most agreeable. It is the ladies who are chiefly concerned about this. In the thick of barbarism the Scythian women, after bathing, are wont to powder and plaster their whole body and face with a certain odoriferous drug that is native to their soil ; and when, having removed this paint, they approach the men, they are both sleek and perfumed.

Whatever the odour, it is marvellous how it clings to me, and how apt my skin is to imbibe it. He that complains that Nature has left man without any vehicle to convey odours to the nose, is wrong, for they convey themselves. But in my particular case it is the moustache, which is thick, that performs that office. If I touch it with my gloves or handkerchief it will retain the scent for a whole day. It will betray the place I come from. Those clinging, fragrant, greedy, long-drawn kisses of youth would formerly adhere to it, and remain for several hours after. And yet I am little liable to contract the prevalent maladies, which are caught by contact and are bred of the infection of the atmosphere ; and I have escaped those of my time, of which there have been several sorts in our towns and our armies. We read of Socrates that, though he never left Athens during the many recurrences of the plague that harassed that city, he alone was never found the worse for them.

Physicians might, I believe, make more use than they do of odours, for I have often perceived that they cause an alteration in me and, according to their nature, act upon my spirits; wherefore I agree with what is said, that the invention of incense and perfumes in churches, the use of which is so ancient and wide-spread among all nations and religions, was intended to cheer us, by exciting and purifying our senses, in order the better to fit us for contemplation.

I should have been glad, in order to form an opinion, to have shared the art of those cooks who are able to blend foreign odours with the savour of their viands, as was particularly remarked in the service of the King of Tunis, who in our time landed at Naples to confer with the Emperor Charles. They stuffed his meats with odoriferous drugs with such extravagance, that the cost of dressing a peacock and two pheasants after their fashion amounted to a hundred ducats; and when they were carved up, not only the banqueting-hall, but all the rooms in his palace, and even the neighbouring houses, were filled with very sweet fumes, which did not vanish for some time after.

My chief care when choosing my lodgings is to avoid a heavy, smelly air. The kindly feelings I have for those beautiful cities, Venice and Paris, is lessened by the acrid smell arising from the marshes of the former and the mud of the latter.

CHAPTER 56

OF PRAYERS

I PUT forward shapeless and unresolved ideas, like those who publish debatable questions for discussion in the schools, not to establish the truth, but to seek it. And I submit them to the judgement of those whose concern it is to direct, not my writings and actions only, but even my thoughts. Condemnation and approbation will be equally acceptable and profitable to me, since I should hold it execrable if I said anything, through ignorance or inadvertence, that is contrary to the holy prescriptions of the Catholic, Apostolic, and Roman Church, in which I am dying,[1] and in which I was born. And therefore, whilst ever submitting myself to the authority of their censure, which has absolute power over me, I thus boldly meddle with every kind of subject. As here.

[1] The use of the present tense here appears odd, but it must be remembered that Montaigne regarded death as being ever present; see Chapter 19 of this Book.

I know not if I am wrong, but since, by particular favour of the divine goodness, a certain form of prayer has been prescribed and dictated to us word for word by the mouth of God, I have always thought that we ought to use it more commonly than we do. And, if I might advise, I would have Christians say the *Paternoster*, if not exclusively, at least at all times : on sitting down and rising from table, on getting up and going to bed, and on all particular occasions that are associated with prayer. The Church may amplify and diversify prayers, according to the need of our instruction : for I know well that it is always the same substance and the same thing. But this one ought to have the privilege of being continually in the mouths of the people. For it is certain that it says all that is necessary and is very proper for all occasions. It is the only prayer that I use on all occasions, and I repeat it rather than make a change. Whence it comes that I remember none so well.

It came into my mind just now to inquire how we came to fall into that error of having recourse to God in all our designs and enterprises, and of calling upon him in every kind of need, and whenever our weakness requires support, without considering whether the occasion be just or unjust ; and of invoking his name and power, whatever condition we may be in, in whatever action we may be engaged, be it never so vicious.

He is indeed our sole and unique protector, and is all-powerful to succour us, but, although he deigns to honour us with this sweet fatherly kinship, yet he is as just as he is good and powerful. But much oftener does he exercise his justice than his power, and his favours are granted in accordance with the dictates of justice, and not according to our requests.

Plato, in his Laws, enumerates three kinds of belief offensive to the gods : 'That there are no gods ; That they do not meddle with our affairs ; That they refuse nothing to our vows, offerings, and sacrifices.' The first error, in his opinion, never remained unchanged in man, from his childhood to his old age. The two others may remain persistent.

His justice and power are inseparable. In vain do we invoke his power in a bad cause. We must have a clean soul, at least at the moment when we pray to him, free of all vicious passions, else we ourselves offer him the rods wherewith to scourge us. Instead of redressing our fault, we redouble it, by showing to one to whom we should sue for pardon, feelings full of hatred and irreverence. Wherefore I am not inclined to commend a man who is so often and habitually on his knees, unless his actions immediately preceding and following his prayers show evidence of some amendment and reform,

> If night and the Santonic hood disguise
> Thy form for some adulterous enterprise. (JUVENAL.)

And the state of mind of one who mingles piety with an execrable life seems somewhat more damnable than that of a man who is in conformity with himself, and in every way dissolute. Wherefore our Church every day denies the grace of entry and fellowship to those of depraved morals who persist in any notorious wickedness.

We pray as a matter of habit and custom, or, more correctly speaking, we read or mutter our prayers. It is after all only a grimace. And I dislike seeing a man cross himself three times at the Benedicite,[1] and as often at the Grace[1] (and I dislike it the more as it is a sign I hold in reverence and continually use, even when I yawn), and meanwhile employing every hour of the day in acts of hatred, avarice, and injustice. To the vices they devote an hour, and an hour to God, as if it were a payment and settlement of accounts. It is wonderful to see actions so unlike following one upon the other with so even a tenor, that one can perceive no interruption and alteration, even upon the confines and transition from one to the other.

What an amazing conscience that must be which can be at ease, whilst harbouring under the same roof, in such peaceful and harmonious fellowship, both crime and judge!

A man whose head is unceasingly domineered by lechery, and who deems it to be most abominable in the divine sight, what can he say to God when he tells him of it? He pulls himself together, but immediately relapses. If the image of the divine justice and its presence did, as he declares, strike and chastise his soul, however short his repentance, his very fear would so often cast back his thoughts to it, that he would forthwith see himself become master of those vices which are habitual and inveterate in him.

---

[1] Grace before and after meat.

But what of those who build their whole life on the fruit and emolument of a sin they know to be deadly? How many trades and professions have we not countenanced whose essence is vicious? And that man who, in confession to me, admitted that he had for quite an age professed and practised a religion which he regarded as damnable and which was at variance with his secret feelings, in order not to lose his credit and his honourable employments, how did he concoct that speech in his heart? With what words can such men converse on that subject before the divine justice? Their repentance consisting in a visible and manifest reparation, they lose the power of pleading it both to God and man. Are they so bold as to sue for pardon without making satisfaction and without repentance? I hold the first to be in the same case as the latter, but their obstinacy is not so easily overborne. These so sudden and violent contradictions and changes of mind which they feign before us savour to me of a miracle. They indicate a state of insoluble struggle.

How fanciful appeared to me the imagination of those who, of late years, were wont to accuse any man who gave evidence of an enlightened spirit, and yet professed the Catholic religion, of being a dissembler; and who thought they were doing him an honour when they maintained that, whatever he might say for appearance's sake, in his heart he could not but hold the reformed faith according to their measure! What a pitiful mania to think your position so strong, and to be convinced that it is impossible to hold the contrary faith! And still more pitiful to persuade oneself that a man so enlightened should put I know not what disparity of present fortune before the hopes and threats of eternal life! They may believe me. If anything could have tempted my youth, the ambition to share the risks and difficulties which accompanied this recent upheaval[1] would not have been the least motive.

It is not, I think, without good reason that the Church forbids the promiscuous, thoughtless, and indiscreet use of the divine and sacred songs which the holy Spirit dictated to David. We must not mingle God with our actions, except with a reverence and attention full of honour and respect. That voice is too divine to be used merely for the

---

[1] The Reformation.

SHOULD THE BIBLE BE TRANSLATED?

exercise of our lungs and to please our ears : it is from the conscience and not from the tongue that it should proceed. It is not consonant with reason that a shop-apprentice, with those empty and frivolous thoughts of his, should entertain and divert himself with such things.

Nor indeed is it reasonable to see the holy book of the sacred mysteries of our faith bandied about a hall or a kitchen. They were once mysteries; now they are sports and pastimes. So serious and venerable a study should not be taken up just by the way and in a hurry. It ought to be a premeditated and sober action, with which should always be associated that preface to our office, *Sursum corda*,[1] and in which even the body should so dispose its demeanour as to evidence a particular attention and reverence.

It is not all the world's study; it is the study of persons who are consecrated to it, who are called to it by God. The wicked, the ignorant, grow worse by it. It is not a story to tell, but a story to revere, to fear and adore. Absurd people they are who, because they have done it into the language of the people, think they have made it easy to be understood by the people! Is it only a question of words, if they do not understand all they find written? Shall I say more? By bringing the people this little step nearer to understanding, they remove them farther away from it. Pure ignorance, and complete dependence upon others, was much more salutary and wise than this vain and wordy knowledge, the nurse of presumption and foolhardiness.

I believe moreover that the liberty given to any one to disperse so sacred and important a word in so many kinds of idioms is much more dangerous than it is profitable. The Jews, the Mohammedans, and almost all others, are wedded to and revere the language in which their mysteries were originally conceived, and any alteration and change in them is forbidden; and that not without reason. Can we be sure that in the country of the Basques and in Brittany there are sufficient men of judgement to establish this translation into their own language? The universal Church has no harder and more solemn task than to decide this matter. In preaching and speaking the interpretation is vague, free, mutable, and piecemeal; so it is not the same thing.[2]

---

[1] Lift up your hearts!
[2] i. e., not the same thing as the text of the Scriptures.

One of our Greek historians justly censured the age in which he lived, because the secrets of the Christian religion were scattered about the market-place and in the hands of the meanest artisans, so that anybody could talk and argue about them according to his lights; and holds that it should be a great shame to us who, by the grace of God, enjoy the pure mysteries of piety, to suffer them to be profaned in the mouths of the ignorant and vulgar, seeing that the Gentiles forbade Socrates, Plato, and the wisest men to investigate and speak of the things committed to the priests of Delphi. And he says, moreover, that the factions of princes are armed, in the matter of theology, not with zeal but with anger; that zeal partakes of the divine reason and justice, when guided by order and moderation; but that, when it is guided by human passion, it turns to hatred and envy and brings forth, instead of wheat and grapes, tares and nettles.

And rightly was it also said by that other, when counselling the Emperor Theodosius, that disputes are less likely to allay the schisms of the Church than to excite them, and to stir up heresies; that they should therefore flee all contentions and dialectical arguments, and frankly rely on the precepts and formulas of the faith established by the ancients. And the Emperor Andronicus, coming upon two great men in his palace engaged in a heated argument with Lopadius,[1] on some point of great importance to us, rated them and even threatened, if they continued, to throw them into the river.

Nowadays the children and women will lecture the oldest and most experienced on the ecclesiastical laws, whereas the first of Plato's laws forbids them to inquire into the reason even of the civil laws, which must be regarded as divine ordinances; and, though he allows the old men to confer among themselves and with the magistracy concerning them, he adds, 'provided it be not done in the presence of young and uninitiated persons'.

A bishop [2] has left in writing that at the other end of the

[1] It seems that Lopadius or Lopadia was the name of a lake, which Montaigne mistook for the name of a man.

[2] Osorius, Bishop of Silves, author of *De Rebus gestis Emanuelis regis Lusitaniae*, which Montaigne read in a French translation. The island is Socotra, in the Indian Ocean. With regard to the chastity of the men, all that was meant was that they were not polygamists.

world there is an island, called by the ancients Dioscorides, accommodatingly fertile in all kinds of fruits and trees, and with a healthful climate, the people of which are Christians, having churches and altars, adorned only with crosses without any other images; great observers of fasts and holidays, exact in paying their tithes to the priests, and so chaste, that no man may know more than one woman in his life. For the rest, so contented with their lot that, surrounded by the sea, they know not the use of ships, and so simple that of the religion they so diligently practise they understand not a word : a thing incredible to such as do not know that the pagans, who are such zealous idolators, know nothing of their gods but merely their names and statues.

The old beginning of *Menalippus*, a tragedy of Euripides, ran thus,

> O Jupiter! for that name alone
> Of what thou art to me is known.

I have also in my time heard people lament the fact that certain writings were purely human and philosophic, without any mingling of theology. Not without reason, however, we might say on the other hand, ' That the divine doctrine better keeps her rank apart, as queen and mistress; That she should be first everywhere, and not subsidiary and suffragan; and That perhaps the examples used in grammar, rhetoric, and logic might more suitably be chosen elsewhere than from so sacred a matter, as well as the subjects for stage-plays, games, and public spectacles; That the divine arguments are treated with greater veneration and respect when by themselves and in their own style, than when coupled with human reasons; That the theologians more often commit the error of writing too humanly, than do the humanists that of writing too untheologically : philosophy, says Saint Chrysostom, has long been banished from the sacred schools as an unprofitable servant, and esteemed unworthy to look, even passing before the entry, upon the sanctuary of the holy treasures of celestial doctrine; That the human language has figures of speech on a lower level, and should not appropriate the dignity, majesty and authority of the divine eloquence.' I for my part permit it to speak, *in undisciplined language* (Saint Augustine), of Fortune, Destiny, Accident, Good Luck, Bad Luck, and the Gods, and other phrases, in its own way.

I put forward human ideas, and my own, simply as human ideas, and considered separately, not as decreed and determined by divine ordinance, beyond doubt and dispute : as matter of opinion, not matter of faith ; as the result of self-communings, and not of my faith in God, as boys show up their essays, not to instruct, but to be instructed ; in a lay, not a clerical style, but still very religious.

And it might also be said, not without a show of reason, that the decree forbidding any but such as make express profession of religion to write about it, except very reservedly, would not lack some colour of utility and justice ; and would perhaps command me among others to hold my peace.

I have been told that even those who are not of our persuasion forbid the use among themselves of the name of God in their ordinary conversation. They will not permit it to be used by way of interjection or exclamation, nor in giving evidence, nor for the purpose of comparison : wherein I think they are right. On whatever occasion we call upon God to accompany and assist us, it should be done seriously and religiously.

There is, I think, in Xenophon, a certain treatise in which he sets forth that we should pray to God less often, seeing that it is no easy matter for us to bring back our minds so often to that calm, chastened, and devotional state necessary for that purpose ; otherwise our prayers are not only vain and unprofitable, but wicked. 'Forgive us, we say, as we forgive those who have offended us.' What do we mean by that except that we offer him our soul free from rancour and ill-will ? Yet we invoke God and his assistance as an accomplice in our sins, and invite him to share our injustice :

Which to impart you draw the gods aside. (PERSIUS.)

The miser prays to him for the safe-keeping of his vain and superfluous treasures, the ambitious man for victories and the guidance of his ruling passion ; the thief implores his aid in surmounting the dangers and difficulties that obstruct the carrying-out of his wicked designs, or thanks him for the ease with which he has been enabled to cut the throat of a traveller. At the foot of the house they intend

THE DEVOUT PRINCE

to scale or blow up they make their prayers, with their hopes and intentions full of cruelty, lust, and greed.

> Well, just ask of
> Staius what you ask of Jupiter;
> He would say, 'By Jove, how dreadful!'
> May not Jove invoke himself so? (PERSIUS.)

The Queen of Navarre, Margaret, tells a tale of a young prince (and, although she does not name him, his rank has made him recognizable enough), that, going to keep an amorous appointment to sleep with the wife of a Paris advocate, and his way taking him through a church, he never passed this holy place, going to or returning from his adventure, but he made his prayers and orisons. With his soul filled with that beautiful design, I leave you to judge for what purpose he employed the divine favour. And yet she cites this as a testimony of singular devotion.[1] But this proof does not stand alone to confirm our belief that women are hardly fit to treat theological matters.

A true prayer and a pious reconciling of ourselves to God cannot light upon an unclean mind, subject at the time to the domination of Satan. The man who calls God to his aid while leading a vicious life acts like the cut-purse who should call justice to his aid, or like those who call upon God to witness a lie.

> In whispered tones we murmur guilty prayers. (LUCAN.)

There are few men who would dare to bring to the light of day the secret requests they make to God:

> It is not every one whose humble whispers
> Within the shrines would bear the light of day. (PERSIUS.)

For that reason the Pythagoreans would have them made public and heard by all the world, that no one might ask any unseemly or unjust thing, like this man,

> He first exclaims aloud, Apollo! Then
> Into a whisper drops his voice again,
> And mutters: O Laverna,[2] fair and bright,
> Grant no suspicion e'er on me alight;
> Make me to seem devout and just, and shroud
> My frauds and follies in a friendly cloud. (HORACE.)

---

[1] See the *Heptameron*, 3rd Day, novel 25. According to the story however, he prayed only on his return from the adventure.

[2] Laverna was the patron goddess of thieves.

The gods cruelly punished the iniquitous vows of Oedipus by granting them. He prayed that his children might determine among themselves by arms the succession to his state. He had the misfortune to see himself taken at his word. We are not to ask that all things shall fall out according to our will, but in accordance with wisdom.

It would seem, indeed, as if the prayers we utter were a mere jargon, like those sacred and divine words which are used in sorceries and deeds of witchcraft; and as if we counted upon their efficiency depending on the form, the sound, and succession of the words, or upon our gestures. For with our souls full of lust, untouched by repentance or any new reconciliation with God, we offer to him those words that the memory suggests to the tongue, and hope by them to atone for our errors. Nothing is so kind, so indulgent, and so gracious as the divine law: she calls us to her, sinful and detestable as we are; she opens her arms and receives us into her bosom, however vile, filthy, and polluted we may be at present and in the future. But then, in return, we must look upon her with a favourable eye. We must receive this pardon with thankfulness, and, at least during the moment when we address her, our soul must be dissatisfied with its errors and at enmity with the passions which have driven us to offend her.

Neither the gods nor the good man, says Plato, accept the gift of the wicked.

> The costliest sacrifice that wealth can make
>   From the incensed Penates less commands
> A soft response, than doth the poorest cake,
>   If on the altar laid with spotless hands. (HORACE.)

CHAPTER 57

OF AGE

I CANNOT accept the way in which we fix the span of our lives. I have observed that the sages hold it to be much shorter than is commonly supposed. 'What! said the younger Cato to those who would prevent him from killing himself, am I now of an age to be reproached with yielding up my life too soon?' And yet he was but forty-eight years of age. He thought that age very ripe and well advanced, considering how few men reach it. And they who flatter themselves that such and such a term, which they call the natural course of life, gives promise of a few years beyond, might be justified, were they privileged to be exempt from the numerous accidents to which each of us, by a natural subjection, is exposed, and which may cut short the term they promise themselves.

What an idle fancy it is to expect to die of a decay of powers brought on by extreme old age, and to propose that as the term of our duration, seeing that that kind of death is the rarest of all, and most seldom reached! That death alone we call a natural death, as if it were contrary to Nature to see a man break his neck by a fall, drowned in a shipwreck, suddenly snatched away by the plague or a pleurisy, and as if it were not our ordinary condition to be exposed to all such calamities. Let us not flatter ourselves with such fine words; we ought perhaps rather to call that natural which is general, common, and universal.

To die of old age is a rare death, singular and out of the ordinary, and hence much less natural than other deaths; it is the last and extreme kind of death: the further it is from us, the less it is to be expected. It is indeed the bourn beyond which we shall not go, and which the law of Nature has prescribed as a limit not to be overstepped; but it is a privilege she rarely bestows to let us live so long. It is an exemption she gives by special favour to one man in the course of two or three centuries, by releasing him from the crosses and difficulties she has cast in the way of this long career.

By this reasoning I have been led to regard the age which we have reached as an age which few people attain to. Since in the ordinary course of things men do not reach that stage, it is a sign that we are well advanced.

And since we have passed the usual limits, which are the true measure of our life, we must not hope to go much beyond. Having escaped so many occasions of death into which we see the world stumbling, we must acknowledge that the extraordinary and uncommon fortune which has kept us alive, is not likely to continue much longer.

It is a fault even in the laws to entertain this false idea: they will not allow a man to be capable of managing his affairs till he is twenty-five years of age; and he will be hard pushed to manage his life till then. Augustus cut off five years from the ancient Roman ordinances, and declared that a man was old enough at thirty to assume the office of a judge. Servius Tullius exempted the knights who had passed the age of forty-seven from the drudgery of war; Augustus released them at forty-five. To send men into retirement before they are fifty-five or sixty years of age seems to me not very reasonable. I should be of opinion that we should continue our professions and occupations as long as possible, for the public good; but I see a fault in the other direction, in that we are not set to business early enough. This emperor had been universal arbiter of the world at nineteen, and would have a man be thirty before he can give judgement about the position of a spout.

For my part, I consider that our minds are developed as far as they are likely to be at twenty and as promising as they can ever be. No mind that has not given evident earnest of its powers at that age, ever gave proof of them after. Then or never do the natural qualities and virtues exhibit the vigour and beauty that is in them:

> If the thorn prick not at its birth,
> Hardly will it ever prick,

as they say in the Dauphiné.

Of all the great human deeds, of whatever kind, that have come to my knowledge, I think I should have a longer task to enumerate those that have been performed, both in ancient and modern times, before the age of thirty, than after. Yea, often in the life of the same men.

May I not with full assurance say so of those of Hannibal and of Scipio, his great adversary? The better half of their lives was lived on the fame they acquired in their youth: great men afterwards, compared with all others, but by no means in comparison with themselves.

With regard to myself, I hold for certain that after that age both my mind and my body have lost rather than gained, and recoiled rather than advanced. It is possible that, in those who employ their time well, knowledge and experience grow with their years; but vivacity, quickness, firmness, and those other qualities which are much more our own, more important and esential, decay and languish.

> Where already
> The body's shattered by master-powers of age
> And fallen the frame with its enfeebled powers,
> Thought halts, tongue wanders, and the mind gives way.
>
> (LUCRETIUS.)

Now it is the body that first surrenders to old age, now the mind; and I have seen a goodly number whose brains were enfeebled before their stomach and legs; and that is the more dangerous, as it is an infirmity that is little felt by the sufferer, and of obscure symptoms. For this once I complain of the laws, not that they keep us at work too late in life, but that they set us to work too late. Considering the frailty of our life, and to how many common and natural reefs it is exposed, we should not, in my opinion, allot so large a share at the beginning of it to idleness and to apprenticeship.

Book the Second

CHAPTER 1

OF THE INCONSISTENCY OF OUR ACTIONS

THEY who make a practice of comparing human actions are never so perplexed as when they try to piece them together and place them in the same light, for they commonly contradict one another so strangely that it seems impossible they should have come out of the same shop. Marius the younger is now a son of Mars, now a son of Venus.[1] Some one said that Pope Boniface the Eighth entered upon his charge like a fox, behaved therein like a lion, and died like a dog. And who could believe that it was Nero, the very image of cruelty, who, when the sentence of a condemned criminal was brought to him to be signed in the usual way, exclaimed, 'Would to God that I had never learned to write!' So grieved was he in his heart to doom a man to death!

The world is full of such examples, nay, any man may provide such an abundance of them out of his own experience, that I sometimes wonder to see intelligent men at pains to sort the pieces, seeing that irresolution is, in my view, the most common and conspicuous defect of our nature: witness that famous line of Publilius the writer of low comedies,

Poor is the plan that never can be changed. (PUBLILIUS SYRUS.)

It seems reasonable to judge a man by the most ordinary acts of his life, but in view of the natural instability of our habits and opinions, I have often thought that even good authors are wrong in obstinately attributing to us a steadfast and consistent character. They hit upon a general feature in a man and arrange and interpret all his actions in accordance with this fanciful conception; and if they are unable to twist them sufficiently, set them down to dissimulation. Augustus has escaped them, for we see in this

[1] 'His martial intrepidity and ferocious behaviour at first procured him the title of the son of Mars, but his conduct afterwards denominated him the son of Venus.'—Plutarch, *Life of Marius*.

man, throughout the course of his life, so manifest, abrupt, and continual a variety of actions, that he has slipped through the fingers of even the most daring critics, and been left undecided. I find nothing more difficult to believe than man's consistency, and nothing more easy than his inconsistency. If we examine him in detail and judge of his actions separately, bit by bit, we shall most often find this true.

Throughout ancient history it would be difficult to choose a dozen men who have steered their lives in one certain and constant course, which is the principal aim of wisdom. For, to comprise it all in one word, as an ancient writer says,[1] and to embrace all the rules of life in one, is ' to wish and not to wish always the same thing. I will not vouchsafe to add, he says, provided the wish be right; for if it be not right, it is impossible it should be always the same '. I once learned indeed that vice is no more than want of rule and moderation, and that it is consequently impossible to associate it with consistency. It is a saying attributed to Demosthenes, ' that the beginning of all virtue is consultation and deliberation ; and the end and perfection, constancy '. If reason directed our course we should choose the fairest ; but no one has thought of that :

> He scorns that which he sought, seeks what he scorned of late ;
> He flows and ebbs, his whole life contradiction. (HORACE.)

Our ordinary practice is to follow the inclinations of our appetite, to right, to left, up hill, down dale, as we are borne along by the wind of opportunity. We do not consider what we wish except at the moment of wishing it, and we change like that animal which takes its colour from what it is laid upon. What we have but now determined we presently alter, and soon again we retrace our steps : it is nothing but wavering and uncertainty ;

> We are led as a puppet is moved by the strings. (HORACE.)

We do not go, we are carried along, like things floating, now smoothly, now perturbedly, according as the water is angry or calm ;

> We see them, knowing not
> What 'tis they want, and seeking ever and ever
> A change of place, as if to drop the burden. (LUCRETIUS.)

[1] Seneca.

Every day a new fancy ; and our humours move with the changes of weather :

> So change the minds of men, like days
> That Father Jove sends down to earth,
> To alternate 'twixt wet and fine.   (HOMER.)

We waver between different minds ; we wish nothing freely, nothing absolutely, nothing constantly. Should any man prescribe and establish definite laws and a definite policy in his own head, he would present throughout his life a shining example of even habits, an order and an unfailing relation of one action to another.

(Empedocles remarked in the inhabitants of Agrigentum this discrepancy, that they abandoned themselves to their pleasures as if they were to die on the morrow, and that they built as if they were never to die.)

The reason will be easily found, as we see in the case of the younger Cato ; he who touches one note of the keyboard touches all : there is a harmony of sounds, all in perfect tune with each other, which is not to be mistaken. With us, on the other hand, the rule is : so many actions, so many particular judgements to be passed. The surest, in my opinion, would be to refer them to the nearest circumstances, without seeking any farther, and without drawing from them any other inferences.

It was told me, during the tumultuous times our poor State had to go through, that a young woman who lived quite near to where I then was, had thrown herself from a high window to avoid the forcible caresses of a poor knave of a soldier who was quartered in her house ; the fall did not kill her, and, repeating the attempt on her life, she would have cut her throat with a knife, but was prevented ; not however without inflicting a serious wound. She herself then confessed that the soldier had done no more than importune her with gifts, entreaties, and solicitations, but that she feared he would in the end proceed to violence. And all this, her words, her mien, and the blood which testified to her virtue, in the true manner of a second Lucretia !

Now I have heard, as a fact, that, both before and after, she was a wench not very difficult to come by. As the tale has it, ' Be as handsome and as fine a gentleman as you will, when you have failed in your pursuit, do not immediately conclude an inviolable chastity in your mistress; it does not follow that the muleteer will not find his opportunity.'[1]

Antigonus, having taken a liking to one of his soldiers, on account of his virtue and valour, ordered his physicians to attend him for a persistent internal malady which had long tormented him, and perceiving that after his cure he went much more coldly to work than before, asked him what it was that had so altered and cowed him. 'You yourself, Sire, he replied, by delivering me from the ill which made me indifferent to life.' A soldier of Lucullus, having been plundered by enemies, devised a bold stroke for his revenge; when he had retrieved his loss with interest, Lucullus, whose good opinion he had gained, tried to induce him, with the best persuasions he could think of, to undertake some risky business;

> With words that might have stirred a coward's heart. (HORACE.)

'Employ, he replied, some wretched soldier who has been plundered;'

> Though but a rustic clown, 'he'll go
> Who's lost his money-belt,' he said; (HORACE.)

and resolutely refused to go.

When we read that Mahomet having furiously rated Chasan, chief of his Janissaries, for allowing his line of troops to be broken by the Hungarians, and bearing himself like a coward in the battle; and that Chasan made no reply but, alone and just as he was with his weapon in his hand, rushed furiously into the first body of enemies that he met with, and was immediately overwhelmed; it was not so much a justification of his conduct as a change of mood, not so much natural prowess as a new spite.

Do not think it strange that the man who was so venturesome yesterday should prove such a poltroon on the morrow; either anger, or necessity, or company, or wine, or the sound of the trumpet had put his heart into his belly; it was not a courage thus formed by reason, but a courage stiffened by those circumstances; it was no marvel if other contrary circumstances made a new man of him.

---

[1] See the host's tale in Ariosto's *Orlando Furioso*, c. 28; La Fontaine's version of the same story, *Joconde*; or the *Arabian Nights* (Introd.).

These so supple changes and contradictions which we manifest have made some to imagine that we have two souls, others, that we have two powers which, each in its own way, accompany and stir us, the one to good, the other to evil, since so abrupt a diversity is not to be reconciled with a single subject.

Not only does the wind of accidents stir me according to its blowing, but I am also stirred and troubled by the instability of my attitude; and he who examines himself closely will seldom find himself twice in the same state. I give to my soul now one face, now another, according to the side to which I turn it. If I speak differently of myself, it is because I regard myself differently. All the contradictions are to be found in me, according as the wind turns and changes. Bashful, insolent; chaste, lascivious; talkative, taciturn; clumsy, gentle; witty, dull; peevish, sweet-tempered; mendacious, truthful; knowing, ignorant; and liberal and avaricious and prodigal: all this I see in myself in some degree, according as I veer about; and whoever will study himself very attentively will find in himself, yea, in his judgement, this discordance and unsteadiness. I can say nothing of myself absolutely, simply, and steadily, without confusion and mixture, nor in one word. *Distinguo* is the most universal member of my logic.

Though I am ever inclined to speak well of what is good, and rather to interpret favourably the things that are capable of such interpretation, yet such is the strangeness of our nature that we are often driven to do good, even by vice; if it were not that well-doing is judged by the intention alone.

Therefore a courageous deed ought not to imply a valiant man: the man who is really brave will be always so, and on all occasions. If valour were a habit, and not a sudden eruption, it would make a man equally resolute for all emergencies, the same alone as in company, the same in single combat as in a battle; for let them say what they will, there is not one valour for the pavement and another for the field. As bravely would he bear sickness in his bed as a wound in camp, nor would he fear death in his own home any more than in an assault. We should not see the same man charge with brave assurance into the breach, and afterwards worrying, like a woman, over the loss of a lawsuit or a son. When, though afraid of infamy, he bears up against poverty; when, though wincing at a surgeon's lancet, he stiffly faces the enemy's sword, the action is praiseworthy, but not the man.

Many Greeks, says Cicero, cannot look upon an enemy, and are brave in sickness. The Cimbrians and Celtiberians, quite the contrary: *For nothing can be consistent that has not reason for its foundation* (Cicero).

No valour could be more extreme in its kind than Alexander's; but it is of one kind only, and is not complete enough, nor universal on all occasions. Incomparable though it be, it has its blemishes. So it is that we see him so desperately disturbed by the slightest suspicions that his subjects may be plotting against his life, and carried away in his investigations to such violent and indiscriminate acts of injustice, and haunted by a fear that upsets his natural good sense. The superstition too with which he was so strongly tainted bears some likeness to pusillanimity. And the excess of his penitence for the murder of Clytus is also evidence of uneven temper.

Our actions are but a patchwork (*they despise pleasure, but are cowardly in pain; they are indifferent to fame, but infamy breaks their spirit*), and we try to gain honour by false pretences. Virtue will not be wooed but for her own sake, and if we sometimes borrow her mask for some other purpose, she will very soon snatch it from our face. When the soul is once steeped in it, the dye is strong and vivid, and will not go without taking the skin with it. Wherefore, to judge a man, we must long and carefully follow his traces. If constancy does not stand firm and wholly on its own foundation, *if the path of life has not been well considered and preconcerted* (Cicero); if changing circumstances make him alter his pace (I should say his route, for the pace may be accelerated or retarded by them), let him go: that man will go *A vau le vent* (down the wind), as the motto of our Talebot has it.[1]

It is no wonder, says an ancient writer,[2] that chance has so

---

[1] *Our* Talebot. Montaigne is probably referring to the Earl of Shrewsbury, who was killed quite near to his château of Montaigne. In the next chapter he refers to *our* Germans, meaning the German troops who were quartered in his neighbourhood.

[2] Seneca.

great a hold over us, since we live by chance. Unless a man has directed his life as a whole to a certain fixed goal, he cannot possibly dispose his particular actions. Unless he have an image of the whole in his mind, he cannot possibly arrange the pieces. How can a painter lay in a stock of colours, if he knows not what he is going to paint ? No man draws a definite outline of his life, and we only think it out in details. The archer must first know at what he is aiming, and then accommodate his hand, his bow, the string, the arrow, and his movements, accordingly. Our plans go wrong because they have neither aim nor direction. No wind serves the ship that has no port of destination.

I cannot agree with those judges who, on the strength of seeing one of his tragedies, declared in favour of Sophocles, when accused by his son of being incapable of managing his domestic affairs. Nor do I hold with the conclusions arrived at by the Parians who were sent to reform the Milesians. Visiting the island, they remarked the best-cultivated lands and the best-kept country-houses, and made a note of their owners ; and then, having called an assembly of the citizens in the town, they appointed these owners the new governors and magistrates, concluding that, being careful of their private affairs, they would be equally careful of those of the public.

We are all made up of bits, and so shapelessly and diversely put together, that every piece, at every moment, plays its own game. And there is as much difference between us and ourselves, as between us and others. *Be sure that it is very difficult to be always the same man* (Seneca). Since ambition can teach a man valour, temperance, and liberality, yea and justice too ; since greed can implant in the heart of a shop-apprentice, bred up in obscurity and neglect, the confidence to entrust himself, so far from the domestic hearth, to the mercy of the waves and angry Neptune in a frail bark ; since it teaches also discretion and prudence ; and since Venus herself can put resolution and temerity into the boy who is still under the discipline of the rod, and embolden the heart of the tender virgin in her mother's arms,

> With Love for guide,
> Alone the maid steps o'er her prostrate guards,
> And steals by night into the young man's arms ; (TIBULLUS.)

it is not enough for a sober understanding to judge us simply by our external actions : we must sound the innermost recesses, and observe the springs which give the swing. But since it is a high and hazardous undertaking, I would rather that fewer people meddled with it.

CHAPTER 2
OF DRUNKENNESS

THE world is all variety and dissimilarity. Vices are all alike in that they are all vices ; and that is perhaps how the Stoics understand it. But though they are equally vices, they are not equal vices. And it is not to be believed that he who has crossed the bounds

> Beyond the which no right path can be found, (HORACE.)

a hundred paces, is in no worse condition than he who has gone but ten ; nor is it to be believed that sacrilege is no worse than the theft of a cabbage out of our garden :

> Nor can right reason prove the crime the same
> To rob a garden, and, by fear unawed,
> To steal by night the sacred things of God. (HORACE.)

In this there is as great diversity as in anything else.

It is dangerous to confuse the order and the measure of sins. The murderer, the traitor, and the tyrant would get off too easily. It is not in reason that they should soothe their conscience with the excuse that some other man is idle, or lascivious, or less assiduous in his devotions. Every man weighs down his neighbour's sin, and makes light of his own. Even our teachers often range them badly, in my opinion.

As Socrates said that the principal office of wisdom is to distinguish between goods and evils, we others, the best of us being ever in a state of sin, should say the same of the knowledge which distinguishes the different sins ; for, unless it be very exact, the virtuous and the wicked will remain confounded and undistinguished.

Now drunkenness, among the others, appears to me a gross and brutish vice. In others the mind has more share : in some vices there is something we may call generous. Some are blended with knowledge, diligence, valour, prudence, skill, and refinement, but drunkenness is all of the body and the earth. And the only nation in the present day among whom it is held in honour is at the same time the grossest. The other vices impair the understanding : this overturns it, and dulls the body.

> When the strong wine has entered into man . . .
> There follows then a heaviness of limbs,
> A tangle of the legs as round he reels,
> A stuttering tongue, an intellect besoaked,
> Eyes all aswim, and hiccups, shouts and brawls. (LUCRETIUS.)

The worst state of man is when he loses the knowledge and control of himself. And among other appropriate things they say that, just as must, seething in a vessel, drives all the lees from the bottom to the top, so does wine, in those who have drunk to excess, uncork the most intimate secrets.

> You make the sage forget his care,
> His bosom's inmost thoughts lay bare,
> And drown his solemn-faced pretence
> Beneath your blithesome influence. (HORACE.)

Josephus tells us how he wormed out the secrets of a certain ambassador sent to him by the enemy, by making him drink too much. And yet Augustus, though he confided his most private affairs to Lucius Piso, who conquered Thrace, was never mistaken in him ; nor was Tiberius in Cossus, to whom he disburdened himself of all his plans ; and yet we know them both to have been so addicted to wine, that they had often to be carried drunk out of the Senate-house.

> His veins were swelled with wine of yesterday. (VIRGIL.)

And Cimber, who was often intoxicated, was as confidently entrusted with the design of killing Caesar, as Cassius, a water-drinker ; as to which he made the witty reply : ' What, I carry a tyrant, who am unable to carry my wine ! ' We see our Germans, drenched with wine, remembering their quarters, their watchword, and their rank.[1]

> Though soaked in wine and reeling drunk,
> No easy task it is to vanquish them. (JUVENAL.)

I could not have believed in a drunkenness so profound,

---

[1] Our Germans ; that is, the foreign mercenaries encamped in his neighbourhood during the Civil wars.

STORY OF THE WIDOW

so dead and senseless, if I had not read the following in history: that Attalus, having invited to supper, with intent to put a singular indignity upon him, that same Pausanias who, for the same reason afterwards killed Philip, King of Macedon (a king whose fine qualities testified to his upbringing in the house and company of Epaminondas), made him drink so much that he could senselessly abandon his beauty, as any hedge-side drab might do her body, to the muleteers and a number of low-born slaves of his household.

And I have been told by a lady whom I hold in singular honour and esteem, that near Bordeaux, towards Castres, where she has her house, a woman of the village, a widow of chaste repute, feeling the first inklings of pregnancy, told her neighbours that she might think she was with child if she had a husband; but when from day to day her suspicion grew into evident certainty, she went so far as to authorize the priest to announce from the pulpit that, if any man should avow himself privy to the deed, she promised to pardon and, if he approved, marry him. A young labourer in her service, emboldened by this proclamation, declared that he had found her one holiday so much under the influence of wine, so fast asleep, and in so indecent a posture by her fireside, that he had been able to ravish without awakening her. They are still living as man and wife.

It is certain that in ancient times this vice was not greatly decried. Several philosophers even touch upon it very tenderly in their writings, and some of the Stoics even advise an occasional excess in wine, even to intoxication, in order to relax the mind.

They say in this too, Socrates the wise,
And great in virtue's combats, bore the prize. (CORNELIUS GALLUS.)

Cato, the censor and corrector of others, has been blamed for hard drinking:

And even old Cato's worth, we know,
Took from good wine a nobler glow. (HORACE.)

One of the reasons why Cyrus, so renowned a king, claimed to be a better man than his brother Artaxerxes, was that he was a much better drinker. And among the best regulated and governed nations this drink test was very prevalent.

I have heard Silvius, an eminent Paris physician, say that to keep the digestive powers from becoming sluggish, it is a good thing, once a month, to prod and rouse them up by this excess, lest they should grow dull.

And we read that the Persians discussed their most important affairs after wine.

My taste and constitution are more hostile to this vice than my reason. For, besides that I am inclined to bow to the authority of the ancients, I certainly look upon it as a weak and stupid vice, but less hurtful and mischievous than the others, which almost all, and more directly, offend public society. And if, as they hold, we cannot take any pleasure but at some cost to ourselves, I am of opinion that this vice costs our conscience less than the others, besides that it is not difficult to get at and to satisfy : a consideration not to be despised.

A man, well advanced in years and dignity, said to me that he counted this among the three main comforts that remained to him in life. [And where can a man more justly expect to find comfort than in the natural pleasures ?] But he looked at it from the wrong point of view. Delicacy and a careful choice of wines is to be avoided. If your pleasure depends upon your drinking to please your palate, you condemn yourself to the penance of sometimes drinking an unpalatable sort. Our taste should be freer and more easily pleased : a good toper should have a less delicate palate. The Germans will drink almost any wine with equal pleasure, their object being to pour it down rather than to taste it. They have the better bargain. Their pleasure is more copious and near at hand.

Secondly, to drink after the French fashion, at the two meals and in moderation, is to restrict too narrowly the favours of the god. It needs more time and more application. The ancients spent whole nights in this practice, often extending their potations to the following day. So we should establish our habits on a broader and firmer basis.

I have seen a great lord of my time, a man who had done great things and earned fame by his successes, who drank, without any effort and in the course of his ordinary meals, seldom less than twenty bottles of wine. And on leaving off was only too wary and knowing, as we knew to our cost.

The pleasure which we account worth while in the course

of our life, should take up more of our time. Like the shop-assistant and the labouring man we should neglect no opportunity to drink, and have this desire always in our mind. It seems to me that we are every day curtailing the indulgence of it; and that the luncheons, snacks, and collations which I remember in my boyhood, were much more frequent and usual in our houses than they are now. Can it be that in some things we are in the way of improvement? Truly, no. But the fact is that we are much more given to lechery than our fathers. These are two occupations that thwart one another in their vigour. On the one hand, lechery has weakened our stomachs, and, on the other, sobriety helps to make us more spruce and more wanton in the exercise of love.

Wonderful are the tales I have heard my father relate of the chastity of the times in which he lived. He was well qualified to speak of it, being well fitted, both by nature and training, for intercourse with ladies. He spoke little and well, and his language was besides sprinkled with picturesque expressions derived from books written in the vulgar tongues,[1] especially Spanish; and among the Spanish his usual reading was that which they call *Marcus Aurelius*.[1]

He bore himself with a pleasing, humble, and very modest gravity. He was singularly careful of neatness and propriety in his person and dress, whether mounted or on foot. He was wonderfully punctilious in keeping his word; conscientious and scrupulous in general to the point of superstition.

For a man of low stature he was very strong, with an upright and well-proportioned figure. Of a pleasing countenance, and a complexion inclining to brown. Nimble and excelling in all kinds of gentlemanly exercises. I still remember seeing some canes filled with lead, with which they tell me he used to exercise his arms when training to throw the bar or the stone, or for fencing; as well as shoes with

---

[1] The vulgar tongues, i.e., the modern languages, as distinct from Latin. *The Golden Book of Marcus Aurelius* was the best-known work of Antonio de Guevara (1490–1545), an historical romance based on the life of that Emperor which, in North's translation, became extremely popular in England. The style resembles what we call Euphuism, which has also been called Guevarism. We see reflections of it in Shakespeare, especially in *Love's Labour's Lost*.

leaded soles, to make him lighter for running or leaping. Of his vaulting they remember little wonders. I have seen him, when past sixty, putting our agility to shame by leaping into the saddle in his furred gown, making the round of the table on his thumb,[1] and scarcely ever mounting the stairs to his room without taking three or four steps at a time.

In the matter I am speaking of he declared that in the whole of a province there was scarcely one woman of quality with an evil reputation. He would tell of strange intimacies, especially his own, with honest women, quite above suspicion. And he solemnly swore of himself, that he was a virgin when he married. Yet he had taken part for a considerable period in the wars beyond the mountains, of which he has left a journal written in his own hand, giving all the details of what happened there, both of general interest and concerning himself in particular.

He consequently married when he was well on in years, at the age of thirty-three, in the year 1528, on his way home from Italy. Let us return to our bottles.[2]

The discomforts of old age, which has need of some support and refreshment, might reasonably beget in me a desire for this faculty of drinking. For it is, we might say, the last pleasure that the course of years robs us of.

The natural heat, so the good fellows say, begins in the feet: that concerns infancy. From thence it mounts to the middle regions, where it long takes root and produces, in my opinion, the only true pleasures of the bodily life. The other pleasures are comparatively dormant. Towards the end, like a rising and exhaling vapour, it arrives at the gullet, which it makes its final resting-place.

I cannot, however, understand how a man can prolong the pleasure of drinking beyond his thirst, and forge in his imagination an artificial and unnatural appetite. My stomach could not go to those lengths: it has enough to do to deal with what it takes for its need. By disposition I care

[1] This feat has greatly exercised the commentators, some of whom suggest impossibilities. What Montaigne really meant must be left to conjecture.

[2] A humorous variant of a favourite phrase of Rabelais, *revenons à nos moutons*, which occurs in the old farce of *Maître Pathelin*. Florio missed the humour of it, or perhaps he did not know his Rabelais. He translates: 'But come we to our drinking again.'

not to drink except after eating, consequently my last draught is almost always the biggest.

[And since in old age our palate is thickened with phlegm or depraved by some ailment, wine tastes the better if our pores are washed and opened; at least it rarely happens that I really relish the first draught.]

Anacharsis wondered at the Greeks drinking from larger glasses at the end than at the beginning of their meals; they did it, I imagine, for the same reason that the Germans do it, who then begin their drinking contests.

Plato forbids the use of wine by children before they are eighteen years of age, and intoxication before the age of forty. But after they have passed that age, he orders them to take a pleasure in it, and to mingle copiously with their convivialities the influence of Dionysos, the kind god who restores cheerfulness to men and youth to the aged, who softens and melts the passions of the soul, as iron is melted by fire. In his Laws he declares these convivial gatherings to have their use, provided there be a master of the feast to enforce rule and restraint; intoxication being, he says, a good and certain test of every man's nature, and at the same time calculated to put heart into the elderly and give them a delight in dancing and music: wholesome pleasures which they dare not indulge in when sober. He adds that wine is capable of making the soul mellow and the body healthy.

He approves, however, the following restrictions, in part borrowed from the Carthaginians: That no wine be drunk on warlike expeditions; That every judge and magistrate abstain from it when about to enter on his duties, and before discussing public business; That we shall not spend the day over it, a time due to other occupations, nor the night which we have reserved for procreation.

It is said that the philosopher Stilpo, weighed down by old age, purposely hastened his end by drinking his wine unmixed. A like cause, but not of his own design, also extinguished the vital spark of the philosopher Arcesilaus, when broken by old age.

But it is an old and absurd question, 'Whether the soul of the wise man is of a nature to yield to the strength of wine?'

Should we lay siege to wisdom's stronghold? (HORACE.)

To what absurdity are we not driven by our self-conceit! The best-regulated soul in the world is hard put to it to keep her feet, and to guard against being thrown to earth through her own weakness. Not one in a thousand is erect and sober for an instant in life. And it may be doubted if, in her natural state, she can ever be so. But if she be steadfast she will attain to the highest state of perfection; provided, I mean, that she be subjected to no shock, which may happen in a thousand ways.

Much good did Lucretius, that great poet, get from his philosophy and his strength of mind, when behold him maddened by a love-philtre! Do you think that Socrates could not be floored by a fit of apoplexy, as well as any porter? Some, under the influence of a malady, have even forgotten their own names, and a slight wound has turned the judgement of others topsy-turvy. Let him be as wise as he will he is after all a man, and what can be imagined more crazy, more miserable, and insignificant? Wisdom does not master our natural disposition:

> Sweats and pallors spread
> Over the body, and the tongue is broken,
> And fails the voice away, and ring the ears;
> Mists blind the eyeballs, and the joints collapse,—
> Aye, men drop dead from terror of the mind. (LUCRETIUS.)

He has to blink his eyes when threatened by a blow; he has to quake like a child on the brink of a precipice, Nature having reserved to herself those slight marks of her authority, which are proof against our reason and stoic virtue, to teach man his mortality and frailty. He turns pale with fear, red with shame: a sharp attack of the colic will make him, if not shout with despair, at least utter a broken and muffled groan:

> From human ills he shall not be exempt.[1] (TERENCE.)

The poets, who invent all things to suit their humour, dare not even acquit their heroes of the weakness of tears:

> Weeping he speaks, and gives his fleet the rein. (VIRGIL.)

Let it be enough if a man curbs and moderates his inclina-

---

[1] *Humani a se nihil alienum putet:* a perversion, to suit the context, of the well-known line, *Homo sum; humani nil a me alienum puto*, 'I am human, and interested in everything human.'

tions, for it is not in him to banish them. Even our Plutarch, so perfect and excellent a judge of human actions, seeing Brutus and Torquatus kill their children, begins to doubt whether virtue could go to such lengths, and whether those men were not rather stirred by some other passion. All actions exceeding the ordinary bounds are liable to a sinister interpretation, seeing that we cannot appreciate what is above us any more than what is beneath us.

We may leave aside that other sect that openly professes a proud spirit,[1] but when, even in that sect which is regarded as the more effeminate,[1] we hear these braggings of Metrodorus : *I have anticipated and caught you, Fortune ; I have cut off every access, so that you cannot reach me* (Cicero) ; When Anaxarchus, lying in a stone trough by command of Nicocreon, tyrant of Cyprus, and belaboured to death with an iron mallet, cries unceasingly, ' Strike, break : it is not Anaxarchus but his shell that you are pounding ' ; When we hear our martyrs, in the midst of the flames, crying to their tyrant, ' This side is sufficiently roasted ; slice it, eat it, it is well done ; begin on the other side ' ; When we hear that boy in Josephus, his flesh torn to pieces by biting pincers, and pierced by the bodkins of Antiochus, still defying him and crying with a firm and assured voice, ' Tyrant, you are wasting your time, I am still at my ease ; where is that pain, where are those tortures you threaten me with ? Is this all you can do ? My fortitude pains you more than your cruelty does me. O poor weakling ! you are giving way, and I am growing stronger ; make me complain, make me yield, if you can ; put heart into your satellites and executioners : see, they are losing courage, they cannot stand it ; arm them, stir them up ! ' When we see all this, we must truly admit that there is some derangement, a sort of frenzy in these souls, how holy soever.

When we come to these stoic outbursts : *I had rather be mad than voluptuous*, a saying of Antisthenes ; When Sextius tells us that he would rather be fettered with pain than with sensuality ; When Epicurus tries to think he is caressed by his gout, and, refusing health and repose, defies his ills with a gay heart ; and when, despising the less acute pains, disdaining to battle and struggle with them, he

---

[1] The Stoics and the Epicureans, respectively.

wishes and calls for others more violent, more painful, more worthy of him,

> No more
> He heeds such timid prey, but longs to hear
> The tawny lion, issuing with a roar
> From forth the lofty hills, or front the foaming boar, (VIRGIL.)

who will not conclude that these are outbursts of a courage thrown off its balance?

Our soul cannot from her seat reach to such a height. She must quit it and rise, and, taking the bit between her teeth, forcibly carry her man so far, that he will afterwards be astounded at his own deeds. So, in the exploits of war, the generous soldier is often impelled in the heat of combat to deeds of so perilous a nature that, having come to himself, he is the first to be struck with amazement.

And so the poet is often rapt in admiration of his own work, no longer recognizing the track along which he ran so fine a race: in him also we call it madness and frenzy. And as Plato says that in vain does a sober-minded man knock at the door of poetry, so Aristotle says that no mind of any eminence is free from a tinge of madness. And he is right in calling madness every transport, however admirable, that transcends our reason and judgement; seeing that wisdom is a well-ordered government of our soul, carried out with measure and proportion, for which she is responsible to herself.

Plato argues thus: 'that the power of prophecy is above us; that we must be beside ourselves when we exercise it: our sober senses must be clouded either by sleep or by some malady, or lifted from its place in a heavenly rapture.'

CHAPTER 3

A CUSTOM OF THE ISLAND OF CEA

IF, as they say, to philosophize is to doubt, then, *à fortiori*, to trifle and indulge in fancies, as I do, must be to doubt. For it is the part of learners to question and dispute, and of the professor to settle the dispute. My professor is the authority of the divine will, which governs us without contradiction, and has its chair above those empty and human wranglings.

Philip having entered the Peloponnesus with an armed force, somebody said to Damidas that the Lacedemonians would greatly suffer unless they committed themselves to his mercy. 'Ah, poltroon! he cried, what can they suffer who fear not death?' Some one also inquired of Agis how a man might live free; 'By despising death,' he replied.

These sayings, and a thousand other such that we meet with to the same purpose, evidently strike a note of something beyond the patient awaiting of death, whenever it shall come to us. For there are many calamities in life that are harder to bear even than death. Witness that Spartan boy, taken by Antigonus and sold for a slave, who, when ordered by his master to perform some menial service, said, 'You shall see whom you have bought; with freedom so near at hand, it would be a disgrace in me to be a slave.' Thereupon he threw himself from the top of the house. Antipater, threatening the Lacedemonians with violence to make them yield to a certain demand of his, they replied, 'If you threaten us with worse than death, we shall die the more willingly.' And to Philip, who had written to them that he would hinder all their enterprises, 'What, will you also hinder us from dying?'

That is what they mean when they say that the wise man lives as long as he ought, and not as long as he can; and that the kindest gift that Nature has bestowed upon us, and which takes from us every excuse for complaining of our condition, is that she has left us the key of the fields. She has ordained only one entry into life, but a hundred thousand outlets. We may lack land to live on, but of land to die upon we can never have any lack, as Boiocatus answered the Romans.

Why do you complain of this world? It does not hold you: if you live in trouble, your cowardice is the cause of it. To die there remains only the will,

> For death is everywhere. A kindly God
> Hath this great law with wisest care ordained:
> That any one can take man's life away,
> But none can stay his death; for countless ways
> Are open unto him who seeks to die. (SENECA.)

Nor is it the remedy for one malady only; death is a remedy for all ills. It is a very sure haven that is never to be feared and often to be sought. It all comes to the same thing whether a man gives himself his quietus, or suffers it; whether he hastens to meet his day, or awaits it; whencesoever it comes, it is still his; wherever the thread may break, it is all there: there is the end of the yarn.

The most voluntary death is the finest.

Life depends on the will of others, death upon our own. In nothing should we follow our inclination so much as in this.

Reputation has no concern with such a design; it is folly to pay regard to it.

Life is a slavery if the freedom to die is wanting.

The ordinary course of cure is carried on at the expense of life: we suffer incisions, or cauterizations, or amputations of limbs, our food and our blood are taken from us; one step more and lo! we are completely cured.

Why is not the jugular vein as much at our command as that in the bend of the arm?[1]

For the most desperate diseases the most desperate remedies.

Servius the grammarian, when suffering from the gout, could think of no better plan than to apply poison to kill his legs. He cared not whether they were gouty, so long as they were without feeling. God gives us permission enough when he reduces us to such a condition that living is worse than dying.

It is weakness to give way to infirmities, but it is folly to cherish them.

The Stoics say that to part with life is, for the wise man, even at the height of happiness, to live in conformity with Nature, if he does it opportunely; and that for the fool it is natural to cling to life, although he be wretched, provided that he possesses most of the things which are said to be according to Nature.

As I do not violate the laws enacted against thieves when I take what is my own and cut my own purse, or those against incendiaries when I burn my own wood, so I am not bound by the law against murderers, if I take my own life.

Hegesias was wont to say that the conditions both of our life and our death should be at our own choice. And

---

[1] i. e., why not cut our throats at once instead of bleeding us?

Diogenes, meeting the philosopher Speusippus, who had been long afflicted with the dropsy and was being carried in a litter, and who called out to him, ' Good health, Diogenes ! ' replied, ' No health to you, who endure life being in such a condition.' Some time after, indeed, weary of living under such painful conditions, Speusippus did make an end of himself.

There is another side to the question. For many maintain, That we cannot quit this garrison of the world without the express command of him who has placed us here ; and That it is for God, who has sent us into this world, not for ourselves only, but rather for his glory and the service of others, to give us our discharge when it pleases him, and not for us to take it ; That we are not born for ourselves, but also for our country ; the law requires us, on her behalf, to render an account of ourselves, and can take action against us for homicide. Otherwise we are punished, both in this and the next world, as deserters from the post of duty :

> And next are those who, hateful of the day,
> With guiltless hands their sorrowing lives have ta'en,
> And miserably flung their souls away. (VIRGIL.)

There is much more fortitude shown in wearing out the chains which bind us than in breaking them, and Regulus gives a better proof of heroism than Cato.[1] It is want of judgement and patience that hastens our steps. No calamities will make live Virtue turn her back : she seeks pain and evils for her aliment. The threats of tyrants, the tortures of the executioners, put life and soul into her :

> Like oak, by sturdy axes lopped
> Of all its boughs, which once the brakes
> Of shaggy Algidus overtopped,
> The loss its glory makes,
> And from the very steel fresh strength and spirit takes. (HORACE.)

And, as another says,

> No virtue 'tis to fear to live,
> As thou dost think, but to withstand,
> And not to turn our backs upon,
> Adversity. (SENECA.)

---

[1] Regulus, after being defeated by the Carthaginians, was a prisoner for five years, and, having been released on parole, was subsequently, on his return from Rome, put to death with torture.

> When Fortune is unkind 'tis easier far
> To laugh at death; the braver man is he
> That is content to live in misery. (MARTIAL.)

It is the part of cowardice, not of virtue, to go and squat in a hollow, under a massive tomb, to avoid the strokes of Fortune. Virtue will not stop her course or slacken her pace, for the wildest storm that blows:

> Yea, if the globe should fall, he'll stand
> Serene amidst the crash. (HORACE.)

Most commonly in our flight from other woes we are driven to this. Nay, sometimes in fleeing from death we run into his arms:

> Can there be greater madness, pray,
> Than to court death through fear of death? (MARTIAL.)

Like those who, in terror of a precipice, throw themselves headlong into it:

> The very fear of ills to come hath sent
> Many to mighty dangers; bravest is he
> Who fearful things to endure is well prepared,
> When they impend, or haply puts them off. (LUCAN.)

> And oft to that degree, from fright of death,
> Will hate of living and beholding light
> Take hold on human-kind that they inflict
> Their own destruction with a gloomy heart—
> Forgetful that this fear is fount of cares. (LUCRETIUS.)

Plato, in his Laws, orders an ignominious burial for the man who has deprived his nearest and best friend, to wit, himself, of life and his destined course, when constrained neither by public judgement, nor by some sad and inevitable vicissitude of fortune, nor by an unbearable disgrace, but by the cowardice and weakness of a timorous soul.

And the idea of disdaining life is ridiculous. For after all it is our being, it is our all. The things that have a richer and a nobler being may condemn ours. But it is contrary to Nature that we should despise and carelessly set ourselves at naught. It is a malady confined to man, and not seen in any other creature, to hate and despise himself. It is on a par with our vanity to desire to be other than we are. We reap no fruit from such a desire, seeing that it contradicts and hinders itself. He that, being a man, desires to be made an angel, does nothing for himself: he would never be the better for it. For, when he is no more, who will rejoice for him or be sensible of this betterment?

> For if woe and ail
> Perchance are toward, then the man to whom
> The bane can happen must himself be there
> At the same time. (LUCRETIUS.)

Security, absence of suffering, impassibility, the privation of the ills of this life, that we purchase at the price of death, bring us no advantage. In vain does he avoid war who cannot enjoy peace, and in vain does he avoid trouble who cannot relish tranquillity.

Among those who held the former opinion, there was much questioning on this point: What occasions are sufficient to justify a man's deciding to kill himself? They call that a *reasonable exit* (Diogenes Laertius). For, although they say that it is often necessary to die for trivial reasons, since those that detain us in life are not very strong, yet there must be some measure. There are fanciful and unreasonable moods which have impelled, not only individuals, but whole nations, to do away with themselves. I have already cited examples. And we further read of the virgins of Miletus that, in a concerted frenzy, they hanged themselves one after another, until the magistracy made an end of it by ordering that those who were found thus hanged should be dragged quite naked through the streets with the same halter.

When Therycion exhorted Cleomenes to kill himself on account of the evil state of his affairs, and, since he had escaped the more honourable death in the battle which he had just lost, to accept this other which was only second in honour to it, and not give the victors an opportunity of making him suffer a shameful death or a shameful life, Cleomenes, with Spartan and Stoic courage, refused this advice as cowardly and effeminate: 'That is a remedy, he said, that can never fail me, and which one should never resort to as long as there is a finger's breadth of hope remaining. To live is sometimes a sign of fortitude and valour. I should wish even my death to be of service to my country, and would make it an act of honour and virtue.' Therycion then followed his own advice and killed himself. Cleomenes afterwards did the same, but not till after he had tasted the extreme bitterness of Fortune.

Not all ills are worth dying to avoid. And besides, there being so many sudden changes in human affairs, it is difficult to decide at what exact point we are at the end of our hope:

> On cruel sand the gladiator lies,
> And, vanquished though he be, he still hopes on,
> In spite of threatening public's hostile thumb. (JUSTUS LIPSIUS.)

All things are to be hoped for, says an old adage, as long as there is life in a man. 'Yes, but, replies Seneca, why should this occur to me, That Fortune can do everything for him who is alive, rather than this, That Fortune has no hold upon him who knows how to die?' We see Josephus involved in a danger so manifest and imminent, a whole nation having risen up against him, that reason could hold out no hope of escape. Yet being advised in this strait by one of his friends, as he informs us, to do away with himself, it turned out well for him that he obstinately clung to hope. For Fortune, against all human reason, so changed the situation that he found himself free and unharmed.

Brutus and Cassius, on the other hand, achieved the loss of the last remnants of Roman liberty, of which they were the protectors, by their rash and precipitate suicide, before the time and occasion.

[At the battle of Sérisolles, Monsieur d'Anguien twice attempted to run himself through the throat with his sword, in despair at the turn the battle was taking in the part of the field where he was engaged; and by his precipitation was within an ace of robbing himself of the fruit of so fine a victory.]

I have seen a hundred hares escape out of the very teeth of the greyhounds; *Many a man has survived his executioners* (Seneca).

> Time—healing Time—and long laborious years
> Oft raise the humble; Fortune in her play
> Lifts those to-morrow whom she lowers to-day. (VIRGIL.)

Pliny says there are but three kinds of maladies to escape which one is justified [1] in killing oneself; the most painful of all is a stone in the bladder, when the urine is retained

---

[1] Pliny wrote 'men are accustomed to', and that was the reading of the earlier editions of the Essays. In the 'Bordeaux MS.' Montaigne wrote 'is justified' and deleted 'the second is a pain in the stomach; the third, a headache'.

by it. Seneca will admit only those which for a length of time disturb the functions of the soul. Some are of opinion that, to avoid a worse death, we may take our life at our discretion. Damocritus, general of the Aetolians, being led captive to Rome, found means to escape by night. But, when pursued by his guards, he ran his sword through his body before they were able to recapture him.

Antinoüs and Theodotus, their city of Epirus having been reduced to extremity by the Romans, advised the people to kill themselves in a body. But the counsel to surrender having won the day, these two sought their death by hurling themselves into the midst of the enemy, with the intention of striking, and not of defending themselves.

When the island of Gozo[1] was stormed some years ago by the Turks, a Sicilian, who had two beautiful daughters of marriageable age, killed them with his own hand, and then their mother who hastened to the spot as they were dying. Having done which, he ran into the street with a cross-bow and an arquebus and with two shots killed the first two Turks who approached his door ; then, with sword in hand, he furiously entered the fray, where he was immediately surrounded and cut in pieces. Thus he saved himself, after delivering his family, from slavery.

To escape the cruelty of Antiochus, the Jewish women, after having their children circumcised, hurled them and themselves into death.

I was told of a man of quality who was imprisoned in one of our conciergeries. His relations, having had certain information that he would be condemned, to avoid the ignominy of such a death, suborned a priest to tell him that the sovereign remedy for his deliverance was to commend himself to a certain saint with such and such a vow, and fast for a week, even if he felt ever so weak and faint. He took this advice on trust and in this way unintentionally rid himself of life and danger.

Scribonia, when she advised her nephew Libo to kill himself rather than await the hand of the law, pointed out to him that it was really playing into others' hands to preserve his life and place it in the power of those who would come to seek it in three or four days ; and that he was serving his enemies' purpose by keeping his blood for them to devour.

---

[1] An island adjoining Malta.

We read in the Bible that Nicanor, the persecutor of God's law, sent his satellites to apprehend the good elder Razis, 'who for his kindness was called a father of the Jews.... Now when the multitude would have taken the tower, and violently broken into the outer door, and bade that fire be brought to burn it, he being ready to be taken on every side fell upon his sword; choosing rather to die manfully, than to come into the hands of the wicked, to be abused otherwise than beseemed his noble birth. But missing his stroke through haste, the multitude also rushing within the doors, he ran boldly up to the wall, and cast himself down manfully among the thickest of them. But they quickly giving back, and a space being made, he fell down into the midst of the void place. Nevertheless, while there was yet breath within him, being inflamed with anger, he rose up; and though his blood gushed out like spouts of water, and his wounds were grievous, yet he ran through the midst of the throng; and standing upon a steep rock, when as his blood was now quite gone, he plucked out his bowels, and taking them in both his hands, he cast them upon the throng, and calling upon the Lord of life and spirit to restore him those again, he thus died.'[1]

Of acts of violence perpetrated against the conscience, the most to be avoided is, in my opinion, that against the chastity of women, seeing that it is naturally attended with some bodily pleasure, and for that reason the want of consent cannot be sufficiently complete, and the force on one side is perhaps not without a little desire on the other.

Of Pelagia and Sophronia, both of whom were canonized, the former leapt into the river with her mother and sisters, to escape the violence of some soldiers; and the latter also killed herself to escape the forced attentions of the Emperor Maxentius. The history of the Church pays reverence to several such examples of devout women who have appealed to death to save them from the outrages planned by tyrants against their [religion and] conscience.

It will perhaps be accounted an honour to us in future

---

[1] 2 Maccabees xiv. 37 ff., in the Apocrypha. I have given the words of the Authorized Version, from which Montaigne's account differs in two particulars: he makes Razis 'pitch directly upon his head', which would probably have been fatal, and ends with making him 'invoke the divine vengeance upon them'.

ages, that a learned author of the present day, and that a Parisian, has been at pains to persuade our ladies to make up their minds to anything rather than adopt that dreadful counsel of despair. I am sorry that he did not know and insert among his tales the good story I heard at Toulouse, of a woman who had passed through the hands of several soldiers. 'God be praised! she said, that at least once in my life I have had my fill without sin!'

In truth such cruelty is unworthy of our tender French ladies. And thank God that our atmosphere is thoroughly cleansed of it since that good hint! Enough if they say *Nenny*[1] (no, no!) while doing it, following the rule of our good Marot.

History is full to overflowing of those who in a thousand ways have exchanged a painful life for death:

Lucius Arruntius killed himself in order, as he said, 'to fly both the future and the past'.

Granius Silvanus and Statius Proximus killed themselves after being pardoned by Nero; whether it was that they would not live by the favour of so wicked a man, or that they feared the irksomeness of a second pardon, on some other occasion, seeing how ready he was to suspect and accuse honest men.

Spargapises, son of Queen Tomyris, taken captive in war by Cyrus, abused the first favour which the King granted him, of releasing him from his fetters, by killing himself; the only fruit he intended to reap from his freedom being to avenge on himself the disgrace of having been taken prisoner.

Boges, governor of Eïon in the name of King Xerxes, besieged by the Athenian army under the leadership of Cimon, refused the terms which enabled him to return in safety to Asia with his goods and chattels, being loath to survive the loss of that which his master had given into his keeping; and, after defending his city to the utmost of its capacity to resist, there being nothing left to eat, he first threw into the river Strymon all the gold and everything else of which he thought the enemy might make booty. Then, having commanded a large wood-pile to be kindled,

---

[1] 'A sweet no, no! with a sweet smile, is so becoming.'—Clément Marot, who lived in the first half of the sixteenth century, a poet whose gift lay in the direction of badinage and graceful satire.

and the throats of his wife, his children, concubines, and household slaves to be cut, cast them on the flames and himself after.

Ninachetuen, an Indian lord, having heard the first rumour of the Portuguese Viceroy's determination to depose him, without any apparent reason, from the charge he filled in Malacca, and transfer it to the King of Campar, resolved to himself on this course of action : He had a scaffold erected, longer than it was broad, supported on pillars, royally hung with tapestries and decked with flowers, with abundance of perfumes. Then, having put on a robe of cloth of gold covered with precious stones of great price, he went into the street and mounted the steps to the scaffold, in one corner of which a pile of aromatic woods was kindled. The people hastened to see what might be the purpose of these unusual preparations. Then, with a countenance expressive of anger and determination, he explained to them how much the Portuguese nation was beholden to him ; how faithfully he had exercised his charge ; that, having so often, with sword in hand, manifested on others' behalf that honour was much dearer to him than life, he was not the man to abandon the care of it on his own behalf ; that, Fortune having denied him any power to resist the insult which was intended to be put upon him, his heart at least commanded him to escape the feeling that he was a laughing-stock to the people and a cause of triumph to men of less worth than himself. Having said which, he threw himself into the fire.

Sextilia, the wife of Scaurus, and Paxea, the wife of Labeo, to encourage their husbands to escape the dangers which were pressing upon them, and in which they had no share but by right of their wifely affection, voluntarily gave their lives in pledge, in order in this extreme necessity to set them an example and keep them company. What they did for their husbands Cocceius Nerva did for his country, with less profit though with equal love. This great lawyer, in the best of health, rich, of good repute and in favour with the Emperor, had no other reason to kill himself but his compassion for the miserable state of the Roman Republic.

Nothing could add to the delicacy of feeling shown in the death of the wife of Fulvius, an intimate friend of Augustus. The latter, having discovered that he had let out an impor-

THE CITIZENS OF CAPUA

tant secret that he had confided to him, one morning, when he waited upon him, gave him a meagre look. He returned home in great despair and said very dolefully to his wife that, having fallen into this disgrace, he was resolved to kill himself. She replied quite frankly, 'It is but right that you should, since, having often enough experienced the incontinence of my tongue, you have not taken warning. But stay till I have first killed myself.' And without more ado she ran a sword through her body.

During the last deliberation of the Senate of Capua, which was being besieged by the Romans, Vibius Virius, having lost all hope of saving the city and of receiving any mercy at the hands of the enemy, after several representations made to that end, came to the conclusion that the noblest way to escape their fate was by their own hands. The enemy would honour them for it and Hannibal would become sensible of what faithful friends he had forsaken. He invited those who approved his counsel to come and eat a good supper that was prepared at his house, where, after making good cheer, they should drink together of what would be offered to him : ' a draught that will free our bodies from torture, our spirits from insults, our eyes and ears from seeing and hearing all the dire ills that the vanquished have to suffer at the hands of cruel and offended conquerors. I have, he added, given orders for our bodies to be thrown on a pyre in front of my door, after we are dead, by men engaged for the purpose.'

A goodly number agreed to this lofty resolution, but few imitated it. Twenty-seven senators followed him, and, after endeavouring to drown their painful thoughts in wine, finished their repast with that fatal dish. And, after embracing one another and jointly deploring their country's misfortunes, some retired to their own houses, and others stayed to be laid with Vibius on his funeral pyre. All were so long dying, the fumes of the wine having congested the veins and retarded the effect of the poison, that some were within an hour of seeing the enemy in Capua, which was taken the next day, and of suffering the miseries they had escaped at such cost.

When the Consul Fulvius was returning after his infamous butchery of the two hundred and twenty-five senators, Taurea Vibellius, another citizen of Capua, fiercely called him by name and, having stopped him, said: 'Command me also to be massacred after so many others, that you may boast of having killed a much braver man than yourself.' Although Fulvius disdained him as a madman, besides having just received letters from Rome condemning the inhumanity of his deed, and tying his hands, Vibellius continued: 'Since, my country being taken and my friends dead, and having killed with my own hands my wife and children, to save them from the desolation of this ruin, I am not permitted to die the death of my fellow-citizens, let me borrow of virtue vengeance on this hateful life.' And, drawing a blade he had hidden, he plunged it into his heart and, falling backwards, died at the Consul's feet.

Alexander was besieging a city in the Indies; the inhabitants, finding themselves hard pressed, manfully resolved to rob him of the pleasure of his victory, and burned themselves in a body together with their city, in spite of his humanity. Whence a new kind of war: the enemy striving to save them and they to destroy themselves and doing, to ensure their death, all that men do to ensure their life.

Astapa, a town in Spain, being too weak in walls and fortifications to withstand the Romans, the inhabitants piled up their valuables and furniture in the public square, and, having placed upon this heap their wives and children, and built it round with wood and very inflammable matter, and left fifty of their young men to carry out their purpose, they made a sally and, in accordance with a vow they had taken, seeing they could not vanquish, suffered themselves to be slain every one. The fifty, after having massacred every living soul scattered about their town and set fire to the heap, leapt into it also, ending their noble liberty in a state of insensibility rather than in pain and ignominy; proving to the enemy that, if Fortune had willed it, they would have had as much courage to rob them of their victory as they had to frustrate it and make it hideous; yea, and fatal too to a good number of them who, enticed by the glitter of the gold melting in the flame, approached too near and were burned or suffocated, their retreat being prevented by the throng that followed.

The citizens of Abydos, besieged by Philip, took the same resolution. But, coming upon them suddenly, the

King, horrified at the frantic haste with which they were carrying out their purpose (the treasures and movables which they had severally condemned to be burned or sunk having been seized), drew off his soldiers and granted them three days in which to kill themselves at their leisure; which time they filled in with blood and murder beyond any cruelty committed by an enemy, so that not a single person escaped who had power over himself.

There are countless examples of the like popular resolutions, which seem the more ferocious in that their effect is more general. They are really less so than when carried out individually. What arguments and persuasions cannot effect in an individual they can do with a body of individuals, since the ardour of men acting in common carries the judgement of the individual along with it.

In the time of Tiberius the condemned who awaited their execution forfeited their property and were denied the rites of sepulture; those who anticipated it by suicide were interred and allowed to make their wills.

But we sometimes desire death in the hope of some greater good. 'I desire, says Saint Paul, to be dissolved, that I may be with Jesus Christ'; and elsewhere, 'Who will deliver me from these bonds?

Cleombrotus of Ambracia, having read the *Phaedo* of Plato, conceived so great a desire for the life to come that, without any other reason, he leapt into the sea. Whence it becomes clear how improperly we apply the word Despair to this voluntary dissolution, to which we are often borne by the eagerness of hope, and often by a calm and sober inclination of judgement.

Jacques du Chastel, Bishop of Soissons, when engaged in the overseas expedition with Saint Louis, seeing the King and his whole army preparing to return to France without having accomplished their devout purpose, resolved rather to go to Paradise. And having said adieu to his friends, charged single-handed, in sight of all, into the midst of the enemy army, where he was cut in pieces.

In a certain kingdom of those newly-discovered regions, upon a day of solemn procession, on which the idol they worship is carried about in public upon a car of prodigious size, besides that many are seen to cut off pieces of their living flesh to offer him, there are numbers of others who prostrate themselves in the place, and are crushed and mangled under the wheels, in order to win, after death, the veneration for holiness, which is paid them.[1] The death of that Bishop with his arms in his hands is more noble and less felt, since the heat of combat distracts some of the feeling.

Some governments have taken upon them to decide the justice and expediency of voluntary deaths. In times gone by there was kept in our city of Marseilles, at the public expense, a supply of poison made from hemlock, for those who wished to hasten their days, after having the motives of their design approved by the six hundred who formed the Senate; since it was not permitted to lay hands on oneself except by leave of the authorities and for lawful reasons. This law also prevailed in other places.

Sextus Pompeius, on his way to Asia, called at the island of Cea of Negropont. It happened by chance, whilst he was there, as we are told by one of his companions,[2] that a lady of great authority, after explaining to her citizens why she was resolved to end her life, entreated Pompeius to be present at her death, in order to lend more distinction to it; to which he assented. After trying long in vain, by the power of eloquence, which he had at his command to a wonderful degree, and of persuasions, to turn her from her purpose, he at length suffered her to have her will. She had spent ninety years in a state of great happiness both of mind and body; but now, reclining on a couch which was more richly adorned than was usual, and supported on her elbow, she said: 'May the gods, O Sextus Pompeius, and rather those that I leave behind than those I go to seek, be kind to you for not having disdained both to advise me in my life and to witness my death! For my part, having ever seen the kinder side of Fortune's face, and fearing lest the desire for too long a life might make me see the other side, I am going, by a happy ending, to dismiss the rest of my days, leaving two daughters of my body and a legion of grandchildren.'

---

[1] The car of Juggernaut. Popular errors die hard: the stories of self-immolation to Jagganath have been conclusively shown to be entirely fictitious.

[2] Valerius Maximus, the historian, who flourished about A. D. 26. The island of Zea or Kea (old Ceos) lies to the south of Negroponte.

Having said this, and after lecturing and exhorting her descendants to preserve peace and concord, she divided her property among them, and commended her household gods to her elder daughter; with a steady hand she took the cup which contained the poison, and, having paid her vows to Mercury and prayed to him to lead her into some happy seat in the other world, she quickly drained the fatal potion. Then she entertained the company by describing the working and progress of the poison, and how she felt the several parts of her body seized one after the other with chill, until at length it reached the heart and bowels. She then called on her daughters to fulfil the last office and close her eyes.

Pliny tells us of a certain country in the Far North where, by reason of the mild temperature of the atmosphere, the lives of the inhabitants are commonly ended only by their own will. When they have reached an advanced old age and are weary and satiated with life, their custom is, after making good cheer, to leap into the sea from a certain high rock appointed for that purpose.

Intolerable pain and the fear of a worse death appear to me to be the most excusable inducements.

CHAPTER 4

TIME ENOUGH FOR BUSINESS TO-MORROW

I AWARD, and I think with good reason, the palm to Jacques Amyot[1] over all our French writers, not only for the simplicity and purity of his language, wherein he excels all others, nor for his perseverance in a work of such length, nor for the profundity of his learning, which enabled him to interpret so happily an author so stiff and thorny (they may tell me what they please about it, for I know no Greek;[2] but I find throughout his translation so beautiful, so well-connected and sustained a meaning, that certainly he has either fathomed the real thoughts of the

[1] Jacques Amyot (1513–93), professor at the University of Bruges, a delegate to the Council of Trent, tutor to the sons of Henri II, afterwards Bishop of Auxerre and translator of Plutarch's *Lives* (1559), and his *Moral Works* (1572). To him chiefly we owe our knowledge of Plutarch through North's translation.

[2] Montaigne evidently means no more than that he does not know sufficient Greek to check Amyot's work.

author, or, having, by such long intercourse with him, deeply implanted in his mind a general idea of Plutarch's mind, he has at least attributed to him nothing that belies or contradicts him); but above everything I owe him gratitude for having had the judgement to pick out and choose so worthy and appropriate a book to present to his country. We other ignoramuses had been lost if this book had not lifted us out of the quagmire; thanks to him, we dare now to speak and write, and the ladies may lecture on him to the school-masters; he is our breviary.

If this good old man be yet alive, I recommend Xenophon to him, to be treated in the same way: it is an easier task and the better adapted to his old age; and besides, it somehow seems to me that, although he gets out of a difficulty very briskly and cleanly, yet his style is more at home when it is not harassed by difficulties, and rolls along at its leisure.

I lighted just now on the passage in Plutarch where he says of himself, that Rusticus, being present at a lecture which he was delivering at Rome, received a packet from the Emperor and put off reading it until the end of the lecture, wherefore, he says, all those present singularly commended the self-control of the man. Indeed, as he was discoursing on the subject of curiosity, and that greedy and gluttonous passion for news, which makes us so indiscreetly and impatiently forsake everything in order to speak with a new-comer, and, neglecting all respect and good behaviour, immediately tear open, wherever we may happen to be, the letters that are brought to us, he had some reason to commend Rusticus' self-control; and he might have applauded him besides for his civility and courtesy in being loath to interrupt the course of his lecture. But I doubt whether he could be commended for his prudence; for by deferring the reading of a letter received unexpectedly, and especially from an emperor, a man might very well come to great harm.

The contrary vice to curiosity is indifference, to which I evidently incline by nature; and I have known several men so extremely negligent that letters received by them three or four days before have been found unopened in their pockets.

I have always refrained from opening, not only letters

entrusted to me, but even such as have by chance passed through my hands. And I feel guilty if, standing near a great man, my eyes inadvertently snatch some knowledge of the contents of an important letter he is reading. No man was ever less inquisitive, or pried less into other people's business, than I.

In the time of our fathers Monsieur de Boutières very nearly lost Turin through having deferred, whilst supping in good company, reading a letter that was handed to him, warning him of treachery brewing against that city, of which he was commander. And from that same Plutarch I have learned that Julius Caesar might have saved his life if, on the way to the Senate on the day he was assassinated by the conspirators, he had read a paper which was handed to him. He tells also a story of Archias, tyrant of Thebes, that on the eve of his intended assassination by Pelopidas, whose object it was to restore his country to freedom, he was informed in a letter, giving all the details, from another Archias, an Athenian, of what was in store for him; but that, the packet having been handed to him during his supper, he put off opening it with these words, which afterwards became proverbial in Greece: 'Business to-morrow.'

A wise man may, I think, in consideration of others, in order, for instance, not to cause an unseemly interruption in company, like Rusticus, or to break off some other business of importance, defer hearing the news brought to him; but to do so in his own interest or for his own particular pleasure, in order not to interrupt his dinner or even disturb his sleep, is inexcusable, especially if he is a man holding public office.

In ancient Rome the most honourable place at table was called *consularis*, being more free from obstruction and more accessible to any one who should come in to speak with the person seated there: a testimony that being at table was not regarded as a reason for evading the interruption of unexpected business.

But, when all is said, it is difficult in human actions to lay down a rule so exact by the discourse of reason that Fortune will not assert her right.

CHAPTER 5

OF CONSCIENCE

TRAVELLING one day, my brother the Sieur de la Brousse and I, during our civil wars, we met with a gentleman of good presence. He was of the opposite faction to ours, but I had no inkling of it, for he pretended to be other than he was; and the worst of these wars is that the cards are so shuffled, your enemy being distinguished from you by no apparent mark, either of language or demeanour, having been brought up under the same laws and customs, and breathing the same atmosphere, that it is difficult to avoid confusion and disorder. This consideration made me afraid, for my own part, of meeting our troops in a place where I was not known, lest I might be placed in the predicament of telling my name or perhaps of incurring some worse danger. As it had befallen me before; for, in a misunderstanding of that kind, I lost both men and horses, and among others a page of mine, a young Italian of gentle birth, whom I was carefully bringing up, was miserably killed; in him died a very fair youth and of great promise.

But this man, every time we met with mounted men or passed through a town that held with the King, was so desperately afraid and looked so dead, that I at length guessed that it was his conscience that was giving him so much alarm. The poor man seemed to fear that the secret intentions of his heart could be read through his disguise and in spite of the crosses on his cassock. So wonderful is the power of conscience! It makes us betray, accuse, and fight against ourselves, and, for want of outside testimony, witness against ourselves.

The tortured mind is struck by invisible scourges. (JUVENAL.)

This tale is in the mouth of children: Bessus, a Paeonian, rebuked for having wantonly knocked down a sparrow's nest and killed the young, said that he had good reason to do so, because these fledglings would keep on accusing him falsely of the murder of his father. This parricide had hitherto lain secret and unknown, but the Furies, conscience's avengers, made him who was to bear the penalty of it bring it to the light of day.

POWER OF CONSCIENCE

Hesiod amends the saying of Plato, 'that punishment follows close on the heels of sin'; for he says, 'it is born at the same instant as the sin'. He who expects punishment, suffers it; he who has deserved it, expects it. Wickedness forges torments against itself:

> He suffers most who plans the evil deed;
> *(Proverb quoted by Aulus Gellius.)*

as the wasp stings and hurts others, but herself most, for she loses her sting and power for ever;

> And in the wound lays down her very life. (VIRGIL.)

The Spanish fly has something about it which, by a contrariety of nature, acts as an antidote to its own poison. So, while we take a pleasure in vice, conscience at the same time breeds a contrary displeasure which torments us, both waking and sleeping, with many painful reflections:

> For many, often babbling in their dreams,
> Or else in sickness raving, have been known
> To drag to light of day long-hidden crimes. (LUCRETIUS.)

Apollodorus dreamt that he was being flayed by the Scythians, then boiled in a cauldron, and that his heart was murmuring: 'I am the cause of all these thy woes.' No hiding-place will serve the wicked, says Epicurus, for they cannot be sure of being hid, whilst their conscience discovers them to themselves:

> This is the first revenge: himself being judge
> No guilty man will ever be acquitted. (JUVENAL.)

As conscience fills us with fear, so does it also fill us with assurance and confidence. And I may say that I have walked in many perils with a much firmer step by reason of the secret knowledge I had of my own will and the innocence of my intentions:

> As a man's conscience is, so hope within
> Or fear prevails, according to his deeds. (OVID.)

Of numerous examples three may suffice, of the same man: Scipio, being one day arraigned before the Roman people on a serious charge, instead of excusing himself or flattering his judges, said: 'It will become you well to sit in judgement on the head of the man by whose means you have power to judge the whole world!' And on another occasion, instead of pleading his cause, all the answer he made to the imputation cast upon him by a Tribune of the people was : ' Come, my citizens, let us go and give thanks to the gods for the victory they granted me over the Carthaginians upon such a day as this ; ' and behold him striding off to the temple with the whole assembly and the accuser himself at his heels !

And when Petilius, instigated by Cato, demanded of him an account of the money that passed through his hands in the province of Antioch, Scipio, having come into the Senate for that purpose, produced the book of accounts which he had under his toga, wherein he said his receipts and disbursements were accurately entered. But, being required to give it into the hands of the registrar, he refused, saying he would not have this shame put upon him, and with his own hands, in the presence of the Senate, he tore it in pieces. I do not believe that a cauterized soul could have counterfeited such assurance. He had a heart too big by nature and his lot had been cast in too high a place, says Livy, that he should play the part of a criminal and stoop so far as to defend his innocence.

The invention of tortures is a dangerous invention ; they seem to be a test of endurance rather than of truth. He who can endure them conceals the truth as well as he who cannot. For why should pain rather make me confess what is, than force me to say what is not ? And, on the other hand, if the man who has not done what he is accused of has the patience to suffer these tortures, why should not the guilty man have that patience, being offered so fair a reward as life ?

I believe that the idea underlying the use of torture is the power of conscience. For in the guilty man conscience would seem to assist the rack to make him confess his guilt, and to weaken him ; and on the other hand to fortify the innocent man against the torture. To tell the truth, it is a practice fraught with uncertainty and danger. What would we not say, what would we not do, to escape such cruel pains ?

Pain will force the innocent to lie. (PUBLIUS SYRUS.)

The effect is that the man whom the judge has put to the torture, that he may not die innocent, is made to die both innocent and tortured. Thousands and thousands have, by means of torture, loaded their heads with false confessions. Among these I place Philotas, considering the circumstances of Alexander's accusations against him, and the progress of his tortures.

And yet it has been said that it is the least evil that weak human nature has been able to invent. Very inhumanly, however, and very little to the purpose, to my mind.[1]

Many nations, less barbarous in this respect than the Greeks and Romans who call them so, esteem it cruel and horrible to torture and pull a man to pieces for a crime of which they are still in doubt. How can he help your ignorance ? Are you not unjust when, because you will not kill him without cause, you do worse than kill him ? That that is so, consider how often he would rather die without cause than undergo that ordeal which is more painful than the execution, and which often by its ruthlessness anticipates the execution and accomplishes it.

I do not know whence I had this story, but it exactly reflects the conscience of our justice. A village woman accused a soldier before an army-general, a great lover of justice, of having snatched from her little children the little broth that she had left to sustain them with, the army having pillaged all the villages round about. Of proof she had none. The general, after charging the woman to take good heed to what she was saying, since if she lied she would be guilty of false witness, and she still persisting, he commanded the soldier's stomach to be opened to find out the truth of the matter. And the woman was found to be in the right. An instructive sentence ![2]

CHAPTER 6

OF PREPARATION

REASON and education, however much we may be inclined to put our faith in them, can hardly be powerful enough to guide us to action, unless we, over and above, exercise and train our mind by experience to go the way we wish ; otherwise, when it comes to actual deeds, it will no doubt find itself at a loss. That is why those among the

[1] The 'question' was not abolished in France till 1789.
[2] The story is to be found in Froissart, iv. 87. The general was Bajazet I, Turkish Sultan (fourteenth century).

philosophers who have striven to attain to some greater excellence have not been content to await, in tranquil security, the rigours of Fortune, lest she should take them unawares, fresh and inexperienced, in the battle of life, but rather have gone out to meet her and purposely come to grips with difficulties. Some of them renouncing their riches to practise a voluntary poverty; others seeking a laborious and painfully austere life, to inure themselves to hardships and fatigue; others again depriving themselves of the most precious parts of their body, such as sight and the organs of generation, lest their too pleasant and easy functions might soften and slacken the strength of their soul.

But when it comes to dying, which is the greatest business we have to do, practice can avail us nothing. We may, by habit and experience, fortify ourselves against pain, disgrace, indigence, and such other accidents of Fortune; but death we can essay but once: when we come to it we are all novices.

In ancient times there have been men who were such excellent husbanders of their time, that they tried, even in death, to taste and relish it, and resolutely set their minds on seeing the nature of this passing; yet they never came back to tell us news of it:

> No man wakes up
> On whom once falls the icy pause of life. (LUCRETIUS.)

Canius Julius, a noble Roman, a man of singular virtue and strength of mind, was sentenced to death by that scoundrel Caligula; besides several other wonderful proofs that he gave of his fortitude, as he was about to suffer at the hand of the executioner, a friend of his, a philosopher, asking him, 'Well, Canius, at what stage is your soul now? what is it doing? what are your thoughts?' he replied, 'I was thinking to hold myself ready, with all my powers bent on seeing if, in that so brief and fleeting moment of death, I can detect the flitting of the soul, and whether it has any consciousness of its going; in order that, if I learn anything, I may hereafter return, if I can, to advise my friends.'

This man philosophises not only up to the moment of death, but in death itself. What an assurance was this, to think his death could teach him anything, and what undaunted courage, to have leisure to cast his thoughts elsewhere at such a great moment!

Such mastery of soul he had in death! (LUCRETIUS.)

I think however that there is some way of becoming familiarized with death, and in some sort of making trial of it. We may have some experience of it, if not perfect and complete, at least such as may not be unprofitable, and may give us more assurance and fortitude. If we cannot grapple with her, we can approach her, we can reconnoitre her; and if we cannot attack her fortress, we shall at least see and become acquainted with the avenues.

Not without reason are we taught to take notice of our sleep for its likeness to death. How easily we pass from waking to sleeping! And how little we suffer by losing consciousness of the light and of ourselves!

The faculty of sleep, which deprives us of all action and all feeling, might perhaps appear useless and contrary to Nature, were it not that by its means Nature teaches us that she has made us to die as well as to live; and even in life itself presents to our view the eternal state she is reserving for us after this life, in order to accustom us to, and remove our fear of, it.

But they who, in consequence of some violent accident, have fallen into a swoon and lost all consciousness have, methinks, come very near to seeing her true and natural face. For, as to the moment of death and crossing over, we need not fear that it will give us any distress or anguish, since we can have no feeling without leisure. Our sufferings need time, which in death is so brief and sudden, that it must necessarily be imperceptible. It is the approaches we have to fear, and these may fall within our experience.

Many things appear to us greater in imagination than they are in fact. I have passed a good part of my life in perfect and sound health: I may say not merely sound, but brisk and exuberant. This state, so full of sap and enjoyment, made the contemplation of sickness so dreadful to me that, when I came to experience it, I found its prickings weak and mild compared with my fears.

This is my everyday experience: when I am warmly sheltered in a good room during a stormy and tempestuous night, I am afraid and grieve for those who are then in the open country ; if I am there myself I do not even desire to be elsewhere. The mere thought of being always shut up in a room appeared to me insupportable. I was suddenly disciplined to endure it a week and a month, a prey to weakness, agitation, and disorders ; and I have found that when I enjoyed good health I pitied the sick much more than I think myself to be pitied when I am one of them ; and that the power of my apprehension magnified by nearly a half the truth and reality of the thing. I am hoping that the same will happen to me in respect of death, and that it will not justify the trouble I take in making so many preparations, and assembling and calling in so many supports to help me sustain the shock. But, hap what may, we cannot give ourselves too many odds.

I was riding out one day during the time of our third civil war, or the second (I do not quite remember which), to a distance of a league from my house, which is situated at the hub of all the turmoil of the civil wars in France. Thinking myself in all security, and being so near to my home, that I had no need of a better mount, I had chosen a very easy-going nag, but not very sure-footed. On my return, having a sudden occasion to use this horse for a kind of service it was not quite accustomed to, one of my men, a tall, strong fellow, mounted upon a powerful cob with a desperately hard mouth, fresh besides and vigorous, eager to show his mettle and outride his fellows, urged his horse at full speed straight across my track, and came down like a colossus on the little man and the little nag, with the weight and velocity of a thunderbolt, sending us both heels over head. There lay the horse prostrate and stunned, and I ten or a dozen paces farther, stretched on my back like a corpse, my face all skinned and bruised, my sword, which I had had in my hand, more than ten yards off, my belt in pieces, with no more feeling or motion in me than a log.

It was the first swoon I had experienced till that hour. Those who were with me, after trying all the means in their power to bring me round, thinking I was dead, took me in their arms and carried me with great difficulty to my house, which was distant about half a French league. On the way, and after I had been for more than two long hours considered past recall, I began to move and breathe ; for such an abundance of blood had fallen into my stomach that Nature had need to regain its powers to discharge it. I was set up on my feet, whereupon I threw up a bucketful of clots of pure blood, and several times on the way I had to repeat the process. By this means I began to recover a little life, but only by slow degrees, and over so long a space of time that at first I felt more dead than alive :

> Because the soul, down-stricken by the shock,
> Is still in doubt of its return to life. (TASSO.)

This reminiscence, which is vividly imprinted on my mind, so naturally brought the face and image of death home to me, that I am in some sort reconciled to her. When I first recovered my sight, it was so blurred, so weak and dead, that I could as yet only distinguish the light,

> Albeit I had no strength to recognise
> E'en nearest objects through the void opaque,
> But saw as one whose overwearied eyes,
> Nor all asleep nor openly awake,
> Close and unclose without the power to take
> Regard or cognisance of things most nigh. (TASSO.)

As to the functions of the soul, they revived at the same rate as those of the body. I was all covered with blood, for my doublet was stained all over with that I had vomited. My first idea was that I had been shot in the head with a musket, and indeed several had been let off around me at the time of the accident. My life seemed to me to be holding on at the point of my lips ; I closed my eyes to help me, as I thought, to thrust it out, and took a pleasure in my listlessness and indifference. It was an idea that floated only on the surface of my soul, as weak and feeble as everything else ; but in truth not only free from distress, but attended by that tranquil feeling we have when we are gently gliding into sleep.

I believe that those whom we see faint with weakness in the agony of death are in the same state, and I think that we have no reason to pity them, and to imagine that they are tormented by grievous pangs and their minds weighed down by painful thoughts. It has always been my belief, contrary to the opinion of many, and especially of Étienne de la Boëtie, that those we see prostrate and drowsy as their end draws near, or crushed by a lingering disease, or by an attack of apoplexy or the falling sickness,

> Often will some one in a sudden fit,
> As if by stroke of lightning, tumble down
> Before our eyes, and sputter foam, and grunt,
> Babble, and twist about with sinews taut,
> Gasp up in starts, and weary out his limbs
> With tossing round ; (LUCRETIUS.)

or wounded in the head, when we hear them moaning and uttering at intervals heart-breaking sighs, although we gather from these signs and from the few movements of their body that they still retain some consciousness ; I have always thought, I say, that their mind and body are buried in sleep :

> He lives, yet is unconscious of his life. (OVID.)

And I could not believe, the limbs being so paralysed and the senses so weak, that the mind could preserve within it sufficient force to be conscious of itself ; and that therefore they had no tormenting reflections that could enable them to feel and measure the wretchedness of their condition ; and that consequently they were not greatly to be pitied.

For myself I can imagine no condition so dreadful and unbearable as to have my soul alive and afflicted, but without any means of expressing itself. As I should say of those who are sent to execution with their tongue cut out, were it not that in these circumstances the most silent death is, in my opinion, the most becoming, as long as the sufferer faces his doom gravely and resolutely ; and of those wretched prisoners who fall into the hands of the brutal and infamous soldiers of these days, who torture them with every kind of cruelty, to force them to pay an excessive and impossible ransom ; kept meanwhile in a condition and in a place where they have no means whatever of expressing and signifying their thoughts and their misery.

The poets have imagined some of the gods as being favourable to the deliverance of those who thus drag on a lingering death :

> This offering unto Dis I bear,
> As bidden, and from thy body set thee free. (VIRGIL.)

The brief and incoherent words and answers we extort

from them by dint of shouting and bawling into their ears, and the movements which seem to correspond with what we ask them to do, are no evidence of their being, at least fully, alive. So it happens to us in the lisping stage of sleep, before it has quite overpowered us, that we are sensible, as in a dream, of what is happening around us, and follow the voices with a confused and uncertain hearing which seems to hover on the outskirts of the soul; and to the last words spoken to us we give answers which are accidentally appropriate rather than sensible.

Now that I have had actual experience of it, I make no doubt that the opinion I have hitherto held is correct. For, in the first place, being quite unconscious, I was striving with all the power of my nails (for I was not in armour) to open my doublet, and yet I know that I did not even imagine that I felt any hurt: for we make many movements which are not the effect of will;

> Thy lopped right hand
> Gropes for its lord, Larides, and half-quick
> The fingers quiver, and clutch the sword anew. (VIRGIL.)

A man who is falling shoots out his arms in front of him, by a natural impulse which makes our limbs lend each other their services, and stirs them quite apart from our reason:

> Stories still are told
> How that scythe-bearing chariots often lop
> Off limbs among the carnage in such haste,
> That they are seen to quiver on the ground,
> While yet the man's mind and his faculty
> Feel nothing, such the swiftness of the stroke. (LUCRETIUS.)

My stomach was oppressed with the clotted blood, my hands went to it of their own accord, as they often do to a part that itches, against the direction of our will.

There are many animals, and even men, whose muscles move and contract after death. Every one of us knows by experience that there are parts which often stir, rise up and lie down, without his leave. Now these feelings, which only touch our rind, cannot be said to be ours. To make them ours we must be entirely bound up with them, and the pains which are felt by the hand or foot whilst we are asleep are not ours.

As we drew near to my house, whither the alarm of my

fall had preceded me, and as the members of my family came to meet me with the outcries usual on such occasions, not only did I give some sort of answer to the questions put to me, but they tell me that I had the sense to bid them give a horse to my wife, whom I saw stumbling and tiring herself on the path, which was uneven and rugged. This thoughtfulness seemed to proceed from a mind that was wide-awake, yet I was not so by any means : my thoughts were idle, in the clouds, stirred by the senses of sight and hearing ; they came not from myself. I did not know, for all that, whence I was coming or whither I was going, nor could I weigh and consider the questions they asked me ; those are slight effects spontaneously produced by the senses, as if from habit. What the mind contributed was in a dream, very lightly touched, and only as it were merely licked and bedewed by the soft impressions of the senses.

Meanwhile my state of mind was, to tell the truth, one of ease and peacefulness : I was grieved neither for others nor for myself ; it was a languor and extreme weakness without any pain. I saw my house without recognizing it. When I was put to bed I had an inexpressible feeling of comfort and repose, for I had been villainously pulled about by those good fellows who had taken the pains to carry me in their arms on a long and very bad road, and had tired themselves out two or three times in relays. I was offered many remedies, none of which I took, making certain that I was mortally wounded in the head. It would have been, without any lying, a very happy death, for the weakness of my understanding prevented my forming any opinion, and that of my body from feeling anything ; I let myself glide so gently, so softly and easily, that I can hardly think of any action less disagreeable than that.

When I came to and resumed my faculties,

> When sense at last its power regained, (OVID.)

which was two or three hours after, I felt myself suddenly replunged into pain, my limbs being all pounded and bruised with the fall, and I was so ill for two or three nights after, that I thought I was dying over again, only a more painful death ; and I still feel the shock of that tumble. I must not forget to mention this, that the last thing I could recover was the remembrance of this accident, and I made them repeat to me over and over again whither I was going, whence I was coming, at what hour it had occurred, before I was able to realize it. And as to the manner of my fall, it was kept from me for the sake of the man who had been the cause of it, and they invented another story. But a long while after, on the next day, when my memory began to open out and picture to me the state I was in at the moment when I perceived that horse bearing down upon me (for I had seen it at my heels and thought I was a dead man; but this thought had been so sudden that fear had no time to enter my head), it appeared to me as if it were a flash of tning that had given my mind that shock, and that I had come back from the other world.

This narrative of so insignificant an event is rather pointless, were it not for the instruction I have derived from it for my own use: for indeed I find that, to become familiarized with death, the only way is to approach it. Now, as Pliny says, every man is a very good subject of study to himself, provided he have the ability to watch himself closely. This is not my teaching, it is my study; it is not a lesson for others, but for myself.

But one should not take it ill if I hand it on. What is of service to me may perchance be of service to another. After all I waste nothing, I only use up what is my own. And if I play the fool, it is at my own cost and prejudices nobody. For it is a kind of folly that dies with me, and has no result.

We hear of only two or three of the ancients who have trod this path,[1] and yet we cannot say that it was quite after this manner, knowing only their names. No one since has followed their track. It is a thorny undertaking, and more so than it seems, to follow so vagrant a course as that of our mind, to penetrate the obscure depths of its inmost recesses, to choose and fix so many most fugitive forms of its stirrings. And it is a new and uncommon pastime which withdraws us from the ordinary occupations of the world, yea, and the most recommended.

For many years now my thoughts have had no other aim but myself, I have studied and examined myself only, and if I study any other things, it is to apply them immediately to, or rather within, myself. And I do not think I go wrong if, as is done in other incomparably less profitable

[1] i. e., who have disclosed things to their discredit.

sciences, I communicate what I have learned in this one, although I am not very well satisfied with the progress I have made therein. There is no description equal in difficulty to a description of oneself, and certainly none in profitableness. Besides, a man must curl his hair, he must trim and pull himself together, to appear in public. Now I am continually doing myself up, for I am continually describing myself.

Custom has made it a fault to speak of oneself, and obstinately forbids it, in hatred of the boasting which always seems to attach to self-testimony. Instead of wiping a child's nose, that is called cutting it off.[1]

> How often we, in eagerness to shun
> One fault, are apt into a worse to run. (HORACE.)

To me there seems to be more harm than good in this remedy. But, though it were true that to talk to people about ourselves is necessarily a presumption, I must not, whilst pursuing my general plan, forbear an action which makes public this morbid peculiarity, since it is in me. I ought not to conceal this fault which I not only practise but profess. At all events, to speak my mind freely, it is the same wrong opinion that condemns wine because some get drunk with it. Only the things that are good can be abused. And I believe that this rule only concern the popular failing. Such rules are bridles for calves, with which neither saints who speak so highly of themselves, nor philosophers, nor theologians will curb themselves. Nor will I, though I am as little the one as the other. If they do not expressly write about themselves, at all events, when the occasion arises, they do not hesitate to push themselves forward into the highest seats.

Of what does Socrates treat more largely than himself? What does he make his disciples talk about more often than themselves—not the lessons of their book, but the essence and motions of their soul?

We devoutly confess to God and our confessor, as our neighbours[2] do to the whole people. 'But, I may be answered, we confess only our sins.' Then we confess all,

---

[1] There is a proverbial expression: *Pour moucher un enfant il ne faut pas l'écraser*, 'wiping a child's nose is no excuse for pulling it'.

[2] The Protestants.

for our very virtue is faulty and repentable. My trade and art is to live. He who forbids me to speak of it according to my understanding, experience, and habit, may as well expect an architect to speak of buildings, not as he himself regards them, but as his neighbour does, not from his own knowledge, but from another's. If it is vainglory for a man spontaneously to cry out his own virtues, why does not Cicero commend the eloquence of Hortensius, and Hortensius that of Cicero?[1]

Perhaps they would rather I gave testimony of myself by works and deeds, not merely by words. I chiefly paint my thoughts: a shapeless subject, and incapable of being translated into acts. It is all I can do to couch it in this airy body of the voice. Wiser men and more devout have lived and avoided all conspicuous actions. My actions would be rather the result of chance than a reflection of my soul. They testify to the part they play, not to the part I play, unless it be conjecturally and uncertainly: samples which show off only the details. I exhibit myself entire: it is a skeleton on which, at one view, appear the veins, the muscles, and the tendons, each in its own place. One part is brought into evidence by a cough, another by pallor or palpitation of the heart, and that dubiously. It is not my deeds that I write of; it is myself, it is my essence.

I am of opinion that we should be cautious in forming an estimate of ourselves, and equally conscientious in expressing it impartially, whether it be high or low. If I thought myself good or wise, or nearly so, I should shout it at the top of my voice. To make ourselves out worse than we are is foolishness, not modesty. To be content with less than we are worth is want of spirit and pusillanimity, according to Aristotle. No virtue is helped by falsehood, and the truth is never subject to error. To declare ourselves better than we are is not always presumption, it too is often foolishness. To be inordinately pleased with oneself, to be inconsiderately in love with oneself, is, in my opinion, the substance of this error. The supreme remedy for curing it is to do the very opposite of what they enjoin who, by forbidding us to speak of ourselves, consequently still more

---

[1] An allusion to a passage in Cicero's *Brutus*, where he compares himself at great length with Hortensius, chiefly to his own advantage.

forbid us to think of ourselves. Pride lies in thought; the tongue can have only a very small share in it.

They imagine that to muse on oneself is to be pleased with oneself, that to associate and converse with oneself is to hold oneself too dear. That may be. But this excess is only bred in those who touch only on their surface, who view themselves according to their circumstances, who call it dreaming and idleness to commune with themselves, and regard the building up and furnishing of one's mind as a mere building of castles in Spain; looking upon themselves as a third person and a stranger.

If any man, looking down on those beneath him, is intoxicated with his own knowledge, let him turn his eyes upwards to the past ages, and he will lower his horns; for there he will find so many thousands of minds that will tread him under foot. If he entertain any flattering conceit of his own worth, let him remember the lives of the two Scipios, and the many armies and nations that leave him so far behind them. No particular virtue will put pride into the heart of him who will at the same time take account of the many other feeble and imperfect qualities that are in him, ending up with the nothingness of man's estate.

Because Socrates alone had honestly bitten into that precept of his God, 'Know thyself', and had by that study come to despise himself, he alone was thought to deserve the title of Sage. Whoever shall so know himself, let him boldly make himself known by his own mouth.

CHAPTER 7

OF REWARDING HONOUR

THEY who write the life of Augustus Caesar observe this point in his military discipline, that he was wonderfully free of gifts to those who deserved them, but that he was just as sparing of mere rewards of honour. And yet he himself had all the military honours showered upon him by his uncle before he had ever been in war.

It was a pretty idea, and has been accepted in most of the governments of the world, to institute certain empty and valueless marks as an honour and reward of virtue, such as wreaths of laurel, oak, and myrtle, a garment fashioned in a certain way, the privilege of riding through the town in a coach or of being preceded by a torch by night, some particular seat in the public assemblies, the prerogative of bearing certain surnames and titles, a certain distinction in the coat of arms, and similar things, which have prevailed and still prevail in different degrees according to the notions prevalent in different nations.

We have for our share, like several of our neighbours, the orders of knighthood which have been founded for this purpose alone. It is in truth a very good and profitable custom to find means of recognizing the worth of men of distinction and eminence, and to please and satisfy them by payments which are no charge on the public and cost the Prince nothing. And there is good reason and justification for what has always been known by long experience in ancient times, and was formerly observed among ourselves, namely, that people of quality were more jealous of such rewards than of those which were attended by gain and profit. If with the prize, which should be purely one of honour, are mingled wealth and other advantages, this mingling, instead of augmenting its value, lessens and degrades it.

The order of Saint Michael,[1] which has so long been held in repute with us, had this advantage above all others, that it was accompanied by no other advantage. With the result that formerly there was no office or rank, of whatever nature, to which the nobility aspired with so great longing and desire as this order, and no quality that carried with it more respect and dignity : since virtue is more inclined to aspire to and embrace a reward that is purely due to it alone, and is attended by glory rather than profit. For indeed other gifts have not the same dignity, seeing that they are bestowed for all kinds of reasons. With money we pay for the services of a valet, the assiduity of a courier, for dancing, vaulting, speaking, and the meanest offices that we receive : nay, even vice is paid for, flattery, pandering, treachery. It is small wonder if virtue is less ready to desire and receive this kind of common coin, than that which is proper and peculiar to it, and altogether noble and generous. Augustus was right to be more sparing and niggardly of this than of the other, seeing that honour is a privilege that

[1] It must be remembered that Montaigne was a knight of this order.

derives its chief essence from its rarity; and virtue the same:

If you think none are bad, then how can one be good?[1] (MARTIAL.)

We do not particularly commend a man for his care in rearing his children, since that is an ordinary action, however right it may be; no more do we admire a tall tree in a forest of tall trees. I do not think that any citizen of Sparta took any credit to himself for his valour, for that was a universal quality in that nation; and he gloried as little in his contempt of riches, and his fidelity. No reward accrues to a virtue, however great, that has passed into a custom; and I know not withal whether we should ever call it great if it were common to all.

Since therefore these distinctions are only prized or esteemed because few enjoy them, it only needs to be lavish of them to bring them to naught. Even though there might be more men deserving our order than there were in former times, yet there was no need to lower it in estimation. And it may easily be that more are deserving of it; for there is no virtue that so easily spreads as military valour.

There is another virtue, true, perfect, and philosophic, of which I do not speak (and I use the word in our acceptation), very much greater and fuller, which is a strength and assurance of soul that equally despises all kinds of adverse fortunes, equable, uniform, constant, of which ours is but a very poor reflection. Use, education, example, and habit can do all that they will in establishing this I speak of, and easily make it common, as the experience afforded by our civil wars has made manifest enough. And if any man could unite us at this hour, and rouse up the whole of our nation to one common enterprise, our old military reputation would again flourish as before.

It is very certain that this order was in times past not bestowed as a reward of virtue alone; it looked further. It was never a payment of a gallant soldier, but of a leader of renown. The quality of obedience did not merit so honourable a wage. In former times they required a more universal expert knowledge of warfare, comprising the most and the greatest qualities of a soldier (*the qualities of a*

---

[1] When every one is somebody,
Then no one's anybody!—GILBERT.

soldier are not the same as those of a general [Livy]) ; and that he should be besides of a rank befitting so great a dignity. But, as I say, though more men should be found worthy of it than formerly, it should not be for that reason more freely bestowed ; and it would have been better to fall short in not bestowing it on all to whom it was due, than to lose for ever, as we have recently done, the advantage of so useful an institution.

No man of spirit deigns to plume himself on what he has in common with many ; and the men of to-day who have least merited this reward make more show of disdaining it, in order thereby to be ranked with those who have been wronged by the unmerited diffusion and degradation of this distinction which was their particular due.[1]

Now to expect, by obliterating and abolishing this order, immediately to renew and restore to honour an institution of the same kind, is to expect a thing not likely to occur in so licentious and sick a period as the present one ; and it may happen that the latest [2] will incur, from its very initiation, the disadvantages which have just ruined the other. The rules for the distribution of this new order would need to be extremely tightened and restricted, if it is to enjoy any consideration ; and this tumultuous period is not capable of being kept under a short and steady rein. Besides that, before this can be brought into repute, it is necessary that the memory of the first, and the contempt into which it has fallen, should pass away.

This might be a fitting occasion to discuss valour, and how this virtue differs from others ; but as Plutarch has often touched upon this theme, it would be a vain meddling in me to repeat here what he has said on the subject. But it is worthy of consideration that our nation has given to valour (*vaillance*) the first rank among the virtues, as indicated by its name, which comes from *valeur* (worth) ; and that, according to our usage, when we say of a man that he is very worthy (*qu'il vaut beaucoup*), that he is a worthy man (*un homme de bien*), in the style of our court and our nobility,

---

[1] It seems that the Order of St. Michael came to be called '*le collier à toutes bêtes*'.

[2] The Order of the Holy Ghost, instituted by Henri III in 1578. It appears from Brantôme that Montaigne's fears were only too well justified.

it means no other than that he is a valiant man (*un homme vaillant*), somewhat after the Roman fashion; for with them the general appellation of virtue (*virtus*) takes its etymology from strength.[1] The proper and only and essential place for the nobility in France is in the military profession.

It is probable that this was the first virtue that manifested itself in man, and gave to one man an advantage over another, enabling the strongest and bravest to become master of the weaker, and acquire a particular rank and reputation; wherefore it was dignified in speech with that honourable name. Or perhaps it was that among the very warlike nations the prize and the most worthy appellation was given to the quality that was most familiar to them.

In the same way our passion and the feverish solicitude we have for the chastity of our women has brought it about that when we speak of 'a good woman' (*une bonne femme*), 'an honest and virtuous woman' (*une femme d'honneur et de vertu*), we mean in fact no more than a 'chaste woman' (*une femme chaste*); as if, to keep them to that duty, we were indifferent to all the others, and left them a free rein to commit any other fault, on condition that they never commit this.

CHAPTER 8

OF THE AFFECTION OF FATHERS FOR THEIR CHILDREN

To Madame d'Estissac

MADAME, if strangeness and novelty, for which things are usually prized, do not save me, I shall never come off with honour out of this foolish undertaking[2]; but it is so fantastic an idea, and so out of the common, that that itself will perhaps enable it to pass. It was a melancholy humour, and consequently a humour very inimical to my natural disposition, brought about by the brooding solitude into which I was plunged a few years ago, that first put into my head this idle fancy of meddling with writing. And then,

[1] Montaigne evidently means that *virtus* is derived from *vis*, strength, which seems not far from the truth, although modern etymologists derive it from *vir*, man.

[2] Of writing the Essays, or perhaps, of portraying himself.

finding myself empty and totally destitute of any other matter, I offered myself for the subject-matter of my essays. It is the only book of its kind in the world, wildly and extravagantly planned. So there is nothing noteworthy in this business but its oddness; for the best craftsman in the world would have been baffled to shape a matter so mean and unsubstantial in such a way as to deserve consideration.

Now, Madame, having decided to draw a lifelike portrait of myself, I should have neglected an important feature if I had failed to depict upon it the honour I have ever paid to your deserts. And I wished to declare it explicitly at the head of this chapter, the more so as among your other good qualities the love you have shown to your children ranks among the first. One who knows at what age you were left a widow by Monsieur d'Estissac, your husband, the great and honourable proposals that have been made to you, which are as many as have been made to any lady of your condition in France, the constancy and fortitude with which you have sustained, through so many years and so many thorny difficulties, the burdensome conduct of their affairs, which have driven you about from one corner of France to another, and still hold you besieged, the happy guidance you have given them by your wisdom alone or your good fortune, will readily agree with me that there is no more conspicuous example of maternal affection to be seen in our days than yours.

I thank God, Madame, that it has been so well applied; for the great promises that your son, Monsieur d'Estissac,[1] gives of himself, are a sufficient guarantee that, when he comes of age, you will reap the obedience and gratitude of a very good son. But since, by reason of his boyish years, he has not been capable of noticing the many and very great services for which he is beholden to you, I wish, if these writings should one day fall into his hands, when I shall no longer have the mouth and speech to express it, that he should receive from me this very true testimony, which will be still more strongly evidenced by the good results which, if it please God, will make him feel that there is not a gentleman in France who owes more to his mother than he; and that he cannot in future give a more certain proof of his

Young M. d'Estissac, with several others, accompanied Montaigne on his travels in 1580.

goodness and virtue, than by his acknowledgement of the same.

If there be a real law of Nature, that is to say any instinct that is universally and permanently rooted in animals and men (which is not beyond dispute), I may say that, in my opinion, next to the anxiety for self-preservation and avoiding what is harmful, which is possessed by every animal, the affection which the begetter has for his offspring takes the second place. And, because Nature seems to have recommended to us this affection, looking to the extension and advance of the successive parts of this her machine, it is not to be wondered at if the love of children towards their parents, since it goes backwards, is not so great.

To which may be added that other Aristotelian consideration, that the man who benefits another loves him better than he is loved by the other; and that he to whom a thing is owing loves better than he who owes. Every artisan loves his work better than he would be loved by the work if it had feeling; since Being is a thing to be cherished, and Being consists in motion and action. Wherefore every one in some sort lives in his work. He who benefits another does a beautiful and worthy deed; he who receives, only a useful one.[1] Now the useful is much less to be loved than the beautiful. The beautiful is stable and permanent, affording him who has exercised it a constant gratification. The useful is easily lost and escapes, nor is the memory of it either so fresh or so pleasing. Those things are most dear to us that have cost us most; and it is more difficult to give than to take.

Since it has pleased God to endow us with some capacity for reason, in order that we may not, like the beasts, be slavishly subject to the common laws, but rather that we should adapt ourselves to them by exercising our judgement and free will, we ought indeed to yield a little to the simple authority of Nature, without being tyrannically carried away by her; reason alone should guide our inclination.

As for me, my tastes are strangely blunted to those pro-

---

[1] The benefited person stands to the benefactor in the relation of a work to the artist, and is regarded with feelings of affection. The benefactor associates an idea of the beautiful with the recipient of his good deeds; the other associates with him only an idea of the profitable.—Aristotle, *Nic. Ethics.*

pensities which arise in us without the direction and mediation of our judgement. For example, on the subject I am speaking of, I cannot understand that passion for dandling scarcely born infants that have neither motion of soul nor recognizable shape of body, by which they can make themselves lovable. And I never willingly tolerated their being nursed in my presence.

A true and well-regulated affection should spring and increase as we come to know them; and then, if they are worthy of it, the natural propensity walking side by side with reason, we should cherish them with a truly paternal love; and, if they be not worthy, use the same judgement, ever submitting to reason, notwithstanding the force of Nature. Very often it is the other way, and we are generally more excited by the kickings, the silly, playful childish movements of our infants, than we are later by their grown-up actions; just as if we loved them for our pastime, as if they were apes and not human beings. And many a man will liberally supply his children with toys who will be close-fisted when it comes to incurring the least necessary expense after they have come to years of discretion. Nay, it would seem as if the jealousy we feel on seeing them make their appearance in society and enjoy life when we are about to quit it, makes us more close and reserved towards them. It vexes us to see them tread on our heels, as if to solicit us to depart. And if that is what we fear, since it is in the order of things that they cannot really be and live but at the expense of our being and our life, we should not meddle with being fathers.

For my part I think it cruelty and injustice not to receive them into a share and partnership of our goods, and admit them as companions in the understanding of our domestic affairs when they are capable of it; and not to retrench and restrict our comforts in order to provide for theirs, since we have begotten them to that end. It is not right that an old, broken-down, half-dead father should enjoy alone, in his chimney-corner, resources that would suffice for the advancement and maintenance of several children, and suffer them meanwhile to waste their best years for want of means to push themselves in public service and the notice of their fellow-men.

They are driven to the desperate course of seeking, by any

means however wrong, to provide for their needs. In my time I have seen several young men of good family so addicted to larceny that no correction could turn them from it. I know one, well-connected, to whom, at the request of a brother of his, a very honourable and brave gentleman, I once spoke to that purpose. He answered me and confessed quite bluntly that he had been driven into that mire by the rigour and avarice of his father; but that now he was so accustomed to it that he could not keep out of it. He had just been caught pilfering the rings of a lady whose levee he, with many others, had been attending.

His case put me in mind of the story I had heard of another nobleman, who from the time of his youth had become so accustomed and so expert in this pretty business that, when he afterwards came into possession of his own property, although resolved to give up this traffic, if he happened to see something he had need of in a shop he was passing, he could not keep his hand from stealing it, on pain of having afterwards to send and pay for it. And I have seen several so habituated and hardened to this vice, that even among their fellows they would commonly purloin things they intended to give back.

I am a Gascon, and yet there is no vice I am so little skilled in as that. I hate it rather more by natural disposition than I condemn it in words. I do not, even in desire, deprive another of what is his. This province is indeed decried a little more in this repect than the other parts inhabited by the French people. Yet we have on divers occasions in our day seen men of good family in other provinces in the hands of justice, convicted of many horrible robberies.

I fear that for this disorder the avarice of fathers must in some sort be held responsible. And if they should answer me as a very sensible nobleman once did, ' that he saved up his money, not to derive any other use and enjoyment from it except to make himself honoured and sought after by his people; and that, age having deprived him of all other powers, it was his only remaining remedy for maintaining his authority in his family, and preventing his falling into contempt and disdain with all the world ' (and indeed not only old age, but every kind of feebleness, according to Aristotle, is the promoter of avarice); that is something. But it is the physic for a disease of which the birth should be prevented.

A father is indeed miserable who holds the affection of his children only through the need they have of his assistance, if that may be called affection. He should make himself worthy of respect by his virtue and abilities, and worthy of love by his kindness and gentle manners. Even the ashes of a rich matter have their price; and we have been accustomed to hold in respect and reverence the bones and relics of persons of honour.

No old age can be so decrepit and musty in a person who has lived an honourable life, but it should be revered, especially by his children, whose minds he should have trained to their duty by reason, not by want and the need that they have of him, nor by harshness and compulsion:

> He greatly errs who thinks a father's rule
> Can be upheld with more stability
> By stern, unbending measures than
> By any loving kindness. (TERENCE.)

I condemn all harsh measures in the bringing-up of a tender soul that is being trained for honour and freedom. There is a something that savours of slavishness in severity and compulsion; and I hold that what cannot be done by reason, by wisdom and tact, can never be done by force. I was brought up in that way. They tell me that in all my early childhood I did not taste the rod but twice, and very gently. I owed the same treatment to the children I have had. I lost them all as infants in their nurses' arms; but Leonor, an only daughter who escaped that misfortune, has reached the age of six years or more, without our ever employing for her guidance and for the chastisement of her childish faults (her mother's indulgence readily conforming thereto), any but words, and very gentle ones. And if I should be disappointed in my hopes of her, there are other causes enough to blame, without condemning my educational methods, which I know to be right and natural. I should in this respect have been much more scrupulous with boys, who are not so much born for service, and of a freer condition. I should have loved to make their hearts big with free and noble sentiments. I have never known any other effect of the rod but to render the soul more cowardly and more deceitfully obstinate.

Do we wish to be loved by our children ? Would we take from them all occasions to desire our death (although no cause for so dreadful a desire can be either right or excusable —*no crime is founded on reason* [Livy]) ? Let us reasonably furnish their lives with what is in our power. To do that we should not marry so young that our age will be almost confounded with theirs. For this inconvenience plunges us into many great difficulties. I refer specially to the nobility, who are of a leisurely condition, living, as they say, on their rents only. For in other classes where they have to earn their living, the plurality and company of children are an additional resource to the household, and so many new tools and instruments wherewith to grow rich.

I married at thirty-three, and concur in Aristotle's opinion, who is said to have recommended thirty-five. Plato would have nobody marry before thirty ; but he rightly ridicules those who perform their connubial functions after fifty-five, and condemns their brood as unworthy to live and be fed.

Thales gave the truest limits, who as a young man replied to his mother who was urging him to marry, ' that it was too soon ', and, when he was getting on in years, ' that it was too late '. We must deny opportuneness to every inopportune action.

The ancient Gauls [1] regarded it as a highly blameworthy action to have had knowledge of a woman before the age of twenty, and recommended especially those men who desired to be trained for warfare to preserve their virginity till they were well on in years, since courage is enfeebled and diverted by intercourse with women.

> But married to a young and beauteous bride,
> His courage melted in her sweet embrace ;
> And, in his babes now placing his chief pride,
> Sad o'er the risks of war the sire and husband sighed. (TASSO.)

Greek history observes of Jecus of Tarentum, of Chryso, of Astylus, Diopompus and others that, to keep their bodies in vigour and serviceable for the races in the Olympic games, for wrestling and other such exercises, they denied themselves, as long as there was need, any kind of venerian act.

Muley-Hassan, King of Tunis, the same whom the Em-

---

[1] The Germans, according to Caesar.

peror Charles the Fifth restored to his estates, upbraided the memory of his father Mahomet, for his frequent intercourse with women, calling him slack, effeminate, a child-maker.

In a certain region of the Spanish Indies the men were not permitted to marry until after they were forty ; and yet the girls were allowed to marry at ten.

For a gentleman of thirty-five it is too soon to make way for his son of twenty : he is yet able to cut a good figure both in warlike expeditions and at the court of his prince. He has need of all his resources, and he ought certainly to share them, but not to the extent of neglecting himself for another. And such a man may rightly make use of the answer that fathers usually have on their lips : ' I have no desire to undress until I go to bed '.

But a father, stricken with years and infirmities, barred by his weakness and poor health from the ordinary society of his fellow-men, wrongs himself and his family by brooding unprofitably over a great hoard of wealth. He has come to that state when, if he is wise, he will wish to strip, not to his shirt, but to a nice warm nightgown, to go to bed. The remaining pomps, for which he has no further use, he should willingly bestow on those to whom, by the order of Nature, they should belong. It is only right that he should leave to them the enjoyment which Nature denies him : otherwise he is surely moved by envy and malice.

The finest act of the Emperor Charles the Fifth was that, in imitation of some of the ancients of his own calibre, he had the discretion to see that reason sufficiently commands us to strip when our gowns become a burden and a hindrance, and to go to bed when our legs fail us. He resigned his possessions, his greatness, and his power to his son, when he felt himself failing in the strength and firmness necessary to conduct his affairs with the glory he had hitherto acquired.

> Set free betimes the ageing nag, before
> He strains his flanks, a laughing-stock for fools. (HORACE.)

This fault in a man of not being able to know himself betimes, and of being insensible to the impotence and the great changes that old age naturally brings with it, both to body and soul, affecting both equally, in my opinion (if indeed it does not affect the soul by more than half), has ruined the reputation of most of the great men of the world. I have in my time seen and intimately known persons of great authority who, as could very easily be seen, had strangely declined from that former efficiency which I knew of by the reputation they had thereby acquired in their best years. I could heartily, for the sake of their honour, have wished them comfortably retired to their homes, freed from public and military occupations which were grown too heavy for their shoulders.

I was at one time intimate with the family of a gentleman, a widower and very old, but still of a sufficiently green old age. This man had several marriageable daughters and a son already old enough to cut a figure : his house was in consequence burdened with many expenses and strange visitors. This gave him little pleasure, not only on the score of economy, but still more because, by reason of his age, he had adopted a manner of life far removed from ours. I said to him one day, rather boldly according to my wont, that it would be more befitting in him to yield place to us younger folk and leave his principal house (for this one alone was well situated and furnished) to his son, and retire to a neighbouring estate of his, where his repose would be undisturbed, since he could not otherwise avoid our troublesome company, seeing the condition of his children. He afterwards took my advice and was the better for it.

I do not mean to say that we should give our property up to them by means of a bond which cannot be recalled. I, who am old enough to play this part, would resign to them the enjoyment of my house and property, but with liberty to repent, if they should give me occasion. I should leave them the use thereof, because it would be no longer convenient to me, but would reserve to myself as much as I thought good of the management of affairs in general, having ever been of opinion that it must be a great satisfaction to an aged father, himself to put his children in the way of managing his affairs, and to have the power, during his lifetime, of controlling their behaviour, giving them instruction and advice according to the experience he has of them, and of personally directing the ancient honour and order of his house in the hands of his successors, and so make himself responsible for the hopes he may conceive of their future conduct.

And to this end I would not fly their company : I would observe them near at hand and join, as far as my age would permit, in their mirth and their pastimes. If I did not live in the midst of them (which I could not do without trespassing on their gatherings, by reason of the peevishness of my old age and the exigencies of my infirmities, and without besides straining and breaking through the regularity of the habits and mode of living that I should then have adopted), I would at least live near them in a corner of my house, not the most showy, but the most comfortable.

I would not live like a certain Dean of Saint Hilary at Poitiers whom I saw a few years ago, reduced to so great solitude by his distressful melancholy that, at the time when I entered his chamber, he had not moved a step out of it for twenty-two years. And yet he was quite free and easy in his movements, his only ailment being a cold in the stomach. Hardly once a week would he permit any one to come in to see him ; he kept himself ever shut up in his room alone, except that a valet brought him food once a day ; but he only came in and went out. His occupation consisted in walking to and fro, reading some book (for he had some slight knowledge of letters), obstinately resolved moreover on dying in this routine, as he did soon after.

I would endeavour, by kindness and familiarity, to cultivate in my children a strong and unfeigned affection and goodwill towards myself. In well-born natures this is easy to win ; for if they be furious brutes, which our age produces in profusion, they should be hated and shunned as such.

I dislike the custom of not allowing the children to use the name of father, and expecting them to address him as if he were a stranger, as being more respectful ; as if Nature had not usually provided us with sufficient authority. We call Almighty God Father, and scorn to have our children call us so. [I have reformed this error in my family.]

---

[1] The last words appear to have been added by the literary executors. In this respect Montaigne must have followed the example of the good King Henri IV who 'did not wish his children to call him Monsieur, a name which seems to make strangers of them and is a mark of subjection, but Papa, a name full of love and tenderness'.

It is also foolish and wrong not to admit them to familiarity with their fathers when they are grown up, and to try to maintain towards them an austere and scornful gravity, hoping thereby to keep them in awe and obedience. For that is a very futile pretence, which makes fathers distasteful and, what is worse, ridiculous to their children. They are in possession of youth and vigour, and consequently enjoy the goodwill and favour of the world; and receive with mockery those fierce and tyrannical looks of a man who has no longer any blood in his heart or his veins: regular scarecrows in a hempfield!

Even though I could inspire fear I would much rather inspire love.

There are so many kinds of faults in old age; there is so much helplessness; it is so fit a mark for contempt, that the best thing we can gain is the love and affection of our family; command and fear are no longer our weapons.

I have known one who in his youth had been kept under very strict control. Having come to man's estate, although in the best possible health, he strikes, he bites, he swears: the most tempestuous master in France. He wears himself out with cares and vigilance. It is all an amusing comedy, which his family even conspires to keep up. Of his storeroom and cellar, nay of his purse too, others have the greater enjoyment, whilst he guards the keys of them in his pouch as if they were more precious to him than his eyes. Whilst he is pleased with the economy and niggardliness of his table, in divers corners of his house there is nothing but dissipation, gambling and waste, attended with amusing tales of his vain choler and his parsimony. Every one is on guard against him. If by chance any wretched servant becomes attached to him, he immediately becomes an object of suspicion, a feeling at which old age is of itself ready to bite. How many times he has boasted to me how well he kept his people in hand, and of the strict obedience and reverence they paid him, and what a clear insight he had into his affairs!

> Alone he knows not what goes on about him. (TERENCE.)

I know of no man who is better qualified, both by nature and training, to uphold the mastery than he, and yet he has fallen off from it like a child. Wherefore I have picked him out from amongst several I know in that condition, as the best example.

This might form the theme of a scholastic dispute, ' whether he is best thus or otherwise ? ' In his presence all bow and submit to him. They allow his fancied authority to run its course, without ever resisting it. They testify their assent, they fear him, they respect him, to his heart's content. Does he dismiss a servant ? he packs up his bundle, and behold him gone ! but only out of his sight. The steps of old age are so slow, its senses are so blurred, that he will continue to live and serve in the same house for a year without being perceived. And when the time is ripe, there will come letters from a distance, supplicating, cringing, full of promises to do better, on the strength of which he is received back into favour. Does Monsieur carry out some transaction or send some message they do not like ? They suppress it and soon after invent reasons enough to excuse the lack of execution or of an answer. No letters from outside being first brought to him, he sees only those which it suits their convenience that he should know. If by any chance he gets hold of them, being accustomed to rely on a certain person to read them to him, this man will on the spur of the moment invent what suits him, and often pretend that so-and-so, who is abusing him in this same letter, is asking his pardon. In short, he sees his own affairs only in a purposely arranged reflection, to himself as satisfactory as they can make it, in order not to arouse his anger and ill-humour. I have seen, in various forms, enough of these household managements, carried on consistently for long periods, with very similar results.

Women have ever a propensity to disagree with their husbands. They will seize with both hands any pretext to thwart them ; the first excuse serves them for a full justification. I have known one who robbed her husband wholesale, in order, as she told her confessor, to give fatter alms. Don't you believe in such charity ! No management of affairs seems to them sufficiently worthy of consideration if it proceeds from their husband's concession. They must needs usurp it, either by cunning or insolence, and always offensively, to lend it grace and authority in their eyes. When, as in the case I speak of, it is against a poor old man and for the sake of the children, then they grasp at this pretext, and triumphantly make it serve their passion ; and, as if they were ordinary slaves, readily intrigue against his rule and authority. If there are grown-up and stalwart sons, they also presently suborn, either by force or favour, both steward and receiver, and all the rest of them.

Such as have neither wife nor sons do not so easily fall into this misfortune, but at the same time they are more cruelly and shamefully treated. Cato the elder said in his time, 'so many slaves, so many enemies'. Consider whether, seeing the difference in purity between his age and ours, he did not intend to forewarn us that 'wife, sons and servants are so many enemies to us'.

It is well for decrepit age to be provided with the sweet blessings of want of perception and ignorance and easy credulity. If we took the bait, how should we fare, especially in such an age as this where the judges who have to decide our quarrels are usually partisans of the young, and interested ones ? Even though I see no evidence of cheating, I am at least quite aware that I could be easily taken in.[1]

And can one ever sufficiently declare the value of a friend, and what a different thing friendship is in comparison with these civil ties ? Even the reflection of it which I see in animals, so unpolluted, how religiously I respect it !

If others cheat me I do not at least cheat myself into thinking I have the power to prevent it, or cudgel my brains to acquire that power. My own bosom is a refuge from such treacheries ; not that I am a prey to uneasy and disturbing cares, but rather from a determination to divert my thoughts.

When I hear of some one's predicament, I do not waste my thoughts on him. I immediately turn my eyes on myself, to see how it is with me. All that concerns him touches me. His experience is a warning to me, and puts me on my guard in that direction. Every day and every hour we say of one another what we should more properly say of ourselves, if we could turn our thoughts on ourselves as well as let them rove to others.

And many authors in this way prejudice their own cause

---

[1] In a manuscript note, afterwards cancelled, but just decipherable, we may read : 'Three and four times happy is he who can trust his pitiable old age to a loving hand.' It has been conjectured that the words were cancelled by some other person and not by Montaigne.

by heedlessly rushing upon the cause they attack, and hurling shafts at their enemies which may [with greater effect] be hurled back at them.

The late Monsieur the Maréchal de Montluc, having lost his son, who died in the island of Madeira, a brave gentleman indeed and of great promise, when speaking to me of it, greatly stressed, among other regrets, the grief and heartache he felt because he had never opened himself out to him; and that by always putting on the stern looks of a parent, he had lost the opportunity of really knowing and appreciating his son, and also of declaring to him the deep love he bore him, and the well-merited opinion he had of his virtue. 'And that poor boy, he said, never saw me but with a sullen and scornful countenance, and is gone with the belief that I was never able to love and esteem him as he deserved. For whom did I reserve the revealing of this singular affection I had for him in my soul? Was it not he that should have had all the pleasure and all the recognition of it? I forced and tormented myself to keep up that empty mask, and have thereby lost the pleasure of his intercourse and of his affection at the same time; for his feelings to me must have been very cool, having never met with anything but harshness and tyranny on my part.'[1]

This lament appears to me reasonable and well-grounded: for, as I know by too certain experience, there is no consolation in the loss of our friends so sweet as that which is given us by the knowledge that we withheld nothing from them, and that we were in perfect and entire communion with them. [O my friend! am I the better off for having tasted this friendship, or am I the worse off? Truly I am much better off; my sorrow for him is a comfort and an honour to me. Is it not a pious and a pleasing service in my life to be for ever mourning him? Can there be any satisfaction equal to this bereavement?][2]

---

[1] Madame de Sévigné remarks, in a letter to her daughter, that she could never read this passage without tears. 'My word! she adds, how full of good sense is this book!' Blaise de Montluc, who died in 1577, was one of the greatest military leaders of the time; very brave but very sensual and very cruel, especially towards the Protestants.

[2] A reference to his great friend, Étienne de la Boëtie, who died of the plague in 1563. See the chapter *On Friendship*. In the 'Bordeaux MS.' this passage, excepting the first three words, is heavily crossed out, it has been supposed by some other hand than Montaigne's.

I am as open with my family as I can be, and very readily signify to them the state of my feelings towards them and my opinion of them, as I do to everybody. I hasten to reveal and make myself known to them, for I do not wish to be misunderstood, or thought either better or worse than I am.

Among other peculiar customs of our ancient Gauls was this, according to Caesar, that sons did not make themselves known to their fathers, nor dare to appear in their company in public, until they began to bear arms; as if to signify that it was now time for their fathers to admit them to their familiarity and acquaintance.

I have observed yet another error of judgement in some fathers of my day, who, not content with having, during their own long life, deprived their children of the share they should naturally have had in their fortunes, leave their wives after them with the same control over their whole property, and with authority to dispose of it at their pleasure. And I have known a certain lord, one of the first officers in our kingdom, who, having in prospect, by right of succession, an income of more than fifty thousand crowns, died in want and overwhelmed in debts, although he was over fifty years of age, whilst his mother, in her extreme old age, was still in the enjoyment of all his property by the will of his father, who for his part had lived till nearly eighty. That appears to be anything but reasonable.

However, I think it is of little advantage to a man in good circumstances to seek a wife who burdens him with a large settlement; there is no outside debt that brings more ruin to a house. My ancestors have generally been of this opinion, and have very fitly acted upon it, as I too have done.

But they who would dissuade us from marrying a rich wife, in the fear of her being less tractable and grateful, are mistaken, since we might lose some real advantage on so frivolous a conjecture. It costs an unreasonable woman no more to override one reason than another. They love themselves most when they are most in the wrong. They are allured by injustice, just as good women are allured by the honour due to their virtuous actions; and the richer they are, the more sweet-tempered are they, just as the more beautiful they are, the greater pride do they take in their chastity.

It is right to leave the administration of affairs to the mother as long as the children are not, according to the laws, old enough to undertake the charge; but that father has brought them up very badly who cannot expect them to be wiser and more efficient, when they have reached that age, than his wife, considering the ordinary weakness of the sex.

Yet it would in truth be more contrary to nature to make the mother dependent on the discretion of her children. She should be liberally provided with the means to keep up her state according to the standing of her house and her age; the more so as want and necessity are much more unsuitable and harder to bear for a woman than a man. I would rather lay this burden on the children than on the mother.

As a general rule the soundest distribution of our property after death is, in my opinion, a distribution according to the custom of the country. The laws have considered the matter better than we; and it is better to allow them to err in their choosing, than rashly to run the risk of miscarrying in ours. The property is properly speaking not our own, since, by a civil prescription and apart from ourselves, it is destined for certain successors. And, although we have some liberty to go outside the law, I hold that we must not, without great and very apparent reason, deprive one of what is his by fortune, and what common justice entitles him to. And it is an abuse of this liberty, and contrary to reason, to make it serve our own frivolous and private whims.

My lot has been kind to me in not offering me occasions to tempt me, and to divert my inclination to follow the usual and lawful practice.

I know of some on whom a long succession of attentions and good services is mere waste of time: a word taken ill is enough to blot out the merit of ten years. Fortunate is he who has the opportunity to oil their humour at this last crossing over! The last action carries the day; not the best and most frequent services, but the most recent and the most present, do the trick. Those are men who trifle with their last wills as we do with apples and rods in the case of children, to reward or punish every action of those who pretend an interest in them. It is a thing of too far-reaching consequence and too much importance to be thus trotted out at every moment; and in which wise men take their stand once for all, having regard to reason and public observance.

We lay these male substitutions too much to heart.[1] And we expect a ridiculous eternity for our names. We also attach too much weight to vain conjectures regarding their future which their childish minds suggest. Perhaps it might have been an injustice to dispossess me of my rank for being the dullest and most leaden-minded, the slowest and most unwilling at my lessons, not only of all my brothers, but of all the boys in my province, whether in mental or bodily exercises. It is foolishness to sift us in that extraordinary way on the faith of prognostics which so often turn out deceptive. If it is permissible to violate the rule and correct the choice which the destinies have made of our heirs, it may be done with more likelihood of reason in consideration of some extraordinary and abnormal physical deformity, some persistent and incorrigible blemish that, according to us who are great admirers of beauty, is likely to do serious harm.

The amusing dialogue between Plato's lawgiver and his citizens may dignify this discussion. 'What, they say, when they feel that their end is near, may we not dispose of our own to whom we please ? Ye Gods ! how cruel that it shall not be lawful for us, according as we have been served by our friends in our sickness, our old age and our affairs, to give them more or less at our own pleasure !' To which the lawgiver replies in this fashion : ' My friends, seeing that you are no doubt soon to die, it is difficult for you both to know yourselves and to know what is yours, according to the Delphic inscription.[2] I, who make the laws, maintain that neither do you belong to yourselves, nor does that belong to you which you enjoy. Both your goods and you belong to your family, both past and future. But still more do your family and your goods belong to the public. Wherefore, if some flatterer in your old age or your sickness should unseasonably solicit you, or if you should be impelled by some passion to make an unjust will, I will guard you against them. But, having regard to the general interest

[1] And yet Montaigne at his death shared the same weakness, in leaving his estates and name to the youngest of his male descendants; which proceeding led to a lawsuit which was only settled two centuries later.
[2] Know thyself.

of the city and that of your family, I will establish laws and make you understand, what is only reasonable, that private interests should yield to the interest of the community. Go your way quietly and cheerfully whither human necessity calls you. It is for me, who regard not one thing more than another, and who, as far as I am able, look after the general interest, to take charge of what you leave behind you '.

To return to my theme, it appears to me, I know not why, that women ought by no means to have the mastery of any kind over men, except the natural mastery of a mother ;[1] unless it be for the punishment of those who, led by some passionate mood, have voluntarily submitted to them. But this does not concern those elderly women of whom we are speaking. It is the reasonableness of this consideration which made us so ready to enact and give force to that law, which no one ever set eyes on, by which women are debarred from succeeding to the crown of France ;[2] and there is hardly a sovereignty in the world where it is not pleaded, as in our case, by probable reasons which authorize it ; but Fortune has given it more credit in some places than in others.

It is dangerous to leave to their judgement the disposal of our succession according to the choice they will make of the children, which is at all times unjust and capricious. For those unruly appetites and morbid tastes which they have at the time of their pregnancy, they have at all times in their soul. Commonly we see them devoted to the weakest and most puny, or to those, if they have such, who are still hanging on their neck. For, not having sufficient force of reason to choose and embrace those who deserve it, they are more likely to be carried away where the impressions of nature are most left to themselves ; like animals who know their young only as long as they hang on to their teats.

Moreover it is easily seen by experience that this natural affection, to which we give so much authority, has very slender roots. For a very small gain mothers every day allow their children to be torn from their arms, in order to take charge of ours ; we make them abandon their own to some wretched nurse to whom we are not willing to commit

[1] This sweeping dictum was slightly modified by Mlle de Gournay : ' it appears to me, on the whole, that few women are born who ought to have mastery, &c.' [2] Known as the Salic Law.

ours, or to some goat, forbidding them not only to suckle their own, whatever danger these may thereby incur, but even to give any care to them, that they may devote themselves entirely to the service of ours. And in most of them we soon see, begotten by habit, a bastard affection more vehement than the natural, and a greater solicitude for the preservation of the foster-children than of their own.

And, speaking of goats, it is common in my neighbourhood to see the women of the village, when they are unable to nurse the children from their own breast, calling in the aid of goats. And I have at this moment two lackeys who never drew woman's milk longer than a week. These goats are very quickly trained to come and feed these little ones, to recognize their voice when they cry and run up to them. If any other but their nurseling is brought to them, they will refuse to feed it; and the child in like manner will refuse to take milk from any other goat. The other day I saw one from whom they had taken away his goat, because his father had only borrowed her from one of his neighbours; he could never take to the other that was brought to him, and died, doubtless of hunger. Animals change and bastardize their natural affections as readily as we.

I believe that when Herodotus tells us that, in a certain district in Libya, the men and women mingle indiscriminately, but that the child, when able to walk, will find out its father in a crowd, natural inclination guiding its first steps, there must be frequent mistakes.[1]

Now, when we consider this simple reason for loving our children, namely that we have begotten them, for which reason we call them our second selves, there is, methinks, a very different kind of production proceeding from us which is no less worthy of consideration. For that which we engender by the soul, the fruit of our mind, our heart and our abilities, is brought forth by a nobler part than that of the body, and is more our own; in this generation we are father and mother at the same time. These cost us much dearer and bring us more honour, if there is any good in them. For the worth of our other children is much more their own than it is ours, the share we have in them being very small; but of these all the beauty, all the charm and

---

[1] Montaigne seems to have misread Herodotus, who says that the man is reputed to be the father whom the child most resembles.

THE FIRST BURNING OF BOOKS

value are ours. For that reason they represent us and reflect us much more vividly than the others.

Plato adds that these are immortal children that immortalize, nay that deify, their fathers, as in the case of Lycurgus, Solon, Minos.

Now, history being full of examples of that common affection of fathers to their children, it seemed to me not inappropriate to pick out one or two of this kind.

Heliodorus, that good bishop of Tricea, chose rather to forfeit the dignity, the profit, and the devout life, of so venerable a prelacy, than to sacrifice his daughter, a very pretty daughter that still lives, who is perhaps however a little too curiously and too wantonly tricked out for the daughter of a churchman and a priest, and in too erotic a fashion.[1]

There was one Labienus at Rome, a man of great worth and authority, who, amongst other qualities, was eminent in every branch of literature. He was, I think, son of that great Labienus, the chief of the captains who served under Caesar in his Gallic war, and who afterwards, having joined the party of the great Pompey, conducted himself so valorously in that conflict, until Caesar defeated him in Spain. This Labienus of whom I am speaking, was an object of jealousy to many, on account of his great qualities, and, as seems likely, counted among his enemies the imperial courtiers and favourites of his day, on account of his independence and his antagonism, inherited from his father, to tyranny, with which we may well believe that his books and other writings were coloured. His adversaries prosecuted him before the Roman authorities, and succeeded in having several of his published works condemned to be burned. It was with him that this new example of penalty was begun, which was afterwards continued against several others at Rome, of punishing with death even writings and studies. As if there were not enough occasions and objects on which to exercise cruelty without bringing in things that Nature has exempted from all feeling and suffering, such as our reputation and the products of our mind, and without applying corporal punishments to teachings and the monuments of the Muses!

---

[1] Meaning the love-tale of *Theagenes and Chariclea*. It seems that Heliodorus was elected to the bishopric on condition that he burned his novel, but preferred to sacrifice the dignity.

Now Labienus could not endure this loss or survive this progeny, so dear to him : he had himself conveyed and shut up alive in the tomb of his ancestors, thus providing for his suicide and burial at the same time. It would be difficult to show a more vehement paternal affection than that. Cassius Severus, a man of great eloquence and his intimate friend, seeing his books being burned, exclaimed that by the same sentence they should have condemned him to be burned alive with them, seeing that he carried and preserved in his memory all that they contained.

The like misfortune befell Cremutius Cordus, accused of having praised Brutus and Cassius in his books. That base, servile, and corrupt Senate, who deserved a worse master than Tiberius, condemned his writings to the flames. He was content to bear them company in death, and killed himself by abstaining from food.

The good Lucan, having been condemned by that scoundrel of a Nero, in the last moments of his life, when his blood was wellnigh spent from out the veins of his arms, which at his request his physicians had lanced to bring on death, and when the cold had seized his extremities and was approaching his vital parts, the last thing he had in his memory was some of the lines from his poem on the Battle of Pharsalia, which he recited; and he died with these last words on his lips. What was this but a tender and fatherly leave-taking of his children, resembling the adieux and close embraces with which we part from ours when we die, and the result of that natural inclination which recalls to our memory, in these last moments, the things we have held most dear in life ?

Can we believe that Epicurus, who, being tormented at his death, as he said, by an acute colic, found his sole consolation in the beauty of the teachings he left to the world, would have felt the same satisfaction in a number of well-born and well-brought-up children, if he had had them, as he had in the production of his pregnant writings, and that, if he had had the choice between leaving behind him a misshapen and ill-born child and a foolish and absurd book, he would not have chosen, and not he alone but any man of like genius, to incur the first misfortune rather than the other ? It would perhaps have been an act of impiety in Saint Augustine (to take an example), if, it being proposed to him to bury either his writings, from which our religion gathers such abundant fruit, or his children, in case he had any, he had not rather chosen to bury his children.[1]

And I do not know that I would not much rather have begotten a perfectly shaped child by intercourse with the Muses than by intercourse with my wife.

To this child, such as he is, what I give I give purely and irrevocably, as one gives to the children of one's body. The little good I have done him is no more at my disposal: he may know many things that I no longer know, and hold from me what I have not retained, and what I should have to borrow of him as from a stranger, if I had need of it.[2]

If he is richer than I, I am wiser than he.

There are few men devoted to poetry who would not be prouder to be the father of the *Aeneid* than of the handsomest boy in Rome; and who would not more easily suffer the loss of the latter than of the former. For, according to Aristotle, of all craftsmen the poet is especially the one who is most in love with his work.

It is difficult to believe that Epaminondas, who boasted of leaving no other posterity but daughters who would one day do their father credit (meaning the two noble victories which he had gained over the Lacedemonians), would willingly have consented to exchange them for the most gorgeously handsome women in all Greece; or that Alexander and Caesar ever desired to be robbed of their great and glorious exploits of war, for the advantage of having sons and heirs, however perfect and accomplished they might be.

Nay I doubt much whether Pheidias, or any other eminent sculptor, would so much desire the preservation and continuance of his natural children as he would that of an excellent statue, which with prolonged labour and study he had perfected according to art. And as to these furious and wicked passions with which fathers have sometimes been kindled for their daughters, or mothers for their sons, the same is also found in this other kind of parenthood: witness what they relate of Pygmalion, who, having built up the statue of a woman of singular beauty, fell so madly

---

[1] Saint Augustine had a son, as he tells us in his Confession, 'the child of his sin', whom he called Adeodatus, 'Not-God-given'.

[2] Montaigne is of course speaking of his Essays.

and desperately in love with his work, that to gratify his infatuation the gods had to inspire it with life :

> The ivory yields,
> Softening beneath his fingers ; nor retains
> Its rigid hardness. (OVID.)

CHAPTER 9

OF THE ARMS OF THE PARTHIANS

IT is a bad habit and mark of great softness in the nobles of our day not to put on armour until the moment of greatest need, and to unburden themselves of it as soon as there is the slightest indication of the danger being past. Whence proceed many irregularities. For when, at the moment of being attacked, all are rushing about and shouting for their arms, some are still engaged in lacing their cuirass whilst their comrades are already routed. Our fathers used to give their sallet, their lance and gauntlets to be held, but did not abandon the rest of their equipment until the day's work was done. Our ranks are now thrown into disorder and confusion by the encumbrance of baggage and officers' servants, who cannot leave their masters' side by reason of being in charge of their armour.

Livy says, speaking of our nation : *Utterly unable to stand fatigue, they were scarce able to bear their arms on their shoulders.*

Some nations formerly went, and still go, into war without covering armour, or with such as was no protection :

Bark helmets guard them, from the cork-tree peeled. (VIRGIL.)

Alexander, the most daring of captains that ever lived, very rarely put on armour. And those of us who despise it very seldom have the worst of the bargain. Though now and then we see one killed for want of harness, there are nearly as many who have lost their lives through the encumbrance of armour, being embarrassed or galled and crushed by its weight or by a counter-blow, or otherwise. For it would seem indeed, considering the weight and thickness of that we wear, as if our only object were to protect ourselves, and we are more burdened than covered by it. We have enough to do, thus impeded and constrained, to support the load, as if we had to fight only with the brunt of our arms, and as if we had not the same obligation to defend them as they have to defend us.

Tacitus gives an amusing description of the warriors among our ancient Gauls, thus armed only to hold their ground, neither able to hurt nor capable of being hurt, nor of regaining their feet when struck down.

Lucullus, seeing certain Median men-at-arms who formed the van of Tigranes' army, in heavy and unwieldy armour, as in an iron prison, concluded that he could easily defeat them, and upon them he commenced his attack and his victory.

And now that our musketeers are so formidable, I believe that a means will be discovered of immuring us to save us from them, and of dragging us into war shut up in bastions, like those carried by elephants in antiquity.[1]

The younger Scipio was very far from sharing this idea, for he bitterly rebuked his soldiers for having scattered caltrops under water, at a part of the moat where the inhabitants of a town he was besieging were able to sally out upon him ; saying that those who attacked should think of their enterprise, and not of being afraid ; and he rightly feared that this cautionary measure might lull the vigilance of his own men when on guard.

He also said to a young man who was showing off his fine buckler, ' It is truly beautiful, my son, but a Roman soldier should trust more to his right hand than his left '.

Now it is only want of habit that makes the burden of our armour intolerable to us :

> Helm on the head and corselet on the breast
> Of both the knights, of whom I sing, was tied;
> By night or day, since they unto this rest
> Had entered, never doffed and laid aside :
> For such to wear were easy as a vest
> To these, so wont the burden to abide. (ARIOSTO.)

The Emperor Caracalla marched through the country on foot, armed at all points, when he led his army. The Roman foot-soldiers not only wore a morion and carried their sword and shield (for, as to armour, says Cicero, they were so accustomed to have it always on their back, that it was no more a hindrance to them than their limbs, *for they say that the arms of a soldier are his limbs*) ; but they carried at the same time a fortnight's provision, and a certain number

[1] Surely a prevision of the modern ' tank '.

of stakes to make ramparts, up to sixty pounds in weight. And the soldiers of Marius, thus laden, were drilled to march five leagues in five hours, and six when there was any haste. Their military discipline was much ruder than ours, and also produced very different results. It is a thing to be marvelled at in this connexion that a Spartan soldier, being on a warlike expedition, was reproved for being seen under cover of a house. They were so inured to hardship that it was a disgrace to be seen under any roof but the sky, in any kind of weather. The younger Scipio, when reforming his army in Spain, commanded his soldiers to eat only standing, and nothing cooked. On these terms we should not lead our men very far!

Moreover Marcellinus, a man bred up in the Roman wars, minutely comments on the manner of arming of the Parthians, and he remarks on it rather for being so different from that of the Romans.[1] 'They had, he says, armour woven in the manner of little feathers, which did not hinder the motion of the body, and yet it was so strong that our spears rebounded when coming into contact with it' (these are the scales so much in use with our forefathers). And he says in another place: 'Their horses were strong and hardy and covered with stout leather; and they themselves were armed from head to foot with strong iron plates arranged so cunningly that at the joints of the limbs they adapted themselves to their movements. One might have thought they were men of iron, for they had head accoutrements so neatly fitted and so naturally imitating the shape and parts of the face, that there was no way of reaching them except through two little round holes corresponding with the eyes, which let in a little light, and slits at the place of the nostrils, through which they breathed with some difficulty.'

> The enclosed limbs put life into the plates;
> They move like living statues, fearsome sight!

[1] The editions published during Montaigne's lifetime had the following quaint passage, which was deleted in the 'Bordeaux MS.': 'Now, by reason of its being very like our own, I was about to quote this passage from its author, having once taken the trouble of making a full comparison, as far as I was able, between our armour and that of the Romans. But because this scrap of my notes was abstracted, with several others, by a man in my service, I will not rob him of the profit he expects to make by it. Besides, I should find great difficulty in chewing the meat twice over'.

Breathing through kindred steel. Like armed, the steeds
With spiky fronts and iron shoulders move,
   Secure from wounds. (CLAUDIAN.)

There we have a description which very nearly recalls the equipment of a French man-at-arms with his bards.

Plutarch says that Demetrius had two coats of mail made, each weighing six score pounds, for himself and for Alcinus, the first warrior next to him, whilst the ordinary harness weighed only sixty pounds.

CHAPTER 10

OF BOOKS

I MAKE no doubt but that I often speak of things which are better treated by the masters of the craft, and with more truth. What I write here is purely an essay of my natural faculties, and by no means of those I have acquired, and whoever shall catch me tripping in ignorance will have no hold over me ; for I could hardly be answerable to others for my dissertations, who am not answerable to myself, nor satisfied with them. Let him who is in search of knowledge fish for it where it lurks ; there is nothing I so little profess. These are fancies of my own, by which I endeavour to make known, not things, but myself : I may haply know them some day, or perhaps I did once know them, whenever I chanced to light upon the passages where they were elucidated. But I remember them no more.

And if I am a man of some reading, I am a man of no retention.

So I promise no certainty, except it be to make known how far my knowledge of things extends at this moment. Let no one confine his attention to the matter, but to the shape I give to it. Let them see, in my borrowings, whether I have been able to choose the means of improving the idea. For I make others say what I am not able to say so well myself, now for want of words, now for want of understanding. I do not number my borrowings, I weigh them. And if I had wished to raise their value by number, I could have laden myself with twice as many. They are all, or very nearly all, of so famous and ancient names, that I think they reveal themselves sufficiently without my naming them.

In respect of the arguments and ideas which I transplant

to my own soil and mix with my own, I have sometimes purposely omitted to name the author, in order to put a spoke in the wheels of those hasty critics who fall foul of all sorts of writings, especially recent writings of men still living, and in the vulgar tongue,[1] which invites all the world to discuss them, and which seems to them a proof that the conception and design are also vulgar. I should like to see them give Plutarch a fillip on my nose, and burn their fingers in abusing Seneca through me. I must hide my weakness behind those great names.

I will love any one who will strip me of my feathers, I mean through clearness of judgement, and by merely distinguishing the force and beauty of the language. For I, who, through lack of memory, am at every moment at a loss to sort them according to the place of their origin, can quite understand, by measuring my powers, that my soil is quite incapable of growing any of the too rich flowers I find planted in it; and that all the fruits of my own growing could not pay for them.

I am bound to hold myself responsible if I entangle myself in my thoughts, and if there are inanities and blemishes in my writings that I am not sensible of, or of which, if pointed out to me, I should still be insensible. For faults often escape our eyes; but the infirmity of judgement consists in not being able to perceive them when discovered by another.

Knowledge and truth may dwell in us without judgement, and judgement also without them; nay, the confession of ignorance is one of the best and surest testimonies of judgement I can think of. I have no other major-general to marshal my troops but chance. As my idle fancies present themselves I pile them up; now they crowd upon me in a body, now they come creeping in single file. I wish to show my natural and ordinary pace, however much I may be off the track. I let myself go as I am. Besides, the subjects I treat here are not of so much importance but that they may be ignored or discussed casually and at random.

I could indeed wish to have a more perfect understanding of things, but I do not wish to buy it as dear as it costs. My aim is to pass the remainder of my life quietly and not

---

[1] i. e., in French; serious works, on philosophy, morals, history, &c., were usually written in Latin.

laboriously. There is nothing over which I would rack my brains, not even knowledge, however valuable it may be.

In books I seek only pleasure through an honest pastime; or, if I study, I seek only the knowledge which tells me how to know myself, and teaches me to die well and to live well:

> This the post my panting steeds shall reach. (PROPERTIUS.)

If I come across any difficulties in my reading, I do not bite my nails over them; after one or two attacks I give them up. If I were to dwell on them too long I should lose both myself and my time; for I have an impulsive mind. What I do not see at the first onset I am less likely to see by persisting. I do everything lightheartedly: too strenuous and continuous efforts daze, sadden and weary my senses. My sight becomes confused and blurred. I am obliged to withdraw it and set to again by fits and starts; just as, in order to judge of the gloss of a scarlet cloth, we are told to glance lightly at it, running the eyes over it several times, quickly and repeatedly.

If this book bores me I take up another, and only give my mind to it at moments when I am weary of doing nothing. I do not take very readily to the moderns, because the ancient authors appear to me fuller and more virile; nor to the Greek, because my mind is not satisfied with a puerile and prentice understanding.[1]

Among books simply amusing I find, of the moderns, Boccaccio's *Decameron*, Rabelais,[2] and *The Kisses*[2] of

---

[1] Because he has not sufficient Greek to read it without difficulty.

[2] It seems odd that Montaigne should class Rabelais among books simply amusing', and one can hardly believe that he did not see the deep meaning underlying that work. In his day there might have been danger in discussing its more serious import. Hence we may believe that the above words are a 'blind'. Johann Everts (Johannes Secundus) was a Dutchman who died at the age of twenty-five. He published a score of Latin poems under the title *Basia*, in the Catullian style. His prefatory 'Epigram to the grammarians; why he writes wantonly' was calculated to appeal to Montaigne's dislike of pedantry:

> You ask me why I sport in wanton strains,
> Why love in every verse luxuriant reigns;
> Because I would not have dull pedants cumber
> My light effusions with their learned lumber.
> If lives of sainted men inspired my lays,
> Or if I sang heroic Caesar's praise,

Johannes Secundus, if they may be classed in this category, worth reading for pastime. As to the *Amadis*, and that sort of book, they did not enjoy the favour of interesting me even in my boyhood. I will say even this, whether boldly or foolhardily, that, not to mention Ariosto, even the good Ovid no longer tickles this old, heavy soul of mine; his facility and his fictions, which once charmed me, have now little power to entertain me.

I speak my opinions freely in all things, even those which perhaps exceed my capacity, and which I do not conceive to be in any wise under my jurisdiction. My opinion of them is intended to show the measure of my sight, not the measure of the things themselves. When I find I have no liking for Plato's *Axiochus*, which with all due respect for such an author, appears to me a work without power, I do not trust my judgement.[1] It is not so fatuous as to set itself against the authority of so many other famous judgements of antiquity, which it regards as its masters and teachers, and in whose company it would rather be content to err. It blames itself, and condemns itself either to stop at the outer rind, not being able to penetrate to the heart, or to view the thing by a false light. It is content with only securing itself from confusion and disorder; as to its own weakness it frankly acknowledges and confesses it. It thinks it gives a right interpretation of things as they appear to it, but its sight is feeble and imperfect.

Most of Aesop's Fables are capable of being understood and explained in several ways. They who moralize them choose some point of view which squares well with the fable, but in most cases it is only a first and superficial point of view; there are others, more alive, more essential, and more inward, to which they have not been able to penetrate: that is my case.

But to continue my journey, I have always been of

> What notes (oppressive weight!) must I endure;
> What comments, obvious readings to obscure;
> What tedious stuff conceived by addled brains,
> To boys the certain cause of future pains!

There are two or three English translations of these poems, which are 'wanton' without being licentious.

[1] The *Axiochus* is no longer regarded as a work of Plato, and Montaigne had no need to distrust his judgement.

opinion that in poetry Virgil, Lucretius, Catullus, and Horace hold the first place by a long way, and especially Virgil in his *Georgics*, which I consider the most accomplished of all poetical works, in comparison with which we may readily admit that there are some passages in the *Aeneid* to which the author, if he had had the leisure to do so, might have given a few more turns with the comb. And the fifth book of the *Aeneid* seems to me the most perfect.

I also love Lucan, and readily seek his companionship, not so much for his style as for his own worth and the truth of his opinions and judgements. As for the good Terence, that personification of the charm and daintiness of the Latin tongue, I think it is wonderful how he depicts to the life the motions of soul and the manners and customs of our own day; at every turn our actions send me back to him. I cannot read him, however often, without discovering in him some new charm and beauty.

Those who lived near Virgil's time protested when some compared Lucretius to him. I am of opinion that they cannot really be placed on a par, but I find it difficult to confirm myself in that belief when I find myself held by some fine passage in Lucretius.[1] If they were so piqued by this comparison, what would they say of the dull and barbarous stupidity of those who now compare Ariosto to him? And what would Ariosto himself say?

An age of coarseness and stupidity! (CATULLUS.)

I think the ancients had still more reason to protest against Plautus being matched with Terence (the latter savours much more of the gentleman) than against the comparison of Lucretius with Virgil. It says much for the estimation and preference of Terence that the father of Roman eloquence[2] has him, alone of his class, so often on his lips; as does also the verdict which the first critic among the Roman poets passes upon his fellow-dramatist.[2]

[1] Lucretius was the apostle of the Epicurean doctrine in his *De Natura Rerum*, a poem written in forcible and often sublime style, unequalled in any other language for vigour of thought and depth of bitter feeling. He had a powerful influence on Montaigne, who quotes him almost as often as any other writer.

[2] The father of Roman eloquence is Cicero, who frequently quotes Terence. The first critic is Horace, who says in his *Art of Poetry*: 'Our fathers praised both the rhythm and the wit of Plautus; their admiration, I say, was too good-natured, not to say foolish.'

It has often struck me that those of our day who meddle with the writing of comedies (including the Italians, who are rather happy in them) use up three or four plots of Terence or Plautus to make one of their own. They will crowd into a single comedy five or six tales of Boccaccio. What makes them thus load themselves with matter is the diffidence they feel in their own power to please; they must needs find a body to lean upon; and not having enough original matter of their own to interest us, they try to entertain us with the story. With my author it is just the other way: the perfections and beauties of his style of language make us lose our appetite for his subject. His daintiness and pretty conceits hold us throughout. He is so amusing all through,

> Clear and like unto a limpid stream, (HORACE.)

and so fills our soul with his charms that we forget those of his plot.

This same consideration carries me further. I observe that the good ancient poets avoided affectation and the diligent search after, not only fantastic sublimities in the manner of the Spaniards and the Petrarchists, but even those milder and more restrained conceits which form the ornament of all the poetical works of the succeeding periods. And yet there is no good critic who misses them in those ancients, and who does not incomparably more admire the even polish and that perpetual pleasingness and flowering beauty of Catullus' epigrams than all the stings with which Martial sharpens the tails of his.

The reason of this is the same I gave a little while ago, and which Martial uses about himself: *He had the less need of any great efforts, since his subject supplied the place of wit.* The former make us relish them without exciting themselves and making frantic efforts; they find matter for laughter everywhere without tickling themselves. The latter have need of outside help: having little wit they need more body; they ride on horseback because they are not strong enough on their own legs.

Just as at our balls those men of low origin who keep dancing schools, unable to copy the dignified bearing of our nobility, try to win our applause with daring leaps and other odd movements and mountebank's tricks. And the ladies find it cheaper to show off in those dances in which they can twist and wriggle their bodies about than in certain other stately dances, in which they need simply to tread a natural measure and adopt an unaffected carriage and their ordinary grace. I have also seen excellent clowns, in their everyday dress and with their ordinary face, give us all the pleasure which they can derive from their art; whilst the novice who has not been so highly trained is obliged to whiten his face and disguise himself, and assume the most ridiculous postures and ferocious grimaces, in order to make us laugh.

This conception of mine is nowhere better seen than in a comparison of the *Aeneid* and the *Orlando Furioso*. The former we see in swift flight on strong and lofty wing, ever intent on his purpose; the latter, fluttering and hopping from tale to tale, as it were from branch to branch, never trusting to his wings but for a very short flight, and alighting every moment, lest his breath and strength should fail;

> As bees essay their wings in brief excursions. (VIRGIL.)

Those then are, in this kind of subject, the authors that please me most. As to my other reading, in which a little more profit is mingled with the pleasure, and which teaches me to bring order into my opinions and morals, the books that serve my purpose are Plutarch, now that he has been turned into French, and Seneca. They both have this notable advantage, so agreeable to my humour, that the knowledge I seek in them is treated in disconnected pieces and demands no prolonged labour, of which I am incapable; such are the minor works of Plutarch and Seneca's Letters, which are the best things he wrote, and the most profitable. It needs no great effort to sit down to them, and I leave them when I please; for they have no sequence or dependence upon one another.

These two authors meet in most of their opinions, when they are true and profitable, and Fortune brought them into the world at about the same period. Both were tutors to two Roman emperors; both came from a foreign country; both were rich and powerful.[1] Their teaching is of the

---

[1] Seneca was born about 4 B.C., Plutarch about A.D. 46; Seneca was tutor to Nero, who afterwards condemned him to death (see chapter 35 of this book), and Plutarch is supposed to have been Trajan's tutor; Seneca came from Cordova in Spain, Plutarch from Boeotia in Greece.

cream of philosophy, and is presented in simple and pertinent fashion. Plutarch is more uniform and steady; Seneca more variable and wavering. The latter labours and strives with all his might to arm virtue against weakness, fear, and vicious appetites; the former appears to regard them as less formidable, and disdains to quicken his pace and stand on his guard against them. Plutarch's opinions are Platonic, moderate and accommodated to polite society; the other's are Stoical and Epicurean, more remote from the ordinary, but, in my opinion, more suited to the individual and more solid. Seneca seems rather to favour the tyranny of the Emperors of his time, for I hold for certain that he forces his judgement when he condemns the cause of those generous assassins of Caesar; Plutarch is free throughout. Seneca abounds in points and sallies, Plutarch in matter. The former moves you and kindles your ardour; the latter satisfies you more and pays you better. He guides, the other drives.

As for Cicero, the works of his which serve my purpose are those which treat of Philosophy, especially Moral Philosophy. But, to confess the truth boldly (for, since we have cleared the barriers of impudence, there is nothing more to curb us), his style of writing appears to me tedious, like the style of others that resemble him. For his prefaces, definitions, divisions and etymologies take up the greater part of his work. What there is of pith and marrow is smothered by these lengthy dressings. When I have spent an hour in reading him, which is a great deal for me, and try to recall what sap and substance I have extracted from it, most of the time I find nothing but wind; for he has not yet come to the arguments which support his proposition, or the reasons which properly touch on the difficulty I am seeking to solve. For me, who only ask to become wiser, not more learned or eloquent, these logical and Aristotelian premisses are not to the purpose: I should like him to begin with the conclusions. I understand well enough what is meant by Death or Pleasure; there is no need to waste time in anatomizing them.

I look for good and solid reasons at the outset, that will teach me to resist their attack. Neither grammatical subtleties nor an ingenious tissue of words and argumentations will serve. I like reasons that charge at once into the heart of the question; his keep on feebly beating about the bush. They are good enough for the school, for the bar or the pulpit, when we have leisure to take a nap, and a quarter of an hour later are in time to pick up the thread of the discourse. It is the kind of talk that is needed to win over a judge, by hook or by crook, or to use with children and the common people, with whom we have to exhaust the subject, in the hope that some of it will stick.

I have no need of any one who strives to arouse my attention and shouts at me fifty times *Or oyez!*[1] after the manner of our heralds. The Romans used to say in their religion *Hoc age!*,[1] and we in ours say *Sursum corda!*[1] These are so many words wasted on me. I come fully prepared from the house. I need neither enticement nor sauce; I can very well eat my meat quite raw, and these preliminaries and *hors d'œuvres*, instead of whetting my appetite, only pall and weary it.

Will the licence of these times excuse my sacrilegious audacity when I say that in my opinion even Plato's Dialogues drag, and that their matter is too much drowned in words; and that I regret the time spent on these long drawn-out and needless preliminary talks by a man who had so many better things to say? My ignorance of the language will be a better excuse for my not appreciating its beauties.

In general I demand books that offer the results of learning, not those that build it up.

The two first mentioned,[2] and Pliny, and their like, have no *Hoc age*; they prefer readers who have already disposed themselves to attention; or if they have, it is a substantial *Hoc age* that has a body of its own.

I am also fond of reading the Letters to Atticus,[3] not only because they contain very full information on the history and affairs of his time, but much more because they disclose his private opinions. For I have a particular curiosity, as I have said elsewhere, to know the soul and the genuine opinions of my authors. From the samples of their writings

---

[1] *Or oyez!* now listen! The old bellmen or town-criers in England used to begin their announcements with 'Oyes, Oyes, Oyes!' *Hoc age*, give heed! was used by the Roman priests when sacrificing, to exhort the people to be quiet and give attention. *Sursum corda*, lift up your hearts! is similarly used in the Roman Catholic mass.

[2] Plutarch and Seneca.   [3] By Cicero.

which they exhibit on the stage of the world we may form an opinion of their talents indeed, but not of their morals or of themselves. I have a thousand times regretted that we have lost the book *Of Virtue* which Brutus wrote; for it is a fine thing to learn the theory from one who is so well up in the practice. But, seeing that the preaching and the preacher are two different things, I am as pleased to see Brutus reflected in Plutarch as I should be to see him in his own book. I would rather have a true report of the familiar chat he had with some one of his intimate friends in his tent on the eve of a battle, than the speech he delivered to his army on the next day; and of what he did in his study or chamber than what he did in the Forum or the Senate.

As to Cicero, I share the common opinion that, except for his learning, he was intellectually not very eminent. He was a good citizen and good-natured, which is usual with fat and jovial men,[1] such as he was; but, without lying, I may say that he had his good share of weakness and ambitious vanity. And yet I am at a loss how to excuse him for having esteemed his poetry worth publishing. It is no great blemish in a man to write bad verse, but it shows a want of judgement in him not to have felt how unworthy his poetry was of the glory of his name.

As to his eloquence, it is entirely beyond comparison; I believe that no man will ever equal him.[2]

The younger Cicero, who resembled his father only in name, one day whilst he was in command in Asia, had a number of strangers at his table, and among others Cestius, who was seated at the lower end, as men often thrust themselves upon the open tables of the great. Cicero inquiring of one of his men who he was, he told him his name; but as one whose thoughts are elsewhere and forgets the answer made to him, he afterwards asked him again two or three times. The servant, in order not to have the trouble of

---

[1] According to Plutarch (G. Long's translation) Cicero 'was lean and had little flesh, and, owing to weakness of stomach, he took little food'.

[2] In the earlier editions we find these words, deleted in the 'Bordeaux MS.': 'And yet he did not stand out so pre-eminent as Virgil did in poetry; for very soon after him there were several who thought they equalled or even surpassed him, though on very false pretences. But no one ever thought to compare himself with Virgil. And in this connexion I will add a story.'

repeating the same thing so often, and to make the stranger known by some circumstance, said, ' It is that Cestius of whom it was told you that he thinks very little of your father's eloquence compared with his own.' Cicero, stung to anger by this, immediately ordered poor Cestius to be seized and had him soundly flogged in his presence. A very uncivil host !

Even among those who, all things considered, esteemed his eloquence to be incomparable, there were some who, notwithstanding, remarked some faults in it, among them that great Brutus, his friend, who spoke of it as a *broken and enervated* eloquence. The orators who lived near his time also reprehended in him his curious habit of bringing in a certain long cadence at the end of his periods, and especially noted the words *esse videatur* (it would seem to be), which he uses so often. For my part, I prefer a cadence that falls shorter, cut into iambics. Yet at times, though infrequently, he very rudely mixes up his measures. My ear took note of this passage : *Ego vero me minus diu senem esse mallem, quam esse senem antequam essem* (I had rather be old a shorter time, than be old before my time).

The historians are my right-hand ball ; [1] they are entertaining and easy, and at the same time man in general, whom I seek to know, appears there more alive and entire than anywhere else ; there we see the diversity and truth of his inward nature, in the gross and in detail, the variety of the means by which he is knit together,[2] and the accidents which threaten him.

Now the writers of biographies are most suited to my purpose, since they dwell on intentions more than on incidents, more on that which proceeds from within than on that which happens without. That is why, in all kinds, Plutarch is the man for me. I am very sorry that we have not a dozen of Laertius,[3] or that he is not more widely known or

---

[1] The right-hand ball in tennis being the easier to play.

[2] i. e., the diversity with which the same good and bad qualities are combined to form different characters.

[3] Diogenes Laertius flourished in the second or third century A. C., and wrote Lives of the Philosophers, a work that contains a mass of interesting information regarding the private life and habits of the most eminent philosophers of antiquity. From this source Montaigne drew nearly all his anecdotes concerning them.

better understood. For I am not less curious to know the fortunes and the lives of these great teachers of the world than to know the diversity of their teachings and ideas.

In this kind of historical study we must peruse without distinction all kinds of authors, both old and new, both gibberish and French, to learn in them the things of which they variously treat.

But Caesar is, in my opinion, particularly deserving of study, not only for the knowledge of history, but for himself: so perfect and eminent is he above all the rest, although Sallust be one of the number. Indeed I read him with rather more reverence and respect than one feels in reading human works, considering him now in himself, through his actions and his miraculous greatness, now in the purity and inimitable polish of his language, wherein he surpassed not only all the historians, as Cicero says, but perhaps Cicero himself. And he speaks of his enemies with such sincerity of judgement that, saving the false colours with which he tries to cover his evil cause and the filth of his pestilential ambition, I think there is nothing to be said against him but that he speaks too sparingly of himself. For he could not have performed so many great things without having had a much greater share in them than he lays claim to.

I like the historians who are either very simple or of the first order. The simple, who have nothing of their own to mix with their story, who only collect carefully and diligently everything that comes to their notice, and faithfully record all things without picking and choosing, leave it entirely to our judgement to discern the truth.

Among these, for example, is the good Froissart, who marches to his undertaking with so frank an artlessness that, when he makes a mistake, he is not at all afraid of acknowledging and correcting the same in the place where it has been pointed out to him. He records even the divers rumours that were current, as well as the different accounts that were given to him. It is the naked and unshaped matter of history; every man may profit by it according to his understanding.

The really eminent ones, having the ability to choose what is worth knowing, are able to sift two different accounts and select that which is the more likely to be true; knowing the characters of princes and their way of thinking they infer their intentions and put fitting words into their mouths. They are right in assuming an authority to direct our belief according to their own; but this gift certainly belongs to few.

Those who lie between the two (comprising the generality of them) spoil all: they will chew our bits for us; they assume the right to judge, and consequently to bend history according to their fancy. For as soon as the judgement inclines to one side, one cannot help twisting and turning the narrative to that bias. They take upon themselves to choose what things are worth knowing, and often conceal from us such and such a word, such and such a secret deed, which might have been more informative; omitting as incredible the things they do not understand, and perhaps also many a thing from their inability to tell it in good Latin or French. Let them boldly display their eloquence and their reasons, let them judge according to their fancy; but let them also leave us something to judge after them, and let them not alter or apportion, by their choosings and their curtailings, anything of the substance of the matter, but rather deliver it to us pure and entire in all its dimensions.

For the most part, and especially in these latter times, the charge of writing history is committed to men picked out from among the humbler classes, who have no other qualification but a command of choice language; as if we sought to learn grammar of them! And they, being only hired to that end and having nothing for sale but their tittle-tattle, are right in making that their principal concern. So with a store of fine words they go and make up a beautiful hotch-potch of reports picked up at the street corners of the cities.

The only good histories are those written by the men themselves who were at the head of affairs, or who shared in the conduct of them, or who at least had the good fortune to conduct others of a like nature. Of this kind are almost all the Greek and Roman histories. For, several eye-witnesses having written on the same subject (as used to be the case at that time when greatness and learning usually met together in the same person), if there is any error, it must be a marvellously slight one, and on a very questionable incident. What can we expect of a physician discussing war, or of a scholar discussing the intentions of princes?

To observe how scrupulous the Romans are in this

respect, we need but quote this example : Asinius Pollio [1] discovered that even Caesar, in his histories, fell into occasional error through not having had eyes in every part of his army, and giving credit to individuals who often reported matters to him that were not sufficiently verified ; or perhaps through not having been carefully enough informed by his lieutenants of things they had conducted in his absence. From this example we may see what a delicate thing it is to search after the truth, when we cannot fully believe the account of a battle given by the man who was in command, nor trust the soldiers to give a true report of what happened in their presence, unless, after the method of a judicial inquiry, we confront the witnesses and hear the opposite views, and accept the facts only when proved in their minutest circumstances. Truly the knowledge we have of our own affairs is very much looser. But this matter has been sufficiently handled by Bodin,[2] and according to my conception.

In order a little to meet the deficiency of my treacherous memory (which is so extreme that I have chanced more than once to pick up a book, thinking it was new and unknown to me, and discovered, from notes I had scribbled in it, that I had carefully read it a few years before),[3] I have for some time adopted the habit of adding a note at the end of each book (that is, of those I do not intend to read again), recording the time when I finished reading it and the opinion I had formed of it as a whole ; in order thereby to recall at least the character and general idea I had conceived of the author's personality when reading it. I will here transcribe a few of these annotations.

Here is what I wrote about ten years ago in my Guicciardini [4] (for, whatever language my book speaks, I speak to it in my own) : ' He is a diligent historiographer from

[1] C. Asinius Pollio, orator, poet, historian, and soldier, 76 B.C.–A.D. 4, very little of whose work has survived.

[2] A reference to a work by Jean Bodin entitled *Methodus ad facilem historiarum cognitionem* (1568).

[3] The present translator can lay claim to exactly the same experience. It seems to be pretty convincing evidence of Montaigne's defective memory, which has frequently been doubted.

[4] Francesco Guicciardini, an Italian statesman and historian, nearly contemporary with Montaigne, who wrote a long and laboured history of his own times. See Macaulay's anecdote in the Essay on Burleigh.

whom we may learn, I think, as accurately as from any other, the truth of the affairs of his time; in most of which, besides, he was himself an actor, holding an honourable position. There is nothing to show that he has disguised matters through hatred, favour, or vanity; this is evidenced by the outspoken judgements he passes upon the great, and especially those from whom he had received advancement and who had employed his services, such as Pope Clement the Seventh. As to the part upon which he seems most to pride himself, his digressions and dissertations, some of them are good and enriched with some fine touches. But he revelled too much in them. For, in order to leave nothing unsaid, having a subject so full and ample and almost inexhaustible, he becomes wearisome; it savours a little of scholastic cackle. I have also remarked this, that in judging so many persons and actions, so many motives and intentions, he never puts anything down to the score of virtue, religion or conscience, as though these qualities were utterly extinct in the world; and, however fine any action may appear in itself, he always discovers for it some wicked motive or some hope of gain. It is impossible to imagine that, among the infinite number of actions that he criticizes, there was not occasionally one which was prompted by reason. Corruption can never infect men so universally but that some will escape the contagion. That makes me suspect that a certain measure of wickedness was to his liking; and it may perhaps be that he judged others by himsel.'

In my Philippe de Commines I find this: 'You will find his language pleasing and agreeable, of a native simplicity; the narrative clear, evidently reflecting the author's sincerity, free from vanity when speaking of himself, and from partiality and envy when speaking of others; his speeches and exhortations accompanied with good zeal and truth rather than with any uncommon talent; and throughout, authority and gravity, which bespeak him a man of good extraction, and brought up to great affairs.'

On the Memoirs of Monsieur du Bellay: 'It is always a pleasure to see things written about by one who knows by experience how they should be conducted; but it cannot be denied that in these two lords [1] we may discover a great

[1] The Memoirs of Martin du Bellay include those of his brother Guillaume de Langey.

falling-off from the outspoken freedom that is conspicuous in the older historians of their sort, such as the Sire de Joinville, the intimate friend of Saint Louis, Eginhard, Charlemagne's chancellor, and, of more recent memory, Philippe de Commines. This is rather a plea for King Francis against the Emperor Charles the Fifth, than a history. I will not believe that they have altered any of the general facts; but they make it their business to twist the judgement of events, often, contrary to reason, to our advantage, and to omit whatever is ticklish in the life of their master. Witness the disgrace and downfall of Messieurs de Montmorency and de Brion, which they ignore; nay, Madame d'Estampes is not even mentioned by name. One may cover up secret actions; but to hush up what all the world knows, and matters that have produced results known to the public, and of such consequence, is an inexcusable fault. In short, whoever would have a full knowledge of King Francis and the happenings of his time, will, if he takes my advice, look elsewhere. The profit to be gained from this work consists in the detailed account of the battles and warlike exploits in which these gentlemen were engaged; in a few speeches and private actions of several Princes of the time; and the intrigues and negotiations conducted by the Seigneur de Langey, which are replete with many things worth knowing, and some dissertations above the common.'

['In this chapter Montaigne reveals himself as the best and the first in date of the literary critics of the sixteenth century. In his ranking of the Latin poets, Virgil, Lucretius, Catullus, and Horace, he expressed views which were new in his day, but are now well established, and which denote a very correct and very sure taste. None of the poets and critics of the period showed the same discrimination in judging the classical works of antiquity.'—Dr. A. Armaingaud.]

CHAPTER 11

OF CRUELTY

I IMAGINE Virtue to be something else and something more noble than the propensity to goodness that is born with us. The well-born and naturally well-regulated mind follows the same path, and produces the same actions as the virtuous mind. But Virtue somehow rings too great and is too active to allow itself, by a happy disposition, to be meekly and calmly led in the train of reason. The man who, by reason of a meek and easy-going nature, despises injuries received, does a very fine and praiseworthy thing. But he who, provoked and stung to anger by an injury, arms himself with the arms of reason against that furious desire for revenge, and, after a great struggle, masters it in the end, without doubt does a great deal more. The former does well, the latter acts virtuously. The first action might be called good, the other, virtuous. For the name of Virtue, I think, presupposes difficulty and contradiction, and cannot be exercised without opposition. It is for that reason perhaps that we call God good, mighty, liberal and just, but we do not call him virtuous. His works are altogether natural and effortless.

Of the philosophers, not only Stoics, but even Epicureans —(for in putting the former on a higher level than the latter I follow the common practice, which is wrong, in spite of the sly witticism with which Arcesilaus answered a man who taunted him with the fact that many men passed from his school to the Epicurean, but never the other way. ' I can quite believe it : cocks are often made capons, but capons are never made cocks.' For, in truth, in strength of mind and austerity of opinions and precepts the Epicurean sect in no wise yields to the Stoic. And it was a Stoic who, more honest than those disputants who, to combat Epicurus and load their own dice, make him say things he never contemplated, twisting his words awry, and, usurping the grammarian's licence, argue into his language a different meaning and a different belief to that which they knew he had in his mind and showed in his morals, said that he gave up being an Epicurean upon this consideration among others, that he found their road too lofty and inaccessible ; *and they who are called lovers of pleasure, being in fact lovers of honesty and justice, cultivate and practise all the virtues* [Cicero]) ;—of the Stoic and Epicurean philosophers, I say, there are some who decided that it was not enough to have the soul in good trim, well-regulated and well-disposed to Virtue. It was not enough that we should be resolute in word and deed, and beyond the reach of Fortune ; but we should also seek occasions to be put to the proof. They think that we should go in quest of pain, indigence and contempt, in order to fight them and keep our souls in breath : *Virtue provoked is greatly strengthened* (Seneca).

That is one of the reasons why Epaminondas, who was also of a third sect,[1] refuses the wealth that Fortune gives into his hands by very lawful means, in order, he says, to have to battle with poverty ; and in these straitened circumstances he held on to the last.

Socrates, I think, put himself upon a much ruder trial, keeping for his exercise his wife's bad temper ; which is to fence with the button off.

Metellus, having, alone of all the Roman senators, taken upon him, by dint of his virtue, to resist the violence of Saturninus, Tribune of the people at Rome, who tried by might and main to pass an unjust law in favour of the plebeians, and having thereby incurred the dreadful penalties that Saturninus had provided for such as refused, talked with those who, in this extremity, were walking with him in the Forum, in these terms : 'To do an ill action is too easy and too base ; to do a good one that involves you in no danger, is quite common : but it is the proper duty of a virtuous man to do great and good things, though he risks everything by it.'

These words of Metellus very clearly set forth what I desired to make out, that Virtue declines the company of Facility ; and that that easy and gentle incline down which are guided the regular steps of a good natural disposition is not the way of true Virtue. She asks for a rugged and thorny path ; she would have either outside difficulties to wrestle with, like those of Metellus, by means of which Fortune delights to break the speed of her career, or internal difficulties that our inordinate appetites and the imperfections of our nature place in her way.

So far my way has been smooth. But at the end of this discussion this fancy comes into my mind that the soul of Socrates, which is the most perfect that has come to my knowledge, should be, according to my reckoning, a soul little deserving of commendation. For I cannot conceive this man to have been besieged by any vicious lusts. I cannot imagine any difficulty or constraint in the way of his virtue. I know his reason to have been so powerful a

---

[1] The Pythagorean.

mistress over him that she would never have allowed a vicious appetite even to arise in him. I have nothing to set against a virtue so sublime as his. I seem to see her marching with a victorious and triumphant step, in state and at her ease, without hindrance or disturbance. If Virtue can shine only through the conflict of contrary desires, shall we therefore say that she cannot dispense with the help of vice, and that to vice she owes it that she is held in honour and repute ? What should we say of that noble and generous Epicurean voluptuousness, which makes such a show of tenderly cherishing Virtue in its bosom, and there makes her frolic, giving her disgrace, fevers, poverty, death, and tortures, for toys to play with ? If I take it for granted that perfect Virtue is known by her combating and patiently enduring pain, by bearing up against the attacks of the gout without being thrown off her balance ; if I allow hardships and difficulties to be her necessary aim : what shall we say of the Virtue raised to such a pitch as not only to despise pain but to rejoice in it, and to feel tickled by the pangs of a violent colic, which is that which the Epicureans have established, and of which many of them by their actions have given us very certain proofs ? As have many others who, I find, have actually exceeded even the rules of their teaching.

Witness the younger Cato. When I see him dying and plucking out his bowels, I cannot be satisfied with simply believing that his mind was then wholly free from distress and horror ; I cannot believe that he merely maintained that attitude which the rules of the Stoic sect prescribed, calm, impassive, emotionless ; there was, it seems to me, in the virtue of this man too much sap and virility to stop there. I believe that without doubt he felt a sensual pleasure in an action so noble, and that he felt a greater satisfaction in it than in any other action of his life : *He departed this life, rejoicing in having found a motive for leaving it* (Cicero).

I am so far advanced in that belief that I begin to question whether he would have wished to be robbed of the opportunity of so heroic an achievement. And, if I were not held in check by consideration of the goodness which made him espouse the public interest more than his own, I could readily fall in with this opinion, that he was grateful to

Fortune for having put his virtue to so noble a test, and for having favoured that brigand [1] in treading under foot the ancient freedom of his country. I seem to read in that action I know not what exultation in his soul, and the expression of an extraordinary pleasure and manly voluptuousness, when she considered the nobility and sublimity of his deed :

> Embracing death with desperate ferocity, (HORACE.)

not goaded by any hope of fame, according to the popular and effeminate opinion of some, for that is too mean a consideration to touch a heart so generous, so haughty and so unbending ; but by the beauty of the thing in itself, which he, who worked the springs of it, discerned much more clearly and in its perfection than we are able to do.

I am pleased to find that Philosophy decided that a deed so heroic would not have been in keeping with any other life than Cato's, and that his alone was fitted to end in that way. Therefore he enjoined, in accordance with reason, both his son and the senators who accompanied him to provide otherwise for themselves. *Cato, whom Nature had endowed with an incredible strength of soul, and who, ever following the path he had traced for himself, had by habit strengthened the firmness of his character, was bound to die rather than look upon the face of a tyrant* (Cicero).

Every death should correspond with its life. We do not become different for dying. I always interpret a death by its life. And if any one tells me of a death, brave in appearance, annexed to a feeble life, I maintain that it is produced by a feeble cause, in keeping with the life.

Must we then say that the easiness of this death, and that facility which he had acquired through the strength of his soul, should abate anything from the splendour of his virtue ?

And what man whose brain is ever so little tinged with the true philosophy can be satisfied with imagining Socrates merely free from fear and emotion when prison, fetters and condemnation fell to his lot ? And who does not discover in him, not only courage and confidence (for that was in his nature), but also I know not what new satisfaction, and a gay cheerfulness in his last words and actions ?

---

[1] Caesar.

INNOCENCE NO VIRTUE

By that thrill of pleasure that he feels when scratching his leg after his irons were removed, does he not betray a like joy and delight in his soul at being unfettered of past discomforts, and prepared to enter into a knowledge of the things to come?

Cato will pardon me, if he please; his death is more tragic and more strained, but this one is somehow still more beautiful.

Aristippus said to one who was lamenting his death, 'May the gods send me one like it!'

We see in the souls of these two men [1] and their imitators (for I very much doubt whether they had their equals) so perfect a habituation to virtue, that it passed into their nature. It ceases to be a laborious virtue, or the result of the precepts of reason, to keep to which the soul needs to brace itself; it is the very essence of their soul, it is its natural and ordinary course. They rendered it such by long practice in the precepts of philosophy, lighting upon a rich and fine nature. The vicious passions which arise in us can find no door of entry into them. The strength and rigidity of their soul stifles and extinguishes the lusts as soon as they begin to stir.

Now I think there is no doubt that it is a finer thing to prevent, by a sublime and divine resolution, the birth of temptations, and so to train oneself to virtue that the very seeds of vice are rooted out, than by main force to stop their progress, and, after being taken unawares by the first stirrings of the passions, to arm oneself resolutely to arrest their progress and vanquish them; and that this second power is still finer than to be simply furnished with an easy and compliant nature, which has a natural distaste for vice and debauchery. For this third and last degree seems indeed to make a man innocent, but not virtuous; free from ill-doing, but not sufficiently capable of well-doing. To which may be added that this condition is so near to imperfection and weakness that I do not quite know how to recognize and distinguish their confines. The very names of Goodness and Innocence are, for that reason, in some sort words of contempt. I can see that some of the virtues, such as chastity, sobriety and temperance, may be due to feebleness of body. Fortitude in face of dangers (if it must

---
[1] Socrates and Cato.

be called fortitude), contempt of death, patience in misfortunes, may often be found in a man through his being unable to rightly calculate such mishaps, and to conceive their nature. Thus, want of apprehension and dullness sometimes counterfeit valorous actions. And I have often chanced to hear a man praised for a thing that deserved blame.

An Italian lord once spoke as follows in my presence, to the discredit of his nation: that the subtlety of the Italians and the vivacity of their imagination were so great, that they foresaw the dangers and accidents that might befall them so far ahead, that it should not be thought strange if they were often seen in war to look to their safety, even before they had clearly seen the peril of it; that we French and the Spaniards, who were not of so fine a grain, are more reckless, and that we must be made to see the danger with our own eyes and touch it with our hands before we take the alarm, and that then we lose all control; but that the Germans and Swiss, who are heavier and coarser, have not the sense to recover their bearings, and hardly even when they are crushed under the blows.

This was perhaps only spoken in jest. Yet it is very true that in the business of war the novice very often hurls himself into hazards with much greater want of consideration than he does after having burned his fingers in it:

> Well I knew
> How potent was the new-born pride in arms,
> And a first onset's all-entrancing spell. (VIRGIL.)

That is why, in judging a particular action, we must consider many circumstances, as well as the whole man by whom it is performed, before we give it a name.

To say a word about myself. I have sometimes known my friends to call prudence in me what was due to chance, and to regard something as being won by courage and patience which was won by thought and judgement; and to apply to me one name instead of another, sometimes to my advantage, sometimes to my detriment. After all, so far am I from having attained to that first and most perfect degree of excellence where virtue becomes a habit, that I have hardly even given any proofs of the second. I have not made any great efforts to bridle the desires by which I have been importuned. My virtue is a virtue, or, to speak more correctly, an innocence that is casual and accidental. If I had been born with a more unruly disposition, I am afraid I should have been in a pitiable way. For I have not experienced much steadfastness in my soul to resist passions, if they were ever so mild. I am unable to cherish quarrels and conflicts in my bosom. Hence I cannot be greatly beholden to myself for being free from many vices:

> And if some trivial faults, and these but few,
> My nature, else not much amiss, imbue,
> Just as you wish away, yet scarcely blame,
> A mole or two upon a comely frame, (HORACE.)

I owe it to my fortune rather than to my reason. To her I owe that I am descended from a race famous for honesty, and that I am the son of a very good father. I know not whether he has passed on to me something of his character, or whether perhaps the home examples and my good education in childhood have insensibly contributed to it, or else whether I was born so:

> Whether 'neath Libra's aspect I was born
>   Or the dread Scorpion's, of the natal hour
> The stormier influence, or of Capricorn,
>   Who sways the Western wave with tyrant power; (HORACE.)

but so much is true that I have a natural horror of most of the vices.

The answer which Antisthenes gave to one who asked him what was the best apprenticeship, 'Unlearn evil', seems to be rooted in this idea.

I hold them in horror, I say, with so natural and so inborn a persuasion, that this same instinct or impression with regard to them that I imbibed from my nurse I have preserved without any occasion having arisen to make me alter it; nay, not even my own reasonings, which, through having deviated from the beaten path in many things, might easily give me a licence to do what my natural inclination makes me hate.

I will tell you something that may appear monstrous, but yet I will tell it: the effect of that is that in many respects there is more order and restraint in my morals than in my opinions; my sexual appetites are less dissolute than my reason.

Aristippus was so outspoken in favour of pleasure and wealth, that all philosophy rose up in revolt against him. But as to his morals, Dionysius the tyrant having offered him three fair young girls to choose from, he replied that he chose all three, for that Paris had got into trouble for preferring one over her companions. But, having taken them to his house, he dismissed them untasted.

When his servant, who was following him, complained that the money he was carrying was too heavy, he ordered him to throw away so much as he found burdensome.

And Epicurus, whose teachings are non-religious and non-ascetic, was very devout and laborious in his way of living. He writes to a friend of his that he lives only on coarse brown bread and water, and entreats him to send him a little cheese, in case he has a mind to make a sumptuous repast. Can it be true that, in order to be thoroughly good, we must be so by an occult, natural and universal quality, without law, without reason or example ?

The excesses in which I have found myself involved are, thank God, not of the worst kind. I have indeed condemned them in myself as they deserved, for my judgement has not been infected by them. On the contrary, I blame them more rigorously in myself than in another. But that is all, for after all I offer too little resistance to them and am apt to incline too much to the other side of the scales, except that I moderate them and prevent them mixing with other vices. For they most generally keep together and become interlocked, in one who is not on his guard. Mine I have cut down and forced to be as single and simple as I could make them ;

> Outside of that no vices I indulge. (JUVENAL.)

For, as to the theory of the Stoics, who say, ' The wise man acts, when he does act, by all the virtues together, although there be one more apparent, according to the nature of the action (and herein the comparison with the human body might serve them in some degree, for anger cannot work without the aid of all the other humours, although anger may predominate); if from thence they would draw a like inference, that when the sinner sins, he sins by all the vices together, I am not so simple as to believe them, or I do not understand them ; for in effect I feel the contrary. Those are minute, unsubstantial subtleties, with which philosophy sometimes busies itself.

Some vices I am addicted to, but others I fly as much as any saint could do.

The Peripatetics, besides, reject this indissoluble connexion and union ; and Aristotle maintains that a wise and just man may be both intemperate and incontinent.

Socrates confessed to those who discovered in his physiognomy a certain inclination to vice that that was in truth his natural propensity, but that he had corrected it by discipline.

And the intimate friends of the philosopher Stilpo used to say that, though naturally fond of wine and women, he had by study become very abstemious in respect of both.

The good that is in me I owe, on the other hand, to the accident of my birth. I owe it neither to law, to precept nor to any other apprenticeship. The innocence that is in me is a natural innocence ; there is little of vigour in it, and no artifice.

Among other vices, I cruelly hate cruelty, both by nature and reason, as the worst of all the vices. But then I am so soft in this that I cannot see a chicken's neck wrung without distress, and cannot bear to hear the squealing of a hare between the teeth of my hounds, although the chase is a vehement pleasure.

They who have to combat voluptuousness are fond of employing this argument, to prove that it is wholly vicious and contrary to reason : 'That when it is at its highest pitch, it masters us to such a degree that reason can have no access.' And they instance the feeling we experience in intercourse with women,

> When now
> Their bodies have sweet presage of keen joys,
> And Venus is about to sow the fields
> Of woman ; (LUCRETIUS.)

in which they think that the pleasure carries us so far beyond ourselves that our reason cannot then perform its office, being crippled by the ecstasy of pleasure.

I know that it may be otherwise, and that we may sometimes, by force of will, succeed in that same instant to bring back our mind to other thoughts. But it needs to be deliberately strained and stiffened. I know that it is possible to master the violence of that pleasure, and I know it from personal experience. For I have not found Venus so imperious a goddess, as many men, and those more chaste than I, testify to her being. I do not regard it as a miracle, as does the Queen of Navarre in one of the tales of her *Heptameron* (which is a pretty book for its matter), nor as a thing of extreme difficulty, to pass whole nights, with every opportunity and in all freedom, with a long-desired mistress, keeping the word one has pledged her to be satisfied with kisses and simple contact.

I think the example of the chase would be more to the point. Though the pleasure be less, we are more carried away by it and more liable to surprises, our reason, taken unawares, having no time to prepare for and resist the onslaught, when, after a long quest, the quarry suddenly starts up and appears in a place where perhaps we least expected to see it. This shock and the eagerness of the hue and cry so strike our senses that it would be hard for those who love this kind of sport to withdraw their thoughts, at the moment, elsewhere.

And the poets make Diana triumph over the torch and arrows of Cupid:

> Who, mid such sports, does not forget his woes
> And all the cares of love ? (HORACE.)

To come back to my subject, I have a very tender compassion for others' afflictions, and could readily weep for company, if I were able to shed tears on any occasion. Nothing draws my tears except tears, not only real ones but of whatever kind, feigned or painted. The dead I can hardly pity, and I should rather envy them; but I very greatly pity the dying.

The savages who roast and eat the bodies of their dead do not scandalize me as much as they who persecute and torture the living. I cannot even look upon executions of the law, however reasonable they may be, with a steadfast eye.

Somebody, having occasion to testify to Julius Caesar's clemency, said, 'He was mild in his vengeance: having forced the pirates to surrender, by whom he had before been taken prisoner and put to ransom, and since he had threatened them with the cross, he condemned them to be crucified, but not until they had been strangled. Philemon, his secretary, who had attempted to poison him, he punished no more harshly than with simple death.' Without revealing the name of that Latin author,[1] who dares to allege as an evidence of mercy the mere killing of those by whom we have been injured, it is easy to guess that he is struck by the horrible and villainous examples of cruelty practised by the Roman tyrants.

For my part, even in justice, all that is over and above a simple death appears to me pure cruelty, and especially with us[2] who ought to make it our duty to dismiss a soul in a state of grace; which cannot be when it has been agitated and driven to despair by insufferable tortures.[3]

In these latter days a soldier, having perceived, from a tower in which he was imprisoned, carpenters busy at work erecting a scaffold and people assembling in the market-place, concluded that it was for himself; in his despair, finding nothing else to kill himself with, he seized upon an old rusty nail out of a cart which chance had thrown in his way, and therewith dealt himself two serious wounds about the throat; but seeing this had no effect on his life, he soon after dealt himself a third in the belly and fell into a swoon. In this state he was found by the first of his jailers who entered to see him. They brought him round and, to take advantage of the time before he expired, they at once read his sentence to him, which was that he was to be decapitated, whereat he was greatly rejoiced, and accepted the wine he had before refused; and after thanking the judges for the unexpected leniency of their sentence, he said that his resolve to kill himself was due to his horror of a more cruel punishment, which the sight of the preparations had increased. The change in the mode of death appeared to him a deliverance from it.

I should recommend that these examples of severity, whereby it is intended to keep the people in awe, be exercised on the dead bodies of criminals. For to see them deprived of burial, boiled and cut in pieces, would affect the populace almost as much as the torments that the living

[1] Suetonius, in his *Life of Julius Caesar*.
[2] Who profess ourselves Christians.
[3] When Montaigne was in Rome in 1581, he was urged by the Papal authorities to suppress the above passage, which however he did not do.

are made to suffer; although in reality that amounts to little or nothing, as God says: *Be not afraid of them that kill the body, and after that have no more that they can do* (Saint Luke).

And the poets singularly dwell upon the horrors of this picture, as something worse than death:

> Ah! that the remnant of a king, half-burnt,
> The bones laid bare, with blood and filth besmeared,
> Should be thus foully dragged along the ground!
>
> (ENNIUS, quoted by Cicero.)

One day at Rome I happened to be on the spot at the moment when they were executing a notorious brigand named Catena. He was strangled without the spectators exhibiting any emotion; but when they came to cut his body in pieces, the hangman dealt no blow that the people did not follow with pitiful cries and exclamations, as if every one had lent his own sense of feeling to that carrion.

Those inhuman excesses should be performed upon the shell, not upon the quick. Thus, in a somewhat similar case, Artaxerxes mitigated the harshness of the ancient laws of Persia by ordaining that those nobles who had failed in their charge, instead of being scourged, as was the custom, should be stripped and their garments flogged in their stead; and, instead of the customary tearing out of the hair, that they should only be stripped of their high tiaras.

The Egyptians, who are so devout, thought they sufficiently satisfied the divine justice by sacrificing effigies and pictures of pigs: a bold idea, to think to pay God, so essential a substance, with picture and shadow!

I live in a time when we abound in incredible examples of this sin, through the licence bred by our Civil wars. And we can read of nothing in ancient histories more extreme than what we may witness any day. Yet that has in no wise reconciled me to it. I could hardly have believed, until I saw it with my own eyes, that there could have been found souls so unnatural that they could commit murder for the mere pleasure they took in it; that they could hack and mangle others' limbs, that they could sharpen their wits to invent unheard-of tortures and new kinds of death, without enmity, without profit, and to the sole end of enjoying the pleasing spectacle of the pitiful gestures and motions, the

CRUELTY TO ANIMALS

lamentable cries and groans, of a man dying in agony. For that is the utmost pitch to which cruelty can reach. *O that a man should kill a man without anger, without fear, only for pleasure in the sight!* (Seneca).[1]

For my part I could not even witness without distress the pursuing and killing of a harmless and defenceless animal, that has done us no injury. And I have always been pained by the common sight of a stag, weak and panting, reduced to surrender and cast itself on the mercy of its pursuers, with tears in its eyes,

Blood-stained, with piteous and imploring eyes, (VIRGIL.)

which has always been to me a very unpleasant sight.

I seldom capture a live animal but I restore it to the fields. Pythagoras used to buy them of the fishermen and fowlers, to do the same:

'Twas slaughter of wild beasts, methinks, that made
Man first with blood to stain his cruel blade. (OVID.)

Men of bloodthirsty nature where animals are concerned display a natural propensity to cruelty.

At Rome, after the people had become accustomed to the spectacle of the slaughter of animals, they proceeded to that of men and gladiators. Nature herself has, I fear, fastened on man a certain instinct to inhumanity. No man finds his recreation in seeing animals playing together and fondling one another, and none fails to take a delight in seeing them tearing each other limb from limb.

And, that no man may jeer at me for my sympathy with them, Theology herself enjoins us to show them some kindness; and, considering that one and the same master has lodged us in this palace for his service, and that they like ourselves are of his family, she is right in commanding us to show them consideration and affection.

Pythagoras borrowed the theory of Metempsychosis of the Egyptians; but it was since accepted by several nations, and notably by our Druids:

The spirit is immortal, cannot die;
It only changes dwelling and survives
In other dwelling, where anew it lives. (OVID.)

---

[1] The above, according to Dr. Armaingaud, is probably an indictment of Charles IX and Catherine de Medici, on account of their treatment of Coligny and other atrocities; in which case Montaigne showed a rare courage.

In the religion of our ancient Gauls it was held that the soul, being eternal, never ceases to move and change from one body to another; which idea was also accompanied with some consideration of divine justice. For, according to the behaviour of the soul, whilst it had been in Alexander, they said that God assigned to it another body to inhabit, more or less painful and suitable to its condition:

> The silent chains of brutes he made them wear:
> Encased in bearish form were cruel souls,
> Robbers in wolves', the sly in foxes' hides;
> Where, after ending, through successive years
> And many thousand shapes, their sad careers,
> In Lethe's stream their souls were duly purged,
> And back to their primeval shape restored. (CLAUDIAN.)

If it had been valiant they lodged it in the body of a lion; if voluptuous, in that of a pig; if timorous, in that of a stag or a hare; if cunning, in that of a fox; and so with the rest, until, purified by this chastening, it resumed the body of some other man.

> Well I remember I was Pantheus's son
> Euphorbus, in the fatal war of Troy.[1] (OVID.)

As to that cousinship between the animals and ourselves, I do not take much account of it; nor of the fact that several nations, and especially some of the most ancient and most noble, have not only received animals into their society and companionship, but have ranked them much higher than themselves, sometimes regarding them as the familiars and favourites of their gods, and paying them a more than human respect and reverence. And others recognized no other god or divinity but them. *Beasts were made sacred by barbarians on account of the benefits they bestowed* (Cicero).

> The crocodile is here adored, and there
> The snake-gorged ibis fills all hearts with awe;
> The long-tailed monkey here is graved in gold;
> Here fish of Nile are reverenced, and there
> The multitude falls down before a dog. (JUVENAL.)

And even the very ingenious explanation which Plutarch gives of this error is to their honour. For he says that it was not the cat or the ox, for example, that the Egyptians

---

[1] These words are put into the mouth of Pythagoras.

worshipped, but that in these animals they worshipped some image of the divine attributes. In the latter, patience and usefulness; in the former, activity, or, like our neighbours the Burgundians, as well as all Germany, intolerance of being imprisoned; whereby they represented Freedom, which they loved and adored above any other divine attribute; and so with the others.

But when, among the most moderate opinions, I meet with arguments which endeavour to demonstrate the close resemblance between us and the animals, and to show how large a share they have in our greatest privileges, and with how much reason they have been likened to us, truly I abate a great deal of our presumption, and willingly renounce that imaginary kingship which we are supposed to have over the other creatures.

But even though all this were an error, there is yet a certain consideration and a general duty of humanity which attaches us not only to those animals that have life and feeling, but even to trees and plants. To men we owe justice, and mercy and kindness to the other creatures that are capable of receiving it. There is a certain commerce and mutual obligation between them and ourselves. I am not afraid of confessing my natural tenderness, which is so childish that I cannot very well refuse my dog when he offers to frolic with me, or appeals to me to frolic with him, at an inopportune moment.

The Turks have almshouses and hospitals for animals. The Romans made the keeping of geese a public care, since by their vigilance the Capitol had been saved. The Athenians ordained that the mules and hinnies which had served them in building the temple which they called Hecatompedon, should be free and allowed to graze wherever they pleased without hindrance.

Among the inhabitants of Agrigentum it was the usual custom to give a serious interment to the animals they held dear, such as horses of rare merit, dogs and birds which had been of some use, or even had helped to amuse their children. And the magnificence they ordinarily showed in all other things was particularly apparent in the number and costliness of the monuments they raised to that end, and which remained in all their pomp many centuries after.

The Egyptians buried bears, wolves, crocodiles, dogs and

cats in consecrated places, after embalming their bodies; and after their death they put on mourning.

Cimon gave an honourable burial to the mares with which he had three times won the prize for the race at the Olympian games. The ancient Xantippus buried his dog on a promontory on the sea-coast, which has since been called after it. And Plutarch tells us that it went against his conscience to sell and send to the slaughter-house, for a small gain, any ox that had long been in his service.

CHAPTER 12

APOLOGY FOR RAIMOND SEBOND.[1]

KNOWLEDGE is truly a great and very useful acquisition; they who despise it bear sufficient witness to their stupidity. Yet I do not value it at so excessive a rate as some have done, as Herillus the philosopher, who sees in it the sovereign good, and maintains that it has the power of making us wise and contented, which I do not believe. No more do I believe what others have affirmed, that knowledge is the mother of all virtue, and that every vice is the result of ignorance. If that be true, it is capable of being widely interpreted.

My house has long been open to men of learning, and is very well known to them. For my father, who controlled it for fifty years and more, inflamed with the new ardour which made King Francis the First espouse Letters and bring them to honour, very zealously and at great expense cultivated the acquaintance of learned scholars, welcoming them to his house as if they were little saints gifted with a peculiar inspiration of divine wisdom; gathering their words and sayings as so many oracles, and with the greater reverence and devotion as he was less qualified to appreciate them; for he had no more knowledge of letters than his ancestors. For my part, I like them indeed, but I do not worship them.

Among these was Pierre Bunel, a man with a great reputation for learning in his day, who, after staying with my

[1] A careful reading of this, the most important and most interesting of the Essays, seems to make it pretty clear, if we keep in mind Montaigne's hint to the wise to 'catch his meaning' and read between the lines, that the title was intentionally misleading, and that the whole chapter is an attack on Christian beliefs in general.

father at Montaigne for a few days, along with a few others of his sort, presented him on his departure with a book entitled : *Natural Theology, or Book of Things Created, by Master Raimond de Sabonde*. And, as my father was familiar with the Italian and Spanish languages, and this book being constructed of a Spanish with Latin terminations,[1] he expressed a hope that with very little assistance he might find it profitable, and recommended it to him as a very useful book, and suited to the time when he gave it to him ; which was when the new teachings of Luther were beginning to gain favour and to shake our old faith in many places.

In this he was very well advised, rightly foreseeing by reasonable inference that this incipient disease might easily degenerate into an execrable atheism. For the common people, lacking the power to weigh things by themselves, and being easily misled by chance appearances, when once they have become possessed with the temerity to despise and criticize the beliefs they once held in the utmost reverence, such as those on which depends their salvation ; and when once certain articles of their religion have been called in question and placed in the scales, they will soon be ready to throw into a like uncertainty all the other articles of their faith, which had no more authority or foundation in their eyes than those which are already shattered ; and will shake off, as a tyrannical yoke, all the impressions they once received from the authority of the laws or the reverence of ancient usage ;

> For, once too dreaded, with more greedy zest
> Trampled beneath the rabble heel ; (LUCRETIUS.)

resolved henceforth to accept nothing to which they have not applied their judgement and given their special sanction.

Now, some days before his death, my father, having by chance come across this book under a heap of other neglected papers, commanded me to turn it into French. It is an easy task to translate an author like this one, where there is little but the matter to be reproduced ; whereas those in which grace and elegance of language are a main factor are dangerous to attempt, especially if they are to be rendered into a weaker idiom. It was for me a new and very strange

---

[1] *Un Espagnol barragoiné en terminaisons Latines.* Sebond's Latin is not very good, but this description is a little too hard.

occupation, but as I chanced to be at the time at leisure, and being incapable of disobeying the command of the best father that ever was, I managed as best I could. He was singularly pleased with the result, and arranged to have it printed, which was done after his death.[1]

The ideas of this author appeared to me excellent, the arrangement of the work consistently carried out, and the intention very pious. Because many people devote their time to reading it, and especially the ladies, to whom we owe it to be more helpful, I have often had occasion to assist them to clear their book of two main objections that have been raised against it. The author's aim is bold and courageous; for he undertakes, by human and natural reasons, to establish and prove against the atheists all the articles of the Christian religion. Wherein, to tell the truth, I find him so strong and successful that I do not think it possible to improve on his arguments; and I believe that no man has equalled him.

As this work appeared to me too fine and rich for an author who is so little known, and of whom all that we know is that he was a Spaniard who professed medicine at Toulouse about two hundred years ago, I once inquired of Adrian Turnebus,[2] who knew everything, what he thought of this book. He replied that he thought it was some quintessence extracted from Saint Thomas Aquinas. For in truth that mind, full of an inexhaustible erudition and of a wonderful subtlety, was the only one capable of such ideas. This much is true, that, whoever may be the author and inventor (and it is not reasonable, without more evidence, to rob Sebond of that title), he was a man of great ability and many fine parts.

The first thing that is criticized in his work is that Christians injure their cause when they endeavour to ground their belief on human reasons, seeing that it can only come by faith and a particular inspiration of the divine grace.

---

[1] In the older editions these words were added, which were deleted in the 'Bordeaux MS.': 'With the carelessness which is seen in the endless number of errors which the printer left, he alone having seen it through the press.' Montaigne evidently became more indulgent to human weakness as he grew older, as shown by this and several other suppressions.

[2] Adrien Turnèbe, a humanist scholar and professor at the College de France.

In this objection there seems to be an over-zealous piety, and for that reason it is our duty to try and satisfy, with the more moderation and respect, those who put it forward.

This is a charge much better befitting a man who is versed in theology rather than myself, who know nothing of it. However, I argue thus, that in a matter so divine and sublime, and so far transcending human understanding as is this Truth wherewith it has pleased God in his goodness to illuminate us, it is very necessary that he should still lend us his assistance, by an extraordinary privilege and favour, in order that we may apprehend it and harbour it within us. And I do not believe that purely human powers are in any way capable of doing so; and if they were, so many rare and eminent minds, so abundantly furnished with natural powers, in olden times, would not have failed, through their reason, to arrive at this knowledge.

It is Faith alone that vividly and with certainty embraces the sublime mysteries of our religion. But that does not mean that it is not a very fine and very laudable undertaking to employ in the service of our faith also the natural and human implements that God has given us. It is not to be doubted that that is the most honourable use that we can put them to, and that there is no occupation or design more worthy of a Christian than to aim, by all his studies and reflections, at embellishing, extending and amplifying the truth of his belief. We are not content to serve God in spirit and with our soul; we also owe him and render him a bodily reverence; we apply our limbs even and our movements and external things to do him honour. We must do the like, and accompany our faith with all the reason that is in us; but always with this reservation, that we must not imagine that it depends upon ourselves, nor that our endeavours and arguments will be able to attain to a knowledge so divine and supernatural.

Unless it enter into us by an extraordinary infusion; if it enter, I will not say by reason alone, but by any human means, it is not in us in its dignity and splendour. And yet I truly fear that we shall possess it only by these means.

If we held fast to God by the mediation of a living faith; if we held to God through him and not through ourselves; if we had a divine foundation and foothold, human accidents would not have the power to shake us as they do. Our fort would not be ready to surrender to so feeble a battery. The love of novelty, the compulsion of rulers, the success of a party, the hasty and accidental change in our opinions, would not have the power to shake and alter our belief. We should not allow it to be disturbed at the bidding of any fresh argument, or yield to the persuasions even of all the eloquence that ever man employed; we should withstand those waves with an unmoved and inflexible firmness:

> As a vast rock repels the dashing waves,
> And scatters with its mass the blustering billows. (ANON.)

If this ray of divinity did in any sort touch us, it would appear throughout: not only our words but our works also would bear its light and lustre. Whatever proceeded from us would be seen illuminated by this noble brightness. We ought to be ashamed to observe that whilst there never was an adherent to any human sect, however strange and difficult his teachings, whose life and conduct did not in some degree conform to them; yet so divine and heavenly an institution as Christianity marks its adherents only by speech.

Do you desire a proof of this? Compare our ways with those of a Mohammedan or pagan; you will always fall short of them. Whereas, seeing the advantage our religion offers us, we ought to outshine them in excellence at an extreme and incomparable distance; and people should be able to say, 'Are they so just, so charitable, so good? Then they are Christians.'

All other outward signs are common to all religions: hope, trust, events, ceremonies, penitence, martyrs; the peculiar mark of our Truth ought to be our virtue, as it is also the most heavenly and difficult mark, and the most worthy product of Truth.

Therefore our good Saint Louis was in the right, who, when that Tartar king who had become a Christian proposed to come to Lyons to kiss the Pope's feet and to witness the sanctity he expected to find in our manners, earnestly dissuaded him from his purpose, for fear lest on the contrary our dissolute way of living might give him a loathing for so sacred a religion. Yet since then it happened quite otherwise to that other person who, having come to Rome with the same intent, and seeing the licentiousness of the prelates and the people of that time, became more firmly established in our religion, when he considered how much divine power there must be in a faith that could maintain its dignity and splendour in the midst of so much corruption and in hands so wicked.[1]

If we had a single drop of faith we should move mountains from their places, says the holy word. Our actions, which would be accompanied and guided by the Divinity, would not be simply human; they would have in them something miraculous, like our belief. *Brief is the way to an honest and happy life, if you believe* (Quintilian).

Some make the world believe that they believe what they do not believe; others, more numerous, make themselves believe it, being unable to penetrate into the nature of belief.

And we think it strange if, in the wars that are at this moment oppressing our State, we see events fluctuating and varying after a common and ordinary fashion.

The reason is that we bring to them nothing but our own. The justice which is in one of the two factions is only there as an ornament and a cloak: it is indeed alleged, but is neither received nor harboured nor espoused. It is there as on the lips of an advocate, not as in the heart or affection of a suitor. God owes his extraordinary succour to faith and religion, not to our passions. Men are the directors therein, and there make use of religion. It ought to be quite the contrary.

Observe if it be not with our own hands that we guide it, and that we mould, as in wax, so many figures at variance with a rule so straight and so constant. When was it more manifest than in France at the present day? They who have bent it to the left hand, they who have bent it to the right, they who call it black, they who call it white, employ it so alike for their violent and ambitious undertakings, progress so equally in riot and injustice, that they make us doubt and unable to believe in the diversity of the opinions they profess, in a matter on which depends the rule and conduct of our life.[2] Is it possible to see actions more uniform and

[1] Montaigne perhaps had in his mind Boccaccio's tale (second of the first day) of the Jew who was recommended to go to Rome, and after witnessing the evil living of the clergy, returned to Paris and was baptized a Christian.

[2] Their crimes are so much alike, that it is difficult to believe that their opinions are so unlike.

more identical proceeding from the same school and the same teaching ?

Observe with what dreadful impudence we bandy divine reasons about, and how irreligiously we have rejected them and taken them back, according as chance has shifted us from place to place in these public storms. This so serious proposition : Whether it be lawful for a subject to rebel and take up arms against his ruler, in the defence of religion, remember in whose mouths, in the year that is just past, the affirmative of this proposition was the buttress of one faction; and of what other faction the negative was the buttress. And hearken now from what quarter comes the voice and the instruction of both the one and the other, and whether the weapons make less of a clatter for this cause than for that. And we burn those people who say that the Truth must be made to bear the yoke of our necessity. And how much more France sins than in saying that ![1]

Let us confess the truth : should any one pick out of the army, even the average loyalist army, all those who march out of pure zeal and affection for religion, as well as those who only think of protecting the laws of their country, or serving their prince, he would be unable to make up a full company of men-at-arms. Whence comes it that there are so few to be found who have maintained the same mind and march at the same pace in our public movements, and that we see them at one time going but a foot-pace, at another riding at full speed, and the same men damaging our affairs, now by their violence and acrimony, now by their coldness, slackness and heaviness ; except it be that they are driven to it by special and accidental considerations, according as they are diversely stirred by them ?

It is evident to me that we do not willingly lend to devotion any other services but those that gratify our passions. There is no hostility that surpasses that of the Christian. Our zeal works wonders when it seconds our propensity to hatred, cruelty, ambition, avarice, detraction, rebellion. Against the grain, towards kindness, good-will, moderation,

---

[1] Before the death of the Catholic King Henry III (assassinated in 1589) the Protestants claimed the right, disputed by the Catholics, to rebel against the throne. When the Protestant King Henry IV succeeded, it was the Catholics who claimed the same right, and the Protestants disputed it.

it will neither walk nor fly, unless borne, as by a miracle, by some uncommon disposition.

Our religion was made for extirpating sins; it screens them, it fosters them, it provokes them.

We must not, as the saying goes, give God chaff instead of corn. If we believed in him, I will not say by faith, but with a simple belief; nay (and I say this to our great confusion), if we believed him and knew him as we do any tale, as we do one of our friends, we should love him above all other things, for the infinite goodness and beauty that shine in him. At least he would march in the same rank of our affections as riches, pleasure, fame and friends.

The best of us is not afraid to insult him as he is afraid of insulting his neighbour, his kinsman, his master. Is there any man of so simple understanding who, having on one side the object of one of our vicious pleasures, and on the other, with the like knowledge and persuasion, the state of an immortal glory, would barter the one against the other? And yet we often renounce it out of pure contempt; for what desire is it that tempts us to blaspheme, if not perhaps the very desire to give offence?

When the philosopher Antisthenes was being initiated into the mysteries of Orpheus, and the priest was telling him that they who vowed themselves to that religion would receive after death perfect and eternal blessings, he said to him, 'If you believe that, why do you not die yourself?' Diogenes, more rudely after his manner, and, though this is not to the point, to the priest who was in like manner exhorting him to join his order, that he might attain to the blessings of the next world, said, 'Would you have me believe that those two great men, Agesilaus and Epaminondas, will be wretched, and that you, who are but a calf, will be blessed because you are a priest?'

If these great promises of eternal beatitude were received with the like authority that we give to a philosophical lecture, we should not hold death in so great horror as we do.

> But were this mind of ours immortal mind,
> Dying 'twould scarce bewail a dissolution,
> But rather go with joy and leave its coat,
> As does a snake its slough, and stag its antlers old. (LUCRETIUS.)

'I would be dissolved, we should say, and be with Jesus

Christ' (Saint Paul). The power of Plato's Discourse on the Immortality of the Soul was such indeed that it impelled some of his disciples to seek death, in order the more speedily to realize the hopes he gave them.

All this is a very evident sign that we only receive our religion after our own fashion, and at our own hands, and no otherwise than the other religions are received. Either we happen to have been born in a country where it is practised, or we regard its antiquity or the authority of the men who have upheld it, or we fear the menaces which attach to unbelief, or are attracted by its promises. These considerations ought to weigh in our belief, but as subsidiaries only; they are human ties. A different region, other witnesses, the like promises and threats, might in the same way imprint upon us a contrary belief.

We are Christians by the same title as we are natives of Périgord or Germany.

And with regard to what Plato says, that there are few men so confirmed in their atheism but that an imminent danger will bring them back to a recognition of the divine power; that is not a part that a true Christian should play. It is for mortal and human religions to be received by human guidance. What kind of faith must that be that is implanted and established in us by cowardice and faintheartedness! What an absurd faith that believes what it believes only through want of courage to disbelieve it! Can a sinful feeling, such as unsteadfastness and perplexity, produce in our souls anything of a well-regulated nature?

The Atheists, says Plato, taking their reason for guide, assert that the stories about Hell and future punishment are fictions. But when an occasion arises to put them to the proof, when old age and sickness bring them near to death's door, their terror of it, and their horror of the future state, fill them with a new belief. And because such impressions put fear into one's heart, he forbids, in his Laws, all teaching of such threats and the belief that any evil can come to a man from the gods, except for his greater good, when it befalls him, and as a medicine.

They tell of Bion that, being infected with the atheistic doctrines of Theodorus, he had long scoffed at religious people; but that, being surprised by death, he gave himself up to the most extreme superstitions; as if the gods would withdraw and come back again to suit Bion's purpose!

Plato, and these examples, would lead us to the conclusion that we are brought back to a belief in God either by love or by force.

Atheism being a proposition, monstrous and unnatural as it were, hard and difficult too to establish in the human mind, however arrogant and unruly it may be, we have seen a goodly number, out of vanity and pride in harbouring opinions not held by the common sort, and which aim at reforming the world, affect to profess it out of ostentation; who, if they are mad enough, are yet not strong enough to have implanted it in their conscience. They will not fail to join their hands and raise them to heaven, if you give them a good sword-thrust in the chest. And when fear or sickness have abated the licentious fervour of that flighty humour, they will not fail to come to their senses and very wisely allow themselves to be directed to the common faith and examples. A doctrine seriously digested is one thing; another thing are those superficial impressions which, born of the dissoluteness of an unhinged mind, heedlessly and uncertainly swim in the imagination. Most miserable and hare-brained fellows who strive to be worse than they can be!

The error of paganism and ignorance of our sacred Truth caused the great soul of Plato, but great only in human greatness, to fall also into this other kindred fallacy, 'that children and old men are most susceptible to religion:' as if it were born of and derived its credit from our imbecility!

The knot which ought to bind our judgement and our will, which ought to closely knit and join our souls to our Creator, should be a knot that takes its folds and its strength, not from our ponderings, from our reasons and feelings, but from a divine and supernatural compulsion, having but one form, one face and one light, which is God's authority and his grace. Now, our heart and soul being ruled and commanded by faith, it is right that she should bring to the service of her purpose all our other faculties, according to their capacity.

And it is not to be believed that this whole edifice has not some marks imprinted on it by the hand of that great architect, and that there is not, in the things of this world, some image that in some sort recalls the artificer who has built and formed them. On these sublime works he has left the stamp of his divinity, and our imbecility is alone to blame if we are not able to discover it. It is what he himself tells us, 'That he manifests his invisible works to us, by those that are visible.' Sebond laboured at this laudable study and demonstrates to us that there is no part of the world that belies its maker. It would be a wrong done to the divine goodness if the universe did not concur in our belief. Heaven, earth, the elements, our body and our soul, all things conspire in this; it only remains to find out the way to use them; they instruct us if we are capable of understanding. For this world is a very holy temple, into which man is led to contemplate therein statues, not fashioned by mortal hand, but such as the divine Thought has made perceptible, the sun, the stars, the waters, and the earth, to represent things that are intelligible. 'The invisible things of God, says Saint Paul, appear by the creation of the world, considering his eternal wisdom, and his divinity by his works.'[1]

> For God himself begrudges not the world
> The sight of heaven; his form and countenance,
> Ever revolving, to our eyes reveals;
> Himself he clear impresses on our minds,
> That we may know him well, and learn
> His ways, by seeing him, and heed his laws. (MANILIUS.)

Now our human reasons and reflections are as it were the dull and barren matter; the grace of God is their mould; it is that which gives them shape and value. Just as the virtuous actions of Socrates and Cato remain vain and unprofitable for having been aimless, having no regard to the love and obedience of the true creator of all things, and because they did not know God, so it is with our ideas and reflections; they have a kind of body, but it is an unformed mass, without shape or light, if faith and the grace of God be not added to it. Faith, giving a tincture and light to Sebond's arguments, renders them firm and solid: they are capable of serving as a first guide and direction-post to

[1] Romans i. 20. The A. V. has: 'For the invisible things of him from the creation of the world are clearly seen, being understood by the things that are made, even his eternal power and Godhead'.

a learner, to put him into the way of this knowledge. They in some sort fashion him and make him capable of receiving the grace of God, by means of which our belief is afterwards consummated and made perfect.

I know a man of authority, nurtured on letters, who confessed to me that he had been reclaimed from the errors of unbelief by the medium of Sebond's arguments. And even if we stripped them of this ornament and of the assistance and approbation of the faith, though we regarded them as mere human fancies, to combat those who have fallen headlong into the awful and horrible darkness of irreligion, they will even then be found as firm and solid as any other of the same kind that may be opposed to them. So that we shall be justified in saying to our adversaries,—

> If you have better, send it here,
> Or else be thankful for my cheer,— (HORACE.)

that they must admit the force of our proofs, or else show us elsewhere, and on some other subject, arguments better woven and stuffed with more matter.

I have already inadvertently half involved myself in the second objection, to which I proposed to reply on Sebond's behalf.

Some say that his arguments are weak and unfitted to prove what he proposes; and undertake to knock them down with ease. These men must be shaken a little more roughly, for they are more dangerous and more crafty than the first. (We are apt to twist the meaning of others' writings to suit the opinions we have prejudged in our own minds. An Atheist flatters himself that he can make every writer out to be an Atheist; infecting the harmless matter with his own venom.) The minds of these men are prepossessed in such a way as to jade their palate for Sebond's reasons. Moreover they think they have an easy game when they are given the liberty to combat our religion with purely human weapons, when they would not dare to attack it in its authoritative and commanding majesty.

The means I take, and which appear to me the fittest, to subdue that frenzy, is to crush and tread under foot human pride and arrogance, to make them sensible of the inanity, the vanity and insignificance of man; to wrest out of their fists the miserable weapons of their reason; to make them bow the head and bite the dust under the authority and reverence of the divine majesty. To it alone belongs knowledge and wisdom ; it alone is able to estimate a thing at its proper value, and from it alone we rob whatever we think is our worth and price. For *God allows no one to have high thoughts but himself* (Herodotus quoting Artabanus).

Let us suppress this self-conceit, the first foundation of the tyranny of the evil spirit : *For God resisteth the proud, and giveth grace to the humble* (Saint Peter). Understanding is in all the gods, says Plato, and in very few men.

Now, it is meanwhile a great comfort to the Christian to see our mortal and fragile implements so fitly suited to our holy and divine faith that, when we employ them upon subjects that are by their nature mortal and fragile, they are not more uniformly and more powerfully appropriate to them. Let us see then if man has at his disposal any reasons more forcible than those of Sebond ; nay let us see if it is in him to arrive at any certainty by argument and reason.

For Saint Augustine, arguing against these people, rightly accuses them of wrongheadedness, in that they hold those articles of our faith to be false which our reason fails to establish. And, in order to show that a good many things may exist and may have existed, whose nature and causes our reason cannot fathom, he puts before them certain well-known and undoubted experiences which man confesses he cannot penetrate. And this he does, as he does everything else, in a diligent and serious search after truth. We must do more, and let them know that there is no need to go picking out uncommon examples, to convince them of the feebleness of their Reason ; and that she is so infirm and so blind that nothing, however clear and easy, is clear enough for her ; that to her the easy and the difficult are all one ; that all subjects equally, and Nature in general, disclaim her jurisdiction and mediation.

What does Truth preach to us, when she preaches to us to fly worldly philosophy, when she so often impresses upon us, That our wisdom is but folly in the sight of God ; That of all vain things the most vain is man ; That man, who presumes on his learning, does not yet know what it is to know ; and That if man, who is nothing, thinks himself something, he deceives and beguiles himself ? [1] These

---

[1] See St. Paul, Colossians ii. 8, 1 Corinthians iii. 19 and viii. 2, and

MAN'S PRESUMPTION

sayings of the Holy Spirit so clearly and vividly express what I wish to maintain, that I should need no other proof against men who would bow with all submission and obedience to its authority. But the others would rather be whipped to their own cost, and will not suffer their reason to be combated except by itself.

Let us then for the nonce consider man alone, without outside assistance, armed only with his own weapons, and destitute of the divine grace and knowledge, which comprise all his honour, his strength and the foundation of his being. Let us see how he will hold out in this fine equipment. Let him explain to me, by the force of his reason, on what foundation he has built those great advantages he thinks he has over the other creatures. What has induced him to believe that that wonderful motion of the heavenly vault, the eternal light of those torches rolling so proudly over his head, the awe-inspiring agitations of that infinite sea, were established, and endure through so many centuries, for his service and convenience ?[1]

Is it possible to imagine anything more ridiculous than that this miserable and puny creature, who is not so much as master of himself, exposed to shocks on all sides, should call himself Master and Emperor of the universe, of which it is not in his power to know the smallest part, much less to command it ? And that privilege which he assumes of being the only creature in this great edifice that has the capacity to know the beauty and the several parts of it, the only one who is able to give thanks to the architect, and to keep an account of the receipts and outlay of the world : who has sealed him this privilege ? Let him show us his letters-patent for this great and noble charge.

Have they been granted in favour of the wise only ? Then few people would be concerned. Are the fools and the wicked deserving of so extraordinary a favour, and, being the worst lot in the world, of being preferred to all the rest ?

Shall we believe the man who says this, *For whose sake shall we then say that the world has been made ? Undoubtedly for those creatures that have the use of reason : these are gods and men, to whom assuredly nothing is superior ?* (Balbus

---

Galatians vi. 3. These texts are inscribed on the joists of Montaigne's library.

[1] Here as elsewhere Montaigne flatly **contradicts** Sebond.

the Stoic, according to Cicero). We could never sufficiently deride the impudence of this coupling of gods and men.

But, poor devil, what is there in him deserving of such a privilege? When we consider the incorruptible life of the heavenly bodies, their beauty, their grandeur, their continual motion by so exact a rule:

> When we gaze aloft
> Upon the skiey vaults of yon great world
> The ether, fixt high over twinkling stars,
> And into our thought there come the journeyings
> Of sun and moon; (LUCRETIUS.)

when we consider the dominion and power those bodies have, not only over our lives and the conditions of our fortune,

> Our lives and actions on the stars depend, (MANILIUS.)

but even over our dispositions, our judgement, our will, which they govern, impel and stir at the mercy of their influence, as our reason discovers and tells us:

> This we learn: the far, far distant stars
> Govern by silent laws; the world is ruled
> By periodic causes, and the turns of destiny
> Observed by certain signs; (MANILIUS.)

when we see that not only a man, not only a king, but kingdoms, empires, and all this world here below, are moved according to the lightest swing of the heavenly motions:

> How great a change each little motion brings!
> So great this kingdom that it governs kings; (MANILIUS.)

if our virtue, our vices, our talents and our knowledge, if even this dissertation of mine on the power of the stars, this comparison between them and ourselves, comes, as our reason supposes, by their means and their favour;

> Maddened by love, Leander swims the strait,
> A Grecian king o'erturns the walls of Troy.
> 'Tis this man's lot to give his country laws.
> Sons kill their fathers, fathers kill their sons,
> And brothers arm themselves in mutual strife.
> Not we have made these wars; tis Fate compels
> To bear such pains with lacerated limbs.
> And Fate it is that makes me ponder Fate; (MANILIUS.)

if this little portion of reason we possess has been allotted to us by heaven, how can reason make us the equal of heaven ? How can it subject its essence and conditions to our knowledge ? All that we see in those bodies fills us with amazement. *What apparatus, what instruments, what levers, what engines, what craftsmen were employed about so mighty a work ?* (Cicero).

Why do we deny them a soul, and life and reason ? Have we discovered in them any stubborn, senseless stupidity, we who have no concern with them but to obey them ? Shall we say that we have seen no other creature but man in possession of a reasoning mind ? Why ! have we seen anything comparable to the sun ? Does it exist the less for our not having seen its like ? Does it move the less because no other movement is to be compared with it ? If what we have not seen does not exist, our knowledge is marvellously short-sighted : *How close the confines of our mind !* (Cicero).

Is it not a delusion of human vanity to make the moon a celestial earth, and to imagine that there are mountains and valleys upon it, as did Anaxagoras ; to set up human habitations and dwellings and establish colonies upon it for our convenience, as do Plato and Plutarch, and to make our earth a bright and shining star ? *Amongst other infirmities of human nature is that mental blindness which not only forces man to err, but makes him hug his errors* (Seneca). *The corruptible body weighs down the soul, and this earthly habitation prevents it from pondering on many things* (The Book of Wisdom, quoted by Saint Augustine).

Presumption is our natural and original infirmity. The frailest and most vulnerable of all creatures is man, and at the same time the most arrogant. He sees and feels himself lodged here in the mud and filth of the world, nailed and riveted to the worst, the deadest and most stagnant part of the universe, at the lowest story of the house and the most remote from the vault of heaven, with the animals of the worst condition of the three ;[1] and he goes and sets himself in imagination above the circle of the moon, and brings heaven under his feet.

With this same vanity of imagination he makes himself the equal of God, assumes to himself divine qualities, selects and separates himself from among the multitude of other creatures, carves out their shares to each of his

[1] Of those that creep on the earth, as distinguished from those that fly and swim.

fellows and comrades, the animals, and allots to them their portion of faculties and powers according as it seems good to him. How can he know, by the force of his understanding, the secret and internal motions of the animals? By what comparison between them and himself does he suppose them to be as stupid as he thinks?

When I play with my cat, who knows but that she regards me more as a plaything than I do her? [We amuse each other with our respective monkey-tricks; if I have my moments for beginning and refusing, so she has hers.]

Plato, in his picture of the golden age under Saturn, numbers, among the chief advantages of the man of that time, his communion with the beasts, of whom inquiring and learning he knew the real attributes and differences of each of them; whereby he acquired a very perfect understanding and wisdom, and in consequence passed his life very much more happily than we are able to do. Do we need a better proof of the impudence of man where the beasts are concerned? That great author opined that, in giving them their bodily shape, Nature for the most part only considered the use they could be put to in the prognostications which were drawn from them in his time.

That defect which hinders communication between us and them, why may it not as well be in ourselves as in them? It is a matter of conjecture with whom the fault lies that we do not understand one another; for we understand them no more than they do us. By the same reasoning they may regard us as beasts, as we do them.

It is no great wonder if we do not understand them, for neither do we understand the Basques and the Troglodytes.[1] Yet some have boasted of understanding them, as Apollonius of Tyana, Melampus, Tiresias, Thales, and others. And since it is the case that, as the cosmographers tell, there are nations that receive a dog for their king, they must needs in some way interpret its voice and actions.

We must observe the parity there is between us. We have some halfway understanding of their meaning, as the animals have of ours, in about the same degree. They cajole us, they threaten us, they entreat us, as we do them. Moreover, it is very evident to us that they are able fully and completely to communicate with one another, that they

---

[1] Cave-dwellers on the Western shore of the Arabian Gulf.

We may see well enough, in most of their works, how much the animals surpass us, and how much we fall short in the art of imitating them. And yet, in our ruder performances, we are sensible of what faculties we employ, and we know that our mind applies to them its utmost powers ; why do we not conclude the same of the animals ? Why do we ascribe to I know not what slavish instinct of nature those works that excel anything we can do by nature or art ? Herein we unconsciously give them a very great advantage over ourselves, in making Nature, with a maternal kindness, to accompany and lead them as it were by the hand, to all the activities and conveniences of their life ; whilst us she abandons to chance and fortune, and forces us to seek by art the things necessary for our preservation ; at the same time denying us the means of attaining, by any education or mental effort, to the natural skill of the animals. So that their brutish stupidity surpasses in all their contrivances everything we are able to do with our divine intelligence.

Truly, by this reckoning, we might with great reason call her a very unjust stepmother ; but that is not so. Our organization is not so formless and unregulated. Nature has been universally kind to all her creatures, and there is none that she has not very amply furnished with all the means necessary for the preservation of its being. For those common complaints that I hear men uttering (as the licence of their opinions now lifts them up above the clouds, now brings them down to the antipodes), that we are the only outcast animal, bare on the bare earth, bound and tied down, with no means of arming or covering ourselves but with others' spoils ; whereas all the other creatures have been clothed by Nature with shells, husks, bark, hair, wool, spikes, leather, down, feathers, scales, fleece, bristles, according to the need of their being ; armed with claws, teeth, horns for attack and defence, and has herself instructed them in what is requisite to each, to swim, run, fly, sing, whilst man cannot even walk or speak, nor eat, nor do anything but weep, without an apprenticeship :

> Then again the babe,
> Like to the castaway of the raging surf,
> Lies naked on the ground, speechless, in want
> Of every help for life, when Nature first

> Hath poured him forth upon the shores of light
> With birth-pangs from within the mother's womb,
> And with a plaintive wail he fills the place,—
> As well befitting one for whom remains
> In life a journey through so many ills.
> But all the flocks and herds and all wild beasts
> Come forth and grow, nor need the little rattles,
> Nor must be treated to the humouring nurse's
> Dear broken chatter; nor seek they divers clothes
> To suit the changing skies; nor need, in fine,
> Nor arms, nor lofty ramparts, wherewithal
> Their own to guard—because the earth herself
> And Nature, artificer of the world, bring forth
> Aboundingly all things for all. (LUCRETIUS.)

These complaints are unfounded; there is in the governance of the world a much greater equality and a more uniform relationship. Our skin is provided as abundantly as theirs with power to resist the inclemency of the weather. Witness the many nations that have not yet tried the use of clothes. Our ancient Gauls wore hardly any clothes, like our neighbours the Irish of the present day, in spite of their cold climate.

But we may judge better by ourselves: for all those parts of our person which we are pleased to expose to the wind and air are adapted to endure it, the feet, the face, the hands, the legs, the shoulders, the head, according to the demands of usage. For if there is in us a tender spot, in which we should seem to fear the cold, it should be the stomach, where digestion takes place; our fathers used to leave it uncovered, and our ladies, soft and delicate as they are, sometimes go half-covered down to the navel.

Nor are the bindings and swaddlings of infants any more necessary. The Lacedemonian mothers reared their children in all freedom to move their limbs, without any wrappings or fastenings.

Our weeping we have in common with most of the other animals; there are hardly any that do not wail and whine long after their birth, seeing that it is a natural effect of their helplessness at that age. As to the habit of eating, it is natural to us as well as to them, and comes without instruction:

> For each creature feels
> By instinct to what use to put its powers. (LUCRETIUS.)

Who doubts but that a child, having acquired the strength to feed himself, is able to seek his food? And the earth yields and offers him enough for his needs, without any cultivation and artifice; and if not at all times, no more does she do it for the animals. Witness the provision we see made by the ants and other creatures, in view of the barren season of the year. Those nations we have lately discovered, so abundantly provided with meat and a natural drink, without care or trouble on their part, have now made us realize that bread is not our only sustenance, and that, without any tilling, our Mother Nature has plentifully provided us with all that we need. Nay, as seems very probable, more amply and richly than she does now that we have taken to meddling with it by our contrivances:

> She first, the Earth, of own accord
> The shining grains and vineyards of all joy
> Created for mortality; herself
> Gave the sweet fruitage and the pastures glad,
> Which now to-day yet scarcely wax in size,
> Even when, aided by our toiling arms,
> We break the ox, and wear away the strength
> Of sturdy farm-hands; (LUCRETIUS.)

the excess and unruliness of our appetite outstripping all the inventions wherewith we seek to satisfy it.

With regard to weapons, we are better provided by Nature than most other animals; we are more able to move our limbs about and to extract service from them, naturally and without being taught. Those who are trained to fight naked are seen to rush into dangers just like our own soldiers. If some of the beasts surpass us in this advantage, we surpass many others in the same. We possess by a natural instinct and teaching the skill to fortify our bodies and protect them by acquired means. That this is so is proved by the example of the elephant who sharpens and grinds the teeth which he makes use of in warfare (for he has special teeth which he saves and employs for this purpose only). When bulls go to battle they throw up and scatter the dust around them; the boars whet their tusks; the ichneumon, when it is about to grapple with the crocodile, fortifies its body by coating it all over with a crust of mud, well kneaded and compressed, as with a cuirass. Why shall we not say that it is as natural to us to arm ourselves with wood and iron?

As to speech, it is certain that, if it is not natural, neither is it necessary. Nevertheless I believe that a child brought up in complete solitude, far from all intercourse (which would be a difficult experiment to make), would have some kind of speech to express his ideas. And it is not to be believed that Nature has denied us this power which she has given to many other animals; for what else but speech is that faculty we observe in them of complaining, rejoicing, calling to one another for succour, inviting to love, which they do by the use of their voice?

Why should they not speak with one another? They speak to us, and we to them: in how many different tones do we not speak to our dogs? and they answer us. We use another language with them, than we do in talking to birds, pigs, oxen and horses, and give them other names; we change the idiom according to the kind.

> So ants amidst their sable-coloured band
> One with another mouth to mouth confer,
> Haply their way or state to understand. (DANTE.)

Lactantius seems to attribute to beasts not only the power of speech but also of laughter. And the same difference of tongues which, according to the difference of countries, is found in human beings, is also found in animals of the same species. Aristotle, writing on this subject, instances the various calls of partridges, according to locality:

> The dappled birds
> Utter at other times far other cries
> Than when they fight for food, or with their prey
> Struggle and strain. And birds there are which change
> With changing weather their own raucous songs. (LUCRETIUS.)

But it is yet to be known what language the supposed child would speak; and what has been conjectured about it has no great probability. If any one declares to me, in opposition to this belief, that those deaf by nature do not speak, I reply that it is not only because they have not been taught to speak by ear, but more because the sense of hearing, of which they are deprived, is related to that of speech, and that they hold together by a natural tie; in such a way that the words we speak must in the first place be spoken to ourselves, and be made to strike upon our own inward ears, before being sent out to others' ears.

I have said all this to establish the resemblance to human conditions, and to bring us back and join us to the majority. We are neither superior nor inferior to the rest. All that is under heaven, says the sage, is subject to one law and one fate :

> Enshackled in the gruesome bonds of doom. (LUCRETIUS.)

Some difference there is ; there are orders and degrees, but under the aspect of one same Nature :

> But each sole thing
> Proceeds according to its proper wont,
> And all conserve their own distinctions, based
> In Nature's fixed decree. (LUCRETIUS.)

Man must be forced and lined up within the barriers of this organization. The poor wretch has no mind really to step over them. He is shackled and entangled, he is subjected to the same obligation as the other creatures of his order, and is of a very mediocre condition, without any real and essential prerogative and pre-eminence. That which he thinks and imagines himself to possess, neither has body nor can it be perceived. And if it be so that he alone of all the animals has this freedom of imagination, this licence of thought, which represents to him that which is, that which is not, that which he wills, the false and the true ; it is an advantage sold to him very dearly, and of which he has very little cause to boast. For from it springs the principal source of all the ills that press upon him, sin, sickness, irresolution, affliction, despair.

I say then, to return to my theme, that there is no reason to imagine that the beasts do, through a natural and enforced instinct, the same things that we do by choice and skill. From like results we must infer like faculties [and from more abundant results, more abundant faculties] ; and we must consequently confess that the same reason, the same method, that we employ in working are also employed by the animals [if not some other and better ones]. Why do we imagine in them that natural compulsion, although we experience no such thing in ourselves ? Besides that it is more honourable, and nearer allied to the Divinity, to be guided and obliged to act rightly by a natural and irresistible condition, than to act rightly by an impulsive and fortuitous liberty; and safer to leave the reins of our conduct in the hands of Nature than to keep them in our own. In the vanity of our presumption we prefer to owe our superiority to our own powers rather than to Nature's bounty. We endow the other animals with natural gifts and renounce them in their favour, in order to honour and ennoble ourselves with acquired gifts. And we do all this, it seems to me, in all simplicity, for I should prize as highly gifts that are purely and naturally my own, as those I had begged and collected from education. It is not in our power to acquire a higher recommendation than to be favoured by God and Nature.

Take the case of the fox, which the inhabitants of Thrace employ before they attempt to cross a frozen river, by letting it loose before them. If we saw him at the edge of the water approaching his ear very near to the ice in order to listen if, at a distance or near by, he can hear the noise of the water running underneath, and recoiling or advancing according as he perceives the ice to be thick or thin, should we not be justified in assuming that the same ideas pass through his head as would pass through ours, and that his natural sense has taught him to reason and conclude somewhat as follows : ' That which makes a noise, moves ; that which moves is not frozen ; that which is not frozen is liquid, and yields under a weight ' ? For to attribute that merely to an acute sense of hearing, without any reasoning or concluding, is an absurd notion, and not to be imagined. We must judge in like manner of the many wiles and stratagems that the animals employ to defend themselves from our attacks upon them.

And if we would claim any superiority from the fact that we have it in our power to seize them, employ them in our service and use them at our pleasure, it is but the same advantage we have over one another. On these terms we have our slaves. Were there not women in Syria called Climacides, who, crouching on all fours, served as footstools or step-ladders to enable the ladies to mount into their coaches ? And the majority of free people, for a very slight consideration, surrender their life and being into the power of others. The wives and concubines of the Thracians plead to be chosen to die upon their husbands' tombs.

Have tyrants ever failed to find enough men pledged to devote themselves to their service, some of whom were besides obliged to accompany them in death as in life? Whole armies have so bound themselves to their captains.

The form of oath in that rude school of men who fought to the bitter end contained this promise: 'We swear to suffer ourselves to be fettered, burned, beaten, killed with the sword, and to endure everything that real gladiators suffer at the hands of their masters; most religiously pledging both body and soul to his service':

> Burn, if thou wilt, my head with fire,
> With sword my body strike, and cut
> My back with twisted thong. (TIBULLUS.)

That was a covenant indeed;[1] and yet there were, in some years, ten thousand who entered into it and rushed to perdition.

When the Scythians interred their king, they strangled on his body the most favoured of his concubines, his cup-bearer, his door-keeper, the groom of his stables, his chamberlain and his cook. And upon his anniversary they killed fifty horses, mounted by fifty pages, whose bodies were impaled up the spine of the back as far as the throat, and thus left planted in state around the tomb.

The men who work for us do so more cheaply and for a less careful and favourable treatment than we mete out to our hawks, horses, and dogs. What anxious care we devote to the comfort of these! I do not think the most obsequious of servants would do willingly for their masters what princes think it an honour to do for those creatures.

Diogenes, seeing his parents at pains to redeem him from slavery, said, 'They are mad; it is the man who feeds and keeps me who is my slave.' And they who keep animals may be said to serve, rather than to be served by them.

And surely the animals are more noble in this respect,

---

[1] The oath is taken from a work of fiction (Petronius' *Satyricon*), and can hardly be put as historical evidence. It was besides not taken seriously, nor by real gladiators, but by the friends of Trimalchio, temporarily disguised as his slaves.

that no lion ever submits to be the slave of another lion, no horse of another horse, for want of spirit. As we go hunting animals, so do tigers and lions go hunting men; and they give chase to one another, dogs to hares, pikes to tench, swallows to grasshoppers, sparrow-hawks to blackbirds and larks:

> Her little ones the stork with serpents feeds,
> And finds them lizards in the devious meads;
> Jove's eagle and the nobler tribes of air
> Pounce on the kid and seize the timid hare. (JUVENAL.)

We share the fruit of the chase, as well as the pains and skill, with our hawks and hounds. And above Amphipolis in Thrace the huntsmen and the wild falcons fairly divide the booty into equal parts; as also, on the shores of Lake Moeotis, if the fisher does not honestly leave the wolves an equal share in his catch, they will forthwith tear his nets.

And as we have a kind of sport conducted more by cunning than by strength, as with gins, hooks and lines, we see the same in animals. Aristotle says that the sepia throws out from its neck a gut, as long as a line, which it lets out at its full length and draws back at its pleasure. On perceiving some little fish approaching, she allows it to bite the end of this gut, and, being the while hidden in the mud or sand, by degrees draws it in until the fish is so near that she can catch it with one leap.[1]

As to strength, no animal in the world is exposed to so many injuries as man. There is no need to mention whales, elephants, crocodiles, or the like, a single one of which is able to destroy many men; lice are sufficient to put an end to Sylla's dictatorship, and the heart and life of a great and triumphant emperor is the breakfast of a little worm.

Why do we call it knowledge and science, built up by art and reason, when a man discriminates those things which sustain life and are helpful in his maladies from those which are not so, and when he knows the virtues of rhubarb and polypody? And when we see the goats of Candia, if wounded by an arrow, picking from among a million herbs

---

[1] This is Aristotle at fourth or fifth hand, for Montaigne no doubt derived this account from some Latin or French translation. Aristotle knew too much about the tentacles and suckers of the cuttle-fish to write such nonsense. Most of the descriptions and anecdotes which follow are taken from Plutarch or Pliny.

the dittany for their cure ; and the tortoise, after devouring a viper, straightway looking for marjoram to purge itself ; the dragon making its eyes clear and bright with fennel ; the storks administering to themselves clysters of sea-water ; elephants pulling out of themselves and their mates, and even out of their masters' bodies (witness the elephant of King Porus, defeated by Alexander) the javelins and darts hurled at them in battle, and extracting them so skilfully that we ourselves could not do so with so little pain ; why do we not also call that science and foresight ? For to assert, to their disparagement, that their knowledge is solely due to the teaching and instruction of Nature, is not to deprive them of their claim to science and foresight, but to attribute it to them, with greater reason than to ourselves, to the honour of so reliable a schoolmistress.

Chrysippus, although in all other respects as scornful a judge of the condition of animals as any other philosopher, pondering over the movements of a dog, who, coming to a cross-road with three ways to choose from, either in search of his master whom he has lost, or in pursuit of some game fleeing before him, goes sniffing one path after another, and, after making sure of two of them and not discovering the scent he is after, darts along the third without any hesitation ; is forced to admit that the dog reasons somewhat in this way : ' I have followed my master's track to this crossing ; he must necessarily have gone one of these ways : it is not this, it is not that ; he must then infallibly have gone this other one ' ; and that, assured by this reasoning and inference, he no longer uses his power of scent to investigate the third, but allows himself to be carried away by the force of reason.

Is not this exercise of pure logic, and this use of propositions, divided and conjoined, and the sufficient enumeration of the parts, which comes to the dog by nature, quite as good as if he had learned it of Trapezuntius ?[1]

And yet animals are not incapable of being instructed after our manner. We teach blackbirds, ravens, magpies, parrots, to speak ; and that facility with which we see them rendering their voice and breath so supple and pliant that it can be formed and confined within a certain number of

---

[1] George of Trebizond, a fifteenth-century logician, who translated and commented Aristotle.

letters and syllables, testifies to their having an inner reasoning faculty which makes them so teachable and willing to learn.

Everybody, I should think, is satiated with the sight of the many tricks which mountebanks teach their dogs; the dances in which they do not miss a single note of the music they hear; the many and varied leaps and movements they make them perform at the word of command. But what I observe with more wonder is the behaviour of dogs in the service of the blind, both in the country and the cities; a common sight enough. I have remarked how they stop at certain doors where they are wont to receive alms; how they avoid contact with carts and coaches, even when, for their part, they have sufficient room to pass. I have seen one, walking alongside the town ditch, leave an even and level path to choose a worse, in order to keep his master away from the ditch. How was it possible to make this dog understand that it was his duty to look to his master's safety only, and to despise his own convenience in order to serve him? And how could he know that such and such a path was broad enough for him but not for a blind man? Can all this be apprehended without reason?

I must not forget what Plutarch tells of a dog he saw with the Emperor Vespasian, the father, in the theatre of Marcellus at Rome. This dog belonged to a tumbler who acted a play in several scenes and with several parts, one of which was taken by the dog. Among other things he had to pretend to be dead for a time, in consequence of having eaten of a certain drug; after swallowing the bread which was supposed to be this drug, he began immediately to tremble and stagger as if dizzy. Finally, stretching and stiffening himself as if dead, he allowed himself to be pulled and dragged from one place to another, as the subject of the piece required. Then, when he knew it was time, he first began to move very slightly, as if he had just awakened out of a deep sleep, and, lifting his head, looked about him in a manner to astonish all the spectators.

In the royal gardens at Susa oxen were employed to water the same, and to turn certain big wheels for drawing the water, to which buckets were attached (such as those we may commonly see in Languedoc). They had been commanded to do as many as a hundred turns a day each, and they were so accustomed to this number, that it was impossible by any force to make them do another turn; but having performed their task, they stopped dead. We are almost out of childhood before we can count to a hundred, and we have recently discovered nations that have no knowledge of numbers.

It needs still more intelligence to teach others than to be taught. Now, setting aside what Democritus held and proved, that most of the arts have been taught us by animals, as the spider has taught us to weave and sew, the swallows to build, the swan and the nightingale music, and many animals, through imitating them, to practise medicine; Aristotle maintains that the nightingales teach their young to sing, and spend time and care over it. Whence it happens that the young birds we keep in cages, which have not had the opportunity to go to school under their parents, lose much of the charm of their song. We may conclude therefrom that it is improved by teaching and study.

And even those that are free do not all sing alike, each one having picked it up according to its capacity; and in their zeal to learn they contend with so brave a rivalry that the vanquished sometimes falls dead on the spot, its breath rather than its voice having failed. The youngest ruminate pensively, and begin to imitate certain snatches of song; the learner listens to the master's teaching and imitates him very carefully; they hold their peace, now one, now the other; one may hear their faults being corrected, and perceive that they are sometimes reproved by their tutor.

Arrianus says that he once saw an elephant with a cymbal hanging on each thigh and another fastened to its trunk, to the sound of which all the others danced around, rising and bowing at certain intervals, as they were guided by the instrument; and that it was a pleasure to listen to this harmony.

In the Roman shows it was usual to see elephants trained to move and dance to the sound of the voice, dances with many coupees and other intricate measures, very difficult to learn. They have been seen in private to memorize their lesson, and practise with care and study, in order not to be scolded and beaten by their masters.

But this other story of the magpie, which is vouched for by Plutarch himself, is strange. She lived in a barber's shop at Rome and could wonderfully imitate with her voice everything she heard. It happened one day that certain trumpeters halted for a considerable time before this shop to blow their instruments. After that, and all the next day, behold this magpie pensive, dumb and melancholy, whereat everybody marvelled. They thought she had been stunned and deafened by the blare of the trumpets, and that she had lost her hearing and voice at the same time. But they discovered at last that she was in a deep study and had retired within herself, and that in her mind she was exercising and preparing her voice to reproduce the sound of the trumpets; and the first time she raised her voice she perfectly imitated their pitch, their changes and repetitions. After this new acquisition she disdained and abandoned all that she had been able to say before.

I will not omit to cite also this other example of a dog which the same Plutarch (for, with regard to the order of the examples, I am well aware that it is confused; but I am no more able to observe order in arranging these examples than in all my other affairs), declares he saw when on a ship. This dog, anxious to get at some oil at the bottom of a pitcher, which he could not reach with his tongue on account of the narrow mouth of the vessel, went in search of pebbles and dropped them into the pitcher until the oil rose nearer to the edge, where he could reach it. What have we there but the workings of a very subtle mind? It is said that the ravens in Barbary do the same thing when the water they wish to drink is out of their reach.

This action is somewhat akin to what Juba, a king of that country, tells of the elephants, that when, through the cunning of the hunters, one of them is entrapped in certain deep pits prepared for them and covered with small brushwood to deceive them, his comrades very promptly bring great store of stones and logs of wood to help him to get out. But this animal shows a capacity akin to that of man in so many ways that, if I related in detail all that experience has taught us about them, I could easily make out a case for my general contention, that there is a greater difference between many a man and many another man, than between many a man and many an animal.

INTELLIGENT ELEPHANTS

In a private house in Syria the keeper of an elephant used, at every meal, to rob his charge of half his allowance. One day his master himself wished to attend to him, and tipped into his manger the full measure of barley he had prescribed for his maintenance; the elephant, regarding his keeper with an evil eye, with his trunk separated and put aside the half of it, thereby intimating the wrong that had been done to him. And another, that had a keeper who mixed stones with his food to increase the measure of it, approached the pot in which he cooked his meat for his own dinner, and filled it with ashes.

Those are particular facts. But everybody has read and knows that in all armies which were brought from the Levant one of the greatest elements of strength was the elephants, from which they obtained results incomparably greater than we now do from our artillery, which has more or less replaced them in a pitched battle (as they may easily understand who know ancient history):

> Their sires warred for Tyrian Hannibal,
> For Roman generals and Molossian kings;
> With cohorts fighting on their bulky backs,
> A tower of strength they moved into the fray. (JUVENAL.)

They must indeed have had good reason to rely upon the fidelity and intelligence of these beasts, in trusting them to go into the vanguard of the battle, where the least stoppage they might have caused by reason of the bulk and heaviness of their bodies, the slightest scare that might have made them face about upon their own people, would have been enough to ruin all. And we do not read of so many examples of their falling back upon their own battalions and routing one another, as occur in our own days. They were charged not merely to carry out simple movements in battle, but to discharge many different functions; and the Spaniards employed their dogs for the same purpose in the new conquest of the Indies, for which they received pay and shared in the booty. And these animals showed so much skill and judgement in following up and deciding the victory, in attacking and withdrawing, as the occasion required, in distinguishing their friends from their enemies, as they did ardour and fierceness.

We are more apt to wonder at and value the things that are strange to us than those we may see every day; but for that I should not have spent so much time over this catalogue of examples. For I think, if we look closely into the habits of the animals that live with us, that we shall have occasion to discover facts as wonderful as those we gather from foreign countries and remote ages. It is one same Nature that rolls its course. If we could form a sufficient estimate of its present state, we might safely infer the whole of its future and the whole of its past.

I once saw some men who had been brought over from distant parts to this country, of whose language we did not understand a word; whose ways, moreover, whose faces and clothing differed totally from ours. Who among us did not look upon them as savage and brutal? Which of us did not put it down to dullness and stupidity to see them dumb, ignorant of the French language, knowing nothing of our handkissings and our grovelling salutations, our deportment and behaviour, which no doubt human nature must take as its pattern?

We condemn everything that appears strange to us and which we do not understand; and we do the same in our judgement of the animals. They resemble us in many ways, and from them we may, by comparison, draw some conclusions; but what can we know of those things that are peculiar to them? Horses, dogs, oxen, sheep, birds and most of the animals that live among us, recognize our voice and allow themselves to be guided by it. So did also Crassus' lamprey, which came to him when he called it; and so do also the eels in the fountain of Arethusa. And I have often enough seen fish in ponds hurrying to be fed, when called in a certain way by their attendant;

> All have their proper names, and every one
> Comes at his master's voice when called upon. (MARTIAL.)

We may judge by that.

Of the elephants it may also be said that they share with us a kind of religion; for they may be seen, after several ablutions and purifications, to raise their trunks, as we do our arms, and, at a certain hour of the day, of their own accord, without any precept or instruction, to stand, with their eyes fixed in the direction of the rising sun, in a long meditation and contemplation. But, although we see no signs of this in any other animals, we cannot conclude that they have no religion, nor explain in any way what is hidden from us.

But we may see something in this action which the philosopher Cleanthes observed, since it somewhat resembles ours. He records that he saw a party of ants leaving their nest bearing the dead body of a comrade, and approaching another ant-hill, out of which several other ants came to meet them, as if to parley with them; and, after having been some while together the second party returned to consult, as we may suppose, with their fellow-citizens, and thus made two or three journeys, by reason of the difficulty of coming to terms. Finally the last comers brought to the first a worm out of their den, as it were for a ransom for the defunct, which worm the first loaded on their backs and carried home, leaving the body of the deceased with the others. That was the interpretation Cleanthes put upon it, testifying thereby that those creatures, though they have no voice, yet have some means of communication and dealing with one another, which through our defect we cannot share; and therefore it is a foolish meddling on our part to discuss them. The ants can do yet other things which are quite beyond our capacity, and which we are so far from being able to imitate that we cannot even conceive or imagine them.

Many hold the opinion that in that great and last naval battle which Antony lost against Augustus, the admiral's galley was arrested in the middle of its course by the little fish that the Latins call *Remora*, by reason of that property it possesses of arresting every kind of vessel which it fastens upon. And when the Emperor Caligula was rowing with a large fleet on the coast of Romania, his galleon was stopped dead by this same fish, which he commanded to be taken, firmly fixed as it was to the keel of his vessel, greatly vexed that so small a creature should resist both the sea and the winds and the strength of all his oars, by simply fixing itself with its beak to his galley (for it is a shell-fish);[1] and was astonished besides, and not without reason, that when brought to him into the boat it no longer had the strength it had when outside of it.

A citizen of Cyzicus once acquired the reputation of a good weather-prophet through having learned the habits of a

[1] The *Remora* as commonly known is not a shell-fish, and has no beak.

hedge-hog. Its burrow is open to different quarters and different winds, and, forecasting the wind that is coming, it stops a hole on the side of that wind; observing which the citizen brought to his town certain predictions of the wind that was about to blow.

The chameleon takes its colour from the spot on which it lies; but the octopus assumes what colour it pleases to suit the occasion, in order to hide from what it fears, and to catch its prey. In the chameleon it is a passive, in the octopus an active, change. We are liable to many changes of colour, caused by fright, anger, shame and other feelings, which alter our complexion; but as with the chameleon it is a passive result. It is in the power of the jaundice to turn us yellow, not in the power of our will.

Now these effects which we observe in other animals, and which are much greater than those we experience ourselves, testify to some pre-eminent faculty in them which is hidden from us; and it may be presumed that they possess many other properties and powers which are not apparent to us.

Of all the predictions in past ages the most certain and the most ancient were those drawn from the flight of birds. We have nothing like it and nothing so wonderful. That rule and order according to which they flap their wings, from which conclusions are drawn with regard to coming events, must necessarily have been established by some superior power to produce so noble an activity. For to attribute that great effect to some law of Nature without the intelligence, consent and reason of the creature which produces it, is evidently to hold a wrong opinion, and to give a meaning to empty words.

This is proved by the following example: the torpedo has the power not only of benumbing the limbs that touch her, but of transmitting, through the nets and seines, a heavy torpidity to the hands of those who finger and disturb her. Nay, they say further, that if one pours water on her one feels that numbness advancing up to the hand, and deadening the sense of touch through the water. This is a marvellous power, but it is not useless to the torpedo: she is sensible of and makes use of it, for in order to catch the prey she is after, she is seen to lie snug in the mud, that other fishes, gliding overhead, struck and benumbed by this coldness of hers, may fall into her power.

The cranes and swallows and other migratory birds, by changing their domicile according to the season of the year, sufficiently manifest the knowledge they have of their divining faculty, and make use of it.

Sportsmen assure us that, in order to pick out the best of a litter of puppies that we wish to keep, it is only necessary to put the mother in the way of choosing it herself. For, if you carry them out of their bed, the first she brings back will always be the best. Or if you pretend to light a fire all round their kennel, it will be the pup she first hastens to rescue. From which it is evident that they have a power of divining which we do not possess, or that they have some hidden virtue which enables them to judge the little ones, which is other and quicker than ours.[1]

The manner of coming into the world, of bringing forth, of feeding, acting, moving, living and dying, of beasts, being so like ours, whatever we subtract from their motive powers and add to our own condition over and above theirs, can in no wise be the result of our reasoning powers. The physicians propose, as a rule of health, that we should follow the example of the beasts and live in their way ; for this saying has from time immemorial been in the mouths of the people,

> Keep warm the head and the feet ;
> In every way live like the beasts.

Generation is the chiefest of natural actions. We have a certain disposition of members which is more suitable for our purpose ; yet they recommend us to fall in line with the brutes and adopt their posture and method, as being more effectual :

> For commonly 'tis thought that wives conceive
> More readily in manner of wild beasts,
> After the custom of the four-foot breeds,
> Because so postured, with the breasts beneath
> And buttocks then upreared, the seeds can take
> Their proper places. (LUCRETIUS.)

And they condemn as harmful those indelicate and insolent motions which the women have introduced into it of their

---

[1] The earlier editions add this strange remark, which seems to show an amazing ignorance of childhood. 'For it is certain that in our children, even when they are well advanced, we have no means of selecting them but by their bodily shape.'

own invention; referring them to the more modest and sedate example and usage of the animals of their sex:

> For thus the woman hinders and resists
> Her own conception, if too joyously
> Herself she treats the Venus of the man
> With haunches heaving, and with all her bosom
> Now yielding like the billows of the sea—
> Aye, from the plowshare's even course and track
> She throws the furrow, and from proper places
> Deflects the spurt of seed. (LUCRETIUS.)

If it be justice to give every one his due, the beasts which serve, love and defend their benefactors, and that pursue and injure strangers and those who hurt them, by doing so reflect some of our notions of justice; as they do also in observing a very just equality in distributing their goods among their young.

With regard to friendship, that of animals is without comparison more passionate and more constant than that of man. King Lysimachus' dog, Hyrcanus, when his master was dead, obstinately remained in his bed, refusing to eat and drink; on the day when the body was burned, he started off and leapt into the fire, where he was consumed. As did also the dog of one named Pyrrhus, who would not budge from off his master's bed after he was dead; and, when his body was removed, let himself be carried with it, and finally flung himself on the funeral pyre on which his master was burned.

There are certain affectionate tendencies that sometimes arise within us without the consent of our reason, which are the result of unreasoning chance which others call sympathy; of this the animals are as capable as ourselves. We may see horses forming a sort of attachment to each other, to such a degree that we have much ado to make them live and travel separately. We may observe them taking a particular fancy to a colour in those of their kind, as we might to a particular type of face, and, when they meet with a horse of that colour, hasten to make its acquaintance with great joy and demonstrations of good-will; at the same time taking a dislike and hatred of some other colour.

Animals, like ourselves, exercise a choice in their amours, and are particular in selecting their mates. Like ourselves they are not free from extreme and implacable jealousy and envy.

Desires are either natural and necessary, as eating and drinking, or natural and not necessary, as intercourse with females ; or again they are neither natural nor necessary. Of this latter kind are almost all those of human beings. They are all superfluous and artificial ; for it is marvellous how little Nature needs for her satisfaction, how little she has left us to desire. Our culinary dressings are not of her ordaining. The Stoics say that a man should be able to subsist on an olive a day. Our delicate choice of wines is no part of her teaching, nor are the additional refinements of our amorous desires :

> Are her kisses sweeter
> Though she be daughter to a mighty consul ? (HORACE.)

Those exotic desires which have crept into us in consequence of wrong ideas and ignorance of the good, are so numerous that they drive out almost all the natural ones. No more nor less than if foreigners had entered a city in such numbers as to thrust out the native inhabitants, or to suppress their ancient authority and power, seizing and usurping it entirely to themselves.

Animals are much more self-controlled than we are, and keep with greater moderation within the limits that Nature has prescribed. Not so strictly however but that they sometimes share our sensualities. And just as we have heard of men being impelled by furious lusts to animal loves, these have sometimes been known to be enamoured of human beings, and to indulge their abnormal affections for others of a different species. Witness the elephant which was a rival with Aristophanes the grammarian in the affection of a young flower-girl in the city of Alexandria, and in no wise yielded to him in the attentions of a very passionate suit ; for, going through the market-place where they sold fruits, this beast would seize some of them with his trunk and offer them to her. He would not lose sight of her more than he possibly could, and would occasionally thrust his trunk into her bosom under her cape to feel her breasts. They tell also of a dragon in love with a maid, of a goose enamoured of a boy in the town of Asopus, and of a ram that danced attendance on Glaucia the flute-player. Barbary apes are constantly known to be madly enamoured of women.

Among certain animals the males are known to be addicted to loving those of their own sex. Oppianus and others cite examples to show how animals, in their marriages, respect the laws of kinship ; but experience very often shows us the contrary :

> The heifer thinks no shame her sire to bear
> On willing back ; the horse his filly leaps ;
> The goat will pair with them he has begot ;
> Birds breed by them by whom themselves are bred. (OVID.)

Can there be a more evident example of sly cunning than that of the mule of the philosopher Thales ? Fording a river, when laden with salt, she chanced to stumble, so that the sacks she carried were saturated with wet. Having observed that by the dissolving of the salt her burden was lightened, she never failed, as soon as she came to a stream, to plunge into it with her load, until her master, discovering her roguery, ordered her to be laden with wool ; after that, finding herself nonplussed, she gave up that trick.

There are some in which our vice of avarice is naively reflected ; for we may see them very diligent to appropriate by stealth and carefully to conceal all they can, although they may have no use for it.

As to husbandry, they surpass us, not only in that foresight which makes them store up and save for the future ; they also possess much of the knowledge necessary to that end. The ants carry their grains and seeds out of their barns and spread them out to air, to cool and dry them, whenever they find they are beginning to turn mouldy and smell rank, lest they should rot and spoil. But the precaution and foresight they exercise in gnawing their grains of wheat exceeds all that can be imagined in man's prudence. Because the wheat does not always remain dry and wholesome, but dissolves, becomes soft and as if steeped in milk, being on the way to sprout and germinate ; lest it should shoot and so lose its nature and property as a store of food, they nibble off the end where it usually sprouts.

With regard to war, which is the greatest and most pompous of human activities, I would fain know whether we should regard it as arguing some prerogative, or, on the contrary, as a testimony of our imbecility and imperfection ; as indeed the science of defeating and killing one another, of ruining and destroying our own race, seems to have little to recommend it to the animals that have it not.

> What lion takes advantage of his strength
> To kill his kind ? What boar will e'er succumb
> To boar with larger tusks ? (JUVENAL.)

They are not however universally exempt ; witness the furious encounters between the bees, and the exploits of the princes of the two hostile armies :

> For oft 'twixt king and king with uproar dire
> Fierce feud arises, and at once from far
> You may discern what passion sways the mob,
> And how their hearts are throbbing for the strife. (VIRGIL.)

I can never read that divine description but I seem to see a true picture of human folly and vanity. For these war manœuvres, which fill us with fright and terror, this storm of cries and shouts,

> There the sheen
> Shoots up the sky, and all the fields about
> Glitter with brass, and from beneath a sound
> Goes forth from feet of stalwart soldiery,
> And mountain walls, smote by the shouting, send
> The voices onward to the stars of heaven ; (LUCRETIUS.)

that terrifying array of so many thousands of armed men, all that fury, ardour and courage, how absurd to consider how frivolous the occasions that give rise to them, and how easily they are quenched !

> The tale of Greece, dashed through long years of strife,—
> All because Paris loved another's wife—
> Against a barbarous foe. (HORACE.)

The whole of Asia ruined and destroyed in war for Paris' bawdry ! The desire of one man, a spite, a pleasure, a family jealousy, causes which should not incite a couple of herring-wives to scratch each other, that was the soul and motive of that great hurly-burly.

Can we believe those same men who are the prime movers and authors of wars ? Listen to the greatest and most victorious Emperor, and the most powerful that ever was, jesting and very cleverly and humorously making a laughing matter of the many perilous battles both by sea and land, the blood and lives of five hundred thousand men who followed his fortunes, the resources and wealth of the two halves of the world exhausted in the service of his enterprises:

> 'Cause Anthony is fired with Glaphyre's charms
> Fain would his Fulvia tempt me to her arms.
> If Anthony be false, what then? Must I
> Be slave to Fulvia's lustful tyranny?
> . . . .
> Declare for love or war, she said, and frowned,
> 'No love I'll grant, so let the trumpets sound!'

(I quote my Latin with a clear conscience, and with the permission you have given me.)[1]

Now this great body, with so many aspects and movements, which seems to threaten heaven and earth;

> Numberless
> As billows that on Libya's sea-floor roll,
> When fierce Orion sets in wintry wave,
> Or thick as clustering corn-ears, that beneath
> The young sun ripen, or on Hermus' plain,
> On Lycia's yellowing fields; their bucklers clang,
> And the earth quakes for terror as they tread; (VIRGIL.)

that furious monster with so many arms and so many heads is still always man, feeble, calamitous and wretched; it is but an ant-hill, stirred and excited;

> In narrow path
> Moves the black column o'er the plain. (VIRGIL.)

A contrary breath of air, the croaking of a flight of ravens, a horse's stumble, the chance passing of an eagle, a dream, a voice, a sign, a morning mist, suffice to overthrow him and bring him to earth. Dart but a sun-beam on his face, he will melt and swoon; blow a little dust into his eyes, as in the case of the bees our poet speaks of, behold all our standards, our legions, and the great Pompey himself at their head, routed and shattered! For it was he, I take it,[2]

---

[1] Montaigne is addressing a lady of quality, by some supposed to have been Queen Margaret of Navarre, who may have urged him to write the Apology. The epigram was written by Augustus, and quoted by Martial to show that even that emperor could surpass him in licentiousness. It may be remarked that the translation, which is Cotton's, is not strictly literal.

[2] Montaigne is not sure; it was not against Pompey that Sertorius made use of this stratagem, but against the Caracitanians, a people of Spain who lived in deep caves cut out of the rocks, where it was impossible to force them. See Plutarch's *Life of Sertorius*.

who was beaten by Sertorius in Spain with those brave arms, which also served others, as Eumenes against Antigonus, and Surena against Crassus :

> Such fiery passions and such fierce assaults
> A little sprinkled dust controls and quells. (VIRGIL.)

Let loose but a couple of bees upon them, and they will have the power and courage to scatter an army. Within recent memory, when the Portuguese were attacking the town of Tamly, in the territory of Xiatine, the inhabitants of the place brought a great number of hives, in which they are rich, upon the wall, and with fire drove the bees so furiously upon their enemies, that they routed them, as they were unable to withstand their attack and stings. Thus they owed their victory and the freedom of their town to this novel reinforcement, with such good fortune that on returning from the fray not a single bee was missing.

The souls of emperors and cobblers are cast in the same mould. When we consider the weight and importance of the actions of rulers, we imagine that they are produced by causes equally weighty and important. We are mistaken : they are pushed forward and pulled back in their movements by the same springs that work within ourselves. The same cause that makes us bandy words with a neighbour will stir up a war between kings ; for the same reason that we flog a lackey a prince will lay waste a province. Their will is as weak as ours, but their power is greater. A mite and an elephant are stirred by the same appetite.

In the matter of fidelity there is no animal in the world so treacherous as man. Our histories tell of the eager pursuit that certain dogs have made on the murderers of their masters. King Pyrrhus, coming upon a dog guarding a dead man's body, and understanding that he had been doing that office for three days, ordered the body to be buried, and took the dog along with him. One day when he was assisting at a general review of his army this dog, perceiving his master's murderers, flew at them with loud barking and furious anger, and this first indication led to the avenging of the murder, which was carried out soon after by way of justice. The same was done by the dog of the sage Hesiod, and led to the conviction of the sons of Ganistor of Naupactus, for the murder committed on the person of his master.

Another dog, set to guard a temple at Athens, perceiving a sacrilegious thief carrying away the finest jewels, began barking at him as loud as he could ; but, being unable to awaken the temple-guardians, he set off to follow him, and, when day broke, kept at a little further distance from him, without however losing sight of him. When the thief offered him something to eat he would not touch it, but wagged his tail at others he met on the way, and took food at their hands. If his thief stopped to sleep, he stopped at the same time and place. News of this dog having come to the guardians of the church, they set off to follow in his track, making inquiries as to the dog's colour, and at last came upon him, as well as the robber, in the town of Cromyon. They were brought back to Athens, where the thief was punished ; and the judges, in recognition of this faithful service, ordered a certain measure of corn for the dog's sustenance at the public expense, and the priests were enjoined to take good care of him. Plutarch testifies to the truth of this story, which happened in his time.

With regard to gratitude (for it seems to me that we have need to bring this word into repute), this one example will suffice, which Apion tells us he himself witnessed : One day, he says, when the Roman people were being gratified with the combats of many outlandish beasts, especially lions of unusual size, there was one among others which, by reason of its furious demeanour and the strength and size of its limbs, and its terrifying and surly roar, attracted the attention of all the spectators. Among the slaves that were offered to the people in this fight with animals was one Androclus of Dacia, who was the property of a Roman lord of consular rank. The lion, perceiving him from a distance, at first stopped dead, as if in wonder, then softly approached in a gentle and peaceable manner, as if trying to recognize an acquaintance. Then, having made sure of what he was seeking, he began to lash his tail in the manner of a dog fawning on his master, and to lick and caress the hands and thighs of this poor wretch, who was quite paralysed and beside himself with fear. When Androclus had recovered his spirits in consequence of the gentle behaviour of the lion, and regained enough assurance to observe and recognize the animal, it was a singular pleasure to see their mutual joy and caresses. The people breaking out into loud acclamations of joy at this sight, the Emperor sent for the slave to know from him the meaning of this strange scene.

He then told a novel and wonderful story : ' My master, he said, being Proconsul in Africa, I was forced by his cruelty and harsh treatment in having me beaten every day, to steal away from him, and take flight. To hide in safety from a person of so great authority in the province the most expeditious way was to gain the solitude of the sandy and uninhabited regions of the country, and I resolved, in case the means of supporting life failed me, to find some way of killing myself. The heat of the sun at noon being extremely fierce and insupportable, I happened to discover a hidden and inaccessible cave, and threw myself down inside it. Soon after there came this lion with a wounded and bleeding paw, moaning and groaning with the pain he was suffering. At his coming I was very frightened, but he, seeing me crouching in a corner of his lair, softly approached, holding out and showing me his injured paw, as if to entreat my help. I then pulled out of it a large splinter, and, growing more accustomed to him, squeezed the wound and let out the accumulated dirt, wiped and cleaned it as well as I could. He, the cause of his hurt being removed, and relieved of the pain, lay down to rest and went to sleep with his paw still in my hand. After that the lion and I lived together for three whole years in that cave, sharing the same food ; for of the beasts he killed in hunting he brought me the best parts, which for want of fire I cooked in the sun for my nourishment. At length, growing weary of that wild and brutish life, the lion being one day gone on his accustomed raid, I departed, and on the third day after was caught by the soldiers, who brought me from Africa to my master in this city. He immediately condemned me to death by being delivered to the wild beasts. Now, by what I see, this lion was also caught soon after, and would now repay me for the good turn I did him in curing his wound.'

This was the story that Androclus related to the Emperor, which he also conveyed from hand to hand to the people. Wherefore, by general request, he was absolved from his sentence and given his freedom, and, by the order of the people, the lion was presented to him as a gift. After that, says Apion, Androclus could be seen leading his lion by quite a small leash, going from tavern to tavern in Rome to receive the money that was given to him, whilst the lion suffered himself to be covered with the flowers that were thrown at him, and all who met them would say: 'There goes the lion, the man's host; there goes the man, the lion's physician.' We often weep for the loss of animals we have loved, and so do they for our loss:

> With big, round tears,
> Stripped of his trappings, in the mournful train,
> Aethon, the warrior's steed, comes sorrowing for the slain. (VIRGIL.)

Whilst in some of our nations wives are held in common, and in others each man has his own, do we not also see this in animals, and that some of them are more faithful in marriage than we? As to societies and leagues they form with one another for mutual assistance, we may observe that when you hurt an ox, a pig or some other animal, all the herd will answer to its cry for help and rally to its defence.

When the parrot-fish has swallowed the angler's hook, its companions will crowd around it and nibble the line; and if by chance one of them has swum into the net, the others from outside will offer their tails, which the prisoner will grip with all the power of its teeth and thus be dragged out. When a barbel is caught, its companion will set the line against its back, and erecting one of the spines, which are toothed like a saw, will saw through and cut the cord.

As to the particular services we render one another in the battle of life, we may see many like examples in animals. It is said that the whale never goes abroad without being preceded by a small fish resembling the sea-gudgeon, which is for that reason called the Guide. The whale follows it, allowing itself to be turned and led as easily as a vessel is turned by its rudder; and in return for this service, whilst every other thing, whether animal or vessel, that enters the awful chasm of this monster's mouth is forthwith engulfed and lost, this little fish retires into it in all security, and sleeps there. During its sleep the whale never stirs, but as soon as it issues forth, starts and follows it unceasingly; and if by chance the guide goes astray, the whale will go wandering about hither and thither, often knocking itself against the rocks, like a ship without a rudder; which Plutarch testifies to having seen at the island of Anticyra.

A similar partnership exists between the little bird called the 'little king' (the wren) and the crocodile. The wren acts as a sentinel to this great brute. And if the ichneumon, her enemy, comes near and shows fight, this little bird, lest she should be caught asleep, by singing and pecking with its beak awakens her and warns her of the danger. The bird lives on the leavings of the monster, who receives him familiarly into her mouth and allows him to peck at her jaws and between her teeth, and gather the bits of flesh that remain there. When about to shut her mouth she first warns him to leave by gradually closing it upon him, but without crushing or hurting him.

The shell-fish called Nacre (the Pinna) lives in the same fellowship with the pinna-guardian, a little creature of the crab family that acts as porter and doorkeeper, sitting at the mouth of the shell which it continually keeps half open, until it sees some little fish enter that is worth catching ; then the pinna-guard enters the pinna, pinches the living flesh of the animal and forces it to close its shell ; then the two together eat the prey entrapped in their fort.

In the life of the tunnies we may observe a singular knowledge of the three parts of mathematics. With regard to astrology they teach it to man, for they stop at the place where the winter-solstice overtakes them, and do not move from thence until the following equinox ; wherefore even Aristotle readily grants them that science. As to geometry and arithmetic, they always assemble in a body like a cube, square on every side, and thus form a close, solid, battalion-like body of six sides, all equal ; they swim in this order, as broad behind as before, in such a way that, if one sees and counts one row, one may easily number the whole troop, since the number of the depth is equal to that of the breadth, and the breadth to the length.

With regard to magnanimity, it could hardly appear more evident than in the case of the large hound that was sent from the Indies to King Alexander. He was first confronted with a stag to fight with, next with a boar, and then with a bear. Of these he made no account, and disdained to stir from the spot ; but when he saw a lion, he straightway rose to his feet, clearly showing that he declared that animal alone worthy to enter the lists with him.

Touching repentance and the acknowledgement of faults, they tell a story of an elephant who, having in the impetuosity of his rage killed his keeper, felt so extremely grieved that he would never after eat, and died of starvation.

As to clemency, it is told of a tiger, the most inhuman of all the beasts, that a kid having been given to him he endured hunger for two days rather than injure it; on the third day he broke the cage in which he was imprisoned to go in search of other prey, being unwilling to touch his friend and guest, the kid.

Concerning the rights of familiarity and agreement, formed by intercourse, it is quite usual to accustom cats, dogs and hares to live in harmony.

But that which experience teaches those who travel by sea, and especially on the Sicilian sea, of the condition of the halcyon or king-fisher, surpasses all human imagination. What kind of animal was ever so honoured by Nature in its breeding, birth and deliverance? For the poets say indeed that one island, that of Delos, being once a wanderer, was made firm for the sake of the lying-in of Latona; but God willed that the whole sea should be arrested, made firm and smooth, without waves, without wind or rain, whilst the halcyon is breeding, which is just about the time of the solstice, the shortest day in the year. And by this privilege of hers we have seven days and seven nights, in the very heart of winter, when we may safely navigate. The female never knows any other male but her own mate; she keeps company with him all her life, and never forsakes him. When he becomes weak and broken with age she will bear him on her back, carry him everywhere and wait on him till death.

No wit of man could ever attain to the knowledge of that marvellous fabric, the nest which the halcyon constructs for its young, nor guess what material it is made of. Plutarch, who saw and handled many of them, thinks it consists of the bones of some fish bound and joined together, and interlaced, some being placed lengthwise, the others laid across, with ribs and hoops added in such a manner as to form a round vessel ready to float. Then, the construction being completed, it is carried to the edge of the sea, where the tide, gently beating upon it, shows where the parts that are not well joined are to be mended, and where those are to be strengthened which are loosened and have come apart through the beating of the waves. On the other hand those parts which are well knit are tightened and closed up by the beat of the sea, in such a way that it cannot break or come to pieces, nor be damaged by the throwing of stones or iron, except with great force. And what is more wonderful is the proportion and the shape of the cavity within ; for it is composed and proportioned in such a way that it cannot receive or admit anything but the bird that had built it. For it is closed, locked and impenetrable to any other thing, so that nothing can enter, not even the sea-water.

There we have a very clear description of this structure, and borrowed from a good source ; yet it seems to me that it does not make the difficulty of the architecture sufficiently clear. Now, what vanity can that be that makes us consider beneath us, and interpret disdainfully, these actions that we can neither comprehend nor imitate ?

To pursue a little further this equality and correspondence between men and animals. The privilege that our soul glories in of reducing to her own condition all that she apprehends, of stripping all things that come to her of their mortal and corporeal qualities, of compelling the things she deems worthy of her notice to put off and divest themselves of their corruptible qualities, and make them lay aside, like so many mean and superfluous garments, their thickness, length, depth, weight, colour, smell, roughness, smoothness, hardness, softness and all palpable properties, in order to make them conform to her own immortal and spiritual condition ; so that the Rome and Paris that I have in my soul, the Paris that I have in my imagination, I imagine and conceive to be without size and without place, without stones, plaster or wood. This same privilege, I say, seems very evidently to be shared by the beasts. For when we see a horse, accustomed to trumpets and battles and the rattle of musketry, shaking and trembling in his sleep while stretched on his litter, as if he were in the fray, it is certain that in his soul he imagines the beat of the drum without noise, an army without body and without arms :

> Thou'lt see the sturdy horses, though outstretched,
> Yet sweating in their sleep, and panting ever,
> And straining utmost strength, as if for prize. (LUCRETIUS.)

This hare that a greyhound imagines in a dream, after which we see him panting in his sleep, stretching out his tail, moving his legs convulsively, exactly reproducing the motion of running, is a hare without skin and bones :

> And hounds of huntsmen oft in soft repose
> Yet toss a-sudden all their legs about,
> And growl, and bark, and with their nostrils sniff
> The winds again, again, as though indeed
> They'd caught the scented footprints of wild beasts;
> And, even when wakened, often they pursue
> The phantom images of stags, as though
> They did perceive them fleeing on before,
> Until the illusion's shaken off, and dogs
> Come to themselves again. (LUCRETIUS.)

The watch-dogs we often see growling in their sleep, then barking outright and waking up with a start, as if they perceived some stranger coming; this stranger seen by their soul is a ghostly and unsubstantial stranger, without dimension, without colour, without being:

> And fawning breed
> Of house-bred whelps do feel the sudden urge
> To shake their bodies and start from off the ground,
> As if beholding stranger-visages. (LUCRETIUS.)

With regard to beauty of body, before proceeding any further, I should need to know if we agree in its description. It is probable that we have little idea of what beauty in Nature and in general is, since to our human beauty we ascribe so many different forms. For if there were any rule or prescription of Nature in respect of beauty, we should all recognize it in common, as we do the heat of fire. We imagine its form as our fancy leads us:

> The Belgian bloom would mar a Roman face. (PROPERTIUS.)

The Indians paint it black and dusky, with big, swollen lips, a broad and flat nose, and they load the cartilage between the nostrils with big rings of gold, to make it hang down to the mouth; as also the lower lip with great hoops enriched with jewels, so that it falls over the chin; since they see a charm in showing the teeth as far as the gums. In Peru the largest ears are the most beautiful, and as far as they are able they stretch them artificially. A man now living declares that, in an Eastern country that he visited, this practise of enlarging the ears is so honoured, and that they weight them with such heavy jewels, that he often thrust his arm, sleeve and all, through the bore of an ear.

Elsewhere there are people who very carefully blacken their teeth, and hold white teeth in contempt; in another country they dye them red.

Not only in the Basque country, but in some other places, and, what is more, in certain Arctic regions, according to Pliny, the women are considered more beautiful with their heads shaven. By the Mexicans a small forehead is regarded as a sign of beauty, and though they remove the hair from the rest of the body they cultivate it on the forehead, and people [1] it by art; and they regard large teats as so great a recommendation, that they aspire to be able to suckle their infants over their shoulders. We should paint ugliness that way.

The Italian's idea of beauty is big and massive, that of the Spaniards is gaunt and hollow. With us, one likes it fair, the other dark; one soft and delicate, another robust and strong; this one looks for sweetness and daintiness, that for a proud and majestic mien.

Just as the preference in beauty is given by Plato to the spherical figure, the Epicureans give it rather to the pyramidal or the square, and cannot swallow a god in the shape of a ball.[2]

But, however that may be, Nature has not privileged us in that any more than in any other respect, above her common laws. And, if we judge ourselves aright, we shall find that, if there be some animals less favoured in that respect than we, there are others, and they are very numerous, that are more so; *many animals surpass us in beauty* (Seneca), even among our terrestrial compatriots. For, as regards the denizens of the sea (leaving aside the shape as a whole, in which there can be no comparison, so much does it differ from ours), in colour, neatness, smoothness, and agility, we sufficiently yield place to them; and no less in all qualities to those of the air. And that prerogative, on which the poets lay so much stress, of our erect stature, which makes us look to heaven, whence it came,

> Whilst other creatures, prone, the earth regard,
> Sublime the front he gave to man, and bade him
> Raise his eyes to heaven's majestic vault
> And contemplate the stars, (OVID.)

[1] What Montaigne means by this is not quite clear; it can hardly be taken in the sense in which the Emperor Julian gloried in his 'populous beard', since the cult of dirt was not practised outside of Christendom. (See Gibbon.) Florio translates it 'make it grow', Cotton 'increase it'.

[2] See Cicero, *Of the Nature of the Gods*, i. 10.

is poetical indeed ; for there are many little creatures whose sight is turned wholly skywards. Camels and ostriches appear to me to have their necks set up straighter and more upright than ours. What animals are there that have not their face high and in front, that do not look forward, as we do, and discover, in their normal posture, as much of heaven and earth, as man ? And what qualities of our bodily constitution, described by Plato and Cicero, are not at the service of a thousand kinds of animals ? Those that most resemble us are the ugliest and meanest of the whole herd : the apes in external appearance and facial shape :

> The Simian how similar, the ugly beast, to us ! (ENNIUS.)

the pig for inward and vital parts.[1]

In truth, when I imagine man quite naked, yea, even in that sex that seems to have the greater share of beauty, his blemishes, his natural limitations, his imperfections, I find that we have more reason than any other animal to cover ourselves. We are to be excused for having borrowed from those that have been more favoured by Nature than ourselves, for having decked ourselves with their beauty, and concealed ourselves under their spoils of wool, feathers, hair, silk.

Observe moreover that we are the only animal that is offended by the defects in our fellow-creatures, and that we alone have to withdraw and hide ourselves in our natural actions, from our kind. It is in truth also a fact worthy of consideration that the masters of the craft prescribe as a cure for amorous passions a full and open sight of the body we desire ; and that, to cool our love, it only needs entire liberty to see the object of it :

> Full oft the man who viewed the secret parts
> Was stayed in full career, and felt his passions cool. (OVID.)

And, although this recipe may proceed from a rather squeamish and frigid disposition, yet it is a wonderful sign of our imperfection that acquaintance and familiarity should make us distasteful to one another. It is not modesty so much as discretion and artfulness that makes our ladies so circumspect in refusing admittance to their boudoir before they are dressed up and painted for public view ;

---

[1] ' if we are to believe the Physicians ', is added in the earlier editions.

And these our Venuses are 'ware of this.
Wherefore the more are they at pains to hide
All the behind-the-scenes of life from those
Whom they desire to keep in bonds of love. (LUCRETIUS.)

Whereas in many animals there is nothing that we do not love, and that does not gratify our senses; so that from their very excrements and discardings we obtain not only dainties to eat, but our richest ornaments and perfumes.

These remarks concern only the common run of mortals, and we are not so sacrilegious as to include in them those divine, supernatural and extraordinary beauties we sometimes see refulgent among us, like stars under a corporeal and terrestrial veil.

Moreover, the very share in the bounties of Nature which, by our own confession, we allow the animals, is much to their advantage. We ourselves assume imaginary and fanciful advantages, advantages which are to come and nonexistent, which human capacity itself cannot guarantee, or advantages which we erroneously attribute to ourselves in the freedom of our opinions, such as reason, knowledge, honour. And to them we leave for their share essential, tangible and attainable advantages, as peace, repose, security, innocence and health: health, I say, the richest and finest gift that Nature can bestow upon us.

Therefore Philosophy, even that of the Stoics, is so bold as to say that Heraclitus and Pherecydes, if they had been allowed to give their wisdom in exchange for health, and by this transaction rid themselves, the one of the dropsy, the other of the lousy disease that afflicted him, they would have done well. By which admission they set a still greater store by wisdom, since they compare it and put it into the scales with health, than they do in this other proposition, which is also one of theirs: They say that if Circe had offered Ulysses two potions, the one to make a madman wise, and the other to make a wise man mad, Ulysses would rather have taken the cup of madness than consent to Circe's transforming his human shape into that of a beast; and they add that Wisdom herself would have spoken to him in this wise: 'Forsake me, let me alone, rather than allow me to dwell in the body and shape of an ass.'

What! will the philosophers then abandon this great and

divine Wisdom for this corporeal and terrestrial covering? Then it is not by our reason, our speech and our soul that we are superior to the animals; it is by our beauty, our fair complexion and the fine symmetry of our limbs, for which our intelligence, our wisdom and all the rest are to be set at naught!

Well, I accept this frank and naïve confession. Assuredly they knew that these qualities that we make such a boast of, are but a vain imagination. Even though the beasts had all the virtue, knowledge, wisdom and perfection of the Stoics, they would still be beasts; and yet they would not be comparable to a poor, wretched, witless man.

In short, whatever is not as we are, is not worth a rap. And God himself, to be any good, must be like us, as we shall presently show. From which it is clear that it is not upon any true ground of reason, but from a foolish arrogance and stubbornness, that we put ourselves before the other animals, and remove ourselves from their condition and fellowship.

But to return to my theme. To us has been allotted inconsistency, irresolution, uncertainty, sorrow, superstition, solicitude about things to come, even after we shall have ceased to live, ambition, avarice, jealousy, envy, inordinate, furious and untamable desires, war, falsehood, disloyalty, detraction and curiosity. We have indeed strangely overrated this precious reason we so much glory in, this faculty of knowing and judging, if we have bought it at the price of that infinite number of passions to which we are continually a prey. Unless we are inclined to pride ourselves, as Socrates does indeed, on that remarkable prerogative over the other animals, that, whereas Nature has prescribed to them certain seasons and limits for the delights of Venus, she has given us the reins at all hours and on all occasions.

As wine is rarely good for the sick, and very often does them harm, it is better not to administer any at all, than to run into manifest danger in the hope of a doubtful benefit. So I know not whether it had not been better for mankind if this quickness of thought, this acumen, this subtlety that we call Reason, had not been given to man at all, considering that it is so baneful to many, and salutary to only a few, instead of having been conferred so bountifully and with so liberal a hand (Cicero).

ARE WE BENEFITED BY LEARNING?

What benefit do we suppose that Varro and Aristotle derived from knowing so many things? Did it exempt them from human ills? Were they freed from the accidental mishaps that threaten any street-porter? Did they extract from their logic any consolation for the gout? Did they feel that humour any the less for knowing that it was located in the joints? Had they made a covenant with Death for knowing that some nations welcome her? Or with cuckoldry, for knowing that in some region or other wives are held in common?

On the contrary, having held the first rank in knowledge, the one among the Romans, the other among the Greeks, and that at a time when science was at its best bloom, we have not heard that they particularly excelled in the conduct of their lives; indeed the Greek is hard put to it to clear himself from some notorious blots on his.

Has any one discovered that pleasure and health have any greater relish for one who knows astrology and grammar?

> Is the illiterate plowman not as fit
> For Venus' service as the wit? (HORACE.)

and that disgrace and poverty are less irksome to him?

> True! you can bid disease and sickness fly,
> Escape from pain, life's every care defy;
> Thy life can be prolonged with better days. (JUVENAL.)

I have in my time seen a hundred artisans, a hundred labourers, wiser and happier than the rectors of the University, and whom I had much rather resemble. Learning, in my opinion, has a place among the things that are necessary to life, like fame, nobility, dignity, or, at the most, like beauty, wealth and such other qualities, which are indeed serviceable to it, but remotely so, and more in fancy than by nature.

We scarcely need more offices, more rules and laws of living in our community than the cranes and ants do in theirs. Nevertheless we observe them to conduct themselves therein in a very orderly manner, without any erudition. If man were wise, he would estimate each thing at its true value, according as it would be most useful and convenient to him in life.

If any man will sum us up according to our actions and behaviour, he will find many more excellent men among the ignorant than among the educated ; I mean as regards any kind of virtue.[1] It seems to me that the older Rome contained men of greater ability, both for peace and war, than that educated Rome that brought on her own ruin. Though equal in all other respects, honesty and innocence at least would remain on the side of the older ; for those qualities dwell in singular harmony with simplicity.

But I will leave this theme, which would drag me further than I should be inclined to follow. I will only say this besides, that humility and submission alone can bring a man to perfection. Not every man should have the knowledge of his duty left to his own judgement ; he should have it prescribed to him, and not be allowed to choose at his discretion. Otherwise, seeing the imbecility and infinite variety of our reasons and opinions, we should in the end forge for ourselves duties that would set us on devouring one another, as Epicurus says.[2]

The first law that God ever gave to man was a law of pure obedience. It was a command pure and simple, which gave man no room to inquire and argue, since to obey is the proper duty of a reasonable soul that acknowledges a heavenly superior and benefactor. From obeying and yielding spring all the other virtues, even as all sin springs from presumption. Contrariwise, the first temptation that came to human nature, through the devil, its first poison, insinuated itself into us through the promises he gave us of possessing knowledge and understanding : *ye shall be as gods, knowing good and evil* (Genesis). And the sirens, in Homer, to gull Ulysses, and draw him into their dangerous and destructive snares, offer him the gift of knowledge.

The conviction of wisdom is the plague of man. That is why ignorance is so much recommended by our religion, as a fitting element of faith and obedience : *take heed lest there shall be any one that maketh spoil of you through his philosophy and vain deceit, after the rudiments of the world* (Saint Paul).

On this point there is a general agreement among all the

[1] Goethe came to the same conclusion early in life. Writing to Frau von Stein, he says : ' What admiration I feel for that class of men which is called the lower, but which in God's sight is certainly the highest ! Among them we find all the virtues together—moderation, contentment, uprightness, good faith, joy over the smallest blessing, harmlessness, innocence, patience—but I must not lose myself in exclamations.'

[2] Not Epicurus, but the Epicurean Colotes.

philosophers of all the schools, that the sovereign good consists in the tranquillity of the soul and body. But where do we find it?

> In fine, the sage unswayed by power and pelf,
> Is only less than sovereign Jove himself:
> Wealth, honour, freedom, beauty, all are his—
> In short a very king of kings he is:
> In wind and limb sound, vigorous and bold,
> Except when troubled by a wretched cold. (HORACE.)

It would seem in truth that Nature, to console us in our wretched and forlorn state, has allotted to us only presumption. This is what Epictetus says, 'That man has nothing properly his own but the use of his opinions'. We have nothing but wind and smoke for our portion. The gods, says philosophy, have health in essence, and sickness through understanding: man, on the other hand, possesses his goods in imagination, his ills in essence. We have had good reason to make the most of our power of imagination; for all our goods are but a dream.

Just listen to the swaggering boast of this poor helpless creature: 'There is nothing, says Cicero, so charming as occupation with letters, those letters, I mean, by means of which the infinity of things, the immense grandeur of Nature, the heavens, even in this world, and the lands and seas are disclosed to us. It is they that have taught us religion, moderation, magnanimity, and have rescued our souls out of the darkness, to show them all things, high and low, first and last, and those between. It is they which furnish us with the wherewithal to live well and happily, and point out the way to spend our lives without displeasure and without suffering.' Would you not think he were describing the condition of ever-living, almighty God? And, as a matter of fact, a thousand little women in their villages have lived more equable, more agreeable, and more uniform lives than his.

> A God was he, great Memmius, a God,
> Who first and chief found out that plan of life
> Which now is called Philosophy, and who
> By cunning craft, out of such mighty waves,
> Out of such mighty darkness, moored our life
> In haven so serene, in light so clear. (LUCRETIUS.)

There we have very grand and beautiful words; but a

very slight accident reduced this poet's understanding to a worse state than that of the meanest shepherd, notwithstanding his godlike teacher and the divine philosophy he speaks of.[1]

Of like impudence is this promise of the book of Democritus, 'I am going to speak of all things'; and that foolish name that Aristotle applied to us of 'mortal gods'; and that assertion of Chrysippus that 'Dion was as virtuous as God'. And my Seneca discovers, as he says, that 'God has given him life, but that he owes to himself that he lives well'; which is of a piece with this other: *we rightly glory in our virtue, which we should not do if we had this gift of God and not of ourselves* (Cicero). This is also of Seneca: 'That the wise man has courage equal with God, but attended with human frailty; wherefore he overtops him.'

Nothing is more commonly met with than such daring expressions. Not one of us is so shocked at hearing himself placed on a par with God as at finding himself levelled to the rank of the other animals: so much more jealous are we of our own interest than of that of our Creator!

But we must tread this silly pretension underfoot, and boldly and strenuously shake the ridiculous foundations on which these false notions are built. So long as man imagines that any strength or any resources he has are due to himself, he will never acknowledge what he owes to his Master; he will always regard his eggs as chickens, as the saying goes. We must strip him to his shirt.

Let us consider a few well-known examples of the effect of his philosophy:

Posidonius, tormented by a malady so painful that it made him toss his arms and gnash his teeth, imagined he was snapping his fingers at the pain by crying out against it, 'You may do your worst, yet will I not say that you are an evil'. He has the same sensations as my footman, but he smites himself on the chest, because he at least restrains his tongue, according to the laws of his school. *For one who brags in words it is unbecoming to succumb in deeds* (Cicero).

---

[1] A philtre given to Lucretius, by his wife or his mistress, disturbed his reason and afforded him only a few lucid intervals, during which he composed his famous poem 'Of the Nature of Things'. He ended by killing himself. The 'godlike teacher' is Epicurus.

Arcesilaus being laid up with the gout, Carneades, who came to see him, was on the point of retiring, greatly vexed, when he called him back, and pointing to his feet and his breast, said, 'Nothing has come from this to this.' He is in a somewhat better state of grace, for he is sensible of his ill, and would be delivered of it; but his courage is neither cast down nor weakened by the pain. The other insists on his inflexibility, which I fear is more in words than in deeds. And Dionysius of Heraclea, afflicted with a grievous smarting of the eyes, was reduced to quit those Stoical resolutions.

But, even though knowledge could really do what they say, blunt the point and lessen the bitterness of the misfortunes that attend us, what more does it do than what ignorance does, much more simply and manifestly? The philosopher Pyrrho, in peril of a great storm at sea, could offer his companions no better example to follow than the serenity of a pig, their fellow-traveller, which was looking at the tempest with perfect equanimity.

Philosophy, having exhausted her precepts, refers us to the example of an athlete and a muleteer, who are usually seen to be much less apprehensive of death and less sensible to pain and other discomforts, and to possess more endurance than ever learning could store a man with who was not born to those hardships, and prepared for them by a natural disposition. What is it that makes it easier to cut and incise the tender limbs of an infant, or those of a horse, than our own, if not ignorance? How many people have not been made ill by the mere force of imagination? It is quite common to see them bled, purged and physicked, in order to be cured of diseases they feel only in imagination. When real infirmities fail us, science provides us with her own. 'That colour and complexion portends some catarrhous inflammation; this hot season threatens you with a feverish disturbance; this cutting of the life-line of your left hand gives you warning of some impending and unusual indisposition.' And finally she shamelessly has a fling at health itself: 'This vigour and sprightliness of youth cannot endure as it is; we must let some blood and deprive you of some of your strength, lest it turn against yourself.'

Compare the life of a man enslaved to such fancies with that of a labourer following his own natural appetites, who measures things only as they actually affect his senses, without either learning or foreboding, who is never ill except when he is ill ; whilst the other often has the stone in his soul before he has it in his bladder. As if it were not time enough to suffer the evil when it comes, he must needs anticipate it in fancy and run to meet it.

What I say of medicine may be generally taken as exemplifying all science. And hence is derived that ancient theory of the philosophers [1] who made the sovereign good to consist in the acknowledgement of the weakness of our judgement. My ignorance affords me as much occasion to hope as to fear ; and, having no other rule of health but that of others' examples and of the results I see elsewhere upon the like occasions, I find that they are of all sorts, and fix upon the comparisons that are most favourable to me. I welcome health, free, full and entire, with open arms, and whet my appetite to enjoy it, and the more so as it is now less usual and more rare with me ; so far am I from disturbing its ease and sweetness with the bitterness of a new and constrained mode of life.

The example of the animals may enlighten us as to how many maladies are brought upon us by mental emotions.

What we are told of the inhabitants of Brazil, that they never die but of old age, is attributed to the tranquillity and serenity of their climate ; I rather attribute it to the tranquillity and serenity of their souls, which are free from all passion, thought, or any absorbing and unpleasant labours. Those people spend their lives in an admirable simplicity and ignorance, without letters, without law, without king, without any manner of religion.

And whence comes this, which we know by experience, that the grossest and most doltish are the most vigorous and desirable in amorous performances ; and that the love of a muleteer often makes itself more acceptable than that of a gentleman, if it be not that in the latter the soul's agitation distracts the bodily vigour, arrests and wearies it, as it also usually distracts and wearies itself ?

What is it that unsettles the mind and most usually throws it into a state of madness, but its quickness, its subtlety, its versatility, and in short its own power ? Wherein consists the most subtle madness but in the most subtle wisdom ? As great enmities are born of great

[1] The Sceptics.

friendships, and fatal diseases of robust health, so do the rarest and most crazy distempers proceed from the most uncommon and active agitations of the soul; it needs but half a turn of the pin from one to the other. The acts of the insane show how strictly madness harmonizes with the most vigorous operations of the mind. Who does not know how imperceptibly near madness is to the wanton flights of an unfettered mind, as well as to the effects of a supreme and extraordinary virtue? Plato says that melancholic persons are the most excellent and the most easily taught; and there are none with so much propensity to madness.

Numberless minds have been destroyed by their own power and versatility. What a fall has just been suffered, through its own restlessness and activity, by the mind of one of the most judicious and inventive of Italian poets, who was more highly trained in the manner of pure and ancient poetry than any other that had lived for a long time! Has he not reason to be grateful to this his murderous vivacity, to this light that has blinded him, to this exact and delicate apprehension of reason, which has left him without reason, to that diligent and laborious search after knowledge, which has brought him level with the beasts, to that rare aptitude in exercises of the mind, which has left him without exercise and without mind?

I felt even more sadness than compassion to see him at Ferrara in so pitiable a state, surviving himself, oblivious both of himself and his works, which, without his knowledge and yet before his very eyes, were published in incorrected and shapeless form.[1]

Would you have a man healthy, would you have him steady and well-balanced in mind and morals? Wrap him in the darkness of sloth and dullness. We must be made like the beasts to be made wise, and blinded before we can guide ourselves. And if you tell me that the advantage of having one's taste indifferent and blunted to pain and other ills, brings the disadvantage along with it, that it also makes us, in consequence, less keen and dainty for the enjoyment

[1] It is generally inferred from this passage that Montaigne paid a visit to the unfortunate poet Torquato Tasso, author of the *Jerusalem Delivered*, who was confined in the Hospital of S. Anna at Ferrara. But as he makes no mention of this visit in his travel diary, although he makes a note of having seen a bust of Ariosto, it seems open to doubt. He often uses the word 'see' rather vaguely with the sense of 'know'.

of the good things and pleasures of this life, that is true; but the wretchedness of our condition is such that we have not so much to enjoy as to avoid, and that the extremest pleasure does not affect us as much as a slight pain. *Men are more dull to feel pleasure than pain* (Livy). We are less sensible of perfect health than of the slightest indisposition;

> The merest scratch will make a body wince,
> When perfect health will be quite unperceived.
> I'm quite content if I be never plagued
> By gout or pleurisy, but pay no heed
> When I am hale and hearty. (LA BOËTIE.)

Our health is but the absence of sickness. That is why the philosophic school which has set the greatest value on pleasure has still only ranked it solely with freedom from pain. The absence of ill is the nearest approach to good that man can hope for, as Ennius said,

> Who feels no ill enjoys too great a good.

For that very titillation and sting we feel in certain pleasures, and that seem to lift us above simple health and insensibility; that active, stirring and, so to say, itching and biting voluptuousness, even that has as its chief end and aim freedom from pain. The craving that carries us headlong to a woman's embraces has no aim but to expel the torment which our ardent and furious desires cause us, and only asks to satisfy them and to be laid at rest and delivered from that fever. And so with the rest.

Therefore I say that if simplicity directs us to the absence of pain, it directs us to a very happy state, conditioned as we are. Yet we must not imagine it so leaden as to be entirely without feeling. For Crantor had good reason to combat the insensibility of Epicurus, if it were built on so deep a foundation that the very approach and birth of evils were to be absent. 'I do not commend, said he, that insensibility, which is neither possible nor desirable; I am content not to be sick, but if I am, I would know that I am; and if they cauterize or incise me, I wish to feel it.' In truth, he who would eradicate the knowledge of evil would at the same time extirpate the knowledge of pleasure, and in short would annihilate man: *an insensibility that is not to be purchased but at the price of the inhumanity of the soul and dullness of the body* (Cicero).

To man evil is in its turn a good. Neither should pain be always shunned by him, nor pleasure always pursued.

It is greatly to the credit of ignorance that knowledge herself throws us into its arms, when she finds herself at a loss to stiffen us to bear the weight of ills; she is constrained to enter into this compromise, to give us the reins, permit us to take refuge in its bosom, and under its protection shelter from the blows and injuries of Fortune. For what else does she mean when she exhorts us 'To withdraw our mind from the ills that possess, and entertain it with thoughts of lost joys; To console ourselves for present ills by recalling past delights; and To call to our aid a vanished contentment to fight against that which oppresses us'? *To banish grief, he says,*[1] *we must avoid brooding over unpleasant things and call up pleasant ideas* (Cicero). What does she mean but that, where strength is lacking, she will use cunning and artfully trick the opponent by tripping him up, when vigour of body and arms begin to fail? For how could, I will not say a philosopher, but any man in his right mind, when he is actually suffering the burning thirst of a high fever, be satisfied with such a coin as the remembrance of the sweetness of Greek wine? He would make a worse bargain than ever:

> Recalling the pleasure will double the pain.

Of the same stamp is that other counsel which Philosophy gives us, 'To keep in mind only past happiness, and blot out from it the troubles we have undergone'; as if we could master the science of forgetfulness. It is a counsel that again leaves us worse off than before.

> Sweet is the memory of evils overpast. (EURIPIDES.)

What! Is Philosophy, who should place weapons in my hands to fight against Fortune, who should steel my heart to tread all human adversities underfoot, reduced to that state of feebleness that she recommends me to bolt like a rabbit, and save myself by such cowardly and ridiculous shifts? For Memory sets before us, not what we choose, but what she pleases. Nay, there is nothing that so vividly imprints a thing on our memory as the wish to forget it; the best way to give our mind something to keep, and to

[1] Epicurus.

impress it upon herself, is to entreat her to lose it. And this is untrue : *It is in our power to bury, as it were, in a perpetual oblivion all adversities, and to retain a pleasant and delightful memory of our prosperities* (Cicero). And this is true : *I remember even what I would not ; I cannot forget what I would* (Cicero).

And who gave that counsel ? *It was the man, who alone of all men durst profess himself wise* (Cicero) ;

> The man in genius who o'ertopped
> The human race, extinguishing all others,
> As sun, in ether risen, all the stars.[1] (LUCRETIUS.)

To empty and dismantle the memory, is not that the real and proper way to ignorance ?

A lifeless remedy for ills is ignorance. (SENECA.)

We hear of many like precepts, which permit us to borrow from the vulgar frivolous make-believes, where Reason, for all her strength and vigour, is powerless, provided they afford us satisfaction and comfort. When they cannot cure the wound, they are content to deaden and alleviate it. I think you will not deny me this, that if, through a weak and disordered mind, they could constantly and regularly live a life of ease and pleasure, they would accept it and say with Horace,

> For my part I'll in future ply
> The wine-cup well, and scatter flowers
> Profusely in my festal hours ;
> Nor shall I care though it be said
> That I have fairly lost my head.

Many philosophers might be of Lycas' mind : though otherwise of very regular habits, living quietly and peacefully in his family, remiss in none of his duties to his own people and to strangers, and very well able to take care of himself, this man had, through some distemper of the brain, become possessed with a fanciful idea, which was this : he imagined that he was perpetually witnessing a stage performance, watching games, spectacular shows and the finest comedies in the world. Being cured of this peccant humour by the physicians, he all but sued them at law to oblige them to restore him to his pleasing fancies :

[1] Epicurus.

> A plague on you for meddling friends, quoth he ;
> Saved ? not a whit ! You've fairly murdered me ;
> You've robbed me of my pleasure, torn away
> The sweet illusion made my life so gay. (HORACE.)

Of a like nature was the delusion of Thrasylaus, son of Pythodorus, who had come to believe that all the ships that put out from the harbour of Piraeus and landed there were working in his interest alone; delighting in the good fortune of their voyages, and welcoming them with joy. His brother Crito having had him restored to his better senses, he looked back with regret at that state of mind in which he had lived in clover and free from all troubles. This is in accordance with the old Greek line, which says that 'there is a great advantage in not being over-wise'.

> The sweetest life consists in taking heed of naught. (SOPHOCLES.)

And the Preacher says, 'For in much wisdom is much grief : and he that increaseth knowledge increaseth sorrow.'

Even in that in which Philosophy in general agrees, that last remedy she prescribes in all kinds of necessities, which is to make an end of life when we are unable to bear it : *Does it please ? Bear it. Does it not please ? Get out of it by whatever way you like* (adapted from Seneca). . . . *Does grief prick you ? nay, does it stab you ? If naked, present your throat ; if covered by the arms of Vulcan, that is fortitude, resist it* (Cicero). And those words of the Greek revellers, *Let him drink or let him quit*, which are to the point but sound more appropriate in the mouth of a Gascon, who usually changes B into a V[1], than in Cicero's :

> If how to live as best befits a man
> You do not know, make way for those who can.
> You've had as much as should your heart content
> Of sport, and meat and drink ; 'tis time you went,
> Lest youth, that fitlier plays the fool than age,
> Should thrust the maudlin toper off the stage. (HORACE.)

What, I say, is this agreement of Philosophy but a confession of her impotence, when she refers us, not only to ignorance, there to be under cover, but even to dullness, to insensibility, to non-existence ?

> Then, too, Democritus, when ripened age
> Admonished him his memory waned away,
> Of own accord offered his head to death. (LUCRETIUS.)

[1] *Bibat*, 'let him drink', would become *vivat*, 'let him live'.

As Antisthenes said, 'We must either provide ourselves with sense to understand, or with a rope to hang ourselves'; and the poet Tyrtaeus, as quoted to the point by Chrysippus,

> If virtue be not in us, let us die.

And Crates said, 'Love is cured by hunger, if not by time; and if these two means do not find favour, by the halter.'

That Sextius of whom both Seneca and Plutarch speak with so high an encomium, having abandoned everything and applied himself to the study of philosophy, and finding the progress of his studies too slow and tedious, resolved to cast himself into the sea. He hastened to death in default of knowledge.

Here are the words of the law on the subject: 'If, perchance, he be overtaken by some great calamity that cannot be remedied, the haven is near, and he may save himself by swimming out of his body, as out of a skiff that leaks; for it is the fear of dying, and not the wish to live, that keeps the fool tied to his body.'

As life is rendered more agreeable by simplicity, so it thereby also becomes better and more innocent, as I was erstwhile beginning to say. 'The simple and ignorant, says Saint Paul, raise themselves to heaven, and take possession of it; and we, with all our learning, plunge ourselves into the infernal abyss.'

I will not stop to consider either Valentinian, the avowed enemy of science and letters, nor Licinius, Roman emperors both, who called them the 'poison and plague of all political states'; nor Mahomet, who, as I have heard, interdicted learning to his followers. But the example of the great Lycurgus, and his authority, should certainly have great weight, as well as the reverence in which that divine Lacedemonian government was held, so great, so admirable, and so long flourishing in virtue and happiness, without any teaching or practise of letters.

The men who return from that new world which was discovered in the time of our fathers by the Spaniards can testify how much more lawful and orderly is the life of those nations, who have neither magistrates nor laws, than that of our own countries, where the lawyers outnumber the other people, and there are more laws than actions.

CURIOSITY THE ORIGINAL SIN

> Her lap was full of writs and of citations,
>   Of processes, of actions and arrests,
> Of bills, of answers and of replications,
>   In Courts of Delegates and of Requests,
> To grieve the simple sort with great vexations.
>   She had resorting to her as her guests,
> Attending on her circuits and her journeys,
> Scriveners and clerks, and lawyers and attorneys. (ARIOSTO.)

It was as a Roman senator said of the later ages, 'That their predecessors had a breath stinking of garlic, and their stomach bemusked with a good conscience; and that on the other hand those of his day only smelled outwardly of perfumes, stinking within of every kind of vice.' That is to say, I take it, that they had great learning and ability, and a great lack of honesty. Incivility, ignorance, simplicity, rudeness, are the usual companions of innocence; curiosity, subtlety, learning, bring mischief in their train; humility, fear, obedience, friendliness (which are the principal qualities for keeping human society together), require a soul that is intact and teachable, without any self-conceit.

Christians have a particular reason for knowing that curiosity is a natural and original sin in man. The desire to increase in wisdom and knowledge was the cause of the first downfall of the human race; it was the way by which they hurled themselves into eternal damnation. Pride is their ruin and corruption; it is pride that turns a man aside from the common path, that makes him embrace novelties and choose to be head of an erring troop, straying into the way of perdition, to teach and inculcate errors and falsehoods, rather than be a pupil in the school of truth, and be led and guided by the hands of another, along the straight and beaten road. That is perhaps the meaning of this old Greek saying, *Superstition follows pride and obeys it as if it were a father* (STOBAEUS).

O presumption, how much dost thou hinder us![1]

When Socrates was informed that the God of Wisdom had bestowed upon him the title of The Sage, he was astonished; and having thoroughly shaken and examined himself, he could discover no ground for this divine verdict. He knew of men as just, as temperate, as worthy, as learned as himself, and more eloquent, handsomer, and more useful to their

---

[1] This is one of the sentences inscribed in Latin on the ceiling of Montaigne's library.

country. At last he concluded that he was distinguished from other people and wise only in not thinking himself so; and that his God considered man singularly stupid for thinking himself knowing and wise, and that the best thing he could learn was his own ignorance, and simplicity his best wisdom.

The holy word declares those of us poor creatures who have a high opinion of ourselves: 'Dust and ashes, it tells them, what hast thou to boast of?' and in another place: 'God made man like a shadow, of which who can judge when by the removal of the light it vanishes?'[1] We are truly a thing of naught.

So unable are we by our own powers to conceive the sublimity of God, that we least understand those works of our creator that best bear his stamp, and are most his. To meet with a thing that is unbelievable is to the Christian an occasion to believe. It is the more according to reason as it is contrary to human reason. If it were in accordance with reason it would no longer be a miracle; and if it were according to some example, it would no longer be singular. *God is better known by not knowing*, says Saint Augustine; and Tacitus, *It is more holy and reverend to believe the works of God than to know them.*

And Plato thinks that there is something impious in inquiring too curiously into God and the world, and the primary causes of things. And *it is difficult to discover the parent of this universe; and when you have discovered him, it is wicked to reveal him to the vulgar*, says Cicero.

We say, indeed, Power, Truth, Justice: they are words that denote something great, but that something we are quite unable to see and conceive. We say that God fears, that God is angry, that God loves,

> Branding with mortal names immortal things. (LUCRETIUS.)

They are feelings and emotions that God is unable to harbour according to our manner of thinking; nor can we imagine them according to his. It belongs to God alone to know himself and to interpret his works.

And in our language he does it improperly in order to stoop and condescend to us, who lie grovelling on the earth. How can wisdom, which is the power of choosing between

---

[1] This sentence, in Latin, is inscribed on the ceiling of Montaigne's library, with a reference to Ecclesiastes.

WISDOM BORN OF IGNORANCE

good and evil, be properly attributed to him, seeing that he has no dealings with evil? How reason and intelligence, which we use to arrive at, by things that are obscure, things that are clear, seeing that nothing is obscure to God? Justice, which distributes to each man what belongs to him, which was created for the fellowship and community of men, how can it be in God? How temperance, which is moderation in bodily pleasures, which have no place in the Deity? Fortitude to endure pain, labours, dangers, just as little appertains to him, since these three things have no access to him.[1] Wherefore Aristotle holds him equally exempt from virtues and vices.

He is susceptible neither of favour nor anger, for they are the effects of weakness (Cicero).

The share we have in the knowledge of truth, such as it is, has not been acquired by our own powers. God has taught us that sufficiently well through the witnesses[2] he chose out of the common people, simple and ignorant men, in order to impart to us his wonderful secrets; our faith is not of our own acquiring, it is purely the gift of another's bounty. It is not by our reasoning or our understanding that we have received our religion, but by outside authority and command. We are therein assisted by the weakness more than by the strength of our judgement, by our blindness more than by our clearsightedness. By means of our ignorance, more than our knowledge, do we become wise in this heavenly wisdom. It is not to be wondered at if our natural and earthly powers are unable to conceive that supernatural and heavenly knowledge; let us bring to it nothing of our own but obedience and submission. 'For, as it is written, I will destroy the wisdom of the wise, and will bring to nothing the understanding of the prudent. Where is the wise? where is the scribe? where is the disputer of this world? Hath not God made foolish the wisdom of this world? For after that in the wisdom of God the world by wisdom knew not God, it pleased God by the foolishness of preaching to save them that believe' (Saint Paul to the Corinthians).

Yet must I consider, in fine, if it be in the power of man to find what he seeks, and if this search he has been making

---

[1] The above passage, from 'How can wisdom, &c.' is transcribed from Cicero, *Of the Nature of the Gods*, iii. 15.   [2] The Apostles.

for so many centuries has enriched him with any new power and any solid truth. I think he will admit, if he speak in all conscience, that all he has gained by his long pursuit is to have learned to acknowledge his own weakness. The ignorance which was naturally in us we have by long study confirmed and verified.

It is with the truly learned as with the ears of corn. As long as they are empty they shoot up and raise their heads, upright and proud; but when they are full and swollen with grain in their ripeness, they begin to humble themselves and lower their crest. Similarly, men have tried all things, and probed all things, and, having found in that accumulation of knowledge and that store of so many diverse things, nothing firm and solid, and nothing but emptiness, they have dropped their presumption and recognized their natural condition.

It is what Velleius impresses upon Cotta and Cicero, 'That they have learned from Philo that they have learned nothing.'

Pherecydes, one of the Seven Sages, writing to Thales from his death-bed, said, 'I have appointed my friends, as soon as I shall be laid in my grave, to bring you my writings. If they satisfy you and the other sages, publish them; if not, suppress them. They contain nothing certain enough to satisfy myself. Nor do I profess to know the truth, nor to be near it. I uncover rather than discover things.'

The wisest man that ever was, when asked what he knew, replied 'that he knew this much, that he knew nothing'. He verified what has been said, that the greatest part of what we know is the least of what we do not know; that is to say, that even that same that we think we know is a portion, and a very small portion, of our ignorance.

We know things in a dream, says Plato, and are ignorant of them in reality. *Almost all the ancients have said that we can know nothing, perceive nothing, understand nothing; our senses are narrowed, our minds are weak, and the course of life is short* (Cicero).

Of Cicero himself, who owed all he was worth to his learning, Valerius said that as he grew old he began to despise letters. And, whilst he cultivated them, he did so independently of any party, following what seemed probable to him, now in one sect, now in another; holding himself ever in academic suspense. *I will speak, but so as to affirm nothing; I shall search into all things, mostly in doubt and distrust of myself* (Cicero).

It would be too easy a task for me to consider man in his average condition and in the gross; yet I could do so by his own rule, which is to judge of the truth, not by the weight but by the number of votes. Let us leave the people on one side,

> For whom already life's as good as dead,
> Whilst yet they live and look; who waste their life
> In sleep, and waking snore; (LUCRETIUS.)

who cannot feel or estimate their powers; who allow most of their natural faculties to lie idle. I will take man in his highest state.

Let us consider him in that small number of eminent and select persons who, having been endowed by Nature with a great and exceptional talent, have brought it to still greater power and acuteness by diligence, study and art, and raised it to the highest pitch of wisdom that it is capable of reaching. They have moulded their soul to every shape and ever pattern, they have strengthened and underpropped it with all suitable outside support, they have enriched and adorned it with everything they were able to borrow, for its advantage, from within and outside the world; in them has human nature reached its zenith.

They have organized the world with laws and constitutions; they have instructed it in the arts and sciences, and further instructed it by the example of their admirable lives. I will take into account only such men as these, their testimony and experience. Let us see how far they have gone, and what they have believed. The infirmities and defects we shall find in this assemblage the world may boldly avow to be its own.

Whoever goes in search of anything must reach this point: either to say that he has found it, or that it is not to be found; or that he is still upon the quest. All Philosophy is divided into these three kinds. Its purpose is to seek out the truth, knowledge and certainty.

The Peripatetics, Epicureans, Stoics and others, thought they had found it. These have established the sciences that we have, and treated them as certain knowledge.

Clitomachus, Carneades and the Academics despaired in their search, and decided that truth cannot be conceived by our capacities. The conclusion they came to was that man is weak and ignorant. This school had the greatest following and the most noble sectaries.

Pyrrho, and other Sceptics or Ephectics, whose doctrines are held by many of the ancients to have been derived from Homer, the Seven Sages, and from Archilochus and Euripides, to whom they join Zeno, Democritus, Xenophanes, say that they are still in search of the truth. These conclude that the others who think they have found it are profoundly mistaken, and that there is, moreover, too daring a vanity in those of the second degree, who affirm that human powers are not capable of attaining it. For to establish the measure of our powers, to know and estimate the difficulty of things, requires the highest degree of knowledge, of which they doubt whether man is capable :

> If one suppose
> That naught is known, he knows not whether this
> Itself is able to be known, since he
> Confesses naught to know. (LUCRETIUS.)

The ignorant man who knows himself to be ignorant, who judges and condemns himself as ignorant, is not absolutely ignorant ; to be that, he must be ignorant of himself. Hence the profession of the Pyrrhonians is to waver, to doubt, and to inquire ; to be sure of nothing, to answer for nothing. Of the three actions of the soul, the Imaginative, the Appetitive, and the Consenting, they accept the two first ; on the last they suspend their judgement and maintain it to be ambiguous, without approving or inclining ever so little either way.

Zeno described by a gesture his idea of this partition of the faculties of the mind. The hand spread out and open was Probability ; the hand half-shut and the fingers a little hooked, Consent ; the closed fist, Comprehension ; with the left hand closing the fist more tightly, Knowledge.

Now this straightforward and inflexible attitude of the Pyrrhonians, taking all things in without conformity or consent, brings them to their Ataraxia, which is a tranquil and composed condition of life, free from the emotions forced upon us by the knowledge and idea we think we have of things. Whence arise fear, avarice, envy, immoderate desires, ambition, pride, superstition, love of novelty, rebellion, disobedience, obstinacy, and the most part of bodily ills. Nay, they thereby become free from doctrinal zeal. For they dispute in a very half-hearted manner. They fear no retort in their debates. When they assert that heavy things descend, they would be very sorry to be taken at their word; and they court contradiction, to create doubt and suspension of judgement, which is their ultimate end. They advance their propositions only to combat those they think we believe.

If you accept their proposition, they will be just as ready to maintain the contrary one: it is all one to them; they have no choice. If you maintain that snow is black, they will argue, on the contrary, that it is white. If you say that it is neither one nor the other, it is their business to maintain that it is both. If you decidedly affirm that you know nothing for certain, they will insist that you do know. Yes; and if you affirm axiomatically that you are sure you are in doubt about it, they will go on arguing that you are not in doubt, or that you cannot decide and prove that you are in doubt.

And in this attitude of extreme doubt, which is self-destructive, they separate and divide themselves from the opinions of many, even those who have in several ways maintained doubt and ignorance.

If, among the Dogmatists, one is allowed to say green, and the other yellow, why, they say, shall they not also be allowed to doubt? Can anything be proposed to you, to admit or deny, which you shall not be allowed to consider as ambiguous? And where others are led, either by the custom of their country, or by the instruction of their parents, or by some chance accident, such as a storm, without judgement and without choice, nay, most often before the age of discretion, to such or such an opinion, to the school of the Stoics or the Epicureans, to which they have become pledged, enslaved and glued, as to a thing they have grasped and cannot let go—*to whatever doctrine they are driven, as by a tempest, they cling to it as to a rock* (Cicero)—why shall these not likewise be allowed to maintain their freedom, and consider things without slavish compulsion? *The more free and independent because their power of judging is intact* (Cicero).

Is there not some advantage in being free from the necessity that curbs others? Is it not better to remain in suspense, than to be entangled in the many errors that the human imagination has brought forth? Is it not better to suspend one's conviction than to get mixed up with those seditious and wrangling divisions?

What am I to choose? 'Choose what you please, as long as you choose.' There you have a foolish answer, which seems to be the outcome, however, of all Dogmatism, which will not allow us to be ignorant of that of which we are ignorant.

Take the most reputed school theory, it will never be so sure but that, in order to defend it, you will be obliged to attack and combat hundreds of contrary theories. Is it not better to keep out of this scuffle? You are permitted to espouse, as if your honour and life were at stake, Aristotle's opinion on the eternity of the soul, and to contradict and give the lie to Plato on that point; and shall they be forbidden to doubt it?

If it be lawful for Panaetius to suspend his judgement concerning auspices, dreams, oracles, vaticinations, of which things the Stoics make no doubt whatever, why shall not a wise man dare, in all things, what this man dares in those he has learned of his masters, and which are established by common agreement of the school which he follows and professes? If it is a boy that judges, he does not know what he he is talking about; if it is a scholar, he is prejudiced.

The Pyrrhonians have reserved to themselves a wonderful advantage in the combat, in having no desire to defend themselves. They care little whether they are struck, so long as they strike; and they make everything serve their purpose. If they vanquish, your proposition limps; if you, theirs. If they fail they confirm ignorance; if you fail, you confirm it. If they prove that nothing can be known, it is well; if they cannot prove it, it is equally well. *So that, finding equal reasons for and against, in the same matter, one may more easily suspend one's judgement on either side* (Cicero).

And they are assured that they can much more easily discover why a thing is false than why it is true; and that which is not than that which is; and that which they do not believe, than that which they do.

Their way of speaking is: 'I settle nothing; It is no

more thus than thus, or than neither one nor the other ; I do not understand it ; Appearances are everywhere equal ; It is equally possible to take either side ; Nothing seems true that may not seem untrue.'[1] Their sacramental word is ἐπέχω, that is to say, ' I hold myself in reserve, I do not budge.' That is the burden of their song, and others of like stuff. The result of it is a pure, complete, and most perfect surceasing and suspension of judgement. They use their reason to inquire and to debate, but not to resolve and choose. If we can imagine a perpetual confession of ignorance, a judgement without bias or leaning, upon any occasion whatever, we can have a conception of Pyrrhonism.

I explain their attitude to the best of my ability, because many find it difficult of comprehension ; and the authors of it themselves express it rather obscurely and diversely.

As concerning the actions of life, they follow in this respect the ordinary course. They give way and submit to their natural inclinations, to the impulse and violence of their passions, to the constitutions of laws and customs, and to the tradition of arts. *For God would not have us know, but only use, those things* (Cicero). They allow their ordinary actions to be guided by those things, without any arguing or laying down the law. For which reason I cannot very well reconcile with this account what is said of Pyrrho. They describe him as dull and impassive, adopting a surly and unsociable mode of life, getting in the way of jostling carts, defying precipices, refusing to conform to the laws. That is to overdo his teaching. He had no wish to make himself a stock or stone ; he wished to be a living, discoursing and reasoning being, enjoying all natural pleasures and amenities, using and bringing all his bodily and spiritual gifts into play, in right and orderly fashion. The fantastic, imaginary and unreal privileges which man has usurped of lording it, of laying down the law and setting up the truth, he honestly renounced and abandoned.

So there is no school of philosophy which is not obliged to permit its sage to follow many things neither comprehended, nor discerned, nor agreed upon, if he desires to live. And when he goes to sea, he acts in accordance with that permission, not knowing whether it will profit him. He

[1] These maxims were inscribed on the joists of the ceiling in Montaigne's library, and the word ἐπέχω on the walls.

relies on the goodness of the vessel, the experience of the pilot, the fitness of the season, circumstances which are only probable, but by which he is bound to be guided, allowing himself to be governed by appearances, provided there be no positive contradiction in them. He has a body, he has a soul; he is impelled by his senses, stirred by his mind. Although he is not conscious of being particularly and individually marked out for deciding, and although he perceives that he must not pledge his consent, seeing there may be something false resembling this true, he none the less carries on the functions of his life fully and commodiously.

How many arts are there that profess to depend more on conjecture than on knowledge; that do not decide on what is true and what is false, and only follow that which seems? There is, they say, a true and a false, and we have in us the means of seeking it, but we have no touchstone by which to test it. It is much better for us to let ourselves go the way of the world, without inquiry. A soul assured against prejudices has made a wonderful advance towards tranquillity. People who judge and find fault with their judges never submit to them as they should.

How much more docile and tractable, both to the laws of religion and to the civil laws, are simple and incurious minds, than those wits who supervise and pedantically hold forth on divine and human causes!

There is no theory invented by man that offers more likelihood and profit.[1] It presents man naked and empty, confessing his natural weakness and ready to receive from on high some power not his own; stripped bare of human knowledge, and all the more fit to harbour within himself divine knowledge; suppressing his own judgement to leave more room for faith; neither disbelieving nor setting up any teaching contrary to the common observances; humble, obedient, docile, zealous, a sworn enemy to heresy and consequently free from the vain and irreligious beliefs introduced by the false sects. He is a blank tablet prepared to take from the finger of God such forms as he shall be pleased to engrave upon it. The more we resign and commit ourselves to God, and

[1] i.e. than Pyrrhonism. The previous passage, from 'So there is no school, &c.', was an interpolation in the 'Bordeaux MS.', and Montaigne overlooked the breach of continuity, as he not infrequently does.

the more we deny ourselves, the better it is for us. 'Receive thankfully, says the Preacher, day by day, the things that are offered to thee to see and enjoy ; the rest is beyond thy knowledge.'[1] *The Lord knoweth the thoughts of man, that they are vanity* (Psalms).

Thus we see that, of the three general schools of Philosophy, two make open profession of doubt and ignorance ; and in that of the Dogmatists, which is the third, it is easy to discover that the greater part of them only put on the mask of certainty to make a better appearance. They thought not so much of establishing any certainty, as to show us how far they had gone in this pursuit after the truth ; *which the learned doctors suppose rather than know*.

Timaeus, having to inform Socrates as to what he knew of the gods and of the world and of men, proposes to speak of them as one man to another, and holds that it is enough if his reasons are as probable as another's ; for exact reasons, he said, were not in his hand, nor in any mortal hand. Which one of his followers has thus imitated : *I will explain as well as I am able ; yet do I not pretend to be a Pythian Apollo, to declare things that are fixed and certain ; I speak but as a manikin that tries to reach probabilities by conjecture* (Cicero). That was in reference to the contempt of death, a subject naturally within everybody's reach. In another place he has translated word for word from Plato : *If perchance when discoursing of the nature of the Gods and the origin of the world, we cannot attain to the end we have in view, do not be surprised. For it is right you should remember that I who am discoursing, and you who are to judge, are men. So, if only probabilities result, do not ask for more.*

Aristotle usually accumulates, for our benefit, a large number of other opinions and other beliefs, to compare with his own, and let us see how far he has gone beyond them, and how much nearer he approaches to likelihood ; for the truth is not to be decided by the authority, nor accepted on the testimony, of another. And therefore Epicurus scrupulously avoided quoting any in his writings. The former is the prince of Dogmatists, and yet we learn of him that much knowledge occasions more doubt. We see him often purposely shrouding himself in so thick and inextricable

---

[1] This verse has not been identified.

an obscurity that we cannot pick out his meaning. It is in fact a Pyrrhonism under an affirmative form.

Listen to Cicero protesting, and explaining the conception of others by his own: *They who would know what we personally think on every matter carry curiosity too far. . . . This practice in Philosophy of discussing everything and coming to no open conclusion, begun by Socrates, resumed by Arcesilaus, confirmed by Carneades, has flourished till our time. . . . We are of those who declare that there is some falsehood mixed with every truth, and that they so resemble one another, that there is no criterion which will allow us either to assent or decide with certainty.*

Why did not only Aristotle, but most of the philosophers, affect obscurity, if not to emphasize the vanity of the subject, and keep our curious minds occupied by giving them, instead of food, this hollow and fleshless bone to pick? Clitomachus declared that from the writings of Carneades he had never been able to discover what opinion he held. For which reason Epicurus, in his, avoided clearness; and Heraclitus, for the same reason, was surnamed The Cloudy. Obscurity is a coin used by the learned as the conjurors use sleight of hand, to conceal the inanity of their art; and human stolidity is quite ready to take it in payment:

> At the head of them
> Comes Heraclitus, famous for dark speech
> Among the silly, not the serious Greeks
> Who search for Truth. For dolts are ever prone
> That to bewonder and adore which hides
> Beneath distorted words. (LUCRETIUS.)

Cicero reproves some of his friends for their habit of bestowing more of their time on astrology, law, logic, and geometry, than those arts deserved; as they were by them diverted from the more profitable and honourable duties of life. The Cyrenaic philosophers equally despised physics and logic. Zeno, at the very beginning of the books of his *Republic*, declared all the liberal studies to be of no use.

Chrysippus said that Plato and Aristotle wrote what they did about Logic only by way of pastime and exercise,[1] and could not believe that they had spoken seriously on so empty a matter. Plutarch says the same of Metaphysics. Epicurus would likewise have said it of Rhetoric, Gram-

---

[1] According to Plutarch he said just the opposite.

mar, Poetry, Mathematics and all the sciences with the exception of Physics. And Socrates equally of all, excepting only that which treats of Morals and the conduct of life. Whatever you might ask him, he would in the first place refer the inquirer to his past and present life, to give an account of it, which he then examined and judged, esteeming any other learning as subsidiary to that and superfluous.

I should think little of that learning which profited not the teachers to become more virtuous (Sallust). Most of the arts have been thus despised by learning itself. But they did not think it foreign to the purpose to exercise and relax their minds in those things in which there was no solid advantage.

Moreover, some have regarded Plato as a Dogmatist, others as a doubter; others, in certain things the one, in certain others, the other. The conductor of his dialogues, Socrates, is ever asking questions and stirring up arguments, never concluding, never satisfying; and professes to have no other art but that of opposing. Homer, their progenitor, equally laid the foundation of all the schools of Philosophy, to show how indifferent he was as to which way we were going.

They say that ten different schools sprang from Plato. And certainly, in my opinion, no teaching was ever wavering and non-committal, if his was not.

Socrates used to say that the wise women,[1] when they take up the business of helping to bring others into the world, themselves give up the business of breeding; that he, by the title of Wise man which the gods had conferred upon him, had also, in his virile and mental love, given up the faculty of begetting, contenting himself with affording help and succour to those who were in labour, opening their organs of generation, oiling their conduits, facilitating the issue of their offspring, appraising the latter, baptizing it, feeding it, strengthening it, swaddling and circumscribing[2] it; exercising and employing his skill in the perils and fortunes of others.

It is the same[3] with most of the authors of this third

---

[1] *Sages femmes*, i. e. midwives.

[2] The 1595 and subsequent editions have *circumcising*, which is perhaps what Montaigne intended to write.

[3] i. e. the same as with Plato.

kind, as the ancients remarked of the writings of Anaxagoras, Democritus, Parmenides, Xenophanes, and others. They have a way of writing, doubtful in substance, and their purpose is to inquire rather than to instruct; although they sprinkle their style with dogmatic phrases. Do we not see this as well in Seneca and Plutarch? How often do they not speak, now from one point of view, now from another, if we examine them closely? And they who reconcile lawyers with one another, should in the first place reconcile each one with himself.

To me it appears that Plato purposely favoured this method of philosophizing in dialogue form, in order more fittingly to put into divers mouths the diversity and variety of his own ideas. To treat of matters diversely is as good as to treat them conformably, and better; to wit, more copiously and with greater profit.

Let us take example from ourselves. Judicial sentences occupy the highest point of dogmatic and decisive speaking. And yet those which our Supreme Courts present to the people, the most exemplary and the best fitted to foster in them the reverence they owe to those dignified bodies, especially by reason of the ability of the persons who represent them, derive their beauty, not so much from the conclusion, which with them is of daily occurrence and common to every judge, as from the discussion and the stirring up of diverse and contrary arguments, which questions of law permit.

And the widest field for mutual reprehensions among the different philosophers is offered by the contradictions and differences in which each of them is entangled; either by design, to show the vacillation of the human mind around every subject, or, in ignorance and in spite of himself, by the mutability and incomprehensibility of all matter.

What is the meaning of this refrain: 'In a smooth and slippery place let us suspend our belief'? For, as Euripides says,

> The works of God in various ways perplex us;

a refrain similar to that which Empedocles here and there scattered over his books, as if stirred by a divine madness, and vanquished by the truth: 'No, no, we feel nothing, we see nothing; all things are hidden from us; there is not one of which we can affirm what it is'; returning to this divine saying : *For the thoughts of mortal men are miserable, and our devices are but uncertain* (Book of Wisdom).

It should not be thought strange that men who have no hope of the quarry yet take a pleasure in the chase ; study being in itself a pleasant occupation, and so delightful that the Stoics forbid, among other pleasures, that which comes from the exercise of the mind, and would put a curb upon it, regarding it as intemperance to know too much.

Democritus, eating figs [1] at his table that tasted of honey, immediately began to search in his mind for the cause of this unusual sweetness ; and to resolve his doubts was about to rise from the table to examine the situation of the place where these figs had been gathered. His servingmaid, when told of his perplexity, said laughingly that he need not trouble himself about it, the reason being that she had put them into a vessel that had contained honey. He was vexed that she had deprived him of an occasion for research, and robbed his curiosity of matter to work upon : ' Go along, he said to her, you have done me an ill turn ; I shall still seek out the reason, as if it were a natural one.' And he did not fail to find some true cause or other for a false and supposed effect.

This story of a great and famous philosopher very clearly illustrates that passion for study which impels us to waste time in the pursuit of a thing that we never hope to gain. Plutarch relates a like example of some man who refused to be enlightened with regard to a thing on which he felt a doubt, in order not to lose the pleasure of investigation ; like that other man who would not allow his physician to allay the thirst of his fever, in order not to lose the pleasure of quenching it by drink. *It is more satisfactory to learn superfluous things than nothing at all* (Seneca).

Just as in all feeding there is often merely the pleasure— and the tasty things we eat are not always either nutritious or wholesome—so what our mind extracts from learning does not fail to be pleasurable, though it be neither sustaining nor healthful.

This is what they say : ' The consideration of Nature is

---

[1] Not figs, but a gherkin, according to Plutarch, who tells this delightful story. The close resemblance between the two Greek words misled the translator.

a proper food for our minds; it elevates and lifts us up, makes us disdain things that are low and terrestrial, by comparing them with higher and celestial things. The mere investigation of great and occult things is very pleasing, even to one who derives from it only a feeling of awe and fear of drawing conclusions from them.' That is their profession in so many words.

The vanity of this morbid curiosity is still more plainly reflected in this other example which they have so often on their lips and make a boast of. Eudoxus desired and prayed the gods to be allowed for once to see the sun near at hand, to take in its shape, its grandeur and beauty, even though he should be immediately burned up. He desires, at the price of life, to purchase a knowledge the use and possession of which will be taken from him in the same instant. And, for the sake of this sudden and fleeting knowledge, he would forgo any other kind of knowledge he possesses or may afterwards acquire.

I cannot be easily convinced that Epicurus, Plato, and Pythagoras gave us their Atoms, their Ideas, and their Numbers for current coin. They were too wise to build their articles of faith upon so uncertain and debatable a foundation. But to this dark and ignorant world each of these great men laboured to bring some semblance of light, such as it was; and walked their minds up and down such theories as might at least offer some pleasing and subtle appearance, provided that, false though it might be, it might hold its own against their opponents. *These systems are the fictions of the genius of each philosopher, not the result of their knowledge* (Seneca).

One of the ancients, to whom it was made a reproach that he professed a philosophy of which he nevertheless, in his own opinion, made no great account, replied 'that that was the true way to philosophize'. Those men went about to consider everything, to weigh everything, and found that occupation well suited to the natural curiosity that is in us. Some things they wrote for the needs of society in general, such as their religious beliefs; and on this account it was but reasonable that they should not desire violently to pull to pieces the opinions of the people, in order not to breed trouble and disobedience to the laws and customs of their country.

Plato treats of these mysteries with his cards on the table. For when he writes his own opinions, he lays down no certain laws. When he plays the legislator, he borrows a domineering and assertive style, and yet boldly brings in the most fantastic of his ideas, which are as useful to persuade the people as they are ridiculous for persuading himself ; knowing how ready we are to receive all sorts of impressions, and above all the wildest and most extravagant.

And therefore, in his *Laws*, he is very solicitous that in public only those poems should be sung whose fabulous fictions tend to some useful purpose ; and, since it was so easy to imprint all sorts of phantasms on the human mind, he thought it was wrong not to feed them rather on profitable untruths than on untruths that were either useless or harmful. He says quite shamelessly, in his *Republic*, ' That for the good of mankind it is often necessary to gull them.'

It is easy to discern that some of the schools have rather followed the truth, others utility, whereby the latter have gained credit. It is the wretchedness of our condition that often what appears to our imagination as the most true, does not appear the most profitable to our life. The boldest sects, the Epicurean, the Pyrrhonian and the New Academic, are yet, when all is said and done, obliged to bow to the civil law.

Other subjects there are which they have sifted and thrown, some to the left, others to the right, each labouring to give them, whether right or wrong, some kind of colour. For, as they find nothing too occult for their discussion, they are often obliged to forge weak and foolish conjectures ; not that they themselves took them for a groundwork, to establish any truth upon them, but for the exercise of their study. *Not that they themselves believed what they said, but they seemed desirous of exercising their ingenuity upon the obscurity of the matter*.

And if this is not the way to take it, how could we excuse so many inconsistent, diverse and shadowy theories, that we see to have proceeded from those eminent and admirable minds ? For, to take an example, what can be more fruitless than to try to divine God by our analogies and conjectures, to measure him and the world according to our capacity and our laws; and to employ, at the expense of the Deity, that little sample of talent which it has pleased him to allot to our natural condition? And, because we are unable to raise our eyes to his glorious throne, to bring him down to the level of our corruption and our miseries?

Of all human and ancient theories concerning religion, that appears to me the most probable and the most defensible which recognized in God an incomprehensible power, the origin and preserver of all things, all goodness, all perfection, graciously taking and accepting the honour and reverence rendered him by human beings, under whatever aspect, whatever name, and in what manner soever.[1]

> Almighty Jove, of kings and Gods and all
> Father and mother. (VALERIUS SORANUS.)

This zeal has been invariably looked upon by heaven with favour. All governments have reaped fruit from their piety; impious men and impious deeds have everywhere been suitably punished. Pagan histories recognize dignity, order, justice, and prodigies and oracles worked for their benefit and instruction, in their fabulous religions; God, in his mercy, vouchsafing perhaps to cherish, by these temporal benefits, the tender beginnings of a brute knowledge of him, such as it was, which our inborn reason has given to us amid the deceptive images of our dreams.

Not only deceptive, but impious and harmful, are those which man has forged of his own invention.

And of all the religions which Saint Paul found in repute at Athens, that appeared to him the most pardonable which they had dedicated to a 'hidden and unknown Deity'.

Pythagoras more nearly outlined the truth when he concluded that the knowledge of this primary Cause, and Being of Beings, must be undefined, unprescribed, unexplained; that it was nothing else but the utmost effort of our imagination towards perfection, each one amplifying the idea of it according to his capacity.

But if Numa attempted to fit the piety of his people to this vague outline, to attach them to a purely intellectual

[1] This was followed, in the 1588 edition, by a sentence which, apparently after some hesitation, was deleted: 'Those deities to whom man of his own invention has tried to give a shape, are injurious, full of error and impiety.'

religion, without any predetermined object or any material admixture, he attempted an unprofitable thing. The human mind cannot keep on rambling in this infinity of shapeless ideas ; it must compile them into a certain image after its own model.[1]

The divine majesty has thus allowed itself in some sort to be circumscribed, as far as we are concerned, within corporeal limits. His supernatural and heavenly sacraments bear the signs of our earthly condition ; his worship finds expression in services and audible words, for it is man who believes and prays.

I leave aside the other arguments employed on this subject. But it would be difficult to make me believe that the sight of our crucifixes, and pictures of that pitiful agony, that the ornaments and the ceremonious movements in our churches, that the chants attuned to the devotion of our thoughts, and that stirring of our senses, do not warm the souls of the people with a religious feeling of very beneficial effect.

Of the religions that give a body to their Deity, as necessity requires in this universal blindness, I should, I think, more readily incline to that of the sun-worshippers.

> The common light that shines indifferently
> On all alike, the world's enlightening eyes ;
> And, if the almighty ruler of the skies
> Has eyes, the sun-beams are his radiant eyes,
> That life to all impart, maintain, and guard,
> And all men's actions upon earth regard.
> This great, this beautiful and glorious sun,
> That seasons gives by revolution ;
> That with his influence fills the universe,
> And with one glance doth sullen clouds disperse ;
> Life, soul of the world, that, flaming in his sphere,
> Surrounds the heavens in one day's career ;
> Immensely great, moving, yet firm and round,
> Who the whole world below has fixed his bound,
> At rest without rest, idle without stay ;
> Nature's first son, and father of the day.   (RONSARD.)

Seeing that, besides its grandeur and beauty, it is the part of this machine that appears most remote from us, and is in consequence so little known, they were to be pardoned for being stirred to wonder and reverence of it.

[1] Dr. Armaingaud sees in this passage a disguised criticism of the Protestant religion.

Thales, the first who inquired into this matter, regarded God as a spirit, that made all things of water.

Anaximander held that the gods died and were newly born at divers seasons, and that they were worlds of infinite number;

Anaximenes, that the air was God, that he was brought forth, immense, ever moving.

Anaxagoras was the first to hold that the disposition and order of all things was directed by the power and reason of an infinite spirit.

Alcmaeon attributed divinity to the sun, the moon, the stars and the soul.

Pythagoras made God a spirit, diffused through the nature of all things, whence our souls were detached;

Parmenides, a circle surrounding the heavens and sustaining the world by the intensity of its light.

Empedocles declared the four elements, of which all things are made, to be gods.

Protagoras declared that it was not for him to say whether they are, or are not, or what they are.

Democritus at one time held that the images and their circular revolutions, at another that that Nature which shoots out those images, and again, that our knowledge and understanding, are gods.

Plato varies in his belief, as we may see in his different writings: in the *Timaeus* he says that the father of the world cannot be named; in the *Laws*, that we must not inquire into his nature; and in other passages in these same books he makes the world, heaven, the stars, the earth, and our souls, gods. And he also accepts those accepted by time-honoured institution in every republic.

Xenophon records a similar confusion in Socrates' teaching: at one time that we must not inquire into the form of God; at another he makes him conclude that the sun is God, and the soul, God; that there is only one; and again that there are several.

Speusippus, Plato's nephew, makes of God a certain power that governs things, and is animate.

Aristotle says at one time that it is the mind, at another the world; now he gives this world another master, and again he makes God the heat of heaven.

Zenocrates makes eight of him: five named among the

planets, the sixth composed of all the fixed stars, as his members, the seventh and eighth the sun and moon.

Heraclides of Pontus just wavers between different opinions, and ends by depriving God of feeling, making him shift from one form to another; and then declares him to be heaven and earth.

Theophrastus, with like indecision, rambles among his various fancies, attributing the superintendence of the world now to the understanding, now to heaven, now to the stars.

Strato says it is Nature, with the power to generate, to increase and diminish, without form or feeling;

Zeno, the Law of Nature, commanding good and forbidding evil; which Law is an animated being. And he abolishes the customary gods, Jupiter, Juno, Vesta.

Diogenes of Apollonia declares him to be Age.[1]

Xenophanes makes God round, seeing, hearing, non-breathing, having nothing in common with human nature.

Aristo thinks the form of God to be incomprehensible, deprives him of senses, and knows not whether he be an animated being or something else.

Cleanthes supposes him to be, now Reason, now the World, now the Soul of Nature, now again the supreme Heat surrounding and enveloping all things.

Perseus, a disciple of Zeno, maintains that the title of gods was given to such as had enriched the life of man with some notable blessings, and even to the profitable things themselves.

Chrysippus made a confused heap of all the preceding declarations, and among the thousand forms of gods that he creates he numbers those men who have been immortalized.

Diagoras and Theodorus flatly denied that there were gods.

Epicurus makes the gods shining, transparent, not air-tight, lodged between two worlds as between two forts, sheltered from blows, invested in human shape and limbs like ours, which are of no use to them.

> There is a race of gods, I've always held;
> They live in heaven, and never give a thought
> To human actions. (ENNIUS.)

[1] No doubt a misprint, overlooked in subsequent editions, for Air.

Now trust to your Philosophy; boast that you have found the bean in the cake,[1] after hearing this racket from so many philosophical brains!

The confusion we see in the ways of the world has had this good effect upon me, that the difference between my conduct of life and ideas and those of the world is to me instructive rather than displeasing. The comparison humbles me instead of raising my pride; and every other choice but that which comes directly from the hand of God seems to me of little advantage. I leave aside those who lead outrageous and unnatural lives. The governments of the world are no less contradictory in this respect than the schools; whence we may learn that Fortune herself is not more variable and fickle than our reason, nor more blind and unthinking.

The things we are most ignorant of are fittest to be deified; wherefore, to make gods of men, as the ancients did, is the height of imbecility. I would much rather have followed those who worshipped the serpent, the dog and the ox; seeing that their nature and being are less known to us, and we can more easily imagine what we please of those creatures, and so ascribe to them extraordinary powers. But to make gods of men of our own condition, whose imperfections we should know, to attribute to them desire, anger, vengeance, marriages, generation and kinships, love and jealousy, our limbs and bones, our fevers and pleasures, our deaths and burials, that must needs proceed from a marvellous intoxication of the human understanding:

> These are so far removed
> From any touch of deity, and seem
> So far unworthy of numbering with the Gods. (LUCRETIUS.)

Their shapes, ages, clothing, ornaments, are known; their descents, marriages, kinships, all translated into a likeness to human weakness. For they are also represented with troubled minds; and we hear of the lusts, maladies and angers of the Gods (Cicero).

The same may be said of the attribution of divinity, not only to Faith, Virtue, Honour, Concord, Freedom, Victory, Piety, but also to Voluptuousness, Fraud, Death, Envy,

---

[1] In the Twelfth Night cake; the person who found the bean became King of the Bean.

Old Age, Misery, to Fear, to the Ague, and to Bad Fortune, and other infirmities of our frail and decrepit lives:

> Why desecrate the temples with vicious words and deeds,
> O souls bound down to earth and void of thoughts divine!
> (PERSIUS.)

The Egyptians, with prudence unashamed, forbade any man, on pain of the halter, to say that their gods Serapis and Isis had once been men; and no one was ignorant that they had been. And their statues, representing them with their finger on their lips, signified to their priests, says Varro, the mysterious command to hush up their mortal origin, which, as a necessary consequence, would nullify the veneration paid to them.

Since man was so desirous to make himself the equal of God, he would have done better, says Cicero, to bring down to earth and to himself those divine attributes, than to send up aloft his own corrupt and miserable condition; but, to look at it rightly, he has in several ways done both, with the same vain conceit.

When the philosophers dissect the hierarchy of their gods, and are so eager to distinguish their alliances, their functions and their power, I cannot believe that they speak seriously. When Plato describes Pluto's orchard, and the pleasures or bodily torments that still await us after the destruction and annihilation of our bodies, and adapts them to the senses and feelings we possess in this life,

> In myrtle groves and alleys hide their woes,
> Nor death itself relieves them of their cares; (VIRGIL.)

when Mahomet promises his followers a paradise all tapestried, bedecked with gold and precious stones, peopled with damsels of surpassing beauty, stored with choice wines and viands, I see very clearly that they are deceivers who pander to our stupidity, in order to sugar the pill for us, and allure us by these hopes and ideas adapted to our mortal appetites.

And yet there are some of our own persuasion who are fallen into the like error, promising themselves after the resurrection a terrestrial and temporal life, accompanied with all sorts of worldly pleasures and comforts.

Can we believe that Plato, the man who had such heavenly thoughts and was so much in touch with the divinity, that the surname of Divine still clings to him, should have thought that man, poor creature, had in him anything comparable to that incomprehensible power; and that he believed that our feeble grip was capable, or our senses strong and robust enough, to participate in the eternal beatitudes or torments? We should say to him, in the name of human reason, 'If the pleasures you promise us in the next life are of the kind I have felt here below, that life has nothing in common with infinity.

'Though all my five natural senses are loaded up with joy and gladness, and this soul were possessed with all the contentments it could desire and hope for, we know what it is capable of; it would still be nothing.

'If there be anything of mine in it, there can be nothing divine.

'If it be nothing other than that which appertains to this our present condition, it cannot be taken into account; every contentment of mortals is mortal.

'If the recognition of our parents, our children and our friends, can move us and gratify us in the next world, if we still care for that kind of pleasure, we are still in earthly and finite conditions.

'We cannot adequately conceive the grandeur of those sublime and divine promises, even if we can conceive them at all; to imagine them at their true worth, we must imagine them unimaginable, inexpressible and incomprehensible, and absolutely different from anything in our miserable experience. "Eye cannot see, says Saint Paul, nor can it enter into the heart of man, the happiness that God prepares for his children."[1]

'And if, to render us capable of it, our being is reformed and our essence changed (as thou sayest, Plato, by thy purifications), it must be so extreme and universal a change, that, according to the teaching of Physics, it will be no more ourselves;

> Hector he was whilst he in battle strove,
> But dragged by Achilles' steeds, no Hector he. (OVID.)

'It will be something else that receives those rewards:

[1] Things which eye saw not, and ear heard not,
And which entered not into the heart of man,
Whatsoever things God prepared for them that love him.
(1 Corinthians ii. 9, Revised Version.)

> For what is changed is so dissolved,
> It dies; the parts are shifted from their place,
> And lose their order. (LUCRETIUS.)

'For, in the Pythagorean Metempsychosis, the change of habitation that he imagines for our souls, do we think that the lion that contains the soul of Caesar espouses the passions that moved Caesar, or that the lion is he? If it were still he, they would be right who, controverting this theory against Plato, point out to him that a son might find himself riding on his mother invested in the body of a she-mule; and the like absurdities.

'And do we think that, in the transmigrations that take place from the bodies of animals to others of the same kind, the newcomers are not other than their predecessors? From the ashes of a phoenix, they say, is bred a worm, and then another phoenix; who can imagine that the second phoenix is not other than the first? The worms that make our silk are seen to die as it were and dry up, and from this same body is produced a butterfly, and from that another worm, which it would be ridiculous to regard as being still the first. What has once ceased to be, is no more:

> And, even if time collected after death
> The matter of our frames and set it all
> Again in place as now, and if again
> To us the light of life were given, O yet,
> That process too would not concern us aught,
> When once the self-succession of our sense
> Had been asunder broken. (LUCRETIUS.)

'And when thou sayest, Plato, in another place, that it is the spiritual part of man that will enjoy the rewards of the next life, thou tellest us of a thing of as small likelihood:

> An eye, from out its socket torn, apart
> From all the body, can nothing more discern,
> So soul and mind, it seems, are nothing able,
> When by themselves. (LUCRETIUS.)

For, by this reckoning, it will be no longer man, nor consequently us, whom this enjoyment will concern; for we are built up of two principal and essential parts, the separation of which is the death and destruction of our being:

> For there hath been
> An interposèd pause of life, and wide
> Have all the motions wandered everywhere
> From these our senses. (LUCRETIUS.)

'We do not say that man suffers when the worms nibble at his limbs, whereby he lived, and when the earth consumes them :

> Yet nothing 'tis to us who in the bonds
> And wedlock of the soul and body live,
> Through which we're fashioned to a single state. (LUCRETIUS.)

'Moreover, what grounds of justice can the gods have for noticing and rewarding the good and virtuous actions of a man, after his death, when it is they themselves who led him to do them, and so brought them about ? And why are they offended with him, why do they avenge upon him his wicked actions, when they themselves have created him in that faulty condition, and when with a single twinkling of their will they can prevent him from erring ? '

Might not Epicurus raise those objections against Plato, with great show of human reason, were it not that he often shelters behind this saying, 'That it is impossible to infer anything certain of immortal nature, from mortal nature.'

Reason ever goes astray in all matters, but especially when she meddles with divine things. Who is more evidently conscious of this than we ? For, although we have given her certain and infallible principles, although we illumine her steps with the sacred lamp of Truth which it has pleased God to communicate to us, we daily see, nevertheless, how, if she stray ever so little from the ordinary path, if she turn aside and wander out of the way marked and trodden by the Church, she immediately loses her way, becomes embarrassed and entangled, whirling around and floating, aimless and unchecked, in that vast, turbulent and undulating sea of human opinions. As soon as she leaves that common high-road she becomes divided, and strays into a thousand different paths.

Man cannot be anything but what he is, nor imagine anything beyond the reach of his capacity. It is a greater presumption, says Plutarch, in a man who is but a man, to take upon himself to speak and discourse about the gods and demigods, than it is in a man who knows nothing of music to criticize a singer, or in a man who was never in a camp to begin to dispute about arms and war, presuming, on the strength of a hazy conjecture, to understand the resources of an art that is beyond his ken.

I believe the ancients thought they were doing the divine greatness a good turn when they gave it the likeness of man, investing it with his faculties, endowing it with his fine whims and his most shameful needs, offering it a share of our viands to eat, our dances, mummeries and farces to amuse it, our garments to cover it, and houses to live in; gratifying it with the odour of incense and the notes of music, with festoons and nosegays, and, in order to make it an accomplice in our vicious passions, giving to its inhuman vengeance the flattering name of justice, delighting it with the destruction and dispersion of things it has created and preserved (like Tiberius Sempronius who, as a sacrifice to Vulcan, burned the rich spoils and arms he had won from the enemy in Sardinia; and Paulus Emilius, who sacrificed those of Macedonia to Mars and Minerva; and Alexander who, on reaching the Indian Ocean, cast into the sea, to propitiate Thetis, many great vessels of gold); besides glutting its altars with a butchery, not only of harmless beasts, but also of human beings, which with many nations, including our own, was an ordinary practice. And I believe there is no people that is free from the charge.

> Eight youths alive he seizes for the pyre,
> Four, sons of Sulmo, four whom Ufens bred,
> Poor victims, doomed to feed the funeral fire,
> And pour their blood in quittance for the dead. (VIRGIL.)

The Getae think themselves to be immortal, and their dying is nothing but a journey to their God Zamolxis. Once in every five years they dispatch one of their number to request necessary things of him. This deputy is chosen by lot. And the manner of dispatching him is this: after informing him by word of mouth of his charge, three of the assistants each hold a javelin upright, on which the others hurl him with all their might. If he is impaled in a vital part and dies at once, it is a certain sign of the divine favour; if he escapes he is accounted wicked and execrable, and they depute another in the same manner.

Amestris, the mother of Xerxes, in her old age had on one occasion fourteen youths of the best families in Persia buried alive, in accordance with the religion of the country, to gratify some god of the underworld.

To this day the idols of Themistitan are cemented with the blood of little children ; no sacrifice satisfies them but that of such pure and childish souls : a justice famishing for the blood of innocence !

> Such are the crimes to which religion leads ! (LUCRETIUS.)

The Carthaginians immolated their own children to Saturn ; and they who had none, bought them, the father and mother being the while obliged to assist at the ceremony with cheerful and pleasant countenance.

It was a strange fancy to think that we purchase the divine goodness with our affliction, like the Lacedemonians, who wheedled their Diana with the torture of young boys, who were scourged for her sake, often to death. It was truly a savage notion, to think to gratify the architect with the subversion of his building, and to compound the penalty due to the guilty by the punishment of the guiltless ; and to imagine that poor Iphigenia, at the harbour of Aulis, could by her death and immolation acquit, in the eyes of God, the Greek army of the crimes they had committed :

> A sinless maiden, sinfully foredone,
> A parent felled her on her bridal day,
> Making his child a sacrificial beast. (LUCRETIUS.)

And those two noble and generous souls, the two Decii, father and son, in order to incline the favour of the gods to be propitious to the affairs of Rome, were forced to go and plunge headlong into the thick of the enemy. *How great was the iniquity of the Gods, that they could not be reconciled to the Roman people, unless such men perished !* (Cicero.)

To which may be added that it is not the part of the criminal to have himself scourged how and when it pleases him ; it belongs to the judge, who accounts nothing as chastisement but the penalty he orders, and cannot regard that as a punishment which is agreeable to the man who suffers it. The divine vengeance presupposes in us an absolute dissent, for its justice and our punishment.

And it was a ridiculous notion of Polycrates, the Tyrant of Samos, who, to break the spell of his continuous good fortune and counteract it, threw into the sea the dearest and most precious jewel he possessed, imagining that by this purposed mishap he was satisfying the fickleness and instability of Fortune. And she, to deride his folly, caused the very same jewel to be returned upon his hands, having been found in a fish's belly.

And then, what is the use of the mutilations and dismemberings of the Corybantes, of the Maenads, and in our own time of the Mohammedans, who slash their faces, their stomach and their members, to please their prophet; seeing that the offence lies in the will, not in the breast, the eyes, the genitals, the shoulders, the throat, and the healthy state of the body? *So great is the fury of a perturbed mind when thrown off its balance, that the Gods are placated in such a way that men could not be more savage!* (Saint Augustine).

The proper treatment of the natural structure of our bodies concerns not only ourselves, but also the service of God and other men; to wound it wilfully is wrong, as it is to kill ourselves under any pretext whatsoever. It seems a great treachery and cowardice to mar and ill-treat the senseless and servile functions of the body, in order to spare the soul the trouble of directing them according to reason. *Wherein do they fear the anger of the Gods, who think to purchase their favour by this means? . . . Some indeed have been castrated to serve the lust of kings; but no man has ever, at the Lord's command, unmanned himself by his own hand* (Saint Augustine).

Thus did they satisfy their religion with many wicked deeds:

> It is that same religion oftener far
> Hath bred the foul impieties of men. (LUCRETIUS.)

Now nothing that is ours can in any way whatever be matched or compared with the divine nature, without branding and tarnishing it with so much imperfection. How can that infinite beauty, power, and goodness, admit of any relation or likeness to a thing so abject as we are, without absolutely damaging and diminishing its divine greatness? *The weakness of God is stronger than men; the foolishness of God is wiser than men* (Saint Paul).

Stilpo the philosopher, being asked whether the gods were gladdened by our homage and sacrifices, replied, 'You are indiscreet; let us go aside if you wish to discuss that matter.'

And yet we prescribe bounds to God, we lay continual

siege to his power with our reasons (I call reason our dreams and fancies, with the dispensation of Philosophy, which says, 'The fool even and the wicked lose their wits by reason; but it is a particular kind of reason'); we would make him subservient to the vain and feeble conjectures of our understanding, him who has made both us and our knowledge.

Because nothing is made of nothing, God could not have built the world without material! What! has God given into our hands the keys and the most secret springs of his power; has he bound himself not to overstep the limits of our knowledge? Put the case, O man, that thou hast been able to observe here some traces of his deeds; dost thou think that he has used all his power, that he has put all his thoughts and ideas into that work? Thou seest only the order and disposition of this little dungeon in which thou art lodged—if thou dost indeed see it. His divinity has an infinite jurisdiction beyond; this fragment is nothing in comparison with the whole:

> All these, with sky and land to boot,
> Are all as nothing to the sum entire
> Of the all-Sum. (LUCRETIUS.)

It is a municipal by-law thou art adducing; thou knowest not what the universal law is. Apply thyself to what thou art subject to, but not him; he is not thy colleague, nor thy fellow-citizen, nor thy mate. If he has in some sort communicated himself to thee, it is not done in order to stoop to thy littleness, nor to give thee the right to criticize his power.

This is for thy consideration: the human body cannot soar up into the clouds; the sun runs its ordinary course without a rest; the bounds of the seas and the earth cannot be confounded; water is unstable and without solidity; a wall without a fracture is impenetrable to a solid body; man cannot keep alive in the flames; he cannot be in the body both in heaven and on earth, and in a thousand places at the same time. It is for thee that he has made these rules; it is thee that they bind. To Christians he has proved that he has overstepped them all, whenever it has pleased him. Why, indeed, omnipotent as he is, should he have restricted his powers within a certain measure? In whose favour do you suppose he has renounced his privilege?

Of nothing can thy reason convince thee with better grounds and more likelihood than of the plurality of worlds:

> Wherefore we must confess on grounds the same
> That earth, sun, moon, and ocean, and all else,
> Exist not sole and single—rather in number
> Exceeding number. (LUCRETIUS.)

The most famous minds of past ages have believed in it, as well as some of our own time, compelled by the evidence of human reason; inasmuch as in this fabric that we see there is nothing single and one:

> Hence too it happens in the sum there is
> No one thing single of its kind in birth,
> And single and sole in growth; (LUCRETIUS.)

and all species are multiplied into some number. Wherefore it seems unlikely that God should have created this work alone without a fellow, and that the matter of this form should have been exhausted upon this single individual:

> Again and again we must confess there are
> Such congregations of matter otherwhere,
> Like this one world which vasty ether holds
> In huge embrace; (LUCRETIUS.)

especially if it be something with life, which its motions make so credible that Plato is assured of it, and many moderns either confirm his belief or do not venture to deny it, any more than they do that ancient belief, that the heavens, the stars and the other parts of the universe, are creatures made up of body and soul, mortal in respect of their composition, but immortal by the decree of the Creator.

Now if there be many worlds, as Democritus, Epicurus and almost all the philosophers have believed, how do we know if the principles and laws of this one in like manner apply to the others? They have perhaps a different appearance and a different constitution. Epicurus imagines them either like or unlike.

In this world we see endless differences and variations, due merely to distance in place. In those new regions of the world discovered by our fathers neither corn nor wine are to be seen, nor any of our animals; there all is different.

And in the past ages consider in how many parts of the world they had no acquaintance with either Bacchus or Ceres. If[1] we are to believe Pliny and Herodotus, there are, in certain regions, species of men who have very little resemblance to our kind.

And there are hybrid and ambiguous forms between the human and brute nature. There are countries where men are born without heads, with their mouth and eyes in their breast. Where all are androgynous. Where they walk on all fours. Where they have only one eye in the forehead, and a head more like a dog's than a man's. Where they are half fish below, and live in the water. Where the women are brought to bed at five years of age, and live but eight. Where their head and the skin of the forehead are so hard, that a sword can make no impression, but loses its edge. Where the men are beardless. There are nations that know not the use of fire; others where they eject a black semen.

What of those who naturally change into wolves or mares, and then into men again? And if it is as Plutarch says, that in a certain region of the Indies there are men without mouths, who feed on the smell of certain odours, how many of our descriptions are wrong! Man would no more be able to laugh, nor perhaps capable of reason or fellowship. The disposition and the cause of our internal structure would be, for the most part, meaningless.

Besides, how many things there are within our knowledge that impugn those fine rules that we have cut out for and prescribed to Nature! And shall we attempt to bind even God to them? How many things there are that we call miraculous and contrary to Nature! For that is done by every man and every nation according to the measure of their ignorance. How many occult properties and quintessences do we not discover! For, to 'go according to Nature' means with us to 'go according to our intelligence', as far as it is able to follow, and as far as we can see. What is beyond is most unnatural and irregular.

Now, by this reckoning, to the wisest and most circum-

---

[1] Observe the conditional 'If'; we must not suppose that Montaigne believed in these travellers' tales, any more than Shakespeare believed in his

> Anthropophagi, and men whose heads
> Do grow beneath their shoulders.

spect everything will be most unnatural. For human reason has convinced them that she has no ground and no foothold whatever, not even enough to assure them that snow is white (and Anaxagoras declared it to be black) ; whether there be anything or nothing ; whether there be knowledge or ignorance (which Metrodorus of Chios denied that man was able to determine) ; or whether we live, of which Euripides is in doubt :

> Who knows but life is that which we call death,
> And death the thing that we call life ?

And not without a semblance of reason. For why do we call that ' existence ', that instant which is but a flash in the infinite course of an eternal night, and so brief an interruption of our perpetual and natural condition ; death occupying all that is before and all that is behind that moment, and a good part besides of that moment ?

Others, as the followers of Melissus, swear that there is no motion, that nothing stirs (for, if there be but one, neither can spherical motion serve it, nor motion from one place to another, as Plato proves) ; that there is neither generation nor corruption in Nature.

Protagoras says, That there is nothing in Nature but doubt ; That we may equally dispute all things, and even this, whether we may equally dispute all things ;

Nausiphanes, That of the things that seem, nothing is more than it is not ; That there is nothing certain but uncertainty ;

Parmenides, That of that which seems there is no one thing in general ; That there is but One ;

Zeno, That even One is not, and that there is Nothing. If One were, it would be either in another, or in itself ; if it be in another, then there are two ; if it be in itself, there are still two, the comprising and the comprised.

According to these dogmas, the nature of things is but a false and empty shadow.

It has always seemed to me that it is altogether unwise and irreverent in a Christian to say this sort of thing : ' God cannot die ; God cannot go back from his word ; God cannot do this, God cannot do that.' I cannot approve of the divine power being thus confined by the laws of our speech. And even if these propositions appear reasonable, they should be expressed more reverently and devoutly.

Our speech has its defects and shortcomings, like all other things. Most of the grounds of the world's troubles are matters of Grammar. Our lawsuits arise only out of disputes as to the interpretation of the laws, and most wars from the inability to express in clear terms the conventions and treaties of agreement among rulers. How many quarrels, and how momentous, have not been caused in this world by doubt as to the meaning of that syllable HOC![1]

Let us take the plainest sentence that even Logic can offer us. If you say, 'It is fine,' and what you say is true, then the weather is fine. Is not that a very certain way of speaking? And yet it will deceive us. That that is so, let us continue the example. If you say, 'I lie,' and what you say is true, then you do lie. The art, the reason, the force of the conclusion of this latter are like the other; yet behold us stuck in the mire!

I can see that the Pyrrhonian philosophers are unable to express their general conception in any kind of speech; for they would need a new language. Ours is all made up of affirmative propositions, which are entirely hostile to them; so that when they say 'I doubt,' we immediately seize them by the throat and make them admit that they at least know and are assured of this, that they doubt. So they have been constrained to save their faces by this medical comparison, without which their habit of thought[2] would be inexplicable: when they declare, 'I know not,' or, 'I doubt,' they say this proposition carries itself off with the rest, no more nor less than rhubarb, which drives out evil humours and carries itself off with them.

This idea is more surely understood by interrogation: WHAT DO I KNOW?[3] which I bear as my motto with the emblem of a pair of scales.

See how the people revel in that most irreverent way of speaking! In our present religious disputes, if you drive your opponents too hard, they will say quite unashamedly

---

[1] In the Eucharist, *Hoc est corpus meum*, &c., 'this is my body', &c. The reference is of course to the different interpretations put upon these words by the Catholics and Protestants.

[2] Literally 'humour'.

[3] The famous 'Que sçay-je?' which is generally supposed to sum up Montaigne's philosophy.

that 'it is not in the power of God to make his body to be in Paradise and on earth and in several places at the same time'. And that ancient scoffer,[1] how he takes advantage of it! 'It is at least, he says, no little consolation to man to see that God cannot do everything; for he cannot kill himself, though he might wish to do so, which is the greatest privilege we possess in our human state; he cannot make mortals immortal, nor make the dead to come to life again, nor him that has lived not to have lived, nor him who has had honours not to have had them; having no other power over the past but that of oblivion. And, that this association of man and God may be coupled with some absurd examples, he cannot make twice ten not to be twenty.'

That is what he says, and what a Christian should take heed not to allow his lips to utter. Whilst, on the contrary, men seem to study this foolish arrogance of speech, to bring God down to their stature:

> Let Jove to-morrow, if he will,
> With blackest clouds the welkin fill,
>   Or flood it all with sunlight pure;
> Yet from the past he cannot take
>   Its influence, for that is sure;
> Nor can he mar or bootless make
>   Whate'er of rapture and delight
> The hours have borne us in their flight. (HORACE.)

When we say, That the numberless centuries, both past and to come, are to God but an instant; That his goodness, wisdom, power, are one with his essence: our tongue speaks it, but our intelligence does not apprehend it. And yet our overweening conceit would make the Deity pass through our sieve. Whence are bred all the delusions and errors with which the world is possessed, when we reduce and weigh in our scales a thing so far above our measure.[2] *It is wonderful to what lengths the wickedness of the human heart will go, when encouraged by the smallest success* (Pliny).

How arrogantly the Stoics reprehend Epicurus when he maintains that a truly good and happy existence belongs

---

[1] Pliny the Elder; the name is given in the earliest editions.

[2] Here and elsewhere Montaigne flatly contradicts the author he translated, and is supposed to be defending. 'Man, says Sebond, is by his nature, and in so far as he is man, the true and living image of God. As the seal impresses its form on wax, so does God impress his likeness on man.'

to God alone, and that the wise man has but a shadow and semblance of it! How airily they bind God to Destiny (let no man that calls himself a Christian do it again with my consent!), and Thales, Plato, and Pythagoras make him a slave to Necessity!

This arrogance of thinking to discover God with our eyes made a great man of our religion [1] give the Deity a bodily shape. And it is the cause of our making God responsible (a thing we do every day) for events of importance, by a special dispensation. Because they weigh with us it would seem that they also weigh with him, and that he pays more undivided attention to them than to events which are of less moment to us, or of ordinary occurrence. *The Gods concern themselves with great matters, and neglect the small* (Cicero). Listen to his example, it will make his reason clear to you: *For Kings in their rule pay no attention to all minor matters* (Cicero).

As if it were a greater or smaller matter to him to stir an empire or the leaf of a tree; and as if he exercised his providence otherwise in deciding the issue of a battle, than the direction of a flea's jump! His guiding hand lends itself to all things, with the same continuity, with the same power and order; our interest does nothing towards it; our movements and measures do not touch him. *God, so great an artificer in great things, is no less so in small* (Saint Augustine).

In our arrogance we are continually putting forward that blasphemous pairing.

Because our occupations are a burden to us, Strato endowed the gods with complete immunity from duties, like their priests. He makes Nature produce and maintain all things, and with her weights and motions constructs the parts of the world; and he relieves human nature of the fear of divine judgements. *That which is blessed and eternal has neither any business itself, nor gives any to another* (Cicero).

Nature wills that in things that are like there be a like relation. Therefore from the infinite number of mortals we may conclude a like number of immortals. The numberless

---

[1] Tertullian, a great theologian of the Western Church, born about A.D. 160 at Carthage. He said, 'Who denies that God is a body, even though he be a spirit?'

things that kill and destroy presuppose as many that preserve and benefit. As the souls of the gods, without tongue, without eyes, without ears, have each in themselves a feeling of what the other feels, and judge our thoughts, so the souls of men, when they are free and severed from the body in sleep or in some ecstatic trance, divine, foretell and see things which they could not see when united to the body.

'Men, says Saint Paul, professing themselves to be wise, become fools; and have changed the glory of the incorruptible God into an image made like to corruptible man.'

Only observe the jugglery of a deification among the ancients. After the grand and stately pomp of the funeral, as the fire began to mount to the top of the pyramid and catch the litter of the defunct, they at the same time let loose an eagle, which, soaring upward, signified that the soul was rising to Paradise. We have a thousand coins, and particularly of that virtuous woman of a Faustina,[1] on which this eagle is represented carrying those deified souls pickaback to heaven. It is a pity that we should fool ourselves with our own fictions and tomfooleries:

Of their own bugaboos they stand in fear and dread; (LUCAN.)

like children who are frightened at the face of their playfellow which they have themselves blacked and besmeared. *As if anything could be more unhappy than man who is dominated by his own figments!*

It is a far cry from honouring him who has made us to honouring him whom we have made. Augustus had more temples than Jupiter, which were served with as much devotion and belief in miracles. The Thasians, in requital of the benefits they had received of Agesilaus, came to tell him that they had canonized him. 'Has your nation, he said to them, this power to make gods of whom they please? Make a god of one of yourselves, as an experiment; then, when I see how he has benefited by it, I will say gramercy to your offer.'

Man is indeed out of his wits! He cannot create a mite, and he creates gods by the dozen!

---

[1] Irony! The whole world knew, except the outraged husband himself, of the shameless debaucheries of this consort of Marcus Aurelius.

Listen to Trismegistus,[1] in praise of our excellence: 'Of all wonderful things, this has surpassed wonder, that man has been able to find out the divine nature and to make it.'

Here are some arguments of the school of philosophy itself,

> To whom alone 'tis given the Gods to know,
> Alone to know that they can ne'er be known: (LUCAN.)

'If God is, he is animal; if he is animal, he has sense and feeling; if he has feeling, he is liable to corruption. If he be without body, he is without soul, and consequently without action; and if he have body, he is perishable. Is that not a triumph?

'We are incapable of having made the world; there is then some more surpassing Nature that has set its hand to it.

'It were a piece of foolish arrogance to esteem ourselves the most perfect thing in this universe: there is then something better; that is God. When you see a rich and stately mansion, though you know not who is the owner of it, yet you will not say that it was built for rats. And that divine edifice of the heavenly palace that we behold, must we not believe that it is the dwelling of some owner who is much greater than we are?

'Is not the highest always the most worthy? And we are placed on the lowest rung.

'Nothing that is without soul and without reason is able to produce a living creature capable of reason: the world produces us; therefore the world has a soul and reason.

'Each part of us is less than we: we are part of the world; the world is therefore equipped with wisdom and reason, and more abundantly than we are.

'It is a fine thing to have a great government; the government of the world is therefore in the hands of some happy nature.

'The stars do us no harm; they are therefore full of goodness.

'We have need of food; so then have the gods, and they feed on the fumes rising from here below.

---

[1] Hermes Trismegistus (Thrice-greatest Hermes), the Greek name of the Egyptian God Thoth; whence the Hermetic Books, the sacred canon of the later Egyptians.

'Worldly goods are not goods to God; therefore they are not goods to us.

'To offend and to be offended are equally evidence of imbecility: it is therefore madness to fear God.

'God is good by his nature; man by his endeavour, which is more.

'The divine wisdom and human wisdom have no other distinction except that the former is eternal. Now duration is no accession to wisdom; wherefore we are fellows.

'We have life, reason, and liberty, and we esteem goodness, charity, and justice; these qualities are therefore in him.'[1]

To sum up, the building and the unbuilding,[2] the conditions of the Deity, are the work of man, according as they bear relation to himself. What a pattern! What a model! Let us stretch, let us exalt and magnify our human qualities as much as we please; blow thyself out, poor man, and again, and again, and again,

> Blow till thou burst, ma'am, frogling cries,
> You'll ne'er be match for him in size. (HORACE.)

Of a truth, it is not God (whom they cannot conceive, conceiving themselves in his place), it is not God they compare, but themselves, not with him, but with themselves (Saint Augustine).

In things of Nature we can only half infer the causes from the effects. What of this cause? It is above the order of Nature; its condition is too elevated, too remote, too supreme, to suffer itself to be tied and bound by our conclusions. It is not through ourselves that we reach them; that way lies too low. We are no nearer heaven at the top of Mont Cenis than at the bottom of the sea; consult your astrolabe to prove it.

They degrade God even to having carnal knowledge of women, noting how many times, how many procreations. Paulina, wife of Saturninus, a highly reputed Roman matron, thinking she was lying with the god Serapis, found herself in the arms of a lover of hers, the priests of his temple being the go-betweens.

---

[1] The above arguments are taken from Cicero, *Of the Nature of the Gods.*
[2] i.e. Theism and Atheism, all these arguments for and against a Deity.

Varro, the most refined and most learned of Latin authors, writes in his books on Theology, that the sacristan of Hercules, casting lots for himself with one hand and with the other for Hercules, staked a supper and a girl against him: if he won, at the expense of the offerings; if he lost, at his own. He lost, and paid for his supper and his girl, whose name was Laurentina. During the night she saw that god in her arms, who told her into the bargain that the first man she should meet on the next day would pay her a heavenly reward. That was Taruntius, a rich young man,[1] who took her to his house, and in course of time left her his heiress. She, in her turn, hoping to do a thing acceptable to the god, made the Roman people her heirs. Wherefore she was granted divine honours.

As if it were not enough for Plato to be originally descended from the gods, both on his father's and his mother's side, and to have Neptune for the common progenitor of his race, it was held for certain at Athens that Aristo, wishing to enjoy the fair Perictione, was unable to do so; and that he was warned by the god Apollo in a dream to leave her intact and unpolluted until she had been brought to bed. They were the father and mother of Plato.

How many such cuckoldries there are in history, procured by the gods against poor humans! And how many husbands outrageously disgraced for the benefit of the children!

In the religion of Mahomet, through the credulity of the people, there are plenty of Merlins, to wit, children without fathers, spiritual, divinely born in the womb of virgins, and bearing a name that signifies as much in their language.[2]

It must be noted that to every creature nothing is dearer and of more account than its own existence (the lion, the eagle, the dolphin, prize nothing above their kind); and each measures the qualities of all other things by its own qualities. Which we may indeed extend or contract, but that is all; for beyond this comparison and this principle our imagination cannot go. It can divine nothing other, nor is it possible for it to escape and pass beyond it. Whence

---

[1] According to Plutarch, he was a man 'far advanced in years'.

[2] If we take the author's previous hint, and read between the lines, these remarks, and those which follow concerning the plurality of gods, &c., might give many grounds for surmise as to Montaigne's beliefs.

arise these time-honoured reasonings : ' Of all shapes the most beautiful is that of man : wherefore God is of that shape. No man can be happy without virtue, nor can virtue exist without reason ; and no reason can dwell elsewhere but in a human form : God is therefore clothed in human form.' *Our minds are so informed and prejudiced, that when a man thinks of God, the human shape at once occurs to his imagination* (Cicero).

Therefore it was that Xenophanes wittily remarked, that if the animals create any gods for themselves, as it is likely they do, they will certainly frame them in their own image, and glorify themselves as we do. For why should not a gosling say thus : 'All things in the world concentrate upon me ; the earth serves me to walk upon, the sun to give me light, the stars to communicate to me their influence ; the winds benefit me in this way, the waters in that. There is nothing the vault of heaven looks upon so favourably as myself. I am the darling of Nature. Does not man keep me, house me, and wait upon me ? For me he sows and grinds. If he eats me, so he does his fellow-man ; and so do I the worms that kill and eat him.' A crane might say the same, and in more magnificent language, by reason of its free flight, and the possession of that lofty and beautiful region. *So flattering and wheedling is Nature to herself* (Cicero).[1]

Well then, by the same train of reasoning, for us are the Destinies, for us is the world ; it shines, it thunders for us ; and the Creator and the created are all for us. We are the end and aim at which the universality of things is directed. Examine the record that Philosophy has kept for two thousand years and more, of celestial affairs. The gods have acted, have spoken only for man ; according to the philosophers we occupy all their thoughts and time.

Here we see them taking part against us in war :

> Nor the earth-born brood Titanic,
> Whom the death-dealing hand of Alcides crushed,
> Though they smote the Saturnian walls with panic. (HORACE.)

[1] Montaigne here really satirizes Sebond, who says : 'The heaven says to thee (man), I give thee light by day, that thou mayest wake ; darkness by night, that thou mayest sleep in peace ; for thy convenience I renew the seasons, and give thee the blooming sweetness of spring, the heat of summer, the fertility of autumn, the cold of winter, &c.'

Here they side with us in our troubles, to repay us in kind for having so often sided with them in theirs:

> Neptune with his vast trident shakes the walls,
> And heaves the deep foundations, from her bed
> O'ertopping all the city. Juno here
> Storms at the entrance of the Scaean gates. (VIRGIL.)

The Caunians, zealous for the supremacy of their own gods, load their backs with arms on the day dedicated to them, scour the outskirts of their city, beating the air on all sides with their swords, thus pursuing to the death and banishing from their territory all strange gods.

The powers of the gods are limited according to our needs. This one cures horses, that one cures men; this the plague, that the scurvy, another the cough; one again cures one sort of itch, another another. *Thus does a corrupt religion drag the gods into the smallest matters* (LIVY). One makes the grapes to grow, another the garlick; this one patronizes lechery, that one trade. Every class of artisan has his god. This one has his province and credit in the East, that in the West:

> Here were shown her arms, and here her chariot. (VIRGIL.)

> Sacred Phœbus, who holdest earth's fixed navel.[1] (CICERO.)

> Pallas by sons of Cecrops is adored,
> Minoan Crete reveres chaste Artemis;
> Lemnos the limping spouse of fair Cythera.
> Mycene and Sparta to Juno's altars bow;
> The Arcadian shepherds worship pine-crowned Pan,
> And Mars is God of mighty Rome. (OVID.)

This one has but one borough and one family under his dominion; this one lives alone, that one in company, either voluntarily or of necessity:

> To grandsire's temples are a grandson's joined. (OVID.)

Some are so mean and common (for their number amounts to thirty-six thousand), that full five or six of them have to be crowded together to produce an ear of corn, and they take therefrom their several names. It takes three to make a door, one for the planks, one for the hinge, and one for the threshold; four to make a child, patrons of his baby-

---

[1] Delphi, where was a celebrated temple of Apollo, was regarded by the Greeks as the navel or centre of the earth.

clothes, his drinking, his eating, and his sucking. Some are certain, others uncertain and doubtful; some are not yet in Paradise:

> For since of Heaven they're not yet worthy deemed,
> We grant them lands of ours to dwell upon. (OVID.)

Among them we find physicians, poets, politicians. Some are by nature half-divine, half-human, mediators and brokers between us and God; worshipped with a sort of secondary and diminutive worship. Infinite in titles and offices, some are good, others bad. Some there are who are old and decrepit, and some are mortal. For Chrysippus was of opinion that in the last conflagration of the world all the gods would come to an end except Jupiter.

Man imagines a thousand absurd fellowships between God and himself. Is he not his fellow-countryman?

> The isle of famed Crete,
> For Jove a cradle meet. (OVID.)

This is the excuse we get, after consideration of the matter, from Scaevola, a Pontifex Maximus, and Varro, a great theologian, in their day: 'That it is needful that the people be ignorant of many things that are true, and believe many that are untrue.' *When he seeks the truth whereby he may be free, let it be thought to his interest that he be deceived* (Saint Augustine).

Human eyes cannot perceive things but in the shape they know them by. And we forget what a fall the wretched Phaeton suffered, when he attempted to guide the reins of his father's steeds with a mortal hand. Our mind has a fall as deep, and is in the same way shattered and bruised through its own foolhardiness.

If you inquire of Philosophy of what material are the sky and the sun, what will she reply but of iron, or, with Anaxagoras, of stone, or such material as we are familiar with? Ask of Zeno what Nature is, he will say, 'An artificial fire, proceeding in a regular way to generation.' Archimedes, master of that science which assumes the precedence before all others for truth and certainty, says, 'The sun is a God of red-hot iron.' Is not that a fine idea, extracted from the beauty and inevitable necessity of geometrical demonstrations? Yet not so inevitable and useful but that Socrates thought that a man knows enough geometry if he is able to measure out the land he gives or receives ; and that Polyaenus, who had been a renowned and eminent teacher of that science, conceived a contempt for those demonstrations, as being full of untruths and manifest foolishness, after he had tasted the sweet fruits of the enervating gardens of Epicurus.

Socrates, in Xenophon, with regard to that assertion of Anaxagoras, who in ancient times was esteemed above all others for his knowledge of celestial and divine matters, says that his brain became unhinged, as happens to all men who probe too deeply into those matters that are not of their province. As to his saying that the sun was a glowing stone, he did not reflect that a stone does not shine in the fire, and, what is worse, that it is consumed by it. In making the sun and fire one, he forgets that fire does not blacken those it looks upon ; that we can look straight into the fire ; that fire kills plants and herbs.

It is Socrates' opinion, and mine too, that the wisest theory about the gods is to have no theory at all.

Plato, in his *Timaeus*, having occasion to speak of the ' Daemons ', says, ' That is an undertaking that is outside our range. We must believe those ancients who said they were begotten by them. It is contrary to reason not to give credit to the children of the gods, though what they say should not be grounded upon necessary or probable reasons, seeing that they warrant us that they are speaking of domestic and familiar matters.'

Let us see if we have any clearer knowledge of human and natural things.

Is it not an absurd presumption on our part to fabricate, for those things which we confess to be beyond the reach of our learning, a different body, and of our own invention to lend them an unreal shape ; as we may see in the movements of the planets, to which, since our minds cannot reach up to them, nor imagine their natural course, we attribute our own material, clumsy, terrestrial contrivances :

> A golden beam, wheels tyred with golden rim,
> About the hub a star of silver spokes. (OVID.)

You might think that we have had charioteers, carpenters, painters, who went up aloft to set up machines with different movements, to arrange the wheelworks and interlockings of the heavenly bodies, in motley colours, around the spindle of Necessity, according to Plato:

> This world, of things the greatest home,
> By five high-thundering zones begirt,
> Which, traversed obliquely by a belt
> Of twice six constellations bright,
> Admits the chariot of the moon. (VARRO.)

Those are all vain delusions and frenzied follies. Why will not Nature one day be pleased to disclose to us her bosom, and plainly reveal to us how she contrives and directs her movements, and prepare our eyes to see them? O Heavens, what mistakes, what blunders we should discover in our poor science! I am mistaken if it has grasped the right end of any single thing, and I shall depart this life more ignorant of everything than of my own ignorance.

Have I not read in Plato this divine word, 'That Nature is nothing more than enigmatic poetry?'[1] as we might say, perhaps, a veiled and shadowy picture, with glimpses here and there of an infinite variety of false lights, to exercise our conjectures. *All those things are hidden and enveloped in so misty an obscurity, that the human mind is not acute enough to penetrate into heaven or pierce the earth* (Cicero).

And truly Philosophy is but sophisticated poetry. Whence do those ancient writers derive all their authority but from the poets? And the first of them were themselves poets, and discoursed upon it in their artistic way. Plato is but a disconnected poet. Timon calls him derisively the 'great forger of miracles'.[2]

Just as the women wear ivory teeth when their natural teeth are wanting, and in place of their true complexion contrive one from some foreign matter; as they make up their hips with cloth and felt, and their embonpoint with cotton, and, in the sight and knowledge of all men, embellish themselves with a false and borrowed beauty; so does science (and our law itself has, they say, its legal fictions, whereon is grounded the truth of its justice). She gives us

---

[1] Montaigne has mistaken Plato's meaning, which was rather, 'All poetry is by its nature enigmatic'.

[2] Apparently a mistranslation. In the Loeb edition of Diogenes Laertius the passage is rendered: 'Then there is Timon (of Phlius) who puns on his name thus: As Plato placed strange platitudes.'

as current coin and as presupposition, things that she herself tells us are imagined ; for those epicycles, eccentric and concentric, which Astrology call to its aid to conduct the movements of her stars, she gives us as the best she has been able to contrive on that subject. So too, Philosophy offers us, in all other things, not that which is, or what she believes, but what she forges, because more probable and attractive.

Plato, on the subject of the state of our body and that of the beasts, ' We should be sure that what we have said is true, if we had the confirmation of an oracle on the point ; of this only are we sure, that it is the most probable that we have been able to say.'

Not to heaven alone does she send her cords, her machines, her wheels. Let us consider a little what she says of ourselves and our framework. There is not more retrogradation, trepidation, accession, recession, conversion, in the stars and heavenly bodies than they have imagined in this poor little human body. Truly they had good reason on that account to call it the *Microcosmos*, the Little World, so many pieces and aspects have they employed to fashion and build it up. To explain the movements they see in man, the divers functions and faculties that we are conscious of in ourselves, into how many parts have they divided our soul ? In how many places have they lodged, into how many orders and stages have they divided this poor creature man, besides those which are natural and perceptible ? And into how many offices and vocations ? They make of him an imaginary republic.

He is an object to be held and handled. They are allowed full power to pull him to pieces, to assemble and rearrange him, and to stuff him out, every one according to his fancy ; and they have not yet mastered him. They cannot, I will not say in reality, but even in imagination, so order him, but that there will be discovered some cadence or some sound that will escape their architecture, prodigious as it is, and patched up with a thousand false and fantastic shreds.

And it is not in reason to excuse them. For we condone a painter if, when drawing the sky, the earth, a mountain, a remote island, he merely gives some slight indication of them, and, since we are unacquainted with the subject, we are content with something shadowy and fictitious, whatever it be. But when he depicts, after nature, a subject we know and are familiar with, we expect of him a perfect and exact representation of the outlines and colours, and we despise him if he fails.

I commend that Milesian [1] girl who, seeing the philosopher Thales continually wasting his time in contemplation of the heavenly vault, and ever gazing upward, placed something in his way to stumble over, thereby to warn him not to give his thoughts to things in the clouds, before he had seen to those at his feet. She indeed counselled him well to look to himself rather than to go star-gazing. For, as Democritus says, by the mouth of Cicero,

> No man regards the common facts of earth,
> But wastes his time in gazing at the stars.[2]

But our condition is such that the knowledge of what is close at hand is as remote from us, and as far above the clouds, as our knowledge of the stars. As Socrates says in Plato, whoever meddles with Philosophy may incur the reproach of that woman to Thales, that he sees nothing of what is in front of him. For every philosopher is ignorant of his neighbour's doings, nay, of what he is doing himself, and knows not what they both are, whether beasts or men.

Those people who think Sebond's arguments too weak, who are ignorant of nothing, who rule the world, who know everything,

> What regulates the ocean's force,
> The seasons in their yearly course;
> If free the constellations roll,
> Or moved by some supreme control;
> What makes the moon obscure her light,
> What pours her splendour on the night;
> Whence concord rises from the jar
> Of atoms that discordant are;   (HORACE.)

have they not sometimes, when absorbed in their books, sounded the difficulties that stand in the way of their knowing their own being? We see indeed that the finger moves, and that the foot moves, that some parts of us stir of themselves, without our leave, and that the others are

---

[1] Thracian, to be exact; and the story goes, according to Plato, that Thales was walking with his eyes fixed on the stars and fell into a well.

[2] Not a saying of Democritus, but a line of poetry directed by Cicero against him.

stirred by our will; that a certain apprehension gives rise to blushing, a certain other to pallor. One imagination acts only on the spleen, another upon the brain. One makes us laugh, another weep. Some other stuns and paralyses all our senses, and arrests the movement of our limbs. One object causes the stomach to rise, another a part that lies lower down.

But how a spiritual impression should so deeply penetrate so massive and solid a thing as the body, and the nature of the connexion and juncture of those wonderful springs of action, that is what man has never known. *All these things are impenetrable to human reason, and hidden in the majesty of Nature*, says Pliny; and Saint Augustine: *The manner in which spirit clings to bodies is altogether wonderful, and cannot be comprehended by man; and this is man himself.*

And yet we are never in doubt, for men's opinions are accepted in obedience to ancient beliefs, by authority and upon trust, as if they were religion and law. What is commonly held about it is an accepted jargon. This truth, with all its elaborate scaffolding of arguments and proofs, is received as if it were a firm, solid and unshakable body, never more to be doubted. On the contrary, all strive in emulation to plaster up and corroborate their accepted belief, with all the power of their reason, which is a supple tool, pliant and adaptable to any figure. Thus is the world filled with, and steeped in, nonsense and lies.

The reason why we doubt so few things is that ordinary impressions are never put to the test. We do not probe the foot of the tree, where the defect and weakness lies; we dispute only about the branches. We do not ask if such and such a thing be true, but whether it has been understood so or so. We do not ask if Galen said anything worth saying, but whether he said thus or otherwise. There was good reason, forsooth, why this curb and restraint upon the liberty of our judgement, and this tyranny over our beliefs, should be extended to the schools and the arts.

The god of scholastic knowledge is Aristotle; to question his laws is as profane as it was to question those of Lycurgus at Sparta. We accept his teaching as if it were magisterial law, when it is perhaps as wrong as any other. But I cannot see why I should not as soon accept the Ideas of Plato, or the Atoms of Epicurus, or the Plenum and Vacuum of Leucippus and Democritus, or the Water of Thales, or the Infinity of Nature of Anaximander, or the Air of Diogenes, or the Numbers and Symmetry of Pythagoras, or the Infinite of Parmenides, or the One of Musaeus, or the Water and Fire of Apollodorus, or the Similar Parts of Anaxagoras, or the Discord and Friendship of Empedocles, or the Fire of Heraclitus, or any other theory in that endless medley of beliefs and judgements that this precious human Reason, with its certainty and acumen, brings to light on all subjects that it meddles with, as I should the opinion of Aristotle on this matter of the principles of the things of Nature.

And these principles he builds up of three parts, Matter, Form, and Privation. And what can be more useless than to make emptiness the cause of the production of things? Privation is a negative; what train of thought could have led him to make it the cause and origin of the things that are? This theory however we must not presume to shake, except as an exercise in Logic. No part of it may be discussed with a view to doubt, but only to defend the founder of the school from foreign objections; his authority is the end and aim, beyond which no inquiry is to be tolerated.

It is very easy, the postulates being admitted, to build whatever we please; for if we follow the rules and authority of this commencement, the remaining parts of the structure are easily carried out, without any discordance. In this way we find that our reasons are well grounded, and we argue without any difficulty. For our masters have seized and occupied beforehand as much place in our belief as they need for subsequently drawing what conclusions they please, after the manner of the geometricians when their postulates are granted. Our consent and approval enable them to drag us to the left or to the right, and whirl us about at their pleasure. Whoever is believed on his hypotheses is our master and our god; he will plan his foundations so easily and spaciously that by them he may, if he pleases, hoist us up to the clouds.

By this practice and treatment of science we have accepted for ready money the saying of Pythagoras, 'That every expert is to be believed in his own trade.' The logician defers to the grammarian for the meaning of words; the rhetorician borrows of the logician the premises of his arguments; the poet of the musician his rhythm; the geometrician of the arithmetician his proportions; the metaphysician takes for his foundation the conjectures of Natural Philosophy. For every science has its presupposed principles, by which human judgement is held in check on all sides. If you happen to attack this barrier where the principal error lies, they immediately give tongue to this maxim, 'That there is no arguing with people who deny first principles.'

Now, there can be no first principles for men, unless the Deity has revealed them to us; of all the rest, the beginning, middle and end are but dreams and smoke. Against those who argue by hypotheses we must presuppose on the contrary the very axiom that is in dispute. For every human presupposition, and every enunciation, has as much authority as any other, unless reason steps in and makes a difference. So we must place them all in the scales; and in the first place those which are general, and those which tyrannize over us. To be convinced of certainty is certain evidence of folly and extreme uncertainty; and there are no more foolish and less philosophical people than the Philodoxes of Plato.[1]

We must know whether fire be hot, whether snow be white, if there be anything hard or soft within our knowledge. And with regard to those answers of which the ancients make up stories, as when the man who doubted heat was bidden to jump into the fire, or when the man who denied the coldness of ice was urged to put some into his bosom; they are most unworthy of the profession of Philosophy. If they had left us alone in our natural state, to receive external impressions as they appear and present themselves to our senses, and left us to follow our simple appetites, as regulated by the conditions of our birth, they might have reason to talk like that, but it is they who have taught us to make ourselves judges of the world. It is through them that we are possessed of this fanciful idea, 'That the human Reason is controller-general of all that is outside of us and within the heavenly arch; that she embraces everything, that she can do everything; that by her means everything is known and understood.'

[1] According to Plato's own definition: 'People who fill their minds with opinions whose grounds they are ignorant of, who are infatuated with words, who see and affect only the semblance of things.'

This answer might hold good with the cannibals, who enjoy the happiness of a long, calm and peaceful life without the help of Aristotle's precepts, and without ever having heard mention of Physics. This answer might perhaps possess greater force and value than any of those which they borrow from their reason and imagination. This answer all the animals might be able to use, as we do, and all who are purely and simply under the sway of the law of Nature; but they for their part have abandoned it.

They need not tell me, 'It is true; for you see and feel that it is.' They must tell me whether I really feel what I think I feel; and, if I do feel it, let them then tell me why I feel it, and how, and what. Let them tell me the name, the origin, the long and the short of heat, of cold, the qualities of him who acts and of him who suffers, or let them renounce me their claim, which is, not to admit or approve of anything but by the way of Reason. That is their touchstone in all kinds of experiments; but it is indeed a touchstone full of falsity, error, weakness and impotence.

How better shall we test her than by herself? If we are not to believe her when she is speaking of herself, she will hardly be fit to judge of things outside of herself. If she knows anything, she will at least know her essence, and her abode. She is in the soul, and a part, or an effect, of the same. For true and essential Reason, whose name we steal by false pretences, dwells in the bosom of God. There is her home and retreat; from there she flows, when it pleases God to let us see some ray of her, as Pallas issued from the head of her father to communicate herself to the world.

Now let us see what human Reason has taught us about herself, and of the soul. Not of the soul in general, which according to wellnigh all the philosophers is allotted to the heavenly bodies and the first bodies; nor the soul which Thales, prompted by the consideration of the magnet, ascribed even to things reputed inanimate; but of that which belongs to ourselves, which we should know best:

> For what the soul may be they do not know,
> Whether it be born or enter in at birth,
> And whether, sustained by death, it die with us,
> Or visit the shadows and the vasty caves
> Of Orcus, or by some divine decree
> Enter the brute herds. (LUCRETIUS.)

Crates and Dicaearchus were taught by their Reason that there is no soul at all, but that the body is thus stirred by a natural movement;

Plato, that it was a substance moving of itself;

Thales, a Nature without repose;

Asclepiades, an exercising of the senses;

Hesiod and Anaximander, a thing composed of earth and water;

Parmenides, of earth and fire;

Empedocles, of blood:

> He vomits up his blood-red soul; (VIRGIL.)

Posidonius, Cleanthes, and Galen, a heat or a heated disposition:

> And fiery vigour, of heavenly source, they share; (VIRGIL.)

Hippocrates, a spirit diffused throughout the body;

Varro, an air received at the mouth, heated in the lungs, moistened at the heart, and dispersed through the whole body;

Zeno, the quintessence of the four elements;

Heraclides of Pontus, the light;

Xenocrates and the Egyptians, a movable number;

the Chaldeans, a virtue without any determinate form:

> It is of body some one vital state,
> By Greeks named 'Harmony'. (LUCRETIUS.)

We must not forget Aristotle, who held it to be that which naturally makes the body to move, which he calls Entelechia:[1] as frigid an invention as any other, for he speaks neither of the essence, nor of the origin, nor of the nature of the soul, but only notices its effect.

Lactantius, Seneca, and the better part of the Dogmatists, confessed that it was a thing they did not understand.

After all this enumeration of theories, *let some God determine which of these opinions is the true one*, says Cicero. 'I know from myself, says Saint Bernard, how incomprehensible God is, since I cannot comprehend the parts of my own being.' Heraclitus, who held that all the universe was full of souls and daemons, nevertheless maintained that man could not advance so far towards knowledge of the soul as to attain to it, so mysterious was its essence.

[1] Constant and continuous motion.

THE SOUL'S ABODE

There is no less discussion and dissension about the place of its abode :

Hippocrates and Hierophilus located it in the ventricle of the brain ;

Democritus and Aristotle, in the whole body :

> As oft the body is said
> To have good health (when health, however, is not
> One part of him who has it), so they place
> The sense of mind in no fixed part of man ;   (LUCRETIUS.)

Epicurus, in the stomach :

> 'Tis fixed in the midmost heart ;
> Here lies dismay and terror ; round these haunts
> Are blandishments of love ; and therefore here
> The intellect, the mind ;   (LUCRETIUS.)

The Stoics, around and within the heart ;

Erasistratus, adjoining the membrane of the epicranium ;

Empedocles, in the blood ; as also

Moses,[1] which is the reason why he forbade the eating of the blood of beasts, with which their soul is united.

Galen believed that every part of the body has its soul.

Strato placed it between the two eyebrows.

What aspect the soul bears, or where it dwells, must not be even inquired into, says Cicero. I gladly allow this man to use his own words ; for why should I mar the language of eloquence ? Besides that there is small gain in stealing the substance of his ideas ; they are neither very frequent, nor very deep, and sufficiently well known.[2]

But the reason why Chrysippus argues it to be around the heart, as do all the rest of his school, is too good to be forgotten : ' It is, he says, because, when we wish to asseverate a thing, we place our hand upon our bosom, and when we utter the word Ἐγώ, which means I, we drop the lower jaw towards the stomach.' This passage should not be passed over without remarking on the flippancy which so great a man can descend to. For, besides that these considerations are extremely flimsy in themselves, the last is only a proof for Greeks that they have their soul in that

---

[1] ' But flesh with the life thereof, which is the blood thereof, shall ye not eat ' (Genesis). The substitution of Moses for ' the Lord ' is curious.

[2] Strange that an author whom he held in such small esteem, except on the head of his eloquence, should have been quoted by him more frequently than any other, with the exception perhaps of Plutarch !

region. No man's judgement is so wide-awake but that he sometimes slumbers.

Why should we be afraid to speak out? Here are the Stoics, the fathers of human wisdom, discovering that the soul of a man, crushed under a ruin and unable to extricate itself, tugs and strives with long-drawn groans to set itself free, like a mouse caught in a trap!

Some hold the opinion that the world was made in order to give a body, by way of punishment, to spirits fallen, through their own fault, from the state of purity in which they had been created; the first creation having been only incorporeal. And that, according as they have more or less departed from their spirituality, so they are more or less heavily or lightly incorporated. Hence the variety in so much created matter. But the spirit which, for its punishment, was invested with the body of the sun, what a very rare and particular measure of thirst it must have had!

When we carry our researches to an extreme point we always become dazed; as Plutarch says of the beginning of histories, that, as in the maps of the world, the farthest margins of known countries are occupied by morasses, dense forests, deserts and uninhabitable places. For the same reason those who treat of the most elevated subjects, and enter most deeply into them, lose themselves in the grossest and most childish nonsense, engulfed in their curiosity and presumption.

The end and the beginning of knowledge are accounted for as foolishly. See Plato soaring aloft into his poetical clouds, observe him using the jargon of the gods! But of what was he thinking when he defined man as a 'featherless biped', providing those who had a mind to deride him with an opportunity of doing so in a humorous way? For, having plucked a live capon, they went and called it 'Plato's Man'.

And what of the Epicureans? What simplicity made them first imagine that their Atoms, which they declared to be bodies with some weight and a natural downward movement, had built up the world, until their adversaries suggested to them that, according to that description, it was not possible for them to unite and cling together, their fall being so straight and perpendicular, producing everywhere parallel lines? Wherefore they had perforce to add afterwards a lateral, fortuitous motion, and moreover to furnish their atoms with bent and hooked tails,[1] to make them capable of joining and hanging together.

And even then were they not driven into a corner by those who followed them up with this other consideration, 'If the atoms have by chance formed so many sorts of figures, why did they never meet together to form a house or a shoe ? Why should we not likewise believe that an infinite number of Greek letters scattered about the place should in the end form the text of the Iliad ? '

That which is capable of reason, says Zeno, is better than that which is not capable of it ; there is nothing better than the world : it is therefore capable of reason. Cotta, by the same reasoning, makes the world an arithmetician. And by this other reasoning of Zeno he makes it a musician and organist : ' The whole is greater than the part ; we are capable of wisdom and are parts of the world : the world is therefore wise.'

In the objections which the philosophers, when they disagree in their opinions and their schools, throw in one another's teeth, we meet with an endless number of similar examples, not merely of unsound but of foolish and irreconcilable arguments, which accuse their authors not so much of ignorance as of thoughtlessness.

If I were to make up a goodly bundle of all the asinine things that have been uttered by *homo sapiens*, I should make you wonder. I feel a satisfaction in collecting them, as samples which, considered from some points of view, are not less instructive than sane and moderate opinions. From them we may judge what we are to think about man, of his sense and his reason, seeing that these great men, in whom human capacity has reached so high a level, commit such gross and manifest errors.

For my part, I would rather believe that they have treated knowledge in a haphazard way, as a toy for all occasions, and have played with Reason as if it were an instrument for vain and frivolous purposes, advancing all sorts of ideas and fancies, more or less precise or vague. This same Plato, who defines man as a fowl, says in another place, after Socrates, ' That in truth he knows not what man is ; and that there is nothing in the world so difficult to know.'

In consequence of this variety and instability of opinions,

[1] A first foreshadowing of the comma bacillus !

they tacitly, as it were, lead us by the hand to this solution of their irresolution. They profess not always to deliver their opinions openly and barefacedly; they have sometimes disguised them in the obscure fictions of poetry, at other times under some other mask. For our imperfection is, moreover, such that raw meat is not always good for our stomach; it must be dried, altered, and corrupted. They do the same; at times they obscure their real opinions and conclusions, and adulterate them to adapt them to public use. They will not frankly confess that human reason is weak and ignorant, in order not to frighten children. But they make it sufficiently evident under a semblance of muddled and uncertain learning.

When in Italy, I suggested to somebody who was at great pains to learn Italian, that, provided he only sought to make himself understood, without being particularly ambitious to excel, he should simply use the first words that came to his tongue, Latin, French, Spanish, or Gascon, and that by adding the Italian terminations, he would never fail to hit upon some dialect of the country, either Tuscan, or Roman, or Venetian, or Piedmontese, or Neapolitan, and so lay hold of some one of the many different forms.

I may say the same of Philosophy; she has so many faces, so much variety, and has said so many things, that they include everything we can dream or imagine. The human fancy can conceive nothing that is not to be found there, whether of good or evil purport. *Nothing can be so absurd but it has been said by some philosopher* (Cicero). I am the more ready to publish my whims, as, although they are my own and after no pattern, I know that they will be found related to some idea in ancient writers, and there will be plenty of people to say, 'That is where he got it.'

My conduct of life is natural; I have not called in the assistance of any learning to build it up. But, feeble as it is, whenever I have had a mind to speak of it, and, to make it appear a little more decent in public, made it my duty to back it up with reasons and examples, I have myself marvelled to find it, by mere chance, to conform with so many philosophical examples and reasons. I did not learn what was the rule of my life until after it was used up and spent. A new figure: an unpremeditate and accidental philosopher!

To return to our soul. When Plato located reason in the brain, anger in the heart, and cupidity in the liver, he probably intended rather to explain the movement of the soul than to divide and separate it, as one divides a body into its several members. And the most probable of their theories is, That it is in any case a soul which, by its faculty, reasons, remembers, understands, judges, desires, and exercises all its other functions with the different instruments of the body (as the mariner steers his ship according to his experience of it, now tightening or slackening a rope, now hoisting the mainyard or moving the rudder ; by a single power carrying out several actions) ; and, That it is lodged in the brain, which is apparent from this, that the wounds and other accidents that affect this part immediately impair the faculties of the soul ; it is not strange that it should thence diffuse itself through the rest of the body :

> Ne'er from his central path does Phoebus stray,
> Yet all things brightens with his golden beams ; (CLAUDIAN.)

as the sun sheds from heaven outwards its light and influence, and fills the world with them :

> The other part, the soul,
> Dispersed throughout the body, still obeys
> The bidding and the movement of the mind. (LUCRETIUS.)

Some have said that there was a general soul, as it were a great body, from which all the individual souls were extracted, and thither again returned, ever remingling with that universal matter :

> For God, they say, is imminent in all,
> Land, sea, and sky's immensity ; from him
> All flocks and herds, wild nature and mankind,
> Each at their birth, draw down their ghostly lives ;
> Then all unto the same are rendered back
> At dissolution, nor give room for death. (VIRGIL.)

Others maintained that they only rejoined and reunited themselves with it ; others, that they were produced from the divine substance ; others again, by the angels, from fire and air. Some, that they existed from all time ; some again, that they were created at the very moment when they were needed. Some make them descend from the moon's orb, and return thither. The generality of the ancients believed that they were engendered from father to son, in the same way in which all other things are produced in Nature ; arguing thus from the resemblance of the children to their fathers :

> Thy father's virtue into thee instilled. (AUTHOR UNKNOWN.)

> 'Tis of the brave and good alone
> That good and brave men are the seed ; (HORACE.)

and from the fact that fathers transmit to their children, not only bodily marks, but also the same disposition, the same constitution and mental tendencies :

> Again, why is't there goes
> Impetuous rage with lion's breed morose,
> And cunning with foxes, and to deer why given
> The ancestral fear and tendency to flee ;
> If not because one certain power of mind
> That came from its own seed and breed
> Waxes the same along with all the body ? (LUCRETIUS.)

that thereupon is based the divine justice, punishing in the children the sins of the fathers ; since the soul of the child is in some degree contaminated by the vice of the father, and is affected by the unruliness of his disposition.

Moreover, if the soul came some other way than by a natural succession ; if it had been some other thing apart from the body, it would have a recollection of its first existence, considering the natural faculties that are proper to it, of discoursing, reasoning, and remembering :

> If soul immortal is, and winds its way
> Into the body at the birth of man,
> Why can we not remember something then,
> Of lifetime spent before ? why keep we not
> Some footprints of the things we did of old ? (LUCRETIUS.)

For, if our soul is to be so conditioned as we would have it, we must presuppose it to be all-knowing when in its natural simplicity and purity. This being so, it would have been such when free from the bodily prison as well as before entering into it, as we hope it will be after it has gone out of it. And this knowledge it should remember while yet in the body, as Plato said, ' That what we learn is only a recollection of what we have known ' ; a thing which every one by experience may hold to be untrue ; because, in the first place, we remember only as much as we have been taught, and, if the memory simply performed its office, it would at least suggest to us some points other than those we have learned. Secondly, that which the soul knew, being in her integrity, was real knowledge, that knows things as they are, through its divine intelligence; whereas here she is made to entertain falsehoods and depravities, if they are taught her. Herein she cannot have used her recollection, such ideas and conceptions having never had a place in her.

To say that the bodily prison so stifles her inborn faculties that they become totally extinct, is in the first place to contradict that other belief, that we acknowledge her powers to be so great, and her workings, which men are conscious of in this life, so wonderful, that they have therefrom concluded her divinity and past eternity, and a future immortality:

> But if so changed hath been the power of mind,
> That all remembrance of the past is gone,
> That is not far removed from death. (LUCRETIUS.)

Furthermore, it is here, in this world, and not elsewhere, that the powers and actions of the soul should be considered; all her other perfections are vain and useless to her. It is for her present state that she is to be rewarded and paid during all her immortality, and it is for the life of the man only that she is held accountable. It would be unjust to strip her of her powers and resources, to disarm her and pass judgement upon her for what she did during the time of her captivity and imprisonment, her weakness and infirmity, during the time when she was under force and restraint, and condemn her to a punishment of infinite and perpetual duration; and to stop at the consideration of so short a time, perhaps an hour or two, or at the worst a century, which has no more proportion to infinity than an instant, in order, from this momentary interval, definitively to settle and dispose of her whole existence.

As also it would be an iniquitous disproportion to receive an everlasting reward following upon so short a life.

Plato, to avoid this dilemma, decides that future payments should be limited to the term of a hundred years, corresponding to the duration of human life; and a good many men of our time have fixed temporary limits.

Thus they concluded that the generation of the soul, as well as the duration of its life, are subject to the ordinary conditions of human things, according to the theory of Epicurus and Democritus, which has been the most widely accepted; in accordance with this fine evidence, That we see it to be born as soon as the body is capable of receiving it; That we see it increase in vigour with that of the body; That we observe its weakness in childhood, and in course of time its vigorous growth and maturity, then its decline and old age, and finally its decrepitude:

> We feel that soul to being comes
> Along with body, with body grows and ages. (LUCRETIUS.)

They perceived it to be capable of divers passions, and agitated by many distressing emotions, causing it to fall into pain and lassitude; capable of change and alteration, of cheerfulness, dullness, and languor; subject to its own infirmities and injuries, like the stomach or the foot:

> We mark the mind itself is cured,
> Like the sick body, and restored can be
> By medicine; (LUCRETIUS.)

dazed and fuddled by strong wine; thrown off its balance by the vapours of a burning fever; laid asleep by the administering of certain medicaments, and roused by others:

> So nature of mind must be corporeal, since
> From stroke and spear corporeal 'tis in throes. (LUCRETIUS.)

They saw how all her faculties are dulled and upset by the mere bite of a distempered dog, and that she had not enough stability of reason, nor strength of mind, nor virtue, nor philosophical resolution, nor resisting power, to exempt her from liability to such accidents. They saw that the saliva of a wretched mastiff, dropped on Socrates' hand, might shatter all his wisdom and all his great and well-regulated ideas, and so annihilate them that there would remain not a trace of his former knowledge:

> He becomes
> Mere fool, since energy of mind and soul
> Confounded is, and, as I've shown, disrupt,
> Asunder thrown, and torn to pieces all
> By that same venom, (LUCRETIUS.)

and that this venom would find no more resistance in that soul than in a child of four; a venom capable of turning all philosophy, if it were incarnate, to fury and madness. So much so that Cato, who twisted the neck both of Death and

Fortune, could not have endured the sight of water or a mirror, and would have been struck down by terror and dismay, supposing he had contracted, through the contagion of a mad dog, the disease that the physicians call Hydrophobia:

> His frame by violence of disease distract,
> He foams, as if to vomit all his soul,
> As on the salt sea boil the billows round
> Under the master-might of winds. (LUCRETIUS.)

Now, as to this particular point, Philosophy has sufficiently armed man, for the enduring of all other misfortunes, either with patience, or, if it costs too dear to acquire, with an infallible expedient, that of totally depriving himself of feeling. But these are resources which are only at the service of a soul that possesses itself and is in its full vigour, capable of reason and deliberation; not against this mishap, which changes the soul of a philosopher into that of a madman, deranged, overturned and destroyed. This state is occasioned by many causes, such as a too violent agitation which, as the result of some strong passion, the soul may beget of itself, or a wound in a certain part of the person, or an exhalation from the stomach, causing a dizziness and lightheadedness:

> In body diseased, oft the mind
> Wanders afield; for 'tis beneath itself,
> And crazed it speaks, or many a time it sinks,
> With eyelids closing and a drooping nod,
> In heavy drowse, on to eternal sleep. (LUCRETIUS.)

The philosophers have, it seems to me, hardly touched this chord.

Nor have they touched another of like importance. They have this dilemma continually on their lips, to console us in our mortal state: 'The soul is either mortal or immortal. If mortal, it will be without pain; if immortal, it will go on changing for the better.' They never touch the other branch, 'What if it goes on getting worse?' and leave to the poets the threats of future punishments. But in that way they deal themselves a good hand. Those are two gaps in their arguments that often meet my eye. I will return to the first.[1]

---

[1] i. e. that the wisest and most vigorous mind may be thrown off its balance.

This soul ceases to care so decidedly for the sovereign good of the Stoics. Our fine wisdom must here surrender and give up her arms. Moreover they also considered, with their futile human reason, that the mingling and association of two things so different as the mortal and the immortal is unimaginable :

> For, verily, the mortal to conjoin
> With the eternal, and to feign they feel
> Together, and can function each with each,
> Is but to dote : for what can be conceived
> Of more unlike, discrepant, ill-assorted,
> Than something mortal in a union joined
> With an immortal and a secular,
> To bear the outrageous tempests ? (LUCRETIUS.)

They felt besides that the soul is involved in death, as well as the body :

> Along with body outworn by weight of years ; (LUCRETIUS.)

which, according to Zeno, is sufficiently proved by the resemblance of sleep. For he regards it as a ' swoon and fall of the soul as well as of the body '. *He thinks the mind is dragged down, and that, as it were, it slips and falls* (Cicero). And when it maintained its strength and vigour to the end of life, as they observed in some cases, they attributed it to a difference in the disease. For we may have seen that in this extremity one man will retain one sense, another another : this man his hearing, that man his sense of smell, without deterioration. And that no debility is so general but that some parts will retain their full vigour :

> Not otherwise than when the foot's in pain,
> And leaves the sick man's head quite unaffected. (LUCRETIUS.)

The sight of our understanding stands in the same relation to the truth as the owl's eye does to the splendour of the sun, as Aristotle says. What could be a stronger condemnation than such gross blindness in so shining a light ?

For the contrary belief, that of the immortality of the soul, which according to Cicero was first introduced, at least by the testimony of books, by Pherecydes of Scyros, in the time of King Tullus (though others attribute the discovery to Thales and others to others), is the part of human knowledge that has been treated of with most reserve and doubt. The boldest Dogmatists have been constrained, chiefly on this point, to shelter in the obscurity of the Academy. No one knows what theory Aristotle propounded on the matter, any more than all the ancients generally, who handle it with a wavering belief: *a thing more gratifying in the promise than in the proof* (Seneca). He hid behind a cloud of words difficult to understand, and left his followers disputing about his decisions as much as about the matter itself.

Two things rendered this theory plausible to them; one, that but for the immortality of the soul there would be no room for the vain hope of glory; a consideration which has a wonderful hold on the world. The other, that a very salutary impression prevails, as Plato says, that when a crime escapes the dim and uncertain sight of human justice, it will still be exposed to the eyes of divine justice, which will pursue it, even after the death of the guilty person.

Man is possessed with an excessive anxiety to prolong his existence; he has made all possible provisions to that end. For the preservation of the body there are tombs; for the preservation of his name there is glory. Impatient of his fortune, he has used all his wits in the rebuilding and underpropping of himself with his productions. The soul, in her anxiety and feebleness, being unable to stand by herself, goes about everywhere seeking consolations, hopes, and foundations in external circumstances, where she may cling and find a firm footing. And, however flimsy and fantastic they may be, as created in her imagination, she more readily and securely relies upon them than upon herself.

But it is a marvel how those who are most obstinately convinced of the immortality of our spirit, which to them appears so sound and clear, have been pulled up short, and how powerless they are to prove it by their human arguments. *They are dreams, not of the teacher, but of the wisher*[1] (Cicero), says one of the ancients.

From this evidence man may know that he owes to Fortune and accident the truth he himself discovers; since, even when it has dropped into his hands, he has not the power to grasp and keep it, and his reason is not strong enough to make any use of it. All the outcome of our own reasoning powers, whether true or not, is subject to doubt

[1] In Shakespeare's words, 'the wish is father to the thought'.

and uncertainty. It was to punish our arrogance, and to teach us our wretchedness and incapacity, that God wrought the chaos and confusion of the old Tower of Babel.

Whatever we may undertake without his aid, whatever we see without the lamp of his grace, is but vanity and folly. The very essence of truth, which is uniform and constant, we corrupt and adulterate by our weakness, when Fortune gives it into our possession. Whatever course a man may follow of his own accord, by God's leave he always comes to that same confusion, which is so vividly reflected in the well-merited chastisement meted out to Nimrod by crushing down his arrogance and frustrating his vain enterprise in building his pyramid. *I will destroy the wisdom of the wise, and bring to nothing the understanding of the prudent* (Saint Paul).

The diversity of languages and tongues by which he confounded that work, what is it other than the constant and perpetual altercation and discordance of opinions and reasons, which attend and embroil the vain structure of human learning? And embroil it to good effect.

What would hold us if we had a grain of knowledge?

I am greatly pleased with Saint Augustine's dictum: *The very obscuring of what is useful to us is either an exercise in humility or a crushing of pride.* To what a pitch of presumption and insolence do we not carry our blindness and our folly!

But to resume my subject. It was truly quite right that we should be beholden to God alone, and to the benefit of his grace, for the truth of so noble a belief, since of his bounty alone we receive the fruit of immortality, which consists in the enjoyment of eternal blessedness.

Let us ingenuously confess that God alone, and faith, have told us so; for it is not a lesson we have learned of Nature or of our reason. And whoever will again and again test his being and his powers, both within and without, without the aid of that divine privilege; whoever will consider man without flattery, will see in him neither efficacy nor faculty that savours of anything but death and earth. The more we give and owe and render to God, the more shall we act as Christians.

What this Stoic philosopher professes to owe to the accidental agreement of the popular voice, had it not been better if he had it of God ? *When we treat of the eternity of souls, the agreement of men who either fear or worship the powers of the underworld is of no small moment. I adopt this general belief* (Seneca).

Now the weakness of human arguments upon this subject is strangely seen in the fabulous details which are added as a consequence of this belief, to determine the nature of this our immortality.

We may leave aside the Stoics (*they grant us long life as do the crows ; they say that souls will endure a long time, but that they will endure for ever they deny* [Cicero]), who grant the soul a life beyond this one, but finite.

The most widely and universally accepted belief, which continues to prevail to this day in various parts of the world,[1] is that of which Pythagoras is made the author ; not that he first conceived it, but because it receives great weight and credit from the authority and approbation he accorded it. It is ' that the soul, when leaving us, only rolls from one body to another, from a lion to a horse, from a horse to a king, thus unceasingly wandering from house to house '. And he himself said that he remembered having been Aethalides, then Euphorbus, after that Hermotimus, and that lastly from Pyrrhus he passed into Pythagoras ; having a recollection of himself for two hundred and six years.

Some added that these same souls at times reascend to heaven, and come down again :

> And must we think,
> Some spirits, father, heavenward mount from hence,
> And to their sluggish bodies back return ?
> Holds them so fond a longing for the light,
> Unhappy souls ! (VIRGIL.)

Origen makes them eternally to come and go from the good to the bad state. The theory that Varro cites is that they rejoin their first body after four hundred and forty years of revolution. Chrysippus held that that must happen after a certain space of time not determined. Plato, who states that he owes to Pindar and the ancient poetry that belief in the endless vicissitudes of change during which the soul is prepared, her punishments and rewards in the other world being only temporary, as her life in this is

---

[1] In Persia, Hindustan, &c.

but for a time, concludes that she has a singular knowledge of the affairs of heaven, of hell and of this world through which she has passed, repassed and sojourned during many peregrinations : a matter for her recollection.

This is her progress elsewhere : ' He who has lived well rejoins the star to which he is assigned ; he who has lived ill passes into a woman. And, if he does not mend even then, he is changed back into an animal of a kind suited to his vicious life ; nor will he see an end to his punishments until he returns to his original state, having by the power of reason thrown off the gross, dull, and elemental qualities that were in him.'

But I must not forget the objection that the Epicureans raise against this transmigration from one body to another. It is amusing. They ask, ' What order would be maintained if the crowd of the dying should happen to be greater than that of those who are being born ? For the souls that were turned out of their lodgings would tread on one another's heels in their eagerness to get the first places in these new shells.' They also ask how they would spend their time when waiting for a lodging to be ready for them. Or, on the other hand, if more animals were born than died, they say that the bodies would be in a sad fix, awaiting the infusion of their souls ; and it might happen that some of these would die before they had been alive :

>   Again, at parturitions of the wild
>   And at the rites of Love, that souls should stand
>   Ready hard by, seems ludicrous enough—
>   Immortals waiting for their mortal limbs
>   In numbers innumerable, contending madly
>   Which shall be first and chief to enter in !   (LUCRETIUS.)

Others have kept the soul in the bodies of the deceased, to animate with them the snakes, worms, and other creatures that are said to be bred of the corruption of our limbs, even of our ashes. Others divide the soul into a mortal and an immortal part. Others make it corporeal and nevertheless immortal. Some make it immortal, without knowledge and without understanding.

There are also some who believed that devils were made of the souls of the damned (and that belief has been held by some of our religion) ; just as Plutarch thinks that gods are made of those which are saved. For there are few things that this author states in such decisive words as this, whilst on other matters he always adopts a doubtful and ambiguous tone. 'We must hold, he says, and firmly believe that the souls of virtuous men, in accordance with nature and divine justice, change from men to saints,[1] from saints to demigods,[1] and from being demigods, after they have been perfectly, as in purgatorial sacrifices, cleansed and purified, being free from all mortal passions, they become, not by any civil decree, but in very truth, in accordance with reasonable probability, entire and perfect gods, and meet with a very happy and very glorious end.'

But if you would see him, who is after all one of the most restrained and moderate of the crowd, laying about him with greater boldness, and telling us his wonderful things on the subject, I refer you to his essays *Of the Moon* and *Of the Daemon of Socrates*,[2] where you may find it made as evident as in any other place, that the mysteries of Philosophy have many strange things in common with those of Poetry; where you may see the human understanding going astray in trying to sound and investigate all things to the depths. Just as, tired and worn out by the long course of our life, we fall back into childishness.

There you have the fine and certain teachings we derive from human science concerning our soul!

There is no less want of thought in what it tells us of our bodily parts. Let us choose one or two examples, for otherwise we should lose ourselves in that vast and troubled sea of medical errors. Let us see whether there is agreement at least on this point, from what matter human beings produce one another. For, with regard to their first production, it is not to be wondered at if, in so sublime and time-honoured a matter, the human understanding is perplexed and distracted.

Archelaus, the natural philosopher, whose disciple and favourite Socrates was, according to Aristoxenus, said that both men and animals were created out of a milky slime pressed out by the heat of the earth;

---

[1] Or 'heroes' and 'genii', according to the English translations of Plutarch.
[2] Perhaps Montaigne refers to Timarchus's account of his visit to Hades in the first essay, and the Myth of Sylla in the second.

Pythagoras says that the semen is the skimming of our best blood;

Plato, that it is the distillation of the marrow of the backbone; which he argues from the fact that this part first feels the lassitude of the labour;

Alcmaeon, part of the substance of the brain; and that that is so, he says, is shown by the fact that the eyes of those become dimmed who labour too excessively at that exercise;

Democritus, a substance extracted from the whole bodily mass;

Epicurus, that it is extracted from the soul and the body;

Aristotle, an excrement drawn from the aliment of the blood, the last that is diffused through our members;

Others, blood cooked and digested by the heat of the genitals, which they conclude from the drops of pure blood that are ejected after excessive efforts; wherein there seems to be more likelihood, if we may derive any probability from such endless confusion.

Now, in trying to bring this seed to do its work, how greatly they contradict each other! Aristotle and Democritus maintain that women have no sperm, and that it is only a perspiration exuding in the heat of pleasure and movement, which contributes nothing towards the generation. On the other hand, Galen and his followers hold that generation cannot take place without the meeting of the seeds.

There you see the doctors, the philosophers, the lawyers, and the theologians at loggerheads and in a regular scuffle with our women on the question, 'For how long a period the women carry their fruit.' And for my part I will back up with my own example those of them who support an eleven months' pregnancy. The world is built up on this experience. No little woman is so simple but she may have her say on all these matters in dispute; and yet we men cannot come to an agreement!

That is enough to show that man knows no more about himself bodily than he does spiritually. We have brought him face to face with himself, and his reason with his reason, to see what it could tell us about him. I think I have made it clear enough how little Reason knows about herself.

And what can he know who knows nothing about him

self? *As if he could really take the measure of any other thing, who cannot take his own!* (Pliny.)

Truly Protagoras stuffed us very nicely when he made man the measure of all things, who never knew even his own. If it be not he, his dignity will not allow any other creature to have that privilege. Now, he being in himself so contradictory, and one opinion unceasingly subverting another, that favourable proposition was but a mockery, and necessarily led us to conclude the futility of the compass and the compasser.

When Thales thinks it very difficult for man to know man, he tells him that the knowledge of any other thing is impossible.

END OF VOL. I

THE ESSAYS OF
MONTAIGNE

THE ESSAYS OF MONTAIGNE

TRANSLATED BY
E. J. TRECHMANN

WITH AN INTRODUCTION
BY THE RT. HON.
J. M. ROBERTSON
*Author of 'Montaigne
and Shakespeare'*

*In two volumes
Volume II*

LITHOGRAPHED IN UNITED STATES OF AMERICA

CONTENTS

BOOK II (*continued*)

12. Apology for Raymond Sebond (*continued*)	1
13. Of judging of another's Death	53
14. How our mind stands in its own way	60
15. That Difficulties increase our desires	61
16. Of Glory	66
17. Of Presumption	80
18. Of giving the Lie	114
19. Of Freedom of Conscience	119
20. That our Enjoyments are never unmixed	123
21. Against Idleness	126
22. Of Riding Post	131
23. Of Evil means employed to a good end	132
24. Of the Greatness of Rome	135
25. Of not Malingering	137
26. Of Thumbs	139
27. Cowardice is the mother of cruelty	140
28. There is a time for all things	150
29. Of Valour	152
30. Of a young Monstrosity	160
31. Of Anger	162
32. Defence of Seneca and Plutarch	169
33. The Case of Spurina	176
34. Observations on Julius Caesar's Methods in War	184
35. Of three Good Wives	193
36. Of the Greatest Men	201
37. Of the Resemblance of Children to their Fathers	208

BOOK III

1. Of the Useful and the Honest 241
2. Of Repentance 257
3. Of three kinds of Intercourse 272
4. Of Diversion 285
5. On some lines of Virgil 296
6. Of Coaches 358
7. Of the Disadvantage of Greatness 377
8. Of the Art of Conversing 383
9. Of Vanity 408
10. Of husbanding one's Will 472
11. Of Cripples 497
12. Of Physiognomy 509
13. Of Experience 540

INDEX 603

Book the Second

CHAPTER 12

APOLOGY OF RAYMOND SEBOND

(continued)

YOU,[1] for whom I have taken the pains, contrary to my usual habit, to stretch out my treatise to such a length, will not hesitate to defend your Sebond with the ordinary methods of argument in which you are every day instructed, and thus you will exercise your wit and learning; for this final fencer's trick should not be employed except as a last resource. It is a desperate thrust, in which you have to abandon your weapon in order to disarm your adversary, and a secret ruse which should be practised seldom and with reserve. It is a very foolhardy thing to lose your life in order to kill another.

We must not wish to die in order to be revenged, as Gobrias did. For, being in close grips with a Persian lord, and Darius coming up with sword in hand, and fearing to strike lest he should brain Gobrias, the latter called him to lunge boldly, even though he should run them both through.

I have heard combats condemned, in which the weapons and conditions offered are so desperate that it was incredible that either could escape. The Portuguese captured fourteen Turks in the Indian Ocean, who, chafing at their captivity, resolved to reduce themselves and their captors and the vessel to ashes, by rubbing some ships' nails together, until a spark fell upon the kegs of gunpowder which they found; and they carried out their resolution.

Here we are shaking the barriers and last fences of knowledge, wherein excess is to be condemned, as in virtue. Keep on the high road; it will not do a crumb of good to be so subtle and clever. Remember the Tuscan proverb: *Chi troppo s'assottiglia, si scavezza*.[2]

---

[1] The lady Montaigne is addressing is supposed by some to have been Margaret of Valois, first wife of Henry IV, but this is uncertain.

[2] A line of Petrarch, which may have become proverbial in Montaigne's time. It might be rendered, using the words of the popular taunt, 'If you try to be too sharp, you will cut yourself.'

I advise you to be sober and reserved in your opinions and expressions, as well as in your conduct of life and all other things, and to flee all novelty and eccentricity. All extravagant ways are a source of vexation to me. You who, with the authority your lofty position gives you, and still more with the advantages derived from your own particular qualities, have all men at your beck and call, could have given this charge to some professional man of letters, who might have supported and enriched this rhapsody with very much better arguments. However, I have lectured you enough on your duty.

Epicurus said, speaking of the laws, that the worst of them were so necessary to us, that without them men would devour one another. And Plato comes near to saying that but for the laws we should live like brute-beasts; and he tries to prove it.

Our mind is an erratic, dangerous and unthinking tool; it is difficult to reconcile it with order and moderation. And in these days nearly all the men of exceptional eminence above their fellows, and of extraordinary quickness of parts, may be seen to get out of hand with their licentious opinions and conduct. It is a miracle if you find one of them sober and fit for society.

Men are right in setting up the strictest possible barriers for the human mind. In study, as in all else, its steps should be counted and regulated; its hunting rights should be artificially prescribed. They curb and fetter it with religions, laws, customs, sciences, precepts, mortal and immortal punishments and rewards; and yet we see it, by its versatility and licentiousness, escape all these bonds. It is a shadowy body with nothing by which it may be seized and directed; a varying and shapeless body, incapable of being either bound or held. Indeed, there are few minds so well-regulated, strong and well-born that they may be trusted with their own guidance, and are able, with moderation and without temerity, to sail in the freedom of their opinions, beyond those of the generality of men. It is more expedient to place them under pupilage.

The mind is a formidable blade, even to its possessor, if he cannot use it with judgement and discretion. And there is no animal that is more in need of blinkers, to control its eyes to look straight ahead, and keep it from gadding about hither and thither, outside of the ruts that custom and the laws have traced.

Therefore it will be more becoming in you to confine yourself within the ordinary routine, whatever it be, than to soar aloft with such unbridled licence. But if any one of these new doctors [1] attempts to show off his cleverness in your presence, at the risk of his salvation and yours, to rid yourself of this dangerous pest, which is daily spreading in your courts, will be your best preservative, in extreme need, and will prevent the contagion of this poison from injuring either you or your environment.

The liberty, then, and wantonness of those ancient wits gave rise, in Philosophy and the Humanities, to several schools differing in their beliefs, each undertaking to choose and decide, in order to take sides. But now that men all go one pace, *who are so bound and devoted to certain fixed beliefs, that they are forced to defend even those they do not approve* (Cicero); now that we receive the arts and sciences in accordance with the decrees of the civil authorities, so that the schools are all after one pattern, and have a uniform and circumscribed system of education and discipline, they no longer regard the weight and value of coins, but every one in his turn accepts them according to the current price put upon them by general approval. They go to law, not about the standard, but the market-price; so all things are regulated in like manner. They accept medicine as they do geometry, and they swallow wizardry, charms, ligatures,[2] correspondence with spirits and the dead, prognostications, domifications,[3] and even that absurd pursuit after the philosopher's stone; all are accepted without question.

It is enough to know that the seat of Mars is in the middle of the triangle of the hand, that of Venus on the thumb, that of Mercury in the little finger; and that when the table-line cuts across the tubercle of the forefinger it is a sign of cruelty; when it falls short under the middle finger, and when the natural middle line forms an angle with the line of life under the same spot, it is a sign of a miserable death. That if, in a woman, the natural line

[1] The Reformers, according to Dr. Armaingaud.
[2] A spell to cause impotence in a man; see the chapter on the Power of the Imagination.
[3] Dividing the heavens into twelve houses, to take a horoscope &c.

be open and does not close the angle with the line of life, it means that she is unchaste. I call yourself to witness, whether a man with this science may not be admitted, find favour and make a reputation in any company.

Theophrastus said that human knowledge, guided by the senses, could estimate the causes of things up to a certain degree; but that, having reached the ultimate and first causes, it must stop and be turned back, by reason either of its own weakness, or by the difficulty of things. It is a belief soothing to the average mind, that our capacities may guide us to the knowledge of some things, but that there is a certain limit to their powers, beyond which it is temerity to employ them. That is a plausible belief, suggested by people who are given to compromise.

But it is not easy to confine our mind; it is curious and insatiable to know, and has no more occasion to stop at a thousand than at fifty paces. Having learned by experience that where one man has failed another has succeeded, and that what was unknown to one century the following century has made clear, and that the arts and sciences are not cast in a mould, but that they are formed and shaped by degrees, by repeated handling and polishing, as a she-bear at her leisure licks her cubs into shape; I do not cease from testing and sounding what I have been unable to discover, and by remanipulating and kneading this new matter, by stirring and heating it, I make it easier for him that shall succeed me, that he may enjoy it more at leisure, and render it more pliable and manageable for him:

> As Hymettian wax grows softer in the sun,
> And moulded by the finger and the thumb,
> Will various forms and several shapes admit,
> Till for the present use 'tis rendered fit. (OVID.)

The second will do as much for the third; for which reason difficulties ought not to make me despair, any more than my own incapacity, for it is only my own.

Man is as capable of all things as he is of some; and if he confesses, as Theophrastus says, ignorance of primary causes and principles, let him boldly give me up all the rest of his knowledge. If he lacks foundation his reason sprawls on the ground. Disputes and investigations have no other aim and limit but principles; if this barrier do not arrest his course, he falls into endless irresolution. *One thing can be neither more nor less comprehended than another, since there is only one definition of the comprehension of everything* (Cicero).

Now it is probable that if the soul knew anything, she would first of all know herself ; and if she knew anything outside of herself, it would be before all things her body and shell.

If to this day we still see the gods of the medical faculty disputing about our anatomy,

> Vulcan against, for Troy Apollo stood ; (OVID.)

when can we expect them to agree ? We are nearer to ourselves than the whiteness of snow and the weight of a stone are to us. If man does not know himself, how should he know his functions and powers ? It cannot be, perhaps, but that we should harbour some real knowledge, but it is by chance. And since errors enter into our soul in the same manner and guided through the same channel, she has no means of distinguishing them, or of choosing between truth and falsehood.

The Academics allowed the judgement to incline a little to one side, and thought it too crude to say ' that it was no more likely that snow was white than black, and that we were no more certain of the motion of a stone thrown by our hand than of that of the eighth sphere '. And to avoid this difficulty and strangeness, which indeed is hard to imagine, although they conclude that we are in no sort capable of knowing, and that the truth is engulfed in deep abysses which human eyes cannot penetrate ; yet they allowed some things to be more likely than others, and granted their judgement the option of inclining to one piece of evidence more than to another. This bias they permitted themselves, but forbade the coming to any conclusion.

The Pyrrhonian attitude is bolder, and at the same time more reasonable. For that bias of the Academics, and their leaning towards one proposition rather than to another, what is it but an acknowledgement that one proposition is more evidently true than another ? If our understanding is capable of taking in the shape, the lineaments, the face and bearing of the truth, it would be just as likely to see it full-grown as half-grown, incipient and imperfect. That apparent probability which makes them bear to the left rather than to the right, you must increase; that ounce of likelihood that turns the scales you must multiply by a hundred, by a thousand. In the end the scales will come to a definite decision, and fix on one choice and one absolute truth.

But how can they allow themselves to incline to a probability if they know not the truth? How can they know the semblance of a thing of which they know not the essence? We can either form an absolute judgement, or none at all. If the faculties of our intellect and senses lack foundation and foothold, if they only hover and are blown about by any wind, in vain do we allow our judgement to be carried away by any part of their operation, however apparent may be that which it sets before us; and the surest and happiest attitude our understanding can take would be one of sobriety, justness, inflexibility, without any wavering and agitation. *As between things seen, whether true or false, it matters nothing to which the mind gives assent* (Cicero).

We can see clearly enough that our mind does not take in things in their form and essence, and that they do not enter therein by their own force and authority. Because, if that were so, we should all receive them in the same shape; wine would taste the same to a sick man as to a sound. To a man with chapped or benumbed fingers the wood or iron he touches would seem as hard as to another. External objects therefore surrender to our mercy; they dwell in us as we please.

Now, if for our part we took in anything without alteration, if the human grip were strong and capable enough to seize the truth by its own powers, these powers being common to all men, this truth would be bandied about from one to another, and there would be found at least some one thing in the world, out of so many as there are, that would be believed by all men with universal consent. But this fact, that there is no proposition that is not, or might not be, disputed and controverted among us, clearly proves that our innate judgement does not very clearly grasp that which it does grasp. For my judgement cannot force my neighbour's judgement to accept it; which is a sign that I have become possessed of it by some other means than by a natural power that is in me and in all men.

We may pass over that endless confusion of beliefs that

we see among the philosophers themselves, and those perpetual and universal disputings concerning the knowledge of things. For this is a very true presupposition, That on no one thing are men in agreement, I mean the best-endowed and most talented scholars, not even that the sky is over our heads; for they who doubt everything, doubt even that. And they who deny that we are able to comprehend anything, say that we have not comprehended that the sky is above our heads: and these two beliefs are without comparison the most widely held.

Without considering this endless diversity and division, it is easy to see, from the confusion that our judgement causes ourselves, and the uncertainty that every man feels in himself, that it has a very insecure seat. How variously we judge of things! How often we change our opinions! What I hold and believe to-day I hold and believe with my whole belief; with all my tools and all my strength I grasp that opinion, and they guarantee it with all the power at their command. There is no truth I could embrace and keep more strongly than that. I am wholly and in very truth possessed by it. But has it not happened, not once, but a hundred, nay a thousand times, and every day, that, with those same implements and under the same conditions, I have embraced something else, which I have since concluded to be false?

We must at least become wise at our own cost. If I have often found myself betrayed marching under these colours; if my touchstone is usually at fault, and my scales uneven and incorrect, what greater assurance can I have now than at other times? Is it not folly to allow myself to be so often misled by one guide?

Nevertheless, though Fortune shift us five hundred times from place to place, though she do nothing but unceasingly empty and pour back into our belief, as into a vessel, other and other opinions, the present and last one is ever the certain and infallible one. For this we must abandon worldly goods, honour, life, salvation, and all:

> But then some later, likely better, find
> Destroys its worth and changes our desires
> Regarding good of yesterday. (LUCRETIUS.)

Whatever they preach to us, whatever we may learn, we

should still remember that it is a man that gives and a man that takes. It is a mortal hand that offers it, it is a mortal hand that accepts it. The things that come to us from heaven have alone the right and authority to persuade, they alone have the stamp of truth, which also we do not see with our own eyes, nor receive by our own powers. That great and holy image could not remain in so mean a habitation, unless God prepared it for that purpose, unless God repaired and strengthened it with his particular and supernatural grace and favour.

Our faulty condition should at least make us behave with more moderation and discretion in our changes. We should remember that whatever we receive into our understanding, we often receive untruths, and that we receive them with the aid of those same tools that often prove false and deceptive.

Now it is no wonder if they prove false, being so easily turned aside and twisted by the slightest events. It is certain that our apprehension, our judgement, and the faculties of our mind in general are affected by the movements and alterations of the body, which alterations are continual. Is not our mind more wide-awake, our memory more prompt, our reason more active, in health than in sickness? Do not things put on quite different faces when we are in a gay and merry mood and when we are melancholy and oppressed by cares? Do you think that the verses of Catullus and Sappho smile upon a crabbed old miser as they do upon a lusty and vigorous young man?

Cleomenes, son of Anaxandridas, being sick, his friends reproved him for his changed and unwonted humours and fancies: 'I quite agree, he replied; I am not the same man I am in health. I being a different man, my opinions and fancies are also different.'

The lawyers in our Palaces of Justice have a customary saying, referring to a criminal who happens to have a judge in good humour and an indulgent mood: *Gaudeat de bona fortuna,* 'let him rejoice in his good fortune!' For it is certain that we meet with judges who are at one time harsher, more captious, more prone to convict, and at another more easy-going, complaisant, and more inclined to pardon. When Justice So-and-so leaves his house suffering from the gout, from jealousy or from resentment against his valet who has been robbing him, his whole soul dyed and steeped in anger, we cannot doubt but that his judgement will be warped accordingly.

That venerable Senate of the Areopagus used to sit in judgement by night, lest the sight of the litigants might corrupt their sense of justice. The very atmosphere and the serenity of the sky have some power to change us, according to these Greek lines, quoted by Cicero,

> The minds of men oft with the weather change,
> As the days, foul or fair, dark or serene. (HOMER.)

Not only do fevers, potions, and serious happenings upset our judgement; the least thing in the world will turn it like a weather-cock. And there is no doubt, though we are not conscious of it, that, if a continuous fever can prostrate our soul, the tertian fever will impair it to a certain extent, in proportion to its severity. If the apoplexy dims and totally extinguishes the light of our intelligence, we cannot doubt but that the influenza will blind it. And, consequently, hardly for a single hour in life will our judgement chance to be in its proper trim, our body being subject to so many continual changes, and stuffed with so many different springs of action that (I take the word of the physicians for it) it will be strange if there is not always one that shoots wide of the mark.[1]

Moreover, this infirmity is not so easily detected, unless it be extreme and quite past remedy; inasmuch as reason always walks crooked, lame and broken-hipped, and in the company of falsehood as well as of the truth. Hence it is difficult to discover her miscalculations and irregularities.

I always call by the name of Reason that semblance of it which every man imagines himself to possess. This kind of reason, which may have a hundred counterparts around one and the same subject, all opposed to each other, is an implement of lead and wax, that may be bent and stretched and adapted to any bias and any measure; it needs but the skill to mould it. However well-meaning a judge may be, if he does not closely hearken to his own conscience, which few waste their time in doing, his leaning towards friendship, kinship, the fair sex and revenge, and not only things so weighty, but that fortuitous instinct which inclines

[1] Montaigne's mixed metaphors are often a little perplexing.

us to favour one thing more than another, and which, without the permission of reason, gives us the choice between two like objects, or some equally empty shadow, may imperceptibly creep into his judgement, and prompt him to allow or disallow a cause, and give a tip to the scales.

I, who watch myself more narrowly and have my eye continually bent on myself, as one that has no great business elsewhere,—

> I care not—not I—not a stiver,
> Who in Scythia, frozen and drear,
> 'Neath the scourge of a tyrant may shiver,
> Or who keeps Tiridates in fear,—(HORACE.)

I should hardly dare to tell of the vanity and weakness I am conscious of in myself. I am so unsteady and shaky on my feet, I am so inclined to trip and so apt to stumble, my sight is so irregular, that when fasting I am quite another man than after a meal. If health, and a fine, bright day smile upon me, behold me quite amiable! If a corn trouble my toe, behold me sullen, disagreeable and quite unapproachable! One and the same pace of my horse may appear to me now hard, now easy, the same road at one time shorter, at another longer, and the same shape now more now less agreeable. At this moment I am for doing anything, at another time for doing nothing. What is now a pleasure to me will sometimes be a drudgery. I am subject to a thousand rash and accidental impulses. I am possessed either by the melancholic or the choleric humour; at this moment sadness predominates in me of its own accord, at another I am blithe and gay.

When I take up a book I may discover a charming and admirable passage, which strongly impresses my mind, whilst if I light upon the same passage on another occasion I may turn it over and over again in my mind, I may twist and bend it, but all in vain; to me it is but a shapeless and unrecognizable mass.

Even in my own writings I cannot always recover the meaning of my former ideas; I know not what I meant to say,[1] and often get into a regular heat, correcting and putting a new sense into it, having lost the first and better one.

---

[1] And no wonder!

I do nothing but come and go. My judgement does not always forge straight ahead; it strays and wanders,

> Like a frail vessel caught on the mighty deep
> By stormy winds. (CATULLUS.)

Many a time having undertaken, by way of exercise or pastime, to support an opinion opposed to one I held (which I am fond of doing), my mind, turning and bending in the new direction, becomes so firmly attached to it, that I can no longer discover the reasons of my former belief, and so abandon it. I am dragged, as it were, the way I incline, whichever it may be, and am carried along by my own weight.

Every one almost could say the same of himself, if he looked into himself as I do. Preachers know that their own fervid eloquence in preaching animates their faith; and that when angry we more hotly defend our proposition, we impress it upon ourselves and espouse it with greater vehemence and approval than we do in our cool and calm moments.

You state your case simply to a barrister, and he will answer you with doubts and hesitations; you feel that it is a matter of indifference to him whether he takes up the one side or the other. If you have tempted him with a good fee to nibble at and take up your quarrel, will he not begin to take an interest in it and warm up his sympathy? His reasoning powers and his learning are warmed up at the same time. See how his intelligence begins to discover an evident and indisputable truth! He will detect an altogether new light thrown upon your case; he honestly believes in it, and is convinced that he does so.

Nay, I know not if the ardour born of pique and obstinacy in his encounter with the violent attack of the law, and of his danger or the concern for his reputation, have not sent many a man to the stake in support of a belief for which, at liberty and among his friends, he would not have been willing to burn the tip of his finger.

The shocks and agitations that our soul receives through the bodily passions have a great influence upon her; but still more have her own feelings, which have so strong a hold upon her, that it is perhaps tenable that she is only moved and propelled by the breath of her own winds, and that, unless stirred by them, she would remain inactive, like a ship becalmed on the open sea, to which the winds have denied their assistance. And whoever should maintain that belief (following therein the Peripatetics) would do us no great wrong, since it is a well-known fact that most of the noblest actions of the soul proceed from, and have need of, this impulsion of the feelings. Valour, they say, cannot become perfect without the aid of anger :

> Ajax was ever brave, but bravest when in wrath. (CICERO.)

And we do not set upon the wicked, or our enemies, vigorously enough, unless we are angry. And they say that the barrister must provoke the judge to anger in order to obtain justice.

Strong passions moved Themistocles, moved Demosthenes, and have spurred the Philosophers to labour night and day, and to travel in distant countries ; they lead us to honour, to learning, to health : useful ends. And that faintheartedness with which we suffer grief and trouble helps to nourish remorse and repentance in the conscience, and make us feel that the scourges of God are for our chastisement, as well as the scourges of public correction.

Compassion acts as a spur to clemency ; and the wisdom to preserve and govern our lives is aroused by our fear. How many fine actions are due to ambition ! how many to presumption ! In short, no conspicuous and gallant valour but is caused by some unruly emotion.

Is it not possible that this is one of the reasons that moved the Epicureans to relieve God of all care and solicitude about our affairs, since his goodness cannot work its effects upon us without disturbing his repose through passions, which are so many spurs and incitements driving the soul to virtuous actions ? Or did they think otherwise, and regard them as tempests which shamefully seduce the soul out of her tranquillity ? *As we imagine the sea to be calm, when not the least breath of air stirs its waves ; so we judge the soul to be tranquil and at rest when no passion can stir her* (Cicero).

How variously our passions react upon our thoughts and reasoning faculties, and change our ideas to their very opposites ! What reliance then can we place in a thing so unstable and shifting, liable by its condition to be domineered by mental disturbances, and never going but a forced and borrowed pace ? If our judgement be at the mercy of sickness and violent emotions ; if folly and madness are bound to influence the impression we receive of things, what reliance can we place in it ?

Is it not very rash on the part of Philosophy to suppose that men perform their greatest actions, and those most nearly approaching to divinity, when they are furious and mad, and beside themselves ? We are thought to become better by the deadening and privation of our reason. The two natural ways by which to enter into the cabinet of the gods, and there to foresee the course of destinies, are madness and sleep. This is a quaint notion, that by the dislocation of our reason through our passions we become virtuous ; that by its annihilation in madness or sleep, the image of death, we become soothsayers and prophets !

I was never more ready to believe it. It is a pure frenzy which the sacred Truth has breathed into the spirit of Philosophy, which wrests from it the confession, contrary to its own standpoint, that the tranquil state of our soul, the composed state, the healthiest state that philosophy can win for her, is not her best state. Our waking state is more asleep than sleep ; our wisdom is less wise than madness. Our dreams are better than our reason. The worst abode we can choose is in ourselves.

But does Philosophy think that we are not wise enough to remark that the voice that renders the spirit, when detached from man, so clear-sighted, so great, so perfect, and, whilst it is in man, so earthly, ignorant, and cloudy, is a voice proceeding from the spirit which is a part of earthly, ignorant, and cloudy man ; and, for that reason, a voice not to be trusted and believed ?

I, who am of a dull and easy disposition, have no great experience of those violent emotions, most of which suddenly take our soul unawares, without giving her time to recollect herself. But that passion which is said to arise in the hearts of young men through idleness, although it walks with a leisurely and measured step, very evidently manifests, to those who have tried to resist its influence, the violence of the alteration and subversion which our judgement suffers.

I have at other times attempted to arm myself to withstand and repel its advances (for I am so far from being one of those who encourage vices, that I would not even follow them, unless forcibly dragged by them). I would feel the beginning, the growth and increase of the passion in spite of my resistance, and in the end, quite alive and with open eyes, I would be seized and possessed by it, to such a degree that, as in drunkenness, things adopted quite a different appearance from the ordinary. The attractions of the desired object would visibly swell and increase; they would be blown out and expanded by the breath of my imagination. The difficulties of the pursuit appeared to be smoothed and levelled, my reason and conscience appeared to withdraw into the background. But, this fire being damped all in an instant, as it were in the brilliance of a flash of lightning, my soul would recover another kind of sight, another state and another judgement; the difficulties of retreat would appear great and insurmountable, and the same things would take on quite a different aspect and taste to that which they offered in the heat of desire.

Which had the more likelihood? Pyrrho cannot tell.

We are never without sickness. Fevers have their hot and cold periods; from the effects of a burning passion we fall back into the effects of a shivery passion.

As far as I had shot forward, so far do I recoil backwards:

> As when, with alternating ebb and flow,
> The advancing sea now rushes to the beach,
> Shoots o'er the crags in torrent foam, and bathes
> With curved billow all the sandy bourne,
> Now, with swift ebb, retreats, and sucking back
> The shingle, leaves the beach with gliding shoal. (VIRGIL.)

Now, being conscious of this my liability to change, I have accidentally cultivated in myself a certain steadfastness of belief, and have hardly altered my original and natural opinions. For, however much new fashions may appeal to me, I do not readily change, for fear of losing by the exchange. And since I am not capable of choosing for myself, I accept the choice of others, and remain in the state wherein God has placed me. Otherwise I could not keep from perpetual rolling. Thus, by the grace of God, I have kept wholly, without being stirred or troubled by conscience, within the ancient tenets of our religion, amidst the many sects and divisions that our times have brought forth.

The writings of the ancients, I mean the good, serious and pregnant works, allure and carry me almost whither they please; the one I am listening to always appears to me the most forcible. I find each one right in his turn, although they contradict one another. The ease with which strong minds lend probability to whatever they please, and the fact that nothing is so strange but that they will try to colour it sufficiently to deceive a simplicity like mine, manifestly shows the weakness of their proof.

The heavens and the stars have been swinging round for three thousand years, as all the world had believed, until Cleanthes of Samos, or, according to Theophrastus, Nicetas of Syracuse, presumed to proclaim that it was the earth that moved, revolving about its axis, through the oblique circle of the zodiac. And, in our days, Copernicus has so well grounded this theory, that he very lawfully uses it for all astronomical conclusions. What can we make of that, except that we need not bother our heads about which of the two theories is right? And who knows but that a third opinion, a thousand years hence, will overthrow the two former?

> Thus it is
> That rolling ages change the times of things:
> What erst was of a price, becomes at last
> A discard of no honour; whilst another
> Succeeds to glory, issuing from contempt,
> And day by day is sought for more and more,
> And, when 'tis found, doth flower in men's praise,
> Object of wondrous honour. (LUCRETIUS.)

Thus, when we are offered some new theory, we have great reason to distrust it, and to remember that before it was introduced the contrary was in vogue; and as that was overthrown by this, a third discovery may start up, in time to come, which may knock the second on the head.

Before the principles which Aristotle introduced were in repute, other principles satisfied human reason, as his satisfy us at this moment. What letters-patent, what special privilege have these, that the course of our discoveries should stop at them, and that they should for all time to come possess our belief? They are no more exempt from being thrust out of doors than their forerunners.

When I am driven into a corner by a new argument, I ought to consider that what I cannot answer satisfactorily, another will answer; for to believe all the likely things we cannot confute is great simplicity. It would follow therefrom that the belief of all common people (and we are all common people) would be as versatile as a weather-cock. For their minds, being soft and unresisting, would be continually forced to receive other and other impressions, the last ever effacing the traces of the preceding one. He who finds himself at a loss must answer, according to the usual practice in law-suits, that he will confer with his counsel; or he will refer to the wisest of those who have been his teachers.

How long has medicine been in the world? It is said that a new-comer, whom they call Paracelsus,[1] is changing and reversing the whole order of ancient rules, and maintaining that to this hour that science has been of no service but to kill men. I believe that he can easily verify that statement. But I do not think it would be very wise to stake my life on the proof of his novel experiments.

We must not believe every man, says the adage, because any man may say anything.

One of those men who profess new and improved methods in physics said to me not long ago that all the ancients had evidently miscalculated the nature and motion of the winds, which he would make very palpable to me if I would give ear to him. After listening with some patience to his arguments, which had all the appearance of likelihood, 'What! I answered, did those who navigated under the laws of Theophrastus go west when they were steering east? Did they go sideways or backwards?' 'That was chance, he replied; at all events they miscalculated.' I then replied that I would rather believe facts than reasons.

Now those are things that often clash, and I have been told that in Geometry (which thinks it has reached the high-water mark of certainty among the sciences) may be found irrefutable demonstrations that subvert the truth of experience. For example, Jacques Pelletier said to me in my house, that he had discovered two lines that started out to meet, which nevertheless he proved could never meet to all eternity. And the Pyrrhonians employ their argu-

[1] Theophrastus von Hohenheim, a Swiss physician who adopted the rather pretentious name of Paracelsus ('greater than Celsus'). 'His method and influence tended in the direction of the immediate observation of nature, the discarding of antiquated theories, the encouragement of independent research, experiments and innovation.'—*Chambers's Encyclopaedia*.

ments and their reason only to wreck the apparent facts of experience; and it is marvellous how far the nimbleness of our reason has followed them in their design to resist the evidence of facts. For they demonstrate that we do not move, that we do not speak, that there is neither weight nor heat, with the same force of arguments with which we prove the most likely things.

Ptolemy, who was a great man, had fixed the limits of our world, and all the ancient philosophers thought they had taken its measure, excepting some remote islands which might have escaped their notice. A thousand years ago it would have been a case of Pyrrhonizing to question the science of cosmography, and its universally accepted conclusions. It was heresy to admit the existence of Antipodes. And behold! in this century of ours there has just been discovered an infinite extent of terra firma, not merely an island or one particular country, but a hemisphere nearly equal in extent to the one we knew! The geographers of our time do not stick at assuring us that to-day all is discovered, everything has been seen:

> For what we have at hand,
> That chiefly pleases and seems best of all. (LUCRETIUS.)

The question is, if Ptolemy, grounding his belief on reason, was once mistaken, whether it would not be foolish on my part now to trust the word of those geographers; and whether it is not more likely that this great body which we call the World is quite another thing than we imagine.

Plato maintains that it changes its aspect in every way; that the heavens, the stars and the sun at times reverse the motion we see, changing east to west. The Egyptian priests told Herodotus that since their first king, who lived eleven thousand and odd years before their time (and they showed him the effigies of all their kings, in the form of statues taken from the life), the sun had four times altered its course; That the sea and the land alternately change into one another; That the birth of the world has not been determined.

Aristotle and Cicero say the same. And some one [1] amongst us affirms, that the world has existed from all eternity; that it is mortal, and comes to life again after

[1] Origen.

many changes, calling Solomon and Isaiah to witness, in order to evade those objections, that God has at some time been a creator without a creature ; that he has been idle ; that he abandoned his idleness by setting his hand to this work ; and that he is consequently subject to change.

In the most famous of the Greek schools [1] the World is regarded as a god made by another and greater god, and is composed of a body, and of a soul situated in the centre of it, spreading, by musical numbers, to its circumference ; divine, very happy, very great, very wise, eternal. In it are other gods, the earth, the sea, the stars, which entertain one another with a harmonious and perpetual motion and divine dance ; now meeting, now parting, hiding, showing themselves, changing their order, sometimes in front, sometimes behind.

Heraclitus declared that the World was composed by fire ; and that, by order of the Fates, it would some day be kindled and resolve itself into fire, and some day would be born again. And of men Apuleius says, *Severally mortal, as a body perpetual*.

Alexander wrote to his mother a story told to him by an Egyptian priest, which the latter had gathered from their monuments, and which evidenced the extreme antiquity of that nation and comprised a true account of the birth and progress of other countries.

Cicero and Diodorus say that in their day the Chaldeans kept a record of four hundred thousand odd years ;

Aristotle, Pliny, and others, that Zoroaster lived six thousand years before the age of Plato.

Plato says that the people of the city of Saïs possess written records of eight thousand years, and that the city of Athens was built a thousand years before the said city of Saïs ;

Epicurus, that whilst the things of this world are as we see them, they are quite alike and after the same fashion in many other worlds. Which he would have said with greater assurance, if he had seen how the conditions of that new world of the West Indies resemble and correspond to those of our own in the present and the past, as shown by such strange examples.

In truth, when we consider the things that have come to our knowledge regarding the course of this terrestrial

[1] The Platonic School.

government, I have often marvelled to see, divided by great distances of time and place, so many coincidences in popular, fabulous ideas, so many uncivilized customs and beliefs, which, from whatever side we may look at them, seem to have no connexion with our inborn reason. The human mind is a great worker of miracles. But in this correspondence there is a something much more anomalous which I am unable to define. It shows itself also in names, in many incidents, and in a thousand other things.

For in that newly-discovered hemisphere were found nations who, as far as we know, had never heard of our world; some that believed in circumcision; regions in which great states were governed by women, without the help of men; where our Lent and fastings were reflected, with the addition of abstinence from women. Where, as with us, the cross, in varying shapes, was held in honour. In one place tombs were adorned with it; in another it was worn by people, especially the St. Andrew's cross, to protect themselves against nocturnal visions, or placed on the beds of children against enchantments. In another place they came upon a very tall wooden cross which was worshipped as the god of rain, and that very far inland.

There they found a very plain likeness of our shriving-priests, besides the wearing of mitres, the celibacy of the priesthood, the art of divining by the entrails of sacrificed animals, abstinence from every kind of flesh and fish in their diet; the custom of the priests, when officiating, to use a special language in place of the vulgar tongue. And that fanciful notion that the first god was ousted by a second, his younger brother. That men were created with all kinds of advantages, which were afterwards taken from them for their sin; that they were removed from their land and reduced to a worse condition.

That they were once submerged by an inundation of waters from heaven; that only a few families escaped, who fled into the caves of high mountains, which caves they stopped up, so that the water could not come in, having shut up therein many kinds of animals; that when they perceived the rain to be ceasing, they drove out some dogs, which returning clean and wet, they concluded that the waters had not yet quite subsided; then sending out other dogs and seeing them return muddy, they issued forth to repeople the world, which they found full of nothing but snakes.

In one place they met with the belief in a Day of Judgement, so that the people took very great offence when the Spaniards scattered the bones of their dead in their search of the tombs for rich spoils, saying that those bones they had dispersed could not easily rejoin. They have trade by barter, and no other kind ; fairs and markets for that purpose ; dwarfs and misshapen persons to grace the tables of their princes ; the practice of falconry according to the nature of their birds ; tyrannical subsidies ; refinements in horticulture ; dancing and tumbling ; the music of instruments ; coats of arms ; tennis-courts, dice and games of chance, at which they often become so excited that they will stake their persons and their freedom ; no medicine but that of charms ; the system of writing in pictures.

The belief of a single first man, father of all the nations ; worship of a God who once lived as a man in perfect virginity, who, with fasting and penitence, preached the law of Nature and religious ceremonies, and who vanished from the world without dying a natural death. The belief in giants ; the custom of drinking to excess and getting drunk with their liquor ; religious ornaments with painted bones and deaths' heads ; surplices, holy water, and sprinklers ; the custom of wives and slaves vying in their eagerness to be burned or interred with their dead husbands or masters ; the law by which the eldest son succeeds to the whole property, the younger having no portion but obedience ; the custom, at the promotion to a certain office of great authority, of the promoted taking a new name and discarding his own ; the custom of strewing lime on the knee of a new-born infant, with these words : ' From dust thou art come, to dust shalt thou return ; ' the art of augury.

These empty shadows of our religion, which are seen in some of these examples, bear witness to its dignity and divinity. Not only has it insinuated itself to some extent into all the infidel nations on this side of the world, by a sort of imitation, but also into those barbarians, as by a universal and natural inspiration. For they also found a belief in a Purgatory, but in a new form : what we give to the fire they give to the cold, and imagine the souls to be both purged and punished by the severity of extreme cold.

And this example reminds me of another amusing diversity; for, as there were some nations who found a satisfaction in unsheathing the end of their member, removing the skin after the manner of the Mahommedans and Jews, there were others who made so great a scruple about laying it bare, that, very carefully stretching the skin, they brought it up and fastened it with little cords, for fear lest the end might see the air.

And this diversity too, that, whereas we, in honour of kings and festivals, dress ourselves up in the handsomest clothes we possess, in some regions, to emphasize their disparity and their submission to their king, his subjects present themselves before him in their meanest attire, or on entering the palace throw some tattered old gown over their good one, that all the lustre and ornament may remain with their lord.

But let us continue. If Nature encloses within the bounds of her ordinary progress, besides all other things, the beliefs, judgements, and opinions of men; if these beliefs have their revolving seasons, their birth, their death, like cabbages; if heaven moves and rolls them about at its pleasure, what magisterial and permanent authority are we to attribute to them? If experience makes it palpable to us that the form of our being depends on the atmosphere, the climate and the soil on which we are born, and not only our complexion, our stature, our constitution and countenance, but also the faculties of our mind—*the climate affects not only the vigour of the body, but also that of the soul*, says Vegetius—; and if the goddess who founded the city of Athens chose for its situation a region whose temperature made men cunning, as the priests of Egypt told Solon:—*the air of Athens is light, wherefore the Athenians are reputed to be more astute; that of Thebes is heavy, wherefore the Thebans are more dull-witted and more robust* (Cicero)—; so that, as fruits and animals are born differing among one another, men are born more or less warlike, just, temperate and docile; here given to wine, elsewhere to theft and lechery; here inclined to superstition, elsewhere to unbelief; here to freedom, there to slavery; capable of one science or one art; dull or clever; obedient or rebellious; good or bad, according as the place where they live inclines them; and assume a new disposition if they change from one place to another, like the trees; which was the reason why Cyrus would not grant the Persians permission to leave their rugged and hilly country and remove to another that was level and mild, saying that a fat and soft soil made men soft, and a fertile land made barren brains; if at one time we see one art, one belief to flourish, at another time another, by virtue of some celestial influence; if we see such or such an age produce such or such natures, and bend humankind to such or such a ply; the minds of men now luxuriant, now lean, like our fields; what becomes of all those fine prerogatives on which we flatter ourselves? Since a wise man may go wrong, and a hundred men, and many nations; nay, since even human nature, in our belief, may for many centuries go wrong in this thing or that; what assurance can we have that it will at some time cease to go wrong, and that in this century it is not on the wrong track?

Among other evidence of our imbecility I think that this deserves not to be forgotten, That even man's desire will not enable him to find out what he needs; That, I will not say by enjoyment, but in imagination and wish, we are unable to agree about what we need for our satisfaction. Let our imagination cut out and sew at its pleasure, it cannot even desire what is meet for it, and be satisfied:

> For when does Reason guide desire or fear?
> What plan dost thou conceive so happily,
> But that thou wilt repent of thy endeavour
> And of the granted prayer? (JUVENAL.)

Therefore it was that Socrates prayed to the gods to give him nothing but what they knew to be good for him. And the import of the Lacedemonian's prayer, both public and private, was simply that he might be granted good and beautiful things, leaving the choice and selection of them to the discretion of the supreme powers:

> We pray for wife and child, but those above
> Are well aware what child and wife will prove. (JUVENAL.)

And the Christian prays to God that 'his will be done', in order not to fall into the calamity that the poets invent for King Midas. He prayed the gods that everything he touched might turn to gold. His prayer was heard. His wine was gold, his bread gold, and the feathers of his bed, his shirt and clothes were all of gold, so that he found himself overwhelmed in the realization of his desire, and gifted with a privilege that proved intolerable. He was fain to unpray his prayer :

> Amazed at this calamity so rare,
> To be so rich, yet pitiably poor,
> He wishes now he could his wealth evade,
> And curses that for which before he prayed. (OVID.)

Take my own case. Being young, I desired of Fortune, as much as anything else, the order of Saint Michael ; for at that time it was the greatest mark of honour with the French nobility, and very rare. She ironically gratified my desire. Instead of raising and lifting me up from my station to reach it, she treated me much more graciously : she debased it and brought it down to the level of my shoulders, and even below that.[1]

Cleobis and Bito, Triphonius and Agamedes, having besought, the former of their goddess, the latter of their god, a recompense worthy of their piety, received death for their gift. So much do the gods differ from us as to what is good for us !

God might sometimes grant us wealth, honours, life and even health, to our prejudice ; for what is pleasing is not always good for us. If, instead of a cure, he sends us death or an aggravation of our ills—*thy rod and thy staff they comfort me* (Psalms)—he does so for providential reasons, for he takes account of what is our due much more unerringly than we can do ; and we must accept it gladly, as from a very wise and a very loving hand :

> Take my advice : allow the Gods themselves
> To weigh what is most meet we should receive,
> And to our state most profitable . . .
> Man is more dear to them than to himself. (JUVENAL.)

For to beg of them honours or offices is to beg of them to hurl you into a battle, or a game of dice, or something of a like nature, of which the issue is unknown to you, and the advantage doubtful.

There is no strife among the Philosophers so violent and so bitter as that which arises over the question of the

---

[1] This order was afterwards superseded as the greatest distinction by the Order of the Holy Ghost, founded by Henri III, and it greatly fell in estimation.

sovereign good of man, which, according to Varro's calculation, brought forth two hundred and eighty-eight sects. *But whoever disagrees with me about the chief good, disagrees with me about the whole principle of philosophy* (Cicero).

> I have three guests to dine. Alas for me,
> Their tastes about no single dish agree!
> What shall I give? What not? You can't abide
> The very thing for which another cried,
> And what I give as a *bonne bouche* to you
> Is sour and odious to the other two. (HORACE.)

Nature should give the same answer to all their disputtings and quarrellings.

Some say that our well-being lies in Virtue, others in Pleasure, others again in conforming to Nature; this man in knowledge, that in freedom from pain, this other in not allowing ourselves to be led away by appearances. (And this last idea seems to come near to that of the ancient Pythagoras:

> To wonder at naught is all the art I know
> To make men happy and to keep them so; [HORACE.]

which is the aim of the Pyrrhonian school.)

Aristotle attributes this being amazed at nothing to greatness of soul. And Arcesilaus said that to suspend one's judgement and to keep it upright and inflexible is good, but to consent and yield is bad and deplorable. It is true that in setting this up as a certain axiom he departed from Pyrrhonism. The Pyrrhonians, when they say that the sovereign good is Ataraxy, which is the immobility of the judgement, do not mean it in an affirmative sense; but the same impulse of their soul which makes them shun a precipice and take shelter from the cool of the evening, itself suggests this fancy and makes them reject any other.

How I could wish that, whilst I live, either another or Justus Lipsius,[1] the most learned man still remaining to us, a man of a most polished and judicious mind, true cousin-german to my Turnebus, had the will, as well as the health and sufficient leisure, carefully and honestly, and according to our lights, to collect and make a divided and classified list of all the theories of ancient philosophy on the subject

[1] Justus Lipsius, a Belgian scholar with whom Montaigne corresponded. He partially fulfilled this wish in a large work on Stoicism, which appeared after Montaigne's death.

of our being and our conduct of life ; their controversies, showing how the different schools succeeded one another and in what repute they were held, how the founders and followers applied their own precepts on memorable and exemplary occasions in their lives ! What a fine and useful work that would be !

Moreover, if we ourselves determine the rule of our conduct, into what a confusion we are thrown ! For the counsel that our reason is most likely to give us is that every man generally shall obey the laws of his country, which was the advice of Socrates, inspired, as he says, by divine counsel. And what does reason mean thereby, if not that our duty is only guided by chance ?

Truth ought to have one face, always and everywhere the same. If a man's justice and equity had any substance and real existence, he would not let it be bound by the conditions and customs of this country or that. It would not be from the ideas of the Persians or Indians that virtue would take its shape.

There is nothing more subject to continual change than the laws. During my lifetime I have known the laws of our neighbours the English to change and change back again three or four times ; not only in political matters, wherein permanence may be dispensed with, but in the most important subject that can be, to wit, religion. Whereat I am the more shamed and grieved as they are a nation with whom the people of my district were once so intimately acquainted, that there yet remain in my household some traces of our old cousinship.[1]

And here at home I have known a thing to become lawful which used to be a capital offence ;[2] and we who hold other opinions may quite possibly one day, so uncertain are the fortunes of war, become guilty of high treason, both against men and God, should our justice fall under the mercy of injustice, and, after a few years' possession, assume a contrary character.

How could that ancient God[3] more clearly accuse human knowledge of ignorance of the divine being, and give men to understand that their religion was but a thing of their own

---

[1] Guienne belonged to England from 1152 to 1453.
[2] Montaigne is perhaps thinking of the Protestant faith.
[3] Apollo.

contrivance, and useful as a social bond, than by declaring, as he did to those who sought instruction of his tripod, 'That the true worship for every man was that which he found observed by the custom of the place where he lived?'

O heavens! how greatly we are under obligation to the goodness of our sovereign Creator for having purged our belief of those vagrant and arbitrary devotions, and fixed it on the eternal foundation of his holy word!

What then will Philosophy tell us in this strait? 'That we must follow the laws of our country?' That is to say, that surging sea of the beliefs of a people or a ruler, who will paint me justice in so many colours, and reshape it into as many forms as there are changes of passion in themselves. I cannot have a judgement so flexible. What kind of goodness can that be that was yesterday held in honour, and will cease to be so to-morrow, and which the mere crossing of a river turns into a crime?

What kind of truth can that be that is bounded by these mountains, and that becomes a lie to the people on the other side of them?

But those people amuse me who, to give some certainty to laws, say that there are some that are fixed, perpetual and immutable, which they call laws of Nature, and which, by the very condition of their being, are imprinted in humankind. And of these some say there are three, some four, some more, some less; a sign that it is a mark as doubtful as the rest. Now, they are in such a hapless case (for what else can I call it but haplessness, that out of so infinite a number of laws there does not happen to be one at least that has been permitted by Fortune and the heedlessness of chance to be universally accepted by the consent of all nations?), they are, I say, so unhappy, that of those three or four selected laws there is not one that is not rejected and disowned, not by one nation, but by many.

Now the only likely token, by which they can argue some laws to be natural, is universality of approval. For what Nature has truly commanded us we should without doubt obey with universal consent. And not only every nation, but every individual, would resent the force and violence that any one should put upon him to drive him to oppose that law. Let them produce me a law of that kind, that I may prove it.

Protagoras and Aristo gave no other justification of the laws than the authority and judgement of the law-giver; and held that, apart from this, the words 'good' and 'honest' would lose their meaning, and become empty names of indifferent things.

Thrasymachus, in Plato, thinks there is no other right but the convenience of the superior.

There is nothing in which the world varies so much as in customs and laws. Many a thing is abominable here that is commended elsewhere; as in Sparta cleverness in stealing. Marriages with near relations are capital offences with us, and are in other countries held in honour:

> Some nations, so 'tis said, there are,
> Where fathers daughters, sons their mothers wed,
> And love is deepened by the double tie. (OVID.)

The murder of infants, the murder of fathers, community of wives, traffic in robberies, licence in all sorts of pleasures; nothing in short is so outrageous but it may be allowed by the custom of some nation or other.

I can quite believe that there are laws of Nature, such as we may observe in other creatures; but in us they have vanished, this fine human reason of ours thrusting itself into everything, commanding and domineering, confusing and distorting the face of things, in its vanity and inconsistency. *Nothing is any longer really ours; what I call ours is the result of art* (Cicero).

Things may be considered from various points of view, which is the chief cause of diversity of opinions. One nation views a thing from one side, and stops there, another from another side.

Nothing more horrible can be imagined than to eat one's father. The people who formerly observed this custom, however, regarded it as evidence of piety and natural affection, as they thought by that means to give their progenitors the most honourable and worthy sepulture, harbouring in themselves, and as it were in their marrow, the bodies and remains of their fathers; in some sort resuscitating and regenerating them by transmutation into their living flesh, by means of digestion and nourishment. We may easily imagine what cruelty and abomination it would have been to men steeped and imbued with this superstition, to throw their parents' mortal remains to the corruption of the earth, and to be food for beasts and worms.

Lycurgus considered theft from the point of view of the quickness, the agility, the impudence and skill with which a neighbour was done out of a thing, and the benefit which redounded to the people in general by every man looking more carefully to the safe keeping of what was his ; and believed that this double instruction in attack and defence was to the advantage of military discipline (which was the principal science and virtue in which he desired to train his people), and of much greater consideration than the disorder and injustice resulting from the purloining of others' property.

Dionysius the Tyrant offered Plato a long, figured, perfumed gown in the Persian fashion. Plato declined it, saying that, being born a man, he would not willingly dress in a woman's gown ; but Aristippus accepted it with this reply, ' that no apparel could corrupt a chaste heart.' His friends taunted him with want of spirit for being so unconcerned when Dionysius spat in his face. ' A fisherman, he said, will suffer himself to be dashed from head to foot by the sea-waves, to catch a gudgeon.' Diogenes was washing his cabbages and, seeing him pass, said, ' If you could live on cabbage, you would not fawn upon a tyrant ' ; to which Aristippus retorted, ' If you could live among men, you would not be washing cabbages.'

Thus does Reason provide a different point of view for different actions. It is a two-handled jug which can be grasped by the left or the right.

> War it is thou bringest,
> O stranger-country ! Steeds are armed for war,
> And war these herds portend us. Yet at times
> The same beasts use to bow them to the car,
> And, yoked together, bear the friendly rein ;
> Yes, there is hope for peace too. (VIRGIL.)

Some one was admonishing Solon not to shed vain and bootless tears for the death of his son. ' It is for that reason, he said, that I more rightly shed them, because they are bootless and vain.' Socrates' wife aggravated her grief by this consideration : ' Oh, how unjust of these wicked judges to put him to death ! ' ' Would you then rather that they should execute me justly ? ' he replied.

We have our ears bored; the Greeks regarded that as a mark of slavery. We retire into privacy to enjoy our wives; the Indians do it publicly. The Scythians immolated strangers in their temples; elsewhere temples are a sanctuary:

> All peoples are with hate and fury filled
> For that their neighbours kneel to other Gods,
> Deeming none others can be recognized
> But their own deities. (JUVENAL.)

I have heard of a judge who, when he came across a sharp conflict between Bartolus and Baldus,[1] or some point discussed with many contradictions, was wont to write in the margin of his book, 'Question for a friend'; that is to say, that the truth was so entangled and debatable, that in a similar case he might favour whichever of the parties he thought fit. It needed but a little more wit and cleverness to write in all cases 'Question for a friend'. The lawyers and judges of our day discover in all cases enough bias to incline them to whichever side they please.

In a branch of learning of such infinite range, depending on the authority of so many opinions, and in so arbitrary a subject, there must necessarily be many conflicting judgements. And so we see that, be a law-suit never so clear, opinions regarding it will be found to differ. The judgement of one court is reversed by another, and on another occasion by itself. As a result of this licence, which is a marvellous blemish on the solemn authority and lustre of our courts of justice, it is quite usual to be dissatisfied with a sentence, and to run from court to court for a decision on the same case.

As to the freedom of philosophical thought concerning Vice and Virtue, that is a matter on which there is no need to expatiate, and on which there are many opinions which it would be better to hush up and not publish abroad for the weaker minds.

Arcesilaus said that in lechery it mattered little on which side or where it was committed. *As to lascivious pleasures, Epicurus thinks that, if nature requires them, we are not to regard birth, place or rank, but age, beauty and person* (Cicero). *Nor do we think virtuous love inconsistent with a wise man* (Cicero). *Let us consider up to what age youths are*

---

[1] Two eminent Italian lawyers of the fourteenth century.

to be loved (Seneca). These two last citations from the Stoics, and the reproach of Dicaearchus to Plato himself on this subject,[1] show what excessive and unnatural licence even the soundest philosophy will tolerate.

The laws derive their authority from possession and use; it is dangerous to trace them back to their origin. They grow and gather dignity as they roll on, like our rivers. Follow them upstream to their source, it is but a little spring of water scarce discernible, which thus grows in pride and strength as it grows older. Look at the ancient motives which gave the first start to this famous torrent, so authoritative, awe-inspiring and venerable; you will find them so trifling and slender that it is no wonder that these people, who weigh and reduce everything to reason, and who accept nothing by authority and on trust, find that their judgements are often very remote from those of the people.

It is no wonder if people who take their pattern from the first image of Nature, in most of their opinions swerve from the common path. As, for instance, few of them[2] would have approved the strict conditions of our marriages; and most of them would have wished wives to be held in common and without obligation. They rejected our proprieties.

[Everybody has heard of the want of shame shown by the Cynic philosophers in their conduct.] Chrysippus said that a philosopher will turn a dozen somersaults in public, even without his breeches, for a dozen of olives. He would hardly have advised Cleisthenes to refuse his daughter, the beautiful Agarista, to Hippoclides, because he saw him stand on his head with his legs apart on a table.

Metrocles broke wind rather indiscreetly while disputing in presence of his school, and kept his house for shame, until Crates went to see him, and, after consoling and reasoning with him, set him an example of licence, urged him to a competition in wind-breaking, and so cured him of his scruples; and besides, drew him over to his freer Stoical sect, from the more urbane Peripatetic school of which he had hitherto been a follower.

What we call Decency—not to dare to do that openly which it is proper to do in private—they call Foolishness; and the affectation of concealing and condemning those of

---

[1] i. e., for countenancing pederasty.
[2] i. e., few of the ancient philosophers.

our actions which nature, custom, and our desire publish and proclaim, they reputed a vice. And they held that it was profaning the mysteries of Venus to remove them from the secluded sanctuary of her temple, and expose them to the people's gaze ; and that to draw her sports from behind the curtain was to cheapen them. (Shame is a weighty coin. Concealment, reservation, limitation, have their share in its estimation.) They held that voluptuousness very ingeniously protested, under the mask of virtue, against being prostituted in the middle of the highways, trodden under the feet and eyes of the crowd, prizing rather the dignity and convenience of its wonted cabinets.

Wherefore some say that to abolish the public brothels is not only to spread about everywhere the fornication that was assigned to those places, but also to spur men on to that vice, by making it difficult :

> Thou, once her husband, art become her lover,
> Now that she is thy rival's spouse ;
> Why should'st thou love another's, and not thine own ?
> Art impotent without the risk ? (MARTIAL.)

This experience is diversified in a thousand examples :

> Scarce one in all the city would embrace
> Thy proffered wife, Cecilian, free to have ;
> But now she's guarded and locked up, apace
> Thy custom comes. Oh, thou art a wily knave ! (MARTIAL.)

A philosopher who was surprised in the act, and was asked what he was doing, replied, 'I am planting a man ;' no more blushing at being so caught than if he had been found planting garlic.[1]

I think it was out of over tenderness and respect that a great writer and monk [2] maintained that this action was so necessarily bound up with concealment and modesty, that he could not be persuaded that those shameless embraces of the Cynics were effectual ; but that they stopped short at imitating lascivious motions, in order to keep up the reputation for shamelessness which their school of philosophy professed ; and that it was still necessary for them to seek the shade to eject what shame had withheld and restrained.

[1] This story of Diogenes has had a wide circulation, but, according to Bayle, has never been traced. Give the devil his due !
[2] Saint Augustine, in his *City of God*.

He had not seen far enough into their debauchery. For Diogenes, behaving indecently in public, expressed a wish, in presence of the bystanders 'that he could as easily satisfy his hunger by rubbing his belly'. To those who asked him why he did not seek a more convenient place for eating than the open street, he answered, 'Because I am hungry in the open street.'

The women philosophers who mixed with their sect also mixed with their persons in all places and without discrimination; and Hipparchia was received into the society of Crates only on condition of following in all things the uses and customs of his order.

These philosophers set an extreme price upon Virtue, and rejected any but a moral teaching. And yet in all their actions they attributed the chief authority to the choice of their sage, as being above the laws; and placed no other check upon sensual pleasures but moderation and the preservation of others' liberty.

Heraclitus and Protagoras argued from the fact that wine seems bitter to the sick man and grateful to the sound, and that an oar appears bent in the water and straight outside of it, and from the like contradictory appearances in other things that all objects had in themselves the causes of their appearances: that in wine there was a certain bitterness which corresponded with the sick man's palate, and in the oar a certain bent quality which corresponds with the person who looks at it in the water. And so with all the rest. Which is as much as to say that everything is in all things, and consequently nothing in any; for where all is, nothing is.

This theory puts me in mind of what we know by experience, that there is no meaning or aspect, either straight, or bitter, or sweet, or crooked, that the wit of man cannot find in the writings he may undertake to dig into. Into the clearest, simplest, and most perfect language imaginable, how many lies and falsehoods have not been read! What heresy has not found in them sufficient grounds and evidence, both for attack and defence? For this reason it is that the originators of such errors will never let go the proof and evidence afforded by their interpretation of words.

A certain dignitary, trying to justify to me by authority

the search for the philosopher's stone, in which he is entirely absorbed, recently quoted to me five or six passages from the Bible, on which he said he relied principally for the discharge of his conscience (for he is an ecclesiastic by profession); and indeed the discovery was not only amusing, but also very properly suited to the defence of that pretty branch of learning.

In this way do the diviners' fables gain credit. There is no prophet of so great authority that people will think it worth while turning over his pages and carefully examining his words from every side and in their remotest meanings, who cannot be made to say whatever we please, like the Sibyls. For there are so many ways and means of interpreting a thing, that it can hardly be but that an ingenious mind will discover in any subject, either obliquely or directly, some meaning that will serve his turn.

Therefore it is that those people have so frequently and from all times employed a cloudy and obscure style. Let the writer succeed in attracting and busying posterity about himself (which he may effect not only by the excellence of his matter, but as much, and more, by the accidental favour it enjoys), he need not care a rap if he expresses himself, either through stupidity or subtlety, somewhat obscurely and contradictorily. There will be any number of minds that will sift and shake him, and squeeze out any number of meanings, either his own, or beside the point, or contradictory, which will all redound to his honour. He will see himself enriched through the means of his disciples, like the tutor by the fees [1] of his scholars.

This it is that has given value to many worthless things, that has made a reputation for many books, and filled them with any kind of matter that the reader is pleased to put into them. One and the same thing may be seen and considered from a thousand different points of view, or as many as we please.

Can it be possible that Homer intended to say all that he has been made to say? And that he lent himself to so many and so different shapes, that theologians, legislators,

---

[1] *Comme les regents du Lendit.* *Lendits,* according to Cotgrave, are 'gate-money, fairings, or yearly presents bestowed by the scholars of Universities (especially those of Paris) on their tutors'; presumably at the time of the *Lendit,* a great fair held annually near St. Denis.

generals, philosophers, people of every kind who treat of sciences, be it ever so diversely and contradictorily, refer to and rely upon him, as the Grand Master of all functions, works and artists, General Adviser in all undertakings? Whoever had need of oracles and predictions found enough of them in his work to serve his turn.

It is marvellous how many and wonderful passages a learned friend of mine has lighted upon in Homer in support of our religion; and he cannot be easily persuaded that it was not the poet's purpose (and yet he is as well acquainted with him as any man of our time). And what he finds in support of our religion many in ancient times found to support theirs.

See how Plato is tumbled and tossed about! Every man, proud to think that he is on his side, bends him to the side he would wish. They trot him about and ingraft upon him all the new theories accepted by the world, and, as things come to differ, make him differ from himself. To suit their purpose they make him to disclaim the licit manners and customs of his age, because they are illicit in ours. And all this with the more keenness and power as the mind of the interpreter is powerful and keen.

From the same ground on which Heraclitus took his stand and gave out his maxim, 'That all things are as we see them,' Democritus drew a quite opposite conclusion, That objects are in no wise as we see them.' And from the fact that honey appears sweet to one and bitter to another, he argued that it is neither sweet nor bitter.

The Pyrrhonians would say that they know not whether it is sweet or bitter, or neither, or both; for they always reach the high water mark of doubt.

The Cyrenaics maintained that nothing was perceptible from outside, and that that only was perceptible which touched us by internal touch, as pain and pleasure; admitting neither tone nor colour, but only certain impressions that we received of them; and that man's judgement had no other seat.

Protagoras believed that 'what seems to every man is true to every man'.

The Epicureans made the senses judges of all, both in the cognisance of things and in pleasure.

Plato decided that the judgement of the truth, and the

truth itself, derived from opinions and the senses, belonged to the mind and thought.

This discussion has brought me to the consideration of the Senses, in which lie the greatest foundation and proof of our ignorance. Whatever is known is doubtless known by the faculty of the knower; for since the judgement comes from the operation of him who judges, it is reasonable to suppose that this operation is performed by his means and will, not by the constraint of others, as would be the case if we knew things by the power and according to the law of their essence.

Now, all knowledge is conveyed to us through the senses; they are our masters:

> Whereby the opened highways of belief
> Lead most directly into the human breast
> And temples of the mind. (LUCRETIUS.)

Knowledge begins through them and resolves itself into them.

After all we should know no more than a stone, if we did not know that there is sound, smell, light, taste, measure, weight, softness, hardness, roughness, smoothness, colour, breadth, depth. There you have the plan and groundwork of the whole edifice of our knowledge. And according to some, knowledge is nothing other than sensation. He who can drive me to confute the senses, has me by the throat; he cannot make me recoil any further. The senses are the beginning and end of human knowledge:

> Thou'lt find
> That from the senses first hath been create
> Concept of truth, nor can the senses be
> Rebutted . . .
> What then than these our senses must there be
> Worthy a greater trust? (LUCRETIUS.)

Allow them as little as we can, we must still grant them this, that all our instruction is conveyed by way of the senses and their agency. Cicero says that Chrysippus, having tried to discount the strength and power of the senses, raised up against himself arguments to the contrary, and such powerful objections, that he could not refute them. Whereupon Carneades, who supported the opposite side, boasted that he would use the very words and weapons of Chrysippus to fight him with, and therefore exclaimed against him, 'O wretched man, your strength has undone you!'

There is no greater absurdity, in our opinion, than to maintain that fire does not warm, that light does not shine, that there is no weight nor solidity in iron, which are things brought to our notice by the senses; nor is there any belief or knowledge in man which can compare with that for certainty.

The first observation I have to make on the subject of the Senses is that I doubt whether man be provided with all natural senses. I see that there are many creatures that live a full and perfect life, some without sight, and others without hearing; who knows whether we too do not lack two, three, or many other senses? For if any one is wanting, our reason cannot discover the want of it. It is the privilege of the senses to be the extreme limit of our perception. There is nothing beyond them that can help us to discover them. Nay, neither can one sense discover another.

> For shall the ears have power to blame the eyes,
> Or yet the touch the ears? Again, should taste
> Accuse the touch, or shall the nose confute
> Or eyes defeat it? (LUCRETIUS.)

They altogether form the extreme limit of our faculties:

> For unto each has been divided off
> Its functions quite apart, its power to each. (LUCRETIUS.)

It is impossible to make a man who is born blind understand that he does not see; impossible to make him wish to see, and to regret his defect. Wherefore we should not take any assurance from the fact that our soul is contented and satisfied with those senses we possess; seeing that it has not the means of feeling its infirmity and imperfection therein, if there be any. It is impossible to convey anything to this blind man, either by reason, argument, or comparison, that can arouse in his imagination any apprehension of light, colour, and sight. There is nothing behind that can push on the senses to evidence. If those born blind wish they could see, it is not because they understand what they require. They have heard us say that they lack something, that there is something in us which is desirable, and which, with its effects and consequences, they call good; yet they know not what that is, and have neither a near or a distant apprehension of it.

I have seen a gentleman of good family, blind from his birth, or at least from such an early age that he knows not what sight is. He has so little understanding of what he lacks, that he makes use, as we do, of words which imply sight, and applies them in a way peculiarly his own. They brought him a boy, who was his godchild, and taking him in his arms he said, 'My word, what a fine boy! it does one good to look at him; what a merry face!' He will say, like any one of us, 'There is a fine view from this room; it is a clear day; the sun is shining bright.'

There is more to tell; for having heard that hunting, tennis, and shooting at the mark are our sports, he takes a pleasure and a keen interest in them, and imagines that he can share in them as we do; he delights in them, he becomes excited, and yet he only knows of them through his ears. Some one will call to him, 'Look, a hare!' when in the open country where he can clap on his spurs. They will tell him that a hare has been caught, and behold him as proud of the catch as he hears others say they are! He will take a tennis-ball in his left hand and strike it with his racket. He will shoot at random with a musket, and is quite pleased when his men tell him that he is over or beside the mark.

Who knows but that mankind is committing a similar absurdity, through want of some sense or other, and that in consequence of this defect the face of things is for the most part hidden from us? Who knows but that that is the reason why we are perplexed by many of the works of Nature, and that many of the actions of animals, which exceed our capacity, are the result of the exercise of some sense or other which we lack, and that some of them by this means live a fuller and more perfect life than we do? We seize an apple wellnigh with all our senses; we find in it redness, smoothness, smell, and sweetness. Besides these it may have other properties, as drying up or binding,[1] to which we have no corresponding sense.

As to what we call hidden properties in some things, as that of the magnet to attract iron, may we not believe that there are sentient faculties in Nature adapted to perceive

---

[1] *Comme d'asseicher ou restreindre.* I give W. C. Hazlitt's translation. Florio has 'either drying or binding'; Cotton 'as to heat or binding'.

and estimate them, and that the want of such faculties is the cause of our ignorance of the real essence of such things ? It is perhaps some special sense that enables the cock to know the morning and midnight hours, and incites him to crow. That teaches a hen, before all knowledge and experience, to fear a sparrow-hawk, and not a goose or a peacock, though birds of larger size. That warns a chicken of the natural hostility of the cat towards itself, and teaches it not to distrust a dog; to be on its guard against the mewing, which is rather a wheedling sound, of the one, and not against the barking, a harsh and quarrelsome note, of the other. That teaches wasps, ants, and rats always to select the best pear and the best cheese before tasting them ; and guides the stag, the elephant, the snake to the knowledge of certain herbs that have curative properties.

There is no sense that does not exercise great dominion, and enable us by its means to know an infinite number of things. If we lacked the apprehension of sounds, of harmony and the voice, it would cause an inconceivable confusion in all our other knowledge. For, besides what attaches to the proper effect of each sense, how many arguments, consequences, and conclusions we draw with regard to other things, by comparing one sense with another! Let an intelligent man imagine human nature to have been originally created without the sense of sight, and then consider how much ignorance and confusion such a defect would bring upon him, into what obscurity and blindness our soul would be sunk. From this we may see what an important difference it would make for the knowledge of the truth, should we be deprived of some other sense, or of two or three of them. We have built up a truth through the consultation and concurrence of our five senses ; but it would perhaps need the agreement and contribution of eight or ten to perceive it with certainty, and in its essence.

The schools that deny that we can know anything ground their denial chiefly on the uncertainty and weakness of the Senses. For, since all knowledge comes to us by and through them, if they fail in their report, if they alter and corrupt what they convey to us from without, if the light which through them shines into our soul be obscured on the way, we have nothing else to go by.

This extreme difficulty has given rise to these ideas :

'That every object has in itself all that we find in it ; That it has nothing of what we think we find in it ' ; and that of the Epicureans, ' That the sun is no bigger than it appears to our sight ' :

> Whichever it be, she journeys with a form
> Naught larger than the form doth seem to be
> Which we with eyes of ours perceive ;   (LUCRETIUS.)

' That if a body appear large to one who is near, and smaller to one who is at a distance, both appearances are real ' :

> And yet in this we don't at all concede
> That eyes be cheated. . . . And so
> Attach thou not this fault of mine to eyes ;   (LUCRETIUS.)

and this bolder idea, ' That there is no deception in the senses ; that we must be at their mercy, and seek elsewhere reasons to excuse the difference and contradiction we find in them ; nay that we must invent any other false or fanciful idea (for they go to that length) rather than accuse the senses.'

Timagoras declared that he might squeeze and turn his eyes ever so much, he had never been able to see the light of a candle doubled ; and that that appearance was due to a defect in the mind, not of the organ.

Of all absurdities the most absurd to the Epicureans is to deny the power and effect of the senses.

> And therefore what
> At any time unto these senses showed,
> The same is true. And if our reason be
> Unable to unravel to us the cause
> Why objects, which at hand were square, afar
> Seemed rounded, yet it more availeth us,
> Lacking the reason, to pretend a cause
> For each configuration, than to let
> From out our hands escape the obvious things,
> And injure primal faith in sense, and wreck
> All those foundations upon which do rest
> Our life and safety. For not only Reason
> Would topple down ; but even our very life
> Would straightaway collapse, unless we dared
> To trust our Senses and to keep away
> From headlong heights and places to be shunned
> Of a like peril.   (LUCRETIUS.)

This desperate and so unphilosophical advice means

nothing more than that human knowledge can support itself only by unreasonable, foolish, and senseless Reason; but that it is still better that man, in order to assert himself, should make use of it, and of any other remedy however fantastic, rather than confess his necessary stupidity: so unpalatable a truth! He cannot run away from the fact that the Senses are the sovereign lords of his knowledge; but that they are uncertain and liable to deception in all circumstances. It is there he must fight to the death, and, if his legitimate forces fail him, as they do, he must employ stubbornness, heedlessness, impudence.

Should it be true what the Epicureans say, namely, 'That we have no knowledge if the senses represent things falsely'; and also true what the Stoics say, 'That the senses represent things so falsely, that they cannot furnish us with any manner of knowledge,' we shall arrive at the conclusion, to the cost of these two great Dogmatic schools, That there is no such thing as knowledge.

With regard to the failure and uncertainty of the operation of the Senses, any man may provide himself with as many examples as he pleases: so commonly do they play us false. The sound of a trumpet re-echoing in a valley appears to come from in front of us, whilst it really comes from a league behind us:

> Between two mountains rising far away
> From midst the whirl of waters open lies
> A gaping exit for the fleet, and yet
> They seem conjoined in a single isle.
>
> And hills and fields
> Seem fleeing far astern, past which we urge
> The ship, and fly under the bellying sails.
>
> When in the middle of the stream
> Sticks fast our dashing horse, and down we gaze
> Into the river's rapid waves, some force
> Seems then to bear the body of the horse,
> Though standing still, reversely from its course,
> And swiftly push up-stream. (LUCRETIUS.)

When rolling a musket-ball under the forefinger, with the middle finger entwined over it, we have to force ourselves to admit that there is only one, so clearly does the sense of touch tell us that there are two. For we may observe at every turn that the senses are many a time masters of our reason, and force it to receive impressions which it knows and judges to be false. I leave aside the sense of touch, whose functions lie nearer, and are more alive and substantial, which so often, through the effect of the pain it imparts to the body, upsets all those fine Stoical resolutions, and compels that man to cry out with the belly-ache who has most resolutely established the doctrine in his soul, 'That the colic, like every other sickness and pain, is an indifferent thing, that has no power to diminish in any way the supreme happiness and felicity, in which the wise man lives by reason of his virtue.'

No heart is so faint that it does not beat the faster at the sound of our drums and trumpets, nor so hard that it will not be stirred and soothed by sweet music. No soul is so stubborn that it will not feel some touch of reverence when beholding the sombre vastness of our churches, the variety of ornaments and the order of our ceremonials, when hearing the devotion-inspiring notes of our organs, the harmony, so religious and solemn, of our voices. Even they who enter there disdainfully feel a certain thrill at their heart, and a certain awe which makes them distrust their opinions.

For my part, I do not feel strong enough to listen with equanimity to the lines of Horace or Catullus, ably sung by a young and beautiful voice.

And Zeno was right when he said that the voice is the flower of beauty.

Some one tried to make me believe that a man, well known to all of us Frenchmen, had unduly impressed me by his reciting of some lines he had composed ; that they were not the same on paper as in the air, and that my eyes would reverse the judgement of my ears : such is the power of utterance to lend value and shape to that which is left to its mercy ! Wherefore Philoxenus was to be excused when, hearing some one badly accentuating something he had composed, he began stamping on and breaking some tiles that belonged to him, saying, 'I break your property as you spoil mine.'

Why was it that those same men who had resolutely determined to die of their own free will would turn away their eyes, in order not to see the stroke they had ordered to be dealt them ; and that others who, for their cure, wish and order an incision or a cauterization, cannot endure the sight of the preparations, the surgical instruments and the operation itself, since the sight is to have no share in the pain ? Do not these examples sufficiently prove how the Senses dominate the reason ?

We may be quite aware that those tresses are borrowed of a page or a footman, that this blush is a product of Spain, and that this pallor and smoothness of skin has come out of the ocean-sea ; [1] yet must our eyes compel us, against all reason, to think the object more pleasing and lovely. For here there is nothing of her own.

> By dress we are beguiled ; defects are hid
> By gold and gems ; the girl is of herself
> The smallest part. And often when you seek
> The one you'd love mid all this outward show,
> Richness deceives the eye with Gorgon shield. (OVID.)

What a power the poets ascribe to the Senses, who make Narcissus distractedly in love with his own reflection !

> All things admires for which he is admired ;
> Fond youth, on self he dotes ; himself the lover,
> Himself alone he loves. He kindles passions
> Which do himself consume ; (OVID.)

and tell of Pygmalion's judgement so disturbed by the sight of his ivory statue, which he loves and worships as if it had life !

> He kisses gives, and thinks they are returned ;
> He speaks, and in his arms his love he strains,
> Believes the flesh to yield to his embrace,
> And fears the livid marks that may ensue. (OVID.)

Let a philosopher be placed in a cage of small thin-set iron wire, and suspend it at the top of one of the towers of Nôtre Dame de Paris ; by evident reason he will see that he cannot possibly fall out of it, and yet (unless he has been brought up to the trade of a steeplejack) he cannot help being paralysed with terror on looking down from that extreme height. For it is as much as we can do to feel secure in the galleries of our steeples, if they are guarded by an open-work parapet, although it be of stone. There are some who cannot bear even to think of it. Let these two towers be bridged by a beam of sufficient breadth to walk upon, no philosophic wisdom is so resolute that it can give

---

[1] Face-powder was perhaps made from the shel lof the cuttle-fish, now used for tooth-powder.

us courage to walk upon it, as we should do if it were on the ground.

I have often experienced this in our mountains on this side of the border (and yet I am not one who is easily frightened by such things), that I could not bear to look down into that bottomless depth without a shudder and a trembling in my hams and thighs; even though I might be quite a body's length from the edge, and could not have fallen, unless I had purposely risked my life.

I have also observed that, however great the height, provided there be a tree or a jutting rock in the side of the precipice to catch the sight a little and break it, we are relieved and assured, as if those things might help to break our fall; but that we cannot even look down a sheer and level precipice without a feeling of dizziness: *not to be looked down without giddiness both of eyes and mind* (Livy); which is an evident imposture of the sight.

That fine philosopher [1] put out his own eyes, to free his soul from the distractions which they caused him, and enable him to philosophize with greater freedom.

But by the same reckoning he should also have had his ears stopped up, which Theophrastus says are the most dangerous organs we have for receiving violent impressions that alter and disturb us; and in short he ought to have deprived himself of all his other senses, that is to say, of his life and being. For they all have this power of overbearing our reason and our soul. *For it often happens that our mind is more vehemently struck by some sight, by a loud voice, or by singing; often also by anxiety and fear* (Cicero).

Physicians hold that there are certain temperaments which are excited even to fury by certain sounds and instruments. I have known some who could not hear the gnawing of a bone under their table without losing patience; and there is hardly a person who is not disturbed by the harsh and grating noise made by some one filing a piece of iron. So too some people are moved to anger and hatred if they hear any one chewing beside them, or speaking with an obstruction in the throat or nose.

Of what use was that piping prompter of Gracchus who softened, steadied, or modulated his master's voice when he

---

[1] Democritus, according to Cicero; but Cicero doubts it, and Plutarch says positively that it was not true.

was haranguing at Rome, if the inflection and quality of the tone had not the power to move and alter the judgement of his audience?[1] Truly a great thing to brag about is that fine firmness of judgement which suffers itself to be handled and swayed by the accidental stirring of so light a wind!

That same trickery with which the Senses deceive the understanding deceives them in their turn. Our soul sometimes gives tit for tat. They compete in lying and being deceived. What we see and hear when stirred by anger we do not hear as it is:

> A double sun, a twofold Thebes appear. (VIRGIL.)

The object we love appears to us more beautiful than it is:

> And thus we see
> Creatures in many a wise crooked and ugly
> The prosperous sweethearts in a high esteem, (LUCRETIUS.)

and that which we loathe appears more ill-favoured. To a man bowed down by grief and affliction the light of day appears dark and overclouded. Our senses are not only corrupted, but often quite deadened, by the passions of the soul. How many things we see which we do not take notice of when our mind is occupied with other thoughts!

> Yet thou canst know that, even in objects plain,
> If thou attendest not, 'tis just the same
> As if 'twere all the time removed and far. (LUCRETIUS.)

The soul seems to retire within itself, and the powers of the senses are kept in abeyance. Thus, both within and without, man is full of weakness and falsehood.

They who have compared our life to a dream were perhaps more in the right than they were aware of. When we dream, our soul lives, acts, exercises all her faculties neither more nor less than when we are awake. But if more inertly and obscurely, the difference is certainly not so great as between night and bright daylight; rather as between night and shade. There she sleeps, here she slumbers. More and less it is always darkness, and Cimmerian darkness.

We wake sleeping, and waking sleep. I do not see so

---

[1] 'To guard against excesses, he ordered his servant Licinius, who was a sensible man, to stand with a pitch-pipe behind him when he spoke in public, and whenever he found him straining his voice or breaking out into anger, to give him a softer key, upon which his violence, both of tone and passion, immediately abated.'—Plutarch, *Life of T. Gracchus*.

clearly in sleep; but as to my waking hours I never find them perfect and cloudless enough. Sleep, moreover, when it is deep, sometimes puts dreams to sleep. But our waking is never so wideawake as to thoroughly purge and dissipate reveries, which are the dreams of the waking, and worse than dreams.

Since our reason and our soul accept those fancies and opinions which arise in her while asleep, and authorize the actions of our dreams with the same approval as she does those of our day-dreams, why do we not question whether our thought and action be not another sort of dreaming, and our waking some kind of sleeping?

If our Senses are our first judges, it is not only our own that must be consulted; for in this faculty the animals are as much, and more, privileged than we are. It is certain that some of them have a more acute hearing than man, others a sharper sight, others a keener scent and others a finer touch and taste. Democritus said that gods and animals had the sensitive faculties much more perfect than man.

Now there is an extreme difference between the effects of their senses and ours. Our saliva cleanses and dries up our wounds; it kills a snake:

> So great the distance and the difference is
> That what is food to one to some becomes
> Fierce poison, as a certain snake there is
> Which, touched by spittle of a man, will waste
> And end itself by gnawing up its coil. (LUCRETIUS.)

What property shall we attribute to saliva? Shall it be from our point of view, or from that of the snake? According to which point of view shall we prove its real essence, which we are seeking? Pliny says that in the Indies there are certain sea-hares [1] which are poison to us, and we to them, so much so that we kill them by a mere touch. Which is really poisonous, the man or the fish? Which are we to believe, the fish about the man, or the man about the fish?

Air of a certain quality infects a man and does an ox no harm; and a certain other quality infects an ox and does a man no harm. Which of the two shall, in reality and nature, be the pestilent quality?

[1] Aplysia: sea-hare; a kind of snail or slug said to be poisonous.

To people who have the jaundice all things appear yellowish, and paler than to others :

> Again whatever jaundiced people view
> Becomes wan-yellow. (LUCRETIUS.)

Those who have the complaint which the physicians call Hyposphagma, which is a suffusion of blood under the skin, see everything red and bloody. How can we know but that these humours, which thus alter the action of our sight, predominate and are usual with animals ? For we may see some with yellow eyes like our jaundice-patients, others with bloodshot eyes. It is quite likely that to them the colour of objects appears other than to us. Which of us judges aright ? For it is not ordained that man alone shall be the referee with regard to the essence of things. Hardness, whiteness, depth, sourness, affect and are distinguished by the animals as they are by us; by nature they exist for them as much as for us.

When we partially close the eye, the bodies we look at appear longer and more distended ; some of the animals have the eye thus half-closed. Those bodies are therefore perhaps really longer, and not as our eye normally perceives them. If we squeeze the eye from below, things appear double to us :

> Twin lights of torches blossoming with flames ;
> Twofold the face of man, and twain his body. (LUCRETIUS.)

If our ears are stopped with anything, or if the auricular passage is contracted, we receive the sound quite otherwise than we usually do. Animals with hair in their ears, or that have only a very little hole in place of an ear, do not consequently hear what we hear, and sounds appear different to them.

On feast-days and in theatres we may observe that when a pane of glass tinted with some colour is held before the candles, everything in the place appears green, yellow, or violet :

> This the crowd surveys
> Often in the theatre, whose curtain broad,
> Bedecked with crimson, yellow, or the tint
> Of steel cerulean, from their fluted heights
> Wave tremulous ; and, o'er the scene beneath
> Each marble statue, and the rising rows
> Of rank and beauty, fling their tint superb. (LUCRETIUS.)

It is likely that the eyes of animals, which we observe to vary in colour, cause bodies to appear to them of the same colour as their eyes.

We should therefore, to estimate rightly the action of the Senses, come to an agreement, in the first place with the animals, and secondly among ourselves. This we in no wise do, but ever and anon we fall to disputing, because one person differs from another as to what he hears, sees, or tastes; and we wrangle about the different images that the senses put before us, as much as about anything else. By the ordinary rule of Nature a child hears, sees, and tastes differently to a man of thirty, and the latter otherwise than a sexagenarian.

In some people the Senses are more dim and cloudy, in others clearer and more acute. We take in things differently according to our nature, and as they seem to us. Now our seeming being so uncertain and open to controversy, it is no longer to be wondered at if we are told that we may admit that snow seems white to us, but that we cannot guarantee to prove that it is white by its essence and in reality; and this principle being shaken, all the science in the world necessarily goes by the board.

What if our senses themselves hinder one another? To the eyes a painting appears raised, to the touch it appears flat. Shall we say that musk, which delights our sense of smell and offends our taste, is agreeable or not? There are herbs and unguents which agree with one part of the body and injure another. Honey is pleasant to the taste, unpleasant to look at. Of those rings which are cut in the form of feathers and are called in heraldry *Feathers without end*, there is no eye that can tell the width or escape the deception which makes them appear to grow wider on one side, and narrower and more pointed on the other, especially when we turn them round our finger; and yet to the touch they appear equal in width and alike throughout.

When those persons who, in ancient times, enhanced their pleasure by using mirrors that enlarged and magnified the objects reflected in them, in order that the members they were about to busy might please the more by the ocular increase, which of the two senses carried the day, the sight which represented those members as big and long as they could wish, or the touch which made them appear small and contemptible?

Is it our Senses that lend these different properties to objects, and have the objects nevertheless but one? As we see in the bread that we eat; it is only bread, but our use makes bones, blood, flesh, hair, and nails of it:

> For just as food, dispersed through all the pores
> Of body, and passed through limbs and all the frame,
> Perishes, supplying from itself the stuff
> For other nature. (LUCRETIUS.)

The moisture sucked up by the roots of a tree becomes trunk, leaf, and fruit; and the air, being but one, driven through a trumpet, is diversified into a thousand kinds of sound. Is it our senses, I say, which in like manner give to those objects their different qualities, or have they really such? And in the face of this doubt, what may we conclude with regard to their real essence?

Moreover, since the conditions of sickness, delirium, or sleep make things appear to us otherwise than they appear to those in health and in their right mind, and to the waking; is it not likely that there is something in our normal state and natural disposition that gives an essence to things corresponding and agreeing with our condition, as there is in our disordered state? That our health, as well as our sickness, is capable of regarding things in its own way? Why should not the temperate man have his own way of looking at things, as well as the intemperate, and in like manner stamp his own character upon them?

The man with a fastidious taste charges wine with being insipid; to the healthy man it has a bouquet; the thirsty finds it delicious.

Now, since our condition accommodates things to itself, and transforms them according to itself, we no longer know things in their reality; for nothing comes to us that is not altered and falsified by our Senses. When the compass, the square, and the rule are untrue, all the calculations drawn from them, all the buildings erected to their measure, are of necessity also defective and out of plumb. The uncertainty of our senses renders uncertain everything they produce:

> As in a building
> If the first plumb-line be askew, and if
> The square deceiving swerve from lines exact,

WHO IS TO JUDGE?

> And if the level waver but the least
> In any part, the whole construction then
> Must turn out faulty—shelving and askew,
> Leaning to back and front, incongruous,
> That now some portions seem about to fall,
> And falls the whole ere long—betrayed indeed
> By first deceiving estimates: so too
> Thy calculations in affairs of life
> Must be askew and false, if sprung for thee
> From Senses false. (LUCRETIUS.)

After all who will be a competent judge in these differences? As we say that in discussions on religion we need a referee who is not attached to either one or the other side, one who has not made his choice and is free from partiality (a thing impossible among Christians); so it is in our case. For, if a man is old, he cannot be a judge of the feeling of old age, being himself a party in the controversy; if he is young, the same; if healthy, the same; the same if sick, sleeping, or waking. We should need one who is exempt from all these conditions, to decide with unprejudiced mind these questions as if they were indifferent to him; and by this rule we should need a judge who never has existed.

To judge the appearances we receive of things, we should need a judicatory instrument; to verify this instrument, we should need demonstration; to rectify this demonstration we should need an instrument: so here we are arguing in a circle!

Seeing that the Senses cannot decide our dispute, being themselves full of uncertainty, we must have recourse to Reason; there is no reason but must be built upon another reason: so here we are retreating backwards to all eternity!

Our ideas are not due to direct contact with outside things, but are formed through the mediation of the Senses; and the senses do not take in the outside objects, but only their own impressions. So the idea and image we form is not that of the object, but only of the impression and the feeling made by it on the senses; which impression and the object are different things. Wherefore whoever judges by appearances, judges by something other than the object.

And if you say that the impressions of the senses convey to the soul the qualities of outside objects by resemblance, how can the soul and the understanding be assured of this resemblance, having of themselves no communication with outside objects? Just as a man who does not know Socrates cannot, on seeing his portrait, say that it is like him.

Now, supposing a man nevertheless desires to judge by appearances. If it be by all, it is impossible; for they hamper one another by their contradictions and discrepancies, as we know by experience. Shall some selected appearances govern the others? We should need to verify the selection by another selection, the second by a third; in this way we shall never make an end.

Finally, there is no permanent existence, either of our being or of that of the objects. And we, and our judgement, and all mortal things, incessantly go flowing and rolling on. So nothing certain can be proved of one thing by another, both the judging and the judged being in continual motion and change.

'We have no participation in Being, because all human nature is ever midway between being born and dying, giving off only a vague image and shadow of itself, and a weak and uncertain opinion. And if you chance to fix your thought on trying to grasp its essence, it would be neither more nor less than if you tried to clutch water. For the more you squeeze and press what by its nature runs through everything, the more surely will you lose what you would lay hold of. Hence, seeing that all things are liable to change from one thing to another, Reason, which seeks in them a real permanence, is deceived, being unable to apprehend anything that is subsistent and permanent. Because everything is either entering into being and does not yet fully exist, or is beginning to die before it is born.'[1]

Plato said that bodies never had existence, but only birth. He conceived that Homer made the Ocean father, and Thetis mother, of the gods, thereby to show us that all things are in a perpetual state of fluctuation, motion and variation; an opinion held in common by all the philosophers before his time, as he says, excepting alone Parmenides, who denied that things had motion, of the power of which he made no small account.

---

[1] The above paragraph is taken word for word (with the exception of one word) from Amyot's translation of an essay of Plutarch; a fact which appears to have escaped the notice of all the editors and commentators of Montaigne, until quite recently.

Pythagoras opined that all matter is flowing and unstable;

The Stoics, that there is no present time, and that what we call Present is only the junction and meeting of the future and the past;

Heraclitus, that no man ever entered twice into the same river;

Epicharmus, that the man who borrowed money some time ago does not now owe it; and that he who was overnight invited to come to dinner this morning, to-day comes unbidden, seeing that they are no longer themselves, but are become others, and 'That no mortal substance can be found twice in the same condition. For, through the suddenness and quickness of its change, it is now scattered, and now brought together again; it comes, and then it is gone. Hence that which begins to be born never arrives at the perfection of being. Forasmuch as that birth is never finished and never stays, as being at an end; but, even in the seed, is evermore changing and shifting from one to another. As the human seed first produces, in the mother's womb, a shapeless fruit, then a fully-formed infant, then, being out of the womb, a suckling, it afterwards becomes a boy, then in due course a stripling, then a full-grown man, an elderly man, and finally a decrepit old man. So that the subsequent age and generation is always undoing and destroying the preceding one':

> For lapsing aeons change the nature of
> The whole wide world, and all things needs must take
> One status after other, nor aught persists
> For ever like itself. All things depart;
> Nature she changeth all, compelleth all
> To transformation. (LUCRETIUS.)

'And then we others foolishly fear one kind of death, when we have already passed and are still passing through so many others. For not only, as Heraclitus said, is the death of fire the birth of air, and the death of air the birth of water; but we may see it much more clearly in ourselves. The man in his prime dies and passes when old age comes along, and youth comes to an end in the prime of the grown man, childhood in youth, and the early age dies in childhood. And yesterday dies in to-day, and to-day will die in to-morrow; and there is nothing that stays and is ever One.

'For, as proof of this, if we always remain one and the same, how is it that we take pleasure now in one thing, now in another ? How is it that we love or hate opposite things, that we praise or blame them ? How is it that we have different affections, and that we do not retain the same feelings and thoughts ? For it is not likely that we should harbour other feelings without changing. And that which suffers change does not remain one and the same. And if it is not one and the same, neither does it then exist. But, with Being all one, it also simply changes its being, ever becoming one thing out of another. And, consequently, the senses by nature deceive and lie to themselves, taking that which seems for that which is, for want of really knowing what that which is, is.

'But what then really is ? That which is Eternal. That it to say, that which never had a birth, and will never have an end ; to which no time ever brings change. For Time is a thing which moves, and appears as in a shadow, with matter ever flowing and running, without ever remaining stable and permanent. Of which we use these words, Before, and After, and Has been, or Will be. Each of which at first sight gives clear evidence that it is not a thing that Is. For it would most evidently be wrong and absurd to say that that Is which is not yet in being, or which has already ceased to be. And as to these words, Present, or Here, or Now, on which our apprehension of time seems chiefly to be founded and to rest, Reason discovers the error and immediately destroys it, for she at once splits it up, and divides it into Future and Past, as though trying to see it of necessity divided into two.

'It is the same with Nature, which is measured, as with Time, which measures it. For no more is there anything in Nature that abides or is permanent, but all things in her are either born, or being born, or dying. According to which it would be a sin to say of God, who alone Is, that he Was, or Will be. For these words are changes, transitions or vicissitudes of that which cannot endure or remain in being. Whence we must conclude that God alone Is, not indeed according to any measure of time, but according to an immutable and immovable eternity, not measured by time nor subject to any decline ; before whom nothing is, nor will be after, neither more new nor more recent ; but one really being, which by one single Now fills the Ever; and there is nothing that truly Is, except he alone, without our being able to say, He has been or He will be, without beginning and without end.'[1]

To this pious conclusion of a pagan I will only join these words of a witness in the same condition, and make an end of this long and wearisome treatise, which would furnish me with endless matter: 'O what a mean and abject thing is man, says Seneca, if he does not rise above humanity!' There we have a good word and a profitable desire, but at the same time an absurd one.[2] For to make the handful bigger than the hand, and the armful bigger than the arm, and to expect to stride further than our legs can reach, that is impossible and contrary to Nature. Neither is it possible for man to rise superior to himself and humanity. For he cannot see but with his eyes, nor grasp more than he can hold. He will rise if God extraordinarily lends him a hand. He will rise by abandoning and renouncing his own proper means, and by suffering himself to be raised and uplifted by purely celestial means.

It is for our Christian faith, and not his Stoical virtue, to aspire to that divine and miraculous metamorphosis.

CHAPTER 13

OF JUDGING OF ANOTHER'S DEATH

WHEN judging of another's assurance at the point of death, which is without doubt the moment in the life of a man that should be most carefully noted, we must take care to remember one thing, That it is difficult for a man to believe that he has reached that stage. Few people, when they are dying, have made up their minds that it is their last hour; and at no point of our lives are we more deluded by deceptive hope. She keeps dinning into their ears,

---

[1] The whole of the above passage in inverted commas is copied, not word for word, as all the editors and commentators assert, but with alterations and omissions, from the aforesaid essay of Plutarch, in Amyot's translation.

[2] This sentence takes the place of the following, which originally stood in the edition of 1588: 'In the whole of the Stoic school there is not a truer word than this.' Seneca was a Stoic, but Montaigne, though he did not like the Stoics, had a great admiration for Seneca.

'Others have been in a much worse condition, and have not died. Your case is not as hopeless as they think ; and, at the worst, God has worked greater miracles.'

And that comes of thinking too much of ourselves. We imagine that the universe will suffer some loss by our annihilation, and that it commiserates our condition. Our sight being disturbed, things appear to it equally disturbed, and we imagine that things are passing from us when we lose sight of them ; as to those who travel by sea, the mountains, fields, cities, heaven and earth appear to be tossed about in the same way as they are :

> From harbour fare we ; lands and cities fade. (VIRGIL.)

Who ever knew an old man who did not praise the past and blame the present, laying his troubles and misery to the charge of the world and the conduct of men ?

> The aged ploughman shakes his head and sighs ;
> And when he puts the present by the past,
> His father's fate he blesses, often prates
> How those of old with piety were filled. (LUCRETIUS.)

We drag everything along with us. As a consequence we look upon our death as a great matter, which does not come to pass lightly, nor without a solemn consultation of the stars ; *so many gods making a stir over one head* (Seneca). And of this we are more convinced the more we prize ourselves : 'What, is so much learning to be wasted, to the great detriment of the world, without the Fates being specially concerned about it ? Does it cost them no more to kill so rare and exemplary a mind than one that is common and of no use to the world ? This life of ours, that shelters so many others, on which so many other lives depend, which employs such a world of people, that fills so many places, is it to be dismissed like one that holds by its one single thread ? '

Not one of us lays it sufficiently to heart that he is but one. Hence those words of Caesar to his pilot, more tumid than the sea which threatened him :

> If thou to sail to Italy decline
> Under the Gods' protection, trust to mine ;
> The only cause thou justly hast to fear
> Is that thou knowest not thy passenger ;
> But I being now aboard, slight Neptune's braves,
> And fearlessly cut through the swelling waves. (LUCAN.)

CAESAR'S ARROGANCE

And these:

> But Caesar now
> Thinking the peril worthy of his Fates:
> 'Are such the labours of the gods? exclaimed;
> Bent on my downfall have they sought me thus,
> Here in this puny skiff in such a sea?'

And that fantastic idea entertained by the people, that the sun for a whole year shrouded its face, in mourning for his death:

> Yea, he it was that showed
> At Caesar's death compassion upon Rome,
> Veiling in umber haze his dazzling head. (VIRGIL.)

And a thousand such, by which the world is so easily gulled, imagining that our loss changes the face of the heavens, and that they, in their infinity, take a keen interest in our paltry distinctions. *We are not so intimate with heaven that the light of its stars should die at our death* (Pliny).

Now it is not reasonable to judge of the resolution and firmness of a man who, though he be in certain danger, is not yet convinced of it; and it is not enough that he dies in this frame of mind, unless he be really prepared for that event. In most cases they put on a brave face and utter brave words in order to acquire a reputation, which they still hope to live long enough to enjoy.

All those whose death I have observed were beholden to chance for their demeanour and not to their own design.

And even in the case of those who in ancient times took their own lives, we should carefully consider whether it was a sudden death, or a death that took time. That cruel Roman Emperor used to say of his prisoners that he wished to make them feel death; and if one made away with himself in prison, he would say, 'That fellow has escaped me.'[1] He would rather he had felt the torments of a lingering death.

> His every limb
> Maimed, hacked and riven; yet the fatal blow
> The murderers with savage purpose spared. (LUCAN.)

It is not indeed so great a matter, in a man in perfect health and in his right mind, to resolve to kill himself; it is very easy to swagger before coming to grips. So we see

---

[1] The first part of the sentence applies to Caligula, the second to Tiberius, whose cruelty a certain Carvilius escaped by suicide.

the most effeminate man that the world has seen, Heliogabalus, amid all his vulgar debaucheries, making preparations for dying artistically, when occasion should force him to do so. And, that his death might not belie the rest of his life, he expressly built a sumptuous tower, the base and front of which was floored with boards enriched with gold and precious stones, from which to hurl himself. He also had cords made of gold and crimson silk threads to strangle himself; a sword forged in gold wherewith to run himself through; and kept poison in vessels of emerald and topaz to poison himself, according as the whim should seize him to choose between these different ways of dying:

> By a forced valour, resolute and brave. (LUCAN.)

Yet in respect of this man, the luxuriousness of his preparations makes it more likely that he would have bled at the nose,[1] had he been put to the test.

But even in the case of those men of stouter heart who have resolved to dispatch themselves, we must consider (I say), whether it was with a stroke which left them no time to feel the effect of it. For it may be questioned whether, on feeling life draining away little by little, the body's senses mingling with those of the soul, and with the means at hand of undoing his action, a man would still obstinately persist in so dangerous an intent.

During Caesar's Civil wars, Lucius Domitius, who took poison after being made prisoner in the Abruzzi, afterwards repented. It has happened in our time that a man, having resolved to die, and not having struck deep enough at the first attempt, the itching of the flesh repelling his arm, afterwards dealt himself two or three very serious wounds, but could never screw up enough courage to thrust home.

Whilst Plantius Sylvanus was on his trial, Urgulania, his grandmother, sent him a poniard with which, having failed to kill himself outright, he made his slaves open his veins.

Albucilla, in the time of Tiberius, attempted to kill herself, but struck half-heartedly, and still gave her adversaries the opportunity to imprison her and put her to death in their own way. The same thing happened to Demosthenes the General, after being routed in Sicily. And C. Fimbria,

---

[1] His courage would have failed him; or, in the familiar phrase, he 'would have got cold feet'.

having struck himself too feeble a blow, entreated his slave to finish him.

On the other hand, Ostorius, unable to use his own arm, and disdaining to employ that of his slave except to hold the poniard with firm and steady hand, hurled himself forward, thrust his throat against the point, and so ran himself through.

It is indeed a meat that must be swallowed without chewing by one whose throat is not lined with paving-stones ; and so the Emperor Hadrian made his physician accurately mark and encircle the spot on his pap at which the man he had charged to kill him was to aim. For this reason it was that Caesar, when asked what death he thought the most desirable, replied, ' The least premeditated and the quickest.'

If Caesar had the courage to say so, it is no cowardice in me to believe it.

' A quick death, said Pliny, is the supreme good fortune in human life.' People are loath to acknowledge it. No man can say he is resolved on death who fears to reflect on it, and cannot bear to look on it with open eyes. They who, under sentence of death, in order to make a rapid end of it, urge and hasten on their execution, do so not because they are resolved, but because they would rather not have time to think it over. It is not death that troubles them, but very much the dying :

> I fear not death, but dying gives me pause. (EPICHARMUS.)

That is a degree of firmness which I know by experience I could attain to, like those who plunge into danger, as into the sea, with eyes shut.

There is nothing, in my opinion, more illuminating in the life of Socrates, than that he had thirty whole days in which to ruminate over his death sentence, and that he digested it all that time in certain expectation of its being carried out, without dismay, without change, his train of words and actions rather depressed and languid than strained and exalted by the weight of such thoughts.

That Pomponius Atticus to whom Cicero wrote his letters, being ill, sent for Agrippa, his son-in-law, and two or three other friends, and said to them that, having found by experience that he gained nothing by trying to cure himself, and that all he did to prolong his life only prolonged and aggravated his pain, he was resolved to put an end to both, and begged them to approve of his determination, or, at the most, not to waste their labour in trying to dissuade him from it. Now, having chosen to die by abstaining from food, behold him accidentally cured of his disease! The remedy he had employed to do away with himself restored him to health. When the physicians and his friends came to celebrate this happy event and rejoice with him, they were greatly disappointed, for, in spite of their efforts, they could not make him change his mind; he said that some day he would in any case have to go through with it, and being now so far on his way, he would save himself the pains of beginning all over again on a future occasion.

This man, having made acquaintance with death at his full leisure, not only is not disheartened, but is eagerly bent on overtaking it; for, being satisfied with the reason which made him enter into the combat, he makes it a point of bravery to see it out. There is a great distance between not fearing death and being ready to taste it and relish it.

The story of the philosopher Cleanthes is very similar. His gums were swollen and decayed. The physicians advised him to be very abstemious. After fasting for two days he is so much better that they pronounce him cured, and permit him to return to his usual diet. He, on the other hand, having already tasted the sweets of faintness, resolved not to go back, and ended the journey on which he was so far advanced.

Tullius Marcellinus, a young Roman, wishing to anticipate the hour of his destiny, to be rid of a disease which tyrannized over him more than he was minded to endure, although the physicians promised him a certain if not a speedy cure, called his friends together to discuss his case. Some, says Seneca, gave him the advice they would themselves have taken through faintheartedness. Others, to gratify him, that which they thought would be most acceptable to him. But a Stoic spoke as follows: 'Do not let it worry you, Marcellinus, as if you were considering a weighty matter. It is no great thing to live; your slaves and animals live. But it is a great thing to die nobly, wisely and firmly. Think how long you have been doing the same things, eating, drinking, sleeping; drinking, sleeping, and

CATO'S EXEMPLARY END

eating. We are continually going the same daily round ; not only evil and intolerable calamities, but the mere satiety of living, make a man wish to die.'

Marcellinus wanted no man to give him advice ; he wanted a man to help him. His slaves feared to meddle, but this philosopher explained to them that domestic slaves fall under suspicion only when it is doubtful whether the death of their master is voluntary ; that otherwise it would be as bad an example to prevent him as to kill him, seeing that

> To save a man against his will
> Is just the same as 'tis to kill. (HORACE.)

He then suggested to Marcellinus that, just as after a meal we give the dessert to the attendants, so when life is ended it would not be unbecoming to distribute something among those who have ministered to our needs. Now Marcellinus was of a free and generous disposition ; he divided a certain sum among his slaves, and comforted them. For the rest he needed neither steel nor blood. He resolved to walk out of this life, not to run away from it ; not to escape death, but to experience it. And, to give himself time to meditate over it, he gave up eating, and on the third day after, having had himself sprinkled with warm water, he became gradually weaker and weaker, and not, as he said, without a certain voluptuousness.

Indeed they who have experienced this failing of the heart due to weakness declare that they feel no pain, but rather a certain pleasure, as when passing into sleep and repose.

Those are studied and digested deaths.

But, in order that Cato alone might furnish an example of virtue in all respects, it would seem as if his kind destiny had injured the hand with which he dealt himself the blow, that he might have opportunity to meet death face to face, and hug him, fortifying his courage in the face of danger instead of abating it. And if it had been my lot to picture him in his most superb attitude, I should have represented him covered with blood and tearing out his bowels, rather than with sword in hand, as did the sculptors of his times. For this second murder was much more relentless than the first.

CHAPTER 14

HOW OUR MIND STANDS IN ITS OWN WAY

IT is an amusing idea, that of a man exactly balanced between two equally strong desires. For it is not to be doubted that he will never make up his mind, since choice and inclination would imply that things were unequally prized; and if we were placed between the bottle and the ham, with an equal desire to eat and drink, there would doubtless be no help for it, but we must die of thirst and hunger.[1]

To provide against this dilemma, the Stoics, when asked how our mind comes to choose between two indifferent things, and why, from a large number of coins, we take one rather than another, when they are all alike, and there is no reason to incline us to any preference, reply that this movement of the soul is out of the common and irregular, coming to us by an outside, accidental, and fortuitous impulsion.

I think we might rather say that nothing meets our eyes which does not show some difference, however slight; and that, either to the sight or the touch, there is always something additional which attracts us, however imperceptibly. Similarly, if we could imagine a piece of string equally strong in every part, it is impossible by all impossibility that it should snap; for where would you have the break to begin? And it is not in Nature that it should break everywhere at the same time.[2]

If we should add to this the geometrical propositions which conclude, by certain proofs, that the contents are greater than the containing, and the centre as great as its circumference; and which discover two lines eternally approaching one another without ever meeting, and the philosopher's stone, and the squaring of the circle, where reason and experience are so opposed; we might perhaps find some argument to support this bold saying of Pliny: *There is nothing certain but uncertainty, and nothing more miserable and arrogant than man.*[3]

[1] The classical instance of irresolution is that of Buridan's ass, which died of starvation standing between two bundles of hay.
[2] Save in fiction; see Holmes's poem 'The Deacon's Masterpiece, or The Wonderful One-Hoss-Shay'.
[3] This is one of the sentences inscribed on the ceiling of Montaigne's library.

CHAPTER 15

THAT DIFFICULTIES INCREASE OUR DESIRES

THERE is no reason but has its opposite, says the wisest school of Philosophers.[1] I was just ruminating over that fine saying which one of the ancients adduces as a reason for despising life, 'No good thing can bring us pleasure but that for whose loss we are prepared:' *Grief for a lost thing and the fear of losing it equally affect the mind* (Seneca); thinking to make clear thereby that we cannot truly enjoy life if we are in fear of losing it.

It might, however, be said, on the other hand, that we clasp and embrace this good thing the more closely and affectionately for seeing it to be less sure, and fearing to have it taken from us. For it is felt to be obvious that, as cold air helps to stir up a fire, our desire is also whetted by opposition:

> Ne'er had Danaë been by Jove embraced,
> Had she not been confined in brazen tower; (OVID.)

and there is nothing that so naturally destroys an appetite as the satiety that comes of facility; nothing that so whets it as rarity and difficulty. *In all things pleasure gains a new attraction from the very danger which should deter us* (Seneca).

> Deny thy favours, Galla; love is cloyed
> When bliss is not with torment blent. (MARTIAL.)

To keep love in breath, Lycurgus decreed that married couples in Sparta should only meet by stealth, and that they should be as much ashamed at being discovered sleeping together as if they had been caught in adultery. The difficulty of assignations, the danger of surprise, the shame of the morrow,

> Silence and listlessness and piteous sighs
> Drawn from the inmost soul, (HORACE.)

these things it is that give piquancy to the sauce. How many most lasciviously pleasant sports are the result of the modest and shamefaced style of books on Love! Lust even seeks an additional zest in pain. The pleasure is sweeter

---
[1] The Pyrrhonian.

when it smarts and scorches. The courtezan Flora [1] used to say that she had never lain with Pompey but she made him carry away the marks of her teeth :

> The parts they sought for, those they squeeze so tight,
> And pain the body; implant their teeth upon
> The lips, and crush the mouth with kisses, yet
> Not unalloyed with joy; for there are stings
> Which goad them on to hurt the very thing,
> Whate'er it be, from whence arise for them
> Those germs of frenzy. (LUCRETIUS.)

So it is in everything; difficulty gives value to things.

The people of the March of Ancona prefer to pay their devotions to Saint James, and the people of Galicia to Our Lady of Loreto.[2] At Liège they have a high opinion of the baths of Lucca, and in Tuscany they think as highly of those at Spa. You rarely see a Roman in the fencing-school at Rome, which is filled with Frenchmen.

The great Cato became as weary of his wife as any of us might do, as long as she was his wife, and desired her when she became another's.

I have turned an old horse into the stud, as he got quite out of hand when he scented a mare. Facility presently sated him towards his own; but at sight of the first stranger that passed along his paddock, he would neigh as impatiently, and become as hot and furious, as ever.

Our appetite despises and looks beyond what is at hand, and runs after what it does not possess :

> He slights what's near at hand, and longs
>   For what's beyond his reach. (HORACE.)

To forbid us a thing is to make us long for it :

> If thou no better guard that girl of thine,
> She'll soon begin to be no longer mine. (OVID.)

To give it wholly into our possession is to breed in us contempt for it. Want and abundance each have their disadvantages :

> You of your superfluity complain,
>   And I of want. (Adapted from TERENCE.)

---

[1] Dictes-moy où, n'en quel pays,
   Est Flora la bele Romaine.—Villon, *Ballade des Dames du temps jadis*.

[2] Saint James of Compostella in Galicia. The Italians go on pilgrimage to Spain, the Spaniards to Italy. Loreto is near Ancona.

THE USES OF CONCEALMENT

Desire and enjoyment make us equally impatient. The severity of a mistress becomes a weariness, but an easy and yielding disposition becomes, to tell the truth, a greater; seeing that dissatisfaction and anger are the result of the value which we put on the desired object, sharpening and kindling love. But satiety breeds distaste; it is a blunt, dull, weary, and drowsy feeling.

> If you would keep your lover at your side,
> Treat him with scorn. (OVID.)

> Treat your mistress with neglect;
> If yesterday she said you nay,
> She'll come to you another day. (PROPERTIUS.)

What was Poppaea's intention, when she hid her beauty behind a mask, but to enhance it in the eyes of her lovers? Why do they veil, even down to the heels, the beauties that every woman desires to show, and every man to see? Why do they cover with so many obstacles, one on top of another, the parts on which are chiefly concentrated our desires and their own? And what purpose is served by those great bastions which our ladies have recently adopted, to fortify their flanks, except to allure our appetites, and attract us to them by keeping us at a distance?

> She hies her to the willows, hoping to be seen. (VIRGIL.)
> Her tunic interposed would ofttimes rouse my passion.
> (PROPERTIUS.)

What is the object of that maidenly modesty, that deliberate coolness, that severe expression, that profession of ignorance of things they know better than we who instruct them, but to increase in us the longing to overcome, bear down, and trample upon all those affected airs and those obstacles to our desire? For there is not only a pleasure, but a source of vainglory, in seducing that meek, mild and childlike bashfulness, in inflaming and goading it into madness, and in subduing to our ardour a cool and calculated sternness. It is a matter for boasting, they say, to triumph over rigour, modesty, chastity and temperance; and whoever dissuades the ladies from those attitudes, betrays both them and himself. We are to believe that their hearts shudder with fright, that the sound of our words offends the purity of their ears, that they hate us for them, and yield to our importunities by a forced constraint. Beauty, all-powerful as it is, has no power to make itself relished without that interposition.

Look at Italy, where there is most beauty on sale, and the most perfect of its kind, and how they are obliged to seek extraneous means and other arts to make it acceptable; and yet, to tell the truth, whatever they may do, being venal and public, it remains feeble and languid. Just as, even in the case of valour, when two deeds are alike, we hold that to be the nobler and more worthy, which offers the most difficulty and risk.

It is the work of divine Providence to suffer its holy Church to be disturbed, as we see it now, by so many troubles and storms, in order that pious souls may be roused up by this strife, and rescued from that drowsy lethargy in which they were plunged during a prolonged period of tranquillity. If we weigh the loss we have suffered by the many who have gone astray, against the gain that accrues to us through having recovered our breath, and resuscitated our zeal and our strength as the result of this strife, I know not whether the profit does not outweigh the loss.

We thought we had tied the knot of our marriages more firmly by removing all means of dissolving them; but the bond of hearts and affections has become more loose and slack as that of constraint has been drawn closer. And, on the other hand, what made marriages to be so long honoured and so secure in Rome was the liberty to break them off at will. They loved their wives the better as long as there was the chance of losing them, and, with full liberty of divorce, five hundred years and more passed by before any took advantage of it.

> What's free we are disgusted at, and slight;
> What is forbidden whets the appetite. (OVID.)

We might here mention the opinion of an ancient writer which is to the point, 'That punishments rather whet than dull the edge of sins; That, instead of making us careful to do good, which is the work of reason and discipline, they only make us careful not to be caught doing ill':

> Though rooted out, the infection of the plague
> Spreads more luxuriantly. (RUTILIUS.)

I do not know whether that be true; but I know this by experience, that never was a civil government reformed by that means. It needs some other power to make us orderly and regular in our morals.

Greek history makes mention of the Argippaeans, neighbours of the Scythians, who live without either rod or stick for striking; yet not only does no one attempt to attack them, but any man who wishes to take refuge among them is safe, by reason of their virtue and sanctity of life, and there is no one who is so daring as to touch him. People of other regions have recourse to them to settle their differences.

There is a country where gardens and fields are made safe by being enclosed by a cotton thread only, which is found to be more firm and secure than our hedges and moats. *Things sealed up invite the thief. The burglar passes by an open door* (Seneca).

The easy access to my house is perhaps a reason among others why it has escaped the violence of our Civil wars. Defence allures the enterprising, and distrust provokes them. I have baffled the designs of the soldiery by depriving the exploit of all danger and all chance of military glory, which have usually provided them with an excuse and a pretext. Every courageous deed is an honourable deed in times when justice is dead. I have thus made the conquest of my house a cowardly action and a treachery. It is closed to nobody who knocks. It is provided with no other safeguard but a porter with old-fashioned ceremonious manners, whose office it is not to forbid my door, but rather to offer it with the more grace and decorum. I have no other sentinel nor watch but what the stars keep for me.

It is a mistake for a gentleman to make a show of defence, unless his defence be perfect. What is open on one side is open on all. Our fathers did not think of building frontier garrisons. The means of attacking, I mean without armies and artillery, and of falling upon our houses by surprise, every day grow greater than the means of guarding them. Men's wits generally are sharpened in that direction. Poor and rich alike are interested in invading, the rich alone in defending.

My house was strong for the time when it was built. I have added nothing to it in the way of strength, and should be afraid that its strength might be turned against me. Besides that a peaceful period would require it to be unfortified; and there is the risk of being unable to recover it. And it is difficult to make sure of being safe. For in the matter of intestine wars, your own footman may be on the side you fear. And where religion serves as a pretext even kinship becomes unreliable, under the cloak of justice. The public exchequer will not support our domestic garrisons; it would be drained thereby. We have not the means of doing so without ruin to ourselves, or, more unfitly and unjustly, without ruin to the people. My loss could hardly be greater.

Moreover, if you should ruin yourself, your friends will even go out of their way, rather than pity you, to accuse you of want of vigilance and caution, of ignorance and carelessness in the exercise of your profession.

The fact that so many strongly guarded houses have been destroyed, whilst mine endures, makes me suspect that they were destroyed because they were strongly guarded. That arouses the assailant's desire, and provides him with an excuse. All defence wears the aspect of war. If God wills it, let them attack me; but in any case I will not invite attack. It is my retreat and resting-place from wars. I try to keep this corner as a haven against the tempest outside, as I do another corner in my soul. Our war may well assume different forms, factions may vary and multiply; for my part, I do not budge. When so many houses were fortified in France, I alone of my rank, so far as I know, simply entrusted mine to the protection of heaven. And I never removed even a silver spoon or a title-deed. I will neither fear nor save myself by halves. If by full gratitude I can gain the divine favour, it will remain with me to the end; if not, I have still survived long enough to make my survival remarkable and fit to be recorded. How long? For quite thirty years.[1]

CHAPTER 16

OF GLORY

THERE is the name and the thing; the name is a sound which sets a mark on and denotes the thing. The name is no part of the thing nor of the substance; it is an extraneous piece added to the thing, and outside of it.

God, who is all fullness in himself and the acme of all

---

[1] i. e., since the beginning of the Civil Wars, 1560 or 1562.

perfection, cannot grow and increase within ; but his name may grow and increase by the blessing and praise we bestow on his external works. Which praise, since it cannot be incorporated with him, because there can be in him no accession of good, we give to his name, which is the thing outside of him that is nearest to him. So it is that to God alone honour and glory are due; and nothing can be more unreasonable than that we should seek them for ourselves. For, being indigent and necessitous within, being imperfect in essence, and continually in need of amendment, we should use all our endeavour to perfect ourselves.

We are all hollow and empty. Not with wind and words must we fill ourselves ; we need a more solid substance for our amendment. A famished man would be very foolish to think of providing himself with a fine coat instead of a good meal ; he should hasten to supply the more urgent need. As we say in our ordinary prayer, *Glory to God in the highest, and on earth peace towards men* (Saint Luke). We are suffering a dearth of beauty, health, wisdom, virtue and the like essential qualities. We must not think of external ornaments until we have provided the necessary things. Theology treats that subject fully and more pertinently ; but I am not well enough versed therein.

Chrysippus and Diogenes were the first to begin, and that most resolutely, to despise glory ; of all the gratifications they said there was none more dangerous, nor more to be avoided, than that which we derive from others' approbation. Indeed experience teaches us that we are often betrayed by it to our hurt. There is no worse poison for a prince than flattery, and nothing whereby a wicked man more easily wins their favour. Nor is there any fitter and more ordinary go-between to corrupt the chastity of a woman than to feed and entertain her with her praises.

The first charm the Sirens employed to seduce Ulysses was of this nature :

> Come here, thou worthy of a world of praise,
> That dost so high the Grecian glory raise. (HOMER.)

Those philosophers said that, to an intelligent man, all the fame in the world was not worth the stretching out of a finger to reach it :

> What's glory in the highest degree,
> If it no more than glory be ? (JUVENAL.)

I mean for itself alone. For it is often attended with many advantages, for the sake of which it may become desirable. It brings us goodwill; it leaves us less exposed to injuries and insults from others, and the like.

It was also among the principal teachings of Epicurus; for this precept of his school, 'Conceal thy life', forbids a man to encumber himself with public offices and affairs, also necessarily presupposes a contempt for fame, which is the world's approval of actions by which we push ourselves into notoriety. The man who commands us to keep in the background and only mind our own business, and who would not have us make ourselves notorious, desires still less that we should seek to win honour and glory. So he advises Idomeneus to regulate his actions with no regard to public opinion or common renown, unless it were to avoid other incidental disadvantages which the contempt of men might bring upon him.

That view is, I should say, profoundly true and in accordance with reason. But we are, I know not how, double in ourselves, as a consequence of which we do not believe what we believe, and are unable to put aside what we condemn. Let us see the last words of Epicurus, written at the point of death; they are great and worthy of such a philosopher, and yet they bear some signs that he was thinking of his renown, and that his mental attitude contradicted his teachings. Here follows a letter which he dictated shortly before breathing his last:

'Epicurus to Hermachus, greeting.

'I write this letter while passing a happy day, which is also the last day of my life. And the pains of my bladder and bowels are so intense that nothing can be added to them which can make them greater. But still I have, to balance this, a joy in my mind, which I derive from the recollection of my philosophical teachings and discoveries. But do you, as becomes the goodwill which from your youth upwards you have constantly shown for me and for philosophy, protect the children of Metrodorus.'

That is his letter. And what makes me interpret the pleasure, which he says his soul feels in his discoveries, in the sense that he had some concern for the renown he hoped for after his death, is the injunction in his will and testament to Amynomachus and Timocrates, his heirs, ' to furnish every year what, in the opinion of Hermachus, shall be enough to keep his birthday in the month Gamelion, with all proper solemnity. And that they shall also every month, on the twentieth day of the month, supply money enough to furnish a banquet for those men who have studied philosophy with him, in order that his memory, and that of Metrodorus, may be duly honoured.'

Carneades was the chief upholder of the opposite view. He maintained that fame was desirable for itself ; just as we espouse the interests of our posthumous heirs, although we do not enjoy their acquaintance. This view has not failed to be more commonly followed, as those are apt to be which agree most with our inclinations.

Aristotle gives it the first place among external goods : ' Avoid, as two vicious extremes, immoderation either in running after it, or fleeing from it.'

I believe that, if we had the books that Cicero wrote on the subject, we should be hugely edified ; for that man was so infatuated with the passion for glory, that if he had dared, he would, I believe, have fallen into the excess into which others fell, who held, That virtue itself was only desirable for the honour which always attended it :

> Valour unsung shows in no nobler dress
> Than cowardice when dead. (HORACE.)

Which is so erroneous a view, that I am sorry it could ever have entered the mind of a man who was honoured with the name of philosopher.

If that were true, there would be no need to be virtuous except in public ; and there would be no object in keeping the operations of the soul, which is the true seat of virtue, in rule and order, except in so far as they might come to the knowledge of others.

Is it then only a question of sinning slyly and cunningly ? ' If you know, says Carneades, that a snake is concealed in a place where a person, by whose death you hope to gain, is about to sit down unsuspectingly, you do wickedly if you do not warn him of the danger. And the more so if the action can be known only to yourself.' If we do not find in ourselves the laws of well-doing, if impunity passes with us for justice, to how many kinds of wickedness shall we not yield every day !

What S. Peduceus did, in faithfully handing over to the widow the sum of money which C. Plotius had entrusted to his sole keeping and knowledge, a thing I have often done myself, seems to me not so praiseworthy as I should think it execrable if we had both failed in our trust.

And I think it a good and profitable thing to remember in these days the example of P. Sextilius Rufus, whom Cicero accuses of having received an inheritance against the grain of his conscience, and not only not contrary to the law, but with the consent of the law.

And M. Crassus and Q. Hortensius, who, by reason of their influence and authority, having been called in by a stranger to participate in the succession of a forged will, in order by that means to establish his own claim to a share, were content with having no hand in the forgery, whilst not refusing to enjoy the fruit of it; feeling secure enough if they were sheltered from accusations, from witnesses and the laws. *Let them remember that they have God to witness, that is (as I understand it) their own conscience* (Cicero).

Virtue is a very vain and frivolous thing, if it derives its recommendation from glory. In vain should we undertake to make it keep its place apart, and separate it from fortune; for what can be more fortuitous than reputation? *Truly Fortune rules over all things; she sheds a lustre on things, or obscures them, according to her own caprice rather than their merits* (Sallust).

It is purely the work of Fortune if actions are seen and become known. It is chance in its heedlessness that fastens glory upon us. I have often seen her marching in front of merit, and often outpacing merit by a long distance. The man who first thought of likening glory to a shadow made a better comparison than he was aware of. They are both pre-eminently empty of substance. The shadow too sometimes goes ahead of the body, and sometimes greatly exceeds it in length.

If you teach the nobility to seek in valour only honour, *as if nothing were virtuous unless noised abroad* (Cicero), what do you gain thereby except that you instruct them never to run into danger unless they are seen, and to take very good care that they have witnesses to carry news of their valour; whilst they may have a thousand occasions to act bravely without being observed? How many noble deeds of individuals are buried in the throng of battle! Should any one in such a fray waste his time in checking the actions of others he cannot be very busy himself, and in giving testimony of his comrades' behaviour he would be furnishing evidence against himself. *The wise and truly great soul places honour, which is the chief aim of our nature, in deeds and not in glory* (Cicero).

All the fame I look for in life is to have lived it tranquilly; tranquilly not as Metrodorus, or Arcesilaus, or Aristippus, understood it, but as I understand it. Since Philosophy has been unable to discover any way to tranquillity that is good for all, let every one seek it for himself.

To what do Caesar and Alexander owe the infinite greatness of their renown, if not to Fortune? How many men has she not snuffed out in the beginning of their career, of whom we have no knowledge, who brought to their work the same courage as they, but whose ill luck stopped them short at the very birth of their enterprises? In the course of the many and extreme dangers to which he was exposed, I do not remember having read that Caesar was ever wounded.[1] A thousand have fallen in lesser dangers than the least of those he passed through.

An endless number of noble deeds must be lost for want of witnesses, before one turns to account. A man is not always at the top of a breach, or in the forefront of an army, in the sight of his general, as on a stage. He is taken unawares between the hedge and the ditch; he must tempt fortune in attacking a hen-roost; he must dislodge four wretched musketeers out of a barn; he must separate from his company, and attack on his own account, as necessity provides the occasion. And if we look into the matter, we shall find by experience that the least brilliant occasions happen to be the most dangerous; and that in the wars of our own times more good men have been lost on slight and unimportant occasions, and in disputing some paltry fort, than in worthy and honourable places.

He who thinks his death wasted except on some signal occasion, instead of throwing a lustre on his death, is more likely to cast a shadow over his life; in the meantime

---

[1] The edition of 1588 adds these words: 'but I know very well that that is said of Hannibal and of Scanderbeg;' i. e., that they were never wounded.

allowing many a fitting opportunity for venturing his life to escape him. And there is lustre enough in every fitting opportunity, each man's conscience sufficiently trumpeting them. *Our glory is the testimony of our conscience* (Saint Paul).

He who is only good because his goodness will be known, and because he will be the better thought of after it is known; he who will only do good on condition of his goodness coming to the knowledge of men, is not one from whom much service is to be expected.

> The remnant of the winter, he with shield
> And spear achieved things worthy to be shown,
> I ween; but these were then so well concealed,
> It is no fault of mine they were not blown;
> For good Orlando was in fighting field
> Prompter to do than make his prowess known.
> Nor e'er was bruited action of the knight,
> Save when some faithful witness was in sight. (ARIOSTO.)

A man must go to the wars as a matter of duty, and expect this reward which cannot fail every noble deed, however hidden it may be, or even a valiant thought, that is, the inward satisfaction that a well-regulated conscience reaps from well-doing. A man must be valiant for himself and for the advantage he derives from having his courage firmly based, and secure against the assaults of Fortune:

> Worth, all indifferent to the spurns
>   Of vulgar souls profane,
> The honours wears it proudly earns,
>   Unclouded by a stain;
> Nor grasps nor lays the fasces down
> As fickle mobs applaud or frown. (HORACE.)

Nor for outward show must our soul play her part, but within ourselves, where no eyes but our own can penetrate. There she will shelter us from the fear of death, of pain, and even of shame; there she will arm us against the loss of our children, of our friends and fortunes, and when opportunity offers, she will also lead us on to the hazards of war; *not for any profit, but for the beauty attached to virtue* (Cicero). This is a much greater gain, and much more worthy of being coveted and hoped for, than honour and glory, which are no more than a favourable judgement passed upon us by others.

We must needs select a dozen men out of a whole nation to decide a question about an acre of land ; and the judgement of our inclinations and actions, the most difficult and important matter that can be, we refer to the voice of the people, to the rabble, the mother of ignorance, injustice, and fickleness. Is it reasonable to make the life of a wise man dependent on the judgement of fools ? *Can anything be more foolish than to rate highly as a body those whom singly we despise ?* (Cicero). Whoever aims at pleasing them will never have done ; it is a butt we can neither see nor hit. *Nothing can be so little counted upon as the mind of the multitude* (Livy).

Demetrius said wittily of the voice of the people that he set no more store by that which issued from above than on that which issued from below. Cicero goes still farther : *My opinion is that, though a thing be not disgraceful in itself, it cannot be free from suspicion when it is commended by the multitude.*

No skill, no mental cunning, could direct our steps to follow so misleading and erratic a guide. In this windy chaos of rumours, reports, and vulgar opinions, in which we are blown about, we can fix upon no road that is likely to lead anywhere.

Let us set up a goal that is not so unsteady and wavering ; let us consistently follow reason. Let public approval then follow us, if it will ; and, as it is entirely dependent on chance, we have no more reason to expect it by any other way rather than that. Even should I not follow the straight road for its straightness, I should follow it because I had learned by experience that at the end of the reckoning it is usually the happiest and most profitable. *Providence has given this gift to mortals, that honesty is the best policy* (Quintilian). The ancient mariner spoke thus to Neptune in a great storm : ' O God, you can save me if you will, and if you will you can destroy me ; yet will I always keep my rudder straight.'

In my time I have seen a thousand supple-minded, double-faced, and equivocating men whom nobody doubted to be more worldly-wise than myself, and who were lost where I was saved :

I laughed to see that wit no better sped. (OVID, altered.)

Paulus Emilius, on setting out upon his famous expedition against Macedonia, especially warned the people of Rome ' to restrain their tongues during his absence with regard to his actions '. What a disturbing element in great affairs is freedom of opinion! seeing that not every one has the firmness of Fabius who, in face of the hostile and abusive tongues of the people, suffered his authority to be pulled to pieces by the idle fancies of men rather than carry out his charge less well, with a favourable reputation and with the approval of the populace.

There is naturally something indescribably pleasant in hearing oneself praised; but we attach far too much importance to it:

> I'm not afraid of praise, I must confess,
> My heart is not of horn, but ne'ertheless
> I must deny the only end and aim
> Of doing well is to hear men exclaim:
> ' O worthy man, O noble deed!' (PERSIUS.)

I care not so much what I am in the opinion of others as what I am in my own. I would be rich of myself, and not by borrowing. Strangers see only actions and outside appearances. Any man can put on a bold face outside, though in a fever of fright within. They do not see my heart, they only see my countenance.

With good reason do people denounce the hypocrisy we see in war-time; for what is easier for the practised soldier than to shirk the dangers, and to bluster, although he may be but a faint-hearted fellow? For the individual there are so many ways of avoiding risks, that we may deceive the world a thousand times before we are involved in a dangerous undertaking; and even then, finding ourselves entangled in it, we are well able for the time being to hide our game behind a bold face and brave words, though our heart be all in a tremble within.

And if they had the use of Plato's ring which made him invisible who wore it on his finger, by giving it a turn towards the palm of the hand, many people would often conceal themselves when they should show themselves most openly, and would be sorry to be placed in so honourable a position, where necessity must make them bold.

> None but knaves and liars can be charmed
> By groundless praise, by slanders be alarmed. (HORACE.)

Thus we see how marvellously uncertain and doubtful are all those judgements that are founded on external appearance; and no witness is so reliable as each man is to himself.

On those occasions how many camp-followers have we to share our glory? When a man stands firm in an open trench, what more does he do than fifty wretched pioneers have done before him, in clearing the way and sheltering him with their bodies for a daily pay of twopence-halfpenny?

> For if thick-headed Rome should aught condemn,
> Pay thou no heed, nor take upon thyself
> To mend her faulty scales. Go thine own way! (PERSIUS.)

To disperse and scatter our name into many mouths we call aggrandizing it; we should like it to be favourably thought of, and profit by this aggrandizement; that is the best excuse for this desire. But this craving is carried to so great an excess that many seek to become notorious in any way whatsoever. Trogus Pompeius said of Herostratus, and Livy of Manlius Capitolinus, that they were more ambitious of a world-wide than of a good reputation.[1] It is a common fault. We are more anxious that people *should* talk about us, than *how* they talk about us; it is enough if our name be on men's lips, whether for good or evil. To be known seems in some sort to have our lives and duration in others' keeping.

For my own part, I consider that I exist only in myself; and of that other life of mine, which lies in the knowledge of my friends, considering it naked and simply in itself, I know very well that I am sensible of no fruit or enjoyment from it, but by the vanity of a fantastic opinion. And when I am dead I shall be still less sensible of it; and so I shall absolutely lose the enjoyment of the real advantages which sometimes accidentally attend it. I shall then have no handle by which to take hold of reputation, nor will it have any means of reaching or touching me.

For, supposing that I should expect my name to become famous: in the first place I have no name which I can sufficiently call my own. Of the two that I have, one is

[1] Herostratus successfully sought to gain immortality by burning the magnificent Temple of Diana, one of the seven wonders of the world. Manlius was ambitious of becoming, by fair means or foul, the greatest man in Rome.

common to all my family, and indeed to other families besides. There is a family with the surname of Montaigne at Paris and at Montpellier, another in Brittany, another in Saintonge, who call themselves La Montaigne. The removal of a single syllable will so entangle our threads that I may share in their glory, and they perchance in my shame. And besides, my family formerly bore the surname Eyquem, a name which still attaches to a well-known house in England.

As to my other name,[1] anybody that pleases is at liberty to take it. So a street-porter may perhaps succeed to the honour that is due to me. And then, though I had a particular mark to myself, what can it mark when I am no more? Can it designate and bring into prominence a thing of no substance?

> What though posterity should laud his name,
> The tomb will press no lighter on his bones.
> No violets will spring from his remains. (PERSIUS.)

But of this I have spoken elsewhere.[2]

After all, in a whole battle, in which ten thousand men are maimed or killed, not fifteen will be noticed. It must be some great and outstanding deed, or one that is accidently followed by important consequences, that will bring into prominence not merely a musketeer's, but a general's exploit. For to kill a man or two, or ten, to face death courageously, is indeed something for each one of us, for we hazard everything. But for the world they are such common and every-day occurrences, and it needs so many of the same kind to produce any noteworthy result, that we cannot expect to be particularly commended for them:

> That fate is shared by many, it is trite,
> As picked at random out of Fortune's heap. (JUVENAL.)

Of so many myriads of valiant men who have died these last fifteen hundred years in France, with their weapons in their hands, not a hundred have come to our knowledge. The memory, not only of the leaders, but of the battles and victories, is buried.

The happenings of more than half the world, for want of record, are confined to one spot, and vanish without duration. If I possessed the knowledge of all unrecorded events,

---

[1] Michel.
[2] In the chapter Of Names, in the First Book.

I think I could very easily furnish examples of every kind that would supplant those that have been recorded.

Why, even of the Romans and Greeks consider how few names have been handed down to us, in spite of the many rare and noble exploits they performed, and all their writers and witnesses!

> Scarcely to our ears
> Floats through the ages a thin breath of Fame. (VIRGIL.)

It will be a wonder if, a hundred years hence, it is remembered in a general way that there were civil wars in our time in France.

The Lacedemonians, on entering into battle, sacrificed to the Muses, that their deeds might be well and worthily written down, thinking it to be a divine and no common favour if their noble actions should find witnesses able to give them life and memory.

Do we imagine that at every musket-shot we receive, and every danger we run into, there will suddenly appear a notary to record it? And a hundred notaries besides may write them down, and their comments will endure only three days and be seen by nobody.

We do not possess a thousandth part of the works of the ancients. Fortune has given them a shorter or longer life, according to her favour; and, not having seen the remainder, we are at liberty to question whether those we have are not the worst. History is not written on every small trifle. A man must have been a leader and conquered an empire or a kingdom; he must have won fifty-two pitched battles, and always with inferior numbers, like Caesar. Ten thousand good fellows and many great captains valiantly and courageously died in his service, whose names endured only as long as their wives and children lived:

> Whom Rumour doth in darkness hide. (VIRGIL.)

Even those whose brave deeds we have witnessed, three months or three years after they are left on the field of battle, are no more spoken of than if they had never been.

If you consider, in due measure and proportion, the people and the deeds whose fame is preserved in the memory of books, you will find that there are very few actions and very few persons in our time that may claim any right to such fame. How many valorous men have we not seen to survive their own reputation, men who have seen and suffered the honour and glory they had justly acquired in their younger days to be snuffed out in their presence ! And for three years of this fanciful and imaginary life shall we throw away our real and essential life, and be plunged into a perpetual death ? The wise man sets up a much fairer and more fitting goal to such an important enterprise as life. *The reward of a good deed is to have done it* (Seneca). *The fruit of a service is the service itself* (Cicero).

It would be excusable perhaps in a painter or any other artist, or even in a rhetorician or grammarian, to labour to make a name by his works ; but the actions of Virtue are too noble in themselves to seek any other reward but from their own worth, and especially to seek it in the vanity of human estimation.

And yet if this erroneous notion is of such service to the community as to keep men within their duty ; if the people are thereby instigated to virtue ; if rulers are moved when they hear the world blessing the memory of Trajan and execrating that of Nero ; if it stirs them up to hear the name of that great scoundrel, once held in such fear and dread, freely cursed and reviled by the first schoolboy who attacks his memory ; let it wax bravely, and let us nourish it to the best of our power !

And Plato, employing every means to make his citizens virtuous, advises them amongst other things not to despise the good repute and esteem of the people. He declares that by some divine inspiration it happens that even the wicked man is often able, not only by words but in thought, to distinguish rightly between the good and the bad. This great man and his schoolmaster [1] are marvellously bold craftsmen in the art of bringing in the operations and revelations of the gods whenever the power of man fails ; *after the example of the tragic poets, who have recourse to a god when they are unable to unravel their plot* (Cicero). That is perhaps why Timon called him abusively ' the great forger of miracles '.

Since man, on account of his shortcomings, will not be satisfied with good money, let us also pay him in spurious coin. This expedient has been practised by all the lawgivers ; and there is no body of laws that is not mixed up

[1] Socrates.

with some empty ceremonies or lying legends, to serve as a curb to keep the people to their duties. For this reason it is that to most legislators is given a fabulous origin and beginning, with a wealth of mysteries and superstitions. It is this that has brought spurious religions into credit, and made them to be countenanced by men of intelligence. For this reason too did Numa and Sertorius, the better to impose on the credulity of their people, feed them with this foolish idea, the one that the nymph Egeria, the other that a white fawn, conveyed to them from the gods all the decisions they adopted.

And the same authority that Numa claimed for his laws, on the pretence of being patronized by the aforesaid goddess, Zoroaster, the legislator of the Bactrians and Persians, claimed for his, in the name of the god Oromazis; Trismegistus of the Egyptians, in the name of Mercury; Zamolxis of the Scythians, in the name of Vesta; Charondas of the Chalcidians, of Saturn; Minos of the Candiots, of Jupiter; Lycurgus of the Lacedemonians, of Apollo; Draco and Solon of the Athenians, of Minerva. So every code of laws has a god as its fountain-head; falsely so the others, but truly so that which Moses established for the people of Judea when they were come out of Egypt.

The religion of the Bedouins, as the Lord of Joinville tells us, taught, among other things, that the soul of any one of them who died for his prince entered into another body that was happier, stronger, and handsomer than the first. This belief made them much more ready to risk their lives:

> They covet wounds and seek their deaths; 'tis base
> To save a life so soon to come again. (LUCAN.)

There we see a very wholesome belief, however groundless it may be. Every nation has many examples of the same kind. But this subject would deserve an essay by itself.

To add a few more words on my first theme, neither will I advise the ladies to call their duty honour. *In ordinary parlance that only is called honourable which enjoys popular favour* (Cicero). Their duty is the pith, their honour is but the rind. Nor do I advise them to give us this excuse for payment of their refusal. For I take it for granted that their intentions, their desire, and their will, with which honour has nothing to do, since they do not appear on the surface, are still better regulated than their deeds :

> She sins who but abstains from fear of sin. (Ovid.)

Towards God and the conscience the desire would be as great an offence as the deed. And, besides, they are actions which are of themselves hidden and secret ; it would be very easy to keep an action, on which honour depends, from the knowledge of others, if they had no other consideration for their duty and the affection in which they hold their chastity for its own sake.

Every woman of honour will choose to lose her honour rather than her conscience.

CHAPTER 17
OF PRESUMPTION

THERE is another kind of glory,[1] which is to have too high an opinion of our own worth. It is an unthinking self-love which we nourish, and which makes us appear to ourselves other than we are ; like the passion of love, which lends charm and beauty to the object it embraces, which disturbs and corrupts the judgement of the man in love, and makes him think his lady other and more perfect than she is.

Yet I would not have a man, through fear of sinning in that direction, mis-know himself, and think himself worse than he is ; the judgement should maintain its rights always and everywhere. It is right that here, as in all things, he should see what the truth sets before him. If he is a Caesar, let him boldly think himself the greatest general the world has seen.

We are all convention ; conventions carry us away, and we neglect the substance of things. We hang on to the branches, and leave the trunk and body. We have taught the ladies to blush at the mere mention of things they have no fear of doing. We dare not call our members by their right names, yet we are not afraid to employ them in all kinds of debauchery. Convention forbids our expressing in words things that are allowed and natural, and we obey her. Reason forbids our doing illicit and wicked things, and

[1] Vainglory.

nobody obeys her. Here I am fettered by the laws of convention; for she allows a man to speak neither well nor ill of himself. We will leave her alone for the time being.

The man whom Fortune (call it good or ill, as you please) has enabled to live in some position of eminence may by his public actions testify to what he is. But he who is only one of the herd (and of whom no man will speak unless he speak of himself) is to be excused if he has the hardihood to speak of himself, especially to those who are interested in knowing him, after the example of Lucilius:

> As unto loyal friends and tried
> He to his notebook would confide
> His secrets; thither turning still,
> Went Fortune with him well or ill;
> Hence all the old man's life is known
> As on a votive tablet shown. (HORACE.)

He committed to his paper his actions and thoughts, and there portrayed himself as he felt himself to be. *Nor did any one doubt the honesty or question the motives of Rutilius or Scaurus in writing their memoirs* (Tacitus).

So I remember that, from my tenderest childhood, there was observed in me a certain indefinable carriage of the body and certain gestures which testified to some empty and silly pride.

I may say this, in the first place, that there is no harm in certain qualities and propensities which are so much a part of ourselves that we have no means of perceiving and recognizing them. And of such natural inclinations the body may easily, without our knowledge or consent, retain a certain bent.

It was a kind of affectation sorting with his beauty that made Alexander carry his head a little on one side, and caused Alcibiades to lisp. Julius Caesar used to scratch his head with one finger, which is the action of a man full of troublesome thoughts; and Cicero, I think, was wont to wrinkle his nose, which is a sign of a scornful disposition. Such motions may arise without our noticing them.

Others there are that do not come naturally, of which I will not speak, such as our bows and salutations, whereby one gains credit, wrongfully for the most part, for being very humble and polite; a man may be humble through vainglory. I am rather prodigal of bonnetings, especially in summer, and never take a salute without returning it, whatever the rank of the person, unless he be in my pay.

I could wish that some princes I know would be more sparing and discriminating in dispensing these marks of courtesy. For, thus unwisely bestowed, they are thrown away ; if they are given without respect of persons, they lose their effect.

Among different kinds of irregular deportment let us not forget the haughty bearing of the Emperor Constantius, who in public always held his head erect, without turning it or bending it this way or that way, not even to look at those who saluted him from the side ; keeping his body rigid and motionless in spite of the jolting of his coach, and daring neither to spit, blow his nose, nor wipe his face before the people.

I do not know whether those gestures they remarked in me were of this first kind, and whether I had indeed some hidden propensity to the fault in question, as may well have been the case. And I cannot answer for the motions of my body ; but as regards the motions of the soul, I will here confess what I think about myself.

This vainglory consists of two parts, namely, To think too highly of ourselves, and Not to think highly enough of other people. With regard to the one, I think that in the first place these considerations should be taken into account :

That I feel oppressed by an error of the soul, which displeases me, both as being unjust, and still more as being troublesome. I try to correct it, but eradicate it I cannot. This fault is that the mere fact of possessing a thing makes me undervalue it, and that I attach too high a value to things that are not mine, that belong to another and are out of my reach. This habit of mind is very common. As the privileged authority which men have over their wives makes some regard their own, and some fathers their children, with a wicked disdain ; so it is with me, and of two works that are equal I should always think less of my own. It is not so much that zeal for my progress and improvement disturbs my judgement and prevents my being satisfied with myself, as that the fact of being master of itself breeds contempt of what we hold and control.

The governments, customs, and languages of distant countries are my delight; and I am aware that Latin, by reason of its dignity, fascinates me more than it should, as it does boys and the common sort of people. My neighbour's husbandry, his house, his horse, though no better than my own, I value more than my own, just because they are not mine. I am besides very ignorant of my own affairs. I admire the cheerful self-assurance and optimism of other people, whilst there is scarcely anything I am sure of knowing, or that I can answer for being able to do. I have no exact idea in advance of the means at my disposal, and only know of them after the event. I am as doubtful of myself as of everything else ; whence it comes that if I happen to succeed in any business, I attribute it more to my luck than to my ability, seeing that in all my plans I am haphazard and diffident.

So another general characteristic of mine is this, that of all the estimates of mankind in the gross expressed by the ancient writers, I most readily embrace and most strongly adhere to those that are most contemptuous, most humiliating and most crushing. To me Philosophy never seems to have so easy a game as when she attacks our presumption and vanity, when she sincerely admits her own indecision, weakness, and ignorance. It seems to me that the nursing-mother of the most erroneous ideas, both of men in general and of the individual, is the exaggerated opinion man has of himself.

Those men who bestraddle the epicycle of Mercury and see so far into the heavens get on my nerves.[1] For when in my studies, whose subject is Man, I find so great a variety of opinions, so inextricable a maze of obscurities one on top of the other, so great variance and uncertainty in the very school of Wisdom, you may judge (since those men have been unable to agree in their knowledge of themselves and their own condition, which is ever present to their eyes, which is within them ; since they do not know how those things move which they themselves set in motion, nor how to describe and explain the springs of action which they themselves hold and manage), you may imagine, I say, how far I can believe them when they explain the causes of the flow and ebb of the river Nile. The curiosity

[1] Lit., pull out my teeth.

to know things has been given to man for a scourge, says Holy Scripture.[1]

But to come to my own particular case, I think it would be very difficult to find a man who has a smaller opinion of himself, nay, a man who has a smaller opinion of me, than I have of myself.

I regard myself as a very ordinary person, except in this respect, that I do regard myself in that light. I plead guilty to the meanest and commonest defects; I neither disclaim nor excuse them. The only value that I set upon myself is that I know my own value.

If I have any vainglory, it is superficially poured upon me, through the treachery of my nature, and has not so much body that my judgement can perceive it; I am sprinkled but not dyed with it.

For indeed, with regard to intellectual achievements of any kind, I never produced anything that filled me with satisfaction. And the approval of others does not repay me. My taste is delicate and hard to please, and especially with regard to my own work. I continually repudiate myself, and feel myself at all times fluctuating and bending by reason of my weakness. I have nothing of my own that satisfies my judgement. My sight is clear and normal enough, but when at work it becomes blurred.

This I experience most evidently in the case of poetry. I am extremely fond of it, and I can form a pretty good judgement of others' work; but when I try to set my hand to it I am indeed but a child, and the result is something I cannot tolerate. We may play the fool in anything else, but not in poetry:

> For Gods and men and booksellers refuse
> To countenance a mediocre Muse. (HORACE.)

Would to Heaven that these lines were inscribed over the doors of all our printers' shops, to forbid the entrance of so many versifiers!

> None more conceited than a sorry poet. (MARTIAL.)

Why are not our people like this? Dionysius the father valued nothing of his so highly as his poetry. At the season of the Olympian games, with chariots surpassing all others

---

[1] A translation of one of the Latin sentences inscribed on the ceiling in Montaigne's library.

in magnificence, he also sent poets and musicians to present his verses, together with tents and pavilions royally gilt and tapestried. When they began to recite his lines, the charm and excellence of the delivery at first attracted the attention of the people; but after considering the inanity of the composition, they first showed disdain, then, becoming more and more exasperated, they soon fell into a fury and angrily rushed his tents and tore them all in pieces. And when his chariots failed to make a show in the races, and the vessel which carried back his people missed the coast of Sicily and was driven before the gale and dashed against the rocks at Tarentum, they took it for a certain sign that the gods, like themselves, were incensed against the badness of his poem. And even the sailors who escaped from the shipwreck backed up the opinion of the people, with which also the oracle that predicted his death seemed in some sort to agree.

This was to the effect 'that Dionysius should be near his end when he had vanquished those who were better than himself'. These he interpreted to be the Carthaginians, whose forces were greater than his own. Being at war with them he often dodged the victory, or qualified it, in order not to incur the fate intended by that oracle. But he misunderstood it; for the God was thinking of the occasion when, by favour and injustice, he gained the advantage at Athens over the tragic poets who were better than he, and in competition with whom he had his play, called 'The Leneians',[1] acted. He died immediately after this victory, partly in consequence of the excessive joy he felt at his success.

What I find tolerable in my own work is not so really and in itself, but by comparison with other and worse things which I observe to be well received. I envy the happiness of those who are able to rejoice and find a satisfaction in their productions; for that is an easy way of indulging oneself, since the source of our pleasure is in ourselves, especially if we are strong in our self-conceit.

I know a poet against whom everybody, the strong and the weak, in the crowd and in the chamber, against whom

---

[1] Not quite accurate. The play had another name, but was acted at the Leneian games. As to Dionysius's death, it was not the excessive joy, but the deep potations with which he celebrated his victory, that brought it on.

heaven and earth cry out that he is no poet. For all that he will not abate a jot of the measure to which he has cut himself; ever beginning again, ever persisting, ever reconsidering, he is all the stronger and more stubborn in his good opinion of himself for being the only one who holds it.

My works are so far from pleasing me that, as often as I peruse them, so often do they annoy me:

> When I re-read I blush at what I've written;
> For many things I see which even I,
> Being judge, account but fit to be erased. (OVID.)

I have always an idea in my mind, a sort of blurred picture, which shows me, as in a dream, a better form than that I have framed; but I cannot grasp it and turn it to account. And yet that idea is but on a middle plane. From this I conclude that the productions of those great and fertile minds of the past are very far beyond the utmost stretch of my imagination and desire. Their writings not only satisfy me to the full, but they excite my astonished and rapturous admiration. I see and appreciate their beauty, if not so far as they are capable of being appreciated, at least so far that I cannot possibly aspire to equal them.

Whatever I take in hand, I owe a sacrifice to the Graces, as Plutarch says of some one, to conciliate their favour:

> If anything should please that I indite,
> Into men's minds if it infuse delight,
> I owe it to the charming Graces. (*Poet unknown.*)

But they always leave me in the lurch. All that I write is rude; it lacks grace and beauty. I am unable to make the most of things. My style adds nothing to the matter.[1] Therefore I need a strong matter, with plenty of grip, and one that shines by its own light. When I take up a popular theme and one of a more sprightly nature, I do so in obedience to my own instinct, as I do not affect a solemn and gloomy wisdom, like the world in general; to enliven myself, not my style, which is rather suited to a grave and austere subject (at least if I may call that a style which is a way of speaking without form or rule, a popular jargon,

---

[1] A commentator points out that Montaigne here seems to flatly contradict what he said in another place: 'Do not look to the matter, but to the shape that I give it. My humour is to regard the form more than the substance.'

proceeding without definitions, without divisions, without conclusions, hazy, like that of Amafanius and Rabirius).[1]

I can neither please, nor delight, nor tickle. The best story in the world becomes dull and dry by my handling. I can only speak in real earnest and am entirely without that facility which I observe in many of my friends of entertaining any chance people and keeping a whole company amused, or of holding the attention of a prince with all kinds of small talk, without boring him. Those people never run short of matter, by reason of their gift in laying hold of the first that comes to hand, and adapting it to the humour and capacity of those they are talking with.

Princes are not very fond of serious talk ; nor am I of telling stories. The first and most obvious arguments, which are usually the most readily accepted, I am unable to hit upon ; a poor preacher for the gentry ! When once I start a subject I am apt to exhaust it.

Cicero thinks that in philosophical treatises the most difficult part is the exordium. If that be so, I confine myself to the conclusion.

And yet we must tune the string to every kind of note ; and the sharpest is that which comes least often into play. It needs at least as much perfection to develop an empty theme as to sustain a weighty one. At times one needs to handle a matter superficially, at other times to dig deeply into it. I know well that most people keep to that lower stage, being unable to see beneath the outer rind. But I also know that the greatest masters, both Xenophon and Plato, often unbend and employ that lower and popular manner of speaking and treating of matters, enhancing them however with the charm that never fails them.

Now in my style there is no ease and polish ; it is harsh and disdainful, disposed to be free and unrestrained. And as such it flatters my inclination, if not my judgement. But I am very sensible of the fact that I sometimes allow myself to go too far, and that by endeavouring to avoid art and affectation, I drop into them on another side :

I grow obscure in trying to be brief. (HORACE.)

Plato says that length and brevity are not qualities that either take from or give value to style.

---

[1] Two men mentioned by Cicero. The former was one of the earlier Roman writers of the Epicurean school. Of the latter nothing is known.

I could not, though I tried, attain to that even, smooth and correct style of other writers. And, although the concise and rhythmic style of Sallust best suits my humour, yet I find Caesar both greater and less easy to copy. And if my inclination prompts me rather to imitate the style of Seneca, I have yet a higher estimation of that of Plutarch.

As in doing, so also in speaking, I simply follow my natural bent; which is perhaps the reason why I am better at speaking than at writing. Movement and action put life into words, especially with those who, like me, move briskly and become heated. Demeanour, face, voice, attitude, and the gown may set off a speech, which in itself is mere twaddle. Messala complains, in Tacitus, of some tight garments or other worn in his time, and of the arrangement of the benches from which the orators had to speak, and which impaired their eloquence.

My French is corrupt, both in pronunciation and in other respects, through the barbarism of my native place. I have never known a man of the hither provinces [1] whose native speech did not show a very perceptible twang, and offend purely French ears. Not however that I am very expert in my Périgord patois, for I can speak it no better than I can German. Nor do I much care; for (like the other dialects around me, going from district to district, those of Poitou, Saintonge, Angoumois, Limoges, and Auvergne) it is a languid, drawling, long-winded language.

There is certainly above us, towards the mountains, a Gascon dialect which I consider singularly fine, blunt, concise, expressive, and indeed a more virile and soldier-like language than any I know; as sinewy, forcible, and direct as the French is graceful, neat, and fluent.

As for Latin, which was given me for my mother-tongue, I have, through want of practice, lost the ready use of it in speaking; nay, in writing too, though at one time I could be called a master-hand at it. There you may see how much I fall short in that direction.

Beauty is a highly commendable quality in human intercourse. It is the first means of winning the favour of other people, and no man is so barbarous and surly as not to feel the attraction of it in some degree. The body has a great part in our being, and holds an eminent place in it; hence

---

[1] i. e., south of the Charente, the boundary of the Languedoc.

its structure and composition are well worthy of consideration.

They are to blame who would disunite our two principal parts and keep them apart. They should on the contrary be coupled and joined together. We should bid the soul, not to stand aside and entertain herself alone, not to despise and forsake the body (nor can she do so, except by some pretence and hypocrisy), but to become allied with him, to embrace him, cherish him, assist him, control him, advise him, correct him and bring him back when he goes astray; in short marry him and become his spouse, that they may not appear to be pulling in different and opposite directions, but to live together in unity and harmony.

Christians have a particular instruction concerning this bond. For they know that the divine justice embraces this union and fellowship of body and soul, to the extent of making the body capable of everlasting rewards; and that God looks at the actions of the whole man, and wills that he shall receive, as one whole, his punishment or his wage, according to his deserts.

The Peripatetic school, of all sects the most sociable, makes this the sole care of Wisdom, to provide for and procure the common good of these two associated parts. And they point out that the other sects, through not giving sufficient consideration to this admixture, took sides, one for the body, another for the soul, with equal error on both sides; and that they lost sight of their subject, which is Man, and their guide, which they generally admit to be Nature.

It is probable that the first of human distinctions, and the first consideration which gave to some men a pre-eminence over others, was the advantage of beauty:

> They portioned out their flocks and fields,
> And gave to each according to his beauty,
> Or strength or sense. For beauty then was prized,
> And strength was valued. (LUCRETIUS.)

Well, I am a little below the middle height. This is not only an ugly defect, but it is also a disadvantage, especially in those who are in office and command. For the authority given by a fine presence and bodily dignity is lacking. C. Marius was unwilling to enlist soldiers under six feet.

The Courtier[1] is quite right when, in the gentleman he is training, he prefers a moderate stature rather than any other; and objects to anything unusual that would make him too noticeable. But if he fails to be of the right middle height, I should prefer, in a military man, that he should exceed it.

Little men, says Aristotle, are very pretty, but not handsome; and as a great soul connotes greatness, so a big and tall body connotes beauty. The Ethiopians and the Indians, he says, when they elected their kings or magistrates, had regard to the beauty and lofty stature of the candidates. They were right. For the sight of a tall and handsome leader marching at the head of his army inspires his followers with respect and his enemies with terror:

> Himself too Turnus, of surpassing mould,
> Amid the foremost moving, arms in hand,
> By a whole head o'ertops them. (VIRGIL.)

Our great, divine, and heavenly King, about whom everything should be carefully, religiously, and reverently remarked, did not despise bodily advantages: *thou art fairer than the children of men* (Psalms). And Plato desires beauty, as well as temperance and courage, in the guardians of his Republic.

It is very humiliating, if you are standing among your servants, to be addressed with the question, 'Where is your master?' and to receive only the fag-end of a salute made to your secretary or your barber. As happened to poor Philopoemen.[2] Being the first of his company to arrive at a house where he was expected, his hostess, who did not know him and received him rather coldly, made use of him to help her maids draw water and stir the fire against Philopoemen's coming. When the gentlemen of his suite appeared, and caught him busily engaged in this pleasant occupation (for he had not failed to obey the lady's orders), they asked him what he was doing there. 'I am paying the penalty of my ugliness,' he replied.

Other kinds of beauty are for the women; beauty of stature is the only beauty of man. When a man is small, neither a broad and round forehead, nor clear and soft eyes,

---

[1] *The Courtier;* see vol. i., p. 286.
[2] The 1580 edition has Phocion, with the remark, 'I can easily mistake a name, but not the substance.'

nor an average nose, nor small ears and mouth, nor white and regular teeth, nor a thick, smooth, auburn beard, nor curly hair, nor a properly rounded head, nor a fresh complexion, nor a pleasant face, nor an odourless body, nor a correct symmetry of limbs, will make him handsome.

As to myself, I have a sturdy, thick-set figure; my face is full without being fat; my disposition between the jovial and the melancholy, moderately warm and sanguine;

> My legs are stiff with bristles,
> And hair is on my chest. (MARTIAL.)

I enjoyed a robust and vigorous health until I was well on in years, and was rarely troubled by illness.

Such I was, for I am not portraying myself now that I have entered the avenues of old age, being long past forty:

> And now by slow degrees
> Years break my strength, my vigorous growth destroy,
> And drag me downward to a dull decay. (LUCRETIUS.)

Henceforth I shall be only half a man, and no longer myself. I escape and steal away from myself every day:

> Then too the years they rob us, as they run,
> Of all things we delight in, one by one. (HORACE.)

Skill and agility I have never had; and yet I am the son of a very nimble father, who retained his sprightliness to an extreme old age. He could scarcely find a man in his station of life to equal him in all bodily exercises; whilst I have hardly come across one who did not surpass me, except in running, at which I was middling good. Of music, either vocal, for which my voice is very ill-adapted, or instrumental, they could never teach me anything. In dancing, tennis, wrestling, I was never able to acquire more than a very slight and ordinary skill; in swimming, fencing, vaulting, and leaping, none at all.

My hands are so awkward, that I cannot even write legibly enough for myself; so that I prefer to re-write what I have scribbled rather than give myself the trouble of deciphering it.[1] And I can hardly read any better. I feel

---

[1] On this point we can at least flatly contradict Montaigne. His handwriting, which is open to all the world to see, never gave anybody any trouble.

that I bore my listeners. Otherwise, a good scholar.[1] I cannot fold a letter correctly, nor could I ever cut a pen, nor carve at table worth a rap, nor saddle and bridle a horse, nor properly carry a hawk and let it fly, nor speak with hound, hawk, or horse.

In short, my bodily and mental faculties are very much on a par. There is no briskness, only perfect strength and vigour. I can stand hard work, but only when it is voluntary, and as long as my desire prompts me,

> Where the zest and the sport
> Makes the labour seem light, and the long hours short. (HORACE.)

Otherwise, unless I am allured by some pleasure, and have no guide except my free will and inclination, I am good for nothing. For I have arrived at that stage when, excepting health and life, there is nothing for which I would bite my nails and that I would purchase at the price of mental torment and constraint:

> For all the sands and all the golden wealth
> That shady Tagus rolls into the sea. (JUVENAL.)

Extremely idle, extremely independent, both by nature and habit, I would as willingly lend my blood as my pains.

I have a soul that belongs wholly to itself and is accustomed to go its own way. Having had, to this hour, neither master nor governor forced upon me, I have gone ahead as far as I pleased, and at my own pace. This has made me slack and unfit in the service of others, and of no use to any but myself.

And, as far as I am concerned, there was no need to force my heavy, lazy, and do-nothing disposition. For, having enjoyed from my birth such a degree of fortune that I had reason to be satisfied with it [a reason, however, which a thousand others of my acquaintance would rather have used as a plank over which to pass in quest of fortune, worries, and anxieties]; and being endowed with as much sense as I felt I had occasion for, I have neither sought nor taken anything:

---

[1] A reminiscence of a well-known line of Marot, who, after enumerating all his vices and shortcomings, ends up with

> Au demourant, le meilleur fils du monde,

'otherwise, the best son in the world.'

> Fair winds we may not have, nor swelling sails,
> Yet neither have we always adverse gales.
> In strength, in worth, in influence, powers of mind,
> In rank and fortune though I were behind
> The very foremost, many yet there be
> That in their turn come lagging after me. (HORACE.)

A sufficiency was all I needed to make me content; that, however, if rightly considered, implies a well-ordered state of mind, equally difficult in every station of life, and, as we see by experience, more often found with want than with plenty. Since, as with our other passions, the hunger for wealth is perhaps whetted more by its enjoyment than by its scarcity, and the virtue of moderation is rarer than that of patience. And all I needed was to enjoy in tranquillity the good things that God in his bounty placed in my hands.

I have never fancied any kind of tiresome labour. I have hardly ever [1] had any but my own affairs to manage; or, if I have, it has been on condition of managing them at my own times and in my own way, when they were committed to me by people who trusted me, who knew me and did not hustle me. For expert horsemen will get some service out of even a restive and broken-winded nag.

Even in childhood my training was relaxed and free, and I was not subjected to a rigorous discipline. All this has produced in me a sensitive disposition that is impatient of anxieties; to such a degree that I prefer any losses or irregularities that concern me to be kept from my knowledge. I put down under the heading of my expenses what it costs me to feed and maintain my negligence:

> Poor is the house wherein there's not a deal
> Which masters never miss, and varlets steal. (HORACE.)

I prefer not to take count of what I have, that I may be the less sensible of what I lose. I pray those that live with me, if they are wanting in attachment to me and treat me accordingly, to cheat me with all outward decency. For want of sufficient fortitude to endure the troubles, misfortunes, and crosses that we are liable to, and being unable to keep up the strain of regulating and managing my affairs,

---

[1] The editions previous to that of 1588 had 'never', which was altered to 'hardly ever' after Montaigne had been Mayor of Bordeaux for four years.

I leave myself entirely in the hands of Fortune, and to the best of my power foster this notion in myself, ' to be prepared for the worst in all things, and to resolve to bear that worst meekly and patiently.' For that alone do I strive ; that is the aim to which I direct all my thoughts.

In face of a danger I do not so much consider how I shall escape it as how little it matters whether I escape it or not. Even though I should succumb, what would it matter ? Not being able to control events, I control myself ; and I adapt myself to them, if they do not adapt themselves to me. I am hardly cunning enough to dodge Fortune, to escape from her or to compel her, and wisely to direct and incline matters to serve my purpose. Still less have I the patience to suffer the hard and painful anxiety needed to do so. And the most painful position for me is to be kept in suspense in urgent affairs, and tossed between fear and hope.

Deliberation, even in the most indifferent things, is a trouble to me ; and my mind is more put to it to suffer the various shocks and shakes of doubt and deliberation than to settle down and acquiesce in any course whatever, after the die is cast. My sleep has been disturbed by few passions ; but the slightest deliberation will disturb it. So too, having the choice of ways, I generally avoid the steep and slippery hill-side, and take the high road, however deep the mud, where I can sink no lower, and feel secure. And I prefer a misfortune pure and simple, in which I am no longer tormented and worried after feeling certain that it cannot be mended ; and which at the first push plunges me directly into suffering :

> The ills that plague me most are those half-known. (SENECA.)

When a thing has happened, I bear myself like a man ; when it has to be carried through, like a boy. The dread of falling throws me into a greater fever than the fall itself. The game is not worth the candle. The miser suffers more from his passion than the pauper, and the jealous man than the cuckold. And it is often better to lose your vineyard than to go to law about it. The lowest step is the firmest. There lies safety. There you have need but of yourself. There it is grounded and rests solely upon itself.

Is there not something philosophical in the attitude of a certain gentleman who was well-known ? He married when he was well on in years, having spent his youth in convivial company; moreover, great at telling merry tales. Remembering how often he had had occasion to laugh at others who 'wore the horns', he resolved to be safe and under cover, and married a woman whom he picked up in a place where any man could have what he needed for his money, and made a match of it with her. 'How d'ye do, Mistress Whore?'—'How d'ye do, Master Cuckold?' And he was always ready to talk openly about his venture to anybody who came to see him, and so took the wind out of the sails of any would-be scandal-monger or tale-bearer, and the point off their sting.

With regard to ambition, which is neighbour, or rather daughter, to presumption, Fortune, to advance me, would have had to come and take me by the hand. For I could never have gone to any trouble for an uncertain hope, or submitted to all the difficulties which attend those who try to push themselves into favour at the beginning of their career:

> I will not purchase hope at any price. (TERENCE.)

I cling to what I see and have, and keep the harbour well in view:

> Into the sea one oar I plunge,
> And with the other rake the sands. (PROPERTIUS.)

And, besides, we seldom advance very far unless we first risk what we have. And I am of opinion that if we have sufficient to keep up the state we are born and accustomed to, it is foolish to let it go in the uncertain hope of increasing it. The man to whom Fortune has denied a foothold and the means of settling down into a calm and peaceful life, may be excused if he risks what he has, since in any case necessity sends him out to seek a living:

> In evil we must take the boldest step. (SENECA.)

And I could more readily excuse a younger son for scattering his portion to the winds, than one who has the honour of his family in his keeping, and cannot become necessitous except by his own fault.

With the advice of my good friends in the past I have

found the shorter and easier way of being rid of that ambition and sitting still:

> Who would not win the palm of victory
> Without the sweat and dust of the arena? (HORACE.)

Besides, having a very sound judgement of my own powers, and knowing that I am not capable of great things, and remembering that saying of the late Chancellor Olivier that 'the French are like apes, climbing up a tree from branch to branch, and, having reached the topmost bough, showing their backsides':

> 'Tis base to take a load one cannot bear,
> And, fainting 'neath it, bend the knee and yield. (PROPERTIUS.)

Even the irreproachable qualities I possess have been useless in this age. My easy-going ways would have been called slackness and weakness; my fidelity and conscientiousness would have been deemed scrupulous and squeamish, my frankness and independence troublesome, rash and inconsiderate.

Ill luck is of some good. It is not amiss to be born in a very depraved age; for, by comparison with others you may earn a cheap reputation for goodness. The man who in our days is only guilty of parricide and sacrilege is a good man, and an honourable:

> If now a friend do not deny a trust,
> If he restore a purse with all its rust,
> His faith is deemed prodigious, fit to be
> Enrolled in sacred books of Tuscany,
> Or celebrated by some sacrifice
> Of lambs with garlands decked. (JUVENAL.)

And there never was a time and place when a ruler could expect a greater and more certain reward for goodness and justice. I shall be much mistaken if the first who makes it his business to push himself into favour and influence by that path, does not easily outstrip his fellows. Force and violence can do something, but not always everything.

We see tradesmen, village justices, artisans, holding their own with the nobles in valour and military knowledge. They give a good account of themselves both in public battles and in private combats; they fight, they defend cities in our wars. A Prince's special qualities are eclipsed in this crowd. Let him shine by his humanity, his truth, his loyalty, his moderation, and especially in his justice: marks rarely seen, unknown and banished. Only by the goodwill of the people can he carry out his functions; and no other qualities gain their affection as do those, being much more beneficial to them than the others. *There is nothing so popular as goodness* (Cicero).

By this standard [1] I should be as great and out of the common as I am dwarf-like and common by the standard of some of the past ages, when, if no other stronger qualities concurred, it was usual to find a man moderate in his revenge, slow to resent an insult, religiously scrupulous in keeping his word, neither double-faced nor cunning, nor accommodating his faith to others' wishes or to every occasion.[2] Rather would I allow a transaction to break its neck than twist my words in order to further it.

For, with regard to this new-fangled virtue of hypocrisy and dissimulation, which is now held in so great honour, I have a deadly hatred of it. Of all vices I know of none that gives more evidence of a mean and craven spirit. It shows a cowardly and servile disposition to disguise ourselves and hide behind a mask, and not to dare to show ourselves as we are. By that means the men of our day train themselves to perfidy. Being accustomed to speak untruths, they make no scruple of breaking their word.

A generous heart should not belie its thoughts, but should be ready to show its inmost depths. It is either all good, or at least all human.

Aristotle regards it as the duty of a great soul to hate and love openly, to judge, to speak in all freedom, and, when the truth is in question, to pay no attention to the approval or disapproval of others.

Apollonius said it was for slaves to lie, and for free men to speak truth.

That is the first and fundamental part of virtue. We must love her for herself. He who tells the truth because he is obliged to do so, and because it serves his turn, and who is not afraid of telling an untruth when it is of no importance to anybody, is not truthful enough.

---

[1] i. e., by comparing myself with my contemporaries.

[2] By these words Montaigne originally intended to characterize himself. The earlier editions have: 'By this standard I should have been moderate in *my* revenge, &c.'

My soul naturally abominates a lie, and hates even to think one. I feel an inward shame and a pricking remorse if one happens to escape me, as sometimes it does, if the occasion is unexpected and I am taken unawares.

It is not always necessary to say everything; that would be foolishness. But what we say should be what we think; the contrary would be knavery. I do not know what advantage people expect who continually feign and dissemble, except it be not to be believed even when they speak the truth. That may deceive men once or twice, but to make a profession of secrecy, and to boast, as some of our rulers have done, ' that they would throw their shirt into the fire, if it were privy to their real intentions ' (which was a saying of the ancient Metellus of Macedon); and ' that the man who cannot dissemble cannot rule ',[1] is to warn those who have to deal with them, that what they say is but lying and deceit. *The more artful and cunning a man is the more is he hated and suspected, when he loses his reputation for honesty* (Cicero).

A man would be very simple who allowed himself to be beguiled either by the looks or the words of one who relies upon never being the same outside and within, as Tiberius did. And I cannot see how such people can share in human transactions, as they never utter anything that can be accepted as current coin.

He who is disloyal to the truth is also disloyal to falsehood.

Those men of our time who, in drawing up the duties of a Prince,[2] considered only his advantage, without any regard for his good faith and conscience, might perhaps have been in the right, supposing the affairs of the Prince had been so disposed by Fortune that he could settle them once for all by a single breach of faith. But that is not the way things happen. He often has occasion to enter upon the same transaction. He has to draw up more than one peace, more than one treaty, in his life. The gain which allures him to the first breach of faith (and gain is almost always the end in view, as it is of every other kind of villainy; sacrilege, murder, rebellion, treachery, are all committed for profit of some kind or other), this first gain is

---

[1] A favourite saying of Louis XI. The other was also attributed to Charles VIII.

[2] Macchiavelli, author of *The Prince*, and his followers.

followed by endless losses, and the Prince, after this example of his faithlessness, is barred from every opportunity of treating and negotiating.

When, during my boyhood, Solyman, of the Ottoman race, a race that is not over-scrupulous in the keeping of promises and pacts, after making a raid with his army on Otranto, was told that Mercurino de Gratinare and the inhabitants of Castro were kept prisoners after having surrendered the place, in contravention of the terms of capitulation, he sent word that they should be released; for, as he said, having some other great enterprises on hand in those parts, such a breach of faith, although it might appear to be a present gain, would in the future bring upon him a disrepute and distrust of infinite prejudice.

Now for my part, I would rather be a troublesome and indiscreet bore than a fawner and dissembler.

I allow that there may be a little touch of pride and obstinacy mixed with my integrity and candour, that takes no consideration of others. And methinks I tend to grow a little more outspoken where I should be less so, and that, where I should show the more respect, I become the more heated in upholding my opinion. It may also be that, for want of tact, I let Nature have her own way. Using the same freedom of speech and demeanour with men in high position that I have used in my own house, I am sensible of how much it inclines to indiscretion and incivility. But, besides that I was born that way, I am not quick-witted enough to dodge a sudden question, and escape by some shift, or to invent a truth. Nor is my memory good enough to keep to a truth I have thus invented, and I certainly lack the assurance to stick to it.

Wherefore through feebleness I put on a bold face. I take refuge in candour and always say what I think, both by nature and design, leaving it to Fortune to guide the issue.

Aristippus said that the best fruit he had gathered from Philosophy was that he spoke freely and openly to every man.

The memory is a wonderfully serviceable implement, without which the judgement does its duty very laboriously; in me it is entirely wanting. If a matter is expounded to me, it must be done piece-meal. For it is not in my power to answer a proposition with several different heads. I cannot carry a message without noting it in my tablets. And if I have to make a long-winded speech of any importance, I am reduced to the poor and miserable necessity of getting by heart, word for word, what I have to say; otherwise I should have neither method nor assurance, being afraid of my memory playing me a trick. But with this expedient I find it no less difficult. It takes me three hours to learn three lines. And besides, in a composition of my own, the freedom and authority whith which I change the order and alter a word, continually varying the matter, makes it the more difficult to keep it in mind.

Now, the more I distrust my memory the more muddled does she become; she serves me best by chance, and I have to woo her unconcernedly. For if I hustle her she is put out; when she once begins to totter, the more I sound her the more perplexed and entangled does she become. She waits upon me at her own time, not at mine.

The same defect I find in my memory I find also in several other parts. I shun all command, obligation, and constraint. What at other times I can do easily and naturally I am unable to do if I strictly and expressly command myself to do it. Even those parts of my body that have any particular freedom and authority over themselves sometimes refuse to obey me, if I intend them to do me a necessary service at a fixed time and place. They spurn such a compulsory and tyrannical order. They shrink through fear and spite, and become paralysed.

One day, being in a place where it is considered a barbarous piece of discourtesy not to pledge those who invite you to drink, although they allowed me every freedom, I tried to play the part of a good boon companion, out of respect to the ladies who were of the company, according to the custom of the country.[1] But there was compensation; for, as I was preparing, under threats, to force myself beyond my habit and inclination, my gullet became so stopped that I was unable to swallow a single drop, and was debarred from drinking even as much as I needed for my meal. And my thirst was fully quenched by the great amount of drink that my imagination had anticipated.

[1] Probably a reminiscence of his travels, which took him through part of Germany.

This effect is most apparent in those who have the most powerful and vivid imagination; yet it is natural, and there is no one who does not in some degree feel it. An eminent archer, who had been condemned to death, was offered the chance of saving his life if he would give a signal proof of his skill; he declined to attempt it, fearing lest the too great strain on his will might misdirect his aim, and that, instead of saving his life, he might also forfeit the reputation he had acquired in shooting with the bow.

A man whose thoughts are elsewhere will not fail, when he is walking, to take every time the same number and length of steps, within an inch; but if he gives his attention to measuring and counting them, he will find that what he did naturally and by chance he will not do so exactly by design.

My library, which is a handsome one among country libraries, is situated at one corner of my house.[1] If anything enters my head that I wish to look up or to write down there, I am obliged, for fear of its escaping me while merely crossing the courtyard, to communicate it to some other person. If, in speaking, I am so bold as to digress ever so little from the thread, I never fail to lose it; for which reason I force myself to be short, concise, and sparing of words. My servants I am obliged to call after the name of their occupation or their province,[2] for I have great difficulty in remembering names. I can tell indeed that it has three syllables, that it has a harsh sound, that it begins or ends with such and such a letter. And if I should live long, I am not sure that I shall not forget my own name, as others have done.

Messala Corvinus was two years without a trace of memory, and the same is said of George of Trebizond. And in my own interest I often reflect what kind of a life was theirs, and whether without this faculty I shall have enough left to support me in easy circumstances. And, if I look closely into the matter, I fear that this privation, if complete, will be attended with the loss of all the functions of the mind.

---

[1] More precisely, in a tower which forms an angle of the large courtyard, where it still stands.

[2] This, however, appears to have been a common practice. In the comedies of Molière and others we find such names of valets as Basque, Champagne, Picard, &c.

It is certain that the memory is the only receptacle, not only of Philosophy, but of all that concerns the conduct of life, and of all the arts (Cicero).

I'm full of cracks, and leak out every way. (TERENCE.)

More than once it has happened to me to forget the watchword which I had given out three hours before, or received from another; to forget where I had hidden my purse, whatever Cicero may say.[1] I help myself to lose what I have carefully locked up.

Memory is the receptacle and coffer of knowledge. Mine being so defective I have no great cause to complain if I know so little. I know in a general way the names of the arts, and of what they treat, but nothing more. I turn over the leaves of books; I do not study them. What I retain of them I no longer recognize as another's. Only my judgement has profited by the thoughts and ideas it has imbibed from them. The author, the place, the words, and other circumstances, are immediately forgotten.

And I am so eminent in forgetfulness that I forget my own writings and compositions no less than the rest. At every turn people quote my Essays to me without my being aware of it. If any one would know where to find the lines and examples I have here accumulated, I should be at a great loss to tell him.[2] And yet I have begged them only at well-known and famous doors, not satisfied with their being rich unless they also came from rich and honourable hands. Authority and reason there co-operate with one another.

It will be no great wonder if my book follows the fortune of other books, and if my memory loses its hold of what I write, as it does of what I read; of what I give as well as of what I receive.

Besides the defect of memory I have others which greatly contribute to my ignorance. My mind is slow and blunt; the least cloud will arrest its point, so that (for example) I never set it any problem, however easy, that it could unravel. Any idle subtlety will perplex me. Of games in

---

[1] 'I have never heard of any old man forgetting where he has hidden his treasure.'—Cicero, *Of Old Age*.

[2] Montaigne gave no references, and his editors, beginning with Mlle de Gournay, have no doubt had great trouble in identifying the twelve hundred and more quotations.

which the intellect has its part, as chess, cards, draughts, and others, I have only the rudest idea.

My apprehension is slow and muddled; but what it once grasps it grasps thoroughly, and embraces very closely, very deeply and very comprehensively, for as long as it does grasp it. I have a long, sound and perfect sight, but it is soon tired by work and becomes dim; for which reason I cannot converse for any length of time with my book except with another's help.

The younger Pliny will tell those who have not experienced it how important [1] is this delay to those who are fond of reading.

No mind is so feeble and brute-like that it does not give plain evidence of some particular faculty; none is so deeply buried but that it will start up at one place or another. And how it comes to pass that a mind that is blind and asleep to all else is found to be clear, wide-awake, and excelling all others in one particular direction, is a question for the masters. But the best minds are those which are far-reaching, open, and ready to embrace all things; if not educated, at least capable of education.

What I say is a condemnation of my own. For, whether from weakness or indifference (and I am far from approving indifference to what lies at our feet, what we have in hand, what most nearly concerns the employment of our time), no mind is so absurdly ignorant as mine of many such ordinary things, of which it is a disgrace to be ignorant. I must relate a few examples.

I was born and bred in the country and among field-labourers; I have had the business of husbandry in my own hands ever since my predecessors in the possession of the property I enjoy left me to succeed to it. And yet I can add up neither with counters nor with a pen. Most of our coins are unknown to me.[2] I cannot differentiate

---

[1] Perhaps Montaigne intended to say 'vexatious' (*importun*), and had in mind an anecdote which Pliny tells of his uncle: 'I remember once, his reader having pronounced a word wrongly, somebody at the table made him repeat it; upon which my uncle asked him if he understood it? He acknowledged that he did: 'Why then, said he, would you make him go back again? We have lost, by this interruption, above ten lines': so covetous was this great man of time.

[2] It must be remembered that coinage was in Montaigne's time not so simple as it is now. Every important city appears to have had its own.

between one grain and another, either in the ground or in the barn, unless the difference be too glaring; and can scarcely distinguish between the cabbages and lettuces in my garden. I do not even know the names of the chief implements of husbandry, nor the rudest principles of agriculture, which the boys know. I know still less of the mechanical arts, of trade and merchandise, of the nature and diversity of fruits, wines, and foodstuffs, of training a hawk or physicking a horse or a hound. And, to complete my disgrace, only a month ago I was caught in ignorance of the fact that leaven is used in making bread, and of the meaning of allowing wine to ferment.

Somebody at Athens once conjectured an aptitude for mathematics in a man he saw cleverly arranging a load of brushwood and making it up into faggots. Truly in my case one could draw quite the opposite conclusion; for give me a whole kitchen-battery and you will see me starving.

From this outline of my confession you may imagine other things to my prejudice. But whatever I make myself out to be, provided it be such as I am, I attain my purpose. So I will not apologize for daring to put in writing such paltry and trivial details as these. The meanness of the subject [1] compels me to do it. You may condemn my purpose, but not my treatment of it. After all I see well enough, without being informed of the fact by another, how unimportant and worthless all this is, and how foolish my design. It is enough if my judgement is not put out, of which these are the essays:

> Be nosy, be all nose, till your nose appear
> So big that Atlas it refuse to bear;
> Though even against Latinus you inveigh,
> Against my trifles you no more can say
> Than I have said myself. Then to what end
> Should you to render tooth for tooth contend?
> You must have meat if you'd be full, my friend.
> Lose not your labour; but on those that so
> Admire themselves your deadliest venom throw.
> That these things nothing are full well I know. (MARTIAL.)

I am not obliged to refrain from saying absurd things, provided I do not deceive myself and know them to be such. And to trip knowingly is so usual with me that I seldom

---

[1] Meaning himself, as stated in earlier editions.

trip any other way; I never trip by accident. It is a slight accusation to attribute my foolish actions to heedlessness, since I cannot deny that I usually attribute my vicious actions to the same.

One day at Bar-le-Duc I saw King Francis the Second being presented with a portrait which King René of Sicily had painted of himself, and sent to him to recall him to his memory. Why should not every one be allowed, in like manner, to portray himself with his pen, as he did with his brush? I will not then omit also this scar, which is very unfit to be published: my want of resolution, a very serious drawback in transacting the business of the world. In dubious enterprises I am at a loss which side to take:

> Nor yes nor no my inmost heart will say. (PETRARCH.)

I can maintain an opinion, but I cannot choose one.

For in human affairs, to whatever side we lean, we are confronted by many probabilities which confirm our opinions (and the philosopher Chrysippus said that he wished to learn of Zeno and Cleanthes, his masters, only their doctrines, for, as to proofs and reasons, he could furnish enough himself); so, whichever way I turn, I can always provide myself with grounds and probabilities enough to keep me there. Hence I hold myself in suspense, with freedom to choose, until the occasion urges me. And then, to confess the truth, I most often throw the feather into the wind, as the saying goes, and commit myself to the mercy of Fortune. A very slight turn and circumstance will carry me along:

> When the mind doubts and oscillates,
> A pin will turn the scales. (TERENCE.)

The uncertainty of my judgement is so evenly balanced on most occasions, that I could readily decide it by a throw of the dice. And, when I ponder over our human disabilities, I note that even sacred history gives examples of that custom of leaving it to chance and Fortune to determine the choice in doubtful cases: *The lot fell upon Matthias* (Acts).

Human reason is a two-edged and dangerous sword. And even in the hand of Socrates, her most intimate and familiar friend, observe that it is a stick with many ends.

Thus I am fitted only for following and am easily carried

away with the crowd. I have not sufficient confidence in my own strength to take upon me to command and lead ; I am quite content to find my steps marked out by others. If I must run the risk of a doubtful choice, I prefer that it be under one who is more assured of his opinions, and espouses them more strongly, than I do mine, the ground and foundation of which I find to be very slippery.

And yet I am not too easily imposed upon, since I perceive a like weakness in the contrary opinions. *The mere habit of assenting seems to be dangerous and slippery* (Cicero). Especially in political matters there is a large field for hesitation and conflict :

> As scales correct and pressed by equal weights,
> Nor rise, nor dip, but keep an even poise. (TIBULLUS.)

Macchiavelli's reasons, for example, were sound enough for the subject they treated of, yet it was very easy to combat them ; and they who did so made it no less easy to combat theirs. In that kind of argument there can never be wanting matter for answers, rejoinders, replications, triplications, quadruplications,[1] and that endless chain of disputes which our lawyers draw out to as great a length as they can in favour of law-suits :

> We lunge and parry, dodging in and out,
> Like Samnites at a tedious fencing-bout ; (HORACE.)

since the reasons have little other foundation than experience, and human actions and passions take on such an endless variety of forms.

A shrewd person of our days says that if, when our almanacs say cold, you say hot, and wet when they say dry, and always put the opposite of what they predict, you might lay a wager upon either event, without caring which side you take ; except in cases that admit of no uncertainty, as if you promised extreme heat at Christmas, or the rigours of winter at Midsummer.

I should say the same about these political controversies ; whatever part they set you to play, you will have as fair a prospect as your adversary, provided that you do not run counter to principles that are too solid and obvious. And yet, according to my way of thinking, in public matters

[1] *Dupliques, répliques, tripliques*, like their English equivalents, seem to be legal terms. Montaigne goes one better and adds a *quadruplique*.

no course of proceeding is so bad, provided it have age and continuity to recommend it, but that it is better than change and uncertainty. Our morals are extremely corrupt, and wonderfully incline to the worse. Many of our laws and customs are barbarous and monstrous; yet, by reason of the difficulty of improving our condition, and the danger of the whole State toppling to pieces, if I could put a spoke into our wheel and stop it at this point, I would do it with a light heart:

> No acts so foul and shameful could I tell,
> But that far worse remain behind. (JUVENAL.)

The worst thing I observe in our State is instability; our laws cannot, any more than our clothes, settle down to any fixed shape. It is very easy to condemn a government for its imperfection, for all mortal things are full of it. It is very easy to generate in a people a contempt for their ancient observances; no man ever attempted it without succeeding. But many have come to grief in their attempt to establish a better state of things in place of what they have destroyed.

I seldom consult my prudence in my conduct; I generally allow myself to follow the ordinary routine of the world. Happy are the people who do what they are commanded better than they who command, without troubling their heads about reasons; who allow themselves gently to roll according to the heavenly rolling. Obedience is never pure and simple in one who talks and argues.

In fine, to return to myself, the only quality for which I take some credit to myself is that in which no man ever thought himself deficient. My self-approbation is common and vulgar, and shared by all; for what man ever imagined he was lacking in Sense? That would be a self-contradictory proposition. It is a disease that never exists where it is seen; it is very strong and tenacious, but at the first glimmer the patient has of it it is seen through and dispersed, as a thick fog is dispersed by the sunbeams.

To accuse oneself in this case would be to excuse, and to condemn oneself would be to absolve. There never was a street-porter or any silly woman who did not think they had enough sense for their needs. We are ready enough to acknowledge others to have the advantage over us in courage, bodily strength, experience, agility, beauty; but the advantage in judgement we yield to none. And we think we could have discovered the reasons which naturally occur to the mind of another, if we had adopted his point of view.

We quite readily admit the learning, style, and such other qualities as we see in the works of another, if he excels us therein; but regarding them as mere products of the understanding, each one of us thinks he could have discovered the same in himself. And he does not easily perceive the importance and difficulty of them, unless they be at an extreme and incomparable distance, and scarcely even then.

[And he who could very clearly discern the height of another's judgement would be able to raise his own to the same pitch.]

So it is a kind of exercise for which I must expect very little praise and commendation, and a kind of composition which promises little reputation.

And then, for whom do you write? The scholars, to whom it falls to sit in judgement on books, value them only for their learning, and will admit no procedure in the mind but along the lines of art and erudition. If you have mistaken one of the Scipios for the other, can you say anything worth saying? According to them, the man who is ignorant of Aristotle is at the same time ignorant of himself. Vulgar and common-place minds, on the other hand, cannot discern the charm and power of a lofty and elegant style. Now, these two classes of people are in possession of the world. The third class by whom it is your lot to be judged, that of men of naturally strong and well-regulated intellect, is so small, that for that reason they have neither name nor position with us. It is time half wasted to aspire and endeavour to please them.

It is commonly said that the fairest portion of her favours that Nature has given us is that of Sense; for there is no man who is not contented with his share of it. Is not that reasonable? He who should see beyond would see beyond his sight.

I think my opinions are good and sound; but who does not think the same of his? One of the best proofs I have of this is the small estimation in which I hold myself. For if I had not been very sure of those opinions they might easily have been led astray by the singular affection I bear myself; as one who concentrates it almost all upon himself, and does not squander much of it on others. All the love that others distribute among an infinite number of friends and acquaintances, upon their glory and their grandeur, I dedicate entirely to the tranquillity of my mind and to myself. If any escapes me in other directions, it is not really with my deliberate consent:

> By instinct trained for self to thrive and live. (LUCRETIUS.)

Well, I seem to be very bold in so persistently condemning my own littleness. It is indeed a subject on which I exercise my judgement as much as on any other. The world always looks over the way; I turn my eyes inwards. There I fix them and keep them fixed. Every one looks in front of him; I look within myself. I have no business but with myself, I continually reflect upon myself, examine and analyse myself. Other men, if they will but see it, always go abroad; they always go straight ahead:

> No man attempts to dive into himself. (PERSIUS.)

As for me, I revolve in myself.

This capacity which I have, whatever it may be worth, for sifting the truth, and my independence in not readily subjecting my belief, I owe chiefly to myself. For the most abiding and general ideas I have are those which, so to say, were born with me; they are natural and entirely my own. When I begat them, with a strong and bold, but rather hazy and imperfect begetting, they were crude and simple; I have since confirmed and established them with the authority of others, and the sound reasonings of those ancient writers with whom I found myself to agree. They strengthened my hold upon them, and enabled me more fully to possess and enjoy them.

Whilst all others seek to recommend themselves by an active and ready wit, I lay claim to steadiness; the satisfaction they seek in conspicuous and signal deeds, or in some particular talent, I find in the order, the consistency, and moderation of my opinions and conduct. *Now it is certain that, if anything in the world is becoming, it is a constant uniformity in our whole lives and particular actions; which it is impossible we should ever maintain so long as we run counter to our inclinations, and follow after those of other people* (Cicero).

Here then you see to what degree I am guilty of what I called the first kind of Presumption. Of the second, which consists in not having a sufficiently high opinion of others, I know not whether I can so fully exonerate myself; for, at whatever cost to myself, I am resolved to speak the truth.

Whether it be perhaps that my continual intercourse with the habits of mind of the ancient writers, and the picture I have formed of those richly-endowed minds of the past, have put me out of humour with others, and with myself; or that we do in truth live in an age which produces only very indifferent things, the fact remains that I see nothing worthy of great admiration. At the same time I know few men so intimately that I am qualified to pass judgement upon them; and those with whom my station in life brings me most frequently into contact are, for the most part, men who pay little attention to their mental culture, and to whom the greatest blessing is honour, and valour the greatest perfection.

Whatever I see that is fine in others I am very ready to praise and esteem. Nay, I often express more admiration than I feel, and that is the extent to which I allow myself to be untruthful. For I am unable to originate anything untrue. I willingly testify to the laudable qualities I see in my friends, and of a foot of merit I generally make a foot and a half. But attribute to them qualities they do not possess I cannot, nor can I openly defend their imperfections.

Even to my enemies I honestly concede the honour that is their due. My feelings may change, but not my judgement. I do not confuse my animosity with other circumstances that are foreign to it; and I am so jealous of the independence of my judgement that I can very hardly part with it for any passion whatever. I do myself more injury by lying than I do the man about whom I lie.

This laudable and generous custom has been observed in the Persian nation, that they speak of their deadly enemies, and at the same time wage war to the death with them, fairly and honourably, in so far as they deserve it by their valour.

I know men enough who have divers fine qualities, the

one wit, the other courage, another skill, another conscience, another eloquence, one, one science, another, another. But as for a man great in all respects, combining all those fine qualities, or possessing one in so eminent a degree as to excite wonder or be comparable with those we honour in the past, it has not been my fortune to meet with him. The greatest I have known in the flesh, I mean for natural qualities of the soul, and of the best disposition, was Étienne de La Boëtie. His was a full mind indeed that appeared beautiful from every point of view, a soul of the old stamp, which would have produced great things if Fortune had so willed it. And he added greatly to his rich nature by learning and study.

But I know not how it is, and it is undoubtedly the case, that there is as much vanity and as little intelligence in those men who lay claim to the highest abilities, who meddle with literary pursuits and bookish occupations, as in any other class of people; whether it is that more is required and expected of them, and common defects are inexcusable in them, or, perhaps, because the conceit they have of their learning makes them bolder to show off and push themselves too far forward, the result being that they betray and give themselves away.

As an artist gives more evidence of his dullness when working upon a rich material that he has in hand, by applying and mixing it stupidly and against the rules of his work, than when using a baser material; and as we are more shocked by a fault in a statue of gold than in a plaster model: so do these men when they quote things which would be good in themselves and in their proper place; for they serve them up without discrimination, doing honour to their memory at the expense of their intelligence. They do honour to Cicero, to Galen, to Ulpian and Saint Jerome, and bring ridicule upon themselves.

I readily return to that subject of our absurd educational system; its aim has been to make us, not good and wise, but learned; and it has succeeded. It has not taught us to follow and embrace Virtue or Wisdom, but has impressed upon us their derivation and etymology. We can decline Virtue, if we cannot love it. If we do not know what Wisdom is by practice and experience, we know it by jargon and by heart. We are not content with knowing the origin of our neighbours, their kindred and their intermarriages ; we wish to be friends with them, to establish some intercourse and understanding with them. This education has taught us the definition, the divisions, and sub-divisions of Virtue, as we know the surnames and branches of a genealogical tree, without further caring to become familiar and intimate with her. It has selected, for our instruction, not those books which contain the soundest and truest opinions, but those which speak the best Greek and Latin ; and with all those fine words has poured into our minds the most unprofitable ideas of the ancients.

A good education changes one's outlook and character, as in the case of Polemo. This dissipated young Greek, happening to hear Xenocrates lecture, was struck not only by the eloquence and learning of the professor, and carried home not only the knowledge of some noble matter, but a more substantial and palpable fruit, which was a sudden change and amendment of his former life. Who was ever affected in that way by our education ?

> Say, will you act like Polemo
> On his conversion long ago ?
> The signs discard of your disease,—
> Your mits, the swathings of your knees,
> Your mufflers too,—as he, 'tis said,
> Slipped off the chaplets from his head
> Which, flushed with revel, still he wore
> When he was stricken to the core
> By the undinner'd sage's lore. (HORACE.)

To me the least contemptible class of people are those who, by reason of their simplicity, stand on the lowest rung ; their relations with each other are better regulated. I generally find the morals and the language of the peasants more in accordance with the teachings of true Philosophy than those of our philosophers. *The common people are wiser, because they are as wise as they need be* (Lactantius).

In my opinion, the most remarkable men judging by outward appearance (for to judge them in my own way I should need more light thrown upon them) have been, for eminence in war and soldier-like qualities, the Duke of Guise,[1] who died at Orleans, and the late Marshal Strozzi ; [1]

[1] François de Guise, 1519–63 ; Piero Strozzi, d. 1558.

for great ability and uncommon merit, Olivier and l'Hôpital, Chancellors of France. Poetry too I think has flourished in our century; we have an abundance of good craftsmen in that trade,[1] Daurat, Bèze, Buchanan, l'Hôpital, Montdoré, Turnebus. As to the French poets, I think they have raised their art to the highest pitch it will ever attain; and in those qualities in which Ronsard and Du Bellay excel, I do not think they fall far short of the perfection of ancient poetry. Adrianus Turnebus knew more, and knew better what he did know, than any man of his time, and long before his time.

The lives of the Duke of Alva, lately dead, and of our Constable de Montmorency were noble lives, and in several respects their fortunes were uncommonly alike. But the beauty and lustre of the latter's death, in the sight of Paris and of his King, and in their service, fighting against his nearest relations, at the head of an army victorious through his leadership, and coming so suddenly in an advanced old age, deserves, in my opinion, to rank among the noteworthy events of my time.

The same may be said of the constant goodness, the gentle manners and the scrupulous affability of Monsieur de la Nouë, who lived all his life surrounded by violent deeds of armed factions (a real school of treachery, inhumanity, and brigandage), a great and most experienced warrior.

[I have taken pleasure in proclaiming, in several places, the hopes I entertain of Marie de Gournay le Jars, my *fille d'alliance*, whom I truly love, with a more than paternal affection, and whom in my solitude and retreat I cherish as one of the best parts of my own being. She is now my chief concern in this world. If I may presage from her youth, her soul will be some day capable of the finest things, and amongst others, of the perfection of that very sacred friendship, to which, as far as my reading goes, none of her sex has yet been able to rise. Her sincerity and steadfast character are quite equal to it. Her affection for me is more than superabundant, and such in short that it leaves nothing to be desired. I could wish, however, that she were not so cruelly troubled by apprehensions of my end, since we first met when I was fifty-five years of age. Her appreciation, as a woman, and of this century, and so

---

[1] Montaigne means writers of Latin poetry.

young, and alone in her district, of the first Essays, and the wonderful impetuosity of her love and desire to make my acquaintance, long before setting eyes on me, merely on the strength of her esteem, are circumstances well worthy of consideration.][1]

Other virtues have been little, if at all, prized in this age; but valour is become common through our Civil wars. And in this respect we have souls brave even to perfection, and so numerous that it is impossible to sift them out.

Those are all I have known hitherto who have shown any extraordinary and uncommon greatness.

CHAPTER 18

OF GIVING THE LIE

YES, but, some will tell me, this idea of using oneself as a subject to write about would be pardonable in a famous and eminent person, whose reputation had aroused a desire to become acquainted with him. That is certain; I admit it. And I know very well that a mechanic will hardly raise his eyes from his work to see a man of the common run; whilst to see a great and distinguished person arriving in a town, shops and workrooms will be deserted. It ill becomes any other to make himself known unless he have qualities worthy of imitation; unless his life and opinions may serve as a pattern.

Caesar and Xenophon had a real and solid foundation whereon to base their histories, in the greatness of their own deeds. And it were to be wished that we had the written journals of the great Alexander, and the commentaries on their exploits which Augustus, Cato, Sylla, Brutus, and others left behind them. One loves and studies the statues of such men, even in bronze and marble.

This objection is very true, but it affects me very little:

> I ne'er recite except to friends; and even from that forbear
> Unless implored; to everyone I can't, nor everywhere.

---

[1] This passage does not appear in the 'Bordeaux Manuscript'; which omission, in the opinion of at least one commentator, casts some doubt upon its authenticity.

> In open Forum some recite their works, and some for choice
> Within the baths, whose vaulted space rings sweetly back the voice.
> (HORACE.)

I am here not erecting a statue to be stuck up at the street corner of a town, or in a church or market-place :

> No aim of mine to swell my page
> With such pretentious trifles . . .
> With you alone I mean to talk
> In secret converse. (PERSIUS.)

It is intended for a nook in the library, and to entertain a neighbour, a kinsman, a friend, who may take a pleasure in renewing his acquaintance and intimacy with me by means of this portrait. Others have taken heart to speak of themselves because they thought the subject worthy and fruitful; I, on the other hand, because I thought it too meagre and barren to incur the suspicion of ostentation.

I am ready enough to judge the actions of others; of my own I give little to judge of, by reason of their insignificance. I do not find so much good in myself that I cannot tell it without blushing.

What a satisfaction it would be to hear somebody thus tell me of the habits, the faces, the behaviour, the everyday words, and the fortunes of my ancestors! How attentively I would listen to it! Truly it would show a bad nature to despise even the portraits of our friends and forbears, the fashion of their clothes and their armour. I treasure the inkstand, the seal, the breviary, and a peculiar sword which they used; and have not banished from my cabinet certain long switches which my father usually carried in his hand. *A father's coat and his ring are the more dear to his children the more they loved him* (St. Augustine).

If my posterity should, however, be of another mind, I shall have the means of being revenged upon them; for they cannot care less for me than I shall then care for them.[1]

All the traffic I have in this with the public is that I borrow the implements of their writing, as being easier to

---

[1] This was probably not intended to be taken seriously, but if it means anything it would mean that he would be beyond caring, since he did not believe in immortality. That his posterity were not of his mind seems certain, as his daughter appears to have soon disposed of his library of about a thousand books, which were afterwards dispersed. Only about seventy of them have since been recovered.

read and more speedy. In requital of it I shall perhaps keep some pat of butter from melting in the marketplace :[1]

> Lest tunny-fish and olives lack a coat. (MARTIAL.)
>
> And mackerel shall have a roomy shirt. (CATULLUS.)

And if nobody reads me, shall I have wasted my time, when I have beguiled so many idle hours with such pleasant and profitable reflections ? In modelling this figure after myself, I have so often been obliged to adjust and compose it, in order to get at myself, that the copy has in some sort become shaped and consolidated of itself. In portraying myself for others I have portrayed myself in more distinct colours than were mine originally. I have no more made my book than my book has made me ; a book consubstantial with its author, concerned with me alone, a part of my life ; not dealing with and aimed at other and third persons, like all other books.

Have I wasted my time in so continually and carefully rendering an account of myself ? For they who only occasionally survey themselves in thought and speech do not examine themselves so closely, they do not penetrate so far beneath the skin, as one who makes it his study, his work and his trade, who is engaged, with all his faith, with all his strength, on a record that will endure.

The most delightful pleasures are indeed digested inwardly, leaving no trace of themselves, and avoiding the sight not only of the public, but of any other person.

How often has not this work diverted me from troublesome thoughts ? And all frivolous thoughts ought to be accounted troublesome. Nature has amply endowed us with the faculty for entertaining ourselves with our own thoughts ; and often invites us to do so, to remind us that we owe ourselves in part to society, but for the best part to ourselves.

For compelling my fancy to indulge even its reveries in some order and according to some plan, and to keep it from wandering aimlessly and losing itself, there is nothing like giving a body to and recording all the trifling thoughts that

---

[1] By the ' implements of their writing ' Montaigne seems to mean the printing-press. He was not a good prophet when he suggested that his books might be used for wrapping butter.

present themselves. I give ear to my reveries because I have to record them.

How many a time, when annoyed by some action which civility and good sense forbade my openly reproving, have I not disgorged myself here, not without an eye to the instruction of the public ? And then these poetical lashes :

> Zon dessus l'euil, zon sur le groin,
> Zon sur le dos du Sagoin ! [1]

make a still deeper impression on paper than on the living flesh. What if I lend ear a little more attentively to books, since I am on the look out to pilfer any little thing, to enamel and prop up my own ?

I have by no means studied in order to make a book ; but I have to some extent studied because I had made one, if we may call it studying to skim and to lay hold, by the head or the feet, now of one author, now another. Not by any means to form my opinions, but certainly to support, confirm, and serve those formed long ago.

But whom are we to believe when speaking of himself in so corrupt an age, seeing there are few, if any, whom we can believe when speaking of others, when there is less to be gained by lying ? The first stage in the corruption of morals is the banishing of the truth ; for, as Pindar said, to be truthful is the beginning of a great virtue, and it is the first article that Plato requires in the ruler of his Republic.

Our truth nowadays is not what is, but what we can persuade others to believe ; just as we call Money not only that which is legal, but also any spurious coin that will pass. Our nation has long been taxed with this vice ; for Salvianus of Massilia, who lived in the time of the Emperor Valentinian, says, ' that with the Franks lying and perjury are not vice, but a way of speaking.' If you would overbid this testimony, you might say that they now regard them as a virtue. We are trained, we are fashioned to it as to an honourable practice ; for dissimulation is among the most notorious qualities of this century.

Wherefore I have often considered whence could have arisen that custom we so religiously observe, of being more

---

[1] ' One in the eye, one on the snout, one on the back of the pig '. From a poem of Marot in reply to a violent attack upon him by a priest named Sagon. Their quarrel, in which others joined, lasted for quite a year.

deeply offended when taxed with this vice, which is so common with us, than with any other; and that to be accused of lying is the last insult that can be put upon us in words. From this it seems to me to be natural to deny most strongly the faults with which we are most strongly tainted. It would seem as if, by hotly resenting the accusation, we in some sort acquit ourselves of the guilt. If we have it in fact, we at least condemn it in appearance.

May it not also be because this reproach seems to imply cowardice and a craven heart? Can there be any more manifest cowardice than to deny what we have said? Then how much more cowardly to deny what we know!

Lying is an ugly vice, which is painted in its most shameful colours by an ancient writer when he says that 'to lie is evidence that we despise God and at the same time fear men'. It would be impossible to declare more fully what a vile, detestable, and outrageous a thing it is. For what more infamous can we imagine than to be a coward before men and to stand up against God? As speech is the only means that men have of understanding one another, the man who violates it is a traitor to society. It is the only instrument for communicating our wishes and thoughts; it is the interpreter of our soul. If it fails us we can no longer hold together, we shall cease to know one another. If it deceives us, it breaks off all our intercourse and dissolves all the ties of our government.

Certain nations of the new Indies (there is no object in mentioning their names, which no longer exist; for the desolation attending their conquest went so far as to utterly abolish the names, and all knowledge of the old places—a monstrous and unheard-of example!) made offerings to their gods of human blood, but only such as was drawn from the tongue and ears, to atone for the sin of lying, both heard and uttered.

That good old Greek [1] said that boys play with knucklebones and men with words.

With regard to the different ways in which we give the lie, and our laws of honour on this point, and the changes which have taken place in them, I will defer saying what I know of them to another occasion. Meanwhile I will learn, if I can, when that habit arose of so exactly weighing and

[1] Lysander

measuring our words, and making it a point of honour to do
so. For we may easily imagine it was not in the time of
the old Romans and Greeks. And I have often thought it
strange and novel to see them abuse and accuse one another
of lying, without any further quarrel. Their laws of duty
steered some other course than ours. Caesar is called, now
a robber, now a drunkard, to his face. We see how free they
were in their mutual invectives ; I mean the greatest war-
lords of both nations, among whom words are only avenged
with words, and that was the end of it.

CHAPTER 19

OF FREEDOM OF CONSCIENCE

IT is a common thing to see good intentions, unless guided
by moderation, driving men to very mischievous acts. In
this conflict which has now stirred up France to civil wars,
the best and the soundest side is no doubt that which up-
holds both the old religion and the old government of the
country. Yet amongst the honourable men who follow that
side (for I do not mean those men who make a pretence of
it, either to wreak their private vengeance, or to gratify
their avarice, or to court the favour of princes ; but those
who follow it out of true zeal to their religion and a godly
desire to maintain the peace and the present state of their
country), among these, I say, we see many who are driven
by passion beyond the bounds of reason, and sometimes
adopting unjust, violent, and even foolhardy measures.

It is certain that in those early days when our religion
first gained authority with the laws, many armed themselves
with zeal against pagan books of every kind, in consequence
of which men of letters have suffered an enormous loss. In
my estimation this devastation has done more harm to
Letters than all the fires of the Barbarians. A good witness
to this is Cornelius Tacitus ; for although the Emperor
Tacitus, his kinsman, had, by express command, furnished
all the libraries in the world with his works, not a single
complete copy was able to escape the careful search of those
who desired to destroy them, on account of five or six insignificant sentences adverse to our religion.

Another characteristic of theirs was their readiness to

lend undeserved praise to all the Emperors who were on our side, and to condemn generally all the actions of those who were hostile to us ; as we may plainly see in the case of the Emperor Julian, surnamed the Apostate.[1]

He was indeed a very great and very uncommon man, with a mind deeply imbued with the teachings of Philosophy, by which he professed to regulate all his actions. And indeed there is no kind of virtue of which he has not left behind some very notable examples. In respect of chastity (of which in the course of his life he gives very clear evidence), they tell of him a similar story to that related of Alexander and Scipio, that of a number of very beautiful captive girls he would not even look at one, although he was then in the prime of life, for he was killed by the Parthians at the early age of thirty-one.

As to his justice, he went to the trouble of personally hearing the parties to a suit ; and, although out of curiosity he would inquire of what religion they were who appeared before him, yet the hostility he bore to ours never weighed down the scales. He himself made sundry good laws and cut down a great number of the subsidies and imposts which his predecessors had levied.

We have two good historians who were eye-witnesses of his actions. One of them, Marcellinus, strongly condemns, in several passages of his history, that edict of his which forbade all Christian rhetoricians and grammarians to keep school and teach ; and he adds that he could wish this action of his to be buried in silence. It is probable that, had Julian adopted any harsher measures against the Christians, Marcellinus would not have omitted to mention them, being very favourably inclined to our religion.

He was indeed a harsh, but not a cruel, enemy to us ; for our own people tell this story of him : One day, as he was walking about the city of Chalcedon, Maris, the Bishop of the place, had the temerity to call him ' wicked traitor to Christ ', to which he merely answered, ' Go, wretched man,

---

[1] The character of the Emperor Julian was censured, when Montaigne was in Rome in 1581, by the Master of the Sacred Palace, who, however, as Montaigne tells us in his Travel journal, referred it to his conscience to alter it. This he did not do, and this chapter supplied Voltaire with the greater part of the praises he bestowed upon that Emperor.—*Note by Leclerc.*

and deplore the loss of your eyes.' To which the Bishop retorted, 'I thank Jesus Christ for having deprived me of sight, that I might not see your insolent face.' Wherein they say he affected a philosophic tolerance. It is at least true that this action cannot be reconciled with the cruelties he is reported to have exercised against the Christians. He was (says Eutropius, my other witness) an enemy to Christianity, but without touching blood.

And, to return to his justice, there is nothing to be brought up against him except the severity he exercised, in the beginning of his reign, against those who had sided with Constantius, his predecessor.

As to his sobriety, he always lived a soldier's life; and even in peace times he dieted himself like a man who is preparing and training for the hardships of war.

His vigilance was such that he divided the night into three or four parts, the least part of which was allotted to sleep; the rest of it was spent either in supervising in person the state of his army and his bodyguard, or in study; for, among other rare qualities of his, he was a very eminent scholar in all branches of literature.

They tell of Alexander the Great that, having gone to rest, lest sleep should divert him from his thoughts and studies, he had a basin placed at his bedside, and grasping a copper ball in one hand held it over the basin, in order that, should sleep overtake him and cause his fingers to relax their hold, the noise of the ball dropping into the basin might awaken him. Our man had his mind so bent on what he was about, and so little disturbed by the fumes of wine, by reason of his singular abstinence, that he was able to dispense with that artifice.

As to his eminence in military matters, he was wonderfully endowed with all the qualities appertaining to a great general, and no wonder, since he was nearly all his life continually engaged in warfare, for the most part with us in France, against the Germans and Franks. We have hardly any record of a man who looked on more dangers, or more often gave proof of his personal valour.

His death has something in common with that of Epaminondas; for he was pierced by an arrow and tried to pull it out, and would have done so but that, the arrow having a sharp edge, he cut and disabled his hand. He incessantly requested to be carried back, as he was, into the thick of the battle, to encourage his soldiers, who very bravely held their own without him, until night separated the armies.

To philosophy he was indebted for the singular contempt in which he held his life and things human. He had a firm belief in the eternity of the soul.

In the matter of religion he was wrong throughout. He was called the Apostate for having abandoned ours; yet there seems to be more likelihood in this explanation: That he never had Christianity at heart, but that, in obedience to the laws, he dissembled until he held the Empire in his own hands.

He was so superstitious in his own religion that even his co-religionists of the time ridiculed him; they said that if he had gained the victory over the Parthians, he would have drained the world of oxen to satisfy his sacrifices. He was also infatuated with the art of Divination, and encouraged all kinds of prognostications.

He said at his death, among other things, that he was grateful to the gods, and thanked them, for having decreed that he should not be surprised by death, since they had long before apprised him of the time and place of his end, and that he should neither die a soft and ignominious death, more suitable to idle and effeminate persons, nor a prolonged, lingering, and painful death; that they had held him worthy of dying in this noble way, in the full tide of his victories and at the height of his fame. He had had a vision like Marcus Brutus, which first threatened him in Gaul and afterwards reappeared to him in Persia, at the point of his death.

These words that they have put into his mouth when he felt himself wounded, ' You have vanquished, Nazarene,' or, according to others, ' Be satisfied, Nazarene,' would not have been forgotten, if they had been believed, by my witnesses, who, being present in the army, observed his slightest movements and words at the end; any more than certain other miracles attached to his name.

And, to come back to the subject of my essay, he had, according to Marcellinus, long cherished Paganism in his heart. But since his army was wholly composed of Christians, he did not dare to disclose it. In the end, when he found himself strong enough to venture to proclaim his change of mind, he caused the temples of the gods to be thrown open, and did his utmost to restore idolatry. To effect his purpose, having found the people at Constantinople at loggerheads, and the prelates of the Christian church divided among themselves, he summoned them to his palace, and earnestly admonished them to suppress their civil dissensions, promising that every man should, without fear or hindrance, follow his own religion. He was very careful to urge this point, in the hope that this liberty would strengthen the factions and the schisms which divided them, and would prevent the people from becoming reunited, and consequently fortifying themselves against him by unanimous concord and mutual understanding; having learned by experience, from the cruelty of some of the Christians, 'That there is no beast in the world so much to be feared by man, as man.'

Those are very nearly his words. Wherein this is worthy of consideration, that the Emperor Julian, to stir up civil troubles and dissensions, uses the same remedy of freedom of conscience that our Kings have lately employed to stifle them. It may be said, on the one side, that to give a loose rein to the factions to hold to their opinions, is to sow and scatter division, and almost to lend a hand to increase it, there being no barrier and restraint of the laws to check and impede its course. But, on the other side, it might also be said that to give the factions the reins to hold to their beliefs is to render them soft and lax through ease and facility, and to blunt the edge which is sharpened by rarity, novelty and difficulty. And so I think it is better, for the honour of the piety of our kings, that, not having been able to do what they would, they have made a show of willing what they could.

CHAPTER 20

THAT OUR ENJOYMENTS ARE NEVER UNMIXED

WE are naturally so feeble that we cannot enjoy things in their native purity and simplicity. The elements we live on are corrupted; and so are the metals: even gold must be debased with some other matter to fit it for our use.

Neither the virtue, simple as it seemed, which Aristo and Pyrrho, as well as the Stoics, made the 'end of life', nor the hedonism of the Cyrenaics and Aristippus, were of any practical use without being compounded.

Of the pleasures and good things we enjoy not one is exempt from some mixture of evil and discomfort:

> Since from the very heart of these delights
> A bitter something springs, something to sting
> Even amid the flowers. (LUCRETIUS.)

Our keenest pleasure appears, as it were, to groan and lament. Would you not think it were dying of anguish? Nay, when we compose a picture of it at its highest point; we deck it out with sickly and painful epithets and qualities, languor, softness, weakness, faintness, *morbidezza*; a great testimony to their consanguinity and consubstantiality.

In profound joy there is more seriousness than gaiety; in the highest and fullest contentment more soberness than merriment. *Even felicity, unless it be tempered, overwhelms* (Seneca). Happiness grinds us down.

That is the meaning of an old Greek line which says that 'the gods sell us all the good things they give us'; that is to say, that they give us none pure and perfect, and that we do not buy at the price of some evil.

Toil and pleasure, very unlike by nature, are however joined together by some sort of natural connexion.

Socrates said that some god tried to mix in one lump and to confound pain and pleasure; but that, unable to succeed, he bethought himself to couple them at least by the tail.

Metrodorus said that in sadness there is some alloy of pleasure. I know not whether he meant something else, but for my part I imagine there is a certain amount of purpose, acquiescence, and satisfaction in nursing one's melancholy; I mean besides the desire for approval which may be mixed up with it. There is a little shade of daintiness and delicacy that smiles upon and flatters us in the very lap of melancholy. Are there not some natures that feed upon it?

> A certain kind of pleasure 'tis to weep. (OVID.)

And one Attalus, in Seneca, says that the memory of our lost friends is grateful to us, like the bitterness of wine that is too old:

> O ministering slave, of old Falernian
> Pour out a bitterer cup; (CATULLUS.)

and like sour-sweet apples.

Nature discloses to us this confusion. Painters hold that we work the same facial muscles and wrinkles both in crying and laughing. In fact, if you watch the progress of a picture before either expression is fully developed, you will be in doubt which of the two the artist is aiming at. And the merriest laughter is mingled with tears. *There is no evil without its compensation* (Seneca).

When I think of a man besieged by every desirable felicity (let us put the case that all the parts of his body are constantly seized with a pleasure equal to that of generation at its highest point), I can imagine him sinking under the weight of his pleasure, and see that he is utterly unable to support a delight so unmixed, so constant and universal. Indeed, he will run away from it when he is in it, and will naturally make haste to escape, as from a place where he can find no foothold, and is afraid of sinking.

When I make a rigorous self-confession I find that the best virtue I have has some taint of vice. And I am afraid that Plato, in his greenest virtue (I who am as sincere and faithful an admirer of it, and of other virtues of the same stamp, as any man can be), if he had lent an attentive ear to it, and he did lend an attentive ear to it, would have detected some sinister note of a human admixture; but it would be a faint sound and perceptible only to himself. In all things and throughout man is but patchwork and motley.

Even the laws of Justice cannot subsist without some blending of injustice. And Plato says that they who imagine they can remove from the laws all their defects and unfairness, are undertaking to cut off the Hydra's heads. *In every exemplary punishment there is a certain amount of injustice towards the individual which is counterbalanced by public utility*, says Tacitus.

It is likewise true that for the ordinary conduct of life and service in public affairs our minds may be too clear and perspicacious. This penetrating clearness of vision is too subtle and curious. These qualities should be weighted and blunted to make them more obedient to example and practice; they should be thickened and obscured to adapt them to this cloudy and terrestrial life.

Therefore it is that commonplace and less highly-strung minds are more proper and more successful in managing affairs. The lofty and exquisite ideas of Philosophy are unsuited to practical purposes. That mental acuteness and vivacity, that supple and restless volubility, are a disturbing factor in our negotiations. Human enterprises must be handled more roughly and superficially; and a good and great part must be left to the guidance of Fortune. It is not necessary to pry so deeply and cunningly into things. We lose our way when we view matters in so many contrary aspects and in such divers shapes. *Turning over in their minds things so contradictory they became quite dazed* (Livy).

This is what the ancients say of Simonides: Because his imagination suggested to him (upon the question King Hiero had put to him, to answer which he had many days to meditate in) so many different subtle and ingenious solutions, that he doubted which was the most probable, and totally despaired of finding the true.[1]

He who inquires into and embraces all the circumstances and consequences, impedes his choice. An average mind will suffice equally well for conducting operations of great or little weight. Observe that the best managers of their own affairs are those who are least able to say how they came to be so; and that those self-sufficient talkers can generally do nothing to the purpose.

I know a man, a great talker and most excellent at describing every kind of husbandry, who has allowed a yearly revenue of a hundred thousand livres to slip through his fingers, more's the pity! I know another who can prate, and give better advice than any man of his counsel, and there is not a man in the world who makes a better show of mental gifts; yet when it comes to deeds, his servants can tell quite a different tale. I mean without taking his ill-luck into account.

CHAPTER 21

AGAINST IDLENESS

THE Emperor Vespasian, though sick of the disease which brought on his death, did not cease to take an interest in the state of the Empire; and, even lying in bed, continually dispatched many affairs of importance. When his physician rated him for it, as a thing prejudicial to his health, he replied, 'An Emperor must die standing.' A fine saying, in my opinion, and worthy of a great ruler!

[1] The question was: 'What is God?'

The Emperor Hadrian afterwards made use of the same expression on a similar occasion, and it ought to be frequently recalled to the minds of kings, to make them feel that the great charge that is laid upon them, of ruling so many men, is not an idle charge. And that there is nothing that can so justly disgust a subject, and make him unwilling to expose himself to hardships and dangers in the service of his Prince, as to see him all the while lolling in idleness, or busy over paltry and frivolous things; and to look after the safety of one who is so neglectful of ours.[1]

If anyone should wish to maintain that it is better for a ruler to conduct his wars through others than himself, Fortune will furnish him with examples enough of princes whose lieutenants have brought great enterprises to a happy issue in their service, and even of kings whose presence in war would have done more harm than good. But no brave and valorous prince could patiently listen to such a shameful suggestion. Under colour of preserving his head, like the statue of a saint, for the happiness of his kingdom, they just degrade him from his office, which lies entirely in military activity, and declare him incapable of it.

I know one who would much rather be defeated than sleep whilst others are fighting for him, and who was never without jealousy when he knew that even his own men were doing great things in his absence.[2]

And Selim the First said very rightly, it seems to me, 'that victories which are won without the master are not complete.' How much more he would have been inclined to say that that same master should blush for shame to claim a share in the honour when he had busied only his voice and his thoughts in the matter! And not even that, since, in that kind of business, the only direction and command which deserve honour are those which are given on the spot and in the midst of the fray.

No pilot can perform his duty on dry land.

The rulers of the Ottoman race, the first race in the world in military fortunes, warmly espoused this opinion. And Bajazet the Second, with his son, who departed from this principle, spending their time in the sciences and other

---

[1] The last word, 'ours', if used intentionally, appears to confirm the view that this was a hint for the reigning monarch, Henry III.

[2] It appears probable that Henry IV was here meant.

stay-at-home occupations, gave to their empire a good slap in the face; and the present ruler, Amurath the Third, following their example, is pretty well beginning to find himself in the same pickle.

Was it not the King of England, Edward the Third, who, speaking of our Charles the Fifth, made this remark, 'There was never a king who armed less; and yet there was never a king who gave me so much to do?' He was right to think it strange, as a result of chance rather than of reason.

Those who would number the Kings of Castile and Portugal among warlike and great-hearted conquerors, because at twelve hundred leagues distance from their abodes of idleness, by the skin of their agents, they made themselves masters of the East and West Indies, may seek some other than myself to agree with them; since it is doubtful whether they would even have had the courage to go in person to take possession of their conquests.

The Emperor Julian said even more, 'that a philosopher and a gallant soldier should not so much as breathe'; that is to say, that they should yield no more to their bodily needs than what cannot be refused, ever keeping soul and body busied about great, noble and virtuous things. He felt ashamed to be seen spitting and sweating in public (which is also said of the Spartan youths and by Xenophon of the young men of Persia), because he thought that exercise, continual labour and sobriety should have burned and dried up all those superfluities. What Seneca said will not be out of place here, that the old Romans kept their young men standing on their feet: 'They taught their boys nothing, he says, that had to be learned sitting.'

It is a noble desire to wish even to die usefully and like a man; but the realization lies not so much in our good resolution as in our good fortune. Thousands have resolved to vanquish or to die in battle, who have failed in either design; wounds, imprisonment, cross their purpose, and force them to live. There are diseases which prostrate even our desires and our understanding.

[Fortune was not allowed to second the vanity of the Roman legionaries who bound themselves by oath to die or vanquish. *I will return a victor from the combat, O Marcus Fabius; if I fail, I call down upon myself the wrath of Father Jupiter, Mars Gradivus, and the other Gods* (Livy).

The Portuguese tell that in a certain part of the conquered Indies they came across soldiers who had doomed themselves, with horrible execrations, to accept no alternative but to be killed or remain victorious; and, as a token of this vow, they shaved their heads and beards. In vain do we obstinately rush into danger. It would seem as if blows avoid those who confront them too cheerfully, and are loath to reach the man who offers himself too willingly and spoils their design.

Many a man, after vainly trying every means to be killed by the hand of the enemy, has been constrained to take his own life in the very heat of the battle, in order to make good his resolution to return with honour or not to return alive. I could cite other examples, but here is one : Philistus, head of the naval forces of Dionysius the younger against the Syracusans, offered them battle, which was fiercely contested, the forces being equal. In this engagement, by reason of his prowess, he had the best of it at the beginning. But when the Syracusans drew up and surrounded his galley, after performing great deeds of valour in his own person, in trying to extricate himself, and despairing of relief, with his own hand he took away the life he had so freely and so vainly exposed to the enemy.]

Muley Moloch, King of Fez, who has lately won, against Sebastian, King of Portugal, that battle made famous by the death of three Kings, and the transference of that great kingdom to the crown of Castile, happened to be seriously ill when the Portuguese invaded his state with an armed force; and he grew daily worse until his death, which he foresaw. Never did a man more strenuously and more gloriously use up his strength. He felt too weak to endure the pompous and ceremonious entry into his camp, which, according to their custom, is attended with much magnificence, and necessitates great activity. This honour he resigned to his brother, but it was the only function of a general that he resigned. All the other necessary and useful duties he carried out very rigorously and with much labour, his body reclining, but his understanding and courage upright and firm to the last gasp, and a little beyond.

He was able to wear down his enemies, who had imprudently advanced into his territory, and it was a great grief to him that for want of a little life and of somebody to replace him in the conduct of this war and the management of a troubled kingdom, he was obliged to seek a doubtful and bloody victory, when he had it in his power to make it clean and sure.

However, he husbanded his strength in miraculous fashion, in spite of his illness, wearing down the enemy, and drawing them far away from their naval forces and the seaports they held on the coast of Africa, until the last day of his life, which he purposely reserved and employed for that great battle.

He disposed his troops in circular form, investing the camp of the Portuguese from all sides, and this circle, bending and closing in, hindered the enemy not only in the battle (which was very furious owing to the valour of the young assailant King), seeing they had to offer a front in every direction, but also prevented their flight after their rout. And, finding all the outlets seized and closed, they were obliged to fall back upon themselves—*piled up not only by the slaughter, but by their flight* (Livy)—and were heaped up one on top of the other, enabling the conquerors to gain a very murderous and very complete victory.

Dying as he was, he had himself borne and hurried from place to place whither necessity called him, and, passing along the ranks, he encouraged his captains and men one after another. But when one wedge of his line of battle was broken, he was not to be kept from mounting his charger with sword in hand. He strove with all his power to enter the fray, his men trying to hold him, some by the bridle, others by his gown or his stirrups. This effort finished the little life that was left in him. They laid him down again. Then, recovering with a start from his swoon, unable in any other way to advise his people to hush up his death, which was the most necessary command he had then to give, that his soldiers might not be driven to despair by the news, he expired with his finger on his closed lips, the usual sign for enjoining silence.

What man ever lived so long and so far into death? What man ever died so erect?

The highest degree, and the most natural, of bravely meeting death, is to look upon her not only without dismay, but unconcernedly, freely continuing one's wonted course of life even into her very lap. Like Cato, who passed his time in sleep and study, all the while having a violent and bloody death in his mind and in his heart, and holding it in his hand.

CHAPTER 22

OF RIDING POST

I HAVE not been among the least able in this exercise, which is suited for men of my build, short and sturdy. But I have given up the business ; it is too trying in the long run.

I was just now reading that King Cyrus, the more speedily to obtain news from all parts of his empire, which was of very great extent, ascertained how far a horse could go at a stretch in one day ; and at that distance from one another he posted men whose business it was to keep horses in readiness to mount those who were coming to him. And some say that this speed amounts to the measure of the flight of cranes.

Caesar says that Lucius Vibulus Rufus, being in haste to bring information to Pompey, rode night and day, changing his horses for greater dispatch. And he himself, according to Suetonius, travelled a hundred miles a day in a hired coach. But he was a furious courier, for whenever a river cut across his road he would swim it, and never turned out of his way to look for a bridge or ford.

Tiberius Nero, going to see his brother Drusus, who was ill in Germany, made two hundred miles in twenty-four hours, having three coaches.

In the war of the Romans against King Antiochus, T. Sempronius Gracchus, says Livy, *with almost incredible speed rode in three days from Amphissa to Pella on relay horses* ; and it appears, looking at the journey, that they were fixed posts, not freshly commanded for that ride.

Cecinna's contrivance for sending news to his family was much speedier ; he carried swallows with him, and released them to fly to their nests when he wished to send back news of himself, having marked them with some colour, according to pre-arrangement with his people, to signify his meaning. At the theatre in Rome the paterfamilias would keep a pigeon in his bosom and tie a letter to it when he desired to send a message to his people at home ; and it was trained to bring back an answer. D. Brutus also employed pigeons when besieged in Mutina ; and others elsewhere.

In Peru they rode post upon men, who carried them on their shoulders by means of litters ; and they were so agile that, in full career, the first porters would transfer their load to the second, without stopping a moment.

I understand that the Wallachians, who are the Grand Sultan's couriers, make wonderful speed, since they are authorized to change mounts with any rider they meet on the way, leaving him their jaded horse. And that, to guard against weariness, they compress their waist very tightly with a broad bandage [as do many others. I have not found it to give any relief].

CHAPTER 23

OF EVIL MEANS EMPLOYED TO A GOOD END

THERE is a wonderful relation and correspondence in that general scheme of the works of Nature, which clearly proves that it is neither accidental nor carried out by divers masters. The diseases and conditions of our body are reflected in states and governments ; kingdoms, republics are born, flourish and decay with old age, as we do. We are subject to a useless and harmful superabundance of humours ; either of good humours (for even this the physicians fear ; and because there is no stability in us, they say that a too brisk, robust and perfect state of health must be artificially reduced and lowered, lest our nature, unable to settle down to any certain condition, there being no room for improvement, might make a disorderly and too sudden retreat ; and therefore they prescribe purgings and bloodlettings for athletes, to save them from that superabundance of health), or a superabundance of evil humours, which is the usual cause of diseases.

We may observe that States are often sick of a like superabundance, and it has been the custom to purge them in different ways. Sometimes a large number of families are allowed to leave a country for its relief, and seek settlements in other regions at the expense of strangers. So it was that our ancestors the Franks came from the heart of Germany, took possession of Gaul, and drove out its first inhabitants. So was created that endless tide of people that poured into

Italy under Brennus and others. So the Goths and Vandals, as well as the people who are now in possession of Greece, quitted their native country to settle elsewhere, where they had more elbow-room ; and there are scarcely two or three corners of the world that have not felt the effects of these removals.

In this way the Romans established their colonies ; for, perceiving their city to be growing beyond measure, they drained it of the least necessary people, and sent them to inhabit and cultivate their conquered territories. At times too they purposely fomented war with some of their enemies, not only to keep their soldiers in breath, lest idleness, the mother of corruption, should bring worse evils upon them :

> A lengthy peace has been our bane, for war
> Is less disastrous than are ease and sloth ;   (JUVENAL.)

but also to bleed their Commonwealth, to vent a little the too exuberant heat of their young men, and to prune and thin out the branches of that too lustily growing stock. To serve this end they once made war upon the Carthaginians.

By the treaty of Bretigny, Edward the Third, King of England, refused to include, in that general peace he made with our King, the difference regarding the Duchy of Brittany, in order that he might keep a place upon which to unload his soldiers, and that the crowd of Englishmen he had employed in his affairs on this side of the Channel might not pour back into England. It was one of the reasons why our King Philip consented to send his son John to war overseas, that he might take along with him a great number of young hot-bloods who were among his armed troops.

There are many nowadays who argue in this manner, and would like the heated and turbulent spirits among us to be drained into some war with our neighbours, lest those peccant humours which are now predominant in our body, if not allowed to flow out in other directions, should keep our fever at its present height, and end by causing our total ruin. And indeed a foreign war is a much milder disease than a civil war. But I do not believe that God would look with favour upon so iniquitous a design as to insult and pick a quarrel with others for our convenience :

> Grant me no fierce desire, Rhamnusian maid,
> To rob a lawful owner of his wealth.   (CATULLUS.)

Yet we are so feeble by nature that we are often driven to the necessity of using bad means to a good end. Lycurgus, the most virtuous and perfect legislator that ever was, contrived this most iniquitous plan for teaching his people to be temperate, of forcibly making the Helots, who were their slaves, drunk, in order that the sight of these men, so lost and buried in wine, might inspire the Spartans with a horror of that vice carried to excess.

They were still more in the wrong who, in ancient times, allowed criminals, whatever kind of death they were condemned to suffer, to be cut up alive by the physicians, in order to see our internal parts in their natural state, and obtain a greater certainty in their art. For if we must run to excess, it is more excusable to do so for the health of the soul than for that of the body ; as the Romans trained the people to valour and contempt of dangers and death by means of those outrageous exhibitions of gladiators, who were pledged to fight to the death, cutting up and killing each other in their presence ;

> What other object has this savage sport,
> This death of youths, this blood-fed lust ? (Prudentius.)

And this custom continued till the time of the Emperor Theodosius :

> Seize now the honour destined for thy reign,
> O Prince, and to the glory of thy sire
> Add all that now remains to thee to gain.
> Henceforth let none in Rome be slain for sport,
> Condemned to please the rabble by his pain.
> Let blood of beasts alone henceforth be shed ;
> No homicides permit with cruel arms. (Prudentius.)

It was, forsooth, a wonderful example, and highly edifying for the populace, to see every day a hundred, two hundred, nay a thousand couples of men armed against one another, hacking each other to pieces, with such intense courage and fortitude, that they were never heard to utter a word indicating weakness or pity, never seen to turn their backs, nor as much as to take one cowardly step to dodge their adversary's stroke, but rather to extend their neck to the sword and offer to receive the death-blow !

Many of them, when covered with wounds and at death's door, sent to ask the spectators whether they were satisfied that they had done their duty, before lying down to give up the ghost in the arena. It was not enough to fight and die bravely, but they must also do it cheerfully ; for if they were seen to show any reluctance to die, they were howled down and cursed.

The very girls egged them on :

> The gentle maid jumps up at every blow ;
> And every time the victor thrusts his blade
> Into his rival's gorge, shrieks with delight,
> And with extended thumb urges him on
> To kill his prostrate foe. (PRUDENTIUS.)

The early Romans employed criminals for this exemplary exhibition. But afterwards they used innocent slaves, and even freemen who sold themselves for the purpose ; nay, Roman senators and knights, and, what is more, women :

> They sell their heads to die in the arena ;
> Though peace prevails, each seeks an enemy. (MANILIUS.)

> Amid these tumults and new sports
> The tender sex, unskilled in arms,
> Immodestly their weakness test
> In fights for men intended. (STATIUS.)

All this I should think very strange and incredible, were it not that we are daily accustomed to see, in our wars, many myriads of foreigners staking, in return for money payment, their blood and their life in quarrels in which they have no concern.

CHAPTER 24

OF THE GREATNESS OF ROME

I WILL say only a word on this inexhaustible subject, in order to show up the simplicity of those who couple the pitiful greatness of these times with that of Rome. In the seventh book of Cicero's *Familiar Letters* (the grammarians may, if they please, drop the epithet 'familiar', for it is not really very appropriate ; those who, in place of 'familiar', have substituted *ad familiares*,[1] may be justified by the fact that Suetonius, in his *Life of Caesar*, states that there was a volume of letters of his *ad familiares*), there is one addressed to Caesar, who was then in Gaul, in which Cicero

---

[1] To his friends.

repeats these words which appeared at the end of another letter that Caesar had written to him: 'With regard to Marcus Furius, whom you have recommended to me, I will make him King of Gaul; and if you want me to advance some other friend of yours, send him to me.'

It was no new thing for a simple Roman citizen, as Caesar was at the time, to dispose of kingdoms; for indeed he deprived King Deiotarus of his to give it to a nobleman of the town of Pergamus, by name Mithridates. And those who write his Life record several other kingdoms sold by him; and Suetonius says that at one stroke he squeezed out of King Ptolemy three million six hundred thousand crowns, which was very like selling him his kingdom:

> So much Galatia cost; so much for Pontus,
> So much for Lydia was paid. (CLAUDIAN.)

Mark Antony said that the greatness of the Roman people showed itself not so much in what they took as in what they gave. And yet, about a century before Antony, they ousted one, among others, with so marvellous a show of authority, that in the whole history of Rome I know of no example that throws so strong a light on her reputation and power. Antiochus possessed the whole of Egypt, and was engaged in the conquest of Cyprus and other appendages of the empire. During the progress of his victories, C. Popilius came to him in the name of the Senate, and at first refused to take him by the hand until he had read the letters he was bringing. The King, having read them and saying he would consider the matter, Popilius with his staff drew a circle around the spot on which he was standing, and said, 'Return me an answer to carry back to the Senate before you step outside of this circle.' Antiochus, astonished at this rude and peremptory command, replied after a little thought, 'I will do as the Senate commands me.' Then Popilius greeted him as a friend of the Roman people.

To give up so great a monarchy and so fortunate and prosperous a career, because of the impression made by three lines of writing! He had good reason indeed to send word to the Senate, as he afterwards did by his ambassadors, that he had received their command with the same respect as if it had come from the immortal gods.

All the kingdoms that Augustus won by the right of war

he restored to those who had lost them, or presented them to strangers.

And, in this connexion, Tacitus, speaking of the King of England, Cogidunus, by a wonderful touch gives us an inkling of this immense power. 'The Romans, he says, had from time immemorial been wont to leave the kings they vanquished in possession of their kingdoms, subject to their authority, *that they might have even kings to be the tools of their slavery.*'

It is very likely that Solyman, whom we have seen generously bestowing the kingdom of Hungary and other states, had more regard to this consideration than the one he was accustomed to allege, 'That he was glutted and overburdened with so many kingdoms and so much power [which had been acquired by his own valour or that of his ancestors.]'

CHAPTER 25

OF NOT MALINGERING

THERE is an epigram of Martial, which is among his good ones (for they are of all sorts), and in which he tells in a humorous way the story of Cælius who, to avoid paying his court to several of the great men in Rome, assisting at their levee, following and attending upon them, pretended to have the gout; and, to make his excuse the more plausible, had his legs rubbed with ointment and swathed, and in all respects assumed the behaviour and looks of a gouty person. In the end Fortune gratified him by making him really so:

> What may not man with care and art obtain;
> He feigned the gout, and now has ceased to feign. (MARTIAL.)

I have read, somewhere in Appian, I think, a similar story of one who, wishing to escape the proscriptions of the Triumvirs at Rome, and to evade recognition by those who were in pursuit of him, disguised and hid himself, pretending in addition to be blind in one eye. When he came to recover a little more liberty, and removed the plaster he had so long worn over that eye, he found that under the disguise he had really lost the sight of it.

It may be that the action of sight had become dulled through having been so long without exercise, and that the visual power had wholly transferred itself to the other eye. For if we keep one eye covered we can very plainly feel it conveying some part of its virtue to its fellow, with the result that the eye which remains free dilates and grows bigger. So also idleness, combined with the heat of the bandages and medicaments, might very well have attracted some podagric humour to the gouty man of Martial's epigram.

Having read in Froissart of the vow taken by a band of young English noblemen to keep their left eye covered until they had crossed over into France and distinguished themselves in fighting against us, I have often been tickled by the idea that they might have been caught, like the above-mentioned, and might have returned with only one good eye to the mistresses for whom they had taken this rash vow.

Mothers are right to scold their children when they mimic blindness, lameness, squinting, and other personal infirmities of the same kind. For besides that their body at that tender age might take on some evil ply, Fortune somehow seems to deride us and take us at our word. I have heard of many instances of people becoming ill after pretending to be so.

I have always been accustomed, when riding or walking, to burden my hand with a switch or stick, even affecting an air of elegance by using it as a support. Several have warned me that Fortune might one day turn this foppery into a necessity. I rely upon the fact that I should be the very first of my clan to have the gout.

But let us prolong this chapter and checker it with another story on the subject of blindness. Pliny tells of a man who, dreaming in his sleep that he was blind, next morning found himself really so, though he had not previously suffered any infirmity. The power of imagination may easily be a contributing cause, as I have explained elsewhere; and Pliny seems to be of that opinion. But it is more probable that the agitation which the body felt within (of which the physicians may, if they please, discover the cause), and which deprived him of his sight, occasioned the dream.

We will add one more story, akin to this subject, which Seneca relates in one of his letters : ' You know, he says, writing to Lucilius, that Harpaste, my wife's idiot, has been thrown upon my hands as a hereditary burden ; for I have a natural aversion to these freaks ; and if I have a mind to laugh at a fool, I have not far to go, for I can laugh at myself. This idiot has suddenly lost her sight. I am telling you something strange but true. She is not conscious of being blind, and keeps urging her keeper to take her out, because she says my house is dark.

'What we laugh at in her I pray you to believe happens to every one of us : no man knows that he is avaricious or covetous. The blind at least ask for a guide ; we go astray of our own accord. I am not ambitious, we say ; but at Rome a man cannot live otherwise. I am not a spendthrift, but the city requires a great outlay. It is not my fault if I am choleric, if I have not yet laid down a certain plan of life ; it is the fault of youth.

'Let us not seek our evil outside of us ; it is within us, it is rooted in our entrails. And the mere fact that we are not conscious of being sick makes the cure more difficult. If we do not begin in good time to look after ourselves, when shall we have time to attend to so many sores and maladies ? And yet we have a very sweet medicine in Philosophy ; for of the others we do not feel the pleasure until after the cure. This one pleases and cures at the same time.'

Those are the words of Seneca, who has carried me away from my theme. But there is profit in change.

CHAPTER 26

OF THUMBS

TACITUS relates that it was the custom of certain barbarian kings, when entering into a firm covenant, to clasp their right hands tightly, with the thumbs interlocked ; and when by dint of squeezing, the blood rose to the tips, they pricked them lightly, and each sucked the other's.

Physicians say that the thumb is the master-finger of the hand, and that the word (*pouce*) is derived from the Latin word *pollere*.[1] The Greeks call it ἀντίχειρ, as who should say ' another hand '. And the Latins sometimes appear to take it in this sense of the whole hand :

> No soft persuasion, whether of voice or thumb,
> Will make him rise to the occasion. (MARTIAL.)

[1] To be strong or powerful.

At Rome, to close and hold down the thumbs was meant to signify approval:

> Admirers now applaud your play
> With both their thumbs turned in. (HORACE.)

and disapproval to raise and turn them up:

> They kill their man to win applause
> When the assembled mob turn up their thumbs. (JUVENAL.)

The Romans excused from military service those whose thumbs were injured, as not having sufficient strength to grasp their weapons. Augustus confiscated the estates of a Roman knight who had cunningly cut off the thumbs of his two young sons, to excuse them from joining the army. And before his time the Senate, during the Italian wars, sentenced Caius Vatienus to perpetual imprisonment, and confiscated all his property, for having purposely cut off the thumb of his left hand, to exempt himself from that expedition.

Some person whose name I no longer remember,[1] having won a battle at sea, ordered the thumbs of all his vanquished enemies to be cut off, to render them incapable of fighting or rowing. The Athenians did the same to those of Aegina, to deprive them of their superiority in the art of navigation.

In Lacedemon the schoolmaster punished his boys by biting their thumbs.

CHAPTER 27

COWARDICE IS THE MOTHER OF CRUELTY

I HAVE often heard it said that cowardice is the mother of cruelty. And I have found by experience that this malevolent and inhuman ferocity and heartlessness are usually accompanied by a feminine weakness. I have observed that some of the most cruel men are easily moved to tears, and for trivial reasons. Alexander, the Tyrant of Pheres, dared not witness a tragedy in the theatre, lest his citizens should see him groaning over the misfortunes of Hecuba and Andromache, although he himself every day cruelly murdered, without any pity, so many of his subjects. Can it be weak-mindedness that makes them so easily liable to every kind of extreme?

---

[1] Philocles, one of the Athenian generals in the Peloponnesian war.

Valour, which only manifests itself when there is resistance to be overcome:

> To fight
> An unresisting bull gives no delight, (CLAUDIAN.)

restrains itself when it sees the enemy at its mercy. But pusillanimity, to be able to say that she too has acted, unable to assume the leading rôle, takes a secondary one, that of bloodshed and massacre. The killing after a victory is usually done by the rabble and the baggage-officials. And what causes so many unexampled cruelties in civil wars is that the dregs of the army become callous, and imagine themselves to be heroes when steeped up to the elbows in blood after ripping up a body at their feet, since that is their only idea of valour:

> The wolves, the filthy bears, and all
> The more ignoble beasts will fall
> Upon the dying foe. (OVID.)

They are like a cowardly house-cur worrying and tearing the skin of a wild beast it would not have dared to attack in the open.

What is it that in these days makes our quarrels altogether deadly; and that, whilst our fathers observed some degrees in revenge, we now begin with the last, and at the very outset speak of nothing but killing? What is that if not cowardice?

Every one is well aware that it needs a more scornful courage to defeat one's enemy than to finish him off, to make him lick the dust than to kill him. Besides that the craving for vengeance is more completely assuaged and satisfied, for it only aims at making itself felt. That is why we do not attack an animal or a stone when they hurt us, since they are incapable of feeling our revenge. And to kill a man is to save him from further injury on our part.

And as Bias called out to a wicked man, 'I know that soon or late you will be punished for it, but I am afraid I shall not be there to see;' and pitied the Orchomenians because the penalty which Lyciscus paid for the treason committed against them was not exacted until there was nobody alive of those who had been injured by it, and who should have been gratified by his punishment; so revenge is to be pitied, when he upon whom it is executed has lost the power of feeling it. For, as the avenger desires to witness his vengeance in order to derive pleasure from it, so must he upon whom it is carried out witness it, in order to suffer pain, and repent.

'He will repent it,' we say. And when we have shot him through the head with a pistol, do we think that he will repent? On the contrary, if we watch him closely, we shall see that he is making a face at us as he falls. He does not even begrudge us our revenge, which is very far from repenting. And we are doing him the greatest favour possible by making him die suddenly and painlessly.

As for us, we are driven to scuttle about and hide like a rabbit, and fly from the officers of justice who are at our heels, whilst he is at rest. To kill a man is a good means of avoiding future injury, but not of avenging one already committed. It is an action dictated by fear rather than bravery, an act of precaution rather than courage, an act of defence rather than of aggression. It is obvious that by that action we abandon both the real object of our revenge, and care for our reputation. We are afraid, if he lives, that he will return to the charge. You rid yourself of him, not to his prejudice, but in your interest.

In the kingdom of Narsinga this expedient would avail us naught. There not only military men but even artisans settle their quarrels with the sword. The king never denies the field to those who wish to fight, and in the case of persons of quality he looks on, and rewards the victor with a gold chain. But to win this chain any man who has a mind to it is at liberty to cross swords with the wearer. So that, having settled with one adversary, he may have several on his hands.

If we thought that by our valour we should always master our enemy and crow over him at our pleasure, we should be sorry for him to escape us, as he does by dying. We desire to vanquish, but with safety rather than honour. And in our quarrel we look to the end rather than the glory.

For an honourable man the case of Asinius Pollio illustrated a like error. Having written an invective against Plancus, he awaited his death before publishing it. That was like 'biting his thumb' at a blind man, casting filthy abuse at a deaf man or wounding one who has no feeling, rather than run the risk of his resentment. And it was in reference to him that somebody said that ' it was only for ghosts to strive with the dead '. As for the man who awaits the death of an author before attacking his writings, what does he do but confess himself a feeble brawler ?

Someone said to Aristotle that a man had spoken ill of him. ' Let him do more, he said, let him flog me, provided I am not there.'

Our fathers were content to answer an insult with a contradiction, a contradiction with a blow, and so on, in regular order. They were brave enough not to fear an adversary, alive and insulted. We tremble with fright as long as we see him with a leg to stand on. And that that is so, is it not shown in our noble practice nowadays of pursuing to the death both the man we have insulted and the man who has insulted us ?

It was also by a kind of cowardice that the custom was introduced of being attended in our single combats by seconds and thirds and fourths. Formerly they were duels ; now they are encounters and battles. Those who initiated this practice were afraid of being alone, *because neither had any confidence in himself*. For naturally any kind of company is a comfort and a solace in danger. Formerly they called in third persons to guard against irregularity and foul play, and as witnesses to the hazard of the combat. But now that it has assumed this form that the witnesses themselves engage with one another, whoever is called upon cannot honourably stand aside as a spectator, for fear lest he might be suspected either of want of feeling or of courage.

Besides the iniquity and the vileness of this action of engaging another strength and valour not your own for the defence of your honour, it seems to me that, for a good man who has full confidence in himself, it is a disadvantage to go and mix up his fortune with that of a second. Each one incurs a sufficient risk for himself without also incurring it for another, and has enough to do to safeguard his own valour in defence of his life, without committing a thing so dear to the hands of a third party. For, unless the contrary has been expressly agreed upon, the four form a combined party. If your second is down, you have two adversaries to deal with, and rightly so. And if you say that it is not fair play, that is indeed so, just as it is unfair, if you are well armed, to attack a man who has only the stump of a sword, or, if you are sound, a man who is already badly wounded. But if these are advantages you have won in the fight, you may use them without fear of reproach.

The disparity and inequality are weighed and considered only from the point of view of the condition of the combatants at the beginning of the fight; as for the rest you must take your chance. And when single-handed you have three men to deal with, your two companions having been killed, you would have no more wrong done you than I should do if, with equal chances in a battle, I cut down an enemy with my sword whom I saw fiercely attacking one of my own side.

It is in the nature of fellowship that, when a body of men is opposed to another (as when our Duke of Orleans challenged King Henry of England, a hundred against a hundred; three hundred against the same number, as in the case of the Argives against the Lacedemonians; three against three, as in the case of the Horatii against the Curiatii), the number on either side is regarded but as a single man. Wherever there is company the hazard is confounded and mixed.

I am interested in this discussion for family reasons. For my brother, the Sieur de Matecoulom, was called upon at Rome to second a gentleman whom he hardly knew and who was the defender, having been challenged by another. In this duel he happened to be matched against one whom he knew better and who was nearer to his heart. (I should like to hear somebody justify by reason these laws of honour which so often contradict and collide with the laws of reason.) Having disposed of his man, and seeing the two principals in the quarrel still on their feet and unhurt, he went to the relief of his own. What less could he do? Was he to keep quiet and look on whilst the man for whose defence he had come was defeated, if Fate had so willed it? What he had so far done had not advanced the business; the quarrel was still unsettled.

That courtesy which you can and certainly ought to show your enemy, when you have brought him to his knees and have a great advantage over him, cannot be exercised, as far as I can see, when another's interest is at stake, when you are only an assistant, when the quarrel is none of yours. He could not afford to be either just or courteous at the risk of the man to whom he had lent his assistance. He was therefore released from the Italian prisons upon a very speedy and solemn recommendation of our King.

What a hare-brained people we are! We are not satisfied with making our vices and follies known to the world by repute, but we must go among foreign nations and let them see them with their own eyes. Put three Frenchmen in the Lybian deserts, and they will not be a month together without annoying and scratching each other. You would imagine that this peregrination of our countrymen were specially organized to give foreigners the satisfaction of witnessing our tragedies, and most often to those who rejoice over and laugh at our misfortunes.

We go to Italy to learn to fence, and practise at the expense of our lives before we have acquired any skill. And yet by the rule of discipline we should put theory before practice. We betray ourselves as mere tyros:

> O bitter first-fruits of a youth so fair!
> O war's stern prelude! promise dashed to scorn! (VIRGIL.)

I know well that it is an art that is very useful for the end it has in view (in the duel between the two Princes,[1] who were cousins-german, in Spain, the elder, says Livy, by skill in the use of his weapon and by cunning, easily got the better of the more reckless strength of the younger); and, as I know by experience, an art the knowledge of which has swelled the hearts of some beyond their natural measure. But it is not valour, properly speaking, since it derives its support from skill, and relies upon something other than itself.

The honour of the combat consists in the jealousy of courage, not of science. And so I have seen a friend of mine, famed as a past master in this exercise, choose in his quarrels weapons which deprived him of the power of exercising this advantage, and wholly depended on good fortune and assurance, in order that his victory might not be put down to his skill in fencing rather than his valour. In my boyhood the nobles shunned the reputation of good fencers as offensive, and retired from public view if they

---

[1] Corbis and Orsua; see Livy, xxviii. 21.

wished to learn the art, as a cunning trade, derogating from true and natural valour :

> They shrink not, trifle not, strive not to smite
> By artificial rules, with wary will;
> Stand not on postures or on points, the night
> And their blind rage forbid the tricks of skill;
> But swords crash horribly with swords, and shrill
> The mountain echo shrieks along the plain ;
> Not a foot stirs,—where stood, there stand they still;
> But aye their hands in motion they maintain ;
> And not a lunge, or foin, or slash descends in vain. (TASSO.)

Shooting at the target, tournaments, tilting-matches and suchlike mimic warfare, were the exercises of our forefathers. This other exercise is the more ignoble since it has only a private end in view, and teaches us to destroy one another against the laws and justice, and in every way produces only harmful results. It is much more meritorious and becoming to practice things which strengthen instead of injuring our government, which tend to public security and the common glory.

Publius Rutilius, the Consul, was the first to instruct the soldier in handling his weapon with skill and science, who joined art and valour ; not to employ them in private quarrels, but in war and the quarrels of the Roman people. An art of fence for the people and the citizen.

And, not to mention the example of Caesar, who commanded his men to aim chiefly at the faces of Pompey's legionaries at the battle of Pharsalia, a thousand other army generals have bethought themselves of contriving new forms of weapons, and new ways of striking and defending, according to the needs of the moment.

But just as Philopoemen condemned wrestling, in which he excelled, since the training for that exercise differed from that appropriate to military discipline, to which he thought that men of honour should alone devote themselves, so it seems to me that this agility to which we now form our limbs, those feints and movements which the young men are taught in this new school, are not only useless, but rather contrary and harmful to the military style of fighting.

Besides, our people commonly use particular weapons specially intended for that purpose. And I have known the time when it was hardly considered the right thing for a gentleman, when challenged to fight with rapier and dagger, to appear in military equipment [or that any should offer to come with his cloak instead of a dagger].

It is worthy of consideration that Laches, in Plato, speaking of an apprenticeship in the handling of weapons agreeing with ours, said he had never known a great soldier to come out of that school, especially from among the masters of it. As to these our experience tells us the same. In any case we may at least maintain that they are talents that have no relation or correspondence with one another. And Plato, in the educational system of his Republic, forbids the art of using the fists, introduced by Amycus and Epeius, as well as that of wrestling, invented by Antaeus and Cercyon, because they have another aim than that of making youths more fit for military service, and do not contribute to it.

But I am straying a little aside from my theme.

The Emperor Maurice, being warned by dreams and several divinations that one Phocas, a soldier then unknown to him, was to kill him, questioned his son-in-law Philip with regard to this Phocas, his disposition, his circumstances and habits; and when Philip told him, amongst other things, that he was cowardly and timorous, the Emperor at once concluded that he was murderous and cruel.

What is it that makes tyrants so bloodthirsty? It is anxiety for their safety, and because their faint hearts can suggest to them no other means of ensuring it than to exterminate those who have the power to injure them; even the women, for fear of a scratch.

> He strikes at all, for every man he fears. (CLAUDIAN.)

The first cruelties are practised for their own sake; thence springs the fear of a just revenge, which afterwards gives rise to a string of fresh cruelties, in order to stifle the first by means of others.

Philip, King of Macedon, the one who had so many bones to pick with the Roman people, moved by horror of the murders committed by his orders, finding himself unable to decide what precautions to take against the many families he had at different times injured, resolved to seize all the children of those he had put to death, in order, from day to day, to destroy them one after the other, and thus set his mind at rest.

A beautiful matter will always be in place, wherever it is sown. I, who am more solicitous about the weight and utility of what I say than of its order and connexion, should not be afraid of bringing in here, though a little out of the way, a very pretty story. [When they are rich in their own beauty and are able to justify themselves only too well, I am satisfied with the end of a hair to join them to my matter.]

Among those condemned by Philip was one Herodicus, a Prince of the Thessalians. After killing him he later put to death also his two sons-in-law, each of whom left a very young son. Theoxena and Archo were the two widows. Theoxena could not be induced to marry again, although she was much sought after. Archo married Poris, the leading man among the Aenians; she had by him a number of children, but died leaving them all very young. Theoxena, spurred by a motherly love for her nephews, in order to take them under her care and guidance, married Poris.

Then came the proclamation of the King's edict. This brave mother, fearing both Philip's cruelty and the excesses of his satellites directed against these fair and tender children, boldly declared that she would rather kill them with her own hands than give them up. Poris, alarmed by this declaration, promises her to convey them secretly to Athens, and place them in charge of some trusted guest-friends of his. They take the opportunity afforded by an annual festival which was celebrated at Aenia in honour of Aeneas, and thither they go. After assisting during the day at the ceremonies and a public banquet, they stole away by night in a ship that lay ready to escape by sea.

The wind was against them, and finding themselves next morning in sight of the land whence they had put to sea, they were pursued by the harbour guards. As these approached, and while Poris was busy urging the sailors to make all speed, Theoxena, frantic with love and revenge, in pursuance of her first resolution, prepared weapons and poison, and showing them to the boys, said, 'Come, my children, death is henceforth the only means of your defence and freedom, and will be an occasion for the Gods to exercise their sacred justice. These drawn swords, and these cups, will open the door to it. Courage! And you, my son, who are the eldest, grasp this blade and die the braver death!'

Having on one side so energetic a counsellor and on the other the enemy at their throats, each of them wildly rushed at the weapon that was nearest at hand, and half dead they were thrown into the sea. Theoxena, proud of having so gloriously provided for the safety of all her children, warmly embraced her husband with the words, 'Let us follow these boys, my friend, and enjoy the same grave with them.' And locked in each others' arms they leapt into the sea, and the vessel was taken back to land without its masters.

Tyrants, in order both to kill and make their anger felt, have used all their wits to find the means of prolonging death. They wish their enemies to be gone, but not so quickly that they may not have leisure to taste their revenge. Herein they are greatly perplexed, for if the tortures are violent, they are short; if they are prolonged, they are not sufficiently painful for their liking. So we see them carefully contriving their implements. We see thousands of examples of this in antiquity; and I do not know whether we have not unwittingly retained some traces of this barbarity.

All that is over and above simple death appears to me pure cruelty.[1] Our justice cannot hope that the man who is not deterred from wrong-doing by the fear of being hanged or beheaded, will be prevented by the idea of a slow fire, or the pincers, or the wheel. And I know not but that he is meanwhile driven to desperation. For what can be the condition of a man's soul, who is awaiting twenty-four hours of death, broken on the wheel, or, after the old fashion, nailed to a cross?

Josephus relates that during the wars of the Romans in Judea, passing by a place where, three days before, several Jews had been crucified, he recognized three of his friends, and obtained permission to remove them. Two of them died, he says, the other lived since that time.

Chalcondylas, a man worthy of belief, in the memoirs that he left of events which happened in his days and in his neighbourhood, records as the worst of punishments that which was often inflicted by the Emperor Mahomet of having a man cut in two, with one stroke of a scimetar, at the diaphragm, just below the ribs; the result being that

---

[1] This sentence was censured by the Papal authorities in Rome, when Montaigne was there in 1581; but he defied the censure by retaining it.

they died as it were two deaths at once. He adds that both parts could be seen long after, full of life and writhing in torment.

I do not suppose that these movements implied that there was much feeling left in those bodies. The most ghastly torments to look at are not always the hardest to endure. To my mind there is more atrocity in those he inflicted, according to other historians, upon some lords of Epirus, who were flayed piecemeal, by a dispensation so malignantly devised, that they endured that agony for fifteen days.

And here are two other examples. Croesus had a nobleman, a favourite of his brother Pantaleon, seized and carried into a fuller's shop, where he was scratched and carded with the cards and combs used in the trade, until he died.

George Sechel, leader of those Polish peasants who, under the cloak of a crusade, did so much mischief, being defeated and taken prisoner in battle by the Voivode of Transylvania, was for three days bound naked to a wooden horse, exposed to all manner of tortures that anybody might devise against him. During this time the other prisoners were given nothing to eat or drink. In the end, while he was still alive and able to see, they gave his blood to drink to his beloved brother Lucat, whom he entreated them to spare, drawing upon himself all the hatred for their misdeeds. Twenty of his most favoured captains were made to feed upon him, tearing his flesh with their teeth and swallowing the morsels. After he was dead the rest of his body, with the entrails, was boiled and given to others of his followers to eat.

CHAPTER 28

THERE IS A TIME FOR ALL THINGS

THOSE who compare Cato the Censor with the younger Cato, who was his own murderer, compare two fine characters that are much akin. The former displayed his in more ways, and surpassed the other in military exploits and in the usefulness of his public services. But the virtue of the younger, besides that it would be blasphemy to compare any other with it in vigour, was much more unblemished. For who could acquit the Censor of envy and ambition, when he presumed to attack the honour of

Scipio, who in goodness and all eminent qualities was very much greater than he and any man of his time?

What they tell of him, among other things, that in his extreme old age he began to learn Greek with a greedy appetite, as if to quench a long-standing thirst, does not appear to me very greatly to his honour. It is properly speaking what we should call falling into second childhood.

There is a time for all things, good and all. I may say my Paternoster at the wrong moment; and T. Quintus Flaminius was denounced for having been seen standing apart, wasting his time in praying to God during the course of a battle which he won as army general.

> The sage sets bounds to even virtuous things. (JUVENAL.)

Eudemonidas, seeing Xenocrates in his old age very busy over his school lessons, said, 'When will this man know, if he is still learning?' And Philopoemen replied to those who were extolling King Ptolemy because he daily hardened his body in warlike exercises, 'It is not commendable in a king of his age to practise them; he should henceforth actually apply them.'

The young should make their preparations; the old should reap the fruits of them, say the sages. And the greatest defect they observe in our nature is that our desires incessantly renew their youth. We are ever beginning to live over again. Our studies and desires should sometimes savour of old age. We have a foot in the grave, and our appetites and pursuits are but new-born:

> So you, upon death's very brink,
> Of cutting marbles only think,
> That yet are in the quarry's womb,
> And, all unmindful of the tomb,
> Rear gorgeous mansions everywhere. (HORACE.)

The most far-seeing of my plans have no more than a year in view; henceforth I think of nothing but the end. I shake off all fresh hopes and enterprises, take my last leave of all the places I shall quit, and every day dispossess myself of my belongings. *For a long time I have neither lost nor gained; I have more than enough provisions for my journey* (Seneca).

> My life is lived; the course by Fortune given
> I have fulfilled. (VIRGIL.)

This is in fact all the comfort I have in my old age, that it deadens in me many desires and cares which trouble our life; care about how the world wags, care for wealth, greatness, knowledge, health, myself. This man learns to speak [1] when he ought to learn to hold his peace for ever.

We may continue our studies at all times, but not our schooling. What a foolish thing is an old man learning his ABC!

> For different things do different men delight;
> And all things are not for all ages right. (PSEUDO-GALLUS.)

If we must study let us take up a study that is suitable to our present condition, that we may answer as he did who was asked for what purpose he was studying in his decrepitude, 'that I may depart this world a better man, and a happier.'

Of this kind were the studies of the younger Cato, when he felt his end to be near and came across Plato's Discourse *Of the Eternity of the Soul*. Not but that, as we may well believe, he had long been furnished with every kind of provision for that departure. Of confidence, a resolute will and learning, he had more than Plato had in his writings. His knowledge and his courage were in this respect ahead of Philosophy. He applied himself to this study, not that it might be serviceable to him in death, but, like a man whose sleep is not even disturbed when important matters are under consideration, he also continued, without choice or change, his studies with the other wonted actions of his life.

The night which followed his rejection for the Pretorship he spent in play; that in which he was to die he spent in reading. The loss of either life or office was all one to him.

CHAPTER 29

OF VALOUR

I HAVE learned by experience that there is a great difference between the flights and sallies of the soul and a firm and constant habit of mind; and very well perceive that there is nothing we cannot do, even, as somebody says,[2] to

---

[1] A reference to the above-mentioned Cato, who learned to read Greek in his old age, in order to improve his eloquence.
[2] Seneca.

surpassing the Deity itself, since it is a greater thing to become immune to passion by our efforts than to be so by our original condition ; and even to be able to combine our human frailty with a godlike firmness and assurance. But it is by fits and starts. And in the lives of those heroes of olden times there are sometimes seen miraculous flashes, which seem by a long way to exceed our natural powers ; but they are indeed flashes, and it is hard to believe that it is possible for the soul to be so dyed and steeped in these exalted conditions that they become usual and as it were natural to her.

It may even befall ourselves, who are but human abortions, that our soul, aroused by others' examples and teachings, will sometimes shoot up far beyond her ordinary range ; but it is some kind of passion which stirs and drives her, and carries her some way outside of herself. For, when that whirlwind has blown over, we see that she unconsciously flags and slackens of herself, if not to the lowest key, at least so far as to be no longer the same ; so that upon any occasion, for a lost hawk or a broken glass, we suffer ourselves to be moved almost like any one of the vulgar sort.

Saving order, moderation and firmness, I think all things are possible to a man who is generally very defective and infirm.

For that reason, say the sages, to form a correct judgement of a man, we must in the first place examine his ordinary actions, and surprise him in his everyday habit.

Pyrrho, who built up such an amusing theory of ignorance, endeavoured, like all other true philosophers, to make his life correspond to his teaching. And, because he held that man's judgement was so extremely weak that he could not make up his mind to choose, and would keep it perpetually on the balance, regarding and accepting all things as indifferent, they say of him that he always preserved the same demeanour and countenance. If he had begun to speak he would not stop till he had finished, when the man he was speaking to was gone. If he was walking he would not be turned from his path for any impediment he came across, and his friends had to save him from precipices, from colliding with carts, and from other accidents. For, to fear or avoid a thing would have been to run counter to his propositions, according to which even the senses were deprived of all choice and certainty. Sometimes he suffered the surgeon's lancet or the caustic with such stolidity that he was never seen even to wink his eyes.

It is something to bring the mind to these ideas. It is something more to translate them into action; yet it is not impossible. But it is almost incredible that a man can do so habitually, in things so far removed from common usage, with so much constancy and perseverance.

So we hear that he was once discovered in his house sharply scolding somebody for his sister, and, when it was pointed out to him that he was sinning against his theory of indifference, he replied, 'What, may I not break my rules in the cause of this weak woman?' On another occasion, when he was seen defending himself from a dog, he said, 'It is very difficult entirely to strip off the man; we must endeavour to make it our duty to combat things, in the first place by deeds, but, as a last resource, by reason and argument.'

About seven or eight years ago, a man living in a village about two leagues from here, who is still alive, having been long plagued by his wife's jealousy, returning one day from his labour, was welcomed with her customary screechings. He became so furious that suddenly, with the bill-hook he still held in his hand, he clean mowed off the parts which were the cause of her heat, and threw them into her face. And it is said that an amorous and lusty young gentleman of our nation, having at length by his perseverance softened the heart of his fair mistress, was thrown into despair because, at the moment of attack, he found that he himself was soft and a weakling, and that

> Languidly the member raised his head. (TIBULLUS.)

When he returned home he immediately stripped himself of it and sent it, a cruel and bloody sacrifice, for the expiation of his offence. If this had been done from religious motives and deliberately, as the priests of Cybele did, what should we not say of so sublime an action?

Not many days ago a woman living at Bergerac, five leagues from my house up the river Dordogne, having been the night before beaten and ill-used by her husband, a surly man of uncertain temper, resolved to escape from his violence at the price of her life. On rising next morning she had a few words with her neighbours as usual, and let fall a few words in recommendation of her affairs; then taking a sister of hers by the hand she took her to the bridge, and after taking leave of her as if in jest, without showing any other alteration of manner she threw herself headlong into the river, where she perished. What is more remarkable in this case is that her plan was maturing a whole night in her head.

But it is quite another thing with the Hindu women. For, it being the custom for the men to have several wives, and for the best beloved of them to kill herself after her husband, each of them makes it the aim of her whole life to gain this point and advantage over her companions; and for the good offices they render their husbands they expect no other reward but to be preferred to accompany him in death:

> For when above the bier the death-fires gleam,
> Round crowd the loving wives with locks astream;
> Strive which shall first her husband's footsteps trace,
> And deem refusal bitterest disgrace.
> The favoured seeks the flames with dauntless breast
> And dies, her scorched lips to her husband's prest. (PROPERTIUS.)

A man still living writes of having observed this custom, which is still held in honour among those Eastern nations, of not only the wives being interred after their husbands' death, but also the slave-girls he has enjoyed. It is done in this manner. The husband being dead, the widow may, if she desires (but few desire it), demand two or three months respite to arrange her affairs. The day being come, decked out as if for her wedding, she mounts a horse, and that with a cheerful countenance, as if going, as she says, to sleep with her spouse, holding a mirror in her left hand and an arrow in her right. After riding about in state, attended by friends and relations and a concourse of people in festal garb, she presently returns to the public place appointed for these shows. This is a large square, in the middle of which is a pit filled with wood, and adjoining it a raised place with four or five steps, to which she is led and served with a sumptuous repast. After partaking of it she begins to dance and sing and, when she thinks fit, gives the word for the fire to be kindled. This being done she steps down, and, taking the nearest of her husband's relations by the hand, they repair together to the river which is near by, where she strips herself naked, and, having distributed her clothes and jewels among her friends, plunges into the water as if to wash away her sins. On leaving the water she wraps herself in a yellow linen cloth about fourteen French fathoms long, and again giving her hand to this kinsman of her husband, they return to the mound, from which she makes a speech to the people, and recommends her children, if she has any. Between the pit and the mound they usually draw a curtain, to shut out the burning furnace from their sight; but some wives forbid it, to show the greater courage. When she has finished her speech a woman presents her with a vessel full of oil to anoint her head and whole body; which done, she throws it into the fire and immediately leaps in after it. The people at once cover her with a great many faggots to prevent a lingering death; and all their joy is converted into sorrow and mourning.

If they are persons of meaner stuff, the body of the defunct husband is taken to the place where it is to be buried, and there placed in a sitting posture; the widow, on her knees before him, closely embraces him and remains there whilst they build a wall around them, and, when it has reached the height of the woman's shoulders, one of her relations, taking hold of her head from behind, wrings her neck. As soon as she has given up the ghost the wall is at once built higher and closed, and there they remain entombed.

A similar custom was observed in the same country by their Gymnosophists.[1] For, not under outside constraint, nor from a sudden impetuous caprice, but by express profession of their order, their custom was, as soon as they had reached a certain age, or if they found themselves threatened by some disease, to have a funeral pile erected, and on the top of it a richly decorated couch. After joyously feasting their friends and acquaintances, they remained lying on this couch with such determination that, when the fire was applied, they were not seen to move either hand or foot.

Thus died one of them, by name Calanus, in presence of the whole army of Alexander the Great. And he who did not thus commit suicide and dismiss his soul purged and purified by fire, after all that was mortal and earthly in him had been

[1] A hermit class of ancient Hindu philosophers, who wore little or no clothing and were addicted to mysticism and asceticism.

consumed, was reputed neither a saint nor blessed. It is this constant premeditation of a whole life that excites our wonder.

Among our other questions under dispute that of *Fatum* has entered in. To bind future events and even our will to predetermined and inevitable necessity, they still employ this time-honoured argument : ' Since God foresees that all things shall happen in such and such a way, as no doubt he does, they must therefore so happen.' To this our masters reply : ' That to see a thing happen, as we do, and God likewise (for, as everything is present to him, he sees rather than foresees), is not to force it to happen ; nay, we see because things happen, and things do not happen because we see. The happening causes the knowledge, and not the knowledge the happening. What we see happen, happens ; but it might have happened otherwise. And God, in the catalogue of the causes of happenings which he has in his prescience also has those which are called fortuitous, and the voluntary ones which depend on the freedom of the will he has given us ; and he knows that we shall sin, because we shall have willed to sin.'

Now I have known a good many men who encouraged their troops with this necessity of Fate. For if our last hour is fixed to a certain point, neither the musket-shots of our enemies, nor our boldness, nor our flight and cowardice, can either advance or retard it.

That is easily said, but find a man who will act upon it. And if it is the case that a strong and lively belief will be followed by actions of a like nature, truly this faith, of which our mouths are so full, is marvellously little in our days. Unless it be that the contempt in which works are held by Faith makes her disdain their company.[1]

So much is true that, apropos of this, the Lord of Joinville, as credible a witness as any other, tells us of the Bedouins, a race associated with the Saracens with whom Saint Louis had to deal in the Holy Land, that in their religion they so firmly believed that every man's days have been from all eternity prefixed and numbered by an inevitable preordination, that they went to war bare of armour except a sword in the Turkish fashion, their bodies covered

[1] An allusion to the question whether salvation is won by faith or by works.

only by a white linen garment. And their strongest curse, which they were always ready to utter when angered by their own men, was : ' Accursed be thou as he who arms himself for fear of death ! ' Here we see a proof of faith and belief very different from ours.

And with this may be classed the faith of those two Florentine monks in our fathers' days. Being engaged in some learned controversy, they both agreed to enter the fire in the market-place in sight of all the people, to prove their argument. All the preparations had been already made, and the matter was about to be carried into execution, when it was interrupted by an unforeseen accident.

A young Turkish lord signalized himself by some feat of arms in full view of the two armies of Amurath and Huniades when on the point of engaging. When asked by Amurath what it was that had filled him, so young and inexperienced (for it was the first war he had witnessed) with such a noble and undaunted courage, he replied that he had learned his best lesson in valour of a hare. ' Being out hunting one day, he said, I descried a hare lying in her forme, and, though I had with me two excellent greyhounds, I thought it advisable, to be sure of my quarry to use my bow, for she offered a very good mark. I began to discharge my arrows and shot as many as forty I had in my quiver, not only without touching, but without rousing her. After all I slipped my dogs upon her, but they were no more successful. From this I learned that she was covered by her Destiny, and that neither arrows nor swords will avail without permission of our fate, which it is not in our power either to retard or to advance.'

This tale may serve to teach us, by the way, how much our reason may be influenced by a sight of any kind.

A man advanced in years, of great repute, dignity and learning, was boasting to me that he had been led to alter his faith on a very important point by a strange incentive, so fantastic and moreover so inconclusive that I thought it a stronger argument to the contrary. He called it a miracle, and so did I, but in a different sense.

Their historians [1] say that the conviction so widely dispersed among the Turks of the fatal and inflexible pre-

[1] i. e., the Turkish historians.

determination of their days visibly helps to inspire them with confidence in danger.

And I know a great Prince who gains by it greatly to his honour [whether it be that he believes in it, or that he makes it an excuse for risking his life to such an extraordinary degree], if Fortune continues to lend him a helping hand.[1]

There has not been seen within our memory a more wonderful example of determination than that of the two who plotted the death of the Prince of Orange.[2] It is a marvel how the second, who dispatched him, could screw up sufficient courage to repeat an attempt in which his fellow-assassin had so miscarried, although he did his utmost. For, following in his footsteps and using the same weapon, he attacked a lord armed with so recent a lesson of distrust, powerful in his friendly following and his bodily strength, in his own hall, in the midst of his body-guards, in a town wholly devoted to him. Assuredly he employed a very resolute hand and a heart moved by strong passion. A dagger is a surer weapon for striking home, but since it needs more movement and strength of arm than a pistol, it is more liable to be turned aside or intercepted. I make little doubt that this man ran the risk of a certain death; for any hopes that might have been held out to him could not have deceived a man of sober intelligence. And the manner of his execution shows that he had no lack of it, any more than of courage. A conviction so powerful may be grounded on various motives, for our imagination does what it will, both with itself and with us.

The assassination which took place near Orleans[3] is not to be compared with it; there was more chance than vigour in it. The stroke was not fatal if Fortune had not made it so; the act of shooting from horseback and from a distance, at a man whose motion followed that of his horse, was the act of a man who would rather have failed in his attempt than failed to escape. This was proved by the sequel. For he was so dazed and intoxicated by the thought of killing so exalted a personage, that he entirely lost his head in

---

[1] Probably an allusion to Henry IV.
[2] Jean de Jaureguy, who wounded the Prince at Antwerp in 1582, and Balthazar Gérard, who killed him in his house at Delft in 1584, both using pistols.
[3] The murder of the Duc de Guise in 1563 by Poltrot.

managing both his flight and his tongue when answering questions.

What more need he have done but rejoin his friends across a river ? It is a means I have often resorted to in lesser dangers, and is of little risk, in my opinion, however broad the crossing, provided that your horse can enter the water easily and that you can calculate upon a safe landing-place on the other bank, taking account of the current. The other, when hearing his dreadful sentence read out to him, said, ' I was prepared for this, and will astonish you by my endurance.'

The Assassins, a people subject to Phoenicia, are reputed among the Mahommedans to be supremely religious and pure in morals. They hold that the surest way to deserve Paradise is to kill someone of a different religion. Wherefore, despising all personal danger in carrying out so useful a purpose, one or two of them have often been known to offer, with the expectation of certain death, to assassinate (we have taken this word from their name) their enemies in their strongholds. Thus was killed our Count Raymond of Tripoli in his own city [during our conduct of the Holy war ; and likewise Conrad, Marquis of Montferrat. The murderers were led to execution, puffed up with pride for their fine masterpiece].

CHAPTER 30

OF A YOUNG MONSTROSITY

THIS tale shall be told quite simply ; for I leave it to the doctors to discuss it. Two days ago I saw a boy that was being carried about by two men and a nurse, who said they were his father, his uncle and aunt, to make a few coppers by exhibiting him on account of his strangeness. In all other respects he was of ordinary shape ; he could stand on his feet, walk and chatter much as other boys of the same age. He had not yet taken to any food except his nurse's milk, and when, in my presence, they tried to put something into his mouth, he chewed it a little and spat it out without swallowing it. There was certainly something unusual in his crying. He was just fourteen months old.

Below the paps he was fast stuck to another boy that had no head, the spinal canal being stopped up ; the rest of the body was entire. One arm was indeed shorter than the other, but it had been broken by accident at birth. They were joined face to face, as if a smaller child were trying to embrace one a little bigger. The juncture and the space where they held together was only four fingers' breadth or thereabouts, so that if you turned up the imperfect child you could see below it the navel of the other; so the joining was between the paps and his navel. The navel of the smaller child could not be seen, but you could see all the rest of his belly. Thus the unattached parts of the imperfect child, as the arms, the rump, the thighs and legs, remained hanging and dangling from the other, and might reach half-way down his legs. The nurse told us besides that he urined from both places; also that the limbs of this other were nourished and living, and throve as well as his own, except that they were smaller and thinner.

This double body and its several limbs corresponding to a single head might indeed serve as a favourable augury to the King, that he will maintain those several parties and factions of our State under the union of his laws. But, lest the issue might belie the prophecy, it will be better to let it go on before; for there is no prophesying except in things already past. *So that, when things have come to pass, we may interpret them as prophecies* (Cicero). So they said of Epimenides that he prophesied backwards.

I have just seen a shepherd at Medoc, thirty years of age or thereabouts, who has no show of genital parts. He has three holes from which he continually drops his water. He is bearded, has desires, and readily seeks contact with women.

What we call monstrosities are not so to God, who sees in the immensity of his work the infinity of shapes which he has comprehended within it; and it may be believed that this figure which arouses our astonishment corresponds to and resembles some other figure of the same kind unknown to man. From his all-wisdom there proceeds nothing that is not good, usual and regular; but we do not see the relationship and the harmony. *What he often sees does not excite his wonder, even though he knows not the cause of it. But if a thing happen that he has not already seen, he regards it as a prodigy* (Cicero).

We call contrary to Nature what happens contrary to

what is customary; there is nothing whatsoever that is contrary to Nature. This universal and natural reason should dispel from our minds the errors and the wonder caused by what is new and strange.[1]

CHAPTER 31

OF ANGER

PLUTARCH is admirable throughout, but especially when he judges human actions. In his comparison of Lycurgus and Numa we may read the excellent things that he says on the subject of our great folly in leaving children in the charge and under the rule of their fathers.

In most of our States, as Aristotle says, the guidance of his wives and children is left to each man, after the manner of the Cyclops,[2] according to his foolish and unthinking caprice; and the Lacedemonian and Cretan are almost the only states where the direction of childhood is entrusted to the laws. Who does not see that everything in a state depends upon their nurture and bringing up? And yet, without any discrimination, they are left to the mercy of their parents, however foolish and wicked they may be.

Among other things, how often have I felt a desire, when passing along our streets, to play some trick, to avenge the little boys I saw being belaboured, knocked down and bruised by some father or mother in a mad frenzy of anger! You may see their eyes flashing with fire and rage:

> By burning fury they are headlong borne,
> As when great rocks are from the mountain torn,
> By which the cliffs deprived and lessened are,
> And their steep sides are naked left and bare,   (JUVENAL.)

(and, according to Hippocrates, the most dangerous diseases are those which disfigure the face), with shrill, piercing voice often directed against a child that has just left its mother's breast. And then see how they are stunned and crippled

---

[1] Nowhere perhaps does Montaigne show how far he is in advance of his age than in his attitude to deformities and monstrosities, which in his day and long after were usually regarded as a judgement of God and a punishment of sins.

[2] 'Each the law gives out to his own wives and children.' Hom., *Od.* ix. 114.

with blows, and our justice taking no notice of it, as if they were not members of our Commonwealth that were being thus maimed and dislocated!

> Most grateful 'tis to people and to State
> To give a citizen, if he be fit
> To till the earth, or serve his fatherland
> In peace or war. (JUVENAL.)

There is no passion that so disturbs the clearness of our judgement as anger. No one would hesitate to punish with death a judge who had sentenced his criminal in anger. Why should fathers and pedagogues be any more allowed to flog and chastise the boys in anger? It ceases to be correction and becomes vengeance. Chastisement takes the place of medicine with children; and should we tolerate a physician who was moved to anger against his patient?

We masters, if we wish to act rightly, should never raise our hand against a servant as long as we are angry. While the pulse beats and we are sensible of passion we should defer the business. The matter will indeed appear to us in a different light when we have recovered and cooled down. It is passion that then rules, it is passion that speaks; it is not we ourselves.

Faults, when seen through passion, appear greater to us, like bodies seen through a mist. A man uses meat to appease his hunger; but when he would use punishment he must neither hunger nor thirst for it.

And besides, a punishment that is administered deliberately and with discrimination is taken in better part by him who suffers it, and with more benefit. Otherwise he will think he has been unjustly condemned by a master who is moved by anger and fury; and will plead, for his justification, the extraordinary conduct of his master, his inflamed countenance, his unaccustomed oaths, his excitement and inconsiderate hastiness:

> With anger faces swollen show,
> The veins turn black with rush of blood,
> The eyes with Gorgon fires glow. (OVID.)

Suetonius relates that, Lucius Saturninus[1] having been condemned by Caesar, what most prevailed with the people

---

[1] More correctly Caius Rabirius, as corrected in all the later editions. L. Saturninus was a Tribune whom he had opposed.

(to whom he appealed) to declare in his favour was the fierce animosity which Caesar had exhibited in that sentence.

Saying is one thing and doing is another. We must consider the sermon apart from the preacher. Those who in our days have tried to shake the truth of our Church by attacking the vices of her ministers, have had an easy game ; she draws her testimony from elsewhere. Theirs is a foolish line of argument which would throw everything into confusion. A man may have an erroneous belief though his morals be good ; and a wicked man may preach the truth, nay, even though he does not believe it. When doing and saying go together it is indeed a beautiful harmony ; and I will not deny that words, when followed by deeds, are of greater authority and efficacy.

As Eudamidas said, on hearing a philosopher holding forth on war, ' The language is fine, but the man who is speaking is not to be believed, for his ears are not accustomed to the sound of the trumpet.' And Cleomenes, hearing an orator declaiming on valour, burst out laughing, at which the other taking great offence, he said, ' I should do the same if I heard a swallow talking of valour ; but an eagle I would readily listen to.'

I think I can gather from the writings of the ancients that the man who says what he thinks drives it home much more forcibly than he who dissembles. Listen to Cicero speaking of the love of freedom, and then listen to Brutus. From the mere written words of the latter you hear the note of a man who was ready to buy it at the price of his life. Let Cicero, the father of eloquence, treat of the contempt of death, and then let Seneca treat of the same ; in the former the words drag feebly, and you feel that he is trying to persuade you of a thing of which he himself is not persuaded. He gives you no heart, for he has none himself. The other excites and inflames you. I never read an author, especially one who treats of virtue and duties, without carefully endeavouring to find out what kind of a man he was.

For the Ephors at Sparta, hearing a dissolute man offering a wholesome piece of advice, ordered him to hold his tongue, and requested a respectable man to appropriate the idea and propound it.

Plutarch's writings, if we taste them aright, sufficiently disclose their author, and I think I am able to see into his soul; and yet I could wish that we had some memoirs of his life. After digressing a little in this Essay I am obliged to Aul. Gellius for having left us in writing this story reflecting on his character, which brings me back to the subject of Anger.

One of his slaves, a bad and vicious man, but whose ears had drunk in a few of the teachings of Philosophy, having been, for some fault or other, stripped and flogged by Plutarch's orders, at first muttered that he was being punished without reason, since he had done nothing. But at last he began to shout and roundly abuse his master, saying, 'that he was no philosopher, as he boasted of being; that he had often heard him say that it was an ugly thing to get angry, and he had even written a book on the subject; and that to have him so cruelly beaten, when plunged in anger, was completely to belie his writings.' To which Plutarch replied quite coldly and tranquilly, 'What, you clown, from what do you argue that I am angry at this moment? Do my face, my voice, my colour, my words give you any indication of my being in a passion? I do not think my eyes are rolling wildly, that my countenance is disturbed, or that I am shouting very terribly. Am I red? Do I foam at the mouth? Have I allowed a word to escape me of which I might repent? Am I shaking and trembling with fury? For these, I may tell you, are the true marks of anger.' Then, turning to the man who was flogging him, 'Go on with your work, he said, whilst he and I are having our little argument.' That is the story.

Archytas of Tarentum, returning from a war in which he had been commander-in-chief, found his household affairs in a state of great disorder, and his lands lying fallow, through the mismanagement of his steward. Having sent for him, he said, 'Go; If I were not angry I should give you a good thrashing.' Plato too, being greatly incensed against one of his slaves, charged Speusippus to chastise him, excusing himself from laying hands upon him on the ground that he was angry. Charillus, a Lacedemonian, said to a Helot whose behaviour was too bold and insolent, 'By the Gods, if I were not angry, I should have you put to death on the spot.'

It is a self-complacent and self-flattering passion. How often, when we have been put out under a wrong impression, and the offending person offers a good defence or excuse, we are vexed even at the truth and his innocence! In connexion with which I remember a remarkable example in antiquity.

Piso, in all other respects a most worthy man, being greatly angered against one of his soldiers because, returning alone from foraging, he was unable to explain the absence of his companion, took it for granted that he had murdered him, and forthwith condemned him to death. He was no sooner on the gibbet than the missing man turned up. The whole army was in high glee, and after much kissing and embracing on the part of the two fellows, the executioner conducts them both into the presence of Piso, all the bystanders expecting that he would be equally pleased. But it fell out quite otherwise; for shame and vexation increased his fury, which was still at its height, and, with a craftiness which his passion instantly suggested to him, he made three guilty men of one, because one had been found innocent, and had them all three dispatched: the first soldier because he was under sentence; the second, who had lost his way, because he was the cause of his comrade's death; and the executioner, because he had not carried out his orders.

Those who have to deal with headstrong women may have experienced how furious they become if we meet their excitement with a cool silence, and disdain to add fuel to their rage.

The orator Celius was by nature exceedingly choleric. Supping in the company of a man of a mild and gentle disposition, who, in order not to excite him, had decided to approve and agree with everything he said, he exclaimed, unable any longer to suffer his ill humour not to be fed, 'By all the Gods, do contradict something I say, that there may be two of us!' So the women only lose their temper in order that we may lose ours, therein following the laws of love.

Phocion, when interrupted in a speech by a man who began to insult him with opprobrious words, merely stopped speaking, to give the man time to exhaust his anger; then, without any mention of the disturbance, he continued his speech at the place where he had left off. There is no retort so stinging as a contempt of that kind.

Of the most hot-tempered man in France (it is always a fault, but more excusable in a soldier, for in that profession there certainly are occasions when it cannot be dispensed with) I often say that he is the most patient man to curb his anger that I know; it stirs him to such violence and fury:

> As when a wood-fire crackles with such fierce roar,
> Heaped round a cauldron, and the simmering stream
> Foams, fumes and bubbles, and at last boils o'er,
> And upward shoots the mingled smoke and steam, (VIRGIL.)

that, to moderate it, he is obliged to exercise a cruel restraint. And, for my part, I know of no passion to conceal and restrain which I were capable of making such an effort. I would not set wisdom at so high a price. I do not so much consider what he does, as what it costs him to do no worse.

Another was boasting to me of his mildness and self-control, which is indeed out of the common. I said to him that it was certainly something, especially in a man of high standing like himself, on whom all eyes are directed, always to show great moderation to the world; but that the main thing was to be well provided inwardly, and that to eat his heart out was not, in my opinion, the right way to husband his resources. And I was afraid that he was doing so in order to keep up that mask and outward appearance of self-control.

Anger, by being concealed, becomes incorporated. Hence Diogenes said to Demosthenes who, for fear of being seen in a tavern, was withdrawing into it, 'The further you retire into it, the more you are in it.'

I should advise you rather to give your footman a slap on the cheek, even though it were undeserved, than to strain your inclination to put on the airs of a sage. I would rather show my feelings than brood over them at my own expense. To vent and give expression to them makes them flag. It is better that their point should be turned away from us than against ourselves. *All vices are less serious when they appear in the open; they are most dangerous when concealed under an appearance of discretion* (Seneca).

I admonish those of my family who are authorized to get angry; Firstly, to husband their anger, and not to pour it out at any cost, since that lessens its effect and weight.

Unpremeditated and continual brawling becomes a habit, and is set at naught by everybody. Your scolding of a servant for theft will lose its effect, if you have scolded him in the same way a hundred times for a dirty glass or a misplaced footstool. Secondly, not to vent their anger at random, but see that their reproof reaches the ears of the delinquent; for people commonly begin to shout before the guilty person has entered their presence, and continue to shout for an age after he is gone:

> And petulant madness contends with itself. (CLAUDIAN.)

They fall out with their shadow and continue their bluster in a place where nobody is punished or affected except by the racket of their voice, which many have to suffer who have done nothing to deserve it. I also condemn those one-sided quarrels in which a man fumes and blusters without any antagonist; he should keep his rodomontades for those they are intended for:

> As when a bull, against some battle-bout
> Uplifts a fearful bellowing, and for proof
> Flings wrath into his horns, and butts against
> A tree-trunk, and provokes the air with blows,
> Or, scattering sand, makes prelude of the fray. (VIRGIL.)

When I get angry my outbursts are quick, but as brief and subdued as I can make them. I am indeed hasty and violent, but I do not so lose my head that I fling about any kind of insulting words, at random and without choice, and without considering whether they are pertinently placed where I think they will hurt most; for my tongue is usually my only weapon. My serving-men come off better in great matters than in small. The small ones take me unawares, and the mischief is that when you are once over the precipice it matters not who has given you the push, you will reach the bottom all the same; the fall accelerates its own speed without any more pushing.

When the matter is important it pays me that my cause is so just that all expect me to be reasonably angry; for I have a sense of triumph in disappointing their expectation. Against the great occasion I brace and prepare myself, for if I give way to it I lose my head and am in danger of going too far. I find it easy to be on my guard against falling into a great rage, and am strong enough to repel its attack if I expect it, however great the cause. But if it takes me unawares and has once got a fair grip on me, it will carry me away, be the cause ever so small.

This is how I bargain with those who are able to stand up against me: 'When you feel that I am the first to get excited, let me have my say, whether I am right or wrong; I will do the same for you in my turn.' The storm is bred only from the clashing of two passions, which usually produce one another, and are not born simultaneously. Let each run its course and we shall always be at peace! A useful arrangement, but difficult to carry out!

It sometimes happens that I simulate anger for the better government of my household, without any real emotion. As I become more crabbed with advancing years I study to resist my temper, and, if I am able, I will try henceforth to be less peevish and hard to please as I shall have more excuse and inclination to be so; although I have hitherto been one of the least impatient.

One more word to close this chapter. Aristotle says that 'anger is sometimes a weapon in the hands of virtue and valour'. That is very likely; yet they who deny it wittily reply that it is a weapon of novel use. For we move the other arms, whilst this one moves us; our hand does not guide it, it guides our hand; it holds us, we do not hold it.

CHAPTER 32

DEFENCE OF SENECA AND PLUTARCH

MY familiarity with these two men, and the help they give me in my old age, and to my book, which is purely built up of their spoils, oblige me to espouse their honour.

With regard to Seneca, among a myriad of pamphlets which the adherents of the religion which calls itself Reformed circulate in defence of their cause (and which sometimes proceed from such good hands that it is a great pity they were not busied upon a better subject), I once read one in which, to supplement and complete the similarity which he thinks he sees between the rule of our late poor King Charles the Ninth and that of Nero, the writer compares the late Cardinal de Lorraine with Seneca; their fortunes, each of them having been at the head of the government of his

Prince, and at the same time their character, their circumstances and their conduct. By this comparison he pays, in my opinion, a very great compliment to the said Lord Cardinal. For, although I am of those who have as high an opinion as anybody of his intelligence, his eloquence, his zeal in the cause of his faith and in his service to his King, as well as his good fortune to have been born at a time when it was so novel and rare a thing, and at the same time so necessary for the public weal, to have a Churchman of such high rank and dignity sufficient and capable of undertaking so weighty a charge; yet, to confess the truth, I do not think that in capability he comes anything near to Seneca, or that his virtue was so entirely strong and pure.

Now, in this book I speak of, the author, to justify his comparison, gives a very opprobrious description of Seneca, having borrowed his strictures of Dion the historian, to whose testimony I attach no importance whatever. For, besides that he is inconsistent in calling him now a very wise man, now a deadly enemy of Nero's vices, and elsewhere makes him out to be a miser, a usurer, ambitious, effeminate, voluptuous and claiming to be a philosopher on false pretences, Seneca's virtues show forth so clear and strong in his writings, and he vindicates himself so clearly from some of these imputations, such as his wealth and his excessive expenditure, that I should believe no testimony to the contrary. And moreover it is much more reasonable in these matters to believe the Roman historians than the Greeks and foreigners. Now Tacitus and the others speak in very honourable terms of his life and death, and depict him in all respects as a very excellent and a very virtuous man. And I will urge no other accusation against Dion's judgement than this, which is irrefutable, that his ideas with regard to Roman affairs are so unsound that he dares to maintain the cause of Julius Caesar against Pompey, and that of Antony against Cicero.

We will come to Plutarch.

Jean Bodin is a good author of our day, who is endowed with much more judgement than the crowd of scribblers of his time, and merits consideration and appreciation. I find him a little bold in that passage of his *Method of History* in which he not only accuses Plutarch of ignorance (on which I should have allowed him to have his say, as that does not

come within my province), but also remarks that that
author often writes of 'incredible and wholly fabulous
things' (those are his words). If he had simply said 'things
otherwise than they are', it would have been no great
reproach, for what we have not seen we take at the hands of
others and on trust, and I have observed that he sometimes
knowingly tells the same story differently, such as Hannibal's opinion as to the three best generals that ever lived,
which appears differently in the Life of Flaminius and in
that of Pyrrhus. But to charge him with having taken for
current coin incredible and impossible things is to accuse
the most judicious author in the world of want of judgement.

And this is his example : ' As, he says, when he tells us
that a Spartan boy suffered all his bowels to be torn out by
a young fox he had stolen and was hiding under his garment,
choosing rather to die than disclose his theft.' In the first
place I think this example is badly chosen, since it is very
difficult to set bounds to the power of the mental faculties,
whereas we are more at liberty to assume a limit to our
knowledge of the bodily powers. And for that reason, if it
had lain with me, I should rather have chosen an example
of this second kind. And there are some that are less
credible, as, among others, what he tells of Pyrrhus ' that,
wounded as he was, he dealt an enemy who was armed at all
points such a stroke with his sword that he clove him from
the head downwards, so that the two parts of the body fell
asunder.'

In Bodin's example I see no great miracle, and I cannot
accept the excuse with which he shelters Plutarch that he
added the words, ' as the story goes ', in order to put us on
our guard and curb our belief. For, except on things received
on good authority, or in reverence to religion or antiquity,
he would not have been willing either himself to accept or
expect us to believe things incredible in themselves. And
it may be easily seen that he does not there use these words
' as the story goes ' for the purpose suggested ; for in connexion with the endurance of the Spartan boys, he himself
tells us, in another place, of other examples which happened
in his own time, and which are much more difficult to
believe. That, for instance, to which Cicero before him also
testified, ' having, as he said, been on the spot,' that even

in their time there were boys who, in the test of endurance to which they were subjected before the altar of Diana, endured being flogged until the blood ran down their whole body, not only without shouting, but without even moaning, and some until they voluntarily gave up their lives.

And there is that other story which Plutarch tells, together with a hundred other witnesses, of a Spartan boy who, as he was burning incense during a sacrifice, suffered a red-hot ember which had fallen into his sleeve to burn his whole arm until the smell of the broiling flesh reached the bystanders.

There was nothing, according to their custom, in which their reputation was more concerned, nor for which they had to suffer more blame and disgrace, than being caught in a theft. I am so impressed by the greatness of those people, that not only does that story of Plutarch not appear incredible to me, as it does to Bodin, but I do not find it even strange and uncommon.

Spartan history is full of a thousand more cruel and more uncommon examples; it is, in this respect, all miracle.

Marcellinus relates, on this subject of theft, that in his time they had not yet discovered any kind of torture that could compel the Egyptians, when detected in this crime, which was very prevalent with them, even to reveal their names.

A Spanish peasant, being put to the rack to make him betray his accomplices in the murder of the Praetor Lucius Piso, exclaimed in the midst of his torments 'that his friends need not stir, but might look on in all security, and that no pain had the power of wresting a word of confession from him.' And that was all they could get out of him on the first day. On the following day, as they were again dragging him to the torture, he vigorously shook himself free from the hands of his jailors and killed himself by dashing his head against a wall.

Epicharis, having exhausted and glutted the cruelty of Nero's satellites by enduring for a whole day their fires, their stripes, their instruments, without a word that could reveal her conspiracy, the next day, as she was being carried back to the torture, her limbs all broken, she tied the girdle of her garment round an arm of her chair with a running knot, and, thrusting her head into it, was strangled by the weight of her body.[1]

Having had the courage to die in this manner after surviving the first torments, does it not appear as if she had purposely lent her life to that test of her endurance, in order to flout the tyrant, and to encourage others to a like attempt against his life?

And if any one will question our mounted musketeers on their experiences in these Civil wars, he will discover deeds of endurance, obstinacy, and stubbornness in this our miserable age, and in this rabble sunk in a more than Egyptian indolence and effeminacy, that will bear comparison with those we have just told of Spartan courage.

I know that there have been simple peasants who have suffered the soles of their feet to be grilled, the ends of their fingers to be crushed with the cock of a pistol, their bleeding eyes to be squeezed out of their heads by means of a thick cord twisted around their brows, before they would allow themselves even to be ransomed. I have seen one, left for dead naked in a ditch, his neck all bruised and swollen from a halter still hanging to it, by which they had dragged him all night at a horse's tail, his body pierced in a hundred places by dagger-thrusts, which had been dealt him, not to kill, but to cause pain and terrify him; who had suffered all this, and even lost all speech and feeling, resolved, as he told me, to die a thousand deaths (and indeed, as far as suffering goes, he had passed through a complete death) rather than make any promise. Yet he was one of the wealthiest labourers in the whole district.

How many of them have been seen patiently to endure burning and roasting for opinions borrowed of others, which they neither knew nor understood!

I have known hundreds of women, for they say that Gascon heads have a certain prerogative in this respect, who would rather bite into red-hot iron than let go their bite of anything they have said in anger. Beating and violence exasperate them only the more. And the man who made up the story of the woman who, in defiance of all threats and cudgellings, kept on calling her husband 'Lousy'; and, when plunged into a pond, and on the point

[1] Montaigne's account of this feat is not very clear; but that of Tacitus is hardly more so.

of drowning, still raised her hands above her head and imitated the action of killing lice, invented a tale that plainly illustrates the obstinacy of woman, as we may see it any day. And obstinacy is the sister of constancy, at least in strength and firmness.

We must not judge of what is possible and what is not so, according to what is credible and incredible in our judgement, as I have said elsewhere;[1] and it is quite an error, into which, however, most men fall (this is no reflexion on Bodin), to make a difficulty about believing of others what they themselves could not, or would not, do. Every man believes that he represents Nature's masterpiece; by this he tests, as if it were the touchstone, all other pieces. The conduct that does not square with his is counterfeit and artificial. What brutal stupidity! [If you tell him something about another person's doings or abilities, the first thing he does is to compare him with himself; as he is, so must the world be. O dangerous, intolerable and asinine folly!]

For my part, I regard some men as very far above me, especially among the ancients, and, although I clearly recognize my inability to follow in their footsteps, I yet follow them with my eyes and can estimate the powers that raise them to such a height, and of which I feel I have some of the seeds in myself; just as I can estimate the depths to which a mind can sink, which I am neither astonished at nor refuse to believe. I can very well detect the proceeding whereby those great souls raise themselves, and wonder at their greatness. I understand their aspirations, which appear to me very noble, and if my strength is not equal to it, my judgement at least readily goes along with them.

The other example which Bodin cites of 'things incredible and entirely fabulous' mentioned by Plutarch is 'that Agesilaus was fined by the Ephors for having drawn to himself alone the hearts and good-will of his citizens'. I know not what mark of falsehood he sees in it, but surely Plutarch is here speaking of things that he must have known much better than we do; and it was no new thing in Greece to see men punished and exiled for being too acceptable to their fellow-citizens. Witness Ostracism and Petalism.[2]

---

[1] Book I, chapter 27.

[2] Ostracism, banishment for ten years from Athens; Petalism, the

There is in the same place another accusation which annoys me on Plutarch's account, namely, that he was honest in his comparison of Romans with Romans, and Greeks with Greeks, but not of Romans with Greeks; witness, he says, Demosthenes and Cicero, Cato and Aristides, Sylla and Lysander, Marcellus and Pelopidas, Pompey and Agesilaus, holding that he favoured the Greeks by giving them such unequal mates. That is really to attack what is most excellent and commendable in Plutarch. For in his parallels (which are the most admirable part of his work, and in which I think he took a particular pride) the fidelity and sincerity of his judgements equals their weight and profundity. He is a philosopher who is teaching us virtue.

Let us see if we can defend him from this reproach of prevarication and falsehood.

What I think may have given rise to this censure is the great and brilliant lustre which in our imagination falls upon those Roman names. It does not appear possible to us that Demosthenes should rival the glory of a man who was a Consul, Proconsul, and Quaestor of the great Republic. But if we consider the truth of the matter, and the men in themselves, and compare their nature, their moral qualities, their genius, rather than their fortunes, which was Plutarch's chief aim, I think, in contradiction to Bodin, that Cicero and the elder Cato fall short of their parallels. For his purpose I should sooner have chosen the example of the younger Cato compared with Phocion; for in this parallel there would have been a more likely disparity, to the advantage of the Roman.

As to Marcellus, Sylla, and Pompey, I quite see that their exploits in war are more inflated, more glorious and pompous than those of the Greeks with whom Plutarch compares them; but the noblest and most valorous actions are not always, either in war or elsewhere, the most famous. I often see the names of generals smothered under the splendour of less meritorious names; witness Labienus, Ventidius, Telesinus, and many others.

And, to adopt Bodin's argument, if I had reason to

same for five years from Syracuse. They were so-called respectively from the earthen tablets and the olive-leaf on which the citizens recorded their votes.

complain on behalf of the Greeks, might I not say that Camillus is much less to be compared with Themistocles, the Gracchi with Agis and Cleomenes, Numa with Lycurgus?

But it is foolishness to try to estimate things at one glance, from so many points of view. When Plutarch compares them, he does not on that account make them equal. Who was able more eloquently and conscientiously to mark their differences? When he comes to parallel the victories, the martial exploits, the forces led by Pompey, and his triumphs, to those of Agesilaus, 'I do not believe, he says, that even Xenophon, if he were alive, though he were allowed to write whatever he pleased to the advantage of Agesilaus, would dare to bring them into comparison.' Does he speak of equalling Lysander to Sylla? 'There is no comparison, he says, either in the number of victories, or in the hazard of battles; for Lysander won only two naval battles, &c.'

This is not robbing the Romans of any glory; by merely confronting them with the Greeks, he can have done them no wrong, whatever disparity there may have been between them. And Plutarch does not weigh them all together; he does not indicate any preference for either as a whole; he compares actions and circumstances, one after another, and estimates them separately. Wherefore, if we would convict him of partiality, we should have to pull one particular judgement to pieces; or we should have to say, in a general way, that he was mistaken in matching this Greek with that Roman, since there were others more suitable for comparison and more resembling each other.

CHAPTER 33

THE CASE OF SPURINA

PHILOSOPHY is not conscious of having made a bad use of her resources in giving Reason the sovereign mastery over our soul, and authority to keep our appetites in check. They who hold that there is no desire more violent than that engendered by love, have this argument in their favour, that it affects both body and soul, and that the whole man is possessed by it; to such an extent that health itself depends on it, and medicine is sometimes obliged to be its broker.

But we might also say, on the other hand, that the interference of the body abates and weakens it; for this desire is subject to satiety and susceptible to material remedies.

Many, wishing to rid their soul of the continual restlessness caused by this appetite, have had recourse to incisions and amputation of the disturbed and ravenous parts. Others have quite subdued its strength and ardour by frequent application of cold objects, as snow and vinegar. The *haire* of our ancestors was applied to this purpose; this was a fabric woven of horse-hair, of which some of them made shirts and others belts to chafe their reins.

A Prince not long ago told me that in his younger days, on the occasion of a solemn festival at the court of King Francis the First, when everybody was dressed in his best, a fancy took him to put on his father's hair-shirt, which is still in his house. But, in spite of his devotion, he had not patience enough to await the night to strip himself of it; and he was ill for a long time after. He added that he did not think that any heat of youth could be so fierce but that the use of this remedy would damp it. It may be, however, that he never felt that heat at its strongest; for experience shows that that disturbance will often survive under rough and beggarly garments, and that the *haire* does not always make him a *hère* who wears it.[1]

Xenocrates went more rigorously about it; for his disciples having, to test his continence, smuggled into his bed the famous and beauteous courtesan Laïs, quite bare but for the arms of her beauty and those philters, her wanton charms; he, feeling, in spite of his teachings and rules, his body, usually so hard, beginning to rebel, had those members burned that had lent ear to this rebellion.

Whereas, when the passions are all in the soul, as ambition, avarice, and the rest, they give the reason much more to do; for she cannot find any help but in herself. Nor are they appetites which are capable of being satiated, but rather become whetted and increased by gratification.

The example of Julius Caesar alone may suffice to illustrate the disparity of these appetites; for no man was ever more addicted to amorous delights. One testimony of this is the meticulous care which he devoted to his person, which

[1] A very bad pun, which Montaigne drags in by the shoulders. *Un pauvre hère* means a 'poor, feeble creature'.

he carried so far as to adopt the most lascivious devices then in vogue, such as having his whole body depilated with tweezers and dressed with exquisitely choice perfumes. And he was naturally a handsome man, fair, tall, and active, with a full face and dark, bright eyes, if we are to believe Suetonius; for the statues we see of him in Rome do not always correspond with this picture.

Besides his wives, whom he changed four times, and without counting his youthful amours with Nicomedes, King of Bithynia, he had the maidenhead of the so renowned Queen of Egypt, Cleopatra; witness the little Cesarion, who was the result of it. He also 'made love' with Eunoë, Queen of Mauritania, and at Rome with Posthumia, wife of Servius Sulpitius; with Lollia, wife of Gabinius; with Tertulla, wife of Crassus; and even with Mutia, wife of the great Pompey; which was the reason, say the Roman historians, why her husband repudiated her, but which Plutarch confesses he does not know. And the Curios, father and son, afterwards, when Pompey married Caesar's daughter, twitted him with becoming the son-in-law of the man who had made him cuckold, and whom he himself was wont to call Aegisthus.[1]

Besides all this crowd he kept Servilia, the sister of Cato and mother of Marcus Brutus, which, as every one supposes, explains the great affection he had for Brutus, because he was born at a time which made it likely that he was the father.

Hence I think I am justified in regarding him as a man who was in a high degree given to that excess, and of a very amorous disposition. But the other passion of ambition, with which he was also afflicted in a very high degree, coming in conflict with the other, soon made it yield the first place.

Recalling to mind, on this subject, Mahomet, the one who subjugated Constantinople and brought about the final extermination of the Greek name, I can think of no case in which these two passions were more evenly balanced; he was equally indefatigable as a lecher and a soldier. But when the two compete with one another in his life, the quarrelsome spirit always dominates the amorous. And the

[1] Lover of Clytemnestra, and murderer of her husband King Agamemnon.

latter (although out of its natural season) did not fully regain the absolute power until he was in his extreme old age, and no longer able to support the burden of war.

What is related, as an example in the opposite direction, of Ladislaus, King of Naples, is noteworthy: That, a good general, brave and ambitious, he made it the chief aim of his ambition to satisfy his sensuality and enjoy some rare beauty. His death was in keeping. Having, after a closely conducted siege, reduced the city of Florence to such straits that the inhabitants were on the point of capitulating, he left them in possession on condition that they delivered up to him a girl of exceeding beauty of that city whom he had heard of. They were forced to grant his wish, and avert the public ruin by a private wrong.

She was the daughter of a physician famous in his day, who, seeing himself reduced to so foul a necessity, resolved on a desperate expedient. As all were busy dressing his daughter and bedecking her with jewels and ornaments, to render her pleasing to this new kind of lover, he also gave her a handkerchief, exquisite in workmanship and perfume, which she was to use at their first embraces. It was an article they seldom neglect to use in those parts. This handkerchief, poisoned with all the skill he was capable of, rubbed over the inflamed flesh and open pores, so quickly infused its venom, that, suddenly converting their warm into a cold sweat, they expired in each other's arms.

I come back to Caesar.

His pleasures never permitted him to steal a single moment of time, nor turn one step aside from any occasion that offered for his aggrandizement. His ambition exercised such sovereign sway over all his other passions, and possessed his soul with such absolute authority, that it carried him wherever it pleased. It vexes me indeed when I consider the greatness, in all other respects, of this man, and the wonderful talents wherewith he was endowed; so eminent was he in every kind of learning, that there was hardly any branch of science on which he had not written. He was so great an orator that many preferred his eloquence to Cicero's; and he himself, as I conceive, did not think he owed him much in that respect. He wrote his two *Anti-Catos* chiefly to counterbalance the fine style that Cicero had used in his *Cato*.

As for the rest, was there ever a mind so vigilant, so active, so patient of labour as his? And without doubt it was adorned with many uncommon seeds of virtue, I mean living, natural, not counterfeit. He was singularly sober, and so far from being dainty in his eating that Oppius relates that one day at table, when he was handed some sauce made with medicinal [1] instead of ordinary oil, he ate of it copiously, in order not to shame his host. On another occasion he had his baker whipped for serving him with other than the ordinary bread.

Cato himself was wont to say of him that he was the first sober man who had set out to ruin his country. And as to the same Cato one day calling him 'drunkard', it happened in this way. Both of them being in the Senate, whilst Catiline's conspiracy was being discussed, in which Caesar was suspected of having a share, some one from outside secretly handed him a note. Cato, thinking it was some warning from the conspirators, challenged him to hand it over, which Caesar was obliged to do to avoid a greater suspicion. It happened to be an affectionate letter from Servilia, Cato's sister. Cato, after reading it, threw it back at him with the words, 'There, drunkard!' That, I should say, was rather a word uttered in anger and contempt than an explicit accusation of that vice; as we often use the first insulting words that come to our lips against one that has angered us, although by no means deserved by the person we apply them to. Besides, that vice that Cato cast in his teeth is wonderfully akin to that in which he had detected Caesar, for Venus and Bacchus, according to the proverb, are usually on good terms.

But with me Venus is much more sprightly when accompanied with sobriety.

The examples of his mildness and clemency towards those who offended him are endless; I mean besides those he gave during the time when the Civil War was still in progress, the purpose of which was, as he himself makes sufficiently clear in his writings, to cajole his enemies, and make them less afraid of his future dominion and victory. Yet we must say that, if those examples are not sufficient evidence

---

[1] This seems to suggest the favourite remedy of the Fascisti; but, according to Suetonius, it was 'stale instead of fresh oil', and according to Plutarch, 'sweet ointment poured upon the asparagus instead of oil'.

of his natural mildness, they prove at least that this man possessed wonderful trust and magnanimous courage. It often happened that he sent back to the enemy whole armies, after vanquishing them, not even deigning to bind them by oath, if not to befriend him, at least to refrain from making war upon him. Three or four times he captured certain captains of Pompey, and as often set them free. Pompey declared all those to be his enemies who did not accompany him to the war; and Caesar proclaimed all those to be friendly who did not stir, and did not actually take up arms against him. If his captains deserted from him to take other service, he sent them their arms, horses, and accoutrements. The towns he had taken by force he left at liberty to follow which side they pleased, leaving them no other garrison but the memory of his mildness and clemency. And on the day of his great battle of Pharsalia, he forbade any man to lay hands on a Roman citizen, except as a last resource.

There we see, in my judgement, some very risky steps; and it is not to be wondered at if, in the Civil Wars we are suffering from, those who, like him, are fighting against the old institutions of their country, do not imitate his example. They were extraordinary methods, which Caesar's fortune alone and his wonderful foresight were allowed to employ successfully. When I reflect upon his incomparable greatness of soul, I can excuse victory for not having been able to shake off his fetters, even in that very unjust and very iniquitous cause.

To return to his clemency, we may see many genuine examples of it at the time of his rule, when, everything being subjected to his power, he had no more need to dissemble. Caius Memmius had published a very biting satire against him, to which he very sharply replied; but that did not prevent him from soon after helping him to the Consulship. Caius Calvus, who had composed several insulting epigrams upon him, having employed some of his friends to reconcile them, Caesar was prompted to write to him first. And our good Catullus, who had given him such a rude dressing under the name of Mamurra, coming one day to make his excuses to him, Caesar invited him to stay to supper at his table. Having been informed of some who spoke ill of him, he merely announced in one of his public speeches that he had been informed of it. If he did not hate his enemies, still less did he fear them. Certain conspiracies and meetings organized against his life having been discovered, he contented himself with publishing by edict that he knew of them, without further prosecuting the ringleaders.

With regard to the consideration he had for his friends, Caius Oppius travelling with him and feeling indisposed, he relinquished to him the only lodging there was, and slept all night in the open on the hard ground.

As to his justice, he put to death one of his freedmen of whom he was particularly fond, for having lain with the wife of a Roman knight, although nobody had made any complaint of it. No man ever showed more moderation in his victory, nor more fortitude in his adverse fortunes.

But all these noble inclinations were stifled and corrupted by that furious passion of ambition by which he was so forcibly carried away, that we may safely declare that it held the rudder and steered all his actions. It turned a generous man into a public robber, to provide for that profusion and liberality, and made him utter that vile and most iniquitous saying, 'that if the most wicked and degraded men in the world had been faithful in serving him towards his aggrandizement, he would cherish and advance them to the best of his power, as well as the most honourable.' It intoxicated him with so excessive a vanity that he dared to boast, in presence of his fellow-citizens, 'that he had made the great Roman Republic a name, without shape and without body', to declare that his answers must henceforth be taken as laws, to remain seated when he received the Senate in a body in his house, and to allow himself to be worshipped, and divine honours to be paid him in his own presence.

To sum up, this single vice, in my opinion, destroyed in him the richest and most beautiful nature that ever was, and made his memory abominable to all good men, since it led him to seek his glory in the ruin of his country and the subversion of the most powerful and flourishing Republic the world will ever see.

We could, on the other hand, find many examples of great men whose sensuality caused them to neglect the conduct of their affairs, as Mark Antony and others; but where love and ambition are equally balanced and clash together with equal forces, I make no doubt but that the latter will win the prize of mastery.

Now, to retrace my steps, it is a great thing to be able to curb our appetites with the arguments of reason, or violently to force our members to keep within the bounds of duty. But as to punishing ourselves for the good of our neighbours ; not only ridding ourselves of that sweet passion that tickles us, of the pleasure we feel in being agreeable to others, and beloved and sought after by all ; but conceiving a hatred and loathing of the charms which are the cause of it, and blaming our beauty because another is inflamed by it, of this I have met with few examples ; but here is one.

Spurina, a young Tuscan,

> Glittering like a gem that cleaves
> The red gold round it, to deck head or throat,
> Or as gleams ivory, cunningly inlaid
> In boxwood or Orician terebinth, (VIRGIL.)

being endowed with a beauty so uncommon and surpassing that the most continent eyes could not continently resist its brilliance, not content to leave so much flame and fever, which he kindled on all sides, without relief, conceived such a furious spite against himself and the rich gifts which Nature had bestowed upon him, as if they were to be blamed for others' faults, that he purposely slashed and disfigured with wounds and scars the perfect proportion and symmetry that Nature had so carefully observed in his face.

To give my own opinion, I do not so much admire as wonder at actions of that kind. Such excesses outrage my sense of order. The purpose was noble and conscientious, but, to my mind, a little wanting in wisdom. What if his subsequent deformity resulted in making others guilty of the sin of hatred and contempt, or of envy of the glory of such uncommon merit, or of calumny, by attributing this whim to a frantic ambition ? Is there anything on which malice cannot, if it will, find an occasion, one way or another, to vent itself ? It would have been better and at the same time more glorious to have made these gifts of God an occasion for exemplary virtue and right conduct.

Those who try to escape from the common duties, and

that endless number of rules, difficult from so many points of view, which bind a strictly honest man to civil life, practise, to my mind, a fine economy, whatever degree of special rigour they impose upon themselves. It is, in a sense, dying in order to avoid the trouble of living well. They may have some other reward, but it never seemed to me that they could have the reward of difficulty. Nor do I think there is anything more difficult than for a man to keep straight amid the rushing waters of this world, loyally responding to and satisfactorily performing every part of his charge.

It is perhaps easier to keep clear of the whole sex than to behave entirely as we should in companionship with our wives. And a man may pass a more easy and careless life in poverty than in a rightly dispensed abundance. To employ one's wealth according to reason is harder than abstinence. Moderation is a virtue that gives us more trouble than suffering does. The right living of the younger Scipio may assume a thousand forms; the right living of Diogenes only one. The latter surpasses in harmlessness the life of the ordinary man as much as it is itself surpassed in usefulness and power by the most perfect and uncommon lives.

CHAPTER 34

OBSERVATIONS ON JULIUS CAESAR'S METHODS IN WAR

IT is told of several war-chiefs that they had a particular regard for certain books, as the great Alexander for Homer; Scipio Africanus for Xenophon; Marcus Brutus for Polybius; Charles the Fifth for Philip de Commines. And we are told that Macchiavelli is still held in repute in other countries. But the late Marshal Strozzi without doubt made a much better choice in adopting Caesar as his favourite; for that book should indeed be the breviary of every soldier, as being the true and supreme model of the art of warfare. And God knows besides with what charm and beauty he has overlaid that rich matter, expressed in so pure, delicate, and perfect a style, that to my taste there are no writings in the world comparable to his on that subject.

I will here record certain individual and uncommon features, in connexion with his warfare, that have remained in my memory.

His army being somewhat intimidated by a rumour which was circulating of the numerous forces which King Juba was leading against him, instead of diminishing the apprehension of his soldiers and minimizing the enemy's resources, having called them together to reassure them and give them courage, he adopted the opposite course to that we are accustomed to. For he told them that they need no more trouble to inquire about the forces the enemy was leading, and that he had very certain information about them. Then he gave them a number greatly exceeding both the truth and the report that was circulating in his army, herein following the advice of Cyrus in Xenophon; since the deception is not so important when it is found that the enemy is in fact weaker than was expected, as when he is found to be very strong after having been reported weak.

He trained his soldiers above all to simple obedience, and not to presume to criticize or even speak of their general's plans, which he never communicated to them until they were about to be carried out. And if they happened to get wind of them, he delighted in changing his mind on the spur of the moment, in order to deceive them. And often, with the same end in view, having fixed upon an encampment at a certain spot, he would pass on and prolong the day's march, especially in bad and rainy weather.

At the commencement of his Gallic wars, the Swiss having sent to ask permission to cross over the Roman territory, although determined to stop them by force, he yet pretended to favour their request, and put off his answer for several days to give himself time to collect his army. Those poor men did not know how excellent a hand he was at husbanding his time; for many a time he repeats that the supreme qualification for a general is to be able to seize his opportunity at the right moment, and to be ever on the spot. And his exploits show that he possessed this quality in an unexampled and incredible degree.

If he did not show much scruple in taking advantage of an enemy under colour of a treaty of agreement, he had as little in requiring in his soldiers no other quality but valour, and he seldom punished any faults except mutiny and disobedience. Often, after a victory, he would give them a free hand to revel at pleasure, releasing them for a time from the rules of military discipline; and, what is more, he had trained his soldiers so well that, perfumed and oiled though they were, they would none the less rush into battle with great fury. Indeed he liked them to be richly armed, and encouraged them to wear engraved, gilded and plated armour, that they might be the more anxious to save it, and consequently more resolute in their defence.

When he spoke to them he called them 'Fellow-soldiers', as we do now, a practice which his successor Augustus discontinued, holding that Caesar had done so when his affairs made it necessary, and to gratify the hearts of men who only followed him as volunteers;

> At crossing of the Rhine great Caesar was
> My general; in Rome he is my fellow.
> So crime does equalize those it pollutes; (LUCAN.)

but that this mode of address was beneath the dignity of an Emperor and army-general; and he revived the custom of calling them merely 'Soldiers'.

With this courtesy, however, Caesar combined great severity in keeping them in check. The Ninth legion having mutinied near Placentia, he ignominiously disbanded it, although Pompey was still afoot at the time, and only after many entreaties did he receive them back into favour. He appeased them more by authority and audacity than by soft words.

In the passage where he speaks of his crossing of the river Rhine into Germany, he says that he thought it unworthy of the honour of the Roman people to convey his army across in boats, and built a bridge that they might pass over firm-footed. It was there that he built that wonderful bridge, the construction of which he describes in all its details. For he never dwells with so much complacency on his exploits as he does in explaining the ingenuity of his inventions in this kind of manual works.

I have also observed this, that he attaches great importance to his addresses to his troops before battle. For when he wishes to show how much he was surprised and hard pressed, he always mentions the fact that he had no time even to harangue his army. Before that great battle with the forces of Tournay, he writes, 'Caesar, having given all necessary orders, immediately hastened to that part of the army whither chance led him, to exhort his soldiers, and coming across the Tenth legion he had only time to tell them to remember their pristine valour, not to be taken aback, and boldly to resist the enemy's onslaught. And, the enemy having already approached to within a dart's throw, he gave the signal for battle; and forthwith proceeding to another part to encourage the others, he found them already engaged in fighting.'

That is what he says there. In truth his tongue did him very notable service in many places, and, even in his own day, his military eloquence was so highly thought of, that several in his army took down his speeches; by this means there arose a collection of volumes that existed long after his time. He had a peculiar charm in speaking, and so characteristic of him, that his familiar friends, among whom was Augustus, hearing those speeches read which had been collected, detected even words and phrases which were not his.

The first time he left Rome with a public command, he reached the river Rhone in a week, having a secretary or two in front of him in his coach, whom he kept continually writing, and behind him the man who carried his sword. And indeed, if one were merely travelling, one could hardly attain the speed with which he advanced from victory to victory. For, leaving Gaul and pursuing Pompey to Brindisi, he subdued Italy in eighteen days; returned from Brindisi to Rome; from Rome he penetrated into the heart of Spain, where he surmounted the greatest difficulties in the war against Afranius and Petreius, and at the prolonged siege of Marseilles. From thence he returned to Macedonia, defeated the Roman army at Pharsalia; passed thence, still in pursuit of Pompey, into Egypt, which he subdued; from Egypt he came to Syria and the region of the Pontus, where he fought against Pharnaces; thence to Africa, where he defeated Scipio and Juba; and again retraced his steps, through Italy, into Spain, where he defeated Pompey's sons:

> Fleeter than flames of heaven, or tigress newly-delivered.
> (LUCAN.)

> As when a boulder, from a hill-top borne,
> Which rains have washed, or blustering winds have torn,
> Or creeping years have loosened, down the steep,
> From crag to crag, leaps headlong, and in scorn
> Goes bounding on, and with resistless sweep
> Lays waste the woods, and whelms the shepherd and his sheep.
> (VIRGIL.)

Writing of the siege of Avaricum he says it was his custom to remain night and day with the workmen he was employing. In every important undertaking he always reconnoitred in person, and never brought his army to a place that he had not first thoroughly explored. And, if we are to believe Suetonius, when he invaded England, he was the first to sound the ford.[1]

He was wont to say that he would rather gain a victory by thought than by strength. And in the war against Petreius and Afranius, when Fortune offered him a very obvious advantage, he refused it, hoping, as he says, to get the better of his enemies with less risk by prolonging the operation.

There too he performed a wonderful feat when he commanded his whole host, without any necessity, to swim the river:

> Eager to fight they plunged into the stream
> They would have feared if close pursued in flight.
> Their armour donned, their frozen limbs restore
> By running to and fro. (LUCAN.)

To me he appears to have been rather more cautious and deliberate in his enterprises than Alexander; for the latter seems to have looked for dangers and rushed headlong into them, like an impetuous torrent which attacks and collides with everything that comes into its way, without choice or discrimination:

> So rolls the flood of horned Aufidus,
>   That flows beside Apulian Daunus' realm,
> When he designs in mood tumultuous
>   With deluge dread the fields of tilth to whelm.
>
>   (HORACE.)

And then too he was busy at that work in the bloom and first ardour of youth; whilst Caesar set about it when he was already mature and well on in years. Besides that Alexander was of a more sanguine temperament, hot and choleric, and he aggravated this disposition by drinking wine, of which Caesar was very abstemious.

But in case of need and when the occasion required it, never did any man hold his life more cheaply. For my own

[1] Montaigne's knowledge of the Channel appears to be a little at fault. Suetonius says 'he did not cross to Britain until he had himself explored the harbours and the navigation, and the access to the island'.

part I seem to read in divers of his exploits a determined resolve to throw his life away, to avoid the shame of being vanquished. In that great battle which he fought against those of Tournay, seeing the vanguard of his army wavering, he hastened to the front of the enemy, without a buckler, just as he was; and the same happened on several other occasions. Hearing that his men were besieged, he passed through the enemy's forces in disguise, to go and encourage them by his presence.

After crossing the sea to Dyrrhachium with a very small force, and seeing that the remainder of his army, which he had left in Antony's charge, was slow in following him, he dared alone to recross the sea in a violent storm, and, the ports on the other side and the whole sea being in Pompey's possession, he slipped through to fetch the rest of his army himself.

As to the expeditions he carried out with armed forces, some of them exceeded in risk all the rules of military art; for with what feeble resources he undertook to subdue the kingdom of Egypt, and afterwards attacked the armies of Scipio and Juba, ten times greater than his own! Men of his kind have had an unaccountable and superhuman confidence in their fortune.

He used to say that one should embark, and not deliberate, upon great enterprises.

After the battle of Pharsalia, having sent his army before him into Asia, and crossing with a single ship the strait of the Hellespont, he met Lucius Cassius at sea, with ten great ships of war; he had the pluck, not merely to await his coming, but to steer straight for him and call upon him to surrender; and he was successful.

Having undertaken that mad siege of Alesia, which was defended by a garrison of eighty thousand men, the whole of Gaul having risen in arms to come down upon him and raise the siege, with an army of 109,000 [1] horse and 240,000 foot, what maniacal foolhardiness it was to refuse to give up the attempt and to be determined to perform two such difficult feats at the same time! And yet he carried them through. After winning that great battle against the army

---

[1] 8,000 according to Caesar himself. The mistake was perhaps due to Montaigne's misreading of Caesar's number *IIX milibus* (*De Bel. Gall.* vii. 76).

outside, he soon brought those he was besieging to their knees.

Lucullus performed a similar feat at the siege of Tigranocerta, against King Tigranes; but the conditions were not the same, considering the want of energy shown by the enemy with whom Lucullus had to do.

I must here note two rare and extraordinary circumstances in connexion with the siege of Alesia. The one is that the Gauls, assembling together for the purpose of encountering Caesar, after a calculation of all their forces, decided in council to cut down a good part of that great multitude, lest they might fall into confusion. This was a new thing, to be afraid of being too many; but looking at it rightly, it is probably true that an army-corps should be of moderate size, and regulated within certain limits, either on account of the difficulty of feeding it, or of the difficulty of handling it and keeping it in order. It would be very easy at least to prove by examples that those immense armies have seldom done anything worth speaking of.

According to the saying of Cyrus, in Xenophon, it is not the number of men, but the number of good men, that gives the advantage. The rest are a hindrance rather than a help.

And Bajazet grounded his decision to give battle to Tamerlane, against the advice of all his captains, chiefly on the consideration that the numberless number of the enemy army gave him an assured hope of throwing them into confusion.

Scanderbeg, a good and very expert judge, was wont to say that ten or twelve thousand reliable fighting-men should suffice a competent leader to guarantee his reputation in any kind of military emergency.

The other circumstance, which appears to be contrary to usage and reason in warfare, is that Vercingetorix, who was elected general-in-chief over all the parts of the revolted Gauls, decided to shut himself up in Alesia. For the man in command of a whole country should never shackle himself except in the extreme case of his last stronghold being in danger, and of there being no hope but in defending it. Otherwise he should hold himself free, in order to have the full power of protecting all the regions under his command.

To come back to Caesar. With advancing years he became rather less active and more deliberate, as his friend Oppius testifies; thinking it wise not lightly to risk the honour of so many victories which a single disaster might cause him to lose. The Italians, when they wish to reprove their young men for their foolhardiness, call them *bisognosi di honore*, 'hard up for honour'. When they still hunger and thirst after fame they are right to seek it at any price; but, having already acquired a sufficiency of it, they should renounce it. There may be some reasonable moderation in this craving for honour, and this appetite, like any other, may be glutted. Many men have had this experience.

He had outgrown the scruples of the ancient Romans, who would take no unfair advantage in their warfare, but relied upon pure and native valour alone; and yet he was more conscientious than we should be in these days, and did not approve of every kind of means to gain a victory. In the war against Ariovistus, whilst he was parleying with him, some trouble arose between the two armies, of which the fault at first lay with Ariovistus' horsemen. This tumult gave Caesar a great advantage over his enemy, yet he would make no use of it, for fear of being accused of bad faith.

When he went to battle he was usually richly dressed, and in bright colours, to make himself conspicuous.

In presence of the enemy he kept a tighter rein on his soldiers, and kept them more strictly in hand.

When the ancient Greeks wished to accuse a man of extreme incompetence, they used a proverbial saying: 'That he could neither read nor swim.' Caesar held the same opinion, that the art of swimming was very useful in war, and it gave him many advantages. When he was in great haste he usually swam the rivers he came across; for he loved to travel on foot, like the great Alexander. In Egypt, having been obliged to save himself by entering a little skiff, and so many men leaping in after him that it was in danger of foundering, he chose rather to commit himself to the sea and gained his fleet by swimming, although it was more than two hundred yards away, holding his tablets above the water in his left hand, with his military cloak, which he held with his teeth, trailing after him, that it might not fall into the hands of the enemy; and he was already well advanced in years.

No general ever inspired such trust in his soldiers. At the beginning of his Civil wars, his centurions offered to pay a horseman each, out of their own purses; and the foot-soldiers offered to serve him at their own expense, those who were better off also undertaking to defray the cost of the more needy.

The late Admiral de Chatillon recently showed us a similar case in our Civil wars; for the Frenchmen of his army furnished the money out of their own purses to pay the foreigners who accompanied him. We could not find many examples of so warm and ready an affection among those who march under the old colours, under the old government of the laws.[1]

Passion rules us much more strongly than reason. And so it happened, in the war against Hannibal, that, after the generous example of the Roman people in the city, the men-at-arms and captains refused their pay; and those who took it in Marcellus' camp were called Mercenaries.

After suffering a check near Dyrrhachium, his soldiers came of their own accord and offered themselves for chastisement and punishment, so that there was more need to comfort than to scold them. A single cohort of his held their own against four of Pompey's legions for more than four hours, until nearly the whole cohort was shot down with arrows, of which 130,000[2] were found in the trenches.

A soldier named Scaeva, who commanded one of the approaches, invincibly maintained his ground, having lost one eye, one shoulder and thigh being shot through, and his shield pierced in two hundred and thirty places. Many of his soldiers, being taken prisoner, chose death rather than promise to join the other side. Granius Petronius, having been captured by Scipio in Africa, the latter, after putting his comrades to death, sent word to him that he gave him his life, as he was a man of rank and a quaestor. Petronius replied that the soldiers of Caesar were wont to grant life to others, not to receive it, and immediately killed himself with his own hand.

---

[1] i.e. in the Catholic army. Montaigne was nothing if not impartial. The Admiral de Chatillon is better known as Gaspard de Coligny.

[2] According to Suetonius; but Caesar himself makes the number 30,000.

Of their fidelity we have endless examples. We must not forget the conduct of the men who were besieged at Salona, a town that held with Caesar against Pompey, on account of an uncommon incident which occurred there. Marcus Octavius held them in siege; those within were reduced to such extreme necessity in all things, that, in order to supply the want of men, most of them having been killed or wounded, they manumitted all their slaves, and were constrained to cut off the hair of all the women to make ropes for their catapults; not to speak of a great shortage of food. Yet they were determined never to surrender.

This siege having dragged out to a great length and Octavius having become in consequence more negligent and less attentive to his operations, they chose a day about noon, and, after ranging the women and children on the walls to make a good show, they sallied out with such fury against the besiegers that, having broken through the first, the second, and the third body of guards, and the fourth, and then all the remainder, and forced them to abandon all their trenches, they drove them to their ships; and Octavius himself escaped to Dyrrhachium, where Pompey was.

I cannot at this moment call to mind another example of the besieged beating the besiegers wholesale, and gaining the upper hand in the campaign; nor of a sortie being converted into a real and entirely victorious battle.

CHAPTER 35
OF THREE GOOD WIVES

GOOD women are not found by the dozen, as everybody knows, and especially in the duties of marriage; for that is a bargain fraught with so many difficulties, that a woman's will is strained to keep to it entirely for long. The men, although they enter into it under somewhat better conditions, yet have enough to do to keep to it.

The touchstone of a good marriage, and its real proof, is the duration of the partnership, and whether it has been constantly pleasant, loyal, and smooth. In our days the women more commonly reserve the display of their good offices and the strength of their affection for their husbands until after they have lost them; then at least they seek to give evidence of their goodwill. A tardy and unseasonable testimony! They prove thereby rather that they only love them when dead.

Life is full of tumult; death, of love and courtesy. As fathers conceal their affection for their children, so the wives likewise are wont to conceal their affection for their husbands, in order to keep up a modest respect. That mystery is not to my liking. In vain do they tear their hair and lacerate their faces; I should go to the lady's maid or the secretary and whisper in their ear, 'How did they get on? how did they live together?'

I am always reminded of that wise saying: *They make most ostentation of sorrow who grieve the least.*[1] Their glum looks are offensive to the living and useless to the dead. We should willingly give them leave to smile after, if only they smile on us during life. Is it not enough to bring one back to life in vexation to find her who spat in his face when alive coming and rubbing his feet when he is hardly dead? If there is any honour in weeping over a husband, it is only for one who has smiled upon him; let those who have wept during his life smile at his death, outwardly as well as inwardly.

Therefore pay no heed to those tear-stained eyes and that pitiful voice; observe rather her bearing, her colour and the plumpness of her cheeks under those thick veils; it is by them that they speak plain French. There are few who do not improve in health, an infallible sign. That ceremonious demeanour looks not so much backward as forward; it means acquisition more than payment. When I was a boy, an honest and very fair lady, the widow of a Prince and still living, dressed a little more ornamentally than is permitted by our laws of widowhood; to those who reproved her for it, she replied, 'The meaning of it is that I am not on the look-out for a new lover, and have no desire to marry again.'

In order not to be quite out of harmony with our customs, I have here made choice of three women whose extreme tenderness and affection also centred around their husbands' death. Yet they are examples of a somewhat different kind, and of a love so convincing that they bravely threw life into the scale.

[1] Altered from Tacitus.

Pliny the Younger had a neighbour living near one of his houses in Italy who was grievously afflicted with ulcers on his private parts. His wife, seeing his prolonged anguish, entreated him to allow her to examine at leisure the condition of his malady, that she might tell him more frankly than any other what hopes he had. His permission being obtained, and having carefully considered his case, she found that a cure was impossible, and that all he could hope for was to drag out a painful and lingering life. Therefore she advised him, as the surest and most sovereign remedy, to kill himself; and finding him a little reluctant to adopt so heroic a measure, she said, 'Do not think, my friend, that the pain I see you suffering does not touch me as much as yourself, and that I am not willing to use, to rid myself of it, the same medicine I am prescribing for you. I will accompany you in the cure as I have done in the disease. Put away your fear, and believe me that we shall derive only pleasure from this passage which is to deliver us from such torments. We will depart happily together.'

Having said that, and warmed up her husband's courage, she resolved that they should leap into the lake [1] through a window of their house that overlooked it. And, to preserve to the last that loyal and vehement affection with which she had embraced him during life, she desired that he should die in her arms. But, lest they should fail her and the closeness of her embrace be relaxed in the fall through fear, she had herself fast bound to him by the waist; and so gave up her own life for the repose of her husband's.[2]

This was a woman of humble origin; and in this class of people it is not so unusual to see occasional acts of uncommon goodness:

> When Justice fled this world of wickedness,
> 'Twas in their midst that last her steps were seen. (VIRGIL.)

The other two are noble and rich, among whom examples of virtue are rarely found.

---

[1] Lake Larius, the modern Como.
[2] Montaigne rather elaborates the story, which Pliny tells in a third as many words; introducing it with the remark: 'How much does the fame of human actions depend upon the station of those who perform them!'

Arria, wife of Cecinna Paetus, a man of consular rank, was the mother of another Arria, the wife of Thrasea Paetus, so renowned for his virtue in Nero's time, and through this son-in-law, grandmother of Fannia; for the resemblance between the names and fortunes of these men and women has led many to confuse them. When Cecinna Paetus, her husband, was taken prisoner by the Emperor Claudius' soldiers, after the defeat of Scribonianus, whose party he had joined, this first Arria entreated those who were leading him captive to Rome, to take her into their ship, where she would be of much less expense and trouble to them than a number of persons they would need to wait upon her husband, since she alone would undertake the whole charge of his cabin, his cooking, and all other services. They refused her request. She embarked in a small fishing-vessel which she hired on the spot, and in this craft followed him from Sclavonia.

One day, when they were at Rome, in presence of the Emperor, Junia, the widow of Scribonianus, having familiarly accosted her on the strength of their similar fortunes, she repulsed her rudely with these words, 'I, speak to you, or listen to anything you say! you, in whose lap Scribonianus was killed, and you still alive!' These words, together with several other indications, made her relations suspect that, unable to endure her husband's fate, she was designing to do away with herself. And when Thrasea, her son-in-law, on hearing those words, entreated her not to throw her life away, saying, 'What! if I incurred the same fate as Cecinna, would you expect my wife, your daughter, to do the same?' 'Would I? she replied, most certainly I would, if she had lived as long and in such harmony with you as I have done with my husband.' These answers increased their solicitude about her, and made them watch her conduct more carefully.

One day she said to those who were keeping guard over her, 'You may do what you please, you may drive me to a much more painful death, but prevent me from dying you cannot;' and thereupon, rushing madly from the chair on which she was seated, she dashed her head with all her might against the nearest wall, so that sorely bruised she fell down in a swoon. After they had with great trouble brought her round, she said, 'I told you that if you refused me some easy way of dying, I would choose another, however painful it might be.'

The end of so admirable a virtue was this: When her husband Paetus was sentenced to death by the Emperor's cruelty, he had not sufficient courage of his own to take his life. One day, among others, after employing all the arguments and persuasions which she thought best calculated to prevail upon him to do her bidding, she snatched the dagger which her husband was wearing and, holding it naked in her hand, said, as a last exhortation, 'Do this, Paetus,' and at the same instant dealt herself a fatal stab in the heart. Then, tearing it out of the wound, she offered it to him, at the same time ending her life with these noble, generous, and immortal words, *Paete, non dolet.* She had only time to utter those three words of such beautiful meaning, 'See, Paetus, it does not hurt me.'

> When from her breast chaste Arria snatched the sword,
> And gave the fatal weapon to her lord,
> ' My wound, she said, believe me, does not smart;
> 'Tis thine alone, my Paetus, pains my heart.'   (MARTIAL.)

The words are much more alive in the original, and richer in meaning; for both her husband's and her own wound and death were so small a matter to her, since it was she who advised and instigated them. But having taken this bold and heroic step solely for her husband's benefit, she had no thoughts except for him in the last gasp of her life, and for removing his fear of following her in death. Paetus immediately stabbed himself with the same blade; ashamed, as I think, of having needed so dear and precious a lesson.

Pompeia Paulina, a young and very noble Roman lady, had married Seneca in his extreme old age. Nero, his precious pupil, sent his satellites to announce to him his death decree, which was done in this wise: When the Roman Emperors of that time had sentenced any man of rank, they sent him word by their officers to choose what death he pleased, and to take his life within such and such a prescribed time, which was shorter or longer according to the temper of their choler; giving him leisure to arrange his affairs during that time, or sometimes making the interval so short that he was deprived of the opportunity of doing so. And, if the condemned resisted the order, they sent special men to execute it, either by cutting the veins of his arms and legs, or forcibly making him take poison. But a man of honour did not abide this necessity and employed his own physician and surgeon to that end.

Seneca heard their charge with calm and confident demeanour, and then asked for paper to make his will; which being refused by the centurion, he turned to his friends. 'Since I cannot, he said, leave you anything else in requital of what I owe you, I leave you at least the best thing I possess, which is the example of my life and character, which I pray you to cherish in your memory, that by doing so you may acquire the name of true and sincere friends.' At the same time, now with gentle words assuaging the bitterness of the grief he saw they were suffering, now hardening his voice to chide them, 'Where, he said, are those brave precepts of philosophy ? What has become of the provisions that for so many years we have laid up against the accidents of Fortune ? Was Nero's cruelty unknown to us ? What could we expect of a man who has killed his mother and his brother, if not that he would also put to death the tutor who has fostered and brought him up ? '

Having spoken these words to the company, he turned to his wife, and, closely embracing her, whose heart and strength were sinking under the weight of her grief, he entreated her for the love of him to bear this misfortune a little more patiently, and said to her that the hour was come when he had to show, no longer by words and arguments, but by deeds, the fruit he had gathered from his studies ; and that he really embraced death, not only without pain, but cheerfully. 'Wherefore, my love, he added, do not dishonour it by your tears, that you may not seem to love yourself more than my reputation ; moderate your grief, and comfort yourself with the knowledge you have had of me and my actions, and pass the remainder of your life in the honest occupations to which you are devoted.'

To this Paulina, having a little recovered her spirits and warmed her great heart by a very noble affection, replied, 'No, Seneca, I am not the woman to leave you without my company in such a need ; I will not have you think that the virtuous examples you have set by your life have not also taught me how to die well; and how could I do so better and more honourably, or more to my own desire, than in your company? So be assured that I am departing with you.' Then Seneca, approving this noble and glorious resolution of his wife, and glad to be delivered of the fear of leaving her after his death at the mercy and cruelty of his enemies, said, 'I have advised you how to lead your life more happily; you prefer then the honour of death. Truly I will not begrudge it you; the fortitude and resolution in our common end may be alike, but the beauty and glory will be greater on your part.'

When he had said that, the veins of their arms were opened at the same time, but Seneca's being shrunk both through old age and abstinence, and the blood flowing too long and too sluggishly, he ordered them also to cut the veins of his thighs; and lest the anguish he was suffering might pierce his wife's heart, and to be delivered from the affliction he felt at seeing her in so pitiable a condition, after taking a very tender leave of her, he prayed her to allow herself to be carried into the adjoining room; which was done.

But all these incisions being still insufficient to cause his death, he ordered his physician, Statius Annaeus, to give him a poisonous draught, which had scarcely more effect; for, by reason of the feebleness and chilliness of the limbs, it could not reach the heart. Therefore they prepared in addition a very hot bath; and then, feeling his end to be near, as long as he had any breath he continued to talk very excellently on the subject of his present condition, his secretaries taking down his words as long as they were able to hear his voice. And his last words were long after treasured and held in honour by men (it is a grievous loss to us that they have not been preserved to this day). As he felt the last pangs of death, with some of the bath-water mixed with blood he wetted his head,[1] saying, 'I make libation of this water to Jove the Deliverer.'

When Nero was informed of all this, fearing lest he might incur the blame of Paulina's death, who was a lady allied to some of the best families in Rome, and towards whom he felt no particular enmity, he sent in all haste to command her

[1] According to Tacitus, who appears to be Montaigne's authority, he did not wet his head, but 'sprinkled' some of his slaves.

wounds to be bound up; which her people did without her knowledge, she being already half dead and unconscious. And, though she continued to live against her design, she lived very honourably and as befitted her virtue; her wan complexion testifying how much life had flowed from her wounds.

Those are my three very true stories, which I find as entertaining and as tragic as any of those that we make up out of our heads to please the public. And I wonder that it does not occur to those who are devoted to that kind of composition to choose rather one of ten thousand very fine stories which are found in books, which would give them less trouble and bring more pleasure and profit. And if any man should wish to build up a whole and connected body of them, he need provide nothing of his own but the link, like the solder of some other kind of metal; by this means he might accumulate a store of true incidents of all sorts, arranging and varying them as the beauty of the work may require, pretty much as Ovid sewed and pieced together, from that great number of different fables, his *Metamorphoses*.

In respect of the last couple, this is also worthy of consideration, that Paulina voluntarily offers to relinquish this life for love of her husband, and that her husband had once also relinquished death for the love of her. To us there is no great equivalence in this exchange, but, according to his Stoic way of thinking, it seems to me that he thought he had done as much for her in prolonging his life for her sake, as if he had died for her.

In one of the letters he wrote to Lucilius, after giving him to understand that, having caught a fever at Rome, he immediately took coach to retire to one of his country houses, against his wife's advice, who tried to make him stay; and that he had replied that his fever was not a fever of the body, but of the place, he continues as follows: 'She allowed me to go, strongly recommending me to look after my health. Now I, knowing that her life is involved in mine, begin to look after myself in order to look after her. I lose the privilege which my old age had given me of being more firm and resolute in many things, when I remember that in this old life there is a young life to which I am of some use. Since I cannot bring her to love me more courageously, she brings me to love myself more carefully; for we must allow something to honest affections. And at times, although occasions urge us to the contrary, we must call back our life, even though it be a torture. We must arrest the soul between our teeth, since with men of honour the law of living is determined not by their pleasure but by their duty.

'The man who does not value his wife or one of his friends sufficiently to prolong his life for them, and obstinately persists in dying, is too squeamish and lax in his love. The soul must command itself to do this, when it is requisite to serve our dear ones. We must sometimes lend ourselves to our friends, and, when we would rather die for our own sake, renounce our intention for theirs. It is evidence of a great heart to return to life out of consideration for others, as many eminent men have done. And it is a sign of a singular good nature to preserve old age (the greatest advantage of which is that it makes us less solicitous about prolonging it, and more courageous and disdainful in the conduct of life), if we feel we are doing some sweet, agreeable, and profitable service to one to whom we are very dear. And we reap a very pleasant reward; for what is sweeter than to be so dear to your wife that for her sake you become dearer to yourself? So my Paulina has charged me not only with her fear, but also with my own. It was not enough for me to consider with how much fortitude I might die, but I have also considered with how little fortitude she might bear my death. I have forced myself to live, and to live is sometimes the mark of a great soul.'

Those are his words, excellent as they always are.

CHAPTER 36

OF THE GREATEST MEN

IF I were asked to make a selection from among all the men who have come to my knowledge, I think I could pick out three who excel all the rest.

The first is Homer. Not but that Aristotle or Varro (for instance) was perhaps as learned as he, and that possibly in his art itself Virgil may be compared with him. I leave that question to be decided by those who know them both.

Knowing only one of them, I can say only this, that as far as my range goes I do not think that the Muses themselves could outstrip the Roman:

> So sweetly to his tuneful lyre he sings;
> His only rival is the Cynthian God. (PROPERTIUS.)

We must not forget, however, in judging him, that it is chiefly from Homer that Virgil derives his inspiration, that he was his guide and schoolmaster,[1] and that a single incident in the Iliad provided both body and matter for that great and divine *Aeneid*. That does not come into my reckoning; I bring in several other circumstances which make this man a source of wonder to me, and almost above human conditions. And in truth I often wonder that he who introduced many gods into the world and by his authority brought them to honour, did not himself gain the rank of a god. Being blind and poor, living before the sciences were reduced to rules by certain observations, he knew them so well, that all who have since taken upon them to set up governments, to conduct wars, and to write either on religion and philosophy, of whatever sect or school, or on the arts, have made use of him as of a very perfect master in the knowledge of all things, and of his books as of a nursery of every kind of excellence:

> Whose rich and storied page
> Better than Crantor or Chrysippus sage
> Shows what is base, what noble, to man's lot
> What is of true advantage, and what not; (HORACE.)

and, as another says,

> From whose perennial spring the poet sips,
> And in Pierian waters wets his lips; (OVID.)

and another,

> 'Mid comrades of the Heliconian maids
> The peerless Homer holds his sceptre high; (LUCRETIUS.)

and another,

> From whose full-flowing lips, all later poets
> Have filched their lines, and turned the mighty stream,
> Sole source of eloquence, into their little
> Rivulets. (MANILIUS.)

---

[1] *Tu duca, tu signor, et tu maestro*, in the words of Dante saluting Virgil in Hell.

His creation of the most excellent work it was possible to produce was against the order of Nature. For ordinarily things are born in an imperfect condition; they increase, and gather strength in their growth. In him, the infancy of poetry and several other sciences is mature, perfect, and accomplished. For this reason he may be called the first and last of the poets, in accordance with that noble testimony which antiquity has left us of him, 'that, as there was no one before him whom he could imitate, so there has been none since who could imitate him'. His words, according to Aristotle, are the only words that have movement and action; they are the only substantial words.

Alexander the Great, having lighted upon a rich casket among the spoils of Darius, commanded it to be kept for him as a receptacle for his Homer, saying that ' he was the best and most faithful counsellor he had in military matters'. For the same reason Cleomenes, son of Anaxandridas, said that ' he was the poet of the Lacedemonians, because he was a very good master for the teaching of warfare'. This singular and remarkable eulogy has also been bestowed upon him by Plutarch, ' that he was the only author in the world who never cloys the appetite, appearing ever new to the reader, and ever blooming with a new charm.' That madcap Alcibiades, having asked one who professed to be a man of letters for a book of Homer, gave him a box on the ear because he had none; as who should find that one of our priests was without a breviary.

Xenophanes one day lamented before Hiero, Tyrant of Syracuse, his being so poor that he had not enough to feed two slaves. ' What! he replied, Homer, who was much poorer than you, can feed more than ten thousand, dead though he be.'

What more could Panaetius say of Plato than to call him the ' Homer of Philosophers ' ?

Besides, what fame can be compared to his ? There is nothing that will live so long on men's lips as his name and his works; nothing will ever be better known or more acceptable than Troy, Helen, and his wars, which perhaps never took place. Our children are still called by the names he invented more than three thousand years ago. Who does not know a Hector or an Achilles ? Not only a few individual families, but most of the nations seek their origin in his fictions. Mahomet, the second of that name, Emperor of the Turks, writing to our Pope Pius the Second, says, 'I wonder that the Italians should league themselves against me, seeing that we have our common origin in the Trojans, and that I, as well as they, have an interest in avenging the blood of Hector on the Greeks, whom they are backing up in opposition to me.' Is it not a noble drama in which kings, commonwealths, and emperors have been playing their parts for so many centuries, and for which all this great world has been the stage? Seven Greek cities disputed the honour of being his birthplace; so much honour did his very obscurity bring him!

Smyrna, Rhodos, Colophon, Salamis, Chios, Argos, Athenae.[1]

The second is Alexander the Great. For, if we consider the early age at which he commenced his career; the small means with which he carried out his glorious designs; the authority which he gained in his boyhood among the greatest and most experienced captains in the world, whom he led; the extraordinary favour with which Fortune embraced and seconded many of his hazardous, I might almost say foolhardy, exploits;

> He bore down all that his high aims withstood,
> And joyed to force a way across the ruins; (LUCAN.)

his greatness in having, at the age of thirty-three, victoriously traversed the whole of the habitable globe, and in having, in half a lifetime, attained to the utmost that human nature is capable of, so that you cannot imagine his full term of life, and the continuation of his growth in valour and fortune until a ripe age, without imagining something superhuman; in having made so many lines of kings to spring from his soldiers, leaving the world after his death allotted among four successors, mere captains in his army, whose descendants have so long remained in possession of that great inheritance.

If we consider his many great virtues, justice, temperance, liberality, integrity in keeping his word, love for his men, humanity to the vanquished; for his character appears to have been indeed above just reproach, although some of his individual actions were uncommon and extraordinary. But

[1] Aulus Gellius. The names are so arranged as to form a hexameter line.

A EULOGY

it is impossible to conduct such great movements according to the rules of justice ; such men as he need to be weighed in the gross, with an eye to the chief end of their actions. The destruction of Thebes [and Persepolis], the murder of Menander and Hephaestion's physician, of so many Persian prisoners at one time, of a troop of Indian soldiers, not without prejudice to his good faith, of the Cosseians, even their little children ; these are outstanding excesses which can hardly be condoned. For, with regard to Clytus, he made amends for his mistake beyond its weight ; and this action, as much as any other, is evidence of the mildness of his disposition : it shows a nature in itself eminently formed for goodness, and it was wittily said of him ' that Nature gave him his virtues, and Fortune his vices '.

As to his being rather boastful, a little too impatient of hearing himself spoken ill of, and with regard to the mangers, weapons, and bridles that he had scattered about the Indies,[1] all these things, it seems to me, may be excused in consideration of his age and the remarkable prosperity of his fortunes.

If we consider withal his many military qualities, his diligence, foresight, patience, discipline, subtlety, magnanimity, resolution, and his good fortune, wherein, even though we had not Hannibal's authority for saying so, he was the first of men ; the uncommon beauty and symmetry of his person, which amounted to the marvellous ; his carriage and imposing mien, in a face so young, ruddy, and radiant :

> As when the dawn-star, washed in Ocean's wave,
> Dearer to Venus than all stellar fires,
> Uplifts in heaven his sacred head and melts
> The darkness ; (VIRGIL.)

his eminent learning and abilities ; his great and enduring fame, pure and untainted, free from blemish and envy ; and the fact besides, that long after his death it was religiously believed that his medallions were lucky to those who wore them, and that more kings and princes have written of his exploits than other historians have written of the exploits of any other king or prince whatever ; and

---

[1] ' He contrived many ingenious devices to impress the natives, as, e. g., he caused arms, bridles and mangers for horses to be made of much more than the usual size, and left them scattered about.'—PLUTARCH.

that to this day the Mahommedans, who despise all other histories, by a special privilege accept and honour his alone.

Considering all these things together, I think it will be admitted that I am right in putting him even before Caesar, who alone could have made me doubtful of my choice. And it cannot be denied that there was more of his own in Caesar's exploits, and more of Fortune's in Alexander's. In many things they were equal, and Caesar perhaps had some greater qualities.

They were two fires, or two torrents, that ravaged the world by several ways:

> Lo, as fierce flames drive in from left to right
> Through woodlands parched and groves of crackling bay;
> As sweep impetuous from a mountain height
> Loud, foaming torrents, that withouten stay
> Cleave to the sea their devastating way. (VIRGIL.)

But, though Caesar's ambition might have been of its nature more moderate, it was so unfortunate in having for its abominable object the ruin of his country and the humiliation of the world in general, that, all things raked together and placed in the scales, I cannot but incline to the side of Alexander.

The third and, to my mind, the greatest, is Epaminondas.

Of fame he has not nearly so much as others (which, for that matter, is not a part of the substance of the thing). Of fortitude and valour, I mean, not that which is whetted by ambition, but that which wisdom and reason may implant in a well-ordered soul, he had as much as it is possible to imagine. Of this particular virtue of his he has, in my opinion, given as many proofs as Alexander himself, and as Caesar. For, although his warlike exploits were not so frequent, nor on so large a scale, they were nevertheless, if duly considered with all their surrounding circumstances, as important and as stoutly carried out, and bear evidence of as much bravery and military genius.

The Greeks have done him the honour, which has not been disputed, to call him the first man of their nation; but to be the first man in Greece is to be an easy first in the world.

With regard to his knowledge and abilities, this estimate of the ancients has come down to us, 'that no man ever knew so much and spoke so little as he.' For he was by sect a Pythagorean. And what he said no man ever said better. An excellent and very persuasive speaker.

But in character and conscience he surpassed by a very long distance all who have ever undertaken the management of affairs. For in this respect, which ought to be considered in the first place, which alone really shows what we are, and which alone I place in the scales against all other things together, he yields to no philosopher, not even to Socrates. In him blamelessness is a natural, dominating, constant, uniform, incorruptible quality, in comparison with which it appears in Alexander subordinate, uncertain, capricious, sentimental, and accidental.

The ancients thought that if you minutely analyse all the other great generals, you will find in each some special quality that makes him illustrious. In Epaminondas alone we see a virtue and excellence everywhere the same and complete, which in all offices of human life leave nothing to be desired, whether in public or private employment, in peace or war, whether in living or in dying greatly and gloriously. I know of no man whom for his personal qualities and his career I look upon with so much love and honour.

It is certainly true that I consider his persistence in poverty, as described by his best friends, as rather too scrupulous. This attitude alone, though lofty and very worthy of admiration, appears to me a little too acid to make me even desire to imitate it [in the same degree].

Scipio Emilianus alone, if we could give him as sublime and magnificent an end, as deep and comprehensive a knowledge and learning, could make me doubtful about the choice. O, what an ill turn Time has done me in withholding from our eyes, at the very time when they are most needed, and among the first, the Lives of this pair of men, precisely the most noble pair in Plutarch, and by common agreement of the world, one the first of the Greeks, the other of the Romans! What a subject! What a craftsman![1]

For a man who was no saint, but rather a man of the world, of average social habits and moderate eminence, the richest life I know of to have been lived among the living, as they say, and stored with more rich and desirable parts

---

[1] It appears that Epaminondas was Plutarch's favourite hero, as he was Montaigne's. His parallel lives of the two men are lost.

than any, was, everything considered, to my mind, that of Alcibiades.

But with regard to Epaminondas, to exemplify his exceeding goodness, I will add here some of his opinions.

He declared that the sweetest satisfaction he had had in all his life was the pleasure he gave his father and mother by his victory at Leuctra. It is saying a great deal that he thought more of their pleasure than of his own, so full and so just, in so glorious an action.

He did not regard it as permissible, even to recover the freedom of his country, to kill a man without just cause. For that reason he was so lukewarm towards the enterprise of his companion Pelopidas, for the relief of Thebes.

He also maintained 'that in battle we should avoid encountering a friend who was on the opposite side, and we should spare him'.

And his humanity, even towards the enemy, having made him suspected by the Boeotians, because, after miraculously forcing the Lacedemonians to open the pass to him which they had attempted to defend at the entrance to the Morea, near Corinth, he contented himself with charging through them without pursuing them to the death, he was deposed from the rank of commander-in-chief: very honourably upon such an account, and for the shame it was to them to be obliged soon after to restore him to his place of honour, and to acknowledge how much their glory and safety depended upon him; victory attending him like his shadow wherever he led. The prosperity of his country died, as it was born, with him.

CHAPTER 37

OF THE RESEMBLANCE OF CHILDREN TO THEIR FATHERS [1]

IN making up this bundle of so many diverse pieces, I never set my hand to it unless driven by an idleness that has become unbearable, and nowhere but at home. So it has built itself up with divers intervals and interruptions, which vary according to my occasional absences, sometimes for months together.

For the rest, I do not correct my first impressions by my

[1] Or, as we should say, Heredity.

second, except perhaps a word or two ; but only to vary the phrase, not to expunge. My intention is to show the progress of my opinions, and that each part may be seen in its original state. I should like to have begun earlier, that I might follow the course of my changes. A valet whom I employed to write at my dictation thought he had made a rich booty by filching several of my essays, chosen according to his liking. I am consoled by the thought that he will gain no more than I lose.

I have grown older by seven or eight years since I began ; not without some new acquisitions. These years have been so generous as to make me familiarized with the stone in the bladder. A long intercourse and acquaintance with Time is not often made without some such fruit. I could have wished that, of the many gifts he has in store for those who have long known him, he had chosen a more acceptable one. For he could not have selected one of which I have had a greater horror since my childhood. Of all the misfortunes of old age it is just the one I dreaded most. Many a time have I thought to myself that I was travelling too far, and that in thus prolonging my journey I should not fail in the end to be involved in some unpleasant adventure. Often enough I felt and protested, That it was time to depart, and that life ought to be cut short when sound and healthy, following the rule of the surgeons when they have to amputate a limb ; That of the man who did not pay in good time Nature was wont to exact a very stiff usury.

But those were idle speculations. So far was I from being ready at the time that in the eighteen months or thereabouts that I have been in this disagreeable plight I have already learned to put up with it. I am already compounding with this colicky existence. I am finding a source of comfort and hope in it. Men are so accustomed to hug their miserable existence, that no state is so wretched that they will not accept it, provided they live.

Listen to Maecenas :

> Though I be lame in hand and foot,
> Though every tooth in my head be loose,
> So long as life remains, 'tis well. (cited by SENECA.)

And Tamerlane cloaked under a foolish kind of humanity the fantastic cruelty which he exercised upon the lepers, by putting to death all he heard of, ' to deliver them, as he said, from the painful life they were living '. For there was not one among them who would not rather have been a leper three times over than not to live.

And Antisthenes the Stoic being very ill and calling out, ' Who will deliver me from these evils ? ' Diogenes, who had come to see him, offered him a knife, saying, ' This, if you mean it, and that very quickly.' ' I do not mean life, he replied, I mean my evils.'

The sufferings that merely affect us through the soul afflict me much less than they do most others. Partly by estimation, for the world deems many things to be dreadful, or avoidable at the cost of life, which to me are wellnigh a matter of indifference. Partly from a dull insensibility to accidents which do not hit me point-blank; and that insensibility I regard as one of the best parts of my nature. But bodily and really essential sufferings I feel very acutely. And yet, when formerly I dimly foresaw them, with a sight enfeebled and mollified by the enjoyment of the happy and prolonged health and repose that God had given me, for the best part of my life, I conceived them in imagination to be so unbearable that in truth my fear of them was greater than my present suffering. Wherefore I am ever more confirmed in this belief, that most of the faculties of the soul, as we exercise them, disturb the peace of life more than they promote it.

I am at grips with the worst, the most sudden, the most painful, the most fatal and most irremediable of all diseases. I have already experienced five or six very long and painful attacks of it. And yet, unless I flatter myself, even in this condition there is something endurable for a man whose soul is free from the fear of death, and free from the menaces, conclusions, and consequences which the doctors keep dinning into our ears. But the pain itself is not so violent, so sharp and piercing, as to drive a sober-minded man to rage and despair. I derive at least this advantage from the colic, that it will accomplish what I had not hitherto been able to bring myself to do, that is, to become wholly reconciled and familiarized with death. For, the more it oppresses and troubles me, the less shall I fear to die. I had already gained this much, that I was attached to life only for the sake of life; my pain will dissolve also this idea

And God grant that, if its violence exceeds my powers, it will not in the end drive me to the other, and not less wicked extreme, to love and desire death!

> Pray not for death, but feel no fear
> When the last hour of life draws near. (MARTIAL.)

Those are two feelings to be dreaded, but the one has its remedy much more ready to hand than the other.

Moreover, I have always regarded as affectation that precept that so sternly and precisely tells us to put on a good face, a disdainful and indifferent mien, when suffering pain. Why does Philosophy, who is concerned only with what is vital and effective, waste her time over these external appearances?[1] Let her leave that charge to actors and teachers of rhetoric, who set so great a value on our gestures. Let her boldly condone this cowardice of the vocal organs, and lay the blame on the pain, as long as it does not come from the heart or the seat of the passions; let her place those voluntary lamentations in the same category with sighs, sobs, palpitations, pallors, which Nature has put beyond our control. As long as the heart shows no fear, words no despair, let her rest content! What matter whether we wring our hands, as long as we do not wring our thoughts? She trains us for ourselves, not for others; to be, not to seem. Let her stop short at governing our understanding, which she has taken upon herself to instruct. During the attacks of the colic let her keep our minds capable of self-control, and of going their accustomed way, combating and subduing pain, and not shamefully grovelling at its feet; excited and heated, not

---

[1] The earlier editions had this passage in place of what follows: As if she were training men for the acts of a comedy, or as if it were within her jurisdiction to hinder the movements and alterations which we are by Nature forced to accept. Let her then prevent Socrates from blushing with shame or emotion, from winking his eyes when threatened by a blow, from shaking and sweating in a fever. The painting of Poetry, which is free and does what it pleases, dares not forbid even tears in the persons she wishes to represent as perfect and accomplished:

> Who are so pained,
> They bite their hands, they bite their lips,
> Bedew their cheeks with plenteous tears. (ARIOSTO.)

They should leave this charge to those who make a profession of regulating our expressions and demeanour.

subdued and overthrown, in the struggle ; able, to a certain degree, to converse and communicate with others.

In so extreme a calamity it is cruelty to expect so composed a bearing. If we play the game it is no great matter that we make a wry face. If the body finds a relief in lamenting, let it lament. If agitation pleases it, let it tumble and toss at its pleasure. If by raising the voice with greater violence the pain appears to evaporate a little (as some physicians say that it helps a woman in child-birth), or if it distracts its anguish, let it shout at the top of its voice. We need not command our voice to shout, but let us not forbid it. Epicurus not only permits his sage to shout in pain, but he advises it. *Even the pugilists groan when they strike with the cestus, because in throwing out the voice the whole body is on the stretch, and the blow is driven home with greater force* (Cicero). We have enough to do to contend with the evil, without labouring over these superfluous rules.

I have said all this in excuse of those we generally see raging and storming under the shocks and attacks of this disease. For my part I have hitherto suffered them a little more patiently [and I stop short at groaning, without braying]. Not, however, that I put any great constraint upon myself to maintain this seemly exterior, for I make little account of such an advantage. In this respect I yield to the pain as much as it requires ; but either my pangs are not so excessive, or I bring more fortitude to them than the average man. I moan, I fret and fume when I am in the throes of a sharp attack, but I never yield to despair, like this man :

> Whose groans, bewailings, and whose bitter cries
> With grief incessant rend the very skies.
> (ATTIUS, quoted by Cicero.)

I watch myself in the thick of the onslaught, and I have always found that I was capable of speaking, thinking, and answering as sanely as at any other time, but not so consistently, the pain disturbing and distracting my thoughts. When those present think I am most stricken, and refrain from troubling me, I often test my powers, and myself broach a subject most remote from my condition. I can do anything by a sudden effort, but it must not continue long.

O why have I not the faculty of that dreamer in Cicero, who, dreaming he was embracing a young girl, found that he had discharged his stone in the sheets! Mine strangely diswenches me!

In the intervals of excessive pain, when my ureters languish without stinging so sharply, I immediately return to my normal condition;[1] since it is only my body and senses that have been alarmed, and not my soul. And this I certainly owe to the care with which, with the help of reason, I prepare my mind for such attacks:

> To me no toil strange or unlooked-for comes.
> All things have I forecast, and in my mind
> Traversed ere seen. (VIRGIL.)

Yet I have been rather rudely tried, for a beginner, and with a very sudden and very violent change for the worse, having dropped all at once, from a very easy and very happy state of life, into the most painful and uneasy that can be imagined. For, besides that it is a disease that is in itself greatly to be dreaded, its beginnings have been much ruder and harder in me than they are wont to be. The attacks recur so frequently that I hardly ever feel in perfect health. Yet I have hitherto kept myself in such good spirits that, so long as they continue so, I am in rather better condition of life than a thousand others, who have neither fever nor any other infirmity except those that, for lack of judgement, they bring upon themselves.

There is a certain kind of subtle humility, which is born of presumption, as for instance, this, That we confess our ignorance in some things, and are so polite as to admit that there are, in the works of Nature, certain properties and conditions that we do not perceive, the means and causes of which we are unable to discover. By this honest and conscientious declaration we hope to gain the advantage of being believed in respect of those things we say we do understand. We have no need to go and sift miracles and things that appear strange and obscure; it appears to me that among the things we commonly see there are some so strange and incomprehensible that they surpass all the mysteries of miracles.

---

[1] The earlier editions add: I talk, I laugh, I study, without emotion or alteration.

What a wonderful thing it is that that drop of seed, from which we are produced, bears in itself the impressions, not only of the bodily shape, but of the thoughts and inclinations of our fathers ! Where can that drop of fluid harbour such an infinite number of forms ? And how do they convey those resemblances, so heedless and irregular in their progress, that the great-grandson shall be like his great-grandfather, the nephew like his uncle ?

In the family of Lepidus, at Rome, there were three, not consecutive but at intervals, who were born with the same eye covered with a cartilage. At Thebes there was a family who from their mothers' womb bore the picture of a lance-head ; and he who was not born so was regarded as illegitimate.[1] Aristotle tells of a certain nation among whom wives were held in common, that they allotted the children to the fathers by their resemblance.

It may be supposed that I owe this stony propensity to my father, for he died grievously tormented with a large stone in the bladder. He was not sensible of his disease until the sixty-seventh year of his age. Before then he had neither menace nor symptom of it, either in his kidneys, sides, or any other part, having lived till that time in a happy state of health, and very little subject to infirmities. He lived another seven years with this malady, dragging out to the end a very painful existence. I was born twenty-five years or more before his disease came on, and during the time of his best state, the third of his children in order of birth.

Where was the propensity to this defect hatching all this time ? And when he was so far from the infirmity, how could that small part of his substance, of which I was constructed, carry for its part so great an impression ? And how did it remain so concealed that I did not begin to be sensible of it until forty-five years after, the only one hitherto among so many brothers and sisters, and all of one mother ? If any man will enlighten me about the course of this mischief, I will believe him in any other miracles he pleases ; provided that he does not put me off with a theory, as they generally do, that is much more obscure and fantastic than the thing itself.

[1] This last touch was evidently imagined by Montaigne, for Plutarch, his authority for the tale, makes no mention of illegitimacy.

MONTAIGNE'S FAMILY HISTORY

I hope the doctors will excuse my freedom a little, for it is by this same fatal infusion and insinuation that I have inherited my hatred and contempt of their science. My antipathy to their art is hereditary. My father lived to be seventy-four, my grandfather sixty-nine, my great-grandfather to nearly eighty, without ever tasting any kind of physic; and with them, whatever was not in ordinary use took the place of a drug.

Medicine is built up on examples and experience; so is my theory.

Is not that a very positive and very serviceable experience? I doubt whether they will find me three on their case-books, who were born and bred, and who died at the same hearth, under the same roof, and lived so long under their directions. They must grant me this, that, if not reason, at least Fortune is on my side. Well, with the physicians, Fortune is stronger than reason. Let them not take me at a disadvantage, let them not threaten me, prostrate as I am at this moment; that would be foul play. Besides, to tell the truth, I have gained sufficient advantage over them by my family examples, although they stop there. In human affairs there is not usually so much constancy.

This experience of ours has endured for two centuries, wanting but eighteen years; for the first of them was born in the year 1402. It is indeed but reasonable that this experience should begin to fail us. They cannot now upbraid me for the calamity that has now seized me by the throat; is it not enough for me to have lived in good health for forty-seven years? Though it should be the end of my career, it is one of the longest.

My ancestors, by some natural and mysterious instinct, loathed physic; for my father was horrified at the very sight of drugs. The Seigneur de Gaviac, my uncle on the father's side, an ecclesiastic, who was delicate from his birth and yet made his sickly life hold for sixty-seven years, having once been taken with a violent and dangerous continued fever, the doctors ordered him to be plainly told that unless he called in their aid (they call Aid what is more often Hindrance), he would infallibly be a dead man. The good man, terrified though he was by that dreadful sentence, replied, 'Then I am a dead man.' But God soon after falsified the prognostic.

The last of the brothers (there were four of them), the Sieur de Bussaguet, and the last by many years, alone submitted himself to their art, by reason, I think, of his connexion with the other arts, for he was a Councillor in the Court of Parliament; but with so little success that, although he seemed to be of a stronger constitution, he died long before the others, with the exception of one, the Sieur de Saint-Michel.

It may be that I have inherited from them this natural antipathy to medicine; but if that was the only reason, I should have tried to overcome it. For all those unreasonable prejudices we are born with are unsound; they are a kind of disease we must combat. It may be that I had this propensity, but I have supported and fortified it by arguments, which have confirmed me in my opinions. For I also hate that idea of rejecting medicine on account of its bitter taste. That would hardly be in accordance with my mental attitude, since I hold health to be worth purchasing at the price of all the most painful cauteries and incisions that can be applied.

And I agree with Epicurus when he says that sensual pleasures are to be shunned if they are succeeded by greater pains, and that those pains are to be sought that are followed by greater pleasures.

Health is a precious thing, the only thing indeed that deserves to be pursued at the expense not only of time, sweat, labour, worldly goods, but of life itself; since without it life becomes a burden and an affliction. Without it, pleasures, wisdom, knowledge, and virtue lose their colour and fade away; and to the most forcible and laboured arguments that Philosophy would impress upon us to the contrary, we have but to oppose the idea of Plato stricken with the falling sickness or an apoplexy, and, on this supposition, challenge him to call to his aid the rich and noble faculties of his mind. To my mind no way that leads us to health can be rugged, no means dearly bought.

But I have several other ways of looking at it, which make me strangely distrustful of all that lumber. I do not deny that there may be some art in it; that there are, among the many works of Nature, things proper for the preservation of our health; that is certain. I know well that there are certain simples that moisten, certain others that dry up ; I know by experience both that horse-radish induces flatulence, and that senna-leaves relax the bowels. I have several other experiences of the same kind, as I know that mutton nourishes and wine heats me ; and Solon said, 'that eating, like the other drugs, is a physic against the disease of hunger'. I do not deny the use we derive from the things of this world, nor do I doubt the power and fecundity of Nature, and that it may be applied to our needs. I can clearly see that pikes and swallows are well off under her protection.

I distrust the inventions of our mind, of our learning and art, for whose sake we have abandoned Nature and her rules, and are unable to keep within the bounds of moderation.

As we call Justice the fortuitous hotch-potch of the first laws that come to hand, and the practical dispensing of them, which is often very foolish and unjust ; and as they who ridicule and condemn the application of them have no intention of disparaging that noble virtue, but only condemn the abuse and profanation of that sacred name, so, in medicine, I indeed honour that glorious name, its intentions, its promises, so useful to the human race ; but, as it is understood with us, I neither honour nor esteem it.

In the first place experience makes me dread it ; for there is no sort of people, as far as my knowledge of them goes, who are so liable to fall ill, and take so long to cure, as those who are under the thumb of medicine. Their very health is impaired and undermined by the constraint of diet. The doctors are not content with dominating sickness ; they make health sickly, to guard against their patients' ever escaping from their authority. Do they not argue that perfect and continuous good health means a great sickness in the future ?

I have been ill pretty often, and without their help my illnesses (and I have experienced nearly every kind) have been as easy to bear and as short as those of any other person ; and yet I have never interfered with them by taking their bitter prescriptions. My health, when I have it, is full and free, without any rules, and without any other schooling than that of my habits and my pleasure. Any place suits me to stay in, for I need no other comforts when ill than those I need when I am well. I am not frightened at the idea of being without a physician, apothecary, and medical aid, which to most men is a greater affliction than the illness. What! do the doctors themselves give any evidence, by living longer and happier, of any manifest effect of their skill?

There is no nation that has not existed many centuries without medicine, and those the first ages, that is to say, the best and happiest. And to this day a tenth part of the world has no use for it. There is a vast number of people who have no knowledge of it, and they live longer and in better health than they do here. And with us the common people can happily dispense with it. The Romans had existed six hundred years before they received it; but after making trial of it they drove it from their city at the instance of Cato the Censor, who demonstrated how easily he could do without it, having lived for eighty-five years and kept his wife alive to an extreme old age, not indeed without physic, but certainly without a physician. For everything we find conducive to a healthy life may be called physic.

He kept his family in health, it seems, according to Plutarch, by the use of hare;[1] as the Arcadians, according to Pliny, cured all maladies with cows' milk. And the Libyans, says Herodotus, generally enjoy an uncommon good health by observing this custom that, when their children have reached the age of four, they cauterize and burn the veins of the head and temples, by which means they cut off all the defluxions of rheum for their whole lives.

And the villagers of this neighbourhood, for all emergencies, use only the strongest wine they can procure, mixed with plenty of saffron and spice; all this with a like result.

And, to tell the truth, what after all is the end and result of all this diversity and confusion of prescriptions but to void the bowels, which a thousand household simples will do? And yet I do not know that this is so beneficial as they declare, and that our nature does not require that the excrements should remain for a certain part, as do the lees

---

[1] I quote, without comment, the passage from Plutarch: He himself had a book full of recipes, according to which he used to physic and regulate the diet of any who fell sick in his house, being careful never to allow the patient to fast, but making him eat salad, with ducks, pigeons and hares, which he said were light food and suitable for sick persons, except that it often happened that those who ate of them suffered from nightmare.

of wine for its preservation.[1] You often see healthy people, through some strange accident, taken with a sudden attack of vomiting and diarrhoea, attended with a copious evacuation of the bowels, without any preceding need and without any succeeding benefit, but rather feeling much the worse for it.

It was from the great Plato that I lately learned that of three kinds of motions that are natural to us, the last and worst is a purge, and that no man who is not a fool ought to undergo it except in the extremest necessity. We disturb and irritate the evil by contrary oppositions. It should be gradually diminished and brought to an end by our manner of living. The violent gripings caused by the drug and the illness are always to our prejudice, since the two fight it out in our bodies, and the drug is an unreliable aid, naturally inimical to our health, and having no access in our domain except through disturbance.

Let us leave things to go their own way. The Order which takes care of fleas and moles will also take care of men, if they have the same patience to allow themselves to be governed as fleas and moles. In vain do we shout ' Gee up ' ; we shall only make ourselves hoarse and not advance a step. That Order is proud and pitiless. Our fear and despair disgust her and keep her from coming to our relief, instead of inviting her. She owes it to the malady, as well as to health, to let it take its course. She will not allow herself to be bribed in favour of the one, to the prejudice of the other's rights ; that would mean disorder. Let us follow, in God's name, let us follow ! She guides those who follow ; those who will not follow she will drag along together with their fury and their physic. Get a purge prescribed for your brain ; it will be better employed than in your stomach.

A Lacedemonian was asked what had made him live so long in good health : ' Ignorance of medicine,' he replied. And the Emperor Hadrian kept exclaiming on his death-bed, ' that the crowd of doctors had killed him '. A poor wrestler took up medicine. ' Bravo, said Diogenes, you are right ; you can now throw those who once threw you.'

But they have this good fortune, according to Nicocles,

---

[1] This is of course rank heresy to the Faculty ; but after nearly seventy years' experience of life the translator has come to the conclusion that there is at least something in what Montaigne says.

that ' the sun shines on their successes, and the earth hides their failures '. And besides, they have a very useful knack of taking advantage of all kinds of happenings ; for it is the privilege of the Faculty to take the credit for the good and salutary things that Fortune or Nature, or some other extraneous cause (and there is an endless number of them) produces in us. All the happy effects that the patient feels, who is under their care, is due to them. The causes which have cured me, which cure a thousand others who do not call in the doctors, they usurp in the case of their subjects.

When an unfortunate accident occurs, either they will disclaim all responsibility, and lay the blame on the patient ; and they take care never to be at a loss for any number of frivolous reasons, such as, ' he must have left his arm uncovered ; he has heard the rattling of a coach,

> The wagons crossing in the narrow streets ; (JUVENAL.)

somebody has opened the window ; he has been lying on his left side ; he has been thinking of something painful '. In short, a word, a look, a dream, appear to them a safe excuse for shifting the blame.

Or, if they so please, they will even take advantage of this relapse and turn it to their account, by this other trick which can never fail them : When the disease has become aggravated by their applications, they put us off with the assurance that it would have been very much worse but for their remedies. If they have precipitated them out of a chill into a quotidian fever, ' he might have had a continued fever, but for me '. There is no risk of their doing their business badly, since the loss turns to their profit. In truth they are right to require their patients to place an implicit trust in them ; and it must indeed be a really very compliant trust that will believe things so hard to swallow.

Plato said very appropriately that Physicians were the only men that might lie in all freedom, since our health depends on the falsity and emptiness of their promises.

Aesop, an author of most rare excellence, of whom few people discover all the charm, humorously illustrates the tyrannical authority which they usurp over poor souls enfeebled and cast down by sickness and fear. He tells of a doctor questioning his patient about the operation of his physic. ' I have been sweating a great deal.' ' That 's good,' said the doctor. Another time, when he asked him how he felt after his medicine, he said, ' I have been very cold and shivery.' ' That's very good,' said the doctor. He asked him a third time how he was. ' I am all swollen and puffed up, as if I had dropsy.' ' That's splendid ! ' said the doctor. One of his friends presently coming to inquire after his condition : ' Really, my friend, I am getting on so well that I am on the point of death.'

In Egypt they had a juster law, which compelled the physician to take a patient under his care, for the first three days, at the latter's risk and chance ; when the three days were over, it was at his own risk. For why was Aesculapius, their patron, struck by a thunderbolt for having brought the dead Helen [1] back to life :

> Then, wroth that mortal should from shades of hell
> Rise to the light of life, the Almighty Sire
> With his own levin-bolt to Stygian wave
> Thrust down the finder of such craft and cure,
> The Phoebus-born ; (VIRGIL.)

when his followers are absolved, who dispatch so many living souls to death ?

A physician was boasting to Nicocles of the great authority of his art. ' It must be so indeed, said Nicocles, when it can kill so many people with impunity.'

For the rest, if they had consulted me, they would have enveloped their art in more sanctity and mystery. They began well enough, but they did not end as well. It was a good beginning to make gods and demons the originators of their science, to adopt a language of their own, and a writing of their own ; although Philosophy may think that it is folly to advise a man for his good by a way that is unintelligible. *As if a physician should order his patient to take ' an earth-born, grass-crawling, house-bearing, bloodless creature '* [2] (Cicero).

It was a good rule of their art, and one that accompanies all fantastic, empty, and supernatural arts, that the patient's faith must anticipate, by good hope and confidence, the

---

[1] The editions published after 1588 substitute Hippolytus, who was brought back to life at the request of Diana. According to another account, Aesculapius was killed by Zeus at the bidding of Pluto, who found that the inhabitants of Hades were dwindling.

[2] i.e. a decoction of snails.

efficacity of their treatment. And they cling so firmly to this rule that they regard the most ignorant and incompetent doctor as more fit to treat one who has confidence in him, than the most experienced, if he is a stranger.

Even the choice of most of their drugs is in some sort mysterious and divine : the left foot of a tortoise, the urine of a lizard, an elephant's dung, a mole's liver, blood drawn from under the right wing of a white pigeon ; and for us who have the stone (so scornfully do they take advantage of our misery !), the pulverized droppings of a rat, and other such tomfooleries that are more suggestive of magic and spells than of a serious science. Not to mention their pills, to be taken in uneven numbers, the setting apart of certain days and festivals in the year, of certain hours for gathering the herbs of their ingredients, the grim scowl, the wise and learned looks and demeanour which they put on, and which even Pliny remarked upon with derision.

But what I mean to say is that, having made so good a beginning, they were wrong in not making their meetings and consultations more mysterious and secret. No profane person should be admitted to them, any more than to the secret ceremonies of Aesculapius. The result of this error is that their irresolution, the weakness of their arguments, their guesses and grounds, the fierceness of their disputes, revealing nothing but hatred, jealousy, and self-consideration, coming to the knowledge of all the world, a man must be marvellously blind not to see that he runs great risks at their hands.

Who ever heard of a doctor using a colleague's prescription without taking something from, or adding something to it ? Thereby they sufficiently betray their practice, and make it plain to us that they consider their reputation, and consequently their profit, more than their patient's interests.

He was a wiser physician who in ancient times laid down the rule that only one doctor should undertake to treat a patient ; for, if he does no good, the failure of a single man cannot be a very great reproach to the medical faculty. And, on the other hand, if he happens to make a lucky guess, his glory will be the greater. Whilst if there are many of them, they bring the profession into disrepute at every turn, since they more frequently do harm than good.

They ought to be satisfied with the perpetual discord we

find in the theories of the chief masters and the ancient writers on this science, which is known only to people who are well read in books, without betraying to the people the controversies and inconsistencies of judgement which they still keep alive among themselves.

Would you like an example of the ancient controversy in medicine ?

Herophilus places the original cause of diseases in the humours ;

Erasistratus, in the blood of the arteries ;

Asclepiades, in the invisible atoms gliding through our pores ;

Alcmaeon, in the exuberance or deficiency of the bodily powers ;

Diocles, in the inequality of the elements of the body, and in the quality of the air we breathe ;

Strato, in the abundance, crudity, and corruption of the food we take ; and

Hippocrates lodges it in the spirits.

There is a friend of theirs, whom they know better than I, who exclaims in this connexion, ' That the most important science we practise, as having charge of our health and preservation, is unfortunately the most uncertain and most confused, and is more disturbed by changes than any other.' [1]

There is no great danger in miscalculating the height of the sun or the fraction of some astronomical computation ; but here, where our whole being is at stake, it is not a mark of wisdom to abandon ourselves to the mercy of so many winds blowing from different quarters.

Before the Peloponnesian war not much was heard of this science. Hippocrates brought it into repute. All that he established Chrysippus overthrew. After him, Erasistratus, Aristotle's grandson, overthrew all that Chrysippus had written about it. After them appeared the Empirics, who adopted quite a different method from that of their predecessors in their practice of the art. When the credit of these latter began to grow stale, Herophilus set another sort of practice on foot, which Asclepiades in his turn combated and annihilated. By turns the theories of Themison gained authority, then Musa's, and after them those of Vectius

[1] Pliny.

Valens, a physician who became famous through his intimacy with Messalina. In Nero's time the empire of medicine fell into the hands of Thessalus, who condemned and abolished all that had been accepted before him. The latter's theories were upset by Crinas of Marseilles, who reintroduced the practice of regulating all medicinal operations by the Ephemerides, and motions of the stars; of eating, drinking, and sleeping at such times as were pleasing to the Moon and Mercury. His authority was soon after supplanted by Charinus, a physician of the same city of Marseilles. This man opposed not only the older science of medicine, but also the hot baths which had been generally in use for so many centuries. He made the men bathe in cold water, even in winter, and plunged his patients into the natural water of streams.

Until Pliny's day no Roman had ever deigned to practise medicine; it was in the hands of foreigners and Greeks, as, among us French, it is practised by Latinists.[1] For, as a very great physician has said, we are loath to take the medicine we understand, or the drugs we gather. If those countries from which we import our guaiacum, sarsaparilla, and China root have any physicians, we may imagine, if they follow our example of valuing a thing for its strangeness, rarity, and dearness, how greatly they must prize our cabbages and parsley. For who would dare to despise things brought from such a distance, at the risk of so long and perilous a voyage?

Since those ancient changes in medicine there has been an endless number of others even to our days, and for the most part complete and universal changes, like those introduced in our time by Paracelsus, Fioravanti, and Argenterius. For they alter not only a prescription, but, as I am told, the whole disposition and order of the body of physic, accusing all who have professed it hitherto of ignorance and imposture. I leave you to imagine where the poor patient comes in.

If only we were sure, when they make mistakes, that they do us no harm, even if they do us no good, it would be quite a reasonable bargain to risk gaining something, without incurring the danger of losing.

---

[1] Perhaps those who assumed Latin names, like Paracelsus—whose real name was von Hohenheim—or who used a Latin jargon.

A DOCTOR'S CONFESSION

Aesop in one of his Fables tells how a man who had bought a Moorish slave, thinking his colour was accidental and brought on by the ill usage of his former master, had him very carefully medicined with many baths and potions. The result was that the Moor was not a whit cured of his swarthy complexion, but entirely lost his previous good health.

How often we hear the doctors charging one another with the death of their patients! I remember an epidemic disease, of a very dangerous and fatal nature, raging in the towns round about me a few years ago. When the storm, which had swept away an endless number of people, had passed over, one of the most reputed physicians of the whole district published a pamphlet on the subject, in which he changed his mind about the blood-lettings which had been practised, and confessed that that was one of the chief causes of the mortality which ensued. Moreover, the writers of the faculty hold that there is no medicine that does not contain some hurtful ingredients; hence, if those which benefit us also do us some harm, what must those do that are totally misapplied?

For my own part, though there were nothing else to be considered, I am of opinion that for those who loathe the taste of medicine, to force it down at such inconvenient times and with so much aversion, must have a very dangerous and prejudicial effect. And I believe it must try the patient's constitution to an alarming degree at a time when he has so much need of rest. Besides, when we consider the grounds on which they generally diagnose the cause of our maladies, they are so slight and so ticklish that I argue therefrom that a very little error in the dispensing of their drugs may do us a great deal of mischief.

Now, if the doctor's mistake is dangerous, we are in a very bad way; for it is very unlikely but he will often fall into the same error. He has too many details and circumstances to consider before deciding upon his treatment: he should know his patient's constitution, his temperament, his humours, his inclinations, his actions, even his thoughts and ideas. He must make sure of external circumstances, of the nature of the place, of the atmospherical and weather conditions, of the position of the planets and their influences. He must know the causes of the disease, the symptoms, the effects, and the critical days.

In the matter of drugs he must know their weight, their strength, the place of their origin, their appearance, their age, and the right way to administer them ; and he must know how all the parts are to be proportioned and related to each other to create a perfect symmetry. Wherein if he makes the slightest error, if there is a single one of these springs that is twisted awry, it is enough to kill us.

Heaven knows how difficult it is to know most of these details ; for how will he discover, for example, the true symptom of the disease, when every disease is capable of showing an infinite number of symptoms ? How often do they not doubt and dispute together about the interpretation of the urine ! Otherwise, why all those continual altercations over the diagnosis of the malady ? How can we excuse the error they so often fall into of taking fox for sable ? In the diseases that I have had, when there was the slightest doubt, I have never found three of them to agree. I am readier to note examples which concern myself.

Recently at Paris a gentleman was operated upon by order of the physicians, and in the bladder they found no more stone than in the palm of his hand. And in the same city a Bishop, with whom I was very friendly, was strongly urged by most of the doctors he consulted to allow himself to be cut ; and I myself helped to persuade him, on the faith of others. When he was dead and opened it was found that he only had kidney trouble. They have less excuse in the case of this malady, since it is in some sort palpable. Hence it appears to me that surgery is much more certain, since it can see and feel what it is doing. There is less conjecture and guess-work ; whereas the physicians have nothing in the way of a vaginal speculum which might enable them to look into our brain, our lungs, and liver.

The very promises of medicine are incredible. For, as they have to provide against different and contrary ills which often afflict us at the same time and are almost necessarily related together, such as inflammation of the liver and a chill on the stomach, they would make us believe that one of the ingredients of the physic will warm the stomach and another cool the liver. One of them has received its orders to proceed directly to the kidneys, nay even to the bladder, without spreading its action elsewhere, and, by its occult property, to preserve its power and virtue on that long journey, fraught with obstacles, until it reaches the place it is intended to benefit. One will dry the brain, another moisten the lungs.

Having made up a potion of all that bundle of ingredients, is it not a kind of delusion to expect that the different virtues will divide and sort themselves from out that mixture and confusion, to hasten on their different errands ? I should very much fear that they would lose or exchange their labels, and mistake their quarters. And who can suppose that in this liquid confusion those properties will not corrupt, disturb, and vitiate one another ? To make matters worse, the making up of this prescription is entrusted to another functionary, to whose mercy and good faith we have again to abandon our lives !

As we have our doublet-makers and our breeches-makers to clothe us, and are the better served by them because each of them meddles only with his own province, and his skill is more restricted and concentrated than that of an all-round tailor ; and as, in the matter of food, the nobles, in order to be better served, have distinct functionaries for making their soups and roasting their meats, which a cook who takes the whole charge could not succeed in doing so perfectly ; so the Egyptians were right to reject this trade of general practitioner, and to break up the profession. To each disease and each part of the body its own workman ; for it was more properly and less confusedly treated when each one was concerned only with his own specialty.

It never occurs to our doctors that he who sees to all sees to nothing ; that the entire government of this little world is beyond their digestion. Whilst they were afraid to arrest the progress of a dysentery, in order not to bring on a fever, they killed me a friend [1] who was better than the whole pack of them put together. They place their own guesses in the scales against the present evils ; and in order not to cure the brain to the prejudice of the stomach, they injure the stomach and make the brain worse by jumbling up their quarrelsome drugs.

With regard to the variety and feebleness of the reasonings of this profession, they are more apparent than in any other :

Aperients are beneficial to a man with the stone, because

[1] Étienne de la Boëtie.

by opening and dilating the passages they help forward the sticky matter of which the gravel and calculi are formed, and convey downward the matter that is beginning to collect and harden in the kidneys.

Aperients are dangerous to a man with the stone, because by opening and dilating the passages they convey the matter that forms the gravel towards the kidneys, which by their nature are apt to seize upon it, so that they must necessarily arrest a great part of that which was carried to them.

Moreover, if there happens to be some body that is a little too big to pass through all those narrows that still have to be passed in order to be expelled, that body, being stirred up by the aperient and thrown into those narrow channels, will stop them up and bring on a certain and very painful death.

Their advice with regard to regimen is equally wobbly :

It is a good thing to pass water frequently, for we know by experience that by allowing it to stagnate, the excrements and lees which form the matter of which the stone is built up in the bladder, have time to settle.

It is a good thing not to pass water frequently ; for the heavy excrements it drags along with it will not be carried away without violence, as we see by experience that a swiftly rolling torrent sweeps and cleans the places it passes over much more effectually than a gently flowing and sluggish river.

Similarly, it is a good thing to have frequent intercourse with women, for that opens the passages and carries away the gravel and sand ; it is also very bad, because it inflames, wearies and weakens the kidneys.

It is a good thing to take hot baths, since that relaxes and softens the places where the sand and stone settle ; it is also a bad thing, because the application of external heat assists the kidneys in baking, hardening, and petrifying, the matter there stored up.

For those who are taking the baths it is more wholesome to eat little in the evening, that the waters they have to drink next morning may act more effectually when the stomach is empty and unhampered.

On the other hand it is better to eat little at dinner, in order not to hinder the action of the water, which has not yet had its due effect, and not to overload the stomach so immediately after that other labour, and to leave the duty of digestion to the night, which is more equal to it than the day, when body and mind are in perpetual movement and action.

That is how they go on trifling and juggling with their reasons at our expense. And they cannot provide me with a proposition to which I could not construct a contrary one of equal force.

Let them no longer rail against those who, in their troubles, allow themselves to be gently guided by their appetites and the counsel of Nature, and resign themselves to the common lot.

In the course of my travels I have seen almost all the famed baths in Christendom; and for some years past have begun to make use of them. For I look upon bathing as generally salubrious, and believe that we suffer in health to no small degree through having left off the custom, which was universally observed in former times by almost all nations, and is still observed by many, of washing the body every day. And I cannot imagine but that we are much the worse for having our limbs so encrusted and our pores stopped up with grime.

And with regard to the drinking of the waters, it is in the first place fortunate for me that they are in no way hostile to my taste; in the second place they are simple and natural, and are at least attended with no danger, even if they do no good. Which is warranted, I take it, by the large number of people of every sort and constitution who are gathered together at the baths. And, although I have not felt any extraordinary or miraculous effects from them, but rather, after investigating a little more carefully than is usually done, I have found all such reports of miraculous cures which circulate in those places, and are believed (the world generally being easily gulled into believing what it wishes to believe), to be ill-grounded and untrue; yet I have hardly met any people who have been the worse for taking the waters, and nobody can, without malice, deny them this, that they stimulate the appetite, help the digestion, and inspire us with fresh energy, unless we go there in too weak a condition, which I would dissuade anybody from doing. They are not supposed to restore a heavy ruin, but they may prop up a slight leaning, or prevent a threatening deterioration.

He who does not bring with him sufficient energy to be able to enjoy the pleasure of the society he will find there, and the promenades and exercises to which the beauty of the places where these springs are usually situated invites us, will no doubt lose the best and surest part of their effect. For this reason I have hitherto selected, for residence and use of the waters, those baths which are most pleasantly situated, and which offer the most advantages in the way of lodging, food and society. Such are, in France, the baths of Bagnères; on the frontier between Germany and Lorraine, those of Plombières; in Switzerland, those of Baden; in Tuscany those of Lucca, and especially those of Della Villa, which I have used most often and at different seasons.

Each nation has its own ideas regarding their use, and their rules and methods of taking advantage of them, all different, and, as far as my experience goes, with about the same result. In Germany the drinking of them is not practised at all; the Germans bathe for all maladies, and will lie in the water like frogs almost from sun to sun. In Italy, when they drink nine days, they will bathe at least for thirty; and they usually drink the water mixed with other drugs, to assist its operation. Here we are ordered to take exercise, to digest the water; there they are kept in bed, where they have taken it, until they have voided it, the stomach and feet being kept continually warm. As the Germans are peculiar in their general practice of blood-letting, by means of leeches or cupping-glasses after scarification, in the bath; so the Italians have their *doccie*,[1] which are certain drops of hot water which are conducted through pipes, and will bathe, for an hour in the morning, another hour after dinner, for the space of a month, either the head or the stomach, or some other part of the body that is under treatment.

There is an endless variety of other customs in each country; or, more correctly speaking, there is hardly any resemblance between the different customs.

So we see that this branch of medicine, to which alone I have submitted myself, although it is the least artificial, yet has its good share in the confusion and uncertainty which is seen in all the other branches of the art.

[1] Anglice, shower-baths.

The poets are able to express all their meaning with greater emphasis and charm ; witness these two epigrams :

> A doctor touched the statue of great Jove ;
> No marble could withstand the awful shock.
> To-day, removed from out the sacred fane,
> They buried him, though God he was, and stone. (AUSONIUS.)

And the other :

> He bathed and dined with me, he seemed so bright.
> Next morn they found him dead, the luckless wight.
> Would'st know what was the cause of his decease ?
> He dreamed he saw the quack Hermocrates. (MARTIAL.)

And now I will tell a couple of stories.

The Baron de Caupene in Chalosse and I share the right of presentation to a benefice in a parish of great extent, called Lahontan, at the foot of our mountains. It is with the inhabitants of this corner of the world as it is said to be with those in the valley of Angrougne. They formerly lived their own life, had their own manners, habits, and dress ; they were ruled and governed by certain particular laws and customs handed down from father to son, to which they submitted without any other compulsion than reverence to established usage. This little state had continued from time immemorial in so happy a condition that no neighbouring judge had ever been put to the trouble of inquiring into their doings, no lawyer had ever been consulted to give them advice, no stranger had ever been called in to settle their quarrels. And no man in the district had ever been known to beg alms.

They avoided any relations or intercourse with the outer world, in order not to impair the purity of their government, until, as the story goes, one of their number, within living memory, his soul spurred by a noble ambition to bring his name into credit and renown, took it into his head to make one of his sons a Maître Jean or a Maître Pierre,[1] and, having had him taught to write in some neighbouring town, succeeded in turning him into a fine village attorney.

This man, having outgrown himself, began to sneer at the old customs, and to fill the heads of his neighbours with

---

[1] *Maître* is the form of address of all lawyers in France.

stories of the magnificence of the world this side the mountains. The first of his cronies whose goat had lost a horn he advised to demand satisfaction at the hands of the royal justices in the neighbourhood ; and, what with one thing and another, he soon had the whole place corrupted.

On the heels of this mischief they say that another presently followed, of worse consequence, through a doctor who conceived a desire to marry one of their daughters and settle among them. This fellow began by teaching them the names of fevers, colds, and abscesses, the situation of the heart, the liver, and the intestines, of all which they had hitherto been very ignorant. And, in place of the garlic with which they had learned to drive away every kind of disease, however violent or extreme, he led them into the way of taking, for any cough or cold, strange mixtures, and began to trade, not only on their health, but on their death. They declare that only since then have they observed that the night air made their heads heavy, that drinking when they were heated was injurious, that the autumn winds were more unhealthy than those of spring ; that since taking physic they find themselves overwhelmed by a legion of unwonted infirmities, that they are conscious of a general decline in their former vigour, and live only half as long as before. That is the first of my tales.

The other is that, before my gravelly tyranny, having heard several people speak highly of the blood of a he-goat as a heavenly manna sent down in these latter ages for the protection and preservation of the life of man, and hearing it spoken of by intelligent people as a wonderful drug and infallible in its action ; having, moreover, always imagined myself to be liable to any accident that may befall any other man, I took a satisfaction, although I was in perfect health, in providing myself with this miracle. I gave orders for a he-goat to be fed on my estate in accordance with the recipe ; for he has to be removed during the hottest days of summer, and be given nothing but laxative herbs to eat and white wine to drink.

I happened to return home on the day he was to be killed. They came and told me that my cook was finding two or three big balls in the paunch, which rattled against each other among the stuff he had eaten. I was curious, and had all this tripe and guts brought to me, and had the large, thick skin opened in my presence. There came out three big lumps, light as sponges, so that they appeared to be hollow; hard and firm however on the outside, and spotted with several dull colours. One was perfectly round, the size of a short bowl;[1] the other two rather smaller, not so perfectly round, but apparently becoming so. Having made inquiries of people accustomed to open those animals, I found that the case was unusual and rare. It is probable that these stones are cousins to ours; and, if that is so, it is very hopeless for those afflicted with gravel to expect a cure from the blood of an animal that is itself about to die of a like disease. For to say that the blood does not share the infection, and that its wonted virtue is not corrupted thereby, is not to be believed, but rather that nothing is engendered in a body but by the concurrence and communication of all the parts. The whole mass works together, although one part may contribute to it more than another, according to the diversity of the action. Wherefore it appears very clear that there was some petrifying property in all the parts of that goat.

It was not so much from fear of the future, and for myself, that I felt a curiosity about this experiment; but it happens in my household, as in many others, that the women store up petty drugs of that kind for the benefit of the people round about, using the same recipe for fifty diseases, and of such a kind that they do not themselves take, and yet are triumphant when they turn out successful.

On the whole I honour the physicians; not in accordance with the precept,[2] because they are necessary (for to this text we may oppose another where the prophet reproved King Asa for having recourse to a physician), but for love of themselves, having met many honest and likeable men among them. It is not them I attack, but their art; and I do not greatly blame them for taking advantage of our folly, for the greater part of the world does so. Many professions, both of greater and less repute than theirs, are built up and rely upon the deception of the public.

---

[1] *Courte boule*, according to Cotgrave 'our round bowle'. Perhaps he means the jack, in the game of bowls.

[2] Honour the physician with the honour due unto him for the use which ye may have of him : for the Lord hath created him.—Ecclesiasticus xxxviii. 1.

I call them in to keep me company when I am ill, if they happen to be near at hand, and expect them to talk to me; and I pay them as others do. I give them leave to order me to cover myself up warm, if I would rather be warm than not; they may, if they please, choose between lettuces and leeks to make my broth, and order me to drink white wine or claret. And so with all other things that are indifferent to my palate or habit. I know very well that I am doing them no favour, since bitterness and strangeness are incidental to and of the very essence of physic.

Lycurgus ordered the Spartans to drink wine when they were ill. Why? because they hated the use of it when well. Like a gentleman, a neighbour of mine, who takes it as a very wholesome drug when he has a fever, because naturally he has a deadly hatred of the taste of it.

How many doctors we see who are of my mind, who despise physic for their own account, who adopt a liberal diet, quite contrary to that they prescribe for others! What is that but shamelessly abusing our simplicity? For their life and health are no less dear to them than ours is to us, and they would adapt their practice to their preaching, if they did not themselves know its falsity.

It is the fear of death and pain, inability to bear sickness, a frantic and unthinking thirst for cure, that so blinds us; it is pure cowardice that makes us so credulous and ready to be imposed upon. Yet most people do not so much believe as merely acquiesce. For I hear them finding fault and speaking of it as we do. But in the end they become resigned. 'What should I do?' As if impatience were of itself a better remedy than patience! Is there any one of those who have submitted to this wretched tyranny who does not equally submit to any kind of imposture, who does not put himself at the mercy of any man who has the impudence to promise a cure?

The Babylonians carried their sick to the public square. The people were the physicians; every one who passed by was obliged by humanity and civility [1] to inquire into their case, and give them some salutary advice according to his experience. We do pretty much the same. We are ready to believe the mumblings and charms of any old woman of the people; and for my own part, if I had to take physic, I

---

[1] Obliged by law, according to Herodotus.

should more readily take this than any other, the more so as there is at least no fear of being harmed by it.

What Homer and Plato said of the Egyptians, that they were all physicians, should be said of all people. There is nobody who does not crack up some remedy and experiment with it upon his neighbour, if he will take his advice. The other day I was in a company where some one or other of my confraternity[1] brought news of a kind of pill made up of a hundred odd ingredients, accurately calculated. There was great rejoicing, and we felt singularly comforted ; for what rock could withstand so numerous a battery ? I understand, however, from those who have tried it, that even the smallest little pebble disdained to be stirred by it.

I cannot take my hand from this paper without adding a word or two upon the claim they make that their experience is a warrant of the infallibility of their drugs. The greater part and, as I think, more than two-thirds of the medicinal virtues consist in the quintessence or occult property of simples, which we can only know by use. For quintessence is no other than a quality of which we cannot, by our reason, find out the cause. Those of their proofs which they say they have acquired by the inspiration of some demon I am content to accept (for, as to miracles, I never touch upon them) ; or again the proofs which are derived from things which we often employ for some other purpose ; as when in the wool in which we are usually clothed they accidentally find some occult dessicative property which cures chilblains on our heels, or when in the radishes we eat for our food they detect some aperient action.

Galen tells us that a leper happened to be cured by drinking some wine out of a vessel into which a viper had crept by chance. In this example we may discover the means and a likely guide to that kind of experiment, as also in those to which the physicians say they have been led by the example of certain animals. But in most of the other experiments to which they say they were led by fortune, and had no other guide but chance, I find it impossible to believe in the progressive course of their investigation.

I imagine a man looking at the endless number of things around him, plants, animals, metals. I cannot think where to make him begin his experiments ; and if his first fancy

[1] The confraternity of sufferers from stone in the bladder.

should light upon an elk's horn, which would need a very pliant and easy faith, he will yet find himself equally perplexed in his second operation. He is confronted with so many diseases and so many circumstances, that, before he has arrived at any certainty as to whither the perfection of his experiments should lead him, human wit will be at the end of its tether. And before he has discovered, among that endless number of things, that it is this horn; among so many diseases, that it is epilepsy; so many constitutions, the melancholic; so many seasons, in winter; so many nations, the French; so many ages, old age; so many celestial changes, the conjunction of Venus and Saturn; so many parts of the body, the finger; [1] being guided in all this neither by reason, nor by conjecture, nor by example, nor by divine inspiration, but solely by the movement of chance, it must be a chance that is perfectly artificial, regular and methodical.

And then, even should the cure be effected, how can he be assured that it was not because the disease had reached its crisis, or that it was not the result of chance, or that it was not due to something else he had eaten or drunk or touched on that day, or to the power of his grandmother's prayers?

Besides, supposing this proof to have been perfect, how many times was it repeated? How often was this long bead-roll of chances and coincidences strung anew, to infer a certain rule therefrom? Should it be inferred, by whom? Among so many millions there will be but three men who trouble about recording their experiments; will chance have lighted upon just one of these three? What if another or even a hundred others have had the contrary experiences? We might perhaps see some daylight if all the reasonings and all the decisions of men were known to us; but that three witnesses, and those three doctors, should lord it over mankind is against reason. They would have to be chosen and deputed by human nature, and declared our judges by express power of attorney.

[1] To understand the above sentence we may suppose that Montaigne was thinking of an imaginary case, namely, that of an elderly Frenchman of a melancholic temperament who is afflicted with epilepsy. The question is, how did the physicians discover that it could be cured by a preparation of elkshorn to be applied to the finger, in winter and at the conjunction of Venus and Saturn?

To Madame de Duras

Madame, you found me at work on this chapter when you came to see me the other day. As these trifles may some day fall into your hands, I wish them also to bear witness that the author feels very highly honoured by the favour you will show them. You will find in them the same air and manner that you observed in his conversation. Even though I had been able to adopt some other than my ordinary garb, and some better and more honourable shape, I would not have done so; for I wish to derive no advantage from these writings but that they shall recall me to your memory as Nature made me. These same qualities and faculties which you are familiar with and have received, Madame, with much more honour and courtesy than they deserve, I will lodge (but without change and alteration) in a compact body which may survive me a few years, or a few days, where you will find them again when you are pleased to refresh your memory of them, without taking too much pains to recall them; for they are not worth it. I desire you to continue the favour of your friendship for me, for the same qualities by which it was acquired.

It is by no means my aim to be better loved and esteemed dead than living. Tiberius's whim was ridiculous, and yet is shared by many: he was more anxious to extend his fame to posterity than to win the goodwill and esteem of his contemporaries.

If I were one of those to whom the world could owe commendation, I would acquit it, and be paid in advance. Let their praises come quick and heaped-up around me, more thick than long, more full than lasting; and let them boldly vanish with my knowledge of them, and when their sweet sound shall no longer reach my ears. It would be a foolish fancy, now that I am about to sever my connexion with humanity, to introduce myself to them by a new recommendation.

I make no account of the gifts I have been unable to employ in the conduct of my life. Whatever I may be I wish to be elsewhere than on paper. My skill and industry have been employed to make myself worthy; my studies, to teach me to do, not to write. I have used all my endeavours to shape my life. That has been my trade and my work. I am less a maker of books than of any other commodity. I have wished for talents in order to gain present and essential advantages, not to store them up and keep them for my heirs.

If a man has any good in him, let it appear in his conduct, in his ordinary talk, in his love affairs and his quarrels, in play, in bed, at table, in the management of his business and household economy. If I saw a man wearing tattered hose and writing good books, I should advise him first to mend his hose. Ask a Spartan whether he would rather be a good speaker than a good soldier; do not ask me, who would rather be a good cook, if I were not provided with one.

Good heavens, Madame, how I should hate to be commended for a clever writer and looked upon as an insignificant fool in other respects! Yet would I rather be a fool, both here and there, than to have made so ill a choice in using my talents. And I am so far from expecting to earn any new honour with these foolish fancies, that it will be as much as I can do not to lose the little I have acquired. For, besides what this dead and dumb picture will take from my natural being, it does not resemble me at my best; it shows me greatly fallen off from my former vigour and sprightliness, and verging on the decayed and mouldy. I have come to the end of the cask, which begins to taste of the lees.

For the rest, Madame, I should not have dared so boldly to stir up the mysteries of medicine, considering the esteem in which you and so many others hold it, if I had not been shown the way by the writers on the art. Among the ancient Latins I think there are only two, Pliny and Celsus. If some day you will look into them, you will find that they treat their art much more roughly than I do. I only pinch it; they kill it outright. Pliny, among other things, twits them with this, that when they are at the end of their tether, they have hit upon this pretty shift, to send the patients they have teased and tormented to no purpose with their drugs and dietings, some to seek assistance in prayers and miracles, others to the hot springs. (Be not offended, Madame, he does not speak of those on this side of the frontier which are under the patronage of your family, and all belong to the Gramonts). They have a third device for getting rid of us and avoiding our reproaches for the small improvement in our infirmities, which they have had so long under their charge that they can think of nothing more to put us off with ; that is to send us for change of air to some other country.

Enough, Madame ; you will give me permission to resume the thread of my discourse, from which I turned aside to talk with you.

It was, I think, Pericles who, being asked how he was, replied, ' You may judge by this,' pointing to the amulets he had tied about his neck and arm. He wished to imply that he was in a very bad way, since he was reduced to have recourse to such vanities, and had allowed himself to be so equipped. I do not guarantee that I may not some day be borne away to this absurd notion of committing my life and health to the mercy and government of the doctors. I may fall into such a frenzy. I cannot answer for my future firmness. I too, should anybody ask me how I am, may answer with Pericles, ' You may judge by this,' showing my hand filled with six drachms of electuary. That will be a very evident symptom of a severe illness. My judgement will be marvellously unhinged. If fretfulness and fright obtain such a hold upon me, you may conclude that my soul is in a very violent fever.

I have taken the trouble to plead this cause, of which I have little enough understanding, to support and fortify a little the natural aversion to drugs and medicine as practised by our physicians, which I have derived from my ancestors ; that it may not appear to be merely a stupid and thoughtless bent, but to have a little better foundation. And also that they who see me standing so firm against exhortations and threats when in the throes of sickness, may not think that it is mere stubbornness ; or in case any one should be so ill-natured as to think that I were being spurred by vainglory. It would be a well-aimed ambition forsooth to try to gain honour by an attitude that I share with my gardener and my muleteer ! My heart is indeed not so puffed up and windy that I should wish to exchange so solid, so fleshy and marrowy a pleasure as health for a pleasure that is imaginary, spiritual and airy. Fame, even that of the four sons of Aymon, is too dearly bought by a man of my humour, if it costs him three good attacks of the colic. Give me health, in God's name!

They who love our medicine may also have their good, great, and strong reasons; I have no hatred of ideas that contradict my own. I am so far from being exasperated by seeing a disagreement between my opinions and others', and from being unfit for the society of men because their sentiments and party differ from my own, that on the contrary (the most general path that Nature has followed being that of variety, and more in minds than bodies, the former being of a more pliant substance and susceptible of taking on more shapes) I have found that opinions and views disagree much more often than they agree. Never in the world were two opinions alike, any more than two hairs or two grains. Their most universal quality is diversity.

Book the Third

CHAPTER 1

OF THE USEFUL AND THE HONEST

NO man is exempt from saying silly things; the mischief is to say them deliberately:

> With all his pains he says most foolish things. (TERENCE.)

That does not touch me; mine slip from me as heedlessly as they deserve. All the better for them. I would part with them at once for the little they are worth. And I neither buy nor sell them except for what they weigh. I speak to my paper as I speak to the first person I meet. That this is true, observe what follows.

To whom should not treachery be detestable, when Tiberius refused it when it was so much to his interest? They sent him word from Germany that, if he approved, they could rid him of Arminius by poison. He was the most powerful enemy the Romans had, since he had treated them so villainously under Varus, and was the only obstacle to the expansion of their dominion in those parts. Tiberius replied, 'that the Roman people were accustomed to take revenge on their enemies by open means, with arms in their hands, not by fraud and stratagem.' He renounced the profitable for the honest.

He was (you will tell me) an impostor. I believe it; it is no great miracle in men of his profession. But the recognition of Virtue carries no less weight in the mouth of one who hates it, since truth forcibly wrests it from him, and, if he will not receive it into his heart, he at least covers himself with it, as with an ornament.

Our structure, both public and private, is full of imperfection. But there is nothing useless in Nature; not even uselessness itself. Nothing has thrust itself into this universe that has not its fitting place. Our being is cemented with diseased qualities: ambition, jealousy, envy, vindictiveness, superstition, despair, quarter themselves upon us with so natural a possession, that we recognize the semblance of them even in animals. Nay, cruelty too, so unnatural a vice ; for, with all our compassion, we feel within us a kind of bitter-sweet pricking of malicious pleasure in witnessing the sufferings of others ; and the children feel it :

> 'Tis sweet when, down the mighty main, the winds
> Roll up its waste of waters, from the land
> To watch another's labouring anguish far. (LUCRETIUS.)

Whoever would root out the seeds of those qualities in man would destroy the fundamental conditions of our life. Similarly, in every government there are necessary offices which are not only base but wicked. Wickedness finds a place there, and is employed in sewing and binding us together ; as poison is used for the preservation of our health. If it becomes pardonable, since we are in need of it and the common necessity blots out its real quality, we must allow that part to be played by the stoutest and least timorous citizens, who will sacrifice their honour and their conscience ; as those others, in ancient times, sacrificed their lives for the good of their country. We others who are more feeble will assume easier and less dangerous parts. The public weal requires men to betray, to lie, and to massacre ; let us resign that charge to men who are more obedient and more compliant.

It has often really angered me to see a judge, by deceit and false hopes of favour or pardon, alluring a criminal to betray his offence, using to that end a shameless trickery. It would be a good service to justice, and to Plato even who countenances that custom, to furnish me with other means more to my liking. It is a mischievous kind of justice, and is wronged, in my opinion, no less by itself than by others. Not long ago I answered that I could hardly betray my Prince for a private individual, since I should be very sorry to betray any private person for the Prince ; and I hate not only to deceive, but I also hate that any one should be deceived in me. I will not even provide matter and occasion thereto.

On the few occasions I have had to negotiate between our Princes, in these divisions and subdivisions by which we are to-day rent in pieces, I have carefully avoided that they should be mistaken in me, or deceived by my face. The men of the trade[1] are the least open; they profess and pretend to be as unbiassed and as near to you as they can. For my part I recommend myself by my readiest opinions and by a manner that is most my own. A mild negotiator and a novice, I would rather fail in the business than be untrue to myself. And yet I have followed that course to this day with so much luck (for indeed Fortune has the chief share in it) that few men have been bandied from one to another with less suspicion and with greater favour and familiarity.

I have an open and easily ingratiating manner that inspires confidence at the first acquaintance. Naturalness and the simple truth will always find their opportunity and pass current, in any age whatever. Besides, the freedom of speech of the man who acts without any self-interest attracts little suspicion and odium. He may truly make use of the answer of Hyperides to the Athenians who complained of the bluntness of his speech: 'Good sirs, do not consider whether I am free-spoken, but whether I am so without accepting anything and without thereby advancing my own affairs.' My candour has also readily cleared me from all suspicion of dissembling by its vigour (leaving nothing unsaid, however painful and bitter; I could not have said worse behind their backs), and by its evident show of simplicity and indifference. I expect no other result from acting than to act, and look to no far-reaching consequences or projects. Every action plays its own particular game; let it strike home if it can.

Moreover I am not swayed by any passion, either of love or hatred, towards the great; nor is my will strangled by offence or obligation for particular favours. I look upon our Kings simply with the loyal affection of a citizen, which is neither stimulated nor cooled by private interest; for which I think the better of myself. To the general and rightful cause I have only a moderate attachment, without any heat. I am not subject to those close and deep-seated pledges and engagements. Anger and hatred go beyond the duty of justice, and are feelings which are useful only to those who are not sufficiently kept to their duty by simple reason. [*Let him employ his passion who can make no use of his reason* (Cicero).] All fair and lawful intentions are of

---

[1] The diplomats.

themselves equable and temperate ; if not, they degenerate and become seditious and unlawful. This it is that makes me walk ever with head erect, with open face and heart.

Indeed, and I am not afraid of confessing it, I could readily, in case of need, follow the example of the old woman and offer a candle to St. Michael and another to his serpent.[1] I will follow the good side as far as the fire, but exclusively, if I can.[2] Let Montaigne [2] be engulfed in the general ruin, if need be ; but, if there is no need, I shall be grateful to Fortune if it escapes, and I will make use of all the length of rope my duty allows me, to save it.

Was it not Atticus who, holding to the right side, which was the losing side, in that general shipwreck of the world, amid so many changes and divisions, saved himself by his moderation ? It is easier for a private citizen, as he was ; and I think one may be justified in not being ambitious to thrust oneself uninvited into that kind of business.

When one's country is disturbed and the people are divided I think it neither handsome nor honourable to be a wobbler and a hybrid, to be unmoved in one's affections and to incline to neither side. *That is not to steer a middle course ; it is to steer no course at all. It is to await events, in order to join the fortunate side* (Livy).

That may be allowed in the case of affairs with neighbours. And so Gelo, Tyrant of Syracuse, in the war between the barbarians and Greeks, so suspended his inclination, keeping an ambassador with presents at Delphi, to be on the watch and see to which side Fortune should turn, and seize the right opportunity to make up to the victors. It would be a kind of treachery to act in this manner in the home affairs of one's own country, in which a man must necessarily and designedly make up his mind to join one side or the other.

But for a man to hold aloof from affairs who is not in public service, or driven by express command, I hold to be more excusable (and yet I do not accept this excuse for my

---

[1] To propitiate both parties. St. Michael, who was presumably Montaigne's patron saint, was usually represented on altar-pieces in the act of slaying a dragon.

[2] Montaigne is not in the habit of striking heroic attitudes, and we must not take him too literally. The words *jusqu'au feu exclusivement* are playfully adopted from Rabelais, who uses them several times. In the next sentence Montaigne means the château of that name.

own part) than not to join in foreign wars, in which, however, by our laws, no one need be engaged against his will. Nevertheless, even those who are wholly engaged in them may conduct themselves with such order and moderation that the storm will pass over their heads without injury to themselves. Had we not reason to expect this in the case of the late Bishop of Orleans, the Sieur de Morvilliers ? And among those who at this moment are valiantly labouring at it, I know some of such even and mild temper that they are likely to remain standing, however great the ruin and desolation that Heaven has in store for us.

I am of opinion that it properly belongs to kings alone to quarrel with kings, and can see the absurdity of those spirited persons who gaily stand up to so uneven a contest. For to march openly and bravely against a Prince in defence of our honour and at the call of duty is not to pick a private quarrel with him. If he does not love such a man, he does better, he esteems him. And especially the cause of the laws and of the defence of the old State has always this privilege, that even those who, for private ends, attack the same, excuse, if they do not honour, the defenders.

But we must not call by the name of duty, as we do every day, a bitterness and asperity of the soul that is born of private interest and passion ; nor must we call a treacherous and malicious conduct by the name of courage. Their mischievous and violent propensities they call zeal. It is not the cause that excites them but their self-interest. They stir up war, not because it is just, but because it is war.

There is nothing to prevent a man acting in an accommodating manner between men who are enemies, without being disloyal. Bear yourself with an affection, if not altogether equal (for it may be of different degrees), at least moderate, and which will not so pledge you to one of them that he can require everything at your hands. Content yourself too with a moderate measure of their favours, and with swimming in troubled waters without trying to fish in them.

The other way, that of offering to do one's best for both parties shows imprudence rather than want of conscience. Does not the man to whom you betray another, who receives you with equal favour, know that you will treat him in the same way, when his turn comes ? He regards you as a scoundrel; meanwhile he will listen to you, he will draw what he can out of you and turn your disloyalty to his own account. For double-dealers are useful for what they bring; but you must take good care that they carry away as little as they can.

I say nothing to the one that I could not say to the other at the right moment, with only a little change of accent; and I report only things that are either indifferent, or known, or which are serviceable to both sides. For no useful end would I permit myself to lie to them. What is entrusted to my silence I religiously keep; but I receive as few secrets as I can. The secrets of princes are an awkward trust to one who has no use for them. I willingly offer them this bargain, that they trust me with little, but that they confidently trust me in what I bring them. I have always known more than I wished.

Open speaking opens the way to another's speaking, and draws it out, like wine and love.

Philippides replied wisely to King Lysimachus, who asked him, 'Which of my goods do you wish me to hand over to you?' 'Whatever you please, provided it is not one of your secrets.' I have observed that men generally grumble if you keep from them the gist of the business on which you employ them, and if you conceal something that lies at the back of it. For my part, I am satisfied if they tell me no more than what they wish me to do; and do not desire that my knowledge of the business should exceed or restrict what I have to say. If I am to serve as a tool of deceit let me at least salve my conscience. I would not be thought either so affectionate or so loyal a servant as to be judged fit to betray any man. He who is untrue to himself is excusably so to his master.

But the Princes I have in my mind will not accept men by halves, and scorn limited and conditional services. There is no way out of it; I tell them frankly how far I will go. For if I must be a slave I will be so to Reason alone; and yet I can hardly compass even that. And they too are wrong to demand of a free man the same submission and obligation to their service, as they do of a man they have created and bought, or whose fortunes are particularly and expressly bound up with theirs.

The laws have saved me great pains; they have chosen

a side for me and given me a master. All other authority and obligation should be relative to that of the laws, and restricted. That does not mean however that, if my affection should otherwise incline me, my hand would immediately obey it.[1] Will and desire make their own laws; actions have to submit to the law of public policy.

My method of negotiating as a whole, as here described, is a little out of harmony with that practised in our country. It would produce neither great nor lasting results. Innocence itself could not negotiate between our parties without dissimulation, nor strike a bargain without lying. And besides, public employments are not in my line; what my profession requires I perform in as private a manner as I can.

As a youth I was plunged up to the ears in public affairs, and that not without success; and yet I let go of them in good time. Since then I have often declined, seldom consented, and never volunteered to meddle with them; keeping my back turned upon ambition, but, if not like rowers who thus advance backwards, yet so that I owe it more to my good fortune than to my resolution that I am not wholly embarked in them. For there are ways less inimical to my taste, and more within my capacity, by which, if Fortune had at one time invited me to take public service and to seek advancement in the world's honours, I know that I should have stepped over my better judgement, and followed her.

Those who usually declare, in contradiction to what I profess, what I call frankness, simplicity, and ingenuousness in my conduct to be art and cunning, and discretion rather than goodness, cleverness than naturalness, good sense than good luck, do me more honour than they rob me of. But indeed they make my subtlety too subtle; and if any one has closely followed and spied upon me, I will own myself beaten, if he does not confess that there is no rule in their school[2] that could, on such various and tortuous roads, produce this natural impulse, and keep up an appearance of freedom and independence so uniformly inflexible; and that all their ingenuity and watchfulness are unable to bring them to it.

The way of truth is one and simple; that of private gain

[1] That if my affections inclined to the Protestants I should act with them.   [2] The school of diplomacy.

and of advantage, in the conduct of affairs a man is charged with, is double, uneven, and accidental. I have often seen that counterfeit and artificial freedom in practice, but for the most part without success. It is often too suggestive of the ass in Aesop's fable who, in imitation of the little dog, quite happily planted his two hoofs on his master's shoulders; but, whilst the little dog received caresses in abundance, the poor ass was treated to twice as many bastinadoes. *That best becomes a man which is most natural to him* (Cicero).

I will not deprive deceit of its place; that would be to misunderstand the world. I know that it has often been of profitable service, and that it supports and feeds most of the avocations of men. There are lawful sins, just as there are many either good or pardonable actions which are unlawful.

True justice, which is natural and universal, is otherwise regulated, and more nobly, than that other special, national justice, which is restricted by the necessities of our governments. *Of true right and real justice we have no solid and positive model; we practise only the shadow and image of it* (Cicero). The sage Dandamis,[1] hearing tell of the lives of Socrates, Pythagoras, and Diogenes, judged them to be great men in every other respect except that they were too much enslaved to reverence of the laws, to justify and support which true virtue must abate much of its original vigour; and added that many wicked actions are done not only with their permission, but by their instigation. *There are crimes authorized by the decrees of the Senate and the popular vote* (Seneca). I follow the ordinary language which makes a distinction between things that are profitable and things that are honest; so that some natural actions, which are not only profitable but necessary, are called dishonest and unclean.

But let us continue our examples of treachery. Two pretenders to the kingdom of Thrace had started a quarrel about their rights. The Emperor[2] prevented their coming to blows; but one of them, under colour of bringing things to a friendly issue by a conference, having invited his competitor to an entertainment in his own house, had him imprisoned and killed. Justice required that the Romans

[1] A Hindu sage who lived in the time of Alexander the Great.
[2] Tiberius; the pretenders were Rhescuporis and Cotys, the brother and son of Rhemetalces, the last King of Thrace.

should demand satisfaction for this crime. There was a difficulty in obtaining it by ordinary means. What they could not lawfully do without war and risk, they attempted to do by treachery. What they could not do honestly they did profitably. For this they found a fit and proper instrument in Pomponius Flaccus. This man, having drawn the other into his nets by feigned words and assurances, instead of the honours and favours he promised him, sent him bound hand and foot to Rome.

Here one traitor betrays another, contrary to the usual custom; for traitors are full of distrust, and it is difficult to catch them with their own wiles; witness the sad experience we have lately had.[1]

Let who will be a Pomponius Flaccus, and there are men enough who are willing. For my part, both my word and my good faith are, like the rest of me, parts of this common body.[2] The best they are capable of is at the public service; I take that as a matter of course. But just as, if I were commanded to take charge of the Palace of Justice and the lawsuits, I should answer, 'I know nothing about them'; or, if commissioned to be a leader of pioneers, I should say, 'I am called to play a worthier part'; so also, if any man proposed to employ me to lie, to betray, commit perjury, not to speak of assassinating and poisoning, for some important end, I should say, 'If I have stolen or robbed from any man, send me rather to the galleys.' For a man of honour may be allowed to say as did the Lacedemonians, when, after their defeat by Antipater, they were arranging terms, 'You may put upon us as many heavy and ruinous burdens as you please, but if you command us to do shameful and dishonourable things, you will waste your time.'

Every man should take to himself the oath which the Kings of Egypt made their judges solemnly take, 'that they would not deviate from their conscience, though they themselves should command them to do so.'

In a command to act dishonestly there is an evident mark of ignominy and condemnation. The man who gives it you, accuses you; and he gives it to you, if you understand him

[1] Montaigne here perhaps refers to the feigned reconciliation between Catherine de' Medici and Henry, Duke of Guise, in 1588.
[2] The State.

rightly, for a burden and a punishment. In the same degree that public affairs are bettered by your action your own state has become worse. The better you do in it, so much the worse do you do for yourself. And it will be no new thing, nor perhaps without some colour of justice, if the very same man who has set you to the work punishes you for it.

If perfidy can ever be excusable it is only so when it is employed to punish and betray perfidy.

There are examples enough not only of treachery being disowned, but of its being punished by those on whose behalf it was practised. Who does not know of Fabricius' denunciation of Pyrrhus' physician ? [1]

But this also we find, that some person has commanded an act of treachery, and has rigorously avenged the victim of it upon the man he had employed to carry it out ; disclaiming such unbridled authority and power, and refusing an obedience so abject, slavish, and unprincipled.

Jaropelc, Duke of Russia, suborned a Hungarian nobleman to betray Boleslaus, King of Poland, either by killing him or by putting the Russians in the way of doing him some notable injury. This man set to work with great cunning; he became more assiduous than ever in that King's service, contriving to become his counsellor and one of his most trusted servants. With these advantages, taking an opportune occasion of his master's absence, he betrayed Vislicza to the Russians, a great and rich city, which was completely sacked and burned by them, with total slaughter, not only of the inhabitants of whatever age or sex, but of a great number of the nobles of the neighbourhood, whom he had assembled to that end.

Jaropelc, his vengeance and anger being assuaged, for which he was, however, not without justification (for Boleslaus had done him great injury, and in the same way), sated with the fruit of this treachery, when he came to consider the foulness of it, naked and by itself, and to look upon it with sane vision no longer blinded by passion, was seized with

[1] When Pyrrhus, King of Epirus, was at war with the Romans, his physician wrote to Fabricius, the Roman Consul, offering to poison the King and so put an end to the war. Fabricius denounced him to Pyrrhus, 'lest your death, he wrote, should bring a disgrace upon us, and we should seem to have put a period to the war by treachery when we could not do it by valour.'

so great remorse and disgust, that he commanded his agent to be blinded, and his tongue and privy parts to be cut off.

Antigonus persuaded the Argyraspides [1] to betray to him Eumenes, their commander-in-chief and his adversary; but no sooner had he put him to death after they had delivered him into his hands, than he himself desired to be the agent of the divine justice, for the punishment of so detestable a crime. He handed them over to the Governor of the province, with most express command to destroy them and bring them to an evil end in any manner whatsoever. So that not one of them, although so numerous a body, ever again saw the air of Macedonia. The better he had been served by them the more wickedly he judged it to be, and the more punishably.

The slave who betrayed the hiding-place of his master, P. Sulpicius, was given his freedom, in accordance with the promise of Sylla's proscription; but in accordance with the promise of public justice, freeman though he was, he was hurled from the Tarpeian rock. They hang them, so to say, with the purse of their payment around their necks. After carrying out their second and special promise, they satisfy their general and primary conscience.

Mahomet the Second, wishing to be rid of his brother, by reason of his jealousy as a ruler, so common in that race, employed for the purpose one of his officers, who choked him by pouring too suddenly a great quantity of water down his throat. That being done, to expiate the murder he delivered the murderer into the hands of the dead man's mother (for they were brothers only on the father's side). She, in his presence, opened the murderer's stomach, and, whilst still quite warm, with her own hands searched for his heart, tore it out and threw it to the dogs to eat.

And our King Clovis, instead of the golden arms he had promised the three slaves of Cannacre, hanged them after they had, at his own instigation, betrayed their master.

And even to the most abandoned person it is so pleasant a feeling, after profiting by a wicked deed, subsequently to be able to sew upon it, in all security, a stitch of goodness and justice, as by way of compensation and conscientious correction. To which may be added that they look upon the ministers of such horrible crimes as a living reproach,

[1] A body of soldiers who carried silver shields.

and seek by their death to smother the knowledge and testimony of such proceedings.

Now, if by chance you are rewarded for it, in order that the public necessity for such extreme and desperate remedies may not be frustrated, the man who rewards you cannot but regard you as an accursed and execrable fellow, unless he be so himself, and as more treacherous than does the man you have betrayed; for he tests the wickedness of your heart by your own hands, which act without disapproval and without object. But he employs you as they do hopelessly degraded men to be the executors of high justice,[1] an office as necessary as it is dishonourable; not to speak of the vileness of such commissions, there is a prostitution of conscience.

Since the daughter of Sejanus could not, by a certain provision of the laws at Rome, be punished with death, because she was a virgin, in order to allow the law to take its course, she was violated by the hangman before being strangled. Not only his hand, but his soul, is a slave to public convenience.

When the first Amurath, to aggravate the punishment of his subjects who had given their support in the parricidal rebellion of his son against him, commanded their nearest relations to lend their assistance in the execution, I think it highly honourable in some of them to have rather chosen to be unjustly thought guilty of another's parricide than to serve justice by parricide of their own.

And when, after the storming of some wretched fortress in my time, I have seen a rascal consenting, in order to save his own life, to hang his friends and comrades, I thought him worse off than the hanged.

It is said that Witolde, Prince of the Lithuanians, once made it a law that the condemned criminal should with his own hand carry out his execution. He thought it strange that a third person, innocent of the fault, should be employed and laden with the guilt of homicide.

When, by urgent circumstances, or some sudden and unexpected event, a ruler is obliged, for reasons of state necessity, to shuffle out of his word and break his faith, or is otherwise forced out of the ordinary path of duty,

---

[1] i.e., hangmen; now sometimes euphemistically referred to as the 'exécuteurs des hautes œuvres'.

he must regard this necessity as a stroke of the divine rod. A sin it is not, for he has abandoned his own reason to a more universal and powerful reason; but it is indeed a misfortune. So that to some one who asked me, 'What remedy?' 'No remedy, I replied; if he was really squeezed between those two extremes—*but let him beware of seeking a pretext for his faithlessness* (Cicero)—he was obliged to do it; but if he did it without regret, if it did not weigh upon his mind, it is a sign that his conscience is in a bad way.'

Even if there were any ruler of so tender a conscience as to think no cure worth so serious a remedy, I should not esteem him the less. He could not ruin himself more excusably and more becomingly. We cannot do everything. In any case we must often entrust the protection of our vessel to the simple guidance of Heaven, as to our last anchorage. For what more justifiable necessity does he reserve himself? What is less possible for him to do than what he can do only at the price of his good faith and honour, things which should perhaps be dearer to him than his own safety, nay, than the safety of his people? Though he should stand with folded arms and merely call God to his aid, may he not hope that the divine goodness will not refuse exceptional favours from its hand to a hand that is so clean and just?

Those are dangerous examples, rare and sickly exceptions to our natural laws. We must yield to them, but with great moderation and circumspection. No private interest is worth so great a strain upon our conscience; public interest certainly, when it is both very apparent and very important.

Timoleon fitly expiated his extraordinary deed by the tears he shed when he called to mind that it was with a brother's hand that he had killed the tyrant; and his conscience justly pricked him that he should have been put to the necessity of purchasing the public weal at so high a price as his honesty of character. Even the Senate, delivered from thraldom by his means, did not venture roundly to pass judgement upon a deed so sublime and split into two so important and contrary aspects. But the Syracusans having, very opportunely at that moment, sent to the Corinthians to solicit their protection by sending them a leader able to restore their city to its former dignity and cleanse Sicily of a number of petty tyrants by whom it was being oppressed, they deputed Timoleon, with this new-fangled quibble and declaration, 'That according as he bore himself well or ill in his charge, they would decide to pardon him as the liberator of his country, or disgrace him as his brother's murderer.' This fantastic decision is somewhat to be excused, by reason of the danger of the example and the seriousness of so singular a deed. And they did well to throw off the burden of passing sentence, and to make it depend on other and extraneous considerations.

Now the conduct of Timoleon on this mission soon made his cause more clear, so worthily and virtuously did he bear himself in every way. And the good fortune which attended him in the difficulties he had to overcome in this noble business seemed to have been sent to him by the gods conspiring in favour of his vindication.

This man's aim was excusable, if ever any could be. But the advantage of increasing the public revenue, which served the Roman Senate as a pretext for that unsavoury decision which I am about to tell of, is not great enough to warrant any such injustice.

Certain cities had by a money payment redeemed themselves and regained their freedom, by the order and permission of the Senate, from the hands of L. Sylla. The matter having come up again for decision, the Senate condemned them to be taxable as before, and decided that the money they had paid for their redemption should remain lost to them.

Civil wars often give rise to such villainous cases, as when we punish private individuals for following the advice we gave them when we were other than we are now, and the self-same judge lays the penalty for his own change of mind upon one who is innocent of it. The master whips his pupil for his docility, and the leader his blind charge. A horrible counterfeit of justice!

There are rules in Philosophy which are both false and weak. The example that is proposed to us to make private advantage to prevail over a given promise, does not receive sufficient weight from the circumstance they mix up with it. Robbers have seized you; they have set you at liberty after extracting an oath from you to pay a certain sum. They are very wrong who say that a man of honour, once out of their power, will be quit of his word without paying. Nothing of the kind. What fear has once made me will I am bound still to will when the fear is past. And even though fear forced only my tongue without my will, I am still bound to pay to the last farthing what I have promised. For my part, when my tongue has sometimes heedlessly outstripped my thoughts, I have yet scrupled to disown it. Otherwise we shall, little by little, come to upset all the claims that a third person has upon us on the strength of our oaths and promises. *As though a man of courage could be wrought upon by force!* (Cicero.)

In this case only does private interest justify us in failing to keep our promise : when we have promised a thing that is in itself wicked and iniquitous. For the right of virtue should prevail over the right of our obligation.

I erstwhile placed Epaminondas in the front rank of great men; and I do not retract it. To how high a pitch this man raised the consideration of his private duty, who never killed a man he had vanquished, who, for the inestimable blessing of restoring freedom to his country, scrupled to put a tyrant or his accomplices to death without the forms of justice, and who regarded him as a wicked man, however good a citizen he might be, who, among the enemy and in battle, did not spare his guest-friend! There we have a richly compounded soul! To the rudest and most violent human actions he wedded goodness and humanity, even the most delicate that may be found in the school of Philosophy.

Was it Nature or Art that softened this heart, so big, so full, so obstinate against pain, death, and poverty, to such an extreme degree of sweetness and gentleness of disposition? A dreaded man of blood and iron, he goes breaking and shattering a people invincible against any but himself, and, in the midst of such a fray, turns aside to avoid an encounter with a guest-friend. Truly he was a fit and proper man to control war, who forced it to submit to the curb of loving-kindness in the very heat of battle, when, all inflamed, it foamed with fury and slaughter. It is wonderful to be able to mingle with such actions any semblance of justice; but only a man as strong as Epaminondas was able to mingle with them the most gentle and affable manners and pure innocence.

And whereas one [1] said to the Mamertines that 'laws were powerless when opposed to armed men'; another,[1] to the Tribune of the People, 'that the time of justice and the time of war were two'; and a third,[1] 'that the noise of arms drowned the voice of the laws': this man was not deaf even to the voice of urbanity and pure courtesy. Had he not borrowed from his enemies [2] the custom of sacrificing to the Muses when he went to war, to dilute its martial fury and fierceness with their sweetness and gaiety?

After so great a teacher let us not be afraid of concluding that there are things which should not be allowed even in fighting the enemy, and that the common interest should not require all things of all men, against their private interest: *the memory of private right continuing even in the midst of public dissensions* (Livy);

> No power on earth can sanction treachery
> Against a friend; (OVID.)

and that not all things are permissible to a man of honour, in the service of his king, the general cause and the laws. *For duty to one's country does not override all other duties; she herself requires that we be dutiful towards our parents* (Cicero).[3]

This teaching befits our times; we have no need to harden our hearts with these steel blades. It is enough that our shoulders are hardened by them. It is enough to dip our pens in ink, without dipping them in blood. If it is the sign of a great heart and the effect of a singular and rare virtue to despise friendship, private obligations, one's word and one's kinsmen, for the common good and obedience to authority, we are truly sufficiently excused from showing it by the consideration that it is a greatness that can have no place in the great heart of Epaminondas.

I abominate those crazy exhortations of this other unruly spirit: [4]

> When weapons flash, let no fond thoughts of love,
> Friendship and piety compassion move;
> But boldly strike the venerable face
> Of your own fathers, if opposed in place. (LUCAN.)

---

[1] Respectively Pompey, Caesar, and Marius.   [2] The Spartans.
[3] The first clause is put interrogatively by Cicero; and his answer does not agree with Montaigne's.
[4] Julius Caesar. It is within the recollection of all how these words

Let us deprive wicked, bloodthirsty, and treacherous natures of this pretence of reason; let us thrust aside that atrocious and insane justice, and imitate more humane examples. How much cannot time and example bring to pass! In an encounter during the civil war against Cinna, one of Pompey's soldiers, having unwittingly killed his brother who was on the opposite side, immediately took his own life for shame and sorrow; and a few years later, in another civil war of the same nation, a soldier demanded a reward from his captains for having killed his brother.

To judge an action to be fine and honourable because it is useful is a poor argument; as also to hold that every man is obliged to perform such an action, and that it becomes him as long at it is useful:

> All things are not alike for all men fit. (PROPERTIUS.)

Let us take that action which is most necessary and useful for human society; which will surely be marriage. And yet the council of the saints has concluded the contrary to be more honourable, and excludes from it the most venerable profession of men; as we destine for our studs the least valuable of our cattle.

CHAPTER 2

OF REPENTANCE

OTHERS[1] form man; I describe him, and portray a particular, very ill-made one, who, if I had to fashion him anew, should indeed be very different from what he is. But now it is done.

Now the features of my painting do not err, although they change and vary. The world is but a perennial see-saw. All things in it are incessantly on the swing, the earth, the rocks of the Caucasus, the Egyptian pyramids, both with the common movement and their own particular movement. Even fixedness is nothing but a more sluggish motion.

---

were re-echoed before the Great War by another and lesser Caesar (pronounced by the Romans *Kaiser*).

[1] The other moralists.

I cannot fix my object;[1] it is befogged, and reels with a natural intoxication. I seize it at this point, as it is at the moment when I beguile myself with it. I do not portray the thing in itself. I portray the passage; not a passing from one age to another, or, as the people put it, from seven years to seven years,[2] but from day to day, from minute to minute. I must adapt my history to the moment. I may presently change, not only by chance, but also by intention. It is a record of diverse and changeable events, of undecided, and, when the occasion arises, contradictory ideas; whether it be that I am another self, or that I grasp a subject in different circumstances and see it from a different point of view. So it may be that I contradict myself, but, as Demades said, the truth I never contradict.[3] If my mind could find a firm footing, I should not speak tentatively, I should decide; it is always in a state of apprenticeship, and on trial.

I am holding up to view a humble and lustreless life; that is all one. Moral philosophy, in any degree, may apply to an ordinary and secluded life as well as to one of richer stuff; every man carries within him the entire form of the human constitution.

Authors communicate themselves to the world by some special and extrinsic mark; I am the first to do so by my general being, as Michel de Montaigne, not as a grammarian or a poet or a lawyer. If the world finds fault with me for speaking too much of myself, I find fault with the world for not even thinking of itself.

But is it reasonable that I, who am so retired in actual life, should aspire to make myself known to the public? And is it reasonable that I should show up to the world, where artifice and ceremony enjoy so much credit and authority, the crude and simple results of nature, and of a nature besides very feeble? Is it not like making a wall without stone or a similar material, thus to build a book without learning or art? The ideas of music are guided by

---

[1] i. e., myself.

[2] Alluding to a popular notion that the human body is entirely renewed every seven years.

[3] Not quite accurate: Demades said, according to Plutarch, that he may have often contradicted himself, but that he had never said anything contrary to the public weal.

art, mine by chance. This I have at least in conformity with rules, that no man ever treated of a subject that he knew and understood better than I do this that I have taken up; and that in this I am the most learned man alive. Secondly, that no man ever penetrated more deeply into his matter, nor more minutely analysed its parts and consequences, nor more fully and exactly reached the goal he had made it his business to set up. To accomplish it I need only bring fidelity to it; and that is here, as pure and sincere as may be found.

I speak the truth, not enough to satisfy myself, but as much as I dare to speak. And I become a little more daring as I grow older; for it would seem that custom allows this age more freedom to prate, and more indiscretion in speaking of oneself. It cannot be the case here, as I often see elsewhere, that the craftsman and his work contradict each other. 'How could a man who shows to such advantage in company write so foolish a book?' or, 'Are these learned writings the work of a man of such feeble conversation?'

When a man of ordinary conversation writes uncommon things, it means that his talent lies in the place from which he borrows them, and not in himself. A learned man is not learned in all things; but the accomplished man is accomplished in all things, even in ignorance.

Here, my book and I go hand in hand together, and keep one pace. In other cases we may commend or censure the work apart from the workman; not so here. Who touches the one touches the other. He who judges the one without knowing the other will wrong himself more than he does me; he who has come to know the work will completely satisfy me. Happy beyond my deserts if I have only this share of public approval, that intelligent persons will be made to feel that I was capable of profiting by learning, if I had had any; and that I deserved more assistance from my memory!

In this place let me offer an excuse for what I often repeat, that I seldom repent, and that my conscience is satisfied with itself, not as the conscience of an angel or a horse, but as the conscience of a man; always with the addition of this refrain, not a formal or conventional refrain, but prompted by a real and natural modesty, 'that I speak as an inquirer and an ignoramus, leaving the decision purely and simply to the common and authorized beliefs.' I do not teach, I relate.

There is no vice, that is really a vice, which is not hurtful and which a sound judgement does not condemn ; for its ugliness and evil consequences are so apparent that they are perhaps right who say that it is chiefly begotten of stupidity and ignorance. So hard it is to imagine that a man may know it and not hate it !

Wickedness sucks in the greater part of its own venom, and poisons itself with it.

Vice, like an ulcer in the flesh, leaves a repentance in the soul, which is always scratching itself and drawing blood. For Reason blots out all other grief and sorrow, but begets that of repentance, which is the more hard to bear since it is born from within ; as the chill and heat of a fever are more acutely felt than those which are external. I regard as vices (but each according to its measure), not only those which are condemned by reason and Nature, but those too which have been created by human opinion, even false and erroneous opinion, if it is authorized by laws and custom.

There is likewise no goodness in which a well-born nature does not delight. We feel indeed a certain self-congratulation when we do a good deed, which gives us inward satisfaction, and that generous pride which accompanies a good conscience. A boldly wicked soul may perhaps arm itself with assurance ; but with that complacency and satisfaction it cannot provide itself.

There is no small pleasure in feeling oneself preserved from the contagion of so corrupt an age, and saying to oneself, ' Should any one look into my very soul, he would yet not find me guilty of the affliction or ruin of any man, or of revenge or envy, of publicly offending against the laws, of innovation or disturbance, or of failing to keep my word. And whatever the licence of the times may permit or suggest to any man, I have laid hands on no Frenchman's property nor dived into his purse. I have never lived but on what is my own, either in war or peace time ; and have never used another man's labour without hire.' These testimonies of a good conscience please ; and this natural satisfaction is a great boon to us, and the only payment that will never fail us.

To ground the reward of virtuous actions on others' approval is to choose a too uncertain and shaky foundation. Especially in an age so corrupt and ignorant as this, the good opinion of the people is harmful. Whom can you trust to see what is praiseworthy? God defend me from being an honest man according to the ideas of honesty which men every day ascribe to themselves! *What was once vicious is now become moral* (Seneca).

Some of my friends have at times attempted to lecture and censure me unreservedly, either of their own accord or at my invitation, as a service which, to a well-regulated mind, exceeds all services of friendship, not only in usefulness but in kindness. I have always welcomed it with the most open arms of courtesy and gratitude. But when I come now to speak of it candidly, I have often discovered in their blame or praise such a want of proportion, that I should hardly have gone wrong if I had sinned, rather than done a good deed, according to their way of thinking.

We especially who live a retired life, not exposed to any view but our own, must have a fixed pattern within ourselves by which to test our actions, and, according to this pattern, now pat ourselves on the back, now kick ourselves. I have my own laws and my own court to judge me, and I appeal to them more than to others. I do indeed restrict my actions according to others, but extend them only according to myself. You alone know whether you are cruel and cowardly, or loyal and devout. Others do not see you, they guess you by uncertain conjectures; they see not so much your nature as your art. Therefore pay no heed to their sentence, pay heed only to your own. *Use your own judgement with regard to yourself ... The conscience weighs heavy in deciding your virtues and vices. Take that away, and all falls to the ground* (Cicero).

But when they say that repentance follows close upon the heels of sin, they do not seem to consider the sin which is in its corslet, which dwells in us as in its own domicile. We may disown and retract the sins that take us unawares, and to which we are carried away by passion. But those which, by long habit, are rooted and anchored in a strong and powerful will, are not capable of being resisted. Repentance is no other but a recanting of our will and an opposition to our fancies, which leads us about in all directions. It makes this man [1] disown his past virtue and continence :

> Alas ! alas !
> Why feel I not to-day
> As in my youthful bloom, when I
> Unmoved heard others moan,
> Or, now that I would win them, why
> Is all my beauty flown ? (HORACE.)

It is a life in a thousand that is consistently well-ordered even in private. Any man may play his part in the mummery, and act the honest man on the scaffolding ; but to be right within, in his own bosom, where all is allowed, where all is concealed—there's the point ! The next step is to be so in our own home, in our ordinary actions, of which we need render no account to any man, where there is no study, no make-believe. Wherefore Bias, describing an exquisite state of family life, says : ' of which the master is the same within, before his own conscience, as he is abroad, under fear of the laws and the tongues of men'. And that was a worthy saying of Julius Drusus to the workmen who offered, for three thousand crowns, to rebuild his house in such a way that his neighbours could no longer overlook him as before : ' I will give you six thousand, he said, to build it in such a way that any one may see into it from all sides.' They make honourable mention of Agesilaus' habit, when travelling, of lodging in the churches, that the people and the gods themselves might see into his private actions.

Many a man has been a wonder in the eyes of the world in whom neither his wife nor his valet have ever detected anything even remarkable. Few men have been admired by their own household.

No man has been a prophet not only in his own house, but in his own country ; such is the experience of history. It is the same in things of no account. In the following humble example you may see a reflection of greater ones. In my clime of Gascony they think it droll to see me in print. The farther from my own home that the knowledge of me extends, the more am I valued. In Guienne I buy the printers ; elsewhere they buy me. On this eventuality do they found their hopes who keep in concealment when alive and present,

---

[1] Horace imagines Ligurinus, when he is old, repenting of not having made a better use of his beauty.

to make a name when dead and absent. I would rather have less. I launch myself upon the world only for the portion of it that I actually gain. When I leave it, I will hold it quit.

This man,[1] after playing his part in public, is escorted to his door by an enthusiastic rabble. With his gown he drops this part; the higher he had risen, the lower does he now fall. Within, in his house, all is confusion and sordidness. And even if order should prevail there, it needs a keen and well-sifting judgement to perceive it in those humble and private acts. Besides, orderliness is a dull and obscure virtue. To enter a breach, conduct an embassy, rule a people, are conspicuous actions. To chide, laugh, sell, pay, love, hate, to live in communion with one's people and oneself, pleasantly and correctly, not to give way to passion, not to contradict oneself; that is more rarely seen, more difficult and less remarked.

Wherefore, whatever they may say, a retired life is burdened with as difficult and strenuous duties, if not more so, than other lives. And private individuals, says Aristotle, do a higher and more difficult service to virtue than those in authority. We prepare ourselves for eminent occasions more for glory than for conscience's sake. The shortest way to arrive at fame would be to do for conscience's sake what we do for glory. And the virtue of Alexander appears to me to reflect much less vigour on his stage, than that of Socrates in his humble and obscure actions. I easily conceive Socrates in Alexander's place; Alexander in that of Socrates, I cannot. If you ask the former what he can do, he will reply, 'Subdue the world;' if you ask the latter, he will say, 'Lead a human life conformably with its natural condition;'[2] a much more general, more important, and more legitimate art.

The worth of the soul lies not in flying high, but in walking in an orderly manner. Its greatness is not brought into play in greatness, but in a middle state. As those who judge and probe our hearts think but little of the brilliance of our public acts, and see that they are but thin threads and sprays of water spurting from an otherwise thick and

---

[1] i.e., the man who is not a hero in his own home. The previous paragraph was an interpolation.
[2] Montaigne here added in the margin, but deleted, the words: 'do for the world that for which he is in the world.'

muddy depth; so likewise those who judge us by this brave outward show conclude the like of our inner nature; being unable to reconcile common faculties, resembling their own, with those other faculties that astonish them, that are so far beyond their vision.

So it is that we give to demons uncouth shapes. And who does not endow Tamerlane with raised eyebrows, open nostrils, a fear-inspiring visage, and a huge stature, in accordance with the imaginary stature we have conceived from report of his fame? At one time, if I had been introduced to Erasmus, I could hardly have believed but that he spoke only in adages and apothegms to his servant and landlady. We can much more fitly imagine an artisan upon his stool or on his wife than a great President, of venerable demeanour and sufficiency. We imagine that from those lofty thrones they will not even condescend to live.

As wicked souls are often stirred by some outside impulse to do a good action, so are virtuous souls to do evil. We must judge them therefore in their settled state, when they are at home, if ever they are; or at least when they are more nearly in repose, and in their natural seat.

Natural inclinations are assisted and strengthened by education, but they seldom change and are seldom mastered. In my time a thousand natures have escaped towards virtue, or towards vice, in spite of a contrary training.

> As jungle beasts, in cages long confined,
> Tamed and subdued to suffer man's control,
> Are by a single taste of blood transformed.
> Their native rage and fury then returns;
> They thirst for more, and scarcely can be stayed
> From onslaught on their trembling lord. (LUCAN.)

These original qualities are not to be extirpated; they may be covered and concealed. Latin is to me like a native tongue; I understand it better than French. But for these forty years past I have made no use of it either for speaking or writing. And yet on two or three occasions in my life, under sudden and violent emotion (once, when my father, although in good health, fell back into my arms in a swoon), the first words I uttered, coming from the depth of my heart, were always in Latin; Nature, in spite of so long a disuse, springing up and finding forcible expression. And this is said to have occurred to many others.

Those who, in my time, have attempted to correct the morals of the world by new beliefs, have reformed the surface vices; the essential ones they have left as before, if they have not increased them; and it is to be feared that they will increase. We are apt to rest from all other well-doing on the strength of these external, arbitrary improvements, which cost less and earn greater esteem. And we thereby cheaply satisfy the other natural, consubstantial, and inherent vices.

Just see what our own experience teaches. There is no man, if he listen to himself, who will not discover in himself a particular nature, a dominant nature, that struggles against his education and against the tempestuous passions that oppose it. For my part I am seldom stirred by fits and starts; I am nearly always in my place, like a heavy and unwieldy body. If I am not at home, I am always very near it. My excesses do not carry me very far. There is nothing extreme or uncommon in them. And besides I have healthy and vigorous recoveries.

The real condemnation, which touches the common run of men in our time, is that even their recantation is altogether corrupt and unclean; their idea of amendment smudged, their penitence as sick and faulty almost as their sin. Some, from being glued to vice either by a natural adhesion or by long habit, have lost all sense of its ugliness. In others (to which regiment I belong) sin is a burden, but they counterbalance it with pleasure, or some other need; they suffer and give way to it, at a certain price; viciously however, and basely. Yet we might perhaps imagine a disproportion of degree so remote that pleasure might with justice excuse the sin, as we say of usefulness; not only if it were accidental and apart from the sin, as in larceny, but in the very exercise of sin, as in intercourse with a woman, where the incitement is violent and, so they say, sometimes unconquerable.

Being the other day at Armagnac, on the estate of a kinsman of mine, I saw a country fellow whom everybody nicknamed the Thief. He gave us this account of his life: That being born a beggar and discovering that, by earning his bread with the labour of his hands, he would never be sufficiently armed against want, he decided to take to thieving; and, being of great bodily strength, he practised that trade in all security throughout his younger days. For he reaped his harvest and vintage on other men's lands, but at such a distance and in so great stacks that it is incredible how one man could have carried away so much on his shoulders in a single night. And he took care besides to equalize and distribute the damage he did, so that the total loss became less serious for each individual.

He is now, in his old age, rich for a man of his rank in life, thanks to this traffic, which he openly confesses. And to make his peace with God out of his winnings, he says that it is his daily task to compensate, in charity, the heirs of those he robbed ; and, if he does not finish his good work (for he cannot see to it all at once), he will charge his heirs to repay them, proportionally to the wrong he did to each, which he alone knows.

From this declaration, whether it be true or false, it appears that this man regards theft as a dishonest action and hates it, but less than he does poverty ; he repents of it very simply, but in so far as it is thus counterbalanced and compensated, he does not repent of it.

This is not a case of that habit by which we are incorporated with vice, when even our understanding is brought into conformity with it ; nor is it the case of an impetuous wind that in gusts disturbs and blinds our soul, and for the time being hurls us, judgement and all, into the power of sin.

What I do I do thoroughly, as a matter of habit, and make one step of it ; and I seldom take any step that steals away and hides from my reason, and that is not very nearly guided by all my faculties in agreement, without division or inner revolt. My judgement takes all the blame or all the praise for it ; and the blame it once takes it takes always, for almost from birth it has been one : the same inclination, the same direction, the same strength. And in the matter of general opinions, I have since my childhood occupied the position I had to hold.

Some sins there are which are impetuous, quick, and sudden ; let us leave them on one side. But with regard to those other sins, so often repeated, deliberately, advisedly, whether constitutional sins, or even professional or vocational sins, I cannot imagine them to have been so long implanted in one and the same heart, unless the reason and conscience of the man who has them constantly wills them, and intends them to be so. And I find it somewhat hard to form a mental image of the repentance which, as he is apt to boast, comes upon him at a certain prescribed moment.

I do not share the opinion of the Pythagorean school, 'that men take up a new soul when they approach the images of the Gods to receive their oracles.' Unless he meant this, that it must be extrinsic, new, and lent for the occasion; since their own soul shows so little sign of the purification and cleanness befitting such an office.

They do just the opposite to what the Stoics teach, who command us indeed to correct the imperfections and vices we know to be in us, but forbid us to grieve and trouble ourselves about them. They make us believe that they feel great regret and remorse within; but of improvement and correction, or of discontinuance, they show no signs. Hence it is no cure, if the disease be not thrown off. If repentance were placed in the scale of the balance, it would weigh down the sin. I know of no virtue that is so easy to copy as piety, if life and morals are not in conformity with it; its essence is hidden and abstruse; the imitation easy and showy.

For my part, I may desire in general to be different; I may dislike and condemn my whole being, and beseech God to reform me throughout and pardon my natural infirmity. But I should not, I think, call that repentance, any more than my being dissatisfied that I am not an angel or a Cato. My actions are orderly, and conformable with what I am and my condition; I can do no better. And repentance does not properly concern the things that are not in our power; but regret certainly does. I can imagine an endless number of natures on a higher plane and better governed than mine, and yet I do not improve my powers; just as neither my arm nor my mind becomes any stronger by conceiving those of another to be so. If to imagine and desire a nobler conduct than ours led to our repenting of our own, we should have to repent of our most innocent actions, since we rightly suppose that a superior nature would have performed them with greater perfection and dignity; and we should wish to do equally well.

When, with the eyes of old age, I look upon the conduct of my younger days, I find that I generally behaved in an orderly manner, according to my lights; that is all that my power of resistance can do. I do not deceive myself; in like circumstances I should always do the same. It is not a smutch, it is rather a universal tincture with which I am stained. I know no superficial, half-way, and formal repentance. It must touch me in every part before I can call it so; it must grip my heart and distress it as deeply and thoroughly as God sees into me.

With regard to business, I have allowed many good ventures to slip through my fingers for lack of successful management. Yet my plans were well chosen, considering the opportunities I was offered. It is my habit to take always the easiest and safest course. I have found that in my former decisions, following my own rule, I proceeded wisely, considering the nature of the matter proposed to me, and I should do the same a thousand years hence on the like occasions. I do not consider what it is at this moment, but what it was when I deliberated upon it.

The importance of every decision lies in the moment; opportunities and matters roll on and change incessantly. I have in my life run into some serious and clumsy mistakes, not for want of good judgement, but for want of good luck. There are hidden and undreamt of springs in objects we have to handle, especially in human nature; mute conditions that make no show, sometimes unknown even to their possessor, that are manifested and aroused by unexpected occasions. If my prudence was unable to penetrate into and foresee them, I cannot blame it in the least; its office is limited. If the issue beats me, and if it favours the course I have refused, there is no help for it; I do not blame myself, I accuse my luck, not my work. That cannot be called repentance.

Phocion had given the Athenians certain advice which was not followed. When, however, the affair turned out happily against his expectation, somebody said to him, 'Well, Phocion, are you pleased that the things have gone so well?' 'Indeed I am pleased, he replied, that it has happened in this way, but I do not repent of having counselled the other course.'

When my friends refer to me for my advice, I give it to them freely and frankly, without being deterred, as most people are, by the consideration that, the matter being risky, it may turn out quite contrary to what I expected, and that I may be blamed for my advice; that does not trouble me in the least. For they will be in the wrong, and I felt obliged not to refuse them that office.

I have generally only myself to blame for my errors or my misfortunes. For, as a matter of fact, I seldom ask another's advice, except formally and as a compliment, saving when I have need of scientific instruction and knowledge of facts. But, in things in which I have but to use my judgement, others' reasons may serve to confirm it, but not often to divert me. I lend a favourable and courteous ear to them all. But I cannot remember to this hour having ever followed any but my own counsel. To me they are but flies and specks that distract my will. I set little store by my own opinions, but I set as little by others'. Fortune pays me as I deserve.

If I take little advice, I give still less. It is very seldom asked, and still more seldom is it followed; and I know of no undertaking, public or private, that has been set right and mended by my advice. Even those who chanced to be somewhat dependent upon it have been more ready to follow the directions of anybody else's brains. And, as I regard the rights of my repose as jealously as the rights of my authority, I would rather have it so; by leaving me in peace they humour what I profess, which is to be set up in myself and wholly self-contained. It is a satisfaction to me to be disinterested in others' affairs and free of responsibility with regard to them.

When an affair is over, however badly it has turned out, I seldom fret. For I am soothed by the reflection that things were bound to happen thus; I see that they follow the great stream of the universe, and are involved in the concatenation of Stoical causes. Your imagination cannot conceive or wish the slightest alteration without upsetting the whole order of things, both past and future.

For the rest, I hate that repentance which is incidental to old age. The man who said of old [1] that he was obliged to his years for having rid him of sensuality was not of my opinion; I can never be beholden to impotence for any good it can do me. *Nor can Providence ever be so hostile to her own work that debility should be ranked with the best things* (Quintilian). Our passions are seldom excited in old age; we are seized with an extreme satiety after the

[1] Sophocles.

act. In that I can see no sign of conscience; vexation and weakness imprint upon us a mean-spirited, rheumatic virtue. We must not allow ourselves to be so wholly carried away by our natural alterations as to warp our judgement. Youth and pleasure did not in former years so overpower me that I did not recognize the face of vice in sensual pleasure; nor does the distaste that years bring with it so overpower me now, that I do not recognize the face of sensual pleasure in vice. Now that I am no longer in it I judge as if I were still in it.

If I rudely shake up my reason and examine it attentively, I find it to be the same as in my most licentious years, except perhaps in so far as it has become enfeebled and impaired by age. And I find that the pleasure it refuses me in the interest of my bodily health, it would not refuse me, any more than formerly, for my spiritual health. I do not esteem her to be any more valiant for being *hors de combat*. My temptations are so broken and mortified that they are not worth being resisted by her. I exorcize them by merely spreading out my hands in front of me. Should she be face to face with that old lust, I fear she would have less power to resist it than she once had. I cannot see that she thinks any differently about it than she did then, or that she has acquired any new light. Wherefore if there is any convalescence, it is a broken-down convalescence.

A miserable kind of cure to owe one's health to disease! It is not the part of our misfortune, but of the good fortune of our judgement, to do this office. Ills and afflictions can make me do no more than curse them; they are good enough for people who can only be stirred up by the whip. My reason runs a nimbler course in prosperity. She is much more absorbed and put to it to digest pains than pleasures. I see much more clearly in fair weather. Health admonishes me more cheerfully and to better purpose than sickness. I approached as nearly as I could to an amended and orderly life when I had health to enjoy. I should feel ashamed and mortified that the misery and misfortune of my shaky old age should be thought more estimable than my good, healthy, sprightly, vigorous years; and that I should be honoured, not for what I have been, but for what I have ceased to be.

In my opinion human felicity lies in the happy life, not

in the happy death, as Antisthenes declared. I never expected to be that monstrosity, a philosopher's tail attached to the head and body of a libertine ; nor that that miserable appendage should disclaim and belie the fairest, fullest, and longest part of my life. I wish to show and present myself uniformly throughout. If I had to live my life over again I would live it as I have lived it ; I neither regret the past nor fear the future. And if I do not deceive myself, I have been nearly the same inwardly as outwardly. It is one of the chief things that I owe to my fortune, that my bodily state has run its course, each part in its due season. I have seen it in the herb, in the flower, and in the fruit ; and now I see it in decay. Happily, however, since it was according to Nature, I bear my present infirmities much the more patiently because they are in season, and because they invoke a more kindly recollection of the long happiness of my past life.

So also my wisdom may well have been of the same stature at the one time as at the other. But it was capable of achieving much more and had a better grace when green, gay, natural, than now that it is broken down, morose, painful. I repudiate therefore those casual and dolorous conversions.

God must touch our hearts. Our conscience must amend of itself, with the reinforcement of our reason, and not through the weakening of our passions. Sensual pleasures are in themselves neither pale nor discoloured because they appear so to dim and bleared eyes. We ought to love temperance for its own sake, and for our reverence to God who commanded it, as well as chastity ; if they are lent to us by a catarrh, or if I owe them to the favour of my stone, they are neither chastity nor temperance. We have no right to boast of despising and combating carnal pleasure, if we cannot feel it, if we know nothing of it, of its charms and power, and its most alluring beauties. I know both, and so have a right to speak.

But it seems to me that in old age our souls are subject to maladies and infirmities more troublesome than those of youth. I used to say so when I was a young man ; at that time they would cast my beardless chin in my teeth. I say so still, now that my grey hairs give me authority to speak. We call by the name of wisdom our austere humours, our distaste for present things. But to tell the truth, we do not so much abandon our vices as change them, and, in my opinion, for the worse. Besides a silly and feeble pride, a wearisome garrulousness, a captious and unsociable temper, and superstition, and a ridiculous anxiety about money after we have lost the use of it, I find there more envy, injustice, and malice. Old age sets more wrinkles on the mind than on the face; and we never, or very seldom, see a soul that does not, as it grows old, smell sour or musty. The whole man waxes and wanes.

When I look at the wisdom of Socrates, and several circumstances connected with his condemnation, I should venture to believe that he in some sort purposely contributed towards it himself by prevarication, seeing that he was so soon, at the age of seventy years, to suffer his richly-endowed mind to become more sluggish, and to see its wonted clearness becoming dimmed.

What metamorphoses I see many of my acquaintances undergoing every day through old age! It is a powerful disease that steals upon us naturally and imperceptibly; it needs a great store of study, and great precaution, to avoid the infirmities that it lays upon us, or at least to retard their progress. I feel that, notwithstanding all my intrenchments, it is gaining upon me foot by foot. I hold out as long as I am able. But after all I do not know to what it will reduce even me. Happen what may, I am satisfied that the world may know from what height I have fallen.

CHAPTER 3

OF THREE KINDS OF INTERCOURSE

WE must not rivet ourselves too firmly to our humours and dispositions. Our chief talent lies in our being able to adapt ourselves to different fashions. To keep oneself tied and bound by necessity to a single course is to exist, not to live. The best minds are those which show most variety and versatility. Here we have an honourable testimony to the elder Cato: *His mind was so equally versatile for all purposes that, whatever he was doing, you would have thought he had been born for that alone* (Livy). If it lay with me to dress myself up in my own fashion,

I should not like to be so firmly modelled to any pattern, however good, as not to be able to get away from it.

Life is an unequal, irregular, multiform movement. To follow incessantly one's own inclinations, to be so held by them as not to be able to deviate from them or twist them out of their course, is to be, not our own friend, still less our own master, but our own slave. I say this now, because I find it difficult to shake myself free from the tyranny of my soul, who cannot interest herself in a thing without being absorbed in it, nor occupy herself with any subject without devoting her full powers to it. However trifling the subject given to her, she is apt to magnify and stretch it to such a point as to require her utmost strength. For that reason her idleness is to me very distressing, and prejudicial to my health.

Most minds need a matter outside of themselves in order to quicken and exercise them; mine needs it rather to enable it to settle down and rest: *the vice of idleness must be shaken off by occupation* (Seneca); for its chief and most laborious study is the study of itself.

Books are for my mind one of the occupations which distract her from her study. At the first thoughts that come to her she is aroused, she makes trial of her vigour in all directions, exercising her power of handling the subject, now in a forcible, now in an orderly and graceful manner; she becomes steady, moderate, and strong. She has the means within her of rousing her faculties. Nature has given her, as to all other minds, matter enough of her own to utilize, subjects enough of her own on which to exercise her imagination and judgement.

Meditation is a powerful and ample exercise for a man who is able to search his mind and employ it vigorously. I would rather fashion my mind than furnish it. There is no exercise that is either more feeble or more strenuous, according to the nature of the mind, than that of entertaining one's thoughts. The greatest make it their profession, *for whom to live is to think* (Cicero). Besides, Nature has gifted it with this privilege, that there is nothing we can do for so long a time, nor any activity to which we can devote ourselves more frequently and easily. It is the business of the Gods, says Aristotle, from which comes their happiness and ours.

Reading serves especially to wake up my reasoning power by suggesting various subjects for meditation; it busies my judgement, not my memory.

Therefore few conversations are able to hold my attention that are carried on without a mental effort. It is true that charm and beauty sometimes hold and satisfy me no less, if not more, than weight and profundity. And since I become sleepy in any other kind of converse, and only give the rind of my attention to it, it often happens that, in such languid and indolent talk, which we keep up for appearances, I say silly things and make absurd replies, unworthy of a child, or, still more rudely and foolishly, observe an obstinate silence. I have a dreamy way of withdrawing into myself, and on the other hand a gross and childish ignorance of many common things. These two peculiarities have earned me five or six anecdotes, true ones, which people tell of me, as silly as those told of any man.

Now, to follow up my subject, this difficult propensity makes me particular in choosing my company. I have to pick them out on the sorting-board. And it unfits me for ordinary actions. We live and deal with ordinary people. If we are bored by associating with them, if we disdain to adapt ourselves to humble and vulgar minds—and the humble and vulgar are often as well regulated as the most refined (and all sapience is insipid that does not adapt itself to ordinary insipience)—we must cease to meddle either with our own or with others' business. And both public and private business has to be negotiated with such people.

The least strained and most natural pace of our soul is the finest; the least forced occupations are the best. Good heavens, how well wisdom serves those whose desires she regulates according to their power! There is no more useful knowledge than this: 'According to one's power,' which was the refrain and favourite saying of Socrates; a word of great substance.

We must direct and fix our desires on the easiest and nearest objects. Is it not a foolish humour in me to be out of sympathy with a thousand to whom I am joined by Fortune, without whom I cannot live, and to cling to one or two who are outside of my circle, or rather, to a fanciful desire for a thing I cannot obtain? My easy-going ways, adverse to all bitterness and austerity, may easily have saved me from envy and hostility; no man ever gave more occasion, I will not say to be loved, but not to be hated. But the coolness of my demeanour towards others has, and rightly so, deprived me of the goodwill of many, who are to be excused if they interpret it in another and worse sense.

I am very capable of contracting and keeping up rare and chosen friendships. Since I grasp so hungrily at any acquaintance that promises to be to my liking, I make such advances, I rush forward so eagerly, that I rarely fail to become attached, and to make an impression where I hit. I have often made happy proof of this. In ordinary friendships I am rather dry and cool; for my motion is not natural if not with full sail.

Besides, Fortune, having in my younger days spoiled me and made me dainty, as the result of a unique and perfect friendship, has in fact given me a slight distaste for others, and has too deeply imprinted on my fancy that, as that ancient [1] said, it is a 'beast of company, not of the herd'. And then I find it naturally hard to communicate myself in a half-hearted and reserved manner, and with that slavish and suspicious caution which intercourse with numerous and imperfect friends enjoins; and enjoins especially in these days when we cannot speak of the world without risk and without dissembling.

I see very well, however, that one who, like me, has the amenities of life (I mean the essential amenities) for his end, ought to avoid like the plague those difficult and particular humours. I should commend a soul of several degrees, that can both wind and unwind itself; that is well wherever its Fortune bears it, that can chat with its neighbour about his building operations, about his hunting and his quarrels, and take a pleasure in talking with a carpenter and a gardener. I envy those who can be familiar with the meanest of their retinue, and begin a conversation among their own staff of servants.

Plato's advice is not to my liking, that we should always speak in a masterful tone to our servants, whether male or female, without any jests, without any familiarity. For, besides the reason I have already given, it is inhuman and unjust to assert so strongly that privilege, such as it is, that we owe to Fortune. And that household dominion

[1] Plutarch.

appears to me the most equitable which admits the least disparity between masters and men.

Others study how to elevate their minds and raise them on stilts; I, to humble mine and bring it low. It is refractory only in expansion.

> The race of Aeacus
> You tell, and wars 'neath Ilion's sacred wall.
> Of Chian wine the cost,
> Who at the fire shall make our water hot,
> When and with whom for host
> To 'scape the cold Pelignian, that you tell not. (HORACE.)

Thus, as the Lacedemonian valour needed moderating and soothing in war by the soft and pleasing notes of the flute, lest it should turn to fury and madness; whereas all other nations generally use loud and shrill sounds and voices, which stir and inflame the hearts of the soldiers to the last degree; so it appears to me, contrary to the usual opinion, that in using our minds, we have for the most part more need of lead than of wings, of coolness and repose rather than of heat and agitation. It is especially foolish, to my mind, to put on wise and knowing airs before simple people, always to speak in a stilted manner, *on the point of a fork*.[1] You must come down to the level of those in whose company you are, and sometimes affect ignorance. Lay aside your strength and cunning; in ordinary converse it is enough to preserve order. For the rest crawl on the ground, if they like it.

The savants generally stumble over this stone; they keep parading their pedantry, and scatter their book-learning right and left. In these days they have poured out so much of it into the boudoirs and ears of the ladies, that if the fair creatures have not retained the substance of it, they at least try to appear as if they had. On every kind of subject and in all conversation, however shallow and commonplace, our womenkind affect a novel and scholarly style of writing and speaking:

> In this same language they express their fears,
> Their anger and their joys, their griefs and troubles,
> And all the secrets of their soul pour out.
> What more? Their love is done in learned style. (JUVENAL.)

They will quote Plato and Saint Thomas as witnesses,

---

[1] As the Italians say, *favellar in punta di forchetta*.

ADVICE TO THE LADIES

when any chance comer could serve as well. The learning that cannot reach their mind remains on their tongue.

If the well-bred ladies will take my advice, they will content themselves with making the best of their own natural wealth. They cover and conceal their beauties under borrowed beauties. It is a great sign of simplicity to extinguish one's own light in order to shine with a borrowed lustre. They are buried and entombed under artifice : *they look as if they had come out of a band-box* (Seneca).

The fact is they do not sufficiently know themselves. The world has nothing more beautiful. It is for them to honour the arts and to paint the lily. What need they do but live beloved and honoured ? They have and know more than enough to do that. They need but revive a little and rekindle the faculties that are in them. When I see them intent on rhetoric, astrology, logic, and the like drugs, so futile and useless for their needs, I begin to suspect that the men who urge them to these studies do so as a means of getting them into their power. For what other excuse can I find for them ?

Enough that they can, without our instruction, train their charming eyes to look merry, severe, or soft, season a ' No, no ' with cruelty, hesitation, or encouragement, and need no interpreter for the speeches we make in our wooing. With this knowledge they can command with the switch and master their schoolmasters and the school.

If, however, it irks them to acknowledge their inferiority to us in anything, and if they insist, out of curiosity, on having their share in book-learning, poetry is a diversion suited to their needs ; it is a wanton, subtle, dressed-up and talkative art, all pleasure and show, like themselves. They will also derive various advantages from history. In Philosophy, that part of it which is useful in the conduct of life, they may choose the dissertations that will teach them to judge of our humours and dispositions, to protect themselves against our treacheries, to regulate the boldness of their own desires, to husband their freedom, to prolong the pleasures of life, and meekly to bear the inconstancy of a lover, the rudeness of a husband, the unwelcome encroachments of years and wrinkles, and the like things. That is the utmost share I should allot to them in the matter of learning.

There are peculiar natures that retire into their own shells. It is of the essence of my nature to be communicative, to come out of myself. I am all outside and in evidence, born for society and friendship. The solitude that I love and preach shows itself chiefly in leading my thoughts and feelings back to myself, in restraining and confining, not my steps, but my desires and cares, in eschewing any solicitude about outside things, in avoiding with mortal dread any subjection and obligation, and not so much the throng of men as the throng of business. Local solitude, to tell the truth, makes me rather expand outwardly and sets me more at large; I am more ready to devote myself to affairs of state and to the world when I am alone. At the Louvre [1] and in the crowd I shrink and retire into my skin; the crowd thrusts me back upon myself, and my thoughts are nowhere so mad, so licentious and so personal as in places where respect, discretion, and ceremoniousness should be observed. It is not human follies that make me laugh, but our displays of wisdom.

By nature I am not adverse to the bustle of courts; I have spent a part of my life in them, and am accustomed to bear myself cheerfully in grand company, provided it be at intervals and at my own times.

But that fastidiousness of taste, of which I was speaking, forcibly attaches me to solitude, even at home, amid a numerous household, where visitors are as frequent as elsewhere. I see enough people there, but seldom of the kind that I like to converse with; and I there reserve, both for myself and others, an unusual liberty. There is a truce to ceremony, dancing attendance on people and showing them off the premises, and such other laborious rites enjoined by politeness (a slavish and tiresome custom!). Every one there behaves as he pleases; whoever likes may commune with his own thoughts. I may hold my peace, dreamy and absorbed, without offence to my guests.

The people whose society and intimacy I court are those they call refined and talented men, the idea of whom puts me out of liking for others. It is, if rightly understood, the rarest type with us, a type that is chiefly due to Nature. The aim of this intercourse is simply frequent and intimate forgathering and conversation; the exercise of wits, with-

[1] The Royal Court.

out any other fruit. In our talks all subjects are alike to me; it matters little to me if there be neither gravity nor profundity in them; charm and pertinency are never wanting. All is tinted with mature and consistent good sense, mingled with kindliness, freedom, gaiety, and friendship. Not only on the subject of substitutions and the affairs of kings does our mind disclose its beauty and power; it shows it no less in intimate chat. I know my sort even by their silence and their smiles, and discover them perhaps more easily at the dining-table than at the council-board.

Hippomachus said truly that 'he could tell a good wrestler by merely seeing him walk in the street'.

If Learning is pleased to intrude into our conversation, she will not be shown the door, provided she be not, as she usually is, overbearing and obtrusive, and does not attempt to lay down the law; but modest and ready to learn herself. We only seek to pass the time; when it is time to be instructed and preached at we will go and seek her on her throne. Let her stoop to our level for the nonce, if she will so please; for, useful and desirable as she may be, I imagine that at a pinch we shall very well dispense with her presence, and manage our business without her. The mind of a well-bred person, who has come into frequent contact with the world of men, is in itself sufficiently agreeable. Art is nothing other than the record and register of the productions of such minds.

I also take pleasure in the society of beautiful and honest women. *For we also have eyes that are learned in the matter* (Cicero). If the mind has not the same enjoyment in this as in the other, the bodily senses, which also have a greater share in this, bring it to a proportion near to, although, in my opinion, not equal to the other. But it is an intercourse in which we men must be a little on our guard, especially those, like myself, in whom the body counts for much. In my youth I burned myself at that fire, and suffered all the torments that, according to the poets, befall those who abandon themselves to it without order or judgement. It is true that that whipping has since taught me better:

> The fleet that once escaped Capharean rocks
> Will evermore avoid Euboean seas. (Ovid.)

It is madness to give one's whole thoughts to it, and

become entangled in a furious and senseless passion. But, on the other hand, to associate with them without any love or bond of affection, after the manner of actors ; to play an ordinary stage-part, assuming the appropriate age and costume, to contribute nothing of our own except the words, is indeed to keep on the safe side, but in a mean-spirited way, like a man who abandons his honour, or his profit, or his pleasure, in fear of danger. For it is certain that those who contract an intimacy of that kind can expect to reap no fruit from it that will move or satisfy a noble mind.

A man must have earnestly desired what he wishes earnestly to enjoy ; I mean when Fortune should unjustly favour their mask, which often happens, for there is not one of them, however ill-favoured she may be, who does not think herself very attractive, who has not some point to recommend her, her age, or her smile, or her graceful movements (for there are no entirely ugly, as there are no entirely beautiful women) ; and the Brahmin maidens who have no other recommendation go to the market-place, after the people have been assembled by the public crier to see them, and show their matrimonial parts, to see if they at least have not the power of procuring them husbands.

Consequently there is not one who is not easily won over by the first vow a man takes to be her lover. Now, the necessary consequence of these common and ordinary betrayals by the men of to-day is, as we already know by experience, either that they rally together and stand upon the defensive in order to avoid us ; or that they too follow the example that we set them, play their part in the comedy, and lend themselves to the transaction, without passion, without care, without love. *Incapable of attachment, she requires none from others* (Tacitus). They think, following the persuasion of Lysias in Plato, that they may the more profitably and advantageously surrender to us the less we love them.

It will be the same as in a stage-play : the spectators will take as much or more pleasure in it than the actors.

For my part, I can no more recognize Venus without Cupid than maternity without offspring ; these are things that mutually lend and owe their essence to one another. So this cheat recoils upon the man who is guilty of it. It costs him little, but he also gains nothing worth having. Those who made Venus a goddess saw to it that her chief beauty was incorporeal and spiritual ; but the Venus that these people are after is not only not human, it is not even animal.

The animals will not have it so gross and earthy. We often see that imagination and desire kindle and excite them, before the body ; we may observe in both sexes that, among the herd, they make a choice and selection in their affections, and that their mutual intimacies and likings are enduring. Even those to whom old age denies bodily strength will still tremble, neigh, and thrill with love. We may see them, before the deed, filled with hope and ardour, and when the body has played its part, still gratified by the sweetness of the remembrance ; and some there are that are afterwards puffed up with pride and, though weary and sated, crow with triumph and glee.

He who has but to relieve his body of a natural necessity, has no need to trouble others with such careful preparations ; it is no meat for a coarse and gross appetite.

As I have no expectation of being thought better than I am, I will tell this of the errors of my youth. Not only on account of the danger to health (and yet I did not manage so well but I have had two touches, slight, however, and transitory),[1] but also out of contempt, I have seldom had recourse to venal and public connexions. I preferred to whet the pleasure by difficulty, by desire, and by some vain-glory. I shared the tastes of the Emperor Tiberius, who in his amours was as much taken with modesty and noble birth as with any other quality ; and the inclination of the courtezan Flora, who gave herself to no man below the rank of a Dictator, a Consul, or a Censor, and found her delight in the dignity of her lovers. No doubt pearls and brocades, titles and retinues, contribute their part to the pleasure.

For the rest, I used to set great store by mental qualities, but only provided that there was no fault to be found with the body. For, to answer conscientiously, if one or the other of these two attractions must of necessity be wanting,

---

[1] We may observe how Montaigne becomes more indiscreet as he grows older. This parenthesis was a marginal addition to the 1588 edition.

I would have chosen rather to renounce the spiritual; it has its use in better things. But in the matter of love, which chiefly concerns sight and touch, something may be done without the charms of the mind, nothing without the charms of the body. Beauty is the real advantage of the ladies. It is so peculiarly their own that ours, though it requires somewhat different characteristics, is never at its best but when confounded with theirs, boyish and beardless. It is said that at the court of the Grand Turk the youths that serve him on the score of beauty, who are of endless number, are dismissed at the latest when they are twenty-two years of age.

Reason, wisdom, and the offices of friendship are found better among men; therefore they govern the affairs of the world.

These two kinds of intercourse are accidental and depend upon others. The one is annoyingly rare, the other withers with age; so they could not sufficiently satisfy the needs of my life. Intercourse with books, which is the third, is much surer and more in our power. To the first two it yields the other advantages, but it has for its share the constancy and facility of its service. This goes side by side with me in my whole course and accompanies me everywhere. It is my comfort in old age and solitude. It relieves me of the burden of a wearisome idleness, and at all times delivers me from unwelcome company. It blunts the edge of grief, unless it be extreme and overmastering. For diverting my troublesome fancies there is no resource like that of books; they easily turn my thoughts to themselves and drive out the others. And yet they do not grumble when they see that I only seek their company for want of those more real, more lively, and natural pastimes; they always receive me with the same welcome.

He may well go on foot, as they say, who leads his horse by the bridle; and our James, King of Naples and Sicily, who, though young, handsome and robust, was carried about the country on a stretcher, lying on a wretched feather-pillow, clothed in a gown of grey cloth and a bonnet of the same, attended at the same time by a numerous retinue and royal pomp, litters, hand-led horses of all kinds, gentlemen and officers, formed a picture of a still delicate and hesitating asceticism.

The sick man is not to be pitied who has his cure in his sleeve.

In my experience and application of this maxim, which is a very true one, lies all the benefit I reap from books. As a matter of fact I hardly make more use of them than those who have no knowledge of them. I enjoy them as a miser enjoys his treasure, knowing that I can enjoy them when I please ; my mind is satisfied to the full with this right of possession.

I never travel without books, either in peace or in wartime. Yet many days, and even months, will pass without my using them. It will be presently, I say, or to-morrow, or when I please. Meanwhile time flies, and is gone, and I am none the worse. For it cannot be imagined what a restful and comforting thought it is to me, that they are at my side to give me pleasure at my own time, and to feel how much they help me in life. It is the best provision I have found for this human journey ; and I greatly pity any intelligent man who is deprived of it. I am more inclined to accept any other kind of diversion, however trivial, since this can never fail me.

When at home I resort a little more frequently to my library, from which I can quite easily overlook my household. It is over the entry, and I see below me my garden, my farm-yard, my court-yard, and into most parts of my house. There I turn over now one book, now another, without order or plan, in a desultory way. At one time I muse, at another I make notes and dictate, walking to and fro, my fancies, such as these.

It is on the third story of a tower ; on the first is my chapel, on the second a bedroom with its accompaniment, where I often lie down, to be alone. Above it is a large wardrobe. Formerly this was the most useless place in my establishment. There I spend most of the days of my life, and most of the hours of the day ; I am never there at night. Adjoining the library is a rather neat study, in which a fire may be kindled in winter, very pleasantly lighted by a window. And if I did not fear the trouble more than the expense, the trouble that drives me from every kind of business, I could easily join to each side, on the same level, a gallery, a hundred paces long and twelve broad, having found all the walls raised, for another purpose, to the necessary height.

Every place of retirement requires a place for walking. My thoughts go to sleep if I sit still. My mind will not move unless stirred by my legs. All who study without a book are in the same plight.

My library is circular in shape, the only flat side being that needed for my table and chair; it being rounded, I can see all my books at a glance, arranged about me on five rows of shelves. From this room I have three open and extensive views; and it offers sixteen paces of empty space in diameter.

In winter I am not there so continually, for my house is perched upon an eminence, as its name implies, and no room is more exposed to the winds than this, which, being rather difficult of access and a little out of the way, I like, both for the benefit of the exercise and because I can keep people at a distance.

Here is my throne; here I endeavour to make my rule absolute, and to sequester this one corner from all society, conjugal, filial, and social. Everywhere else my authority is only verbal, and doubtful in reality.

Miserable, to my mind, is he who has not in his home a place to himself, where he may give all his attention to himself; where he may hide! Ambition is forsooth a great satisfaction to its devotees, since it keeps them always in evidence, like a statue in a market-place. *A great fortune is a great slavery* (Seneca). Not even their privy is private. Nothing appears to me so intolerable in the austere life which our monks affect as the rule I have observed in one of their communities of being perpetually in company, and performing no action whatever except in presence of numbers of others. I find it rather more supportable to be always alone than never to be able to be alone.

If any one tells me that it is degrading to the Muses to use them only for a toy and pastime, he does not know, as I do, the value of pleasure, sport, and pastime. I can hardly help saying that any other aim is ridiculous. I live from day to day, and, speaking in reverence, I live only for myself; I aim no further.

In my youth I studied for ostentation; after that a little to gain wisdom; now for diversion; never for gain. I have long given up a vain and expensive hobby I had for acquiring that kind of furniture, not only to supply my needs, but to go a little further, to cover and adorn my walls.

Books have many charming qualities for those who know how to choose them. But no good thing without a drawback: it is no more than any other a pure and unadulterated pleasure. It has its disadvantages, and very weighty ones. The mind is exercised by them, but the body, the care of which I have likewise not neglected, meanwhile remains inactive, and becomes heavy and dull. I know of no excess more prejudicial to me, and more to be shunned, in these my declining years.

Those are my three favourite and particular occupations. I will not speak of those civil duties I owe to the world.

CHAPTER 4

OF DIVERSION

I WAS once engaged in comforting a lady who was really afflicted; for most of their mourning is put on and formal:

> A plenteous gush of tears is ever at hand,
> Ready to flow at will. (JUVENAL.)

We go the wrong way to work when we oppose this grief; for opposition goads them and drives them further into their sadness. The heat of discussion exasperates the evil. We may observe, in ordinary conversation, if I have made a casual remark and somebody disputes what I say, I resent his contradiction and stoutly defend what I have said; and still more so that in which I take an interest.

And besides, by proceeding in this way, you enter upon your task too abruptly; whereas the first greeting of a patient by his physician should be pleasant, cheerful, and encouraging. A grumpy and disagreeable doctor never did any good. On the contrary, then, we must at first encourage and second their grief, and appear to approve and excuse it. By this understanding you will be authorized to proceed further, and, by easy and imperceptible degrees, you will pass over to more solid arguments, and such as are more likely to cure them.

My chief desire being to delude the bystanders who had their eyes upon me, I bethought myself of palliating the evil. And I have found by experience that I am a poor and unsuccessful hand at persuading. My reasons are offered too dryly and pointedly, or too brusquely, or too carelessly.

After having for some time touched upon her anguish, I did not attempt to cure her by strong and powerful reasons, because I have a lack of them, or because I thought I could better effect my purpose in a different way. Nor did I choose the different methods of consolation which Philosophy prescribes: That what we complain of is no evil, with Cleanthes; That it is a slight evil, with the Peripatetics; That this lamenting is neither a right nor a praiseworthy action, with Chrysippus; nor that of Epicurus, more near to my style, That we should shift our thoughts from unpleasant to pleasant things; nor that of Cicero, To make a bundle of all this mass of cures, and dispense them as occasion offers.

But, quite imperceptibly changing our subject and diverting it gradually to more adjacent ones, and then to others a little more remote, according as she gave me more attention, I insensibly drew her out of her painful thoughts, and kept her in good spirits and quite calm as long as I was there. I made use of diversion.

Those who succeeded me in the same service found no improvement, for I had not laid the axe to the roots.

I have perhaps touched elsewhere upon some kinds of diversion in public affairs. And the use of it in military matters by Pericles in the Peloponnesian war, and by a thousand others at other times, for enticing hostile forces from their own country, is too frequent in history.

That was an ingenious shift with which the Sieur d'Himbercourt saved both himself and others in the city of Liège, which the Duke of Burgundy, who held it besieged, had commanded him to enter, to carry out the terms of surrender agreed upon. The people of the town, assembled together by night to take the necessary measures, began to revolt against those agreements which had been passed, and a number of them decided to fall upon the negotiators whom they had in their power. He, getting wind of the first wave of people who were coming to storm his lodgings, immediately let loose upon them two of the inhabitants of the town (for some of them were on his side), charged with fresh and milder terms to be proposed in their council, which in his need he had there and then invented. These two arrested the first storm and led back the excited rabble to the town hall to hear their message and discuss it. The discussion was short, and now a second storm burst loose, as violent as the other ; and he immediately dispatched four new mediators of the same kind to meet them, with protestations that they now had fatter terms to offer them, which would absolutely content and satisfy them. By this means the people were again turned back to their conclave. In fine, by thus dispensing out delays, diverting their fury and dissipating it in fruitless discussions, he at length laid it to sleep until daylight appeared, which was his main purpose.

This other story falls into the same category. Atalanta, a maiden of exceeding beauty and marvellously agile, to be rid of the throng of a thousand suitors who sought her in marriage, issued this decree, ' that she would accept the man who was her match in running, on the understanding that those who failed should lose their lives.' There were many who thought the prize was worth the risk, and who suffered the penalty of the cruel bargain.

Hippomenes, whose trial was to come after that of the others, addressed himself to the tutelary goddess of this amorous ardour, and invoked her aid ; and she, lending a favourable ear to his prayers, provided him with three golden apples, with instructions how to use them. The race-track being cleared, as Hippomenes perceived that his mistress was gaining upon him, he dropped, as if by accident, one of these apples, and the girl, beguiled by the beauty of it, did not fail to step out of her way to pick it up :

> The maiden, dazzled by the glittering gold,
> Stops in her course to seize the rolling fruit. (OVID.)

He did the same, when he saw his opportunity, with the second and the third, until, by thus diverting her and making her lose ground, he won the race.

When the doctors are unable to purge the catarrh, they divert it and guide it into some less dangerous part. I have observed that that is also the most usual cure for mental ailments. *Sometimes the mind should be guided to other interests, other preoccupations, other cares, other business ;*

often it will be cured by change of place, as in the case of sick people who are slow in recovering (Cicero). Little good is done by making a direct onslaught on the disease ; we do not make the patient sustain or ward off the attack, we draw it off and turn it aside.

This other lesson is too high and too difficult. It is only for men of the highest order to dwell simply upon the thing, to consider and estimate it. It belongs to a Socrates alone to meet death with an everyday countenance, to become familiar and trifle with it. He seeks no consolation outside of the thing. Dying appears to him a natural occurrence and a matter of indifference ; he just fixes his eyes upon it, he is prepared for it without looking elsewhere.

The disciples of Hegesias who, inflamed by the splendid eloquence of his lectures, starved themselves to death, and so thickly that King Ptolemy forbad him again to entertain his school with these homicidal discourses, do not consider death in itself ; they do not appreciate it. It is not on death that they fix their thoughts ; they aim and rush at a new existence.

These poor wretches we see on the scaffold; filled with a burning piety, doing their utmost to devote all their senses to it, their ears to the instructions given to them, their eyes and hands lifted up to heaven, their voices in loud prayers, under violent and continual excitement, no doubt do a thing very commendable and proper in such a strait. We ought to commend their devotion, but strictly speaking not their fortitude. They shun the struggle, they turn their thoughts from death, as we try to amuse children when they are about to be lanced. I have seen some who, if they happened to cast their eyes on the dreadful preparations for death going on around them, became paralysed, and frantically cast their thoughts elsewhere.

We recommend those who are passing along a dreadful precipice to close their eyes or turn them aside.

When Subrius Flavius, sentenced by Nero's command to lose his life, and that at the hands of Niger (both commanders in war), was led to the place of execution, he observed that the hole that Niger had had dug for his burial was badly and unevenly made, and said, turning to the soldiers present, ' Not even this is according to military discipline.' And to Niger, who exhorted him to keep his head steady, 'I only wish that you may strike as steadily.' And he divined correctly, for Niger's arm trembled so that he needed several blows to sever it. This man appears to have had his thoughts directly fixed upon the matter in hand.

The man who dies in the fray, sword in hand, does not then give his mind to death; he does not feel it, or even think of it. He is carried away in the heat of battle.

A gentleman of my acquaintance, having fallen to the ground when fighting in the lists, and feeling himself stabbed nine or ten times with a dagger by his enemy, whilst every one present was calling upon him to think of his conscience, told me afterwards that, although those voices reached his ears, they did not move him in the least, and that he thought of nothing but how to disengage and avenge himself. He killed his man in this same combat.

The man who brought L. Silanus his death-sentence did him a good turn in that, having heard his reply, 'that he was indeed ready to die, but not at the hands of a criminal,' he hastened with his soldiers to lay forcible hands upon him, and when Silanus, unarmed as he was, offered a stubborn defence with fists and feet, he killed him in the struggle, thus drowning in a sudden and tumultuous rage the painful apprehension of the lingering death that was in store for him.

Our thoughts are always elsewhere; we are stayed and supported by the hope for a better life, or by the hope that our children will turn out well, or that our name will be famous in the future, or that we shall escape the evils of this life, or that vengeance threatens those who are the cause of our death:

> I hope indeed that on the mid-sea rocks,
> If aught the good powers can, thy lips will drain
> The cup of suffering, and oft cry aloud
> On Dido's name. O graceless, thou shalt rue it,
> And I shall hear thereof, yea, for the tale
> Will reach me, even among the nether dead. (VIRGIL.)

As Xenophon was sacrificing, crowned with a garland, news was brought to him of the death of his son Gryllus, killed at the battle of Mantinea. On first hearing the news he threw his wreath to the ground; but when they subsequently told him of the manner of his death, which was most brave, he picked it up and replaced it on his head.

Epicurus himself, drawing near to his end, is comforted by thoughts of the immortality and usefulness of his writings. *All labours are easy to bear, if followed by fame and reputation* (Cicero). And the same wound, the same fatigue, says Xenophon, does not bear so hard upon an army general, as upon a common soldier.

Epaminondas accepted his death much more cheerfully when he was informed that the victory remained with him. *This is a solace, this is a fomentation in the greatest sorrow* (Cicero). And other like circumstances delay, divert, and turn our thoughts from the consideration of the thing in itself.

Nay, even the arguments of Philosophy keep on skimming over and dodging the matter, hardly ever rubbing the crust of it. The first man of the first school of Philosophy, which superintended the others, the great Zeno, against death: 'No evil is honourable; death is honourable: therefore death is no evil.' Against drunkenness: 'No man entrusts his secret to the drunkard; every one entrusts it to the wise man: therefore the wise man will not be a drunkard.' Is that hitting the bull's eye? I love to see that those leading minds cannot escape our common lot. Perfect men as they are, they are still men in a very dull and heavy way.

A sweet feeling is revenge, and deeply implanted in our nature. I can see that well enough, although I have no experience of it in myself. Endeavouring recently to turn a young Prince's thoughts from revenge I did not tell him that he should turn his other cheek to the man who had struck him, for charity's sake; nor did I picture to him the tragic results that poetry attributes to that passion. I did not touch that string; but I tried to make him relish the beauty of a picture of a contrary kind, the honour, the favour, the goodwill he would gain by goodness and clemency. I diverted his thoughts to ambition. That is how it is done.

When passion in love gets the better of you, disperse it, they say; and they say true, for I have often tried it with advantage. Break it up into several desires, of which one may be ruler and master, if you please; but lest it be domineering and tyrannical, weaken it, arrest its progress, by dividing and diverting it:

> When fretful throbs the vein, then vent the sperm
> Within thee gathered, into sundry bodies.
>
> (PERSIUS and LUCRETIUS.)

And look to it in good time, lest it torment you when once it has taken hold of you:

> Unless thou dost destroy even by new blows
> The former wounds of love, and curest them
> While yet they're fresh, by wandering freely round
> After the freely-wandering Venus. (LUCRETIUS.)

I was once stricken with an overpowering grief for one of my nature; and yet it was more justified than powerful. I might perhaps have sunk under it, if I had simply trusted to my own strength. Having need of a powerful diversion to take my thoughts from it, I made myself, by art and study, fall in love, wherein I was assisted by my youth; love solaced me and withdrew me from the evil caused by friendship.

It is the same in all things. A painful fancy takes possession of me; I find it shorter to change than to subdue it; if I cannot replace it by another contrary idea, I replace it at least by a different one. Variety always solaces, dissolves, and scatters. If I cannot combat it, I run away from it; and in running away I double and change my direction. By changing place, occupation, company, I escape into the crowd of other thoughts and diversions, where it loses my trace, and leaves me safe.

In this way does Nature proceed, with the help of inconstancy; for Time, which she has given us for the sovereign physician of our passions, chiefly obtains its result in this way: by supplying our imagination with other and still other matter, it dissolves and destroys the first feeling, strong as it may be.

A wise man has a hardly less vivid picture of his dying friend after twenty-five years [1] than in the first year; and according to Epicurus it is no less vivid. For he attributed no alleviation of afflictions either to the anticipation or to the age of his grief. But so many other thoughts cross this one, that in the end it languishes and wearies.

To turn aside the stream of popular gossip, Alcibiades cut

---

[1] This was written about twenty-five years after La Boëtie's death.

off the ears and tail of his handsome dog, and drove him into the market-place, in order that the people might have something to talk about, and leave his other actions in peace. I have also observed that, for the same purpose of diverting people's suspicions and conjectures and putting the gossips off the scent, some women conceal their real amours by pretending to be in love with some other man. But I knew one who, whilst merely making believe, became seriously smitten, and left the real and original lover for the pretended one. She taught me that the man who has found a soft place is a fool to acquiesce in this dissimulation. When the lady keeps her smiles and favours in public for this suborned wooer, believe me when I say that he is not very clever if he does not in the end usurp your place and dismiss you to his. This is properly speaking to cut out and sew a shoe for another to put on.

It takes very little to divert and turn us aside; for it takes little to hold us. We seldom consider things in the gross and singly; it is the minute and superficial surroundings and pictures that strike us, and the empty husks that peel off from the things:

> As nowadays in summer tree-crickets
> Do leave their shiny husks. (LUCRETIUS.)

Even Plutarch bewails his daughter on account of her pretty childish tricks. The recollection of a farewell, of an action, of a particular charm, of a last recommendation, will revive our sorrow. Caesar's toga stirred all Rome as his death had not been able to do. The mere sound of a name buzzing in our ears: 'My poor master! or My good friend! Alas, my dear father! or My kind daughter!' When I am distressed by these repeated lamentations, and look closely into them, they appear to me nothing but words and phrases. The word and the tone offend me, as the shouting of a preacher will often arouse his congregation more than his reasons, and as we are moved by the piteous cries of an animal killed for our use; so that I am meanwhile unable to weigh and penetrate into the true and solid essence of my subject:

> With these incitements Grief provokes herself. (LUCRETIUS.)

These are the foundations of our mourning.

The obstinacy of my stones, especially as affecting the

penis, has sometimes caused so long a suppression of the urine, for three, even four days, and brought me so near death, that, considering the cruel strain this state puts upon me, it would have been madness to hope, nay to desire, to avoid it.

O what a past master in the hangman's trade was that good Emperor [1] who had the yards of his criminals tied fast, that they might die through being unable to pass water!

When I found myself in this plight, I would reflect how trivial were the reasons and objects that imagination fed me with to make me cling to life; what atoms go to the building up in my soul of the importance and difficulty of departing this life; for how many frivolous thoughts we find room in so great an affair. A dog, a horse, a book, a glass, and what not, counted for something in my loss. With others it is their ambitious hopes, their purse, their learning, no less foolishly to my mind. I looked upon death with indifference when I saw it in a general way, as the end of life. I master it in the lump; in detail it worries me. The tears of a lackey, the disposing of my old clothes, the touch of a well-known hand, a commonplace word of comfort, make me soft and sorry for myself.

In like manner our hearts are touched by the laments of fiction; the tears of Dido and Ariadne strongly affect even those who do not believe in their existence in Virgil and Catullus. It is the sign of a hard and unbending nature not to be stirred to emotion by them, as is related of Polemon, as if it were a something to wonder at; but he did not even turn pale when bitten by a mad dog that carried away the calf of his leg. And no man is wise enough to picture in his mind the cause of so sharp and overwhelming a grief, that it will not be enhanced by its actual presence, when eyes and ears have a share in it; parts which are not to be moved only by unreal incidents.

Is it reasonable that even the arts should take advantage of and profit by our natural stupidity and feebleness of mind? The barrister, says Rhetoric, in that farce they call pleading, will be moved by the sound of his own voice and his feigned emotion, and will suffer himself to be cozened by the passion he is acting. He will affect a real and substantial grief in this mummery he is playing, to transmit

[1] Tiberius.

it to the jury who are still less concerned in the matter than he. Like those men who are hired at funerals to assist in the ceremonial of mourning, who sell their tears and grief by weight and measure ; for, although they are stirred by borrowed emotions, it is certain that, through the habit of settling their countenance to suit the occasion, they are often quite carried away and affected with genuine melancholy.

I assisted, with several others of his friends, in escorting the body of Monsieur de Grammont to Soissons, from the siege of La Fère, where he was killed. I observed that, in all the places we passed through, the people we met with were moved to tears and lamentations by the mere solemn pomp of our convoy ; for they did not know even the name of the departed.

Quintilian relates that he saw actors who entered so deeply into a tragic part that they still wept after reaching home ; and of himself he tells that, having undertaken to work upon others' feelings, he was so carried away by his own that he detected himself not only in tears, but with the paleness of countenance and behaviour of a man really overwhelmed with grief.

In a region near our mountains the women play the part of Prester Martin,[1] for whilst magnifying their grief for their deceased husband by recalling his good and agreeable qualities, in the same breath they summon up and proclaim his imperfections ; as if to strike a balance with themselves and turn away from pity to contempt. This they do with a much better grace than we who, on losing any chance acquaintance, take a pride in praising him for newly discovered and unreal qualities, and make him out quite another man when we have lost sight of him than he appeared when we saw him in the flesh ; as if grief were something instructive, or as if tears cleared up our understanding by washing it.

For my part I renounce from this time forward the testimony any man will give in my favour, not because I shall deserve it, but because I shall be dead.

If you ask this man, 'What interest have you in this siege ?' he will say, 'The interest of example and of

[1] Some legendary priest who when celebrating Mass took the parts both of priest and clerk.

common obedience to the Prince ; I expect to gain nothing whatever by it, and as for glory, I know how small a share will fall to an individual like myself. I have neither feeling nor quarrel in the matter.' And yet look at him on the following day, quite another man, red and boiling with fury, in the battle-ranks and ready for the attack. It is the gleam of so much steel, the fire and din of our cannon and drums, that have cast this new hardness and hatred into his veins.

A frivolous cause, you will say. Why a cause ? None is needed to stir our souls ; any idle fancy, without body or object, will rule and stir them. Let me take to building castles in Spain, my imagination will invent pleasures and delights in them, by which my soul will be really tickled and rejoiced. How often we darken our minds with anger and sadness by means of such shadows, and give ourselves up to chimerical feelings which alter both our body and soul !

What astonished, grinning, perplexed grimaces we put on when we indulge in day-dreams ! How limbs and voice start and tremble ! Would you not think that this man, although all alone, falsely imagines that he is conversing with a crowd of other men, or that he has some devil inside him and persecuting him ?

Search within yourself where is the object of this change. Is there anything in Nature except man that feeds on unrealities, and upon which they have any power ?

Cambyses, because he dreamed in sleep that his brother was to become King of Persia, put him to death ; a brother whom he loved and had always trusted ! Aristodemus, King of the Messenians, killed himself for some fancied ill-omen which he drew from the meaningless howling of his dogs. And King Midas did the same, being disturbed and upset by some unpleasant dream he had dreamed.

To abandon life for a dream is to appraise it at its true value. And yet listen to our soul exulting over the wretchedness of the body and its weakness, and because it is exposed to every kind of injury and corruption ! Truly it has a right to speak !

O wretched clay, first by Prometheus shaped !
How little wisdom showed he in his work !
In moulding body he heeded not the soul,
The soul which should have been his art's first care. (PROPERTIUS.)

CHAPTER 5

ON SOME LINES OF VIRGIL

AN edifying thought is engrossing and burdensome in proportion to its fullness and substance. Sin, death, poverty, disease, are solemn and depressing subjects. Our minds should be taught the means to support and combat evils, and the rules of right living and right thinking, and should be often stirred up and exercised in that noble study. But by a mind of ordinary stamp it should be done intermittently and with moderation; if it is too continually strained it will become deranged.

In my younger days I needed self-exhortations and urgings to keep myself in moral trim; a cheerful and healthy nature does not go very well, so they say, with such wise and serious reflexions. I am now differently situated; the conditions attending old age are only too ready to give me warnings and preach me wisdom. From an excess of high spirits I have dropped into the more regrettable excess of seriousness.

For that reason I now purposely indulge myself a little in licence, and sometimes occupy my mind, to give it a rest, with youthful and wanton thoughts. I am at this age only too sober, too heavy and too mature. Every day my years read me lessons in coldness and temperance. This body flees irregularities and dreads them. It is taking its turn in guiding my mind towards reformation. In its turn it is beginning to domineer, and that more rudely and imperiously. It leaves me not an hour of respite, either sleeping or waking, from preaching to me about death, patience, and repentance. I am now on the defensive against temperance, as I was once against sensuality. It pulls me back too much, to the extent of making me insensible.

Now, I desire to master myself in every way. Wisdom has its excesses, and, no less than folly, needs to be moderated. So, lest I should dry up and wither, and be weighed down with prudence, in the intervals that my infirmities allow me,

        Lest mind be too intent upon my ills, (OVID.)

I gently turn aside, and avert my eyes from that stormy and cloudy sky that faces me, which, thanks be to God, I can regard indeed without terror, but not without effort and study ; and I divert my thoughts with recollections of my youthful follies :

> My Soul would have again what she has lost,
> And revels but in memories of the past. (PETRONIUS.)

Let childhood look ahead, and old age behind it ; was that not the meaning of Janus' double face ? Let years drag me along, if they will, but backward ! As long as my eyes are able to distinguish that lovely expired season of life, I turn them off and on in that direction. If it escapes from my blood and my veins, I will not at least tear the picture of it out of my memory :

> The man lives twice who can the gift retain
> Of memory, to enjoy past life again. (MARTIAL.)

Plato recommends old men to look on at the exercises, dances and games of youth, to enjoy in others the beauty and suppleness of body which they no longer possess, and recall to their mind the gracefulness and charm of their prime ; and would have them award the honour of victory in those sports to the youth who has provided most recreation and amusement to the greatest number of people.

Formerly I used to mark the dull and cloudy days as extraordinary ; these are now almost ordinary with me, and the extraordinary are the fine and bright days. I shall soon have come to such a pass that I shall leap for joy, and regard it as an unwonted favour, to be without pain. Though I tickle myself I cannot force a poor laugh out of this wretched body. I am merry only in fancy and in day-dreams, to divert by artifice the chagrin of old age. But, in faith, it would require another remedy than that of a dream. A feeble struggle of art against nature !

It shows great simplicity to prolong and anticipate human discomforts, as most men do. I would rather be old for a shorter time than be old before my time. I eagerly grasp even the slightest occasions for pleasure that I meet with.

I know indeed, from hearsay, several kinds of delights that are discreet, powerful, ostentatious ; but I am not such a slave to public opinion as to wish to acquire an appetite for them. I prefer them not so much grand, brilliant and showy as luscious, easy and ready to hand. *We depart from Nature; we follow the people, who are never a good guide* (Seneca).

My philosophy lies in action, in natural and present practice; little in imagination. O that I could take a pleasure in playing at cobnut or spinning a top!

> For he regarded not the foolish prate
> Of idle people—but his own good health. (ENNIUS adapted.)

Pleasure is an unambitious pursuit; it is rich enough in its own estimation without adding to it the reward of fame, and prefers to be in the shade. A young man who spends his time in acquiring a taste for choice wines and sauces deserves a thrashing. There is nothing I have known so little about and valued so little. I am now beginning to learn. I am greatly ashamed of it, but what can I do? I am still more ashamed and vexed at the occasions which drive me to it.

It is our part to dote and trifle; it is for the young to gain a reputation and climb the ladder. They are going into the world and the world's opinion; we are withdrawing from it. *Let them keep arms, horses, spears, clubs, tennis, swimming, and races. Of so many sports let them leave the dice-box to us old men* (Cicero). Even the laws send us home. I cannot do less, to gratify this wretched condition into which my age is forcing me, than to provide it with toys and playthings, as we do children; and after all it is a second childhood that we fall into. And wisdom and folly will have a hard task to prop and succour me with alternate services in this calamity of old age:

> Mingle your wisdom with glimpses of folly;
> 'Tis delightful at times the fool to play. (HORACE.)

And I try to escape the lightest punctures; and those that once would not have left a scratch now pierce me through and through. My habit of body begins to be so easily susceptible to pain. *To a frail body every shock is intolerable* (Cicero):

> A sickly mind can suffer nought that's hard. (OVID.)

I have always been delicately sensitive and susceptible to injuries: I am now still more tender and exposed to them on all sides:

> It needs no force to break a dish that's cracked. (OVID.)

My judgement certainly keeps me from kicking and murmuring against the discomforts that Nature commands me to suffer ; but it cannot keep me from feeling them. I, who have no other aim but to live and be merry, would travel from one end of the world to the other in search of one good year of agreeable and cheerful tranquillity. A dull and melancholy tranquillity may suffice me, but it benumbs and stupefies me ; and that is not to my liking. If there is any person, any good company, in country or town, in France or elsewhere, whether stay-at-home or travellers, who like my humours, whose humours I like, they have but to whistle in their palms, and I will come and provide them with Essays in flesh and bone.

Seeing that it is the privilege of the mind to escape from old age, I advise mine to do so to the best of its power ; let it bud, let it flower meanwhile, if it can, like the mistletoe on a dead tree !

But I fear my mind is a traitor ; he has formed so close a tie with the body that he forsakes me at every turn, and leaves me to follow him in his need. I take him aside to coax him, I make up to him, but to no purpose. In vain do I try to wean him from this intimacy, and offer him Seneca and Catullus, the ladies and royal dances ; if his comrade has the colic he seems to have it too. Even the activities which are peculiarly and essentially his own cannot then be stirred ; they so evidently smack of a cold in the head. In his productions there is no joy if it is not shared by the body.

Our masters are wrong in this : when seeking the causes of the extraordinary soarings of our soul, besides those they attribute to a divine rapture, to love, to martial fierceness, to poetry, to wine, they have not given its due share to health ; a full, lusty, exuberant, lazy health, such as once the verdure of youth and the feeling of security provided me with in increasing measure. That fire of good humour kindles in the mind bright and vivid flashes beyond our natural capacity, and some of the most joyous, not to say extravagant, enthusiasms.

It is no wonder then if a contrary state depresses my spirits, nails them down, and produces a contrary effect :

When body flags 'twill rise to no achievement. (PSEUDO-GALLUS.)

And yet my mind expects me to be grateful to it because, as it tells me, it acquiesces much less in this languor than is usual with most men. Let us at least, while we are under truce, drive away the evils and difficulties of our partnership:

> While yet we may,
> We'll drive old age with clouded brow away. (HORACE.)

'Tis good to sweeten black cares with pleasantries (Sidonius Apollinaris). I love a gay and sociable wisdom, and steer clear of all sour and austere morality; I suspect a forbidding mien,

> The arrogant gloom of a scowling face. (BUCHANAN.)
> Austerity hides many a debauchee. (MARTIAL.)

I heartily agree with Plato when he says that an easy or difficult humour contributes much towards making a soul either good or wicked. Socrates had a settled expression, but serene and smiling; not settled like that of the elder Crassus, who was never seen to laugh.

Virtue is a pleasant and cheerful quality.

I know well that very few people will frown at the looseness of my writings who will not have more reason to frown at the looseness of their own thoughts. My sentiments agree with theirs, but I offend their eyes.

It shows a nice habit of mind indeed to cavil at Plato's writings, and glide over his supposed relations with Phaedo, Dion, Stella,[1] Archeanassa! *Let us not be ashamed to say what we are not ashamed to think.* I hate a gloomy and dismal person who allows the pleasures of life to pass him by, and fastens and browses on its miseries. Like flies that cannot fasten on a very smooth and polished surface, but fix and rest on rough and uneven places; or like leeches that suck and crave only for bad blood.

For the rest I have made it a rule to dare to say all that I dare to do; and I dislike even unpublishable thoughts. The worst of my actions and qualities does not appear to me so ugly at it appears ugly and base not to dare to own it.

Every man is discreet in confession; we should be the same in action.

Boldness to sin is somewhat compensated and curbed by the boldness to confess it. If a man forced himself to tell

---

[1] i.e., Aster, of which Stella is the Latin equivalent.

everything, he would force himself not to do anything that he is obliged to conceal.

God grant that my extreme outspokenness should induce our men to be more free, and to be above those timorous and affected virtues, born of our imperfections; that at the cost of my immodesty I may lead them on to the point of good sense!

A man must see and study his faults before he can criticize them. They who conceal them from others usually conceal them from themselves. And they do not think them sufficiently hidden if they can see them; they disguise them and withdraw them from their own consciousness.

Why does no man confess his faults? Because he is still a slave to them. We must be awake to tell our dreams (Seneca).

The diseases of the body become more distinct as they increase. What we thought was a cold or a sprain turns out to be gout. The diseases of the mind become more obscure as they increase; the most sick are least sensible of them. Therefore we must often, with pitiless hand, bring them to the light of day, lay them bare, and tear them out of the hollow of our bosom.

As in the case of good deeds, so also in the case of evil deeds, the mere confession is sometimes a reparation. Is any sin so ugly that one can be excused the duty of confessing it?

It is so painful to me to conceal anything that I shun being trusted with another's secrets, not having the assurance to deny what I know. I am able to keep it to myself; but deny it I cannot without effort and great reluctance. To be really secretive, one must be so by nature, and not by obligation. In the service of a prince it is of little use to be secretive if one is not also a liar.

If the man who asked Thales of Miletus whether he should solemnly deny having committed adultery had referred to me I should have told him not to do so. For lying appears to me still worse than adultery. Thales advised him quite otherwise, that he should swear in order to shield the greater by the lesser sin.[1] Yet he advised him not so much a choice as a multiplication of sins.

---

[1] Either Montaigne's memory here played him false, or he was misled, as Coste suggests, by the absence of a note of interrogation in his Greek

Whereupon let us say this by the way, that we make it easy to a conscientious man when we offer him some difficulty to counterbalance a sin; but when we hem him in between two sins, we put him to a rude choice, as in the case of Origen. He was given the alternative of either practising idolatry or suffering himself to be carnally enjoyed by a big ruffian of an Ethiopian who was brought before him. He submitted to the former condition; and sinfully, according to one writer. On this assumption, those ladies would not be in the wrong, according to their erroneous views, who *protest* to us in these days that they would rather charge their conscience with ten men than one mass.[1]

If it is an indiscretion thus to publish abroad one's errors, there is no great danger that it will become a precedent and custom; for Aristo said that the winds that people fear most are those which uncover them. We must tuck up this silly rag that covers our manners. They send their conscience to the brothel and preserve a starched countenance. Even traitors and murderers observe the laws of decorum, and make it a matter of duty. Yet neither can injustice complain of incivility[2] nor knavery of indiscretion. It is a pity that a wicked man is not at the same time a fool, and that outward decency should palliate his sin. Such a rough-cast is only suitable to a good and sound wall, that deserves to be preserved or whitewashed.

In common with the Huguenots, who condemn our auricular and private confession, I confess in public, simply and scrupulously. St. Augustine, Origen, and Hippocrates published the errors of their belief; I, besides, those of my morals. I am hungering to make myself known; and I care not to how many, provided I do so truly; or, to speak more correctly, I hunger for nothing, but I have a deadly fear of being thought other than I am by those who come to know me by name.

What does that man who will do anything for honour text of Diogenes Laertius. His answer was, 'Is not perjury worse than adultery?'

[1] Montaigne will have his little joke, though it may not be in the best taste. He felt, however, neither ill-will nor intolerance towards the Protestants.

[2] i.e., perhaps: a man who violates the laws is not entitled to rebuke a man for rude behaviour.

and glory think to gain by showing himself to the world with a mask, hiding his real nature from public knowledge? Praise a hunchback for his handsome figure, and he must take it for an insult. If you are a coward and some one compliments you on being a man of valour, is it you he is speaking of? He takes you for another. I should as soon commend him who was pleased with the bonnetings that somebody bestowed upon him, thinking he was master of the company, when he was the meanest of the retinue.

As Archelaus, King of Macedon, was passing along the street, some one poured water upon him; his attendants said he ought to be punished. 'Yes, but, said he, it was not me he poured the water upon, but the man he took me for.'

Socrates said to one who informed him that people were speaking ill of him, 'Not of me; there is nothing in me of what they say.'

For my part, if any man commended me for a good pilot, or as very modest, or as very chaste, I should owe him no thanks. And, on the other hand, if one called me a traitor, a thief, a drunkard, I should just as little take offence. Those who misknow themselves may feed on undeserved approbation. Not I, who can see myself, who can search my very heart, and know very well what is due to me. I am content to be less commended, provided I be better known. I might be thought wise in such a sort of wisdom as I take to be folly.

It annoys me that the ladies use my Essays merely as a common piece of furniture, furniture for the reception-room. This chapter will make me suitable for the boudoir. I love their society when it is a little private; in public it is without favour or savour.

In taking farewell we warm up, more than ordinarily, our affection for the things we are leaving. I am taking my last leave of the sports of the world. These are our last embraces. But let us come to my theme.

What harm has the genital act, so natural, so necessary, and so lawful, done to humanity, that we dare not speak of it without shame, and exclude it from serious and orderly conversation? We boldly utter the words, *kill, rob, betray*; and the other we only dare to utter under our breath. Does this mean that the less of it we breathe in words, the more are we at liberty to swell our thoughts with it? For it is amusing that the words which are least used, least written, and most hushed up, should be the best known and the most generally understood. There is no person of any age or morals but knows them as well as he knows the word *bread*. They are impressed upon each of us, without being expressed, without voice and without form. [And the sex that does it most is charged to hush it up.]

It is also amusing that it is an action we have placed in the sanctuary of silence, from which to tear it by force is a crime, even for the purpose of accusing it and bringing it to justice. And we do not dare to scourge it but in roundabout and figurative terms. A great favour indeed for a criminal to be so execrable that justice thinks it wrong to touch and see him; free and saved by the favour of the severity of his sentence! Is it not the same as with books, that sell better and become more public for being suppressed? For my part I will take Aristotle's word for it, who says, 'To be shamefaced is an ornament of youth, but a reproach to old age.'

These lines are preached in the old school, a school with which I hold much more than with the modern; its virtues appear to me greater, its vices less:

> Who strives too much to shun fair Venus' wiles
> Sins equally with him who is too keen
> In her pursuit. (AMYOT after PLUTARCH.)

> Thou, Goddess,
> Dost rule the world alone, and without thee
> Naught rises to the shining shores of light,
> Nor aught of joyful or of lovely is born. (LUCRETIUS.)

I know not who could have set Pallas and the Muses at variance with Venus, and made them cool towards Cupid; but I know of no deities that agree so well together, and are more indebted to one another. Take from the Muses their amorous fancies and you will rob them of the best entertainment they have, and of the noblest matter of their work. And if you deprive Cupid of the society and service of Poetry you will blunt his best weapons. In this way you charge the god of sweet intimacy and amity, and the patron goddesses of humanity and justice, with the sin of ingratitude and forgetfulness.[1]

---

[1] In writing the above, Montaigne might have been reminiscent of a

I have not been so long cashiered from the staff and retinue of this god but that I still retain a memory of his power and worth :

> Too plain
> I know the traces of the long-quenched flame. (VIRGIL.)

There is still some remnant of heat and emotion after the fever :

> In wintry age let not this love grow cool ! (JOHANNES SECUNDUS.)

Withered and drooping though I be, I still feel a few tepid remains of that past ardour :

> As the deep Aegean, when no more blow the winds,
> That rolled its tumbling waves with troublous blasts,
> Doth yet of tempests passed some show retain,
> And here and there its swelling billows casts. (TASSO.)

But, if I understand the matter, the power and importance of this god, as portrayed in poetry, are much greater and more alive than they are in reality :

> And Poetry has fingers too
>   To titillate and please. (Adapted from JUVENAL.)

Her pictures are somehow more amorous than Amor himself. Venus is not so beautiful, quite naked and alive and panting, as she is in these lines of Virgil :

> The Goddess ceased, and with the soft embrace
> Of snowy arms about his body wound
> Fondled him as he faltered. Quick he caught
> The wonted fire ; the old heat pierced his heart,
> Ran through his melting frame : as oftentimes
> A fiery rift, burst by the thunder-clap,
> Runs quivering down the cloud, with flash of light.
> . . . . So saying, he gave
> The embrace she longed for, on her bosom sank,
> And wooed calm slumber to o'erglide his limbs.[1] (VIRGIL.)

pretty passage in Rabelais : 'I remember having read that Cupid on a time being asked of his mother, Venus, why he did not assault the Muses, his answer was, That he found them so fair, so neat, so modest, so virtuous, and so continually occupied, that approaching near unto them he unbent his bow, shut his quiver and extinguished his torch, through mere shame and fear that he might do them some hurt. Which done he thereafter put off his fillet wherewith his eyes were bound, to look them in the face, and to hear their melody and poetic odes. There took he the greatest pleasure in the world, that many times he was transported with their beauty and pretty behaviour, and charmed asleep by the harmony ; so far was he from assaulting them, or interrupting their studies.'

[1] As probably no translation can do full justice to the original, another

What strikes me is that he depicts her a little too passionate for a married Venus. In this sober contract the desires are not generally so wanton; they are dull and more blunted. Love hates to be held by any tie but himself, and goes feebly to work in intimacies formed and continued under a different name, such as marriage. Family and fortune are there rightly accounted as important, or more so, than charm and beauty. We do not marry for ourselves, whatever they may say; we marry as much, or more, for posterity, for the family. The custom and interest of marriage concern our stock, long after we are dead.

For this reason I approve of its being arranged by a third hand rather than by our own, by others' good sense rather than our own. How totally different is all this to a love compact! Besides, it is a kind of incest in this sacred and time-honoured alliance to employ the extravagant actions of amorous licence, as I think I have said elsewhere.[1] We should, says Aristotle, approach our wives discreetly and soberly, lest the pleasure of being touched too lasciviously should transport them beyond the bounds of reason. What he says upon the account of conscience the physicians say upon the account of health, 'that an over-heated, voluptuous and assiduous pleasure corrupts the seed and hinders conception.' They say, on the other hand, 'that in a languid intercourse, as this is by its nature, the man should offer himself rarely and at considerable intervals, in order that a proper and fertile heat may be stored up':

> To eagerly absorb
> Their fill of love, and deeply entertain. (VIRGIL.)

I know of no marriages that are so soon troubled and that version may be appended, that of the late E. Fairfax Taylor. The translation in the text is by Mr. James Rhoades:

> She spoke, and both her snowy arms outflung
> Around him doubting, and embraced the Sire,
> And, softly fondling, kissed him as she clung.
> Through bones and veins her melting charms inspire
> The well-known heat, and reawake desire.
> So, riven by the thunder, through the pile
> Of storm-clouds runs the glittering cleft of fire.
> . . . . He said,
> And gave the love she longed for; on her breast
> Outpoured at length he slept, and loosed his limbs with rest.

[1] Book I, chapter 30.

so soon come to grief as those which are contracted on account of beauty and amorous desires. It needs more solid and permanent foundations, and we should proceed circumspectly ; such an exuberant vivacity serves no purpose.

They who think to do honour to marriage by the addition of love are in the same case, it seems to me, as those who, thinking to honour virtue, maintain that virtue and nobility are the same thing. They are qualities which have some affinity, but there is a great difference between them. There is no need to confuse their names and titles, whereby both of them are wronged. Nobility is a fine quality and introduced with good reason ; but as it is a quality dependent on others, and may fall to the share of any vicious or worthless person, in estimation it falls far short of virtue. If it can be called a virtue, it is an artificial and visible virtue, depending on time and fortune, varying in its nature according to country, of this life and mortal, with no more source than the river Nile, genealogical and common to many, a thing of succession and resemblance, derived by inference, and a very weak inference.

Knowledge, strength, goodness, beauty, wealth, all other qualities, have their value in intercourse and commerce ; this is self-centred, and of no use in the service of others.

One of our kings was offered the choice of two competitors for the same office, one of whom was a nobleman, and the other not. He ordered them to elect the man of greatest merit, without regard to that kind of quality ; but in case of their being of exactly equal merit, that they should take nobility into consideration. This was to give it its proper place.

Antigonus said to a young man who was a stranger to him, and who entreated him to be allowed to succeed to his father's command, a man of valour, lately dead, ' My friend, in such preferments I regard not so much the noble birth of my soldiers as their prowess.'

In truth it should not be as with the functionaries of the Kings of Sparta, trumpeters, musicians, cooks, who were succeeded in their office by their sons, however incompetent they might be, in preference to the most experienced in the profession.

The people of Calicut look upon their nobles as a super-human species. They are forbidden to marry, or adopt any profession except war. Of concubines they may have their fill, and the women as many gallants, without any mutual jealousy. But it is a capital and unpardonable crime to mate with a person of different rank to their own. They think themselves contaminated if they have been merely touched by them in passing, and, as their nobility is damaged and injured thereby to a remarkable degree, they will kill any who have only come a little too near them. So the ignoble are obliged to shout as they walk, like the gondoliers at Venice, at the street-corners, for fear of collisions; and the nobles order them, as they choose, to step to one side or the other. By this means the one avoids what they regard as a perpetual disgrace, and the other a certain death. No length of time, no princely favour, no office, no virtue, no wealth, can ever make a noble of a plebeian. To which the custom contributes that marriages between different trades are forbidden. A girl of shoemaker stock may not marry a carpenter; and the parents are rigorously obliged to train a son to his father's calling, and to no other, by which means the distinction and continuity of their fortunes is preserved.

A good marriage, if there is such a thing, rejects the company and conditions of love. It tries to imitate those of friendship. It is a sweet partnership for life, full of constancy, trust, and an endless number of useful and substantial services and mutual obligations. No woman who relishes the taste of it,

On whom the nuptial torch has shed a welcome light, (CATULLUS.)

would like to hold the position of her husband's mistress or leman. If she is lodged in his affections as a wife she is much more honourably and securely lodged. Even if he is paying ardent attentions to another, let any one ask him 'on which of the two, his wife or his mistress, he would rather a disgrace should fall? whose misfortune would grieve him most? for whom he would desire the greatest honour?' These questions would admit of no doubt in a sound marriage.

It is a sign of the value and excellence of marriage that we see so few good ones. If rightly established and properly understood, there is no better institution in modern society. We cannot dispense with it, and we continue to dishonour it. It may be compared to a cage; the birds outside are desperately anxious to get in, and those that are in it are equally anxious to get out.

Socrates, when asked whether it was better to take a wife than not, replied, 'Whichever you do, you will repent it.' It is a compact to which the saying fitly applies, ' Man is to man either a god or a wolf.' It needs the conjunction of many qualities to build it up. In these days it is better adapted for simple souls, those of the people, who are not so much disturbed by pleasures, curiosity and idleness. Men of loose morals, like myself, who hate any kind of tie or obligation, are not so well fitted for it:

To me 'tis sweeter far to live with neck unyoked. (PSEUDO-GALLUS.)

If I had followed my own bent, I would have shunned wedlock with Wisdom herself, if she would have had me. But, say what we please, custom and the uses of everyday life carry us along. Most of my actions are guided by example, not by choice. In any case it was not properly at my own prompting that I married. I was led and brought to it by outside occasions. For not only inconvenient things, but anything, however offensive, wicked and repulsive, may be rendered acceptable by some condition or circumstance; so unsteady are we on our feet!

And I certainly was drawn into it at the time more ill-prepared and more reluctantly than I should be at present, after having made trial of it. And, however loose I may be thought, I have in truth observed the laws of wedlock more strictly than I either promised or expected. It is too late to kick when once we have been hobbled. We must manage our freedom wisely; but, having once submitted to bondage, we must keep within the laws of common duty, or at least make an effort to do so.

Those men who enter into this bond with the intention of behaving with hatred and contempt act wrongly and improperly; and this pretty rule which passes from hand to hand among the ladies, like a sacred oracle,

Serve your husband as a master;
Trust him not, for he betrays you,

which is as much as to say, ' Bear yourself towards him with a constrained, hostile and distrustful reverence,' as if it were a war-cry and a challenge, is equally hard and unjust.

I am too mild to harbour such repellent intentions. To tell the truth, I have not yet arrived at such perfection of cleverness and refinement of wit as to confound reason with injustice, and make a mockery of all rule and order that does not fall in with my desires. Though I may hate superstition I do not forthwith take refuge in irreligion. If we do not always do our duty, we should at least always love and acknowledge it. To marry without being wedded is treachery. Let us proceed.

Our poet depicts a marriage in which there is perfect harmony and propriety, in which there is, however, not much loyalty. Did he mean to imply that it is not impossible to yield to the power of love, and yet reserve some duty towards marriage ; and that it may be bruised without being altogether broken ? Many a serving man shoes his masters' mule[1] without necessarily hating him. Beauty, opportunity, fate (for Fate also has a hand in it),

> There is a Fate that rules our hidden parts ;
> For if the stars be not propitious,
> Virility will not avail thee aught, (JUVENAL.)

have attached her to a stranger ; not so wholly perhaps but that there remains some tie by which she is still held to her husband. It is like two plans, with distinct routes, not to be confounded with one another. A woman may surrender to a certain man whom she would in no case have married ; I do not mean on account of the state of his fortune, but for his personal qualities. Few men have married their mistresses without repenting it.

And even in the other world, what a poor match Jupiter made of it with the wife whom he had first seduced and enjoyed in love's dalliance ! That is, as the proverb puts it, ' to cack in the basket, and then put it on your head.'

I have seen in my time, in a good family, love shamefully and indecently cured by marriage ; the considerations are too different. We love, without pledging ourselves, two different and contradictory things.

Isocrates said that the city of Athens pleased after the manner of the ladies we serve for love. Every man loved to go there, to saunter and pass the time ; but no one loved it so well as to marry it, that is to say, to reside and settle there.

---
[1] Pilfers from him.

MAN'S INJUSTICE TO WOMAN

I have been annoyed to see husbands hate their wives merely because they themselves have wronged them. We should at all events not love them less for our own faults; pity and repentance should at least make them more dear to us.

They are different ends, he says,[1] and yet in some sort compatible. Marriage has, for its share, usefulness, justice, honour and constancy; a stale but more durable pleasure. Love is grounded on pleasure alone, and it is indeed more gratifying to the senses, keener and more acute; a pleasure stirred and kept alive by difficulties. There must be a sting and a smart in it. It ceases to be love if it have no shafts and no fire. The liberality of the ladies is too profuse in marriage, and blunts the edge of affection and desire. Observe what pains Lycurgus and Plato take, in their Laws, to avoid that disadvantage.

Women are not by any means to blame when they reject the rules of life which have been introduced into the world, seeing that it is the men who made them without their consent. Intrigues and wranglings between them and ourselves are only natural; the closest agreement we enjoy with them is still attended with tumults and storms.

In the opinion of our author we treat them without consideration in this respect: After knowing that they are incomparably more capable and ardent in the sexual act than we, of which that priest of antiquity was a witness, who was first a man and then a woman:

> Tiresias must decide
> The difference, who both delights has tried; (OVID.)

after hearing moreover from their own lips the proof that was given, in different centuries, by an Emperor and an Empress of Rome,[2] both famous master-workers in the art (he indeed deflowered in one night ten Sarmatian virgins, his captives, but she actually suffered in one night twenty-five assaults, changing her company according to need and liking:

> Still burning with unconquerable lust,
> Weary she gave up, but still unsatisfied; [JUVENAL].)

and after the dispute which took place in Catalonia, when a woman complaining of her husband's too unremitting

---
[1] Isocrates.   [2] Proculus and Messalina.

attentions, not so much, I take it, because she was inconvenienced by them (for I believe in no miracles, except in matters of faith), as, under this pretext, to restrict and curb, in this the most fundamental act of marriage, the authority of husbands over their wives, and to show that their perverseness and ill-will extend beyond the nuptial couch and tread under foot even the sweets and delights of Venus; and the husband, certainly an unnatural brute, replying that even on fast-days he could not do with less than ten, the Queen of Aragon interposed with that notable sentence, by which, after mature deliberation with her Council, that good Queen, to establish for all times a rule and example of the moderation and modesty required in a rightful marriage, prescribed as a lawful and necessary limit the number of six per diem; thus renouncing and surrendering a great part of her sex's needs and desires, to set up, as she said, ' an easy and consequently permanent and immutable formula;' against which the doctors exclaim, ' what must be the appetite and lust of women, when their reason, their amendment and virtue are taxed at such a rate!'

Considering these varying estimates of our sexual needs, and seeing that Solon, head of the school of lawgivers, assesses this conjugal intercourse, if we are not to be found wanting, at no more than three times a month; after believing and preaching all this, we have gone and allotted them continence for their particular portion, at the risk of the last and extreme penalties.

There is no passion more exacting than this, which we expect them alone to resist, as being not simply an ordinary vice, but an abominable and accursed thing, and worse than irreligion and parricide; whilst we men at the same time yield to it without blame or reproach. Even those of us who have tried to master it have often enough had to admit how difficult, or rather how impossible it was, by the use of material remedies, to deaden, to weaken and cool the body.

On the other hand, we expect them to be healthy, robust, plump, well nourished and chaste at the same time; that is to say, both hot and cold. For marriage, whose function we say it is to keep them from burning, brings them but little relief, as we live nowadays. If they take a husband who is still exuberant with the vigour of youth, he will make a boast of expending it on others :

> If you don't mend your ways, we'll go to law.
> Your vigour, bought with many thousand crowns,
> No longer's yours, my Bassus ; you have sold it. (MARTIAL.)

The philosopher Polemon was rightly haled before justice by his wife, for sowing in a barren field the fruit that was meant for the genital field.

If on the other hand, they take one of the worn-out kind, behold them in full wedlock worse off than virgins and widows ! We think they are well provided for because they have a man at their side. By the same reasoning the Romans held Clodia Laeta, a Vestal virgin, to have been violated, because Caligula had approached her, although it was averred that he had no more than approached her. Their need is, on the contrary, thereby redoubled, since the contact and company of any male whatever excites their heat, which in solitude would remain more dormant.

And, in order, in all probability, to render their chastity the more meritorious by this circumstance and consideration, Boleslas and Kinge, his wife, King and Queen of Poland, by mutual agreement consecrated it by a vow, while lying together on their very wedding-night, and kept it in the teeth of conjugal opportunities.

We train them from childhood in the service of love ; their charm, their dressing up, their knowledge, their language, all their instruction, have only this end in view. Their governesses keep suggesting amorous ideas to them, though always with the intention of exciting their disgust. My daughter (who is the only child I have) is at an age when the most precocious of them are allowed by the laws to marry ; she is constitutionally backward, thin and delicate, and has accordingly been brought up by her mother in a retired and particular manner, so that she is only now beginning to put off her childish naïveté.

She was reading a French book when I was present, and came across the word *fouteau*, the name of a well-known tree (beech). The woman to whose care she was entrusted rather rudely stopped her short and made her pass over the danger spot. I let her have her way in order not to disturb their rules, for I never meddle with that government ;

feminine policy has a mysterious procedure, and we must leave it to them. But, if I am not mistaken, the conversation of twenty lackeys could not, in six months, have implanted in her imagination, the meaning and use and all the consequences of the sound of those criminating syllables, as this good old lady did by her reprimand and interdict.

> The ripening virgin joys to learn
> In the Ionic dance to turn
>   And bend with plastic limb ;
> Still but a child, with evil gleams
> Incestuous love's unhallowed dreams
>   Before her fancy swim. (HORACE.)

Let them but drop their formal modesty a little, give them occasion to talk freely ; compared with them we are but children in that science. Only hear them describing our pursuits and our conversation ; they will very soon let you know that we can bring them nothing they have not known and digested without our help. Can it be, as Plato says, that they have once been dissolute boys ?

My ear once happened to be in a place where it was able, without being suspected, to snatch a little of their talk. Why cannot I repeat it ? By our Lady, said I, what need is there to study the phrases of Amadis and the books of Boccaccio and Aretino, and think ourselves so knowing ? It is a mere waste of time. There is no word, no example, no proceeding, that they know not better than our books ; it is an instruction that is born in the veins,

> By Venus herself inspired of old, (VIRGIL.)

which those good schoolmasters, Nature, Youth and Health, continually breathe into their souls. They have no need to learn it ; they breed it :

> Not more delighted is the snow-white dove,
> Or if there be a thing more prone to love,
> Still to be billing with her male than is
> Woman with every man she meets to kiss. (CATULLUS.)

If the natural violence of their desire were not held a little in check by the fear and honour with which they have been provided, we should be shamed. The whole movement of the world resolves itself into and leads to this pairing ; it is a matter infused throughout ; it is a centre to which all things are directed. We may still see some of the laws of old and wise Rome, drawn up for the service of Love ; and Socrates' precepts for the instruction of courtezans :

> On silken cushions they love to lie,
> Those little books the Stoics write. (HORACE.)

Zeno, amongst his laws, gives rules for the spreading and the attack in deflowering. What was the drift of the philosopher Strato's book, Of Carnal Conjunction ? Of what did Theophrastus treat in those he called, one The Lover, the other Of Love ? Of what Aristippus, in his work Of Ancient Delights ? What was the aim of Plato's so lengthy and lively descriptions of the boldest amours of his time ? And of the book Of the Lover, by Demetrius of Phalera ? And Clinias, or the Ravished Lover, of Heraclides of Pontus ? And Antisthenes' Of Begetting Children, or Of Weddings, or his other, Of the Master or the Lover ? And Aristo's Of Amorous Exercises ? Those of Cleanthes, one Of Love, the other Of the Art of Loving ? The Amorous Dialogues of Sphaerus ? And the Fable of Jupiter and Juno, by Chrysippus, which is shameless beyond all bearing, and of his fifty so lascivious Epistles ? For I must omit the writings of the philosophers who followed the Epicurean school [the protectors of sensuality].

In ancient times fifty deities were subservient to this business. And there were countries where, to assuage the lust of those who came to pay their devotions, they kept girls and boys in the churches for enjoyment, and it was a ceremonious act to use them before going to service. *Doubtless incontinence is necessary for continence, as a fire is extinguished by fire.*

In most parts of the world that part of the body was deified. In one and the same province some flayed off the skin to offer and consecrate a piece of it, and others offered and consecrated their semen. In another province the young men publicly pierced and opened it in several places between the flesh and skin, and through the openings thrust skewers, as long and thick as they could bear them ; and of these skewers they afterwards made a fire, as an offering to the gods. They were reputed weak and unchaste if they were dismayed by the force of this cruel pain. In another place the most sacred magistrate was revered and known by that member; and in some ceremonies an effigy of it was carried about in state, to the honour of various divinities.

At the festival of the Bacchanals the Egyptian ladies carried about their necks a wooden effigy of it, exquisitely carved, big and heavy according to their capacity; besides which the statue of their god exhibited one which exceeded in size the rest of the body.[1]

In my neighbourhood the married women twist their kerchief over their forehead into the shape of one, to boast of the enjoyment they have out of it; and when they become widows they turn it behind them and hide it under their coif.

The most sedate of Roman matrons thought it an honour to offer flowers and garlands to the god Priapus; and the virgins at the time of their nuptials were made to sit upon his least seemly parts. And I know not but that I have seen something of the like devotion in my time.

What was the meaning of that ridiculous part of the hose our fathers wore, and which is still seen on our Swiss?[2] What is the idea of the show we still make of our pieces, in effigy under our galligaskins; and, what is worse, often, by falsehood and imposture, above their natural size?

I am inclined to think that a dress of this kind was invented in the best and most conscientious ages in order not to deceive the world, and that every man might, publicly and boldly, render an account of his capacity. The most simple nations still have it, nearly corresponding to the real thing. In those days the workman was taught the art, as it is practised in taking the measure of an arm or a foot.

That good man who, when I was young, castrated so many beautiful and antique statues in his great city, that the eye might not be offended, following the advice of that other ancient worthy ·

> The censure of this shame [3] to those is due
> Who naked bodies first exposed to view,
> (ENNIUS, quoted by Cicero.)

---

[1] More correctly, according to Herodotus, 'nearly as large as the rest of the body.'
[2] Probably the Swiss mercenaries quartered in the neighbourhood.
[3] The 'shame' Ennius refers to is the widely prevailing vice of sodomy.

should have considered that, as in the mysteries of the Good Goddess [1] all male semblance was precluded, nothing would be gained unless he also had horses and asses, and in short nature, castrated:

> All things terrestrial, whether man or brute,
> The ocean tribes, tame beasts, gay-feathered birds,
> Rush on to passion's pyre. (VIRGIL.)

The Gods, says Plato, have furnished us with a disobedient and tyrannical member, which, like an animal in its fury, attempts, in the violence of its desire, to subdue everything to its power. So also to the women they have given a greedy and voracious animal which, if denied its food in due season, goes mad in its impatience of delay; and, breathing its rage into their bodies, stops up the conduits, arrests breathing, and causes a thousand kinds of ills, till, having imbibed the fruit of the common thirst, it has copiously bedewed and sown the ground of their matrix.

Now my legislator [2] should also have considered that it is perhaps a more chaste and salutary practice to let them know betimes the living reality, than to leave them to guess it according to the licence and heat of their imagination. In place of the real parts their desire and hope substitute others triply magnified. And a certain man of my acquaintance ruined his chances by openly disclosing his in a place where he was not yet enabled to put them to their proper and more serious use.

What mischief is not done by these pictures of enormous size that the boys scatter all over the galleries and staircases of the royal houses! From them they derive a cruel contempt for our natural capacity.

How do we know that Plato had not an eye to this when he ordained, following other well-established republics, that men and women, young and old, should appear naked in view of one another in his gymnasiums?

The Indian women, who see their men undressed, have at

---

[1] The *Bona Dea*, worshipped by the women of Rome as the goddess of chastity and fidelity, whose temple no man was permitted to enter. In later times it became the resort of unchaste women, and the scene of licence.

[2] The 'good man' who treated the statues at Rome in the aforementioned manner, supposed to have been Pope Paul III.

least cooled their sense of sight. And, although the women of that great kingdom of Pegu, who have nothing to cover them below the waist but a cloth slit in front, and so skimp that, however much modesty they may try to observe, they reveal themselves at every step they take, may tell us that is a device for attracting the men to their sides and wean them from intercourse with their own sex, a practice to which that nation is universally addicted, we might reply that they lose thereby more than they gain, and that a complete hunger is sharper than one that has been satisfied at least by the eyes.

Besides, Livia said 'that to an honest woman a naked man is no more than a statue'.

The Lacedemonian women, more virginal as wives than our maidens are, every day saw the young men of their city stripped for their exercises, and were not very particular themselves to cover their thighs as they walked, esteeming themselves, as Plato says, sufficiently covered by their virtue without a farthingale.[1]

But those men, mentioned by Saint Augustine, who raised a doubt whether the women, at the universal judgement, will rise again in their own sex, and not rather in ours, lest they should tempt us in that holy state, have ascribed a wonderful power of temptation to nudity.

In short we lure and flesh them by every means; we incessantly heat and excite their imagination, and then we shout when we are hurt. Let us confess the truth: there is hardly one of us who does not fear the disgrace his wife's misdeeds may bring upon him more than his own; who does not look more tenderly after his good spouse's conscience than his own (wonderful charity!); who would not rather be a thief and guilty of sacrilege, and that his wife were a heretic and murderess, than that she should be less chaste than her husband.

And they would willingly offer to seek a livelihood in the law-courts, or a reputation in war, rather than be obliged, in the midst of pleasures and idleness, to keep so difficult a guard. Do you think they do not see that there is not a

---

[1] *Assez couvertes de leur vertu sans vertugade.* This pun perhaps suggested the ingenious derivation *vertugarde*, 'virtue-guard'. The farthingale (actually a corruption of *vertugade*, which is of Spanish origin) was certainly well contrived to keep men at a distance.

tradesman, or an attorney, or a soldier, who will not leave his business to run after this other; nor even a street-porter or cobbler, weary and jaded as they are with labour and hunger?

> For all that did Achaemenes possess,
>   Or wealth Mygdonian of rich Phrygia,
> Or Arab treasure-house, would'st give one tress
>   Of thy Licymnia,
>
> While to thy burning kiss her neck she bends,
>   Or with feigned cruelty that kiss denies
> Which ravished then the thief she more commends,
>   Sometimes to ravish tries? (HORACE.)

What an iniquitous balancing of sins! Both we and they are capable of a thousand more mischievous and unnatural depravities than lasciviousness. But we create and weigh sins not according to Nature, but according to our interest; wherefore they assume such unequal shapes. The harshness of our decrees makes the addiction of the women to that sin more serious and sinful than its nature admits of, and involves it in consequences which are worse than their cause.

I doubt if the achievements of an Alexander or a Caesar surpass in difficulty the steadfastness of a handsome young woman, brought up after our fashion, in the open view and in contact with the world, assailed by so many contrary examples, keeping herself entire in the midst of a thousand powerful and persistent solicitations. There is no activity more abounding in thorny difficulties, nor more active, than this inactivity. I should think it easier to wear a suit of armour all one's life than a virginity. And the vow of chastity is the most noble of all vows, as being the hardest. *The power of the Devil is in the loins*, says Saint Jerome.

Certainly the most arduous and rigorous of human duties is that we have resigned to the ladies, and we leave them the glory of it. That should serve them as a particular spur to persist in it; it offers them a fine occasion to challenge us, and to tread under foot that vain pre-eminence in courage and valour that we claim over them. They will find, if they take notice, that they will be not only very highly esteemed for it, but also better loved.

A gallant man does not give up his pursuit for a refusal, provided it be a refusal of chastity, not of choice. Though we swear and threaten and complain ever so much, we lie; we love them the better for it. There is no greater allurement than a chastity that is not hard and forbidding. It is stupid and vulgar to persist obstinately in the face of hatred and contempt; but to do so against a virtuous and constant resolution, accompanied by a grateful disposition, is the action of a noble and generous spirit. They may gratefully accept our services to a certain degree, and with due modesty make us feel that they do not disdain us.

For it is indeed a cruel law, if only for its difficulty, which commands them to abhor us because we adore them, and hate us because we love them. Why should they not listen to our offers and requests, so long as they keep within the bounds of modesty? Why should they try to detect the note of some more licentious meaning under our words? A Queen of our time wittily said that 'to repel these approaches was a testimony of weakness, and an accusation of her own facility; and that a lady who had not been tempted could not vaunt her chastity'.

The bounds of honour are not by any means cut so closely; it is quite able, without transgressing, to relax its severity, and give itself a freer rein. Beyond its frontier there is some expanse of land, free, indifferent and neuter. He who has hunted and forcibly run it home, even into its corner and stronghold, is wanting in tact if he is not satisfied with his fortune. The prize of victory is estimated by its difficulty.

Would you know what impression your assiduity and your merit have made on her heart? Judge of it by her character. Many a woman may give more without giving so much. The obligation of a benefit is entirely in proportion to the will of him who gives. Other circumstances which accompany the conferring of a benefit are dumb, dead and fortuitous. This little may cost her dearer to give than it may cost her companion to give her all. If ever rarity was a sign of esteem it must be so in this case; do not consider how little it is, but how few have it. The value of a coin changes according to the stamp and the place where it is minted.

Whatever the spite and indiscretion of some men, at the height of their discontent, may drive them to say, virtue and truth always recover their ground. I have known women, whose reputation had long been unjustly compromised, to recover their good name in the eyes of the world by their constancy alone, without any effort or cunning. All did penance and took back what they had once believed. From being a little under suspicion as girls they have risen to the first rank among good and honourable ladies.

Somebody said to Plato, 'All the world is maligning you.' 'Let them say, he said, I will live in such a way that they shall change their tone.'

Besides the fear of God and the reward of so rare a fame, which should incite them to keep themselves unspotted, the corruption of the world we live in compels them to do so; and if I were in their place, there is nothing I would not rather do than entrust my reputation in such dangerous hands.

In my time the pleasure of telling (a pleasure which in sweetness falls little short of that of doing) was only permitted to those who had some trusty and unique friend. Nowadays, when men come together at table or elsewhere, their ordinary talk consists of boasts of favours received and the secret liberality of the ladies. Truly it shows too mean and vulgar a spirit to allow those tender charms to be so cruelly followed up, pounded and tumbled about by ungrateful, indiscreet, and empty-headed fops.

This our intemperate and unjustifiable exasperation against that sin is born of the most futile and turbulent disease that afflicts the mind of man, which is Jealousy.

> Who'd shrink from torch to take a light?
> Whate'er they give, they nothing lose. (OVID and another.)

She and her sister Envy appear to me the most foolish of the tribe. Of the latter I can say little; though described as a strong and powerful passion, she has had the good grace never to come my way. As to the other, I know her, at least by sight. The animals have a sense of it: the shepherd Crastis, having become enamoured of a goat, her ram, in a fit of jealousy, came and butted his head as he was asleep, and crushed it.

We have exceeded in this passion, after the example of some barbarian nations; the best disciplined have not escaped, which is reasonable, but they have not been driven to extremes by it :

> Ne'er did adulterer, by sword of husband slain,
> The purple blood of Stygian waters stain. (JOHANNES SECUNDUS.)

Lucullus, Caesar, Pompey, Antony, Cato, and other brave men were cuckolds and knew it without making a fuss about it. In those times there was only a fool of a Lepidus who died of grief for that reason :

> Ah, wretch! if you are taken in the act,
> They'll drag you feet first through the open door,
> And make you food for turnips and red mullets. (CATULLUS.)

And the god of our poet, when he surprised one of his fellow-gods with his wife, was satisfied with putting them to shame ;

> And one of the Gods, not of the most austere,
> Wished he could share the shame ; (OVID.)

yet none the less is he warmed by the sweet caresses she offers him, and complains that for such a trifle she should distrust his affection :

> Why, Goddess mine, invent
> Such far-fetched pleas ? Dost thou thy faith remove,
> And cease to trust in Vulcan ? (VIRGIL.)

Nay, she asks a favour of him for a bastard of hers,

> Thine arms I ask, a mother for her son ; (IBID.)

which is generously granted by him ; and Vulcan speaks honourably of Aeneas :

> Arms for a hero must the forge prepare. (IBID.)

Truly a superhuman humanity ! And I am willing to leave this excess of kindness to the gods :

> Nor is it meet to equal men with Gods. (CATULLUS.)

With respect to the confusion of children, besides that the most thoughtful legislators consider it desirable and ordain it in their republics, it does not trouble the women, in whom, however, that feeling[1] is, for some reason or other, still more justified :

> Even the stately Juno, Queen of heaven,
> Was maddened by the oft-repeated faults
> Of her poor erring spouse. (CATULLUS.)

---

[1] Jealousy.

JEALOUSY IN WOMEN

When jealousy seizes those poor weak and unresisting souls, it is pitiful to see how cruelly it catches them in its toils and masters them. It worms itself into them under the cloak of affection, but when it once possesses them, the same causes which served as the foundation of kindness, serve as the foundation of a deadly hatred. Of all mental diseases it is the most easily fed and the most difficult to cure. The virtue, the health, the merit, the reputation of the husband are the firebrands of their fury and malevolence :

No hate implacable except the hate of love. (PROPERTIUS.)

This feverish passion disfigures and corrupts all that is otherwise good and beautiful in them ; and there is no act of a jealous woman, however chaste and however good a housewife she may be, that does not reveal a bitter and nagging spirit. It is a furious perturbation of mind, which will drive them to an extreme the very opposite to its cause.

This was absurdly exemplified by one Octavius in Rome : Having lain with Pontia Posthumia, his affection was so much increased by enjoyment, that he pestered her with entreaties to marry him. Being unable to persuade her, his excessive love hurled him to the opposite extreme of the most cruel and deadly hatred, and he killed her.

In like manner the ordinary symptoms of that other love-malady are intestine hatreds, plots, and conspiracies :

We know what frantic woman scorned can do, (VIRGIL.)

and a rage which eats into itself the more it is obliged to shield itself under the cloak of kindness.

Now the duty of chastity is far-reaching. Is it their will that we would have them curb ? That is a very supple and active thing. It is too nimble to be stayed. What if dreams sometimes carry them so far that they cannot deny them ? It is not in them, nor perhaps in Chastity herself, since she is a female, to guard against lust and desire. If their will alone had the power of injuring us, where should we be ? Imagine the great scramble, supposing any man had the privilege of being borne, fully equipped, without eyes to see or tongue to tell, to every one who had the opportunity to receive him !

The Scythian women put out the eyes of all their slaves

and prisoners of war, to make use of them more freely and more secretly.

O what a tremendous advantage is opportunity! Should any one ask me what is the first advantage in love, I should reply that it is to be able to make one's opportunity; likewise the second, and the third as well. There you have the key to everything.

I have often wanted luck, but sometimes I have also wanted enterprise; God shield him from harm who can laugh at this! It needs greater temerity in these days, which our young men excuse under the name of ardour; but if the ladies looked closely into it, they would find that it rather proceeds from contempt. I used to be scrupulously afraid of giving offence, and am inclined to respect where I love. Besides, in this traffic, if you leave out the esteem, you will destroy the glamour. I like the lover to be something of a boy, timid, and a slave. If not quite in this, I have in other situations something of the foolish bashfulness that Plutarch speaks of, and which at various times in the course of my life has been to me a blemish and a source of harm. It is a quality that is not in keeping with my nature as a whole.

But what are we if not a bundle of rebellions and discrepancies? My eyes are as sensitive to suffer a refusal as they are to refuse; and it troubles me so much to be troublesome to others, that, on occasions where duty compels me to ask a favour of another when the granting of it is doubtful and would put him to any cost, I do so sparingly and reluctantly. But if it is for my own particular benefit (although Homer truly says, ' that in a poor man bashfulness is a foolish virtue ') I usually commission a third person to blush for me. And if another requests a favour of me, I find it equally difficult to show him the door; so that I have sometimes had the inclination, but not the strength of will, to deny.

It is folly therefore to try to curb in women a desire that is so acute and so natural to them. And when I hear them boast of having so cold and virginal a disposition, I laugh at them; I tell them they are too backward. If she is a toothless and decrepit old woman, or, if young, sapless and consumptive, though it is not altogether credible, there may at least be a semblance of truth in it. But those who still move and breathe only make the matter worse, seeing that he who excuses himself incautiously accuses himself. Like a gentleman of my neighbourhood who was suspected of impotence,

> Whose dagger, hanging limp as well-cooked beet,
> Could never rise to middle height. (CATULLUS.)

Three or four days after his wedding, to vindicate his reputation, he went about boldly declaring that he had ridden twenty stages the night before. His own words were afterwards used to convict him of pure ignorance, and to unmarry him.

Besides, when the women make the aforesaid boast they prove nothing; for there can be neither continence nor virtue where there is no temptation to resist. 'That is true, they should say, but I am not one to make an easy surrender.' Even the saints say the same. I am speaking of those who boast in good earnest of their coldness and insensibility, and expect to be believed with a serious countenance. For when they say it with an affected air, when their eyes belie their words, when they talk the cant of the profession, which must be taken against the grain, I find it amusing. I am a great admirer of naturalness and plainness of speech; but there is no hope for them. If it is not wholly simple and childish, it is improper for ladies, and out of place in that kind of intercourse; it very soon inclines to effrontery.

Only fools are taken in by their masks and faces. Lying is there in the seat of honour; it is a roundabout way, and leads to the truth by the postern-gate. If we cannot curb their imagination, what do we expect of them? Deeds? There are enough of these that avoid all outside communication, by which chastity may be corrupted:

> That's often done that's done without a witness. (MARTIAL.)

And the people we fear least are perhaps the most to be feared; their silent sins are the worst:

> I confess,
> A simple prostitute offends me less. (MARTIAL.)

There are acts which, without immodesty on their part, may cost them their virginity, and, what is more, without their intention. *Sometimes a midwife, on pretence of examin-*

ing a virgin's integrity, by evil-mindedness, unskilfulness or accident, has destroyed it (St. Augustine). Many a one, in seeking her maidenhead, has lost it ; many a one has killed it in sport.

We cannot precisely circumscribe the actions we would forbid them. Our rules must be worded in general and ambiguous terms. The very idea we create of their chastity is ridiculous ; for, among the extreme patterns I have are Fatua, wife of Faunus, who never allowed any man to see her after her wedding, and the wife of Hiero, who did not realize the fact that her husband had a stinking breath, thinking it was a characteristic of all men. To satisfy us, they must become invisible and devoid of senses.

Now we must confess that our difficulty in estimating this duty lies chiefly in the disposition. There have been husbands who have suffered that mishap, not only without blaming their wives or feeling injured by them, but under a sense of singular obligation and acknowledgement of their virtue. Many a woman there has been who, though she loved honour more than life, has prostituted herself to the furious appetite of a deadly enemy, to save her husband's life ; doing for him what she would never have done for herself. This is not the place to enlarge upon these examples : they are too sublime and too precious to be set off by this foil ; let us reserve them for a nobler setting.

But for examples of more commonplace distinction, are there not women amongst us who every day lend themselves out for their husbands' sole benefit, and by their express command and mediation ? And, in ancient times, Phaulius of Argos offered his wife to King Philip out of ambition. The same was done out of civility by that Galbus, who, entertaining Maecenas to supper, and seeing his wife and him beginning to conspire together by signs and oglings, sank down upon his couch, pretending to be overcome with sleep, in order to help on their understanding. And he very graciously gave himself away ; for when, at this point, one of his slaves made bold to lay hands on the plate which was on the table, he called out, ' Don't you see, you rascal, that I am only asleep for Maecenas ? '

This woman may be of loose conduct, and yet of a more moral disposition than that other whose behaviour appears more correct. As we hear some lamenting the fact that they had made a vow of chastity before the age of discretion, I have also heard others truly complain of having been given over to a dissolute life before the age of discretion. This may be due to the sin of the parents, or to the force of necessity, who is a rude counsellor. In the East Indies, although chastity was there held in singular esteem, yet custom permitted a married woman to abandon herself to any man who presented her with an elephant; and it reflected a certain glory to have been valued at so high a price.

Phaedo the philosopher, a man of good family, after the capture of his country Elis, made it his trade to prostitute his youthful beauty, as long as it endured, to any man who would pay the price, and thereby gained a livelihood.

And Solon is said to have been the first in Greece who by his laws gave women the liberty, at the cost of their chastity, to provide for the necessities of life; a custom which Herodotus asserts to have been usual, before his time, in several states.

And then, what do we gain by this painful anxiety? For, however justified this feeling [1] may be, it still remains to be considered whether it carries us very far. Does any man think he can confine them, with all his ingenuity?

> Hang bolts and bars; keep her in close confinement.
> But who will watch the guards? The crafty wife
> Begins with them. (JUVENAL.)

Will they ever lack opportunities in so knowing an age?

Curiosity is mischievous in all things; but here it is fatal. It is madness to seek enlightenment on a disease for which there is no physic that does not aggravate it and make it worse, the disgrace of which grows greater and becomes public chiefly through jealousy; revenge for which wounds our children more than it heals us. You will pine away and die whilst searching in the dark for proofs.

How pitifully they have fared who in my time have succeeded in this quest! If the informer does not offer a remedy and relief together with the information, he will only make mischief, and deserves the poniard more than if he kept back the truth. The man who is at pains to prevent it is laughed at no less than the man who is in

[1] Jealousy.

ignorance. The mark of cuckoldry is indelible; the man who is once stamped with it will always carry it; the punishment makes it more visible than the guilt. It is a fine thing to see our private misfortunes dragged out of doubt and obscurity, to be trumpeted on the tragic boards; and especially misfortunes that only pinch us by being told. For we say ' Good wife ' and ' Happy marriage ' not of those that are so, but of those no man speaks of.

We must exercise our ingenuity to prevent that awkward and useless knowledge from reaching us. It was customary with the Romans, when returning from a journey, to send a messenger before them to the house, to give their wives notice of their coming, in order not to surprise them. And for the same reason a certain nation arranged that the priest should ' open the ball ' with the bride on the wedding night, to relieve the bridegroom of doubt and curiosity, on his first trial, as to whether she comes to him a virgin, or bruised by another's love.

But the world will be talking. I know a hundred respectable men who are cuckolded, respectably and not discreditably. A gentleman is pitied for it, but not held in less esteem. See to it that your worth drowns your misfortune, that good men curse the occasion; and that he who wrongs you trembles at the mere thought of it. And besides, does any one escape being talked of in that sense, from the little man to the greatest?

> Many a man who mighty empires ruled,
> And was by far a better man than you
> In many things, you miserable wretch! (LUCRETIUS.)

When you hear so many decent men involved in this reproach in your presence, remember that neither will you be spared in other quarters. But even the ladies will laugh at it; and what are they more ready to laugh at in these days than a tranquil and well-settled married life?

There is not a man of you [1] who has not made some one a cuckold; now, Nature runs quite on parallel lines, in compensation, and turn for turn.

The frequency of this mishap must by this time have

---

[1] Montaigne originally wrote on the margin of the 1588 edition, ' There is not one of *us*,' but he deleted *us*, and substituted *you*. A significant alteration!

tempered the bitterness of it ; it will soon have become the rule.

A miserable passion ! which has this also, that it is incommunicable :

> And spiteful Fortune too denies
> An ear to our laments. (CATULLUS.)

For where will you find a friend to whom you dare confide your doleful complaints, who, if he does not laugh at them, may not use them as a stepping-stone and an instruction to take his share in the quarry ? Both the bitter and the sweet of marriage the wise man keeps to himself. And among its other awkward conditions one of the chief, to a communicative man like myself, is this, that custom makes it improper and prejudicial to confide to anybody all we know and feel about it.

To give the women the same advice, in order to disgust them with jealousy, would be a waste of time ; their nature is so steeped in suspicion, vanity, and curiosity, that to cure them by legitimate means is not to be expected. They often recover from this infirmity by a form of health much more to be feared than the malady itself. For, as there are spells which cannot remove a disease except by laying it upon another, so they are apt, when they lose this fever, to transfer it to their husbands.

Yet I know not, to tell the truth, that a man can suffer worse at their hands than jealousy ; it is the most dangerous of their conditions, as the head is of their members. Pittacus said, ' that every man had his trouble, and that his was his wife's jealous temper, but for which he would be perfectly happy.' It must be very hard to bear, when a man so just, so wise, so valiant, felt his whole life poisoned by it ; what are we other little fellows to do ?

The Senate of Marseilles was right to grant the request of the man who asked permission to kill himself, that he might be delivered from his wife's tempestuous temper ;[1] for it is a disease which is only removed by removing the whole piece, and has no effectual remedy but flight or suffering, both, however, very difficult.

---

[1] The example seems to be of Montaigne's invention ; but it is recorded that the Senate of Marseilles permitted that course to any who was the victim of adversity or too great prosperity.

That man, I think, knew something about it who said
'that a happy marriage might be arranged between a blind
wife and a deaf husband.'

We must also see to it that that great and violent strictness
of obligation we lay upon them does not produce two results
that may run counter to our purpose ; to wit, that it may
spur on the followers, and make the women more ready to
surrender. For, as to the first point, by enhancing the value
of the fortress, we enhance the value and desire of conquest.
Might not Venus herself have thus cunningly raised the
price of her wares by making the laws her brokers ; knowing
how insipid a pastime it would be, if not heightened by the
imagination and by its dearness ? In short, it is all swine's
flesh, varied by sauces, as Flaminius' host said. Cupid is a
rogue of a god, who makes it his sport to wrestle with religion and justice ; it is his glory that his power battles with
every other power, and that all other laws give way to his :

> He ever seeks out victims for his guilt. (OVID.)

And with regard to the second point : Should we not be
less often cuckolded if we were less afraid of it, considering
the nature of woman ? For prohibition incites and invites
them :

> You will, they won't ; you will not, they insist. (TERENCE.)

> They think it shame to go where we permit. (LUCAN.)

How could we better interpret Messalina's behaviour ? At
first she conceals her amours from her husband, as they
commonly do ; but finding that, by reason of his dullness,
she could carry on her intrigues too easily, she soon disdained that customary way. Behold her then making love
openly, owning her admirers, entertaining and favouring
them in the sight of all. She wished to make him resent it.
When that animal was not to be roused by all this ; when
her pleasure was rendered flat and tasteless by his weak and
easy-going nature, which appeared to authorize and legalize
her conduct, what did she do ? Wife of an Emperor still
living and in good health, and at Rome, the theatre of the
world, at full noon, with public pomp and ceremony, and
to Silius, whom she had already long enjoyed, she is married
on a day when her husband was outside the city.

Does it not appear as if she were on the way to becoming

chaste through her husband's nonchalance, or as if she were seeking another husband who might whet her appetite with his jealousy and rouse her by opposition? But the first difficulty she encountered was also the last. The beast woke up with a start. We often drive the worst bargain with those who appear to be deaf or asleep. I have found by experience that this extreme long-suffering, when once dissolved, will vent itself in the most cruel acts of revenge; for anger and fury, being heaped up in a mass and suddenly taking fire, discharge all their energy at the first attack:

> And so let loose the reins of wrath. (VIRGIL.)

He put her to death, together with a large number of those who were intimate with her; even some who had been guilty against their will, having been invited to her bed with scourges.

What Virgil says of Venus and Vulcan, Lucretius more fitly said of a stolen enjoyment between her and Mars:

> Thou on whose breast, consumed with eager love,
> Mars throws himself, who rules with powerful sway
> O'er war's wild works, and then with gaze upturned
> All open-mouthed, with shapely neck flung back,
> Feeds his love-greedy eyes on thy dear face,
> While all his soul hangs quivering on thy lips.
> Oh, while he lies within thy fond embrace,
> With all thy godlike charms around him shed,
> Pour low sweet words from thy sweet lips.

When I reflect upon those words *rejicit* (throws), *pascit* (feeds), *inhians* (open-mouthed), *molli* (soft), *fovet* (fondles), *medullas* (marrow), *labefacta* (melting), *pendet* (hangs), *percurrit* (runs through), and that noble *circumfusa* (shed around), mother of the pretty *infusus* (infused),[1] I despise those little conceits and verbal triflings, which have since cropped up. Those simple poets had no need of that clever and ingenious playing upon words; their language is quite full-bodied, and big with a natural and constant vigour. They are all epigram; not only the tail, but the head, stomach, and feet. There is nothing far-fetched, nothing that drags; it all proceeds at an even pace. *It is a texture of manly beauties; they are not concerned about flowers of rhetoric* (Seneca).

[1] Some of these words occur in the passage from Virgil which forms the theme of the chapter.

It is not merely a tame eloquence, where nothing offends. It is nervous and substantial, and does not so much please the palate, as it fills the mind with rapture, and especially the greatest minds. When I see those bold forms of expression, so vivid, so deep, I do not say 'This is well said', but 'This is well thought'. It is the healthy freshness of the imagination that elevates and swells the words. *It is the heart which makes one eloquent* (Quintilian). We moderns confound language with judgement, and fine words with full conceptions.

This painting is not so much the result of manual dexterity as of having the object more vividly imprinted on the soul. Gallus[1] speaks simply because he conceives simply. Horace is not content with a superficial expression; it would betray him. He sees more clearly and more deeply into the matter. His mind unlocks and ransacks the whole storehouse of words and figures wherewith to express itself; and he needs them beyond the commonplace, because his conceptions are beyond the commonplace.

Plutarch said that he saw the Latin language through things.[2] It is the same here; the sense illuminates and brings forth the words, which are not mere wind, but flesh and bone. They mean more than they say. Even the feeble-minded show some reflection of this; for when I was in Italy I could say what I pleased in ordinary talk, but in serious conversation I should not have dared to trust myself with an idiom that I could not wind and turn out of its ordinary course. I like to be able to introduce something of my own.

It is the use and the handling of language by men of genius that sets it off; not so much by innovations as by putting it to more vigorous and varied services, by stretching and bending it. They do not contribute words to it, but they enrich their own, giving more weight and depth to their meaning and their use, teaching them unaccustomed movements, but discreetly and skilfully.

---

[1] Cornelius Gallus or the Pseudo-Gallus, an elegiac poet, a friend of Virgil and Propertius.

[2] 'In the reading of Latin books, singular as it may appear, I did not find that the words assisted me to discover the meaning, but rather that my knowledge of the history enabled me to find out the meaning of the words.'—Plutarch, *Life of Demosthenes.*

And how little that is given to all may be seen in the numerous French writers of our time. They are so bold and disdainful that they will not follow the common high-road; but want of inventiveness and of judgement is their ruin. We see in them only a miserable affectation of singularity, of frigid and absurd disguises which, instead of elevating, lower the matter. As long as they can strut about in new things, they care little about the effect; if they can grasp at a new word, they will drop the usual one, which is often more forcible and energetic.

In our language I find plenty of stuff, but rather a want of style. For there is nothing that might not be done with our jargon of the chase and our military terms, which are a fruitful soil to borrow from. And forms of speech, like plants, improve and grow stronger by being transplanted. I find it sufficiently abundant, but not sufficiently pliable and vigorous. It usually succumbs under a powerful conception. If you try to strain it you will often feel it drooping and bending under you; and when it fails you, Latin comes to your aid, as Greek does to others.

Of some of those words I have picked out we find it harder to realize the energy, because the frequent use of them has somewhat debased and vulgarized their beauty for us; as in our vernacular we meet with excellent phrases and metaphors whose charm has withered with age, and whose colour is tarnished by too general handling. But that does not take away from their flavour for one who has a good nose, nor does it lessen the glory of those old authors who in all probability brought these words to their present prominence.

The scholars treat of things too subtly, in too artificial a manner, differing from the common and natural. My page makes love, and understands it. Read to him Leo Hebreus and Ficino;[1] they speak of him, his thoughts and actions, and yet he will not understand a word of it. I do

---

[1] Juda Leon, or Leo Hebreus, a Portuguese Rabbi, who lived under Ferdinand the Catholic, author of *Dialoghi d' Amore*, translated from Italian into French, and evidently widely read in the sixteenth century. Four dialogues between a youth and a maiden, in which there is more subtlety than love-making. Marsilio Ficino, who lived about the same time, was an Italian philosopher and theologian who entered the Church rather late in life. He translated from Plato and other classical works, and wrote on metaphysics and theology, but I have seen no mention of any work on Love that he wrote.

not recognize in Aristotle most of my ordinary motions; they have been covered and clothed in another gown, for the use of the school. God grant that they be right! If I were of the trade, I should naturalize art as much as they artialize nature. Let us leave Bembo and Equicola [1] alone.

When I write I can dispense very well with the company and remembrance of books, lest they should interfere with my style. Also because, in truth, the good authors humble me too much, and dishearten me. I would gladly do like the painter who, having made a wretchedly bad picture of some cocks, gave his boys strict injunctions to allow no natural cock into his shop. And to set myself off a little, I should rather have to adopt the idea of Antigenidas the musician, who, when he had to perform, took care that, before or after him, his audience was drenched by some other poor singers.

But I can more hardly do without Plutarch. He is so universal and so full, that on all occasions, and however extravagant the subject you have taken in hand, he will thrust himself into your business, and hold out to you a liberal, an inexhaustible handful of treasures and ornaments. I feel vexed that he should be so exposed to plunder by those who resort to him. I can hardly come near him without purloining a leg or a wing.

And it suits my present purpose to write at home, in these uncivilized parts, where I have nobody to assist or correct me; while I associate with no man who understands the Latin of his Paternoster, and who does not know even less French.[2] I might have done it better elsewhere, but the work would have been less my own; and its chief aim and perfection is to be precisely my own. I might indeed correct an incidental error, and these abound with me whenever I run on carelessly; but the imperfections which are common and constant with me it would be a treachery to remove.

---

[1] Cardinal Pietro Bembo (1470–1547), a celebrated Italian scholar who wrote among other things *Gli Asolani*, supposed to be a licentious dialogue on Platonic love. Equicola, a theologian and philosopher of the sixteenth century, wrote a book *Della Natura d' Amore*.

[2] Montaigne probably means the French of Paris, which would be very different from that of Gascony.

When another tells me, or I say to myself, 'You are too thick in metaphors; here is a word of Gascon growth; there is a risky expression' (I avoid none that are used in the streets of France; those who would oppose grammar to usage are queer people); 'this is ignorant reasoning; that is paradoxical reasoning; this is too foolish; you often jest; people will think you are serious when you are pretending.' 'Yes, I reply, but I correct the faults of inadvertence, not those which are customary with me. Do I not speak like that throughout? Do I not portray myself to the life? Enough. I have done what I intended; all the world will recognize me in my book, and my book in me.'

Now it is in my nature to ape and copy. When I presumed to write verse (and I never wrote any except in Latin), they openly betrayed the poet I had last been reading; and some of my first Essays smell rather exotic. At Paris I speak a language somewhat differing from that I speak at Montaigne. If I look upon any one attentively I easily take some impression of him. What I consider I usurp: a foolish deportment, a disagreeable grimace, a ridiculous way of speaking. Still more vices; as soon as they prick me they stick, and will not let go without shaking. I have more often been heard to swear by imitation than naturally.

It is a murderous imitation, like that of those terribly big and strong apes that King Alexander came across in a certain region of the Indies, and which he would have found it difficult to master if they had not afforded him the means by that propensity of theirs to copy everything they saw done. For this gave the hunters the idea of putting on shoes when they were looking, and tying them with many laces and knots, of wrapping their heads in some contrivance provided with running nooses, and pretending to anoint their eyes with bird-lime. So these poor beasts incautiously followed their ape-nature to their own ruin: they glued up their own eyes, hobbled their own feet and strangled themselves.

That other accomplishment of cleverly and purposely mimicking the words and actions of another, which often affords amusement and is much admired, I have no more than a log.

When I swear in my own way, it is only *Perdy*, which is

the most straightforward of all oaths. They say that Socrates swore by a dog, that Zeno used the same interjection now used by Italians, *Cappari*, and that Pythagoras swore by water and air.

I am so apt unthinkingly to take those superficial impressions that if I have had the words 'Sire' or 'Your Highness' on my lips for three days in succession, they will slip from me for a week after instead of 'Your Excellency' or 'Your Lordship'. And if I begin to say a thing in sport or jest, I am likely to say it next day in earnest. Wherefore in writing I am more loath to choose a thrashed-out subject, lest I should treat of it at another's expense.

Every theme is equally pregnant for me. A fly will serve my purpose; and God grant that this I have now in hand has not been taken up at the bidding of too flighty a disposition! I need only begin with a subject that I fancy, for all subjects are linked to one another.

But I am dissatisfied with my mind in that it usually brings forth its profoundest ideas, as well as its maddest and those I like best, unexpectedly, and when I least look for them, for they will instantly vanish if I have no means at hand for fixing them; on horseback, at table, in bed, but mostly on horseback, where my thoughts wander most widely.

When speaking I am rather sensitively jealous of attention and silence, if I am speaking forcibly; whoever interrupts me, stops me. When travelling, the necessities incidental to the road will cut conversation short; besides that I most frequently travel without company fit for connected discourse. Wherefore I take every opportunity to commune with my own thoughts.

It is the same with my dreams; when dreaming I recommend them to my memory (for I am apt to dream that I am dreaming); but next morning I can indeed call to mind what colour they were of, whether gay, or sad, or strange, but as to what they were besides, the more I labour to recover them, the more deeply do I plunge them into oblivion. So of those ideas that come accidentally into my mind I retain only a vague outline; only enough to make me worry and fret in pursuit of them, and all to no purpose.

Well then, setting books aside and speaking more materially and simply, I find after all that Love is nothing else but the thirst for enjoying the desired object, and that Venus is but the pleasure of discharging one's vessels [like the pleasure Nature gives us in discharging other parts], which becomes vicious by immoderation or indiscretion. For Socrates Love is the appetite for generation, by the mediation of beauty.

And when I think, as I have done many a time, of the ridiculous titillation of this pleasure, the absurd, giddy, crack-brained emotions which it stirs up in Zeno and Cratippus, of that unreasonable rage, that countenance inflamed with fury and cruelty at the most delightful moment of love, and then that solemn, stern, ecstatic mien in so extravagant an action; when I consider besides that our joys and excrements are lodged together pell-mell, and that sensual pleasure at its height is attended, like pain, with faintness and moaning, I believe it is true what Plato says, that man is the plaything of the gods:

> Truly a cruel way to sport with us! (CLAUDIAN.)

and that Nature was in a mocking mood when she left us that most common and most disturbing of our actions to make us all alike and put us on the same level, wise men and fools, men and beasts. The most contemplative and wisest of men, when I picture him in that attitude, appears to me a humbug with his wise and contemplative airs; it is the peacock's feet that humble his pride:

> Why may not truth in laughing guise be dressed? (HORACE.)

Those who refuse to discuss serious matters playfully act, as somebody says, like the man who fears to worship the statue of a saint unless it has an apron.

We eat indeed, and drink like the animals; but these are not actions that hinder the workings of the mind. In these we maintain an advantage over them; the other brings every other thought under its yoke, brutifies and bestializes, by its imperious authority, all the theology and philosophy that is in Plato; and yet he does not lament it. In all other things you may observe some decorum. All other operations may be subjected to the rules of decency; this one cannot even be imagined other than vicious and ridiculous. Try to find, if you can, some modest and sober way of doing it.

Alexander said that he knew himself to be mortal chiefly by this action, and by sleeping. Sleep stifles and suppresses the faculties of our mind. The sexual act similarly absorbs and dissipates them. Truly it is a mark, not only of our original corruption, but also of our inanity and deformity.

On the one hand Nature pushes us on to it, having connected with this desire the noblest, most useful, and pleasant of all her operations; and on the other hand she allows us to condemn and fly from it as from a shameless and immodest action, to blush at it and recommend abstinence.

Are we not indeed brutes to call brutish the operation that makes us?

The nations, in their religions, have met together in a number of conventions, as sacrifices, candles, incense, fasts, offerings and, among other things, in their condemnation of this action. All opinions tend that way, as well as to the widespread custom of cutting off the foreskin, which is a punishment of it.

We are perhaps right in blaming ourselves for producing so foolish a thing as man; in calling the action shameful, and shameful the parts that serve that purpose. (At present mine are really shameful and shamefaced.)

The Essenians, of whom Pliny speaks, kept up their numbers for several centuries without nurses or baby-clothes, through the influx of foreigners who, following that pretty humour, continually joined them: a whole nation risking extermination rather than become entangled in a woman's embrace, and breaking the continuity of men rather than create one.

It is said that Zeno never had to do with a woman but once in his life, and then only out of civility, that he might not seem too obstinately to disdain the sex.

Every one avoids seeing a man born; every one runs to see him die. For his destruction they seek out a spacious field, in the full light of day; for his construction they creep into some dark little corner. It is a duty to hide and blush when making him; and it is a glory, and the source of many virtues, to be able to unmake him. The one is offence, the other is grace; for Aristotle says that in a certain phrase of his country, to benefit some one is to kill him. The Athenians, to equalize the disgrace of these two actions, having to purify the island of Delos and justify themselves to Apollo, forbade at once all burials and births within its territory. *We are ashamed of ourselves* (Terence); we regard our being as a sin.

There are countries where they cover themselves when they eat. I know a lady, and one of the greatest, who holds the same view, that a woman masticating is an unpleasant sight, as it takes away much of her charm and beauty; and she does not care to appear in public with an appetite. And I know a man who cannot bear to see another, or to be seen, eating, and is more shy of company when filling than when emptying himself.

In the empire of the Turk there are many who, to show their superiority over others, are never seen at their meals, and only take one a week; who cut and disfigure their face and limbs; who never speak to any man: all of them [fanatic] people who think they honour their nature by de-naturalizing themselves, who prize themselves for their misprision, and think they become better by becoming worse. What an unnatural animal to be a horror to himself, to grieve at his pleasures, to regard himself as a misfortune!

There are some who conceal their lives,

> And change the sweets of home
> For exile kingdoms 'neath an alien sky; (VIRGIL.)

and withdraw from the sight of other men; who shun health and cheerfulness as if they were hurtful enemies. There are not only many sects, but many nations, that curse their birth and bless their death. There are countries where the sun is abominated and the darkness worshipped.

We show no skill except in ill-treating ourselves; that is the true quarry for our powerful intellect: a dangerous tool when misapplied!

O wretched men, whose pleasures are a crime! (PSEUDO-GALLUS.)

Alas, poor human! you have sufficient necessary evils, without adding to them by your own invention; you are miserable enough by nature without being so by art. You have real and essential deformities in abundance without forging imaginary ones. Do you think you are too well off unless you find [the half of] your well-being an affliction? Do you think you have fulfilled all the necessary duties to which Nature binds you, and that she is wanting and idle

in you, if you do not force yourself to create fresh duties ?
You are not afraid of sinning against her universal and
unquestionable laws, and spur yourself to obey your own,
which are partial and fanciful ; and the more partial, uncertain and questionable they are the more do you persist in
obeying them. You are possessed and bound by the positive
orders of your own invention and the rules of your parish ;
those of God and the world leave you unconcerned. Consider for a moment the examples of this kind ; all your life
is reflected in them.

The lines of these two poets, treating lasciviousness as
they do with so much reserve and discretion, appear to me
to disclose it more fully and cast a strong light upon it. The
ladies cover their bosoms with open-work lace, the priests
keep many sacred things hidden, painters put shadows
into their work to set off the light, and they say that the
sun's rays and the wind are harder to bear when reflected
than direct. The Egyptian who was asked, ' What are you
hiding under your cloak ? ' answered discreetly, ' I am
hiding it under my cloak that you may not know what it
is.' But there are certain other things that are hidden to
be shown. Listen to this man, who is more unreserved :

> And pressed her naked body unto mine.[1] (OVID.)

I feel as if he were caponizing me. Let Martial gather up
Venus's skirts as high as he pleases, he will not succeed in
making her appear so entire. He who says all sates and
disgusts us. He who fears to be explicit leads us on to thinking more than is meant. There is treachery in this kind of
modesty, and especially when they half open, as these do,
so fair a path to imagination. And the action and the
painting should smack of theft.

I like the Spanish and Italian methods of making love,
which are more respectful, more timid, more affected and
discreet. Somebody in ancient times, I forget who, wished
for a gullet as long as a crane's neck, that he might the
longer relish what he was gulping down. This wish is more
appropriate to this quick and hasty pleasure, especially in

---

[1] The commentator Coste, after quoting Cotton's translation of this
line, remarks, ' We cannot say the same thing so openly in French ; and
if more disguised, it would form a ridiculous contrast with what Montaigne
adds immediately after.'

a nature like mine, whose failing it is to be too sudden. To arrest its flight and lengthen out the preliminaries, everything serves as a favour and recompense between them : a look, a nod, a word, a sign. If we could dine off the steam of a roast joint, what an expense we could save !

It is a passion in which very little solid reality is mingled with much more unreality and feverish imagination ; it should be paid and served accordingly. Let us teach the ladies to make the most of themselves, to observe self-respect, to keep us in suspense and fool us. We begin with the final attack, and always show our French impetuosity. When they spin out their favours and spread them out in small portions, each of us, even miserable old age, will find a little to glean, according to his substance and merit.

He who finds no enjoyment except in enjoyment, who wins nothing unless he sweeps the stakes, who loves the chase only for the sake of the quarry, has no business to intrude into our school. The more steps and degrees there are, so much higher is the uppermost seat, and so much more honourable it is to reach it. We should take a pleasure in being led to it, as into a magnificent palace, through divers porticoes and passages, long and pleasant galleries and many turnings. This dispensation would turn to our advantage ; we should dwell there the longer, and love the longer. Without hope and without desire we can make no progress worth a rap.

They should infinitely dread our mastery and entire possession of them. As soon as they have wholly surrendered to the mercy of our fidelity and constancy, their position is a little too risky ; for those virtues are rare and hard to find. No sooner are they ours than we are no more theirs.

> The lust of greedy soul once satisfied,
> Nor oaths nor promises they reck. (CATULLUS.)

And Thrasonides, a young Greek, was so much in love with his love that, having won his mistress's heart, he refused to enjoy her, that he might not thereby deaden, sate, and weaken that restless ardour on which he fed and so prided himself.

Dearness gives relish to the meat. See how the form of salutation, which is peculiar to our nation, spoils by its cheapness the charms of the kiss which, as Socrates says, is so powerful and dangerous a stealer of hearts. It is a disagreeable and offensive custom for a lady to have to lend her lips to any man, however disgusting, who has three lackeys at his heels : [1]

> As from his snout, so like a dog's,
> Hangs the rime of frozen fogs,
> And the beard it fairly clogs
>   Around his throat. . . .
> A hundred times I'd rather kiss his ——.   (MARTIAL.)

And we ourselves do not gain much by it ; for the world is so divided that for three pretty women we must kiss fifty plain ones. And for a tender stomach, such as we have at my age, a bad kiss is too high a price to pay for a good one.

In Italy they act the part of the languishing suitor even with the ladies who are for sale, and defend this practice as follows : ' that there are degrees in enjoyment, and that by paying them homage we try to procure for ourselves the most complete. For these ladies sell only their bodies ; their good will cannot be on sale, it is too free and too much at its own disposal.' Hence they say that it is the will they lay siege to ; and they are right. It is the will we must serve and win by our attentions. To me it is a horrible idea that a body void of affection should belong to me. It can only be compared to the mania of that youth who defiled by his love the beautiful statue of Venus that Praxiteles made ; or of that raving Egyptian whose lust was kindled by a dead body he was embalming and shrouding, which was the occasion of the law since made in Egypt, which ordained that the bodies of beautiful young women and those of good family should be kept for three days before being delivered into the hands of the undertakers. Periander acted still more unnaturally by carrying his conjugal affection (although more regular and lawful) to the point of enjoying his wife Melissa after she was dead.

Does it not appear a lunatic humour in Luna, when she could not otherwise enjoy her darling Endymion, to put him to sleep for several months, and browse in the enjoyment of a youth who stirred only in his dreams ?

---

[1] Sir John Falstaff, with his three retainers, is a case in point ; see *Merry Wives*, Act I. sc. i. Evidently the custom was not peculiar to France.

So I say that we love a body without a soul, or without feeling, when we love a body without its consent and desire. All enjoyments are not alike ; some are hectic and some languid. A thousand other causes besides goodwill may win us this favour of the ladies ; it is not a sufficient evidence of affection. Treachery may lurk there, as elsewhere ; sometimes they respond with only one buttock :

> As cool as at a sacrifice, you'ld think
> Her marble, or in quite another place. (MARTIAL.)

I know some who would rather lend that than their coach, and who have nothing else to communicate. You must observe whether she enjoys your company on any other account, or on that alone, as if you were some burly stable-boy ; in what degree of favour or esteem you are housed :

> Whether she gives herself to thee alone,
> And marks thy day out with the whiter stone. (CATULLUS.)

What if she eats your bread with the sauce of a more pleasing imagination :

> She holds you in her arms,
> But sighs for other loves. (TIBULLUS.)

What ! Have we not heard of some one, in our time, who turned this action to a horrible revenge, to poison and kill, as he did, an honest woman ? They who know Italy will never think it strange if, in this connexion, I do not go elsewhere for examples. For that nation may be said to be the schoolmaster of the world in this practice.

Handsome women are more commonly met with in that nation, and fewer plain ones than here ; but in rare and surpassing beauties I think we are on a par. And I judge the same of their intellects ; of commonplace minds they have many more. A brutish stupidity, as may be plainly seen, is with them incomparably more rare. In exceptional minds and those of the highest degree we can hold our own with them.

If I were to carry this comparison further, I think I may say, on the other hand, that, as compared with them, valour is common and natural with us ; but sometimes we may see it on their side in so full and powerful a degree, that it exceeds all the boldest examples we can produce.

The marriages in that country are lame in this respect :

their custom commonly imposes so rude and slavish a law upon the wife, that the most distant acquaintance with a stranger is for her as capital an offence as the most intimate. The result of this law is that every approach is necessarily of a substantial nature ; and, since all comes to the same with them, they have a very easy choice. And, once they have broken through this partition, you may imagine that they catch fire. *Lust, like a wild beast, angered by its chains, breaks loose* (Livy).

We must give them a little more rein :

> Of late I saw, with firm bit held, a colt
> Rush headlong like a mighty thunderbolt. (OVID.)

The desire for company is assuaged by giving it a little liberty.

We are pretty much in the same case ; they go too far in restraint, we in licence. It is a pleasing custom we have in this country that our sons are received into good families to be brought up and trained as pages, as in a school of nobility ; and it is regarded as a piece of discourtesy and an affront to refuse one of gentle birth.

I have perceived (for so many houses, so many different styles and methods) that those ladies who have tried to lay down the strictest rules for the maids of their retinue have not had the best luck. It needs moderation, and we must leave a good part of their conduct to their own discretion ; for, taking all in all, there is no discipline that will curb them at every point. But it is most true that one who has come safe, with bag and baggage, out of a free schooling, inspires much more confidence than one who comes safely out of a school in which she has been kept a strict prisoner.

Our fathers trained their daughters to look bashful and timid (hearts and desires were the same) ; we train ours to put on an air of assurance. We understand nothing of the matter. That is all very well for the Sarmatian women, who are not allowed to lie with a man until they have with their own hands killed another in war.

For me, who have no authority over them except through the ears, it is enough if they retain me for their counsel, in accordance with the privilege of my age. So I counsel them, as well as ourselves, abstinence ; but, if this generation is too hostile to it, at least discretion and modesty.

For, as Aristippus, according to the tale, said to some young men who blushed to see him enter the house of a courtesan, 'The sin is not in entering, but in not coming out again.' If she has no care for her conscience, let her have some regard to her good name. Though the substance be not worth much, let the appearance hold good.

I commend gradation and delay in the dispensation of their favours. Plato points out that in every kind of love an easy and prompt surrender is forbidden in those who hold the fort. It is a sign of gluttony, which they should conceal with all their cunning, to surrender so heedlessly and impetuously all they have. By observing order and measure in granting their favours, they fool our desire the better, and conceal their own. Let them ever flee before us. I mean even if they wish to be caught. They will conquer us the better in flight, like the Scythians. Indeed, according to the law that Nature has given them, it is not properly their part to will and desire; their part is to suffer, obey, and consent. That is why Nature has given them a perpetual capacity; to us a rare and uncertain one. They always have their hour, that they may always be ready for ours; *born to be passive* (Seneca). And, whilst she has decreed that our appetites should show and declare themselves prominently, she has arranged for theirs to be hidden away and inward, and has provided them with parts fitted simply for the defensive, and not for show.

They must leave pranks like the following to Amazonian licence: when Alexander was marching through Hyrcania, Thalestris, Queen of the Amazons, came to see him with three hundred troopers of her own sex, well mounted and well armed, having left the remainder of a large army that was following her beyond the neighbouring mountains, and said to him aloud and publicly, 'that the reports of his victories and his valour had brought her thither to see him and offer her power and resources to help him in his enterprise; and that, seeing he was so handsome, young and strong, she, who was perfect in all his qualities, proposed to him that they should cohabit, that there might be born, of the most valiant woman in the world and the most valiant man then living, something great and rare for the time to come.' Alexander thanked her for the rest; but to gain time for the accomplishment of her last request, he stayed thirteen days at that place, which he spent in feasting and jollity to the best of his powers, to welcome so courageous a princess.

We are, in almost all things, unjust judges of their actions, as they are of ours. I confess the truth when it tells against me as when it is on my side. It is an infamous and badly ordered state of things that so often drives them to change, and prevents them from fixing their affections on any object whatever; as we see in that goddess to whom we attribute so much fickleness and so many lovers. Yet it is true that it is contrary to the nature of love not to be violent, and contrary to the nature of violence to be constant. And they who wonder at it, who exclaim against it and look for the causes of this frailty in them, as if it were unnatural and incredible, why can they not see how often they themselves share it, without being amazed and crying 'miracle'? It would perhaps be more strange to see them attached to one object. It is not a merely bodily passion. If there is no end to avarice and ambition, neither is there to lechery. It still lives after satiety; and neither constant satisfaction nor limit can be set to it; it ever outlives possession.

And besides, inconstancy is perhaps rather more pardonable in them than in us. They may plead, as we do, the inclination to variety and novelty common to both sexes; and secondly they may plead, as we do not, that they buy a cat in a poke.

Joan, Queen of Naples, had her first husband Andreasso hanged at the bars of her window with a cord of silk and gold thread twisted with her own hands, because in the matrimonial fatigue-duties she found that neither his parts nor his performances answered the expectations she had formed of him when she saw his stature, his beauty, his youth and activity, by which she had been caught and deceived.

They may plead that the active part needs more effort than the passive, so that on their part the effort is always equal to the occasion, whilst on our part it may fall out otherwise. For this reason it was that Plato wisely made a law that, in order to decide upon the expediency of a marriage, the judges should see the youths who contemplated it stark naked, and the girls nude only down to the girdle.

DISAPPOINTED EXPECTATIONS

When they come to try us they do not perhaps find us worthy of their choice :

> All efforts vain to excite his vigour dead,
> The married virgin flies the unjoyous bed. (MARTIAL.)

It is not enough that the will should drive straight. Weakness and incapacity lawfully dissolve a marriage :

> A lover much more vigorous she needs
> To undo her virgin zone. (CATULLUS.)

Why not ? and, according to her standard, a more licentious and more active capacity for love :

> Lest to his pleasing toil he prove unequal. (VIRGIL.)

But is it not a great impudence to bring our imperfections and weaknesses where we desire to please and leave a good opinion and recommendation of ourselves ? For the little that I now need,

> —For one encounter only am I fit,—(HORACE.)

I would not trouble a person I have to respect and fear :

> Let me not suspicion rouse
> Who now, alas, have passed my fiftieth year. (HORACE.)

Nature should be satisfied with making this age miserable, without also making it ridiculous. I should hate to see it, for one inch of pitiful vigour that inflames it three times a week, strutting and swaggering as fiercely as if it had some big and lawful day's work in its belly : a regular straw-fire. What wonder if, after leaping up into a sudden and crackling flame, it dies down in a moment and becomes cold and lifeless !

That desire should only be found in the prime of youth and beauty. Trust your age, if you would be convinced, to back up that indefatigable, full, constant and courageous ardour you feel in yourself ; it will leave you nicely in the lurch. Better to boldly hand on your experience to some nerveless, wide-eyed, ignorant boy, who still trembles under the rod, and will blush at it :

> A crimson blush her glowing face o'erspread,
> As Indian ivory, when stained with red,
> Or lilies mixed with roses in a bed. (VIRGIL.)

He who can await, in the morning, without dying of

shame, the contempt of those beautiful eyes that have witnessed his slackness and impertinence,

> And truly eloquent with dumb reproof, (OVID.)

has never felt the satisfaction and pride of wearying them and setting dark rims around them by the vigorous exercise of an active and busy night.

When I have seen one dissatisfied with me, I did not at once accuse her of fickleness; I began to wonder whether I should not rather blame Nature, who has certainly treated me unfairly and unkindly:

> He is not very tall, and not very stout. (PRIAPEA.)
>
> The very matrons look with much disfavour
> Upon a man with little parts; (IBID.)

and done me a most enormous hurt. Every part of me makes me what I am, as much as any other. And no other makes me more properly a man than this.

I owe it to the public to give them my full-length portrait. The wisdom I have learned lies wholly in truth, freedom of speech, reality. It disdains to include in the catalogue of its real duties those petty, invented, customary provincial rules. It is entirely natural, constant, universal. Its daughters, but bastard daughters, are civility and conventionality.

We shall easily get the better of the sins of appearance when we have conquered those of reality. When we have done with the latter, we may run full tilt at the others, if we find it necessary to run at them. For there is danger of our setting up new duties in our imagination, to excuse our neglect of our natural duties, and to obscure them. As a proof of this we may see that in places where faults are crimes, crimes are no more than faults; that with the nations where the laws of propriety are more uncommon and more laxly kept, the primitive and common laws are better observed; since the innumerable crowd of so many duties stifles, deadens, and scatters our attention. Our application to little things withdraws us from more urgent ones.

O what an easy and pleasant path do those superficial men take, in comparison with ours! They are shadowy things wherewith we plaster our conscience and pay one another's debts. But we do not pay, but rather pile up, our debts to that great judge, who pulls up our rags and tatters around our shameful parts, and does not pretend not to see through us, even to our inmost and most secret impurities. Our virginal modesty would be usefully covered if it could keep this discovery from him.

In short, whoever could sharpen the wits of man and rid him of these over-nice verbal superstitions would do the world no great harm. Our life is part folly, part wisdom. He who only treats of it reverently and canonically will leave more than half unsaid. I do not indulge in self-excuses, and if I did, I should rather excuse myself for my excuses than for any other fault. I excuse myself to those of a certain way of thinking, whom I hold to be more numerous than those on my side. For their consideration I will say this besides—for I wish to please every one; though it is a difficult thing *for a single man to conform to that great variety of manners, discourses and wills* (Q. Cicero)—that they ought not strictly to blame me for the things I quote from authorities accepted and approved by many centuries; and that there is no reason why, because I do not write in verse, they should deny me the freedom that is enjoyed, in our days, even by church dignitaries, and those of our nation and the most tufted. Here are two specimens:

Rimula, disperearm, ni monogramma tua est.[1]

Un vit d'ami la contente et bien traite.

And what about so many others? I love modesty, and it is not judgement that prompts me to choose this scandalous way of speaking. It is Nature who has chosen for me. I do not commend it any more than I do all methods that are contrary to accepted custom; but I excuse it, and, by particular and general circumstances, lighten the accusation.

[1] Which a commentator translates: 'Que je meure si ta fente n'est pas légère.' The line is by Theodore de Bèze, born 1519 in Burgundy, one of the most influential of the Genevese reformers, who in his youth wrote witty but indecent poetry, the publication of which caused him bitter regrets in his after days. The second line is by Mellin de Saint-Gelais, who was Chaplain to the Dauphin, and whose poems, published after his death, were remarkable only for the absence of poetic feeling, and for the continual blending of pious and erotic phrases. The meaning of the word *vit* may be guessed.

But to proceed. Whence too comes that sovereign authority you usurp over one who grants you favours at her own cost,

> Who in the dead of night has given you
> Many a little present; (CATULLUS.)

and whom you immediately treat with the self-interest, coolness, and authority of a husband? It is a free compact; why do you not keep it as you would hold her by it? There is no law to bind voluntary actions.

It is contrary to custom, but it is true none the less that in my time I have carried out this bargain, as far as the nature of it would permit, as conscientiously as any other bargain, and with some appearance of justice; that I never pretended more affection than I felt; and that I gave simple expression to its decline, its vigour and birth, its outbursts and slack periods. One does not always go at the same pace. I was so sparing of promises that I think I did more than I promised or owed. They found me faithful to the point of serving their interest when they were inconstant to me, I mean avowedly and sometimes repeatedly inconstant. I never broke with them as long as I was attached to them even by a thread; and whatever cause they may have given me I never broke with them so far as to hate and despise them. For those intimacies, even when gained on the most shameful terms, still oblige me to have some kindly feeling for them.

At times I have given way to anger and somewhat unwise impatience on detecting their tricks and shifts, and in our quarrels; for I am naturally liable to sudden fits of temper which, though fleeting and soon over, are often prejudicial to my interest. If they were minded to test the freedom of my judgement, I did not shirk giving them some sharp paternal advice, and pinching them where they smarted. If I gave them any cause for complaint, it was rather because they found me too foolishly conscientious in my love, compared with modern ways. I have kept my word when I might easily have been excused from doing so; they would then sometimes surrender with credit to themselves, and on conditions which they would readily have allowed the victor to break.

More than once I have made the pleasure at its highest

point to yield to the interest of their honour. And when urged by reason I have armed them against myself, so that they acted more securely and decorously by my rules, when they freely submitted to them, than they would have done by their own.

As often as I could I took upon myself all the risks of our rendezvous, to relieve them of responsibility; and always contrived our meetings at the most difficult and unexpected times and places, because they arouse less suspicion and are besides, I think, more accessible. A place is chiefly open at a spot which is supposed to be of itself covered. The less we fear a thing the less are we on the defensive and on the watch for it. You may more easily dare a thing that nobody thinks you will dare, so that it becomes easy through its difficulty.

No man ever acted with more regard to consequences.[1] This way of loving is more correct; but who knows better than I how ridiculous it appears nowadays, and how little it is practised? Yet I shall not repent of it; I have nothing more to lose there:

> My votive tablet, in the temple set,
> Proclaims that I to Ocean's God have hung
> The garments from my latest shipwreck wet.   (HORACE.)

I can now speak openly about it. But, just as I might perhaps say to another, 'My friend, you are dreaming; love, these days, has little to do with faith and honesty':

> Now if you try to make unstable counsel
> Stable by reason's rules, you only add
> To madness, and are reasonably mad;   (TERENCE.)

so, on the contrary, if I had to begin anew I should certainly pursue the same path and the same course of proceeding, however fruitless it might be to me.

Incapacity and folly are praiseworthy in an unpraiseworthy action. The further I depart from their point of view in this, the nearer I keep to my own.

For the rest, in this traffic, I did not let myself go entirely; I took pleasure, but I did not forget myself, in it; I kept entire the little sense and judgement that Nature has given

---

[1] On the margin of the edition of 1588 was written, and then deleted: 'The desire to generate should be purely legitimate.'

me, for their sake as well as for my own ; a little excitement, but no delirium. My conscience was also involved to the point of making me licentious and dissolute ; but ungrateful, treacherous, malicious or cruel, never. I was not reckless in pursuing the pleasure of this vice, but bought it for what it cost and nothing more. *There is no vice that is self-contained* (Seneca).

I hate a stagnant and sleepy idleness almost as much as a toilsome and thorny activity ; the latter pinches me, the other makes me drowsy. I like a wound as well as a bruise, a cut as well as a dry blow. I found in this traffic, when I was fitter for it, a right moderation between those two extremes. Love is an excitement, wideawake, lively and gay ; it did not disturb or afflict me, but it made me warm and thirsty for more. One should stop there ; it is hurtful only to fools.

A young man asked the philosopher Panaetius whether it was becoming in a wise man to be in love. 'Let us leave the wise man out of the question, he replied ; but you and I, who are far from being wise, must not become entangled in so violent and exciting a business, which enslaves us to another and makes us contemptible to ourselves.' He spoke truth, that a soul is not to be trusted that has not the strength to withstand the attack of a thing that comes so suddenly, and that is not able practically to disprove the saying of Agesilaus 'that wisdom and love cannot go abreast'.

True, it is a vain pastime, unbecoming, shameful and unlawful ; but, conducted in this fashion, I regard it as salubrious, proper to enliven a dull body and soul. And, as a physician I would prescribe it for a man of my temperament and condition as readily as any other remedy, to stir him up and keep him robust till well on in years, and to ward off the attacks of senility. Whilst we are yet but in the suburbs and the pulse still beats ;

> Whilst hair is yet but grey, and age still stands upright,
> While yet remain some threads for Lachesis to spin,
> While on my feet I walk and need no staff to help,   (JUVENAL.)

we need to be solicited and tickled by some such biting excitation as this. See what youth, vigour and sprightliness it put into the wise Anacreon. And Socrates, when older than I now am, said, speaking of a girl he fell in love with, ' With her shoulder touching mine, and my head near to hers, as we were looking together into a book, I suddenly felt a pricking in the shoulder, if you will believe me, like the bite of an insect ; and for more than five days it tingled, and through my heart ran a continual itching pain.' What! a touch, and that an accidental one, and of a shoulder, disturb and kindle a soul cooled and weakened by age, and of all human souls the most chastened ! Why not, in heaven's name ? Socrates was a man, and desired neither to be nor seem anything else.

Philosophy does not strive against natural pleasures, as long as due measure be observed ; she preaches moderation, not flight. Her power of resistance is used against exotic and bastard pleasures. She says that bodily desires must not be heightened by the mind, and wittily warns us not to try to excite hunger by surfeiting, not to stuff instead of merely filling the belly ; to avoid all enjoyment that may bring us to want, and all food and drink that makes us thirsty and hungry.

So in the service of love she bids us to choose an object that simply satisfies the body's need, that does not stir the soul, which must not look to its own satisfaction, but should simply follow and assist the body.

But am I not right in thinking that these precepts, which by the way are in my opinion a little too rigorous, concern a body that is equal to its functions ; and that when a body is in a low condition, like a disordered stomach, it is excusable to warm and sustain it artificially, and by means of the imagination to restore the appetite and cheerfulness which it loses when left to itself ?

May we not say that there is nothing in us, during this earthly imprisonment, that is purely either corporeal or spiritual ; that we wrongfully tear a living man to pieces, and that it seems but reasonable that we should look upon pleasure with at least the same favour as upon pain ? The latter (for example) was violent to the point of perfection in the souls of the Saints, by means of penitence ; the body naturally, by virtue of their alliance, shared the pain, and yet could have little share in the cause. And still they were not satisfied that it should simply follow and assist the ill-used soul ; they tormented the body itself with atrocious and appropriate tortures, in order that soul and body might vie together in plunging man into anguish, the more cruel, the more salutary.

So in the case of bodily pleasures, is it not wrong to cool the soul with regard to them, and to say that she must be dragged to them as to some enforced and slavish obligation and necessity ? It is her part rather to cherish and promote them, to offer and invite herself to share them, since it is her office to rule. As it is also, I think, her part, in respect of her own pleasures, to breathe and instil into the body all the feeling they are capable of arousing, and study to make them sweet and wholesome. For it is reasonable, as they say, that the body should not follow its appetites to the prejudice of the mind.

But why is it not also right that the mind should not follow hers to the prejudice of the body ?

I have no other passion to keep me in breath. What avarice, ambition, quarrels, lawsuits, do for other men who, like myself, have no fixed occupation, love would do more beneficially. It would wake me up again, make me more sober, pleasing and careful of my person ; it would recompose my countenance and prevent the grimaces of old age, those ugly and pitiful grimaces, from spoiling it ; it would bring me back to wise and healthy studies, whereby I might become better loved and esteemed, driving from my mind its hopelessness in itself and its employment, and restoring it to itself ; it would divert me from a thousand troublesome thoughts, a thousand melancholy humours, which idleness and the poor state of our health impose upon us at this age ; would warm up, at least in dreams, this blood that Nature forsakes, would raise the chin and stretch out a little the nerves and the vigour and the gaiety in the soul of this poor man who is moving full speed towards disintregration.

But I know well that it is a blessing very hard to recover. Through failing strength and long experience our taste has become more delicate and fastidious. We demand more when we can bring less ; we are more anxious to choose when we least deserve to be accepted. Knowing ourselves for what we are, we are less confident and more distrustful of our powers ; nothing can make us sure of being loved, knowing our condition and theirs.

I am ashamed of being found in the midst of these green and exuberant young people,

> In whom undaunted vigour stands more firm
> Than sapling on the mountain-side. (HORACE.)

Why should we go and intrude our misery into that gay throng,

> That fervid youngsters may behold,
> With laughter loud and long,
> The burnt-out torch into the ashes flung? (HORACE.)

They have strength and reason on their side; let us give place to them; we can only look on.

And that germ of budding beauty will not be touched by such stiff old hands, nor won by mere material means. For, as the old philosopher replied to the man who jeered at him for being unable to win the good graces of a tender lass he was pursuing, 'My friend, the hook will not bite in such fresh cheese.'

Now, it is an intercourse that needs reciprocity and mutual exchange. The other pleasures we receive may be acknowledged by returns of a different nature; but this can only be paid for in the same kind of coin. Indeed in this pastime the pleasure I give tickles my imagination more agreeably than that which I feel. Now there is no generosity in the man who can receive pleasure where he confers none; it is a mean soul that would be beholden for everything, and is content to keep up relations with a person to whom he is a charge. There is no beauty, favour or intimacy so exquisite that a gentleman should desire it at that price. If they can be kind to us only out of pity, I would much rather not live, than live on alms. I would like to have the right to ask it of them in the way in which I heard them beg in Italy: *Fate ben per voi*;[1] or after the manner of Cyrus exhorting his troops: 'Who loves himself, follow me!'

You may tell me to consort with persons in my own state, who, sharing the same fortune, will be more easy of access. O foolish and insipid compromise!

> I will not pluck the beard of lion dead. (MARTIAL.)

Xenophon makes it the ground of his objection and accusation against Menon, that in his amours he set to work on faded flowers.

---

[1] Charity, for the good of your soul.

I find more sensual pleasure in merely witnessing, or even in only imagining, the sweet and honest pairing of two fair young people, than in myself making a second in a pitiful and imperfect conjunction. I leave that fantastic appetite to the Emperor Galba, who preferred his meat when it was old and tough; and to this poor wretch:

> O that the Gods would grant me yet to see
> And kiss thy own dear self with changed locks,
> And clasp thy withered body to my arms![1]

And among the chief disfigurements I count a forced and artificial beauty. Emonez, a young boy of Chios, thinking by pretty ornaments to acquire the beauty that Nature had denied him, appeared before the philosopher Archesilaus and asked him whether a wise man might fall in love. 'Yes, by heaven, he replied, as long as it is not with a dressed up and sophisticated beauty like yours.' The confessed ugliness of old age is less old and less ugly, to my mind, than when it is painted and polished.

Shall I say it? Provided you do not seize me by the throat. Love, in my opinion, is not properly and naturally in season except in the age next to childhood:

> Him should you, with dishevelled hair
> And that ambiguous face bring in
> Among a troop of pretty girls,
> He would deceive the subtlest there,
> So smooth, so rosy is his skin. (HORACE.)

Nor beauty either. For while Homer extends it until the chin begins to be shaded, Plato himself remarked that that was rare. And the reason is notorious why the Sophist Bion so wittily called the downy hairs of adolescence Aristogeitons and Harmodians'.[2] In manhood I think it already out of date; not to speak of old age.

> Ruthless is Love, for past the withered oak
> He flies. (HORACE.)

And Margaret, Queen of Navarre, being a woman, greatly extends the privileges of her sex, ordaining that thirty is the season for them to exchange the name of 'beautiful' for that of 'good'.

---

[1] Ovid, writing in exile to his wife at Rome.
[2] As Harmodius and Aristogeiton delivered their country from the tyrant, so the first signs of virility delivered the Greek youth from a persecution of a different kind.

The shorter the possession we grant Cupid over our lives, the better we are for it. Look at his bearing, and his boyish chin! Who knows not how, in his school, all goes backward, against all rule? Study, exercise, use, are the ways that lead to inefficiency; there the novices are the teachers. *Love knows no order* (St. Jerome). Truly his conduct is much more charming when blended with heedlessness and irregularities; mistakes and checks give point and grace to it. Provided it be eager and hungry, it matters little whether it be prudent. See how he goes reeling, tripping and wantoning; you put him in the stocks when you guide him by art and discretion, and he is restrained in his divine freedom when put under those hirsute and callous hands.

For the rest, I have often heard the ladies describing this intercourse as entirely spiritual, and disdaining to consider the part the senses play in it. Everything serves, and I may say that I have often observed that we pardon their intellectual shortcomings in consideration of their bodily charms; but I have not yet observed any of them to be willing to favour intellectual beauty in us, however wise and mature, when joined to a body that shows the least signs of decay. Why does not one of them feel a desire to make that noble Socratic exchange of body for soul, purchasing a spiritual and philosophical generation and intelligence at the price of her thighs, the highest rate at which she can value them?

Plato, in his Laws, ordains that one who has performed a signal and useful exploit in war shall, as long as it is being waged, not be denied, however old or ill-favoured he may be, a kiss or any other amorous favour from any woman he may choose. Can that which he thinks so fair in consideration of military worth not also be fair in consideration of some other kind of worth? And why does not one of them seek to forestall her sisters and win the glory of so chaste a love? I may well say chaste:

> A horse grown old,
> Slow kindling unto love, in vain prolongs
> The fruitless task, and, to the encounter come,
> As fire in stubble blusters without strength,
> He rages idly. (VIRGIL.)

The vices that are confined to thought are not the worst.

To conclude this remarkable commentary, which has slipped from me in a torrent of babble, a torrent sometimes impetuous and hurtful:

> Like the red apple, her lover's secret gift,
> In the chaste bosom of the maiden fair,
> Where hidden it lies in tunic soft forgot;
> Soon as she hears her mother's step she starts;
> Away it rolls, and conscious of her crime
> Her cheeks are steeped in red. (CATULLUS.)

I say that male and female are cast in the same mould; saving education and habits, the difference is not great. Plato, in his Republic, invites all indiscriminately to share all studies, exercises, charges and occupations, in peace and war; and the philosopher Antisthenes rejected all distinction between their virtue and ours. It is much easier to accuse one sex than to excuse the other; it is, in the words of the proverb, 'the poker calling the shovel black'.

CHAPTER 6

OF COACHES

IT may very easily be verified that the great authors, when they write of causes, make use not only of those they think true, but also of those they do not believe in, provided there be some originality and beauty in them. They speak truly and usefully enough, if they speak judiciously. We cannot make sure of the master-cause; we accumulate a number of them, to see if by chance it may not be found among them:

> There are besides some things
> Of which 'tis not enough one only cause
> To state—but rather several, whereof one
> Will be the true. (LUCRETIUS.)

Do you ask me whence comes that custom of saying 'God bless you!' when a person sneezes? We produce wind of three sorts. That which comes from below is too foul; that which issues from the mouth brings with it some reproach of gluttony. The third is the sneeze, and because it comes from the head and is without offence we give it that civil greeting. Do not smile at this subtle distinction; it is said to have been made by Aristotle.

I think I have read in Plutarch (who, of all writers I know, has best blended art with nature, and judgement with knowledge) that he gives as a reason for the heaving of the stomach in those who travel by sea, that it is caused by fear ; having first discovered some reason by which he proves that fear may produce some such effect. I, who am very liable to sea-sickness, know very well that that is not the case with me ; and I know it, not by reasoning, but by necessary experience. Not to mention, what I have been told, that the same thing often happens to animals, and especially pigs, that have no idea of danger ; and the testimony of an acquaintance of mine, that, though very subject to it, on two or three occasions, being in a very stormy sea and very much afraid, the inclination to vomit passed away. So it happened to that ancient writer : *I was too much upset to think of danger* (Seneca).

I have never had any fear on the water, nor indeed anywhere else (and I have often enough had just cause to be afraid, if death be one), at least to such a degree as to be disturbed or bewildered by it.

Fear is sometimes due to want of judgement, as well as to want of courage. All the dangers I have seen, I have seen with open eyes, with free, sound, and entire sight ; besides, it needs courage to be afraid. Mine once stood me in good stead, compared with others, in conducting my flight in an orderly manner, since it was done, if not without fear, at least without alarm and dismay ; I was excited, but not stunned or distracted.[1]

Great souls go yet much further, and offer us a picture of flight not merely correct and steady, but proud. I will quote what Alcibiades relates of Socrates, his comrade in arms : ' I found him (he says), after the rout of our army, him and Lachez, among the last of the fugitives, and I was able to observe him at leisure and from a safe place, for I was mounted on a good horse, and he on foot, as we had been in the battle. I noted first how much presence of mind and determination he displayed when compared with Lachez, and then how boldly he marched, never exceeding his ordinary pace ; how firm and steady his glance when

---

[1] Montaigne is here perhaps referring to the time when the plague was ravaging the district, and he found great difficulty in finding a refuge for his family.

observing and taking in the situation, looking now at one, now at another, friends and enemies, in such a way as to encourage the former and signify to the latter that he was the man to sell his blood and life very dearly to any who had a mind to take them. And so they got away; for men like that are not readily attacked; it is the terrified who are pursued.'

There we have the testimony of that great captain, and it teaches us, what we may learn any day by experience, that nothing is so likely to bring us into danger as a frantic eagerness to escape from it. *Where there is less fear there is generally less danger* (Livy).

Our common people are wrong to say 'so-and-so fears death', when they mean to say that he ponders over it and foresees it. Foresight is equally proper in all that concerns us, whether for good or ill. To consider and appreciate the danger is in some sort the reverse of being alarmed by it.

I do not feel myself strong enough to withstand the force and impetuosity of that passion of fear, or of any other violent passion. If I were once vanquished and beaten down by it, I should never entirely recover. Whoever should make my soul lose her footing would never again set her upright. She probes and searches herself too deeply and too closely, and therefore would never allow the wound that has pierced her to close up and heal. It has been fortunate for me that no sickness has yet prostrated her. To every attack made upon me I stand up and defend myself in my corslet. So the first that should sweep me off my feet would leave me without resources. I have no second defence. Wherever the torrent should break my dike I should be defenceless and drowned without help.

Epicurus says that the wise man can never pass into a contrary state. Reading it backwards I rather agree with that sentence, and say, That he who has once been a very fool, will never after be very wise.

God tempers the wind to the shorn lamb, and gives me passions in proportion to my means of resistance. Nature, having uncovered me on one side, has covered me on the other: having disarmed me of strength, she has armed me with insensibility and a moderate or dull power of apprehension.

Now, I cannot bear for any length of time (and much less could I bear them in my younger days) either coach, or litter, or boat, and I hate any other conveyance but on horseback, both in town and country. But I can bear a litter less than a coach ; and for the same reason I can more easily bear a rough tossing on the water, which usually causes fear, than the motion we feel in calm weather. That slight concussion caused by the oars, that makes the craft slip from under us, somehow disturbs my head and stomach ; neither can I endure a tottering chair under me. When the sail or the current carries us along smoothly, or when we are towed, the even motion causes me no discomfort whatever. It is an intermittent motion that upsets me, and more so when it is slow. I cannot exactly describe its effect. The doctors have recommended me to bind and compress the bowels with a towel, to remedy the discomfort ; but I have not tried it, being accustomed to wrestle with my defects and overcome them by self-control.

If my memory were sufficiently stored, I would not spare my time in telling here of the infinite variety that history offers of the use of coaches in the service of war, varying according to nations and according to the age ; of great effect, in my opinion, and very necessary, so that it is a wonder that we have lost all knowledge of them. I will only say this, that quite recently, in the time of our fathers, the Hungarians worked them to great advantage against the Turks ; each of them occupied by a targeteer and a musketeer, a number of muskets lying in a row, ready loaded, wholly protected by a fence of shields, like a galiot. These coaches formed the battle-front to the number of three thousand, and, after the cannon had played, they were made to advance, and the enemy had to swallow that volley before tasting the rest, which was no small advantage. Or they rushed them into the squadrons to break them and open a way ; besides the assistance they could derive from them by flanking in a ticklish place the troops marching into the field, or by hastily covering a camp and fortifying it.

In my time a gentleman on one of our frontiers, who was unwieldy of body and unable to find a horse equal to his weight, having a feud, used to travel the country in a coach like those described above, and felt quite safe. But enough of these war-coaches. [As if their sloth had not been sufficiently notorious by better proofs,] the [last] kings of our first dynasty travelled the country in a cart drawn by four oxen.

Mark Antony was the first who had himself drawn in Rome by lions harnessed to a chariot, with a female musician at his side. Heliogabalus did the same later, calling himself Cybele, mother of the gods; he was also drawn by tigers in imitation of the god Bacchus, and on occasion had a pair of stags harnessed to his chariot; and again, four hounds; and again he was dragged in state by four young nude girls, he also being naked. The Emperor Firmus had his chariot drawn by ostriches of prodigious size, so that it seemed to fly rather than roll.

The strangeness of these inventions has put this other idea into my head, That it is a kind of small-mindedness in a monarch, and a sign that he is not sufficiently sensible of his power, when he labours to enhance his importance, and show off by excessive expenditure. It might be excusable in a foreign country; but among his own subjects, where he is all-powerful, he derives from his dignity the highest degree of honour he is able to reach.

So it appears to me superfluous in a gentleman to dress with studied elegance in his own home. His household, his retinue, and his table are sufficient guarantee of his station.

The advice that Isocrates gave to his king appears to me not unreasonable, ' That he may be sumptuous in furniture and utensils, since he spends on durable things that are handed on to his heirs; but that he should avoid all extravagance on things that will presently drop out of use and memory.'

When I was a young fellow I was fond of dress, for want of other attractions; and it sat well on me. There are some on whom fine clothes weep.

We have wonderful tales of the frugality of our kings in regard to their person and their gifts, kings great in renown, in valour and fortune.

Demosthenes fought tooth and nail against the law of his city which allotted public money to be spent on ostentatious games and feasts; he thought the greatness of the city should show itself in the number of well equipped ships and good, well furnished armies. And Theophrastus was rightly condemned for setting up a contrary opinion, in his book on Riches, and maintaining that an expenditure of that kind was the true fruit of opulence. 'Those are pleasures, says Aristotle, that only appeal to the meanest of the people, and vanish from memory as soon as they have been satiated with them. No serious and sensible man can value them.'

The expense would, it seems to me, be more royally as well as more justly, usefully and durably devoted to ports, harbours, fortifications, and walls ; to sumptuous buildings, churches, hospitals, colleges, the improvement of streets and roads, for which Pope Gregory the Thirteenth is held in praiseworthy memory in my time, and wherein our Queen Catherine might for many long years testify to her natural liberality and munificence, if her means were sufficient to satisfy her bent.

Fortune has greatly spited me in interrupting the noble structure of the new bridge of our great city, and robbing me of the hope of seeing it in full use before I die.

Moreover, to the subjects, spectators of these triumphs, it appears to be their own wealth that is displayed before them, and that they are feasted at their own expense. For the people are apt to suppose of kings, as we do of our servants, that they should make it their care to provide us in abundance with all that we need, but that for their part they should never lay hands on it. And therefore it was that the Emperor Galba, pleased with the performance of a musician whilst he was at supper, sent for his casket and gave him a handful of coins which he fished out of it, with these words, 'This is not out of the public purse, but my own.'

At all events, it most often happens that the people are right, and that their eyes are feasted on what should go to feed their bellies.

Liberality itself is not in its right setting in the hands of a sovereign ; private individuals have more right to be liberal. For, precisely speaking, a king has nothing that is properly his own ; he owes even himself to others.

Justice is administered, not in favour of him who administers it, but of him to whom it is administered. A superior is never appointed for his own benefit, but to benefit the inferior ; and a physician for the patient, not for himself. All authority, as every art, has its end outside of itself ; *no art is concerned with itself* (Cicero).

Wherefore the governors of young princes, who make it a point to instil into them this virtue of lavish generosity, and preach to them that they should be unable to deny anything, and to think nothing so well spent as what they give (an instruction that in my time I have heard highly commended), either look to their own profit rather than that of their master, or they do not quite realize to whom they are preaching. It is too easy a matter to inculcate liberality into one who has ample means to practise it at others' expense. And as the esteem in which he is held is proportioned, not to the measure of the gift, but to the measure of the means of him who bestows it, it comes to nothing in hands so powerful. They become prodigal before they are liberal.

Therefore it is a virtue little to be recommended in comparison with other royal virtues ; and it is the only one, as Dionysius the Tyrant said, that goes well with tyranny itself. I would rather teach him this little saying of the ancient labourer, *To obtain a good crop, you must sow with the hand, not pour out of the sack* (Plutarch). He must scatter the seed, not spill it ; and since he must give, or, more properly speaking, since he must pay and restore to so many people according to their deserts, he ought to be a fair and discreet dispenser. If the liberality of a prince is without measure and discrimination, I would rather he were a miser.

Royal virtue seems to consist chiefly in Justice ; and, of all the branches of justice, that best stamps a king which is accompanied by liberality. For this they have particularly taken into their own keeping, whilst every other kind of justice is generally administered through others.

Extravagant liberality is a feeble means of acquiring goodwill ; for it alienates more people than it wins. *The more you have formerly obliged, the fewer you will be able to oblige in the future. What greater folly is there than to disable yourself ever after from doing that which you delight in?* (Cicero.) And if it is exercised without regard to merit, it shames him who receives, and is received ungraciously. Tyrants have been sacrificed to the hatred of the people by the hands of the very men they have unjustly advanced ;

for that kind of man thinks he will secure himself in the possession of property received without being earned, by showing hatred and contempt for the man from whom he holds it. Thereby he rallies to the opinion and judgement of the majority.

The subjects of a ruler who is lavish in gifts become lavish in asking; they assess themselves, not according to reason, but to example. We have indeed often cause to blush for our impudence; in justice we are overpaid when the reward equals our service, for do we owe nothing to our princes, by natural obligation? If he bears our expenses, he does too much; it is enough if he contributes to them. The surplus is called benefit, and cannot be exacted; for the very name Liberality suggests Liberty.

From our point of view, he has never done; what we have received is no longer taken into account. We love only liberality to come; wherefore the more a prince exhausts himself in giving, the poorer he grows in friends. How can he assuage desires that grow the more they are fulfilled? He whose thoughts are bent on taking no longer thinks of what he has taken. Nothing is so properly allied to greed as ingratitude.

The example of Cyrus will not be amiss in this place, to serve the kings of our time as a touchstone to know whether their gifts are well or ill bestowed, and make them see how much more happily that Emperor invested them than they do; whereby they are reduced to borrowing of unknown subjects, and rather of those they have wronged than those they have benefited, and receive aid that is gratuitous only in name.

Croesus blamed him for his extravagance, and calculated what his treasure would amount to if he had been less open-handed. Cyrus desired to justify his liberality, and sent dispatches in all directions, to the grandees of his State whom he had particularly advanced, begging each one to assist him with as much cash as he could afford, for an urgent necessity, and send him particulars. When all these notes were brought to him, he found that each of his friends had considered it insufficient to offer him no more than he had received through Cyrus's munificence, but had added much more of what was his very own; so that the total amounted to very much more than Croesus' estimate of what he would have saved by being less generous. Whereupon Cyrus said, 'I am not less in love with riches than other princes; rather I am more careful of them. You see at how small a cost I have gained the inestimable treasure of so many friends; and how much more trusty treasurers they are to me than any mercenary fellow, without obligation, without affection, would have been. And my fortune is better harboured than in chests, that would call down upon me the hatred, envy and contempt of other princes.'

The Emperors found some excuse for the superfluity of their public games and shows in the fact that their authority depended to some extent (at least in appearance) on the will of the Roman people, who had from time immemorial been accustomed to be flattered by extravagant spectacles of that description. But it was the private individuals who had kept up this custom of gratifying their fellow-citizens and friends, chiefly out of their own purse, by that great profusion and magnificence. It had quite a different flavour when it was the masters who came to imitate them. *The transferring of property from its rightful owners to others who have no claim to it should not be regarded as liberality* (Cicero).

Philip taunted his son in a letter, for trying to purchase the goodwill of the Macedonians with gifts, in these words, 'What, do you wish your subjects to regard you as their purse-bearer and not as their king? Would you bribe them? Bribe them with the benefits of your virtue, not with the benefits of your coffers.'

It was, however, a fine thing to transport and plant in the amphitheatre a great number of big trees with all their branches in full verdure, to represent a large and shady forest, disposed in fine symmetry, and on the first day to let loose into it a thousand ostriches, a thousand stags, a thousand wild boars, and a thousand fallow deer, and leave them to be scrambled for by the people; on the next day to have a hundred big lions, a hundred leopards, and three hundred bears butchered in their presence; and for the third day to make three hundred pairs of gladiators fight to the bitter end, as did the Emperor Probus.

It was also a fine thing to see those great amphitheatres faced with marble on the outside, adorned with statues and ornaments, the interior glittering with many rich and rare gems :

> The circle here behold with gems inlaid,
> The porches all in gold! (CALPHURNIUS.)

all the sides of this vast space filled and environed, from top to bottom, with three or fourscore tiers of seats, also of marble, covered with cushions :

> ' Out you go, for very shame, he says ;
> These cushioned seats are only for the Knights
> Who pay the lawful tax ' ; (JUVENAL.)

where a hundred thousand people could dispose themselves and sit in comfort.

The arena, where the shows took place, would be in the first place artificially opened and split into chasms, representing caves that vomited forth the animals intended for the spectacle ; then, secondly, it would be flooded with a deep sea, wherein swam store of marine monsters, and laden with armed vessels, to represent a naval battle ; and thirdly, dried and levelled again for the combat of the gladiators ; and for the fourth show, strewn with vermilion and storax instead of sand, arranged for a ceremonial banquet for all that endless number of people ; the last act of a single day.

> How oft have we beheld the floor sink in,
> When from the open chasm there emerged
> Wild beasts ; and from the same retreat there grew
> Forests of trees with gold and saffron bark.
> And sylvan monsters not alone we saw,
> But seals and bears locked in a deadly strife ;
> And, though no horse, yet horse-like is he named,
> The huge and shapeless hippopotamus. (CALPHURNIUS.)

Sometimes they created a high mountain covered with fruit and other trees in full leaf, from the summit of which gushed a rivulet, as from the mouth of a living spring. At other times they sailed on it a big ship, which opened up and came to pieces of itself, and, after vomiting from its belly four or five hundred fighting beasts, closed up again and vanished without assistance. Again from the floor of the place they caused springs and spurts of water to shoot up into the air, and, at that immense height, sprinkled and perfumed the great multitude.

To shelter themselves from harm by inclement weather, they stretched over that immense space awnings made of purple and worked with the needle, or of silk of one colour or another, which were drawn back or forward in a moment, as they had a mind:

> The awnings, though the sun doth scorch the skin,
> Are, when Hermogenes appears, drawn in.[1]

The nets too which were hung before the spectators to protect them from the violence of the animals that were let loose, were worked in gold:

> The woven nets refulgent are with gold. (CALPHURNIUS.)

If there is anything excusable in these extravagances, it is that the inventiveness and the novelty excite our wonder, more than the expense.

Even in those vanities we discover how fertile those ages were in wits differing from those of our time. It is with this kind of fertility as with all other productions of Nature. That is not to say that she exhausted all her resources in those times. We do not move forwards; we rather prowl about, turning this way and that. We retrace our steps. I fear that our knowledge is deficient in all directions; we do not see very far ahead, nor very far behind us. It embraces little and is shortlived; short in extent of time and extent of matter:

> For many have lived who were valiant in fight,
>   Before Agamemnon; but all have gone down,
> Unwept and unknown, in the darkness of night,
>   For lack of a poet to hymn their renown. (HORACE.)

> Long, long before the Theban war, and Troy
> And its sad fall, were there not other bards
> To sing of those old days? (LUCRETIUS.)

And Solon's account, which he had from the Egyptian priests, of the long life of their State, and their manner of learning and recording the history of other countries, is not, I think, a testimony to be despised in this connexion. *If we could view that unbounded extent of space and time into which the mind, plunging and spreading itself, travels so far and wide that it can find no end, no extremity to arrest its*

---

[1] From an epigram of Martial. Hermogenes was a notorious thief and picker-up of unconsidered trifles, as handkerchiefs, table-cloths, awnings.

course, we should, in that immensity, discover an endless number of forms (Cicero).

Even if all that has been handed down and reported to us concerning the past, until our own time, were true and known to some person, it would be less than nothing compared with what is unknown. And of this same image of the world which glides along while we live upon it, how limited and contemptible is the knowledge even of the most curious! Not only of particular events, which by chance often become exemplary and important, but of the condition of great governments and nations, a hundred times as many escape us as come to our knowledge. We raise our hands in admiration over the miracle of our invention of artillery and our printing-press; other men, at the other end of the world, in China, used them a thousand years before us. If we saw as much of the world as we do not see, we should perceive, as may well be believed, a perpetual multiplication and vicissitude of forms.

There is nothing single and uncommon as regards Nature, but there is indeed with regard to our knowledge, which is a poor foundation for our rules, and is apt to give us a very wrong idea of things. As vainly as we now conclude the decline and decrepitude of the world, from arguments based on our own weakness and decay:

> This age is broken down, the earth outworn; (LUCRETIUS.)

so vainly did that poet argue its birth and youth from the vigour he saw in the minds of his time, abounding in novelties and inventions in the different arts:

> The truth I think is this:
> The universe is new, quite fresh the world,
> Nor long ago begun. Why, there are arts
> Which even now receive the final touch,
> Even now advance; how much is now being learned
> Of ships! (LUCRETIUS.)

Our world has of late discovered another (and who will warrant us that it is the last of its brothers, since the Demons, the Sibyls, and we moderns had been hitherto ignorant of this one), no less big and full-limbed than himself, yet so fresh and infantile that he is still being taught his ABC. It is not fifty years since he knew neither letters, nor weights and measures, nor clothes, nor corn, nor vines.

He was still quite naked at the breast, and lived only on what his nursing mother provided.

If we are right in our conclusions with regard to the end of the world, and this poet is right with regard to the youth of his own age, this other world will be only coming into the light as we are leaving it. The universe will fall into paralysis; one limb will be shrunken, the other in full vigour.

I very much fear that we shall have greatly hastened the decline and downfall of the latter by our contact; and that we shall have made him pay us very dearly for our ideas and our arts. It was an infant world, and yet we have not whipped it and subjected it to our discipline, with all our advantages in valour and natural strength; nor have we won it over by our justice and goodness, nor subdued it by our magnanimity. Most of their replies in our dealings with them are witness that they were by no means behind us in native clearness of wit and pertinence.

The astounding magnificence of their cities, Cuzco and Mexico, and among many other like things, that King's garden where all the trees, fruits, and all the herbs were exquisitely formed in gold, of the same size and so arranged as in an ordinary garden, as well as, in his cabinet, all the animals that are native to his states and in his seas; and the beauty of their workmanship in jewellery, feathers, cotton, and painting, prove that neither did they yield to us in industry. But with regard to their piety, observance of the laws, goodness, liberality, loyalty, and openness, it served us well that we had not as much as they; by this advantage over us they lost, sold, and betrayed themselves.

In respect of hardihood and courage, of firmness, steadfastness, fortitude in bearing pain and hunger and death, I should not fear to oppose the examples I could find amongst them to the most famous examples in ancient times that we find recorded in our hither world. For, take away from their conquerors the tricks and artifices which they practised to deceive them, and the natural amazement of those people on seeing the so unexpected arrival of men with beards, differing from them in language, religion, shape and countenance, from so remote a region of the world, where they had never imagined that there could be any inhabitants, mounted on big, strange monsters, opposed to men who had never seen, not only a horse, but any animal whatever trained to carry and support a man or any other burden ; provided with a hard and shining skin and a sharp and glittering weapon against men who, for the marvel of a shining mirror or a knife would barter great wealth of gold and pearls, and who had neither the knowledge nor the material with which, even with time at their disposal, they could pierce our steel ; add the thunder and lightning of our cannon and musketry, enough to disturb even Caesar, if he had been surprised with so little experience and at that hour, against people who were naked, except where they had risen to the invention of some sort of cotton tissue, with no other arms, at the most, but bows, stones, staves, and wooden bucklers, people taken at a disadvantage, under colour of friendship and good faith, by curiosity to see strange and unknown things. Place to the account of the conquerors, I say, all this superiority, and you will deprive them of all credit for so many victories.

When I look upon the indomitable ardour with which so many thousands of men, women, and children so often came forward and plunged into inevitable dangers, in defence of their gods and their liberty, their noble stubbornness in suffering every extreme hardship and even death, rather than submit to the dominion of those who had so shamefully deceived them ; some of them, after being captured, choosing to waste away with hunger and fasting rather than accept food at the hands of their enemies who had been so basely victorious ; I can foresee that if any one had attacked them on equal terms in respect of arms, experience, and numbers, it would have been as hazardous, or more hazardous, a war than any we know of.

Why did not so noble a conquest fall to the lot of Alexander, or the ancient Greeks and Romans ; why did not this great change and transformation of so many empires and nations fall into hands that would have gently refined and cleared away all that was barbarous in them, and fostered and propagated the good seeds that Nature had there produced ; not only mingling with the cultivation of their lands and the adorning of their cities the arts of our hemisphere, so far as might have been necessary, but also blending the Greek and Roman virtues with those of the natives of that continent ?

What a compensation it would have been, and what an improvement for the whole of this earthly globe, if the first examples of our conduct offered to those people had called them to the admiration and imitation of virtue, and established between them and us a brotherly fellowship and understanding! How easy it would have been to turn to profit minds so fresh, so hungry to learn, which had, for the most part, naturally made so good a beginning!

On the contrary, we took advantage of their ignorance and inexperience, to bend them more easily to treachery, luxury, avarice, and to every kind of inhumanity and cruelty, by the pattern and example of our manners. Who ever set so high a value on the utility of trade and commerce? So many cities razed to the ground, so many nations exterminated, so many millions of people put to the edge of the sword, and the richest and most beautiful part of the earth turned upside down, for a traffic in pearls and pepper! Wretched machine-made victories! Never did ambition, never did national enmities impel men one against the other to such horrible acts of hostility and such miserable calamities.

Certain Spaniards, coasting the sea in search of their mines, put to shore in a pleasant and fertile region, thickly peopled, and made their usual professions to the inhabitants: 'That they were peaceable men, come from distant countries by sea, sent on behalf of the King of Castile, the greatest Prince on the habitable globe, to whom the Pope, representing God on earth, had given the lordship over all the Indies. That if they would be tributary to him, they should be treated very kindly.' They demanded of them provisions for their sustenance, and some gold to use in some medicine or other. They besides expounded to them their belief in one God, and the truth of our religion, which they advised them to accept; to this they added a few threats.

The reply was as follows: 'That, as to being peaceable, if that was so they did not look like it. As to their King, since he begged he must be needy and indigent, and the man who parcelled out things in that way must be fond of broils, to go and give to another person what did not belong to him, and set him by the ears with the ancient possessors. With regard to provisions, they would supply them; of gold they had little, and it was a thing they valued not at all, since it was of no use to them in their daily life, their only care being to pass it happily and pleasantly. They might, however, boldly take all they could find, except what was used in the service of their Gods. As to the one God, what they had said pleased them well; but they had no wish to change their religion, which had so long served them so well; and they were not accustomed to take counsel but of their friends and acquaintances.

'As to their threats, it was a sign of want of judgement to go threatening those with whose nature and means they were unacquainted. So let them make all speed to quit their territory, for they were not wont to take in good part the professions and civilities of armed and strange men; if not, they would treat them as they had treated these others,' showing them the heads of some men executed around their city.

There we have an example of the babbling of these children. But so it is, neither here nor in several other places where they did not find the merchandise they were in search of, did the Spaniards make any stay or attempt any violence, in spite of any other advantages they found there; witness my Cannibals.

Of the two most powerful monarchs of that hemisphere, and perhaps of this, kings of so many kings, the last they drove out, the King of Peru, having been taken in a battle, and put to so excessive a ransom that it surpasses all belief, and this having been faithfully paid, and he having in negotiation shown signs of a frank, liberal and undaunted spirit, and a clear and logical mind, the desire seized the victors, after extorting a million three hundred and twenty-five thousand five hundred weight of gold, besides silver and other things that amounted to no less, so that their horses never went but shod with solid gold, to discover besides, by any treacherous means they could think of, what the remainder of this King's treasures might come to, and freely to take possession of what he had in reserve. They set up a false accusation and false proofs that he was plotting to raise an insurrection in his provinces to set him free. Whereupon, in a delightful judgement pronounced by the very men who had contrived this treachery, he was condemned to be publicly hanged and strangled, after making him buy off the torment of being burned alive, by the baptism they gave him at the moment of execution. A dreadful and unprecedented crime, which he, however, suffered without betraying himself either by look or word, with truly royal demeanour and gravity ! And then to soothe the people, alarmed and bewildered by such strange doings, they counterfeited great sorrow at his death, and appointed him a sumptuous funeral.

The other, the King of Mexico, after a prolonged defence of his beleaguered city, during which he showed what endurance and perseverance are capable of, if ever prince or nation did so, had the misfortune to fall alive into his enemies' hands, it being stipulated that he should be treated as a King (nor did he in his captivity exhibit anything unworthy of that title). When, after this victory, they did not find all the gold they had promised themselves, after turning up and ransacking everything, they set about to obtain information, by inflicting the most cruel tortures they could think of upon the prisoners in their power. But, having got nothing out of these, and finding that the courage of the victims was stronger than their torments, they became at last so enraged that, against their given word and every human right, they condemned the King himself and one of the chief lords of his court to be put to the torture in each other's presence.

This lord, finding himself overcome with the pain, surrounded by red-hot braziers, at last turned piteous eyes towards his master, as if to ask his pardon for not being able to endure it. The King, proudly and sternly fixing his eyes upon him, to reprove his cowardice and pusillanimity, spoke only these words, with rude and firm voice, ' Do you think that I am in a bath ; do you think that I am more comfortable than you ? ' The other immediately succumbed to his anguish, and died on the spot. The King, half roasted, was carried from thence, not out of pity (for what pity ever touched the soul of a man who, for the dubious revealing of some gold vessel to be pillaged, had a man grilled before his eyes, not to speak of a King so great in fortune and merit), but because his fortitude made their cruelty more and more shameful. They hanged him afterwards, for having bravely attempted to deliver himself by force of arms from so long a captivity and subjection ;

and he ended his life in a manner worthy of a great-souled Prince.

On another occasion they made a fire in which they burned alive, at one time, four hundred and sixty men; the four hundred being of the common people, the sixty being the principal lords of the province, mere prisoners of war.

We have the accounts of these atrocities from themselves; for they not only admit them, but they boast of them and preach them abroad. Can it be for a testimony of their justice, or zeal for their religion? Truly those are ways and means too contrary and hostile to so sacred a purpose. If it was their purpose to spread our faith, they should have considered that it does not spread by possession of territory but by possession of men, and they should have been more than satisfied with the murders that war's necessity brings with it, without adding an indiscriminate butchery, as of so many wild beasts, and as universal as fire and sword could attain to; since they purposely kept alive only so many as they meant to make miserable slaves of, for the working and service of their mines.

So far did they exceed that many of the captains were punished with death on the scene of their conquests by command of the Kings of Castile, who were justifiably shocked by their horrible crimes; and almost all of them were hated and despised. God justly rewarded them by allowing those great spoils to be swallowed up by the sea in transit, or by the intestine wars in which they devoured one another; and the most part of the men buried one another on the scene of their crimes, without enjoying any fruits of their victory.

With regard to the fact that the revenue, even in the hands of a thrifty and prudent King,[1] answers so little to the expectations given of it to his predecessors, and to that abounding wealth which they originally came across on landing in that new world (for, although they obtain a great deal from thence, we can see that it is nothing compared with what they should expect), the reason is that the use of money was quite unknown, and that their gold was consequently all collected together, since it was of no use except for show and ostentation, as if it were a piece of

[1] Philip II, who was then ruling in Spain.

furniture preserved from father to son by many powerful kings, who were ever draining their mines for creating that vast heap of vessels and statues to adorn their palaces and temples. Whereas our gold is all in circulation and trade. We cut it up small and adulterate it in a thousand ways, then we scatter and disperse it.

Imagine our Kings accumulating in that way all the gold they could lay hands on during several centuries, and keeping it idle!

The inhabitants of the kingdom of Mexico were somewhat more civilized and artistic than the other nations of that continent. They too believed, with us, that the world was nearing its end, and accepted as a sign of it the desolation we brought upon them. They believed that the existence of the world was divided into five ages, and into the life of five consecutive suns, four of which had already run their time, and that the one that gave them light was the fifth. The first perished with all other creatures by a general inundation of water. The second by the heavens falling upon us and stifling every living thing; to which age they assigned the giants, whose bones they showed to the Spaniards, according to the proportions of which the stature of men amounted to twenty handbreadths. The third by fire, which burned and consumed all. The fourth by an agitation of air and wind which levelled even many mountains; the human beings did not die therein, but were changed into baboons (what ideas will not human credulity accept in its imbecility!). After the death of this fourth sun the world was for twenty-five years in perpetual darkness, in the fifteenth of which a man and woman were created, who restored the human race. Ten years later, on a certain day of their calendar, the sun appeared newly created, and from that day begins the reckoning of their years. On the third day after its creation the old gods died; the new ones have been born since, from day to day. In what manner they think this last sun is to perish my author did not learn. But their number of this fourth change coincides with that great conjunction of the stars which produced, some eight hundred years ago, according to the calculation of the astrologers, many great alterations and innovations in the world.

With regard to the pomp and magnificence which led me

to this subject, neither Greece nor Rome nor Egypt has any work to compare, either in usefulness or difficulty or grandeur, with the road which is seen in Peru, levelled by the kings of the country, which connects the cities of Quito and Cuzco (three hundred leagues in length), straight, even, twenty-five paces wide, paved, enclosed on either side by fine, high walls, and running alongside, within the walls, two perennial streams of water, bordered with handsome trees which they call *Molly*. When they met with rocks and mountains, they cut through and levelled them, and filled up the valleys with stone and chalk. At the end of each day's journey there were fine palaces, furnished with provisions, clothes and arms, both for travellers and for the armies that had to pass that way.

In calculating this work I have considered the difficulty of it, which is unusually formidable in that place. They built with stones no less than ten feet square, and had no other means of transporting them but the strength of their arms, to draw their loads; they had not even the art of scaffolding, knowing no other cunning but to raise so much earth against the building as it gradually rose, and afterwards removing it.

Let us return to our coaches. Instead of these or any other kind of vehicle, they had themselves carried by men, and on their shoulders. That last King of Peru, on the day when he was taken, was thus carried in the midst of his battle-army, seated in a gold sedan-chair, supported on golden shafts. As many of these carriers as they killed, to bring him to earth (for they wished to take him alive), so many others strove in emulation to take the place of the dead; so that they could never bring him down, however many of his men they massacred, until a horseman seized him round the body and pulled him to the ground.

CHAPTER 7

OF THE DISADVANTAGE OF GREATNESS

SINCE we cannot reach it, let us avenge ourselves by disparaging it. Yet to find defects in a thing is not absolutely to disparage it; there are defects in all things, however beautiful and desirable.

Greatness has as a rule this evident advantage, that it

can descend from its height when it pleases, and can well-nigh choose between either condition. For one does not fall from every height; there are more from which one can descend without falling.

It really seems to me that we think too highly of it, and that we also think too highly of the resolution of those men who, in our own experience or from hearsay, have despised it and laid it down of their own accord. Its advantages are not so essentially manifest that one may not refuse it without performing a miracle.

I should think it needs great strength to bear adversity; but in being content with a mediocre degree of fortune and avoiding greatness I can see nothing to make a stir about. That is a virtue to which I think I myself, who am but a noddy, could attain without a great effort. What effort can it need in those who also consider the glory attending such a refusal, wherein there may lurk more ambition even than in the desire for and enjoyment of greatness; since ambition never better follows its own bent than along out-of-the-way and unused paths?

I urge on my heart to patience; I rein it in to desire. I have as much to wish for as another, and allow my wishes as much freedom and indiscretion; and yet it has never occurred to me to wish for empire or royalty, nor for the eminence of those high and commanding fortunes. My aim lies not in that direction; I love myself too well. When my thoughts are bent on growth, it is a humble growth, a restricted and mean-spirited growth, of a more personal nature, towards firmness, wisdom, health, beauty, and even wealth. But such renown, such mighty authority, crushes my imagination. And, quite contrary to that other,[1] I would perhaps rather see myself the second or third at Périgueux than the first in Paris; at least, without feigning, rather the third than the first in authority in Paris. I would neither wrangle, a wretched nobody, with a door-keeper, nor have a crowd of worshippers make room for me. I am

---

[1] There is a story that as Caesar was crossing the Alps, he passed through a wretched barbarian town with very few inhabitants. When his companions humorously observed that they did not suppose there were any contests for honours in such a place, Caesar replied seriously, 'I would rather be the first man here than the second in Rome.'—Plutarch, *Life of Julius Caesar*.

accustomed, both by lot and by inclination, to a middle station. And I have shown, in the conduct of my life and my undertakings, that I have rather avoided, than not, climbing beyond the degree of fortune at which God placed me at my birth.

Everything that is constituted according to Nature is equally right and easy.

My soul is so indolent that I do not measure good fortune by its height ; I measure it by its facility.

But if my heart is not big enough, it is proportionably open, and commands me boldly to publish its defects. Should any one ask me to compare the life of L. Thorius Balbus, a gentleman, handsome, learned, healthy, intelligent, with a superfluity of all kinds of pleasures and opportunities, leading a peaceful existence quite at his own disposal, his mind fully armed against death, superstition, grief, and other obstacles to human needs, ending his life in battle with sword in hand, in the defence of his country, on the one hand ; and on the other, the life of M. Regulus, so great and eminent that it is known to all men, and his admirable end : the one without a name, and without honours, the other so exemplary and famous as to excite wonder, I should certainly speak of them as Cicero does, if I could speak as well as he.[1]

But if I had to measure them by my standard, I should also say that the first is as much within my reach, and according to my desire, which agrees with my reach, as the second is far beyond it ; that to the latter I can only attain by veneration ; the former I could easily attain in practice.

Let us return to our temporal greatness, from which we started.

I have a dislike for mastery, either active or passive. Otanez, one of the seven who had a claim to the throne of Persia, took a step which I could easily have taken : he renounced to his competitors his possible right to come to it by election or by lot, provided that he and his family might live in that empire free from all subjection and mastery,

---

[1] 'You call this man happy ? As for me, I will not venture to name the man I prefer to him. Virtue herself shall speak for me, and she will not hesitate to rank Marcus Regulus before this happy man of yours.'— Cicero, *De Fin*, ii. 20.

saving that of the ancient laws, and could enjoy every freedom that was not prejudicial to these; averse either to commanding or being commanded.

The hardest and most difficult trade in the world is, to my mind, to play the part of a King worthily. I can excuse more of their faults than people usually do, in consideration of the terrible weight of their burden, which confounds my reason. It is difficult to observe measure in a power so unmeasured.

And yet, even in men of a less excellent nature, it is a singular incitement to virtue to be seated in a place where you can do no good action that is not recorded and placed to your account; where the smallest good action affects so many people, and where your excellence, like that of a preacher, chiefly appeals to the people, no very exacting judges, easy to deceive and easily satisfied.

There are few things on which we can pass a sincere judgement, because there are few things in which we have not, in one way or another, a particular interest.

Superiors and inferiors, masters and subjects, are bound to be naturally envious of and hostile to one another; they must be perpetually robbing one another. I trust neither, when the rights of the other party are in question. Let us leave the decision to Reason, who is inflexible and impassive when we can get at her.

Less than a month ago I was perusing two books written by Scotchmen, who were debating this subject. The democrat makes the King out to be in a worse plight than a carter; the monarchist lodges him a few fathoms above God in power and sovereignty.

Now the disadvantage of greatness, which I have been led to discuss here by an event that has lately put me in mind of it, lies in this: There is perhaps nothing more pleasing in human intercourse than those trials of strength we make against one another, in rivalry of honour and worth, whether in exercises of the body or those of the mind, in which those in supreme power can have no true share. Indeed it has often seemed to me that through over-much respect princes are in this regard treated contemptuously and insultingly. For what used to offend me mightily as a boy, namely that those who competed with me in bodily exercises refused to take me seriously, because they thought

I was not worth their exerting themselves for, is what we see every day happening to princes, since every one thinks himself unworthy to use his best efforts against them. If they are observed to have the least desire to gain the victory, there is no man who will not do his best to let them have it, and who will not rather betray his own honour than offend theirs; he only exerts his strength so far as is necessary to save his reputation.

What share can they have in the fray in which every one fights on their side? They remind me of those Paladins of olden times who entered the tournaments and battles with enchanted bodies and weapons.

Brisson, running a race against Alexander, only pretended and hung back; Alexander scolded him for it, but he should have had him flogged.

In this connexion Carneades used to say 'that the sons of kings learn nothing well except the management of horses; since in every other exercise every man gives way to them and yields them the victory. But a horse, who is neither a courtier nor a flatterer, will throw the son of a king as soon as the son of a porter.'

Homer was constrained to consent to Venus, so sweet a saint and so frail, being wounded at the battle of Troy, to show her courage and daring, virtues which never fall to the share of those who are immune against danger. The gods are made to show anger, to fear and run away, to give way to jealousy, grief, and passion, in order to honour them with the virtues which, in human beings, are built up on these imperfections.

He who does not share in the danger and difficulty can claim no interest in the honour and pleasure which attend dangerous actions.

It is a pity when a man is so powerful that everything gives way to him. His fortune removes him too far from the society and company of his fellow men; it plants him too far out of the way. That ease and facility, that needs no effort, in making everything bow to you is an enemy to every kind of pleasure. It is to slide, not to walk; to sleep, not to live. Imagine a man accompanied by omnipotence, you engulf him; he must entreat of you, as an alms, impediments and opposition; his being and substance lie in indigence.

Their good qualities are dead and wasted; for these are only felt by comparison, and they are disqualified from competing. They can little know true praise, being deafened with such perpetual and uniform approval. If they have to deal with the most stupid of their subjects, they have no means of gaining an advantage over him. If he says 'it is because he is my king', he thinks he has given a sufficient reason for lending a helping hand to his own defeat. That royal quality stifles and consumes the other real and essential qualities; they are drowned in royalty. And it leaves them nothing to recommend themselves by but those actions which directly concern and interest it, the duties of their charge.

It is so much to be a king, that he only exists as such. That external light that surrounds him hides and steals him from us; our sight is broken and dissipated by it, being filled and arrested by this strong glare.

The Senate allotted the prize of eloquence to Tiberius; he refused it, judging that he could derive no honour from so unfree an award, even if it had been just.

As we yield to them every advantage of honour, so we encourage and authorize their vices and defects, not only by approval, but even by imitation. Every one of Alexander's followers carried his head on one side, as he did; and the flatterers of Dionysius used to collide with one another in his presence, and kick and upset things at their feet, to make believe that they were as shortsighted as he. Even a rupture of the bowels has at times served as a recommendation to favour. I have known deafness to be affected. And Plutarch saw courtiers who repudiated their wives, although they loved them, because the master hated his.

What is more, we have known lechery to be in fashion for that reason, and every kind of dissoluteness, as well as disloyalty, blasphemy, cruelty, nay heresy, superstition, irreligion, cowardice, and worse, if worse there can be. Their example was even more dangerous than that of the flatterers of Mithridates who, when their master was most anxious to be reputed a good physician, brought him their limbs to be slashed and cauterized; for the others allowed their souls to be cauterized, a nobler and more delicate part.

But to end where I began. When the Emperor Hadrian was disputing with the philosopher Favorinus about the interpretation of some word, the latter soon yielded him the victory ; and to his friends who expostulated with him, he said, ' You cannot be serious ; would you not have a man be more learned than I who can command thirty legions ? '

Augustus wrote some lines against Asinius Pollio. ' And I, said Pollio, will hold my tongue ; it is not wisdom to enter the links as a scribe with one who has the power to proscribe.' And they were right ; for Dionysius, because he was no match for Philoxenus in poetry and Plato in prose, condemned the one to the quarries, and sent the other to be sold for a slave in the island of Aegina.

CHAPTER 8

OF THE ART OF CONVERSING

IT is a custom of our justice to condemn some as a warning to others.

To condemn them because they have done wrong would be stupidity, as Plato says. For what is done cannot be undone. But they are condemned that they may not go wrong again in the same way, or that others may avoid following their example.

We do not correct the man we hang ; we correct others through him. I do the same. My errors are sometimes natural and incorrigible ; but whereas honest men benefit the public by setting an example, I may perhaps benefit them by making them avoid my example :

> Look, boy, he'ld say, at Albius' son,
>   Observe his sorry plight ;
> And Barrus, that poor beggar there !
>   Say, are they not a sight
> To warn a man from squandering his patrimonial means ?
> (HORACE.)

If I disclose and publish my imperfections, some will learn to fear them. The qualities I most value in myself derive more honour from my self-accusation than from my self-commendation. That is why I so often fall back and dwell upon them. But when all is summed up, a man never speaks of himself without losing thereby. His self-accusations are always believed ; his self-praise disbelieved.

There may be some who are constituted like me, who

learn more by avoiding the faults of others than by imitating their example; by flight than by following. That was the kind of teaching that the elder Cato had in mind when he said that the wise have more to learn of fools, than fools of the wise; and that ancient player on the lyre, of whom Pausanias tells us, that he used to make his pupils go to hear a bad performer who lived over the way, where they might learn to hate his discords and faulty phrasings.

The horror of cruelty impels me more to clemency than any model of clemency could draw me on. A good rider does not improve my seat as well as an attorney or a Venetian on horseback; and a bad style of speaking improves mine more than does a good one.

Every day the foolish demeanour of another warns and admonishes me. That which irritates will affect and arouse us more than that which pleases. These times are only good for reforming us backwards; more by disagreement than by agreement; more by difference than by similarity. Since I learn little by good examples, I make use of the bad, which give me daily lessons. I have tried to make myself as agreeable as I see others disagreeable; as energetic as I see others feeble; as mild as I see others fierce; [as good as I see others wicked]. But I set up unattainable standards.

In my opinion the most profitable and most natural exercise of our mind is conversation. To me it is a more agreeable occupation than any other in life; and for that reason, if I were at this moment obliged to choose, I would sooner consent, I think, to lose my sight than my hearing or speech. The Athenians, and still more the Romans, held this practice in great honour in their Academies. To this day the Italians preserve some traces of it, and greatly to their benefit, as may be seen if we compare ourselves with them in intelligence.

The study of books is a feeble and languid action which does not warm us, whilst conversation instructs and exercises us at the same time. If I converse with a man of strong mind and a stiff jouster, he will press on my flanks, prick me to right and left; his ideas will give an impetus to mine. Rivalry, vainglory, strife, stimulate me and lift me above myself. And agreement is an altogether tiresome element in conversation.

As our mind is strengthened by communication with

vigorous and well regulated minds, it is not to be imagined how much it loses and deteriorates by continual intercourse and association with vulgar and feeble-minded people. There is no infection which spreads like that. I know well enough by experience how much a yard it costs.

I love to discuss and dispute, but in a small company of men, and in private. For to exhibit oneself before great people, and to parade one's wit and cackle in rivalry with others, is to my mind a trade very unbecoming a gentleman.

Foolishness is an unfortunate quality; but to be unable to endure it, to be vexed at and worry over it, which is my case, is another kind of infirmity that is not much less tiresome than foolishness. And it is this that I am about to condemn in myself.

I can enter into a conversation and debate with great freedom and ease, since opinions find in me a soil very hard to penetrate and strike deep roots. No propositions astonish me, no belief offends me, however much opposed to my own. No idea is so frivolous or so extravagant but it appears to me naturally produced by human wit. We others,[1] who deny our judgement the right of deciding, look indulgently upon opinions differing from our own; and if we do not lend credence, we readily lend an ear to them.

When one scale of the balance is entirely empty, I let the other waver under the weight of some old woman's superstitious fancies. And it appears to me excusable if I accept an odd rather than an even number; if I prefer a Thursday to a Friday; if I would rather make a twelfth or a fourteenth than the thirteenth at table; if, when I am travelling, I am more pleased to see a hare skirting than crossing my path; and rather offer my left than my right foot to be booted first.

All such idle fancies, which obtain credit around us, deserve at least a hearing. For me they weigh just more than nothing, but they do weigh. Vulgar and unfounded opinions are besides, as regards weight, other than nothing in nature. And one who will not yield so far may perhaps, whilst avoiding the error of superstition, fall into that of opinionativeness.

Opinions then that are opposed to mine do not offend or estrange me; they only arouse and exercise my mind.

[1] We Pyrrhonians.

We dislike correction ; we should meet it half-way and welcome it, especially if it comes in the form of conversation and not of a school-lesson. At every contradiction we do not consider whether it be just, but by what means, fair or foul, we may get rid of it. Instead of extending our arms, we extend our claws to it.

I could endure hard knocks from my friends : ' You are a fool ; you are dreaming ! ' Among gentlemen I like bold expressions of opinion, and to have them speak as they think. We must fortify and harden our ears against that delicate and ceremonious sound of words. I love a strong and manly fellowship and familiarity, a friendship that delights in the rudeness and vigour of its intercourse, as love does in bites and scratches that draw blood.

It is not vigorous and generous enough if it is not quarrelsome ; if it is all civility and art ; if it fears a shock and walks in constraint. *For there can be no discussion without reprehension* (Cicero).

When a man opposes me he arouses my attention, not my anger ; I meet him half-way if he contradicts and corrects me. The cause of truth ought to be the cause common to both of us. What will he reply ? The passion of anger has already knocked his judgement on the head. Confusion has usurped the place of reason.

It would be a boon if our disputes were decided by way of wager, and if there were a substantial mark of our losses, that we might keep them in mind ; and if my serving-man could say to me, ' Your ignorance and wilfulness on twenty occasions last year cost you a hundred crowns.'

I hail and welcome the truth, in whatever hand I find it ; I cheerfully surrender and tender my vanquished sword to her, as soon as I see her approach in the distance.

And, as long as it does not come with too overbearing and schoolmasterly a mien, I encourage criticism of my writings ; and I have often altered them more from civility than because they were improved by it ; preferring, by readily giving way, to gratify and foster their freedom to admonish me ; yea, even at my own expense.

And yet it is difficult to draw the men of my time into it ; they have not the courage to correct because they have not the courage to suffer correction, and always speak with dissimulation in presence of one another. I take so much pleasure in being known and criticized that it is almost a matter of indifference to me which of the two forms it takes. My imagination so often contradicts and condemns itself that it is all one to me if another do it, chiefly in view of the fact that I allow his criticism only as much authority as I please. But I shall fall out with him who holds his head too high, as does one man I know, who thinks his advice is thrown away if it is not taken seriously, and takes it as an insult if you do not immediately follow it.

That Socrates always welcomed with a smile the contradictions offered to his arguments was due, we might say, to his strength; and that, the advantage being certain to fall to his side, he accepted them as occasions for fresh triumphs. But we may, on the other hand, observe that there is nothing that makes us so delicately sensitive to contradiction as the feeling we have of our adversary's superiority, and his contempt of us; and that, in reason, it is the part of the weaker rather to accept with a good grace the opposition which corrects and sets him right.

In fact I seek the society of those who drub me rather than of those who fear me. It is a flat and harmful satisfaction to have to do with people who admire and give way to you. Antisthenes recommended his children 'never to regard with gratitude or favour the man who praised them'. I feel much prouder of the victory I gain over myself when, in the very heat of the combat, I make myself give way to the force of my adversary's argument, than I feel gratified by the victory I gain over him through his own weakness.

In short, I accept and admit any kind of blow that is delivered according to the rules of the game, however weak it may be; but I am much too intolerant of those that are given irregularly. I care little about the matter, and all opinions are the same to me; and I am pretty indifferent as to who wins. I can argue peaceably for a whole day, if the debate is carried on according to the rules.

It is not so much force and subtlety that I expect, as order; the order that we may see any day in the altercations of shepherds and shop-boys, never with us. If they go wrong, it is in want of civility; and so it is with us. But their turbulence and impatience never put them off their theme; their argument keeps its course. If they speak out of their turn without waiting for the other to finish, they at least understand one another.

To my mind a man answers only too well if he answers to the purpose. But when the discussion becomes confused and disorderly, I leave the subject to take care of itself, and, losing my temper and my head, I cling to the form; I fall into a testy, spiteful, and overbearing style of debate, for which I have afterwards to blush.

It is impossible to deal honestly with a fool; not only my judgement but also my conscience is vitiated at the hands of so impetuous a master.

Our wranglings ought to be forbidden and punishable like other verbal crimes. How much vice they always stir and pile up, when ruled and governed by anger! We quarrel, first with the reasons, and then with the men. We learn to debate only that we may contradict; and when every one contradicts and is contradicted, it follows that the fruit of debate is to suppress and nullify the truth. So Plato, in his Republic, forbids debates among fools and ill-bred people.

What is the good of starting in quest of truth with one who has no pace and no walking-power to speak of?

We do no wrong to the subject when we leave it in order to find a better method of treating it; I do not mean a scholastic method, a method according to the rules, but a natural method, carried out with a sound understanding.

What will be the end of it all? One will go East, the other West; they drop the main point and lose sight of it among a crowd of incidental questions. After an hour's storming they forget what they are after; one shoots low, the other high, the other wide. One catches at a word and a simile. Another forgets his opponent's point, so intent is he on steering his own course; he can only think of following up his own reasons instead of yours. Another, finding he is weak in the back, is afraid and declines all argument; at the very outset he mixes up and confuses the issues. Or, in the thick of the debate, he stops dead, holds his tongue and sulks, in spiteful ignorance, affecting a proud contempt, or a silly modesty in giving up the struggle.

Provided that he gets in his blow, one man does not care how much he lays himself open. Another counts his words and weighs them as if they were so many reasons. Another only takes advantage of his voice and lung-power. Here we have one who sums up against himself, and another who deafens you with futile preambles and digressions. This one arms himself with downright insults, and seeks a Dutch quarrel to rid himself of the society and conversation of a wit who presses too hard upon him. This last can see nothing in reason, but keeps you enclosed within the barriers of his logical clauses and the formulas of his art.

Now who will not begin to distrust the sciences and doubt if he can derive any substantial gain from them for the needs of life, when he considers the use we put them to? *Learning which cures nothing* (Seneca). Who has ever gained any intelligence from Logic? Where are her fine promises? *She teaches neither to live any better, nor to reason any more pertinently* (Cicero). Do you hear any worse jumble in the cackle of herring-wives than in the public debates of the professors of Logic? I would rather my son learned to speak in the taverns than in the talking schools.

Take a Master of Arts,[1] converse with him; why does he not make us sensible of excelling in those arts, and captivate the ladies and ignoramuses like ourselves with admiration for the solidity of his reasons and the beautiful arrangement of his matter? Why can he not use his powers of persuasion and guide us at his pleasure? Why is a man with all his advantages in learning, and in conducting a debate, unable to fence without getting furiously angry and insulting his opponent? Let him put away his hood and gown and his Latin, and cease to beat his quite raw and undigested Aristotle about our ears, and you will take him for one of us, or worse.

When they become entangled and involved in the words with which they drive us into a corner, they remind me of a juggler; their sleight of hand imposes upon and vanquishes our senses, but it does not by any means shake our belief. Leave out their legerdemain, and what they do is but commonplace and mean. They may be more learned than we, but they are none the less fools.

I love and honour learning as much as those who possess it; and, if rightly used, it is the noblest and most powerful

[1] i. e. a professor of the Humanities and Philosophy.

human acquisition. But in those (and there is an endless number of their kind) who make it the ground of their worth and excellence, who appeal from their understanding to their memory, *covering under the shelter of others* (Seneca), who are powerless without their book, I hate it, if I may venture to say so, a little more than I do stupidity.

In my country, and in my time, learning often enough mends the purse, but rarely the soul. If it lights upon a mind that is dull and heavy, like a crude and undigested mass it makes it duller and heavier, and chokes it up ; if upon an acute mind, it usually purifies, clarifies, and subtilizes it, even to exhaustion. It is a thing of almost indifferent quality ; a very useful accessory in a naturally gifted mind, pernicious and harmful to another. Or rather it is a thing of very precious use, which is not to be purchased at a low price ; in some hands it is a sceptre, in others a fool's bauble.

But to proceed. What greater triumph can you expect than to teach your enemy that he is not your match ? When you gain the advantage by the substance of your argument, it is the truth that wins ; when you gain the advantage by your method of conducting it, it is you who win.

I am of opinion that, in Plato and Xenophon, Socrates debates more for the sake of the debaters than for the sake of the debate, and more to teach Euthydemus and Protagoras to know their own irrelevance than the irrelevance of their art. He lays hold of the first matter that comes to hand, as one who has a more useful purpose than to clear it up, namely, to clear up the minds he undertakes to direct and exercise.

The excitement of the chase is properly our quarry. We are not to be pardoned if we carry it on badly or foolishly ; to fail to seize the prey is a different matter. For we are born to search after the truth ; to possess it belongs to a greater power. It is not, as Democritus said, hidden in the depths of chasms, but rather raised to an infinite height in divine knowledge.

The world is but a school of research. The question is not who shall hit the ring, but who shall run the best course. He can be as great a fool who speaks true, as he who speaks false ; for we are concerned with the manner, not the matter, of speaking. It is my nature to regard the form as much as the substance, the advocate as much as the cause, as Alcibiades ordained that we should.

And every day I spend time in dipping into authors without any care about their learning ; in searching their style, not their matter. Just as I eagerly seek the society of any man renowned for his intellectual qualities ; not that he may teach me, but that I may know him [and knowing him, imitate him, if he is worthy of it].

Any man may speak truthfully ; but to speak methodically, with wisdom and talent, is given to few. So the errors that proceed from ignorance do not offend me ; it is the foppery of it. I have broken off several transactions which might have profited me, because of the impertinent protestations of those with whom I was transacting.

I do not once in a year excite myself over the faults of those over whom I have authority ; but when they stupidly and obstinately persist in their brutish and asinine assertions, excuses and defences, we are every day ready to fly at each other's throats. They neither understand what is said to them nor why, and reply accordingly ; it is enough to drive one to despair.

My head only hurts when it comes into rough contact with another. And I can sooner put up with the vices of my men than their want of thought, their unreasonableness and stupidity. Let them do less, provided they are capable of doing. You live in hopes of warming up their willingness. But we cannot hope to get any good out of a log.

But what if I take things otherwise than they are ? It may be so ; and therefore I condemn my intolerance and hold, firstly, that it is equally a blemish in one who is right and in one who is wrong. For it is always a sign of an arbitrary and sour nature to be unable to suffer any way of thinking differing from our own ; and besides, there can be no worse, no more obstinate and more eccentric fatuity than to be annoyed and exasperated by the fatuities of the world. For it irritates us chiefly with ourselves. And that philosopher [1] of olden times would never have lacked an occasion for shedding tears as long as he had himself to look at.

Miso, one of the Seven Sages, who was of a Timonian and

[1] Heraclitus, called the 'weeping philosopher'.

Democritian[1] humour, being asked why he was laughing to himself, replied, 'Because I am laughing to myself.'

How frequently I make remarks and replies every day that appear foolish to myself; therefore how much more commonly and frequently they must appear so to others! If I bite my lips over it, what must they do.

In short, we must live among the living, and let the river flow under the bridge, without caring, or at least without being upset by it.

True, but why can we meet a man with a crooked and deformed body without being moved, when we cannot bear to meet with an illogical mind without getting angry? The hardness of the judge is here more to blame than the fault.

Let us ever keep that saying of Plato on our lips: 'If I find a thing unsound, is it not because I am myself unsound? Am I not myself at fault? May not my observations reflect upon myself?' A wise and divine refrain, which scourges the most common and universal error of mankind! Not only the blame we cast at one another, but also our reasons and arguments and matters in dispute may usually be turned against us; we wound ourselves with our own weapons. Of which antiquity has left me pregnant examples enough. This was cleverly said, and much to the purpose, by him who first thought of it:

> Every man's ordure well
> To his own sense doth smell.[2]
>
> (ERASMUS, slightly altered.)

Our eyes can see nothing behind us. A hundred times a day we laugh at ourselves when we laugh at our neighbours; and we detest in others the faults which are much more glaring in ourselves, and with marvellous impudence and thoughtlessness we express our astonishment at them. Only yesterday I had the opportunity to hear a man, an intelligent and well-mannered person, ridiculing with as much humour as aptness, the fatuity of another who pesters everybody with his pedigrees and his alliances, which are more than half imaginary (for they are most ready to pounce upon this silly subject whose quality is most doubtful and least certain). And this man, if he had retired within him-

---

[1] The humour of Timon of Athens, the Misanthrope, and Democritus, the Laughing Philosopher.

[2] A good specimen of Florio's doggerel rhymes.

self, would have seen that he was hardly less extravagant and tedious in publishing and extolling his wife's family prerogatives. Oh, the meddlesome presumption with which the wife sees herself armed by the hands of her own husband!

If they understood Latin we might say to them:

> As if she were not mad enough already,
> You now provoke her to a greater madness. (TERENCE.)

I do not mean that no man should judge unless he himself be spotless, for then no man could judge; not even if he were free from the same kind of blemish. But I do mean that our judgement, when laying blame on another who is in question, should not save us from self-judgement. It is a charitable office in one who cannot rid himself of a fault to endeavour none the less to rid another of it, in whom it may have taken less deep and stubborn root.

Nor do I think it a proper answer to one who apprises me of a fault, to say that he also has it. What of that? The warning is still true and useful. If our sense of smell were good, our ordure should stink the more in our nostrils because it is ours. And Socrates is of opinion that if a man and his son and a stranger were guilty of some violence and injustice, he should begin by offering himself to be condemned by justice, and implore, for his purgation, the help of the executioner's hand; secondly for his son and in the last place for the stranger. If this precept strikes rather too high a note, he should at least present himself first for punishment to his own conscience.

The senses are our first and proper judges, which perceive things only by external accidents; and it is not to be wondered at if in all the parts of the service of our social life there is so perpetual and universal a mingling of ceremonious and superficial appearances; so much so that therein consists the best and most effective part of our regulations. It is, after all, man with whom we have to do, whose condition is wonderfully corporeal.

Let those who, in these latter years, have tried to establish for us so contemplative and immaterial a practice of religion,[1] not wonder if there are people who think that it would have melted and slipped through their fingers, if it had not held together amongst us as a mark, title, and

---

[1] The Protestant Reformers.

instrument of division and faction, more than by its own power.

So in conversation the gravity, the gown, and the fortune of the speaker often gain credit for his empty and foolish remarks. It cannot be supposed that a gentleman so formidable and with such a following should not have inside him more than ordinary talents ; and that a man so arrogant and supercilious, who has been trusted with so many offices and missions, is not more able than this other who salutes him from afar, and whom nobody will employ. Not only the words, but even the grimaces of these people are pondered and weighed, and every one labours to discover some fine and deep meaning in them. If they condescend to familiar talk, and if you do not approve and bow to everything they say, they will knock you down with the authority of their experience : they have heard this, they have seen that, they have done the other ; you are crushed with examples. I should be inclined to say to them that the result of a surgeon's experience is not the history of his patients, and the recollection that he has cured four plague-stricken and three gouty people, unless from that experience he has been able to draw conclusions wherewith to form his judgement, and has given us reason to believe that he has become the wiser in the practice of his profession.

So in an instrumental concert we do not hear a lute, a spinet, and the flute ; we hear a general harmony, the effect of the blending of the whole band.

If their travels and their experience in office have improved them, they should make it apparent in the product of their intelligence. It is not enough to sum up their experiences, they should weigh and sort them ; they should have digested and distilled them, in order to extract from them the reasons and conclusions they admit of.

There were never so many historians. It is always good and profitable to give ear to them, for they keep us fully provided with good and commendable instruction from the store-house of their memory ; they assist us no doubt, for a great part, in the conduct of life. But that is not what we ook for at present ; we seek to know if those tellers and gatherers are themselves commendable.

I hate any kind of tyranny, whether of words or deeds. I commonly battle against those unreal surroundings that delude our judgement through our senses ; and, when I keep a strict watch on those who have risen to any extraordinary eminence, I find that they are for the most part only men, like the rest of us :

> In those high places common sense
> Is rarely to be found. (JUVENAL.)

Perhaps in our estimation they appear smaller than they are, by reason of their attempting more and being more in evidence than others ; they are not equal to the burden they have taken on their shoulders. There must be more strength and power in the porter than in the load. He who has not fully tried his strength leaves you to guess if he has any power left, and if he has been tested to his utmost ; he who sinks under his burden, betrays his measure and the weakness of his shoulders. That is why we see so many incapables among the scholarly, outnumbering the capable. They might have made good husbandmen, good tradesmen, good artisans. Their natural powers were cut out to those proportions.

Knowledge is a thing of great weight, and they sink under it. Their mental machine is not powerful nor manageable enough to spread out and distribute that noble and powerful matter, to use it and derive help from it. It can only dwell in a strong nature, and strong natures are very rare. And the weak, says Socrates, by their handling mar the dignity of philosophy. It appears not only useless but harmful when it is badly encased. See how they prejudice and undo themselves !

> As when an ape, the counterfeit of man,
> By grinning schoolboy dressed in silken coat,
> Leaving his backside bare, is ushered in
> To amuse the dining guests ! (CLAUDIAN.)

So too it is not enough for our rulers and administrators, who hold the world in their hands, to have no more than an ordinary intelligence, no more ability than we. They are very much below if they are not very much above us. As they promise more, so they owe more.

And therefore their silence not only gives them an air of solemnity and gravity, but it is often profitable and economical. For Megabysus, visiting Apelles in his studio, stood a great while without speaking a word. Then he began to deliver his opinion of the painter's work, and received this rude snub, ' As long as you held your tongue, I thought you somebody out of the common, because of your chains and your fine clothes ; but now that I have heard you speak, there is not a boy in my workshop who does not despise you.' His gorgeous attire, his elevated rank, were no excuse for being ignorant with a common ignorance, and for speaking impertinently of painting. He should have kept his external and presumptive abilities under a mask of silence.

For how many foolish souls, in my time, has not a frigid and taciturn demeanour served as a mark of wisdom and capability !

Dignities, offices, are necessarily conferred more by fortune than according to merit ; and we are often wrong when we blame the King for it. Rather is it a marvel that they are so successful, when they have so little skill in it :

A Prince's virtue is his folk to know. (MARTIAL.)

For Nature has not given them eyes to take in so many people, to discern our pre-eminence and penetrate our bosoms, where lies the knowledge of our intentions and our greatest worth. They must sift us by conjecture and experiment, by family, wealth, learning, the voice of the people : very feeble testimonies. If any man could discover a means of judging and choosing men correctly and rationally, he would, by that act alone, establish a perfect form of government.

' Yes, but he has conducted this great business with success.' That is something, but it is not enough ; for this is a maxim which is rightly accepted : ' That we must not judge the plan by the issue.'

The Carthaginians punished the badly-laid plans of their generals, although they were set right by a happy issue ; and the Roman people often refused a triumph for a great and very advantageous victory, because the conduct of the commander did not correspond with his good fortune.

We may commonly observe, in the actions of this world, that Fortune, to apprise us of her power in all things, and because she takes a pleasure in confounding our presumption, being unable to make a blockhead wise, makes him successful, to spite the virtuous ; and she is fond of stepping in and favouring those actions in which she has done most of the weaving. Hence we may see every day that the simplest of us may successfully carry through an important affair, either public or private. And, as Siramnez the Persian replied to some one who wondered that his affairs should turn out so badly, seeing that he planned them so wisely: 'That he was sole master of his plans, but that of the success of his affairs Fortune was mistress;' these may answer the same, but with a contrary bias.

Most part of the things of this world work themselves out of their own accord:

> For the Fates will find a way. (VIRGIL.)

The issue often justifies a very foolish conduct. Our intervention is little more than a routine, and most commonly we consult custom and example rather than reason. Being once astonished at the greatness of some affair, and having learned from those who carried it through their motives and their proceedings, I found that their schemes were no more than commonplace. And the most commonplace and time-worn are perhaps also the surest and most adapted to the purpose, in practice if not in appearance.

What if the shallowest reasons are the most suitable; the loosest, most commonplace and threadbare the best adapted for affairs? For the king's Council to maintain its authority, outsiders should not be allowed to join it, or to see further than the nearest barrier. It must command respect on trust and in the lump, if it would keep up its reputation.

In my deliberations I outline the matter a little, and consider it cursorily in its first aspect; the main and chief part of the business I usually entrust to heaven:

> All else unto the Gods I leave. (HORACE.)

Good and bad fortune are, in my opinion, two sovereign powers. It is folly to imagine that human wisdom can play the part of Fortune. And vain is his undertaking who has the presumption to embrace both causes and consequences, and to lead the progress of his affair by the hand; especially vain in military deliberations.

There was never more caution and circumspection in military matters than is observed at times in this country. Can it be that they are afraid of losing themselves on the way, and reserve themselves for the catastrophe of that drama? I go further, and say that our wisdom itself and our deliberation follow, for the most part, whither chance leads them.

My will and my reason are stirred now by one breath, now by another; and many of these movements take place without my guidance. My reason is impelled and stirred by accidental causes varying from day to day:

> The phases of their minds are changed; their breasts
> Conceive emotions now far otherwise
> Than when the storm-wind drove the scudding clouds. (VIRGIL.)

If you will observe who are the most influential people in the cities, and who are most successful in business, you will usually find that they are the least talented. It has fallen to the lot of women, of children and madmen, to rule great states equally well with the most able princes; and the gross-witted, according to Thucydides, are usually more successful than the clever. We attribute to their wisdom the results of their good fortune.

> He makes his way who uses Fortune right,
>   And all the world calls, 'What a clever man!' (PLAUTUS.)

Wherefore I confidently say that in every way results are a poor testimony of our worth and ability.

Now I was about to say that we have but to look at a man who has been raised to dignity. Although we knew him three days before as a man of very little account, there steals imperceptibly into our minds a picture of greatness and excellence, and we are persuaded that, having grown in pomp and reputation, he has grown in merit. We estimate him, not according to his worth, but after the manner of counters, according to the prerogative of his rank. Let his luck turn, let him fall again and mingle with the crowd, every one will ask with wonder what it was that lifted him to such a height. 'Is this the man, they will say; did he know no more about it when he was there? Are princes so easily satisfied? We were in good hands, forsooth!'

That is a thing I have often seen in my time. Yea, and the mask of greatness they put on in stage-plays affects and deludes us to a certain degree.

What I myself reverence in kings is the crowd of their reverers. All obeisance and submission is due to them except that of the understanding; my reason is not trained to bow and bend, it is only my knees.

Melanthius, being asked what he thought of Dionysius' tragedy, said, ' I did not see it, it was so obscured by words.' So most of those who judge a great man's speeches might say, ' I did not understand his meaning, his discourse was so obscured by solemnity, grandeur and majesty.'

Antisthenes one day advised the Athenians to order their asses to be used for field-labour, as well as their horses; whereupon somebody replied that that animal was not born for such service. ' That does not matter, he replied ; your order will be sufficient, for the most ignorant and incapable man you appoint to a command in your wars, immediately and invariably becomes most worthy of it, just because you appoint him.'

Which comes very near the custom in so many nations of canonizing the King they have elected from among themselves ; not satisfied with honouring, they must also worship him. The Mexicans, as soon as the ceremony of crowning their King is over, dare no more look him in the face ; nay, as if his royalty had raised him to the gods, with the oaths they make him take to maintain their religion, their laws, and their liberties, to be valiant, just, and mild, he also swears to make the sun run its course with its accustomed light, to make the clouds drop their water at the proper seasons, to make the rivers flow in their channels, and cause the earth to bring forth all things necessary for his people.

I am opposed to this common way of treating them, and I am inclined rather to doubt a man's ability when I see it attended by exalted fortune and the popular favour. We must be on our guard and think how much it means, when a man is able to speak at his own time, to choose his points, to interrupt the course of a discussion or to change it, with a magisterial authority, to defend himself against opposition of others by a motion of the head, by a smile or by silence, in the presence of an assembly trembling with reverence and respect.

A man of prodigious fortune, putting in his word in a certain trifling discussion that was running its even course at his table, began with these very words, ' He can only be a liar or an ignoramus who says otherwise than, &c.' Follow up this philosophical point with a dagger in your hand !

Here is another observation which I find very useful :

That in discussions and conversations, not all the sayings which we approve of should be immediately accepted. Most men are rich in borrowed excellence. It may very well happen that a man will make a good point, give a good answer, cite a good maxim and put it forth, without perceiving the force of it.

(That a man does not possess all that he borrows may perhaps be verified in my case.)

We must not always grant it, whatever truth or beauty it may contain. Either we must oppose it seriously, or retire under colour of not understanding it, to feel on all sides how it came into the head of the man who gave utterance to it. We may happen to run upon the point of his sword and assist his stroke, although we were out of his reach.

Sometimes, when forced to it and hard pressed in the combat, I have employed a riposte that told beyond my intention and expectation. I only gave it by measure, and it was received by weight. Just as, when disputing with a strong man, I delight in meeting his conclusions half-way, relieving him of the trouble of explaining himself, and anticipating his idea whilst still unformed and nascent (the order and precision of his understanding warning and threatening me from afar) ; in the case of those others I do quite the contrary : I am obliged to understand and presume nothing but what they say. If they give their opinion in general terms, ' This is good, that is not good,' and they happen to hit the mark, see if it is not Fortune that hits it for them. Let them circumscribe and limit their judgements a little : why it is so, how it is so.

Those sweeping judgements which are so common are meaningless. They are like men who salute a whole crowd of people in the mass. Those who really know them salute and take notice of them individually and by name. But it is a hazardous experiment. For I have observed, more often than every day, that a man with a poor intellectual foundation, trying to show off his cleverness when reading a book, by remarking upon some fine passage, will fix his admiration with so poor a choice, that instead of showing up the excellence of the author, he only betrays his own ignorance.

After hearing a whole page of Virgil, it is safe to exclaim, ' That is fine ! ' In that way the artful save their faces.

But when you attempt to follow him line by line, and, with positive and discriminating judgement, to point out where a good author surpasses himself, where he rises to sublime heights, weighing his words, phrases, ideas, one after the other, away with you ! *We must consider not only what each one says, but what he thinks, and why he thinks it* (Cicero).

Every day I hear stupid people saying things that are not stupid.

They say [1] a good thing ; let us know how far they understand it ; let us see whereby they grasp it. We assist them when they use this fine maxim and that fine argument, which is none of theirs ; it is only in their keeping. They will have brought it out at a venture and diffidently ; it is we who give it value and credit. You lend them a hand. What is the good ? They do not thank you for it, and only become more foolish. Do not back them up, let them go ; they will handle this matter like people who are afraid of burning their fingers ; they dare not alter its setting and light, nor probe its meaning. Shake it ever so little, and it will escape them ; they will give it up to you, be it never so strong and beautiful. They are fine weapons, but they are ill-hafted.

How often I have had this experience !

Now, if you happen to enlighten them and corroborate them, they will catch at it and forthwith rob you of the advantage of your interpretation : ' That is what I was about to say ; that was exactly my idea, and if I failed to make myself so clear, it was only for want of words.' Blow your hardest ! One must employ even cunning to correct this arrogant stupidity.

Hegesias' dogma, ' That we should neither hate nor condemn, but instruct,' is reasonable in other cases, but in this case it is unjust and inhuman to help and set him right who stands in no need of it, and is the worse for it. I like to leave them sticking in the mud and becoming more entangled than ever, and so deeply, if it is possible, that they will at last come to acknowledge their error.

Stupidity and a confused mind are not to be cured by a word of admonition ; and we may fitly say of this kind of correction what Cyrus replied to one who urged him to harangue his army when on the point of entering into

---

[1] i. e. those who are ' rich in borrowed excellence ' ; see the last paragraph but six.

battle, ' That men are not suddenly made brave and warlike by a fine harangue, any more than a man immediately becomes a musician after hearing a good song.' It needs a preliminary apprenticeship, a long and continued education.

This attention, this assiduity in correcting and instructing, we owe to our families; but to go preaching to the first passer-by, to be schoolmaster to the ignorance and stupidity of any chance person, is a thing I greatly grudge. I rarely do so even in private conversation with another; and rather give up the whole thing than impart pedantic instruction to such backward people. I am naturally no more adapted to speak than to write for beginners. But when things are said in company or before others, however false and absurd they may appear to me, I never interfere either by word or sign.

Moreover, nothing exasperates me so much in a stupid person as that he is more self-satisfied than any reasonable person can reasonably be. It is a pity that wisdom forbids you to be satisfied with yourself and to trust your own judgement, and always dismisses you discontented and diffident; whilst a bold opinionativeness always fills its possessors with delight and assurance. It is the most empty-headed who look at other men over their shoulders, and always return from the combat full of glee and triumph. And besides, as a rule their arrogant language and cheerful looks make them the victors in the eyes of the audience, who are usually of weak intelligence and incapable of judging and discerning on which side the advantage really lies.

Obstinacy and heat in sticking to one's opinions is the surest proof of stupidity. Is there anything so cock-sure, so immovable, so disdainful, so contemplative, so solemn and serious as an ass?

May we not include under the heading of conversation and intercourse the quick and smart repartees that mirth and intimacy introduce among friends, pleasantly and wittily chaffing and poking fun at each other? A sport for which my natural gaiety makes me fit enough. And if it is not so strained and serious as the other exercise I have spoken of, it is no less subtle and intellectual, and, as Lycurgus thought, no less profitable.

For my part I contribute to it more licence than wit, and have therein more luck than originality. But in patience

I am perfect, and can bear a retaliation that is not only rude but impertinent, without being moved. And when attacked, if I have not a brisk retort ready to hand, I do not waste time in following up that point with feeble and tiresome persistence, bordering on obstinacy; I let it pass, cheerfully letting my ears drop and deferring my revenge to some better opportunity. There is no merchant who always gains.

Most people change countenance and raise their voices when their strength begins to fail; and with unreasonable anger, instead of getting their revenge, only betray their weakness and their impatience at the same time. In this mirthful mood we sometimes pluck some secret string of each other's imperfections, which, in a more sober mood, we cannot touch without offence. And we profitably give one another a hint of our defects.

There are other kinds of rough play, which are unwise and cruel, after the French manner, for which I have a deadly hatred; for I have a tender and sensitive skin. I have seen in my time two Princes of our royal blood brought to their graves as a consequence of them.[1] It is an ugly thing to fight in play.

For the rest, when I wish to size up a man, I ask him how far he is satisfied with himself, how much he is pleased with his conversation and his work. I will have none of those fine excuses : ' I only did it in play ;

> This work unfinished from the anvil comes ; (OVID.)

I was not an hour over it ;[2] I have not looked at it since.' Well then, I reply, put this piece aside; give me one that does you full justice, by which you would like to be measured. And then, what do you consider best in your work ; is it this passage, or this ? Is it the charm, or the matter, or the idea, or the judgement, or the learning ?

---

[1] According to Motheau this can only refer to King Henry II and to Henry de Bourbon-Montpensier, both of whom died of wounds received in the last two tournaments that were held in France, one at Paris in 1559, the other at Orleans in 1560.

[2] *Oronte.*   Au reste, vous saurez
    Que je n'ai demeuré qu'un quart d'heure à le faire.
  Alceste. Voyons, Monsieur ; le temps ne fait rien à l'affaire.

Molière, no doubt, remembered this passage when he wrote that wonderful ' sonnet scene ' in the *Misanthrope*.

For I observe generally that men are as wide of the mark in judging their own work as in judging that of others, not only by reason of the affection that creeps in, but for want of capacity to know and discriminate it. The work, by its own power and fortune, may second the workman, and outstrip him, beyond his own inventiveness and knowledge.

For my part; I do not judge of the value of another's work less clearly than my own ; very changeably and hesitatingly I rate the Essays now low, now high.

There are many books that are useful by reason of their subject, for which the author earns no praise ; and there are good books, as well as good works, which shame the workman. I may write of the fashions of our dinner-parties and our clothes, and write without enthusiasm ; I may publish the edicts of my time, and the letters of Princes, which will pass into the hands of the public ; I may make an abridgement of a good book (and every abridgement of a good book is a foolish abridgement), and the book itself may be lost ; and the like things. Posterity may derive singular benefit from such compositions ; but what honour shall I gain, except through my good fortune ? A good number of famous books are in this plight.

When, some years ago, I read Philip de Commines, truly a very good writer, I noticed this for no common remark : 'That we must take good care not to serve our master so well as to make it difficult for him to requite us adequately for our services.' I ought to have commended the idea, not the writer. I came across it, not long ago, in Tacitus : *Benefits are only so far acceptable as they appear capable of being returned ; if they pass much beyond that limit, they reap hatred rather than gratitude.* And Seneca says with vigour : *The man who thinks it disgraceful not to pay back, would rather have no man for a creditor.* And Q. Cicero,[1] from a meaner point of view : *The man who thinks he cannot requite you can in no way be your friend.*

The subject, according to its nature, may gain a man a reputation for learning and a good memory ; but in order to appreciate those qualities in the book which are most original and most valuable, the power and beauty of the writer's mind, we must know how much of it is original, how

[1] Quintus Cicero, brother of the great orator, known for the letter of advice he addressed to the latter, ' On Standing for the Consulship '.

much not. And, with respect to what is not original, how much we owe him in consideration of the choice, the disposition, embellishment and style which he has contributed to it. What if he has borrowed the matter and impaired the form, as so often happens? We others who have little acquaintance with books are in this strait that, when we come across some beautiful idea in a new poet, some forcible argument in a preacher, we dare not commend them for it until we have been informed by some man of learning whether that element is their own, or some other's. Till then I always stand on my guard.

I have just run through Tacitus' *History* without a break (a thing that seldom happens with me; it is twenty years since I have devoted a whole hour at a time to a book); I did so at the instigation of a gentleman who enjoys great esteem in France, both for his own worth, and for a consistent kind of excellence and goodness which he shares with several brothers.

I know no writer who introduces into the annals of public affairs so many reflections on the manners and dispositions of private persons. And I totally disagree with him when he says that, having made it his special task to trace the lives of the Emperors of his time, so abnormal and so outrageous in every direction, and to tell of the many remarkable deeds which their cruelties in particular called forth in their subjects, he had a more solid and attractive material on which to build his narrative and his reflections, than if he had had to tell of battles and general insurrections. So that often I find him sterile, hurrying over those noble deaths, as if he feared to weary us with their number and length.

This form of history is by far the most useful. Public movements are more dependent on the guidance of Fortune; private ones on our own.

It is rather a summing up than an historical narrative; there are more precepts than stories. It is not a book to read, it is a book to study and learn; it is so full of maxims, that they seem to have been brought in by hook and by crook. It is a nursery of ethical and political dissertations, for the benefit and improvement of those who hold a place in the management of the world.

He always pleads with strong and solid reasons, in pointed

and subtle fashion, in accordance with the affected style of that age; they were so fond of inflated language that when they could find no point or subtlety in things they borrowed them of words.

He writes not unlike Seneca; he appears to me more fleshy, Seneca more pointed. His services were better adapted to a sick and disturbed state, as ours is at present; you might often think he were describing us and criticizing us.

They who doubt his sincerity plainly betray themselves as ill-disposed to him on some other account. His opinions are sound, and he leans to the right side in Roman affairs. Yet I blame him a little for having judged Pompey more harshly than is consistent with the opinion of the honest men who lived at the time and had dealings with him; and for placing him entirely on a par with Marius and Sylla, except in so far as he was more close. In aiming at the government of affairs he was not acquitted of ambition and a feeling of revenge; and even his friends feared that victory would have carried him beyond the bounds of reason, but not to so unbridled a degree.[1] There was nothing in his life to suggest a threat of such purposeful cruelty and tyranny. Besides we should not weigh suspicion against evidence; so I do not agree with Tacitus in that matter.

That his narrative is simple and straightforward may perhaps be argued even from this, that it does not always fit in with the conclusions his judgement comes to, which he follows according to the bias he has taken, often beyond the matter he is presenting to us, which he has not deigned to twist in the least degree.

He needs no excuse for having countenanced the religion of his time, in accordance with the laws which commanded him to do so, and of having been ignorant of the true faith. That was his misfortune, not his fault.

I have considered chiefly his judgement, and am not very clear about it in every case. For example, those words in the letter which Tiberius, sick and aged, sent to the Senate: 'What to write, Conscript Fathers; in what terms to express myself, or what to refrain from writing, is a matter of such perplexity, that if I know how to decide, may the just Gods and the Goddesses of Vengeance doom me to die

[1] As Marius and Sylla.

in pangs worse than those under which I linger every day!' I cannot see why he so positively attributes them to a poignant remorse tormenting Tiberius' conscience; at least I did not see it when I was best able to do so.[1]

This too appeared to me a little mean-spirited, that having occasion to mention a certain honourable office that he filled at Rome, he excuses himself by saying that it is not out of ostentation that he mentions it. This seems to me a cheap thing to say, coming from a mind like his; for not to dare to speak roundly of oneself betrays some want of spirit. A man of staunch and lofty judgement, who judges soundly and surely, will unhesitatingly use himself as an example, as if he were some other person, and give as frank testimony of himself as of anything else. He should override those common rules of politeness for the sake of truth and liberty.

I dare not only to speak of myself, but to speak only of myself; when I speak of other things I wander away and escape from my subject. I am not so inordinately in love, so wholly bound and mixed up with myself, that I cannot consider and distinguish myself apart, as I do a neighbour or a tree. Not to see how much we are worth is as great a fault as to tell more of ourselves than we are able to discover. We owe more love to God than to ourselves, and we know him less well; and yet we speak of him to our heart's content.

If the writings of Tacitus in any way reflect his character, he was a great man, upright and courageous, not of a superstitious, but of a philosophic and generous virtue. We may think him venturesome in his testimony, as when he tells of a soldier, who was carrying a load of wood, that his hands were so stiffened by cold, that they stuck to the wood, and there remained fixed and dead, having come away from his arms. In such matters I usually bow to the authority of such great witnesses.

And when he says that Vespasian, by the grace of the god Serapis, cured a blind woman of Alexandria by anointing her eyes with his spittle, and I know not what other miracle, he follows the example and duty of all good historians. They keep a record of important events, and among matters of public interest are to be numbered popular

[1] 'When I read the text', is perhaps what Montaigne meant.

rumours and ideas. It is their part to cite common beliefs, not regulate them. That part concerns divines and philosophers, the directors of consciences.

Very wisely too his fellow-historian, a great man like himself, said: *Indeed I set down more things than I believe; for I neither affirm things I doubt, nor suppress what I have heard* (Quintus Curtius). And this other: *These are things we need not be at pains either to affirm or refute; we must abide by report* (Livy). And, writing in an age when the belief in prodigies was beginning to decline, he says he will not on that account forbear to insert in his *Annals* and lend currency to things accepted by so many worthy men, and with so much reverence for antiquity. That is very well said. Let them deliver history as they receive it rather than as they believe it.

I, who am monarch of the matter I treat of, and am accountable for it to no man, yet do not trust myself with regard to everything; I often venture on intellectual flights of fancy which are suspicious to myself, and certain verbal quibbles at which I shake my ears. But I let them run their chance. I observe that some are praised for such things; it is not for me alone to judge. I present myself standing and lying, front and back, right and left, and in all my natural attitudes.

Minds, even if alike in strength, are not always alike in tastes and inclinations.

That is what my memory of Tacitus pictures to me in the gross, and with uncertainty enough. All generalizations are loose and imperfect.

CHAPTER 9

OF VANITY

THERE is perhaps no more manifest vanity than to write of it so vainly. What the Deity has so divinely said of it ought to be carefully and continually meditated by intelligent people.[1]

Who does not see that I have chosen a path along which I shall wander, without cease and without labour, as long as there is ink and paper in the world? I cannot keep a record

---

[1] See Ecclesiastes, or the Preacher.

of my life by my actions; Fortune places them too low. I keep it by my ideas. So I knew a gentleman who only communicated his life by the operations of his bowels; at his house you might have seen on view a row of chamber-pots of seven or eight days' use. That was his study, his conversation; all other talk stank in his nostrils.

Here, a little more decently, you have the excrements of an old mind, now hard, now loose, and always undigested. And when shall I have done reflecting a continual movement and change in my thoughts, whatever the matter they light upon, seeing that Diomedes filled six thousand books with nothing but grammatical subjects?[1] What should be the output of garrulity, since the untying of the tongue and mere prattle stifled the world under such a horrific load of volumes! So many words for mere words! O Pythagoras, why did you not conjure this tempest![2]

One Galba[3] of olden times was reproved for living idly; he replied, 'Every man should render an account of his actions, not of his leisure-hours.' He was mistaken, for justice also notices and censures those who keep holiday.

But there should be some kind of coercion on the part of the laws of those who write futile and unprofitable things, as there is of vagrants and idlers. Both I and a hundred others would be banished from the hands of the people.

I am not jesting. The mania for scribbling appears to be one of the symptoms of an unruly age. When did we write so much as in these disturbed times? When did the Romans write so much as at the time of their downfall? Besides, intellectual subtlety does not imply a greater wisdom in a government; that busy idleness proceeds from this, that every man takes a lax interest in the duties of his office, and is easily led away from them.

The corruption of the times is made up of the individual contributions of each one of us; some contribute treachery, others injustice, irreligion, tyranny, avarice, cruelty, according as they are more or less influential; the weaker sort

[1] According to Seneca, Didymus (not Diomedes) the Grammarian wrote four thousand books on futile questions connected with literature, such as 'Who was Aeneas' real mother?' 'Was Anacreon more a lecher than a drunkard?'

[2] Pythagoras is supposed to have imposed a silence of two or five years on his disciples.

[3] According to Suetonius, the Emperor Galba.

bring to it folly, vanity, idleness : of these am I. It would seem as if unprofitable things were in season, when the hurtful weigh heavily upon us. At a time when wicked deeds are so common, merely unprofitable deeds are almost praiseworthy.

I find comfort in the reflection that I shall be one of the last on whom they must lay hands. Whilst they see to the more urgent cases, I shall have leisure to mend. For I think it would be contrary to reason to hunt down the petty evil-doers when the country is infested with great ones.

The physician Philotinus said to one who came to him to have his finger dressed, but who, as he perceived from his complexion and his breath, had an ulcer on his lungs, ' My friend, this is no time to busy yourself with your nails.'

And yet, speaking on this subject, a few years ago I saw that a man whose memory I hold in particular esteem, at the height of our great disorders, when there was no more law or justice, nor any magistrate who did his duty, than there are at this moment, publicly suggested some pitiful reforms or other in our dress, cookery, and law-practice. Those are diversions with which they feed an ill-used people, to make them believe that they are not entirely forgotten.

It is the same with those others who zealously waste their time denouncing forms of speech, dancing, and games, in a people abandoned to all sorts of execrable vices. It is no time to wash and clean up when we are attacked by a high fever. Only the Spartans could afford to set about combing and dressing their hair when about to rush headlong into some extreme danger to their lives.[1]

For my part, I have this other worse habit, that if one of my pumps is trodden down, I am equally neglectful of my shirt and my cloak ; I scorn to mend by halves. When I am in evil plight, I revel in my misfortune ; I abandon myself to despair, and let myself go to the dogs, throwing, as the saying is, the helve after the hatchet. I persist in growing worse, and no longer think myself worth caring for ; either entirely well or entirely ill.

It is in my favour that the desolation of this State coincides with the desolation of my age ; I can more readily suffer that my ills should be increased, than that my well-being should be disturbed by it. The words I utter in

[1] An allusion to the battle of Thermopyle.

misfortune are words of anger; my courage bristles up instead of drooping.

And, contrary to others, I am more devout in good than in evil fortune, following Xenophon's precept, if not his reason,[1] and more generally make eyes at Heaven to give thanks than to beg.

I take more pains to improve in health when it smiles upon me, than to recover it when I have mislaid it.

Prosperity is my teacher and instructor, as adversities and rods are to others.

As if good fortune were incompatible with a good conscience, men never become good but in evil fortune.

Good fortune is to me a singular spur to temperance and humility.

A prayer wins me, a threat repels me; favour makes me bend, fear stiffens me.

Among human attributes this is common enough, that we are better pleased with things of others than with our own, and that we love change and motion:

> The day flows onward in a grateful stream,
> Because the steeds are changed at every hour.[2] (PETRONIUS.)

I have my share in it. Those who go to the other extreme, of being satisfied with themselves, of valuing what they possess above all other things and admitting nothing to be more beautiful than what they see, are indeed happier if not wiser than we. I do not envy their wisdom, but certainly their good fortune.

This greedy craving for the new and unknown greatly helps to foster in me the desire to travel; but there are enough other circumstances that contribute to it. I am content to turn aside from the ruling of my household. There is a certain gratification in being in command, though it were only of a barn, and in being obeyed by one's people; but it is too dull and humdrum a pleasure. And besides, it is necessarily attended by many tiresome considerations; now it is the indigence and oppression of your tenants, now

---

[1] 'The most likely person to obtain favour from the Gods (as well as from men) is not he who, when he is in distress, flatters them servilely, but he who, when he is most prosperous, is most mindful of them.'—Xenophon, *Cyropedia*.

[2] There appear to be two metaphors involved in this Latin quotation, that of the water-hourglass, and of Apollo's steeds.

a quarrel among your neighbours, now the trespasses they make upon you, that give you trouble :

> Whether your vines be smit with hail;
> Whether your promised harvest fail,
>   Perfidious to your toil;
> Whether your drooping trees complain
> Of angry winter's chilling rain,
>   Or stars that burn the soil; (HORACE.)

and that God hardly once in six months sends you a season that fully satisfies your steward, and which, if good for the vines, does not harm the meadows :

> The sun above with burning heat destroys,
> Or sudden showers and icy frosts lay low,
> And blasts of storms with furious whirlwinds vex. (LUCRETIUS.)

Add to this the new and well-shaped shoe of the man of olden times that hurts your foot.[1] And that a stranger does not understand what it costs and how much you sacrifice to keep up that show of order that is seen in your household, and which perhaps you pay too dearly for.

I was late in taking up husbandry. Those whom Nature sent into the world before me for a long time relieved me of that burden. I had already taken another bent, more suitable to my humour. However, so far as my experience goes, it is an absorbing rather than a difficult occupation ; whoever is capable of anything else will be easily capable of this. If I sought to become rich, that way would seem to me too long ; I might have served kings, a more fertile traffic than any other. Seeing that I only aspire to the reputation of having acquired nothing, as I have wasted nothing, conformably to the rest of my life, being unable to do any good or any ill, and that I only desire to pass, I can do that, thank God, without any great exertion.

If it comes to the worst, always hasten to meet poverty half-way by retrenching your expenses ; that is what I strive to do, and to mend my ways before I am forced to it. I have, moreover, sufficiently thought out in my mind the different stages of doing with less than I have ; I mean

---

[1] A certain Roman having divorced his wife, his friends remonstrated and asked him, ' Was she not chaste ? Was she not fair ? Was she not fruitful.' He held out his shoe and replied, ' Is it not handsome ? Is it not new ? Yet no one knows where it pinches but he that wears it.'— Plutarch, *Life of Paulus Emilius*.

contentedly. *Not by your income, but by your living and style, is your wealth really to be calculated* (Cicero).

My real need does not so wholly take up all I have but that Fortune may find something in me to nibble at, without biting to the quick.

My presence, in spite of my ignorance and apathy, affords great help in my domestic affairs; I busy myself with them, but grudgingly. Besides that in my house, although I burn the candle at my end, the other end is by no means spared.

Travelling does me no injury except in regard to the expense, which is great and beyond my means; and I am accustomed to travel with not merely a necessary, but a handsome retinue. I am obliged to make my journeys the shorter and less frequent, and spend on them only the skimmings and the reserve fund, delaying and putting off according as they come in.

I do not wish the pleasure of my wanderings to spoil the pleasure of my retreat; on the contrary I intend that they shall nourish and favour one another. Fortune has been helpful to me in this, that, since my chief aim in this life was to live comfortably and idly rather than busily, she has relieved me of the necessity of multiplying riches to provide for a multitude of heirs. As for the one I have, if that does not suffice her which has so plenteously sufficed me, so much the worse for her; if she is improvident she will not deserve that I should wish her any more. And, after the example of Phocion,[1] every man sufficiently provides for his children who provides for them in so far as they are not unlike him. I should certainly not agree with Crates, or do as he did. He left his money in the hands of a banker, with this condition: 'If his children were fools, he was to give it to them; if they were clever, he was to distribute it among the most foolish of the people;' as if fools, for being less able to do without riches, were more capable of using them!

At all events, the loss that is caused by my absence does not, as long as I am able to bear it, appear to deserve that I should refuse to seize any opportunity that offers of taking a holiday from the labours that my presence entails.

There is always something that goes wrong; you are

[1] 'If my children are like me, my little estate will be enough for them; if not I will not encourage and increase their expensive habits at my cost.'—Cornelius Nepos, *Phocion*.

plagued by business, now about one house, now about another. You pry too closely into everything; your perspicacity is harmful to you in this, as it often enough is in other things. I avoid any occasions for annoyance, and try to ignore things that go amiss; and yet I cannot manage so well but that at every hour when at home I experience some unpleasant jar. And the rogueries they most carefully keep from me are those I know best. There are some we must ourselves help to conceal, that we may suffer less. Harmless pin-pricks; harmless sometimes, but still pin-pricks. The pettiest and minutest troubles are the most keenly felt; and as small letters hurt and tire the eyes most, so do little matters most irritate us. The petty ills that crowd upon us are more worrying than a single big one, however severe. Coming thick upon us with their delicate points, these domestic thorns prick us the more sharply and without warning, easily taking us unawares.

I am no philosopher; evils crush me according to their weight; and they weigh as much in proportion to their form as to their matter, and often more. I have more insight into them than the vulgar, and so suffer them more patiently. In short, if they do not wound me, they hurt me.[1]

Life is a delicate thing, and easily disturbed. From the moment that I am inclined to be ill-humoured—*for after yielding to the first impulse we cannot resist it* (Seneca)— however absurd the cause of it, I incite my humour in that direction; it then nurses[2] and exasperates itself of its own accord, attracting and accumulating matter upon matter whereon to feed:

The drippings from the eaves will scoop the stone. (LUCRETIUS.)

These frequent little droppings eat into my soul. Everyday annoyances are never light. They are continual and irreparable, especially if caused by the continual details inseparable from household management.

---

[1] The edition of 1588 had this passage in place of the last paragraph:
'Now Homer shows us well enough the power of surprise, when he makes Ulysses weep at the death of his dog and not at his mother's (wife's ?) tears. The first accident, trivial as it was, got the better of him since it attacked him unawares; he bore the second and more violent attack because he was prepared for it. They are slight causes, which however disturb our lives.'

[2] 'Nursing her wrath to keep it warm.'—BURNS.

When I consider my affairs from a distance and in the lump, I find, perhaps because I do not remember them very exactly, that they have till now continued to prosper beyond my expectation and calculations. I seem to get more out of my estate than there is in it ; the success of my affairs is deceptive. But when I am in the midst of the drudgery, when I see all those little things in progress,

> Then is my soul with care on care distraught, (VIRGIL.)

a thousand things give me cause to desire and fear. To forsake them entirely I find very easy ; to give my attention to them without anxiety, very hard. It is a pitiful thing to be in a place where everything you see gives you concern and trouble. And I think I enjoy with a lighter heart and with a purer relish the comforts of another man's house.

Diogenes answered according to my humour when, being asked what sort of wine he liked best, he said, ' Another man's.'

My father loved building at Montaigne, where he was born ; and in the management of all my domestic affairs I love to follow his example and his rules ; and I will interest my successors in them as far as I am able. If I could do more for him, I would. I make it my boast that his will is in active operation through me. God forbid that I should fail to repay so kind a father by resembling him in any way whatever !

Whenever I have taken in hand to complete some bit of old wall, or rectify some badly-squared farm-building, I have thought more of his intentions than of my own satisfaction. And I blame my indolence that I have not gone any further towards completing the things he so handsomely commenced in his house, the more so as I am in all likelihood the last possessor of my race, and the last to put a finishing hand to it.

For, with regard to my own inclinations, neither this pleasure of building, which is said to have so much fascination, nor the chase, nor gardening, nor any of those other pleasures of a secluded life, are much of a pastime to me. That is a thing for which I blame myself, as I do for all other notions that I find inconvenient. I do not care so much whether they be vigorous or learned, so long as they are easily adaptable to life ; they are true and sound enough, if they are useful and pleasing.

They do me a mortal wrong who, when they hear me declare my incompetence in matters of husbandry, whisper into my ears that it is disdain, and that I am careless about knowing the implements of field labour, its season, its order, how my vines are dressed, how they are grafted, the names and shapes of plants and fruits and the preparation of the viands on which I live, the names and prices of the materials with which I am clothed, because my heart is set upon some higher knowledge. That would be folly and stupidity rather than vanity. I would rather be a good horseman than a good logician:

> Why not apply yourself to useful tasks,
> Plait wicker crates and baskets of soft reeds? (VIRGIL.)

We entangle our thoughts with general questions, universal causes and the conduct of universal affairs, which will go forward very well without our assistance, and we neglect our own business, and Michael, who concerns us much more nearly than man in general.

Now I do indeed stay at home for the most part; but I should like to take more pleasure in staying at home than in going abroad:

> May it the haven be, I pray,
> For my old age to wear away;
> Oh, may it be the final bourne
> To one with care and travel worn! (HORACE.)

I know not whether I shall bring it about. I could wish that instead of some other part of his possessions, my father had left me that passionate love he had in his old age for his household. He was very happy in being able to adapt his wishes to his fortune, and to be satisfied with what he had. I care not how much political philosophy may condemn the meanness and sterility of my occupation, if I can once take a liking for it, as he did. I am of this opinion, that the most honourable occupation is to serve the public, and to be useful to many. *We best employ the fruits of genius, virtue and all excellence, when we are able to bestow them on our fellow-men* (Cicero). For my part, I stand aside; partly for conscience' sake (for whenever I consider the weight of obligation attaching to such employments, I also perceive how little I am able to bear it; and Plato, a master-worker in all political government, none the less kept aloof from it); partly through indolence. I am content to enjoy the world, without busying myself with it; to live no more than an excusable life, a life that will be no burden to myself or others.

Never did any man more fully and weakly allow himself to be cared for and ruled by another than I should do, if I could find somebody. One of my wishes at this moment would be to find a son-in-law who would comfortably spoon-feed me in my old age, and rock me to sleep; to whose hands I might entrust, with full power, the management and use of my property, that he might dispose of it as I do, and get at my expense what I get, provided he did so with a truly grateful and loving heart. But no, we live in a world where loyalty in our own children is unknown.

Whoever has charge of my purse when I travel, has it purely and without control; and so he might cheat me in the reckoning. And if he is not a devil, my reckless trust obliges him to deal honestly by me. *Many, in their fear of being cheated, have taught how to cheat; and by their suspicions have justified another's crimes* (Seneca). My trust in my people is generally founded on my ignorance of their faults; I do not presume any vice in them until I have seen it, and I place more trust in the younger, whom I consider to be less corrupted by evil examples.

I would rather be told, at the end of two months, that I have spent four hundred crowns, than to have my ears drummed every night with three, five, seven. Yet I have as seldom as any man been a victim to this kind of petty larceny. It is true that I lend a helping hand to my own ignorance; I purposely keep my knowledge of my money somewhat uncertain and muddled; up to a certain point I am quite content to be able to doubt. You must leave a little margin for the disloyalty or improvidence of your servant. If on the whole we have enough to make ends meet, let that overplus of Fortune's liberality run a little more at her mercy: the gleaner's portion. After all I do not so much prize the fidelity of my people as I despise the injury they can do me.

O what a vile and ridiculous study it is to study one's money, to take a pleasure in fingering, weighing, and counting it over and over again! That is the way by which avarice makes its approach.

During these eighteen years that I have governed my estate, I have not been able to bring myself either to look at a title-deed or to examine my principal affairs, which have necessarily to pass under my knowledge and attention. This is not a philosopher's contempt for transitory and mundane things; my taste is not so clarified, and I appreciate them at least at their true value; but it is certainly inexcusable and puerile sloth and negligence.

What would I not do rather than read a contract, rather than go and disturb those dust-laden documents, a slave to my business, or, still worse, to another's business, as so many are for money payment? Nothing costs me so much as trouble and anxiety; and I only seek to throw off care and live in idleness.

I believe I was better adapted to live on another man's fortune, if that were possible without obligation and subjection. And yet I know not, on looking more closely into it, whether, with my disposition and my lot, what I have to suffer from business and at the hands of servants and familiars, does not bring more humiliation, trouble, and bitterness, than I should feel in the retinue of a man, of higher birth than myself, who would steer my course for me in comfort. *Slavery is the subjection of a broken, abject mind, lacking free will* (Cicero).

Crates did worse, who took refuge in the freedom of poverty, to rid himself of the cares and drudgery of household management. That I could not do (I hate poverty equally with pain), but what I could do is to exchange this kind of life for another less showy and less busy.

When absent from home I can throw off all such thoughts, and would feel the ruin of a tower less than I do, when present, the fall of a tile. My mind easily becomes free at a distance, but when at home it suffers like that of a vine-grower. A bridle wrongly adjusted, a stirrup-leather beating against my leg, will keep me in bad humour a whole day. I screw up my courage well enough against discomforts, my eyes I cannot.

The senses, ye Gods, the senses!

At home I am responsible for all that goes amiss. Few masters (I mean those of medium condition like mine, and if there be any such, they are more fortunate) are able to rely so much upon a second, but that a good part of the burden will still rest upon their shoulders. That generally makes me less gracious in entertaining any chance visitors (and some perhaps have been induced to stay for the sake of my good table rather than my gracious manners, as is the way with bores), and takes away much of the pleasure I should derive from the visits and meetings of my friends in my house.

The most absurd figure a gentleman cuts is to be seen in his own house worrying over the details of housekeeping, whispering to one footman, threatening another with his eyes. Things should glide smoothly and imperceptibly and reflect their ordinary course.

And I think it a hateful custom to talk to your guests about the fare you are providing for them, whether to excuse it or to boast of it.

I love order and cleanliness,

> Your cup and salver such that they
> Yourself unto yourself display, (HORACE.)

as much as I do abundance; and at home I am very particular about the needful, and care little for display.

If in another man's house a footman begins fighting, if a dish is upset, you merely laugh at it. You go to sleep while Monsieur is arranging with his butler about your to-morrow's entertainment.

I speak of these things as I myself think, not omitting to consider, in a general way, what a pleasure to certain natures it is to have a peaceful, thriving household, carried on with order and regularity: and not wishing to fasten my own errors and defects to the matter, or give Plato the lie, who esteems it the happiest occupation for every man ' to carry on his own affairs without wronging others '.

When I travel, I have only myself to think of, and the employment of my money; that is disposed of by a single precept. For amassing wealth too many qualities are needed; I have no skill in it. I understand a little how to spend, and how to make the most of what I spend, which is indeed its chief use. But I set about it too ambitiously, which renders it unequal and distorted, and immoderate besides in both respects.[1] If it makes a show and accomplishes

---

[1] In economy and prodigality.

its purpose, I let myself go injudiciously; and just as injudiciously do I tie up my purse-strings if it does not shine and does not please me.

Whatever it be, whether Art or Nature, that implants that idea in our minds that we must defer to others as to how we live, does us much more harm than good. We defraud ourselves against our own interest, in order to make appearances fit in with public opinion. We care not so much what we are in ourselves and in reality, as what we are in the estimation of other people. Even intellectual advantages and knowledge appear fruitless to us, if we alone enjoy the benefit of them, if they are not displayed to the eyes and approval of others.

There are some men whose gold flows in broad streams, through underground places, imperceptibly; others hammer it all out into thin plates and leaves, so that to the one a farthing is worth a crown, to the other the reverse; and the world judges of the use and the value according to the show. All anxious care about wealth savours of avarice; so also does the spending and lavishing of it, when it is too systematic and artificial. It is not worth such painful vigilance and solicitude. He who tries to be too exact in his spending makes it pinched and narrow. Hoarding and spending are in themselves indifferent things, and assume no colour of good or bad but according to the application of our will.

The other cause that invites me to these excursions is that I cannot put up with the present moral condition of our State. I could readily console myself for this corruption as far as regards the public interest:

> Times more evil than the Iron age,
> Whose misdeeds even Nature cannot name,
> Or find a metal to compare them to; (JUVENAL.)

but in regard to my own, no. I in particular suffer too much from them. For in my neighbourhood we are, through the long-continued licence of our civil wars, almost grown old in so riotous a form of government,

> A place where right and wrong unseat each other, (VIRGIL.)

that it is in truth a marvel how things can hold together:

> In arms they plough the furrow, and evermore
> Amass new plunder, and by rapine live. (VIRGIL.)

In short I can see by our example that human society will hold and keep together at whatsoever cost. In whatever position you place human beings, they will shake up and arrange themselves in stacks and heaps, just as uneven bodies, bundled into a sack without any order, will themselves find the means of uniting and settling down together, often better than they could have been arranged by art.

King Philip made a collection of the most wicked and incorrigible men he could find, and settled them all in a city which he had built for them, and which took its name from them.[1] I imagine that out of their very vices they established among themselves a civil constitution, a regular and decent society.

I see not one action, or three, or a hundred, but a commonly accepted state of morality so unnatural, especially as regards inhumanity and treachery, which are to me the worst of all sins, that I have not the heart to think of them without horror; and they excite my wonder almost as much as my detestation. The practice of these egregious villainies bears as much the mark of strength and vigour of soul as of error and disorder.

Necessity reconciles men and brings them together. This accidental union afterwards takes shape in laws. For there have been laws as ferocious as any that the human mind could give birth to, which have yet been as healthy in body and as long-lived as any that Plato and Aristotle could draw up. And indeed all those outlines of government as imagined by art [2] are found to be absurd and unfit to be put into practice.

Those long and tedious debates on the best forms of society, and on the most suitable laws for binding us, are only adapted for exercising the mind; as in the liberal arts there are many subjects which have their being only in discussion and controversy, outside of which they have no existence. Such a description of a form of government might be in place in a new world; but we are assuming people already bound and brought up to certain customs. We do not create them, like Pyrrha or like Cadmus.[3]

Though we may have the power, by some means, to im-

---

[1] Poneropolis, the City of Rogues.   [2] Such as Plato's *Republic*.
[3] Pyrrha, after the deluge, repeopled the world by throwing stones; Cadmus sowed dragon's teeth, from which sprang men ready-armed.

prove and redispose them, we can hardly twist them out of their accustomed bent without breaking all. Some one asked Solon if he had drawn up the best possible laws for the Athenians. 'Yes, indeed, he replied; the best they were capable of receiving.'

Varro excused himself in like manner: 'That if he had to write of religion, if it were quite new, he would say what he thought of it; but seeing that it is already formed and accepted, he will speak of it according to custom rather than according to nature.'

Not in theory only, but in truth, the best and most excellent form of government for every nation is that under which it has maintained itself. For its form and essential suitability it is dependent on custom. It is usual for men to be discontented with their actual condition. I maintain, however, that to wish to replace a Republic by an Oligarchy, or a Monarchy by a different kind of government, is foolish and wrong :

> The government approve, be it what it will;
> If it be Royal, then love Monarchy;
> If a Republic, yet approve it still,
> For God himself thereto subjected thee. (PIBRAC.)

Good Monsieur de Pibrac,[1] whom we have recently lost, a man of so noble a mind, such sound opinions, such pleasing manners! His death, and that of Monsieur de Foix, which fell about the same time, were a grievous loss to our crown. I doubt whether there remains in France another couple to be compared to these two Gascons in honesty and ability, to supply their places in our King's Council. Theirs were beautiful souls in different ways, and truly, as the times go, rare and beautiful, each in its kind. But how did they come to be set down in this age, being so out of proportion and harmony to these our corrupt and tempestuous times?

Nothing presses so hard upon a state as innovation; mere change gives scope to injustice and tyranny. When some part becomes loosened, it may be propped; we may guard against the alteration and corruption natural to all things carrying us too far from our beginnings and prin-

[1] Guy du Faur de Pibrac, 1529–84, author of *Quatrains Moraux* and a few other poems. He defended the Protestants in Parliament, and was imprisoned in the Bastile; but afterwards wrote a political apology for the massacre of St. Bartholomew. Good M. de Pibrac!

ciples. But to undertake to put so great a mass back into the melting-pot, to renew the foundations of so great an edifice, is to efface a picture in the cleaning, to reform particular defects by a general confusion, to cure a disease by killing the patient, *to be not so much for changing as for overturning everything* (Cicero).

The world is incapable of curing itself; it is so impatient of the weight that oppresses it, that it only aims at getting rid of it without considering the cost. We may see by a thousand examples that it usually cures itself to its own prejudice. To throw off a present evil is no cure, if there be not an all-round improvement in condition.

The surgeon's ultimate aim is not to kill off the diseased flesh; that is but the first step in his cure. He looks beyond, to make the natural flesh grow again and to restore the limb to its normal state. Whoever purposes to remove only what galls him will fall short, for the good does not necessarily succeed the evil; another evil may succeed it, and a worse one, as happened to Caesar's assassins, who brought the Republic to such a pass, that they had reason to repent having meddled with it. The same thing has since happened to many, even down to our times. The French, my contemporaries, could indeed tell a tale about it.

All great changes shake up a state and throw it into confusion.

If any man should aim straight at a cure and take counsel with himself before taking action, he would be likely to cool down about setting his hand to it. Pacuvius Calavius corrected the fault of such a method by a signal example: His fellow-citizens had risen up in revolt against their magistrates. He, a person of great authority in the town of Capua, one day contrived to imprison the Senate in the palace, and, calling the people together in the market-place, he said to them that the day was now come when they were at full liberty to take their revenge on the tyrants who had so long oppressed them, and whom, isolated and disarmed, he had at his mercy. He gave them this advice, that, after being drawn by lot, these men should be let out one after another, that the case of each should be considered separately, and that the decision they came to should be executed on the spot; with this additional proviso, that they should at the same time appoint some honourable man to fill the place of the condemned, that there might be no vacancy in the office.

They had no sooner heard the name of one Senator, when there arose a general outcry of dissatisfaction against him. ' I very well see, said Pacuvius, that this man must be dismissed ; he is a wicked man ; let us have a good man in exchange.' There was a prompt silence, every man being at a loss whom to choose. When the first man, with more effrontery than the rest, nominated his candidate, there was a still louder and more unanimous chorus of rejection ; they found a hundred imperfections and just causes for refusing him. These contradictory humours growing more heated, it fared still worse with the second Senator, and the third ; as much disagreement in the election as agreement in the dismissal.

Having fruitlessly worn themselves out in this disturbance, they began gradually, one here, one there, to steal out of the meeting, each one having come to this conclusion in his mind, ' That the oldest and best known evil is after all more bearable than one that is new and untried.'

Because I see that we are pitifully agitated (for what have we not done ?)

> O we repent us of our scars and sins
>   And brothers' blood. What wickedness unplanned
> Has our hard generation left ? Within
>   What bounds restrained itself ? Whence did its hand
> Our youth in reverence for the Gods refrain ?
>   What altar spare ? (HORACE.)

I do not immediately jump to the conclusion that

> The very genius of Success
> Could not this household save. (TERENCE.)

Yet we are not perhaps at our last term. The preservation of States is a thing that in all likelihood surpasses our understanding. A civil government is, as Plato says, a mighty thing, and hard to dissolve. It often holds out against fatal and internal diseases, against the mischief of unjust laws, against tyranny, against the encroachments and ignorance of the authorities and the licence and sedition of the people.

In all our fortunes we compare ourselves with what is above us, and look towards those who are better off ; let us measure ourselves with what is below. There is no one so ill-starred but he will find a thousand examples to comfort him.

It is a human weakness that we are not so pleased to see a man going ahead of us as we are pleased to see one lagging behind us.

Solon said that 'if we were to heap together all the ills, there is no man who would not rather take back with him his own ills than agree to a lawful division with all other men, and take his share.'

Our government is in a bad way; yet others have been in a more advanced stage of sickness without dying.

The gods play at ball with us, and knock us about in all directions:

> Truly the Gods play with us as with balls. (PLAUTUS.)

The stars fatally destined the Roman State for an exemplar of what they could do in this way. In it are comprised all the forms and vicissitudes that affect a state; all that order can do, and disorder, and good and evil fortune. What state need despair of its condition, seeing the shocks and commotions by which Rome was disturbed? And yet she withstood them. If extent of dominion be the health of a state (of which I am by no means persuaded; and Isocrates pleases me when he instructs Nicocles not to envy princes who have wide dominions, but rather those who are well able to keep those they have inherited), the State of Rome was never so well as when it was least well. She was happiest when she was at her worst.

Under the first Emperors we can hardly distinguish the face of any kind of government; it was the darkest and most dreadful confusion conceivable. And yet she endured it, and continued in it, preserving, not a monarchy confined within its boundaries, but all those many nations, so diverse, so remote, so ill-affected, so loosely governed and unjustly conquered:

> For to no nation Fortune gives the task
> To vent her hate against the Roman people,
> Masters of land and sea. (LUCAN.)

Not everything that totters, falls. The frame of so great a body is held together by more than one nail. It is held together even by its antiquity; like an old building whose foundations are worn away by age, without cement and mortar, which yet lives and is supported by its own weight ;

> Or, like a mighty trunk, with no firm roots,
> Safe in its own bulk. (LUCAN.)

Moreover it is not a good plan to reconnoitre only the flank and the moat ; to judge of the security of a fortress, we must know from which side an approach can be made, and the condition of the attacking party.

Few ships sink of their own weight, without outside violence.

Now let us turn our eyes in all directions ; all is crumbling around us. In all the great States that are known to us, whether of Christendom or elsewhere, use your eyes and you will discover evident menace of change and ruin :

> For they too have their ills ; the storm hath swept o'er all.
> (Adapted from VIRGIL.)

The astrologers have an easy game when they warn us, as they do, of great and imminent changes and revolutions ; their prophecies are present and palpable ; no need to go to the stars for that.

There is not only consolation to be derived from this universal aggregation of evils and menaces, but even some hope for the duration of our State ; since naturally where all falls, nothing falls. Universal sickness is individual health ; conformity is antagonistic to dissolution. For my part, I am not going to despair about us, and I think I see ways of saving ourselves :

> Perhaps a God, by happy change,
> May yet our bliss restore. (HORACE.)

Who knows but that God intends it to be as with bodies, that are purified and restored to a better state of health by long and grievous maladies, which will bring them to a cleaner and more perfect health than that they took from them ?

What troubles me most is that, in counting up the symptoms of our malady, I see as many that are due to natural causes, and sent by Heaven itself, as of those attributable to our disorders and our human unwisdom.

It would seem as if the very stars have ordained that we

have endured long enough beyond the ordinary term. And this too troubles me, that the evil which most nearly threatens us is not an alteration in the entire and solid mass, but its dissipation and disintegration; the extremest of our fears.[1]

In these rhapsodies too I fear the treachery of my memory, lest by inadvertence it has made me record a thing twice over. I hate seeing my own reflection, and never, unless compelled, read again what has once escaped me. Now I bring here no new discoveries. They are common ideas, and, having perhaps conceived them a hundred times, I fear I have already set them down. Repetition is tiresome everywhere, even in Homer; but it is disastrous in things that have only a superficial and transitory appearance. I dislike the habit of rubbing things in, even wholesome things, as Seneca does; and I dislike that habit of his Stoical school of reiterating on every matter, and in all their length and breadth, the principles and postulates of general bearing, and of restating over and over again their common and universal reasons and arguments.

My memory grows cruelly worse every day:

> As though with thirsty throat I'd quaffed
> The cups which bring Lethean sleep. (HORACE.)

Instead of seeking time and opportunity, as others do, to think over what I have to say, I must henceforward (for hitherto, thank God, nothing much amiss has happened) avoid all preparation, for fear of binding myself to something I have to depend on. To be tied and bound puts me quite out, as well as to depend on so weak a tool as my memory.

I never read the following story without indignation, and a natural feeling of personal resentment: Lyncestes, accused of conspiracy against Alexander, on the day when he was brought before the army, according to custom, to be heard in his own defence, had in his mind a studied speech of which, stammering and hesitating, he uttered a few words. As he became more and more confused and was struggling with his memory and trying to jog it, the soldiers

---

[1] The note of pessimism in this last paragraph, which is a manuscript addition, appears out of harmony with the more optimistic view expressed a few lines above.

nearest to him charged him and killed him with their pikes, concluding that he had convicted himself. His confusion and silence was to them a sign of confession. Having had so much leisure to prepare himself in prison, it was not in their opinion his memory that failed him ; it was conscience that tied his tongue and robbed him of its power.

That is all very fine, indeed ! The place, the audience, their expectation, have a paralysing effect, even when it is only a question of ambition to make a good speech. What can a man do when life or death depends on the speech ?

For my part, the very fact of being tied to what I have to say is enough to put me off it. When I wholly trust and commit myself to my memory, I lean so heavily upon her that I bear her down ; she is dismayed at the weight. As long as I rely upon her, I lose my head and am put out of countenance ; and on some days I have been at pains to conceal my slavish dependence upon her, whereas my object in speaking was to appear perfectly cool and collected, using casual and unpremeditated gestures suggested by the occasion. I would as soon make an insignificant speech as make it evident that I have primed myself with a good one : a thing unbecoming especially in a man of my profession,[1] and which arouses too many expectations for a man who cannot satisfy them. Preparation raises more hopes than it can fulfil. A man often foolishly strips himself of his doublet, to leap no further than he would have done in his cassock.

There is nothing so unfavourable to those who wish to please as to raise expectation (Cicero). It is recorded of the orator Curio that when he declared his intention of dividing his speech into three or four parts, or announced the number of his arguments and reasons, it often happened that he forgot one or two, or added one or two more. I have always carefully guarded against falling into that awkward situation, being loath to promise or tie myself in that way ; not only because I distrust my memory, but because that method savours too much of the artificial. *A simple style becomes a soldier* (Quintilian). Enough that I have henceforward decided with myself not again to undertake to speak on ceremonious occasions. For, as to reading one's speech, besides that it is unnatural, it is very disadvantageous

[1] As a knight Montaigne was a soldier, though he was not properly speaking of the military profession.

to those who are naturally able to give effect to it by action and gesture. And I am still less able to cast myself at the mercy of my improvisation; my mind works slowly and confusedly, and is not equal to sudden and momentous emergencies.

Reader, permit this test-piece also to pass muster, and this third addition to the other parts of my portrait.[1] I add, but I do not correct. Firstly, because it appears reasonable that one who has handed his work over to the world has no further claim on it. Let him state his views better elsewhere, if he can, and not adulterate the work he has sold. If he does so, nothing of his should be bought until after his death. Let him thoroughly think out his subject before publishing. Why such haste?

My book is always one. Except that at every new edition (that the buyer may not go away quite empty-handed) I take the liberty to add an occasional ornament over and above, since it is only a piece of badly-joined marquetry. They are but over-weights, which do not contradict the first form but, by a little ambitious subtlety, impart some particular value to each of those that follow. Whence, however, some transposition of chronology may easily slip in. My stories take their place according to their opportuneness, not always according to their age.

Secondly, because, as concerns myself, I fear to lose by the change; my understanding does not always advance, it also goes backwards. I do not distrust my thoughts less because they are the second or third, than because they are the first, or my present less than my past thoughts. Besides, we often correct ourselves as foolishly as we correct others.

My first Essays were published in the year 1580. I have since grown older by a long stretch, but I have certainly not grown an inch wiser.[2] Myself now, and myself a little while ago, are indeed two. But whether I am better I really cannot say. It would be a fine thing to be old if we only progressed towards betterment. It is a drunkard's walk,

[1] i.e. the third book, first published in 1588. When Montaigne says that he does not correct, he is not strictly accurate; but most of his corrections were made after 1588.
[2] In the 1588 edition we read 'but I doubt whether I have grown an inch wiser'. Montaigne becomes more modest as he grows older.

reeling, giddy, uncertain ; or the motion of reeds stirred by the wind at its pleasure.

Antiochus had written strongly in favour of the Academy ; in his old age he adopted a different view. Whichever opinion I followed, should I not still be following Antiochus? To attempt to establish the certainty of human opinions after doubting it, was not that to create doubt and not certainty, and to give promise that, had he been given another life to live, he would always have been likely to change his mind, not so much for the better as for something different ?

My favourable reception by the public made me a little bolder than I expected. But what I fear most is to surfeit my readers ; I would rather provoke than weary them, as a learned man of my time has done.

Praise is always agreeable, let it come from whom, or on what account it will ; and yet, if our satisfaction is to be justified, we must find out why we are praised. Even imperfections have a way of recommending themselves. Vulgar and popular favour is seldom seen to be happy in its choice ; and in my time I am much mistaken if it is not the worst writings that have been borne highest by the breath of popular applause.

Truly I render thanks to those good-natured people who are pleased to approve of my feeble efforts.

Nowhere are the faults of style so apparent as in a matter which in itself has nothing to recommend it.

Do not blame me, reader, for the errors that slip in here through the caprice or inadvertence of others ; every hand, every workman [1] contributes his own. I do not meddle either with orthography, only suggesting that the old spelling be followed, or with punctuation ; I am little expert in either.

When they wholly break the sense, I am little concerned, for at least they relieve me of responsibility ; but when they substitute a false one, as they so often do, and twist my

[1] Presumably every compositor. The earlier editions of the Essays were, it seems, very carelessly printed, and full of errors. Montaigne did not approve of the spelling ' reform ' of the etymologists, who overloaded words with unnecessary letters found in the (often supposed) Latin originals. He himself adopts a simple spelling, but most of his editors did not fall in with his views, so that, for example, when Montaigne writes *avec* we almost invariably find *avecques* in the printed editions.

meaning to their own conception, they ruin me. However, when the thought is not vigorous and proportioned to my capacity, a sensible man must decline to take it as mine. Any one who knows how little laborious I am, how framed after my own fashion, will easily believe that I would rather reindite as many more essays than subject myself to the toil of reading these through again, for so puerile a correction.

I was recently saying then, that, being planted in the deepest mine of this new metal,[1] not only am I deprived of any great familiarity with men of opinions and ways differing from my own, in which they are bound together by a tie that flees every other tie;[2] but I am besides not free from danger among men to whom everything is equally permissible, and most of whom cannot henceforth make their case worse in the eyes of our justice; so that licence is now carried to its extreme. Summing up all the particular circumstances concerning myself, I know no man of my country who pays more dearly for the defence of the laws, both in *cessant gain* and *emergent loss*, as the lawyers say, than I do. And many there are who boast of their zeal and fortitude who, if weighed in a correct balance, do much less than I.

As a house that has always been free, very accessible, and at the service of all (for I could never be induced to make it an implement of war, in which I would rather be engaged when it is as far as possible from my neighbourhood), mine has sufficiently deserved the affection of the people round about; and it would be a very difficult matter to defy me on my own dunghill. And I regard it as a wonderful and exemplary masterpiece that it still continues a virgin from blood and pillage under so prolonged a storm, with so many changes and disturbances round about me. For, to tell the truth, it was possible for a man of my nature to escape one constant and continued form of danger, whatever it might be; but the invasions and incursions, first by one side and then by the other, and the alternations and vicissitudes of Fortune, around me, have hitherto more exasperated than mollified the temper of the country, involving me over and over again in insuperable dangers and difficulties.

I escape; but it is unpleasant to think that this is due to

---

[1] The unknown new metal that should characterize this wicked age; see p. 420.   [2] The tie of religion.

chance, nay also to my own prudence, rather than to justice; and it makes me sad to think that I am outside the protection of the laws, and under any other safeguard than theirs. As matters stand, I more than half live by the grace of others; which is a hard obligation. I am loath to owe my safety either to the goodwill and kindness of the great, who approve of my respect for the laws and my independence, or to the easy-going manners of my predecessors and my own.

For, supposing I were different? If my conduct and my open dealings lay my neighbours or my kinsmen [1] under obligation, it is cruel that they should be able to pay off their debt by allowing me to live, and to say: 'We freely pardon him for continuing his divine service in the chapel of his house, after all the churches round about have been ruined and laid waste by us; and we grant him his life and the use of his property, since he shelters our wives and our cattle in times of need.'

For a long while past my house has shared the praise given to Lycurgus the Athenian, who was depositary-general and guardian of his fellow-citizens' purses.

Now I maintain that we should live by right and authority, not as a reward and a favour. How many gallant men have preferred losing their lives to being indebted for them! I would rather not subject myself to any kind of obligation, but especially one that binds me by a duty of honour. Nothing appears to me so dearly bought as what is given me, and that for which my will is pledged under the name of gratitude; and I am more willing to accept such services as are for sale. I think I am right; for the latter I give only money, for the others I give myself.

The tie that holds me by the law of honesty appears to me more insistent and binding than that of legal constraint; a bond drawn up by a notary binds me more loosely than I do myself. Is it not right that my conscience should be much more strongly pledged when it has been trusted in all simplicity? In other cases my fidelity owes nothing, for nothing has been lent to it; let them use the assurance and security they have taken by outside means. I should much sooner break the prison of a wall or of the laws than that of my word.

---

[1] Some of Montaigne's relations, including his mother and one of his brothers, were of the Protestant faith.

I am scrupulous, even to superstition, in keeping my promises, and in all matters I prefer to make them vague and conditional. To those of no great weight I give weight by adhering jealously to my rule, which plagues and burdens me with its own interest. Nay, even in actions in which I alone am concerned and in which I have a free hand, if I once say a thing I feel as if I were bound by it, and that to make it known to another is to command myself to do it. When I say a thing I feel as if I had promised it. Therefore I seldom divulge my plans.

The sentence I pass upon myself is stronger and stiffer than that of any judge, who only considers my case from the point of view of an ordinary obligation; that which my conscience imposes upon me is more strict and severe. I lag behind in those duties to which I should be dragged if I did not go to them. *The most just action is only just in so far as it is voluntary* (Cicero). If the action have not some glamour of freedom it has neither grace nor honour.

Where law commands, my will is in abeyance. (TERENCE.)

When necessity draws me I am content to let the will go. *For what is imposed by a higher power is imputed to him who commands rather than to him who obeys* (Cicero). I know some who follow this rule even to injustice, who will sooner give than restore, sooner lend than pay; who are more niggardly in doing good to one to whom they are beholden. I do not go so far as that, but I come very near it.

I am so disposed to throw off debts and obligations, that I have sometimes counted as profit the ingratitude, the affronts and indignities put upon me by men to whom, by nature or accident, I owed some friendly duty; seizing upon this occasion of their offence as an acquittance and discharge of my debt. Although I continue to pay them the outward civilities reasonably enjoined by society, I find it a great saving to do in the name of justice what I once did through affection, and to relieve myself a little of the tension and solicitude of my inward will—*It is the part of a wise man to restrain, as he would a chariot, the first impulse to friendship* (Cicero)—which in me is a little too urgent and pressing when I take to a person, at least for a man who has no wish to force his friendship. And this husbanding of my feelings consoles me a little for the imperfections of those in whom I am interested. I am very sorry that they are less worthy, but the fact remains that I am spared some of my attentions and obligations towards them.

I do not blame the man who loves his son less for being scurfy and hunchbacked, and not only when he is ill-tempered, but also when he is ill-favoured and ill-born (God himself abated that much from his natural value and estimation); provided that in his coolness towards him he bears himself with moderation and strict justice. With me nearness of blood does not lessen imperfections, but rather aggravates them.

After all, as far as I understand the science of benefits and gratitude, which is a complicated and very useful science, I know of no man who is freer and less indebted than I have been hitherto. What I owe I owe by ordinary and natural obligations. In other respects no one is more absolutely clear:

> The gifts of Princes are to me unknown. (VIRGIL.)

Princes are liberal to me when they take nothing from me, and do me sufficient good when they do me no ill; that is all I ask of them. Oh, how much I am beholden to God that he was pleased that I should receive all I possess immediately by his grace, and that he specially reserved to himself my whole debt of gratitude! How earnestly I beg of his holy mercy that I may never owe thanks to any man for the essentials of life! Blessed liberty which has carried me so far! May it continue to the end!

I endeavour to have no express need of any one:

> All my hope is in myself. (TERENCE.)

It is a thing that any man may do for himself, but more easily one whom God has sheltered from natural and urgent necessities. It is a very pitiful and hazardous lot to be dependent on another. We ourselves, on whom we can most justly and surely rely, have not made ourselves sufficiently sure. I have nothing of mine except myself, and yet the possession is in part defective and borrowed. I fortify myself, both in courage, on which is the strongest reliance, and also in fortune, in order to have enough to satisfy me, though all else should forsake me.

Hippias of Elis furnished himself not only with learning,

that he might in the lap of the Muses dispense gaily, at need, with all other company; not only with the knowledge of philosophy, to teach his soul to find contentment in herself and manfully to do without outward comforts, when Fate would have it so. He was so careful besides as to learn how to cook, to shave himself and cut his own hair, to make his own clothes and shoes, and his rings, to be as self-dependent as he could, and dispense with all outside help.

We enjoy borrowed goods much more freely and more heartily when the enjoyment is not forced and constrained by want, and when we have, in our will and fortune, the power and means to live without them.

I know myself well; but I find it difficult to imagine any so pure liberality, any so free and genuine hospitality in any person, but that I would think it disastrous, tyrannical and tainted with reproach, if I were entangled in it by necessity.

As giving denotes ambition and a wish to rise to pre-eminence, so taking is a mark of submission: witness the insulting and aggressive manner in which Bajazet refused the presents that Timour sent him. And those that were offered in the name of the Emperor Solyman to the Emperor of Calicut so angered him, that he not only rudely declined them, saying that neither he nor his predecessors were accustomed to take, and that it was their part to give; but he even had the ambassadors sent for that purpose cast into a dungeon.

When Thetis, says Aristotle, flatters Jupiter; when the Lacedemonians flatter the Athenians, they do not refresh their memory with the good they have done them, which is always a hateful thing to be reminded of, but recall the benefits they have received from them. Those whom I see so freely making use of all and every man, and laying themselves under obligation to them, would not do so [if they relished, as I do, the sweetness of a pure liberty, and] if they considered, as much as a wise man should do, the weight of an obligation; it is perhaps sometimes repaid, but it is never dissolved. A cruel bondage for one who loves free elbow-room on all sides.

My acquaintances, both above and below me in station, are able to say whether they have known a man [less importuning, soliciting, entreating and] who is less of a burden to others. If I surpass all present-day examples in this respect, it is no great wonder, seeing how many characteristics I have that contribute thereto: a little natural pride, inability to bear a refusal, moderate desires and projects, incapacity for all kinds of business, and my most favoured qualities, idleness and freedom. From all these together I have contracted a deadly hatred of being bound to another or by another than myself. Before enjoying another's favours I should leave no stone unturned to do without them, however slight or important the occasion.

It is to me an intolerable nuisance to be asked by a friend to ask of a third person. And I think it hardly less costly to acquit one who is indebted to me, by making use of him, than to become indebted for a friend to one who owes me nothing. With that exception, and provided also that they do not desire anything of me that requires negotiation and anxiety, for I have declared war to the death against all anxiety, I am accommodating and ready to help any one in need.[1]

I have oftener avoided receiving than sought occasions for giving; and that is much easier, according to Aristotle. My fortune has seldom allowed me to benefit others, and what I have given has met with little thanks. If I had been born to take a high rank among men, I should have been ambitious to be loved, not to be feared or admired. Shall I put it more arrogantly? I should have thought as much of the pleasure I gave as of the good I was doing.

Cyrus, very wisely, and by the mouth of a very good general and a still better philosopher,[2] places his bounty and good deeds far above his valour and his conquests in war. And the first Scipio, whenever he tries to set himself in a favourable light, lays more stress on his mild and humane qualities than on his prowess and victories; and ever has this boast on his lips: 'That he has given his enemies as much cause to love him, as his friends.'

I mean to say then, if we must owe something in this way, it ought to be by a more lawful title than that of which I speak, to which the necessity of this wretched war pledges

---

[1] The edition of 1588 also contained this passage, which was afterwards deleted: 'I have very gladly sought occasions for doing good and attaching others to myself; and it seems to me that we cannot make any better use of our money.'

[2] Xenophon.

me; and not of so big a debt as that of my total preservation; that is too crushing.

I have a thousand times gone to bed in my own house, with an apprehension that I should be betrayed and struck dead that same night, compounding with Fortune that it might not be a terrible and lingering death. And after my Paternoster I would exclaim:

> Shall these my fields, so fairly dressed,
> By godless soldiers be possessed? (VIRGIL.)

Where is the remedy? It is my birthplace, and that of most of my ancestors; on it they fixed their affection and their name.[1] We become inured to everything we are accustomed to. And, in a wretched state such as ours, habit has become a very kind gift of Nature, which benumbs our senses to the suffering of many ills. A civil war is worse than other wars in this, that it makes each of us turn his house into a watch-tower:

> How sad with gate and wall our life to guard,
> And scarce be safe! (OVID.)

It is an extreme hardship to be threatened in one's very household and domestic peace. The district in which I live is always the first and last battle-ground in our disturbed times, where peace never shows her full face:

> Even when peace is here, we quake in fear of war. (OVID.)

> So often as Fortune breaks the peace, 'tis here
> War stalks apace. O better had it been
> To dwell beneath the scorching Eastern vault,
> Or wander homeless in the frozen North! (LUCAN.)

At times I seek the means of combating these thoughts in indifference and carelessness. They also lead some way to fortitude. With a kind of pleasure I often imagine myself in danger of death and awaiting it; in a dull stupor I plunge headlong into it, without considering or recognizing it, as into a dark and silent abyss that swallows me up at one leap, and in an instant wraps me in a profound slumber, without pain or feeling of any kind.

And in this kind of sudden and violent death I am more comforted by the reflexion of what follows after it, than alarmed by the fear of dying.

---

[1] Not quite correct; his family took their name of Montaigne from the place, and not vice versa.

They say that as life is no better for being long, death is the better for not being long. I am not so averse to the idea of being dead but that I meet death itself with confidence. I wrap myself up snugly in this catastrophe which must blind and carry me away with the fury of an attack so sudden that I shall not feel it.

If it were only true, as some gardeners say, that roses and violets spring up more fragrant in the proximity of garlic and onions, since these suck and imbibe the bad odours of the soil; and that those depraved natures also absorb all the venom of my air and climate, and make me so much better and purer by their proximity that I should not be wholly a loser! That is not so; but there may be something in this, that goodness is more beautiful and attractive when it is rare; and that contrariety and diversity stiffen and compress well-doing within itself, and kindle it by the jealousy of opposition and the desire for approbation.

Thieves, when left alone, have no particular spite against me. Have I any more spite against them? I should have to hate too many people. The like consciences abide under different kinds of fortune, the like cruelties, disloyalties, robberies. And they are all the worse for being more meanly and securely hidden under the shadow of the laws. I hate a wrong done openly less than one done treacherously; under the cloak of war than in peace. Our fever [1] has attacked a body that is not much the worse for it. The fire was there, it has burst into flames; the noise is greater, not so much the evil.

To those who ask me why I travel I usually reply, ' I know well what I am fleeing from, but not what I am in search of.' If they tell me that there may be just as little health among foreigners, and that their ways are no better than ours, I reply firstly, that that is hardly likely:

> Wickedness assumes a thousand forms
> Where wars are raging. (VIRGIL.)

Secondly, that there is always gain in changing an evil for an uncertain state; and that others' misfortunes should not affect us as painfully as our own.

I will not forget to mention this, that I am never so

---

[1] The Civil Wars.

exasperated against France that I cease to have a kindly feeling for Paris; she has had my heart since my boyhood. And, as in the case of all excellent things, the more I have since seen of other fine cities, the more does the beauty of this one impress me and gain on my affection. I love her for herself, and more in her own being than overladen with foreign pomp. I love her tenderly, even her warts and blemishes. I am a Frenchman only through this great city, great in its people, great in the happiness of its site; but above all great and incomparable in variety and diversity of amenities, the glory of France and one of the noblest ornaments of the world. May God keep our discords far from her![1] Entire and united, I think she will be safe against all other violence. I warn her that of all parties the worst will be that which sets her at variance. For her I only fear herself; and truly I fear for her as much as for any other part of this State. As long as she endures, I shall not want a retreat wherein to give up the ghost, sufficient to compensate me for the loss of any other retreat.

Not because Socrates has said it, but because it is really in my nature, and perhaps a little more than it should be, I look upon all men as my fellow-citizens, and would embrace a Pole as I would a Frenchman, subordinating this national tie to the common and universal one. I am not enamoured of the charms of my home atmosphere. Quite new and quite personal friendships appear to me fully as good as those other chance acquaintances with one's neighbours, that are shared by all. Friendships that are purely of our own acquiring usually carry the day against those which join us by the common tie of blood and climate.

Nature has given us to the world free and unfettered; we imprison ourselves in certain narrow districts, like the Kings of Persia, who bound themselves to drink no other water but that of the river Choaspes, foolishly renouncing their right to the use of any other stream, and turning the rest of the world, as far as they were concerned, into a waterless desert.

As to what Socrates did towards his end, in regarding a sentence of banishment against him as worse than a death sentence, I shall never, I think, be so broken up or so

[1] Montaigne's prayer was not fulfilled; after 1588 the discord was more violent in Paris than anywhere else.

closely wedded to my country as to agree with him. The lives of such divine men offer sufficient models which I can embrace by esteem rather than affection. And some are so sublime and wonderful that they are even above my esteem, since they are above my conception.

That was a very tender feeling in a man who looked upon the world as his city. It is true that he disdained travel, and had hardly even set foot outside Attic territory.

What are we to think of his grudging his friends' money to buy off his life, and his refusing to leave his prison with the help of others, that he might not disobey the laws, and that at a time when they were so corrupt ? These examples are of the first kind for me ; of the second there are others that I could discover in this same person. Many of these rare examples exceed my power of action, but some even exceed my power of imagination.

Besides the reasons I have given, travel appears to me a profitable exercise ; the mind is continually exercised by observing new and unknown things. And I know no better school, as I have often said, for modelling one's life, in that it continually brings us face to face with so many other lives, ideas, and customs, and gives us a relish for human nature in so perpetual a variety of forms. The body is therein neither idle nor fatigued ; and that gentle excitement keeps it in breath.

In spite of my colic I can keep in the saddle, without dismounting and without weariness, for eight or even ten hours,

> Beyond the strength and ordinary lot of eld. (VIRGIL.)

No season is hostile to me except the fierce heat of a burning sun. For umbrellas, which have been in use in Italy since the time of the old Romans, weary the arm more than they relieve the head.[1]

I should like to know by what contrivance the Persians, so long ago and when they first fell into luxurious ways, obtained fresh air and shade at their pleasure, as Xenophon tells us.

I love rain and mud as much as the ducks do. Change of air and climate does not affect me ; every sky is the same to me. I am only vanquished by the changes in my

---

[1] It seems that they weighed about five pounds. Umbrellas did not come into use in France until the end of the seventeenth century.

internal arrangements ; and these are not so frequent when I travel.

I am not easy to move, but once on the way, I go as far as you please. I shy as much at a little as at a great undertaking, and at preparing for a day's excursion or to visit a neighbour, as for a real journey. I have learned to arrange my day's journey after the Spanish fashion, making one stage of it : long and reasonable journeys ; and in excessive heat I make them by night, from sunset to sunrise. The other method of stopping to bait and dining on the way, in hurry and confusion, is inconvenient, especially when the days are short.

My horses are the better for it. Never did any horse fail me that was able to hold out the first day's journey with me. I water them everywhere, and only see to it that they have time enough after their last watering to work it off.

My laziness in rising gives my attendants time to dine in comfort before starting. For my own part it is never too late for me to eat ; my appetite comes with eating, and not otherwise. I am never hungry but at table.

Some people blame me for continuing to take a pleasure in this exercise, now I am married and well on in years. They are wrong. The best time to leave your family is when you have put them in the way of carrying on without you ; when you have left the home in such good order as to correspond with its former government. It is much more unwise to depart and leave your house to a less faithful guardian, who is less careful to provide you with the needful.

The most useful art, and the most honourable occupation for a woman, is the art of housekeeping. I know some who are miserly, but very few good managers. It is her mistress quality, which one should seek before any other, as the only dower that helps to ruin or save our houses.

Don't tell me ! Experience has taught me to value in a married woman, above every other virtue, the housekeeping virtue.

I give my wife an opportunity of bearing me out by leaving her, during my absence, in full control of my affairs. It vexes me to see, in many households, Monsieur coming home about noon, fretful and worried by business troubles, to find Madame still doing her hair and titivating herself in her dressing-room. That is all very well for a Queen ; and yet I am not so sure. It is absurd and unfair that our wives should be kept in idleness by our sweat and toil.

No person, if I can help it, shall enjoy my goods more easily, more tranquilly, and more free of obligation, than I. If the husband provides the matter, Nature herself ordains that the wife shall provide the form.

As to the duties of marital love being prejudiced by my absence, as some people think, I do not agree with them. On the contrary, it is a relationship that a too continual presence is easily liable to cool, and that is impaired by too assiduous attentions. Every strange woman appears to us agreeable to associate with. And we all find by experience that being continually together cannot equal the pleasure of parting and meeting again at intervals. These interruptions fill me with a fresh love for my family, and make the resumption of my home-life more pleasurable. The alternation warms my appetite for the departure, and then for the return.

I know that the arms of friendship are long enough to reach and join from one end of the world to the other, and especially this kind, in which there is a continual interchange of services, which reawaken its obligations and memory. The Stoics say truly that there is so close a bond and relation between the sages, that one who dines in France nourishes his friend in Egypt ; and that if one of them merely holds out a finger, wherever he may be, all the sages in the habitable globe will feel its help.

Enjoyment and possession are chiefly a matter of imagination. It embraces more warmly what it is in quest of than what we hold, and more continually. Cast up your daily musings and you will find that you are most absent from your friend when he is in your company ; his presence releases your attention and gives your thoughts freedom to absent themselves at any time and for any occasion.

From distant Rome I hold and control my house and the goods I have left there ; I see my walls, my trees, and my rents growing, and diminishing as well, within an inch or two, as when I am there :

> Before mine eyes the vision of my home
> Hovers, and all the once familiar spots. (OVID.)

If we enjoy nothing but what we touch, farewell our

crowns when they are in our coffers, and our boys when they are gone a-hunting. We would have them nearer. In the garden, is that far? Half a day's journey away? What about ten leagues, is that far or near? If it is near, how about eleven, twelve, thirteen? and so on, step by step. Truly if there be a woman who prescribes to her husband the howmanieth step that ends the near, and the howmanieth step that begins the far, I advise her to fix it between the two:

> Name some fixed term, all cavil to arrest...
> Myself of the concession I avail;
> As from a horse's tail we pluck out hairs,
> I take off one league, then another league,
> Till you are vanquished by the very force
> Of my sorites. (HORACE.)

And let them boldly call Philosophy to their aid, in whose teeth it might be cast that, since she sees neither one end nor the other of the joint between the too much and the little, the long and the short, the light and the heavy, the near and the far; since she recognizes neither the beginning nor the end of it, she is a very uncertain judge of the middle. *Nature has given us no knowledge of the limits of things* (Cicero).

Are those not still wives and mistresses of the deceased, who are not at the end of this, but in the other world? We embrace both those who have been, and those who are not yet, not only the absent. We did not bargain, when we married, to be continually joined together by the tail, like some little insects or other that we see, or like the bewitched people of Karenty,[1] in canine fashion. And a wife should not have her eyes so greedily fixed on her husband's front that she cannot endure to see him turn his back upon her, if need be.

But may not these words, by so excellent a painter of their humours, be aptly quoted here, to show the cause of their complaints?

> Your wife, if you should stay out late,
> At once thinks you are toying with a girl,
> Or she with you; that at the public-house
> Or elsewhere you enjoy yourself; in short
> That you have all the fun, and she has all the cares.
> (TERENCE.)

---

[1] A reference to a passage in the *History of Denmark* of Saxo Grammaticus.

Or may it not be that opposition and contradiction are in themselves meat and drink to them; and that they are comfortable enough if they can make you uncomfortable?

In true friendship, of which I am a good judge, I give myself to my friend more than I draw him to me. Not only would I rather benefit him than that he should benefit me, but also that he should benefit himself rather than me; he benefits me most when he benefits himself. And if absence be either agreeable or profitable to him, it is much more acceptable to me than his presence. And you cannot rightly call it absence when you have the means of communicating with one another.

I used to find our separation profitable and agreeable. We possessed our lives more fully and more extensively by keeping apart; he lived, he enjoyed, he saw for me, and I for him, as fully as if he had been present. One part of us remained idle when we were together; we were blended into one another. The distance of place made the conjunction of our wills richer. That insatiable hunger for the bodily presence rather betrays weakness in the enjoyment of souls.

With regard to my old age which they urge against me, it is, on the contrary, for the young to subject themselves to public opinion, and constrain themselves for others. They are able to satisfy the demands of both the public and themselves. We have only too much to do to satisfy ourselves. As our natural resources fail us let us maintain ourselves by artificial means. It is unfair to excuse youth for pursuing its pleasures and forbid old age to seek them. When I was young, I concealed my gay passions by caution; now that I am old I dispel my joyless ones by distractions. Besides, the Platonic laws prohibit travelling before the age of forty or fifty, in order that travel may be more profitable and instructive. I should more readily [1] agree to that other second article of the same laws, which forbids it after sixty.

'But at such an age you may never return from so long a journey.' What do I care? When I start upon it I think neither of the return, nor of the goal. I only undertake it to keep myself on the move, as long as I like movement.

---

[1] Coste suggests that Montaigne meant to write *plus mal volontiers*, 'less readily', instead of *plus volontiers*, in consideration of the following sentence.

I only ride for the sake of riding. Those who run after a benefice or a hare do not run; they only run who run in prisoner's base, or to practice running.

My design is divisible throughout: it is not grounded on any great hopes; each day's journey forms the end of them. And my life's journey is carried on after the same manner. And yet I have been in many distant places where I could have wished that I had been induced to remain. Why not, if Chrysippus, Cleanthes, Diogenes, Zeno, Antipater, so many wise men of the most surly school,[1] left their country, without any reason for being dissatisfied with it, and only for the enjoyment of a different atmosphere? Indeed what displeases me most in my peregrinations is that I cannot bring myself to decide on settling in a place that takes my fancy; and that I must always make up my mind to return, to fall in with conventional ideas.

If I were afraid to die in any other place but that of my birth, if I thought I should die less comfortably away from my family, I should hardly go out of France; I should not go outside my parish without terror. I can feel death continually clutching me by the throat or the reins. But I am differently made; death is the same to me everywhere. Yet if I had the choice I think I would rather die in the saddle than in a bed, away from my home, and far from my people.

There is more heart-break than comfort in taking leave of our friends; I willingly neglect that social duty. For of friendly offices that is the only unpleasant one, and I could as willingly dispense with that great and eternal farewell. If there is any advantage in being surrounded by your friends, there are a hundred disadvantages. I have seen some die very piteously, besieged by all those dependants; the crowd stifles them. They think it contrary to duty and a testimony of little affection and little care, to allow you to die in peace; one torments your eyes, another your ears, another your tongue; there is not a sense or a limb that they do not shatter. Your heart is wrung with pity to hear your friends' lamentations, and perhaps with vexation to hear the feigned and counterfeit laments of others.

---

[1] The Stoic school. These philosophers all came from distant parts and settled in Athens.

When a man has always had delicate sensibilities, they are still more so now that he is in this weak state. In this great extremity it needs a gentle hand, in accordance with his feelings, to scratch him just where he itches; otherwise touch him not at all. If we need a wise woman[1] to bring us into the world, we have great need of a still wiser man to help us out of it. The services of such a man, and a friend to boot, are worth buying at any cost on such an occasion.

I have not reached that pitch of disdainful vigour that finds fortitude in itself, that nothing can either assist or disturb; I am a peg lower. I shall try to steal away and hide from this manner of passing out, not through fear, but by artifice. I have no intention, in this act of dying, to give a proof or make a show of fortitude. For whom should I do so? At that moment all my right and interest in making a reputation will cease. I shall be satisfied with a calm, collected, and solitary death, all to myself, in harmony with my retired and private life.

Quite contrary to the superstition of the Romans, who esteemed a man ill-fated who died without speaking and had not his nearest relations at his side to close his eyes, I shall have enough to do to comfort myself without having to console others, enough thoughts in my brain without need of others suggested by the circumstances, enough matter to reflect upon without borrowing.

To die is not to play a part in society; it is the act of a single person. Let us live and laugh among our friends; let us die and sulk among strangers. For money payment you will find some one to turn your head and rub your feet, who will not press you more than you wish, who will turn indifferent eyes upon you, and leave you to your own reflections and allow you to groan as much as you please.

Every day I try to conquer by reason that puerile and unfeeling disposition that makes us wish to stir the compassion and sympathy of our friends for our misfortunes. We exaggerate our ills beyond measure, to draw their tears. And the fortitude to support their adverse fortune which we commend in all others, we blame and condemn in our friends, when the misfortune is our own. We are not content that they should be sensible of our woes, unless

[1] *Une sage-femme*, the French term for a midwife.

they are also grieved by them. We should spread joy, but, as far as we can, repress sorrow.

He who excites pity without cause deserves not to be pitied when there is cause. To be ever complaining is the way to be never pitied; to put on piteous airs so often is to be pitiable to none. He that makes himself out to be dead when he is alive is in danger of being thought alive when he is dying. I have known some who would take it in dudgeon to be told that they had a ruddy complexion and a steady pulse; restraining their mirth because it betrayed their recovery, and hating health because it did not arouse pity. And, what is much more strange, they were not women!

I describe my ailments at the most as they are, and avoid words of evil omen and made-up exclamations. If not gaiety, at least a serene countenance is appropriate in those attending on the sick sage; he does not pick a quarrel with health because he is in the opposite condition; he likes to contemplate it sound and robust in others, and to enjoy at least its company. Though he finds himself sinking, he does not entirely put away all thoughts of life, nor avoid ordinary conversation.

I am prepared to study sickness when I am well; when it is present it will make its impression real enough, without the help of my imagination. We make our preparations beforehand for the travels we are about to undertake, and have made up our minds about them; we leave it to our attendants to decide when we are to take horse, or we put it off for their convenience.

I have felt this unexpected advantage from the publication of my conduct of life, that in some sort it serves me as a rule. I sometimes consider whether it would not be better not to disclose the history of my life. This public disclosure of it obliges me to keep to my path, and not to give the lie to the picture I have drawn of my qualities, which are usually less distorted and contradictory than the malicious and unhealthy judgements of these times will admit of. The uniformity and simplicity of my character makes it appear easy of interpretation; but the shape of it being rather novel and unusual, calumny has an easy game. Yet so it is, that to any one who is inclined to abuse me by legitimate means, my known and avowed imperfections will, I think, afford sufficient opportunity to bite me to his heart's content, without skirmishing with the wind. If he thinks I am drawing his teeth by anticipating his revelation and condemnation of them, it is but reasonable that he should exercise his right of amplifying and extending (offence has its rights outside of justice); of magnifying the roots of the vices which I reveal in myself until they have become trees, and of using for that purpose not only those that possess me, but also those that merely threaten me: prejudicial vices, both in quality and number; let him belabour me with them.

I could frankly follow the example of the philosopher Bion. Antigonus was beginning to taunt him on the subject of his origin. He stopped his mouth with these words: 'I am the son of a slave, a butcher, branded, and a prostitute, whom my father married by reason of her humble lot. They were both punished for some misdeed. An orator who took a liking for me as a boy, bought me, and at his death left me his whole fortune. Having transferred my possessions to this city of Athens, I devoted myself to philosophy. Historians may save themselves the trouble of seeking information about me; I will tell them how the case stands.'

A free and generous confession takes the sting out of reproach and disarms calumny.

Yet it is true that, taking one thing with another, it seems to me that I am as often praised as dispraised beyond reason; it also seems to me that from my youth up I have been given a rank and degree of honour rather above than below what was my due.

I should be more at home in a country where those orders of precedence were either regulated or despised. Among men, as soon as an altercation on precedence in walking or sitting exceeds three replies, there is an end of politeness. I am not afraid of ceding or preceding out of my order, to avoid such tiresome disputes; no man ever desired to precede me but I permitted him to do so.

Besides the benefit I reap from writing about myself, I hope for this other advantage, that if there happens to be any worthy man who approves and agrees with my humours, he will endeavour before I die to come into touch with me. I am giving him a great advantage over me;

for, all the knowledge he might have gained by a long acquaintance and intimacy during several years, he will obtain in three days from this record, and that more surely and accurately.[1]

An amusing idea! Many things that I would not say to a single person I say to the public; and for my most secret knowledge and thoughts I send my most faithful friends to a bookseller's shop!

> My very heart I open to men's view. (PERSIUS.)

If I knew for a certainty of a man who was of the same mind with me, truly I would go a very long way to find him out; for we cannot, I think, pay too much for the delight of having a companion who is in sympathy and agreement with us. O for a friend! How true is this old saying, 'that the possession of a friend is sweeter and more necessary than the elements of fire and water.'

To return to my story. There is no great evil in dying away from home and alone. Do we not consider it a duty to withdraw apart for natural actions that are less unsightly and less ghastly than this? Besides, those who are reduced to dragging out a prolonged and lingering existence should not perhaps wish to involve a large family in their miseries. For that reason the Indians of a certain region thought it right to kill a man who had reached that unfortunate state; and in another region they abandoned him to himself, to survive as best he could.

To whom do they not in the end become tiresome and insupportable? Ordinary duties do not go to that length. You forcibly teach your best friends to be cruel; by long familiarity with your ailments your wife and children become hardened and cease to feel for you and pity you. The groans that my colic forces from me have ceased to alarm anybody. And though we may derive some pleasure from their company (which is not always the case, by reason of the disparity of conditions, which easily begets contempt or envy for anybody whatever), is it not too much to abuse their good nature for such an age? The more I saw them cheerfully putting a restraint upon themselves for my sake,

---

[1] Montaigne's hope was partially fulfilled by Mademoiselle de Gournay, who called upon him when, for the purpose of seeing his new edition of the Essays through the press, he went for the last time to Paris.

the more sorry should I be for their pains. We are justified in leaning, but not in lying so heavily, upon others, and propping ourselves to their detriment. Like the man who had the throats of little children cut, to make use of their blood to cure some disease he had.[1] Or that other who was provided with young and tender virgins to keep his old limbs warm at night, and mingle the fragrance of their breath with his own rank and fetid exhalations.[1]

I could willingly choose Venice for my retreat when reduced to that feeble condition of life.

Decrepitude is a condition that requires solitude. I am sociable to excess. And yet it appears to me reasonable that I should henceforth withdraw my troublesome person from the eyes of the world, and brood over it in solitude; that I should shrink and retire into my shell, like a tortoise. I am learning to see people without clinging to them; that would be outrageous in so steep a pass. It is time to turn my back on the company.

'But on so long a journey you may be miserably detained in some hole of a place where you will lack everything.' Most of the necessary things I carry about with me. And then we cannot run away from Fortune, if she resolves to attack us. When I am ill I need nothing out of the common; if Nature has no power over me, I have no mind to trust to a pill. At the very beginning of my agues and the maladies that lay me low, whilst I am yet whole and near to health, I reconcile myself with God by means of the last Christian offices; and I feel the more easy and relieved, and seem to have got the better of the malady.

Of notaries and their advice I have less need than of doctors. If I have not settled my affairs when quite well, I cannot be expected to do so when ill. What I wish to do for the service of death is always done; I would not venture to defer it for a single day. And if nothing is done, it means either that hesitation kept me from making a choice (for sometimes not to choose is to choose well), or that I had quite resolved to do nothing.[2]

---

[1] Tiberius, according to one commentator, Louis XI, according to another. The second example is obviously King David.

[2] We have an example of Montaigne's foresight in one of the very few notices of him in contemporary records. In a Commentary on the customs of Bordeaux, under the heading of *Wills*, Bernard Anthoine

I write my book for few people, and for few years. If I had expected a long life for my Essays, I should have committed them to a more settled language.[1] Seeing the continual changes that have taken place in our tongue to this day, who can expect that fifty years hence it will be used in its present form? Every day it slips from our hands, and during my lifetime it has altered by one half. We say that at this moment it is perfect; every century says the same of its own. I hesitate to believe that, as long as it escapes us and changes its forms as it does. It is for the good and useful writings to rivet it to themselves, and its credit will follow the fortunes of our State.

Therefore I do not fear to insert a few private items, interest in which will be confined to people now living, and which deal with things known to certain individuals who will see further into them than the ordinary intelligence. After all I do not wish to be discussed in the way I often hear people raking up the memories of the dead, saying: 'This is what he thought; this is how he lived; this is what he meant; if he had spoken when he was dying, he would have said this, he would have given that; I knew him better than any man.' Now, as far as decency permits I here make my inclinations and feelings known; but I do it more freely and readily by word of mouth to any one who wishes to know them. In any case, if any one examines these memoirs, he will find that I have said everything, or hinted at everything. What I cannot express I point at with my finger:

> But for the keen eye these mere footprints serve
> Whereby thou mayest know the rest thyself. (LUCRETIUS.)

I leave nothing concerning myself to be desired or to be guessed at. If people must be talking about me, I would have it to be truthfully and justly. I would willingly return from the next world to contradict any man who described me other than I was, although he did it to honour me. I have observed that even the living are always

writes: 'The late Montaigne, author of the Essays, feeling his end drawing near, got up in his shirt, put on his dressing-gown, opened his cabinet, called all his servants and legatees, and paid them the legacies he had left them by his will, foreseeing the difficulty his heirs would make in paying them.'

[1] Latin, which, being a dead language, is not liable to change.

misrepresented. And if I had not with all my power upheld the reputation of a friend I have lost, he might have been torn to pieces and represented in a thousand contradictory lights.[1]

To make an end of speaking of my poor humours, I confess that in my travels I seldom reach my night's lodging but the thought comes into my mind whether I could be ill or die there in comfort. I prefer to be lodged in a place which has been appropriated to my own particular use, neither noisy, nor dirty, nor smoky, nor stuffy. I endeavour to flatter death by these trivial details; or, to be more exact, to rid myself of all other encumbrances, that I may give my whole mind to it, since it will probably lie heavy enough upon me without any other load. I would like death to have her share in the ease and comforts of my life. Death is a great and important piece of life, and I hope from this day that mine will not belie the past.

Death assumes shapes of which some are easier than others, and takes on different properties according to each one's imagination. Among natural deaths that which results from weakness or stupor appears to me gentle and pleasant. Among violent deaths I can less easily fancy falling down a precipice than a ruin crushing me, and dying by a sword-cut than by a musket-shot. And I would sooner have drunk Socrates' potion than stabbed myself as Cato did. And, although it all comes to the same thing, yet my imagination sees as much difference between leaping into a fiery furnace and into the channel of a shallow river, as between death and life. So foolishly does our fear regard the means more than the end! It is but an instant; but it is of so much importance that I would willingly give many days of my life to pass it in my own way.

Since every one's imagination discovers a more or a less in its bitterness; since every one has some choice in the manner of dying, let us try a little further to find one that is free from all pain. Might we not make it even voluptuous,

---

[1] The friend was presumably La Boëtie. The edition of 1588 had this passage: 'I know well that I shall not leave behind me any man who will take my part with anything like the same affection and the same understanding of me as I do his. There is no man whom I would fully trust to represent me faithfully; he alone possessed my true portrait, and took it away with him. That is why I reveal myself so carefully.'

as did the 'companions in death' of Antony and Cleopatra? I will not speak of the cruel deaths which are the result of philosophy and religion, and which are held up as examples. But among men of little mark there have been found some, such as a Petronius and a Tigellinus, at Rome, who, pledged to take their own lives, lulled death to sleep as it were by the luxury of their preparations. They made it pass and glide away amid their customary effeminate pastimes, in the company of girls and boon companions; no words of consolation, no mention of wills, no ambitious affectation of fortitude, no talk about their future state, but amidst games, feastings, jestings, ordinary conversation on topical subjects, music and erotic poetry.

Could we not imitate that resoluteness in a more seemly fashion? Since there are deaths good for fools and deaths good for wise men, let us discover some that are good for those who are neither the one nor the other. My imagination suggests to me one or two forms of death that are easy and, since we must die, desirable.

The Roman tyrants considered that they were giving a criminal his life when they gave him the choice of his death. But was not Theophrastus, so delicate, modest, and wise a philosopher, obliged by his reason to dare to say this line, which was latinized by Cicero:

Fortune, not Wisdom, rules the life of man?

How greatly Fortune has helped me to keep with ease the bargain of my life by placing me in such a position that it is henceforth neither necessary nor cumbersome to anybody! It is a condition that I would have accepted at any season of my life, but now that I am ready to pack up for good and turn up my toes, I find a more particular satisfaction in the thought that I shall not give anybody either much pleasure or much pain by dying. By an artistic compensation she has brought it about that those who may expect some material benefit from my death will at the same time suffer some material loss. Our death often bears hard upon us because it is painful to others, and brings us almost as much harm through the harm it does them, and sometimes even more.

Among the comforts I look for in mine inn I include neither magnificence nor abundance; I hate them rather;

but a certain simple neatness which is more often met with in places where there is less of art, and which Nature has adorned with some charm entirely her own. *A meal in which not abundance but cleanliness prevails* (quoted by Nonius). *More wit than luxury* (C. Nepos).

And then, it is those who are compelled, in the depth of winter, to travel on business through the Grisons who are overtaken on the way by those extreme discomforts. I, who most often travel for my pleasure, do not steer myself so badly. If it is unattractive on the right, I take the left turning. If I feel unfit to ride, I stay where I am. And by so doing I really cannot see that it is not as pleasant and commodious as being at home. It is true that I always find superfluity superfluous, and notice that even dainty food and abundance occasion trouble.

If I have left anything unseen behind me, I go back; it is still on my way. I draw no fixed line, either straight or crooked. If I do not find, at the place I go to, what I have been told of, as it often happens that others' opinions do not agree with mine and have generally turned out to be erroneous, I do not regret my trouble; I have learned that what I was told of was not there.

My bodily nature is as adaptable, and my tastes are as catholic, as those of any man living. The different customs I find in one nation after another please me by their very diversity; each custom has its reason. Whether the plates be of tin, of wood, or of earthenware, whether the meat be boiled or roast; whether they give me butter or oil, whether nut-oil or olive-oil; whether dishes be hot or cold, it is all one to me; and so much one that, as I grow older, I find fault with this liberal disposition, and feel the need of a more discriminating choice to arrest my immoderate appetite, and sometimes to ease my digestion.

When I have been outside of France, and people have asked me, out of politeness, whether I would like to be served with French dishes, I laughed at the idea; and I always sought the tables that were most thick with foreigners.

I am ashamed when I see my countrymen steeped in that silly prejudice which makes them fight shy of any customs that differ from their own; when they are out of their village, they seem to be out of their element. Wherever they go they keep to their own ways, and abominate those of foreigners. If they come across a fellow-countryman in Hungary, they celebrate the happy meeting. See them hobnobbing and joining forces, and railing at all the barbarous customs they see around them ! Why not barbarous, since they are not French ? And yet those are the cleverest, who have taken sufficient notice of them to revile them. Most of them start on their travels with no thought but to return. They travel reserved and self-centred, wrapped in a taciturn and unsociable caution, on the defensive against the infection of any strange atmosphere.

What I say of these reminds me of what I have sometimes observed in our young courtiers, in similar circumstances. They associate with none but those of their own kidney, regarding us with contempt or pity, as people of another world. Deprive them of the opportunity of talking of court intrigues, and they are like fish out of water ; as green and ignorant to us as we appear to them. It has been very well said that a well-bred man is an all-round man.

I, on the other hand, start on my wanderings very much fed up with our ways. I do not look for Gascons in Sicily (I have left enough of them at home) ; I would rather meet Greeks and Persians. With these I enter into conversation, and I study them. To them I offer and lend my services. And, what is more, I seem to have met with few customs that are not as good as ours.

I do not risk much ; for I have hardly lost sight of my weathercocks.[1]

For the rest, most of the company one casually meets with on the road causes more embarrassment than pleasure ; I do not cultivate their acquaintance, and less so now that old age makes me particular and somewhat inclined to avoid the customary formalities. You feel for others, or others feel for you ; both are painful discomforts, but the latter seems to me the ruder.

It is a rare chance, but of inestimable solace, to meet with a well-bred man, of solid good sense, agreeing with you in tastes, who takes a pleasure in your company. I have been greatly in need of such a man on all my travels. But

[1] As this was written after Montaigne had been as far as Rome, it must be taken metaphorically ; perhaps he means that he sees many familiar objects in foreign parts.

such company must be chosen and acquired before you leave home.

I relish no pleasure that I cannot communicate. I never have even a merry thought without being vexed at having to keep it to myself, with nobody to share it. *If I were offered wisdom on condition that I must keep it to myself, and not communicate it to others, I would have none of it* (Seneca). This other has tuned it to a higher note: *If the life of a wise man were so arranged, that with an abundance of all things he might have full leisure to consider and contemplate all things worth his study, yet if his solitude were such that he could see no man, he must give up his life* (Cicero).

I agree with Archytas when he says 'that it would be undesirable to be even in Heaven, and to wander about those great and divine celestial bodies, without the companionship of a friend'.

But it is still better to be alone than in stupid and tiresome company. Aristippus preferred to live a stranger everywhere.

> Had Fate vouchsafed me of mine own free will
> My course to shape, (VIRGIL.)

I should choose to pass my life with my seat on the saddle,

> Where scorching suns the long day fill,
> Where mists and snows and tempests chill
>   Hold reckless bacchanal. (HORACE.)

'Have you no more restful pastimes? Of what have you any lack? Is not your house in a beautifully airy and healthy situation, sufficiently furnished and more than sufficiently capacious? Royal majesty with its train has more than once found room in it.[1] Are there not more families below yours in orderliness than there are above you in eminence? Is there any local, extraordinary, indigestible thought that eats into your heart,

> That is now burning in thy troubled breast,
> And ne'er will suffer thee to be at rest? (ENNIUS.)

Where do you expect to live without constraint, and undisturbed? *Fortune's favours are never unmixed* (Q. Curtius). Do you not see that you alone stand in your own way, and

---

[1] King Henry of Navarre stayed at the Château of Montaigne on two occasions.

that you will follow your own inclination everywhere, and that you will grumble everywhere ? For there is no satisfaction here below except for brutish or divine souls. With so much just cause to be contented where do you think to find contentment ? How many thousands of men there are who limit their wishes to such a condition as you enjoy ! You must just amend your own ways, for you are able to do that to any extent ; whereas you have no right but to be patient in the face of Fortune. *There is no peace and quiet except that which Reason has conferred* (Seneca).'

I see the reasonableness of this homily, and I see it very clearly ; but it would have been briefer and more pertinent to have said in one word, ' Be wise.' Such a resolution is beyond wisdom ; it is she that brings about and produces that state. It is like the physician who keeps shouting after a poor lingering patient, ' Be cheerful ; ' his advice would not sound quite so foolish if he said, ' Be well.' For my part, I am but a man of the baser sort. This is a wholesome precept, sure, and easily understood, ' Be content with what you have,' that is to say, with your reason. But to carry it out is no more in the power of the wisest than it is in mine. It is a popular saying, but terribly far-reaching ; what does it not comprehend ? All things are subject to discrimination and qualification.

I know well that, to speak by the letter, this pleasure in travelling is a testimony of restlessness and instability ; and indeed these are our ruling and predominating qualities. Yes, I confess to it, I see nothing, not so much as in a dream, in a wish, whereon I could set up my rest ; variety alone satisfies me, and the enjoyment of diversity, at least if anything satisfies me. When I travel I am sustained chiefly by this idea, that I can give up travelling without inconvenience, and that I have a place where I can comfortably dispense with it.

I love a private life, because it is by my own choice that I love it, not because I am unfit for public life, for which I am perhaps by nature just as well suited. I can serve my Prince the more cheerfully because I can do so by the free choice of my judgement and reason, without any particular obligation ; and because I am not thrown back upon it or forced to it in consequence of being inadmissible and unwelcome to any other party. So of the rest. I hate the morsels that necessity carves for me. Any commodity on which I had solely to depend would stick in my throat:

> Let me in water plunge one oar,
> And with the other rake the shore. (PROPERTIUS.)

One cord will never hold me fast enough. 'There is vanity, you will say, in this amusement.' But where is there not ? And those goodly precepts are vanity, and all wisdom is vanity. *The Lord knoweth the thoughts of the wise, that they are vain* (Paul to the Corinthians). Those fine-spun subtleties are only for the pulpit; they are admonitions that would send us ready saddled into the next world. Life is a material and corporeal movement, an action imperfect in its own essence and irregular ; I make it my business to serve it in its own way.

> We suffer each our ghostly punishments. (VIRGIL.)

We must act in such a way as not to contravene the universal laws of Nature ; that rule being observed, we must follow our own nature (Cicero). What end is served by those lofty heights of Philosophy, on which no human being can sit, and those rules which exceed our strength and our use ?

I often hear a man proposing an ideal form of life, which neither he nor his hearers have any hope, or what is more, any desire to follow. From the same sheet of paper on which he has just written the sentence delivered upon an adulterer, the judge will tear a scrap for a billet-doux to his colleague's wife. The lady with whom you have just been in illicit contact will presently, even before you leave her, abuse her friend for the same fault more bitterly than a Portia[1] might have done. And many will condemn men to death for crimes which they do not even regard as faults.

In my younger days I have known a gentleman offer the public with one hand poems excelling in beauty and licentiousness, and with the other, at the same moment, the most contentious work on theological reform that the world had breakfasted upon for many years.

So it is with men. They let the laws and precepts follow their own way ; we take another road, not only because we are of dissolute habits, but often because we disagree with them. Listen to a lecture on Philosophy ; your mind

[1] Portia, daughter of Cato of Utica, killed herself on hearing of the death of her husband Brutus at the Battle of Philippi.

is at once stirred and affected by the originality, the eloquence, the pertinence of the remarks, but they have no power to tickle and prick your conscience. It is not your conscience that is spoken to. Is that not true ? And so Aristo says ' that neither a hot bath nor a lecture is of any avail unless it cleans away and removes the dirt '. One may busy oneself about the rind, but not till after the pith has been extracted ; just as after draining the good wine out of a beautiful cup we examine the engraving and workmanship of it.

In all the workshops of ancient Philosophy we shall find this, that one and the same worker will publish rules of temperance, and at the same time publishes erotic and licentious writings. And Xenophon, in the bosom of Clinias, wrote against Aristippic sensuality. It is not a question of a miraculous conversion stirring them by fits and starts. But it is as with Solon, who portrays himself now in his own person, now in the shape of a law-giver ; now he speaks for the multitude, now in his own name. And for himself he adopts free and natural rules, feeling assured of perfect and robust health.

> For dubious maladies call in
> A doctor of repute. (JUVENAL.)

Antisthenes permits the sage to love, and do in his own way what he thinks convenient, without paying any attention to the laws ; since he is better advised than they, and has a greater knowledge of virtue. His disciple Diogenes said : ' To agitation oppose Reason ; to Fortune, confidence ; to the laws, Nature.'

For delicate stomachs are needed precise and artificial prescriptions. A good digestion simply follows the prescriptions of its natural appetite. So do our doctors, who eat melon and drink new wine, whilst they keep their patients tied down to syrups and slops.

' I know nothing about their books, said Laïs the courtesan, or their wisdom, or their philosophy ; but I know that these men knock at my door as often as any others.' Since our licence always carries us beyond what is lawful and permitted, the precepts and laws which rule our lives have often been made stricter than universal reason requires.

> No man is satisfied if he transgress
> No further than the laws permit. (JUVENAL.)

It were desirable that there were more proportion between the command and the obedience ; and it seems unjust to set the goal further than we can reach. There is no man, good as he may be, who, if all his thoughts and actions were submitted to the scrutiny of the laws, would not deserve hanging ten times in his life ; yea, many a man whom it would be a very great loss and very unjust to punish with death.

> It is no business of yours
> What he or she do with their skins. (MARTIAL.)

And many a man who has never offended against the laws not only does not deserve to be commended for honesty, but would be very justly scourged by Philosophy. So confused and unjust is the proportion !

We take no heed to be good men according to God's laws. We cannot be so according to our laws. Human wisdom never yet came up to the duties she has prescribed for herself, and if she did come up to them, she would prescribe others beyond them, to which she would ever aim and aspire ; so hostile to consistency is our human condition !

Man has ordained that he shall necessarily be at fault. He does not show much discrimination when he carves out his duties to the measure of another being than his own. For whom does he prescribe that which he expects no man to do ? Is he wrong in not doing what it is impossible for him to do ? The laws which condemn us not to be able, themselves accuse us of not being able.

At the worst this distorted liberty of presenting ourselves in two ways, the actions after one manner, the reasonings after another, may be allowable in those who speak of things, but it cannot be so for those who speak of themselves, as I do ; I must walk with my pen as I do with my feet. The life of the public man ought to have some relation to other lives. The virtue of Cato was vigorous beyond the measure of his time ; and for a man who took upon himself to govern others, a man dedicated to the public service, the rightness of it may be said to have been, if not wrong, at least a vain and unseasonable rightness.

My own conduct of life, which hardly deviates by the width of an inch from that of the generality of people, yet makes me somewhat shy and unsociable to my age. I do not know if I am unreasonably disgusted with the world I frequent ; but I know well that it would be unreasonable for me to complain of the world being more disgusted with me than I am disgusted with the world.

The virtue assigned to the affairs of the world is a virtue with many bends, angles, and elbows, to join and adapt itself to human frailty ; mixed and artificial, not straight, clear, constant, nor purely harmless. Our annals to this day blame one of our Kings for yielding too simply to the conscientious persuasions of his confessor. Affairs of state have bolder precepts :

> Let him who would be pure from courts retire. (LUCAN.)

I once tried to adapt to the service of conducting public affairs ideas and rules of life as rude, fresh, unpolished, and unpolluted as they were either born with me, or derived from my education, which serve me, if not commodiously, at least safely, in my private concerns : the virtue of a schoolboy and a novice. I found them unsuitable and dangerous in such matters. A man who enters a crowd must go now this way, now that, keep in his elbows, retreat or advance, nay he must quit the straight path, according to what he encounters. He must live not so much according to himself as according to others ; not according to what he proposes to himself, but according to what is proposed to him, according to the times, according to the men, according to the business in hand.

Plato says that the man who escapes with clean hands from the management of the world's affairs, escapes by a miracle. He also says that when he places his philosopher at the head of a government, he has not in mind a corrupt government like that of Athens, and still less a government like ours, in which Wisdom herself would lose her Latin. Since a herb, transplanted to a soil differing greatly from that which suits it, rather adapts itself to the soil than corrects the soil to suit itself.

I feel that if I had to direct my mind entirely to such occupations, I should need a great deal of change and reclothing. And even though I could prevail upon myself to do so (and why could I not, with time and diligence ?), I would not. The little experience I have had in that trade disgusted me with it. At times I feel a certain temptation to ambition arising like vapour in my soul; but I stiffen myself obstinately to resist it:

> Be thou, Catullus, firm unto the last! (CATULLUS.)

I am seldom called upon, and as seldom do I offer myself. Independence and laziness, which are my ruling qualities, are qualities diametrically opposed to that trade.

We are unable to distinguish between the faculties of different men; they are minutely divided and limited, and difficult to choose between. To conclude that, because a man is competent in private life, he will be competent in public service, is to conclude badly. Many a man guides himself well who cannot guide others well; and produces Essays who cannot produce deeds. A man will direct a siege well who would badly direct a battle; and discourse well in private who cannot address a crowd or a prince. Nay, to be able to do the one is perhaps rather evidence, than not, that he is unable to do the other.

I observe that great minds are hardly more fitted for little things than little minds for great things. Can it be believed that Socrates gave the Athenians food for laughter at his expense, because he had never been able to count up the votes of his tribe, and report upon them to the Council? Truly the veneration I have for that great man's perfections deserves that my chief imperfections should be excused by the magnificent example which he was fated to set me.

Our talents are cut up into small pieces; mine have no breadth and are miserably few. Saturninus[1] said to the men who had set him at the head of the army, 'Fellow-soldiers, you have ruined a good captain to make a bad general.'

If any man flatters himself that, in a diseased age like the present, he can employ in the service of the world a pure and spotless virtue, he either does not know what virtue is, since morality and our ideas of morality deteriorate in the same ratio (indeed, hear them describing virtue, listen to most of them glorying in their conduct and laying down the law; instead of painting virtue they paint injustice and vice pure and simple, and offer this false image as an example for princes); or, if he does know, he flatters

---

[1] One of the thirty tyrants who rose up in the time of the Emperor Gallienus.

himself wrongfully, and, whatever he may say, he does a thousand things of which his conscience accuses him.

I would willingly take Seneca's word with regard to his experience on a like occasion, provided that he would speak candidly. The most honourable mark of uprightness in such a difficulty is freely to acknowledge one's error, and that of others ; to restrain and resist with all one's might the inclination to evil, to follow that bent reluctantly, to hope and desire something better.

I observe, in this dismemberment of our country and these divisions into which we are fallen, that every man labours to defend his cause, but even the best of them does so with lies and dissimulation. Whoever should write bluntly about them would be a bold man, and vicious. The most just party is still a member of a putrid and worm-eaten body ; but in such a body the member that is least diseased calls itself sound, and with good reason, since our qualities have no name except by comparison. Political innocence is measured according to places and times.

I should like to have seen Xenophon commending Agesilaus for this action :[1] Being entreated by a neighbouring Prince, with whom he had once been at war, to allow him to pass through his territory, he granted him permission, giving him free passage through the Peloponnesus, and not only did he not imprison or poison him when he had him at his mercy, but he received him courteously [as bound by his promise], and did him no harm. To a man of Xenophon's way of thinking there was nothing remarkable in this ; elsewhere and in another age such an action will be specially recorded for its generosity and magnanimity. Our wretched schoolboys would have laughed it to scorn ; so little does Spartan innocence resemble the French kind.

We have no lack of virtuous men ; but it is according to our standard. If there be a man whose morals are tuned to a higher key than that of his age, let him either twist or blunt his rules of conduct, or (which I would rather advise him to do) let him retire into private life, and not mix with us. What could he gain by it ?

> An upright and a blameless man appears
> More wondrous than a boy with double limbs,

[1] This is written ironically ; but it seems that Xenophon did commend Agesilaus in his Life of that King.

> Than fishes found by ploughing husbandman,
> Or mule that's big with foal. (JUVENAL.)

We may regret better times but we cannot flee from the present; we may wish for different men in authority, but we must nonetheless obey those we have. And there is perhaps more merit in obeying the bad than the good. As long as a reflexion of the old and accepted laws of this monarchy shines in any corner, there will I abide. If they unfortunately happen to thwart and contradict one another, and produce two factions of doubtful and difficult choice, I shall readily choose to avoid and escape the storm. In the meantime Nature or the hazards of war may lend me a helping hand. Between Caesar and Pompey I could have openly declared myself. But with those three robbers who came after,[1] either I should have had to hide, or follow with the wind; which I consider permissible when Reason is no longer at the helm.

> Whither from the course so wide? (VIRGIL.)

This padding has carried me a little away from my theme. I go out of my way, but rather through licence than inadvertance. My ideas follow one another, but sometimes at a distance; and they look at one another, but askance.

I have cast my eyes over a certain dialogue of Plato,[2] divided into two halves like a fantastic motley garb, the upper part treating of love, all the lower part of eloquence. They are not afraid of these quick changes, and with wonderful charm they allow themselves thus to roll before the wind, or they seem to.

The headings of my chapters do not always embrace the matter of them; often they only indicate it by some mark, like those other titles, the 'Maid of Andros', 'The Eunuch'[3] or these other names, Sylla, Cicero, Torquatus.[3]

I love the poetic gait, by leaps and bounds. It is, as Plato says, a light, fleet-footed, divinely inspired art.

In some of his dissertations Plutarch forgets his theme; and the drift of his argument is only incidentally found, quite drowned in foreign matter. See how he wanders in

---

[1] Octavius, Antony, and Lepidus.   [2] The *Phaedrus*.
[3] The first are the names of two comedies of Terence; the latter respectively personify the Dictator, the Orator and the Cruel father.

the 'Daemon of Socrates'. My word, what charm there is in those frolicsome sallies and those digressions! And the more charming, the more careless and casual they appear to be!

It is the negligent reader who mislays my subject, not I; a word or two on it may always be discovered in some corner, which will not fail to be sufficient, though it may be hard to find.

I am fond of change and variety, unwisely and impetuously fond, and my style and mind have the same vagabond nature.

A man must be a little mad if he would not be more foolish,[1] as the precepts of our masters tell us, and still more their examples.

A thousand poets flag and languish prosaically; but the best ancient prose (and I scatter it here indifferently as if it were verse), shines throughout with the vigour and boldness of poetry, and reflects some touch of poetic frenzy. And we must certainly allow that poetry has the mastery and pre-eminence in speaking. The poet, says Plato, seated upon the tripod of the Muses, in his frenzy pours out whatever rises to his lips, like a spouting fountain, without weighing and ruminating it; and things escape him of varied hues, of contrary substance, and in a broken stream. Plato himself is poetic throughout, and the old theology is poetry, so the scholars tell us, and the first philosophy. It is the original language of the gods.

I would have my matter distinguishable of itself; that it should sufficiently show where it changes, where it concludes, where it begins, where it is resumed, without interlacing it with joining and connecting words introduced for the benefit of feeble or inattentive ears; and without my having to write my own glosses.

Where is the man who would not rather not be read than read sleepily or hastily? *Nothing, however useful it may be, can be useful when treated negligently* (Seneca). If to take up a book were to take it in, if to look at it were to consider it, if to run through it were to grasp it, I should be wrong to profess to be quite as ignorant as I do.

---

[1] *Il faut avoir un peu de folie qui ne veut avoir plus de sottise.* Hazlitt translates, ' He must fool it a little who would not be deemed wholly a fool.'

Since I am unable to fix the reader's attention by the weight of it, it is a point gained if I chance to fix it by my intricacies. 'True, but he will afterwards repent of having puzzled over them.' No doubt; but after all he will have puzzled over them. And besides, there are men of that nature, who despise what is intelligible, who will think the better of me for not understanding what I say; they will infer the depth of my meaning from its obscurity, which, to tell the truth, I very much hate, and would avoid if I could avoid myself. Aristotle somewhere boasts of affecting it; a mistaken affectation!

As the cutting up of my work into so many chapters, a method which I adopted at the beginning, appeared to me to break and destroy, before arousing, the reader's attention, since it would disdain to settle down and collect itself for so little, I have taken to making them longer, and such as need a firm determination and leisure on his part. In this kind of occupation, to a man to whom you will not give a single hour you will give nothing. And you do nothing for a man for whom you do only whilst you are doing something else. Besides which I have perhaps some particular reason for speaking only by halves, for speaking confusedly and discordantly.

I was about to say that I am out of humour with that kill-joy Reason; and as to those extravagant ambitions that torment one's life and those superfine opinions, if there is any truth in them, I think it too dearly bought and too inconvenient. I am rather out to champion the cause of vanity even, and asininity, if they bring me any pleasure; and let myself follow my natural inclinations, without examining them too closely.

I have seen elsewhere ruined houses, and statues, both of heaven and the earth;[1] they are men, when all is said. All that is true; and yet I cannot so often revisit the tomb of that great and powerful city,[2] but it always excites my wonder and awe.

Care for the dead is a duty imposed upon us. Now I was brought up from childhood with these dead; I was familiar with the affairs of Rome long before I was with those of my own house. I knew the Capitol and its position before I knew the Louvre, and the Tiber before the Seine. I have

---

[1] i.e. of gods and men.   [2] Rome.

meditated more on the conditions and fortunes of Lucullus, Metellus, and Scipio than I have about any of our own men. They are dead. So indeed is my father ; he is as absolutely dead as they, and as far removed from me and life, after eighteen years, as they are after sixteen hundred. And yet I do not cease to cherish and keep alive his memory, his love and companionship in a perfect and very living union.

Nay, I am naturally inclined to be more serviceable to the departed ; they cannot help themselves, and therefore seem to be more in need of my help. It is just here that gratitude shows in its best light. A benefit is less generously bestowed where there is hope of its being returned and reflected.

Arcesilaus, going to see Ctesibius who was ill, and seeing that he was poorly off, softly slipped the money he had intended giving him under his pillow ; by concealing it he besides acquitted him from acknowledging his thanks.

Those who have deserved love and gratitude at my hands never lost it through being no longer on the spot ; I have repaid them better and more carefully in spite of their absence and ignorance of my gratitude. I speak more affectionately of my friends when they have no longer any means of knowing it.

Now I have started a hundred quarrels in defence of Pompey and for the cause of Brutus. This friendship still endures between us ; we have no hold even on present things except through the imagination. Finding myself of no use to this age, I hurl myself back into that other, and am so infatuated with it, that the state of that ancient Rome, when free, just and flourishing (for I love her neither at her birth nor in her old age) arouses my passionate interest. Wherefore I cannot so often revisit the sites of their streets and houses, and those deep ruins extending to the Antipodes, but I must muse over them.

Is it by nature or through an error of the imagination that the sight of places we know to have been frequented and inhabited by men whose memory is held in honour, affects us somewhat more strongly than to hear tell of their deeds or to read their works ? *Such is the power of places to call up memories ! And in this city they are endless ; for wherever we tread we set our foot on some piece of history* (Cicero).

I take a delight in reflecting on their faces, their bearing and their clothes. I ruminate those great names between my teeth and make them resound in my ears. *I pay reverence to them, and always rise in honour to such great names* (Seneca). Of things that are in some part great and admirable I admire even the common parts. I should delight in seeing them talk together, taking their airing, and at supper. It would be ungrateful in me to despise the remains and statues of so many honourable and valorous men whom I have seen live and die, and who by their examples give us so many good instructions, if we but knew how to follow them.

And then, this same Rome that we see deserves our love, having been so long and by so many ties allied to our own crown: the only common and universal city. The supreme authority who rules there is equally acknowledged in other countries; it is the metropolitan city of all Christian nations. Spaniard or Frenchman, every one is at home there. To be one of the Princes of that state, it is but necessary to be of Christendom, wherever it may be. There is no place on this earth that has been so much and so constantly under the protection and influence of Heaven. Her very ruins are replete with glory and pomp:

> The dearer for her memorable ruins. (SIDONIUS APOLLINARIS.)

In her very tomb she still retains the marks and reflexions of empire. *That it may be clearly manifest that in this place of all others Nature rejoiced in her handiwork* (Pliny).

Some would reproach themselves and feel an inner revolt at their being tickled by so vain a pleasure. Our inclinations are not too vain if they are agreeable. Let them be what they may, if they constantly satisfy a man capable of common sense, I should not have the heart to find fault with him.

I owe much to Fortune, in that to this day she has done me no great wrong, at least not more than I was able to bear. May it not be her way to leave those in peace who do not trouble her?

> The more a man himself denies,
> The more to him the Gods will give.
> Naked I seek the camp of those
> Who covet nought...
> Much they lack who much demand. (HORACE.)

If she continues, she will dismiss me very well contented and satisfied:

> I importune the Gods for nothing more. (HORACE.)

But beware the shock! There are thousands who go to pieces in the very harbour.

I can easily console myself for what will happen here when I am gone; present things keep me sufficiently busy:

> The rest I leave to Fortune. (OVID.)

Besides, I have not that strong tie that is said to attach men to the future through the children who bear their name and honour.[1] And I ought perhaps to desire them the less if they are so desirable. I am too much attached as it is to the world and to this life, through myself. I am content to be in the clutches of Fortune with regard to the circumstances that are properly necessary to my existence, without in other ways extending her authority over me; and I have never thought that being without children was a drawback that should render life less complete and less contented. A sterile occupation also has its advantages. Children are among the things that are not strongly to be desired, especially in this age when it would be so difficult to make them good men. *Nothing good can be brought forth now, so corrupt are the seeds* (Tertullian). And yet they are just the things whose loss, when they have been acquired, is to be regretted.

He who left me in charge of my house prophesied that I was likely to ruin it, considering how little I had of the stay-at-home disposition. He was mistaken; here I am as I was when I first entered into possession, if not a little better off. And yet I have neither official position nor church living.

For the rest, if Fortune has done me no violent or extraordinary injury, neither has she done me any particular favour. All the gifts she has bestowed on my house go back more than a hundred years. For my own part I am not beholden to her liberality for any essential and solid benefits. She has granted me a few airy favours, of an honorary and titular nature, without any substance; and these she did not, to tell the truth, grant, but offer to me;

---

[1] Montaigne means that he has no sons.

to me who am, God knows, grossly material, who am only satisfied with realities, and very massive realities; and who, if I dared to confess it, would think avarice rather more pardonable than ambition, and pain more to be shunned than disgrace, and health more desirable than learning, and wealth than nobility.

Among her empty favours there is none that gives so much pleasure to this silly conceit of mine which feeds upon it, as an authentic patent of Roman citizenship, which was granted me on my recent visit to that city, magnificent with its seals and gilt letters, and granted with all gracious liberality. And as these patents are worded differently, in more or less gracious style; and as I myself, before I set eyes on one, would have been very glad to be shown a formula of it, I will, for the satisfaction of any person who is suffering from the same curiosity as I, transcribe it here in full:

'On the report made to the Senate by Orazio Massimi, Marzo Cecio, Alessandro Muti, Conservators of the city of Rome, concerning the right of Roman citizenship to be granted to the most illustrious Michel de Montaigne, Knight of the Order of St. Michael, and Gentleman of the Chamber in ordinary to the Most Christian King, the Senate and People of Rome have decreed:

'Considering that, by ancient usage, those have ever been adopted amongst us with ardour and eagerness, who, distinguished by virtue and nobility, have served and honoured our Republic, or might do so in the future; We, full of respect for the example and authority of our ancestors, consider that we should imitate and follow this laudable custom. Wherefore, the most illustrious Michel de Montaigne, Knight of the Order of St. Michael, and Gentleman of the Chamber in ordinary to the Most Christian King, most zealous for the Roman name, being by the rank and distinction of his family, and by his personal qualities, highly worthy to be admitted to the rights of Roman citizenship by the supreme judgement and suffrage of the Senate and People of Rome: it has pleased the Senate and People of Rome, that the most illustrious Michel de Montaigne, adorned with every kind of merit, and very dear to this noble People, should be inscribed as a Roman citizen, both in regard to himself and his posterity, and admitted to enjoy all the honours and advantages reserved for those who were born Citizens and Patricians of Rome, or who have become such by right of their good title thereunto. And herein the Senate and People of Rome consider that they are less conferring a gift, than paying a debt, and that it is less a service they render than a service they receive from him, who, in accepting this Citizenship, honours and gives lustre to the City itself. The Conservators have caused this Senatus-Consultus to be transcribed by the secretaries of the Roman Senate and People, to be deposited among the archives of the Capitol, and have drawn up this act, sealed with the common seal of the City. A. U. C. 2331, A.D. 1581, 13th March.

Orazio Fosco,
Secretary of the Sacred Senate and of the Roman People.
Vincente Martoli,
Secretary of the Sacred Senate and of the Roman People.'

Being a burgess of no town, I am very pleased to be one of the noblest city that ever was and ever will be. If others were to examine themselves attentively, as I do, they would, as I do, find that they are full of vanity and foppery. I cannot do away with it without doing away with myself. We are all steeped in it, one as much as the other; but those who are sensible of it are in a better way; and yet I am not so sure.

That common habit of mind of looking elsewhere than at ourselves has stood us in good stead. We are an object that fills us with discontent; we see nothing there but misery and vanity. In order not to discourage us, Nature has very fittingly thrown the action of our sight outwards. We go forward with the current; but to turn our course back upon ourselves is a painful movement; thus the sea, when thrown back upon itself, falls into confusion and gets in its own way. Observe, says every one, the motions of the heavens, observe the people, the quarrel of this man, the pulse of that, the last testament of another; in short, keep on observing, high or low, on one side, or before, or behind.

It was a paradoxical command that was given us in ancient times by that God at Delphi. ' Look into yourself; know yourself; lay hold on yourself; call back your mind and will, which are expending their powers elsewhere, to themselves; you are running out, you are diffusing yourself; concentrate yourself; resist yourself; you are being betrayed and dispersed and robbed of yourself. Dost thou not see that this world keeps its sight concentrated upon itself, and its eyes open to contemplate itself? It is always vanity for thee, within and without; but it is less vanity when less extended. Saving thyself, O man, said that God, each thing studies itself first, and, according to its need, sets limits to its labours and desires. There is not a single thing so destitute and needy as thyself, who embracest the universe. Thou art the searcher without knowledge, the magistrate without authority and, when all is said, the fool of the comedy.'

CHAPTER 10

OF HUSBANDING ONE'S WILL

BY comparison with the common run of men, few things give me concern, or, more correctly speaking, gain a hold upon me. For it is reasonable that they should concern, provided they do not possess us. I do my best, by study and argument, to increase this privilege of insensibility, which I have by nature in a high degree. There are consequently few things that I passionately espouse. My sight is clear, but fixed on few objects; my sensibilities are soft and tender. But my powers of apprehension and application are dull and hard. I find it difficult to pledge myself to a thing.

As far as in me lies, I give all my attention to myself; and even here I would willingly curb my feelings and keep them from plunging too deeply into an object that I possess by the favour of others, and over which Fortune has more right than I. So that even as regards health, which I value so highly, it would be well if I did not so passionately desire and dote upon it as to make sickness insupportable.

We should find a mean between hatred of pain and love of pleasure; and Plato prescribes a middle course of life between the two.

But to the feelings that draw me away from myself and attach me elsewhere, I certainly offer all the resistance in my power. My maxim is ' that we should lend ourselves to others, and give ourselves only to ourselves'. If I were easily led to pledge and devote myself, I should not hold out against it; I am too soft, both by nature and habit:

> Averse to all affairs and born
> In idleness and ease. (OVID.)

Obstinately contested disputes in which my adversary in the end had the better of me, the shame of having pursued my point too hotly to an issue, would perhaps rankle too cruelly within me. If I rose to the bait as readily as others do, my soul would never have the strength to bear the terrors and emotions which attack those who espouse so many things. It would be straightway unhinged by that inward excitement.

If at times I have been driven to take up the management of other people's affairs, I have promised to take them in hand, but not into my lungs and liver; to take them upon my shoulders, not to identify myself with them; to look after them, yes; to take them passionately to heart, certainly not. I give my attention to them, but I do not brood over them. I have enough to do to order and dispose the throng of domestic cares which I foster in my bowels and veins, without harbouring and being crushed by a throng of other men's affairs; and am sufficiently concerned with my own natural and necessary affairs, without inviting others that are foreign to me.

Those who know how much they owe to themselves, how much they are in duty bound to themselves, discover that Nature has given them this charge, which will keep them fully enough occupied: 'Thou hast ample business at home; do not abandon it.'

Men hire themselves out. Their faculties are not exercised for themselves, but for those to whom they become slaves. Their lodgers make themselves at home in their house, not they themselves. This common humour is not to my liking. We must husband the freedom of our soul, and not let it out except on lawful occasions, which are very few, if we judge sanely. Observe the people who are accustomed to let themselves be seized and carried away; they do so on all occasions, in little matters as well as great, in those which do not concern them as well as in those that do. They thrust themselves forward indiscriminately wherever there is work to do and anything to bind them. Not to be in a state of bustle and excitement, is to them death. *They seek business only for business' sake* (Seneca).

Not that they wish to be on the move so much as that they cannot keep still; any more or less than a stone which, started on its downward course, does not stop until it comes to its resting-place.

To be busy, for a certain class of people, is a mark of efficiency and dignity. Their minds seek repose in the swing, like infants in the cradle. They may be said to be as serviceable to their friends as they are troublesome to themselves.

No man deals out his money to others; every man deals out his time and his life. Of nothing are we so prodigal as of those things in which alone avarice would be useful and commendable.

I am of quite the opposite disposition. I retire within myself; what I desire, and that is little, I generally desire with no great ardour. So too I am rarely busy and occupied, and then calmly.

Whatever they will and carry out they do with all their will-power and intensity. There are so many slippery places that, for greater safety, we must glide rather lightly and superficially over this world; we must slide over it, and not break through. Even sensual pleasures are painful when they are intense:

> You tread on fires that lurk beneath the treacherous ashes.
> (HORACE.)

Messieurs [1] of Bordeaux elected me Mayor of their town when I was far from France, and still farther from any such thought. I begged to be excused, but they told me I was wrong, since the King also intervened with his command. It is a charge that should appear the more honourable as there is no remuneration or profit attached to it, other than the honour of administering it. The duration of the office is two years, but it may be extended by a second election, which very rarely happens. It was so extended in my case, and only twice before: a few years previously in the case of Monsieur de Lanssac, and recently of Monsieur de Biron,

---

[1] The *Jurats* or Aldermen. Montaigne was at the time at the baths of Lucca in Italy.

Marshal of France, to whose place I succeeded ; and I left mine to Monsieur de Matignon, likewise Marshal of France. Smart in such noble company !

> Both able ministers in peace and war. (VIRGIL.)

Fortune desired to have a hand in my promotion by that particular circumstance which she put in of her own. By no means vain ; for Alexander flouted the Corinthian ambassadors who offered him the citizenship of their town. But when they proceeded to explain to him that Bacchus and Hercules were also on that register, he graciously thanked them.

On my arrival I portrayed myself faithfully and conscientiously, such as I feel myself to be : without memory, without vigilance, without experience and without energy ; without hatred too, without ambition, without avarice, and without strong passions ; that they might be informed and advised of what they were to expect of my service. And since in their choice of me they had only been instigated by their knowledge of my late father and the honour in which they held his memory, I further gave them very clearly to understand that I should be very sorry that anything should affect my feelings as strongly as his had formerly been affected by their municipal affairs, whilst he was administering them in this same office to which they had called me.

I remembered as a boy having seen him, in his old age, his soul cruelly distressed by those bickerings over public affairs, neglecting the sweet atmosphere of his home, to which he had long before become attached in his declining years, his household affairs and his health ; and truly thinking little of his own life, which he came near losing in consequence, obliged as he was to make long and laborious journeys on their behalf. Such was he, and this devotion of his proceeded from his great natural goodness of heart ; there never was a more benevolent and public-spirited soul.

This proceeding, which I commend in others, I am not inclined to follow ; and I am not without excuse. He had been told that we ought to forget ourselves for others ; that the individual was of no importance whatever when the general public interest was concerned.

Most of the rules and precepts of the world aim at pushing

us out of ourselves, and driving us into the market-place, for the benefit of public society. Their authors imagined they had done a great thing in diverting and distracting us from ourselves, assuming that we were but too firmly and naturally wedded to ourselves; and they have not been sparing of words to tell us so. For it is no new thing for the wiseacres to preach things as they serve, not as they are.

Truth has its hindrances, disadvantages, and incompatibilities with us. We are often obliged to deceive, lest we deceive ourselves, and to seal our eyes, deaden our understanding, in order to redress and amend them. *For it is the ignorant who judge and must often be deceived, lest they fall into error* (Quintilian).

When they command us to love three, four, or fifty degrees of things before ourselves, they reflect the skill of the archer, who, to hit the mark, takes his aim far above the bull's eye. To straighten a bent piece of wood we bend it the other way.

I believe that in the Temple of Pallas, as we may see in all other religions, there were open mysteries to be shown to the people, and others, more occult and sublime, to be shown only to the initiated. In these is to be found, in all likelihood, the right degree of love that every man owes to himself. Not a false love that makes us embrace glory, knowledge, wealth, and such things, with a paramount and immoderate affection, as parts of our being; nor a languid and indiscriminate love, whose effect we see in the ivy, that decays and ruins the wall it clasps; but a healthy and well-regulated love, equally beneficial and agreeable.

He who knows the duties of this love and practises them is truly of the cabinet of the Muses; he has reached the summit of human wisdom and human happiness. Such a man, knowing exactly what he owes to himself, finds it written down in his part that he should make the ways of other men and the world serve his purpose; and to do this, that he must contribute to public society the duties and services that he owes to it.

He who does not live in some degree for others, hardly lives for himself. *Know that he who is his own friend is a friend to all the world* (Seneca).

The principal charge we have is 'to every one his own conduct'; and it is for that that we are here.

As the man who should neglect to live a good and godly life, thinking he was discharging his duty by guiding and training others to do so, would be a fool ; so the man who, for his own part, abandons a healthy and cheerful life to help others to live it, takes, in my opinion, a wrong and unnatural course.

I would not have a man, when he takes up an office, spare his attention, his pains, his eloquence, his sweat, and his blood, if need be :

> Not he for his friends whom he loves, or the land
> Of his fathers, will dread to surrender his breath ;   (Horace.)

but only by way of loan, and incidentally, his mind being ever at rest and in health, not indeed inactive, but unaffected by excitement and strong emotions. To be simply acting costs the mind so little, that it is active even in sleep. But it should be set going discreetly. For the body receives the loads laid upon it just as they are ; the mind makes them greater and heavier, often at its own cost, giving them what proportion it pleases.

The same things are done by different men with different degrees of effort and exertion of will-power. The one goes very well without the other.[1] For how many men every day risk their lives in a war which is of no concern to them, and rush into the dangers of a battle the loss of which will not disturb their next night's sleep ! Many a man in his own home and far from those dangers, which he would not have had the courage to face, will be more passionately interested in the issue of that war, and more harried in his soul, than the soldier who gives his life and blood to it.

I was able to discharge public duties without departing from myself a nail's breadth, and to give myself to others without robbing myself of myself.

Those eager and passionate desires hinder rather than advance the execution of what we undertake ; they fill us with impatience when things do not turn out or progress as we wish, and with bitterness and suspicion against those with whom we have to deal. We never carry out a thing well that entirely possesses and rules us :

> In all things passion is an unsure guide.   (Statius.)

The man who uses only his judgement and his discretion

---
[1] The action goes very well without the passion.

in those matters proceeds more cheerfully. He dissembles, he gives way, he puts off very readily, according to the need and the occasion. When he fails to attain his purpose he is neither grieved nor worried, unscathed and ready for a fresh attack. He always walks with the reins in his hand.

In the man who is drunk with purposes so passionate that they tyrannize over him we necessarily observe much unwisdom and wrongheadedness. He is carried away by the impetuosity of his desires. They are reckless movements and, unless Fortune lends a strong helping hand, of little fruit.

Philosophy wills that we put away anger in punishing for injuries received; not that the vengeance may be less, but, on the contrary, that it may be better directed and fall more heavily; which, she thinks, will be frustrated by such impetuosity. Not only does anger turn aside, but of itself it also wearies the arm of him who chastises. This passionate heat benumbs and wastes its strength. As in hastiness, *more haste, less speed* (Q. Curtius). Haste trips itself up, shackles and arrests itself. *Speed gets in its own way* (Seneca). To give an example from what I have observed in everyday life, greed has no greater disturbing element than itself. The more it strains its powers, the less fertile it is. Commonly it grasps wealth more quickly when hidden under the mask of liberality.

A gentleman, a very worthy person and my friend, was in danger of going out of his mind by a too passionate affection and too assiduous attention to the interests of his master, a Prince. This master thus portrayed himself to me: 'That he can estimate the gravity of misfortunes as well as any man; but when he sees there is no remedy, he decides at once to bear them. In other cases, after giving the necessary orders, which he is enabled to do promptly by reason of the quickness of his intellect, he calmly awaits the issue.'

Indeed I have seen him at work, very cool and collected, maintaining his freedom of action and his serenity in the midst of very great and thorny affairs. He appears to me greater and more capable when Fortune frowns than when she smiles upon him. His defeats are more honourable to him than his victories, and his sorrows than his triumphs.

Consider that even in actions that are vain and frivolous,

in chess, tennis, and similar games, the ardent and eager intrusion of passionate desire straightway throws the mind and the limbs into a state of disorder and a disability to discriminate ; we are blinded and hampered by our action. The man who bears himself more soberly towards gain and loss has always his wits about him ; the less excited and impassioned he is over the game, the more safely and advantageously will he play it.

For the rest, we hinder the mind's hold and grip by giving it too many things to seize. Some things should be merely presented to her, others fastened upon her, others incorporated with her. She may see and feel all things, but she must feed only on herself ; and she must be taught what properly concerns her, and what is properly of her having and substance.

The laws of Nature teach us exactly what we need. When the sages have told us that no man is poor according to Nature, and that every man is poor in the opinion of the world, they thus make a subtle distinction between the desires which are natural and those which are the result of our disorderly imagination. Those whose bounds are in view are Nature's ; those which flee before us and which we cannot catch up with, are ours.

Poverty in worldly goods is easily cured ; poverty of the soul is impossible of cure :

> If what for man's enough enough could be,
> It were enough ; but that not being so,
> How can I e'er believe that any wealth
> Will ever fill my mind with real content ? (LUCILIUS.)

Socrates, seeing a great quantity of riches, jewels, and costly furniture, being paraded through his city, remarked, ' What a number of things there are for which I have no desire ! '

Metrodorus lived on twelve ounces a day, Epicurus on less. Metrocles slept in winter among the sheep, in summer in the porticoes of the temples. *Nature provides for all that Nature needs* (Seneca). Cleanthes lived by the labour of his hands, and boasted that Cleanthes, if he would, could maintain yet another Cleanthes.

If that which Nature exactly and originally requires of us to keep us alive is too little (and indeed, how little it is, and how cheaply our life may be supported, cannot be better expressed than by this consideration, that it is so little that by its littleness it escapes the grip and shock of Fortune), let us allow ourselves something over and above. Let us also call the habits and condition of each one of us, Nature ; let us rate and treat ourselves by this standard ; let us stretch our appurtenances and our calculations thus far. For thus far, it seems to me, we have some excuse. Habit is a second Nature, and no less powerful. What my habit lacks, I seem to lack myself. And I would almost as soon be deprived of life as that the style of living which I have so long enjoyed should be greatly diminished and curtailed.

I am no longer in a condition for a great change, nor inclined to plunge into a new and untried course of life, not even a better one. It is too late for me to become other than I am. And as, if some great windfall were at this moment to drop into my hands, I should feel aggrieved that it had not come at a time when I was able to enjoy it :

> Of what advantage wealth to me,
> If I to use it am not free ? (HORACE.)

so I should deplore any inward acquisition.

It were almost better never to become an honest man than so late, or to have learned to live well when there is no life left in us. I, who am about to take my departure, would readily resign to any man who came to me all the worldly wisdom I am acquiring for human intercourse. Mustard after dinner !

I have no use for the blessings I am no longer able to turn to account. What is the use of knowledge to one who has no head left ? It is wrong and unkind of Fortune to offer us gifts which fill us with righteous anger that they failed us in their due season. Guide me no more, I can go no further.

Of all the qualities of an excellent character patience is enough for us.

Give the capacity of an excellent treble voice to a singer with rotten lungs, and eloquence to a hermit consigned to the deserts of Arabia !

It needs no art to fall ; the end is found of itself at the conclusion of every affair. My world is at an end, my form emptied ; I belong entirely to the past, and am bound to authorize it and conform my departure to it.

I mean this [by way of example], that the recent eclipse of ten days by the Pope [1] has so taken me aback, that I cannot quite become reconciled to it. I belong to the years in which we counted differently. A custom so ancient and time-honoured claims me and calls me back to it. I am constrained to be something of a heretic on that point, unable to tolerate any innovation even for the better. My imagination, in spite of my teeth, keeps thrusting me ten days forward or backward, and grumbling into my ears, 'This rule concerns those who are to come.'

Even if health, sweet as it is, happens to revisit me now and again, it is rather to give me cause for regret than possession of it; I have now no place to harbour it. Time forsakes me, without which nothing can be possessed. O how little account I should make of those great elective dignities which I see in the world, and which are given only to men who are about to leave it, in which the chief consideration is not how fit they are to fulfil their duties but how short a time they will do so! At their very entry others look to their exit.

In short, here I am in course of finishing this man, not remaking another. By long habit this form of mine has passed into substance, and Fortune into Nature.

I say then, that every one of us feeble creatures is excusable for regarding as his own that which is comprised under this measure. But beyond those limits too all is confusion; it is the largest extent we can grant to our claims. The more we enlarge our needs and our possessions, the more do we expose ourselves to the blows of Fortune and adversity. The range of our desires ought to be circumscribed and restricted to a short limit of the nearest and most contiguous commodities; and their course ought, moveover, to be directed not in a straight line that ends elsewhere, but in a circle, the two points of which, after a short circuit, meet and terminate in ourselves.

Actions which are performed without this reflexion, I mean near and essential reflexion, like those of the avaricious and ambitious and so many others who run straight ahead, whose course bears them ever forward, are erroneous and diseased actions.

---

[1] An allusion to the reform in the calendar made by Pope Gregory XIII in 1582.

Most of our professions are histrionic. *All the world's a stage.*[1] We must play our part as we should, but as the part of a borrowed personage. We must not make a reality out of a mask and outward appearance, nor of a strange person, our own. We cannot distinguish between the skin and the shirt. It is enough to paint[2] the face without painting the heart. I see some who transform and transubstantiate themselves into as many new shapes and new beings as the offices they take upon themselves; who strut and swell to the very liver and bowels, and carry their dignity even to their closet. I could not teach them to distinguish between the bonnetings intended for their person and those intended for their office, or their retinue or their mule. *They are so wrapt up in their fortunes that they unlearn their nature* (Q. Curtius). They swell and puff up their souls and their natural speech to the height of their seat of authority.

The Mayor and Montaigne have always been two, very distinctly separated. Though we are lawyers or financiers we must not ignore the knavery there is in those callings. An honest man is not accountable for the vices or the follies of his profession, and therefore need not refuse to practise it. It is the custom of his country, and there is profit in it. We must live by the world and make the best of it, such as we find it. But the judgement of an Emperor ought to be above his imperial power, and should look upon and consider it as an extraneous accident; and he himself ought to know how to enjoy a separate existence and reveal himself like any Jack or Peter, at least to himself.

I cannot pledge myself so deeply and so entirely. When my will has commanded me to take a side I am not so forcibly bound to it that my understanding is infected. In the present broils of our State my interests have not made me blind to the laudable qualities of our adversaries, nor the reprehensible qualities in the leaders of my own party. It is usual to worship everything on one's own side; for my part I do not even pardon most of the things done on mine. A good work does not lose its charm for arguing against my cause.

---

[1] Mundus universus exercet histrioniam (Petronius).

[2] Literally 'whiten with flour', after the manner of the stage Pierrots.

Except with regard to the knot of the controversy[1] I have kept myself in a state of equanimity and absolute indifference. *And beyond the requirements of war I bear no special hatred.* Which is a source of satisfaction to me, since I observe that most men sin in the opposite direction. *Let him who cannot appeal to reason appeal to the passions* (Cicero). Those who extend their anger and hatred beyond the dispute in question, as most people do, show that it is due to some other, some personal, reason; just as, when a man has been cured of an ulcer, and the fever continues, it is clear that it must have another more hidden cause.

The fact is that they have no feeling against the cause in general, and in so far as it injures the interest of all and of the State. But they hate it only in so far as it galls them in their private interests. That is why they are stung to a particular passion, to a degree beyond justice and common sense. *They did not agree in blaming all things, but each carped at such as interested him personally* (Livy).

I would have the advantage on our side, but I am not beside myself with anger if it is not. I adhere firmly to the soundest of the parties, but I have no ambition to be specially remarked as an enemy of the others, and more hostile than is consistent with common sense.

I very strongly condemn this vicious form of reasoning: 'He is of the League, for he admires the charm of Monsieur de Guise; He is astonished at the King of Navarre's activity, therefore he is a Huguenot; He picks holes in the King's morals, so he must be a rebel at heart.'[2] And I did not even admit the authorities to be right in condemning a book, because the author classed a heretic among the best poets of this century.[3]

Dare we not say of a thief that his hair is nicely parted? And because she is a prostitute, must she also be syphilitic? Did they, in the wisest ages, revoke the proud title of Capitolinus, which they had previously given to Marcus Manlius, as the preserver of public religion and liberty? Did they suppress the memory of his liberality and his feats of arms, and the military rewards granted to his

---

[1] The religious question.   [2] Montaigne was guilty of all three crimes.
[3] Montaigne evidently means the Papal authorities in Rome, who dragged him over the coals for having spoken so highly of a French poet who was not a Catholic.

valour, because he afterwards aspired to royalty, to the prejudice of his country's laws?

Take a dislike to a barrister and to-morrow you will deny his eloquence. I have elsewhere touched upon the zeal which drives good people to similar faults. For my part I am quite able to say, 'He does this wickedly, and that virtuously.' So too, when prognostics are falsified and affairs turn out unluckily, they will have it that every one, in his own cause, is blind and dull-witted; that our convictions and judgements should subserve, not the truth, but our plans and desires. I would rather err towards the other extreme; so greatly do I fear to be misled by my desires. Besides, I am rather tenderly distrustful of the things I wish.

I have in my time been astounded to see with what wonderful and indiscriminating ease the people have allowed themselves to be led by the nose and manœuvred into believing and hoping whatever has pleased, and served the purpose of, their leaders, in spite of a hundred mistakes one on top of the other, despite dreams and phantasms. I am no longer astonished at those who were cozened by the tomfooleries of Apollonius [1] and Mahomet. Their sense and understanding are entirely drowned by their passions. Their judgement leaves them no choice but that which smiles upon them and flatters their cause.

I had observed this in a supreme degree in the first of our feverish factions. The other,[2] which has since been born in imitation of it, surpasses it. From which I conclude that it is an attitude inseparable from popular errors. When the first error has started on its course others follow, and they drive one another forward, like the waves following the wind. Whoever is able to gainsay them, and does not wander with the common herd, is not a member of the body.

But, indeed, we wrong the just side when we try to bolster it up with fraud. I have ever been against that practice. That is a remedy that is of no avail except for sick brains;

---

[1] 'Apollonius of Tyana was born about the same time as Jesus Christ. His life is related in so fabulous a manner by his disciples that we are at a loss to discover whether he was a sage, an impostor, or a fanatic' (Gibbon). Froude also gives a short account of him in his *Short Studies*.

[2] Respectively, the Protestants and the League.

for the healthy there are not only more honest but surer ways for keeping up our spirits and explaining away mishaps.

Heaven has not seen, and will not again see in the future, so serious a discord as that between Caesar and Pompey. Yet in those noble souls I observe, if I am not mistaken, great moderation in their dealings with one another. It was a rivalry in honour and power, which did not transport them to a blind and furious hatred, and was free from malice and detraction. In their sharpest encounters I can discover some remnant of respect and goodwill; and so I conclude that, if it had been possible, each of them would have liked to effect his purpose without, rather than with, the downfall of his competitor.

How different is the case of Marius and Sylla! Think it over!

We must not pursue our passions and interests so madly. As in my younger days I used to resist the progress of love which I felt to be gaining too rapidly upon me, and strove to prevent it becoming so pleasing as in the end to vanquish and hold me at its mercy; so I do likewise on all other occasions whenever desire gets the better of my will. I lean to the opposite side of its inclination, as I see it plunging ahead and making itself drunk with its own wine. I avoid feeding its pleasure to such a degree that I cannot get the better of it without cruel loss.

The souls that, through their dullness, only half see things, enjoy this happiness, that noxious things are less hurtful to them; it is a spiritual leprosy that has some semblance of health, and such health as Philosophy does not in any way despise. That is no reason, however, for calling it wisdom, as we often do. And so somebody, in ancient times, made sport of Diogenes who, in the depth of winter and stark naked, was hugging a snow-figure to test his endurance. Seeing him in this attitude the man said, 'Are you very cold now?' 'Not a bit,' replied Diogenes. 'Then why do you think it so difficult and so exemplary to do what you are doing?'

To measure fortitude we must necessarily know suffering.

But as for those souls which are to meet with adversities and the outrages of Fortune in all their depth and sharpness, to feel all their weight and taste their natural bitterness, let them do their best to avoid piling up the causes, and to parry their advances.

What did King Cotys do ? He paid liberally for the beautiful and costly vessel that had been offered to him : but seeing that it was particularly fragile he straightway broke it himself, to remove betimes so easy an occasion for anger against his servants. In like manner I have generally avoided having my affairs mixed up with others', and have not been anxious to have my estate adjoining those of my relations and others with whom I am to be linked in close friendship ; which usually gives rise to estrangement and disagreement.

I used to be fond of games of chance with cards and dice. I have long given them up for this sole reason that, however well I appeared to bear my losses, I could not help feeling inwardly annoyed.

A man of honour, who must take to heart a contradiction or an affront, who is not ready to take a foolish answer as payment and consolation for his loss, should avoid being mixed up with any dubious affair and any dispute that might lead to a quarrel.

I avoid any man of melancholy disposition and a surly temper as I would the plague ; and, unless forced by duty, I do not meddle with a subject that I cannot discuss disinterestedly and without excitement. *It is easier not to begin than to stop* (Seneca). The surest way then is to be prepared beforehand for every occasion.

I know well that some wise men have chosen another way and have not feared to clutch and come to grips with many subjects. Those men are confident in their strength, under which they take shelter in all kinds of adverse fortunes, making their power of endurance wrestle with disaster :

> Even as a rock
> That juts far out into the mighty main,
> Bare to the winds' brunt, a target for the sea,
> All stress, all menace both of sky and deep
> Outfaces, and itself remains unmoved. (VIRGIL.)

Let us not attempt to imitate these examples ; we should not succeed. They will steadfastly and resolutely, without any emotion, witness the destruction of their country, which once commanded and possessed all their affection. That is too difficult and rude a task for ordinary souls like ours. Cato gave up to it the noblest life that ever was. We other little men must fly the storm long before it comes; we must obey our apprehensions and not trust to endurance, and dodge the blows we cannot parry.

Zeno, seeing Chremonides, a youth whom he loved, approaching to sit beside him, immediately started up. When Cleanthes asked him the reason he said, 'I have heard that the doctors especially prescribe tranquillity, and forbid excitement, for all kinds of risings.'

Socrates does not say, 'Do not surrender to the charms of beauty; resist it, do your best to oppose it. Fly from it, he says, avoid either seeing or meeting it, as if it were a powerful poison that darts and strikes from a distance.' And his good disciple,[1] imagining or recounting, but I think recounting rather than imagining, the rare perfections of the great Cyrus, makes him distrustful of his power to withstand the attractions of the divine beauty of that illustrious Panthea, his captive, and charging another, who had less liberty than he, to visit and guard her.

And the Holy Ghost in like manner: 'Lead us not into temptation.' We do not pray that our reason may not be combated and vanquished by lust, but that it shall not even be put to the proof; that we may not be brought to a pass in which we have even to suffer the approaches, the solicitations and temptations of sin. And we entreat our Lord to keep our conscience at peace, fully and completely delivered from all dealings with evil.

Those who say that they have gained the mastery over their passion for revenge, or some other kind of troublesome passion, often tell the truth as things are, but not as they were. They speak to us now that the causes of their error have been developed and advanced by themselves. But go further back; recall those causes at their beginning; there you will take them unawares. Do they mean to say that their sin is less for being of longer duration, and that of a wrong beginning the sequel can be right?

Whoever desires the good of his country, as I do, without fretting or pining, will be pained, but not stunned, to see it threatened either with ruin or with a no less ruinous

---

[1] Xenophon.

continuance. Poor vessel, that the waves, the winds, and the pilot toss and worry with such contrary intention!

> Dragged in different ways
> By master, waves and winds. (BUCHANAN.)

He who does not gape after the favour of Princes, as after a thing he cannot do without, is not greatly piqued by the coolness of their reception and countenance, nor by the inconstancy of their affections. He who does not brood over his children or his honours with slavish fondness, will manage to live comfortably after he has lost them.

He who does good chiefly for his own satisfaction will not be much put out when men judge his actions contrary to his merit. A quarter of an ounce of patience will be a sufficient remedy against such troubles. I find that recipe effectual, making up for the beginnings as cheaply as I can; and by its means I find I have escaped much trouble and many difficulties. With very little effort I arrest the first swing of my emotions, and abandon the subject which begins to be troublesome, and before it carries me away.

He who does not arrest the start has no power to arrest the course. He who cannot shut them out will not expel them once they are in. He who cannot accomplish the beginning will not accomplish the end. Nor will he resist the fall who has not been able to resist the push. *For, once severed from reason, the passions rush headlong; human frailty trusts in itself, heedless it ventures into the open sea, and can find no harbour in which to anchor* (Cicero).

I feel betimes the low winds, forerunners of the storm, rumbling and searching for an entry into me. *The soul is shaken long before it is vanquished.*

> As rising winds that, in the forest caught,
> Murmur, and, rolling a dull roar along,
> Bode storm to sailors. (VIRGIL.)

How often have I done myself a very manifest injustice, to avoid the danger of having a worse done me by the judges after an age of vexations, of vile and dirty practices, more hostile to my nature than fire and torments! *We must shun lawsuits by all legitimate, and even a little less than legitimate, means. It is not only generous, but sometimes even profitable, to yield a little of our right* (Cicero).

If we were really wise we should rejoice and boast, like

a certain young gentleman of very noble family, whom I one day heard, very naïvely and with great glee, telling everybody that his mother had lost her lawsuit, as she might have lost her cough, her fever, or some other thing very troublesome to keep. Even the favours which Fortune may have bestowed on me, through my being related to or friendly with people of supreme authority in such things, I have to the best of my powers carefully and conscientiously avoided employing to the prejudice of others; and I have never rated my pretensions above their real value.

In short, I have laboured so hard that (may I say with the help of luck!) I am to this day virgin of lawsuits, though on many occasions I have been tempted to make use of the law, having very good rights on my side, if I had been inclined to give ear to the temptation; and virgin of quarrels. I shall soon have spent a long life without having either given or received serious offence, and without ever hearing worse than my own name; a rare grace of Heaven!

Our greatest disturbances have ridiculous springs and causes. How disastrous to our last Duke of Burgundy was a quarrel about a cartload of sheepskins![1] And was not the engraving of a seal the primary and principal cause of the most dreadful upheaval that this machine has ever suffered? For Pompey and Caesar are only the offshoots and the sequel of the other two. And I have seen in my time the wisest heads in this realm meeting, with great ceremony and at great public expense, to discuss treaties and agreements which were meantime really and absolutely decided by the chattering ladies in a boudoir, and the whim of some little woman.

The poets very well understood this when they put Greece and Asia to fire and sword for an apple.[2]

Ask this man why he stakes his honour and life on his sword and dagger; let him tell you where is the source of the quarrel; he cannot do so without blushing, so frivolous is the occasion.

Before beginning a thing, only a little discretion is needed; but once you are embarked, all the tackle is on

[1] A reference to the war between Charles the Bold and the Swiss in 1476. The next sentence refers to the civil war between Marius and Sylla.
[2] Allusion to the Judgement of Paris, which was the primary cause of the Trojan war.

the stretch. Greater, more difficult and important measures are then needed.

How much easier it is not to enter in, than it is to come out again!

Now, our proceeding should be the opposite of that of the reed, which at its first springing sends up a long straight stem, but afterwards, as if it were weary and out of breath, forms frequent and thick knots, as it were so many pauses, which show that it has lost its first vigour and firmness. We must rather begin coolly and leisurely, and keep our breath and strenuous efforts for the stress and completion of the business.

We guide a business at the beginning, and hold it at our mercy; but afterwards, when set going, it is the business that guides us and drags us along, and we have to follow.

Yet I do not mean to say that this plan of conduct has relieved me of all difficulty, and that I have not often been at pains to curb and bridle my passions. They are not always to be ruled according to the magnitude of the causes, and often enter into us violently and unexpectedly. In any case one may save and gain a great deal by it, except those who, in doing good, are not content with any gain, if there is no reputation to be made by it. For in truth such a result is only valued by each one in himself. You are better contented, but not more esteemed, for having reformed before joining in the dance, and before the matter was in sight. Yet not in this only, but in all other duties of life, the path of those who aim at honour is very different to that followed by those whose aim is order and reason.

I see men who rashly and furiously enter the lists, and slacken as they run. As Plutarch says that those who, owing to bashfulness, are weak and ready to grant whatever may be asked of them, and afterwards as ready to break their word and recant; so he who enters lightly into a quarrel is apt to get out of it just as lightly. This same difficulty which keeps me from cutting in would spur me on when I was once in the swing and heated. It is a bad principle: when once in it, go on or die miserably.

'Undertake coldly', said Bias, 'but pursue hotly.' For want of prudence, men are in danger of wanting heart, which is still less tolerable.

Most of the settlements of our quarrels nowadays are disgraceful and full of deceit; we only seek to save appearances, and at the same time we betray and disown our true intentions. We plaster the fact; we know how and with what meaning we have declared it, and those who are present know it, as well as our friends whom we wanted to make aware of our advantage. At the expense of our sincerity and honour and courage we disown our intention and seek to hide our heads in falsehood in order to come to an agreement. We give ourselves the lie to save a lie we have given.

You must not consider whether your action and your word may admit of another interpretation; you must henceforth uphold your true and sincere interpretation, whatever it may cost you. Your virtue and your conscience are appealed to; they are not things to be hidden behind a mask. Let us leave those mean shifts and expedients to the chicanery of the Law Courts.

The excuses and reparations I see made every day to purge away the want of judgement appear to me more hateful than the want of judgement itself. It would be better to offend your adversary a second time than to offend yourself by giving him such reparation. You defied him when excited and angry, and you are about to appease and flatter him in your cooler and better mood; thus you give way to him more than you had advanced.

Nothing a gentleman can say appears to me so wicked as his unsaying of it appears discreditable to him, when it is a recantation that is wrested from him by authority; since obstinacy is more excusable in him than pusillanimity.

I find it as easy to avoid passions as I find it difficult to moderate them. *They are more easily rooted out of the soul than held in check*. If a man cannot attain that noble impassibility of the Stoics let him take refuge in the bosom of this vulgar callousness of mine. What those men did through virtue I bring myself to do by temperament. The middle region harbours storms; the two extremes, those of the philosophers and rustics, concur in tranquillity and happiness:

> Happy was he whose wit availed to grasp
> The origin of things, who trampled low
> The thronging horrors of unpitying Fate,
> And roarings of unsated Acheron!
> Blest too is he who knows the rural Gods,
> Pan and grey-haired Sylvanus and the Nymphs,
> Sweet sisters! (VIRGIL.)

All things are weak and tender at their birth. Wherefore we should have our eyes open to the beginnings of a thing. For, as in its littleness we can discover no danger, so when it is grown it is too late to discover the remedy. I might have found it harder to digest a million troubles that I should have encountered every day in an ambitious career, than to arrest the natural inclination which bore me to it:

> I shrink with dread
> From raising too conspicuously my head. (HORACE.)

All public actions are liable to be interpreted uncertainly and differently, for there are too many heads to judge them. Some say of this civic function of mine (and I am glad to say a few words about it, not that it is worth mentioning, but to serve as an example of my conduct in such matters), that I behaved as one who is not easily enough stirred to action and shows too languid an interest; and they were by no means far wrong. I endeavour to keep my soul and my thoughts at rest. *At all times calm by nature, and more so as the result of age* (Q. Cicero). And if at times they break out into a rude and cutting attack it is, indeed, against my will.

Yet from this natural listlessness it would be wrong to infer any proof of incapacity (for lack of diligence and lack of sense are two different things), and still less any want of recognition or ingratitude towards those citizens, who did their very utmost to testify their goodwill to me both before and after they had come to know me, and did me much more honour by my re-election [1] than by their first conferring that office upon me. I wish them all possible good, and, indeed, if opportunities had offered I should have spared no pains to be serviceable to them. I have been as active in serving them as on my own behalf. They are good people, warlike and generous, therefore amenable to obedience and discipline, and, if well guided, capable of being made good use of.

They also say that my term of office passed without leaving any trace or mark. That is good! They accuse me of inaction at a time when almost everybody else was convicted of doing too much. I have an impatient activity when

---

[1] On the expiration of his first term of office, Montaigne was re-elected Mayor in 1583.

my will carries me along. But that kind of eagerness is hostile to perseverance. If a man would expect a service of me in conformity with my character let him employ me in a business that needs vigour and freedom, where a direct, short, and even hazardous conduct is necessary; there I might do something. If it is to be a lengthy business, needing cunning, labour, artifice, and tortuous methods, he would do better to apply to some other.

Not all important offices are difficult. I was prepared to be a little more energetic if there had been great need of it. For it is in my power to do something more than I do, or than I care to do. So far as I know I never neglected to move in a matter when duty really required it of me. I readily neglected those things in which ambition mingles with, and hides under the name of, duty. Those are the things that most often fill the eyes and ears of people, and satisfy them. Not the thing but the semblance pays them. If they hear no noise they think we are asleep.

My humour is the opposite of a noisy humour. I could easily check a disturbance without being disturbed, and punish a piece of irregularity without changing countenance. Do I stand in need of anger and heat? I borrow it and put it on like a mask. My manners are blunt, rather tame than fierce. I do not condemn a magistrate when he goes to sleep, provided that those under his charge sleep with him. The laws sleep too. For my part I commend a gliding life, without bustle or glitter, *neither abject and submissive, nor puffed up* (Cicero). My fortune will have it so. I was born of a family which has lived quietly, without brilliance and without bustle, and from all times particularly ambitious of a character for probity.

The men of our day are so bred up in excitement and ostentation that goodness, moderation, equability, steadiness and such unobtrusive and obscure qualities are no more appreciated. Uneven bodies make themselves felt; the smooth and polished may be handled without feeling them. Sickness is felt; health, little or not at all, nor are the things which relieve us, compared with those which grieve us.

We work for our own reputation and private advantage, not for the public weal, when we reserve for the public square what we can do in the Council-chamber, and in the full glare of noonday what we might have done the night before; and when we are jealous of doing ourselves what our colleague can do equally well. So some of the surgeons in Greece were wont to perform the operations of their art on platforms in sight of the passers-by, to attract more custom and patients. They imagine that good rules cannot be heard except to the blare of trumpets.

Ambition is not a sin for little fellows, and for such endeavours as ours. Some one said to Alexander, 'Your father will leave you a great empire, easy to govern and peaceful.' The boy was envious of his father's victories, and of the justice of his rule. He would not have wished to possess the whole universe in peace and inactivity.

Alcibiades, in Plato's Dialogue, prefers to die young, handsome, rich, noble, and eminently learned, rather than not to advance beyond his present condition.

This malady is perhaps excusable in so strong and full a soul. When these puny and dwarfed little souls flatter themselves, baboonlike, and think to spread their name for having delivered a correct judgement or continued to change the guards at the city gates, the more they hope to raise their heads the more do they show their backsides. These petty services have neither body nor life; they vanish in the first telling, and are only carried from one street corner to another. Tell it boldly to your son and your valet, like that ancient who, having no other auditor of his praises and witness of his valour, boasted to his housemaid, exclaiming, 'O Perrette, what a brave and excellent man is your master!'[1] Tell yourself of it, for want of a better, like a councillor of my acquaintance who, having disgorged a boatload of paragraphs, with as much effort as inappropriateness, retired from the Council-chamber to the Palace urinal, and was heard mumbling very devoutly between his teeth, *Not unto us, O Lord, not unto us, but unto thy name give glory* (Psalms). If he cannot get it out of another, let him pay himself out of his own purse.

Fame does not prostitute herself so cheaply. The rare and exemplary deeds which deserve her would not tolerate the company of that numberless crowd of little everyday actions. The marble will exalt your titles as much as you

[1] 'Dionysia, see how I am no longer proud and vainglorious!' Plutarch, according to Amyot.

please for having patched up a bit of old wall or cleaned out a public gutter ; but men who have any sense will not. Renown does not follow all good actions unless they are accompanied by rarity and difficulty. Nay, according to the Stoics esteem is not even due to every action born of virtue ; and they will not admit that we should even approve a man who, from temperance, abstains from a blear-eyed old woman.

Those who have known the admirable qualities of Scipio Africanus deny him the honour that Panaetius gives him of having kept his hands off money gifts, since it was an honour that he shared with all his age.

We have the pleasures suitable to our lot ; let us not usurp those of greatness. Ours are more natural, and the more substantial and sure for being more humble. Since we do not refuse ambition for conscience' sake let us at least refuse it for ambition's sake. Let us despise that low and beggarly craving after honour and renown that makes us cringe for it to all sorts of people. *What praise is that which is to be sought in the market-place* (Cicero), by abject means and at any price however degrading ? It is dishonour to be so honoured.

Let us learn not to be more greedy than we are deserving of fame. To be puffed up with every useful and harmless deed is good enough for people with whom such deeds are uncommon and extraordinary ; they will value them at the price they cost them.

According as a good deed is more brilliant I discount its goodness, since I suspect that it has been performed for its brilliance rather than for its goodness ; displayed is half sold. Those works are more graceful which slip from the hands of the workman, heedlessly and noiselessly, and which are afterwards picked up by some honest man and rescued from obscurity, to be thrust into the light for their own sake. *To me all things appear more praiseworthy that are done without vainglory and unwitnessed by the people* (Cicero), said the most vainglorious man in the world.

I had but to continue and conserve, which are noiseless actions, passing unperceived. Innovation makes a great show but it is out of the question in these days when we are hard pressed and when innovation is just what we have to stand up against.

Abstention from doing is often as noble as doing, but is less exposed to the light of day ; and the little good there is in me lies almost entirely in that direction.

In short, in my term of office as Mayor, opportunities were in keeping with my disposition, for which I am very thankful to them. Is there any one who wishes to be ill that he may see his physician at work, and would not a physician deserve corporal punishment who wished the plague upon us that he might practise his art ? I never shared that wicked and common enough feeling that would desire a disturbed and diseased state of affairs in the city, that my administration might be magnified and honoured ; I heartily lent a shoulder to relieving and lightening them.

If any man refuses to give me credit for the order, the even and silent tranquillity which accompanied my administration, he cannot at least deprive me of the share that belongs to me by right of my good fortune. And I am so built that I would as soon be lucky as wise, and as soon owe my successes purely to the grace of God as to the intervention of my action.

I had explained elaborately enough to the world my unfitness for such public duties. There is something in me worse than my unfitness, which is that I hardly regret it, and hardly try to cure it, in view of the course of life I have mapped out for myself. I did not satisfy myself any more than I did others in this business ; but I almost succeeded as far as I had promised myself, and greatly exceeded the promises I had given to those with whom I had to deal. For my promises are usually of such a nature that I can keep them better than I expected, and perform more than I promise.

I am sure that I left no cause for offence or hatred behind me. As for leaving regret and desire, at the very least I know well that I did not greatly aspire to it :

> Would'st thou have me put faith in such a monster,
> Mark not the sea's smooth face and tranquil waves ? (VIRGIL.)

CHAPTER 11
OF CRIPPLES

TWO or three years ago the year was shortened by ten days in France. How many changes were expected to follow this reform ! It was literally moving heaven and earth at the same time. And yet nothing has budged from its place : my neighbours find the right moment for sowing and reaping, for their business opportunities, their harmful and lucky days, at the very same times that had been assigned to them from time immemorial. We were not sensible of any error in our habits, nor are we now sensible of any improvement. So much uncertainty is there in all things ; so gross, obscure, and obtuse is our perception !

They say that this correction might have been carried out in a less inconvenient way by following the example of Augustus and leaving out, for several years, the bissextus, which in any case is an awkward and troublesome day, until we had made a full settlement of the debt (which has not even been done by this correction, for we still remain a few days in arrears). And so by the same means we could provide for the future by arranging that after the revolution of so many years that supernumerary day might be eclipsed for good ; then our miscalculation would henceforth not exceed twenty-four hours.

We have no other computation of time but by years. The world has employed it so many centuries, and yet it is a measure we have not yet succeeded in fixing, and of such a nature that we are every day in doubt what form other nations have variously given to it, and what used to be their custom.

What if it be true, as some say, that the heavens, as they grow older, contract and come nearer to us, throwing us into an uncertainty even of hours and days, and of months, since Plutarch says that even in his time Astrology had not been able to determine the motion of the moon ? We are in a pretty way to keep a record of past events !

I was just ruminating, as I often do, on this theme, What a free and vague instrument is the human reason ! I generally observe that, when a matter is set before them, men are more ready to waste their time in seeking the reason of it than in seeking the truth of it. They leave the things to take care of themselves and trifle over the causes. Amusing triflers![1]

The knowledge of causes concerns only him who has the guidance of things, not us who only have to suffer them, and have the full and absolute use of them according to our nature, without penetrating into their origin and essence. And wine is not any more agreeable to the man who knows its primary properties. On the contrary; both body and soul disturb and sophisticate their right to enjoy the world by bringing in the pretensions of science. [We are concerned with effects, not at all with means.] To determine and to know is the part of the ruler and master, as well as to give; that of the inferior, the subject, the learner, is to enjoy and accept.

Let us return to our habit. They stride over facts, but they diligently investigate their consequences. They usually begin thus, 'How can that be?' They should say, 'But is it so?' Our reason is capable of furnishing a hundred other worlds and discovering their beginnings and structure. It lacks neither matter nor foundation. Let it run on. It will build as well on the void as on the full, out of nothingness as out of matter:

> Fit but to give solidity to smoke. (PERSIUS.)

I find that in almost every case we might say, 'That is not so.' And I should often make use of that reply, but I dare not; for people will exclaim that that is an attempt to avoid discussion, the result of mental feebleness and ignorance. And I am generally reduced to join the company in juggling with words and discussing trivial subjects and tales which I entirely disbelieve. Besides that it is certainly rather rude and aggressive to flatly deny a stated fact. And few men will resist the temptation, especially when they find a difficulty in persuading, to declare that they have seen the thing, or to cite witnesses whose authority will put a stopper on our contradiction.

In this way we know the foundations and causes of a thousand things that never were; and the world skirmishes

---

[1] *Ils laissent là les choses et s'amusent à traiter les causes. Plaisants causeurs!* Montaigne's fondness for playing on words sometimes leaves the translator stranded.

with a thousand questions of which both the *pros* and the *cons* are false. *The false is so much akin to the true that a wise man should not trust himself in so dangerous a position* (Cicero).

Truth and falsehood are alike in face; they walk and carry themselves alike, and they taste alike; to us they appear the same. It seems to me that we are not only loosely on our guard against deception but that we court and invite its trammels. We love to embroil ourselves in unreality, as being conformable to our being.

I have witnessed the birth of many miracles in my time. Even though they are smothered as soon as born we are none the less able to foresee the course they would have taken if they had lived to their full age. For it is only a matter of finding the end of the string, then we may unravel as much as we please. And the distance is greater from nothing to the smallest thing in the world than from this to the greatest.

Now the first who are imbued with the strangeness of the thing, when they begin to circulate their story, find, from the opposition they meet with, where the difficulty of persuasion lies, and proceed to caulk up that place with some spurious piece. Besides that, *through the appetite innate in man industriously to feed rumours* (Livy), it naturally goes against our conscience to give back what has been lent to us without a little interest, and some addition of our own. The private error first creates the public error, and in its turn the public error afterwards creates the private error.

Thus it comes about that this whole edifice goes on being built up and shaped by one hand after another in such a way that the remotest witness knows more about it than the nearest, and the last informed believes it more firmly than the first. It is a natural progression. For whoever believes a thing thinks it a work of kindness to persuade another to believe it; and for that purpose he is not afraid to add out of his own invention as much as he sees to be necessary to his tale to meet the resistance or the lack of imagination he expects in others.

I myself, though I am singularly conscientious about lying, and am not particularly anxious to give credibility and authority to what I say, observe none the less that, when I become excited over some matter in hand, either through another's opposition or my own heat in the telling, I magnify and inflate my theme by voice and gesture, by the force and energy of words, as well as by extension and amplification, not without prejudice to the naked truth. On the understanding however that, for the first who pulls me up and asks for the plain and unvarnished truth, I straightway drop my ardour and give it to him without exaggeration, without bombast or padding. A lively and noisy style of speaking, as mine is usually, is apt to run into hyperbole.

There is nothing to which men are ordinarily more prone than to push their beliefs; when ordinary means fail us, we add command, violence, fire, and sword. It is a misfortune to have come to such a pass that the best touchstone of truth is the multitude of believers, in a crowd where the fools so much outnumber the wise. *As if there were anything so common in the world as error!* (Cicero.) *A fine evidence of sanity is the multitude of the insane!* (St. Augustine.)

It is a difficult thing to set up a decided judgement in the face of commonly prevailing opinions. The first persuasion, taken from the subject itself, seizes the simple; from them it spreads to the clever, under authority of the number and antiquity of the testimonies. For my part, in a matter on which I would not believe one, I would not believe a hundred and one. I do not judge opinions by age.

It is not long since one of our Princes, in whom the gout had spoiled a fine nature and a cheerful disposition, allowed himself to be so strongly persuaded, on the strength of a report which had reached him of the marvellous operations of a priest who, by means of words and gestures, cured all maladies, that he made a long journey to see him, and, by the power of his imagination, so persuaded his legs that he sent them to sleep for some hours, and obtained from them the service they had long forgotten.

If Fortune had allowed five or six such incidents to accumulate, they were capable of making this miracle a natural thing. They afterwards found so much simplicity and so little cunning in the architect of those works, that he was thought too contemptible to be punished.[1] As

[1] He was probably in danger of being accused of witchcraft.

would be thought of most such things, if we traced them back to their home. *We wonder at the things that deceive us by their distance* (Seneca). So our sight often presents us strange phenomena at a distance, which vanish as they come nearer. *Rumour is never quite cleared up* (Q. Curtius).

It is wonderful from what unreal beginnings and trifling causes such widespread ideas usually proceed! That alone makes investigation difficult. For whilst we seek out solid and weighty causes and purposes, worthy of so great a fame, we miss the real ones; they escape our view by reason of their littleness. And, indeed, such researches need a very wise, diligent and keen inquirer, one who is impartial and unprejudiced.

To this hour all those miracles and strange phenomena have hidden from me. I have seen no more evident monstrosity and miracle in the world than myself. By use and time one becomes familiar with all things strange; but the more I associate with and know myself the more does my deformity astonish me and the less do I understand myself.

It is a privilege chiefly reserved to chance to bring such incidents to light and into repute. As I was passing, the day before yesterday, through a village about two leagues from my house, I found the place still quite warm with a miracle that had lately failed of success, which had kept the neighbourhood talking for several months and was beginning to excite the adjoining provinces; all sorts of people were flocking thither in great numbers. A young fellow of the place had one night amused himself by counterfeiting the voice of a spirit in his own house, with no more thought or aim than to enjoy his joke for the moment. Having succeeded rather better than he expected he took a girl of the village, a very stupid and silly lass, into partnership to help him extend his operations. In the end there were three of them, all of the same age and equally intelligent; and after preaching to their families they preached to the public, hiding under the church-altar, speaking only at night, and forbidding any light to be brought.

From words aiming at the conversion of the world and threatening a day of judgement (for those are the subjects under whose authority and reverence imposture most easily lurks) they proceeded to apparitions and actions, more silly, ridiculous and clumsy almost than anything you could imagine in the playing of children. Yet if Fortune had favoured them ever so little who knows how far their foolery would have gone.

These poor devils are now in prison, and will probably bear the penalty for the foolishness of the community; and who knows but some judge will take vengeance on them for his own folly?

Here the imposture, which has been discovered, is clearly seen; but in many things of a like nature, which have escaped our knowledge, it seems to me that we must suspend our judgement before either rejecting or accepting.

Many of the delusions of the world, or to speak more boldly, all the delusions in the world, are begotten of our being taught to be afraid of professing our ignorance, and thinking ourselves bound to accept everything we cannot refute. We speak of all things in an authoritative and dogmatic style. It was distinctive of the Roman style that even that which a witness deposed to having seen with his own eyes, and what a judge decided of his most certain knowledge, was drawn up in this form of speech: 'It seems to me.' It makes me hate accepting things that are probable when they are held up before me as infallibly true. I prefer these words which tone down and modify the hastiness of our propositions: 'Perhaps, In some sort, Some, They say, I think,' and the like. And if I had had to train children I should have so accustomed them to adopt this inquiring, doubting mode of reply: 'What does that mean? I do not understand; It might be so; Is that true?' that they would rather have kept up the appearance of learners at the age of sixty than put on the airs of a learned doctor at ten, as they do.

Whoever will be cured of ignorance, let him confess it.

Iris is the daughter of Thaumas.[1] Wonder is the foundation of all philosophy; research, the progress; ignorance, the end. There is, by heavens, a strong and generous kind of ignorance that yields nothing, for honour and courage, to knowledge: an ignorance to conceive which needs no less knowledge than to conceive knowledge.

In my younger days I read of a trial which Corras, a

[1] i. e., the Rainbow is the daughter of Wonder. 'For she is so wonderfully beautiful, that she is rightly said to be the daughter of Thaumas.' (Cicero.)

Counsellor of Toulouse, had printed, concerning a strange incident, in which two men personated one another. I remember (and that is all I remember) that he seemed to me to have made out the imposture of the man he judged to be guilty, so marvellous and so far surpassing all our knowledge and his, who was judge, that I thought it was a very rash sentence that condemned him to be hanged. Let us accept some form of sentence which says, 'The Court understands nothing of the matter;' more freely and ingenuously than the Areopagites did who, finding themselves perplexed by a case they could not unravel, ordered the parties to appear again after a hundred years.

The witches of my neighbourhood are in danger of their lives when any one brings fresh witness to bear to the reality of their visions. To reconcile the examples which Holy Writ gives us of such things, most certain and irrefutable examples, and to bring them into comparison with those that happen in modern times, since we can see neither the causes of them nor the means by which they took place, needs a greater ingenuity than ours. That allmighty witness is perhaps alone able to say to us, 'This is a miracle, and that; but not this other.' God must be believed; that is, indeed, very reasonable. Not however one of ourselves, who is amazed at his own telling (and he must necessarily be amazed, if he is not out of his wits), whether he is denouncing another or witnessing against himself.

I am dull-witted, and rather stick to what is substantial and probable, avoiding the reproaches of the ancients: *Men bring a stronger faith to the things they do not understand* (Anon.). *By a mental twist we are more ready to believe what is obscure* (Tacitus). I see, indeed, that people get angry; and I am forbidden to doubt upon pain of execrable punishment:[1] a new kind of persuasion!

Thank God I am not to be cuffed into believing. Let them rail at those who condemn their opinions as false; I only condemn them for being rash and hard to believe,

---

[1] This may be aimed at Jean Bodin (for whom, by the way, Montaigne had great admiration) who, in his *Démonomanie* (1580), having proved the existence of sorcerers from the Bible, called down the utmost rigours of the law, not only upon those who practised witchcraft, but upon those who disbelieved in it. Montaigne had the courage of his opinions.

and am quite as ready as they to condemn those who affirm the opposite, if not so imperiously. *Let it be said that they appear likely; only let them not be affirmed positively* (Cicero).

The man who tries to establish his arguments by domineering bluster shows that his reasoning is weak. In a wordy and scholastic altercation they may appear to be as much in the right as their contradictors; but in the actual conclusions they draw the latter have greatly the advantage.

When it is a question of killing people a clear and shining light is needed; and our life is too real and essential to warrant these supernatural and fantastic chances. As to drugs and poisons, I leave them out of my reckoning; they are homicidal, and of the worst kind. However, even in this matter they say we must not always attach too much weight to the confessions of those people against themselves, for they have sometimes been known to accuse themselves of having killed persons who turned out to be alive and in good health.

In regard to those other extravagant accusations I should be inclined to say that it is as much as we can do to believe a man, however high he may stand in our estimation, on human matters; in matters that are beyond his conception and of a supernatural kind, we should believe him only when he has supernatural sanction and approval. This privilege that God has been pleased to give to some of our testimonies ought not to be cheapened and lightly communicated.

My ears are assailed by a thousand tales such as these: 'Three saw him on such and such a day in the Levant, three saw him next day in the West, at such and such a time, in such and such a place, and dressed in such and such a way.' To tell the truth I would not believe my own eyes in such a case. How much more natural and likely it seems to me that two men are lying than that a man could travel with the wind in twelve hours from the East to the West! How much more natural that our judgement should be misled by the flightiness of our disordered mind, than that one of our kind, in flesh and bones, should be borne away by a strange spirit up the chimney on a broomstick.

Let us not look for outside and strange delusions, when

we are perpetually disturbed by our own home delusions. I think we may be pardoned for disbelieving in a prodigy, at least as long as we are able to turn down and avoid the supernatural explanation. And I agree with Saint Augustine when he says 'That it is better to lean towards doubt than towards assurance, in matters hard to prove and dangerous to believe.'

Some years ago I was passing through the territory of a ruling Prince, who, as a favour to me and to beat down my incredulity, graciously allowed me to see, in his presence and in a private place, ten or a dozen prisoners of that kind,[1] and among others an old woman, a regular witch in ugliness and deformity, whose reputation in that profession was of long standing. I saw both proofs and free confessions, and some hardly perceptible mark or other [2] on that miserable old creature. I questioned and talked as much as I pleased, giving the soundest attention I could to their replies; and I am not the man to allow my judgement to be captivated by preconceived ideas. In short and in all conscience I should rather have prescribed them hellebore [3] than hemlock. *With them it seemed to be a case of madness rather than crime* (Livy). Justice has its corrections proper for such maladies.

With regard to the objections and arguments which honest men have raised up against me, both on this subject and often on others, I have not heard any that could put me to silence, and that do not always admit of a more likely solution than their conclusions. Very true it is that the proofs and reasons that are founded on experience and fact I do not attempt to unravel; they have in fact no end, and I often cut them as Alexander did his knot.[4] After all it is rating one's conjectures at a very high price to roast a man alive on the strength of them.

Among divers other examples it is related by Prestantius of his father that, having fallen into a coma deeper and heavier than an ordinary sleep, he imagined he was a mare, and was being used by some soldiers as a pack-horse; and what he imagined, he was. If the sorcerers dream in this

---

[1] Persons, probably women for the most part, accused of witchcraft.
[2] Witches were supposed to have some mark or stigma on their bodies, imprinted by the Devil.
[3] Hellebore was supposed to cure insanity.
[4] The Gordian knot, tied by the Phrygian King Gordius. The oracle declared that the man who untied it should rule all Asia.

material way; if dreams can thus sometimes assume a body and become realities, still I cannot believe that our will should be accountable to justice.

This I say, neither as a judge nor as an adviser of kings, of being which I esteem myself very far from worthy, but as a man of the common sort, naturally pledged to obey common sense, both in words and deeds. If any man should take my idle talk seriously and act upon it to the prejudice of the pettiest law, belief or custom of his village, he might get himself into trouble, and me just as much. For in what I say I guarantee no other certainty, except that that is what I had in my mind at the time; a turbulent and vacillating mind!

When I speak of all kinds of things it is by way of chat, and by no means to impart information. *And I am not ashamed, as they are, to confess ignorance of what I do not know* (Cicero). I should not speak so boldly if it were likely that people would follow my advice; and this was the answer I gave to a great man who complained that my preachings were too harsh and arbitrary: 'Seeing you bent and prepared to go in one direction, I propose to you the other, with all the diligence and care I am capable of, to enlighten your judgement, not to force it. God holds your heart in his hands, and he will provide you with the means of choosing. I am not so presumptuous as even to wish that my opinions should turn the scale in a matter of such importance; I was not fated to direct them to such high and influential decisions.'

Truly, I have not only a great many propensities, but also enough opinions, which I would gladly make my son dislike, if I had a son. What if the truest opinions are not always the most suitable to man; so untamed is his disposition!

Apropos, or malapropos, it matters not which, it is a common proverb in Italy that he does not know Venus in her perfect sweetness who has not lain with the cripple. Chance or some particular incident has long ago put this saying into the mouths of the people; and it applies to males as well as females. For the Queen of the Amazons replied to the Scythian who invited her love, '*The lame do it best*' (Greek proverb). In that feminine State, to escape the domination of the males, they used to cripple them in their earliest childhood; arms, legs, and other parts which gave them an advantage, were lamed, and the men were only used for the purpose for which we use the women over here.

I might have said that the disjointed motions of the cripple add some new kind of pleasure to the business, and a certain agreeable titillation to those who try it. But I have lately learned that the old Philosophy had even decided the question. It says that, as the legs and thighs of the lame woman do not, by reason of their imperfection, receive their due aliment, it follows that the genital parts, which lie above, are fuller, better nourished and more vigorous. Or perhaps that, as this defect prevents them taking exercise, those who are tainted with it do not waste so much strength and come fresher to the sports of Venus. Which is also the reason why the Greeks denounced the women-weavers as being hotter than others, by reason of their sedentary occupations which they perform without much bodily exercise. What can we not prove by arguing at this rate ? Of the latter I might also say that the tremor which their work imparts to them, while thus seated, arouses and excites their feelings, as the shaking and jolting of their coaches does the ladies.

Do not these examples serve to make good what I said at the beginning: That our reasonings often anticipate the fact, and extend their jurisdiction so infinitely far that they judge and meddle even with things that have no substance and no existence ? Besides the versatility of our invention in forging reasons for all sorts of delusions, our imagination is equally ready to take false impressions from very trifling outward signs. For example, on the mere authority of the ancient and general use of that proverb, I once made myself believe that I received more pleasure from a woman because she was not straight, and accordingly put down that deformity among the number of her charms.

Torquato Tasso, in the comparison he draws between France and Italy, says he observed that we have more slender legs than the Italian gentlemen, and attributes this to the fact that we are continually on horseback. From the same fact Suetonius draws quite the opposite conclusion; for he says, on the contrary, that Germanicus' legs became thicker through continual exercise of that nature.[1]

[1] Which Holland, in a note to his translation of Suetonius's *Life of*

Nothing is so supple and erratic as our understanding; it is the shoe of Theramenes,[1] fitting both feet. And it is double and diverse; and the matters are double and diverse. 'Give me a silver drachma,' said a Cynical philosopher to Antigonus. 'That is not a kingly gift,' he replied. 'Then give me a talent.' 'That is not a gift for a Cynic.'

> Or whether the heat unlocks
> New passages and secret pores, whereby
> Their life-juice to the tender blades may win;
> Or that it hardens more and helps to bind
> The gaping veins, lest penetrating showers,
> Or fierce sun's ravening might, or searching blast
> Of the keen North should sear them.[2]

Every medal has its reverse (Italian proverb). That is why Clitomachus said of old that Carneades had exceeded the labours of Hercules, in that he had eradicated assent, that is to say, opinionativeness and rashness in forming judgements, out of men's minds. This so vigorous idea of Carneades was, in my opinion, suggested by the impudence of those men who in olden times professed to know, and by their inordinate overweeningness.

Aesop was exhibited for sale with two other slaves. A buyer asked the first of them what he could do; and he, to enhance his price, promised mountains and marvels, saying he could do this and that and the other. The second promised as much, and more. When it came to Aesop's turn to answer what he could do he replied: 'Nothing, for these two have forestalled me, and can do everything.'

So it happened in the school of Philosophy: the arrogance of those who attributed to the human mind the capacity to know all things gave rise in others, through spite and emulation, to the belief that it is capable of nothing. The one side go to the same extreme of ignorance as the other of knowledge; so making it undeniable that man is immoderate in all things, and can never stop but of necessity and through his inability to proceed further.

Caligula (1606), explains as follows: 'For they used then no stirrops, therefore the bloud and humours wold descend to the legges.'

[1] According to Plutarch, Theramenes was nicknamed *Kothornos* or 'the Buskin' on account of his liability to change sides; the buskin being a boot that would fit either foot.

[2] Virgil's reasons for setting fire to the barren fields and burning the stubble; see *Georgics*, I. 89.

CHAPTER 12

OF PHYSIOGNOMY

ALMOST all the opinions we hold are taken on authority and trust. There is no harm done ; we could not make a worse choice than our own in so feeble an age. The sayings of Socrates, as reflected in the works which his friends [1] have handed down to us, gain our approval only out of respect to the universal approval that has been accorded to them, not as the result of our own knowledge. They are not in accordance with our way of thinking. If at this moment anything of the same kind should appear there are few men who could appreciate it.

We can perceive no beauties that are not emphasized, puffed out and inflated by artificial means. Those which glide in their native purity and simplicity easily escape so gross a sight as ours. It is a delicate and hidden beauty ; it needs a clear and well-purged sight to discover their hidden light.

Is not simplicity, as we conceive it, germane to silliness, and an object of scorn ? Socrates makes his mind move with a natural and familiar motion. A peasant says this, a woman says that. He never speaks but of charioteers, joiners, cobblers and masons. His inductions and similes are drawn from the most common and best-known activities of men ; everybody understands him. Under so humble a form we should never have recognized the nobility and splendour of his admirable ideas ; we who think all ideas mean and shallow that are not set off by learning, and can perceive no riches but in pomp and show. This world of ours is only formed for ostentation ; men only puff themselves up with wind, and move by leaps and bounds, like balloons.

Socrates' purpose was not vague and fanciful ; his aim was to furnish us with things and precepts that are really and more directly serviceable to life,

> Observe due measure, keep one's end in view,
> And ever follow Nature's course. (LUCAN.)

He was besides always one and the same, and raised him-

---

[1] Plato and Xenophon.

self not by fits and starts, but by his natural temperament, to the highest pitch of vigour. Or, to speak more correctly, he raised nothing, but rather brought down, reduced and subjected vigour to his natural and original pitch, as well as all asperities and difficulties. For, as regards Cato, we see very clearly that he goes a strained pace, far beyond the ordinary ; in the brave exploits of his life, and in his death, we always feel that he is riding the high horse. The other skims the ground, and, at a gentle and ordinary pace, treats of the most useful matters ; and, both in the face of death and over the thorniest obstacles that may come in his way, follows the ordinary course of human life.

It has turned out fortunate that the man most worthy to be known, and to be offered to the world as an example, is the man of whom we have most certain knowledge. He has had a clear light thrown upon him by the most clear-sighted men that ever lived ; the testimonies we have of him are admirable for fidelity and fullness.

It is a great thing to have been able to put such order into ideas as pure as those of a child that, without altering or stretching them, he produced from them the finest results of our mind. The mind he shows us is neither exalted nor richly furnished, only healthy, but assuredly with a health that is very brisk and sound. With those common and natural resources, with those ordinary and everyday ideas, without being animated or excited, he erected not only the best regulated, but the most sublime and vigorous set of beliefs, actions and morals that ever were.

It was he who brought human Wisdom down again from heaven, where she was wasting her time, and restored her to man, with whom her most normal and most laborious and most useful business lies.

Hear him pleading his causes before his judges. See with what reasons he rouses his courage in the hazards of war ; with what arguments he fortifies his patience in the face of calumnies, tyranny, death and against his wife's temper. There is nothing borrowed from art and science ; the simplest may there discover their own means and strength ; it is not possible to mount higher and descend lower. He has done human nature a great kindness by showing how much it can do of itself.

We are, every one of us, richer than we think, but we are

trained to borrow and beg ; we are accustomed to make more use of what is another's than of our own. Man can never stop and be satisfied with the needful ; of pleasure, wealth, power, he grasps at more than he can hold ; his greed is not capable of being moderated.

I have observed that he is the same in his curiosity to know ; he cuts out much more work for himself than he can do, and much more than he needs to do, imagining that the utility of knowledge extends as far as its matter. *In learning, as in all things else, we observe no moderation* (Seneca). And Tacitus is right in commending the mother of Agricola for curbing in her son a too eager appetite for learning. If we look at it steadily it is a blessing in which, as in other blessings enjoyed by man, there is much trifling and weakness, proper and natural to itself, and it costs very dear.

The purchase of it is far more dangerous than that of any other food or drink. For, in the case of other things, what we have bought we carry home in some vessel or other, and there we have leisure to examine its worth, and to consider how much of it, and when, we shall consume. But learning we can at the outset stow into no other vessel but our mind ; we swallow it at the moment of buying, and leave the market-place already either contaminated or improved. Some of it, instead of nourishing us, only clogs and overloads our stomach ; and some of it besides, under colour of curing, poisons us.

I was once delighted to meet, in some place or other, men who had, in the name of religion, taken a vow of ignorance, as well as of chastity, poverty and penitence. That too is a castration of our unruly appetites, a muzzling of that cupidity which spurs us on to the study of books, and depriving the mind of the voluptuous complacency which tickles us with the idea that we know something. And it is abundantly carrying out the vow of poverty to add to it that of the mind.

We need but little learning to live happily. And Socrates tells us that we have it in us, and instructs us how to find it and make use of it. All these acquisitions of ours that exceed the natural are well-nigh vain and superfluous. It is enough if they do not burden and cumber us more than they do us good. *Little learning is needed to form a healthy mind* (Seneca). They are feverish excesses of our mind, which is a restless and meddlesome instrument.

Concentrate your thoughts; you will find in yourself the true arguments of Nature against death, and the fittest to serve you in times of necessity. It is they which enable a farm-labourer, and whole nations, to die with as much fortitude as a philosopher.

Should I have died less cheerfully before I had read the *Tusculans* ?[1] I think not. And when I think it over I feel that my tongue is the richer, but certainly not my heart. This is as Nature forged it for me, and it arms itself for the conflict in a natural and ordinary way. Books have been of service to me not so much for instruction as to exercise my mind.

What if knowledge, whilst trying to arm us with new defences against natural misfortunes, has rather impressed our mind with the magnitude and weight of them than furnished it with arguments and sophistries to shelter us from them ? They are sophistries, indeed, with which she often alarms us to little purpose. Look at even the wisest and most concise writers, how many frivolous and, if we examine them closely, bodyless arguments they scatter around a single good one. They are but wordy quibbles, made to deceive us. But as long as they do so profitably I will not sift them any further. There are enough of that kind in divers parts of this book, either borrowed or imitated.

So we ought to be a little on our guard against calling power what is mere prettiness, or solid what is merely acute, or good what is only beautiful, *which is pleasanter to taste than to swallow* (Cicero).

Not all that pleases, appeases, *when it is a question of the soul, and not the wit* (Seneca).

To see how Seneca strives to prepare himself for death, to see him sweating with anguish to stiffen himself, and struggling so long to gain assurance on his pedestal, I should be inclined to shake his reputation if he had not very valiantly maintained it at his death. His agitations, so burning and frequent, show that he was naturally impetuous and passionate. *A great soul expresses itself more calmly and cheerfully. . . . The soul and the intellect are not differently*

[1] Cicero's *Tusculan Disputations*, the first Book of which deals with the 'Contempt of Death'.

coloured (Seneca). He has to be convinced at his own cost. They also show in some sort that he was hard pressed by his enemy.

Plutarch's style, though more offhand and less strained, is in my opinion the more virile and convincing; I could easily believe that his soul's movements were more confident and more orderly. The one, sharper, pricks and makes us start up; he touches the spirit more. The other, more sober, consistently forms us, sets us up and comforts us; he touches the understanding more. The former carries off our judgement, the latter wins it.

I have likewise seen other writings, still more honoured, which, in depicting the conflict they sustain against the goads of the flesh, paint them so sharp, so powerful and invincible that even we, who are of the dregs of the people, cannot help wondering as much at the strangeness and uncommon vigour of their temptation, as at their resistance.

To what purpose do we go arming ourselves with this laboriously acquired learning? Let us look down there, at the poor people we see scattered about on the face of the earth, their heads bowed over their labours, who know neither Aristotle nor Cato, neither example nor precept; from them Nature every day extracts deeds of fortitude and endurance, purer and more vigorous than those we study so diligently in the schools. How many I see every day who ignore poverty, how many who wish for death, or who meet it without fear and without distress! This man who is digging my garden has this morning buried his father or his son.

Even the names by which they call their maladies mitigate and sweeten their bitterness; phthisis is to them a cough, dysentery a looseness of the bowels, pleurisy a cold; and as they mitigate their names so they support them more easily. It must be a very serious ailment that will interrupt their ordinary labours; they take to their beds only to die.

This simple virtue, that is within the reach of all, has been converted into an obscure and mysterious science (Seneca).

I was writing this about the time when a great load of our troubles had for months descended straight upon me with all its weight. On the one hand I had the enemy at my gate, on the other the freebooters, a worse kind of enemy:

they fight not with arms but with crimes: and I had a taste of every kind of outrage inflicted by the soldiery at the same time:

> To right and left the dreaded foe appears,
> And present danger threatens all around. (OVID.)

A monstrous and unnatural war! Other wars act outwardly, this also against itself, eating away and destroying itself with its own venom. It is of so malignant and ruinous a nature that it ruins itself together with everything else; in its fury it tears itself limb from limb. More frequently we see it dissolving of itself than through any dearth of necessary things, or by the power of the enemy. All discipline flies from it. It comes to cure sedition, and is full of it; it professes to chastise disobedience and sets an example of it. And, being employed for the protection of the laws, plays its part in rebelling against its own laws. To what a pass we have come when our medicine carries infection!

> Our evil mounts the more, grown worse with healing. (VIRGIL.)
> All right and wrong, with awful frenzy blent,
> Estranged from us the righteous-minded gods. (CATULLUS.)

In the beginning of these diseases that attack the people we can distinguish the sick from the sound; but when they come to stay, as ours does, the whole body is infected from head to heels; no part is exempt from corruption. For there is no air that is inhaled so greedily, that so spreads and penetrates, as the air of licence. Our armies no longer join and hold together except with a foreign cement; no longer is it possible to form a regular and reliable army-corps of Frenchmen.

O the shame of it! There is no discipline but that we see in borrowed soldiers; as to ourselves, we follow our own lead, not that of the leader. Every one goes his own way. The general has more to do within than without. It is his part to follow, to pay court and crook his back. He alone obeys; all the rest are free and dissolute.

I am not sorry to see that ambition is reduced to such unmanly and mean-spirited, such abject and servile actions, to attain its end. But this I am sorry to see, that good and generous natures, capable of uprightness, are every day corrupted in their administration and guidance of this confused State.

Prolonged toleration begets habit; habit, consent and imitation. We had ignoble souls enough without spoiling the good and generous. Wherefore, if we continue at this rate, there will hardly be left a man to whom we may entrust the health of this State, in case Fortune should restore it.

> This youthful Prince forbid ye not at least
> To save a fallen generation.[1] (VIRGIL.)

What has become of that old precept, 'That soldiers ought to fear their general more than the enemy'? And that wonderful example of the apple-tree which happened to be enclosed within the precincts of a Roman army-camp, and was found the day after the army had broken up, leaving the owner in possession of the full tale of his ripe and delicious apples?

I could wish that our young men, instead of spending their time in less profitable peregrinations and less honourable apprenticeships, would put in the half of it in witnessing naval warfare under some good Captain-commander of Rhodes, and the other half in observing the discipline of the Turkish armies; for it differs greatly from ours, and greatly to its advantage. For example, our soldiers become more licentious on warlike expeditions, whilst the Turkish soldiers become more restrained and timid; for the offences or thefts committed upon the poor, which in times of peace are punished with the bastinado, become capital offences in war-time. For an egg taken without payment the penalty is, according to a fixed tariff, fifty strokes with a stick. For any other thing, however small, not necessary for food, they are impaled or beheaded without delay.

I was astonished to read in the history of Selim, the most cruel conqueror that ever was, that when he subjugated Egypt the wonderful gardens, abounding in delicious fruits, surrounding the city of Damascus, were left virgin of the hands of the soldiers, unenclosed and open to all as they were.

But is there any disease in a State so bad that it deserves to be fought with so fatal a drug[2]? Not even, said Favonius, the usurping of possession of the State by a tyrant.

---

[1] Virgil refers to Augustus, and no doubt Montaigne had in his mind the King of Navarre, afterwards Henry IV of France.
[2] As civil war.

Plato too will not consent to have the peace of his country violated in order to cure it, and will not accept reformation at the cost of the blood and destruction of the citizens. He lays it down as the duty of a good man in that case to leave things alone, only entreating God to lend extraordinary aid; and he seems to be angry with his great friend Dion for having gone about it somewhat differently.

I was a Platonist on this point before I knew there had been a Plato in the world. And if such a man is to be absolutely barred from our fellowship, who, for the clearness of his conscience, deserved at the hands of the divine favour to penetrate so deeply into the light of Christianity, through the universal darkness in which the world of his time was involved, I do not think it fitting that we should be taught by a Pagan, how great an impiety it is not to look to God for any succour simply his own, and without our co-operation.

I often doubt whether, among so many men who meddle in such a business, any one is to be met with of so weak understanding as to be seriously convinced that he was on the way to reformation through the worst of deformations; that he was advancing towards his salvation by roads that most positively lead to certain damnation; that by overthrowing the government, the authorities and the laws, under whose protection God has placed him, by dismembering his mother and giving her limbs to be devoured by her old enemies, by filling the hearts of brothers with fratricidal hatred, by calling devils and furies to his aid, he could assist the most holy sweetness and justice of the divine word.

Ambition, avarice, cruelty, revenge, have not sufficient natural fury of their own; let us set a match to them and fan the flames under the glorious pretext of justice and religion! It is not possible to imagine a worse outlook than when wickedness becomes lawful and, with the permission of the authorities, puts on the cloak of virtue. *Nothing is more deceptive in appearance than a false religion, in which the will of God is made a cloak for crimes* (Livy).

The extreme of wrong, according to Plato, is reached when what is wrong is held to be right.

The lower classes suffered very largely at that time, not only present losses,

> Such wide confusion fills the countryside; (VIRGIL.)

but also future losses. The living had to suffer, and so had those who were yet unborn. They robbed them, and consequently myself, even of hope, snatching from them all the means they had for providing for their livelihood for many years to come :

> All that they cannot bear or lead away
> The brutal horde maliciously destroys ;
> And harmless cottages are burnt to ashes. (OVID.)
>
> In walls there is no trust, and fields
> Lie all untilled and desolate. (CLAUDIAN.)

Besides this shock I suffered others. I incurred the penalties that moderation brings with it in that kind of epidemic. I was fleeced on all hands. To the Ghibelline I was a Guelph, and to the Guelph a Ghibelline. One of my poets has put that very well, but I do not remember where it is. The situation of my house and my intimacy with the people in my neighbourhood made me appear with one face, my life and my actions with another.[1]

They made no formal accusations, for there was nothing they could lay their teeth on. I never go outside the laws ; and if any man had proceeded against me he might have found that he was more guilty than I. There were only mute suspicions moving under the surface, for which there is never a lack of apparent grounds in so mixed and confused a state of affairs, any more than there is of envious and foolish minds.

I myself generally lend a hand to the offensive presumptions that Fortune scatters abroad against me, by a way I have always had of being loath to justify, excuse and explain my actions ; thinking that to plead on behalf of my conscience was to endanger it. *For the clearness of a case is clouded by argument* (Cicero). And, as if every one could see as clearly into me as I do myself, instead of withdrawing from an accusation I advance towards it, and rather improve upon it by an ironical and scornful confession, if I do not absolutely hold my tongue, as if it were something unworthy of reply.

But those who regard this attitude as too arrogant and self-confident show me hardly less ill-will than those who

[1] M. Villey explains that in the Périgord the majority were Protestants, and Montaigne was by some taken for a Protestant.

look upon it as the weakness of an indefensible cause; especially the Great, in whose eyes want of submission is the great sin; hard upon all self-conscious rectitude that is not humble, servile and suppliant. I have often run my head against that pillar.

However that may be, what I suffered then would have made an ambitious man hang himself; and a miser would have done the same. I have no anxiety whatever to acquire wealth:

> Let me possess
> The goods that now I have, or even less;
> Live for myself the days I have to live,
> So please the Gods a few more days to give! (HORACE.)

But the losses that befall me through others' wrongdoing, whether by theft or violence, hurt me almost as much as they would a man who is sick and tormented with avarice. The injury is infinitely more bitter than the loss.

A thousand different kinds of misfortune assailed me in single file; I could more cheerfully have suffered them in a throng.

I was already considering to which of my friends I could commit a needy and ill-fated old age; after turning my eyes in all directions I found myself stripped to my shirt. When a man falls plumb, and from so great a height, it must be into the arms of a strong and firm affection that is favoured by Fortune; such an affection is rare, if there be any. In the end I saw that it was safest to rely upon myself in my distress; and if it should so fall out that Fortune was too cold in offering me protection, to entrust myself more to my own and fix my eyes and thoughts more firmly on myself.

On all occasions men are too ready to throw themselves into other people's arms, to save their own, which alone are reliable and powerful, if they can make use of them. Every man rushes elsewhere and into the future, because no man has turned to himself.

And I came to the conclusion that my misfortunes were beneficial, since, Firstly, a bad learner must be taught with the rod, when reason is insufficient; as by means of heat and the force of wedges we restore a piece of warped timber to straightness. I have so long been urging myself to rely on my own strength and be independent of strangers, and yet I still keep turning my eyes to one side. The favour of a great man, a gracious word, a condescending glance, tempt me; and God knows how little scarcity there is of such in these days, and how little they mean! I can still listen without wrinkling my brows to the flattering offers that are made me to draw me into the open; and I resist them so feebly that I appear rather willing than not to be vanquished by them. Now so indocile a spirit needs a beating; and when this cask begins to split, and crack, and leak, and fall to pieces, it needs some good sound strokes of the mallet to force down and tighten the hoops.

Secondly, this misfortune might be to me a profitable experience, to prepare me for a worse, in case I, who hoped through the kindness of Fortune, and as a consequence of my own attitude, to be among the last, should be one of the first to be caught in the storm; that I might learn betimes to restrict my mode of life, and set it in order for a new state of things.

True liberty is to be able to control one's own actions. *The most powerful man is he who has power over himself* (Seneca).

In ordinary peace times we prepare for ordinary and reasonable accidents, but in this state of confusion which has existed for these last thirty years every Frenchman, whether as an individual or as a member of the community, may expect at any moment an entire upheaval of his fortune. All the more reason why he should keep his heart well stored with strength and courage. Let us be grateful to Fate that we do not live in an effeminate, idle and languid age. Many a man who could never have become so by other means may become famous by his misfortune.

As I seldom read in history of those upheavals in other States without regretting that I had not been present, to have a better view of them, so my curiosity makes me congratulate myself in some sort for being able to witness with my own eyes this notable spectacle of our public death, its form and symptoms. And, since I am unable to prevent it, I am pleased that I was destined to be a spectator of it, and gain instruction from it.

Thus do we eagerly desire to see, even in pictures and in dramatic fictions, the tragedies of human fortune performed before our eyes. Not that the things we hear do not excite our compassion ; but, those pitiable events being so uncommon, we take a pleasure in having our feelings worked upon by them.

Nothing tickles without hurting. And the wise historian skims over the accounts of peaceful events as he would stagnant water and dead sea, to come back to wars and seditions to which he knows that we beckon him.

I doubt whether I can honestly enough confess with how very mean a sacrifice of my peace of mind and tranquillity I have lived more than half my life whilst my country was in ruins. I exercise my patience a little too cheaply over the misfortunes that do not affect me personally ; and when I feel inclined to pity myself, I think less of what I have been robbed of than of what I have saved, both inwardly and outwardly. There is some comfort in dodging now one, now another of the evils that are successively taking aim at us, and that hit others round about us. Also in this, that when public interests are concerned the more widely my sympathy is scattered the weaker does it become. To which may be added that this is almost certainly true, *that we only feel public calamities in so far as they affect us personally* (Hannibal, according to Livy) ; and that the health with which we parted was so poor that any regret we might feel for the loss of it is lessened. It was health, but only by comparison with the sickness that followed.

We have not fallen from a very great height. The corruption and brigandage that is found in high quarters and is the order of the day seems to me the least supportable. Robbery is less offensive in a wood than in a place of safety. It was a universal conjunction of limbs severally diseased, and each one more so than the other, and for the most part with inveterate ulcers, which no longer admitted of cure or desired it.

This general collapse then certainly stimulated me more than it crushed me, with the help of my conscience, which was not only at peace but bore itself proudly ; and I found no reason to be dissatisfied with myself. Besides, as God never sends us mortals either good or evil quite unmixed, my health at that time held out unusually well ; and, as I can do nothing without health, there are few things that I cannot do with it. It afforded me the means of calling up all my resources to ward off the plague, which might possibly have come nearer to me. And I found that with my endurance I could keep a firm seat against the attacks of Fortune, and that it would need a great shock to throw me out of the saddle.

I do not say this in order to provoke her to make a more vigorous attack upon me. I am her humble servant, and hold out my hands to her and entreat her, in God's name, to be satisfied.

Do I feel her attacks? Yes, indeed. As one who is possessed and stricken with grief will yet at intervals be tickled by some witticism and coaxed into a smile, I too can control myself sufficiently to keep my mind usually in a state of equanimity and free from painful ideas; yet every now and again I am suddenly bitten by those unpleasant thoughts, which attack at the moment when I am putting on my armour to struggle with and repel them.

But now came another aggravation of evils which arrived on top of the others. Both outside and in my house I was welcomed by the plague, virulent above all others. For, as robust bodies are liable to more serious maladies, which alone have any power over them, so the very salubrious air around me, where no infection had within living memory gained a foothold, although it had come very near, became poisoned, and produced uncommon results:

> Old and young promiscuous crowd the tomb;
> No head is spared by ruthless Proserpine. (HORACE.)

I was reduced to that absurd state [1] that the sight of my house became terrible to me. All that was in it was unguarded, and left to the mercy of any man who had a mind to take it. I myself, who am so hospitable, was reduced to the painful necessity of begging for a retreat for my family, a lost and wandering family, a source of fear to their friends and even to themselves, bringing terror wherever they sought to settle, obliged to shift their abode as soon as one of the company began to complain of a sore finger. At such times every malady is concluded to be the plague; people

---

[1] *Cette plaisante condition.* Most of the French commentators, headed by Coste, are scandalized that Montaigne could make a jest of so serious a matter. But the word *plaisant* has various shades of meaning in Montaigne, such as 'amusing', 'ridiculous', 'humorous', 'witty'. My predecessors ignore any difference, and generally translate it 'pleasant'.

do not waste time to investigate it. And the irony of it was that, in accordance with the rules of the faculty, whenever the danger approaches, you are for forty days in a panic terror of that sickness ; imagination meanwhile makes havoc of your feelings in its own way, and even turns your health into a fever.

All this would have affected me less if I had not had to feel for the sufferings of others, and for six miserable months to pilot this caravan. For I carry my antidotes within myself, which are resolution and patience. I am not greatly troubled by apprehensions, which are particularly to be dreaded in this disease. And if I had been alone and allowed myself to catch it, it would have been a much more cheerful and distant flight.[1] It is not one of the worst kinds of death in my opinion ; it is usually short, numb, painless, comfortable by reason of being shared by many ; no fuss, no mourning, no crowd of onlookers.

But, with regard to the people about us, not a hundredth part of the inhabitants had any hope of escaping :

> Behold the shepherds' realms a waste,
> And far and wide the fields untenanted. (VIRGIL.)

In this place the best part of my revenue depends on manual labour ; the land that a hundred men cultivated for me long lay fallow.

What an example of fortitude did we not then see in the simplicity of all these people ! All and every one gave up caring about life. The grapes remained hanging on the vines, which form the principal wealth of the country. All unconcernedly prepared for and expected death that evening or the morrow, showing so little alarm, either in countenance or voice, that they seemed to have resigned themselves as to a necessity, and regarded it as an inevitable and universal sentence of death.

Death is always inevitable. But on how little depends the resolution to die ! Distance and a few hours' difference, the mere consideration of having company, makes one feel quite differently towards it. Look at these people : because they die in the same month, children, young people, old

[1] Meaning, I think, that he would have died cheerfully. M. Villey apparently takes the sentence to mean, 'If I had wished to run away I should have done so cheerfully, and well out of danger.' But the words that follow seem to agree better with my interpretation.

men, are no longer alarmed by it, they cease to lament for themselves. I saw some who dreaded being left behind, as in a dreadful solitude ; and I generally observed them to have no other anxiety than about their burial. They were troubled to see the bodies scattered about in the fields, at the mercy of wild animals that immediately swarmed thither.

How the ideas of men diverge ! The Neorites, a nation subdued by Alexander, throw the bodies of their dead into the deepest parts of their forests, there to be devoured ; the only happy sepulture in their eyes.

Here and there a man, still in good health, was already digging his own grave ; others, still alive, lay down in theirs. And one of my day-labourers, as he was dying, scraped the earth over himself with his hands and feet ; was that not like covering himself up in order to sleep more comfortably ? A heroism almost as sublime as that of the Roman soldiers who, after the Battle of Cannae, were found with their heads thrust into holes, which they had made and filled in with their own hands whilst they smothered. In short, a whole nation was, by habit, soon reduced to adopt a course which for doggedness yields in no wise to any studied and premeditated determination.

Most of the teachings of the learned which are intended to put heart into us are more showy than forcible, more ornamental than effectual. We have abandoned Nature and presume to give lessons to her who used to guide us so happily and surely. And meanwhile from the traces of her teaching, and what little remains of her image, by the favour of ignorance, imprinted on the lives of these unpolished rustics, learning is constrained every day to borrow for its disciples, to serve as models of fortitude, innocence and tranquillity. It is edifying to see how these disciples, with all their fine knowledge, are reduced to copying those foolish and simple people, and to copying them in their elementary actions of virtue ; and how our sapience may derive from the very animals the most useful teachings for the greatest and most necessary concerns of our life : how to live and how to die, how to husband our property, how to love and bring up our children and how to maintain justice : a singular testimony of human infirmity; and how our reason, which we use as it suits us, ever finding something different and something new, leaves in us no apparent trace of Nature.

And men have treated Nature as perfumers treat oil: they have sophisticated her with so many arguments and far-fetched reasons, that she has become variable and individual to every man, and has lost her own constant and universal look; so that we must seek in animals any evidence of her that is not liable to favour, corruption or diversity of opinions.

For it is, indeed, true that even they do not always strictly follow the path of Nature, but they swerve so little from it that you can always perceive her tracks. So a horse that is led by hand indulges in much kicking and plunging, but no further than the length of its halter, and yet always follows the steps of the man who is leading it; and so a hawk takes its flight, but under restraint of its leash.

Meditate upon exile, tortures, wars, diseases, shipwreck, that no disaster may find you a novice (Seneca).

What good will it do to anticipate so carefully all the ills of human nature, and prepare ourselves with so much pains to encounter even those which will perhaps never come our way? *The possibility of suffering makes us as unhappy as the suffering itself* (Seneca). We are frightened not only by the blow, but by the wind and the crack. Or why must you go this very moment, like the most fanatic, for, indeed, it is fanaticism, and ask to be birched, because Fortune may some day have a rod in pickle for you? Why take to your furred gown in Midsummer because you will need it at Christmas?

'Make haste and try the evils that may befall you, especially the worst of them; test your powers, they say, and make sure that you can bear them.'

On the contrary, the easiest and most natural way would be to banish them even from your thoughts.

'They will not come soon enough, and will not afflict you long enough in their true essence; your mind must prolong and magnify them and become united with them beforehand, and make much of them, as if they were not sufficiently painful to our senses.'

'They will be painful enough when they come, said one of the masters, not of some tender sect, but of the hardest.[1]

[1] Seneca the Stoic.

Meantime, indulge yourself ; believe what you like best. What good can it do you to welcome and anticipate your ill-fortune, and to lose the present through fear of the future ; to make yourself miserable now, because you are to be so in time.' Those are his words.

Learning does us a great service, forsooth, in telling us the exact dimensions of evils,

> Whetting the minds of men with care on care. (VIRGIL.)

What a pity that any part of their magnitude should escape our sense and knowledge !

It is certain that to most men the preparation for death has been a greater torment than the suffering of it.

It was once said very truly by a writer of great judgement : *the senses are less affected by physical suffering than by the apprehension of it* (Quintilian).

The feeling that death is present sometimes of itself inspires us with a sudden resolution not to evade a thing that is quite inevitable. Many gladiators in olden times, after fighting faint-heartedly, were seen to swallow death bravely, offering their throat to the adversary's sword and inviting it.

The prospect of death in the future needs a courage of long duration, and consequently hard to acquire.

If you do not know how to die, do not let it trouble you ; Nature will give you full and sufficient instructions when the time comes. She will do the business for you at the precise moment ; do not burden your mind with the thought of it :

In vain, O mortal man, you seek to know
The hour when death shall come, and by which way. (PROPERTIUS.)

Less painful 'tis to suffer sudden death ;
Much harder then to live in constant dread ! (MAXIMIANUS.)

We trouble our life by the thought of death, and death by the thought of life. The one gives us a feeling of regret, the other terrifies us.

It is not for death that we prepare ; that is too momentary. A quarter of an hour of suffering, without any hurtful consequences, does not deserve any particular instruction. If we would confess the truth, it is for the preparations for death that we prepare.

Philosophy exhorts us to keep death ever before our eyes, to foresee and meditate upon it before the time comes, and then gives us rules and precautions to provide against that foresight and meditation doing us any hurt. That is what those physicians do who bring sickness upon us in order to have a subject on which to practise their skill and test their drugs.

If we have not known how to live it is wrong to teach us how to die, and to make the end differ from the whole. If we have known how to live bravely and tranquilly we shall know how to die bravely and tranquilly. They may brag as much as they please, that *the whole life of a Philosopher is a meditation on death* (Cicero). But it seems to me that it is, indeed, the end, but not the aim of life;[1] it is its finality, its extremity, not however its object. It ought to be its own drift, its own purpose; its rightful study is to order, to direct, to suffer itself.

Among the many other duties comprised under this general and important heading of 'Knowing how to live' is this article of 'Knowing how to die'; and one of the lightest, if our fear did not weigh it down.

Judging them by their usefulness and by the naked truth, the lessons of simplicity yield little to those which learning teaches to the contrary. Men differ in inclination and power; they must be guided to their own good, according to their nature, and by different ways.

Where wind and weather waft me, there I'm borne. (HORACE.)

I never met a farm-labourer in my neighbourhood who meditated how, and with what face and assurance, he should spend his last hours. Nature tells him not to think of death until he is dying. And then he will do so with a better grace than Aristotle, whom death oppresses with a double weight, both with itself and with so long a foresight. Therefore it was Caesar's opinion that the happiest and easiest death is the least premeditated. *He grieves more than is necessary who grieves before it is necessary* (Seneca).

The bitterness of this imagination springs from our curiosity. So we always shackle ourselves when we try to outdistance and control what Nature prescribes. It is only

---

[1] *C'est bien le bout, non pourtant le but, de la vie.* As remarked, Montaigne is fond of playing on words.

for the doctors, when in good health, to look glum at the spectre of death and to dine with less enjoyment. The common people have no need of physic or of comfort except when the blow falls, and they think of it no more than just as they feel.

Is it not as we say, that it is the dullness and want of apprehension of the common people that gives them that power to endure present ills, and that profound indifference to the mishaps that may be impending in the future; that their souls, through being gross and obtuse, are not so easily penetrated and moved? If that is so let us in God's name henceforth keep a school of stolidity. This result to which stolidity so imperceptibly guides its disciples is the utmost that learning can promise us.

We shall not lack good teachers, interpreters of the simplicity of Nature. Socrates shall be one. For, as far as I can remember, he speaks something to this purpose to the judges who are about to dispose of his life:

'I fear, my friends, that if I entreat you not to put me to death, I shall involve myself in the indictment of my accusers, which is that I claim to know more than others, as if I had some more secret knowledge of things that are above and below us. I have had no association or acquaintance with death, nor have I known any one who has had experience of its nature, and could give me information. They who fear it presume that they know it. As for me, I neither know what it is nor what the other world is like. Death may be an indifferent thing, or it may be desirable.

'We may believe however that, if it is a migration from one place to another, it will be a gain to go and live with so many departed great ones, and to have nothing more to do with unjust and corrupt judges. If it is an annihilation of our being, it will still be a gain to enter upon a long and peaceful night. Nothing in life is sweeter than a deep and tranquil rest and sleep, without dreams.

'The things I know to be wicked, such as wronging our neighbour and disobeying our superior, whether it be God or man, I carefully avoid. Those as to which I do not know whether they be good or evil, I cannot fear.

'If I am to depart and leave you alive, the Gods alone can see which of us, you or I, will fare the better for it. Wherefore, as far as I am concerned, you may dispose of me as you please. But, following my custom of advising just and profitable things, I will yet say that, for the sake of your conscience, you will do better to set me free, unless you can see further than I do into my case. And, if you consider my past actions, both public and private, if you consider my intentions, if you consider the profit that so many of our citizens, young and old, derive every day from my conversation, and the good I have done you all, you cannot duly repay me for my deserts except by ordering that, in view of my poverty, I be maintained at the public cost at the Prytaneum, a privilege I have often known you, with less reason, to grant to others.

'Do not impute it to obstinacy or disdain if I do not follow the custom of supplicating you and trying to move you to pity. I have friends and kinsmen (not being, in the words of Homer, born of stocks and stones, any more than others) who might appear before you in mourning and tears, and I have three disconsolate children to move you to compassion. But I should disgrace our city, at my age and with the reputation for wisdom of which I am accused, to demean myself so abjectly. What would be said of the other Athenians?

'I have always admonished my hearers not to redeem their lives by a dishonourable action. And in the wars of my country, at Amphipolis, at Potidaea, at Delium, and others in which I took part, I proved by deeds how far I was from securing my safety by disgracing myself. Moreover, I should make you depart from your duty and invite you to do hateful things; for not my entreaties, but pure and solid reasons of justice, should persuade you.

'You have sworn to the Gods to bear yourselves thus. It would seem as if I were suspecting and retorting upon you that you do not believe there are Gods. And I should testify against myself that I did not believe in them as I should, if I mistrusted their guidance and did not commit my affair entirely to their hands. I wholly rely upon them, and hold for certain that they will dispose of this matter as will be best for you and for me. No good man, either in life or after death, has any cause to fear the Gods.'

Is not that a sound and sober pleading, but at the same time artless and familiar, inconceivably highminded, candid, truthful and honest beyond all example? And in what a pressing need it was spoken! Truly he was right to prefer it to that which the great orator Lysias had written for him, which was admirably couched in forensic style, but unworthy of so noble a criminal. If we had heard from the lips of Socrates a single supplicating note that proud virtue would have struck sail at the height of its fame.

And should his rich and powerful nature have entrusted its defence to cunning, and, in its greatest ordeal, renounced truth and simplicity, the ornaments of his speech, to deck and disguise itself with the embellishments and pretences of a discourse committed to memory? He acted very wisely, and in accordance with his character, not to corrupt the tenor of an incorrupt life, and so sanctified a model of human nature, in order to prolong by a year his old age, and impair the immortal memory of that glorious end. He owed his life, not to himself, but, as an example, to the world. Would it not have been a public disaster if he had ended it in idleness and obscurity?

Assuredly, this carelessness and indifference to his own death deserved that posterity should make more of it on his behalf; as, indeed, they did. And no justice was ever so just as that which Fortune had in store for him, to his glory. For the Athenians held those who had been the cause of his death in such abomination, that they shunned them as excommunicated persons. Everything they had touched was looked upon as polluted. No man washed with them at the baths, no man saluted or accosted them, so that at last, unable any longer to support the general hatred, they hanged themselves.

If any one should think that, among so many examples of the sayings of Socrates I had to select from to suit my purpose, I have made a bad choice; and if he judges this speech to be too exalted for ordinary conceptions, I may say that I have purposely selected it. For I judge otherwise, and regard it as a speech that ranks, in naturalness, far behind and below common conceptions. It reflects with unstudied and artless boldness and a childlike assurance the simple and primitive idea and ignorance of Nature. For it may be believed that we are naturally afraid of pain, but not of death in itself. Death is a part of our existence, no less essential than life.

Why should Nature have engendered in us a hatred and

horror of it, seeing that it ranks so highly with her for its usefulness in fostering the continuance and alternation of her works, and that, in this universal republic, it conduces more to birth and increase than to loss or destruction?

> For evermore is thus renewed
> The total sum of things. (LUCRETIUS.)
> A thousand lives are born of one decease. (OVID.)

The decay of one life is the passage to a thousand other lives.

Nature has implanted in animals an instinct to look after themselves and keep out of harm's way. They go no further than fear of injury, of knocks and wounds, of being fettered and beaten by man, accidents which their senses and experience teach them to avoid. But they cannot fear being killed by us, nor have they the faculty to imagine and conclude such a thing as death. So it is also said that they not only suffer it cheerfully (most horses neigh at their death, and swans celebrate it in song), but that, when urged by necessity, they seek it, as has been often exemplified in the case of elephants.

Besides, is not the method of arguing that Socrates adopts in this case equally admirable for its simplicity and its power? Truly it is much easier to speak like Aristotle and to live like Caesar than to speak and live like Socrates. There lies the extreme degree of perfection and difficulty; art cannot attain to it. Our faculties have not been trained to such a pitch. We neither test them nor do we know them; we invest ourselves in those of others, and let our own lie idle.

Any one might therefore say of me that in this book I have only made up a bunch of other people's flowers, and that of my own I have only provided the string that ties them together. I have certainly given way to public opinion in wearing these borrowed plumes. But I have no intention that they shall cover me and hide me; that is the very opposite of my purpose, for I wish to make a show of nothing but what is my own, and what is my own by Nature; and if I had followed my own inclination I should at all hazards have drawn entirely on my own resources. I burden myself with them more and more every day, going beyond my intention and my original practice, following the fashion of the day and other people's advice. If it is unbecoming

HOW BOOKS ARE COMPILED

in me, as I think it is, no matter; it may be of use to some other person.[1]

Many a man quotes Plato and Homer without ever having seen the originals; and I have often enough taken passages elsewhere than from their source. Without trouble and without learning, being surrounded by a thousand volumes of books in the room in which I am writing, I could presently, if I pleased, borrow from a dozen such patch-makers, men whose books I seldom look into, the wherewithal to enamel this treatise on Physiognomy. I need only turn to the preliminary epistle of some German to stuff myself with quotations. In this way we go begging a dainty reputation, and tricking a silly world.

Those pasties of commonplaces, with the help of which so many men economize their studies, are of little use except for commonplace themes; and they only help us to show off our learning, not to regulate our conduct: a ridiculous outcome of learning which Socrates belabours so humorously when arguing against Euthydemus. I have seen books compiled on subjects neither studied nor understood by the writer, who deputed various learned friends of his to look up this and that matter to build it up with, being content, for his share, with planning the work and industriously piling up that heap of undigested material; the ink and paper at least are his. That is in all conscience to buy or borrow a book, not to make one. That is the way to teach men not that you can write a book, but that you cannot write one, about which they may have been in doubt.

A President boasted in my presence that into one of his presidential judgements he had packed two hundred and so many passages from foreign sources. By publishing this fact to all and sundry he was, it seems to me, robbing himself of the glory he might have gained by it. A fatuous and ridiculous boast, to my mind, for such a feat and such a person!

[I do the contrary]; and when so many things are borrowed, I am glad to be able to filch a thing now and then, disguising and altering it for some new purpose. At the

---

[1] It may be noted, in explanation of the foregoing, that the original editions of the Essays, published in 1580 and 1582, contained very few quotations. Many of them were added when the third Book appeared in 1588, and more subsequently.

risk of its being said that I failed to understand its original application, I give it some particular turn of the hand, that it may be less purely inappropriate. The others make a show of their pilferings and take credit for them, and so are more pardonable for them than I.[1]

We followers of Nature think that the honour of invention is greatly and incomparably to be preferred to the honour of quotation.

If I had wished to speak learnedly I should have spoken earlier ; I should have written at a time nearer to my study-period, when I had more wit and memory, and I should have trusted more to my vigour at that age than at this, if I had wished to become a writer by profession.

Moreover, such kind favour as Fortune perhaps offered me through the mediation of this book would then have lighted upon a more propitious season.[2]

Two of my acquaintances, great men in this profession, have in my opinion lost by half through refusing to publish at forty years of age and waiting till they were sixty. Maturity has its drawbacks, as well as the green years, and worse. And old age is as unfit a time for this kind of work as for any other. He who puts his decrepitude under the press plays the fool, if he hopes to squeeze out of it any ideas that do not smack of the disagreeable, the drowsy and visionary. Our brains, as they age, become constipated and stagnant.

I dispense my ignorance abundantly and ostentatiously, my learning meagrely and sparingly ; the latter accidentally and secondarily, the former positively and authoritatively. The only things I treat adequately are things of no account, and all my knowledge betrays want of knowledge.

I have chosen the time when my whole life, which I have to portray, lies before me ; what remains of it is more allied to death. And of my death I should probably give an

---

[1] In the 1588 edition we read here : ' Like a horse-thief I paint the mane and tail, and sometimes blind them in one eye ; if the first owner used it as an ambler I make a trotting horse of it ; and if it was a saddle-horse I turn it into a pack-horse.'

[2] This is taken to be an allusion to Montaigne's friendship with Mademoiselle de Gournay, whom he met in Paris in 1588, when he was seeing his book through the press. In all the printed editions it appeared in an altered form.

account to the public only if I happened to be loquacious, as others are, at the time of my departure.

It grieves me that Socrates, who was a perfect model of all great qualities, chanced to have so ill-favoured a body and face, as they say he had, and out of harmony with the beauty of his soul; when he was so enamoured of, so infatuated with beauty. Nature did him an injustice.

There is nothing more likely than the conformity and relation of the body to the spirit. *It is of no little consequence in what body the soul is lodged; for there are many things which depend on the body that give an edge to the soul, and many which blunt it* (Cicero). Cicero is thinking of an unnatural ugliness and deformity of limbs. But we also call ugliness an incongruity that is visible at the first glance, which lies chiefly in the face, and which often arouses our dislike on very slight grounds: the complexion, a scar, a rugged countenance, some inexplicable cause, whilst the limbs are symmetrical and perfect.

The ugliness which clothed a very beautiful soul in La Boëtie was in this category. This superficial ugliness, which is however very impressive, affects the state of the mind less prejudicially, and makes people uncertain about it. The other kind, which is more properly called deformity, is more material, and more generally strikes inwardly. Not only every shoe of soft leather, but every well-shaped shoe, shows the shape of the foot within.

So Socrates said of his, that it would have betrayed just as much ugliness in his soul, if he had not corrected it by training. But in saying that I think he was jesting, according to his wont; and never did so excellent a soul fashion itself.

I cannot often enough repeat how much I look upon beauty as a quality that gives power and advantage. He called it 'a short tyranny'; Plato, 'Nature's privilege'. Man has no quality that stands in higher repute. It ranks highest in human intercourse; it is the first that attracts notice, it seduces and prepossesses our judgement, exercises great influence, and makes a wonderful impression.

Phryne would have lost her case, although conducted by an eminent counsel, if she had not torn open her tunic and corrupted her judges by her dazzling beauty.

And I observe that Cyrus, Alexander and Caesar, those three masters of the world, did not disdain it in carrying out their great enterprises ; nor did the elder Scipio. One and the same word in Greek embraces both the good and the beautiful ; and the Holy Ghost often calls those good whom it would call beautiful.

I would readily agree to range the blessings of this life in the order in which Plato found them in a song, taken from some ancient poet, which he says was current in his time : Health, Beauty, Wealth.

Aristotle says that to the handsome belongs the right to command, and, if there are any whose beauty approaches that of our idea of the Gods, that veneration is also their due. To one who asked him why one associated longer and more frequently with handsome people, he replied, 'That question could be asked only by one who is blind.'

Most of the Philosophers, and the greatest of them, paid for their schooling, and acquired wisdom, by the favour and mediation of their beauty.

Not only in the men who serve me, but also in animals, I regard it as within two fingers' breadth of goodness. Yet it seems to me that that cut of the face, those features and lineaments from which they argue a certain inner disposition, and foretell our future fortunes, are not things that may be simply and directly classed under the heading of beauty and ugliness. No more can we say that every good odour and clearness of atmosphere promise health, and every closeness and offensive smell bode infection, in times of pestilence.

Those who accuse the fair sex of contradicting their beauty by their character do not always hit the truth; for in a face that is not too well fashioned there may dwell an air of honesty that inspires confidence ; as, on the other hand, I have at times read in a lovely pair of eyes threats of a dangerous and mischievous nature. There are physiognomies that promise friendliness, and when surrounded by victorious enemies you will immediately choose from among a number of strangers one rather than another to whom you will surrender and trust your life ; and not exactly in consideration of his beauty.

The face is a weak surety ; yet it deserves some consideration. And if I had the punishment of the wicked I would more severely lash those who belie and betray the promises that Nature has implanted on their brows ; I would more harshly chastise knavery under a meek and mild aspect.

It seems as if some faces were happy, and others ill-starred. And I believe that it needs some skill to distinguish between the gentle and the silly, the stern and the rugged, the ill-natured and the downcast, the contemptuous and the melancholy, and such other bordering qualities. There are types of beauty that are not only proud but repellent ; there are others not only sweet but, beyond that, insipid. As to foretelling from them their future fortunes, that is a matter I leave undecided.

As I have said elsewhere, I have for my part adopted, very simply and crudely, this ancient rule, 'That we cannot go wrong if we follow Nature', and that the sovereign precept is, 'To conform to her'. I have not, like Socrates, by the force of reason, corrected my natural propensities, and have not in the least interfered with my inclinations by art. I let myself go as I have come ; I combat nothing. My two ruling qualities live, of their own accord, in peace and harmony ; but my nurse's milk was, thank God, passably wholesome and temperate.

May I say this by the way, that I observe that we attach an undue value to a certain conception, almost the only one in vogue with us, of scholastic probity, a slave to precepts, cramped by hope and fear ? I would have it, not formed, but perfected and authorized by laws and religions, sensible of being able to stand without help, springing up within us from its own roots, from the seed planted by universal reason in every man not corrupt by nature. This reason, which straightens Socrates from his vicious bend, makes him obedient to the men and gods who rule in his city, brave in death, not because he has an immortal soul, but because he is a mortal man. It is a teaching that is destructive to all government, and much more harmful than ingenious and subtle, which persuades the people that religious belief alone, without morality, is sufficient to satisfy the divine justice. Experience tells us that there is an enormous difference between piety and conscience.

My bearing is friendly, both in itself and as interpreted by others :

Is, did I say ? Nay, Chremes, it once was. (TERENCE.)

Alas ! of this old worn-out body
Thou seest but the bones ; (MAXIMIANUS.)

and offers an example that contrasts with that of Socrates. It has often happened that, on the strength of my looks and presence only, people who had no knowledge of me have placed great confidence in me, whether in their own affairs or in mine; and in foreign parts they have won me particular and unusual kindness. But the two following experiences perhaps deserve telling in detail.

An individual who shall be nameless planned to make a surprise attack upon me and my house. His scheme was to arrive alone at my gates and rather earnestly request to be let in. I knew him by name and had reason to trust him, since he was a neighbour and distantly related to me by marriage. I opened to him, as I do to everybody. There I found him in a great state of terror, his horse panting and worn out. He entertained me with this fiction: 'That he had just had an encounter, half a league away, with an enemy of his, whom I also knew, and I had heard of their feud; that his enemy had made him clap on his spurs to some purpose, and having been taken unprepared and inferior in numbers, he had sought safety at my gate; that he was very troubled about his men, whom he concluded to be either taken or dead.'

In my innocence I tried to comfort and reassure him, and put new heart into him. Presently four or five of his soldiers turned up with the same look of terror, and were let in, and then more and still more, well armed and mounted, until there were twenty-five or thirty of them, all pretending that the enemy were at their heels.

This mystery was beginning to arouse a little suspicion. I did not forget in what age I was living, how greatly my house might be coveted; and I remembered several examples of others of my acquaintance who had had similar misadventures. However, seeing that there was nothing to be gained by beginning to use them kindly if I did not go through with it, and that I could not get rid of them without bringing matters to a head, I took the most natural and simple course, as I always do, and bade them come in.

Besides, to tell the truth, I am by nature little given to suspicion and mistrust, and am easily inclined to admit excuses and the most favourable interpretation. I take men to be pretty much all alike, and, unless I am forced to do so by overwhelming evidence, I cannot believe in such perverse and unnatural intentions, any more than I believe in prodigies and miracles. And I am, moreover, a man who readily trusts to Fortune and throws himself heedlessly into her arms. And I have hitherto had more reason to applaud than blame myself for so doing, having found her more prudent and more friendly to my affairs than I am myself.

There have been several actions in my life the conduct of which might justly be called suspicious, or, if you prefer it so, circumspect; of these same, supposing the third part may be set down to my credit, the other two-thirds are abundantly due to her. It seems to me that we sin in that we do not sufficiently trust ourselves to Heaven, and expect more from our own conduct than we are entitled to. Therefore it is that our plans so often miscarry. Heaven is jealous of our yielding so much to the claims of human wisdom, to the prejudice of its own; and the more we extend them the more does it cut them down.

These men remained on horseback in my courtyard, whilst the leader was with me in my hall; he would not have his horse stabled, saying he would have to depart as soon as he had news of his men. He saw that he was master of the situation, and nothing remained but the execution of his enterprise. He has since often said, for he was not ashamed to tell the tale, that it was my face and my ingenuousness that snatched the treachery out of his hands. He remounted his horse, whilst his men continually had their eyes upon him to see what signal he would give them, greatly astonished to see him depart and abandon his advantage.

On another occasion, relying upon some truce between our armies that had just been proclaimed, I started upon a journey through an uncommonly ticklish part of the country. My departure was no sooner winded than three or four parties of horsemen started from different points to seize me. One caught me up on the third day, when I was attacked by fifteen or twenty gentlemen with masks, followed by a swarm of troopers. There I was captured and surrendered, drawn into the thick of a neighbouring forest, dismounted, rifled, my coffers searched, my moneybox seized, horses and armour divided amongst new masters. We were a long time in this thicket, disputing the matter of my ransom, which they rated so high that it was very evident that they did not quite know who I was. They had a lively dispute over my life. Indeed, there were many threatening circumstances which showed the danger I was in:

> Now, Trojan, for a stalwart heart and true,
> Firmness and steadiness! (VIRGIL.)

I persisted in standing on my rights under the truce, only relinquishing the gain they had made in despoiling me, which was not to be despised, without promise of any other ransom. After we had been there two or three hours, and after they had set me on a nag of whose escape there was no danger, and committed me to a special escort of fifteen or twenty musketeers, my men being divided among others, and orders given that we should be led prisoners by different routes, and I being already two or three musket-shots on the way,

> Invoking the aid of the Heavenly Twins, (CATULLUS.)

behold a sudden and very unexpected change of mind in my captors! I saw the leader return to me with milder words, taking the trouble to collect my scattered belongings from among the company, and restoring to me as many as he was able to recover, including even my money-box. The best present they made me was after all my freedom; the rest did not give me much concern at that time.

The true cause of so strange a change of mind and conduct, due to no apparent impulse, and of so miraculous a repentance at such a time, in an enterprise that had been deliberately planned beforehand, and which by custom had become quite the right thing to do (for at the outset I openly confessed to them what party I belonged to, and what road I was going), I cannot, indeed, understand to this day. The most conspicuous among them, who removed his mask and told me his name, repeated to me several times that I owed this deliverance to my face, my freedom and firmness of speech, which made me undeserving of such ill-treatment, and asked to be assured of a like treatment if occasion should offer.

It may be that the divine goodness willed to make use of this trivial means for my rescue. It also protected me the very next day from still worse ambushes, against which those men themselves had warned me.

The latter is still above ground to tell the tale; the former was killed not long ago.

If my face did not answer for me, if the innocence of my intentions were not to be read in my eyes and voice, I should not have survived so long without quarrels and without harm, seeing the indiscreet freedom with which I say, right or wrong, whatever comes into my head, and give utterance to rash opinions on things. This habit may reasonably appear uncivil and little in keeping with our usage, but I have never met any one who thought it insulting or ill-natured, or who took offence at my candour, if he had it directly from my lips. Repeated words have a different sound and a different sense.

Nor do I hate any man; and I am so disinclined to do any one a wrong, that I cannot do so even should reason require it. When occasions required me to sentence a criminal I rather sinned against justice. *Whilst I would not have crimes committed, I lack the heart to punish them when they have been committed* (Livy).

It is said that Aristotle was blamed for having been too merciful to a wicked man. 'It is true, he said, that I was merciful to the man, but not to his wickedness.'

The judgement of the ordinary man is provoked to exercise vengeance by the horror of the misdeed. That itself is enough to cool mine. Horror of the first killing makes me fear a second; and hatred of the first cruelty makes me hate any imitation of it. To me who am but a knave of clubs,[1] may be applied what was said of Charilaus, King of Sparta: 'He cannot be good, since he is not hard on the wicked.' Or rather thus, for Plutarch puts the matter in these two ways, as he does a thousand other things, variously and contradictorily: 'He must needs be good, since he is good even to the wicked.' As I am loath to proceed even lawfully against a man who would resent my action, so, to tell the truth, I am not sufficiently conscientious to refrain from an illicit action with one who acquiesces in it.

---

[1] A person of no importance. The expression *valet de carreau*, knave of diamonds, is also used in the sense of a 'contemptible fellow, mean wretch'.

CHAPTER 13

OF EXPERIENCE

THERE is no more natural desire than the desire for knowledge. We try all ways that may lead us to it. When reason fails we resort to experience:

> By various proofs Experience art has made,
> Example pointing out the way; (MANILIUS.)

which is a more ineffectual and less worthy means. But the truth is so great a thing that we should despise no means that may lead us to it. Reason has so many shapes that we know not which to lay hold of: experience has no fewer. The inference we try to draw from the likeness of events is uncertain, because they are always unlike.

No quality is so universal, in the appearance of things, as diversity and variety. To express the highest degree of similarity, both the Greeks and Latins, as well as ourselves, use eggs as an example. Yet there have been men, and notably one at Delphi,[1] who could distinguish marks of difference in different eggs so well that he never mistook one for another. And although he had a great number of hens he was able to tell which of them laid a particular egg.

Dissimilarity intrudes of itself into our works; no skill can attain similarity. Neither Perrozet[2] nor any other can smoothe and whiten the backs of his cards so carefully that no gamester can distinguish between them on merely seeing them slipping through another's hands. Resemblance does not make things so much alike as difference makes them unlike. Nature has obliged herself to make nothing other that was not unlike.

Therefore I do not much like the opinion of the man[3] who thought that to multiply the laws was to curb the authority of the judges, by cutting up their meat for them. He did not realize that there was as much liberty and latitude in interpreting the laws as in the making of them. And they fool themselves who think they can lessen and put a stop to our disputes by referring us to the actual words of the

---

[1] A slight inaccuracy: Cicero, who was probably the source of Montaigne's information, notes that there were many people at Delos who had this power.

[2] Presumably the name of a maker of playing-cards.

[3] Justinian, Emperor and legislator.

Bible, since our mind finds the field no less spacious for controverting another's meaning than for urging its own. As if we showed less animosity and tartness in commenting than in inventing!

We see how much he was mistaken. For in France we have more laws than all the rest of the world together, and more than necessary to rule all the worlds of Epicurus. *As formerly we suffered from crimes, so now we suffer from the laws* (Tacitus). And yet we have left so much to the opinions and decisions of our judges that there has never been such complete liberty and licence.

What have our legislators gained by selecting a hundred thousand particular cases and actions, and applying to them a hundred thousand laws? This number is quite out of proportion to the infinite variety of human actions. By multiplying our invented cases we shall never arrive at the number and variety of possible cases. Add to them a hundred times as many more, and yet no future case will ever be found so to tally with, so exactly to fit and match another of the many thousands of selected and registered cases, that there will not remain some circumstance and diversity that will require a separate consideration and decision.

There is little relation between our actions, which are perpetually changing, and fixed and unchangeable laws. The most desirable laws are those which are most rare, most simple and general; and I still believe it would be better to have none at all, than to have them in such numbers as we have.

The laws that Nature gives us are always happier than those we give ourselves. Witness the Golden Age as depicted by the poets, and the condition in which we see those nations to be living which have no other laws.

Here we have a people who have no judges, but call upon the first traveller who passes through their mountains to decide their quarrels for them.[1] And these others elect one from among themselves, on market-days, to settle all their suits on the spot.

Where would be the danger if the wisest should thus

---

[1] According to Coste, Montaigne was thinking of the little community of San Marino in Italy, which was enclosed within the Papal States. In the Middle Age the custom mentioned prevailed generally in the republics of Lombardy.

settle ours, according to the circumstances and at sight, without being tied to precedents and issues? To every foot its shoe.

When King Ferdinand sent colonists to the Indies he wisely provided that they should take with them no men learned in the law, for fear lest law-suits might breed in that new world, since it is a branch of learning that of its nature generates altercations and divisions; deciding, with Plato, that 'lawyers and doctors are a bad provision for a country.'

Why is it that our common language, so easy for all other uses, becomes obscure and unintelligible in wills and contracts, and that this language that can express itself so clearly, whatever it may say or write, here finds no way of declaring its meaning that does not involve doubt and contradiction? Unless it be that the princes of that art, applying themselves with a particular attention to picking out solemn words and contriving artful formulas, have so carefully weighed each syllable and so accurately analysed every kind of combination that we see them trammelled and embroiled in the endless number of figures and such minute partitions that they cease to fall within any rule and prescription, and to convey any definite meaning. *Whatever is beaten into powder becomes confused* (Seneca).

Have you ever seen a boy attempting to divide a quantity of quicksilver into a certain number of parts? The more he works and squeezes it, and tries to bring it under control the more does he provoke the freedom of that noble metal; it escapes his ingenuity, and keeps dispersing into small particles beyond all reckoning. So it is here; for by subdividing those subtleties they teach men to increase their doubts; they put us into a way of magnifying and diversifying the difficulties; they lengthen them out and disperse them. By scattering questions abroad and cutting them up they make the world to fructify and abound in uncertainties and quarrels; as the earth is made more fertile the more deeply it is dug up and crumbled. *It is learning that creates difficulties* (Quintilian).

We are perplexed by Ulpian; we are still perplexed by Bartolus and Baldus.[1] We should blot out all traces of these

---

[1] Ulpian, a jurist of the second and third centuries; Bartolus and Baldus, Italian jurists of the fourteenth century, all commentators of Justinian.

innumerable differences of opinion, instead of using them to show off our learning and swelling the heads of posterity with them. I know not what to say to it, but experience tells us that so many interpretations disperse the truth and destroy it.

Aristotle wrote to be understood; since he was expressing his own ideas, if he did not succeed, still less will another succeed who is not so clever as Aristotle. We open the matter, and spread it out by diluting it; of one subject we make a thousand, and by multiplying and subdividing fall again into the infinity of atoms of Epicurus.

Never did two men judge alike on the same matter; it is impossible to find two opinions exactly agreeing, not only in different persons, but in the same person at different times. I commonly find matter for doubt in a thing of which the commentator has disdained to take notice. I am most apt to trip on smooth ground, like certain horses that I know, that more often stumble on a level road.

Who would not say that glosses increase doubt and ignorance, since there is no book about which the world busies itself, whether of human or divine origin, of which the difficulties evaporate by interpretation? The hundredth commentator hands it on to his successor, more knotty and slippery than the first had found it. When did we ever agree that 'this book has been sufficiently commented upon, that there is henceforth nothing more to be said about it?'

This is best seen in law-practice. We attribute legal authority to an endless number of doctors, an endless number of judgements and as many interpretations. And yet do we see any end to the need of interpreting? Do we see any progress and advance towards peace? Do we need fewer lawyers and judges than when this great body of law was yet in its first infancy? On the contrary, we darken and bury the understanding; we discover it only hidden behind so many hedges and barriers.

Men do not realize the natural infirmity of their mind; it does nothing but ferret and hunt around, incessantly wheeling about, contriving, involving itself in its own work, like a silkworm, and there suffocating. *A mouse in a barrel of pitch* (Latin proverb).

It thinks it sees in the distance something like a glimmer of light and imaginary truth; but, while it is hastening thither, its path is crossed by so many difficulties, so many obstacles and so many new quests, that it goes off the track and becomes dazed. Not much unlike the dogs in Aesop's fable who, discovering something resembling a dead body floating on the sea, and unable to come near it, set to work to drink up the water and lay the passage dry, and choke themselves.

What a certain Crates said of the writings of Heraclitus may be aptly quoted, ' that they needed a reader who was a good swimmer,' if, owing to the depth and weight of his learning, he is not to sink and drown.

It is only particular weakness that makes us content with what others, or we ourselves, have discovered in this pursuit of knowledge. A more able man will not rest content with it. There is always room for a successor, yea and for ourselves, and another road to travel. There is no end to our researches. Our end is in the other world. It is a sign of contraction of the mind when it is content ; or of lassitude. No noble spirit stays within itself ; it ever aspires and rises above its strength. It soars beyond its deeds ; if it does not advance and does not press forward, and does not back and does not clash with itself, it is only half alive. Its pursuits are boundless and formless, its food is wonder, the chase, ambiguity.

This was sufficiently declared by Apollo, who always spoke to us with a double, obscure and oblique meaning ; not satisfying us, but keeping us always occupied and busy. It is an irregular, perpetual movement, without model and without aim. Its inventions excite, pursue and produce one another :

> So in a running stream one wave we see
> After another roll incessantly.
> And as they glide, each will successively
> Pursue the other, each the other fly :
> By this wave that is e'er pushed on, and this
> By that continually preceded is :
> The water still does into water go,
> Still the same brook, but different waters flow. (LA BOËTIE.

It is more of a business to interpret the interpretations than to interpret the things, and more books have been written on books than on any other subject ; we do nothing but gloss one another.

All the world swarms with commentaries; of authors there is a great dearth.

Does not the chief and most reputed learning in our present age consist in learning to understand the learned? Is not that the universal and final end of all studies?

Our opinions are grafted one upon the other. The first serves as a stock to the second, the second to the third. Thus, we mount stairwise from step to step. So it comes about that he who has mounted highest has often more honour than he deserves, for on the shoulders of the last but one he is only one barley-corn higher.

How often, and perhaps foolishly, I have enlarged my book to make it speak of itself! Foolishly, if for no other reason than this, that it should remind me of what I say of others who do the same, that their so frequent oglings of their own work testify that their heart thrills with love of it, and that even the offhand roughness with which they beat it is only the mincing dissembled love of a fond mother; according to Aristotle, for whom prizing and misprizing of self often have their origin in the same arrogance. For, as to my excuse, that I ought herein to have more elbow-room than others, since I write specifically of myself and my writings, as well as of my other actions, and that my theme turns upon itself, I doubt whether it will be generally accepted.

I have observed that in Germany Luther had left as many divisions and disputes concerning the uncertainty of his beliefs, and more, as he raised concerning the Holy Scriptures.

Our disputes are about words. I ask what are Nature, Pleasure, Circle and Substitution. The question is one of words, and with words it is answered. A stone is a body, but if you urge any further, 'And what is a body?'—'Substance.'—'And what is substance?' and so on, you will end by driving the respondent to exhaust his dictionary. We exchange one word for another, and often for a less-known word. I know better what Man is than I know what Animal is, or Mortal, or Rational. To satisfy one doubt they give us three; it is the Hydra's head.

Socrates asked Meno, 'What is virtue?'—'There is, replied Meno, the virtue of a man and the virtue of a woman, the virtue of a magistrate and the virtue of a private individual, the virtue of a boy and the virtue of an old man.'—'This is very fine, said Socrates; we were in search of a virtue, and here you bring us quite a swarm of them.'

We put a question, and they give us a hive-full. As no event and no shape exactly resembles another, neither do they entirely differ; an ingenious mixture on the part of Nature. If our faces were not similar we could not distinguish man from an animal; if they were not dissimilar, we could not distinguish one man from another. All things hold together by some similarity or other; every example limps, and the connexion that is drawn from experience is always faulty and imperfect. And yet comparisons join at some corner or other. And so do the laws serve and adapt themselves to each of our affairs, by the same wrested, forced and biased interpretation.

Since the ethical laws, which are concerned with the individual duties of every man in himself, are so difficult to establish, as we see them to be, it is no wonder if those which govern so many individuals are more so. Consider the form of this justice which rules us; it is a true testimony of human feebleness, so full is it of errors and contradictions. What we regard as partiality and severity in justice—and we find so much of them, that I doubt whether impartiality is as often met with—are sickly parts and unjust members of the very body and essence of justice.

Some countrymen recently informed me in great haste that they had just left, in a wood that belongs to me, a man with a hundred wounds, still breathing, who entreated them for pity's sake to give him water and help him to rise. They said they did not dare to go near him, and ran away for fear the officers of justice might catch them there, and (as happens with those who are found near a murdered person) they should be made accountable for that mischance, which would be their undoing, since they had neither the ability nor the money to defend their innocence. What could I say to them? It is certain that that act of humanity would have brought them into trouble.

How many innocent people we have known to be punished, I mean without the fault of the judges; and how many are there that we have not known of! This happened in my time: Certain men are condemned to death for murder; the sentence, if not pronounced, is at least decided and fixed.

At that point the judges are informed, by the officers of an inferior court near by, that they hold several men in custody who openly confess to that murder, and are able to throw a light on the whole business that admits of no doubt. And yet they deliberate whether they shall interrupt and defer the execution of the sentence passed upon the first accused. They consider the novelty of the case, and its consequence for suspending judgements; that the sentence is juridically passed, and the judges have no reason to repent of it. To sum up, those poor devils are sacrificed to the forms of justice.

Philip, or some other, dealt with a like dilemma in this way: He had pronounced judgement on a man and condemned him to pay a heavy fine to another. The true facts of the case having come to light some time after, it was found that he had condemned him wrongfully. On the one side was the right of the cause, on the other the right of judicial forms. He in some sort satisfied both by allowing the sentence to stand, and making up the loss to the condemned out of his own purse.

But he had to do with a retrievable miscarriage; my men were irretrievably hanged. How many condemnations I have witnessed more criminal than the crime!

All this brings to my mind these ancient theses: That he must needs do wrong in detail who would do right wholesale, and injustice in little things if he would achieve justice in great;

That human justice is formed after the model of medicine, according to which all that is profitable is also right and honest;

That, as the Stoics hold, Nature herself, in most of her works, goes against justice;

That, as the Cyrenaics contend, there is nothing just of itself; that customs and laws make justice;

That, according to the Theodorians, the wise man is right to commit theft, sacrilege, every kind of lechery, if he knows it to be profitable to him.

There is no remedy. I agree with Alcibiades, and will never, if I can help it, place myself in the power of a man who can dispose of my head, when my honour and life depend on the skill and activity of a solicitor more than on my innocence. I would risk a kind of justice that would take account of my good actions as well as my bad ; that would give me as much cause to hope as to fear. To be indemnified is not sufficient coin for a man who does better than not to go wrong. Our justice offers us only one of her hands, and that is the left. Let him be who he may, he comes off with loss.

In China, a kingdom whose governments and arts, having had no contact with or knowledge of ours, offer examples that surpass ours in many excellent features ; from whose history I learn how much wider and more diverse the world is than either the ancients or we moderns have been able to conceive, the officers deputed by the ruler to inspect the condition of the provinces, whilst punishing those who are guilty of corruption in administering their office, also reward, from pure liberality, those whose conduct has been more than ordinarily honourable, and more so than mere duty required. These men come forward not only to answer for their conduct but to gain ; not to be simply paid but to receive a present.

No judge has yet, thank God, spoken to me as a judge in any cause whatsoever, whether my own or another's, whether criminal or civil. No prison has ever received me, not even as a visitor.[1] Imagination makes even the outside of a jail odious to me. I am so hungry for freedom that if any one were to forbid me access to some corner of the Indies I should feel my life to be a little more constrained. And as long as I can find earth and air free and open elsewhere, I will never lurk in a place where I must hide.

Good heavens, how I should chafe if I were reduced to the condition of so many people I know of, riveted to a district of this kingdom, deprived of the right to enter the chief towns and courts and to make use of the public roads, for having quarrelled with our laws ! If those laws I observe were to threaten only the tip of my little finger I should immediately go in search of others, wherever they may be. All the little caution I possess, in these Civil wars in which we are engaged, is exercised to prevent their curtailing my freedom of coming and going.

---

[1] In 1588 Montaigne did actually become acquainted with the inside of the Bastile, having been arrested at the instigation of the Duc d'Elbeuf as a reprisal for some wrong done to a kinsman, but after four hours' detention he was set free by authority of the Queen-mother.

Now the laws maintain their credit not because they are just but because they are laws. That is the mystic foundation of their authority, and they have no other. And that is, indeed, their advantage. They are often made by fools; more often by men who, in their hatred of equality, are wanting in equity; but always by men, vain and unsteadfast authors. Nothing is so clumsily and widely, nor so ordinarily, faulty as the laws. Whoever obeys them because they are just does not obey them for the reason for which they should rightly be obeyed.

Our French laws, by their irregularity and formlessness, rather lend a helping hand to the confusion and corruption that we see in their administration and execution. Their authority is so confused and inconsistent that in some sort it excuses both disobedience and mistakes in their interpretation, administration and observance. Whatever then may be the fruit of experience, that which we derive from foreign examples will make us little wiser if we profit so little from that which we have of ourselves, which is more familiar to us, and certainly sufficient to tell us what we need.

I study myself more than any other subject; that is my Metaphysics, that is my Physics;

> With how much skill this mighty world is ruled;
> Whence comes the rising moon, and where she sets;
> How 'tis she joins her horns, and every month
> Comes to the full; where winds surmount the sea;
> What regions Eurus seizes with his blast;
> Why waters turn to clouds; if ever a day
> Will come, when all these earthly towers
> Are overthrown: let them inquire whose minds
> Are moved to know the secrets of the world.
>
> (PROPERTIUS and LUCAN.)

In this universe of things I allow myself to be ignorantly and carelessly guided by the general law of the world. I shall know it well enough when I feel it. My learning cannot make it alter its course. It will not modify itself for my sake. It is folly to expect it, and greater folly to be disturbed about it, since it is necessarily the same for all of us. The goodness and capability of our Pilot must relieve us fully and absolutely from all anxiety about steering.

The researches and meditations of the philosophers only

serve to feed our curiosity. The philosophers very rightly refer us to the laws of Nature ; but these laws are not concerned with such sublime knowledge. The philosophers falsify them, and show us Nature with a painted face, too high in colour and too sophisticated ; whence spring so many different portraits of so uniform a subject. As she has provided us with feet to walk with, so she has given us wisdom to guide us through life : a wisdom not so ingenious, robust and showy as that they have devised, but correspondingly easy and wholesome, which very well performs what the other promises, if we are fortunate enough to be able to live it simply and fitly, that is to say, naturally. To trust to Nature most simply is to trust her most wisely.

O what a soft and easy and wholesome pillow is ignorance and freedom from care to rest a well-screwed-on headpiece !

I would rather know myself well by studying myself than Cicero. The experience I have of myself I find sufficient to make me wise if I were a good scholar. He who calls to mind the excess of his past anger, and remembers how he was carried away by his passion, will see the hatefulness of it better than in Aristotle, and will have more reason to hate it. He who remembers the evils he has suffered, and those which have threatened him, the slight causes which have disturbed his state of mind, is by them prepared for future changes, and for the knowledge of his condition.

The life of Caesar can offer us no more examples than our own ; and whether it be the life of an Emperor or that of a proletarian, it is still a life that is subject to all human accidents. Let us only give ear to it ; we tell ourselves all that we chiefly need. If a man remembers how many and many a time he has been mistaken in his own judgement, is he not a fool if he does not ever after distrust it ? When I have been convinced by another's arguments that I have held a wrong opinion ; what I have learned is, not so much the new thing he has told me, and the fact that I was ignorant in one particular (that would be no great gain), but that I am generally feeble-minded and that my understanding is a treacherous guide ; whence I draw the conclusion that my whole mental process needs reforming. I do the same in the case of all my other errors, and find this a very profitable rule in life. I regard not the species and the individual, as I should a stone over which I have stumbled ;

I learn to distrust my steps throughout, and am careful to place them aright.

To learn that we have said or done a foolish thing, that is nothing ; we must learn that we are but fools : a much fuller and more important lesson.

The mistakes that my memory has so often led me into, even when it was most confident of itself, have not been wasted upon me ; she may swear to me at this moment, and assure me to her heart's content, I shake my ears. The first opposition her testimony meets with will give me pause ; I would not dare to trust her in a matter of importance, nor answer for her in another's concerns. And were it not that what I do for lack of memory others do still more often through want of good faith, I should always accept the truth, concerning a matter of fact, from another's lips rather than from my own.

If every one would closely watch the effects and circumstances of the passions that sway him, as I have done of the one that has fallen to my lot, he would see them coming, and would a little break their course and impetuosity. They do not always fly at one's throat with one leap ; they threaten us by degrees :

> As when a wave beneath the rising gale
> 'Gins whiten, slowly heaves the sea, and rears
> Its billows higher, then from lowest deep
> Mounts in one mass to heaven. (VIRGIL.)

The judgement holds a masterful sway with me ; at least it carefully endeavours to do so. It leaves my feelings to go their own way, both hatred and love, even the love which I bear to myself, without change or corruption. If it cannot convert the other parts as it would, at least it does not allow itself to be perverted by them ; it plays its own game by itself.

The advice given to every man, ' Know thyself ', should have very great influence, since the God of light and learning had it engraved on the front of his temple,[1] as comprising all that he had to counsel us.

Plato says besides that wisdom is no more than the carrying out of this command, and Socrates, according to Xenophon, proves it in particular cases.

The difficulties and obscurities of every science are only

[1] The temple of Apollo at Delphi.

perceived by those who have entered upon it. For it still needs some degree of intelligence to be able to remark our ignorance; we must push a door before we know it is closed. Whence arises this Platonic subtlety, 'Neither those who know need inquire, since they know, nor those who know not, since in order to inquire they must know what they are inquiring about.'

So in the matter of 'knowing oneself', the fact that every man is so cocksure and self-satisfied, and thinks he knows enough about himself, shows that he does not know himself in the least; as Socrates, in Xenophon, impresses upon Euthydemus.

I, who make no other profession, find in myself such infinite variety and depth, that the only result of my learning is that I feel how much I still have to learn. I owe it to my weakness, which I so often admit, that I am inclined to be modest, to bow to the beliefs that I have been taught, to be consistently cool and moderate in my opinions, to hate that overbearing and quarrelsome arrogance that causes a man to believe and trust entirely to himself; a deadly enemy of learning and truth.

Hear them laying down the law; as soon as they open their mouths to utter some foolish thing, you would think they were prophets and legislators. *Nothing can be more discreditable than to assert and acquiesce in a thing before we know and understand it* (Cicero).

Aristarchus said that in former times there were scarcely seven wise men in the world, and that in his own time he could scarcely find seven ignorant men. Could we not say the same with more reason of our times?

Affirmation and opinionativeness are positive signs of stupidity. This man may have fallen on his nose a hundred times in one day, and yet here we see him riding the high horse, as positive and headstrong as ever. You would think he had since been inspired with some new soul and intellectual vigour, and that, like that old son of the earth, he renewed his strength and courage with each new fall: [1]

> Whose weakened limbs, touching his Mother Earth,
> Forthwith exult in renovated strength. (LUCAN.)

[1] The giant Antæus, a famous wrestler who could not be thrown, as he regained his strength whenever he touched his Mother Earth; eventually defeated and killed by Hercules, who suspended him in mid air.

Does not this incorrigibly pig-headed fellow think he has picked up a new wit because he has picked up a new argument ? It is personal experience that makes me accuse the world of ignorance, the consciousness of which is, in my opinion, the surest means of schooling the world. Those who will not conclude their ignorance from so vain an example as mine, or as theirs, let them acknowledge it with Socrates. He was the teacher of teachers ; for the philosopher Antisthenes said to his pupils, ' Come, you and I will go and hear Socrates ; there I shall be a pupil with you.' And, maintaining this doctrine of the Stoic sect, ' that virtue sufficed to make a life completely happy, wanting nothing whatever,' he added, ' excepting the strength of Socrates.'

Having so long and attentively studied myself I am also qualified to form a passably good estimate of others ; and there are few matters on which I can speak more happily and pardonably. I am often able to observe and discern the nature of my friends more accurately than they do themselves. I have surprised one or two by the aptness of my description ; and I have warned them against themselves. Through having trained myself from youth up to see my own life reflected in that of others, it has become a natural propensity to study that subject ; and when I give my mind to it, there are few things in the faces, humours and talk of the persons around me that escape my notice, if they are likely to be instructive to me.

I study everything : what I must flee, what I must follow. So from the outer manifestations of my friends I discover their inner natures ; not in order to marshal those infinitely varying, motley and disconnected actions under fixed headings and categories, to distribute my lots and sections into distinct and recognized classes and degrees ;

> How many kinds, and what their names,
> There is no telling. (VIRGIL.)

It is only learned scholars who divide and mark off their ideas more specifically and in detail. I, who see no further into things than I have been taught by using my eyes, and that without any method, present my ideas in the gross, and tentatively. As in this : I express my meaning in disjointed clauses, as a thing that cannot be said all at once and in the lump. A mean and commonplace mind like ours is unable to connect and relate. Wisdom is a complete and substantial structure, each part of which keeps its place and bears its mark. *Wisdom alone is contained wholly in itself* (Cicero). I leave it to artists, and I know not whether they will bring it about, in a matter so mixed, so subtle and uncertain, to marshal into bands that endless variety of aspects, to resolve our inconsistencies and arrange them in order. I find it not only difficult to reconcile our actions with one another, but I find it difficult, taking each one singly, to properly designate it by some leading quality, so ambiguous and motley do they appear from different points of view.

What is remarked as uncommon in Perseus, King of Macedon, ' That his mind, fixing itself to no one condition, wandered through every kind of life, reflecting a character so flighty and erratic, that neither he himself nor any other knew what kind of a man he was,' seems to me to apply to nearly the whole world.

And above all I know another of his kidney, to whom I think this description would still more fittingly apply: no middle attitude, being always carried away from one extreme to another by causes not to be guessed at; steering no kind of course without being crossed, and changing its direction in a surprising manner; no one simple and unmixed quality; so that the likeliest supposition that may be some day put forth about him is that he affected and studied to make himself known by being unknowable.

It needs very strong ears to hear yourself frankly criticized; and since there are few who can bear it without being mortified, those who boldly venture to censure us show their friendship in a remarkable degree. It is a sign of a healthy affection to undertake to offend and wound us for our good. It taxes my powers to give my opinion of a man in whom the bad qualities outnumber the good.

Plato requires three qualities in a man who undertakes to examine another's soul: Knowledge, Benevolence, Boldness.

I was once asked what I thought I was fit for, if any one had thought of employing my services whilst I was young enough to be of use:

> While better blood gave strength, before the snow
>   Of envious age was sprinkled on my brows. (VIRGIL.)

' For nothing,' I said. And I generally excuse myself by

saying that I can do nothing that would enslave me to another. But I would have told any master of mine the plain truth, and would have watched over his conduct, if he had allowed me. Not in the gross, by lecturing him like a schoolmaster, which I cannot do (and I do not observe that those who can do so effect any real improvement), but by observing him step by step, at every opportunity, keeping a close watch upon him, bit by bit, simply and naturally, letting him know what the public thought of him, and opposing his flatterers.

There is not a man of us who would not be worse than a king, if he were continually being pampered, as a king is, by those rapscallions. What can we expect when Alexander, so great both as king and philosopher, was unable to resist them?

I should have had fidelity, judgement and candour enough for that. It would be a nameless office, else it would lose its effect and its grace. And it is a part that cannot be played by all indiscriminately. For even the truth is not privileged to speak at all times and in every kind of way; the exercise of it, noble as it is, is limited and circumscribed. It often happens, as the world wags, that the truth slips into the ears of a Prince, not only fruitlessly, but prejudicially and even wrongfully. And no one will make me believe that a righteous remonstrance cannot be viciously administered; and that the interest of the substance must not often yield to the interest of the form.

For this business I would have a man who is content with his fortune,

> Who likes that present state of his,
> And would not be but what he is,   (MARTIAL.)

and of middle rank by birth, because, on the one hand, he would not be afraid of touching his master's heart to the quick or of deeply offending him, and so losing his chance of preferment; and on the other hand, being of middle station, he would more probably be in communication with all classes of people. I would have him to stand alone, for to spread the privilege of this freedom and intimacy among several would beget a harmful irreverence. And certainly in that man I would require above all things the fidelity of silence.

A king is not to be believed when, for fame's sake, he

boasts of his bravery in standing his ground against the attack of the enemy, if he cannot, for his own good and improvement, stand the liberty of speech of a friend, which has no other power but to penetrate his ear, the rest of its effect being in his own hand. Now there is no kind of man that stands in such great need of true and sincere warning as a king. He has to endure to live in the public eye, and to satisfy the notions of so many onlookers, that, as those about him are wont to conceal from him everything that frustrates his plans, he finds himself involved, without being conscious of it, in the hatred and detestation of his people, often on grounds he might have avoided, even without prejudice to his pleasures, if he had been informed and set right in time. His favourites commonly look to their own interests more than to those of their master; and it answers them well, since, indeed, most of the duties of true friendship towards the sovereign are put to a rude and dangerous test; so that there is need, not only of great affection and freedom, but also of courage.

In fine, all this farrago that I am scribbling here is nothing but a record of the experiences of my life, which, in regard to spiritual health, is exemplary enough if the instruction to be derived from it is reversed. But in regard to bodily health no man can furnish more useful experience than I, since I offer it unadulterated, quite uncorrupted by art and theory. In the realm of medicine experience is, so to say, a cock on his own dunghill, since reason must entirely give way to it.

Tiberius used to say that the man who had lived twenty years ought to be responsible to himself for all the things that were harmful or wholesome for him, and be able to take care of himself without medical aid.[1]

He might have learned this of Socrates, who recommended his pupils to look carefully after their health as a most important study, and added that an intelligent man who took exercise, and was careful about his eating and drinking, could not fail to know better than a physician what was good or bad for him.

---

[1] According to both Suetonius and Tacitus, Tiberius said, in other words, that ' a man at thirty is either a fool or a physician '; Plutarch makes him say that ' the man is a fool who offers his pulse to a doctor after sixty '.

And, indeed, medicine always professes to make experience the touchstone of its actions. So Plato had reason on his side when he said that to be a genuine physician it would be necessary for the practitioner to have passed through all the diseases he professes to cure, and to be familiar with all the accidents and circumstances on which he is to give an opinion. It is but right that he should catch the pox if he would know how to treat it.

I should certainly trust such a man. For the others guide us like a man who should paint seas and rocks and harbours seated on his table, with the model of a ship passing in all safety before his eyes. Put him to the real thing and he will not know how to set about it.

They describe our diseases like a town-crier trumpeting the loss of a horse or a dog : such and such colour, such and such a height, such and such ears ; but bring it to him he will not recognize it.

By heavens ! if only medicine should some day give me real and perceptible relief, you should see how I would exclaim in good earnest :

>At length to potent science I surrender. (HORACE.)

The arts that promise to keep our body in health and our soul in health promise much ; but at the same time there are none that keep their promise less. And in our time and our country the men who profess these arts can show fewer results than any other. The best we can say for them is that they sell medicinal drugs ; but that they are medical men we cannot say.

I have lived long enough to be able to give an account of the habits that have carried me so far. For any man who has a mind to try them I have tasted them as if I were his cupbearer. Here follow a few details, as my memory shall supply me with them. I have no habits that I have not varied according to circumstances, but I record those that I have oftenest observed to prevail, and that have hitherto taken most hold of me.

My mode of life is the same in sickness and in health : the same bed, the same hours, the same food and even the same drink, serve my purpose. I make no change whatever except that I observe more or less moderation, according to my strength and my appetite. With me health means keeping up my accustomed way of living without discomfort. I find that sickness upsets my balance in one direction; if I take the advice of the doctors they will upset it in the other; so what with fortune and art I have quite lost my way.

Of nothing am I more certain than of this, that nothing harms me that I have been so long accustomed to.

It is the part of habit to shape a man's life according to its pleasure; in this it is all-powerful. It is Circe's draught that varies our nature as seems good to her.

In how many countries, and only three steps from here, it is regarded as a ridiculous fancy to dread the night-dew which appears so hurtful to us! And our watermen and peasants laugh at it.

You will make a German ill if you give him a mattress to sleep on, as you will an Italian on a feather-bed, and a Frenchman without curtains or a fire. A Spaniard's stomach cannot stand our way of eating, nor ours to drink like the Swiss.

A German at Augsburg amused me by arguing against the disadvantages of our open fire-places with the very same reasons for which we condemn their stoves. For, indeed, that stifling heat, and the smell of the heated material of which they are made, give most of those who are not accustomed to them a headache; but not me. After all, this heat being even, constant and general, without light, without smoke, and without the draught that is caused by our open chimneys, it may very well bear comparison in other respects with ours.

Why do we not copy the Roman architecture? For it is said that in ancient times the fires were made, not inside the houses but on the outside, and at the foot of them, whence the heat was drawn through the whole dwelling, through pipes which were contrived in the thick walls and embraced the rooms that were to be warmed; which I have seen plainly described somewhere in Seneca.

My German, hearing me praise the beauties and amenities of his town, which certainly deserve the praise, began to pity me because I had to leave it; and among the chief disadvantages he mentioned to me was the heaviness of head that the fire-places elsewhere would cause me. He had heard somebody complain of this discomfort, and fixed it upon us, habit having made him unable to detect it at home.

All heat that comes from a fire makes me feel weak and heavy. And yet Evenus said that fire was the best condiment of life.[1] I prefer any other way of escaping the cold.

We are afraid of the wine at the bottom of the cask; in Portugal they commend it for its delicious bouquet, and call it the drink of princes. In short, every nation has many habits and customs which to any other nation are not only strange but amazing and barbarous.

What can we do with those people who will admit of no evidence that is not in print, who will not believe a man who is not in a book, or the truth unless it is of suitable age?

We dignify our stupidities when we send them to the printers.

To say 'I have read it' carries very much more weight with them than if you say 'I have heard it'. But as for me, who would no more disbelieve a man's mouth than his hand, who know that people write with as little judgement as they speak, and who esteem this age as highly as one that is past, I would as soon quote one of my friends as I would Aulus Gellius or Macrobius, and what I have seen as what they have written.

And, as some have said of Virtue that it is no greater for being of long standing, so I hold of the Truth that it is no wiser for being older.

I often say that it is mere foolishness that makes us run after outlandish and bookish examples. They flourish quite as well at this moment as in the time of Homer and Plato. But is it not true that we seek to gain more credit for the action of quoting than for the truth of what we quote? As if it were more to the purpose to borrow our proofs at the shop of Vascosan or Plantin,[2] than from what we may see in our village.

Or is it not rather true that we have not the wit to pick out and turn to account the things that pass before our eyes, nor the acumen to estimate their fitness to serve as examples? For if we say that we lack authority to win belief for our testimony, we say so without reason; since, in my

---

[1] Or, according to Amyot's translation 'the best sauce in the world', no doubt on account of its culinary properties.
[2] Two well-known printers of the day.

opinion, if we could set them in their proper light, the most ordinary, trite and commonplace things might form the subject of the greatest wonders in Nature, and provide us with the most surprising examples, especially in the matter of human actions.

Now, in this connexion, setting aside the examples I know from books, and the case of Andro of Argos, who, according to Aristotle, crossed the sandy deserts of Libya without drinking, a gentleman, who had acquitted himself very creditably in several charges, said in my presence that he had travelled from Madrid to Lisbon in the middle of summer without drinking. He is very robust for his age, and there is nothing extraordinary in his mode of life except this, that he will go two or three months, and even a year, so he told me, without drinking. He feels the thirst, but he allows it to pass, and maintains that it is a craving that easily becomes weaker of itself; and he drinks more from caprice than from need or for pleasure.

Here is another: Not long ago I found one of the most learned men in France, and a man of no mean fortune, studying in the corner of his hall which had been partitioned off by tapestries, whilst his servants, under no restraint whatever, were creating a regular hubbub around him. He told me, and Seneca says pretty much the same about himself, that this pandemonium suited him. It would seem that, stunned by the noise, he could better retire within himself, become more collected and meditate the better; as if this storm of voices drove his thoughts inward. When he was a scholar at Padua, he studied so long in a room that was exposed to the rattle of coaches, and the tumult of the market-place, that he had trained himself not only to ignore the noise but to find it necessary for his studies.

Socrates replied to Alcibiades, who wondered how he could stand the perpetual din of his wife's scolding tongue, 'I am like those who are accustomed to the regular sound of the water-drawing wheels.'

I am quite the contrary: my mind is sensitive, and is apt to wing its flight; when it is absorbed in itself the mere buzzing of a fly will torment it to death.

Seneca, in his youth, being sorely bitten by the example of Sextius to eat nothing that had been killed, abstained from animal food for a year, and with pleasure, as he said. He left off the habit only because he did not wish to be suspected of borrowing that rule of some new religions that were propagating it. At the same time he followed the precept of Attalus not to lie on any bedding that gave way under his weight, and continued even in his old age to sleep on a bed that did not yield to his body. What was accounted an austere habit in his day would now be put down to effeminacy.

Look at the difference between the life-habits of my hinds and my own. The Scythians and Indians are not more remote from me in ways and capabilities. I remember having rescued boys from a life of beggary and taken them into my service, who soon after left me and gave up my kitchen and their livery, only to return to their former life. And I found one of them afterwards picking up mussels out of the midden for his dinner, whom neither by entreaties nor threats I could reclaim from the relish and delight he took in want.

Beggars have their sumptuousness and their sensual pleasures as well as the rich, and, so they say, their civil ranks and orders.

These are the results of Habit. She can not only mould us into any shape she pleases ('wherefore, as the sages say, choose the best, and habit will soon make it easy for you'), but also teach us to change and vary, which is the noblest and most useful thing we can learn from her.

The best thing about my physical constitution is that it is pliable and not very stubborn. Some of my inclinations are more personal and usual, and more agreeable than others; but I can depart from them with very little effort and easily glide into the opposite habit.

A young man should break in upon his rules, to stir up his energy and keep it from becoming mouldy and lazy; for no course of life is so foolish and feeble as that which is carried out according to rules and discipline:

> Before she takes a drive of half a mile
> Her almanac must tell the proper hour;
> If she but chafes the corner of her eye,
> No salve must touch it ere she can consult
> Her horoscope. (JUVENAL.)

If he will take my advice, he will occasionally even run into excess; otherwise the least dissipation will upset him, and he will become disagreeable and unfit for company. The most repugnant quality in a gentleman is to be over-fastidious and tied down to certain particular ways; and they are particular if they are not yielding and pliable. It is a disgrace for a man to refrain from what he sees his friends doing, because he cannot or dare not follow their example. Let such a man keep to his own kitchen. It is unbecoming in every other man, but in a soldier it is an intolerable fault; for, as Philopoemen said, he should harden himself to all the changes and ups and downs of life.

Although I was trained, as far as possible, to be easily pleased and independent, yet so it is that, having, through indifference as I grew older, become more settled in certain habits (at my age I am beyond learning, and I have henceforth no other prospect but to keep my course), habit has already unconsciously impressed its stamp upon me, in certain things, to such a degree that I call it excess to deviate from it. And I cannot, without trying myself, either sleep by day, or take snacks between meals, or breakfast, or go to sleep without a long interval, of about three hours at least, after supper, or procreate except before sleep, or standing, or carry my sweat, or quench my thirst with either water or wine unmixed, or remain long bareheaded, or have my hair cut after dinner; and I should be as uncomfortable without my gloves as without my shirt, or without washing when I rise from table or get up in the morning, or without a canopy and curtains to my bed; which to me are all very necessary things.

I could dine without a table-cloth, but very uncomfortably without a clean napkin, in the German fashion; I soil them more than they or the Italians do, as I make little use of spoon or fork. I am sorry they did not keep up the fashion which was begun in my day, following the royal example, of changing the napkin with the plates at every course.

We are told by that hard-working soldier, Marius, that he became dainty in his drinking as he grew older, and that he drank only out of one particular cup of his own. I too have dropped into the habit of using a glass of a certain shape, and do not care to drink out of a common glass, nor when served by a common hand. I dislike all metal in comparison with a clear and transparent material. My eyes must also taste to the best of their capacity.

I owe many such weaknesses to Habit. Nature, on the other hand, has also brought me her share of them, such as being unable to bear two full meals a day without overloading my stomach, or abstaining entirely from one of those meals without becoming flatulent, drying up my mouth and taking the edge off my appetite; and suffering from long exposure to the night air. For during the last few years, in the drudgeries of the war, when they continue all through the night, as they often do, after five or six hours my stomach begins to give me trouble, with violent headache, and before daybreak I am obliged to vomit. When the others go to breakfast I go to sleep, and after that I am as fresh as ever.

I had always understood that the evening dew only fell at nightfall, but having during these latter years been long and intimately acquainted with a lord who was imbued with the belief that the evening air is keener and more dangerous towards the decline of the sun, an hour or two before it sets, when he carefully avoids it whilst despising the night air, he has almost communicated to me not so much his belief as his feeling.

What if our imagination should even be so affected by doubt and inquiry as to cause a change in our health? Those who suddenly yield to these fancies will entirely ruin their health. And I pity several gentlemen who, through the foolish advice of their doctors, though still young and in perfect health, have made close prisoners of themselves.[1] It would after all be better to suffer from a cold than by disuse to forfeit for ever the pleasures of life in common by giving up so widespread a habit.[2]

What a disagreeable science to run down the most agreeable hours of the day! Let us hold on to the utmost of our powers. Most often we may harden ourselves by persistence, and correct our constitutions, as Caesar did his epilepsy by dint of despising and fighting it.

We should adopt the best rules, but not become slaves to them; except to those, if there are such, to which obligation and slavery are beneficial.

Kings and philosophers obey Nature's call, and ladies too.[3]

---

[1] *Se sont mis en chartre;* which might also mean, as Florio translates it, 'fallen into a decline or consumption'.

[2] The habit of going out at night.

[3] *Les Roys et les philosophes fientent, et les dames aussi.*

A man who lives in the public eye is obliged to observe the conventions; I, who am an obscure and private individual, enjoy every dispensation that Nature allows. As a soldier and a Gascon I may be allowed a little indiscretion. Wherefore I will say of that action that it must be relegated to certain fixed and night hours, to which we should force and subject ourselves by habit, as I have done; but not, as I have done in my declining years, pamper ourselves by being tied for this function to a particularly comfortable place and seat, and make it a burden by prolongation and luxury.

And yet in the dirtiest functions is it not in some measure excusable to require more care and cleanliness? *Man is by nature a cleanly and dainty animal* (Seneca). It is the one function of Nature that I can least bear to put off. I have known many soldiers to be inconvenienced by the irregularity of their bowels; whilst I and mine never miss the moment of our assignation, which is on leaping out of bed, unless we are disturbed by some urgent occupation or some serious malady.

I cannot think therefore, as I said before, where a sick man can better find safety than in quietly continuing the course of life to which he has been reared and trained. Change of every kind is disturbing and hurtful. Will any man believe that chestnuts will hurt a native of Périgord or Lucca, or milk and cheese a mountain-dweller?

They keep ordering us not merely a new diet, but the very opposite to that we are accustomed to; a change that not even a healthy man can suffer. Order a Breton of seventy to drink water; shut up a sailor in a hot-house; forbid a Basque footman to walk: you deprive them of movement, and in the end of air and light.

> Is mere existence then so very sweet? (ANON.)
> We must perforce renounce our dearest things,
> And give up life that we may merely live.
> Can he be said to live to whom we grudge
> The air we breathe and light that gives us life? (MAXIMIANUS.)

If they do no other good they do this at least, that they prepare their patients betimes for death, by gradually undermining and cutting off their enjoyment of life.

Both in health and sickness I have generally yielded to

my urgent appetites. I allow my desires and inclinations to have a great say in the matter. I have no wish to cure one ill with another; and hate the remedies which are more unpleasant than the malady. To be subject to the stone, and to subject myself to abstaining from the pleasure of eating oysters, are two evils instead of one. The disease twinges us on the one side, the rule on the other. Since we risk making a mistake let us rather risk the pursuit of pleasure. The world goes the contrary way to work, and thinks nothing beneficial that is not painful; it is suspicious of facility.

My appetite has in many things happily enough adapted itself of its own accord, and fallen in with the health of my stomach. Sharp and pungent sauces were agreeable to me when I was younger; my stomach having since then turned against them, my palate has forthwith followed suit. Wine is hurtful to the sick; it is the first thing my mouth takes a dislike to, and an invincible dislike. Whatever I take that is disagreeable to me, disagrees with me.

Nothing disagrees with me that I do greedily and heartily. I have never taken harm from any action in which I found great pleasure. And so I have made every medical decision to yield very largely to my pleasure. And as a young man,

> When young Dan Cupid, gay in saffron shift,
> Would hover round me with his playful wiles, (CATULLUS.)

I yielded, as wantonly and thoughtlessly as any other, to the desire that held me captive;

> And, not without some glory, held my own. (HORACE.)

My love, however, was more constant and enduring than vigorous;

> I scarce remember once attaining six. (OVID.)

It is, indeed, distressing and wonderful to me to have to confess at what a tender age I first chanced to come under Cupid's subjection. It was, indeed, a chance, for it was long before the age of choice and knowledge. I cannot remember so far back. And my lot may be wedded to that of Quartilla,[1] who had no recollection of her maidenhood.

> Precocious hairs and beard soon blossomed forth,
> A mother's admiration. (MARTIAL.)

[1] See Petronius's *Satyricon*.

The physicians modify, usually with good results, their rules according to the vehemence of their patients' cravings. The great desire in question must be put down to Nature, however monstrous and vicious we may imagine it to be. And then, how much does it need to satisfy the imagination? In my opinion that faculty is all-important, at least more so than any other. The most grievous and the most common ills are those that fancy puts upon me. I like this Spanish saying from several points of view, *God defend me from myself*.

When I am ill I am sorry not to have some craving that will give me this pleasure of satisfying it; medicine would find it hard to turn me from it. I feel the same when I am well; I see hardly anything more to hope and wish for. It is pitiful when even the power of wishing becomes weak and languid.

The medical art is not so cut and dried that we cannot find some authority for doing whatever we please. It changes according to climate and according to the moons; according to Fernel and l'Escale.[1] If your doctor does not think it good for you to sleep, to drink wine, or to eat of a particular dish, do not worry; I will find you another who will not agree with him.

The various medical arguments and opinions assume every kind of form. I saw a wretched sick man faint and dying with thirst, for his cure, who was afterwards laughed at by another doctor, who condemned that treatment as hurtful. Had he not had all his torments for nothing?

One of the faculty recently died of stone in the bladder, who resorted to starvation to combat his malady; his colleagues say, on the other hand, that his fast had dried him up and baked the gravel in his kidneys.

I have observed that when sick, or wounded, talking excites me and hurts me as much as any other irregularity that I may commit. The use of my voice tires me, and I have to suffer for it, for it is loud and strong; so much so that when I used to entertain the ears of eminent men with weighty affairs, they would often anxiously entreat me to moderate my voice.

This story deserves a digression: Some one in a certain

[1] Fernel or Farnel and l'Escale, better known as Scaliger, two famous physicians of the day.

Greek school was speaking in a loud voice, as I do ; the master of the ceremonies sent him a request to speak lower. ' Let him send me, he said, the tone in which he wishes me to speak.' The other replied, ' That he should take his tone from the ears of him he was speaking to.' That was well said, provided it was meant in this way : ' Speak according to the matter you have to discuss with your hearer.' For if he meant, ' Let it be enough that he hears you,' or ' Adapt your voice to his hearing,' then I do not agree with him. The tone and movement of the voice help to express and signify my meaning ; it is my part to govern it in order to make myself understood.

There is a tone for teaching, a tone for wheedling, a tone for scolding. I wish my voice not only to reach him, but perhaps to impress him, to force its way into him. When I rate my footman in a sharp and bitter tone, it would be a fine thing if he said to me, ' Master, speak lower, I can hear you very well.' *There is a kind of voice adapted to the hearing, not so much by reason of its volume, as its quality* (Quintilian). Speech is half his who speaks, and half his who hears. The latter must prepare to take it according to the impetus it receives. As with tennis players, he who takes the ball must shift his position and make ready according to the movement of the striker, and according to the nature of the stroke.

Experience has also taught me this, that we undo ourselves by impatience. Misfortunes have their life and their limits, their sickness and their health.

Maladies are constituted after the model of living creatures. Their destiny and their length of days are limited from their birth. He who arbitrarily and forcibly attempts to cut them short in the middle of their career, will prolong and multiply them, and will incense instead of appeasing them. I agree with Crantor, that we should neither obstinately and frantically oppose them, nor weakly succumb to them ; but naturally give way to them, according to their condition and our own.

We ought to give maladies free access to us ; and I have found that they stay a shorter time with me, who give them a free hand. And some have left me, even of those reputed among the most tenacious and stubborn, dying of their own decay, without the help of the art of medicine, and in spite of its rules. Let us allow Nature a little free play ; she knows her business better than we do.

'But so and so died of it.' So will you, if not of that disease, of some other. How many have died in spite of having three doctors at their backsides !

Example is a clear looking-glass, universal and all-embracing.

If the physic is pleasant, take it ; it is always so much present gain. I will not boggle at the name or the colour, if it is delicious and appetising. Pleasure is one of the principal elements in the benefit.

I have allowed colds, gouty discharges, looseness, palpitations, megrims, and other ailments to grow old in me and die a natural death ; they would leave me when I had half accustomed myself to keep them. They are better conjured by courtesy than by defiance.

We must meekly endure the laws of our nature. We are born to grow old and weak, to fall into sickness, in spite of all medicine. It is the first lesson that the Mexicans read their children, when they thus salute them after they have come out of their mother's womb : ' Child, you have come into the world to endure ; endure, suffer, and hold your peace.'

It is wrong to complain that a thing happens to any one of us that may happen to all of us. *You may complain if anything is unjustly decreed against you alone* (Seneca).

Look at an old man praying to God to keep him in perfect and robust health, that is to say, to restore his youth :

Why prayest thou, fool, such childish prayers in vain ? (OVID.)

Is it not madness ? His state does not admit of it. The gout, the stone, indigestion, are symptoms of a long life, as heat, rain and winds of a long voyage.

Plato does not believe that Aesculapius would have taken the trouble to treat a wasted and crazy body and prolong the life of one who was of no use to his country, unequal to his calling, and unable to beget healthy and sturdy children ; nor does he think it consistent with divine justice and wisdom to concern itself with such matters, its duty being to direct all things to usefulness. My good man, it is all over with you. You cannot be set up again ; at the most you may be a little patched up and propped; your misery may be prolonged for an hour or two:

> Like one who, eager to defer a while
> Impending ruin, props the tottering pile,
> Till in short space the house, the props and all
> Together in awful devastation fall. (MAXIMIANUS.)

What cannot be cured must be endured. Our life is made up, like the harmony of the world, of contrary things, also of different notes, soft and loud, sharp and flat, high and low. What could the musician express who liked only the one kind? He must be able to use them in common and blend them. And we too must take the evil with the good, which are consubstantial with our life. We cannot exist without that blending, and the one set is no less necessary to it than the other. To try to jib against the law of Nature is to copy the folly of Ctesiphon, who tried to match his mule in kicking.

I seldom consult the doctor when I feel myself getting worse, for those gentlemen take advantage of you when they have you at their mercy; they deafen you with their forebodings. Formerly, taking me unawares when I was weakened by my ailment, they would deal harshly with me, what with their dogmatic assertions and their masterful airs, threatening me now with acute pain, now with approaching death. Though they knocked and pushed me, they could not upset me and make me lose my balance. If my power of judgement was not impaired or disturbed, it was at least troubled; there is always agitation and a struggle.

Now I treat my imagination as gently as I can, and would relieve it, if I could, of all trouble and conflict. It must be helped and coaxed, and cheated when possible. My mind is well fitted for that service. It has no lack of good reasons for all things. If it could convince as well as it preaches, it would be a very happy assistance to me.

Would you like an example? My mind says to me, ' It is for your good that you have the stone; at your age the edifice has naturally to suffer some leakage. It is the season when it begins to become loose and give way. That is the common lot, and you cannot expect a new miracle to be worked in your favour. In this way you pay the tribute due to old age, and you could not have got off more cheaply.

'You must find comfort in the idea that you are in company, since you have fallen into the most common infirmity of men of your time of life. On all sides you see men afflicted with the same kind of disease, and it is an honourable fellowship, since it most commonly attaches itself to great people. There is something noble and dignified in it.

'Few men who are afflicted with it get off more cheaply; and then they have to pay the penalty of an offensive diet, and the daily swallowing of loathsome medicinal drugs; whilst you owe your better state purely to your good fortune. For a few ordinary decoctions of eryngo and rupture-wort that you have swallowed three or four times, to oblige the ladies who, with more kindness than your pain was sharp, offered you the half of theirs, seemed to you as easy to take as they were ineffectual. The others have to pay a thousand vows to Aesculapius and as many crowns to their doctor for an easy and abundant ejection of gravel, which you often owe to the kindness of Nature.

'Even your decent behaviour in everyday company is not disturbed by it; you can carry your water ten hours, and as long as another.

'You used to be terrified by this disease, says my mind, before you were acquainted with it; the shouts of despair of those who aggravated it by their impatience begot a horror of it in you.

'It is a malady that chastises those of your members through which you have most sinned; you are a man of conscience.

> That punishment alone should be resented
> That we have least deserved. (OVID.)

'Look at the punishment; it is very mild compared with that of others, and inflicted with a paternal tenderness. Consider how late in life it has come; it only seizes and troubles you at a time of your life that, in any case, will be henceforth barren and wasted, having, as if by agreement, left your youth free to enjoy its wanton pleasures.

'The fear and sympathy that people feel at the sight of this malady is for you a cause of vainglory, a feeling of which, even if you have purged your judgement and cured your words of it, your friends will yet discover some tincture in your disposition. It is gratifying to hear people say of you: there is strength of mind indeed, there is patience! They see you sweating in agony, turning pale, red, trembling, vomiting your very blood, suffering strange contractions and convulsions, your eyes sometimes dropping big tears, passing water that is thick, black and dreadful to look at, or having it stopped by some rugged and sharp-edged stone that pricks you and cruelly flays the neck of your penis; meanwhile talking to the bystanders in your usual way, jesting at intervals with your servants, taking your share in a connected conversation, making excuses for your pain and minimizing your sufferings.

'Do you remember those men of olden times who so greedily courted pain, to keep their virtue in breath and exercise? Put the case that Nature is bearing and forcing you into that vainglorious school, which you would never have entered of your own accord. If you tell me that it is a dangerous and fatal disease, what others are not so? For it is a trickery of the doctors to make exception of some, which they say do not make a bee-line for death. What matter if they lead thither by accident, and if they easily glide and turn into the path that takes you there?

'But you do not die because you are ill; you die because you are alive. Death will kill you right enough without the help of sickness. And maladies have kept death away from some who have lived the longer for thinking they were dying. Besides, there are maladies, as there are wounds, that are medicinal and health-bringing.

'The stone is often no less tenacious of life than you. We see men with whom it has stayed from their childhood to their extreme old age; and if they had not left it in the lurch, it was ready to accompany them still further. You kill it more often than it kills you. And though it should confront you with the idea of imminent death, would it not be a kind service to a man at that age to bring him to meditate upon his end?

'And, what is worse, you have no longer any reasons for desiring to be cured. In any case the common lot will call you away at the first opportunity.

'Consider how artfully and imperceptibly she makes life distasteful to you and detaches you from worldly things. She does not subject you to a continual tyranny, like so many other infirmities that afflict old people, which keep them perpetually shackled, without any relaxation of weakness and pain; but by warnings and instructions, repeated at intervals, interrupted by long pauses of rest, she seems to give you the opportunity to repeat and meditate over her lessons at your leisure.

'To give you the means of forming a sound judgement and of resigning yourself like a brave man, she brings before you every different condition of health, at its best and its worst. On one and the same day your life may be at one moment of the gayest, and the next moment quite unbearable.

'Once a month, if you do not embrace death, you at least shake hands with him. Wherefore you will have more reason to expect that he will one day catch you without any warning, and that, being so often led to the port, trusting you are still in your usual state, you and your trust will some morning find that you have unexpectedly crossed the water.[1]

'We have no reason to complain of a disease which loyally divides the time with health.'

I am beholden to Fortune for having so often attacked me with the same kind of weapons; she fashions and trains me by use to resist them, she hardens and habituates me. Henceforth I know within a little how much it will cost me to be quit of them.

For want of a natural memory I make one of paper; and, as any new symptom appears in my ailment, I write it down. Wherefore now, having had experience of almost every kind, if I am threatened by some unforeseen disaster, by turning over these little disconnected notes, like the Sibylline leaves, I never fail to find, in my past experience, some favourable prognostic to comfort me.

Habit is also of use in giving me better hopes for the future. For these ejections having so long continued at the same rate, it may be taken for granted that Nature will not change the rate, and that nothing worse will happen than what I have already experienced. Besides, this infirmity is of such a nature that it is not out of keeping with my hasty and impetuous temper. When the attack is mild it makes me afraid, because then it has come to

[1] The river Styx.

stay for some time. But normally the attacks are brisk, vigorous and extreme; they shake me to pieces for a day or two.

My kidneys held out for an age [1] without any change for the worse; it is nearly another age [1] since their condition did change. Evil things as well as good have their periods; perhaps this infirmity is drawing near its end. Age diminishes the heat of my stomach; the digestion being the less perfect, it passes this crude matter on to my kidneys. Why cannot the heat of my kidneys be likewise diminished, in definite rotation, that they may cease to petrify my phlegm, and Nature find some other way of purging me? Age has evidently caused some of my rheums to dry up. Why not the excrements which provide matter for the gravel?

Moreover, is there anything so delightful as the sudden change, when, after extreme pain, by ejection of the stone I recover, as in a flash of lightning, the beautiful light of health, so full and so free, as happens in our sudden and sharpest attacks of colic? Can the agony we have suffered for a moment counterbalance the pleasure of such a sudden improvement? How much more beautiful health appears to me after the illness, when they come so near and are in such close contact, that I am able to confront them in their full armour; when they appear as two rivals defying and opposing one another.

Just as the Stoics say that vices have been beneficially introduced into the world as a set off and an aid to virtue, we may say, with better reason and less bold conjecture, that Nature has given us pain that we may the better appreciate pleasure and painlessness.

When Socrates, after being relieved of his irons, felt the dainty and pleasurable itching in his legs caused by their weight, he was delighted to think what a close alliance there was between pain and pleasure, how they are linked together by a necessary connexion, so that they follow and beget one another by turns. And he exclaimed to the good Aesop that this consideration might have provided him with a fitting theme for a fine fable.

The worst of other maladies that I know is that their immediate effects are not so serious as their consequences.

[1] The edition of 1588 has respectively 'forty years' and 'fourteen years'.

It takes a year to recover from them, always a year of weakness and dread. There is so much risk, there are so many stages before one is brought back to safety, that there is no end to it. Before you have doffed your kerchief, and then your skull-cap, before you are again allowed to enjoy the fresh air, wine, your wife, and melons, you are lucky if you do not have a relapse into some new misery. My malady has this privilege, that it carries itself clean off, whilst the others always leave their mark and some change for the worse, which renders the body susceptible to catching a new disease; they lend a hand to one another.

These diseases may be pardoned that are content with immediate possession of us, without extending their tyranny and introducing their sequelae; but courteous and gracious are those whose passing benefits us in some way. Since I have had the stone I find myself free from other ailments, more so I think than before; and I have not since then had any fevers. I conclude that the frequent and violent fits of vomiting that I suffer purge me; and on the other hand, my loss of taste and appetite, and the unusual fastings I keep, digest my peccant humours, and Nature ejects in the form of these stones the superfluous and hurtful matter.

Do not tell me that the physic is too dearly sold; for what will you say of all those stinking draughts, those cauteries, incisions, sudorifics, setons, dietings, and all those methods of cure which, being more powerful and violent than we can bear, often bring us to death's door? So, when I have an attack I take it as a physic; when I am free I take it as being a full and certain deliverance.

Here is another benefit peculiar to my malady: that it almost plays its game by itself, and allows me to play mine, unless I lack the courage to do so. When I have been in the greatest throes I have held out for ten hours in the saddle. If you can only support it you have no need of any other regimen: play, dine, run, do this and do that if you can; your dissipation will do you more good than harm. You cannot say the same of one who has the pox, the gout or a rupture.

The other maladies impose a more general constraint; they fetter our actions much more strongly, they disturb all our arrangements, and their consideration involves the whole condition of our life. Mine only pricks the skin; it leaves the understanding and the will wholly at your disposal, as well as the tongue, the feet and the hands. It rouses rather than dulls your faculties. The mind is affected by a burning fever, struck down by an epileptic fit, and dislocated by a violent sick-headache, and in short turned upside down by all the maladies that hurt the main body and the noblest parts of it. In this case the mind is not attacked. If it goes wrong it has itself to blame; it betrays, abandons, breaks itself up.

Only fools allow themselves to be persuaded that that hard and solid body that is baked in our kidneys can be dissolved by drinking; therefore, once it is shaken up, there is nothing to be done but to give it passage; and for that matter it will make one for itself.

I have also observed this particular advantage, that it is a disease that gives little scope for guessing. We are relieved of the uneasiness which other infirmities give us by reason of our uncertainty with regard to their cause, their condition and progress; an extremely painful uneasiness. We have no need to consult the doctors and listen to their explanations; our senses tell us what it is, and where it is.

By such arguments, both weak and strong, I endeavour to lull and beguile my imagination and anoint its wounds, as Cicero did the infirmity of his old age.[1] If to-morrow they become worse, to-morrow we will provide other loop-holes.

For proof of what I say, since I wrote the above,[2] this new development has taken place, that the slightest movement forces the pure blood out of my kidneys. What of that? I move about no less than before, and I gallop after my hounds with the ardour and arrogance of youth. And I find that I make great capital out of so momentous an accident, which costs me only a dull heaviness and uneasiness in that region. It is some big stone that bruises and consumes the substance of my kidneys and my life, which I void by degrees, not without some natural pleasure, as an excrement that is now troublesome and superfluous.

Do I feel a little shaky? Do not suppose that I waste

[1] In his treatise *On Old Age*.
[2] This paragraph is one of the marginal additions to the edition of 1588.

my time feeling my pulse and inspecting my urine, in order to take some tiresome precautions or other ; I shall feel the pain soon enough, without prolonging it by the pain of fear.

He who fears he will suffer, already suffers because of his fear.

Moreover, the uncertainty and ignorance of those who presume to interpret the workings of Nature and her inner progress, and explain away all the wrong prognoses of their art, should make it clear that her ways are infinitely inscrutable. There is great uncertainty, variety and obscurity in both her promises and threats. Saving old age, which is an undoubted sign of the approach of death, I can detect few signs in any other of our ills on which to found a forecast for the future.

I only judge of my condition by actual sensation, not by reasoning. What would be the good, since I intend to do nothing but wait patiently ? Would you know how much I gain thereby ? Look at those who act otherwise and are swayed by so many different opinions and counsels ; how often they are plagued by their imagination, in which the body has no share. Many a time when I felt safe and free from those dangerous attacks, I have felt a malicious pleasure in communicating the symptoms to the doctor, as if they were just beginning. Most cheerfully did I suffer the dreadful doom to which their conclusions condemned me, and was the more beholden to the grace of God, and the more convinced of the futility of the art of medicine.

There is no better recommendation to youth than to be active and wide-awake. Our life is all movement. I am hard to move, and am slow in all things : in rising, going to bed, and at meals. Seven o'clock is early for me, and where I have a say in the matter I never dine before eleven nor sup till after six. I used to attribute the fevers and other ailments to which I was subject to the dullness and heaviness caused by long hours of sleep, and always repented dozing off again in the morning.

Plato disapproves of excess in sleep more than he does of excess in drinking.

I like to sleep hard and alone, even without my wife, in regal style, and rather well covered up. My bed is never warmed, but since I have grown old they give me, when I need it, woollen wraps to warm my feet and stomach.

They used to upbraid the great Scipio with being a sluggard ; for no other reason, I think, than because it vexed them that he was the only man in whom they could find no fault.

If I am at all particular in my manner of living, it is in this matter of sleep more than in anything else ; but as a rule I am able to adapt myself and yield to necessity as well as any other. Sleep has absorbed a good part of my life, and I still continue, at my age, to sleep eight or nine hours at a stretch. I am weaning myself with advantage from this lazy propensity, and am visibly the better for it. I find the change a little hard ; but in three days it is done. And I know of few men who can live with less sleep when necessary, or who take more constant exercise, or who are less affected by prolonged hard work.

My body is capable of enduring constant, but not violent and sudden movement. From now I avoid violent exercises, and such as make me perspire ; my limbs grow tired before they are heated. I can stand a whole day long, and do not tire of walking ; but on paved roads I have always, from my earliest days, preferred to ride. When on foot I am splashed up to the buttocks with mud ; and in our streets a little man is apt to be jostled and elbowed, for want of presence. And I have preferred to rest, either lying or sitting, with my legs as high or higher than my seat.

There is no more agreeable calling than that of the soldier ; a profession noble in its exercise (for valour is the highest, most generous and superb of all the virtues) and noble in its cause. No service is more useful, better justified and more universal than that which is devoted to the protection of one's country's peace and greatness. You take a pleasure in the society of so many noble and active young men, the often recurring tragic sights, the freedom of intercourse without any artificiality, the manly and unceremonious way of living, the many and varying feats of arms, the stirring harmony of the martial music which delights your ears and rouses your soul, the honour of the service with all its hardships and difficulties, of which Plato makes so light that, in his *Republic*, he makes women and boys share them. As a volunteer you may yourself offer to play your part in particular exploits and hazards, according to their importance and the kudos that you think you may derive from them; and you may see, when life itself is staked for good reasons, that

> 'Tis beautiful to die with sword in hand. (VIRGIL.)

To fear the risks that are shared in common by so great a number, not to dare what is dared by so many men of all classes, is the mark of an incalculably mean and craven spirit. Even children are reassured by company. If others surpass you in knowledge, in charm, in strength, in fortune, you have other causes to blame for it; but if you yield to them in stoutness of heart you have only yourself to blame.

Death is more despicable, more lingering and painful in bed than in battle; fevers and catarrhs are as distressing and fatal as a musket-shot. One who is equal to enduring bravely the accidents of everyday life would have no need to swell his courage to become a soldier. *To live, my Lucilius, is to fight* (Seneca).

I do not remember ever having been troubled with the itch. Yet to scratch oneself is one of Nature's most agreeable gratifications, and as ready to hand as any. But repentance follows too intrusively upon its heels. I mostly scratch the insides of my ears, which are at times liable to itch.

I came into the world with all my senses sound and almost perfect. My digestion is good enough for ordinary purposes, as well as my head and my breathing, and they generally hold out all through my fevers. I shall soon have passed my fifty-sixth year, an age which in some countries was, not without reason, fixed upon as so reasonable a term of life that they allowed no one to exceed it. Yet I still have occasional, though brief and fickle, returns of youthfulness, so bright that they fall little short of the health and freedom from pain of my young days. I do not mean vigour and sprightliness; it is not to be expected that they should accompany me beyond their limits:

> No more can I endure the wind and rain
> To serenade my mistress 'neath her casement. (HORACE.)

My face, and my eyes too, immediately reveal the state of my health; all the changes I undergo begin there, and they appear rather worse than they are in reality. My friends often pity me before I am sensible of the reason. My looking-glass does not alarm me, for even in my youth I have more than once put on a muddy complexion and look that boded mischief, without anything serious happening ; so that the doctors, finding no internal cause to account for the outward change, ascribed it to the mind and some secret passion that was gnawing at my heart. But they were mistaken. If I could control my body as well as I do my soul, we should get along together a little more comfortably. My mind was then not only free from troubles, but full of glee and contentment, as it commonly is, half by disposition, half by design :

> No sickness of the mind did e'er
> Affect my body's health. (OVID.)

I am of opinion that this temperament of my soul has many a time lifted the body after a fall. The latter is often in a low state ; but the other, if not gay, is at least tranquil and at rest. I had a quartan fever for four or five months, which quite disfigured me ; the mind held its course, not only calmly but in good humour. If the pain is outside of me, the weakness and languor do not much sadden me.

I have observed that there are many bodily infirmities the very name of which excites horror, but which I should fear less than a thousand mental sufferings and troubles which I see around me.

I have made up my mind that I cannot run any more ; it is enough if I crawl along. And I no more complain of the natural decay that holds me back,

> We marvel not in Alpine heights to see
> The tumid goitre ; (JUVENAL.)

than I regret that my life is not as long and as sound as that of an oak.

I have no reason to complain of my imagination. I have seldom in my life had thoughts which even interrupted the course of my sleep ; except perhaps desires which would excite without distressing me.

I seldom dream ; if I do, I dream of extravagant and grotesque things, usually the result of humorous and absurd, rather than distressing, thoughts. And I believe it to be true that dreams are faithful interpreters of our inclinations ; but it needs some skill to sort and understand them :

> No wonder 'tis if in our dreams
> The acts and thoughts, the cares and sights
> That occupy our waking hours
> Appear again. (ACCIUS, quoted by Cicero.)

Plato says, moreover, that it is a wise precaution to draw from them hints for divining the future. I see nothing in that, if it were not for the marvellous experiences on the subject of dreams related by Socrates, Xenophon, Aristotle,[1] men of unimpeachable authority.

Historians tell us that the Atlantes never dream, and that they eat nothing that has been killed. I add this detail, since that is perhaps the reason why they do not dream; for Pythagoras prescribed certain preparations of food to induce appropriate dreams.[2]

My dreams are mild and make me neither restless in body nor talk in my sleep. I have known of many in my time who have been strangely disturbed by them. Theon the philosopher walked in his sleep; as did also Pericles' slave, on the very roof and tiles of the house.

I exercise little choice at table, and take the first and nearest thing; and I do not readily change from one flavour to another. I dislike a crowd of dishes and courses as much as I do any other crowd. I am easily satisfied with few dishes, and I entirely disagree[3] with Favorinus when he says that at a feast a dish should be removed as soon as you have taken a fancy to it, and a fresh one substituted; that it is a niggardly supper at which the guests have not had their fill of the 'pope's nose' of different birds, and that the beccafico is the only bird that deserves to be eaten whole.

I often eat salt meats, and yet I prefer bread with no salt in it, and my baker at home serves me with no other at my table, contrary to the custom of the country. In my childhood the chief fault they found to correct in me was my refusal to eat the things that children commonly love best at that age, sweetmeats, preserves, pastry. My tutor would combat this aversion to dainty things as if it were a form of daintiness. And, indeed, it is nothing more than a kind of fastidiousness, whatever be the object of it. If you cure a child of a particular and obstinate liking for

---

[1] As related by Cicero, *De Divinatione*, i. 25.

[2] See Cicero, *De Divinatione*, ii. 58, who tells us that among other things Pythagoras advised his disciples to abstain from beans. Cicero adds: 'In short I know nothing so absurd as not to have found an advocate in one or other of the philosophers.'

[3] Montaigne should have said that he agreed with Favorinus, who condemned the practices mentioned.

brown bread, bacon or garlic, you cure him of a kind of epicurism.

There are some who put on the patient airs of a martyr if deprived of beef and ham when partridges abound. They are well off: that is the daintiness of the dainty; it is the taste of an easy fortune that is palled by usual and accustomed things, *by which luxury would escape the tedium of wealth* (Seneca). Not to make good cheer where another does so, to be very particular about what you eat and drink is the essence of this vice:

> And if you fear not homely fare
> Served up on plainest earthenware. (HORACE.)

There is, indeed, this difference, that it is better to restrict your desires to the things that are easiest to procure; but still it is wrong to restrict them. I once called a kinsman of mine fastidious who had in our galleys learned to dispense with a bed and go to sleep without undressing.

If I had sons I should like them to have the same advantages that I enjoyed. The good father that God gave me, whom I can only repay with gratitude, but certainly a very hearty gratitude, for his goodness, sent me to be reared from my cradle in a poor village of his,[1] and kept there as long as I was at nurse, and longer. I was trained to the humblest and most common mode of life. *A well-behaved stomach is a great part of liberty* (Seneca).

Never take upon yourselves, and much less give up to your wives, the charge of bringing up infants. Leave them to be shaped by Fortune, subject to the laws of Nature and the people; let them be trained to frugal and austere habits, that they may rather come down from hardships than rise to them.

His whim had yet another aim, to unite me with the lower class and that condition of people who need our assistance, holding that I was in duty bound rather to look to the man who extends his arms to me than to the one who turns his back upon me. And for this reason I was held over the baptismal font by people of the lowliest fortune, that I might feel obliged and attached to that class.

His plan succeeded by no means badly. I generally feel

---

[1] According to tradition the village of Papessus, about three kilometres from the Château of Montaigne.

drawn towards the lower class, whether on account of the greater credit, or by a natural compassion, a feeling which has great influence with me. The faction which I should condemn in our wars I should much more severely condemn when it is flourishing and prosperous; it will somewhat reconcile me to it when I see it miserable and crushed.

How greatly I admire the generous spirit of Chelonis, daughter and wife of Spartan kings! As long as Cleombrotus her husband had the better of her father Leonidas during the civil war of her city, she played the part of the dutiful daughter, and joined her father in his exile and poverty, in opposition to her victorious spouse. Did Fortune turn? We see her affections changing with Fortune; she bravely stands at her husband's side, whom she attended whithersoever his ill-fortune led him, having, as it seems to me, no other choice but to join the side where she was most needed, and where she could best show her compassion.

I am more naturally inclined to follow the example of Flaminius, who gave himself to those who had need of him instead of to those who could benefit him, than that of Pyrrhus, who was given to cringe to the powerful and to be arrogant with the weak.

Long drawn-out meals are irksome to me, and disagree with me; for, perhaps because I acquired the habit as a boy, for want of something better to do, I eat as long as I am at the table. Therefore, when at home, although the meals are of the shortest, I generally sit down a little time after the others, after the manner of Augustus. But I do not copy him in rising from table before the others; on the contrary, I like to rest a good while after and listen to the conversation, as long as I take no part in it. For it tires me and disagrees with me to talk on a full stomach, whilst I find that to shout and argue before a meal is a very wholesome and pleasant exercise.

The ancient Greeks and Romans had more sense than we in setting apart for eating, which is an important action in life, several hours and the better part of the night, unless they were prevented by some other unusual business; eating and drinking less hastily than we do, who perform all our actions post-haste, prolonging this natural pleasure with more leisure and with greater benefit, and combining therewith various social duties of a profitable and agreeable nature.

Those whose duty it is to look after me could cheaply deprive me of what they think will do me harm; for in such things I never covet nor feel the absence of what I do not see. But again, they waste their time if they preach abstinence from the things that are set before me. Therefore, if I wish to fast they must keep me away from the supper-table, and put before me just so much as is necessary for the small repast that has been prescribed; for if I sit down to table I forget my resolution. When I order any dish to be prepared differently my family know what it means: that my appetite is gone and that I shall not touch it.

The meat that will admit of it I like underdone, and very tender; and some I like high, even smelling. Toughness alone I cannot endure as a rule (with regard to any other quality I am as indifferent and long-suffering as any man I have known), so much so that, contrary to prevailing tastes, I even find some kinds of fish too fresh and firm. Not that my teeth are at fault, for they have always been exceptionally good, and are only now being threatened by age. From childhood I have been accustomed to rub them with my napkin, both in the morning and on sitting down and rising from table.

God is kind to those from whom he takes life by degrees; that is the only blessing of old age. The final death will be less complete and hurtful; it will dispatch only the half or quarter of a man.

Here is a tooth that has just come out without any pain and without an effort; it was the natural term of its duration. And this part of my being, and several others, are already dead, others half-dead, even of those that were most active and ranked highest during my years of vigour. Thus do I melt and steal away from myself. What a folly it would be in my understanding to feel the height of this fall, already so far advanced, as if it were from the very top! I hope it will not.

Indeed, when I think of death I derive my best comfort from the reflexion that it will be normal and natural, and that any favour I may henceforth require or hope from Destiny will be undeserved.

Men hug themselves with the belief that in olden times

they were taller and longer-lived. But Solon, who belongs to those times, cuts down the extreme duration of life to seventy years. How can I who have in all things been such a devotee of the *golden mean* of ancient times, and have regarded the average measure as the most perfect, how can I expect an immeasurable and unnatural old age? Whatever runs contrary to the course of Nature may be disagreeable, but whatever is in accordance with her should be ever pleasing. *All things that are done according to Nature should be accounted good* (Cicero).

Wherefore Plato says that the death that is brought on by wounds or disease may be accounted violent, but that which, guided by old age, overtakes us, is the easiest of all, and in some ways pleasant. *Young men are taken away by force, old men fall like ripe fruit* (Cicero).

Death even mingles and is confounded with all our life; decay anticipates its hour and thrusts itself even across the course of our progress. I have portraits of myself taken at twenty-five and thirty-five years of age, and compare them with that taken at the present moment. In how many ways they are no longer myself! How much more remote is my present face from those, than it will be from that of my end! What an abuse of Nature to drag her along so far that she will be obliged to quit us, to leave our guidance, our eyes, our teeth, our legs, and the rest, to the mercy of assistance begged of others, and, weary of accompanying us, resign us to the hands of art!

I am not excessively fond of salads or fruit, with the exception of melons. My father hated every kind of sauce; I like them all. Eating too much makes me uncomfortable; but in respect of its properties I am not yet very certain that any kind of food disagrees with me. Nor have I noticed that I am affected by full or new moons, by autumn or spring.

We are subject to fickle and inexplicable changes. For example, radishes, which I first found to agree with me, afterwards disagreed, and now they agree again. In several things I have found my stomach and palate to vary in the same way: I have changed more than once from white wine to claret, and back again from claret to white wine.

I have a dainty tooth for fish, and the meatless days are my meat-days; my fasts are my feasts. Besides, I believe that it is, as some people say, more easily digested than meat. As it goes against my conscience to eat meat on fish-days, so my taste rebels against mixing meat and fish; the difference seems to me too wide.

From my youth up I have occasionally skipped a meal; either to sharpen my appetite for the next day (for, as Epicurus used to fast and make lean meals in order to accustom his greed to dispense with plenty, I do so, on the contrary, in order to train my greed to take better advantage of plenty and to enjoy it more cheerfully); or I used to fast to keep my strength for the performance of some mental or bodily action; for both my body and mind are made cruelly sluggish by repletion. (And especially do I hate the foolish idea of coupling so healthy and active a goddess with that little pot-bellied, belching god, all swelled up with the fumes of his liquor). Or again, to cure my ailing digestion; or for want of congenial company; for with that same Epicurus I say that we should not so much look to what we eat as to whom we eat with. And I applaud Chilo, who would not promise to accept Periander's invitation to a feast until he was informed who were the other guests.

To me no dressing is so acceptable, and no sauce so appetising, as that derived from good company.

I think it is more wholesome to eat more at leisure, and less, and to eat oftener. But I would give hunger and appetite their due; I should take no pleasure in dragging through three or four wretched repasts a day, restricted by doctors' orders. Who will assure me that I can recover at supper-time the good appetite I had this morning? Let us old men especially take the first opportunity that comes our way. Let us leave the making of dietaries to doctors and almanac-makers.

The best fruit of my health is sensual pleasure; let us seize the first that is present and known. I avoid consistency in these laws of fasting. He who wishes to benefit by a habit, let him avoid continuing it. We become hardened, our powers are dulled by it; six months after your stomach will be so inured to it, that all the advantage you have gained will be to have lost the freedom of doing otherwise except to your prejudice.

I do not cover my legs and thighs more in winter than in

summer: simple silk hose. For the relief of my colds I gave way to the habit of keeping my head warmer, and my belly on account of the colic. But in a few days my ailments became accustomed to them and scorned my ordinary precautions: from a cap I advanced to a kerchief, and from a bonnet to a lined hat. The wadding of my doublet is now only ornamental. All that would be of no avail unless I added a hare's skin or a vulture's plumage, with a skull-cap for the head. Continue this gradual progress and you will go a long way. I shall take care not to do so, and would gladly go back to where I began, if I dared.

'Have you developed a new ailment? Is the remedy no longer of any avail? You have grown accustomed to it? Then try another.' In this way they ruin their health who allow themselves to be fettered by enforced rules, and superstitiously adhere to them; they need more and more, and after that more again. There is no end.

To suit our occupations, and for pleasure, it is much more convenient to lose one's dinner, as the ancients did, and defer making good cheer till the time of retirement and rest, instead of cutting up the day: that is what I used to do. For health's sake, on the other hand, I have since found by experience that it is better to dine, and that I digest better when awake.

I am not very subject to thirst, whether I am well or ill; in the latter case I very often have a dry mouth, but without thirst, and as a rule I only drink from the desire which comes with eating, and when the meal is well advanced. I drink pretty well for a man of ordinary build; in summer, and with an appetizing repast, I not only exceed the limits of Augustus, who drank only three times and no oftener, but, in order not to violate Democritus' rule, which forbade stopping at four as an unlucky number, I slide on, if need be, to the fifth: about three half-pints. For little glasses are my favourites, and I like to drain them, a thing which others avoid as unbecoming.

As a rule I dilute my wine with half, sometimes a third part of water. And when at home, following an old custom which my father's doctor recommended to him and himself followed, the wine I need is mixed in the buttery, two or three hours before it is served.

It is said that Cranaus, King of the Athenians, first introduced the custom of mixing wine with water; whether beneficially or not has been a matter for debate. I think it more seemly and more wholesome for children not to take wine before they are sixteen or eighteen years of age.

The best mode of life is that which is most usual and common; I think all singularity should be avoided. And I should hate to see a German putting water into his wine as I should to see a Frenchman drinking his pure. General use lays down the law in such things.

I fear a confined atmosphere, and have a mortal dread of smoke (the first repairs I set about in my house were those of the chimneys and the privies, which are commonly defective in old buildings, and not to be tolerated); and among the discomforts of war I include the thick clouds of dust in which we are buried in the hot weather for a whole day's march.

My breathing is free and easy, and my colds generally pass off without a cough, and without injury to the lungs.

The rigour of summer is more hostile to me than that of winter; for, besides the discomfort caused by the heat, which is less easily to be remedied than that of cold, and the force of the sunbeams that strike upon my head, my eyes are afflicted by any dazzling light. I cannot even now sit down to dinner opposite a brightly burning fire.

To counteract the whiteness of the paper, when I used to read more than I do now, I laid a piece of glass upon my book, and felt great relief from it. To this moment[1] I am ignorant of the use of spectacles, and can see as far as I ever did, and as any other person. As the day declines my eyes certainly begin to feel a little dim and weak when reading, an exercise that has always tried them, but especially at night-time.

That is a step backwards, but very hardly perceptible. I shall be retiring another step, from the second to the third, from the third to the fourth, so softly that I must needs become really blind before I feel the age and decay of my sight. So cunningly do the Fates unwind our life's thread!

And so I doubt whether my hearing is hesitating on its way to hardness, and you will see that, before I have half lost it, I shall still blame the voices of those who are speaking

[1] The edition of 1588 adds: 'at fifty-four years of age'.

to me. We must, indeed, put great pressure on the soul to make it feel how it ebbs away.

My step is quick and firm ; and I know not which of the two, my mind or my body, I have had most difficulty in arresting at the same point. The preacher who can hold my attention during a whole sermon is very much my friend. On solemn occasions, when the faces of all are so rigid, and when I have seen ladies keep even their eyes so steady, I could never succeed in keeping some part or other of me from ever wandering ; though I may be seated, I am anything but settled.[1]

As the house-slave of Chrysippus the philosopher said of her master that he was only drunk in his legs (for he had the habit of moving them about, in whatever position he was in ; and she said it when the others were excited by wine and he felt no effects from it), it might have been said of me too that from my childhood I had madness in my feet, or quicksilver, so restless and fidgety are they, wherever I place them.

It is unmannerly, besides being prejudicial to health and even to one's pleasure, to eat greedily, as I do. I often bite my tongue in my haste, and sometimes my fingers. Diogenes, meeting a boy who was eating in that way, gave his tutor a box on the ear. There were people at Rome who taught others to masticate, as well as to walk,[2] gracefully. This habit leaves me no time for talking, which gives so agreeable a relish to the dinner-table, provided that the conversation be in keeping, agreeable, and brief.

There is jealousy and envy between our pleasures ; they clash and counteract one another. Alcibiades, a man who understood the art of entertainment, banished even music from his tables, lest it should disturb the pleasure of conversation, for the reason that Plato ascribes to him, ' that it is the custom of vulgar men to call singers and instrumentalists to their feasts, for want of good conversation and agreeable entertainment, with which intelligent men know how to regale each other.'

Varro makes the following requirements for a banquet :

---

[1] The edition of 1588 adds : ' And as to gesticulation, I am never without a switch in my hand, riding or walking.'

[2] *A mascher comme à marcher.* Montaigne cannot keep away from his *jeux de mots.*

'A company of persons of handsome presence and pleasing conversation, who must be neither dumb nor loquacious; cleanliness and daintiness in the food and in the chamber; and fine weather.' It needs no little skill to provide good entertainment, and it is attended with no little pleasure. Neither great generals nor great philosophers have disdained the knowledge and practice of good eating. My imagination has given three repasts to my memory's keeping, which chanced to be particularly pleasant to me, at different times of my greater prime. For each of the guests brings the principal charm with him, according to the good temper of body and mind in which he happens to be at the time. My present condition excludes me from those pleasures.

I who am but of the earth earthy, dislike that inhuman sapience which would have us despise and hate the care of the body. I think it equally wrong to be out of love with natural pleasures and to be too much in love with them.

Xerxes was a coxcomb who, lapped in all human delights, offered a prize to the man who should invent others; but not much less of a coxcomb is a man who cuts himself off from those that Nature has invented for him. We must neither pursue nor flee them; we must accept them. I accept them a little more generously and graciously, and allow myself more readily to follow the bent of Nature.

We have no need to exaggerate their emptiness; it makes itself sufficiently felt and manifest, thanks to our morbid, kill-joy mind, which disgusts us with them as well as with itself. It treats both itself and all that it takes in, now well, now ill, according to its insatiable, erratic and versatile nature.

> Unless the vessel you would use be sweet,
> 'Twill sour whatever you may pour therein. (HORACE.)

I who boast of embracing so eagerly and particularly all amenities of life, find in them, when I look at them thus closely, little more than wind. But what would you have? We are all wind throughout. And the wind too, more wisely than we, loves to bluster and shift about, and is content with its own functions, with no desire for stability and solidity, which are none of its properties.

The unmixed pleasures of the imagination, as well as its unmixed pains, are, as some say, greater than all others, as hinted at by Critolaus and his scales.[1] It is not to be wondered at, since she composes them at her own sweet will, and cuts them out of the whole cloth. Of this I see every day notable and perhaps desirable examples. But I, who am of a mixed and coarse grain, cannot so fully bite at this single and so simple object presented by the imagination, but that I let myself go, in all my grossness, after the present pleasures prescribed by human and universal laws, intellectually perceptible and perceptibly intellectual.

The Cyrenaic philosophers hold that, like bodily pains, so also bodily pleasures are the more powerful, as being both twofold[2] and more rational.

There are some who with savage stupidity, as Aristotle says, express disgust of pleasures; I know some who do so from ambition. Why do they not also forswear breathing? Why do they not live on their own breath, and refuse the light, because it shines gratis, and costs them neither invention nor strength? Let them try to find sustenance in Mars or Pallas or Mercury, and see what happens, instead of Venus, Ceres, and Bacchus. Are not those the sort of people who will try to square the circle when perched on their wives?

I hate to be told that my spirit should be in the clouds whilst my body is at table. I would have the spirit not nailed down to it, nor sprawling upon it, but attending to it; it should sit at it, and not lie upon it.

Aristippus stood up for the body alone, as if we had no soul; Zeno embraced only the soul, as if we had no body. Both of them mistakenly. They say that Pythagoras followed a philosophy that was all contemplation, Socrates one that was all conduct and action; Plato found the adjustment of it between the two. But they say that to make up a tale. And the true adjustment is found in Socrates, and Plato is much more Socratic than Pythagorean; and it becomes him better.

When I dance, I dance; when I sleep, I sleep. Aye, and

---

[1] 'Supposing all the goods of the mind to be put into one scale, and the goods of the body into the other, Critolaus thought the goods of the mind would outweigh the others so far, that they would require the whole earth and sea to equalize the balance.'—Cicero, *Tusc. Quaes,* v. 17.

[2] i. e., both physical and mental.

when I take a solitary stroll in a beautiful garden, if some part of the time my thoughts dwell on outside events, for some other part I recall them to my walk, to the garden, to the sweetness of the solitude and to myself.

Nature has, with motherly care, observed this rule, that the actions she has laid upon us for our need should give us pleasure ; and she invites us to them, not only through our reason but also through our desire. It is wrong to infringe her rules.

When I see both Caesar and Alexander, in the thick of their great labours, so fully enjoying natural, and therefore necessary and reasonable pleasures, I do not call it a relaxing of their minds ; I call it a stiffening of their minds to subordinate, by strength of spirit, their strenuous occupations and heavy thoughts to the usages of everyday life. Wise they would have been if they could have believed that the latter was their ordinary, the former their extraordinary vocation.

What fools we are ! 'He has spent his life in idleness,' we say ; 'I have done nothing to-day.' What, have you not lived ? That is not only the fundamental but the most honourable of your occupations. 'If I had been given an opportunity to manage great affairs, I might have shown what I can do.' Have you been able to meditate and manage your own life ? Then you have performed the greatest work of all. In order to show herself and get to work, Nature has no need of a great destiny ; she will show herself equally in all ranks, both behind a curtain and without one.

It is our duty to compose our character, not to compose books, and to win, not battles and provinces, but order and tranquillity for our conduct of life.

Our great and glorious masterpiece is to live to the purpose ; all other things, ruling, laying up treasures, building, are at the most but appendicles and adminicles.

I delight in contemplating an army-general, at the foot of a breach he is about to attack, devoting himself entirely and free from cares to his dinner and to his table-talk among his friends. And Brutus, with heaven and earth conspiring against him and Roman liberty, stealing an hour or two from his nightly rounds, to read and epitomize Polybius in all security. It is the part of a little soul, buried

under the weight of business, not to be able to get clean
away from it, to lay it aside and take it up again:

> Now ye brave hearts that have weathered
> Many a sorer strait with me,
> Chase your cares with wine—to-morrow
> We shall plough the mighty sea! (HORACE.)

Whether it be in jest or in earnest that the wine of the
Divines[1] and the Sorbonne has become proverbial, like
their banquets, I think it reasonable that they should dine
more agreeably and cheerfully for having been usefully and
seriously employed in the morning teaching their classes.
The consciousness of having made good use of the other
hours is the right savoury sauce for the table.

Thus did the Sages live. And that inimitable straining
after virtue which excites our admiration in both of the
Catos, that austere turn of mind that is carried to obtrusive-
ness, has thus tamely and complacently submitted to the
laws of human nature, and of Venus and Bacchus; in
accordance with the teachings of their school, which require
the perfect sage to be as skilled and experienced in the
enjoyment of natural pleasures, as in any other of life's
duties. *A wise palate should go with a wise judgement*
(Cicero).

The power to relax and assume easy manners is highly
honourable, I think, and the most becoming trait in a strong
and generous soul. Epaminondas never imagined it to be
derogatory to the honour of his glorious victories and the
perfect purity of his morals to mingle with the dance of
the boys in his town, and to sing, play an instrument, and
give his whole mind to these recreations.

And among the many admirable actions of Scipio, the
grandfather,[2] a man worthy to be reputed of celestial
origin, there is none that shows him in such a charming light
as to see him strolling along the beach with Laelius, playing
the fool like a careless boy, picking up and selecting shells
and playing ducks and drakes; and in bad weather amusing

---

[1] *Vin Théologal*: notable good and strong wine; or the best wine, of
what kind soever.—Cotgrave.

[2] The original reading of the 1588 edition was ' of the younger Scipio
(when all is considered, the first of the Romans) '. Montaigne seems to
have forgotten that it was the younger Scipio who was contemporary
with Laelius and Terence.

and tickling himself with reproducing in written comedies the commonest and most vulgar actions of the people;[1] and, with his thoughts taken up with that wonderful expedition against Hannibal and Africa, visiting the schools in Sicily and attending lectures in Philosophy, thus arming the teeth of the blind envy of his enemies at Rome.

And there is nothing more remarkable in the life of Socrates than that he found time in his old age to learn to dance and play on instruments, and thought it was time well spent.

This same man was once seen standing for a whole day and night in a trance, in the presence of the whole Greek army, his mind caught and carried away by some deep thought. He first, among so many valiant men of the army, ran to the help of Alcibiades, when the latter was overwhelmed by the enemy, covered him with his body and by main force of arms extricated him from the throng. And he first, among all the Athenians, who, like him, were incensed by so shameful a sight, came forward to rescue Theramenes, who was being led to his death by the satellites of the Thirty Tyrants. And, although he was joined by only two other men, all told, only at the instance of Theramenes himself did he desist from this bold undertaking. Although he was run after by a fair lady with whom he was in love, he was known, in spite of pressing need, to observe strict chastity. At the battle of Delium he was seen to pick up and save Xenophon, who had been thrown by his horse. He was always seen to march to war and tread the ice barefoot, to wear the same gown winter and summer, to surpass all his comrades in enduring hardships, and to eat no more at a banquet than at his ordinary. He was seen for twenty-seven years to endure, with unchanged countenance, hunger, poverty, the perverseness of his children, his wife's clawings, and in the end, calumny, tyranny, imprisonment, fetters, and poison.

But if ever he was challenged to a drinking-bout, he

[1] Montaigne was quite convinced that Scipio and Laelius wrote the comedies of Terence; see Book I, ch. 4. The 1588 edition had this passage, afterwards deleted. 'I am exceedingly vexed that the lives of those two great men, Epaminondas and the younger Scipio, by common consent of the world, the one the first of the Greeks, the other the first of the Romans, the finest pair of lives that Plutarch wrote, should have been among the first to be lost.'

accepted as a matter of civility, and of all the army he was the man who came off best. And he never disdained to play at knuckle-bones with the boys or to ride with them on a hobby-horse, and he did it all gracefully; for all actions, says Philosophy, are equally becoming and honourable in a sage. We have material enough, and we should never weary of presenting the picture of this great man as a pattern and ideal of perfection in all things.

There are very few examples of a pure and perfect life, and our education is all wrong when every day we are shown such crazy and defective models, scarce to be commended for any quality, which rather pull us backward; corrupters rather than correctors.

People generally go wrong: it is much easier to go along the side-path, where the boundary serves as a check and guide, than by the broad and open middle way, to be guided by art rather than by Nature; but also much less noble and less commendable.

Greatness of soul consists not so much in soaring high and in pressing forward, as in knowing how to adapt and limit oneself. It regards as great all that is sufficient, and shows its distinction in choosing the mean things rather than the eminent.

There is nothing so noble and so right as to play the man well and fitly, nor anything so difficult to learn as how to live this life well and according to Nature; and the most inhuman of our diseases is to despise our being.

If you would send your soul abroad, do so by all means, if you can, when your body is in a bad way, in order to escape the contagion. At other times, however, let her be kind and helpful to the body, and, with wifely sympathy, not disdain to share his natural pleasures; bringing moderation to them, if she be the wiser of the two, for fear lest, through want of discretion, they be confounded with pain.

Intemperance is the bane of sensual pleasure, and temperance is not its scourge but its seasoning. Eudoxus, for whom pleasure was the sovereign good, and his fellow-philosophers, who set so high a value upon it, savoured it in all its charm and sweetness, by reason of their temperance, which they practised in an uncommon and exemplary degree.

I bid my soul to look upon pleasure and pain with a sight equally well-balanced—*for the dilation of the soul in joy is as blameworthy as its contraction in sorrow* (Cicero)—and equally firm ; but to regard the one gaily, the other severely, and, as far as in her lies, to be as anxious to extinguish the one as to extend the other.[1]

To take a sane view of good naturally means to take a sane view of evil. And pain has something unavoidable in its gentle beginnings, as pleasure has something to be avoided in its excessive end. Plato couples them together and holds that it is equally the duty of courage to fight against pain and against the immoderate charms and blandishments of pleasure. They are two springs, at which all who draw, whence, when and how much they need, whether they be city, man or beast, are very fortunate. The first must be taken in the way of physic and when needed, but more sparingly ; the other for thirst, but not to intoxication.

Pain, pleasure, love, hatred, are the first things a child feels ; and if they conform to Reason, when she comes, that is Virtue.

I have a vocabulary all my own. I ' pass the time ' when it is wet and disagreeable.[2] When it is fine I do not wish to pass it ; I ruminate it and hold on to it. We should hasten over the bad, and settle upon the good. Those ordinary phrases ' pastime ' and ' pass the time ' reflect the habit of those wiseacres who think they cannot make a better use of their life than to let it slide and to escape from it, to while it away, to dodge it, and as far as in them lies to ignore it and run away from it, as if it were an irksome and contemptible thing.

But I know it to be otherwise, and find it agreeable and worthy to be prized, yea even in its last stage, in which I now enjoy it. Nature has given it into our hands, trimmed with so many and such happy surroundings, that we have only ourselves to blame if we feel it a burden, and if we waste it unprofitably. *The life of the fool is joyless, agitated, and wholly given to the future* (Seneca).

And yet I am resigned to lose it without regret ; but as

---

[1] *D'en esteindre l'une que d'estendre l'autre.*

[2] *Je passe le temps quand il est mauvais, &c.* The word *temps* means both ' time ' and ' weather '.

a thing that is by its nature losable, not as if it were a troublesome burden.

Not to hate the idea of death is properly becoming only in those who enjoy life.

It needs good management to enjoy life. I enjoy it doubly as much as others, for the measure of enjoyment depends upon the more or less attention we give to it. Especially now that I feel mine to be so brief in time I try to increase it in weight; I try to arrest the speed of its flight by speedily laying hold of it, and, by the zest of my enjoyment to make up for its hasty ebbing. The shorter my possession of life the fuller and deeper must I live it.

Others feel the sweetness of contentment and well-being; I feel it as well as they, but not in letting it pass by and slip away. Rather should we study, relish and ruminate it, in order to give adequate thanks to him who bestows it upon us.

They enjoy other pleasures, as they do that of sleep, unconsciously. I used to enjoy being disturbed in my sleep in order to get a glimpse of it, and not allow it so senselessly to slip away.

I meditate over a thing that gives me pleasure; I do not skim over it, I go to the bottom of it and force my reason, now grown peevish and hard to please, to welcome it. Am I in some situation where I feel at rest? Is there some sensual pleasure that tickles me? I do not allow my senses to cheat me of it. I make my soul to share in it, not in order to be drawn into it, but to find it acceptable; not to lose, but to find herself in it. And I induce her, for her part, to mirror herself in this fortunate state, to weigh and appreciate its happiness, and to magnify it. She will estimate how far she owes it to God that she is at peace with her conscience, free from other inner passions, that her body is in its natural healthy state, fitly and properly enjoying the exercise of the agreeable and soothing functions with which he of his grace is pleased to compensate her for the afflictions with which his justice chastises us in its turn; how much it means to her to be so situated that, whithersoever she casts her eyes, the heavens around her are serene; that no desire, no fear or doubt disturbs her atmosphere; that there is no difficulty, past, present, or future, over which her imagination may not roam without harm.

Much light is thrown upon this consideration by comparison of my state with that of others. Thus, I can picture to myself in a thousand aspects those who are carried away and tossed about by Fortune or their own errors, as well as those who, more like me, so languidly and indifferently accept their good fortune. Those are the people who really 'pass their time'; they overpass the present and what they possess, to be slaves to hope, and for the shadows and vain images that their imagination dangles before their eyes,

> Like phantoms that, folk say, flit after death,
> Or visions that befool the slumbering sense; (VIRGIL.)

which speed and prolong their flight the more they are pursued. The fruit and aim of their pursuit is to pursue; as Alexander said the end of his labour was to labour;

> Thinking naught is done, if aught is left to do. (LUCAN.)

For my part then, I love life and cultivate it such as it has pleased God to grant it to me. I do not go about wishing that it might be relieved of the necessity of eating and drinking, and I should think it no less pardonable a sin to wish that necessity to be doubled—*the wise man eagerly desires the treasures of Nature* (Seneca);—or that our life could be sustained by merely putting into our mouth a little of that drug with which Epimenides took away his appetite, and kept himself alive; or that we could obtusely beget children by the fingers or heels (nay, in reverence be it spoken, that we could rather beget them voluptuously by the fingers and heels); or that the body should be without desire and incapable of being titillated.

Those would be ungrateful and wicked complaints. I accept heartily and gratefully what Nature has done for me; and I am proud and well pleased with myself that I do so. For we wrong that great and all-powerful giver when we reject, destroy, and disfigure her gift. Being all good, she has made all things good. *All things that are according to Nature are worthy of esteem* (Cicero).

Of philosophical opinions I more readily embrace those which are most solid, that is to say, most human and most our own; my words, in keeping with my actions, are mean and humble.

Philosophy appears to me very childish when she rides the high horse, and preaches to us that it is a barbarous alliance to marry the divine with the earthly, the reasonable with the unreasonable, the severe with the indulgent, the honest with the dishonest; that sensual pleasure is a brutish thing, unworthy to be enjoyed by the sage; that the only pleasure to be derived from the enjoyment of a fair young bride is the conscientious pleasure of performing an orderly action, like putting on one's boots for a business ride. May her followers have no more right or nerve or sap in ravishing their wives than in learning her lessons!

That is not what Socrates, her master and ours, says. He prizes, as he should, the pleasures of the body; but he prefers those of the mind, as being more powerful, more enduring, more easy to come by, more varied and dignified. The latter by no means go alone, according to him (he is not so fanciful), but only come first. With him temperance is the moderator, not the enemy of pleasures.

Nature is a gentle guide, but not more gentle than she is wise and just. *We must penetrate into the nature of things, and see exactly what it demands* (Cicero). I try to follow her footsteps in all things; we have confounded the traces by artificial means. And the sovereign good of the Academics and the Peripatetics, which is to 'live according to her', becomes for that reason difficult to limit and explain; as does also that of the Stoics, which, related to the other, is to 'acquiesce in Nature'.

Is it not a mistake to regard some actions as less worthy because they are necessary? Yet they will not knock it out of my head that the marriage of pleasure with necessity (with which, as an ancient says,[1] the Gods always conspire) is a very proper marriage. Why do we dismember by divorce a fabric woven of so close and brotherly a correspondence? Rather, let us knit it again by mutual offices. Let the mind rouse and quicken the dulness of the body, and the body check and steady the levity of the mind. *He who exalts the nature of the soul as the sovereign good, and condemns the nature of the flesh as an evil thing, truly both carnally desires the soul and carnally flees the flesh; since he is inspired by human vanity, not by divine truth* (Saint Augustine).

In this gift of God there is no part that is unworthy of our attention; we must account for it even to the last hair.

[1] Simonides.

And it is not a merely formal charge to man to direct man according to his nature ; it is positive, simple, and of prime importance, and the Creator has given it to us seriously and sternly.

Authority alone has any weight with an ordinary intellect, and weighs still more heavily in a foreign tongue. Let us here renew the attack. *Who will not say that it is the nature of the fool to do lazily and reluctantly what is to be done ; to urge the body one way and the soul another ; to be divided between wholly different movements* (Seneca).

Come now, to prove it, let such a man some day tell you the diversions and fancies he fills his head with, for which he diverts his thoughts from a good meal, and regrets the hour he spends over his eating. You will find that there is nothing so insipid in all the dishes on your table as the fine things with which he is entertaining his mind (for the most part it would be better fairly to go to sleep than to keep awake for the thoughts of our waking hours) ; and you will find that all his talk and all his aspirations are not worth your savoury stew.

Though they were the raptures of Archimedes himself, what of it ? I am not here concerned with that riff-raff of men that we are, or those aimless desires and thoughts that divert us from more serious things, nor am I confounding them with those venerable souls, lifted by pious and religious ardour to a constant and conscientious meditation on divine things, who, anticipating, by dint of a lively and passionate hope, the enjoyment of the heavenly food, the final aim and last step of Christian desires, the only constant and incorruptible pleasure, scorn to give their minds to our beggarly, fleeting, doubtful goods, and readily leave it to the body to provide and enjoy sensual and temporal fodder. It is a study for the privileged.[1]

Between ourselves, I have ever observed that super-celestial ideas and subterrestrial conduct are singularly suited to each other.

Aesop, that great man, saw his master making water as he walked. 'What ! he said, must we void ourselves as we run ? ' Use our time as best we may, yet a great part

[1] In 1588 the following was added and deleted : ' Our studies are all of this world, and of the things of this world the most natural are the most right.'

of it will still be idly and ill spent. Our mind has probably not enough other time to spare in which to do its business, unless it dissociates itself from the body for that brief space that it requires for its needs.

People try to get outside of themselves, and escape from the man. That is foolishness: instead of transforming themselves into angels, they transform themselves into beasts. Instead of raising they degrade themselves.

Those transcendental fancies overawe me, like high and inaccessible places; and nothing is for me so hard to swallow in the life of Socrates, as his trances and his possessions by his daemon; and nothing in Plato is so human as that for which they say he was called Divine.

And of our sciences those appear to me most terrestrial and low which have soared to the greatest heights. And I can see nothing more contemptible and mortal in the life of Alexander than his fancies about his immortalization. Philotas taunted him wittily in his rejoinder. He had congratulated him by letter on his elevation to the Gods by an oracle of Jupiter Ammon. 'For your sake I am glad; but those people have reason to be pitied who will have to live with and obey a man who exceeds and is not satisfied with human proportions.'

> You rule the world because that you
> Confess the God's supremacy. (HORACE.)

I quite agree with the pretty inscription with which the Athenians welcomed Pompey on his entering their city:

> So far you may be deemed a God
> As you confess yourself a man. (PLUTARCH.)

A man who can rightly and truly enjoy his existence is absolutely and almost divinely perfect.

We seek other conditions because we know not how to enjoy our own; and go outside of ourselves for want of knowing what it is like inside of us. So it is no use raising ourselves on stilts, for even on stilts we have to walk on our own legs. And sitting on the loftiest throne in the world we are still sitting on our behind.

The most beautiful lives, in my opinion, are those which conform to the model of common humanity, with order, but with nothing wonderful or extravagant.

Now old age needs to be treated a little more tenderly. Let us commend it to that tutelary God[1] of health and wisdom, but a gay and sociable wisdom:

> Give me but health, Latona's son,
>   To enjoy what I possess;
> Give me but this, I ask no more,
>   This and a mind entire—
> An old age not unhonoured, nor
>   Unsolaced by the lyre! (HORACE.)

[1] Apollo.

THE END

INDEX

Absence: advantages of, ii. 442
Advice to ladies, ii. 277, 344; to a lady of high degree, ii. 2; to young men, ii. 561
Aesop's fables: appreciation of, i. 400
Age: Bk. I, ch. 57
Agesilaus: his defeat, i. 269
Affectation: to be avoided, i. 172; examples of, ii. 81
Alcibiades: his adaptability, i. 167; as host, ii. 588
Alexander: his cruelty, i. 6; education, i. 163; sleeps before battle, i. 266; his charger, i. 282; valour and superstition, i. 325; preventing sleep, ii. 121; compared with Caesar, ii. 188, 206; greatness, ii. 204; with the Amazons, ii. 345; his deification, ii. 600
Amasis and Laodice, i. 95
Ambassadors: discretion of, i. 67
Ambition: hypocrisy of, i. 234; counsels of, i. 244; petty, ii. 494
Amulets, ii. 239
Amyot: appreciation of, i. 351
Ancients: their writings lost, ii. 77
Androclus and the lion, i. 470
Animals: cruelty and kindness to, i. 427; deified, i. 427; communication with, i. 444; reasoning powers, i. 451; affection, i. 464; imagination, i. 475; advantages of, i. 479; keener senses, ii. 45; selection in, ii. 281
Anticipating evils, ii. 524
Antigonus and the soldier, i. 323
Ants: their human traits, i. 461, 466
Apelles and Megabysus, ii. 395
Archimedes turns practical, i. 132
Aretino: criticism of, i. 300
Ariosto and Virgil compared, i. 403
Aristotelian, the complete, i. 149
Aristotle: his authority, i. 540

Armless man, i. 105
Armour: sumptuous, i. 276; wearing of, i. 394; of the Parthians, i. 396
Arria and Cecina Paetus, ii. 196
Artillery and printing: invention of, ii. 369
Asceticism, i. 54; of Cardinal Borromeo, i. 56; not for Montaigne, ii. 589
Assassins, the: ii. 160
Atalanta's race, ii. 287
Ataraxy, ii. 24
Atheism and Atheists, i. 436, 439
Athens: compared with Sparta, i. 141; compared to a mistress, ii. 310
Atlantis, i. 202
Atoms of the Epicureans, i. 546
Atticus: his suicide, ii. 57
Augustine on the Cynics, ii. 31
Augustus: and Cinna, i. 121; his power of sleep, i. 267; variability, i. 320; lavish of honours, i. 368
Authority of printed matter, ii. 559

Babel: tower of, i. 556
Barbarism: what is it? i. 202
Bathing in Rome, i. 290
Baths: medicinal, ii. 229
Bayard, Chevalier: his death, i. 14
Beauty: different ideas of, i. 476; advantages of, ii. 88, 533; and goodness, ii. 534
Bedouins: belief in transmigration, ii. 79; in fate, ii. 157
Bees: at war, i. 467; rout an army, i. 469
Bible: not to be translated and popularized, i. 311
Bion: not ashamed of his origin, ii. 448
Birds: intelligence in, i. 446, 455, 457
Blind, the: not sensible of blindness, ii. 37

INDEX

Blossius: friendship with Gracchus, i. 189
Bodin criticizes Plutarch, ii. 170
Body and soul: union of, ii. 89
Books: essay on, Bk. II, ch. 10; occupation with, i. 242; burning of, i. 391, intercourse with, ii. 282; how to compile, ii. 531
Borgia and the poisoned wine, i. 219
Borromeo's asceticism, ii. 56
Borrowed emotions, i. 293
Brazilians: description of, i. 206; their poetry, i. 214; at Rouen, i. 214; die of old age, i. 486
Bridegroom, the diffident, i. 94
Brutus: his lost book, i. 406
Buchanan, George, i. 174, 177

Caesar: as engineer, i. 66, 186; his trustfulness, i. 128; as historian, i. 409; clemency, i. 422; ii. 180; arrogance, ii. 53; amours, ii. 177; ambition, ii. 179; his warfare, Bk. II, ch. 34; compared with Alexander, ii. 188, 206; and Pompey, ii, 181, 485
Calendar: alteration of, ii. 481, 497
Callousness: examples of, i. 55
Canius led to execution, i. 358
Cannibalism: i. 209; ii. 27
Cannibals: *see* Brazilians
Capuans: bravery of, i. 347
Carrier pigeons, ii. 131
Cassius, Severus: his ready speech, i. 34
Castration: i. 521
Catholics: surrendering their beliefs, i. 182; spreading the faith, ii. 375
Cato the Censor: his economy, i. 300; compared with his grandson, ii. 150; learning Greek, ii. 151; his panacea, ii. 218
Cato the Younger: praise of, i. 230; his power of sleep, i. 266; his virtue, i. 415; his suicide, i. 59; compared with Cato the Censor, ii. 150; at his end, ii. 152; compared with Socrates, ii. 510

Catullus; appreciation of, i. 402
Causes and effects, ii. 489, 498
Celibacy, ii. 257
Central heating in Rome, ii. 558
Ceremony: banned by Montaigne, i. 42; ii. 278
Chance: we live by, i. 326; *see* Fortune
Change: of mood, i. 323; of opinion, ii. 7; in all things, ii. 51
Charles V: at Rome, i. 67; and Leyva, i. 252; his resignation, i. 379
Chasan: the coward turned brave, i. 323
Chastity: in women, i. 372; difficulty of, ii. 318; spurious, ii. 325
Cheating, i. 105
Chef, the eloquent, i. 298
Chelonis, faithful wife and daughter, i. 582
Chess: a childish game, i. 295
Childbirth: endurance in, i. 52
Children: are they desirable? ii. 469
Children of the mind, i. 390
Choice in wines not desirable, i. 330
Chop-logic, i. 530; ii. 290
Christian: obedience, i. 117; converts, i. 432
Christians on Socotra, i. 313
Cicero: his ambition, i. 246; criticism of, i. 404; his eloquence, i. 406; his boast, i. 483; love of fame, ii. 69; his letters, ii. 135; compared with Brutus and Seneca, ii. 164
Cicero the younger: anecdote of, i. 406
Civility: rules of, i. 41
Civil war: in France, ii. 514; condemned by Plato, ii. 516
Classes: disadvantage of large, i. 148
Cleanthes: his suicide, ii. 58
Cleomenes rejects suicide, i. 341
Climate: effects of, ii. 21
Clothes: Bk. I, ch. 36; are they natural or necessary? i. 224; do not make the man, i. 255
Coaches and chariots, ii. 361
Cod-pieces: their absurdity, i. 114; origin of, ii. 316

INDEX

Cold: severity of, i. 226
College education: defects of, i. 136, 165, 168
Colonizing, ii. 132
Colour in eyes, ii. 46
Commentaries: too many, ii. 543
Commines: criticism of, i. 411
Concealment: uses of, ii. 63; of natural actions, ii. 338
Condoling with grief, ii. 285
Confession, ii. 302
Conrad and the Dames of Weinsberg, i. 4
Conscience: result of custom, i. 111; makes cowards, i. 354
Conspiracy: guarding against, i. 129
Contentment, i. 62
Convention, ii. 80
Conversation, ii. 384
Corporal punishment condemned, i. 165, 377
Counselling kings, ii. 555
Courage defined, i. 39
Cowardice: punishment of, i. 64; the mother of cruelty, ii. 147
Crassus and the engineer, i. 68
Credulity, i. 179; religious, i. 215; of patients, ii. 234
Cripples: tradition concerning, ii. 506
Crocodile and wren, i. 473
Cruelty: in children, i. 104; in the Civil wars, i. 424; beginnings of, ii. 147; of the Spaniards, ii. 373
Cuckold, the philosophical, ii. 94
Cuckoldry: ii. 328
Curiosity: the original sin, i. 493; morbid, i. 508; too much, ii. 511
Custom and habit: Bk. I, ch. 23; in clothes, i. 114
Customs: strange, i. 107; ancient Roman, i. 290; South American, ii. 19
Cynics: shamelessness of, ii. 30
Cyrus: his education, i. 140; liberality, ii. 365

Death: Bk. I, ch. 20; sudden, i. 9, 79; contempt of, i. 44, 217; judge of the past, i. 74; euphemisms for, i. 78; apprehension of, i. 80; from old age unusual, i. 317; a cure-all, i. 337; to gain future bliss, i. 349; should correspond with life, i. 416; unexpected, ii. 53; the best, ii. 57; different kinds of, ii. 452; preparing for, ii. 525; gentle approach of, ii. 583
Death-bed scenes, i. 90
Decency, ii. 30
Defeats, glorious, i. 212
Degeneracy, modern, i. 292
Deifications, i. 514, 529
Democritus: the laughing philosopher, i. 295; and the figs, i. 507
Depreciation of the great, i. 229
Despising the enemy, i. 277
Diary: on keeping a, i. 223
Diet: change of, ii. 564
Different standards of morality, ii. 463
Difficulty increases desire, ii. 61
Diocletian in retirement, i. 262
Diogenes: his shamelessness, ii. 31; his misanthropy compared with Timon's, i. 296
Diomedon's brave speech, i. 16
Dionysius: his cruelty, i. 5; and the miser, i. 60; and the stranger, i. 129; at the Olympian games, ii. 84
Diplomacy: secret, i. 427
Discipline: in armies, ii. 514
Disdaining life, i. 340
Diseases: causes of, ii. 223; should run their course, ii. 567
Disguise of generals, i. 277
Disinheriting, i. 386
Disputes: unreasonableness of, ii. 387; verbal, ii. 545
Dissembling, ii. 97
Diversion: in war, ii. 286; of passion, ii. 290
Divination: decline of, i. 35; abuse of, i. 208; from flight of birds, i. 462
Divorce laws, ii. 64
Dizziness: cause of, ii. 42
Doctor's confession, ii. 225
Dodging the shot, i. 40

Dogs: intelligence in, i. 455, 463; affection, i. 464, 469; vigilance, i. 470
Dream: life compared to a, ii. 44
Dreams, ii. 295
Drink: going without, ii. 560
Drinking in Germany, i. 167; ii. 100
Drugs: magic, ii. 222, 235; outlandish preferred, ii. 224
Drunkenness, i. 327; Plato on, i. 333
Du Bellay, Memoirs of, i. 411
Du Bellay, poet, i. 171
Duels: seconds in, ii. 143
Duras, Mme de: dedication to, ii. 237
Dying among strangers, ii. 445
Dying, the: do they suffer? i. 361

Eccentric Frenchman, i. 106
Eccentricity to be avoided, i. 166
Ecclesiastical licence, ii. 349
Education: early, i. 104; misdirected, i. 136; in Persia, i. 140; at Athens and Sparta, i. 141; of boys, Bk. I, ch. 26; compulsion in, i. 377; defects of, ii. 111
Edward I: his dying command, i. 13
Edward III and the Treaty of Bretigny, ii. 133
Edward the Black Prince and the three knights, i. 3; at Crécy, i. 253
Egmont, Count: his obligation, i. 25
Elephants: intelligence in, i. 457; religion, i. 460; in love, i. 465
Eloquence: a deceitful art, i. 297
English laws: changes in, ii. 25
Enjoying life, ii. 596
Epaminondas: and Pelopidas, i. 4; his greatness, ii. 206, 255; opinions, ii. 208; relaxations, ii. 592
Epicharis the courtezan: death of, ii. 172
Epicureans and Stoics compared, i. 413
Epicurus: on solitude, i. 244; his simple life, i. 420; last letter and will, ii. 68

Equality of the sexes, ii. 358
Essays: publication of, ii. 429; favourable reception of, ii. 430
Estissac, Mme d', i. 373
Etiquette, i. 41
Eudamidas and his friends, i. 191
Evidence: value of, i. 410
Examinations rightly conducted, i. 138
Excitement kills fear, ii. 289
Expenditure by kings, ii. 362
Experience, ii. 540
Extempore speaking, i. 34
Extremes meet, i. 303

Fabulous creatures, i. 524
Faith better than knowledge, i. 494
Faith cure, ii. 500
Fame and glory: mania for, i. 252; vanity of, ii. 67; due to chance, ii. 70; undeserved, ii. 75; cheaply bought, ii. 495
Family pride: foolishness of, i. 272
Fanaticism: examples of, i. 335
Fascination: power of, i. 100
Fashions: changing, i. 289
Fasting: benefit of, ii. 585
Fate: belief in, ii. 157
Fathers and sons, i. 375
Fear: effects of, i. 69
Fencing: on learning, ii. 145
Feraulez: his renunciation, i. 61
Fighting bishop, the, i. 254
Fish: intelligence in, i. 472
Flattery: forms of, ii. 382
Flight: warfare by, i. 39
Flippancy in face of death, i. 44
Folk-poetry, i. 214, 305
Fortitude: examples of, ii. 172
Fortune: mutability of, i. 72; freaks of, i. 219; in war, i. 280; in worldly affairs, ii. 396
Foster-mothers, i. 389
Fox: intelligence in, i. 452
Francis I and the ambassador, i. 31; in Provence, i. 279
Francis, Duke of Brittany: on women, i. 138
Freedom of thought, i. 114
French children: their charm, i. 164
Frenchmen abroad, ii. 145, 454

INDEX

French language: limitations of, ii. 333
French nobility: independence of, i. 261
Friendship: Bk. I, ch. 28; in women, i. 186; Greek, i. 187; cannot be divided, i. 191; not for kings, i. 261; absence in, ii. 444
Fright: effects of, i. 40
Froissart: appreciation of, i. 408
Fugitive Roman, i. 129
Funerals: ordering of, i. 15
Futile labours, i. 238

Gallio in exile, i. 200
Gall-stones: advantage of having, ii. 569
Germans: drinking habits, i. 167, 330; ii. 100; at the baths, ii. 230
Ghost story, ii. 501
Gladiators, i. 453; ii. 134
Goat, story of the, ii. 232
God: taking his name in vain, i. 314; incomprehensible, i. 510; what is he? i. 512; made in man's image, i. 519, 528; limiting his powers, i. 522; cannot do all things, i. 527; Montaigne's theory, i. 536; knows best what we need, ii. 22; the only reality, ii. 52
Gods: multiplicity of, i. 534
Good and evil a matter of opinion: Bk. I, ch. 14
Good conscience: boon of, ii. 260
Good repute not to be despised, ii. 78
Gournay, Marie de: eulogy of, ii. 113
Gouty gentleman: story of, i. 17
Government: the best, ii. 421
Governor, the irresolute, i. 127
Gracchus and his prompter, ii. 43
Great events from little causes, ii. 489
Greatness: disadvantages of, ii. 380; rarity of, ii. 110
Greek and Latin too dearly bought, i. 173
Grief, contagion of, ii. 294
Guicciardini: criticism of, i. 410

Guise, Charles de: his sorrow, i. 7
Guise, Duke of: and the conspirator, i. 120; at Dreux, i. 268; assassination of, ii. 159
Gymnosophists: ii. 156

Habit: force of early, ii. 264; a second nature, ii. 480; force of, ii. 561
Hair-shirt: wearing of, ii. 177
Halcyon, the, i. 474
Hangman: degrading office of, ii. 252
Health: causes of, i. 486; a precious thing, ii. 216
Heliogabalus: his preparations, ii. 55
Henry III of France: probable allusions to, i. 197; ii. 127
Henry IV of France: probable allusions to, ii. 127, 159, 478
Henry VII: his treachery, i. 24
Heraclitus, the weeping philosopher, i. 295
Heredity: mystery of, ii. 214
Hiero on disadvantages of kingship, i. 259
Hilary and his daughter, i. 218
Historians, i. 407
History: on reading, i. 67, 155; on writing, i. 101
Homer among the prophets, ii. 33; his greatness, ii. 201; compared with Virgil, ii. 201
Honesty the best policy, ii. 73; difficult in public affairs, ii. 460
Honour, i. 252; rewards of, i. 368
Horace, i. 401
Horses: Bk. I, ch. 8; fighting on, i. 283
Housewifery, ii. 441
Human arrogance, i. 484, 508, 531
Humanity, i. 427
Human sacrifices, i. 201, 520
Humility and submission, i. 482
Hypocrisy: forms of, i. 309, 314 meanness of, ii. 97

Idleness, i. 26; in rulers, ii. 126
Ignatius, father and son, i. 222
Ignorance: and knowledge, i. 304; confession of, ii. 502; vow of, ii. 511

Imagination: force of, Bk. I, ch. 21; i. 485; in animals, i. 19, 475; magnifies things, i. 359
Impiety: folly of, i. 19
Impotence: fear of, i. 93; results of, ii. 154
Inclination too readily followed, i. 321
Inconsistency: Bk. II, ch. 1
Inconstancy in women, ii. 346
Incredulity condemned, i. 179
Innocence not virtue, i. 417
Innovation: dangers of, i. 115; ii. 423
Instinct, i. 374, 446, 530
Intolerance, religious, i. 310
Iphigenia's father, i. 8
Irresolution: causes of, ii. 60
Isabel of England favoured by fortune, i. 221
Ischolas' honourable defeat, i. 212
Italian: how to learn, i. 548
Italians: as letter-printers, i. 250; compared with others, i. 418; love-making, ii. 340; marriage, ii. 343

Jealousy, ii. 321, 327; in women, ii. 323
Jews: persecution of, i. 46
Johannes Secundus: his *Kisses*, i. 399
Judges: partiality in, ii. 29; evil methods, ii. 242
Judging others, i. 127: ii. 174, 393
Judgement: uncertainty of, Bk. I, ch. 47; upset by fear, i. 69; affected by health, ii. 8
Juggernaut, car of, i. 350
Julian and his courtiers, i. 262; the Apostate, ii. 120
Julius, Pope, and the ambassador, i. 32
Jupiter and Juno, i. 199
Justice: miscarriages of, ii. 546; in China, ii. 548; and the Laws, ii. 549

Keeping faith with outlaws, ii. 254
Kings: are but men, i. 257; lead the fashions, i. 264; should be active, ii. 126; their hard task, ii. 380; need of advice, ii. 556

Kissing as a salutation, ii. 342
Kleptomania, examples of, i. 376
Knowing oneself, i. 368; ii. 551
Knowledge: is it a blessing? i. 481; pre-natal, i. 550

Labienus: his works burned, i. 391
La Boétie, i. 155, 183, 188, 194; ii. 444; his Sonnets, i. 195; his greatness, ii. 111
Ladislas and the physician's daughter, i. 179
Laïs and the philosophers, ii. 177, 459
Latin compared with French, ii. 332
Laughing and crying together, Bk. I, ch. 38
Laws: objection to Latin, i. 113; of honour and justice, i. 114; changing, i. 115; necessity of, ii. 2; diversity of, ii. 26; origin of, ii. 30; fabulous origin, ii. 79; too many in France, ii. 541; often made by fools, ii. 549
Law-suits to be avoided, ii. 488
Learning: expands the mind, i. 131; second-hand useless, i. 135; value of, i. 147; bookish valueless, i. 150; a doubtful blessing, i. 481
Legal jargon, ii. 542
Legislators: divine authority claimed by, ii. 79
Leonor, Montaigne's daughter: her up-bringing, i. 377; and the governess, ii. 313
Letters: of Epicurus and Seneca, i. 249; of the Italians, i. 250; of Cicero, ii. 135
Letter-writing, i. 249
Liberality in kings, ii. 364; example of Cyrus, ii. 365
Lies and untruths, i. 29
Life and death should correspond, ii. 526
Ligatures, i. 93
Living: for self, i. 239; the main thing, ii. 591
Lord's prayer should be more often used, i. 308
Louis IX and the convert, i. 432
Love: unnatural, i. 112; on

INDEX

feigning, ii. 292 ; what is it? ii. 336 ; ridiculous in old men, ii. 347 ; beneficial effects of, ii. 354 ; reciprocity in, ii. 355 ; Platonic, ii. 357 ; youth the season of, ii. 358

Lucan : his swan-song, i. 392 ; appreciation of, i. 401

Luck : in medicine, i. 123 ; in poetry and war, i. 124 ; *see also* Fortune

Lucretia, a modern, i. 322

Lucretius, i. 334 ; and Virgil compared, i. 401 ; his madness, i. 484

Lucullus and the soldier, i. 323

Lust : suppression of, ii. 177 ; unnatural, ii. 342

Lycurgus : neglects learning, i. 140 ; on thieving, ii. 28 ; his marriage law, ii. 61

Lying : Bk. I, ch. 9 ; ii. 97 ; in France, ii. 117, ; accusation of, resented, ii. 117

Macchiavellism criticized, ii. 98

Magpie, the studious, i. 458

Malingering : Bk. II, ch. 25

Marcellinus : his suicide, ii. 58

Marcellinus the historian on Julian, ii. 120

Marcius : his cunning, i. 19

Margaret of Navarre on civility, i. 42

Marie Germain, the transformed maid, i. 92

Maris, bishop, and Julian, ii. 120

Marot : his advice, i. 345

Marriage : by lot, i. 37 ; and friendship, i. 186 ; between relations, i. 198 ; right age for, i. 378 ; and love, ii. 306 ; in Italy, ii. 343

Martial : criticism of, i. 402

Mary Queen of Scots, i. 73

Matecoulon, Montaigne's brother : involved in duel, ii. 144

Maximilian's modesty, i. 14

Medicine : luck in, i. 123 ; criticism of, ii. 216 ; origin and progress, ii. 223 ; specialists advocated, ii. 227 ; Pliny on, ii. 238 ; should be based on personal experience, ii. 557

Messalina and Claudian, ii. 330

Metellus : his dictum, i. 414

Mexicans, ii. 370 ; their traditions, ii. 376 ; and customs, ii. 399

Mexico, king of : his sacrifices, i. 201 ; his cruel death, ii. 374

Microcosmos, i. 538

Midas : his prayer, ii. 22

Military profession : praise of, ii. 577

Mimicking infirmities, ii. 137

Miracles, i. 93, 107, 181 ; birth of, ii. 499

Moderation : Bk. I, ch. 20 ; in marriage, i. 198

Monomaniacs, the happy, i. 490

Monstrosities, ii. 161, 524

Montaigne, Michel de : his modesty, i. 14, 398 ; ii. 552 ; defective memory, i. 27, 410 ; ii. 99, 427, 551 ; money affairs, i. 57, 417 ; date of birth, i. 70 ; ever prepared for death, i. 81 ; his counterspell, i. 94 ; inability to write history, i. 101 ; hatred of deceit, i. 105 ; fearlessness, i. 128 ; ii. 359 ; his borrowings, i. 134, 145, 397 ; ii. 530 ; reading, i. 143, 176, 399 ; early education, i. 173 ; goes to school, i. 175 ; a good actor, i. 177 ; hastiness and anger, i. 233 ; ii. 168 ; on his style and language, i. 248 ; ii. 88, 334 ; on his letter-writing, i. 249 ; coat of arms, i. 272 ; want of method, i. 294 ; submission to the church, i. 307 ; changeability, i. 324 ; ii. 10 ; not inquisitive, i. 352 ; apprehension of sickness, i. 359 ; at death's door, i. 360 ; his critical judgement, i. 400 ; virtue, i. 418 ; humanity, i. 421, 529 ; as translator, i. 429 ; rule of life, i. 548 ; in love, ii. 13, 485 ; immunity from attack, ii. 65, 431 ; on his names, ii. 75 ; diffidence, ii. 82 ; self-criticism, ii. 85 ; dislike of obligations, ii. 100, 433 ; ignorance, ii. 103 ; his gall-stones, ii, 209, 569 ; ancestors, ii. 215 ;

aversion to medicine, ii. 216, 239; tolerance, ii. 240; as negotiator, ii. 242; portrays himself, ii. 91, 103, 258; not a prophet in his own country, ii. 262; Latin his native tongue, ii. 264; unrepentant, ii. 267; neither offers nor takes advice, ii. 268; in company, ii. 274; capable of friendship, ii. 275; at home, ii. 278; intercourse with ladies, ii. 279; and books, ii. 282; his library, ii. 101, 283; affected by old age, ii. 296, 480; outspokenness, ii. 99, 300; hatred of secrecy, ii. 301; on his marriage, ii. 309; as lover, ii. 324, 350; likes to communicate his thoughts, ii. 336; treatment of mistresses, ii. 350; dislikes vehicles, ii. 361; want of of ambition, ii. 95, 378; loves conversation and argument, ii. 385; intolerance of fools, ii. 391, 402; devout in prosperity, ii. 411; contentment, ii. 412, 596; laziness, ii. 415; dislike of business, ii. 417; reception by the public, ii. 429; tribulations, ii. 431; independence, ii. 434; apprehension of death, ii. 437; cosmopolitanism, ii. 439; not afraid to die abroad, ii. 445; needs little sympathy, ii. 447; indifference and adaptability, ii. 454; on his chapter-titles, ii. 464; no intention to write obscurely, ii. 466; knowledge of Rome, ii. 467; Roman citizenship, ii. 470; Mayor of Bordeaux, ii. 474, 482, 492; not blinded by partiality, ii. 483; never went to law, ii. 489; kept his promises, ii. 433, 496; not authoritative, ii. 506; in adversity, ii. 517; during the plague, ii. 520; his physiognomy, ii. 536; his house attacked, ii. 536; adventure with freebooters, ii. 537; love of liberty, ii. 548; knowledge of men, ii. 553; mode of life and habits, ii. 557, 562; early loss of virginity, ii. 565; personal characteristics, ii. 578; tastes, ii. 580; reared by poor people, ii. 581; drinking habits, ii. 586; not an ascetic, ii. 589

Montaigne, Pierre de: a man of ideas, i. 173; invents advertising, i. 222; his method, i. 223; described, i. 331; patronizes scholars, i. 428; afflicted with stone, ii. 214; fond of building, ii. 415; mayor of Bordeaux, ii. 475

Montluc on the loss of his son, i. 385

Montmorency: his death, ii. 113

Mule, the wily, i. 466

Muley Moloch: his brave end, ii. 129

Names: Bk. I, ch. 46
Natural death, i. 317
Nature: her lesson on life and death, i. 86; laws of, ii. 26; her teachings, ii. 523, 550; the best doctor, ii. 568; a gentle guide, ii. 598
Nero and the soldiers, i. 11
News miraculously transmitted, i. 180
Night air not harmful, ii. 563
Ninachetuen: his suicide, i. 346
Niobe: her grief, i. 8
Nobility not virtue, ii. 307
Nobles of Calicut, ii. 307
Notoriety: mania for, ii. 75
Nudity: offensive, i. 478; is purity, ii. 317

Obedience the first law of God, i. 482
Oblivion the fate of most things, ii. 76
Obscurity in Aristotle, i. 504
Obstinacy: in defence, i. 63; in women, ii. 173
Old age, ii. 272
Opportunity: advantage of, ii. 324
Orange, Prince of: his assassination, ii. 159
Order of St. Michael, i. 369; ii. 23
Orders of Knighthood, i. 369
Originality, ii. 404
Otho: his power of sleep, i. 266

INDEX

Outspokenness, ii. 303

Pacuvius quells a sedition, ii. 423
Pagans more consistent than Christians, i. 432
Pain: is it an evil? i. 50; contempt of, i. 49, 53, 335, 484
Palmistry, ii. 3
Panic terror, i. 71
Paracelsus revolutionizes medicine, ii. 16
Paradise: Mahomet's, i. 315; arguments against, i. 516
Pardon better than revenge, i. 125
Parental affection, i. 374, 381
Parents a hindrance to education, i. 151
Paris: Montaigne's love of, ii. 439
Parleying: danger of, i. 21
Parochialism, i. 156
Parsimony of the ancients, i. 300
Parthians: their armour, i. 396
Passing the time, ii. 595
Passions: effects of, ii. 12, 478
Paulina and Seneca: their suicide, ii. 197
Paulina and Serapis, i. 531
Pausanias: his drunkenness, i. 329
Pedantry: Bk. I, ch. 25
Penance, i. 54
Persian education, i. 140
Persian kings: custom of, i. 199
Peru, king of: his cruel treatment, ii. 373
Phallic worship, ii. 315
Pharsalia: Pompey and Caesar at, i. 278
Philip of Macedon: his cruelty, ii. 147
Philopoemen: his strategy, i. 268; anecdote of, ii. 90
Philosophers and pedants, i. 131
Philosophy: three kinds of, i. 498; a gay study, i. 159; may be taught to children, i. 162; on pleasure, ii. 353
Physicians: disagreement among, ii. 566
Physiognomy, ii. 534
Piety without morality, ii. 535
Pious prince: tale of a, i. 315
Piso's iniquity, ii. 166

Plagiarisms, i. 144; Montaigne's, i. 397
Plato: called divine, i. 299; on drinking, i. 333; his origin, i. 532; on marriage, ii. 346; on bequeathing, i. 388
Plato's man, i. 546
Plautus and Terence compared, i. 401
Pleasure: two kinds of, i. 75; due to virtue, i. 76; mingled with pain, ii. 124; of mind and body, ii. 590, 598
Pliny: his credulity, i. 181
Pliny the younger on Solitude, i. 241
Plurality of worlds, i. 523
Plutarch: recommended for boys, i. 155; his credulity, i. 180; and Rusticus, i. 352; compared with Seneca, i. 403; ii. 413; and his slave, ii. 165; criticized by Bodin, ii. 170; parallel lives compared, ii. 175
Poetic language, ii. 331
Poetic licence: when permitted, i. 153
Poetry: definition of, i. 170; barbaric, i. 214; influence on Montaigne, i. 230; and prose, ii. 465
Poets: five Latin compared, i. 230; the first philosophers, i. 537; ii. 465; and madness, i. 330; French, ii. 113
Poisons: relativity of, ii. 45
Polemo reformed, ii. 112
Pompey: his changeability, i. 5; and Caesar, i. 181, 278, 485
Pomposity, ii. 394
Poor: patience and stoicism of the, ii. 513, 522, 527
Popilius and Antiochus, ii. 136
Portuguese cruelty, i. 46, 209
Posting: Bk. ii, ch. 22
Poverty: contempt of, ii. 479
Poyet's unreadiness, i. 33
Prayers: Bk. I, ch. 56; often incantations, i. 316
Preparedness for death: Bk. II, ch. 6; ii. 525
Presumption a human disease, i. 441
Principles: first, i. 542

Private interests: claims of, ii. 256
Private life: joys of, i. 262
Procrastination: Bk. II, ch. 4
Professional jargon, i. 299
Profit and loss, i. 102
Promises in children disappointed, i. 146
Prophecies: ambiguity of, i. 38; ii. 33
Prostitutions: honourable, ii. 326
Protagoras and his pupils' fees, i. 136
Protestants and the League, ii. 484
Protogenes favoured by chance, i. 221
Prudery, ii. 303, 313
Psalms of David, i. 310
Psammenitus and Cambyses, i. 7
Pseudo-scholar, a: i. 134
Public spectacles at Rome, ii. 366
Purging, ii. 219
Pursuing one's advantage, i. 275, 485
Pyrrho: and the pig, i. 48, 485; his consistency, ii. 153
Pyrrhonism, i. 498, 526
Pyrrhus: his ambitions, i. 262

Rabelais, i. 399
Raisciac falls dead from grief, i. 8
Razis and Nicanor, i. 344
Reason: disadvantage of, i. 48; not enough, i. 440; overrated, i. 480; not to be trusted, i. 543
Reasoning power in animals, i. 451
Reasons, forging, ii. 498, 507
Recluse dean, the, i. 381
Reformers: tribute to the, i. 231
Regulus and Balbus, ii. 379
Religion: not confirmed by success, i. 216; disputes on, i. 312; induced by fear, i. 436; wars of, ii. 514
Religious subjects unsuitable for stage, &c., i. 313
Religious zeal lacking, i. 434
Remora, i. 461
Repentance: ii. 261; of old age and sickness, ii. 269
Repetitions: tiresome, ii. 427
Reputation: of rulers, i. 11; of women, ii. 319
Resisting evil, ii. 485

Restitution, belated, i. 25
Retiring, i. 379; Charles V, i. 379
Revenge: misdirected, i. 18; of a king, i. 18; posthumous, i. 25; object of, ii. 141
Rewards and punishments: future, i. 435, 518, 551; in China, ii. 548
Rhetoric: a deceitful art, i. 297; effect on Rome, ii. 298
Rich wife: on marrying, i. 386
Riding feats, i. 288
Roman customs: i. 290, 353, 582; colonizing, ii. 133; shows, ii. 366; state, ii. 425
Romans: discourage treachery, i. 19; greatness of, Bk. II, ch. 24
Rome: execution in, i. 424; glory of, ii. 467
Ronsard, i. 171
Royalty: disadvantages of, i. 260; ii. 380
Rusticus at Plutarch's lecture, i. 352

Sacrifices, i. 520; human, i. 201
Saint-Martin, Montaigne's brother: his death, i. 79
Salusses, Marquis de: his superstition, i. 36
Scaevola and Porsenna, i. 53
Scanderbeg and the soldier, i. 3
Schoolmasters, the two, i. 168
Science: in animals, i. 454; progress of, ii. 15
Scipio: his assurance, i. 355
Scipio and Laelius at play, ii. 592
Scythians: their warfare, i. 39
Sea-sickness, ii. 359
Sebond, Raymond: criticism of, Bk. II, ch. 12
Secret sins, ii. 69
Secrets: on keeping, ii. 246
Self: living for, i. 239; speaking and thinking of, i. 366; writing of, ii. 114; duty to, ii. 473
Self-mutilations, i. 54, 521; ii. 154
Self-torture, i. 140
Semen: nature of, i. 560
Seneca: his advice to Lucilius, i. 218, 244; compared with Plutarch, i. 403; ii. 413; refuted, ii. 53; letter on Harpaste, ii. 138; and the Cardinal of Lorraine, ii. 170; his death, ii. 198;

unselfishness, ii. 200 ; vegetarian, ii. 560

Sense : nobody admits want of, ii. 107

Senses : ii. 35 ; deception of, ii. 40 ; keener in animals, ii. 45 ; affected by disease, ii. 46 ; contradiction of, ii. 47

Servants : i. 383 ; treatment of, ii. 275

Sexual act, ii. 336

Sex-works of the ancients, ii. 315

Shame : confined to man, i. 478

Showing off : ii. 276

Simple language commended, i. 172

Simple life corrupted, ii. 231

Simplicity commended, i. 304

Sleep : power of, Bk. I, ch. 44 ; prepares for death, i. 359 ; going without, i. 267

Smells and odours : Bk. I, ch. 55

Sneezing, ii. 358

Society : formation of, ii. 421

Socotra : Christians on, i. 313

Socrates : his dæmon, i. 38 ; his virtue, i. 414 ; why called wise, i. 493 ; as accoucheur, i. 505 ; under sentence, ii. 57 ; susceptibility, ii. 353 ; in retreat, ii. 359 ; his wisdom, ii. 509 ; before his judges, ii. 527 ; his ugliness, ii. 533 ; pluck and endurance, ii. 593

Soldier : story of a condemned, i. 243

Soldiers : arming of, i. 276

Solitude : Bk. I, ch. 39 ; Epicurus and Seneca on, i. 244

Solon : his maxim, i. 12, 72

Solyman keeps faith, ii. 99

Sophocles and Pericles : anecdote of, i. 199

Soul : nature of, i. 544 ; seat of, i. 545 ; origin of, i. 549 ; and body, i. 552 ; ii. 89 ; mortal or immortal ? i. 517, 554

South Americans : parallel customs and traditions, ii. 19 ; civilization, ii. 370

Sovereign good, ii. 24

Spaniards in S. America, ii. 372 ; treatment of Indians, ii. 373

Spartan endurance, i. 53

Speech : readiness of, i. 33 ; plainness recommended, i. 172 ; by signs, i. 445 ; not necessary, i. 450 ; shared by animals, i. 450

Spurina : story of, ii. 183

Stage-plays should be encouraged, i. 178

Stature : advantages of, ii. 89

Stoicism : at fault, i. 49 ; of Posidonius, i. 49, 484 ; of Arcesilaus, i. 485 ; vanity of, ii. 211

Stoics : on fright, ii. 40 ; and Epicureans compared, i. 413

Stoves and fire-places, ii. 558

Studying under difficulties, ii. 560

Submission : to the church, i. 182, 307 ; to authority, i. 540

Success and ability : ii. 398

Suicide : reasons for and against i. 338 ; discouraged by Plato, i. 340 ; examples of heroic, i. 46, 343 ; to escape dishonour, i. 344 ; from wifely devotion, i. 346 ; of masses, i. 347 ; for a better life, i. 349 ; from weariness of life, i. 350 ; half-hearted, ii. 56 ; determined, ii. 57 ; of Philistus, ii. 129 ; to escape ill-treatment, ii. 154 ; from devotion, ii. 195

Sumptuary laws : Bk. I, ch. 43

Sun-worship : i. 511

Supernatural : belief in, ii. 504

Suspension of judgement, i. 501

Suttee : description of, i. 45 ; ii. 155

Tacitus : loss of his works, ii. 119 ; criticism of, ii. 405

Tasso at Ferrara, i. 487

Temperance : to be loved for itself, ii. 271

Temptation : resisting, i. 420 ; ii. 487

Terence : his comedies written by Scipio and Laelius, i. 246 ; compared with Plautus, i. 401

Thales : makes a fortune, i. 133 ; star-gazing, i. 539

Theft in Sparta, ii. 28

Theology : language of, i. 313

Theory and practice, ii. 458

Theoxena : her heroism, ii. 148

Thief : story of the repentant, ii. 265

Thumbs : Bk. II, ch. 26
Tiberius : refuses treachery, i. 241; letter to the Senate, ii. 406
Timoleon : attempted assassination of, i. 221; his remorse, i. 234; and expiation, ii. 253
Torpedo : i. 462
Torture condemned, i. 356; ii. 149
Transmigration of souls : i. 425, 517, 557; Bedouin belief in, ii. 79
Travel : advantages of, i. 151; reasons for, ii. 413
Travelling companions, ii. 455
Treachery : examples of, i. 22; ii. 248
Troubles : should not be anticipated, ii. 524
Trust : breeds trust, i. 126; accepting on, i. 540; ii. 509
Truth : and falsehood, i. 29; and error, Bk. I, ch. 27; choosing between, ii. 4
Truthfulness : ii. 97
Turkish justice, i. 357; discipline, ii. 515
Turnèbe, Adrien : a real scholar, i. 137; ii. 113
Tutor : choice of, i. 147
Tyrants : cruel and cowardly, ii.147

Undeserved praise, ii. 303
Unknown : search after the, i. 301
Unknown Deity : i. 510
Useless accomplishments, i. 303

Vain-glory : ii. 80
Valour : has its limits, i. 63; of the Spartans, i. 128; true and false, i. 211; the highest degree of virtue, i. 371; not confined to nobles, ii. 96
Venus : without Cupid, ii. 280; and Vulcan, ii. 305; and Mars, ii. 331
Vespasian dies in harness, ii. 126
Vibius Virius : his suicide, i. 347
Vice : repented, ii. 260
Victory : not divinely ordained, i. 216
Virgil : compared with Lucretius, i. 401; with Ariosto, i. 403; with Homer, ii. 201
Virgin births : i. 532
Virtue : the aim of philosophy, i. 160; may be carried to excess, i. 196, 335; extinct, i. 228; presupposes difficulty, i. 412; in women, i. 372; ii. 320; its own reward, ii. 72; the true, ii. 152; mingled with vice, ii. 125; of Socrates and Cato, ii. 417
Vivisection : human condemned, ii. 134
Voice : tone of, ii. 567
Vulcan : and Venus, ii. 305; his jealousy, ii. 322

War : should it be declared ? i. 20; iniquity of, i. 467
Wealth : the true, i. 237
Weapons : missile, i. 284; natural, i. 449
Whale and guide, i. 472
White for mourning : i. 293
Widow : story of the pregnant, i. 329; of Cea, i. 350
Widows : behaviour of, ii. 193
Will : control of, i. 98
Wills : making of, i. 78, 387
Wisdom : born of ignorance, i. 495
Witches and witchcraft : ii. 503, 505
Wives : plurality of, i. 213; can tankerous, i. 383
Wives : stories of devoted, Bk. II, ch. 35
Women : as mothers, i. 389; their obstinacy, ii. 173; no need of learning, ii. 277; intercourse with, ii. 279; more capable than men, ii. 311; treated unreasonably, ii. 311; nothing to learn, ii. 314; Italian, ii. 342; advice to, ii. 344; injustice to, ii. 346; equality of, ii. 358
World : what is it ? ii. 18; a new one discovered, ii. 17, 369
Writing : too much, ii. 409; too late in life, ii. 532

Xenocrates and Laïs : ii. 177
Xenophon hears of his son's death : ii. 289
Xerxes : his emotion, i. 233

Zaleucus : his sumptuary laws, i. 264
Zealous : on being too, ii. 477
Ziska : his command, i. 13